Carol Fomery

DEVELOPMENTAL PSYCHOPATHOLOGY

DEVELOPMENTAL PSYCHOPATHOLOGY

Second Edition

Thomas M. Achenbach

Departments of Psychiatry and Psychology
University of Vermont

John Wiley and Sons, Inc.

New York   Chichester   Brisbane   Toronto   Singapore

Library of Congress Cataloging in Publication Data:

Achenbach, Thomas M. 1940–
      Developmental psychopathology.

      Bibliography: p.
      Includes indexes.
      1.   Child psychopathology.   2.   Adolescent psycho-
pathology.   I.   Title.
RJ499.A32   1982   618.92′89   82-2838
ISBN 0-471-05536-0   AACR2

Printed in the United States of America

10 9 8 7 6 5 4 3 2 1

Once again, to Susan.

PREFACE

In the first edition of this book, I tried to convey the basic concepts of a developmental approach to psychopathology. Although the relevance of these concepts seemed obvious, they were not generally evident in efforts to help troubled children. Since then, the study of child and adolescent disorders has become more sophisticated. New data have challenged old myths and unfounded assumptions, while specialized knowledge of several disorders has increased. These are signs of progress.

On the other hand, the flurry of activity evoked by certain topics often masks a need for closer links between the study of particular disorders and development in general. Interest in a momentarily fashionable disorder rises to a crescendo and then fades away, not because the problems are solved but because another disorder comes into vogue. An example is the shift of interest to childhood depression from what has been variously called minimal brain dysfunction (MBD), hyperkinesis, and attention deficit disorder. Although intensive research helped to dispel certain myths about MBD-hyperkinesis-attention deficit disorder, this research might have made a more basic contribution if it had shown how the disorder (if there is one) relates to other aspects of development rather than viewing it largely as a circumscribed disease entity.

The specifics of such disorders are discussed in Chapter 11, but the general point is that children and adolescents are programmed for change. They are continually changing in many ways at once. A developmental perspective shows specific disorders in relation to the individual's previous experience, the developmental tasks the individual faces, other problems and competencies the individual displays, and what is likely to happen in later developmental periods. For now, this perspective tells us more about where to look than what to find. But, even when interest inevitably shifts from one disorder to another, a developmental perspective may help us find links from which to forge a more enduring and unified approach to childhood and adolescent disorders.

However, a developmental perspective on psychopathology does not offer a ready-made theory or set of answers. Because disorders of childhood and adolescence are so diverse and multidetermined, we need help from multiple theories, none of which provides all the answers. Many of the theories, therapies, and findings do not reflect a "developmental" approach. Yet, in some areas, these "nondevelopmental" efforts may be the best we have at the moment. One of the challenges of a developmental view of psychopathology is to integrate various kinds of truth into a comprehensive picture of development and its deviations. Because we cannot yet weave all the important strands into a single, seamless whole, we must avoid dogmatic judgments about what is or is not "developmental."

This book is intended for readers acquainted with the basic concepts of general psychology, abnormal psychology, or developmental psychology. Chapters 1 to 7 deal mainly with the application of basic concepts to developmental psychopathology in preparation for more intensive concentration on specific disorders and interventions in Chapters 8 to 14. Chapters 15 to 17 presuppose familiarity with key concepts, specific disorders, and interventions. The book is organized so that it can be used as a main text in courses for advanced undergraduates, graduate students, and clinical trainees, but most chapters are sufficiently self-contained to be used alone.

For this edition, I have had the benefit of critiques from diverse perspectives on both development and psychopathology. I am deeply indebted to Professors William Kessen of Yale, Brendan Maher of Harvard, Fred Rothbaum of Tufts, and John Weisz of the University of North Carolina, who provided invaluable commentaries on the entire manuscript. I am also deeply indebted to Professor Barry Nurcombe, Director of Child, Adolescent, Family, and Community Psychiatry at the University of Vermont, who critiqued portions of the book, who debated the rest of it with me, and who facilitates the inquiry needed to advance our knowledge of the developmental course of psychopathology. To my wife, Susan, I offer my gratitude for the sacrifices this kind of effort entails.

Thomas M. Achenbach

CONTENTS

CHAPTER 1

A Developmental Approach to Psychopathology

"This is a book about a field that hardly exists yet." So began the first edition of *Developmental Psychopathology*. It is both gratifying and frustrating to undertake a revision: Gratifying because more sophisticated research is expanding our knowledge of the developmental aspects of psychopathology; frustrating because the burgeoning literature on child and adolescent psychopathology continues to reflect problems that prompted me to write the first edition. It is also frustrating because the sheer volume of literature makes it harder to do justice to all the important findings while still exposing the gaps in our knowledge and pursuing alternative conceptions that go beyond current findings.

In stressing a developmental approach, I must point out that it is more a way of looking at problems than a total solution to the problems. Unlike the "simple and sovereign" theories of an earlier day, a developmental approach to psychopathology does not offer all-encompassing terminology or explanations. Instead, it poses *questions* about the developmental course of adaptive and maladaptive behavior, and it offers *guidelines* for answering these questions. As we will see, no one set of variables and no one theory holds all the answers.

There is not now (and probably never will be) a *single* developmental theory of *all* psychopathology. Instead, the role of a developmental approach is to help us understand troublesome behavior in light of the developmental tasks, sequences, and processes that characterize human growth. A developmental approach can shed light on all phases of the life cycle, but the dramatic changes occurring from birth to maturity make it especially crucial for understanding problems of childhood and adolescence. The following case history illustrates the need for developmental perspectives.

JERRY C., JR.

Jerry was Mr. and Mrs. C's only child. He was born while Mr. C. was away on assignment as a foreman for a nationwide construction company. Mrs. C. was quite ill during pregnancy and the birth was difficult, but Jerry was reported to be in good condition at birth. Jerry's arrival was welcomed by his mother, who longed for company during her husband's frequent absences. Mr. C. was less happy about the birth but did favor naming Jerry after himself. Mr. C.'s career had been a sequence of ups and downs in which promotions earned through seniority were revoked after he disappeared on drunken binges.

Young Jerry was an exceptionally easy baby, usually quiet, placid, and affectionate, and his early development appeared normal. He crawled at eight months and walked at 14 months. His mother devoted a great deal of time to him, absorbing herself completely in caring for him when she became depressed during her husband's absences.

When Jerry had not begun speaking by the age of three, he was taken to a pediatric clinic for a complete medical checkup. Jerry was extremely upset by the medical procedures, but no organic abnormalities were found. An attempt at psychological testing failed because Jerry was too distractible to attend to the tasks. Intelligible speech was completely absent. Speech therapy was tried, but was given up after it appeared to have no effect.

Because Mrs. C. was also concerned about other children's teasing and refusal to play with Jerry, she applied to a child guidance clinic. She was put on the clinic's waiting list, but the family moved away from the area before she was given an appointment.

When Jerry was five, a school official inquired as to why he was not attending kindergarten. Confronted with the need for action, Mrs. C. brought Jerry to the pediatric clinic of another hospital. Here she was told he was retarded, that this was incurable, and that he should be taken to a state institution. Mrs. C. was extremely upset by this suggestion and applied instead to another child guidance clinic. The clinic had a seven-month waiting list, but Mrs. C. persevered.

By the time the C.'s were given an appointment at the clinic, Jerry had begun to speak and appeared able to read a number of words. Interviews with Mrs. C. showed that, while she was very threatened by the possibility of retardation, she had long recognized that her son was not normal. Jerry was not a problem at home. But, besides failing to speak, he showed little interest in other children, did not engage in games, and spent much of his time either watching TV or rolled up in a ball under a table in his favorite corner of the living room. Mrs. C. reported that Jerry displayed a phenomenal memory for TV commercials. To support her contention that he was not retarded, she also said that he read street signs along familiar routes. However, she acknowledged that his speech was difficult for anyone but her to understand.

When Jerry was first seen at the child guidance clinic, he was noted to be a solidly built boy, big for his age, with a pale, puffy, expressionless face, and very bright blue eyes. He showed no reluctance to separate from his mother. In the playroom, he walked around looking at various toys and uttering sounds in a singsong manner. When spoken to, he repeated the sounds of the therapist's voice, but words were almost entirely unintelligible. However, after several interview sessions, the therapist began to recognize words consistently distorted by the substitution of certain sounds for other sounds. Jerry mechanically read aloud and repeated words he saw printed in the building, such as ''Fire Exit.'' He demonstrated a moderate-sized reading vocabulary by reading words printed by the therapist and words he found on the labels of games and toys.

Jerry soon made up his own abbreviation for the therapist's name, repeated it often at home, and seemed eager to come for his weekly appointments. However, he never engaged in conversation, tending instead to repeat over and over the therapist's name, his own name, TV commercials, and the names of places he had visited. His speech was often interrupted with peals of laughter. He also repeated words of the therapist, but scrupulously avoided using the first-person pronouns ''I'' and ''me'' and referred to himself only as ''Jerry.'' He avoided looking the therapist in the eye and, though he seemed to like being hugged and tickled, he stood very rigidly and felt like a heavy inanimate object when the therapist lifted him.

Jerry showed exceptional speed, sensory-motor coordination, and dexterity on a nonverbal formboard test in which the child is to replace wooden geometric shapes in their proper openings. On a vocabulary test requiring the child merely to point to a picture corresponding to a word spoken by the examiner, Jerry obtained an IQ equivalent of 100, despite so little interest in the task that the examiner had to hold him and continually prod him to attend. When induced to draw a human figure, he drew one that scored slightly below average for his age according to standardized norms.

During therapy sessions, Jerry usually picked out a toy vehicle and lay rolling it on the floor, humming or echoing barely recognizable TV commercials. He occasionally drew maps of places he had visited and named the various streets on the maps. Sometimes he set up simple scenes with dolls in the doll house. Information from Mrs. C. showed that these were usually reenactments of rather routine events at home. Certain deviations from routine, such as the therapist's failure to wear a necktie, upset Jerry so much that he would not accompany the therapist. Jerry kept repeating, ''Daddy leave necktie in Florida,'' a reference to a time when his father mentioned having left a necktie where he had been staying during his last job. Attempts to probe with Jerry his association between the tieless therapist and his father elicited only repetitions of ''Daddy leave necktie in Florida.'' When the therapist donned a tie, Jerry resumed his usual cooperative behavior. Other changes in routine seemed to have no effect.

Since it appeared that at least some of Jerry's abilities were in the normal range, the therapist sought a school placement for him. His mother was asked to place him in groups of children whenever possible—such as Sunday school—in order to see how well he could mix with his agemates. While he seemed happy in these situations, he was content to watch the other children and did not interact with them in any way. Since the family could not afford private schooling, the public schools were asked to provide a homebound teacher who visited Jerry's home several times weekly. Arrangements were then made with an especially cooperative kindergarten teacher to have the homebound teacher accompany Jerry to a kindergarten class for an hour a day. Jerry expressed eagerness to go to school and the homebound teacher, who had never been comfortable with Jerry, soon asked to withdraw.

In kindergarten Jerry played by himself and did not partake of group activities, although he did conform to the teacher's instructions and occasionally surprised her with his reading skill and knowledge of maps. After a year of negotiations with the school system, Jerry was admitted to a special class for the emotionally disturbed. Here his social isolation continued, but he showed some academic progress.

Meanwhile, Jerry's father quit his job and deserted the family, although he occasionally called from distant places or reappeared unexpectedly, always promising to mend his ways. Mrs. C. tried to make a new life for herself without her husband, but she now had to depend on public welfare, which barely provided subsistence for her and Jerry. Jerry responded to his father's disappearance by becoming preoccupied with mailboxes and telephones, the sources of the occasional messages from Mr. C. He also talked of Mr. C. and showed affection whenever he reappeared. Jerry's speech and academic skills continued to improve slowly, but, after several years in the special class, it appeared that he was destined to remain significantly handicapped academically as well as socially. He was especially unable to take everyday responsibilities such as crossing streets.

Jerry is not typical of all children needing help, but he illustrates the need for developmental understanding.

Obtaining Help

Unlike adults, children almost never seek mental health services for themselves. Jerry would not have been seen for assessment or treatment if his mother had not sought it. He played no part in making the arrangements; his mother simply took him to the clinic. It was Mrs. C.'s perseverance during the seven-month wait for an appointment, rather than any discomfort on Jerry's part, that resulted in his eventually being seen. This is typical: Mental health services are usually sought for a child because of an adult's discomfort, and not the child's. And the adult's discomfort often results from an accumulation of problems rather than a single event.

Greater initiative is usually needed to get mental health services than other services for children—Mrs. C.'s odyssey included two hospitals, a speech therapist, contacts with school officials, and the waiting lists of two child guidance clinics before Jerry received treatment. Had she lived in other areas of the country, she might never have obtained services for Jerry. Once assessment and treatment finally began at the second clinic, she and Mr. C.—whenever he was available— had to accompany Jerry for interviews with a social worker during Jerry's weekly sessions over a period of two years. Parent motivation is thus a primary factor in continuing as well as obtaining treatment.

Most children lack realistic concepts of mental health services and many actively resist being taken for help. Their preconceptions are often conveyed by their parents. In Jerry's case, his mother had told him that the clinic was a "school," ostensibly to allay his anxiety.

When brought to a mental health professional, children do not readily assume the "patient" role that enables workers with adults to begin by asking clients about their problems. Young children are typically reluctant to leave their parents and go with a stranger, especially in the quasi-medical atmosphere of many mental health settings. It may have been significant that Jerry did *not* seem reluctant to separate from his mother, despite an unhappy previous experience with medical examinations and his general lack of social experience.

Even children suffering subjective discomfort are seldom able to tell a strange adult about it and its possible causes. Mental health workers must adapt to children's communication level and must rely on direct observations of their behavior and on data from other observers, such as parents and teachers. Because office contacts seldom elicit representative samples of children's behavior, it is usually essential to obtain data on behavior in other settings as well.

Family Functioning

Because they are so dependent on their family, children's behavior is usually a more direct function of their family situation than adults' behavior. No families are without problems. Mrs. C.'s depression, Mr. C.'s erratic behavior, and the threatened, and then actual, breakup of the C.s' marriage were bound to affect Jerry. Did they cause Jerry's problems?

Jerry's gratifications and frustrations were intimately tied to those of his parents. Their ways of communicating, interacting, and meeting stress taught Jerry most of what he knew about human behavior. On the other hand, Jerry's birth changed the balance of his parents' marital relationship. When Jerry's abnormalities became apparent, Mrs. C. may have become so concerned that she withdrew from her husband, who then reacted with progressively more infantile behavior. Any biological vulnerabilities on Jerry's part may have been aggravated by the reactions he elicited from his parents. Rather than family problems directly *causing* Jerry's problems, it is thus more likely that a sequence of *transactions* between Jerry's characteristics and those of his parents shaped his behavior.

Developmental Level

Another essential difference between the study of child and adult psychopathology is the importance of developmental milestones. Mrs. C. first sought help when Jerry failed to speak by the usual age. Although she had previously noticed differences between him and other children, the contrast between his lack of speech and the speech of his agemates became so compelling that she could no longer deny the need for action. When no organic cause was found for his lack of speech, it was his failure to achieve another milestone expected for all children, entry into school, that prompted further action.

The onset of speech is a milestone established by the observed uniformity of children's development. School entry is a milestone established by social custom. Both types of milestones are important for children's adaptive development. Jerry's delayed speech may have resulted merely from slow, but not defective, maturation of the speech areas of his brain. He may have begun talking later than average simply because of this one unusual characteristic of his biological makeup. Yet, his failure to talk at the typical age had broad ramifications for his social and intellectual development. Being ostracized by other children for his lack of speech may have caused him to withdraw from social relationships. This, in turn, could hinder development of the cooperative and competitive skills necessary for dealing with others. His handicap may also have evoked further overprotection from his mother, who desperately needed someone to hold close while her husband was absent and her marriage crumbling.

Failure to achieve the developmental milestone of school entry at the usual time has consequences of its own. Most children who start school late will be bigger than their classmates, which can lead to being ostracized. They may therefore develop coping strategies, such as withdrawal or physical force, that hinder further adaptation. When Jerry entered kindergarten, he was already bigger than his classmates. He was further distinguished by his lack of social skills and the special attention of the homebound teacher and regular teacher.

Just as a child's deviation from developmental norms is an important factor in getting parents to seek help, precise comparison with developmental norms is an essential part of diagnostic assessment. Jerry's poor speech led the physician in the second pediatric clinic to diagnose Jerry as mentally retarded and to recommend referral to an institution for the retarded. However, subsequent assessment showed that his sensory-motor functioning, understanding of words, and drawing skills were within the normal range for his age. Uniform mental retardation was not, therefore, an appropriate diagnosis, despite Jerry's deviant speech and social functioning.

Although the question of mental retardation may sometimes arise in the assessment of adults, adults already have a long history of development that includes important developmental milestones. This history usually indicates the adult's attained level of development.

While it was not clear *why* Jerry's speech and social behavior were so deviant, he seemed to have the cognitive ability to acquire academic skills. Unlike adult treatment, which aims to facilitate self-understanding and remove discomforting symptoms, interventions with children must help them reach developmental milestones and acquire needed skills without which they will be forever handicapped, no matter what the other outcomes.

Diagnostic Assessment

Traditional diagnostic practices are oriented toward identification of diseaselike entities in adults, such as schizophrenia and hysteria. Yet, children's problems seldom resemble these disorders. One of the most striking aspects of Jerry's case, for example, was his *failure to progress* in certain areas, such as speech and social behavior, despite adequate cognitive ability. As we will see, the inadequacies of traditional diagnosis often hinder communication and research concerning troubled children. Certain childhood disorders may be properly viewed as disease entities and some may be forerunners of adult disorders, but most childhood disorders do not fit the models provided by adult diagnostic categories. We therefore need to seek ways of assessing childhood disorders in their own right rather than as miniature versions of adult disorders.

Goals of Preventive and Therapeutic Interventions

It is often assumed that adult disorders have their roots in childhood. Interventions with children should therefore be simpler and more promising than adult treatment, because they can nip problems in the bud before there is so much to undo. Yet children's dependence on their parents and other adults makes interventions more complex than treatment of adults. Not only do interventions with children depend on the cooperation of adults, but adults must often change their own behavior before there is much hope for change in children. Thus, the targets of child interventions typically include the interlocking behaviors of people other than the target child. Moreover, a satisfactory outcome may be disrupted by changes in family circumstances beyond the child's control, such as Mr. C.'s desertion and erratic reappearances. Treatment may have more durable effects on adults, thanks to their greater control over their life situations.

Much adult therapy aims to undo pathological past influences. This aim has often been extrapolated to children and adolescents. Yet, the importance of developmental advancement makes mastery of developmental tasks an essential goal of all interventions with children and adolescents. Whatever else it accomplishes, an intervention that fails to help children and adolescents achieve their potential for continued development cannot be considered successful. Systematic comparisons of interventions over lengthy follow-up periods are needed to determine which ones are truly the most effective with what kinds of problems.

THEORIES AND CONCEPTS

Adoption of a single all-encompassing theory would greatly simplify our task. Largely as legacies from the study of adult psychopathology, there are numerous theories of psychopathology in children and adolescents. Some workers place their faith in a single viewpoint to the exclusion of all others. As a result, much that has been written reflects a single viewpoint rather than an integration of diverse views.

To advance our knowledge, however, we must recognize that important questions often require a convergence of thinking from multiple perspectives. Adherents of various approaches may describe Jerry C. in their own languages and prescribe their own favorite treatments for him. Yet in Chapter 12 we will see how much remains to be discovered about problems like Jerry's and how to treat and prevent them.

Human behavior is complex and can seldom be specified with total objectivity. In Jerry's case, for example, how can we best describe what the problem was? His speech? His lack of eye contact? His failure to interact with other children? His absorption in an Oedipal conflict, as revealed in his preoccupation with sexually symbolic mailboxes? Castration fears symbolized by his distress when the therapist failed to wear a necktie? Even when we agree on the important behavior, the potential determinants of the behavior must include concepts at many levels of analysis—genes, anatomical structures, physiological processes, cognitive structures, past experience and learning, motives, and the immediate stimulus situation, to name a few.

If a developmental approach to psychopathology requires bringing diverse ideas together, how can we choose among them? Can we simply grant each idea equal status and be satisfied with it in the form we find it? Such an approach would yield no more than a survey of various schools of thought. Instead, our approach will emphasize scientific criteria for separating the wheat from the chaff. Scientific criteria for the study of behavior will be discussed in Chapter 5, but it will often be necessary to go beyond these in suggesting new ways to formulate and test ideas at the frontiers of our knowledge.

Related to the use of scientific criteria is a distinction between two phases of scientific activity. This distinction, made by philosophers of science and discussed further in Chapter 5, is between the *context of discovery* and the *context of confirmation*. Briefly, the context of discovery refers to the initial generation of ideas and hypotheses in whatever subjective, personal, serendipitous, creative, or accidental way in which an individual happens to think. There are neither rules nor formulas for this stage of science. However, in order to be useful, the products of this phase must be tested by observing phenomena in the real world. It is to this latter context, the *context of confirmation*, that scientific standards of logic and verifiability apply.

The fact that an idea has not yet fully proven itself in the context of confirmation will not keep us from considering it. I will emphasize those that are the most testable, however, even if a "test" is an indirect one requiring considerable inference from data that only instruments or experts can detect.

STRUCTURE OF THE BOOK

I will not tempt the reader with the comfortable dogmas of any single, all-inclusive viewpoint. One reason for the diversity of views is that none can fully explain many of the disorders we will consider. Whenever possible, a viewpoint will be presented in detail where it is most powerful in explaining significant phenomena. In many cases, disagreement over what *are* the significant phenomena requires extended discussion of more than one approach. As we will see in Chapters 9 and 10, for example, the psychoanalytic and behavioral approaches offer contrasting explanations for similar behavior. Amid the diversity of views, however, a common reference point will be the developmental dimension: the sequence of tasks and accomplishments humans follow as they grow.

Because it is not feasible to gather all our topics under one theoretical umbrella, I will try to ferret out important questions that lurk beneath the surface of prevailing custom. Instead of accepting partial solutions for immediate application, I will explore the possibilities for more comprehensive answers. The selection of topics and the suggested reading following each chapter are intended to help the reader pursue as many different questions as possible.

As preparation for understanding specific disorders, Chapters 2 through 7 present the historical context from which the developmental study of psychopathology is emerging, perspectives on development, basic issues that hinder formulation of answerable questions, scientific strategies for studying psychopathology, genetic factors, and neurobiological development. Chapters 8 through 14 are organized around specific disorders, while the final three chapters—on taxonomy, diagnostic assessment, and issues in prevention and treatment—serve an integrative function after the reader is familiar with the material of the earlier chapters.

SUMMARY

A developmental approach to psychopathology is more a way of looking at problems than a total solution to the problems. The role of a developmental approach is to help us understand troublesome behavior in light of the developmental tasks and processes that characterize human growth. The dramatic changes occurring from birth to maturity make a developmental approach especially crucial for understanding problems of childhood and adolescence. The study of psychopathology in children and adolescents is distinguished from the study of adult psychopathology by the way in which help is obtained, the effects of family functioning, the importance of developmental level, diagnostic assessment, and the goals of interventions.

Because no one theory seems able to fully encompass all the phenomena of developmental psychopathology, concepts are drawn from many sources. Scientific criteria are needed for evaluating the adequacy of the various concepts. Instead of accepting partial solutions for immediate application, we will explore the possibilities for more comprehensive answers.

CHAPTER 2

Historical Context

In the words of philosopher George Santayana, "He who forgets the past is condemned to repeat it." Nowhere is this more apparent than in the history of attitudes toward disordered behavior. This history displays some remarkable cycles that have been constantly repeated in one form or another. Examining the historical context from which the developmental study of psychopathology is emerging may help us avoid repeating these cycles, as well as clarifying relevant ideas from diverse sources.

EARLY THEORIES OF MENTAL DISORDERS

From at least the time of Hippocrates (460?–377 B.C.), the ancient Greeks and Romans held organic theories of mental disorders. These dealt mostly with the balance of humoral substances in the body, but also included the belief that hysteria (Greek *hystera* = womb) is caused by wanderings of the womb. Somatic treatments, such as bloodletting and laxatives, were presumed to restore the humoral balance, but kindness and restful environments were also prescribed.

During the medieval period, insanity was sometimes viewed with fear and suspicion as the work of the devil, although there is evidence for more humane attitudes as well (Neugebauer, 1979). In the late eighteenth century, humane treatment of mental patients was increasingly promoted. The change has often been dated from 1793, when Phillipe Pinel, head of Paris's Bicêtre Hospital, supposedly ordered the hospital's inmates unchained. However, long lost documents show that

Pinel mainly followed practices begun slightly earlier (Weiner, 1979). Furthermore, the unchaining at the Bicêtre reflected the widespread reforming spirit of the Enlightenment. During the same period, for example, English Quakers led by William Tuke planned a "retired Habitation," known as a "Retreat" to avoid the stigma of the prevailing terms "asylum" and "madhouse." Opened at York, England, in 1796, the Retreat was to provide a family environment, employment, exercise, and the treatment of patients as guests.

That the change in the treatment of the insane was more a product of social attitudes than of new knowledge or theories about mental disorders is evident in the writings of Benjamin Rush (1745−1813). Known as the "father of American Psychiatry," Rush and other Philadelphians, including Benjamin Franklin, advocated humanitarian reforms in prisons, the treatment of debtors, education, and medical care for the poor. Improving care for the mentally disturbed was a natural byproduct of the spirit of reform. Yet Rush's medical theory was that "madness" was caused by engorgement of the blood vessels of the brain. To relieve the engorgement, Rush prescribed purges, enemas, and, above all, bloodletting, boasting that he had taken as much as 470 ounces of blood from one patient! He also advocated deprivation of food, terrifying punishment, and mechanical restraining devices, such as a "tranquilizing" chair he invented. The wide acceptance of these methods, which may indeed have "calmed" excited patients, is indicated by the popularity of his book, *Medical Inquiries and Observations upon the Diseases of the Mind* (1812), which remained the only systematic American textbook in psychiatry until 1883.

The Rise and Fall of Moral Treatment

Although changes in medical thinking did not *instigate* better care for mental patients, the new humane attitudes did crystallize into a therapeutic system. This was known as *moral treatment,* with *moral* referring to "psychological" as well as having ethical connotations. As Bockoven (1963) describes it, "The moral therapist acted toward his patients as though they were mentally well. He believed that kindness and forebearance were essential in dealing with them. He also believed in firmness and persistence in impressing on patients the idea that a change to more acceptable behavior was expected (p. 76)."

Improvement in patients unchained by Pinel showed that cruel conditions could themselves be responsible for maintaining abnormal behavior. However, this discovery that psychological factors could affect the insane did not contradict the primitive organic theories, because organic changes were often blamed on psychological factors, such as disappointment and bereavement.

The combination of a spirit of reform, the apparent efficacy of moral treatment, and the compatibility of the new ideas with some aspects of prevailing theory led to a movement in the United States that by 1824 established several private retreats modeled on the York Retreat in England. Some were built with state aid and took a few paupers, but they were generally designed for those who could pay (Grob, 1973).

Reports of up to 90 percent cure rates in the early retreats gave rise by 1830 to a "cult of curability" that replaced the former pessimism with a boundless optimism (Deutsch, 1949). This optimism spawned efforts to extend the benefits of moral treatment to the poor by building state hospitals modeled on the private retreats. Beside the humane concept of public responsibility for the insane, a weighty argument with state legislatures was that many people could be quickly cured and become taxpayers who would otherwise have to be supported in prisons and poorhouses for life.

The first success of the movement for state hospitals was the State Lunatic Hospital at Worcester, Massachusetts, opened in 1833. It became a nationally known prototype for other states to follow. In 1841, the movement found in a former school teacher, Dorothea Dix (1802–1887), a militant crusader who canvassed the country exposing the cruelty suffered by the insane poor and campaigning for state hospitals. Dix and her allies got numerous legislatures to build hospitals. By 1844, the hospital movement grew to the point where the Association of Medical Superintendents of American Institutions for the Insane (now the American Psychiatric Association) was founded. It is significant that the Association's members were more concerned with the general management of institutions—building plans, heating and ventilating systems, and food distribution—than with advancing theory, research, or treatment (Grob, 1973).

The "cult of curability" had thus given birth to a new system of interests vested in the operation of large state hospitals. Had the construction of hospitals alone been able to fulfill the hopes raised by the cult of curability, these vested interests would have been all for the best. However, three factors, which were recognized only later, prevented the new hospitals from fulfilling their promise of wholesale cure.

The most basic factor was that the claims of 90 percent cure rates by the early hospitals were invalid. In an 1875 review, published after deep pessimism had returned, Dr. Pliny Earle exposed fallacies in the hospital statistics. Many of the "cures," for example, involved successive releases of the same patient from one or more hospitals. An especially outstanding contributor to the statistics was a woman who had been cured six times in one year and a total of 47 times before she finally died in an insane asylum (Deutsch, 1949).

The second obstacle to wholesale cure was the failure of the state hospitals to provide the good features of early retreats that may indeed have optimized their success. The argument that state hospitals would save tax money by curing the insane poor was translated into the quick erection of cheap buildings by cost-conscious legislatures. Worse yet, legislatures mandated commitment of the insane to the hospitals, but failed to provide funds for adequate care (Grob, 1973). As a consequence, little provision was made for the essential ingredients of moral treatment: family environment, employment, exercise, and treatment of patients as guests.

The third factor working against the state hospitals was the difference between their patients and those in the private retreats. Patients of the retreats came in small numbers from financially secure backgrounds to which they could return as they improved. By contrast, the new state hospitals were filled with paupers, often foreign-born, who came straight from prisons, poorhouses, and other degrading circumstances, and who lacked secure homes to return to, should they improve. Even with impeccable moral treatment, state hospitals could hardly have transformed many of these patients into healthy, self-sufficient citizens.

By the 1860s, the pendulum had again swung back from wild optimism to bleak pessimism about mental illness. The same medical leaders who had been so optimistic in the 1840s now pronounced most forms of insanity incurable. State institutions became grimly custodial.

Neither the early swing to a psychological emphasis when humane treatment was introduced, nor the reaction against it were dictated by advances in scientific knowledge or theory. Indeed, advances were occurring in European research on organic brain pathology, and Wilhelm Griesinger's (1845) textbook stressing organic research helped give psychiatry a scientific orientation. Likewise, Darwin's (1859) *Origin of Species* and Galton's (1869) *Hereditary Genius* provided ammunition for hereditarian arguments. But, in America, these scientific contributions provided *rationalizations* for a change of professional attitudes that had already occurred. Until the end of the nineteenth century, American views of mental disorders remained pessimistically centered on custodial care. This picture was transformed radically by certain forces emerging at the beginning of the twentieth century. These included psychoanalysis, the mental hygiene movement, and behaviorism, which we will discuss later in the chapter.

But what about children up to this point? A few references to children can be found in nineteenth-century works on adult psychopathology, and in Europe at least three books were written primarily on mental disturbances in children (cf. Harms, 1967). Yet there were no facilities for the treatment of children and there was little concern with disorders unique to childhood that fell short of the extreme kinds of "insanity" observed in adults. To find a nineteenth century historical strand that is clearly continuous with our concern for *developmental* psychopathology, we must turn to the mentally retarded.

Discovery and Care of the Mentally Retarded

Distinctions were often made between people who had lost their reasoning (madmen, lunatics) and those who had never developed reasoning (fools, idiots). Yet, the first systematic attention to the retarded, albeit inadvertent, is usually credited to Jean Itard's attempt to educate the Wild Boy of Aveyron, who was found in a forest in 1799.

Like the movement for humane treatment of mental patients, Itard's experiment was as much a product of Enlightenment attitudes of rational humanitarianism as of any theory about retardation per se. In fact, Itard only tried to train the boy, Victor, because he thought he was merely an untutored savage who could be civilized through proper instruction. Applying techniques of sensory-motor instruction already in use with the deaf, Itard had moderate success. But after several years, he concluded that Victor was fundamentally retarded. Nevertheless, he had demonstrated that even a retarded child could be trained to some extent.

Itard's beginning was extended by Edward Seguin (1812–80). First in France and after 1848 in the United States, Seguin did research on the causes, nature, and treatment of retardation. He believed retardation was curable through "physiological" education that would bring all senses and organs to their peak levels of functioning. The functions to be trained depended on the individual's specific weaknesses, but lower functions, such as perception, had to be developed before mental training could proceed.

In contrast to earlier periods when the retarded were neglected or indiscriminately put in mental hospitals, the early 1840s saw the establishment of several European institutions designed specifically to train the retarded. In the United States, the first schools for the retarded were begun in 1848. After 1850, the official census distinguished between "feebleminded" and insane persons. As with the mental hospital movement, initial enthusiasm triggered a flurry of school construction. *Unlike* mental hospitals, the first state schools (in Massachusetts, 1848, and New York, 1851) for the retarded were usually set up for a well-defined *experimental* period.

Another feature that distinguished state care for the retarded from the cult of the curability of the insane was the temperate belief that nonexistent intellectual abilities could not be created; the goal of the special schools was merely to develop "dormant" abilities as much as possible.

By 1876, however, when the Association of Medical Officers of American Institutions for Idiots and Feebleminded Persons was founded, the early educational model for the retarded and the optimism about making them self-supporting had yielded to a custodial model like that for the insane. By the beginning of the twentieth century, attitudes toward the retarded had moved beyond pessimism to outright hostility that lasted until the 1920s. During this "alarmist period," the retarded were blamed for most crime and social ills; it was considered essential to segregate and sterilize them to prevent reproduction (Deutsch, 1949).

Like the vacillation in attitudes toward the mentally ill, the violent change in attitudes toward the retarded was not dictated by new knowledge. Although Darwin's (1859) *Origin of Species* and the rediscovery of Mendel's laws of heredity in 1900 strengthened genetic theory, there was little evidence for genetic causes of mental retardation. Instead, the social Darwinism that glorified dominance by the rich and powerful, the eugenics movement for eliminating "bad stock," and the exclusively hereditarian interpretations of family histories—ranging from *The Jukes* (Dugdale, 1877) to *The Kallikak Family* (Goddard, 1912)—all reflected social attitudes that were unjustly generalized to the retarded.

THE TWENTIETH CENTURY

Systematic research and theory have played a greater role in twentieth century concepts of psychopathology than those of earlier eras. But this does not mean that general social attitudes, historical events, fads, and cycles no longer affect beliefs about psychopathology. On the contrary, these factors continue to stimulate trends and countertrends. More intensive study of disordered behavior, however, has generated such diverse ideas that recent history must be written in terms of the coexisting traditions spawned by these ideas.

Oddly enough, the divergent traditions of the twentieth century originated at a time when the study of psychopathology acquired its first unified classification system or *taxonomy*. Classification of disorders became important only when hospital care spread in the early nineteenth century. The need to separate patients who required different kinds of management, such as the violent and the depressed, demanded a taxonomy that could predict the course of a patient's behavior.

In 1845, Wilhelm Griesinger's influential textbook established the dogma that "mental diseases are brain diseases." Accordingly, it was hoped that classification of mental disease entities could begin with the *description* of symptom syndromes and culminate in the eventual discovery of a specific organic cause for each syndrome. The prototype syndrome was *general paralysis* (later called *paresis,* i.e., "incomplete paralysis"), which received progressively more precise descriptions between 1798 and the 1840s. What became the defining feature of this syndrome was the *combination* of *mental* symptoms, such as forgetfulness and irrationality, with *physical* symptoms of general motor impairment, usually ending in death.

Once syndromes had been precisely described, theories and research could focus on their causes. Intensive research from the 1840s through the 1870s revealed inflammation in the brains of nearly all patients who died of general paresis. Hypothesized causes were gradually narrowed to syphilitic infection. This hypothesis was confirmed experimentally in 1897 when Krafft-Ebing showed that paretics did not manifest secondary symptoms of syphilis when innoculated with syphilis spirochetes—they were already infected. Further confirmation was obtained in 1906 when the Wassermann test revealed syphilis in nearly all paretics. In 1917, the high fever caused by malaria was found to cure paretics, although malarial treatment was ultimately replaced by penicillin. Systematic description thus led to the successful identification of a disease entity whose specific cause was ultimately found and could be treated.

The taxonomy that exemplified "descriptive diagnosis" and provided a unifying framework for psychiatry was the work of the German psychiatrist Emil Kraepelin (1856–1926). Published in 1883, Kraepelin's first edition was based on the conviction that all mental disorders, like paresis, reflect brain pathology. Kraepelin's taxonomy replaced a hodgepodge of idiosyncratic terms and concepts with a comprehensive system for describing disorders in terms that could be widely shared.

By its sixth edition (1899), Kraepelin's system had won general acceptance and had changed in several respects. Beside describing symptoms assumed to reflect brain pathology, Kraepelin now distinguished among disorders partly on the basis of psychological processes, studied via Wilhelm Wundt's experimental techniques (Maher & Maher, 1979). The course of a disorder from beginning to end was also added to symptomatic descriptions and psychological processes as a defining feature. For example, *dementia praecox* ("insanity of the young," renamed "schizophrenia" by Bleuler in 1911) was distinguished from manic-depressive psychosis largely on the basis of psychological characteristics and the differing courses of the two disorders. Thus, in ambiguous cases, recovery argued for a diagnosis of manic-depressive psychosis; failure to recover, on the other hand, was evidence for *dementia praecox*. By 1915, when the fourth volume of his eighth edition appeared, Kraepelin included a full-fledged category of psychogenic disorders and a category of personality disorders bordering between illness and ordinary eccentricity.

Against this newly unified taxonomy of adult psychopathology, five new forces emerged before the developmental study of psychopathology began to take shape. These were Freudian psychoanalysis, the "common sense" psychiatry of Adolf Meyer, the mental hygiene movement, behaviorism, and the systematic study of children.

Freudian Psychoanalysis

The progress of neurology as a new medical speciality in the mid-nineteenth century augmented the tendency to blame disordered behavior on organic pathology. By the end of the nineteenth century, however, certain discoveries by European neurologists were to lead in a very different direction. These discoveries came about largely through scientific interest in hypnosis, which had been popularized in the eighteenth century by Friedrich Anton Mesmer as "mesmerism." It became a respectable scientific topic when the English surgeon James Braid (1795–1860) published *Neurypnology, or, the Rationale of Nervous Sleep,* in 1843. While the behavioral phenomena differed little from those induced by Mesmer, Braid's new medical term, *neurypnology* (soon shortened to *hypnosis*), his quasi-scientific rationale in terms of nervous sleep, and his demonstration of the anesthetic potential of hypnosis laid the foundations for later work by neurologists.

Neurologists were intrigued by similarities between hypnotic behavior and the behavior of hysterical patients who had dramatic physical symptoms, such as paralyses and convulsions, with no discernible organic pathology. In 1878, a leading French neurologist, Jean Martin Charcot (1825–1893), began using hysterical patients to demonstrate these similarities at the Salpêtrière Hospital, Paris. In 1882, he convinced the French Académie des Sciences, which had thrice previously rejected mesmerism, that hypnotic phenomena were real and that they were closely related to hysteria. Another French neurologist, Hippolyte Bernheim (1840–1919), agreed on the authenticity of the phenomena, but contended that they reflected normal suggestibility. Although he employed hypnosis to treat a variety of disorders, he eventually found that the same effects could be obtained by suggestion in the waking state, a procedure his group called *psychotherapeutics*.

Charcot and Bernheim's work with hypnosis sparked interest in the psychological processes that seemed to underlie the physical symptoms of hysteria. Charcot's student, Pierre Janet (1859–1947), sought to understand the mixture of bodily and mental symptoms of hysteria in terms of general principles of psychological functioning, thereby bringing together the study of psychology and clinical disorders. Janet proposed that hysterical symptoms arose when certain *complexes* of ideas became split off or *dissociated* from the rest of the personality. Dissociated complexes concerning a particular limb might cause the limb to become paralyzed, for example. Other dissociated complexes might activate behavior the patient could not remember later, as in amnesia. Janet thought hysterical symptoms might be alleviated by helping patients remember the dissociated complexes of ideas, but he assumed that the basic cause of hysteria was a constitutional vulnerability to dissociation.

The most significant figure to emerge from the new trend in neurology was Sigmund Freud (1856–1939). Trained in Vienna as a physiologist and later as a neurologist, Freud studied with Charcot in 1885–1886 and spent a few weeks with Bernheim. Although his first scientific publications culminated in 1891 with a distinguished neurological monograph on organic causes of speech problems, he turned increasingly toward psychological theory.

Freud's older colleague, Josef Breuer (1842–1925), had from 1880 to 1882 hypnotically treated a hysterical patient, Anna O., whose recollections of unpleasant thoughts seemed to relieve her physical symptoms. Freud and Breuer collaborated on an article in 1893 that was expanded into a book and published as *Studies in Hysteria* (1895). Regarded as the first important document in psychoanalysis, it included a theory of the psychological mechanisms of hysteria, case histories, and a chapter on psychotherapy. Unlike Janet, Freud held that dissociation occurred because the dissociated ideas were incompatible with the individual's conscious values. Freud hypothesized that the unacceptable ideas were forced out of consciousness by a process he dubbed *repression*.

By 1900, Freud had replaced hypnosis with free association as a tool for revealing unconscious thoughts. He had also formulated the basic ideas of defense, resistance, and repression, and had become convinced that childhood sexual experiences contributed to neurosis. He outlined many other elements of psychoanalytic theory in *The Interpretation of Dreams,* published in 1900. This book was ridiculed in some medical circles, but overt hostility greeted the publication of *Three Essays on the Theory of Sexuality* (1905), where Freud argued that children have sexual desires toward their parents. Nevertheless, reactions were not as uniformly negative as Freud later implied (Dekker, 1977). His work won recognition, especially in the United States where he received an honorary doctorate from Clark University in 1909.

Psychoanalytic theory will be discussed further in Chapter 9, but it is important to note here that Freud's ideas continued to change almost until his death in 1939, by which time psychoanalysis was a major force in psychological theory. Child psychoanalysis began by 1920 and was promoted by Anna Freud and Melanie Klein, among others. The psychoanalytic theory of childhood psychosexual development also shaped the views of nonanalysts as well as analysts.

The Psychoanalytic Movement. Besides the development of Freudian thought, it is instructive to consider the "History of the Psychoanalytical Movement," as Freud (1914) titled one of his own works. The first regular meetings for the discussion of psychoanalysis began at Freud's home in Vienna in 1902, as the "Psychological Wednesday Society." In 1908, the group became the Vienna Psychoanalytical Society. The International Psychoanalytical Association was founded in 1910, with Carl Gustav Jung, who met Freud in 1907, designated by Freud as president. Member societies were later founded in several European and American cities.

Ernest Jones (1953, 1955, 1957) eloquently documents the atmosphere in Freud's early group, although others have painted less reverential pictures (Clark, 1980; Sulloway, 1979). Having felt rejected by official medicine, Freud's group acquired the aura of a social movement in which personalities and personal conflicts played a big role. Freud, of course, was at the center, but rivalries among his followers and disagreements on theoretical issues led to schisms among competing factions inside and outside the official psychoanalytic societies. Alfred Adler, Wilhelm Stekel, and Jung were early followers who all broke with Freud between 1911 and 1913.

In response to these defections, Jones, a member of the inner circle since 1908, proposed that "a small group of trustworthy analysts" be formed "as a sort of Old Guard around Freud." Jones (1955, pp. 152–153) quotes Freud as approving the "idea of a secret council composed of the best and most trustworthy among our men to take care of the further development of psychoanalysis and defend the cause against personalities and accidents when I am no more." In 1913, Freud presented the six members of the resulting "Committee," as it was known, with antique Greek intaglios which they then had mounted in gold rings. There was considerable success in maintaining a theoretical orthodoxy, but schismatic tendencies continued and even two memebers of the Committee eventually broke with Freud: Otto Rank in 1926 and Sandor Ferenczi in 1929.

Psychoanalytic theory was extended beyond Freud's ideas by some who broke with Freudian orthodoxy and some who remained loyal. Among those who broke with Freud, Adler became known for his theory of the inferiority complex and drive for power; Jung for his theory of the collective unconscious and the problem-solving function of dreams; and Rank for his theory of the psychological impact of the birth trauma. Neo-Freudians who minimized the role of sex pathology and emphasized social learning included Karen Horney (1950), Erich Fromm (1947), Harry Stack Sullivan (1953), and Erik Erikson (1963). Among those remaining loyal to the orthodox tradition, Anna Freud (1946, 1965) elaborated the theory of ego processes and defense mechanisms, and Heinz Hartmann (1939) and David Rapaport (1951) the theory of ego psychology.

The Practice of Psychoanalysis. Beside the splits over personal and theoretical differences, strains arose within the psychoanalytic movement over professional qualifications for doing psychoanalytic therapy. Some of Freud's early nonmedical adherents began to practice analysis by 1920. They were followed by others who became prominent, including Otto Rank, Anna Freud, August Aichorn, Theodor Reik, Ernst Kris, Robert Waelder, and Erik Erikson. Freud himself clearly believed that psychoanalysis was a general psychology with implications far beyond psychiatry and should not be reserved for medical practitioners. He maintained that psychoanalytic treatment required medical consultation, but that a broad grounding in anatomy, physiology, pathology, biology, embryology, evolution, mythology, the psychology of religion, and classical literature was better than medical education as preparation for analytic training.

As institutes for analytic training were founded, restrictions evolved that contrasted markedly with the informal approach Freud took to training analysts. During the 1920s, the New York Psychoanalytical Society vehemently rejected all practice by nonmedical analysts, leading to friction with Europeans who had trained many of the nonmedical analysts in America. Freud (1926b) firmly defended nonmedical analysis. Despite later rumors of a change in his position, he wrote in 1938, ". . . I have never repudiated these views and I insist upon them even more intensely than before, in the face of the obvious American tendency to turn psychoanalysis into a mere housemaid of Psychiatry (Jones, 1955, p. 301)."

The conflict sharpened in the late 1930s and early 1940s as numerous nonmedical analysts fled Nazi persecution to America. The American Psychoanalytic Association continued to restrict nonmedical analysts, although policies vary among psychoanalytic institutes and restrictions have been less pronounced in child psychoanalysis. Several other psychoanalytic associations and training groups have not restricted nonmedical analysis.

Adolf Meyer's "Commonsense Psychiatry"

Although born and trained in Switzerland, Adolf Meyer (1866–1950) did more than any other single figure to shape American psychiatry in the early twentieth century (cf. Lief, 1948). Like Freud, Meyer moved from training and research based on organic theories of mental disorder to an increasingly psychological perspective. However, his influence was as a teacher, synthesizer, and organizer, not as an advocate of new theories or treatments. Moreover, Meyer's work was closely tied to state hospitals and services for a broad range of disturbed people, rather than a select group who could afford expensive private treatment.

Shortly after arriving in the United States, Meyer in 1893 became one of the first pathologists employed in a state hospital. His job was to perform autopsies, but he soon found that inadequate life histories and diagnoses made it hard to draw conclusions from tissue pathology alone. He urged hospital physicians to obtain life histories as they examined patients and to assess patients' mental conditions instead of merely collecting physical facts. His interest in precursors of mental disorders also led him to join the Illinois Association for Child Study in 1894, with an eye toward getting schools to collect statistics on childhood disorders.

In 1895, Meyer went to Worcester, Massachusetts, State Hospital, still as a pathologist, but now with the opportunity to start a research and training program. His program stressed careful study of patients' needs and symptoms by requiring physicians to make standardized mental and physical examinations, plus detailed follow-up observations. Meyer also worked closely with the developmental psychologist G. Stanley Hall at Clark University and taught graduate students who were later among the first clinical psychologists. In 1896, he instituted Kraepelin's taxonomy at Worcester, but modified it according to his belief that the life history and dynamic characteristics of each patient were more important than the classification of disease entities.

In 1902, Meyer became head of the New York State Pathological Institute, founded to do organic research on the patients of state mental hospitals. He first established basic standards for examinations and records in New York's 13 mental hospitals. With the standardized data thus made available, he soon discovered that autopsies seldom revealed organic causes, except in patients known to be organic before they died. This led him to focus on psychological factors and to move away from Kraepelin's "descriptive" psychiatry toward "dynamic" case formulations stressing comprehensive understanding of each patient's behavior.

To learn more about patients' prehospital surroundings, Meyer's wife interviewed patients' relatives in their own homes. She soon started helping relatives prepare for the return of patients after hospitalization and helping with follow-up care. She thus created a model for the new profession of psychiatric social worker.

By 1906, Meyer had been favorably impressed by Freud's work and saw in it a kinship to his own version of "dynamic psychiatry." Both emphasized specific experiential history and the dynamic balance of psychological forces within the individual. However, Meyer objected to Freud's sharp division of mind into conscious and unconscious. He also objected to analysts' tendency to create a new cult within psychiatry, their contention that symptoms had only symbolic significance, and the popularizations that exploited sex and advocated unrestrained self-indulgence.

Reaction Type of the Psychobiologic Unit. As a substitute for descriptive psychiatry's concept of disease entities, Meyer proposed the *reaction type of the psychobiologic unit*. This is the particular way an individual adjusts to life situations, both mentally and physically. According to this concept, symptoms are faulty reactions that an individual may need help in correcting. To modify these reactions, we must understand the conditions producing them and foster new habits to replace those that have been disrupted.

Meyer sought to replace the term *insanity* with *forms of unsuccessful adjustment*. His view was quite compatible with behavioristic psychology: in 1914, now heading the Phipps Clinic of Johns Hopkins University, he started the first course in psychology for medical students, with John B. Watson teaching part of it. Meyer also had great hope for preventive measures to help people in trouble before their faulty reactions reached symptomatic proportions. Accordingly, he was active in the mental hygiene movement, for which he suggested the name.

Meyer's efforts to standardize and upgrade psychiatric training contributed to the formation in 1934 of the American Board of Psychiatry and Neurology, which certifies psychiatrists and neurologists. His influence was also evident in the first edition of the American Psychiatric Association's (1952) *Diagnostic and Statistical Manual*, where disorders were called "reactions of the psychobiologic unit." Although the 1968 revision of the *Manual* dropped this term, the basic concept remained evident, especially in the childhood disorders. The drug therapies that emerged in the 1950s are also consistent with Meyer's teaching, at least insofar as they help to promote successful overall adjustment rather than being considered panaceas.

The tradition that Meyer established was known by the 1930s as "the American point of view." It had links with the Freudian, mental hygiene, and behaviorist traditions, but was not a systematic amalgam of these. It emphasized behavioral facts, practical understanding of the individual, mind—body unity, and "adjustment." It offered no clear-cut theoretical basis for understanding the psychodynamics of individual patients, but stressed the therapeutic value of sound advice, commonsense counseling, and social service.

The Mental Hygiene Movement

Unlike the professional traditions stemming from Freud and Meyer, the mental hygiene movement stemmed from the excruciating experience of a mentally disturbed layman. Shortly after his older brother developed epileptic seizures,

Clifford W. Beers (1876–1943) became obsessed with the idea that he, too, would have epilepsy; in 1900, he became convinced that epilepsy was beginning. Preferring death to the miserable decline he witnessed in his brother (soon to die of a brain tumor), Beers attempted suicide by jumping from a fourth-story window. Perhaps betraying his ambivalence about suicide, he hung momentarily from the window by his fingertips and dropped feet first, missing a stone pavement by inches. He was not badly hurt, but was hospitalized and his obsession with epilepsy was replaced by delusions of persecution.

Beers spent the next three years in three mental hospitals representing a cross-section of care: a private profit-making hospital, a private nonprofit hospital, and a state hospital. None offered much treatment. He concluded that the doctors simply depended on physical improvement to bring recovery. Insensitive doctors and attendants alike used threats and punishment to control patients.

As Beers recovered from his depression and delusions of persecution, he hatched grandiose plans for a worldwide movement to protect the insane. After his release from the last hospital in 1903, he became so excited about his project that he voluntarily returned to one of the hospitals for a month. This time, he recovered completely and his plans for a movement to help mental patients grew more realistic. In 1907, he began writing *A Mind that Found Itself*, an autobiographical book that he hoped would launch the movement, just as *Uncle Tom's Cabin* had stimulated the antislavery movement.

Before publishing his book, Beers sought the support of leaders in psychology, psychiatry, and other fields. William James donated to the cause and wrote an introduction. Adolf Meyer lent his support and suggested the name "mental hygiene" for the proposed movement. Published in 1908, *A Mind that Found Itself* recounted Beers's personal saga and an exposé of hospital conditions, but also provided realistic proposals for needed reforms. It is a humane, witty, and moving document that immediately became popular and is still a joy to read.

The mental hygiene movement began shortly thereafter with the founding of the Connecticut Society for Mental Hygiene in Beers's home town of New Haven. In 1909, the National Committee for Mental Hygiene was organized, with Beers as executive secretary, and there were soon many state and local societies.

The goal of the first society was to "work for the conservation of mental health" by preventing mental disorders and mental defects, raising standards of care, disseminating reliable information, and cooperating with agencies related to mental hygiene. The National Committee spent eight years making local, state, and national surveys of community needs. In 1917, it helped devise the government's system for detecting and treating emotional disturbances among soldiers. The numerous emotional casualties of World War I revealed the need for trained psychiatric social workers, and the National Committee helped set up the first training school for them, at Smith College, in 1918.

Although social work had existed as a profession in the United States since the

1870s, the concept of mental hygiene now offered a quasi-theoretical framework for psychiatric social workers. This concept replaced the former emphasis on economic and sociologic sources of human problems with psychological explanations and the goal of promoting healthy personalities through individual adjustment. The mental hygiene societies themselves did not espouse any particular theory, however, and the Depression of the 1930s brought a renewed emphasis on the impact of general economic factors on behavior.

Child Guidance. It was the National Committee for Mental Hygiene that first drew public attention to children's disorders. The earliest clinic for children had been founded in 1896 by Lightner Witmer at the University of Pennsylvania. Coining the term *clinical psychologist*, Witmer used educational methods to help children with school problems.

Special court procedures for children began with the establishment of a juvenile court in Chicago in 1899. A clinical approach to delinquency was taken when Dr. William Healey in 1909 founded the Juvenile Psychopathic Institute (now the Institute for Juvenile Research), to work with the Chicago juvenile court.

It was not until 1915, however, when the National Committee's surveys of school children revealed how widespread emotional problems were and how meager the facilities, that clinics for children were organized on a significant scale. Even then, it was only the Committee's own programs and demonstration projects, beginning in 1922, that sparked a movement for child guidance clinics and for liaisons of mental health workers with courts and schools.

Very much a product of the mental hygiene movement's role in child guidance, the American Orthopsychiatry Association was founded in 1924 as a professional organization of psychiatrists, psychologists, and social workers who worked with disturbed children. The term *orthopsychiatry* was coined by analogy with orthopedics to refer to the promotion of "straight-mindedness" through early intervention. In the original child guidance clinics, children were tested by a psychologist, parents were interviewed by a social worker, and treatment was conducted by a psychiatrist, although there are many variations on this model today.

The National Committee on Mental Hygiene sponsored federal legislation establishing the National Institute of Mental Health in 1949, intended to fund research, training, and community services. In 1950, the Committee combined with the National Mental Health Foundation and the Psychiatric Foundation to form the National Association for Mental Health, which continues to play an active role in mental health programs.

Success of the Mental Hygiene Movement. Apart from its contribution to public attitudes and social services, the significance of the mental hygiene movement is best understood in its sociohistorical context. Like earlier reform movements, it was not a direct product of new knowledge or theory. The term *mental hygiene*, with connotations similar to the modern ones, had been used in Germany in the early nineteenth century. An American, William Sweetster, had published a book in 1843 entitled, *Mental Hygiene or an Examination of the Intellect and Passions Designed to Illustrate their Influence on Health and Duration of Life*. Organizations for the protection of the insane had also sprung up in the nineteenth century, but the first American version, the National Association for the Protection of the Insane and the Prevention of Insanity (1880) died quickly when the Association of Medical Superintendents of American Institutions for the Insane opposed its efforts to change hospital conditions.

One factor that may have been crucial to Beers's success was a new belief in the *preventability* of disease through public health measures. The control of several organic diseases sparked great enthusiasm for public health movements, as reflected in the founding of the National Tuberculosis Association (1904), the American Child Health Association (1909), and the American Federation for Sex Hygiene (1910). Convinced that his own breakdown could have been prevented, Beers made *prevention* a cornerstone of the mental hygiene movement from its inception.

A second factor in Beers's success may have been the emergence of new forces within psychiatry and psychology that would not have spawned the mental hygiene movement, but that were highly receptive to it. These included the personal influence of Adolf Meyer and his commonsense psychiatry, Freud's emphasis on psychological processes, the rise of behaviorism, and the generally optimistic environmentalism that peaked in the 1920s.

Behaviorism held the strongest convictions about environmental influences, but nearly all views on child rearing shared the terminology of mental hygiene and emphasized the efficacy of early intervention to promote healthy personality adjustment. Even Arnold Gesell, whose faith in maturation dominated child study in the 1930s and 1940s, enthusiastically endorsed the prospects for mental hygiene offered by child guidance clinics and new nursery schools that were infused with the same spirit (Gesell, 1930).

Behaviorism

The behaviorist tradition was formally launched by John B. Watson's manifesto in the 1913 *Psychological Review*, "Psychology as the behaviorist views it." Watson (1878–1958) attacked the dominant schools of academic psychology for their preoccupation with the study of consciousness. He advocated that consciousness be taken for granted and that behavior, the actions by which organisms adjust themselves to their environment, become the subject matter of psychology.

Watson's conviction that a scientific psychology need deal only with behavior grew out of studies of animal learning where ascribing consciousness to animals seemed superfluous. His first public advocacy of this viewpoint, in a 1908 lecture, had received little notice. But by 1913, behavioristic terminology and attitudes won a sympathetic reaction from a wide audience. Terms like *habit, stimulus,* and *response* had come into popular vogue after a long history in associationistic psychology, while the then dominant psychology of introspectionism had reached a point of diminishing returns.

The compatibility between Watson's behaviorism and the new views on mental hygiene was apparent in many ways. Watson (1919) dedicated his book, *Psychology from the Standpoint of a Behaviorist*, to J. McKeen Cattell, who initiated mental testing in America, and to Adolf Meyer. Strongly endorsing Meyer's emphasis on detailed life histories, Watson held that most problems of the day were due to faulty personality adjustment. He repeatedly appealed to common sense, practicality, mental hygiene, and prevention. Watson also approved of the psychoanalytic advocacy of freer attitudes about sex and the discussion of personal problems. In his 1924 textbook, *Behaviorism*, however, he contended that behavioristic studies of the child were replacing psychoanalysis, which was "based largely upon religion, introspective psychology, and Voodooism" (1924, p. 18).

Acknowledging the importance of general hereditary equipment, Watson nonetheless believed that nearly all important personality characteristics could be shaped for better or worse during infancy and early childhood. He prescribed rigid parenting schedules designed to mold children who would have no unnecessary fears, be independent, require little affection, and fit efficiently into the niches provided by society. Direct forerunners of contemporary behavior therapy were evident in the experimental creation and removal of phobias in young children.

"Habit clinics," sounding very Watsonian but begun by a psychiatrist, D. A. Thom in 1921, also sought to eliminate undesirable habits among preschoolers. By no means exclusively Watsonian in orientation, they did share the behaviorist view that early bad habits would lead to more serious personality problems later, when they would be much harder to treat.

Starting with his Harvard doctoral thesis in 1931, B. F. Skinner carried on the behaviorist fight against "mentalism." He viewed conditioned responses as the basic units of behavior and went further than Watson in rejecting not only mentalism but also the use of physiologic explanations to link stimuli and responses. By studying rats and pigeons, he sought to establish general behavioral laws independent of what was inside the organism.

Skinner applied his principles to the construction of a controlled modular environment for infants ("Baby in a box," 1945) and a fictional portrayal of a scientifically planned world in his novel, *Walden Two* (1948). He regards most current applications of his principles to education and therapy as nothing more than extrapolations from his animal research.

Another major contributor to the behaviorist tradition was Clark L. Hull (1884–1952). Like Skinner, Hull developed principles mainly from animal learning, but was willing to infer unobservable physiologic, and in humans, even mental phenomena. Hull's research on learning was done between 1930 and 1952, with his most important books being *Principles of Behavior* (1943) and *A Behavior*

System (1952). His general strategy of formulating hypothetical constructs from which testable deductions could be made, the specific constructs he proposed, and the interdisciplinary atmosphere he fostered at Yale's Institute of Human Relations attracted followers from diverse specialities. Through his many prominent students, Hull's influence spread to personality, social, clinical, and physiological psychology.

A major outgrowth of the Hullian tradition was John Dollard and Neal Miller's book *Personality and Psychotherapy* (1950), where they joined the traditions of psychoanalysis, learning theory, and social science. They accepted many Freudian concepts, but reinterpreted them in terms of Hullian learning theory. It thus appeared that a unified science of behavior, especially of personality and psychotherapeutic behavior change, was emerging.

As we will see in Chapter 10, behavior therapies based on Watsonian, Skinnerian, and Hullian principles have become widespread since the 1950s. Joseph Wolpe, Hans Eysenck, Arnold Lazarus, Albert Bandura, Donald Baer, Sidney Bijou, O. Ivar Lovaas, Gerald Patterson, and many others have adapted behavioral principles to therapy in new ways. Behavioral approaches have also been incorporated into the assessment and study of almost all aspects of disordered behavior.

Child Study

Like behaviorism, the child study tradition initially focused on normal functioning, but has often been extended to the abnormal. To assess abnormality in children, we need to study normal child behavior for two reasons.

First, children are always changing. It is therefore hard to judge whether new behavior is "abnormal" merely because it deviates from a child's previous behavior. Data on representative samples of normal children are needed to provide a standard against which to judge the behavior of a particular child.

Second, children seldom judge their own behavior as abnormal: parents, teachers, or others decide, often against the child's wishes, whether a child will receive special help. Unlike treatment of adults who help to specify their own goals, treatment of children aims to restore a developmental course defined by behavioral norms. For these reasons, the study of normal child behavior is essential for defining "pathology" in children, as well as for understanding how it comes about and can be corrected.

Interest in children *per se* began with theory and philosophic argument long before it led to systematic observation. For example, John Locke (1632—1704) argued that the mind of the newborn is a *tabula rasa*, or blank slate, whose development is determined by experience. Jean Jacques Rousseau (1712—1778) maintained that children are innately good and that their own natural activities follow an optimal course. Baby biographies were published in 1774 by Johann Heinrich Pestalozzi and in 1787 by Dietrich Tiedemann, but the first one with scientific significance was not published until 1877, when Charles Darwin sought to show that infant development revealed adaptive mechanisms paralleling those in the evolution of the human species.

G. Stanley Hall (1844−1924), founder of the first psychological journal in America (1887) and the first president of the American Psychological Association (1892), avidly promoted child study in the United States. Although his organizing and research activities had many facets, he focused mainly on *genetic* psychology. This referred not to genes but to the *genesis* or origins of behavior. It was virtually a synonym for the now more common term *developmental* psychology. As Hall and other genetic psychologists conceived it, genetic psychology is the study of how organisms develop and adapt to their environments, as viewed from an evolutionary perspective. In his early research, Hall used questionnaires to find out what children thought and knew at various ages. His monumental book on adolescence (1904) was especially popular, because it appealed to the new belief that psychology could produce a scientific system of education.

Many of Hall's students became prominent in the intelligence testing movement that followed publication of the Binet-Simon tests in 1905. One was Lewis Terman (1916), who developed the Stanford-Binet IQ test, the most popular American version of the Binet. Terman also undertook one of the first long-term studies of child development. This began in 1921 with 1,000 intellectually gifted children whom he then followed for 35 years (Terman & Oden, 1959), and Sears (1977) followed for an additional 15 years. Besides supporting the stability of IQ, the study debunked the myth that very bright children become adult misfits. Two other early longitudinal studies that are continuing to yield data on normal development are the Berkeley Growth Study, begun in 1928 (Bayley, 1968), and the Fels Institute Study, begun in 1929 (Kagan & Moss, 1962).

Research on mental testing reached a peak between 1914 and 1925, while other kinds of child study showed a sharp rise after 1920 (cf. Goodenough, 1934). Curiously, the belief in a genetically fixed IQ coexisted for many years with the environmentalist faith in the total malleability of personality. Although the environmentalism of the behaviorists continued to be a prominent force, Arnold Gesell (1880−1961), another of Hall's students, made maturationist views popular as well. From 1911 until 1948 at the Yale Child Development Clinic and after 1948 at the Gesell Institute, he and his colleagues amassed observational data supporting their view of development as a process of embryologic unfolding. In contrast to the behaviorist and psychoanalytic tendencies to blame children's problems on parents, Gesell argued that most child behavior reflects particular stages of development. Thus, the 2½-year-old "acts that (aggravating) way because he is built that way (Gesell & Ilg, 1943, p. 178)."

After World War II, child study diversified further. Research on socialization and personality development became popular, followed by new interest in infancy, language acquisition, cognitive processes, and social cognition. Methodological emphasis has also shifted from an almost exclusive reliance on observational and correlational approaches to more experimentation, multivariate analyses, a search for processes and mechanisms underlying behavioral change, and the direct testing of theoretical propositions.

At another level, twentieth-century interest in child study is reflected in the popularity of child care manuals and in the government's roles in relation to children. An early child-care manual, Holt's *The Care and Feeding of Children*, went through 13 editions between 1894 and 1929. It was called a "catechism" because it consisted of a long series of mother's questions and Holt's answers. The most popular later manual, Dr. Spock's *Baby and Child Care*, first appeared in 1945 and underwent continual revision thereafter.

The U.S. Government's official role in child care began when President Theodore Roosevelt called the first White House Conference on Children in 1910. Similar conferences of experts were called every ten years to make recommendations concerning child welfare. The United States Children's Bureau was founded in 1912 to compile statistics and literature on children. The successive editions of its *Infant Care Bulletin*, first issued in 1914, reflect cyclical changes in child-rearing attitudes since then. Compare, for example, the advice on masturbation in the 1914 and later editions:

> 1914: Masturbation—This is an injurious practice which must be eradicated as soon as discovered . . . as it easily grows beyond control. . . . If the mother discovers the baby rubbing its thighs together or rocking backward and forward with its legs crossed, she should divert him at once to some other interest. . . . Children are sometimes wrecked for life by habits learned from vicious nurses, and mother can not guard too strictly against this evil. . . . In the case of babies, the treatment consists in mechanical restraints. A thick towel or pad may be used to keep the thighs apart, or at night the hands may have to be restrained by pinning the nightgown sleeves to the bed, or the feet may be tied one to either side of the crib [p. 62].

> 1929: Frequently at an early age . . . children learn that pleasurable sensations can be aroused by handling or rubbing the genitals, squeezing the thighs tightly, riding on someone's foot, or in other ways accidently discovered. . . . This early period of what may be called sex awareness will pass away unless it is emphasized by unwise treatment on the part of adults. . . .
>
> Punishment and physical restraint are of little value in dealing with this habit, as they tend to fix the baby's attention on what he is doing and may strengthen the habit rather than stop it. . . . The best method of treatment is occupation and diversion. [p. 60].

> 1963: The baby explores his mouth and ears, and toes and hair with interest, learning about himself and how he feels. In similar fashion, he's going to explore other sensitive areas of his body, too. The baby is not bad when he does so. As he grows, his interests will move beyond his own body to the interesting world about him [p. 31].

Changes in recommendations about feeding have followed a parallel course from extremely strict four-hour scheduling of all babies to stressing the needs of the particular baby, and then to renewed emphasis on the benefits of scheduling. Recommendations on toilet training have shown one of the clearest cycles. In the 1914 edition of *Infant Care*, recommendations for bladder training were relatively mild and bowel training was hardly mentioned. By the 1920s, however, *Infant Care* recommended forcing strict regularity on the child's bowel movements, beginning in the first month of life. If the baby did not have bowel movements on schedule, they were to be induced by inserting a stick of soap into the rectum. Training was to be completed by the age of 8 months, at the latest. By the 1940s, the emphasis had shifted to catching the baby when it was ready to be trained, and soap sticks were considered harmful. By the late 1960s, however, Dr. Spock (1968) viewed the main source of training problems as modern mothers' fear of antagonizing their children, causing them to give up training at the first sign of resistance from the child.

During the early 1960s, the federal role expanded to include more active intervention on behalf of children. This new role was manifest in the founding of the National Institute of Child Health and Human Development (1963) to fund research and services, in expanded federal aid to education, and in special education programs for the disadvantaged, such as Head Start and Follow Through. In 1963, the federal government also launched a network of community mental health centers designed to replace reliance on large and distant state hospitals with treatment in people's home communities. The aim was to prevent the effects of institutionalization by enabling people to retain their family, work, and other community ties. It was not until 1975, however, that community mental health centers were mandated to serve children, and lack of funds has hindered development of children's services. The 1970s also saw massive deinstitutionalization of mental patients and the return of children with special needs to regular school classes (''mainstreaming''). Yet like many earlier innovations, these were often welcomed more for their promise of saving money than for their demonstrated efficacy in practice.

SUMMARY

Attitudes toward disordered behavior have followed a cyclical course in which innovations inspiring great hope have been adopted without careful assessment of how to optimize their effects. Haphazard application of the innovations has, in turn, led to bleak pessimism when they proved not to be panaceas. The innovations were then rejected without a fair test of what was worth keeping. Awareness of the historical context from which the developmental study of psychopathology is emerging may help us avoid repeating these cycles.

Figure 2-1 outlines the alternation of optimism and pessimism in relation to important ideas, therapies, and people since the late eighteenth century. The fluctuation of attitudes was seldom dictated by new knowledge.

The study of psychopathology became unified around Kraepelin's descriptive taxonomy at the end of the nineteenth century, but five new traditions led to a new

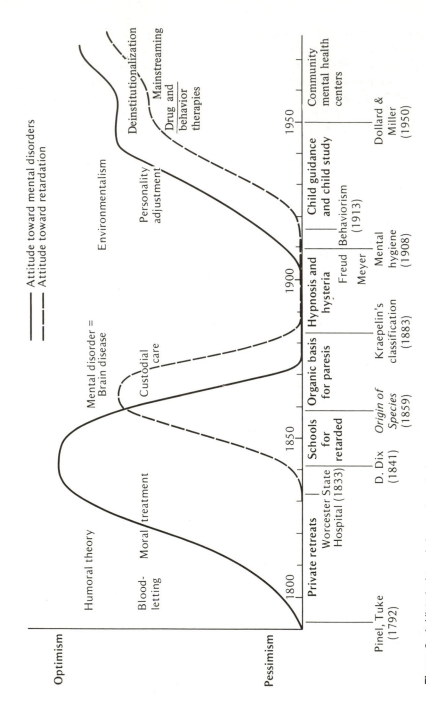

Figure 2–1. Historical trends in psychopathology.

30

diversity in the twentieth century: psychoanalysis, Adolf Meyer's commonsense psychiatry, the mental hygiene movement, behaviorism, and systematic study of children. Although these traditions have many things in common, they have spawned different viewpoints that have coexisted rather than being united in a systematic synthesis. Cycles are still occurring, but the current diversity of approaches makes it harder to identify a single common thread. No approach yet commands enough knowledge to sweep aside the others or to provide a synthesis that could be accepted by all.

SUGGESTED READING

Historical. Deutsch (1949) presents a readable, thorough, and authoritative history of the care and treatment of the mentally ill in America beginning in colonial times. Books by Bockoven (1963, 1972) and Grob (1973) also document the cyclical characteristics of practices and attitudes toward the mentally ill during the nineteenth century, with implications for the present and future. Maher and Maher (1979) depict the development of experimental research on psychopathology over the past century.

Psychoanalysis. Psychoanalytic theory will be discussed further in Chapter 9, but Ernest Jones's (1953, 1955, 1957) "official" biography of Freud is recommended for its appealing, though reverential, insider's account of the development of psychoanalysis and of Freud himself. An excellent one-volume abridgement by Lionel Trilling and Steven Marcus (1963) is available in a paperback. Contrasting perspectives on Freud and the psychoanalytic movement should also be read, such as those provided by Clark (1980) and Sulloway (1979).

Mental Hygiene. Clifford Beers's (1908) autobiographical *A Mind that Found Itself* has been reissued many times, most recently by Doubleday, with later editions updating the history of the mental hygiene movement. The book is worth reading not only for its historical significance and account of Beers's own psychotic experience, but for its intrinsic charm as well.

Behaviorism. Ullmann and Krasner (1975) provide a comprehensive behavioristic treatment of psychopathology that contrasts behavioral and other views, especially the medical and psychoanalytic. Beside behavioral techniques for dealing with disordered behavior, they present the historical context of diverging approaches to abnormality.

Child Study. Kessen (1965) reprints readings representing important views on children from the eighteenth century through Freud, Watson, Gesell, and Piaget, plus eloquent commentary on the historical trends they represent. An updated example of Gesell's approach is available in a book by Ames, Gillespie, Hains, and Ilg (1979). Wolfenstein (1953) documents the amusing cycles of childrearing advice given by the Children's Bureau's *Infant Care Bulletin* between 1914 and 1951.

CHAPTER 3

Perspectives on Development

In Chapter 2, we considered the historical diversity of views on children and their problems. In later chapters, we focus on particular disorders, theories, and therapies. Before we do, however, we need a framework within which to view these specific topics. Because no theory offers a total framework, we will seek an overview of development from birth to maturity as seen from several perspectives. These perspectives concern the biological, cognitive, social-emotional, and educational aspects of development. After a glimpse from each perspective, we consider the developmental tasks, problems, and competencies marking successive developmental periods. We conclude with an outline of issues arising at each period and the problems we face in tracking the developmental course of psychopathology.

THE BIOLOGICAL PERSPECTIVE

The most obvious developmental changes are biological. Neurobiological development and dysfunctions will be detailed in Chapter 7, but here we consider the role biological variables play in our overall developmental framework. All aspects of children's organic makeup can affect their behavior. Children's physical size, maturity, and attractiveness, for example, affect other people's reactions to them. People's reactions to a child's appearance, in turn, help to shape the child's self-image. Children who look much younger than their agemates may feel inferior or behave immaturely because they see themselves as falling short of their peers.

Physical handicaps can also affect children's self-images, as well as hindering their adaptation.

Even when children grow normally, biological changes continually raise new challenges. As detailed in Chapter 6, genes received from both parents determine not only the general growth plan, but also individual variations in physical features and in ways of reacting to the environment. From conception onward, genetic programming and experience both shape the organism's transactions with its environment. Each transaction with the environment shapes the assets and liabilities brought to subsequent transactions. Before birth, the quality of the intrauterine environment and the effects of maternal nutrition, disease, and medication affect the unfolding of the genetic growth plan. The ultimate impact of early hazards depends on the child's adaptive capacities and help from the environment. It has been found, for example, that congenital damage increases the risk of later behavioral problems in children having poor home environments more than in those having better environments (Werner & Smith, 1977).

In the first months after birth, survival requires the baby to progressively adapt its basic biological processes to the extrauterine existence. Human newborns are well equipped to learn from their environment (Lancioni, 1980), but they are far more dependent on adult caretakers than the young of other species. Mutual adjustment between the baby and its caretakers is needed to facilitate basic survival processes such as eating, elimination, sleeping, and temperature control. Individual differences in needs, sensitivities, biological rhythms, and communication patterns shape the adaptive tasks faced by infants and their families, as well as the specific resolutions of these tasks.

Temperament and Adaptive Style

Temperament and adaptive styles evident in infancy can affect the reactions a child evokes from others and the resulting conflicts and resolutions. This was shown in a longitudinal study of relations between infant temperament and childhood behavioral disorders (Thomas & Chess, 1977, 1980; Thomas, Chess, & Birch, 1968). Temperament was defined as:

> a general term referring to the *how* of behavior . . . the *way* in which an individual behaves . . . the *behavioral style* of the individual child. . . . Like any other characteristic of the organism, its features can undergo a developmental course that will be significantly affected by environmental circumstances (Thomas, Chess, & Birch, 1968, p. 4.)

The researchers rated babies on nine aspects of temperament: activity level, rhythmicity (regularity) of biological functions, approach to new stimuli, adaptability to new situations, threshold of responsiveness, intensity of reactions, positive vs.

negative mood, distractibility, and attention span-persistence. Of the 136 children in the study, 42 developed behavioral disturbances between the ages of 2 and 9 years. It was found that certain early temperamental patterns were overrepresented among the children who later developed behavioral disorders. For example, behavioral disorders occurred in 10 (71 percent) of the 14 children who initially showed what was called the *difficult child pattern*. This involved irregularity in biologic functions, withdrawal from new stimuli, slow adaptation to environmental changes, frequent expressions of negative mood, and high intensity of reactions. Although parents' behavior did not seem to *cause* these characteristics, parents differed greatly in their *reactions* to the demands placed on them by the difficult children.

> A frequent [parental] tendency . . . was to seek explanations based on psychodynamic theories that try to account for a baby's behavior in terms of the mother's attitudes. In these theories, a loving and accepting mother should have a happy and contented child, from which it follows that an unconscious maternal attitude of rejection could be the only explanation for a difficult screaming child. As a result . . . it was not unusual for the mother of a difficult infant who screamed frequently and who made all routines a crisis, to develop self-doubts and feelings of guilt, anxiety, and helplessness . . . .
>
> In attempting to eliminate her infant's frequent periods of loud crying, one mother with such feelings of guilt and helplessness redoubled her efforts to help him—walked him at night, spent long periods of time with him, and responded to his needs as soon as they were expressed. . . . The mother's attempts to quiet the child whenever he cried appeared at first to make the child happy and serene. However, such "happiness" lasted only as long as the mother continued to respond immediately to the child's demands. Once she failed to do so, the child's loud protests and slowness to adapt to demands made upon him made it clear that the mother's previous efforts had not served any constructive purpose. Rather, they had reinforced and perpetuated the child's negative and intense reactions by rewarding them each time they occurred (Thomas, Chess, & Birch, 1968, pp. 79–80.)

Even though parental behavior was not to blame for the difficult child pattern, differences in parental reactions did seem to affect the development of behavior disorders in these children. Compare, for example, the different outcomes in two children initially manifesting similar patterns:

> Both youngsters, one a girl and the other a boy, showed similar irregular sleep patterns, constipation and painful evacuations at times, slow acceptance of new foods, prolonged adjustment periods to new routines, and frequent and loud periods of crying. Adaptation to nursery school in the fourth year was also a problem for both children. Parental attitudes and practices, however, differed greatly. The girl's father was usually angry with her. In speaking of her, he gave the impression of disliking the youngster and was punitive and spent little or no recreational time with her. The mother was more

concerned for the child, more understanding, and more permissive, but quite inconsistent. There was only one area in which there was firm but quiet parental consistency, namely, with regard to safety rules. The boy's parents, on the other hand, were unusually tolerant and consistent. The child's lengthy adjustment periods were accepted calmly; his strident altercations with his younger siblings were dealt with good-humoredly. The parents waited out his negative moods without getting angry. They tended to be very permissive, but set safety limits and consistently pointed out the needs and rights of his peers at play.

By the age of five and a half years . . . the boy's initial difficulties in nursery school had disappeared, he was a constructive member of his class, had a group of friends with whom he exchanged visits, and functioned smoothly in most areas of daily living. The girl, on the other hand, had developed a number of symptoms of increasing severity. These included explosive anger, negativism, fear of the dark, encopresis [bowel incontinence], thumb-sucking, insatiable demands for toys and sweets, poor peer relationships, and protective lying. It is of interest that there was no symptomatology or negativism in the one area where parental practice had been firmly consistent, i.e., safety rules. (pp. 82–83)

Despite their importance, temperamental patterns often show marked changes during infancy (Kronstadt, Oberklaid, Ferb, & Swartz, 1979). It would therefore be wrong to label a child as intrinsically "difficult." Instead, certain features—such as chronically negative mood and intense reactions—may indicate a need for special care but should not brand a child for life (Terestman, 1980).

Beside increasing the risk of behavioral disorders, individual differences in adaptive style can affect the *types* of behavior problems manifested. The most universally identified dimension of adaptive style involves a contrast between *introversion* at one extreme and *extroversion* at the opposite extreme. As discussed further in Chapter 6, there is evidence for genetic influences on these adaptive styles (Matheny, 1980). Many studies have also revealed two broad syndromes of children's behavior problems that reflect pathological exaggerations of the introversive and extroversive styles (Achenbach & Edelbrock, 1978; Quay, 1979). The syndrome corresponding to the introversive style includes such problems as fears, bodily complaints, worrying, and social withdrawal. Because this syndrome mainly involves problems within the self, we will call it *internalizing,* but it has also been called "overcontrolled," "overinhibited," "shy-anxious," and "personality disorder." The syndrome corresponding to the extroversive style includes such problems as disobedience, aggression, delinquency, temper tantrums, and overactivity. Because it mainly involves conflicts with the environment, we will call this syndrome *externalizing,* but it has also been called "undercontrolled," "aggressive," "acting-out," and "conduct disorder." The internalizing and externalizing patterns may be shaped by environmental as well as biologic factors, and they come in various subtypes and mixtures. However, the two major patterns reflect pervasive differences in children's reactions to stress; these patterns, in turn, evoke very different reactions from people who deal with the children.

Maturational Course

Biological maturation poses many challenges for the developing child. These arise as changes in the central nervous system, endocrine system, sensory systems, musculoskeletal system, and specific organs foster new levels of behavioral organization. Motor milestones, such as reaching for objects, sitting, crawling, and walking, mark children's expanding control of their body and environment. These advances also enlarge children's perspectives on the world. Yet, each advance brings new risks as children's ability to harm themselves and their surroundings outruns their ability to foresee the consequences of their acts. From infancy onward, children's need to exercise their new accomplishments often conflicts with the need for protection against excessive challenges to their well-being.

Accompanying the motor advances that transform children's relations to the physical world are biologically based changes that transform social relationships. The baby's smile and gaze into people's eyes may be important survival mechanisms, for example, because they reward caretaking behavior by adults. During the middle of the first year, the emergence of anxiety in response to strangers and to separation from familiar caretakers also seems part of a biologically based system of attachment. This attachment system probably aids the survival of our species as well as fostering social development by keeping babies near their caretakers. Proximity is maintained both by babies' efforts to stay with their caretakers and by the effects of their distress cries in getting attention (Bowlby, 1980). A lack of these behaviors may herald deviant social development thereafter.

The emergence of speech and the ability to control sphincter muscles during the second year are additional biologically based advances with major consequences for social development. Failure to speak or control sphincters by about the age of 3 can bias a child's exposure to subsequent socializing experiences. Whether the child responds with aggression, withdrawal, or other behavioral problems, it would be wrong to blame slow maturation alone. Instead, slow maturation may contribute to behavioral disorders merely because it creates a gap between a child's abilities and those of the peer group. The psychological consequences of this gap, such as the ridicule, pity, overprotection, sense of failure, frustration, and inferiority feelings it engenders, are more direct causes of the behavior disorders. Exceptionally slow or rapid maturation of motor abilities, physique, and secondary sex characteristics can also bias later socializing experiences.

Specific physical handicaps can have diverse effects, even when the handicap itself is minor. Middle ear infections (*otitis media*), for example, can cause mild hearing loss during the preschool and early elementary school years. The infections are readily treatable with antibiotics; but because the Eustachian tubes of children's ears do not drain freely, fluid can accumulate to the point where it reduces the transmission of sound. This condition is usually reversible by medication or a minor operation. Yet when unnoticed, it can cut the child off from the more subtle aspects of normal communication. Beside hindering learning and school performance, this may make the child seem inattentive. Unless the real reason for the child's unresponsiveness is detected, negative interaction patterns may arise if others find the child responsive only when they raise their voices in anger. Undetected visual and perceptual-motor deficits can likewise hinder the acquisition of skills and, in turn, social interaction.

As biologic development proceeds, it brings challenges that, when successfully mastered, greatly enlarge the child's sphere of competence and interaction with the physical and social worlds. From the helpless infant emerges an organism capable of such complex activities as speech, roller skating, bicycling, dancing, and driving. Mastery of motor skills is so rewarding as to motivate amazing persistence in most children. Physical size and mastery of skills are also powerful status symbols that play a vital role in children's self-concepts and their capacities to withstand adversities and frustrations.

THE COGNITIVE PERSPECTIVE

Less obvious but just as important as physical maturation is cognitive development. In Chapter 8, we will discuss *rate* of cognitive development, but here we focus on cognitive *styles* and *levels*.

Cognitive Style

Like individual differences in temperament and adaptive style, there are individual differences in information processing. Differences in information processing that are not solely a function of ability or developmental level are known as *cognitive styles*.

One dimension of cognitive style is *impulsivity versus reflectivity*. This refers to the contrast between quick, careless responding to information versus slow, careful responding.

A second cognitive style dimension is *field independence versus dependence*. This marks a contrast between great independence from the influence of distracting cues in a perceptual context or "field" surrounding a target stimulus (field independence) versus great dependence on contextual cues.

Both these dimensions of cognitive style correlate with a variety of personality attributes. Reflective children, for example, generate more hypotheses in a learning task than impulsive children do (Achenbach & Weisz, 1975). Field-dependent people are especially sensitive to social cues, whereas field independent people are better at cognitive analysis (Witkin & Goodenough, 1980).

Both cognitive styles also correlate with developmental level, as indexed by chronological age (CA) and mental age (MA). In some groups, nearly *all* the variation in these cognitive styles can be accounted for by measures of cognitive level, such as MA (Achenbach & Weisz, 1975; Weisz, O'Neill, & O'Neill, 1975).

This means that conclusions about individual differences in cognitive style can be drawn only after the effects of cognitive *level* are separated from the effects of cognitive style.

Among children matched for cognitive level, however, it has been found that the impulsive-reflective dimension is related to the behavior problem patterns described earlier as *internalizing* and *externalizing*. Weintraub (1973), for example, found that disturbed boys manifesting internalizing problems were significantly more reflective than disturbed boys who manifested externalizing problems. Similarly, the introversion-extroversion dimension which parallels the internalizing-externalizing dichotomy, is related to cognitive stylistic differences in psychological defenses: Introverts tend to be sensitive to psychological threats, whereas extroverts tend to repress or ignore threatening material (Bauer & Achenbach, 1976). Because people's ways of cognizing experience may greatly affect moods and behavior, therapies have been devised to change aberrant cognitions (Beck, 1976). These therapies seem more effective than traditional psychotherapy and medical treatment for certain types of depression (Rush, Beck, Kovacs, & Hollon, 1977).

The Course of Cognitive Development

There are many ways of analyzing thought processes. *Information-processing* models, for example, portray thought processes as mechanical functions like those that computers employ to process information. To test a model's accuracy, the model is used to predict how human subjects should behave in an experiment if their thinking actually follows the steps specified by the model. Confirmation of the predictions supports the model.

The information-processing approach has stimulated experimental studies of thought processes that had previously eluded empirical investigation. However, these studies have focused mainly on attained levels of functioning. When *changes* in functioning have been studied, they have generally been changes occurring in response to experimental situations, although efforts have also been made to specify the changes required to account for developmental differences in information processing (e.g., Pascual-Leone, 1974).

Our most comprehensive theory of cognitive development—that of Jean Piaget—portrays cognitive functioning as an aspect of biological functioning. Although Piaget did not deal much with deviant development, his theory deserves our extended attention here, because it highlights so much that is central to human adaptive development.

According to Piaget, thought processes, like other adaptive processes, follow a maturational course rooted in the evolutionary history of the species. This means that cognition is at least partly structured according to a *genetically transmitted* plan. However, Piaget hypothesized that cognitive development is also shaped by three other factors. These are *experience* gained through interactions with the physical world; *transmission of information* by other people via language, modeling, and teaching; and a process Piaget called *equilibration*.

Three of the four contributors to development—maturation, experience, and social transmission of information—have counterparts in most theories. But the fourth contributor—equilibration—is unique to Piaget's theory. The central role of equilibration highlights aspects of development that most information-processing models fail to capture, even though Piaget agreed that thought processes form integrated systems resembling computers.

Piaget's (1977) concept of equilibration is based on his contention that cognitive development cannot be explained solely as a product of genetic programming and environmental contingencies. Instead, it involves progressive *construction* of new ways of knowing. One of the most striking characteristics of young children is their curiosity. This is evident when babies scrutinize their fingers, toes, and toys; when toddlers force their way into all kinds of forbidden but fascinating places; and when preschoolers incessantly question adults about the origin and meaning of things they encounter.

Although equilibration is hard to define, it signifies a crucial aspect of cognitive activity. The essence of this activity is a struggle to overcome gaps and contradictions in what is already known in order to gain more consistent, complete, and integrated knowledge. Because any problem can be conceptualized at many different levels, a cognitive equilibrium is often only temporary. Like scientists, children may be satisfied that they understand a phenomenon, but then find that new information requires new theories.

Why do humans struggle so for equilibration and then undermine their own solutions by seeking new information? We do not know. In fact, some children and many adults seem too readily satisfied with superficial solutions. Yet, *most* children (and at least some adults) derive great joy from cognitive mastery and will work hard for it. At the beach one day, for example, my 3-year-old daughter crouched for a long time at the edge of the retreating waves, occasionally tossing in a pebble with great care. At last, she jumped to her feet, clapped her hands over her head, and squealed with glee. When asked what she was doing, she replied, "I saw the water move some stones. And then I threw in stones to see if it always moves them. And it does! It *always* carries the stones away!" Here was a discovery that could delight a 3-year-old, even though her conclusion would eventually be undermined and revised as she became aware of the multitude of variables involved.

To understand each level of cognitive functioning, we need to view it in relation to the overall course of development. Using Piaget as a guide, we can divide cognitive development into the four periods outlined below. These periods are marked by major transitions in children's thinking. The transitions are gradual, however, and reflect developmental processes that are continuous rather than jumping suddenly from one level to another. Because thought processes typically advance *within* each period as well as during the transitions, the systems of thought hypothesized to characterize each period are far from static. But each developmentally early system lacks certain qualities that the more advanced systems possess.

The Sensory-motor Period. Piaget called the first 2 years the *sensory-motor* period, because cognitive functioning centers in motor responses to sensory inputs. Yet, even babies experiment with their world. At first, the baby focuses on its own body, waving its arms and wiggling its fingers and toes. Later, the baby focuses on other objects, banging them together to repeat interesting effects. As babies gain control of more aspects of their environment, they advance from efforts to repeat effects they have noticed by chance to more deliberate manipulation of their environment in order to see what will happen. As they expand their interactions with the world around them, babies progress from behavior based mainly on reflexes, to behavioral organizations that are precisely adapted to familiar stimuli, to behavior guided by thought.

Piaget described cognitive functioning in terms of *schemes*. A scheme is an *organized action* that can be applied to a variety of related contents. The first schemes are little more than reflexes to specific stimuli, but these rapidly grow into more refined and flexible procedures for attaining specific goals. In their first hours after birth, for example, babies suck reflexively at almost anything that touches their lips. As soon as they can coordinate their vision, actions, and sucking, however, they react to the sight of the breast or bottle with an organized sequence of head turning and reaching that culminates in sucking only when the appropriate object reaches their lips.

Piaget maintained that such overt behavioral schemes as sucking are prototypes of later mental activities. By the end of the sensory-motor period, children use mental schemes. These schemes are evident in children's use of physical actions to picture problem situations before they try solutions. As an illustration, Piaget described his 16-month-old daughter Jacqueline as she figured out how to extract a watch chain from the drawer of a matchbox that was almost completely closed:

> She gazed at the box with great attention, then opened and closed her mouth several times in succession, at first only slightly and then wider and wider. It was clear that the child, in her effort to picture to herself the means of enlarging the opening, was using as a 'signifier' her own mouth . . . (Piaget, 1962, p. 65)

At last, Jacqueline put her finger into the small slit and pulled the drawer open. Picturing the drawer's action by opening her mouth thus helped her understand the problem without manipulating the box itself.

Did Jacqueline merely imitate the drawer's action? Children may show imitation as early as the first weeks of life (Meltzoff & Moore, 1977). Yet, Jacqueline's act differed from earlier forms of imitation: She did *not* directly replicate an observed action. Instead, she enacted a mechanical principle that served to represent a problem situation. This helped her solve the problem. Piaget viewed behavior like Jacqueline's as a forerunner of mental representations that children normally achieve between the ages of about 18 and 24 months. During this period, replications of mechanical actions become independent of concrete stimulus inputs, to the point where children generate mental images that are not mere replicas of perceptual experiences, but that include strikingly original creations.

The Preoperational Period. Once children achieve mental representation, further cognitive development consists largely of changes in the types of mental schemes that can be constructed. Between the ages of about 2 and 6, mental schemes mainly embody physical actions, although actions can apply to imaginary notions, as well as realistic ones. Preschoolers' capacity for mental representation sets them off dramatically from children in the sensory-motor period. Mental representation enables preschoolers to recapture previous experiences at will. They can also transform their world through play and pretense, use language for symbolic communication, engage in mental problem solving, and envision future goals. Yet, preschoolers' mental representation lacks the systematic logic that emerges between the ages of about 5 and 7.

Because preschoolers lack interrelated logical operations, Piaget referred to the period from about 2 to 6 as the *preoperational period*. Lacking the logical operations and the faith in logic that enable older children to resolve contradictions between fantasy and logic in favor of logic, preoperational children can be overwhelmed by their own mental creations. This is when imaginary companions, monsters, witches, and dreams seem real, and when children cannot yet master them by means of logical "reality testing." Even fantasies originating in children's own minds or stimulated by well-meaning adults may get out of hand merely because children do not clearly distinguish between imagined dangers and the realities of the external world.

Yet, preschoolers' imaginative capacities often help them master frightening fantasies through the same processes that trigger the fantasies in the first place. This is illustrated by one 2-year-old's solution to the monsters he feared were under his bed. Chris's parents noticed that he stopped complaining of monsters after he began taking a big toy frog to bed with him. Strangely, though, he disliked the frog: He never cuddled it, and, after demanding it be put in his bed, he abruptly pushed it toward his feet. Finally asked why he wanted the frog so much and then pushed it away, he casually explained: "Dat fwoggie so ugly . . . it keep da monsters fwom comin' up da wall by me bed!" The conviction that the ugly frog would keep the monsters cowering beneath the bed sprang from the same cognitive system that spawned the monsters in the first place!

Fantasy companions are another product of the preschooler's cognitive system that can aid in emotional equilibration. Far more controllable than the real people in the child's life, such companions can be used to play out and master interpersonal stresses. They also play a key cognitive role in the mental dialogue that is first manifest when young children talk aloud to themselves but that becomes progressively more covert with age.

Preoperational thought opens worlds unknown to the sensory-motor child. The preoperational child masters the structure and function of language, an enormous vocabulary, a wealth of data about the physical and social worlds, and a vast array of problem-solving techniques. Yet the preoperational child still lacks the integrated logic that enables older children to reason about underlying relationships rather than being swayed by surface appearances. The transformation that ends the preoperational period between the ages of about 5 and 7 is not as obvious as the transition from the sensory-motor period; but a major advance is evident on many learning and problem-solving tasks.

The Concrete Operational Period. A mathematician friend of Piaget (1964) recalled a childhood experience of playing with some pebbles. First, he placed the pebbles in a row and counted them. Then he put the pebbles in a circle and counted them again. No matter how he rearranged them, he discovered that the number was always the same. He was fascinated by the regularity with which the number of pebbles remained the same despite changes in their arrangement. Yet, his discovery that the number of objects was independent of their dispersal upset his accustomed way of thinking about quantities.

The future mathematician's resolution of the problem illustrates an especially crucial transition in cognitive development. He realized that, no matter how the pebbles were arranged, their number *must* always be conserved. He had grasped what Piaget called *conservation of number*. *Conservation* refers to the ability to distinguish quantitative properties from aspects of appearance that do not affect quantity. A child's understanding of conservation is one sign of abilities that Piaget calls *concrete operational*. These abilities normally emerge between about the ages of 5 and 7.

Through hundreds of simple but provocative experiments, Piaget showed that preoperational children think that quantitative properties are altered by changes in superficial aspects of stimuli, such as when pebbles are rearranged or when the level of a liquid rises higher when it is poured from a wide to a narrow container. Concrete operational children, by contrast, insist that a quantity remains the same despite superficial changes in appearance. More importantly, they also give logical explanations for their judgment. When the level of liquid is higher after transfer to a narrower container, for example, they argue that the amount *must* still be the same because nothing has been added or taken away. Or they say that the higher level is due to the narrower diameter.

According to Piaget, concrete operational thought embodies a *system* of interrelated logical operations. This system enables children to think of phenomena in terms of quantitative relations. Although children are not consciously aware of this system, their ability to apply consistent logic to diverse domains distinguishes them sharply from preoperational children, whose thinking seems dominated by appearances and idiosyncratic associations.

Just as mental imagery challenges the toddler with imagined dangers, however, the advent of a powerful system of logic can spawn problems of its own. As the power of their concrete operational logic grows, children detect fallacies and inconsistencies in what their parents tell them. No longer accepting their parents' omniscience, children's discovery of parental fallibility may foster disappointment, defiance, and a sense of superiority toward their parents that they do not hesitate to express in argument and criticism. Because their new found logic helps them poke holes in parental pronouncements, concrete operational children may develop what Elkind (1979) calls *cognitive conceit* about their superiority to their parents. Yet, in calling this period *concrete* operational, Piaget stressed that the logic is limited almost exclusively to concrete, empirical relationships. It is only in the next period of cognitive development that this limitation is overcome.

The Formal Operational Period. Most adolescents can analyze problems in terms of complex hypotheses from which to deduce testable solutions. To illustrate this ability, Piaget gave adolescents four glasses of colorless liquid and a small bottle of liquid with a medicine dropper. Next, he showed them that drops from the small bottle would turn the liquid in another glass yellow. He then told them there was a way to produce the yellow color by using the liquid in the small bottle and the liquid in the four glasses.

Adolescents who have reached the formal operational period—about the age of 11 or 12—usually hit on a general strategy for trying out all possible combinations of the liquid in the bottle with the liquid in the glasses. They start by trying the liquid from the bottle with the liquid in Glass 1, Glass 2, Glass 3, and Glass 4. Then they use combinations, such as glasses 1 and 2 together, 2 and 3, and so on until they produce the yellow color. They thus translate the problem into an exhaustive array of combinations and deduce that trying out all the combinations will yield the solution.

Concrete operational children may grasp the principle of trying out combinations of the chemicals, yet they fail to see the problem as an *exhaustive* array of possible combinations. As a result, they mix the chemicals randomly. Or they systematically try only a few of the possible combinations. The adolescent's approach, by contrast, reflects an awareness of formal rules of logic in the abstract, rather than being restricted to the concrete relations between specific stimuli.

Abstract logic is also evident in adolescents' preoccupation with ideals, moral issues, philosophical questions, and social values. Whereas concrete operational children detect fallacies in their parents' pronouncements, formal operational adolescents question the whole system of values represented by their parents and society.

THE SOCIAL-EMOTIONAL PERSPECTIVE

People's emotions and interactions with others have always been central topics in the study of psychopathology. Psychoanalytic theory, for example, focuses on inferred mechanisms of emotional functioning, whereas social learning theory emphasizes behavior acquired via interactions with others. In later chapters, we will discuss the psychoanalytic and learning theories in detail, but neither approach offers an empirically based mapping of social-emotional development comparable to those available for biologic and cognitive development. Following a concentration on cognitive development during the 1960s and 1970s, however, research efforts turned toward the mapping of social and emotional development.

Social Cognition

A common approach is to apply what is known about cognition to social functioning. Under the general term *social cognition,* this approach focuses on how people think about themselves and other people, as opposed to how they think about impersonal phenomena. Because concepts of emotions, motives, rules of social behavior, and other people's perspectives require inferences at least as abstract as concepts of physical phenomena, cognitive operations like those hypothesized by Piaget have served as models for social cognition (Flavell & Ross, 1981). It appears that children's cognitive developmental level shapes their social cognition and that some aspects of social cognition develop in stages like those manifest in cognitive development. Moral judgment, for example, has been hypothesized to develop in a sequence of six stages, each of which presupposes progressively more advanced cognitive operations (Kohlberg, 1976). The understanding of psychological defense mechanisms also seems to require cognitive operations that emerge in a developmental sequence. For example, *projection,* whereby one's own motives are imputed to others, does not seem to be understood by children lacking formal operations (Chandler, Paget, & Koch, 1978).

Social-emotional development may involve processes very much like those underlying cognitive development. If we think in terms of Piaget's equilibration model, we can see how certain crisis situations simultaneously promote cognitive and social-emotional development. Consider, for example, Edward, a fourth-grader in a longitudinal study who had long idolized his older brother (Kraus, 1973, pp. 92–93):

> Edward's teacher asked the class to write on the theme 'My Happiest Day.' Edward wrote, 'My happiest day was when my mother came home with my brother. My brother almost died in an accident in Ottowa. And he came back on a train.'
>
> It was only then that we learned that during the previous summer, Edward's brother had married, and on a honeymoon trip had been involved in a severe accident in which his bride was killed and which hospitalized him for several months. When

questioned, Edward spoke of his brother glowingly, 'My brother came out of the hospital. He's home now. He's teaching me how to play the piano and gives me a lesson every Sunday.' A few weeks later, Edward's teacher was absent because of the death of her grandfather. When she returned she found the following note on her desk:

Dear Mrs. ⎯⎯⎯⎯⎯⎯,

     We know what happened from the principal. I know how you feel from when they called us from Canada about my brother. You still have yourself to think of so don't worry and come back soon.

Sincerely yours,
Edward

What must have been an extremely painful experience for Edward had apparently taught him not only to empathize with the feelings of people facing the loss of a loved one, but also to *think* about these feelings, to adopt the perspective of a person who might have them, and to take constructive action to help that person. Perhaps the main difference between the cognitive equilibration described by Piaget and social-emotional equilibration is that the major cognitive advances—involving principles of physical reality to which everyone is exposed—are more uniform and clearcut than are social-emotional advances. These involve aspects of experience that are more subtle and more varied from one person to another.

The Course of Social-Emotional Development

Without pinpointing the exact mechanisms, we can note advances in the social-emotional development of children in our culture. One of the best studied advances was already mentioned in connection with biologic maturation. This is the *attachment bond* between the baby and its caretakers during the first year. During their first year, most babies show behaviors that sustain caretaking, protection, and proximity by adults. The earliest of these behaviors are directed toward almost anyone who tends to the baby. They begin during the first few months with the making of eye contact and the "social smile" in response to attention. By about the age of 7 months, however, attachment behaviors focus more exclusively on familiar caretakers, especially the mother. These person-specific attachment behaviors include *separation anxiety*—distress evoked by the departure of a familiar caretaker; *stranger anxiety*—distress evoked by unfamiliar people; and reluctance to go very far from a familiar caretaker when crawling and walking enable the child to do so. Figure 3-1 depicts age changes found in the relation between indiscriminate early attachment behaviors and later attachment behaviors toward the mother and other familiar figures.

    Attachment is not a one-way street, however. Many of the baby's attachment behaviors, as well as the "cute" facial and body proportions characteristic of mammalian young, elicit caretaking behaviors from most adults. Variations in

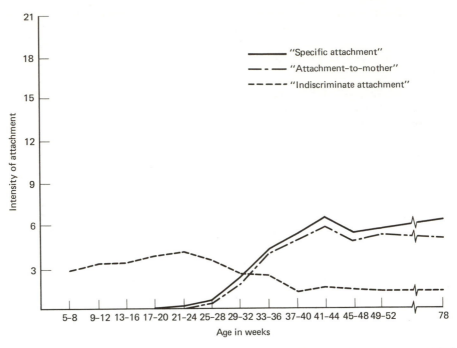

Figure 3–1. Developmental course of attachment behaviors. (From Schaffer & Emerson, 1964.)

parenting may in fact be caused as much by the intensity and timing with which babies elicit particular behaviors from their parents as by preexisting characteristics of the parents. Later parental socialization practices are also affected by specific characteristics of the children being socialized (Bell & Harper, 1977; Buss, 1981).

It has been hypothesized that failure to develop a secure sense of attachment during infancy hinders later social-emotional development (Bowlby, 1980). Consistent with this hypothesis, ratings of babies' attachment have been found to correlate with effective social interaction with peers during the preschool period (Lieberman, 1977). However, this does not necessarily mean that poor attachment *prevents* later competence, as features of the child, mother, or environment that hinder attachment may hinder later social behavior as well.

Following infancy, the child's social world expands to encompass more and more contacts with a widening circle of people under increasingly diverse circumstances. Social behavior grows more differentiated and sophisticated in ways that reflect a decline in egocentrism. During the preschool period, this is especially evident in children's play and speech. In their play, children progress from a preoccupation with their own activity that is minimally affected by the presence of other children, to parallel play in which peers pursue similar activities side-by-side, to cooperative play in which they carry out shared fantasies or work together on joint projects.

After the preschool period, continued social advancement is evident in sports and games involving complex rules, teamwork, and disciplined competition. By adolescence, most young people play a wide range of social roles in relation to their family, school, and peers of the same and opposite sex. In their speech, children advance from short utterances not adapted to their listeners, to progressively longer utterances of far greater grammatical complexity. These are finely tuned to the listener's age, kinship status, social role, familiarity with what the speaker is talking about, and history of social interactions with the speaker.

Increasing differentiation of interpersonal relations accompanies increasing differentiation of children's concepts of themselves. Increasingly differentiated self-concepts stem both from cognitive abilities to form articulated concepts and from the incorporation of social mores that set standards for self-evaluation. The increasing differentiation of the self-concept increases discrepancies between realistic self-appraisals and idealized aspirations. Thus, self-concept measures show increasing disparity between real-self and ideal-self concepts with advancing age, intelligence, and other aspects of development in both children and adults (Achenbach & Zigler, 1963; Katz & Zigler, 1967; Leahy & Huard, 1976).

The Family Context

The long span from birth to adult independence gives the family a crucial role in human development. The family is a major source of most children's early learning about emotions and social relationships. Emotional disorders are therefore often blamed on parent behavior. However, different children show very different responses to the same adult behavior, and adults respond very differently to different children, even when the adults try to be perfectly consistent (Yarrow, Waxler, & Scott, 1971). Furthermore, the entire family system develops and changes as parents and children age, economic circumstances change, and life crises are faced. Correlations obtained between child and parent characteristics are thus ambiguous with respect to the causal relations involved: They could reflect parents' responses to their children, the children's responses to their parents, or the similar ecological and genetic influences operating on parents and their children. When seeking the causes of social-emotional disorders, we must therefore be extremely cautious about assigning blame.

Early separation from parents has often been blamed for psychopathology (e.g., Spitz, 1950). There is no doubt that separation from parents can cause adverse emotional reactions in children, especially during the growth of attachment. Because separations are sometimes necessitated by hospitalization of children or loss of parents, the important question is whether separation per se inevitably harms children. Many hospitals now cushion the adverse effects of medically necessary separations by encouraging parents to room with their children and by providing "child life" programs staffed by people who play with child patients and attend to their emotional needs. Follow-up studies have shown that single hospitalizations of up to a week do not raise the risk of later disturbance, but that repeated hospitalizations may, especially in disadvantaged children (Quinton & Rutter, 1976).

The deprivation of parenting incurred in orphanages is likely to have greater effects. However, the effects depend on the quality of the institution, and most unadopted orphans in this country are now placed with paid foster families rather than in institutions. Because such children are often shifted from one family to another, they may not actually receive any more benefits of a family environment than in an orphanage. British studies have shown that young children reared in orphanages have no more behavior problems than working class children living with their biological parents. Yet orphans who were *adopted* had fewer problems than either group, and most of the children remaining in orphanages failed to form close attachments to adults (Tizard & Rees, 1975). A loving, stable, and intact family is unquestionably preferable to most of the alternatives. However, as single parent families are becoming more common, norms for social-emotional development based on traditional family structure may change.

THE EDUCATIONAL PERSPECTIVE

Every human society educates its young in self-care, survival skills, adult roles, and social customs. Until recently, few children in the world received any of their education in schools. Yet they were no less subject to the educational influences of their society, and only a fraction of the education of those who attend school is contributed by the official curriculum. In fact, the word *educate* and its Latin root (*educare* = to rear, to bring up) originally referred to a general fostering of development not confined to schooling. This broad concept of education underlines the important relations between individual development and society's practices toward its young.

Almost all interactions of children with other people can affect their educational progress. The archbehaviorist John B. Watson claimed that infant training practices decisively shape a personality for life. Watson may have overstated the case, but children certainly learn basic attitudes and behavior through interactions with their parents. Although children often react against parental values, they continue to show the effects of their parents' influence. Parents typically shape children's behavior pertaining to self-control, concern for others, acquisition of skills, and preparation for adult roles, including parenthood. They also help to determine how children react to the more formal educational institutions of their society.

In industrialized societies, the spread of preschool programs and the increasing proportion of the population obtaining advanced formal education give schooling an ever expanding role in personal development. Besides extending over a longer period and becoming a more decisive determinant of occupational roles, American schools have become arenas for political and ideological battles. The 1954 Supreme Court decision against segregated schools sparked the civil rights revolution, and the continuing ramifications have made schools the most sustained and bitter focus of the struggle. Conflicts over sex education, open classrooms, "back to basics," competency testing, funding of parochial schools, prayer in the classroom, homosexual teachers, and school taxes reflect major schisms in the larger society. These inevitably affect children.

On the other hand, schools have also been the focus of some of the most ambitious efforts to improve our society by enhancing the development of the young. The success of the first Russian Sputnik touched off massive efforts to reform mathematics and science education in the 1950s. In the 1960s, Project Head Start was the most widely acclaimed Great Society program and one of the few to survive the demise of Great Society legislation. The central role of schooling is underlined by the use of Head Start and related programs for health, nutritional, and social services to disadvantaged children and their families.

Following the example of Head Start, preschool education is now widely offered children who have any handicaps, including mental retardation, emotional disturbance, developmental lags, and physical disabilities, that may interfere with their educability. The effectiveness of such programs varies, but they are a reaction against piecemeal special services for specific disabilities that often went unattended until children had suffered several years of school failure. Another reaction against traditional special education is *mainstreaming:* this involves placing handicapped children in the same classes as their normal peers. In later chapters, we will consider the effects of mainstreaming and other educational approaches in relation to the different adaptive problems children have.

Schools also affect children through the role models and images of adult behavior they impart. Other than parents, teachers are the adults with whom children have the most contact, especially in relation to adult occupational roles. Children's perceptions of these roles, whether they reflect a love of learning, personal kindness and understanding, cynicism, incompetence, or whatever, can affect the children's views of their own futures as adults. Here too, the school functions as a microcosm of the larger society. During the 1950s and 1960s, for example, the educational system expanded in a spirit of optimism and innovation. This has been followed by a period of shrinking resources, school closings, and pessimism about the future. Schoolchildren of the earlier period could see education as a secure profession, whereas children of the later period who hope to follow in the footsteps of a respected teacher must face the prospect of being jobless. For children unfamiliar with other occupational options, the change in school atmosphere and opportunities may well affect their perspectives on adulthood.

Despite chronic criticism of schools, they nevertheless serve as a key focal point for children, even among the disadvantaged whose schools suffer the severest criticism. Some touching expressions of such children's feelings were recorded by Kraus (1973) when an inner city New York school he had been studying burned down. Even though the building was old and its pupils were disadvantaged, they were saddened by the loss of their school. A spontaneous outpouring of concern from parents, the local community, and the staff and pupils of neighboring schools showed how important their attachment to school was. As Kraus comments,

> This was a so-called inner-city, ghetto school with an 85% black pupil population. . . . How can we reconcile the (attachment) described here with Silberman's (1970) description of schools? These children did not respond as victims of a 'grim, joyless' place, 'oppressive and petty, . . . intellectually sterile and esthetically barren, . . . an appalling lack of civility . . . on the part of teachers and principals, (with) contempt they unconsciously display for children as children.'
>
> One must conclude that children do not see their schools in the same perspective as do adults. Adults have frequently overlooked the fact that the organization and structure of the school give many disadvantaged children a sense of stability and security to a degree which they do not enjoy in their homes. For the most part, expectations are clear and limits have been delineated. For those who are achievement motivated, the school is an avenue to the fulfillment of aspirations. (pp. 137–138)

DEVELOPMENTAL PERIODS

The biologic, cognitive, social-emotional, and educational perspectives discussed in the preceding sections cut across the entire span of development. Another way to view development is by dividing it into periods. Developmental theorists do this in several ways. Piaget defined developmental periods according to levels of cognitive functioning. Freud defined periods in terms of the inferred distribution of *libidinal* (sexual) energy, whereas Erikson placed more emphasis on psychosocial interactions. From marked changes in children's learning, behavioral theorists have inferred stagelike advances in covert mediating responses (Kendler & Guenther, 1980). Gesell (1954) described developmental stages in terms of the motor and social behaviors observed at each chronological age.

Each theorist has responded to a different aspect of functioning and has divided development into segments marked by changes in that aspect. Unfortunately, the various theories cannot be smoothly blended into a single comprehensive theory of development. As an alternative, we will consider the main tasks and problems characterizing periods that are demarcated by major transitions in the biologic, cognitive, social-emotional, and educational development of most children. The age intervals are merely rough approximations—deviations from them are common and most of the transitions are neither sudden nor uniform across all areas of functioning.

We will use the age of 2 years to mark the end of the earliest period—infancy—because it is about this age that increasing linguistic competence revolutionizes the child's relations with the surrounding world. The very word *infant* reflects the importance of language. It comes from the Latin *in* (not) *fari* (to speak). The attainment of linguistic competence is by no means an isolated achievement, however, as it depends on biologic (Lenneberg, 1967) and cognitive (Piaget, 1962) development, as well as social experience. Yet once language is acquired, it radically changes the way the child is viewed and the learning and social interactions that are possible.

The age of 5 marks the end of the next period—the preschool period—because it heralds another major advance in social status: the start of obligatory school attendance. It is also followed by changes in functioning that Piaget interprets as the onset of concrete operations, behavioral theorists interpret as advances in verbal mediation, and Freudians interpret as the latency period. The age of 11 is the next demarcation point, because it is followed by the biologic changes of puberty, formal operational thought, and more adult responsibilities in the educational and social spheres. Our final demarcation point is the age of 20, by which time most people are expected to face the world as adults.

Infancy: Birth to 2 Years

Despite their helplessness, babies master a phenomenal range of adaptive tasks. Research has revealed impressive perceptual and behavioral organization in very young babies, and their survival in the face of fantastically diverse childrearing customs attests to their adaptability. Figure 3-2 illustrates some of the emotional expression already evident at 4 weeks of age. Yet their adaptive progress depends on mutual communication with caretakers to obtain feeding, cleaning, and protection from danger, heat, and cold. Perhaps equally important are the development of a secure sense of attachment to caretakers (Bowlby, 1980), a sense of "basic trust" (Erikson, 1963), and concepts of permanent objects (Piaget, 1970). Human babies' dependence on caretakers is an outgrowth of an evolutionary history that has produced progressively larger but slower maturing brains, as well as adaptive behaviors that require social interaction, communication of symbolic reasoning, and long-term tutelage by adults (Freedman, 1974). In the course of development, human adaptive behaviors become more complex and powerful than those of any other species. However, the need for mutual adjustment between infants and their caretakers makes a certain amount of frustration almost inevitable.

At first, most frustrations arise from mismatches between the baby's biorhythms and its caretakers' abilities to understand and meet its needs. Typical problem areas include eating, especially adverse reactions to particular foods, vomiting, and digestive discomfort known as *colic*; defecation, especially constipation, painful bowel movements, and diarrhea; sleeping, especially failure to sleep

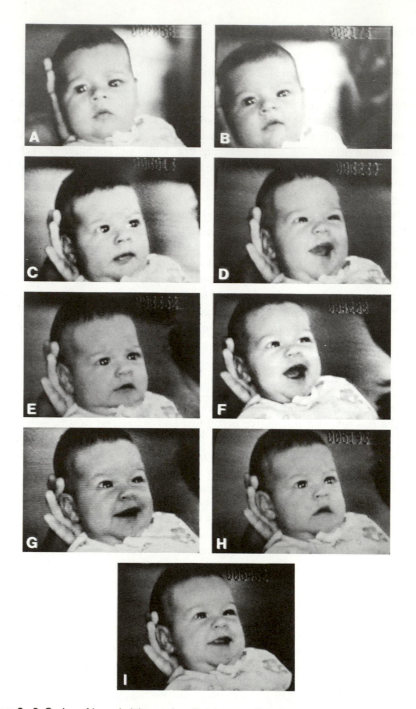

Figure 3−2. Cycles of brow knitting and smiling in infant E, at 4 weeks. A & B−looking to her mother's left; C-I−looking at her mother. (From Oster, 1978, p. 64.)

for extended periods at night; and excess crying without known cause. No baby is totally free of such problems. Yet, even when temporary, they can make parents feel guilty about causing them, overwhelmed by their inability to help their child, or angry for the trouble the child causes, occasionally to the point of child abuse. As a consequence, early problems in biologic functioning can establish conflictual patterns of parent—child interaction that persist long after the biologic irregularities are outgrown.

Toward the end of the first year, the sources of frustration shift to conflicts over efforts at socialization in the face of the child's increasing mobility and mastery of the physical world. Conflicts typically arise from parents' efforts to regulate dangerous and destructive behavior, aggression, feeding, bedtimes, and toileting. A survey of behavior problems encountered by a representative sample of California mothers, for example, showed that temper tantrums and stubbornness become increasing problems as children resist attempts at socialization (Heinstein, 1969). Both types of problem were reported for about 30 percent of children between the ages of 6 and 11 months, but they rose steadily to about 60 percent by the ages of 18 to 23 months. Toilet training problems also became prominent between 18 and 23 months of age, when they were reported for 55 percent of the boys and 51 percent of the girls.

Characteristic Syndromes. Beside the normal problems of infant biologic and behavioral adaptation, several distinctive syndromes become apparent during this period. Some have specific organic causes, including genetic abnormalities and damage sustained during pregnancy, the birth process, or the postnatal period. Many of the disorders known to have organic origins are manifested by a combination of physical abnormalities and mental retardation. Among these are *Down syndrome* (mongolism), which results from failure of the parental sex cell to divide properly and which causes a distinctive physical appearance and retarded mental development. *Rubella* (German measles) infections during the first months of pregnancy can also cause mental retardation, accompanied by deafness and blindness in the child. Several genetically transmitted metabolic disorders likewise cause mental retardation and physical defects evident in infancy. Examples are *phenylketonuria* (PKU) and *galactosemia*. Fortunately, these can now be prevented from causing retardation if they are diagnosed soon enough after birth to exclude from the child's diet those substances that cannot be metabolized. Brain damage caused by mechanical pressures, drugs, deprivation of oxygen, infections, and toxic chemicals during pregnancy or birth can also cause behavioral abnormalities, either with or without noticeable physical defects. Chapters 6 and 7 will deal with these disorders in more detail.

Beside syndromes having known organic causes, a second category consists of those that may involve organic predispositions but that are as yet diagnosable only in terms of behavioral abnormalities. Among these are the "difficult child syndrome" of temperament described earlier in the chapter, as well as developmental lags of unknown origin in social, cognitive, and motor functioning.

Perhaps the most mysterious behavioral syndrome originating in infancy is *early infantile autism*. Although extremely rare, its strangeness has made it the subject of controversy, speculation, and research far out of proportion to its frequency. Autistic children lack certain fundamental features of social development: They fail to look into other people's eyes, do not smile at other people, do not adopt appropriate body positions when held, do not cuddle, and do not show distress at separation from familiar caretakers. The later behavioral peculiarities of autistic children may result partly from their lack of the behaviors with which normal infants elicit parenting responses from adults. Specific theories, research, and treatment will be discussed in Chapter 12.

Other syndromes may result mainly from environmental factors, although biological factors and developmental level determine how a child will react to the environment. Children who lose their primary attachment figure at the age of 6 to 8 months, for example, become apathetic and withdraw their interest in people, food, and the environment. This syndrome is known as *anaclitic depression* (from the Greek *anaklinein* = to lean upon), because it results from losing the person on whom the child depends. If the attachment figure returns after an extended separation, the depressed child may turn away and avoid him or her, as if in anger for having been abandoned (Bowlby, 1973). Single separations for periods up to about a week do not appear to have long-term consequences, however (Quinton & Rutter, 1976).

Institutionalized babies who lack stimulation and attachment to individual caretakers also show apathy, disinterest in their surroundings, and slow motor development (Provence & Lipton, 1962). *Failure to thrive* and *psychosocial growth retardation* are somewhat similar conditions characterized by stunting of physical growth despite adequate nutrition. This stunting sometimes occurs in home-reared children who suffer neglect, inadequate stimulation, or abuse. Normal physical growth can be restored by an improved environment, but long-term follow-ups show high rates of educational and behavioral problems after such children go home, where conditions typically remain poor (Elmer, Gregg, & Ellison, 1969). This finding epitomizes a general dilemma raised by disorders caused by poor parenting: Even when a disorder can be alleviated, altering harmful home conditions or finding better homes is far harder.

The Preschool Period: Ages 2 to 5

By the age of 2, integration into a social world beyond the immediate family circle begins to replace rudimentary physical and social adaptation as a focus of developmental tasks. Advances in motility, self-care, thought, and play expand the child's social contacts and awareness. Despite conflicts over their inclinations to be either more or less grown-up than adults happen to wish, preschoolers normally make tremendous strides in acquiring social customs, self-control, motor skills, and concepts of cooperation and competition. They also develop pride in their own creations, learn to avoid danger, and become sexually curious and stimulated, often leading to sex play thinly veiled as games of "doctor" or "baby."

A powerful capacity for mental imagery, uninhibited as yet by logic, enables preschoolers to imagine themselves in many roles. They also create fantasy companions, mentally transform their world at will, and animate it with all sorts of creatures, both friendly and frightening. Highlighting preschoolers' talent for imaginatively shaping their world, Fraiberg (1959) has dubbed this period *the magic years*. The magic is evident both in the irrational problems preschoolers create for themselves and in their imperviousness to more formal logic. Thus, the child may create elaborate rituals for warding off imaginary dangers, but not accept the logic of parental prohibitions against crossing busy streets. Or parental prohibitions coexist comfortably with the prohibited behavior, as shown by 30-month-old Julia, whose mother found her dropping eggs on the kitchen floor while scolding herself sharply: "No No No. Mustn't dood it. No No No. *Mustn't dood it.*" (Fraiberg, 1959, p. 135).

A grasp of language is the preschooler's most obvious ticket of admission to the social world. The first word usually appears between about 12 and 18 months of age, with two-word combinations emerging between about 15 and 28 months. The timing varies widely, however, and children's capacities for mental representation and nonverbal communication often outrun their verbal skills. This was evident, for example, in a 2-year-old boy who was not yet using communicative speech at all. One day, he went to his great grandmother carrying a magnifying glass equipped with a built-in light that he had seen her use for reading. Holding the magnifying glass in front of his mouth, he pointed to the glass and made little coughing noises. It took awhile to get his message across, but then it became clear. He had been showing some cold symptoms, and a look through the lighted magnifying glass revealed a sore throat. Even though he could not speak, the boy could clearly conceptualize and communicate his problem.

As socialization becomes more dependent on language, failure to develop communicative speech by about the age of 3 can become a significant handicap. Speech abnormalities are often early signs of emotional, behavioral, or cognitive problems. However, most speech problems are merely with articulation of difficult sounds. The *j, fl, rp, rn,* and *shr* sounds, for example, are not mastered by 75 percent of normal children until the age of 5, and certain other sounds are not mastered by most children until the age of 7 or 8 (Templin, 1957). Difficulty in being understood and ridicule for "baby talk" can cause children to avoid particular words, stop speaking altogether (*elective mutism*), or respond with general withdrawal or aggression. Stuttering also emerges during the preschool period; although it usually subsides, it is sometimes a life-long affliction that is very hard to overcome.

Of the problems reported by mothers of normal preschoolers in Heinstein's

(1969) survey, most involved conflicts over socialization. Contrary and stubborn behavior were the most common, being reported for approximately 60 percent of 2- to 5-year-olds. Temper tantrums declined steadily from their high point of about 60 percent between 18 and 23 months to 41 percent for boys and 27 percent for girls at age 5. Problems in toilet training showed a much steeper decline, from about 50 percent around the age of 2, to 11 percent at age 3, and 5 percent at age 5. Disobedience, resistance to bedtime, wanting too much attention, and feelings that were easily hurt were all reported for 30 to 50 percent of 2- to 5-year-olds. Another study reported that 67 percent of 3-year-old girls had significant fears (Macfarlane, Allen, & Honzik, 1954). This dropped to 36 percent by age 5, whereas fears were reported for about 45 percent of the boys throughout the preschool period.

Characteristic Syndromes. Infantile autism is often not diagnosed until the preschool period when a child either fails to speak or shows peculiarities of speech such as a mechanical repetition or "echoing" (known as *echolalia*) of other people's speech. The echoing is so literal that autistic children call themselves "you" and other people "I". Although the reasons are poorly understood, the development of speech during the preschool period is related to the long-term outcome of autism. Autistic children who still lack communicative speech by age 5 generally show the least improvement later (discussed further in Chapter 12).

More common than the peculiarities of autistic children, however, are disorders that affect speech in other ways. Severe congenital deafness, for example, prevents language development. Milder hearing loss may go unnoticed until poor speech and inattention to the speech of others become evident during the preschool period. How severely a hearing loss handicaps language and personality development hinges on whether the loss is noticed and remediated. Too great a reliance on the philosophy of "he'll grow out of it" may cause neglect of impaired hearing that hinders learning.

In children with normal hearing, speech can be impaired by defective neural functioning. Partial impairment is called *dysphasia*, whereas total impairment is called *aphasia*. The impairment may be in the comprehension of speech (*receptive* dysphasia or aphasia) or the production of speech (*expressive* dysphasia or aphasia). In some cases, impairment reflects a developmental lag that is eventually overcome, but it can also reflect progressive neurologic disease or a permanent defect.

Where peculiarities of speech accompany deviant social and emotional functioning, the speech problems may be but one facet of emotional disturbance or environmental deprivation. Where they accompany general lags in other adaptive functions and cognition, the cause may be mental retardation.

Speech problems are a common focus of referrals for psychological assessment in the early preschool period, but behavioral problems become the main focus of referrals by the age of 4 or 5. At this point, the increased referrals of children to mental health services enable us to distinguish more clearly between behavior problems that characterize referred children and nonreferred children. As an example, 73 percent of referred 4- and 5-year-old boys are reported to be *nervous, highstrung, or tense,* as compared to only 17 percent of nonreferred boys (Achenbach & Edelbrock, 1981). By contrast, certain other behaviors, such as showing off and clowning, are reported for about the same percentage of referred and nonreferred boys (80 percent versus 77 percent).

Referral of a child for mental health services is usually a culmination of much distress rather than a response to a single isolated behavior. Knowing which behaviors are more typical of referred than nonreferred children should therefore help us distinguish between behaviors that are relatively normal for a particular age and those associated with significant maladjustment. Table 3-1 lists the 10 problems

Table 3-1   Problems Showing the Biggest Differences Between Clinically Referred and Nonreferred 4- and 5-year-olds

	Boys		Girls	
Problem	Referred (%)	Nonreferred (%)	Referred (%)	Nonreferred (%)
Can't concentrate	81[a]	35	66	24
Can't sit still, restless, or hyperactive	87	44	72	38
Cries a lot	59	16	66	20
Destroys things belonging to others	61	14	(29)	(12)
Disobedient at home	(92)	(56)	81	48
Disobedient at school	54	16	43	6
Doesn't get along with other children	65	20	59	15
Doesn't feel guilty after misbehaving	65	25	(49)	(26)
Nervous, highstrung, or tense	73	17	56	18
Screams a lot	57	16	51	15
Sudden changes in mood	63	19	66	18
Sulks a lot	(48)	(12)	51	11

[a]Numbers indicate the percent of children for whom the problem was reported. Children in the referred and nonreferred groups were matched for race and socioeconomic status. Parentheses indicate that the item was not among the 10 showing the biggest differences in percent for that sex.
Source: Data from Achenbach & Edelbrock, 1981.

showing the greatest differences in the percentage of referred and nonreferred 4- and 5-year-olds for whom parents reported the problems. Most of the problems reflect conflicts with the advancing standards of conduct expected of children as they age.

As an example, 5-year-old Andrew was referred for psychological assessment by the preschool program he was attending. His main problems in the preschool were temper tantrums, impulsivity, aggression, and an inability to concentrate, despite impressing people with his brightness. When seen at the clinic, Andrew was distressed by the disorder of the toys in the playroom, remarking that some "bad person" must have done it. Overconcern with neatness was also evident during psychological testing, when he became so upset with his drawing performance that he tore up his work. Marred by his impulsivity, the drawings that he did complete scored at a much lower level of ability than he achieved on a vocabulary test.

Concern over sexual and toilet matters was inferred from Andrew's activities with Play Doh. He first made a tall tower and then said "That's *not* a tower, it's a *cave* where an old witch lives." He then hollowed out its base. As the tower toppled over, he remarked how soft it was, like wax, and brought a piece to the psychologist, pointing out how very soft it was. He suddenly had to go to the toilet, "*Really* this time (he had urinated earlier), to make a pie. Like if you're out in the woods and there's no bathroom and you have to find some place or do it in your pants so nobody will see." While on the toilet, he said, "It's so soft."

Andrew's behavior clearly seemed to reflect a struggle over conformity to the perfectionistic demands of his mother. His unmanageable behavior seemed likely to become more debilitating as further educational and social development required more effective self-control.

The Elementary School Period: Ages 6 to 11

When children reach the age of compulsory education, the school becomes a central arena for both achievement and conflict. School vastly expands children's social contacts and exposure to social customs, as well as their opportunities for acquiring academic skills and knowledge. The cognitive advances described by Piaget in terms of concrete operations are displayed on many fronts. Not only can children solve problems like those posed by Piaget, but they also delight in exercising their new reasoning powers. Unlike younger children's play, their play is full of complex rules, whether in the realm of team sports such as baseball, individual competition such as marbles, lengthy board games such as Monopoly, or neighborhood clubs. New abilities are also evident in children's eager pursuit of skills, collections, and money with which to buy cherished possessions. Recognition of the principles of monetary exchange can further stimulate children to use their maturing organizational abilities in entreprenurial ventures such as lemonade stands, neighborhood carnivals, and light jobs.

School expands children's sphere of action, but it also imposes demands for conformity to its routines and to an age-graded sequence of academic achievement.

Despite individual differences in motivation, adaptive style, home environment, cognitive development, and maturation of perceptual-motor functions, children must master the complex skills of reading, writing, and arithmetic within a few short years. Even when the initial causes are temporary, failure to progress academically can instill inferiority feelings and fear of intellectual challenges. It is not surprising, therefore, that mental health referrals rise sharply during the elementary school years and that many of the referrals are precipitated by school problems. This is especially true for boys, who are referred to mental health clinics more often than girls during the elementary school period, particularly at ages 8 and 9 (Rosen, 1979; Rosen, Bahn, & Kramer, 1964). Of the problems reported during the elementary school period, Table 3-2 shows that the biggest difference between referred and nonreferred boys is in *poor school work*, while the second biggest difference is in *disobedient at school*. The difference in *poor school work* for referred and nonreferred girls ranked third behind the difference for *unhappy, sad, or depressed* and *doesn't get along with other children*. Other problems of this period, especially those showing big differences between referred and nonreferred boys, also reflect failure to adapt successfully to the school culture, and it is in relation to school that the most characteristic syndromes of the period emerge.

Characteristic Syndromes. Hyperactivity (also known as *hyperkinesis*) has been the most widely publicized and controversial syndrome of the elementary school period. Under the assumption that attention problems are primary, the term *attention deficit disorder with hyperactivity* is also used (American Psychiatric Association, 1980).

At one time believed to reflect brain damage, hyperactivity is often treated with stimulant drugs. Yet, many children labeled hyperactive show little evidence of brain damage. Other treatment approaches have therefore been tried, including behavior modification, special educational programs, and special diets. Because the label has encompassed such diverse children, there may, in fact, be subgroups who have different causes and require different treatments. We will discuss research on causes and treatments in Chapter 11, but it is worth considering the developmental context of hyperactivity here.

Children's activity levels typically decline from the preschool to the elementary school period (Routh, Schroeder, & O'Tuama, 1974). Among those labeled hyperactive, however, inattention and nonconformity to school routines is often more crucial than overactivity in winning them the label. Organic dysfunction can contribute to the problem behavior in some children; but in others the behavior may reflect a failure to learn how to replace the spontaneous activity tolerated in preschoolers with the quiet attentiveness expected in elementary school. This failure may be due partly to temperamental characteristics that hinder sustained attention. It may also be due to lack of motivation to master academic skills, lack of parental modeling and reinforcement of behavior necessary for academic achievement, or school demands that conflict too sharply with a child's abilities. In some cases, slow

Table 3-2   Problems Showing the Biggest Differences Between Clinically Referred and Nonreferred 6- to 11-year-olds

Problem	Boys		Girls	
	Referred (%)	Nonreferred (%)	Referred (%)	Nonreferred (%)
Can't concentrate	(87)[a]	(45)	72	29
Can't sit still, restless, or hyperactive	83	35	(67)	(32)
Demands a lot of attention	82	33	86	42
Disobedient at home	85	39	82	39
Disobedient at school	72	19	(50)	(10)
Doesn't get along with other children	66	16	66	13
Feels worthless or inferior	66	16	62	14
Lying or cheating	65	19	(61)	(19)
Nervous, highstrung, or tense	69	23	69	21
Not liked by other children	(47)	(7)	50	7
Poor school work	70	15	57	6
Temper tantrums or hot temper	(68)	(32)	64	21
Unhappy, sad, or depressed	57	8	67	10

[a]Numbers indicate percent of children for whom the problem was reported. Children in the referred and nonreferred groups were matched for race and socioeconomic status. Parentheses indicate that the item was not among the 10 showing the biggest difference for that sex.
Source: Data from Achenbach & Edelbrock, 1981.

but not defective organic maturation may delay a child's readiness to sustain attention to unstimulating tasks. In other cases, what is labeled "hyperactivity" may include aggressive, demanding, or manipulative behavior, where high activity is a minor aspect at most. Such behavior may be labeled hyperactive merely because this has become a popular wastebasket term for unmanageable behavior.

No matter why a child is labeled hyperactive, failure to acquire age-appropriate social and academic skills indicates a need for help. Follow-ups of hyperactive children have shown that learning and behavioral problems often persist, even when medication reduces overactivity (Loney, Kramer, & Milich, 1979). Reducing overactivity thus does not ensure normal social and educational development. In fact, treatment may sometimes harm a child's self-image without helping the child master developmental tasks, as illustrated by young David Hill's complaint:

> Last year my teacher was always saying, 'Did you take your pill David?' and pretty soon that dumb Susan Neilson wrote her poem on me and this is the poem. I heard it a million times already:
> David Hill
> Did you take the pill
> That makes you work
> And keeps you still?
> Take your pill, Hill. (Ross & Ross, 1976, p. 102)

Learning problems that are not just byproducts of behavioral problems also prevent children from meeting school standards. Academic failure can result from such diverse factors as lack of self-control, lack of motivation for school learning, delayed maturation of the perceptual-motor functions involved in reading and writing, emotional problems, mental retardation, and specific learning disabilities.

Teachers are in a good position to detect learning problems, and their response can be a major factor in the outcome. Slow maturation or mild mental retardation can lead to fear of failure unless expectations are adjusted to a child's abilities and the child is helped to use those abilities without feeling inferior because he or she is slower than other children. Yet, teachers cannot singlehandedly alleviate all obstacles to academic achievement. Where emotional or behavioral problems persist, either as a cause or a result of learning problems, teachers can point them out to parents and initiate referrals for help. But the major responsibilities will typically rest with the family and mental health workers.

Where learning problems are confined to a particular skill, such as reading, writing, or arithmetic, they may reflect organic abnormalities that make certain types of information processing difficult despite normal intelligence. These disorders can be diagnosed through cognitive, perceptual-motor, and neurological tests, and usually require special educational programs to teach the afflicted skill.

> Sometimes minor organic deficiencies contribute to problems of social adaptation as well. Nine-year-old Danny, for example, was referred for assessment because of sudden angry outbursts at his teacher and classmates. These contrasted sharply with the shy, withdrawn, overpolite pattern he had long displayed.
>
> During the assessment interviews, Danny appeared very stiff, anxious, and ill-at-ease. He initiated no conversation whatever. In response to questions, he often wrinkled his brow, seemed to struggle with an answer, and then produced a brief, uninformative reply. Sometimes, after wrinkling his brow and moving his mouth, he lost the struggle entirely and produced no answer at all, settling back with an empty gaze as if no one had spoken to him.

Interviews with school personnel revealed that Danny had always been a social isolate, had problems learning arithmetic, and seemed to forget things he had previously learned. His major classroom problem was during group music, however, where his inability to stay with the group in songs led to his outbursts.

Psychological testing revealed perceptual-motor deficits that could account for his difficulty in music and might be indicative of organic problems interfering with arithmetic as well. It also appeared that Danny's longstanding social withdrawal masked a great deal of anger at others. This anger boiled over when his perceptual-motor problems made it impossible for him to cope with group singing.

School can also evoke severe anxiety. Most children fear school at some time in their lives, especially after absences for illness or holidays. However, when children are so afraid as to panic or show physiologic reactions such as vomiting, fear of school is known as *school phobia*. We will discuss treatment in later chapters, but most views are similar on two points: (1) the phobia may reflect fear of separation from parents more than fear of school per se; and (2) the child must be returned to school as soon as possible, because resistance increases with the length of successful avoidance of school. There is also evidence that school phobias—as well as other phobias—tend to be more easily treated in elementary schoolchildren than in adolescents, for whom phobias may be a sign of severe personality disorder (Kennedy, 1965; Miller, Barrett, & Hampe, 1974). When accompanied by other fears and expressions of anxiety, unhappiness, and inhibition, a school phobia may indicate a persisting pattern of internalizing problems. However, follow-up studies have shown that children manifesting such patterns are better adjusted in adulthood than children who show more antisocial, externalizing problem patterns during the elementary school period (Robins, 1979).

Adolescence: Ages 12 to 20

Portrayals of adolescence often center on the physiologic changes of puberty. There is no doubt that these changes confront adolescents with major adaptive tasks. Not only the growth of sex organs and sex drive, but also changes in voice and body shape, body hair, acne, and sudden growth spurts saddle adolescents with new self-images that can evoke bewilderment, ambivalence, or distaste. The upsurge in sex hormone production can have more subtle effects on emotional and cognitive functioning as well (Ehrhardt & Meyer-Bahlburg, 1975; Petersen & Wittig, 1979). Because the timing of the major physical changes normally varies from about the age of 10 to 17, adolescents can suddenly seem very different from their friends. Those who mature very early or late may feel like misfits and seek companions who are more like them in biological development than age. Acute sensitivity to peer opinion may also spur withdrawal or antisocial behavior, as well as desperate efforts to win acceptance via extreme styles of dress and behavior.

Sexual maturation and its social-emotional byproducts are often blamed for the turmoil and rebellion ascribed to adolescents in modern western societies. Freud, in particular, portrayed the adolescent upsurge of sexual drives as shattering a period of quiescence and as reawakening the Oedipal conflicts imputed to the preschool period. Erik Erikson (1963) broadened the psychoanalytic perspective by stressing identity crises in adolescents. According to Erikson, not only the massive bodily changes of puberty but also the need to forge a stable adult role trigger a conflict that he labels *identity versus role confusion*. The long lag between physical maturity and full adult social status and the lack of clearcut social roles for adolescents in western societies make it hard to adopt well-integrated identities with respect to sex role, occupation, and personal values. From both the psychosexual and psychosocial perspectives, then, adolescence is viewed as an inherently stressful period.

Relatively neglected in psychoanalytic theories have been the contributions of cognitive advances to both the problems and competencies of adolescence. Adolescents apply complex logic to previously unquestioned moral, religious, social, and political conventions. This can contribute to identity problems provoked by puberty and increasing awareness of role alternatives in relation to sex, school, and vocational preparation.

> Adolescent conflicts between personal values, sexual urges, and intricate logic are illustrated by 14-year-old Charles. Brought to a mental health clinic at the urging of his parish priest, Father Riley, Charles had been making ever longer and more elaborate confessions, repeatedly returning to the confessional to correct his earlier confessions. He also spent hours after confession trying to explain to Father Riley the "escape hatches" he detected in the confessional procedure.
>
> When interviewed, Charles reported that his problems had started when he realized that the normal confessional did not cover sinful intentions that had been held back in previous confessions. This raised problems of grammatical tense in confessing sins. The many possible permutations of tense, intention, category of behavior, category of sin, and degree of sinfulness could leave escape hatches for sins which could not be properly confessed. The possible permutations were so numerous that Charles envisioned them stretching out in front of him to infinity. Looking at obscene pictures and getting erections were the sins that concerned him the most.

Despite the problems raised by new reasoning abilities, these abilities also equip adolescents to appreciate literary and dramatic portrayals of the issues they face and may instigate a quest for ideals beyond the ken of younger children. Adult privileges and responsibilities can provide additional incentives to strive for mature modes of adaptation.

Although both cognitive and psychosocial factors can contribute to adolescent problems, they are more varied than the cognitive and psychosocial components of the preceding periods. Higher levels of formal operational thought, for example, may be affected more by individual differences in ability and experience than earlier cognitive levels; and the *application* of formal operational thought to social and personal questions may vary even more. Likewise, the adolescent identity crises so exquisitely portrayed by Erikson (1963) may not affect youth lacking occupational and social role choices. Longitudinal studies show that many adolescents do not experience severe turmoil and that psychopathology does not mushroom as an outgrowth of adolescent developmental conflicts (Offer & Offer, 1975; Rutter, Graham, Chadwick, & Yule, 1976).

Mental health referrals do rise during adolescence, however. The rate for girls is substantially higher than at earlier ages, but still below that for boys, whose rate differs little from their earlier peak at age 9 (Rosen, 1979; Rosen et al., 1964). Yet Table 3-3 shows that many of the problems differentiating best between referred and nonreferred early adolescents are like those reported earlier. In addition, many clinically referred adolescents have longstanding problems that merely take on new forms (Rutter et al., 1976).

Toward late adolescence, several major disorders emerge in significant numbers for the first time, including adult forms of schizophrenia, depression, and antisocial behavior. Furthermore, maladaptive behavior spreads beyond the purview of school and mental health agencies to include criminal activity, chronic drug and alcohol abuse, suicide, unwed pregnancy, and "dropping out."

Characteristic Syndromes. Adolescent delinquency has traditionally received the most public attention. Some offenses (known as *status offenses*) are not necessarily antisocial but are illegal because of the age status of the individual. Examples of behaviors prohibited because they are considered harmful to the young include truancy, running away from home, drinking, and sexual relations. On the other hand, delinquencies such as theft, vandalism, illicit drug use, and assault would be illegal at any age.

Spurred by peer pressure, feelings of anger or rebellion, or just a quest for thrills, many adolescents commit isolated delinquencies without adopting delinquent values or life-styles. For other adolescents, delinquent behavior is but one aspect of definite psychopathology. Still others, however, develop a coherent delinquent identity that sets them at odds with the official values of their society. In Chapter 13, we will discuss causes and outcomes of the different types.

Depression is another problem often ascribed to adolescence. Clinical syndromes of depression include pervasive sadness, slowing of activity, withdrawal of interest, suicidal thoughts, sleep problems, and a sense of guilt. Syndromes of this sort have also been identified in children (Achenbach & Edelbrock, 1978), although they are less common than in adults. Especially rare in children are adult forms of manic-depressive disorders in which depression alternates with euphoria, flight of ideas, and heightened energy levels. In adolescents, depressed feelings are often associated with other problems, although these feelings do not necessarily signify a depressive disorder. Likewise, occasional manic feelings do not necessarily indicate a manic disorder.

Many adolescent depressive episodes are brief, but some are serious enough to

Table 3-3   Problems Showing the Biggest Differences Between Clinically Referred and Nonreferred 12- to 16-year-olds

	Boys		Girls	
Problem	Referred (%)	Nonreferred (%)	Referred (%)	Nonreferred (%)
Can't concentrate	79[a]	29	(60)	(24)
Can't sit still, restless, or hyperactive	69	26	(46)	(18)
Disobedient at home	(73)	(32)	79	20
Disobedient at school	64	20	(57)	(11)
Doesn't feel guilty after misbehaving	66	19	(58)	(13)
Feels or complains that no one loves him/her	(48)	(12)	66	16
Feels worthless or inferior	61	11	62	13
Hangs around children who get in trouble	52	8	(54)	(7)
Impulsive or acts without thinking	(71)	(34)	72	24
Lying or cheating	64	17	72	12
Nervous, highstrung, or tense	74	21	74	21
Poor school work	78	19	65	9
Sudden changes in mood or feelings	(61)	(21)	76	26
Sulks a lot	(43)	(10)	61	10
Unhappy, sad, or depressed	60	10	77	12

[a]Numbers indicate the percent of children for whom the problem was reported. Children in the referred and nonreferred groups were matched for race and socioeconomic status. Parentheses indicate that the item was not among the 10 showing the biggest differences in percent for that sex.
Source: Data from Achenbach & Edelbrock, 1981.

warrant clinical concern. Suicide attempts in particular almost always precipitate mental health referrals. These attempts vary greatly in motivation and earnestness, but there is a rapid increase with age in completed suicides during adolescence: from about 170 per year at ages 10 to 14, to about 1,600 at ages 15 to 19, and more than 3200 at ages 20 to 24 in the United States (Holinger, 1979). This means that no suicide attempt should be taken lightly. However, it is usually possible to distinguish between attempts motivated mainly by a specific experience such as the break-up of a love affair, those that are intended to affect others by winning sympathy or inducing guilt, and those that involve breaks with normal reality. Females appear more prone to the first two types, whereas males, who actually complete three times as many suicides as females, appear more prone to the latter type.

By contrast, another disorder that emerges in adolescence reaches life-threatening proportions much more often in females than males (Bemis, 1978). This is a cessation of eating known as *anorexia nervosa* that can be fatal in extreme cases. Anorexia has been hypothesized to reflect a fear of sexual maturation. According to this view, eating is shunned to prevent normal pubertal changes. Biologic factors have also been implicated in severe food aversions, however (Bemis, 1978).

Many adolescents experience feelings of unreality and *depersonalization,* that is, of being outside oneself. These feelings can be symptoms of schizophrenia. But in schizophrenia, they are also accompanied by a weakening of "reality testing" to the point where subjective experiences are not distinguished from external reality and where distortions coalesce into irrational belief systems (*delusions*) and unreal perceptual experiences (*hallucinations*). Schizophrenia is also characterized by a flattening of the emotions, withdrawal from other people, absence of pleasurable experience, and occasionally by unusual sleep cycles and suicide attempts. Some of these symptoms can appear before adolescence, but severe preadolescent disorders that are sometimes labeled schizophrenia are not necessarily related to adolescent or adult schizophrenia (discussed further in Chapter 12).

A DEVELOPMENTAL FRAMEWORK

We have considered the course of development from the biologic, cognitive, social-emotional, and educational perspectives, as well as from the perspectives of successive developmental periods. It may now be helpful to have a summary of the various aspects of development. Table 3-4 outlines the major cognitive periods hypothesized by Piaget. It also shows the psychosexual phases postulated by Freud and the psychosocial conflicts postulated by Erikson, whose theories will be detailed in Chapter 9. Along with these theoretical outlines of cognitive, psychosexual, and psychosocial development, Table 3-4 lists the important competencies normally acquired, the behavior problems reported most often, and some of the clinical disorders arising in each period.

Table 3-4 A Developmental Overview

Approximate Age	Cognitive Period	Psychosexual Phase	Psychosocial Conflict	Normal Achievements	Common Behavior Problems[a]	Clinical Disorders
0–2	Sensory-Motor	Oral	Basic Trust vs. Mistrust	Eating, digestion, sleeping, social responsiveness, attachment, motility, sensory-motor organization	Stubborn-ness, temper, toileting	Organically based dysfunctions, anaclitic depression, autism, failure to thrive
2–5	Pre-Operational	Anal	Autonomy vs. Shame and Doubt	Language, toileting, self-care skills, safety rules, self-control, peer relationships	Argues, brags, demands attention, disobedient, jealous, fears,[c] prefers older children, overactive, resists bedtime, shows off, shy,[c] stubborn, talks too much, temper, whines	Speech and hearing problems, phobias, unsocialized behavior
		Phallic-Oedipal	Initiative vs. Guilt			
6–11	Concrete Operational	Latency	Industry vs. Inferiority	Academic skills, school rules, rule-governed games, hobbies, monetary exchange, simple responsibilities	Argues, brags,[b] can't concentrate,[b] self-conscious, shows off, talks too much[c]	Hyperactivity, learning problems, school phobia, aggression, withdrawal
12–20	Formal Operational	Genital	Identity vs. Role Confusion	Relations with opposite sex, vocational preparation, personal identity, separation from family, adult responsibilities	Argues, brags[b]	Anorexia, delinquency, suicide attempts, drug and alcohol abuse, schizophrenia, depression

[a]Problems reported for at least 45% of children in nonclinical samples.
[b]Indicates problem reported for ≥45% of boys only.
[c]Indicates ≥45% of girls only.
Source: Achenbach & Edelbrock, 1981; Heinstein, 1969.

To provide a more detailed picture of the ways in which behavior problems vary in relation to children's age, sex, and clinical status, Figure 3-3a presents behavior problem scores computed from behavior checklists filled out by parents of clinically referred and nonreferred children (Achenbach & Edelbrock, 1981). The scores consist of the sums of *0*'s, *1*'s, and *2*'s assigned by parents to 118 behavior problems, where *0* = *not true* of their child, *1* = *somewhat or sometimes true,* and *2* = *very true or often true.* As Figure 3-2a shows, the total behavior problem scores of clinically referred children average about three times as high as scores of nonreferred children.

Figures 3-3b through 3-3d show the percentage of children for whom parents reported each of three specific problems as present (i.e., the parents scored them either 1 or 2). These particular problems were selected from the 118 because they illustrate three different patterns: *Fears* (Figure 3-3b) show a general decline with age but minimal differences between groups. *Impulsivity* (Figure 3-3c) shows a general decline for clinically referred boys but the opposite trend for clinically referred girls. Reports of alcohol or drug use (Figure 3-3d) were negligible until the age of 12 and 13, when they began climbing for referred adolescents, especially girls. The different patterns evident in Figures 3-3b through 3-3d demonstrate that the clinical significance of a particular problem depends on the age and sex of the child. Furthermore, some problems, such as specific fears, have often been considered ominous but may be more characteristic of particular developmental periods than of disorders severe enough to warrant clinical referral (Miller et al., 1974). Other problems that have come to be expected of particular developmental periods, such as alcohol and drug use, may, by contrast, be more indicative of maladaptation severe enough to warrant referral than of normal developmental phases, at least during early and midadolescence.

To depict relations between behavior problems and children's age and sex from yet another angle, Figure 3-4 shows referral rates to three different agencies for children aged 2 through 16 in Aberdeen, Scotland (Baldwin, Robertson, & Satin, 1971). Although the absolute rates may differ in other times and places, these data are of particular value because in Aberdeen these agencies were responsible for virtually all children, and all children served by each agency could be identified through a centralized case register. We can therefore see the overall rate of referral, as well as the rate of referral to each type of agency. The *guidance* group consisted mainly of children with significant educational problems; the *probation* group consisted of first offenders appearing before the juvenile court; and the *psychiatry* group consisted of children referred for emotional and behavior problems, excluding the mentally retarded.

In comparing the male and female rates per thousand children, note that the scale on the vertical axis ranges from 0 to 30 in intervals of 5 for males in Figure 3-4a but from 0 to 12 in intervals of 2 for females in Figure 3-4b. The much higher rates for males are typical of those found in most places. Psychiatric referrals

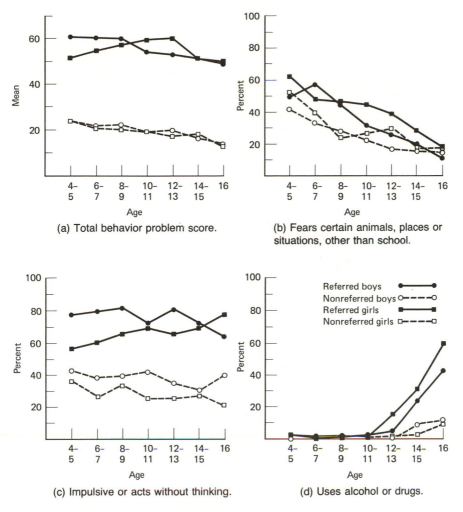

(a) Total behavior problem score.

(b) Fears certain animals, places or situations, other than school.

(c) Impulsive or acts without thinking.

(d) Uses alcohol or drugs.

Figure 3-3. Behavior problems reported by parents of clinically-referred and nonreferred children aged 4-16. (From Achenbach & Edelbrock 1981.)

increased for females during adolescence, but remained below those for males until the end of adolescence. The higher referral rate for males is especially clear when all types of referrals for behavior problems are combined. Referral rates for mental retardation, learning disabilities, disorders of speech, hearing, and vision, neurological impairment, and many other organic conditions are generally higher for males as well (Mumpower, 1970). We will explore reasons for these sex differences in Chapter 6.

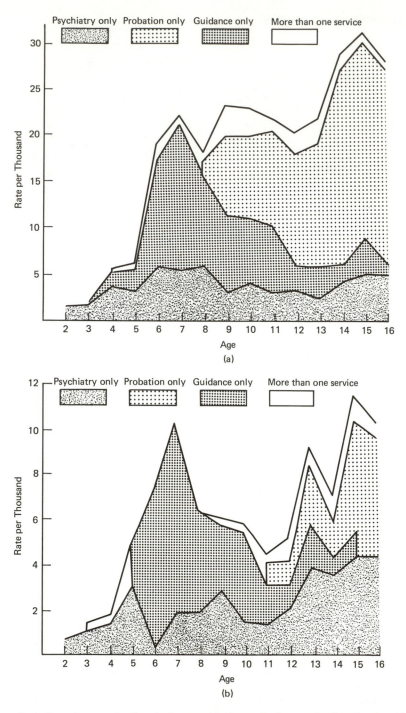

Figure 3-4. Annual rate of referrals for psychiatric, probation, and educational guidance services in Aberdeen, Scotland. *(a)* Annual rate of referrals per 1000 males, *(b)* Annual rate of referrals per 1000 females. (From Baldwin, Robertson, & Satin, 1971.)

Because Aberdeen children having educational problems were referred for educational guidance, we can see from Figure 3-4 that most referrals during the early elementary years concerned school. Schools are therefore especially important foci for intervention during this period. However, the rise in probation cases during the later elementary and adolescent years shows that the juvenile court plays an increasingly central role in handling deviant behavior during these years.

The Longitudinal Course of Disorders

The foregoing overviews reflect the behavior of children of different ages. Yet the behavior of individual children does not necessarily follow the course implied by these age differences. In Figure 3-4, for example, most referred 6-year-olds had primarily educational problems and most referred 15-year-olds were delinquent; but this does not *necessarily* mean that 6-year-olds with educational problems are typically delinquent at the age of 15. Nor are the age differences necessarily the same across time and locality. The proportion of girls brought to juvenile court for delinquency has been increasing faster than for boys, for example (Adler, 1977).

To learn more about the *course* of disorders, we need to study the same individuals *longitudinally* as they develop. As we will see in Chapter 5, this is hard to do. Yet it is important to supplement our cross-sectional overviews with longitudinal findings, even though they are far from definitive.

How do childhood disorders turn out? Follow-ups of children referred for mental health services concur in showing that externalizing behavior is more often followed by poor outcomes than internalizing behavior (Robins, 1979).

Nevertheless, the long-term implications of particular behaviors vary greatly from one developmental period to another. Certain *changes* in behavior from one period to the next may also predict adult status better than straight-line predictions from a single period taken in isolation (Peskin, 1972). The search for precursors of disorders is therefore focusing increasingly on developmental sequences that may either be early manifestations of particular disorders or that may predispose people to later disorders. However, until we know more about the relations between successive developmental periods, we will continue to face discontinuities in the definitions of disorders from one period to another.

SUMMARY

This chapter outlined a developmental framework within which to view specific disorders, theories, and treatments. We first considered the course of development from the *biological, cognitive, social-emotional,* and *educational* perspectives. Each perspective highlights a particular series of developmental challenges, hazards, and advances, as well as persisting patterns of adaptation that shape individual development.

Beside viewing the course of development from the various perspectives, we also viewed it in terms of four developmental periods that are demarcated by changes in biological, cognitive, social-emotional, and educational functioning. During *infancy,* the major developmental tasks involve basic biological and social adaptation. Problems often reflect mismatches between the infant's biorhythms and its caretakers' abilities to meet its needs, as well as conflicts over socialization. Many infant disorders stem from either specific organic roots or general organic predispositions, although environmental deprivation can also impair behavioral and organic development. During the *preschool period,* integration into the larger social world becomes the major focus of developmental tasks. Linguistic competence becomes a particularly important achievement, and speech disorders often instigate clinical referrals.

During the *elementary school period,* school becomes the central arena for both achievement and conflict. School learning and behavior problems instigate sharp increases in mental health referrals, especially for boys. During *adolescence,* major biological and cognitive changes, new social roles, and the need to make vocational choices raise a host of challenges to personal identity. Schizophrenia, antisocial behavior, certain depressive conditions, drug and alcohol abuse, and suicidal tendencies make their appearance for the first time on a significant scale during adolescence, although they are not necessarily direct byproducts of the stresses of adolescent development.

Behavior problems and educational, psychiatric, and court referrals show differing patterns by age and sex. Longitudinal data generally show worse outcomes for children who manifest antisocial, "externalizing" behavior than for children who manifest "internalizing" problems of inhibition and anxiety. However, we need longitudinal research on developmental sequences to assess the precise course and outcome of each disorder under various conditions.

SUGGESTED READING

Temperament. Thomas, Chess, and Birch's (1968) longitudinal study of infant temperamental styles has given temperament an important place in developmental views of psychopathology. The implications have been amplified by Thomas and Chess (1977, 1980) and have led to studies of genetic influences (Matheny, 1980) and variability in temperament (Kronstadt, et al., 1979).

Cognitive and Social Development. Ginsburg and Opper (1979) provide a good overview of Piaget's theory of cognitive development. Interfaces of cognition with social and emotional development are presented in books edited by Collins (1980) and Flavell and Ross (1981). Elkind (1979) illustrates ways in which cognitive development affects children's interactions with their families and society. Bowlby (1973, 1980) has synthesized psychodynamic, ethological, and cognitive approaches into a theory of the role of early attachment in social-emotional development and psychopathology. Selma Fraiberg's (1959) *The Magic Years:*

Understanding and Handling the Problems of Early Childhood is a sensitive, psychoanalytically oriented guide to the first six years of life that highlights the delightful role of magical thinking in social-emotional development. Maccoby (1980) provides a comprehensive overview of social development, especially the parent-child relationship.

CHAPTER 4

Basic Issues in Developmental Psychopathology

The study of psychopathology can evoke sharp disagreements. These are sometimes due to different theoretical allegiances. But disagreements also stem from differences in values, professional training, and responsibilities. In this chapter, we consider sources of disagreement in views of children and their problems. Then we consider issues arising from contrasting models of psychopathology and from different ways of defining disorders, their causes, and their outcomes.

ON DOING YOUR OWN THING

Educators, guidance counselors, nurses, police, probation officers, judges, psychiatrists, psychologists, pediatricians, social workers, child-care workers, foster parents, neighborhood paraprofessionals, and recreation workers all work with troubled children. They differ in training, responsibilities, social roles, and attitudes toward children. Their work settings determine the ages and kinds of children they see, the duration of their contacts, and their relations with the children and other occupational groups.

Let's take a child named Sammy as an example. A teacher has Sammy in class every day and may refer him to a guidance counselor or school psychologist. Sammy may commit a crime and be held by the police. He may be placed under the supervision of a probation officer. He may undergo a court-ordered psychological or psychiatric examination, along with family casework by a social worker. He may receive psychological testing and outpatient psychotherapy at a clinic with a psychiatrist, psychologist, or social worker as therapist. If his family situation is very bad, Sammy may be placed in a foster home. If his crime is serious or he seems badly disturbed, he may be sent to a reform school, state hospital, or residential treatment center. Here he may see mental health professionals, but he will probably have more contact with house parents or child-care workers. This sequence may sound far-fetched, but many children experience one just like it.

Even the most objective, sensitive, and consistent observers would see different behavior if they saw Sammy in all the different settings. Each setting and Sammy's expectations about it affect his behavior. He would also be affected by the way he sees the observers, whether as disciplinarian, teacher, cop, parent figure, or shrink, for example.

Various occupational groups have developed very different views of children. Even if Sammy's behavior is consistent, different workers would describe him differently. This can cause them to work at cross-purposes when dealing with a child. Later, we will discuss differences that have crystallized into theoretical models for psychopathology, but first we consider some practical sources of disagreement about children's problems.

Personality of the Worker

Memories of their own childhoods—as happy, sad, recent, or remote, their relations with parents, siblings, and other children—shape adults' reactions to children. These reactions may lead to the extremes of using the way things were "when I was a kid" as a standard for the way things *ought* to be, or of wanting children "to have all the things I never had." Childhood memories also spark feelings about particular children: Adults identify with some children or certain problems while reacting against others as they did when they were children. Family roles of spouse and parent further affect reactions, producing either oversensitivity or "blind spots" to factors important in their own lives. And our own offspring have an especially powerful impact on our picture of children's hour-by-hour development, joys, and conflicts.

Types and Ages of Clients

Concepts of psychopathology are shaped by the kinds and ages of clients served. Professionals working with very young children, for example, cannot conclude much from verbal interviews with the children, from their peer relations, or from school performance. Instead, judgments of young children are typically based on norms for physical maturation, language skills, and sensory-motor abilities. In thinking about psychopathology, these workers emphasize organic maturation much more than, for example, workers dealing with adolescents in a residential setting. Here, such concepts as impulsivity, ego weakness, and need for structure seem more pertinent. Contradictory views often arise when broad generalizations are based on experience with a narrow range of ages or types of problems.

Types of Settings

Disturbed children are treated in diverse settings. These settings differ greatly in goals, the conditions under which children come to them, and their relations to society at large. They also differ in staff and whether their primary obligations are to parents, government, social agencies, or the children themselves. These differences shape attitudes toward psychopathology. Settings that depend on parents to bring their children, for example, usually emphasize ongoing family dynamics more than those where parents are less involved. The principal types of settings are described next.

Child Guidance Clinics. These were long the primary agencies for troubled children. Most receive public funds and have fee scales adjustable to their clients' incomes. In the traditional model, dating from about 1915, parents are interviewed by a psychiatric social worker, diagnostic testing is done by a psychologist, and psychotherapy by a psychiatrist. However, all three professions do therapy in most clinics, and other approaches, such as behavior modification, parent training, conjoint family therapy, and group therapy, are widespread. The child guidance model is also followed by some private practitioners and community mental health centers that offer children's services.

Treatment typically involves weekly visits for several weeks to several years. Guidance clinics treat a wide range of disorders, but their emphasis is on fairly specific and limited problems. Since children's disorders are often viewed as reactions to parental behavior, the parents are a primary focus of treatment. School consultations are also common. Most children seen in guidance clinics are between 4 and 16 years of age. Younger children are less often referred to mental health settings. Their disorders are handled more by pediatricians and child development clinics. Adolescents over 16 are often referred to adult services unless specialized adolescent services are available.

Residential Settings. Residential treatment centers are designed to provide a therapeutic milieu for severely disturbed children. They are staffed by child-care workers, teachers, social workers, psychologists, psychiatrists, and recreation workers. Treatment models vary, but most emphasize gradual socialization within a protective environment. Unfortunately, there is a shortage of good centers and most are extremely expensive. Some residential settings for disturbed children are sections of adult mental hospitals that provide little more than custodial care.

Institutions for the severely retarded also range from strictly custodial to those with active training programs for returning the retarded to society. An innovation dating from the 1960s is the community-oriented regional center. Regional centers are designed to serve the retarded in their home communities by offering sheltered workshops, recreation, day care, and temporary residential care.

Medical Hospitals. Some medical hospitals, especially children's hospitals and those connected with universities, have child psychiatric wards. These are generally for diagnostic, emergency, and short-term residential care. Other medical hospitals house disturbed children on pediatric wards. In many places, hospitals offer the only refuge for such emergencies as suicide attempts, traumatic experiences, or sudden breakdowns. Yet their antiseptic, illness-oriented atmosphere is frightening and may be insensitive to the special needs of disturbed children.

Educational Settings. Probably more troubled children are dealt with in educational settings than all other settings combined. This is partly because schools must take responsibility for many who never receive help elsewhere. Most schools now have special services for retarded, learning disabled, emotionally disturbed, and perceptually handicapped children. Many also employ school psychologists, social workers, and consulting psychiatrists to back up teachers, the frontline personnel. However, specialized school services for troubled children face opposition due to cost-cutting, resistance to labeling children as deviant, and pressures to keep children in regular classes (mainstreaming).

Disturbed children usually have academic problems and academic problems themselves can lead to disturbance. Hence, the educational process looms large in developmental psychopathology, and the school is a key agency. Yet, there has been a tendency to use "emotional disturbance" as a label absolving schools of further responsibility for a child.

Beside special services within regular schools, there are also special schools—both public and private—to serve children having fairly serious problems. Schools exist for children with brain damage, behavior disorders, perceptual-motor handicaps, retardation, reading problems, and learning disabilities. Some residential centers for disturbed children are called schools and emphasize educational techniques.

Correctional Settings. Another group of facilities includes detention centers and "reform schools," although they are known by various euphemisms. Generally punitive, some are still controlled by police and correctional agencies.

Detention centers provide short-term incarceration of juveniles caught by the police. The best among them employ mental health personnel to diagnose problems and help juvenile courts make decisions. Many, however, are merely cell blocks for holding juveniles, sometimes for months on end. Juvenile courts are intended to be flexible in deciding how to help youngsters instead of simply meting out punishment. Yet, options are often limited by inadequate treatment facilities and lack of well-tested alternative placements. Judges are therefore often left to choose between supervision by probation officers or incarceration in reform school.

Most reform schools employ some mental health workers, but few are really organized around therapeutic or educational goals. Evidence reviewed in Chapter 13 shows that inmates often leave prepared more for a life of crime than for continuing their education or coping constructively with society.

Training and Career Orientation

Not only differences between professions and between settings, but also the training and career orientations of individual workers shape their views of children's problems and the approaches they adopt. A key factor is the relative dominance of interests in teaching, research, or practice. Those not interested in teaching or research are most likely to be found in private practice or service agencies. Workers interested in teaching or research may carry on some practice or consulting but have primary appointments in educational or research settings. Various combinations of interests occur, however, and most workers pursue different combinations at different stages in their careers.

A key difference in the training of mental health professionals is that Ph.D. programs in psychology provide research training, whereas master's degrees in psychological testing, school psychology, special education, and social work, as well as medical and psychiatric training, are oriented mainly toward practice. However, many Ph.D. psychologists are practitioners, and nonresearch Doctor of Psychology (Psy.D.) programs are offered by independent schools of professional psychology and some universities. Conversely, some psychiatrists and social workers undertake research.

CONCEPTUAL MODELS FOR PSYCHOPATHOLOGY

A conceptual model is an analogy. It may use a theory established in one science to depict the subject matter of another science. Or it may be a set of concepts developed especially to describe a particular phenomenon. The model of atomic structure as an array of physical particles, for example, has been especially useful. Most models of psychopathology have not provided very explicit links to observable phenomena, however. Instead, they serve mainly as sources of concepts, metaphors, and technical terms. Despite disagreements among adherents of different models, the models are not mutually exclusive. Each may enhance our understanding of some facet of developmental psychopathology.

The Medical Model

The medical model represents disordered behavior by analogy with physical disease. It helped free psychopathology from demonology in the eighteenth century and justified scientific study of disordered behavior in the nineteenth century. This model fostered the use of such terms as *pathology, treatment, symptom, cures,* and *patient,* as well as *mental health, hygiene,* and *illness.* Psychiatric taxonomy still reflects Kraepelin's (1883) medical model of mental disorders as disease entities with organic causes.

But how far should the medical analogy be carried? Most "mental illness" is observed as disordered or unusual behavior, and few think this behavior is caused only by physical malfunctions. It is, therefore, argued that the concepts of illness, patient, and treatment are misleading when used in this way (Szasz, 1970). Even where organic factors cause mental retardation, for example, educational and psychological methods are used to optimize behavior. Similarly, hyperactive children are sometimes diagnosed as having "minimal brain dysfunction," but the brain dysfunction is seldom proven, and modifying their behavior is the main goal.

The medical model may be apt for some disorders. But too broad an application implies that all disorders have organic causes or that psychological factors are not important. It can also imply that disordered behavior is merely a sign of underlying disease, and that troubled youngsters should be regarded as helpless "patients" until "cured" by "treatment."

The Psychodynamic Model

As will be detailed in Chapter 9, Freudian psychoanalysis is the chief source of the psychodynamic model. But many nonanalysts use it too.

In Freud's early theory, *psychodynamic* referred to psychological forces arising from *psychic energy.* Freud theorized that this energy was continually redistributed within the person in response to arousal, displacement by other psychological forces, and conversion into other forms. *Conversion hysteria,* for example, was thought to involve conversion of repressed sexual energy (*libido*) into physical energy that, in turn, afflicted some part of the body; for example, by paralyzing a limb. As psychoanalytic theory grew, the concepts of *id, ego,* and *superego* came to designate classes of conflicting forces.

The psychodynamic model is like a hydraulic system in which a force applied at one point pushes on other parts of the system. It holds, for example, that abnormal behaviors, slips of the tongue, and dreams are disguised expressions of conflicts between psychological forces. Projective tests, such as the Rorschach inkblot test and the Thematic Apperception Test (TAT), and many kinds of psychotherapy are based on the assumption that unconscious motives are expressed in disguised form. The psychodynamic model resembles the medical model in viewing behavioral symptoms as expressions of underlying processes that constitute the real pathology. Yet it differs in emphasizing psychological causes and treatment.

The Behavioral Model

Several approaches (detailed in Chapter 10) share a behavioral model for psychopathology. Unlike the medical and psychodynamic models, the behavioral model takes the disordered *behavior* as the central focus of treatment. Disordered individuals are seen not as patients who must be cured but clients who can be helped to modify their troublesome behavior. Consequently, even with children, behavior therapists try to enlist the client's aid in changing the problem behavior.

Most behavioral approaches rely on principles of learning to explain deviance and foster new modes of adaptation. Biological and social influences are important, but the focus is on modifying the behavior. Abnormal behavior is viewed as an outcome of the same determinants as normal behavior and as modifiable by manipulating the same variables.

The Nondirective Model

The nondirective model stems from Carl Rogers's (1951) client-centered nondirective psychotherapy. Rogers's basic tenet is that psychotherapy should simply help people become what they really are or have the potential to be. Therapists do this by conveying unconditional positive regard for their clients and by reflecting clients' own feelings back to them as they are expressed. A key assumption is that clients possess a potential for growth that will reconcile their self-image with the image of how they would ideally like to be.

Virginia Axline (1969) has extended this approach to children. Her assumptions are the same as for adult clients, but, because verbal self-expression may be less meaningful for children, the child's play serves as a medium of expression. Play therapists do not entirely reject psychodynamic and behavioral concepts, but they feel that neither the interpretations of inferred psychodynamics nor the manipulation of behavior help the child. Instead, they believe the therapist must demonstrate complete acceptance of the child as a person and reflect back the feelings the child reveals. Children are thus encouraged to recognize their feelings, accept themselves, and grow toward their own personal identity.

The Sociological Model

The clearest expression of this model is found in theories of the relation between delinquency and social class (discussed in Chapter 13). Sociological and social psychological models, however, also apply to family dynamics, family therapy, milieu therapy, community mental health, and work with the disadvantaged.

Sociological concepts imply that much behavior judged pathological is really quite appropriate for the individual's social circumstances. Thus, juvenile gangs can be viewed as subcultures. They can be classified and their functions within the larger culture analyzed. Within a gang, members' behavior can be described in terms of their specific social roles. Likewise, within a family, one member may be the scapegoat who bears the brunt of family tensions, another may be the unchallenged leader, and so on. Sociological models may be especially useful for analyzing entire social units such as the gang or family; patterns that are troublesome within the unit or between it and other social units can then be targeted for change.

Yet groups are comprised of individuals, and the behavior of individuals is our basic subject matter. Each individual functions in multiple social units, and we can often treat only the individual. Nevertheless, we should keep subcultural differences in mind when evaluating the behavior of individual children. Deviance must always be assessed in its cultural context; certain problems may be impossible to remedy by treating individuals one by one.

Other Models

Advocates of the models just described are apt to interpret all psychopathology in terms of their own model. Those who hold the medical model, for example, may think of retardation, neurosis, psychosis, delinquency, and other problems in terms of sickness, symptoms, treatments, and cures. Likewise, those favoring the psychodynamic model may view neurosis in terms of unconscious conflicts, psychosis as failure of early ego individuation, and delinquency as reflecting superego inadequacies. The approaches described next do not offer such broad models but have important applications in certain contexts.

Educational Models. These emphasize educational interventions for developmental deviations and disabilities in reading, perceptual-motor functioning, and learning. Personality support is typically offered, because educational deficits are often accompanied by emotional and behavioral problems. Educational approaches are also used to help seriously disturbed children master elementary aspects of socialization.

Statistical Models. Statistical models are approaches to research, description, and taxonomy rather than theories of psychopathology. One approach uses statistical methods to find out what kinds of behavior tend to occur together. Suppose, for example, we make a list of specific behaviors. We then rate many children on the behaviors. Next we compute correlations of each behavior with every other behavior. We might find, for example, that fire-setting and bed-wetting have a correlation of .80. This means that most children who set fires also wet their beds and vice versa. We then subject the correlations to other statistical procedures, such as *factor analysis,* that identify patterns among the correlations. Each pattern is composed of several behaviors: fire-setting, bed-wetting, poor school work, and stealing, for example.

We can study children who share a particular pattern to find out what produces the pattern and how they can be helped. Statistically identified patterns can also be used to derive theories about psychopathology. These approaches are not limited to behavioral items. They can be applied to test scores, psychodynamic inferences, or organic measures, as well as to combinations of these variables. Statistical methods differ from other approaches in their use of mathematical criteria for combining observations that other approaches combine subjectively.

Developmental Models. There is as yet no completely comprehensive developmental model for psychopathology. One developmental model—that of Arnold Gesell (1954)—defined pathology in terms of deviations from age norms. This approach remains dominant for assessing children up to about the age of 5 and for some kinds of developmental retardation at more advanced ages.

Freud and Erikson stressed the psychological conflicts thought to characterize successive developmental periods. Anna Freud (1965) proposed a "developmental profile" for describing children in terms of the developmental levels of their psychological functioning, fixations, and conflicts (detailed in Chapter 9). Efforts have been made to reconcile Freudian ideas of development with Piaget's theory (Gouin-Décarie, 1965; Greenspan, 1979). Statistical approaches are also used to identify developmental differences in the prevalance and patterning of behavior problems (Achenbach, 1981). As we saw in Chapter 3, however, a developmental understanding of psychopathology requires coordinating multiple perspectives on specific disorders. Because no single model is as yet comprehensive enough to do this, we will rely on diverse developmental concepts and research strategies to help us understand specific disorders.

THE "WHOLE CHILD" ISSUE

How do we keep sight of the whole child when thinking in terms of disorders and their diagnosis, causes, and treatment? Children are not disembodied diseases, egos, or response systems. Yet, selectivity is inevitable when we make judgments and decisions, communicate to others, and form hypotheses about children's behavior. A psychoanalyst, for example, may report observing an oral fixation in a child. A behaviorist, on the other hand, would argue that the analyst had merely observed behavior from which an "oral fixation" was inferred.

Overlaps among diagnostic categories also make it hard to decide what aspects of a child should take priority. The same child could be simultaneously diagnosed as brain-damaged and retarded, and as having an undersocialized aggressive conduct disorder, an attention-deficit disorder with hyperactivity, and a schizoid disorder. This is because brain damage is a physical defect regardless of its behavioral correlates; retardation is defined mainly by performance on an IQ test; conduct and attention deficit disorders are defined by problem behaviors; and the schizoid disorder is defined by lack of social involvement (American Psychiatric Association, 1980).

Nomothetic versus Idiographic Approaches

Allport (1937) argued for a distinction between nomothetic and idiographic methods in the study of personality. The *nomothetic* (Greek *nomos* = law) approach seeks general laws such as those in the physical sciences. The *idiographic* (Greek *idio* = personal, separate) approach seeks to portray the behavior of a particular individual.

According to the idiographic view, general principles of behavior may exist, but the specific variables affecting an individual make that individual's behavior unique. Because we cannot assess all the specific variables and their interactions, we should try to predict the individual's behavior by identifying laws or patterns unique to him or her. Even if we cannot always make precise predictions, we will at least gain a descriptive understanding of the individual's personality. After long contact with a child, for example, we detect consistent responses to particular situations without knowing the reasons. We may then try to change the responses by using other knowledge about this child, although we have never treated another child exactly like this one.

The nomothetic versus idiographic distinction highlights two contrasting trends in the study of psychopathology. But, as Allport suggested, nomothetic and idiographic principles are both important. An engineer constructing a building, for example, faces a situation that is as unique because of ground conditions, structural requirements, and available techniques as the situation we face in treating a particular child. Yet, no matter how unique the building problem, the engineer could not produce a solution that violated the general laws of physics. By the same token, even though we do not fully know the general laws of behavior, we must understand specific behaviors by generalizing from past experience. We cannot avoid nomothetic principles, whether or not they are well validated.

High regard for individuality is an asset in treating children, but no approach completely dispenses with generalized concepts or principles, no matter how strongly it espouses idiographic values. The psychoanalyst may portray a child idiographically in terms of ego strength, defenses, and fixations, while the behaviorist portrays the child in terms of habits and reinforcers. However, the concepts of ego, defense, fixation, habit, and reinforcers are all nomothetic. Their validity and interrelations are assumed to apply to everybody.

Training, diagnosis, treatment, theory, and research are all nomothetic enterprises, seeking generalizable knowledge no matter how individualistic the applications may seem. The common quest is for the nomothetic principles that yield the best ways of helping *all* individuals.

SUBCULTURAL OR INDIVIDUAL DEVIANCE?

To assess deviance, we need a standard for the normal. Unlike adults, children seldom seek help for themselves. The decision that a child needs help is usually made by parents, educators, physicians, and other adults whose decision may reveal more about themselves than about the child's needs.

When children are judged deviant, what standards do they deviate from? Surprisingly high rates of troublesome behavior have been revealed by studies of "normal" children, that is, those not referred for mental health services (Achenbach & Edelbrock, 1981). If we assessed a random sample of these children, would we diagnose them normal or abnormal? Studies have shown that psychopathology tends to be overestimated when behavior is judged from traditional clinical perspectives (Langer & Abelson, 1974; McCoy, 1976). This *pathological bias* in clinical judgments is especially relevant to children, because they seldom decide for themselves whether they need treatment.

We must therefore be aware of subjective standards involved in labeling behavior pathological and in deciding what to do about it. We can begin by distinguishing between (1) behavior that nearly everyone, including a child's family and peers, regards as deviant, and (2) behavior that deviates from dominant social norms but harmonizes with the child's immediate social environment.

Subcultural Deviance

Ethnic, social class, and neighborhood groups have their own norms for certain behaviors. Precocious sexual behavior, certain delinquencies, and academic nonachievement deviate from middle-class norms, but may be normal for children growing up in subcultures expecting these behaviors or failing to foster alternatives. If a behavior is damaging to the child or to others (e.g., physical assault), it may be a proper concern for mental health workers no matter how typical of the subculture it is. Yet, we should not attribute such behavior to the same causes or try to change it in the same way in a subculture where it is typical as where it is very atypical. Cultural relativity may also dictate that certain behaviors considered deviant in the dominant culture should be left alone if they are adaptive in the child's own subculture.

A particular family's antisocial or bizarre norms for behavior may encourage deviance that can also be considered subcultural. If evaluated separately, individual family members might be viewed as seriously disturbed, but the child's deviant behavior may represent successful adaptation to unusual circumstances. In extreme cases, we would be foolish to try changing the child's behavior without changes in the family. Because even mild behavior problems may reflect family stresses, a child brought for treatment is often seen as the "symptom" or "messenger" of a disturbed family.

Individual Deviance

Since almost all child behavior is reactive to the family subculture, most child deviance is to some extent subcultural. Yet most children are brought for treatment because their parents acknowledge that something is wrong. Even when parents foster the problem behavior, they may not see it as being in harmony with their family subculture.

In judging a child's behavior as deviant, parents and other adults tend to apply three general standards. One is a comparison of the child's *enduring traits* with the way adults think children *ought* to behave. This is often revealed in complaints that a child has been very fearful "since he was born," that "he's *always* been terribly destructive and now it's reached the point where . . . ," or the like. The parent's standards may be realistic, but we must ask what the parent expects. Has the parent's perception been unduly affected by the child's behavior in infancy? Does a child's resemblance to a disliked relative produce a self-fulfilling prophecy? Does the parent have expectations that no child could meet? Or is the parent's own behavior so difficult that the child cannot react compatibly?

A second standard for comparison is the child's *previous* behavior. Thus, a perceived *change* in behavior may be the problem. Has the child reached a new developmental stage or temporarily regressed from one not yet firmly achieved? A parent's awareness of developmental changes may be clouded not only by lack of sophistication, but also by a preference for behavior of a particular stage. Some parents prefer the behavior of late childhood to that of early adolescence, for example. Or has there been a change in life situation, such as a birth, death, or move to which the child is reacting? This can work two ways: The change may really affect the child; or it may affect the parents so much that they treat the child differently or exaggerate changes in the child.

A third standard of comparison is the *developmental dimension*. Here the complaint may be that the child does not act like other children of the same age, or is not meeting the parent's expectations for the child's age. Although the range of normal behavior is very broad at all ages, fairly precise developmental standards can be applied to physical growth, behaviors like walking and talking, and intellectual functioning. Developmental norms for social competencies and behavioral problems are somewhat less precise, but can offer important standards of comparison (Achenbach & Edelbrock, 1981).

Being subjective, judgments of deviance are vulnerable to distortions of pertinent information. Such distortions have been amply documented by comparing data gathered longitudinally on children's early development with reports obtained later when parents requested psychiatric evaluation of their children (Chess, Thomas, & Birch, 1966). Despite the fact that the children were only three to seven years old at the time of the psychiatric evaluations, the following distortions were found in parental reports:

1. Distortion of timing that made the sequence of developmental events conform to popular theories of causation, such as those found in childrearing guides.
2. Denial or minimization of problems, especially of their earlier existence.
3. Inability to recall pertinent past behavior.
4. Blaming the child for continuing behavior the parent had earlier encouraged.

It is also hard to assess individual deviance among youths who belong to groups with behavior deviant from both the dominant culture and the environment in which they were raised. Examples include drug, "street people," and religious cults, although youth subcultures are not a new phenomenon. These subcultures may play important roles in the psychosocial development of relatively normal youth, but the more bizarre groups often attract those already quite deviant. In such cases, it is hard to distinguish the individual's personal deviance from the group norms. Sometimes the needs of a disturbed youngster are partially met by a group that then reinforces ever more deviant and self-destructive behavior.

WHAT'S WRONG?

In asking what's wrong, we need to separate three issues: One is the *definition* of the disorder: What is the problem, what is troubling the youngster, how can we understand it here and now? A second is the *cause* of the problem: Why does this particular youngster have this particular problem? How did the youngster get this way and how could it have been prevented? A third is the *remedy:* How can we help?

All approaches use observation and inference, but they differ markedly in how they use observations and inferences to define disorders. Medical and psychodynamic models define psychopathology in terms of inferred states, whereas behavioral and sociological models define it in terms of observed behavior. These differences inevitably affect the causes sought, the therapeutic preferences, and the desired outcomes.

As an example, psychoanalysts argue that behavioral problems represent compromises among conflicting intrapsychic forces. They therefore contend that suppressing behavioral symptoms without relieving the underlying conflicts may produce new symptoms, representing more strained compromises. Behavior therapists, by contrast, argue that the "symptomatic" *behavior* is the main problem and can be solved by altering the contingencies supporting it or by strengthening alternative behaviors.

ETIOLOGY

Organic or Psychological?

A common question is whether the *etiology* (cause) of a child's problem is organic or psychological. The etiologies of some disorders are solely organic. Among these are gross defects that create bodily malformations, behavioral symptoms, mental retardation, and, often, premature death; an example is a disorder of fat metabolism known as Tay-Sachs disease. Short of this extreme, many physical afflictions affect behavior in varying degrees. These include other metabolic disorders, hormone abnormalities, vitamin deficiencies, and brain damage.

Because problem behavior is seldom caused solely by physical defects, the question of etiology should not be posed in either/or terms. To illustrate problems in sorting out psychological and organic contributions, let's briefly consider *epilepsy, minimal brain dysfunction,* and *psychophysiological disorders,* which Chapter 7 discusses in more detail.

Epilepsy is defined by the fact that a person has seizures (convulsions, fits) attributable to brain dysfunction. Psychological factors also play a role because emotional stresses help to precipitate seizures. Moreover, the experience of having seizures, restrictions on certain activities, and social myths and stigmas attached to epilepsy mean that psychological help and special occupational training are often needed.

Similar problems are raised by *minimal brain dysfunction* (MBD). This is sometimes inferred from hyperactive behavior and equivocal signs of neurologic dysfunction without firm evidence of brain damage. As it is often unclear what aspects of behavior reflect organic or nonorganic factors, some MBD children may not actually have malfunctioning brains. In some cases, the contributing organic factors may merely be slow development or constitutional characteristics at the low end of the normal distribution. In other cases, hyperactive behavior may reflect psychological factors, such as anxiety.

Even when warranted, the diagnosis of brain damage should never preclude precise evaluation of a child's psychological functioning and efforts to improve it. Most brain damage does not have unmodifiable effects on behavior. We must also realize, however, that failure to recognize organic handicaps may result in unrealistically high expectations for a child.

Psychophysiological disorders (popularly known as "psychosomatic") involve physical symptoms triggered by psychological stresses. "Psychosomatic" sometimes connotes imaginary or solely psychological discomforts; certain apparent physical malfunctions (usually diagnosed as *hysterical*) may indeed have no verifiable organic component. However, psychophysiological disorders are real and may even be fatal. Among the most dangerous are hypertension (high blood pressure), asthma, ulcerative colitis (inflammation of the large intestine), stomach ulcers, and anorexia nervosa (extreme food avoidance).

Various causes have been hypothesized, but most psychophysiological disorders probably involve an interplay of different causal variables. Such an interplay is well documented for ulcers: They are often caused by a combination of (1) predisposing biological factors such as excess stomach acid; (2) certain personality dispositions; and (3) precipitating stress (Weiner, Thaler, Reiser, & Mirsky, 1957).

Heredity or Environment?

Heredity and environment are familiar opponents in arguments over the origins of behavior. When posed as alternatives, however, they imply a false dichotomy like that of the organic versus psychological concepts of etiology. Although genes directly determine only biochemical processes, these processes ultimately affect psychological variables. The significance of a particular environmental event depends on the child's genetically shaped biology. Normal development, for example, cannot be explained only in terms of events impinging on a child; bombarding one 2-year-old with verbal stimuli may not have the same effect as bombarding another, and certainly will not for a 1-year-old or an 8-year-old. Development always involves transactions between organic structures—whose general form is determined by genetically transmitted plans—and environmental stimuli.

Genotype and Phenotype. Genetically transmitted codes affect behavior in many ways. Long before we could study genes directly, hypotheses about genetic transmission of physical characteristics were rigorously tested. This was done by observing the proportions of offspring having each variant of a trait. Another dimension was added when *chromosomes,* composed of thousands of genes, could be viewed microscopically. Unusual configurations of chromosomes were then found in some disorders, such as Down syndrome (mongolism), that have obvious physical and behavioral abnormalities.

The genetic basis for a particular trait is known as the *genotype* for that trait, whereas the observable expression of the trait is the *phenotype*. The study of genetic influences on behavior (*behavior genetics*) is complicated by the difficulty of defining and measuring phenotypic behavioral traits. This is especially hard because behavior is affected so much by the situation in which it is assessed. Behavior genetics has nevertheless made substantial progress in research on intelligence and personality traits. Its applications to developmental psychopathology are described in Chapter 6.

Hereditary mechanisms seldom operate via one-to-one relations between a gene and a specific physical or behavioral trait. Although some phenotypic traits are determined by single genes, most traits reflect multiple genetic factors. These may be especially important in shaping the general constitutional tendencies with which the child meets the world and to which the world reacts.

PROGNOSIS: CURABLE OR INCURABLE?

A *prognosis* is a forecast about the outcome of a disorder. Attitudes toward prognosis often arise from assumptions about causes of disorders instead of firm knowledge about their outcomes. Assessing outcomes of psychopathology in children is an arduous enterprise: It requires objective identification and classification of disorders in the first place, plus long-term follow-ups of children having particular disorders but different therapies.

Prognosis is not intrinsic to the disorder itself, but hinges on particular interventions. Many organic illnesses that once had poor prognoses now have favorable outcomes as a result of new treatments. An example is *phenylketonuria* (PKU), a severe form of mental retardation caused by an inborn error in the metabolism of phenylalanine, a protein present in most foods. PKU can be diagnosed through biochemical tests soon after birth; removing phenylalanine from the child's diet can then prevent retardation.

TAXONOMY

Persons or Disorders?

Classification is often regarded as a pastime for grammarians, librarians, and butterfly collectors that sheds little light on the phenomena classified. Yet, any act of judgment involves classification, whether or not we recognize it. Judgments of what is wrong with particular children, if they can be helped, and what treatment to use all entail classification. Our understanding of many disorders is hampered by our inability to objectively differentiate among them. A recurring problem in the study of infantile autism, for example, is the lack of agreement as to which children are autistic. Conclusions drawn by one worker are of no value unless other workers can recognize the target children.

Chapter 15 deals with classification systems (*taxonomies*). For now, we should note that taxonomies are valuable if their classes have important correlates and can be applied consistently by different workers. The correlates considered important depend on the *function* the taxonomy is to serve. Thus, a taxonomy of children according to height might be useful in forming basketball teams, but not very helpful in communicating about the causes and appropriate treatment of their behavioral disorders.

Disagreements on classifying psychopathology arise from (1) disagreements about what the pathology is, and (2) the different functions taxonomies are to serve. Because taxonomies are justified only by the functions they serve, there can never be a single "correct" taxonomy. For something that involves people in as many different ways as psychopathology, multiple taxonomies are needed. For mentally retarded children, medical personnel need a taxonomy based on the organic causes they are asked to identify or treat. Psychologists may prefer a taxonomy based on cognitive level, patterns of ability, or behavioral skills and deficits. Institutional personnel may wish to classify children according to whether they need nursing care, are toilet trained, can feed themselves, are subject to seizures, or are potentially dangerous to others. School personnel may identify children according to the kinds of instruction and educational programs they need.

Taxonomic needs also differ according to how well we understand particular disorders. Research to identify causes or develop effective treatment often requires trying out a variety of taxonomic schemes in order to pinpoint attributes that reflect differences in etiology or outcome.

The "Whole Child" Issue in Taxonomy

Taxonomies deal with disorders or other attributes of people, instead of whole individuals. But, because whole individuals are, in fact, classified, it is tempting to identify everything about a person with the disorder he or she is said to have. This is reflected in such terms as "the schizophrenic" and "the obsessive-compulsive." As Adolf Meyer put it, the implication is that the disorder " 'has' the patient," not that "the person 'has' a certain disorder" (cf. Kanner, 1957, pp. 726−27).

No taxonomy can possibly take account of *all* human attributes. A taxonomy simply provides explicit rules for grouping individuals with respect to *some* of their attributes that are related in important ways to the aims of the classifier, for example, selecting those who will benefit most from a particular treatment. Once treatment begins, some therapists (such as the followers of Carl Rogers), believe they are most effective when they forget classification and react only to what clients express. Yet, Rogers (1955) himself tried to identify elements of personality and therapy that would improve the prediction of outcomes.

Diagnostic and Statistical Manual of Mental Disorders

The American Psychiatric Association's *Diagnostic and Statistical Manual of Mental Disorders* (DSM) provides the taxonomy used by most clinical and government agencies for tabulating disorders. Most medical taxonomy, known as *nosology* (Greek *nosos* = disease), is based on physical properties of disorders at whatever level they are currently understood. Tumors, for example, are classified according to their physical characteristics and locations until specific causes are discovered.

The DSM generally follows medical principles regarding disorders with known physical causes. Because most mental and behavioral disorders have no known organic etiologies, however, their classification is subject to much debate, confusion, and revision.

The first edition of the DSM (DSM-I, American Psychiatric Association, 1952) contained only two categories of children's disorders having no known organic etiologies: These were *schizophrenic reaction childhood type* and *adjustment reaction (of infancy, childhood, or adolescence)*, with the subcategories of *habit disturbance, conduct disturbance*, and *neurotic traits*. Although adult diagnoses could also be applied to children, most children seen in mental health clinics were either diagnosed as having adjustment reactions or were undiagnosed (Achenbach, 1966; Rosen, Bahn, & Kramer, 1964).

The second edition of the DSM (DSM-II, American Psychiatric Association, 1968) made more distinctions between child and adult disorders and included the following behavior reactions of childhood: *hyperkinetic reaction, withdrawing reaction, overanxious reaction, runaway reaction, unsocialized aggressive reaction, group delinquent reaction*, and *other reaction*. However, DSM-II did not state specific diagnostic criteria, and diagnoses of adjustment reaction remained common (Cerreto & Tuma, 1977).

The third edition of the DSM (DSM-III, American Psychiatric Association, 1980) made several major departures from earlier editions, as well as adding many more specific disorders of infancy, childhood, and adolescence. A basic departure is the provision of five diagnostic dimensions or *axes*. This *multiaxial* approach is intended to broaden diagnostic assessment beyond clinical syndromes.

Axis I includes clinical syndromes, plus conditions for which people may be referred to mental health professionals but are not necessarily disorders, such as marital problems and bereavement.

Axis II comprises adult personality disorders and childhood developmental disorders that may be accompanied by Axis I syndromes. An adult, for example, may receive an Axis II diagnosis of Paranoid Personality and an Axis I diagnosis of Brief Reactive Psychosis. Similarly, a child may receive an Axis II diagnosis of Developmental Language Disorder and an Axis I diagnosis of Separation Anxiety Disorder. Multiple Axis I and Axis II diagnoses can also be made when needed for a complete clinical picture. Table 4-1 shows the major categories of child and adolescent disorders.

Axis III is for specifying physical disorders. Axis IV is a seven-point scale for rating psychosocial stresses in a person's life. For example, a change of school teacher is rated *three* (mild stress), whereas multiple family deaths is rated *seven* (catastrophic stress). Axis V is a five-point scale for rating the person's highest level of adaptive functioning during the past year. A child who does poorly in school and with peers is rated *five* (poor), whereas a child who does exceptionally well in school, other activities, and social relations is rated *one* (superior). Axis III and IV thus indicate detrimental physical and psychosocial factors that may contribute to a disorder, whereas axis V indicates the level of positive competency expected of a person. Table 4-2 shows the Axis IV and V rating scales as applied to children and adolescents.

Child or Miniature Adult?

This question is nowhere more crucial than in the definition and taxonomy of psychopathology. Although the DSM-III has added several new categories of childhood disorders, most diagnostic and taxonomic concepts originated with the study of adult disorders. Starting with Freud, adult disorders have been assumed to stem from childhood maladjustment. As a result, childhood problems are often viewed in light of the adult disorders they are believed to culminate in, instead of being studied in their own right. Can disorders identified in adults be validly attributed to children? In chapters on specific disorders, we will see that the use of adult terms for childhood disorders may exaggerate similarities and obscure important differences between disturbed adults and children.

Table 4-1   Major Child and Adolescent Diagnostic Categories of the *Diagnostic and Statistical Manual, 3rd Edition*

Axis I	
Mental Retardation	**Eating Disorders**
Mild mental retardation	Anorexia nervosa
Moderate mental retardation	Bulimia
Severe mental retardation	Pica
Profound mental retardation	Rumination disorder of infancy
Attention Deficit Disorder	Atypical eating disorder
With hyperactivity	**Stereotyped Movement Disorders**
Without hyperactivity	Transient tic disorder
Residual type	Chronic motor tic disorder
Conduct Disorder	Tourette's disorder
Undersocialized, aggressive	**Other Disorders with Physical**
Undersocialized, nonaggressive	**Manifestations**
Socialized, nonaggressive	Stuttering
Atypical	Functional enuresis
Anxiety Disorders	Functional encopresis
Separation anxiety disorder	Sleepwalking disorder
Avoidant disorder	Sleep terror disorder
Overanxious disorder	**Pervasive Developmental Disorders**
Other Disorders	Infantile autism
Reactive attachment disorder of infancy	Childhood onset pervasive developmental
Schizoid disorder	disorder
Elective mutism	Atypical
Oppositional disorder	Developmental reading disorder
Identity disorder	Developmental arithmetic disorder
	Developmental language disorder
	Developmental articulation disorder
	Mixed specific developmental disorder
	Atypical specific developmental disorder

Source: American Psychiatric Association 1980, p. 15.

We have evidence on the continuity of a few disorders from follow-ups of children seen in clinics who were assessed again when they were adults. Poorly differentiated childhood diagnoses made it hard to find more continuity in diagnosis, but descriptions of the children's behavioral problems offer a good basis for comparison. In one of the most thorough follow-up studies, Robins (1974) reported: "The shy, withdrawn personality sometimes thought to be predictive of schizophrenia did not predict it. . . . None of the (adult) schizophrenics had been described as a shy or withdrawn child, and only one-sixth as avoiding others or seclusive" (p. 258). On the other hand, Robins found considerable continuity

Table 4-2   Axis IV and V of the *Diagnostic and Statistical Manual*

Axis IV. Severity of Psychosocial Stressors

Code	Term	Child or Adolescent Examples
1	None	No apparent psychosocial stressor
2	Minimal	Vacation with family
3	Mild	Change in schoolteacher; new school year
4	Moderate	Chronic parental fighting; change to new school; illness of close relative; birth of sibling
5	Severe	Death of peer; divorce of parents; arrest; hospitalization; persistent and harsh parental discipline
6	Extreme	Death of parent or sibling; repeated physical or sexual abuse
7	Catastrophic	Multiple family deaths
0	Unspecified	No information, or not applicable

Axis V. Highest Level of Adaptive Functioning in Past Year

Levels	Child or Adolescent Examples
1 Superior—Unusually effective functioning in social relations, occupational functioning, and use of leisure time.	A 12-year-old girl gets superior grades in school, is extremely popular among her peers, and excels in many sports. She does all of this with apparent ease and comfort.
2 Very Good—Better than average functioning in social relations, occupational functioning, and use of leisure time.	An adolescent boy gets excellent grades, works part-time, has several close friends, and plays banjo in a jazz band. He admits to some distress in "keeping up with everything."
3 Good—No more than slight impairment in either social or occupational functioning.	An 8-year-old boy does well in school, has several friends, but bullies younger children.
4 Fair—Moderate impairment in either social relations or occupational functioning, *or* some impairment in both.	A 10-year-old girl does poorly in school, but has adequate peer and family relations.
5 Poor—Marked impairment in either social relations or occupational functioning, *or* moderate impairment in both.	A 14-year-old boy almost fails in school and has trouble getting along with his peers.

Source: American Psychiatric Association 1980, pp. 27, 29.

between antisocial behavior in childhood and the diagnosis of sociopathic (antisocial) personality in adulthood.

SUMMARY

In this chapter, we explored conflicts among views of psychopathology in children. One type of conflict stems from "doing your own thing." Workers' personalities, the types and ages of children they work with, their work settings, and training and career orientations all affect the way they perceive particular children and the causes and remedies for pathology in general.

Disagreements also stem from differing conceptual models for psychopathology. These include medical, psychodynamic, behavioral, nondirective, and sociological models, plus approaches that were described in terms of educational, statistical, and developmental models.

Additional issues arise because we see a whole child in practice but must be selective in assessing the child's problems, communicating about them, providing treatment, and doing research. Some approaches espouse *idiographic* values, but all seek *nomothetic* principles to guide the understanding of individual children.

Several other issues were posed in terms of questions often raised about children's disorders. One question was, what standards are applied in judging behavior as deviant? Some children deviating from the standards of a dominant culture may nevertheless conform to their own subculture: a social class, ethnic, neighborhood, or family group, for example. Beside cultural standards, other common bases for judgment are views on how children *"ought"* to behave; how a particular child *previously* behaved; and how children of a given developmental level *typically* behave.

A second question, "What's wrong?" concerns how we define pathology and whether we emphasize *inference* or *observation*. Different definitions imply different causes, different therapies, and different outcome goals.

The question of *etiology* was raised in two forms: "Organic or psychological?" and "heredity or environment?" These questions are seldom valid in strictly either/or form, since many disorders involve combinations of organic, psychological, hereditary, and environmental factors. We need to know how these factors jointly influence the *phenotypic* outcome.

The *prognosis* of a disorder (its expected outcome) is determined less by the disorder itself than by the state of our knowledge about it. We need long-term follow-up studies to show how disorders respond to different interventions.

Our final question concerned the role of classification in all our judgments. The value of a particular *taxonomy* depends on how effectively it groups people according to attributes related to the aims of the taxonomy. The taxonomy embodied in the *Diagnostic and Statistical Manual of Mental Disorders* follows a medical model, but nonmedical principles are needed for disorders having no known physical cause. Viewing childhood behavior disorders as forerunners of particular adult disorders may exaggerate the similarities and obscure the differences between child and adult disorders.

SUGGESTED READING

The "Whole Person" Issue. Carl Rogers's nondirective approach to psychotherapy emphasizes the whole person. Yet, he developed objective methods for assessing aspects of behavior and beliefs that change during psychotherapy (Rogers & Dymond, 1954). In an article entitled "Persons or science?: A philosophical question" (1955), he contrasts the subjectivity needed in doing therapy with the objectivity needed for evaluating it and communicating about it. Virginia Axline's (1969) extension of nondirective therapy to children reflects the same dual regard for subjective acceptance of the child as a whole person and for objectivity in studying the therapeutic process.

Taxonomy. Scientific and methodological issues related to taxonomy are discussed in greater detail in Chapter 15, but perusal of the *Diagnostic and Statistical Manual of Mental Disorders* (American Psychiatric Association, 1980) provides a taste of the official vocabulary and categories. Achenbach (1980b) summarizes relations between the DSM-III and empirically derived syndromes of child psychopathology, while other articles in the same special issue of the *Journal of the American Academy of Child Psychiatry* discuss the DSM-III from other perspectives. Lee Robins's (1974) classic study, *Deviant Children Grown Up,* focuses mainly on relations between antisocial behavior in childhood and adulthood, but also includes good evidence on relations between other child and adult disorders. Her later review paper adds data from other studies (Robins, 1979).

CHAPTER 5

Scientific Strategies

Most people associate the word science with the physical sciences. However, *science* (from Latin *scire* = to know) literally refers to knowing, or obtaining knowledge. The knowledge needed to deal with psychopathology differs from that needed to cure cancer, but in both cases the goal is mastery of debilitating afflictions. Guesswork is a part of all scientific efforts, but to solve problems like these, we need to advance knowledge beyond personal hunches so that it can be used by others. This chapter outlines criteria and strategies for advancing our knowledge of developmental psychopathology.

DISCOVERY AND CONFIRMATION

Philosophers of science have distinguished two general stages in scientific activity (Popper, 1961). At one stage, called the *context of discovery,* ideas are generated in whatever subjective, intuitive, creative, or accidental way people happen to think. Even the most completely formalized sciences have no rules for generating these inspirations and no standards of scientific respectability for the thought processes involved.

Ideas can emerge from naturalistic or laboratory observations, analogies from other fields, and impressions that someone weaves into a guess about the way things actually work. Ideas may come suddenly or may emerge from a long period of mental trial-and-error. They may be progressively modified by systematically gathering data. The context of discovery is the aspect of science that is subjective. It concerns the knowledge seeker's choice of problems and speculations on solutions, but not the systematic procedures needed to verify and communicate knowledge.

The other stage of science is the *context of confirmation* or *context of justification*. It is at this stage that ideas emerging from the context of discovery are systematically tested. The particular form of hypotheses and the procedures for testing them vary among sciences. Yet, for an idea to be scientifically acceptable, it must have testable implications. The more consistently we confirm the implications, the more confidence the idea deserves.

Discovery and confirmation are not completely separate, nor do they always occur in a particular sequence. There is continual interplay between observation, imagination, exploration, and the generation and testing of hypotheses. Subjectivity in generating ideas and objectivity in testing them play complementary roles in creating useful knowledge.

Context of Discovery

The distinction between discovery and confirmation is especially pertinent to psychopathology, because the treatment of complex individuals is both a major source of hypotheses and a target for knowledge acquired. Observations of patients yield expectations about characteristics that tend to occur together and about causes of these patterns. For example, Freud's (1905) observations that hysterical patients had repressed sexual memories led to his hypotheses about psychosexual development. The term *clinical method* refers to the subjective generation of hypotheses in this way. It may also refer to systematic probing or questioning and to procedures for testing hypotheses during therapy.

Forming hypotheses via clinical observation and intuition is not very different from generating hypotheses in other sciences. Acute observation and effective questioning of patients require special skills, but the data obtained are subjectively woven into hypotheses. To confirm these hypotheses, we must systematically test them. The special requirements for confirming knowledge, discussed below, make it impossible to confirm hypotheses via clinical experience alone.

The distinction between discovery and confirmation is also important for psychopathology, because clinicians, like scientists, face a mass of potential observations from which to derive hypotheses. To treat a patient effectively, clinicians, like scientists, must test their hypotheses against new observations of the patient's behavior. Hypotheses that are not confirmed should be modified or dropped. Trial-and-error may be needed to find the best mix of procedures for helping a particular person. Like scientific theories, clinical formulations of individual cases are most useful when they can be tested and confirmed.

Context of Confirmation

Because knowledge is a mental construction, it can never be perfectly objective. To help us understand or modify events in the real world, however, our knowledge must be related as accurately as possible to those events. Procedures for confirming ideas vary from science to science. I will emphasize those that guide the confirmation of knowledge in the behavioral sciences. Unless we evaluate ideas evolved in the context of discovery according to these criteria, we can never distinguish between genuine discoveries and wrong guesses.

Testability. To evaluate hypotheses, we must state them in a testable form. If our hypothesis concerns the relation between two characteristics, we must first assess them as objectively as we can. Since all characteristics can exist in degrees—even if the "degrees" are just "present versus absent"—they are referred to as *variables;* that is, they are attributes whose values can vary.

We can maximize objectivity by giving each variable on *operational definition.* This is a measurement procedure or *operation* that specifies the value of the variable in a certain situation. For example, if we want to test a clinical impression that aggressive boys have punitive fathers, we must decide what to accept as operational definitions of aggression and punitiveness.

To define aggression operationally, we must specify the age range involved, target behaviors, and norms from which behavior must deviate to be considered aggressive. Suppose we focus on 6- to 10-year-old boys. As our definition of aggression, we select scores on observers' ratings of fighting and efforts to hurt others. To be considered aggressive, let's say a boy's score must exceed that of 90 percent of boys in representative samples from similar ethnic and socioeconomic backgrounds.

An objective definition of paternal punitiveness is more difficult but not impossible. Direct observations would, of course, be desirable but might affect the fathers' behavior. Interview reports by mothers, fathers, and their sons could be used to find fathers who appeared consistently punitive or not, although each informant's report might be too biased to use alone. To avoid contaminating interviewers' judgment, the interviewers should not know which fathers have aggressive sons. In short, before we test our hypothesis, we must specify the variables as objectively as possible.

Once we have operationally defined "aggression" and "punitiveness," we must decide whether we think paternal punitiveness *causes* boys' aggression, or whether the two are correlated for other reasons. Even if most aggressive boys have punitive fathers, while unaggressive boys do not, this alone does not prove that fathers' punitive behavior *causes* aggression. The causal relation could be exactly the opposite: because a boy is aggressive, his father becomes punitive. Or both could result from a third factor: both could be reactions to maternal hostility, for example.

Finding a correlation between operationally defined variables is a key step in most research on psychopathology. But prevention and treatment usually require that causes be verified. We discuss strategies for pinpointing causes below, but first we need additional criteria for objectively confirming knowledge.

Reliability. A key facet of objectivity is the *reliability* of assessment. This is the *consistency* with which a procedure produces certain results. One form of reliability is agreement among observers' ratings of a variable. In determining which boys are aggressive, *interobserver reliability* is high if two observers seeing boys at the same time agree on which ones are aggressive. If they fail to agree, their ratings of aggression would not deserve much confidence.

Training is often needed to obtain high interobserver reliability, but some behaviors cannot be judged reliably even after extensive training. Such factors as the observers' influence on subjects' behavior also contribute to unreliability. We may therefore have to find other ways of assessing variables. One alternative is to devise a test or behavioral inventory of items that assess the target variable in slightly different ways. The variable is viewed as a *trait* whose strength is operationally defined by summing scores on all the items.

Constructing psychological tests is an art and science that involves two further forms of reliability. One is *test-retest reliability,* which is the agreement between a person's scores on the same test when administered on two occasions. Because people are always changing and because they are affected by conditions at the moment of testing, we need to know whether the score obtained on one occasion reflects stable characteristics or momentary conditions. If scores obtained on two occasions agree, this indicates that the test reflects stable characteristics.

Sometimes reliability cannot be properly estimated by retesting, because the subjects are influenced by taking the test, they try to find out answers between testing, and so forth. In these situations, an *alternate form* of the test is needed to measure exactly the same trait as the original form. We can then estimate reliability from correlations between scores on the two forms. Agreement between scores obtained on two occasions is important not only for tests, but also for data obtained by other means, such as interviews and observations.

Another kind of reliability is known as *internal consistency* or *split-half reliability*. This is the consistency with which all items on a test, rating scale, or behavior inventory assess the same trait. Each item serves as a minature test of the trait. Consistency among items can be assessed by correlating people's performance on half the items with their performance on the other half, for example, their performance on the odd-numbered items with that on the even-numbered items. If internal consistency is low, the total score probably does not measure a unitary trait.

A measure's worth is judged by how well it fulfills its intended function. Test-retest reliability and internal consistency are important, but some measures must reflect *changes* in people. A test of anxiety, for example, would not be useful for studying the effects of treatment if it only had items on which people's responses never change. Reliability does not inhere in the measure itself, but depends on characteristics of the subjects and conditions under which they are assessed.

Validity of Assessment. An assessment procedure is *valid* if it accurately reflects its target variable. Reliability is a measure's agreement with *itself,* but to judge validity, we need to know how well the measure agrees with a *different* index of the target variable. A test or diagnosis of brain damage, for example, is judged valid if it agrees with another way of assessing brain damage, such as autopsy. However, validity often depends on partial agreement among several kinds of assessment, all of which are known to be imperfect. The impracticality of autopsy as a validity criterion requires us to validate measures via partial agreement with various procedures that each reflect different aspects of damage. These could include neurologic exams, perceptual-motor tests, electroencephalograms (EEGs), and computerized axial tomography (an x-ray procedure known as a CAT scan).

The validity criteria for assessing a particular variable may change as new methods are invented. For example, teachers' ratings of children's ability served as a criterion for judging the validity of early intelligence tests. However, because the test scores were more reliable and correlated better with other kinds of "intelligent" behavior than teachers' ratings, the tests themselves became a criterion against which new intelligence tests were validated. Likewise, in developing a method for diagnosing schizophrenia, we may begin with the pooled judgment of several clinicians as a criterion against which to validate the method. But if the method proves more reliable or otherwise desirable than the judgments of clinicians, we may use it as a criterion against which clinical diagnoses of schizophrenia are validated.

Validity of Inference. Beside applying to the accuracy of assessment, validity also applies to the accuracy of inferences drawn from data. Two kinds of inferential accuracy are especially important. The first concerns conclusions about the *reasons* for findings. Because data are affected by many variables, we must be certain that findings are not the result of unrecognized variables such as the subjects' own hypotheses about the research, faulty research equipment or data analysis, or logical errors in design or conclusions. Inferences about the *reasons* for findings have *internal validity* only when alternative explanations of this sort can be ruled out.

Once we establish the internal validity of our conclusions from a particular study, can we generalize these conclusions to other people or situations? It depends on how well our study reflects the conditions to which we want to generalize. Biased sampling of subjects and unnatural research settings, for example, limit the ability to make generalizations. Inferences drawn from a particular study have *external validity* only when they can be accurately *generalized* to other people and situations assumed to involve the same variables.

Comparison Groups and Control Groups. To see whether a particular relation exists between two variables, we must compare the relation at different values of the variables. One way to do this is to compare the variables in two or more groups.

Suppose we find that all aggressive boys have punitive fathers. Does this verify a correlation between the two variables? No; not unless we also find that *un*aggressive boys have *non*punitive fathers. To establish a correlation between aggression and paternal punitiveness, we can *compare* fathers of aggressive and unaggressive boys.

To be sure the relation between aggression and punitiveness was not caused by some extraneous third factor, our *comparison* group of unaggressive boys and their fathers should be as similar as possible to our aggressive group. Otherwise, all the aggressive boys may come from a population where fathers are punitive and aggression is encouraged, while the comparison group comes from a population where fathers are not punitive and where aggression is also directly discouraged. If we merely wished to know whether aggression is more common among boys with punitive fathers than boys in general, we would select a comparison group representative of the general population to establish a *base-rate* of aggression. We can then see whether aggression among sons of punitive fathers exceeds the base-rate for the general population.

Where we can manipulate our target variable, comparison groups are called *control groups*. To test a therapy, for example, we give one group (the *treatment* group) the therapy. A second group (the *control* group) receives exactly the same conditions except the aspect of therapy we want to test.

The classical form of this procedure was developed to test drugs. The treatment group receives a new drug while the control group receives an inert substance called a *placebo* (Latin "I shall please"). Since researchers' expectations can affect their observations and the patients' actual behavior, those administering the drugs and observing the effects, as well as the patients, are ignorant of ("blind to") who gets the drug and who gets the placebo. This is called a *double-blind placebo control* procedure.

Where a well-matched control group is not feasible, a person may serve as his or her *own control*. An example is where a base-rate for a child's problem behavior (e.g., frequency of aggression) is obtained before treatment and compared to behavior during treatment. If the target behavior subsides, treatment is temporarily halted to see if the behavior reappears. If it reappears and can be reduced again by resuming treatment, the treatment rather than the passage of time or other extraneous factors probably caused the improvement.

THEORIES AND HYPOTHETICAL CONSTRUCTS

Almost any system of ideas that provides conceptual order can be called a theory. A theory only becomes scientifically useful, however, when it leads to testable statements. Because theories consist mostly of inferences, they can seldom be totally proved or disproved. When deductions from theories are verified, the theories earn credibility. But disconfirmation of specific deductions seldom leads to complete rejection of a theory, because the deductions may be logically incorrect or inappropriately tested. Disconfirmation of a few specific deductions often leads to further research guided by the original theory but the theory is modified to accommodate the results actually found.

The more-or-less formal rules of science apply to objectifying and confirming knowledge; but its intellectual life blood consists of ideas and theories. As Kuhn (1970) has shown, scientific revolutions have resulted as much from new modes of scientific thinking as from empirical discoveries.

Hypothetical constructs are concepts conceived to explain observations and to suggest new testable statements about reality. The gene, for example, was a hypothetical construct conceived by Gregor Mendel to explain patterns of inheritance he observed in peas. Although genes can now be studied directly, genetic research still depends on testable deductions from hypothetical constructs as well as on observations of genes themselves. "Intelligence" and most other psychological traits are constructs that are useful when they suggest testable relations among objectively specified variables. Disease "entities" can also be useful hypothetical constructs, but they should not prevent us from continually trying to view psychopathology in ways that may prove more useful.

In short, theories and constructs are not simply true or false. They are ideas whose worth depends on their ability to foster new knowledge.

CONCEPTS OF CAUSATION

"What causes X?" is a nearly universal scientific question. However, what qualifies as a cause differs according to the phenomena of interest, how far back we trace the causal train, and so on. In psychopathology, the question usually concerns the *etiology* of maladaptive behavior, but we can seldom pinpoint simple, one-to-one causes. It is therefore helpful to distinguish the following four concepts of causation.

Necessary Condition

A *necessary condition* is a factor that must be present for a phenomenon to occur. Without that factor, the phenomenon cannot occur. But the factor may not guarantee that the phenomenon will occur. For a gasoline engine to start, gasoline must be available to the carburetor. Gasoline is, therefore, a *necessary* condition for the operation of the engine. It does not, however, insure that the engine will start, because other factors, such as oxygen, are also necessary. Analogously, Meehl (1977) has hypothesized that a certain genetic factor is a necessary condition for schizophrenia, but this alone does not guarantee that a person will develop schizophrenia, because other factors, such as certain life experiences, also play a role.

Sufficient Condition

A *sufficient condition* is a factor that will produce a particular phenomenon *without* the contribution of any other factors. If the hypothesized genetic factor in schizophrenia *always* led to schizophrenia, regardless of environment, the genetic factor would be a *sufficient* condition for schizophrenia. However, being a sufficient condition does not mean it is also a necessary condition. Schizophrenia might result from brain damage or poor environment in people without the genetic factor. The genetic factor, brain damage, and poor environment could thus each be a sufficient condition, but none would be a necessary condition, that is, a condition required for schizophrenia.

Necessary and Sufficient Condition

This is a factor that (1) *must* be present for a particular phenomenon to occur, *and* (2) *always* leads to the phenomenon. If schizophrenia can occur *only* in the presence of a certain genetic factor and *always* occurs when that factor is present, then the factor is both a necessary *and* sufficient condition for schizophrenia.

Contributory Causes

These factors *contribute* to a certain phenomenon but are neither necessary nor sufficient to produce it. If a genetic factor is a necessary but not sufficient condition for schizophrenia, brain damage may be a *contributory* factor that triggers schizophrenia in people possessing the genetic factor. However, poor environment may be a separate factor that also contributes to schizophrenia in people having the genetic factor but no brain damage.

RESEARCH METHODS

Methods for studying psychopathology can be ordered along several dimensions. No one method is inherently the best for all purposes, and most problems are best studied with a combination of methods. The knowledge necessary for preventing and treating psychopathology requires a convergence of methods on specific testable questions. The following sections summarize some of the dimensions along which research methods vary and show how these methods can complement one another.

Exploratory Versus Hypothesis-Testing Research

One aim of research is to test hypotheses. For example, "If condition X exists, then result Y will be observed." Or, "If X increases, then Y will increase." Condition X

is an *independent variable,* one whose value is established at the start. Y is a *dependent variable;* its value is expected to *depend* on the value of X. An example of the first version of the hypothesis is: "If a boy's father is punitive (condition X), then the boy will be aggressive (result Y)." An example of the second version, where the variables are quantified, is "The more punitive the behavior of a boy's father, the more aggressive the boy will be." To test these hypotheses, we must choose operational measures of the independent and dependent variables and then do a systematic study to see whether aggression in boys varies with the punitive behavior of their fathers.

Testing hypotheses is a key goal of research but seldom the only goal. Much research is designed to detect relations among several variables, with no hypotheses more specific than "if relations are found among these variables, they will be valuable in formulating other research."

Exploratory research of this type requires decisions about what is important, how to define it objectively, and what significance the findings will have. Good exploratory research requires as much sophistication about how knowledge can be confirmed as testing hypotheses does. But it contributes more to forming new ideas than confirming the statements to which these ideas lead.

As an example of exploratory research, suppose we think fathers' behavior is related to their sons' aggression. (This is already a general hypothesis.) We therefore wish to examine differences in the behavior of fathers of aggressive and unaggressive boys. We then develop interview and observation techniques for rating fathers' behavior on several dimensions (e.g., warm-cold, directive-nondirective, punitive-nonpunitive), and we train observers to make the ratings. Since we want to know the relation between fathers' behavior and sons' aggression, our raters must not have their judgments contaminated by knowing which sons are aggressive. We must thus deal with many of the same problems as when testing the specific hypothesis that fathers' punitive behavior is correlated with their sons' aggression.

In the long run, a broad exploratory effort might yield more information than testing a specific hypothesis. If we test only the hypothesis that punitive behavior is related to aggression and fail to confirm it, what would we do next? Well, if it had been just an isolated hypothesis not dictated by a theory or if we learned only that the hypothesis was unsupported, the study would have dispelled an incorrect impression, but we would be starting from scratch again if we wanted to find out whether paternal behavior is related to aggression. The most effective research, therefore, combines exploration with hypothesis testing, either in the same study or in closely related ones. Thus, if we studied other aspects of fathers' behavior, we might find relations between their behavior and sons' aggression suggesting new testable hypotheses or a revision of the theory behind our original hypothesis.

Well-designed studies can yield valuable and often unanticipated findings even when they fail to confirm a hypothesis. Most well-designed studies have both an exploratory aspect and a hypothesis-testing aspect. Both aspects aim to objectify and systematize knowledge through controlled observation.

Correlational versus Experimental Research

In a broad sense, all research is correlational; it seeks to detect correlations among variables. Yet, as Figure 5-1a illustrates, a *correlation* between two variables does *not* necessarily imply that one *causes* the other. Fathers' punitive behavior might correlate with sons' aggression because both are caused by a third variable, such as maternal hostility to males. If so, reducing fathers' punitive behavior would not reduce their sons' aggression.

Another case where we cannot infer causation from a correlation between two variables is where the two variables are both measures of another, more fundamental variable. Figure 5-1b illustrates this. For example, a finding that children getting the best grades in a special educational program also get the best scores on a standardized achievement test does not prove that success in the program *caused* the good test performance. Good performance in both situations reflects good academic functioning, and both could be measures of academic ability.

A *causal* relation between the program and performance on the achievement test could be inferred only if we show that the correlation between them was not merely the result of the variance they both share with a third variable. Effects of a third variable can sometimes be extracted with statistical techniques such as *partial correlation* (McNemar, 1969, provides details). Partial correlation subtracts or "partials out" of the correlation between two variables the components of their correlation with each other that result from their correlations with a third variable. In

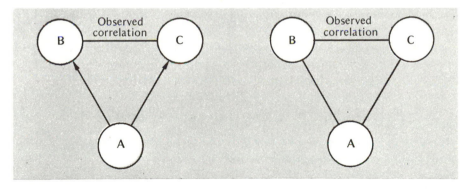

(a) Variable A is a cause of both B and C.   (b) B and C are both measures of A.

Figure 5-1. Two situations in which a correlation between variables B and C does not reflect a causal relation between B and C.

the present example, we can infer causation only if the correlation between performance in the program and on the achievement test remained high after academic ability and similar variables are partialed out.

Developmental and Trait Variance. A special problem of developmental research is that almost all characteristics of children are correlated with their developmental level. Consequently, when we find a correlation between two measures of children's behavior, we must always ask if it reflects anything beside the variance each measure shares with developmental level. For example, as pointed out in Chapter 3, cognitive styles such as impulsivity and field dependence correlate (negatively) with chronological and mental age. Because developmental level accounts for much of the variance in these cognitive styles, we must partial developmental variance out of their correlation with other variables before we can draw conclusions about the roles of the cognitive styles per se. Otherwise, we face a proliferation of "traits" that merely reflect differences in developmental level, which we could more directly assess in terms of general indices of development, such as mental age.

Experimental Research. This is the most direct way to identify causal relations. In an experiment, we *manipulate* an independent variable to see if the value of a dependent variable depends on the independent variable. To confirm the effect of a drug on hyperactivity, for example, we can use a double-blind placebo control procedure and vary the drug (the independent variable) to see if hyperactivity (the dependent variable) varies accordingly.

Some independent variables are impossible to manipulate. We can, however, look for *natural experiments* where naturally occurring differences in independent variables allow us to study the effects on dependent variables. Unfortunately, we seldom find conditions under which only the independent variables of interest vary. If we want to study the behavioral effects of a brain disease, for example, we can compare diseased children with healthy children of similar age and backgrounds. However, conditions relating to the disease, such as treatment and parental solicitude, may also affect the diseased children. We could perhaps control for these variables by comparing diseased children not only with healthy children but also with children having a different kind of brain disease. Natural experiments seldom offer the precision of experiments in which we manipulate the independent variables while holding all others constant. Yet they may be the only way to study certain variables in humans.

Correlational and experimental research both seek to identify relationships between variables and to derive inferences about causation. We often need well-confirmed correlations to help us define a problem precisely enough for effective experimentation. A relation between a dependent variable and an experimentally manipulated independent variable usually supports causal inferences better than strictly correlational research does. Many important variables cannot be manipulated, however, and experimental manipulation often creates unnatural conditions that distort other relevant variables. Since their advantages and disadvantages differ, experimental and correlational methods are best used to supplement each other.

Cross-sectional versus Longitudinal Research

In *cross-sectional* research, we take a sample or "cross section" of a phenomenon at a single point in time. For example, we use a test, interview, or naturalistic observation to obtain a sample of behavior. Sampling the behavior of 5-, 7-, and 9-year-olds at one point in time would also be cross-sectional, even where the goal is to infer behavioral change across these ages.

By contrast, *longitudinal* research assesses the same subjects at several points in time. The focus is on the process of change and relations between particular variables at different ages. Some questions cannot be answered without longitudinal research: "Is early behavior X correlated with later behavior Y?" "Is early event X a necessary condition for later behavior Y?" There is no way to know unless we get data on the same individuals at both time X and Y.

Retrospective Approach. Sometimes we can study relations between earlier and later variables *retrospectively* by finding people who now show behavior Y and similar people who do not show Y and then checking to see who showed or experienced X when they were young. Since the record of X is compared with current behavior Y, the retrospective approach may fulfill the aims of longitudinal research without requiring us to wait from the occurrence of X until the subsequent occurrence of Y. Because retrospective research starts with the current status of a variable and follows its history backwards, it is called a *follow-back* strategy.

Unfortunately, this very tempting strategy is plagued by certain weaknesses. The most obvious is that important early behavior and events are not recorded objectively and uniformly when they occur unless systematic procedures are adopted for doing so. Parents' recollections of even such objective facts as when their children first crawled, walked, and talked are notoriously vulnerable to distortion (Robins, 1963). Studies show that early characteristics potentially related to later personality or problems are still less likely to be remembered accurately, even if such characteristics are objectively defined (Yarrow, Campbell, & Burton, 1970).

A second problem with retrospective research arises when the Y behavior is deviant and comparisons are made with the histories of nondeviant people. If parents are the source of retrospective data, their child's current deviance may cause them to focus on the pathological aspects of the early history more than parents of nondeviant children. We can avoid this *pathological bias* in memory by using information not affected by knowledge of current status, such as early records or informants ignorant of the subjects' current status.

A third problem is bias in the *selection* of people currently showing or not showing behavior Y. Suppose we start with hospitalized adolescents diagnosed as schizophrenic (a summary term for a certain collection of Y behavior). Suppose we find that the second-grade school records (unaffected by current status) of 80 percent of the schizophrenics reported shyness, while the records of 20 percent of normal adolescents (a non-Y comparison group) reported shyness. Can we conclude that shyness is a more common forerunner of schizophrenia than of normal adolescence? The correlation may be useful, yet perhaps the schizophrenics who were not shy in second grade tend not to be hospitalized in adolescence. They may be in reform schools, may die young, or for other reasons may be absent from our hospital sample, even though they fit the Y category of schizophrenia.

Prospective Approach. The best way to overcome these problems is through *prospective* longitudinal research in which we obtain data as our subjects age. Because prospective longitudinal studies demand so much time and effort, they warrant exceptionally careful preliminary planning and research (which may be cross-sectional or retrospective).

Studying subjects as they age does not automatically avoid all the problems of retrospective studies, however. Just as *recent* impressions affect *recall* of previous observations in a retrospective study, observers' *first* impressions of a child may affect their *later* observations in a prospective study. Hence, observations at successive time periods should be made independently of one another—by using different observers at each data collection point, for example, especially for behavior difficult to score objectively. The observational techniques themselves must also be carefully designed to avoid affecting subjects' behavior and development.

Another problem of prospective research is the formation and retention of subject samples. Since continued cooperation and availability are needed, most long-term prospective studies employ middle-class children from stable families. Findings on these children cannot be readily generalized to those from other backgrounds, but long-term studies can seldom be designed to get data on fully representative samples. Even if we start with large samples representative of all important socioeconomic, ethnic, and urban-suburban-rural segments of a population, differential attrition will cause sampling biases in some groups by the study's end. Broadly representative samples are especially impractical for studying psychopathology, because the rate of psychopathology is low in most populations. No generalizations about the development of schizophrenia can be made, for instance, from a sample of 200 children in which only one eventually becomes schizophrenic.

Because broadly representative samples yield few major disorders, researchers often seek samples having especially high rates of a disorder. To study antecedents of schizophrenia, we may look for children who have a *high risk* of becoming schizophrenic, for example, the children of schizophrenic parents. Since many high-risk children never become schizophrenic, we can compare our longitudinal data on those who ultimately become schizophrenic and those who do not. Exactly this strategy is being pursued in a longitudinal study of schizophrenia in Denmark, where national medical services keep track of even the most unstable families (Mednick, Schulsinger, & Venables, 1979; discussed further in Chapter 12).

Another approach is the *follow-up* strategy. Here individuals known to have certain early characteristics are sought out later to identify differential outcomes. However, when subjects are not continously monitored, biases can arise in finding subjects for follow-up; there are also gaps in information linking early variables to later outcomes.

Longitudinal studies are sometimes launched under the illusion that everything important about a child will be recorded and then meshed with later observations to answer every question about development. Unhappily, this is unrealistic, because selectivity is unavoidable in choosing observations and procedures for making them. Moreover, certain important data can only be obtained by designing special situations for testing hypotheses, instead of merely extracting information after-the-fact from the ongoing stream of behavior.

Combining Longitudinal and Cross-sectional Strategies. Longitudinal and cross-sectional research are both vulnerable to biases arising from the confounding of *cohort* and *time-of-assessment* effects with developmental effects. *Cohort effects* reflect similarities among individuals born at about the same point in history, for example, during the same year. As they age, members of a cohort experience conditions differentiating them from cohorts born earlier and later. As a result, their behavior at a particular age reflects not only characteristics typical of that age but also some that are unique to their cohort. When we make conventional cross-sectional comparisons between children who differ in age *and* cohort, we may wrongly attribute certain differences to age when they actually arise from differences between cohorts. In longitudinal research on a single cohort, age changes in behavior may reflect changes unique to that cohort as it grows older, instead of age changes that occur in all cohorts. Cohorts born in the 1930s, for example, had lower delinquency rates than those born in the 1940s. Age changes in delinquent behavior would therefore differ in the earlier and later cohorts.

Time-of-assessment effects are a related source of bias. They arise because every cohort reaches a particular age at only one point in history. Since the relation between age and historical time is unique to each cohort, the effects of historical conditions are intertwined with the age of subjects in developmental studies. For example, Nesselroade and Baltes (1974) found that 16-year-olds declined in superego strength over a 2-year period. However, because they also studied 13-, 14-, and 15-year old cohorts over the same 2 years, they discovered that the decline in superego strength was not specific to the developmental period traversed by the 16-year-olds. Instead, it occurred in all four cohorts, apparently as a result of cultural conditions.

To make the roles of age, cohort, and time-of-assessment more explicit, life-span developmental psychologists have proposed hybrid research designs combining aspects of conventional cross-sectional and longitudinal designs (Baltes, Reese, & Nesselroade, 1977). Table 5-1a depicts two hybrid designs. In the *longitudinal sequential* design, several cohorts of subjects are studied longitudinally over the same period. We can then determine if changes occurring with age in one cohort are unique to the ages spanned in that cohort or if similar changes occur in other cohorts spanning other ages. If similar changes occur in several cohorts despite age differences, this suggests that the changes arise from cultural-historical factors, not just aging alone.

A second hybrid design, the *cross-sectional sequential* design, parallels the longitudinal sequential design. As Table 5-1b shows, however, the cross-sectional sequential design uses a *new sample* from each cohort at each assessment point. We can thereby assess changes occurring with age in each cohort without risking the effects of retesting and attrition. On the other hand, we cannot trace individual development or compare the development of subjects who initially differ on particular variables.

The hybrid designs alone cannot completely disentangle all possible influences on development (cf. Achenbach, 1980a). Instead, combinations of exploratory, hypothesis-testing, correlational, experimental, cross-sectional, and longitudinal research are needed to elucidate complex relationships obscured by reliance on any single approach.

Extensive versus Intensive Research

Most research on psychopathology makes comparisons either among groups or of one group with itself at different times. When differences between groups or within a group over time are found, these differences are often assumed to characterize each member of the group.

Suppose one group of hyperactive children receives a new drug while a control group gets a placebo in a double-blind procedure. If the experimental group becomes less hyperactive than the control group, we conclude that the drug reduces hyperactivity. This is an example of *extensive* research: The procedures, evaluation of results, conclusions, and consequences are all *extended* over many individuals grouped by the hyperactivity they have in common.

Nearly all generalizations about behavior depend on group findings, because no one individual can serve as a test case for everyone else. Humans vary in so many ways that generalizations about a particular variable are justified only when findings are based on many people *and* these findings substantially exceed the random variation among the people. Statistical tests show whether a finding sufficiently exceeds random variation among observations to assure us that the finding would recur if we made new observations under similar conditions. As a

Table 5-1   Longitudinal Sequential and Cross-sectional Sequential Designs

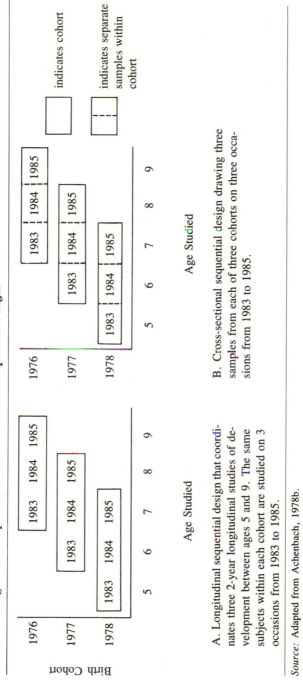

A. Longitudinal sequential design that coordinates three 2-year longitudinal studies of development between ages 5 and 9. The same subjects within each cohort are studied on 3 occasions from 1983 to 1985.

B. Cross-sectional sequential design drawing three samples from each of three cohorts on three occasions from 1983 to 1985.

Source: Adapted from Achenbach, 1978b.

111

standard practice, we accept a finding as reliable if there is a "statistically significant" *probability* (symbolized by p) that the finding would occur by chance less than 5 times in a hundred repetitions of similar conditions. In other words, $p <$ .05 indicates that a particular difference found between groups would occur by chance less than five times in a hundred and is, therefore, likely to be repeatable. To conclude that a drug *significantly* reduces hyperactivity, for example, the decrease in hyperactivity for the treated group must exceed that for the placebo group by an amount that would occur by chance less than five times in a hundred.

We must nevertheless look closely at the findings of group differences. A statistically significant decrease in hyperactivity in a group receiving a drug does not mean that all members benefited uniformly. Some may improve greatly, causing a drop in mean hyperactivity scores for the whole group, but others do not change or get worse. A look at individual scores may disclose subgroups who had opposite responses. Detecting *interactions* between child characteristics and drug responses can help us pinpoint the drug's effects according to who gets it.

The purest form of this strategy involves studying variation in one individual under various conditions. This *intensive* (or *single case,* or *ipsative*) approach may be particularly appropriate for discovering what variables affect a particular child and/or what treatment is most effective. First, we keep a record of the child's behavior for several weeks. When we detect relations between events in the child's life and behavior, we can form hypotheses about the contingencies supporting the behavior. We can test these hypotheses by waiting to see if they predict the child's reactions to new events or by manipulating the relevant contingencies.

Effects of therapies, such as drugs and behavior modification, may be tested by applying the therapy and then stopping to see if the problem behavior returns, and so on, until we can confirm therapeutic benefits. As discussed in Chapter 10, experimental manipulation of contingencies for single cases is the preferred method of operant conditioners. Although intensive procedures cannot completely replace extensive methods, they can help change a question like, "Does treatment X work?" to a more appropriate one: "Which combination of procedures helps this child most?"

EXPLANATION, PREDICTION, AND CONTROL

Is explanation, prediction, or control the most central aim of science? Because "science" refers to obtaining knowledge, explanation is probably the most universal aim. However, the nature of explanation varies with the topic. The ultimate value of most explanations depends on whether they help us solve problems.

Because the study of psychopathology is directed toward prevention and treatment, explanations can be evaluated according to their potential for prediction and control. Prediction may take the following forms: "Genotype X is more likely to result in schizophrenia than genotype Y." "Early experience X is more likely to result in schizophrenia than early experience Y." "Treatment procedures AB will probably help a person diagnosed schizophrenic more than procedures CD." "Child A is likely to become more seriously disturbed as she grows older unless treatment T is started now." "The parents of child A will probably not cooperate in treatment X." "Child C's cognitive growth is likely to progress no further."

We express the goal of controlling behavior in the following ways: "To prevent schizophrenia in child X, implement procedures Y and Z." "To help retarded child C use all of his ability, provide him with educational procedure X." "To relieve child A's depression, provide treatment S."

Clinical versus Statistical Prediction

Although methods of control (prevention and treatment) will be discussed in other chapters, efforts at prediction raise issues important here. Paul Meehl (1954) formulated the prediction problem in terms of clinical and statistical approaches. In the *clinical* or *case-study* method of prediction, we predict an individual's behavior from a hypothesis about that person's personality and an expectation about the environmental events he or she will encounter. A clinician who interviews a client, studies the client's life history, and combines everything known about the client and situation into a guess about a probable outcome is employing clinical prediction.

In *statistical* or *actuarial* prediction, by contrast, we combine data according to a predetermined formula that computes the probability of a certain outcome. The information may be similar to that considered by the clinician, but the procedure for combining it into a prediction involves weighting it according to a formula based on known outcomes for similar people.

A common statistical prediction procedure is the table actuaries use to set life insurance rates. Insurance companies maintain precise tables of death rates for people at each age. Within each age group, tables are further broken down by sex, occupation, and health history. The life insurance premium for a person of a given age, sex, occupation, and health history is then set according to the known death rate for similar people. Actuaries need not know *why* particular individuals die. Instead, the accuracy with which this year's table portrays the distribution of next year's deaths tests the table's predictive power. Prediction from a table is not a precise statement of outcome for individual clients: It is a statement of the proportion of a particular class of clients who will show a particular outcome.

A similar approach is used to predict juvenile delinquency from tables based on psychological test scores, family characteristics, and ratings of character traits (Glueck & Glueck, 1970). Accurately identifying children at high risk for delinquency can help us develop prevention programs. As in all statistical methods of prediction, the accuracy of a prediction table for delinquency must be *cross-validated* (tested) with a sample of children other than those on whom the table was developed. Otherwise, the prediction formula may capitalize on idiosyncracies of the original sample that are absent in new samples.

Statistical prediction requires precise specification of variables relating to the target outcomes in samples large enough for computing prediction formulas. Predictors may include subjective judgments based on clinical impressions, but these judgments must be specified precisely enough to include in the prediction formula.

Clinical prediction can also use data that can be precisely categorized (e.g., marital status) and are even quantitative (e.g., IQ, age). However, the data are combined and weighted subjectively by the clinician for the individual client. Unlike clinical judgments used for statistical prediction, those used for clinical prediction need not be specified precisely enough for categorization. They can remain intuitions in the clinician's mind as he or she develops hypotheses from which to make predictions.

In reviewing comparisons of clinical and statistical predictions of behavioral outcomes, Meehl (1954) found the accuracy of statistical prediction equal or superior to that of clinical prediction in almost all studies. Later studies have likewise shown greater accuracy for statistical than clinical prediction (Wiggins, 1981).

Clinical Versus "Mechanical" Modes of Data Collection

Making accurate predictions depends as much on procedures for *obtaining* data about a client as on procedures for *combining* the data. Data consisting entirely of a clinician's impressions differ from data collected in a more "mechanical" way: by using structured psychological tests, by getting answers to specific factual questions, by making behavioral ratings, and so on.

Because data collected either clinically or mechanically can be combined either clinically or statistically, at least six separate prediction strategies are possible:

1. Clinical data combined clinically.
2. Clinical data combined statistically.
3. Mechanical data combined clinically.
4. Mechanical data combined statistically.
5. Clinical and mechanical data combined clinically.
6. Clinical and mechanical data combined statistically.

As an example, a clinician who derives intuitions from an interview and scores from a test, then combines these clinical and mechanical data mentally to make a prediction, is using Strategy 5. Strategy 6 is exemplified when a clinician's impressions are scored and used with test scores to assign a client to a particular cell of an actuarial table; the client's outcome is expected to be like that of other people assigned to the same cell.

Sawyer (1966) reviewed 45 studies in which predictions made from the six possible strategies could be compared. Table 5-2 shows the percentage of studies in which one strategy was more accurate than another strategy, plus one half the percentage of studies in which a strategy equaled the accuracy of another strategy. The specific percentages should be taken with a grain of salt, as Holt (1978) has pointed out problems in aggregating the findings.

Like Meehl, Sawyer concluded that statistical methods for *combining* data produced more accurate predictions than clinical methods for combining data. Statistical methods were superior whether the data were clinical, mechanical, or both. Thus, in Table 5-2, the strategies in the right-hand column (cells 2, 4, and 6) were each superior to the corresponding strategies in the left-hand column (cells 1, 3, and 5). Table 5-2 also shows that the mechanical mode of *data collection* was superior to the clinical mode whether the data were combined clinically or statistically (cells 3 and 4 versus cells 1 and 2).

When we look at the interface of each mode of data collection with each method of combining data, however, we see that the most accurate predictions were made using clinical *and* mechanical data combined statistically; that is, the most accurate predictions occurred in cell 6. Clinicians' judgments thus improve the accuracy of predictions made with purely mechanical data, but only when stated explicitly enough to be combined statistically. For example, a clinician's *ratings* of clients' likelihood of violent behavior can improve statistical prediction more than a global impression of whether a client might or might not be violent.

None of the studies that Sawyer reviewed dealt with young children, although 13 dealt with college applicants or students, 10 with military servicemen, and two with delinquents or former delinquents. The lack of studies comparing prediction

Table 5-2   Strategies for prediction.[a]

	Method of Data Combination	
Mode of Data Collection	*Clinical*	*Statistical*
Clinical	1. Intuitive (20%)	2. Trait ratings (43%)
Mechanical	3. Subjective interpretation of scores (38%)	4. Actuarial (63%)
Both clinical and mechanical	5. Mental combination of intuition and scores (26%)	6. Actuarial combination of trait ratings and scores (75%)

[a]Figures in parentheses are the percentage of studies in which a prediction strategy was more accurate than another strategy, plus one-half the percentage of studies in which two strategies were equal.
Source: Adapted from Sawyer (1966, p. 192). © 1966 by the American Psychological Association and reproduced by permission.

strategies for children's behavior reflects the lack of controlled research on the outcomes of child psychopathology rather than any intrinsic differences between prediction problems for child and adult behavior.

Despite the superiority of statistical methods of prediction, even these are quite inaccurate, inconsistently used, and applied to narrow problems. Moreover, there are situations in which we cannot obtain data on groups large enough to permit statistical predictions. Consequently, both clinical and statistical approaches to prediction deserve further research and development. We must constantly test predictions against actual outcomes to improve both approaches.

Outcome Research

Helping troubled children requires knowledge of the outcome of children's disorders under various conditions. Unless we know which problems interfere with long-term development and which do not, we have little basis for deciding who should receive help. To intervene effectively, we must also know which interventions improve the prognosis, make it worse, or leave it unchanged.

Explanation, prediction, treatment, or prevention is not possible without knowledge of outcomes. In considering specific disorders, we repeatedly face the question of what happens to children who have each disorder. Because the characteristics of the children and the effects of particular interventions both affect outcomes, we need to study *interactions* between child and treatment characteristics to answer the question "What works best for whom?"

SUMMARY

This chapter introduced criteria and strategies for gaining knowledge about psychopathology in children. We distinguished two aspects of scientific activity: the *context of discovery,* wherein ideas are generated, and the *context of confirmation,* wherein ideas are tested. A parallel was drawn between the scientist in the context of discovery and the clinician forming impressions of clients. Both must confirm their hypotheses via systematic observation.

The following criteria guide the confirmation of knowledge: *testability* of hypotheses, which is best achieved when variables are *operationally defined; reliability* of observations, including *interobserver* reliability, *test-retest* reliability, and *internal consistency; validity* of observations, tested via other assessments of the same variables; *internal* and *external validity* of inferences from data; and detection of relations between variables by assessing the variables when they have different values, for example, by means of *comparison* or *control* groups, or using individuals as their *own controls.* Proper controls often require *placebo* and *double-blind* procedures.

Theories provide conceptual order for observations. We can seldom prove or disprove theories, but we can choose among them according to their yield of confirmed statements. *Hypothetical constructs* are theoretical concepts formulated to explain observations and suggest new testable statements about reality.

Causes of psychopathology seldom involve simple one-to-one relations of mechanical cause and effect. Instead, causes are better viewed in terms of *conditions* that are *necessary, sufficient, necessary and sufficient,* or *contributory* to particular outcomes.

Research methods in psychopathology can be ordered along the following dimensions: *exploratory* versus *hypothesis-testing; correlational* versus *experimental,* according to whether *independent variables* are manipulated; *cross-sectional* versus *longitudinal,* including *retrospective* and *prospective* variants of longitudinal approaches; and *extensive* versus *intensive,* according to a focus on variation extending across individuals versus within single individuals. Various combinations of approaches, such as *longitudinal sequential* and *cross-sectional sequential* designs, are needed to reduce biases inherent in each approach used alone.

Prediction and control (i.e., prevention, treatment) are both goals of research on psychopathology. Comparisons of *clinical* and *statistical* methods of *prediction* and *clinical* and *mechanical* modes of *data gathering* show that statistical prediction and mechanical data collection generally yield more accurate predictions than purely clinical methods. No approach is completely accurate, however, and prediction procedures must be improved. This requires research on *interactions* between child and treatment variables in the determination of outcomes.

SUGGESTED READING

Scientific Thinking. Thomas Kuhn's (1970) short book, *The Structure of Scientific Revolutions,* is acclaimed for its analysis of how major changes in scientific thinking occur. Kuhn's portrayal of the precedence that theories or conceptual "paradigms" often take over facts is especially apt for the the study of psychopathology. The need for theory and the risks of overcommitment to theories are both well documented. In a later work, Kuhn (1977) sheds further light on these issues, including his second thoughts on paradigms.

Strategies for Developmental Research. Baltes, Reese, and Nesselroade (1977) present life-span research designs intended to separate the contributions of cohort effects and time-of-assessment effects from developmental effects. A second book, on concepts, strategies, and methods of developmental research (Achenbach, 1978b), emphasizes the broad core of concepts and research tools common to most developmental research and its applications to practical problems such as the treatment of child psychopathology. Achenbach (1980a) also appraises some intrinsic handicaps to developmental research that are not resolved by life-span designs and may require compromise and alternative strategies.

Clinical Assessment and Research. The fact that discussions of developmental and child clinical concerns are seldom found together reflects the dearth of developmental research on psychopathology. However, methodological problems have been analyzed in articles by Achenbach (1978a) and O'Leary and Turkewitz (1978), both published in a special issue of the *Journal of Consulting and Clinical Psychology* devoted to problems of clinical research. Robins (1979) presents applications of longitudinal methods to normal and pathological development. Several series, such as *Advances in Clinical Child Psychology* (Lahey & Kazdin, 1982), demonstrate a growing sophistication about child psychopathology. Although not directed toward work with children, Chassan (1978) provides detailed comparisons of extensive and intensive research designs, while Kazdin (1980) gives a comprehensive introduction to research design in clinical psychology.

Clinical versus Statistical Prediction. Meehl (1954) first formulated this issue in terms that became the focus of extended controversy, while Sawyer (1966) extended Meehl's analyses to methods for collecting data. Holt (1978) states clinicians' arguments against conclusions favoring statistical prediction, and Wiggins (1981) offers additional evidence for its superiority.

CHAPTER 6

Genetic Factors

Most views of psychological development are rooted in biological assumptions. Before considering genetic factors in behavior, we need to consider biogenetic aspects of the psychoanalytic, learning, Piagetian, and ethological views of development.

VIEWS ON HUMAN BEHAVIORAL DEVELOPMENT

Psychoanalysis

Freud's concept of an innate, organically based motivational force has been a cornerstone of psychoanalytic theory from its inception. His original German word for the psychological aspect of this force was *Trieb* (drive), but it was widely translated as "instinct." Confusion has arisen because, outside psychoanalysis, "instinct" refers to innately determined *behavior patterns*, whereas Freud's term referred to *motivation*. Among psychoanalysts, *instinctual drive* has generally replaced "instinct" as a term for inborn motivational forces (cf. Moore & Fine, 1968).

The two main instinctual drives are the *libidinal* (sexual) and *aggressive* drives. The motives they represent are assumed to be organically based, but psychoanalysis deals with them mainly in terms of *psychic energy*. This is a hypothetical motivational force analogous to physical energy. *Psychodynamics* refers to the distribution of this energy within the personality.

Freud evidently believed that psychosexual development was determined more by biological than cultural factors. Environmental factors helped explain particular outcomes, but biological maturation, instinctual drive development, and various constitutional factors determined the developmental sequence.

Later analysts theorized that certain ego functions develop independently of instinctual drives. These functions thus have *primary autonomy* from the drives. The autonomous ego functions include perception, motility (walking, use of hands, etc.), intention (planning, anticipation), thinking, and language. Their rate and final level of development are assumed to depend on biogenetic determinants other than the instinctual drives (Moore & Fine, 1968).

Learning Theories

There are many learning theories, but most share certain biologic assumptions. One assumption is that some important behaviors are not solely a result of environmental contingencies. These behaviors include reflexes that are available at birth or become available through maturation. Just as learning is viewed as a process whereby individuals adapt themselves to particular environments, reflexes are viewed as inborn adaptive procedures evolving in each species through natural selection.

The sucking reflex is of obvious importance for infant survival. But numerous other reflexes also have survival value or did earlier in the evolution of our species (Kessen, Haith, & Salapatek, 1970). Reflexes are especially emphasized in Soviet psychology where the Pavlovian study of learning is known as *reflexology*, because it mainly concerns the conditioning of reflexive responses.

Most learning theorists acknowledge innately determined complex behaviors but minimize their role in favor of behavior shaped by the environment. Even the founder of behaviorism, John B. Watson (1924), acknowledged that human babies innately fear loud sounds and loss of support. But he held that all other fears are learned via experiences associated with innately feared stimuli or pain.

Like psychoanalysts, learning theorists grant motivation stemming from organic needs a central role in development. Hunger, thirst, sex, and physical discomforts are postulated as *primary drives*; early learning consists mainly of acquiring responses that reduce these drives. If a response reduces discomfort, this *reinforces* the response, that is, it increases the probability or strength of the response in similar situations. Exploration and other forms of behavior not readily explained by reduction of organic discomfort have suggested additional motives such as curiosity (Berlyne, 1960) and competence or "effectance" (White, 1959).

Learning theories also assume similar laws of learning across species. Thus, for example, particular reinforcement schedules are expected to have similar effects on bar pressing by rats, key pecking by pigeons, and social behaviors in humans.

This assumption reflects a belief in the biologically based adaptive function of learning.

Piagetian Theory

As we saw in Chapter 3, Piaget viewed the child's procedures for building knowledge as techniques for adapting to the environment. Just as anatomic structures serve specific physical functions, cognitive structures serve to process specific kinds of information. Cognitive structures are shaped by two types of hereditary influence: *Specific heredity* and *general heredity*.

Specific Heredity. Cognitive development is assumed to follow the same principles as physical development. Genes carry codes or basic plans for the structures characterizing a species. The *specific heredity* of humans, for example, does not include wings, sense organs for detecting infrared light, or fins for swimming, but it does include equipment for walking upright, precise control of vocalization, and developing cognitive structures for quantity.

General Heredity. Besides species-specific characteristics, all organisms inherit similar modes of adaptation. Piaget viewed this *general heredity* in terms of two complementary processes: *assimilation* and *accommodation*. *Assimilation* is activity by which organisms transform environmental inputs for their own needs. A physiologic example is the process of eating, whereby an organism extracts nutriment from food. Cognitive examples are evident in young children at play. Through make-believe, children assimilate objects and situations to their own fantasy. A delightful example of playful assimilation is Piaget's (1962) 16-month-old daughter gleefully pretending the tail of her toy donkey is a pillow on which she is about to sleep.

Accommodation is activity by which organisms change themselves as they adapt to their environment. In digestion, the stretching of the stomach as it receives food is accommodation coordinated with the assimilatory process of extracting nutriment. An elementary behavioral accommodation is the baby's progressive modification of its sucking reflex until it sucks directly on the nipple instead of the surrounding area. At a higher level, accommodation is exemplified by children imitating other people, that is, molding their behavior to copy models in their environment.

In play and imitation, we can see assimilation and accommodation in pure form. But successful adaptation requires coordinating assimilation and accommodation. Some maladaptive functioning, such as psychotic thinking, may involve excessive assimilation of input to the individual's way of construing it. Other problems, such as extreme conformity, may be seen as an excess of accommodation.

Animal Ethology

All three major theories of human behavioral development use biologic assumptions and concepts. A fourth viewpoint, that of animal ethology, also applies to human behavioral development, both normal and abnormal (Eibl-Eibesfeldt, 1975).

Ethology is the study of the natural unfolding of animal behavior. Ethological studies typically start with observations of animal behavior in its natural habitat, but often manipulate environmental conditions to pinpoint the stimuli triggering genetically programmed behaviors.

Ethologists have demonstrated intriguing phenomena in numerous species: imprinting in fowl, fighting and courtship rituals in fish, and social organization in insects, for example. Mother−infant attachment has been an especially central topic of human ethological research (Bowlby, 1980). However, innately determined behaviors in one species seldom justify inferring that other species' behavior is caused in the same way. Extrapolation of animal findings to humans deserves special skepticism. Still, ethological views and research can help us understand human behavior. As Hess (1970) puts it:

> Fundamentally, it is the ethological *attitude* which is most valuable in the analysis of human behavior, rather than merely the use of particular *terms* used by ethologists. An investigator does not need to be an ethologist or even to have had any direct contact with ethology to make behavior analyses which are congruent with ethological thinking. He merely must approach his subject with a concern for the *complete* context in which observed behaviors occur, including biological bases and adaptive functions [p. 24].

An ethological attitude is helpful in integrating the major psychological views with biological concepts. Psychoanalysis, learning theory, and Piagetian theory all see behavioral development as a process by which organisms adapt biologically to their environments. They agree that particular strategies of adaptation occur because they have been successful over the course of evolution. However, we must judge each view in light of findings on relations between behavior and biology.

MECHANISMS OF GENETIC TRANSMISSION

Genetic research is increasingly important in the study of development. We turn now to basic genetic concepts and disorders for which the genetic mechanisms are understood.

Chromosomes

The nucleus of every human cell contains tiny threadlike bodies know as *chromosomes* (from Greek *chroma* = color, because they selectively absorb certain colors of stain). The normal human body cell has 46 chromosomes, arranged in 23 pairs. Chromosomes are studied by photographing them through a microscope. Each chromosome is then cut out of a photographic enlargement and arranged into pairs in a standard order according to features such as length. This arrangement is known as a *karyotype*. Chromosomal abnormalities are detected by comparing a person's karyotype with standardized normal karyotypes. Figure 6-1 shows a normal human karyotype.

Mitosis. When a typical body cell prepares to reproduce itself to form another body cell, each of its 46 chromosomes doubles. Each chromosome than divides in half, yielding two groups of 46 chromosomes each. The two groups of 46 chromosomes migrate to opposite sides of the cell. A wall forms between them and the cell splits, yielding two new cells. Each new cell contains one group of 46 chromosomes identical to the original group of 46. The splitting of the 46 chromosomes to form two new cells, each having 46 chromosomes, is known as *mitosis*.

Meiosis. Sex cells or *gametes*—male sperm cells and female egg (ovum) cells—are not produced like body cells. Instead, they are produced by *germ cells* located in the gonads, through a process called *meiosis*. Unlike mitosis, there is no doubling and splitting of the 46 chromosomes in meiosis. On the contrary, the members of each pair of chromosomes in the germ cell separate from each other. Each set of 23 migrates to the opposite sides of the original cell, a wall forms between them, and two new cells result. Each new cell has just 23 of the original chromosomes.

Genes

Chromosomes are readily seen with a microscope. But genes, the actual units of hereditary transmission, are much tinier. Thousands of genes comprise each chromosome. All an individual's genes together are called the *genome*. Until a single gene was isolated through biochemical research, the gene was a hypothetical construct. Although some genes are now studied directly, hypothetical constructs continue to guide theory and research on the genetic transmission of *phenotypic* traits, the observable characteristics of the organism.

As Watson and Crick (1953) deduced, genes are composed of deoxyribonucleic acid (DNA) molecules shaped like two chains coiled around each other in the shape of a double helix. Structures like the rungs of a ladder join the two chains in a form resembling a spiral staircase. Some species have nonchromosomal genes located outside their cell nuclei (Sager, 1965), but human genetics focuses on genes located on the chromosomes.

When chromosomes double during mitosis, the two chains of the DNA molecule unwind while portions of each runglike structure separate. Part of each rung remains with each chain. From raw materials in the cell nucleus, a new chain forms along the ends of the rungs remaining with each original chain of the DNA molecule. The result is a pair of new double-helix DNA molecules just like the

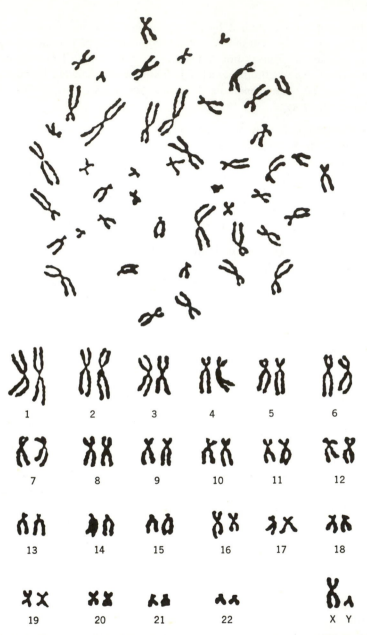

Figure 6–1. A photomicrograph of the chromosomes in a normal human cell (above) and their arrangement into a standard order known as a *karyotype* (below). Note that the members of the twenty-third pair of chromosomes (lower right-hand corner) differ from one another—since this is the cell of a male, one of these chromosomes is a male (Y) chromosome, white the other (X) chromosome is like that found in the cells of females as well as males. (From Penrose, 1961.)

original one. The two new molecules become components of the two new chromosomes resulting from mitosis.

Information coded in the DNA molecule must be transmitted to the point in a cell where it triggers a biochemical chain reaction. This transmission occurs in two steps. First, the information from the DNA molecule is copied onto a ribonucleic acid (RNA) molecule, which is molded into a shape like the helical chain of the DNA molecule. Second, this *messenger RNA* molecule enters the region of the cell where the genetic information it carries guides protein synthesis. The chemical reaction regulated by the messenger RNA molecule determines what organ arises from a cell and how the organ will function.

Creation of a New Individual

When a sperm penetrates an ovum at conception, the 23 chromosomes in the sperm's nucleus join the 23 chromosomes in the ovum's nucleus to form 23 pairs. The normal fertilized ovum, called a *zygote*, thus has a full complement of 46 chromosomes. Each pair of chromosomes contains one member from each parent. Miraculous as it may seem, the paternal chromosomes align themselves with the maternal chromosomes so that each gene on a paternal chromosome is next to the gene on the maternal chromosome controlling exactly the same trait. The different variants of genes that control a particular trait and occupy corresponding loci on the paired chromosomes are called *alleles*. For example, one allele, or variant, of the gene for eye color causes blue eyes, while a different allele causes brown eyes. The paternal and maternal alleles for eye color are aligned beside each other in two adjoining chromosomes of the offspring.

Mendel's Laws

The genetic principles formulated by Gregor Mendel in 1866 concern traits having only two possible alleles. Suppose, for example, a boy inherits blue-eyed alleles from both his mother and father. He is therefore *homozygous* for eye color; both alleles are the same, so the *zygote* is *homogeneous* for eye color. The boy will have blue eyes and can pass only an allele for blue eyes to his own offspring.

If the boy mates with a girl who has alleles only for brown eyes, she can pass only a brown-eyed allele to their child. Since this child receives the blue allele from one parent and the brown allele from the other, the child is *heterozygous* for eye color. The alleles are different, so the *zygote* is *heterogeneous* for eye color.

According to Mendel's laws, one allele dominates the other in the phenotypic expression of a heterozygous genotype. We represent dominant alleles with a capital letter and recessive alleles with a small letter. Brown (B) eye color happens to be dominant over blue (b). Consequently, the heterozygous (Bb) child of the homozygous blue-eyed parent (bb) and the homozygous brown-eyed parent (BB) will have brown eyes. Yet, since half the child's chromosomes carry the blue allele and half the brown allele, this Bb offspring will pass a blue allele to approximately half its own offspring. The eye color of these offspring will be determined by whether they get a blue or brown allele from their other parent. But the offspring who get the brown allele will have brown eyes, no matter what allele they get from their other parent.

Figure 6-2 shows this sequence of Mendelian heredity. Whenever one or both parents are heterozygous for a trait, as often occurs, their children are not all likely to inherit the same genotype. Moreover, because so many different gene combinations can arise from two parents, two siblings seldom have the same genes, unless they come from the same zygote. Then they are identical twins.

Exceptions to Mendel's Laws

Mendel's laws are enormously powerful in predicting and controlling the heredity of many traits in many species. But exceptions occur that require new principles. The exceptions are especially important for detecting genetic effects on human behavioral disorders, since these disorders seldom conform to Mendelian formulas. Because some exceptions involve deviations from the principle of dominance-recessiveness, we symbolize the different alleles of a gene with letters and numbers (e.g., A_1 and A_2) instead of capital and small letters. This shows that neither allele necessarily dominates the other.

Partial Dominance. One exception to Mendelian principles is the lack of complete dominance by one allele over another. For some traits, one allele is only *partially dominant* over the other. That is, someone who has both the dominant and recessive alleles (A_1A_2) for a trait is phenotypically more like the dominant (A_1A_1) version of the trait than like the recessive (A_2A_2) version, but is not as extreme as someone who has only dominant alleles.

As an example, a dominant allele is responsible for the normal metabolism of phenylalanine. The recessive allele of the same gene fails to promote normal metabolism. Children who get the recessive allele from both parents cannot metabolize phenylalanine; they become retarded unless phenylalanine is excluded from their diet. People who are heterozygous—have one dominant and one recessive allele—have been found to metabolize phenylalanine less well than those who have only dominant alleles, but they seem normal otherwise (Fuller & Thompson, 1978).

Additivity. Another deviation from Mendel's dominant-recessive model occurs with alleles having *additive* effects. In such cases, each allele (A_1 and A_2) contributes a different degree of the phenotypic trait. The strength of a phenotypic trait of a heterozygote (A_1A_2) is halfway between the strength for a homozygote whose alleles are both of one type (A_1A_1) and the strength for a homozygote whose alleles

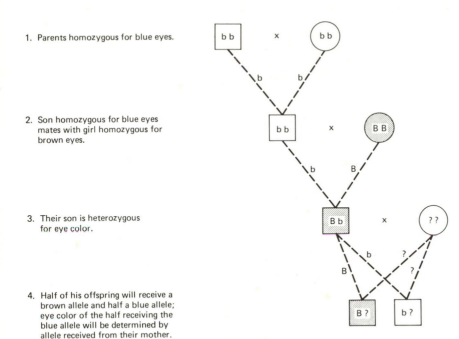

1. Parents homozygous for blue eyes.

2. Son homozygous for blue eyes mates with girl homozygous for brown eyes.

3. Their son is heterozygous for eye color.

4. Half of his offspring will receive a brown allele and half a blue allele; eye color of the half receiving the blue allele will be determined by allele received from their mother.

b = Blue allele
B = Brown (dominant) allele
▨ = Brown-eyed phenotype

Figure 6-2. Illustration of Mendelian principles of genetic transmission.

are both of the opposite type (A_2A_2). Height, for example, is hypothesized to be affected by alleles having additive properties: A person who inherits one tall allele and one short allele measures halfway between people who inherit two short alleles (A_1A_1) and those who inherit two tall alleles (A_2A_2).

Figure 6-3 shows relations between genotypes and phenotypes for classical *dominant* and *recessive* alleles, *partially dominant* alleles, and alleles having *additive* effects. Three genotypes are listed on the horizontal axis according to the number of A_2 alleles present (0, 1, or 2). Phenotypic values are listed on the vertical axis: 0 stands for the value expected for an A_1A_1 genotype and 2 the value for an A_2A_2 genotype. You can see that traits involving partial dominance and additivity are manifest in *degrees*, rather than in "either-or" fashion.

Polygenes and Major Genes. Another exception to Mendelian principles is the *joint control* of a phenotypic trait by more than one gene. Such genes are known as *polygenes*, in contrast to *major genes*, those that determine a trait by themselves.

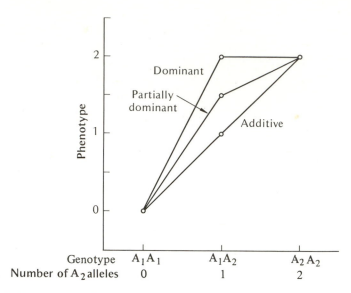

Figure 6–3. Relationships of phenotype to genotype for alleles having dominant-recessive, partially dominant, and additive characteristics. (Adapted from McClearn, 1970.)

Like partial dominance and additivity, *polygenic* (or *multifactorial*) determination causes a trait to occur in degrees instead of an either-or fashion. Even a few polygenes can yield a broad range of variation in a trait. Traits that vary continuously over a broad spectrum (e.g., height, hair color) are probably affected by polygenes whose alleles have additive effects.

Penetrance. *Penetrance* refers to the *percentage of cases* having a particular genotype in which the genotype is phenotypically manifested. For example, a trait (T) governed by a gene with Mendelian dominant (T) and recessive (t) alleles is *completely penetrant* if it is manifest in all TT and Tt individuals. Some traits are *partially penetrant*, however: They are manifest in less than 100 percent of TT and Tt individuals. A trait manifest in 90 percent of TT and Tt individuals is called "90 percent penetrant." Note how partial penetrance differs from partial dominance and additivity: Partially penetrant traits appear *only* in *either* T or t forms. The deviation from Mendelian principles involves the lack of perfect predictability of *which* phenotype (T or t) will result from a given genotype, instead of a trait's tendency to occur in degrees, as with partial dominance and additivity. Some have hypothesized that schizophrenia, for example, is caused by a partially penetrant dominant gene (Gottesman & Shields, 1972).

Expressivity. *Expressivity* refers to the *degree* of a trait's phenotypic expression in individuals having the genotype for that trait. A *partially expressed* trait fails to be fully manifest in everybody having the appropriate genotype. Thus, some TT and Tt individuals manifest a mild degree of a trait or only some aspects of the trait even though they carry genes that usually cause complete expression of the trait. Like partial dominance and additivity, partial expression produces intermediate degrees of a trait. The failure of genes to be completely penetrant or completely expressive may reflect environmental factors or other genes that moderate or counteract their effects.

Sex Chromosomes and Autosomes

In the human karyotype, the chromosomes designated as the 23rd pair control the sex of the offspring. In males, the two sex chromosomes differ markedly from each other (see Figure 6-1). One member of the pair is the *X chromosome*, which is the same as both members of the 23rd pair of chromosomes in females. The other member is the *Y chromosome*, which is considerably shorter than the X chromosome.

When testes produce sperm, each sperm gets *either* an X chromosome *or* a Y chromosome. If a sperm containing an X chromosome fertilizes an ovum, the zygote is XX because the ovum can get only an X chromosome from the mother. The offspring will be female. On the other hand, if a sperm containing a Y chromosome fertilizes an ovum, the zygote will be XY and the offspring will be male, because the Y chromosome carries the genetic information for male sex characteristics. The 44 chromosomes (22 pairs) that are not sex chromosomes are called *autosomes*.

Sex-linked Traits. Beside information for sexual development, genes on the X and Y chromosomes differ in other information they carry. This explains why some traits are sex-linked. For example, boys inherit color blindness only through their mothers, even when the mother herself is not color blind. This is because the gene for color vision occurs only on the X chromosome. Most women who carry the recessive color-blind allele on one of their X chromosomes have a dominant allele for normal color vision on their other X chromosome. Their dominant normal allele produces phenotypically normal color vision. However, half their ova have X chromosomes with the color-blind allele. If a sperm containing a Y chromosome fertilizes one of these ova, the offspring will, of course, be male because of the XY combination. And the male will be color blind, because the Y chromosome has no gene for color vision.

On the average, 50 percent of the sons of a woman heterozygous for color blindness will be color blind. None of her daughters will be color blind unless her husband is also color blind; that is, unless his X chromosomes contain the color-blind allele. If her husband is color blind, then about half her daughters will be color blind, because they get the color-blind allele on the X chromosomes they inherit from each parent. Sex-linked traits transmitted in a similar way include hemophilia, baldness, some forms of muscular dystrophy, and Lesch-Nyhan syndrome. This is a metabolic disorder interfering with neurologic functioning and causing compulsive self-mutilation such as biting the self (Reed, 1975).

Genes on the X chromosome affect many aspects of physical and behavioral adaptation. This helps to explain the higher male death rates beginning prenatally (McMillen, 1979) and higher male rates of neurological impairment, speech, hearing, vision, and health problems, educational retardation, and emotional disturbance (Mumpower, 1970). When a male has a maladapative mutant or recessive allele on his X chromosome, his lack of a second X chromosome gives him no chance of having the normal allele as well. But because a female has two X chromosomes, she has a good chance of offsetting a maladaptive allele on one X chromosome with an adaptive allele on the other (Hamburg, 1977).

GENETIC CONTRIBUTIONS TO DEVELOPMENT

Figure 6-4 illustrates genetic and other biological contributions to development. The bottom contributions are *hereditary*. These include only the information transmitted by intact genes from the parents, although hereditary traits can also be affected by nonhereditary factors. *Tay-Sachs disease (infantile amaurotic idiocy)* and *PKU* are examples of hereditary disorders of development. Both involve defects in metabolism caused by recessive genes, and both can cause severe mental retardation.

The next category in Figure 6-4 is designated as *innate*. It encompasses not only hereditary genetic factors but the effects of mutation and regrouping of genes as they are formed in the germ cells of the parent and transferred to the gametes. Drugs, disease, radiation, and other factors can cause mutations. Many mutations are lethal, but some cause specific nonlethal traits. Certain mutations can have effects like those of inherited genes. An example is *tuberous sclerosis (epiloia)*, characterized by tumors of the brain and skin. It is transmitted by a rare dominant gene but may also be caused by new mutations (Penrose, 1963).

Chromosomal anomalies are another source of nonhereditary genetic influence. In Down syndrome, for example, a sperm or ovum contributes an extra chromosome similar to the normal 21st chromosome. This extra chromosome results from the failure of the two 21st chromosomes to separate from each other during meiosis. When fertilization occurs, the two chromosomes are joined by a third from the other parent. This condition is called *trisomy 21*. Exactly how the extra chromosome causes mongoloid features, furrowed tongue, and defective intelligence is not known. Other forms of extra chromosomal material are also found in some individuals having Down syndrome features.

The next category of biological contributions is designated *congenital* in Figure 6-4. It includes genetic factors, plus conditions arising between conception and birth. The topmost category in Figure 6-4 is labeled *constitutional* and includes

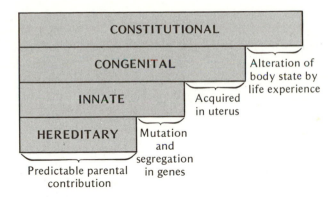

Figure 6—4. Categories of biological contributions to phenotypical development. (From Cattell, 1950.)

all factors based on the biological structure of the person. These include the effects of disease or injury after birth, as well as hereditary factors, nonhereditary genetic factors, and factors arising between conception and birth. Nongenetic congenital and constitutional contributions are discussed in later chapters.

Although their contributions are placed at the bottom of Figure 6-4 and become part of the organism at conception, many genes have effects not evident until long after birth. For example, *Huntington's chorea,* a neural degenerative disease leading to psychotic behavior and death, is caused by a rare dominant allele whose symptoms do not appear until middle adulthood, although effects on IQ are detectible earlier (Lyle & Gottesman, 1980). Other genetic effects end at certain developmental periods, for example, effects on growth.

Activation and Repression of Gene Action

How are certain genetic effects confined to particular developmental periods? It is believed that there are mechanisms for activating and repressing the transcription of information from DNA molecules onto messenger RNA molecules (Caplan & Ordahl, 1978). Two types of genes are hypothesized: One type (*structural genes*) carries codes for specific phenotypic traits; the other type (*regulator genes*) regulates the transcription of information from structural genes.

One explanation is that the transcription of information from structural genes is selectively turned on and off by regulator genes keyed to the developmental stage of the organism. A second explanation is that information can be transcribed from structural genes at the earliest developmental stages, but there is selective repression of particular structural genes as development proceeds. This would explain why in the earliest stages of embryonic development all cells can differentiate into any type of specialized cells, whereas at later stages each part of the organism becomes more specialized and produces only cells of a particular type (Caplan & Ordahl, 1978). Although similar, the two explanations have different implications for how diseases, chemicals, and genetically transmitted abnormalities affect development. The developmental study of genetics is still in its infancy, but genetic research already offers rich possibilities for understanding normal and abnormal development.

BEHAVIOR GENETICS

There are no genes *for* behavior or any other phenotypic trait. Genes exert their influence on behavior through their effects at the molecular level of organization. Enzymes, hormones, and neurons may be considered as the sequence of complex path markers between the genes and a behavioral characteristic. (Gottesman, 1968, pp. 60–61)

For physical as well as behavioral traits, the sequence from transmission of parental genes to their expression in a phenotypic trait is shaped by the environment and chain reactions triggered by other genes.

Special Problems of Behavior Genetics

A primary problem of behavior genetics is operationally defining the target behavior. Unlike anatomic features, behavioral traits are not static, potentially visible entities. Instead, they are abstractions like "schizophrenia," "intelligence," "aggressiveness," and "extroversion" that we must define in terms of observable behavior.

To study genetic effects on schizophrenia, for example, we must identify those who have the phenotypic trait. A common criterion is the diagnostic consensus of clinicians who interview patients and review their test scores and life histories. The clinicians' experience and training presumably enable them to group people consistently into schizophrenic and nonschizophrenic categories. However, most studies also include an in-between category of people for whom clinicians cannot agree. Studies of genetic effects on intelligence use IQ test scores, while studies of aggression and extroversion may use personality test scores and behavioral ratings.

Reliability and Validity of Assessment. The study of genetic effects on behavior must face the same issues as other studies of behavior. Among the most fundamental are the *reliability* and *validity* of assessment discussed in Chapter 5.

There is no point in seeking genetic effects on traits like schizophrenia, intelligence, aggression, or extroversion unless we can assess them *reliably;* that is, unless two separate assessments of someone's behavior yield the same conclusion about whether the person is schizophrenic, intelligent, aggressive, or extroverted.

Likewise, unless our assessment of a trait is *valid* with respect to other criteria for the trait, our evidence for genetic effects is confined to the measure we employ; this measure may not have the same meaning for all workers. For example, if we use crossed eyes as a criterion for schizophrenia, our assessment may be very reliable and we may be able to demonstrate genetic influences on it. However, unless we show that crossed eyes correlate with other criteria for schizophrenia (such as delusions, hallucinations, and bizarre behavior), other workers may object that we have shown nothing about *their* concepts of schizophrenia. By the same token, genetic effects on IQ test scores apply to the test used and behavior correlated with it, but not other concepts of intelligence.

Situational Effects. Elaborate techniques may be needed for observing anatomical structures that are tiny or tightly integrated with other structures, but, once formed, anatomical structures exist as part of the body. Behaviors do not have this static quality. They "exist" only under special conditions. A child who is hostile under some conditions may not be hostile under other conditions. Experience with certain conditions can also change behavior under those conditions.

The complexity of situational effects has led genetic researchers to concentrate on behaviors that are stable under varying conditions. Consequently, major forms of mental disorder, plus traits like IQ and extroversion that can be reliably tested are the most commonly studied. Yet, genetic factors are also likely to affect behaviors that are more subtle or specific to certain situations.

Advantages of Animal Research

Most genetic research is done on nonhuman species. The fruit fly (*Drosophila*), mouse, and rat offer several advantages.

One advantage is that we can control the mating of these species. By mating brothers with their sisters and repeating this over several generations, we can form *inbred strains* whose members have virtually identical heredity. This enables us to manipulate environmental effects while holding heredity constant.

Two inbred strains can also be crossbred. We can then trace in their offspring the interactions of alleles known to differ in the two parent strains. Control over mating also permits *selective breeding* of animals to detect genetic effects. Figure 6-5 illustrates a classic example. Rats that performed exceptionally well in a complex maze were bred with one another. The best performing offspring were also bred with one another, and so on over several generations. The same was done with rats that performed poorly in the maze. By the eighth generation of offspring, there was virtually no overlap in the number of maze errors made by members of the maze-bright and maze-dull strains, thus indicating a strong genetic effect on performance in that particular maze.

Another advantage of animal research is that we can control the subjects' environments. We can expose *genetically identical* animals to *different environ-*

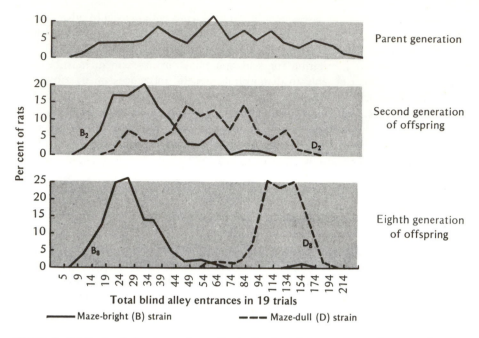

Figure 6–5. Effects of nine generations of selective breeding on maze performance by rats. (From Tryon, 1934.)

ments to see if environmental variation alone produces phenotypic differences. The reverse strategy is also possible. We can expose *genetically different* animals to *identical environments* to see if phenotypic differences arise from genetic factors.

Where total genetic control is difficult or undesirable, naturalistic methods like those in human genetic studies may be applied to animals. A common method is the *pedigree study*: Here, a phenotypic trait is traced through several generations of a family. The distribution of the trait in each generation can suggest hypotheses about possible genetic mechanisms such as dominance, penetrance, sex-linkage, and so forth.

Two further advantages make nonhuman species desirable for pedigree studies as well as for controlled breeding. One is the short period between generations; many generations of animals can be bred in the time required for a single human generation.

The other advantage stems from larger litter sizes. On the average, for example, a Mendelian recessive trait (t) is manifest in one out of four offspring whose parents are both heterozygous (Tt) for the trait, because: Tt × Tt = TT + Tt + Tt + tt. But even traits governed by such a simple mechanism are hard to trace in humans: In families with four children, for example, random deviations from the expected 3:1 ratio are common. As a result, none, one, two, or even four of the offspring may show the trait. The larger size of animal litters makes random deviations less likely to obscure the basic pattern.

Limitations of Animal Research

For traits that are similar in humans and animals, genetic research is typically done with animals until hypotheses are well tested. Unfortunately, few human behavioral traits and disorders have precise analogs in other species. Where analogs do exist, animal research has shown genetic influences and gene-environment interactions that are strongly suggestive for human behavior.

Yet, close analysis often reveals limitations on the application of animal findings to humans. Tryon's (1934) experiment cited above, for example, showed strong genetic effects on rat "intelligence." Further research, however, revealed that the superior performance of "bright" rats was restricted to the maze that was the criterion for selective breeding. The "dull" rats equaled or bettered the "bright" rats in three out of five other maze tests. Distractibility, low food motivation, and fear of the apparatus were the genetically influenced traits that hindered the "dull" rats' performance in the criterion maze (Searle, 1949).

Furthermore, Figure 6-6 shows that the genetically influenced behavioral differences between bright and dull rats are subject to environmental modification. The maze errors of the two strains differed greatly when both were reared under

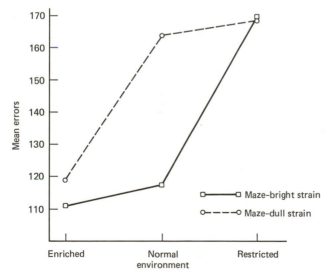

Figure 6–6. Effects of different rearing environments on maze errors by two strains of rats. (Data from Cooper & Zubek, 1958.)

normal laboratory conditions. However, when both strains were reared under very restricted, unstimulating conditions, the bright rats made far more errors, whereas the dull rats made only a few more errors than after normal rearing. As a result, the bright rats performed no better than the dull rats.

On the other hand, when reared under very stimulating conditions, dull rats made many fewer errors than after normal rearing, bright rats made somewhat fewer errors, and the result was a small difference favoring bright rats.

These findings highlight two aspects of relations between genetic and environmental determinants: (1) The different impact of environmental variations on the two strains illustrates the *interaction* between genetic and environmental influences—a particular environment does not necessarily have the same effect on all genotypes; and, (2) environmental *threshold* conditions may have to be surpassed before genetic effects are manifest—genotypic differences between the strains were evident only under certain conditions of rearing.

Studies of rats have also shown genetic effects on other behaviors, such as "emotionality" measured by defecation in open field situations (Fuller & Thompson, 1978). Yet, beyond suggesting genetic models for human behavior, animal studies tell us little about *how* genetic and environmental effects actually *do* interact in humans. For this reason, we need special variations on animal methods.

HUMAN BEHAVIOR GENETICS

Chromosomal Analysis

Since the 1950s, direct analysis of human chromosomes has revealed abnormal *karyotypes* in people with certain physical and behavioral abnormalities, such as Down syndrome.

Like Down syndrome, *Klinefelter syndrome* was known long before its victims were found to have an extra chromosome. In this syndrome, an extra X chromosome is present in an individual who is otherwise male—he has *sex chromosome trisomy,* XXY. The condition may remain undiagnosed until the boy shows incomplete sexual development at puberty. The characteristic physical traits of small testicles, tallness, thinness, long arms and legs, and sterility are often accompanied by personality instability and below average intelligence (Money, 1970; Witkin, et al., 1976). Longitudinal research has shown personality and cognitive differences between XXY and other boys starting in infancy (Walzer et al., 1978).

Turner syndrome in females also involves a sex chromosome abnormality: partial or complete absence of one of the two X chromosomes. In certain cases, some cells of the body lack an X chromosome while others have two X chromosomes. Chromosomal variations among an individual's body cells, like those in some cases of Turner syndrome, is called a *mosaic* condition.

Girls with Turner syndrome are short in stature, have extra skin (webbing) around their necks, and lack pubertal development. Psychological studies show average to superior IQ, deficient spatial abilities, and exceptional emotional stability (Baekgaard, Nyborg, & Nielsen, 1978; Money & Mittenthal, 1970; Silbert, Wolff, & Lilienthal, 1977). These traits may be less pronounced in girls with the mosaic pattern. Since pubertal development can be induced through estrogen treatment, girls with Turner syndrome marry and can live fairly normal lives.

A syndrome first revealed via chromosomal analysis is the *XYY syndrome* in males. It sparked legal controversy and questions of free will versus determinism. Perhaps because an extra male chromosome was imagined to double a man's aggressive "maleness," the discovery of XYY karyotypes among inmates of a maximum security prison hospital suggested that XYY men may be genetically prone to criminal behavior (Jacobs, Brunton, Melville, Brittain, & McClement, 1965). This raised arguments that such men should not be held legally responsible for their crimes. Preoccupation with the XYY syndrome even inspired press claims that a murderer of eight nurses, Richard Speck, was an XYY, although he was not (Engel, 1972). Studies of XYY males, including young boys, have revealed the following characteristics: Unusual tallness, behavior problems beginning in childhood, below-average range of IQ, excessive daydreaming, social isolation, unstable occupational history, and above average rates of criminal convictions (Owen, 1972; Witkin et al., 1976). However, their intellectual inadequacies may account for the elevated rate of criminal convictions among XYY men (Witkin et al., 1976).

If the extra Y chromosome does affect behavior, it may be via certain behavioral reactions to normal stimuli. Environments that lead to normal behavior in XY males may thus lead to criminal behavior in some XYY males. Longitudinal studies of XYY infants might identify environmental inputs leading to criminal and noncriminal outcomes. Knowing how environments interact with XYY genetic factors to produce criminal behavior could suggest preventive measures analogous to the low phenylalanine diet used to prevent retardation in PKU babies. However, research of this kind has been fought as a self-fulfilling prophecy that may cause behavior problems in children with the XYY karyotype (Beckwith et al., 1975).

Biometrical (Quantitative) Genetics

Most genetic factors in psychopathology are probably not discernible through chromosomal analysis. Chromosomal abnormalities, some of which have no known effects, occur in about one out of every 200 births (Lubs & Ruddle, 1970). This rate is too low to explain many of the pathologic conditions probably affected by genetic factors.

Because chromosomal studies, controlled breeding, and pedigree studies cannot tell us much about genetic effects on most important human behavior, statistical techniques have been developed for estimating the effect of heredity on phenotypic traits. In contrast to the Mendelian approach of tracing the distribution of traits manifest in an all-or-none fashion, this approach is known as *biometrical* or *quantitative* genetics. It is especially necessary for studying traits involving polygenic mechanisms.

To calculate the effects of heredity and environment on a trait, we code the trait in a form amenable to quantitative analysis. Traits like IQ, numerically scored personality test performance, height, and weight are obvious candidates, because they yield continuous distributions of scores rather than one or two qualitatively distinct phenotypes. However, even a trait expressed in an all-or-none fashion can be analyzed quantitatively. We do this by giving individuals manifesting the trait a score of 1 while those without it are scored 0.

Heritability. After we score a phenotypic trait, we calculate the proportion of variation among the scores that reflects genetic variation. The *total* variation in scores reflects both genetic and environmental factors. It can be expressed as $V_{\text{phenotypic}} = V_{\text{genetic}} + V_{\text{environmental}}$. (To keep it simple, we will ignore correlations and interactions between genetic and environmental effects.)

We can think of the proportion of phenotypic variation due to genetic variation in terms of *heritability*. The actual formulas for estimating heritability depend on the specific problems and assumptions. However, for conceptual purposes,[1] we can express our heritability estimate (*H*) as

$$H = \frac{V_{\text{genetic}}}{V_{\text{phenotypic}}}$$

Note that estimates of heritability refer to *proportions* of variation among scores rather than *absolute* values. A heritability estimate says nothing about how much an IQ of 100, for example, could be raised or lowered by changing the environment. Even with traits yielding high heritability estimates, a genotype is assumed to determine only a *range* of possible phenotypic reactions to different environments. Thus, an individual's score depends on how much the environment has maximized his or her genotypic potential for that trait.[2]

[1]H is often represented as h^2, because h is the symbol for the *correlation* between genotypes and phenotypes for a trait. The correlation between two variables is the square root of the variance that one variable has in common with the other. Thus, if the heritability estimate (written as either H or h^2) is 0.49, the correlation between the genotypes and phenotypes will be $\sqrt{0.49} = 0.70$.

[2]The variation in scores is operationally defined as statistical *variance*, written as σ^2 ("sigma squared"). Variance is a quantitative index of how much the scores are scattered around the mean of their distribution. It is the square of the standard deviation (σ) of the distribution. Accordingly, the quantitative estimate of heritability is the amount of variance due to genetic variance (σ_g^2), divided by the total phenotypic variance (σ_p^2): $H = \sigma_g^2/\sigma_p^2$.

Because heritability is the *proportion* of variance in scores ascribed to heredity, it cannot be estimated from an individual score. Instead, it can be estimated only from a group of scores having a variety of values. We cannot calculate the heritability of one score or scores that are all the same, because the phenotypic variance in the denominator of the proportion would be zero. The numerator would also be zero, because it is always a portion of the denominator's variance. If, for example, everyone in a sample has an IQ of 100, we cannot estimate heritability, because the scores have zero variance and H would equal zero/zero.

The concept of heritability eliminates the artificial dichotomy between heredity and environment. Since heritability estimates assume that the total phenotypic variance is a sum of both genetic and environmental effects, any change in either genetic or environmental variance changes H. This means that heritability always depends on the *specific range of environmental and genetic* factors existing in the group on which it is calculated. Heritability is *never* an *absolute* index of genetic determination for a trait under all conditions. It is *always relative to particular genetic* and *particular environmental* conditions.

Some Illustrations. To illustrate the complementary roles of heredity and environment in the heritability estimate, imagine that 100 unrelated boys have exactly the same environment. We might find that their IQs range only from 99 to 101. At first glance, this would suggest that genetic differences do not affect IQ much. However, if we calculate the ratio of genetic variance to phenotypic variance, we would obtain a heritability estimate of 1.00 (100 percent), indicating that all the variance in IQ is due to genetic factors. This, of course, is correct: By making the boys' environment identical, we prevent it from contributing anything to the *variation* among their IQs. All the phenotypic variation, small as it is, is due to nonenvironmental factors. We might conclude that the genetic effects on IQ are not very *important*; but we cannot escape the conclusion that *all* the variation in IQ is due to genetic factors.

The reverse situation also shows how heritability estimates are governed by the complementary relation between genetic and environmental effects. If we take 100 boys having identical heredity (the equivalent of identical twins multiplied by 50), and give them 100 different environments, we may also find that their IQs range only from 99 to 101. If we calculate the ratio of genetic to phenotypic variance, we would find that the heritability of IQ is 0.00. Since all subjects are genetically the same, only environmental differences affect phenotypic variance.

Of course, genotypically *different* people never have *identical* environments; and the only genotypically *identical* people having *different* environments are identical twins. But the point is that a heritability estimate applies only to people having a particular distribution of genotypes and environments. Heritability is a statistic for a phenotypic trait *within a particular population, exposed to a particular range of environmental variation*. It is not intrinsic to a trait independent of population or environment.

The relativistic nature of heritability can lead to some surprising conclusions. For example, if middle class environments enable children to reach their full genotypic potentials in IQ, then the heritability of these children's IQ should approach 1.00, because the aspects of environment that affect IQ are uniformly favorable.

On the other hand, if the environments of disadvantaged children do not maximize their genotypic potentials, the heritability of their IQ should be much less than 1.00, because the aspects of environment that affect IQ are not uniform for them.

If disadvantaged children's environments are improved, however, the heritability of their IQ should increase. In effect, certain environmental *threshold* conditions may have to be reached before genetic effects become evident, just as genetic differences between rat strains become evident only under certain conditions of rearing (see Figure 6-6).

In summary, environmental factors affect heritability estimates in at least two ways. First, certain environmental threshold conditions may be required before genetic effects become evident on a particular trait in a particular population. Second, once environmental conditions surpass the necessary threshold, heritability estimates are highest for groups whose environments are the most uniform, because when environmental variance is eliminated, only genetic variance remains.

ESTIMATING HUMAN HERITABILITY

The heritability of human behavioral traits is estimated by comparing family members grouped according to genetic similarity. For example, on the average, 50 percent of the genes of same-sex siblings are identical, because each sibling inherits half the alleles carried by one parent and half the alleles carried by the other parent. Of course, it is theoretically possible for some siblings to have *no* genes in common because each received from each parent exactly the *opposite* set of alleles received by the other. Conversely, some siblings may have *identical* heredity, because both get exactly the *same* alleles from each parent. However, these extremes are very rare.

The difference between siblings' scores on a trait can be compared with the difference between scores of family members having less or more genetic similarity. Same-sex half siblings, for instance, are identical in 25 percent of their genes, on the average. If full siblings who have similar environments differ much less than half siblings who also have similar environments, our estimate of heritability will be high.

Twin Studies

We can make more precise heritability estimates by comparing differences between identical (*monozygotic* or *MZ*) twins, who have identical genes, with differences between same-sex fraternal (*dizygotic* or *DZ*) twins. Like other full siblings, DZ twins are identical in only 50 percent of their genes, on the average. A major advantage of this approach is that twins usually have more similar environments than nontwin siblings. Detailed comparisons of blood types can show whether same-sex twins are MZ or DZ. If co-twins are identical on a large number of blood factors, they are assumed to be MZ.

The rationale for twin studies is that DZ co-twins differ for both genetic and environmental reasons but MZ co-twins differ only for environmental reasons. We can therefore estimate the strength of genetic effects by subtracting the *difference* in MZ co-twins' scores from the *difference* in DZ co-twins' scores:

$$D_{DZ} = \text{Genetic} + \text{Environmental Effects}$$
$$\underline{- D_{MZ} = \qquad\qquad\qquad \text{Environmental Effects}}$$
$$\qquad = \text{Genetic Effects}$$

where D_{DZ} stands for difference between DZ co-twins' scores
D_{MZ} stands for difference between MZ co-twins' scores

The statistical formulas for translating this rationale into heritability estimates vary with the specific problem and assumptions (Fuller & Thompson, 1978).

DZ co-twins are not unrelated, but have, on the average 50 percent identical genes. Perhaps we should therefore double our estimate of genetic effects obtained by comparing DZ and MZ twins. Some formulas for heritability do exactly this. On the other hand, the environmental histories of MZ co-twins tend to be more similar than those of DZ co-twins (Scarr & Carter-Saltzman, 1979). This could reduce environmentally caused differences between MZ co-twins. Yet, it has been shown that much of the difference in the environmental histories of DZ twins results indirectly from their genetic dissimilarities, because DZ co-twins evoke different reactions from their environments (Lytton, 1977: Scarr & Carter-Saltzman, 1979). For these reasons, plus the fact that heritability estimates are not automatically generalizable to other populations, the exact size of a heritability estimate is less important than its statistical significance, its size relative to other estimates obtained in the same way, and its agreement with hypothesized genetic models.

Dichotomous Traits. If we score a trait dichotomously, we can estimate genetic effects by comparing the percentage of DZ twin pairs in which both members show the trait (are *concordant* for it), with the percent of MZ twin pairs in which the members are concordant for the trait. (This compares the *similarity* instead of the *difference* between co-twins, but the results are the same as if we compare *discordance*—dissimilarity—between co-twins in an analogous formula.)

As an example, Kallmann and Roth (1956) compared concordance rates for schizophrenia in DZ and MZ twin pairs having at least one member who became schizophrenic in childhood. Both twins eventually became schizophrenic in 22.9 percent of the DZ pairs and 88.2 percent of the MZ pairs. This difference was statistically significant and led the authors to infer genetic causes for childhood schizophrenia.

Traits Scored Quantitatively. For traits amenable to continuous quantitative scoring, we can make heritability estimates by comparing the correlation (symbolized by r) between MZ co-twins' scores with the correlation between DZ co-twins' scores. [The intraclass correlation rather than the well-known Pearson product-moment correlation is usually used. See McNemar (1969) for the differences between these correlations.]

As an example, Table 6-1 averages the correlations found in three studies of MZ and DZ co-twins' scores on 10 scales of the Minnesota Multiphasic Personality Inventory (MMPI). One study used adult twin pairs in Connecticut (Reznikoff & Honeyman, 1967), while two used adolescent twin pairs in Minnesota (Gottesman, 1963b) and Massachusetts (Gottesman, 1966). The precise heritability estimates derived from the data vary somewhat with the formula used. From looking at the differences between MZ and DZ correlations for each trait, however, we can see that genetic factors account for more variance in the topmost scores than in the bottom scores. Thus, genetic factors affect social introversion, depression, psychasthenia (anxious obsessiveness), psychopathy, and schizophrenia scores more than hypochondriasis, hypomania, or masculinity-femininity.

A 12-year follow-up of Gottesman's (1966) sample of adolescent twins illustrates another aspect of estimates of genetic variance. Some of the MMPI scales showing higher MZ than DZ correlations in adolescence no longer showed these differences when the subjects were in their late twenties (Dworkin, Burke, Maher,

Table 6-1   Values of r_{MZ} and r_{DZ} for MMPI Scores Based on Combined Data of Three Twin Studies.

MMPI score	r_{MZ}	r_{DZ}	$r_{MZ} - r_{DZ}$
Social introversion	.45	.12	.33
Depression	.44	.14	.30
Psychasthenia	.41	.11	.30
Psychopathic deviate	.48	.27	.21
Schizophrenia	.44	.24	.20
Paranoia	.27	.08	.19
Hysteria	.37	.23	.14
Hypochondriasis	.41	.28	.13
Hypomania	.32	.18	.13
Masculinity-feminity	.41	.35	.06
Number of pairs	120	132	

Source: Data from studies by Gottesman (1963b, 1965) and Reznikoff & Honeyman (1967). Table adapted from Vandenberg (1967, p. 78).

& Gottesman, 1976). Conversely, on some scales, small differences between adolescent MZ and DZ correlations grew much larger in adulthood. Even though the genome is formed at conception, changes in genetic variance can reflect many factors such as: (1) developmental changes in activation or repression of genes affecting a trait; (2) the impact of experience on behavior whose initial onset involves genetically based individual differences; and (3) increases or decreases in environmental variance that in turn change the proportion of phenotypic variance reflecting genetic variance.

Adoption Studies

Another way to assess genetic factors is by studying people of known genetic similarity who, because of adoption, grow up in different environments. Just as twin studies capitalize on the naturally occurring genetic difference between MZ and DZ twins, adoption studies capitalize on the environmental difference between genetically related children raised in different homes.

Twins Reared Apart. When MZ twins are raised by different parents, we can compare their similarities with those of MZ twins reared together. Table 6-2 shows personality test correlations for MZ twins reared together, MZ twins reared apart, and DZ twins reared together. Note that the correlations for MZ twins reared apart were actually *higher* than for MZ twins reared together and substantially higher than for DZ twins reared together.

How could MZ twins reared apart be *more alike* than those reared together? It has often been noted that twins living together influence each other to adopt complementary social roles. This could make them less similar than if they were not living together.

Nontwin Adoption Studies. Hard as it is to find MZ twins reared apart, it is harder still to study disorders such as schizophrenia in MZ twins reared apart, because each disorder has a low base rate. Other approaches have therefore been devised for assessing genetic effects on disorders like schizophrenia in people raised in different environments. Rosenthal (1970) has outlined some of these approaches as they have

Table 6-2   Correlations of Personality Test Scores for Twins Reared Together and Apart.

	Adjustment score[a]	Extroversion[b]	Neuroticism[b]
MZ twins reared together	.56	.42	.38
MZ twins reared apart	.58	.61	.53
DZ twins reared together	.37	−.17	.11

[a]Woodworth-Matthews Personal Data Sheet (Newman, Freeman, & Holzinger, 1937).
[b]Self-Rating Questionnaire (Shields, 1962).

been used in Denmark, where comprehensive public health services and centralized records keep track of people who manifest serious disorders.

One approach is called the *cross-fostering* research design. It assesses individuals assumed to have one genotype raised by parents of a different genotype. We can thus see whether the genotype of the child outweighs the environmental impact of parents in producing a trait. As an example, people with a schizophrenic biologic parent but raised by nonschizophrenic parents are compared with those having nonschizophrenic biologic parents but raised by a schizophrenic foster parent. This cross-fostering design is shown in Figure 6-7a.

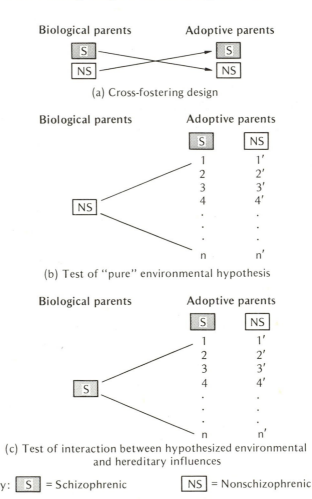

(a) Cross-fostering design

(b) Test of "pure" environmental hypothesis

(c) Test of interaction between hypothesized environmental and hereditary influences

Key: S = Schizophrenic   NS = Nonschizophrenic

Figure 6-7. Three designs for estimating the strength of hereditary and environmental influences on the development of schizophrenia in adopted children. (Adapted from Rosenthal, 1970.)

Figure 6-7b illustrates a test of a "pure" environmental hypothesis. In this design, we compare children of nonschizophrenic biological parents who are raised by schizophrenic or nonschizophrenic foster parents. If only the children adopted by schizophrenic parents become schizophrenic, this indicates that environmental conditions can produce schizophrenia.

Figure 6-7c illustrates a method of testing interactions between a hypothesized schizophrenic genotype and the environmental impact of schizophrenic parents. Children having schizophrenic biological parents but raised by nonschizophrenic foster parents are compared with children having schizophrenic biological parents and raised by schizophrenic foster parents. If other findings show genetic effects on schizophrenia, this design can tell us if the environmental impact of schizophrenic parents further raises the risk to genetically vulnerable children.

HERITABILITY OF PERSONALITY

Here we consider the heritability of behavioral traits other than those discussed in detail later, such as IQ (Chapter 8), mood disorders (Chapter 11), and schizophrenia (Chapter 12).

Infant Behavior and Temperament

Genetic effects are evident in various aspects of infant behavior. As an illustration, Freedman (1965) compared MZ and DZ co-twin differences on 22 items of the Bayley Infant Behavior Profile over the first year of life. Each infant was filmed several times. Observers rated the behavior of one twin of each pair while other observers rated the second twin. Using separate observers avoided "halo" effects potentially arising from co-twins' similar appearance. Awareness of zygosity could not bias results either, because zygosity was determined by blood grouping only after the behavioral data were analyzed.

MZ co-twins differed less than DZ co-twins on all 22 items, significantly so on 10. Freedman (1974) stresses the evolutionary significance of the heritable behavior: Social orientation, especially smiling, during the first five months of life, and fear of strange people and objects above the age of five months play key roles in the survival of the species. Like imprinting in fowl, these behaviors help maintain a close bond between the baby and its mother. Smiling rewards the mother for taking care of the baby, while fear of strangeness makes the baby resist separation from its mother. Early members of the species having genes leading to these behaviors survived to reproduce. Fear of strangeness may no longer enhance survival, but social responses such as smiling still affect the care a child gets. The baby's social responses elicit behaviors from caretakers that can, in turn, shape the child's personality. Children who smile a lot, for example, usually experience warmer social environments than those who do not. Consequently, those who smile a lot may grow up expecting more rewarding social interactions than those who smile less.

The strength of genetic factors in early smiling is shown by Freedman's (1965) findings that even blind babies smile, as Figure 6-8 illustrates. Not only is the blind girl's smile innately organized, but her eyes fixate on her mother's face, just as the eyes of sighted babies do.

Other research has shown that genetic effects on social behavior vary with the stimuli and age. Plomin and Rowe (1979), for example, found stronger genetic effects on the social behavior of 1- and 2-year-olds toward strangers than toward their mothers. Table 6-3 summarizes the behaviors toward strangers for which MZ twins were significantly more alike than DZ twins, whereas the same behaviors toward mothers did not show significant MZ-DZ differences.

Genetic effects on social behaviors show developmental changes during the first and second years of life. In longitudinal analyses of MZ and DZ correlations on Bayley infant test items, cognitive items showed strong and increasing genetic effects, but social items showed decreasing genetic effects (Matheny, Dolan, & Wilson, 1976). However, a general extroversion dimension showed significant genetic effects over most of the first two years (Matheny, 1980).

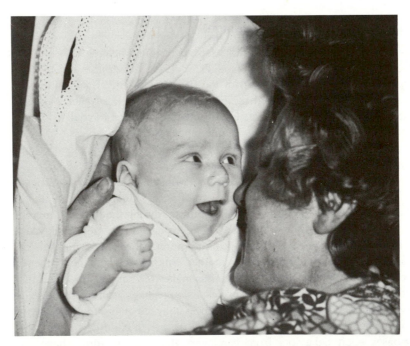

Figure 6–8. Yvonne, aged 2 months, 20 days, congenitally blind, smiling with eyes toward mother. (From Freedman, 1965; reproduced by permission.)

Table 6-3   Some Heritable Social Behaviors of Infancy

	r_{MZ}	r_{DZ}	$r_{MZ} - r_{DZ}$
Looking at stranger	.67	.08	.59
Approaching stranger	.50	−.05	.55
Proximity to stranger	.40	−.03	.43
Positive vocalization to stranger	.49	−.03	.52
Smiling at stranger	.58	.03	.55

Source: Adapted from Plomin & Rowe, 1979, p. 67.

   Increasing genetic influence during the first year has been detected for the nine dimensions of infant temperament studied by Thomas and Chess (1977) in relation to later behavior problems (discussed in Chapter 3). Torgerson and Kringlen (1978) found significantly greater similarity between MZ co-twins than DZ co-twins on only three of the dimensions at two months of age but on all nine dimensions at nine months. By the age of four years, however, genetic effects on cognitive ability seem to outweigh those on temperament (Goldsmith & Gottesman, 1981).

   The changing genetic effects on infant behaviors in different situations and at different ages highlight the interplay between environmental, developmental, and genetic variables. As behavior responds to experience, maturation, and the onset or offset of gene action, genetic effects on phenotypic variance change. Behavior thus has no permanent heritability independent of the environmental situation, range of variation in a population, and variables such as developmental level. Furthermore, some genetically influenced behaviors shaped by strong selective biases over the course of evolution may show little genetically based variation among individuals, because most possess them to the same degree.

   On the other hand, behaviors initially affected by genetic differences, such as social responsiveness, increasingly reflect experience with particular people. Genetic factors may thus affect babies' responses to their mothers when they first recognize their mothers, but then be submerged by the massive experience they accumulate with their mother. Yet, genetic factors may continue to affect relations toward strangers with whom the child has no experience.

Introversion-Extroversion

Genetic effects have been repeatedly found on measures of introversion-extroversion (Fuller & Thompson, 1978). As an example, Eysenck (1956) administered personality, intelligence, and autonomic tests to British MZ and DZ twins aged 11 to 15 years. Factor analysis of all the measures yielded three factors: intelligence, introversion-extroversion, and autonomic functioning (e.g., pulse rate, blood pressure). Table 6-4 shows that correlations between MZ twins were significantly higher than between DZ twins on all three dimensions. Although the

Table 6-4   Correlations of Three Factor Scores for MZ and DZ Twins

	r_{MZ}	r_{DZ}	$r_{MZ} - r_{DZ}$
Intelligence	.82	.38	.44
Extroversion	.50	−.33	.83
Autonomic	.93	.72	.21

Source: Adapted from Eysenck, 1956.

MZ twins' correlation for extroversion was smaller than for intelligence or autonomic functioning, it was actually negative for DZ twins.

Eysenck suggested that the negative correlation for DZ twins was merely a chance deviation from a true correlation of about zero. But Shields (1962) also found a negative correlation on extroversion for DZ twins reared together and a lower correlation on extroversion for MZ twins reared together than reared apart (see Table 6-2). The findings of Shields and Eysenck suggest that twins living together become less similar in introversion-extroversion than expected from their genetic similarities. This hypothesis received further support in another British study: DZ twins living together had negative correlations for extroversion, and both MZ and DZ twins living apart at least five years had higher co-twin correlations than twins living together (Claridge, Hume, & Canter, 1973). This study also revealed sex differences in heritability, as shown by larger differences between MZ and DZ correlations among females than males on sociability and impulsivity, two component traits of extroversion. However, sex differences in heritability differ from trait to trait and may partly reflect sex differences in environment.

Neuroticism

In a study resembling Eysenck's (1956) study of introversion-extroversion, Eysenck and Prell (1951) administered personality tests to MZ and DZ twins aged 11 to 14 years. Neuroticism was viewed as a trait dimension extending from emotional stability and integration at one extreme to instability and lack of integration at the other extreme. Neuroticism scores correlated .85 for MZ co-twins, but only .22 for DZ co-twins.

Two studies by Shields have also shown genetic effects on neuroticism. In one, Shields's (1954) primary data were parents' reports of neurotic behavior in their 12- to 15-year-old twins. The reports were used to rate children on a four-point scale ranging from well-adjusted to neurotic enough to warrant referral for help. Co-twins received identical ratings in 69 percent of MZ pairs and 31 percent of DZ pairs. The parents' reports were also used to rate concordance between co-twins: 69 percent of the MZ pairs but only 12 percent of the DZ pairs were rated completely or essentially concordant, whereas 69 percent of the DZ pairs and only 17 percent of the MZ pairs were rated completely discordant.

In his second study, Shields (1962) used neuroticism scores from a self-report questionnaire, thus avoiding possible biases in parental reports. Co-twins' scores correlated .38 for MZ twins reared together and .11 for same-sex DZ twins. As with extroversion, scores of MZ twins reared apart correlated higher (.53) than MZ twins reared together (.38). However, the genetic effects on a *personality trait* of neuroticism do not necessarily prove genetic determination of specific neuroses or neurotic behaviors (Pollin, 1976).

GENETIC SCREENING

Early detection of genetically based disorders has helped prevent psychopathology, as exemplified by the diagnosis of PKU through blood and urine tests after birth. Other disorders can be diagnosed through *amniocentesis* prior to birth. This is done by inserting a needle into the uterus and extracting a sample of amniotic fluid surrounding the fetus. Fetal cells in the fluid are analyzed to detect chromosomal abnormalities, such as those causing Down syndrome, and enzyme deficiencies, such as those found in Tay-Sachs disease, Lesch-Neyhan syndrome, and galactosemia, a disorder which prevents metabolism of a carbohydrate contained in milk. Amniocentesis is safe and reliable, but is usually used only when risks of a specific disorder are high, as with older mothers having an elevated risk of bearing Down syndrome children and couples carrying the recessive gene for Tay-Sachs disease (Omenn, 1978). Genetic counseling can also help by informing prospective parents of the risks to their offspring.

SUMMARY

Psychological theories, including those of psychoanalysis, Piaget, and the learning theorists, are based on assumptions about biological and genetic aspects of development. The ethological viewpoint also concerns relations between biology and behavior.

Much is known about the transmission of genetic material from parent to offspring. *Chromosomes* can be photomicrographed and arranged into *karyotypes* for study. *Meiosis,* the process by which pairs of chromosomes in the germ cells divide to form sex cells, can also be seen through a microscope. Much knowledge about *genes,* however, the actual molecules of DNA that carry the coded information for development of a new individual, is inferred from distributions of *phenotypic* traits.

We can view biological contributions to development in four broad categories, each of which includes the ones before it: *hereditary, innate, congenital,* and *constitutional.* Hereditary disorders include *galactosemia, Lesch-Nyhan syndrome, Tay-Sachs disease,* and *phenylketonuria (PKU). Down syndrome (mongolism)* and some cases of *epiloia* are innate but not hereditary, since they result from nonhereditary genetic aberrations. Because many genetic influences do not appear until long after birth (e.g., *Huntington's chorea*), activation and repression mechanisms have been proposed to explain the triggering of gene effects at specific developmental periods.

Behavior genetics is more complex than the study of genetic influences on physical traits because it is hard to define behavioral traits, reliably and validly assess them, and control for situational influences. Nonhuman species offer advantages of convenience and control for genetic research, but the paucity of precise analogs between human and animal behavior, especially pathological behavior, limits the value of animal research for human behavior genetics.

Chromosomal analysis has revealed chromosomal anomalies in *Down syndrome, Klinefelter syndrome, Turner syndrome,* and the *XYY syndrome.*

Biometrical (quantitative) genetics uses statistical techniques to estimate *heritability*—the *ratio* of *genetic* to *phenotypic variance* in phenotypic traits. Heritability estimates refer only to the proportion of variance in a phenotypic trait that is attributable to heredity in a *particular population*. These estimates say nothing about how much the trait can be changed by environment nor about the heritability of the same trait in other populations or environments.

We can estimate the heritability of human behavioral traits by comparing the correlation between *monozygotic* (identical) co-twins' scores with the correlations between *dizygotic* (fraternal) co-twins' scores. We can also compare trait correlations for twins reared apart with those for twins reared together and compare the effects adoptive parents differing in phenotypic characteristics have on adopted children who are hypothesized to have a certain genotype.

Evidence of heritability has been found for infant behavior and temperament, introversion-extroversion, and neuroticism. Different heritabilities of behavior in different stimulus situations and at different ages reveal the interplay between environmental, developmental, and genetic variables in shaping behavior.

Genetic screening by means of prenatal *amniocentesis* and postnatal biochemical tests can help prevent genetically-based disorders.

SUGGESTED READING

The Ethological Viewpoint. As an approach to the biological function and genetic basis of behavioral development, ethology offers concepts, strategies, and data of potential importance for the understanding of developmental psychopathology. *Ethology: The biology of behavior* (Eibl-Eibesfeldt, 1975) provides an overview of the field with applications to human behavior, while Freedman (1974) places human infant behavior in an evolutionary context, Hess (1970) relates ethology directly to human developmental psychology, and Plomin (1982) relates both to behavior genetics.

Behavior Genetics. Textbooks by McClearn and DeFries (1973) and Fuller and Thompson (1978), and chapters by diverse authors in a book edited by Kaplan

(1976) introduce the genetic study of human behavior, both normal and pathological. DeFries and Plomin (1978) review research literature, while McClearn (1970) provides links to developmental psychology. Pauls and Kidd (1981) focus on the genetics of childhood behavior disorders. Prospects for integrating developmental genetics with developmental psychology to produce a discipline of developmental behavior genetics are outlined by various authors in a book edited by Schaie, Anderson, McClearn, and Money (1975).

CHAPTER 7

Neurobiological Development and Dysfunctions

The "developmental dimension" becomes especially vivid when we consider organic growth. We can easily see the course of organic development by comparing organisms of different ages. Moreover, environmental effects on organic functioning clearly depend on attained levels of organic development. Certain diseases and traumas, for example, drastically alter a young child's development but have little effect on an older child. Other diseases and traumas show exactly the opposite pattern.

Also clear in organic development is the tendency for gradual developmental processes to bring about new levels of organization and function. From conception onward, each new body cell arises from processes taking place in existing cells. Each step along a developmental pathway depends on steps before it and paves the way for later steps. Yet, when a series of steps culminates in a new organ or a communication network among organs, a new level of functioning emerges.

The continuity of organic development is unduly masked by counting a child's age from birth. The individual's developmental history begins at conception. Babies are born at different developmental ages and differ markedly in maturity.

Despite developmental continuity from the prenatal through the postnatal period, the dramatic change from the intrauterine to the extrauterine environment makes it convenient to separate the prenatal, perinatal, and postnatal periods. Since we are concerned with *risks* to normal development, the environmental change occurring at birth deserves special attention. Many risks in the intrauterine environment are absent after birth and vice versa. Furthermore, the child's own behavior affects the risks encountered after birth more than before. We therefore start with prenatal development and the prenatal risks that can lead to later psychopathology. We then consider risks accompanying the birth process and later development. We conclude by considering organically based behavioral problems, psychophysiological disorders, and psychopharmacology.

PRENATAL DEVELOPMENT

After conception, the fertilized egg (*zygote*) takes about seven days to drift down the Fallopian tube and implant itself in the wall of the uterus. By the time it reaches this point, the *blastocyst,* as it is now called, has several dozen cells. After implantation in the uterine wall, the blastocyst's outer layer forms the placenta while part of its inner layer forms the *embryo.*

The period from two weeks to eight weeks after fertilization is called the *period of the embryo.* During this period, the embryo becomes differentiated into regions such as the head and limbs, and cells become differentiated into specialized tissues such as muscle and nerve. By the eighth week, the child, now about an inch long, is already recognizably human. Known from this point until birth as a *fetus,* it has a beating heart, arms, legs, and a nervous system that shows reflexive responses to tactile stimuli. Most nerve and muscle cells are present by six months after fertilization. The growth of these tissues during the remaining life span consists mainly of developing and enlarging existing cells rather than adding new cells. The brain grows especially fast during the fetal period; by birth it averages about 25 percent of its adult weight, a considerably higher proportion than most other organs.

Growth slows when the fetus nears the capacity of the maternal uterus, generally at 34 to 36 weeks after fertilization, but it accelerates again after birth. Maternal size controls fetal size, as shown by mating a large stallion with a small Shetland mare and a small Shetland stallion with a large mare: The first foal was small at birth, while the second was very large. Yet, both foals were the same size after a few months; at maturity, both were about half way between their parents in size (Tanner, 1970).

Endocrine Functioning

Starting in the fetal period, hormones secreted by the endocrine glands help actualize the growth plan coded in the genes. Hormones that cross the placenta from the mother's bloodstream may be the first to affect fetal growth, but by about the eighth week after conception the fetal pituitary gland begins secreting growth hormone. By about the thirteenth to eighteenth week, the fetal thyroid gland secretes *thyroxine,* which affects protein synthesis in the brain. If thyroxine production is inadequate, nerve cells fail to grow normally, resulting in irreversible neurological defects.

The sexual differentiation of the fetus involves hormones that affect later behavior. In the seventh week after fertilization, genes located on the Y chromosome of a male fetus cause the as yet undifferentiated gonads to start developing into testes. The Leydig cells of the newly formed testes start secreting the male hormone *testosterone* after the ninth week. The testosterone then causes the external genitals to develop into a penis and scrotum beginning in the tenth week. Without testosterone, the sex organs take on female form.

Besides affecting genital development, the male hormone apparently affects parts of the brain that later affect emotions and sexual behavior (Ehrhardt & Meyer-Bahlburg, 1981). Animal evidence indicates that the male hormone affects the brain only within a very short critical period. If the right amount of male hormone is not present at the appropriate time, the brain of a male rat, for example, fails to differentiate in the usual male manner. Instead, it develops along female lines, and normal male sexual behavior is absent in adulthood. Stressing a pregnant rat can cause this abnormality in her male fetus (Ward & Weisz, 1980). Injecting a female rat fetus with male hormone during the critical period causes her brain to develop along male lines, preventing later female reproductive cycles and sexual behavior (Tanner, 1970).

Although the exact neurologic mechanism is unknown, Goy (1968) showed that prenatally administered sex hormones affect the later behavior of rhesus monkeys. Genetically female monkeys getting male hormones prior to birth later behaved more like males than normal females: They made many more threatening facial gestures, initiated more play, engaged in more rough-and-tumble play, and withdrew less from the threats and approaches of other monkeys. They also sexually mounted untreated females and made pelvic thrusts when mounting.

We cannot ethically inject humans with sex hormones to test their effects on postnatal behavior. However, an unanticipated natural experiment occurred when synthetic hormones were used to save the pregnancies of women prone to miscarriages. The chemical structure of these hormones resembles that of male sex hormones (*androgens*). But they function like the female hormone *progesterone* in protecting pregnancy. Since they resemble both progesterone and androgens, they are called *progestins*.

It was discovered that daughters born to some women receiving progestins were masculinized: They had an enlarged clitoris, labial fusion, and, in rare cases, a penis with an empty scrotum. Surgery was used to form female genitals in cases recognized as female because of incomplete genital masculinization. No further treatment was needed, and the girls' ovaries functioned normally, feminizing their bodies and inducing menstruation at puberty.

Did prenatal androgenization affect later behavior? Money and Ehrhardt (1972) interviewed 10 of the girls and their mothers and tested the girls' sex-role preferences. As a control group, they also assessed 10 normal girls. According to their mothers and their own reports, significantly more of the androgenized girls were "tomboys." They took part in vigorous athletics, preferred boys as playmates and male toys to dolls, chose utilitarian over feminine clothing, and gave priority to career plans over marriage. However, the androgenized girls were not dissatisfied with being girls, did not want to be boys, and did not show signs of lesbianism. The same is true of girls prenatally androgenized via genetically based overproduction of androgens by their own adrenal glands, a condition called the *adrenogenital syndrome* (Ehrhardt & Meyer-Bahlburg, 1981). Both sons and daughters of mothers taking progestins during pregnancy are also more disposed to physical aggression than their siblings not exposed to progestins (Reinisch, 1981). Prenatal androgenization thus affects the postnatal behavior of humans as well as monkeys, although it does not determine sex object choices nor preclude normal gender roles.

PRENATAL RISKS FOR NEUROBIOLOGICAL DEVELOPMENT

General Condition of the Mother

Malnutrition. The effects of maternal malnutrition are studied in several ways. The most direct is to study the brains of fetuses whose mothers were malnourished. This can only be done with precision in nonhuman species where the diets of pregnant animals can be manipulated experimentally and the fetuses removed for analysis.

Studies of rats have shown that maternal malnutrition slows fetal brain growth. Part of the growth retardation is in the *size* of the brain cells. Yet, later malnutrition also reduces cell size and size can be increased again if nutrition improves. More crucial is that fetal malnutrition, occurring when most nerve cells are being formed, can cut the *number* of cells by about 15 percent. Furthermore, if malnutrition continues postnatally, the reduction in nerve cells is greater than would result from summing the separate reductions caused by pre- and postnatal malnutrition occurring alone (Winick & Rosso, 1975). Prenatal malnutrition also retards formation of *myelin*, a fatty protective covering on nerve fibers that facilitates the transmission of nerve impulses (Benton, Moser, Dodge, & Carr, 1966).

A second approach to studying prenatal malnutrition is to compare newborns having well-nourished mothers with those having poorly nourished mothers. Several studies show that mothers' diets during pregnancy correlate with the condition of their babies at birth (Suskind, 1977). However, a study of Dutch children born during a famine caused by the Nazis in World War II showed that, at age 19, their ability scores and rates of mental retardation did not differ from those of children unaffected by the famine (Stein, Susser, Saenger, & Marolla, 1975). Although the famine increased infant mortality, and the surviving children may have suffered in undetected ways, other studies have shown that the long-term nutritional status of mothers *before* pregnancy is a critical variable (Birch & Gussow, 1970). Furthermore, good educational and social environments can reduce cognitive deficits found in prenatally malnourished children raised in poor environments. For example, prenatally malnourished children receiving an intensive educational daycare program later had significantly higher IQs than control children, even though both groups got special medical and nutritional services (Zeskind & Ramey, 1981).

Certain specific dietary deficiencies in the mother lead to specific disorders in her offspring. For example, vitamin D deficiency causes congenital rickets (Montagu, 1962), while iodine deficiency causes *cretinism,* a syndrome including mental retardation and dwarfing (Stanbury, 1977). Like general malnutrition, the effects of these deficiencies are less reversible when they occur during the fetal or neonatal period than later.

Maternal Age. The risks of congenital defects, infant mortality, and complications of pregnancy and delivery are elevated for mothers below the age of 20 and above 35 (Ferreira, 1970). Immaturity of the reproductive system may be the cause in the younger group, whereas aging processes may be to blame in the older group.

Down syndrome is particularly associated with maternal age. Rates of mongoloid births range from less than 1 in 1000 for mothers under 30 to over 40 in 1000 for mothers over 45 (Zarfas & Wolf, 1979). Most cases result from the failure of the 21st pair of chromosomes in the mother's egg cell to divide during meiosis, but the reason is unknown.

Maternal Emotions. Strong emotions increase cortisone, adrenalin, and other hormones in the mother's bloodstream. These, in turn, pass through the placenta and affect the fetus (Thompson, 1957). In addition, maternal stress reduces oxygen to the fetus, at least as demonstrated in rhesus monkeys (Myers, 1975). The mother's emotional state can also affect mechanical aspects of the birth process.

Although the specific causes are unknown, it has been found that pregnant women scoring high on anxiety measures later had more complications of delivery and more children with congenital abnormalities than women low in anxiety (Davids, DeVault, & Talmadge, 1961; Davids & DeVault, 1962). The anxious women did not seem to have reasons for expecting more birth complications than the nonanxious women, but other research has shown that women with negative emotions about pregnancy get high doses of medication during labor (Yang, Zweig, Douthitt, & Federman, 1976).

Unfortunately, as with many other prenatal variables, our most precise evidence comes from nonhuman species. Thompson (1957), for example, conditioned female rats to fear a shuttlebox by shocking them in it. After the rats became pregnant, they were repeatedly placed in the box without being shocked, but with the door of the previously unlocked side of the box locked, presumably raising their anxiety. The offspring were raised by foster mother rats who had no fear conditioning. Compared to control rats also raised by foster mothers, the experimental animals were more emotional, as shown by reduced activity in an open-field situation and slow responses to food. Hockman (1961) also found more maternal deaths, abortions, stillbirths, and refusals to raise their young among fearful rats.

Maternal Illness

Certain infectious diseases can be transmitted from mother to fetus, sometimes without the mother herself showing symptoms. These diseases include smallpox, scarlet fever, measles, typhoid fever, anthrax, tuberculosis, and malaria. Syphilis infection in early fetal life causes abortion, whereas a fetus infected later will survive to be born with syphilis, often causing mental defects. In some cases, the symptoms emerge long after birth in the form of general paresis. There is some evidence that prenatal mumps can cause congenital malformations (Penrose, 1963), and conclusive evidence that *rubella* (German measles) in early pregnancy causes deafness, blindness, heart malformation, and mental retardation.

Nontransmissible disorders in the mother during pregnancy can also affect the fetus. Maternal diabetes, for example, causes babies to be large and mature looking at birth, although they are actually quite fragile and immature in their functioning. For women whose diabetes is not well controlled with insulin, fetal mortality is high, as is the risk of neonatal respiratory distress, which is occasionally fatal (Gellis & Hsia, 1959). Fetal and maternal mortality are also high among women with high blood pressure (Montagu, 1962).

Toxemia is a common disorder of pregnancy that involves swelling of the mother's limbs and dysfunctions of her kidney and circulatory systems. Its cause is unknown, although its elevated incidence in lower socioeconomic women suggests that nutrition may play a role. Pasamanick and Knobloch (1966) found increased rates of cerebral palsy, epilepsy, retardation, reading disability, motor tics, and hyperactivity in children whose mothers had a toxemia or unexplained vaginal bleeding during pregnancy. They hypothesized that toxemia and bleeding cause brain damage by depriving the fetus of oxygen. Moreover, as they point out, any disorder of pregnancy that severely harms some offspring may cause undetected damage that increases later behavior disorders in others.

Blood-type Incompatibility

If a fetus inherits blood factors differing from those of its mother, reactions in the maternal and fetal bloodstreams can occur that damage the fetus. The best known incompatibility is when a woman whose blood is negative for the Rh (*Rhesus*) factor carries a fetus having Rh positive blood, inherited from its father. Rh positive blood contains substances called *antigens* that cross the placenta into the mother's blood. Here they trigger antibodies that in turn cross the placenta into the fetal bloodstream where they destroy red blood cells.

The wholesale destruction of the fetal red blood cells (*erythrocytes*) is called *erythroblastosis*. Toxic products from the destruction of red blood cells cause severe jaundice at birth. Many children suffering from erythroblastosis can now be saved by blood transfusions before or immediately after birth, but brain damage may still result. First pregnancies are seldom affected, however, because the mother has not yet developed antibodies. The mother's immunologic reaction can be inhibited by other blood factors and by injections to kill Rh positive cells in her blood resulting from an Rh positive pregnancy (Clayton, 1973). Still, genetic counseling is advisable when a woman is Rh negative and her husband is Rh positive.

Drugs

Any chemical that crosses the placenta can affect the fetus. Many drugs crossing the placenta affect the fetus more than the mother, because the fetus is immature and its small size and small blood supply permit a drug to become more concentrated than in the mother.

The drug thalidomide was responsible for one of the most tragic episodes in modern medical history. Thalidomide was present in sedatives prescribed by Canadian and European physicians in the 1950s. Many birth defects occurred in the babies of women who took thalidomide while pregnant, and the drug was ultimately implicated. The thalidomide syndrome includes absence or shortening of the leg and arm bones, wide-set eyes, low and occasionally deformed ears, depressed bridge of the nose, and malformation of the heart and digestive tract. Psychological study of thalidomide babies has shown somewhat retarded behavioral development (Gouin-Décarie, 1961).

The heart rate of the fetus increases when its mother smokes, apparently because of oxygen deprivation (Quigley, Sheehan, Wilkes, & Yen, 1979). Furthermore, nicotine in mothers' milk produces signs of nicotine poisoning in nursing babies, and there is animal evidence of prenatal damage by carbon monoxide levels in the maternal bloodstream like those produced by smoking (Fechter & Annau, 1977). Prenatal growth retardation is also associated with maternal smoking during pregnancy (Tuchmann-Duplessis, 1975).

Heavy alcohol consumption during pregnancy can cause mental retardation and physical malformations known as the *fetal alcohol syndrome* (Streissguth, Landesman-Dwyer, Martin, & Smith, 1980). The most common features include slitlike eyes, low nasal bridge, short nose, narrow upper lip, small chin, and flat face. Heart defects, brain abnormalities, severe growth retardation, hyperactivity, and poor attention span are also common. Withdrawal symptoms may interfere with the newborn's adaptive behavior (Abel, 1980).

Maternal morphine, heroin, and methadone addictions cause congenital dependency on these drugs which, in turn, produces withdrawal symptoms and other behavioral effects at birth (Strauss, Lessen-Firestone, Starr, & Ostrea, 1975).

Mescaline and LSD cause very high rates of fetal malformation and death in animals (Becker, 1970), and LSD has been implicated in abnormalities found in the offspring of human users (Maugh, 1973).

Most anesthetics and analgesics given mothers at delivery can affect their babies. Their precise effects are not well documented, but there is evidence for an adverse impact on babies' sociability and behavioral organization during the weeks after birth (Murray, Dolby, Nation & Thomas, 1981).

Radiation

Radiation is another potential source of damage during the prenatal period. It probably accounts for few birth defects under normal conditions, but unusual conditions, such as irradiation of the mother's pelvis by an excess of x-rays or exposure to nuclear reactions, cause fetal malformations and mental retardation. The Hiroshima and Nagasaki atomic bomb blasts, for example, were followed by increased fetal, neonatal, and infant mortality, as well as retardation and malformation in the surviving babies (Tuchmann-Duplessis, 1975).

THE BIRTH PROCESS

The risk of brain damage rises during and immediately after birth, often because the brain's oxygen supply is blocked. Deprivation of oxygen, called *anoxia*, can quickly damage or kill brain cells. The effects on later development depend on the exact location, extent, and timing of the damage. Anoxia in a baby may have its greatest effects on functions very different from those in the adult.

Cerebral palsy is a general term for a variety of motor defects caused by early brain damage. Specific effects of brain damage at birth include limb paralysis, tremors of the face and fingers, and lack of speech control. Birth damage to the cerebral cortex can cause later retardation of bone growth on the side opposite the brain damage. For example, damage to the left hemisphere of the cortex may stunt the right arm (Lenneberg, 1968).

One cause of anoxia during birth is the rupture of blood vessels in the brain by excessive pressure on the head. The pressure can result from a difficult or prolonged passage through the birth canal; from improper positioning of the fetus in the birth canal, as, for example, in a *breech delivery,* where the buttocks (''breech'') instead of the head emerge first from the mother's vagina, squeezing the base of the head; and sometimes from the use of instruments such as forceps to extract the baby when it does not emerge smoothly.

When blood vessels in the brain break, they can no longer carry oxygen to their appointed brain cells. The blood from the broken vessels may form clots around other cells, depriving these cells of oxygen as well. Injuries from direct pressure can also cause over- or underdevelopment of myelin on nerves and scar tissue that hinders later brain growth and function (Lenneberg, 1968). Prematurely born babies may be especially vulnerable because (1) their physical structures are more fragile, and (2) nerve cell growth may be hampered before the point of near-completion normally reached at birth.

Another cause of anoxia is prolonged delay between the time the baby stops getting oxygen through the placenta and the time it breathes on its own. An abnormal suspension of breathing is called *apnea*. While apnea can damage the brain, sometimes fatally, the newborn seems able to survive loss of oxygen longer than older people. Rather than being exclusively a *cause* of damage, neonatal apnea may also be a *symptom* of preexisting damage (Tanner, 1970).

Whatever its cause, perinatal anoxia is sometimes followed by deficits in later functioning. A longitudinal study has shown that children who had sustained anoxia *either* postnatally or *both* prenatally *and* postnatally obtained significantly lower IQs than control children at age 3; but the IQ deficit among those sustaining *only* prenatal anoxia was not statistically significant (Corah, Anthony, Painter, Stern, & Thurston, 1965; Ernhart, Graham, & Thurston, 1960). By the age of 7, the IQ differences between the first two anoxic groups and the control group became statistically insignificant. Significant evidence for a perceptual-motor deficit was found at age 7, but not at age 3, whereas examinations by neurologists showed significant signs of neural damage at age 3 but not at age 7 for the anoxic children.

The greatest behavioral deficit among 7-year-old anoxic children was in social competence, as measured by the Vineland Social Maturity Scale. They were especially poor in "self-help" behavior like eating and dressing, in age-appropriate skills, and in socialization. Psychological examiners also rated the anoxic children as significantly more impulsive and distractible than control children at age 7. A national study of 36,000 children revealed elevated rates of mental retardation in children who had perinatal anoxia plus other signs of neurological damage, but only small deficits in anoxic children lacking other signs (Broman, 1979).

We have more precise evidence on the organic and behavioral effects of neonatal anoxia from studies of rhesus monkeys. Monkeys born by cesarean section and then deliberately asphyxiated for 8½ to 11 minutes before breathing did not show significant behavioral retardation, but autopsies revealed brain lesions. Monkeys asphyxiated for 12 to 17 minutes before being resuscitated lagged behind normal monkeys in visual depth perception, visually guided behavior, and independent locomotion; but once these functions developed, they took on normal form. However, the asphyxiated monkeys had lasting defects in learning and memory, and autopsies revealed major degeneration of brain cells beside those killed by the neonatal asphyxiation (Sechzer, Faro, & Windle, 1973). Some effects of severe neonatal anoxia thus disappear with development; others persist or are not even evident until later stages of development, perhaps because the damaged areas are normally used only at later stages.

Early Birth and Low Birth Weight

The term *premature* has traditionally referred to babies born before the usual 40-week gestational period or weighing less than 2500 grams (5½ pounds) at birth. Many babies under 2500 grams, however, especially those between 2000 and 2500 grams, have gestated for 40 weeks, are healthy, and are small merely because the mother is small (Tanner, 1970). Similarly, many babies born after less than 40 weeks are of normal size and health. On the other hand, babies gestating for 40 weeks but still remaining below 2000 grams often have defects hindering development and not overcome later. The more specific terms *low birth weight* for babies under 2000 grams and *short gestation period* for babies born early are therefore more appropriate than "premature" (Tanner, 1970).

Figure 7-1 shows that low birth weight is related to childhood neurologic abnormalities: Abnormalities were four times as common in children weighing under 1501 grams as in those over 2500 grams. Many of the abnormalities were minimal, however, and became milder with age.

The effects of low birth weight on behavioral adaptation vary with environ-

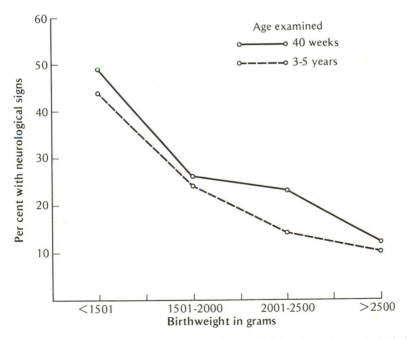

Figure 7-1. Percent of children of various birthweights with later signs of neurological abnormalities. (Data from Harper, Fischer, and Rider, 1959.)

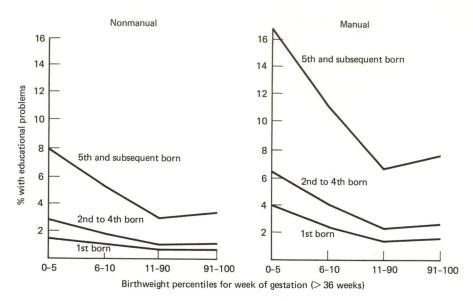

Figure 7-2. Relations between birth weight, birth order, socioeconomic status, and educational problems in British 7-year-olds. Nonmanual and manual indicate the occupation of the family breadwinner. (From Davie, Butler, & Goldstein, 1972, p. 171.)

mental quality. When children are grouped according to percentile of birth weight for their gestational age, low birth weight raises the risk of later educational problems much more for children of low socioeconomic status and late birth order than for those of higher socioeconomic status and/or earlier birth order. Figure 7-2 depicts these relations between birth weight, birth order, and socioeconomic status as found in a large sample of British children (Davie, Butler, & Goldstein, 1972). Longitudinal research on other perinatal risk factors has also shown socioeconomic status to be the best overall predictor of educational and cognitive functioning in childhood (Rubin & Balow, 1977). The success of systematic tactile-kinesthetic stimulation in enhancing the development of low birth weight, short-gestation babies further underscores the importance of postnatal environment (Sostek, Quinn, & Davitt, 1979).

Aside from its correlation with various complications, short gestation period does not seem to slow the development of later functions such as walking, if we calculate onset from the date of conception rather than the date of birth. Douglas (1956), for example, found that short-gestation children walked at later ages than normal children when age was calculated from birth, but the groups were about equal when age was calculated from conception.

POSTNATAL DEVELOPMENT

Brain Development

In proportion to its adult weight, the brain is one of the most advanced organs of the body at birth and throughout childhood. At birth, it averages about 25 percent of its adult weight, at 6 months 50 percent, at 2½ years 75 percent, and at 5 years 90 percent.

Growth rates are not uniform for all parts of the brain, however. At birth, the *midbrain, pons,* and *medulla—brain stem* structures responsible for basic reflex activities like breathing—are the most advanced in terms of proportion of final brain volume. The *forebrain,* or *cerebrum,* which includes the *cerebral cortex* and *thalamus* and is needed for higher mental processes and voluntary movements, is the next most advanced in size. The *cerebellum*—important for coordinating complex motor activity—is the least advanced in size, although it quickly catches up during the first year. Figure 7-3 schematically shows the three major regions of the brain: the *brain stem, cerebrum,* and *cerebellum.*

Growth in brain size is needed for some aspects of development, but neither weight nor size are sufficient indices of brain maturity. In fact, even *nanocephalic*

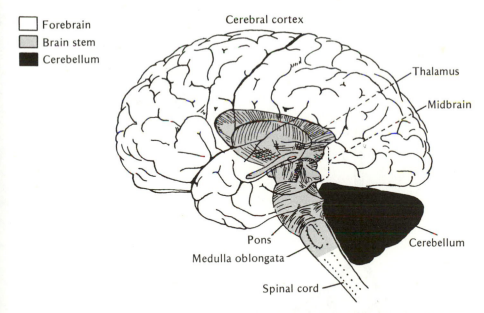

Forebrain
Brain stem
Cerebellum

Cerebral cortex

Thalamus

Midbrain

Cerebellum

Pons

Medulla oblongata

Spinal cord

Figure 7-3. Side view of three major regions of the human brain. The *brain stem* (including *midbrain, pons,* and *medulla*), the *thalamus,* and the *cerebellum* are normally hidden beneath the *cerebral cortex.* (Adapted from Penfield and Roberts, 1959.)

("bird-headed") *dwarfs,* who at adulthood average 30 inches tall and have brains the size of a newborn, develop speech and some other higher mental functions (Lenneberg, 1967).

During postnatal brain development, nerve cells become increasingly inter-connected and able to influence one another. Changes in the cerebral cortex are especially crucial for behavioral development. Neural cells grow and their *dendrites* and *axons*—the fibers carrying impulses *toward* and *away from* the cells, respectively—lengthen, forming synaptic connections with other nerves and various parts of the body. The axons also accumulate myelin, a fatty insulation that speeds conduction of nerve impulses (Jacobson, 1978).

Beside nerve cells, the brain has many *glial cells,* also known as *neuroglia,* which make up the supporting tissue that continues to form around nerve cells after birth. By maturity, glial cells comprise about 90 percent of the brain's cells (Tanner, 1970). Figure 7-4 illustrates typical nerve and glial cells.

The maturing cortex shows many changes: nerve cell bodies grow; dendrites

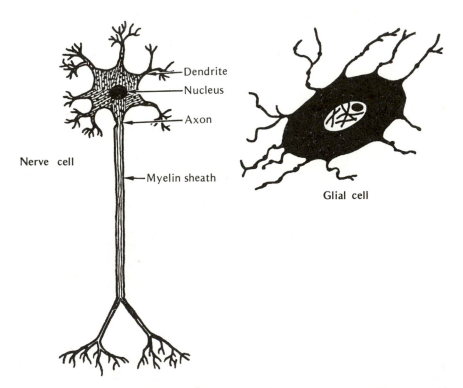

Figure 7-4. A nerve cell and a glial cell typical of those found in the brain and other parts of the nervous system. (Adapted from Scott, 1973.)

and axons lengthen; the number of nerve cells per unit volume of cortex decreases as nerve cell bodies and their dendrites and axons grow; and myelination increases.

According to these criteria, the cortex is very immature at birth. Most behavior of the first postnatal month probably does not require cortical control, because even babies born without cortex show reflexes (Jung & Hassler, 1960) and associative learning (Tuber, Berntson, Bachman, & Allen, 1980).

EEG Evidence. Electrical potentials (''brain waves'') produced by the brain's electrochemical activity can be recorded from electrodes placed on the scalp. The recording, called an *electroencephalogram* (EEG), is traced out on graph paper by a polygraph. The quantitative features of EEG data can be extracted automatically by computer and compared with data on normative samples, an approach known as *neurometrics* (Baird, John, Ahn, & Maisel, 1980).

In normal adults, the EEG shows clearcut rhythms during waking and light sleep. These rhythms are replaced by slow, irregular pulsations during unconsciousness and deep sleep. Although the EEG shows some differences between sleep and wakefulness as early as the eighth fetal month, both the sleeping and waking EEGs are diffuse and irregular until at least a month after birth. This agrees with other evidence that the newborn is ''precorticate''; that is, cortical functions underlying the rhythmic patterns of adult waking EEGs are very minimal in the newborn.

Cerebral Dominance

The cerebrum of mammals forms two nearly symmetrical halves, the *cerebral hemispheres*. One of the most significant aspects of human brain development is *cerebral dominance,* that is, the leading role played by one hemisphere in certain functions. *Lateralization of function* is another way of saying that certain functions depend more on one side of the brain than the other.

Hand preference and speech have long been thought to reflect cerebral dominance. Because the motor neurons connected to one side of the body are controlled by the cerebral hemisphere on the *opposite* side, it was assumed that the *left* hemisphere is dominant in *right*-handers, whereas the *right* hemisphere is dominant in *left*-handers. Since the brain centers controlling speech were known to be in the left hemisphere of right-handers, it was thought that the speech centers of left-handers were in the right hemisphere. However, the effects of brain lesions and surgery show that handedness does not directly reflect the localization of speech. Speech seems centered in the left hemisphere of some left-handers as well as right-handers, although right cerebral dominance and *incomplete lateralization* of speech—where both hemispheres play a role—seem more common in left than right-handers (Satz, 1980).

Anatomic studies show that cortical areas responsible for language are larger in the left hemisphere of most brains at birth (Witelson, 1980). This suggests that the left hemisphere is the "normal" seat of speech and that right hemisphere localization usually arises from abnormalities of the left hemisphere.

Development of Lateralization. Despite the left hemisphere's usual primacy in speech functions, the two hemispheres evidently do not function differently until after the age of 1 and do not become irrevocably specialized until much later. The two cortical areas mainly responsible for speech, *Broca's area* and *Wernicke's area*, seem to mature in both hemispheres around the age of 17 to 20 months (Peiper, 1963), correlating well with the onset of language in most children (Lenneberg, 1967).

Broca's area is involved in speech production, while Wernicke's area is involved in speech comprehension. The division of speech functions between these two areas means that, when one matures before the other, speech comprehension and production may be at very different levels. Lenneberg (1962), for example, described a boy who, by the age of 8, still could not speak, although tests showed good comprehension. An organic defect prevented the motor skills needed for speech but did not prevent comprehension. Disruption of speech production like this is called *Broca's aphasia,* whereas disruption of comprehension is *Wernicke's aphasia.*

The developmental course of speech lateralization can be deduced from the behavior of children who had a cerebral hemisphere surgically removed. Known as *hemispherectomy,* this is done when damage to one hemisphere causes persistent seizures and *hemiplegia,* which is paralysis of one side of the body, always the side opposite the damaged hemisphere. The results of hemispherectomies suggest that both hemispheres participate in speech development before the usual lateralization to the left hemisphere is completed (Basser, 1962). Other evidence indicates that more subtle aspects of lateralization may not normally be completed until adolescence (Tomlinson-Keasey, Kelly, & Burton, 1978) and that females remain less completely lateralized than males (Inglis & Lawson, 1981). In some children, however, early malfunction of one hemisphere may cause lateralization of speech in the other hemisphere right from the start. Early symmetrical damage to *both* hemispheres, by contrast, can delay lateralization and speech development (Dreifuss, 1963).

Endocrine Functioning

Starting with the fetal period, hormones from the endocrine glands help translate genetically coded information into body growth, as well as affecting neural and behavioral functioning. Because of the complexity of the endocrine system, we will consider only some highlights of development and pathology. Figure 7-5 shows the locations of endocrine glands.

The *pituitary gland*, located below the brain, is the "master gland" of the endocrine system. It is so called because it secretes hormones carried in the

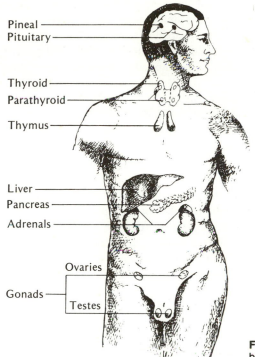

Pineal
Pituitary

Thyroid
Parathyroid

Thymus

Liver
Pancreas

Adrenals

Ovaries

Gonads

Testes

Figure 7-5. The endocrine glands of the body. (Adapted from Maher, 1966.)

bloodstream to other glands. The pituitary hormones, in turn, stimulate these glands to produce their own secretions. The pituitary has multiple effects on development. For example, its hormones stimulate the production of *thyroxine* by the *thyroid* gland; *cortisone* and *adrenal androgens* by the *adrenal* glands; *testosterone* by the *Leydig cells* of the male *testes*; and *estrogens* by the female *ovaries*. All these are needed for normal growth. The pituitary also makes a growth hormone of its own, and its hormones may directly affect the brain, which itself "has many characteristics of a gland: it contains hormones, it is bathed in hormones, it has hormone receptors, hormones may serve as its synaptic neurotransmitters, and hormones modify the brain's main function, behavior" (Bergland & Page, 1979, p. 23).

Just as pituitary hormones regulate other glands, the pituitary itself is stimulated to release these hormones by *releaser* substances from the brain, which are switched on and off in response to specific stimuli. A change in the level of the relevant hormone in the blood, for example, is sensed by specialized *sensor* cells that trigger the cells producing the releasers. There is thus a complex feedback circuit: A sensor, releaser, pituitary hormone, and hormone secreted by a gland in response to the pituitary hormone, which in turn regulates the sensor.

Normal development requires different amounts of hormones at different stages. For example, the Leydig cells of a male fetus must start secreting testosterone 10 weeks after conception to instigate development of the male genitals. However, testosterone drops to negligible levels from birth until puberty, when it must increase again to instigate development of adult sexual characteristics.

Hormone production varies in response to nerve impulses from various parts of the brain that alter sensors in the feedback circuit (Tanner, 1970). From birth to adolescence, for example, the sensor for testosterone in males is set to keep testosterone levels much lower than prenatally or at puberty. Similarly, thyroid hormone drops during the first two years and rises again at adolescence. The many hormone-caused changes in physique and emotions can cause psychosocial adjustment problems for teenagers.

Biochemical abnormalities, dietary deficiencies, and disease can disrupt the endocrine system. Brain lesions and genetic defects, for example, can prematurely increase sex hormones, triggering precocious puberty. An extreme example is a girl who reached menarche at the age of 3½ (Gesell, 1940). Accidental ingestion of sex hormones has shown that sex organs can mature in direct response to hormonal stimulation long before normal puberty, without any other physiological preparation (Tanner, 1970).

A defective pituitary or releasers that stimulate it can cause *pituitary dwarfism*. There is also evidence that extreme emotional deprivation can cause pituitary dysfunction. The pituitary dysfunction reduces growth hormone production and results in severe growth retardation (*psychosocial dwarfism*), as well as behavioral disturbance (Money, 1977).

Endocrine Reactions to Stress. Beside helping to actualize the genetic growth plan, the endocrine glands help the organism cope with threats to its well-being. An especially crucial part of the body's physiological defense is an alliance of the pituitary and adrenal glands, called the *pituitary-adrenal axis*. When we experience stress, such as a local injury, our pituitary secretes a hormone that prompts our adrenal glands to secrete *corticoids*. These serve as part of an "alarm reaction" that alerts tissues to resist effects of the injury. Byproducts of the corticoids can be measured in the blood and urine to assess the strength of physiological reactions to stress.

Emotional stressors, such as a simulated plane crash, affect the level of corticoid byproducts in the same way as physical stressors (Berkun, Bialek, Kern, & Yagi, 1962; Handlon, 1962). As we see later in this chapter, individual differences in the intensity and pattern of physiological stress reactions may contribute to disorders such as ulcers, asthma, and skin eruptions. Experience and constitutional factors may both shape these reactions. For example, periodic removal of baby rats from their nest has been shown to increase their physiological responsiveness to stress such as shock and extreme cold in adulthood, as indicated by corticoid byproducts and behavioral measures. However, the same animals are relatively unresponsive to nonthreatening environmental changes (Levine & Mullins, 1968).

Effects of Sex Hormones on Behavior. We saw earlier that sex hormones affect prenatal development of the genitals and brain as well as sexual maturation. But they have other developmental effects, too. Testosterone, for example, increases muscle and bone growth and activity. It also establishes the noncyclical male pattern of gonadal stimulation by pituitary hormones, in contrast to the cyclical female pattern (Hamburg, 1977). In adolescent boys, it is correlated with self-reported aggressive responses to provocation (Olweus, Mattson, Schalling, & Löw, 1980).

Sex hormones are hypothesized to affect cognitive functioning by activating and inhibiting the central nervous system (Broverman, Klaiber, & Vogel, 1980). They are believed to facilitate the action of *neurotransmitters*, which are chemical substances that help transmit nerve impulses across *synapses*, the points at which nerve endings approach each other. Estrogens and testosterone are both hypothesized to facilitate neural impulses, but estrogens more than testosterone. Greater neural activation improves *automatization* behavior, that is, speedy, accurate performance of well-learned tasks. However, high neural activation may hinder behavior requiring delay or inhibition of familiar responses, reversal of habits, or problem solving. Apparently thanks to the superior activating effects of estrogen, females are faster than males on such tasks as naming colors, crossing out letters and numbers, reading, writing, typing, and simple calculations. Conversely, males are superior on tasks like mirror tracing, maze performance, and counting backwards, all of which require inhibiting quick, habitual responses.

Reflecting estrogen effects, EEG patterns signifying high activation are seen before ovulation and vanish after ovulation, when another hormone, *progesterone*, inhibits estrogen effects. Furthermore, women taking estrogen for disrupted menstruation show activated EEGs like those normally *preceding* ovulation; when taking progesterone, they show less activated EEG patterns like those normally *following* ovulation.

Like estrogens in females, testosterone affects EEGs and facilitates automatization in males. Adolescent males having a cognitive style characterized by "strong automatization"—they are better at automatization than perceptual restructuring—show physical signs of high androgenization, such as heavy body hair and large chests and biceps. Testosterone byproducts in the urine also correlate with the automatization cognitive style, and testosterone treatment improves automatization in androgen-deficient boys. Besides normal cognitive and behavioral functioning, certain reading disabilities may involve poor automatization, which, in turn, results from low sex hormone production (Vogel, Broverman, Klaiber, Kobayashi, & Clarkson, 1976).

The hypothesized relations between sex hormones and automatization have not gone unchallenged, however, as Parlee (1972) objects to lumping together various abilities in terms of automatization versus perceptual restructuring. Furthermore,

Dawson (1972) compiled evidence that differences in socialization interact with hormones to shape male and female cognitive styles and abilities.

Gender Identity Problems. As we have seen, there is good evidence that male and female sex hormones have different effects on behavior. Yet, hormonal differences do not directly determine an individual's choice of sex object or gender identity, which are the psychosocial aspects of sex roles. Even where children born with internal gonads of one sex are reared as the opposite sex owing to ambiguous external genitals, the sex of rearing is usually decisive in determining sex object choices and gender identity (Ehrhardt & Meyer-Bahlburg, 1981). Then why do some people with normal genitals develop gender identity roles discordant with their physical sex and sex of rearing? And why do some people prefer individuals of their own sex as lovers?

We do not really know. However, there is evidence that early gender discordance persists into adulthood, at least in boys who very firmly want to be girls. Money and Russo (1979), for example, periodically reassessed boys who were initially referred for gender identity problems during their elementary school years:

> it was not simply girlish or androgenous behavior that brought the boys to medical attention. Rather it was the pervasive discordance between the sex of the genitalia and the sex of the mind, so pervasive that each boy had developed a conviction that he should change into a girl, and that he should be able to do so by somehow or other losing his penis, for example, by praying to God to perform the miracle of having it wither and drop off. Other evidence of identification with girls and of adopting their socially coded roles, including their dress, was secondary to this rejection of the male anatomy. (p. 38)

When followed up at ages 23 to 29, the boys no longer wished to be female. One had begun a test preliminary to sex-reassignment surgery by dressing and presenting himself socially as a woman but quit after six weeks. Yet all those on whom adequate data were obtained were predominantly homosexual in erotic behavior.

Despite problems caused by discordance with social norms for erotic behavior, the boys generally showed good educational and occupational achievement, as well as satisfactory mental health. They expressed appreciation for the nonjudgmental help offered by the researchers in the longitudinal study; this may have helped minimize psychopathology resulting from the ridicule they got from others.

Although homosexuality and discordant gender identity are not necessarily disorders in themselves, the hardships they inflict on children and adolescents often argue for intervention. Assessment procedures have therefore been developed to determine the extent of a child's gender disturbance; these show consistent preferences for cross-sex-typed toys and rejection of own-sex-typed toys in such children (Zucker, Doering, Bradley, & Finegan, 1982). Behavior therapy has successfully increased the proportion of gender-appropriate behaviors in gender-disturbed boys, but long-term follow-ups are needed to assess adult outcomes (Rekers, 1981).

POSTNATAL RISKS FOR NEUROBIOLOGICAL DEVELOPMENT

Lack of Environmental Stimulation

The role of environmental stimulation in human development has provoked extensive controversy. But "stimulation" has many meanings. No human environments totally lack stimulation. Abnormally uniform stimulation, as produced in sensory-deprivation experiments, causes discomfort for most adults but no physical harm, at least over several days (Solomon et al., 1961).

Animal Evidence. Animals can be subjected to more extreme sensory deprivation than permissible with humans. To study the role of visual stimulation in neural development, for example, Wiesel and Hubel (1963) sewed shut one eyelid of newborn kittens. At three months of age, nerve cells fed by the deprived eye were much smaller than those fed by the normal eye. Sewing the eyelids of two-month-old, visually experienced kittens for a period of three months had similar but less severe effects. No changes occurred in the nerve cells of an adult cat whose eyelid was sewn shut for three months. A translucent contact lens placed over one eye of newborn kittens—admitting light but no patterning—inhibited the development of nerve cells, but less than sewing the eyelids. To develop normally, nerve cells fed by sensory receptors evidently require input from those receptors, with patterned input a stronger growth force than unpatterned.

Rosenzweig (1976, 1979) studied the effects of environmental stimulation on rat brains. Rats chosen from the same litters—thereby roughly equated for genes—were raised under three conditions:

1. *Enriched Condition* (EC): Rats lived together in a large cage furnished with toys, had daily experience exploring an open-field apparatus, and were trained on mazes.
2. *Standard Colony* (SC): Rats lived a normal colony life.
3. *Impoverished Condition* (IC): Rats lived alone, unable to see or touch others.

The brains of rats raised in the enriched condition were significantly heavier, had thicker cerebral cortex, and more glial cells than those of rats in the impoverished condition. *Acetylcholinesterase*, the enzyme that metabolizes the synaptic neurotransmitter *acetylcholine*, was also more plentiful in the brains of EC rats, as was cortical RNA and dendritic growth.

As for behavior, EC and IC rats did not differ on simple discrimination problems; but the EC rats were superior on complex problems. The SC rats, raised in normal laboratory rat environments, tended to be between the EC and IC rats on all measures, both behavioral and physical. Stimulation thus had a positive effect and isolation a negative effect as compared to the normal environment. These effects were found in adult as well as juvenile rats. They could be modified by changing stimulation, although Levine and Mullins (1968) showed that early stimulation has lasting effects on later endocrine functioning in rats.

Early stimulation also increases cell growth in monkey brains (Floeter & Greenough, 1979) and lateralization of function in rat brains (Dennenberg, Garbanati, Sherman, Yutzey, & Kaplan, 1978). Perhaps the clearest message of the animal studies is that poor environmental stimulation can inhibit development but that the specific effects depend on the species, the nature and timing of deprivation, and the animals' subsequent experience (St. James-Roberts, 1979).

Human Evidence. It is clear that extreme variations in early stimulation *can* affect the neurobiological development of nonhuman species. But do the variations actually experienced by *human* children affect their neurobiological development? We earlier considered evidence that extreme *emotional* deprivation hinders pituitary functioning. There is no other direct proof that sensory restriction experienced by humans irreparably harms neurobiological development (Clarke & Clarke, 1976).

Yet, babies raised in nonstimulating institutions do show physical, cognitive, and emotional retardation. Provence and Lipton (1962), for example, poignantly described the daily routine of babies in an orphanage which used to be typical in this country. The environment was almost as monotonous as a sensory deprivation experiment. The babies lay all day in their cribs, fed from bottles propped beside them, and handled only for routine washing and changing. Unable to create stimulation for themselves, the babies may have been even more sensorially deprived than adults in the deprivation experiments.

In reviewing findings on institutionalization, Casler (1968) concluded that the sensory deprivation hindered children's neurobiological development just as it does in animals. Another view is that institutionalization hinders attachment to a primary mothering figure (Bowlby, 1980). These views are not mutually exclusive, however, as the traditional institutional setting reduces both sensory stimulation and opportunities for attachment. Moreover, a responsive mothering person is one of the best imaginable sources of sensory stimulation closely tuned to variations in a child's needs.

Despite retardation on measures of infant development, the effects of early institutionalization may be remediable. Dennis and Najarian (1957), for example, reported that foundlings in an extremely depriving institution were significantly retarded on infant tests but normal on nonverbal intelligence tests between the ages of 4½ and 6 years. Perhaps the early effects of sensory and maternal deprivation are at least partially overcome when children can move around on their own. Sayegh and Dennis (1965) also found that an hour of experience in sitting and manipulating objects each day for 15 days markedly improved the infant test performance of foundlings, but the gains ceased when the supplementary experience ended.

Even without conclusive evidence of biological harm from environmental deprivation, however, socialization, motivation, and learning are probably hindered by extreme early deprivation.

Malnutrition

Over 50 percent of the world's people have suffered early malnutrition (Graham, 1967). To make matters worse, promotion of commercial formulas causes women in developing countries to abandon breast feeding despite a lack of sanitary water for mixing the formulas. Although harmful at any time, malnutrition during the fetal and infant periods has the worst effect on brain development because that is when most nerve cells are formed.

Compared to babies dying of other causes, the brains of babies dying of malnutrition contain markedly fewer cells, especially in the cerebrum and cerebellum, but also in the brain stem (Winick & Rosso, 1975). Children malnourished during their first year but better nourished later show persisting deficits in head circumference (Graham, 1967; Stoch & Smyth, 1968), which is a good index of brain growth. Continuing deficits on infant and IQ tests are also found in impoverished children experiencing early malnutrition, even after better nutrition overcomes the obvious physical effects (Mönckeberg, 1975).

The effects of malnutrition on cognitive development depend partly on the social environment. Malnutrition harms children in adverse social environments more than those in better environments (Townsend et al., 1978). Nutritional supplements can improve cognitive functioning even in poor social environments (Freeman, Klein, Townsend, & Lechtig, 1980), but environmental enrichment improves cognitive functioning still further (Zeskind & Ramey, 1981).

Brain Lesions

Brain lesions have diverse causes and effects. Auto accidents, falls, and direct blows can damage brain tissue just as they damage other tissue. Some diseases cause *encephalitis*, inflammation of brain tissue; or *meningitis*, inflammation of the *meninges*, the membranes enveloping the brain and spinal cord. These can leave temporary or permanent damage. Among such diseases are measles, mumps, "lethargic" or "epidemic" encephalitis ("sleeping sickness"), various bacterial and viral infections, scarlet fever, and tuberculous of the nervous system (Ford, 1973). Others, known as *degenerative diseases*, cause progressive deterioration of the nervous system.

Neoplasms (tumors) and cysts can destroy brain tissue or interfere with its functioning by exerting direct pressure. *Hydrocephalus*, an excess of cerebrospinal fluid in the head, usually caused by injury or disease, can do the same. Although more common in old age than childhood, hemorrhaging of weakened blood vessels can deprive brain cells of oxygen. The immature brain may also be damaged by poisons, including household cleaning fluids and insecticides, medications, alcohol, narcotics, and carbon monoxide. Lead poisoning from lead-based paint and the fumes of leaded gasoline has sometimes reached epidemic proportions in city slums and can damage the brain to the point of mental retardation or death. Certain allergic reactions can also damage the growing brain (Ford, 1973).

Effects of Brain Damage. Although all of the above can damage the brain, the victim's age and general health affect the outcome. Because of this and because we can seldom pinpoint the damage very precisely, most information on the effects of brain damage is highly inferential. The difficulty of directly assessing the brain means that most research is done with groups that are heterogeneous with respect to the location and type of damage.

Despite the inevitable heterogeneity of the children studied, Teuber and Rudel (1962) demonstrated some general relations between age and the effect of brain damage on certain psychological functions. Three perceptual tasks showed three different patterns of relations between behavior and age in cerebral-palsied children suffering brain damage before the age of 1.

In one task, the child sat in a chair that could be tilted to the right and left. A device emitting clicking sounds was then moved over the child's head where he or she could not see it. The child was to report when the sound was directly overhead. Five-year-old children, both normal and brain-damaged, accurately located the sound, even when they were sharply tilted to one side. Older normal children made large errors, however, because they tried to compensate for the tilt of the chair. These errors peaked in adolescence and remained large among normal adults. Older brain-damaged children, by contrast, made *small* errors of overcompensation: By the age of 11, brain-damaged children were *more* accurate than normal children; like younger children, they were not biased by the tilting of their bodies.

In a second task, the sound was gradually moved from a position on the child's left or right toward a position directly overhead. The child was to report when the sound reached this position. Unlike body tilt, the starting position of the sound—to the left or right—had its biggest effect on 5-year-old children: Their judgments of center were displaced toward the starting position. This *starting position effect* diminished as children got older, but it biased brain-damaged children more than normal children at all ages.

In a third task, the child was blindfolded and the chair was tilted to the left or right. It was then brought slowly toward the vertical until the child felt upright. Five-year-olds reported feeling upright when still tilted markedly to the starting side, whereas older children made progressively smaller errors. Brain-damaged children made larger errors than normal children at early ages, but their errors decreased more with age than those of normal children. By age 12, brain-damaged children were as accurate as normals. Figure 7-6 summarizes the contrasting relations between age and brain damage for the three tasks.

These findings show that the effects of brain injury depend on the *age* of the child. Some aspects of functioning, evident in the starting position effect, are affected at all ages. For other aspects of functioning, which are evident in the self-righting effect, the child can ''grow out'' of the abnormality. For still others, evident in the constant errors of sound localization, the child may ''grow into'' the abnormality.

Some kinds of damage are also more detrimental if they occur early than if later, because they interfere with acquisition of basic skills. For example, damage causing deafness in early childhood hinders language development, whereas the same damage occurring later does not cause loss of language. Conversely, some forms of damage are more handicapping when they occur later: the right hemisphere, for example, takes over speech functions when the left hemisphere is damaged early in life, but not later. We must, therefore, avoid stereotyping the ''brain-damaged child'' without considering the child's developmental level, the specific functions involved, and the prospect of compensation via further development or special education.

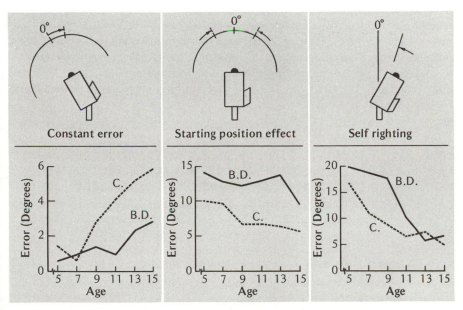

Figure 7-6. Contrasting effects of early brain damage on perceptual functioning at various ages. B.D. signifies brain-damaged group; C. signifies control group. (From Teuber and Rudel, 1962.)

SOME DISORDERS WITH PRESUMED ORGANIC ETIOLOGIES

Certain symptoms can be traced to specific organic dysfunctions. But disorders are sometimes diagnosed as "organic" because of a combination of behavioral symptoms, neurologic "signs" (such as defective reflexes), and organic and psychological test patterns, without pinpointing a specific organic dysfunction. This has often led to broad diagnostic groupings that may encompass very different etiologies.

Brain Damage and the "Brain-Damaged Child"

The Strauss Studies. During the 1930s and 1940s, Alfred E. Strauss, Heinz Werner, Laura Lehtinen, and their colleagues developed methods for diagnosing and educating brain-damaged children (Strauss & Lehtinen, 1947). For example, the patterns in Set I of the Tactual-Motor Test shown in Figure 7-7 are formed by raised rubber thumbtacks placed among rows of flat thumbtacks. The patterns in Set II are carved out of smooth wood. Children were asked to feel the patterns with their fingers without seeing them. Brain-damaged children were found to have difficulty drawing the Set I patterns because the backgrounds distracted them from perceiving the patterns separately, but they had no problem drawing the Set II patterns, because the smooth backgrounds were not distracting.

Normal children, retarded children without brain damage, and retarded children assumed to be brain-damaged were tested on the perceptual tasks and various cognitive tasks. Differences between the performance of the brain-damaged and other children were then used to diagnose children suspected of being damaged.

Largely from this pioneering research, a stereotype of the "brain-damaged child" emerged. The stereotype featured hyperactivity, impulsivity, distractibility,

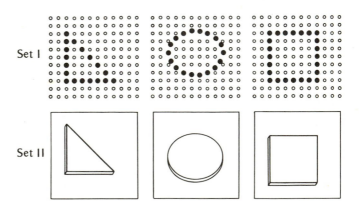

Figure 7-7. Tactual-Motor Test used by Werner and Strauss to identify brain-damaged children. (From Strauss and Lehtinen, 1947.)

short attention span, emotional lability, poor perceptual performance, and clumsiness. The terms *Strauss syndrome, diffuse brain damage, minimal brain damage, minimal brain dysfunction,* and *minimal cerebral dysfunction* have been used for children diagnosed brain damaged from these behaviors. As we will see when we consider this syndrome in Chapter 11, however, blaming these behaviors on brain damage is a gross oversimplification.

The Concept of "the Brain-Damaged Child." The popularity attained by organic diagnoses is illustrated by a survey of 99 consecutive admissions to a child guidance clinic: 37 were diagnosed as having organic abnormalities—31 were called "brain-injured" while six received other organic diagnoses, mainly of convulsive disorders (Lezak & Dixon, 1964). Ten of the "brain-injured" children took EEGs, and five of these were abnormal. All the children had neurological examinations, but abnormalities were detected in only three. The diagnoses thus rested largely on behavioral observations. However, as Birch (1964) pointed out:

> the *fact* of brain damage in children and the *concept* "the brain-damaged child" are quite different matters. As a *fact*, brain damage refers to any anatomic or physiologic alteration of a pathologic kind present in the nerve tissues of the brain . . . The *concept* "the brain-damaged child" . . . has been used to designate a certain pattern or set of patterns of behavioral disturbance . . . .
>
> One major obstacle to knowledge has been the tendency to consider the problem of the "minimally brain-damaged child" as a problem in the singular. The essential inadequacy of the term "brain damage" for purposes of classification derives from the contradiction between its singular form and the plurality of content which it seeks to embrace [pp. 4—6].

Supporting Birch's objections, a study of preschool children known to be brain damaged showed that hyperactive behavior was not a consistent sign of brain damage (Ernhart, Graham, Eichman, Marshall, & Thurston, 1963). Parents' ratings of hyperactivity, aggressiveness, emotionality, and demandingness did not significantly discriminate brain-damaged from normal children. Instead, parents rated their brain-damaged children as more *inactive*, infantile, negativistic, and compulsive. Brain-damaged and normal children generally differed little on personality ratings by parents and psychological examiners. Cognitive and perceptual-motor measures revealed deficits among the brain-damaged children, but not the patterns reported for brain-damaged adults and often imputed to brain-damaged children. Instead of being concentrated in perceptual functioning, the deficits were fairly uniform across all measures, including vocabulary. A prospective study of children following head injury showed that only those suffering quite severe injuries (indicated by amnesia lasting 7 days or more) later had elevated rates of behavior problems (Brown, Chadwick, Shaffer, Rutter, & Traub, 1981). Contradicting stereotypes of the brain-damaged child, these problems showed no uniform pattern.

Problems in Diagnosing Brain Damage. If hyperactive behavior and psychological test deficits are not inexorable products of brain damage, what can we do about the many children in whom it is suspected but not confirmed? The EEG, CAT scan, neurological examination, and developmental history provide clues. Neurological examinations test motor reflexes including knee jerk and Babinski, sensory acuity, and pupillary reflexes. *Hard signs* of neurological damage, such as paralysis, anesthesia (lack of sensation), and major reflex changes, are usually present when damage is severe enough to be apparent in other ways. However, diagnosis is harder when children have only *soft signs* of damage, such as poor fine-motor coordination, impaired visual-motor coordination, poor balance, clumsiness, and *choreiform* (jerky) movements.

Unfortunately, numerous studies show poor correlations among the various diagnostic signs. Comparisons between hyperactive and other children also reveal numerous abnormal EEGs and other signs in *nonhyperactive* children (Boll & Barth, 1981).

Another approach to diagnosing minimal brain damage is via the effects of stimulant drugs, which have been found to reduce hyperactivity. Paul Wender (1971) has interpreted this effect as indicating that hyperactivity is caused by an organic abnormality. We will consider this diagnostic strategy further in the section on psychopharmacology. However, it has certainly not solved the problem of relations between behavior and organic dysfunction.

Unless we can advance our understanding of relations between brain function and behavior, some children having *no* organic dysfunction may be treated as if they are organically defective, with the often unjustly pessimistic connotations of such diagnoses. Others having organic dysfunctions may be wrongly treated as if solely psychological factors are to blame.

Central Processing Dysfunctions

Another category of presumed organic dysfunctions involves difficulties in acquiring normal skills. These disorders are often grouped under the heading of central processing dysfunctions. Reading and speech problems get the most attention, but general learning disabilities, difficulties with writing (*dysgraphia*) and math (*dyscalculia*), and problems in integrating sensory inputs are also viewed as central processing dysfunctions (Chalfant & Scheffelin, 1969). Like the "brain-damaged child" syndrome, most research and theory concerns the numerous children for whom no organic dysfunctions are directly confirmed.

Reading Problems. Emotional problems, poor instruction, low motivation, and environmental disadvantages can all interfere with learning to read. But these factors do not explain all reading problems. Some poor readers are diagnosed as having *specific developmental dyslexia,* defined as: "A disorder manifested by difficulty in learning to read despite conventional instruction, adequate intelligence, and sociocultural opportunity. It is dependent upon fundamental cognitive disabilities that are frequently of constitutional origin'' (Research Group on Developmental Dyslexia of the World Federation of Neurology, quoted by Critchley, 1970, p. 11).

Theories of dyslexia abound. Most emphasize a basic, possibly hereditary, inability to assimilate information from written words and relate it to spoken words. The condition was once known as *word blindness,* implying a ''blindness'' to the meaning of written words. Critchley (1970) sees developmental dyslexia as a distinct syndrome because of the following observations:

1. Its persistence into adulthood.
2. Peculiar errors made in reading and spelling.
3. Elevated incidence in some families.
4. Greater incidence among males (although most disorders are more common among males than females).
5. Absence of signs of serious brain damage or perceptual defects.
6. Absence of psychological origins.
7. Continued failure to read despite conventional instruction.
8. Presence of normal intelligence.

As we will see in Chapter 11, the exact causes and best treatments for dyslexia and other specific learning disabilities have not been clearly identified.

Speech Problems. One type of speech problem involves poor articulation (*dysarthria*). Some articulation problems reflect central processing dysfunctions, but most are due to defects or immaturity in the motor apparatus for forming sounds.

A second type of speech problem involves an inability to understand or produce speech. Total inability is called *aphasia;* partial inability is called *dysphasia.* Inability to *understand* speech is called Wernicke's or *receptive* aphasia (or dysphasia); inability to *produce* speech is called Broca's or *expressive* aphasia (or dysphasia).

Brain damage occurring after speech develops can cause temporary or permanent aphasia (or dysphasia) of the receptive or expressive type. Young children's recovery from speech loss is usually better than adults' because the healthy hemisphere of the child's brain more readily acquires speech functions.

Beside loss of speech, there are *congenital* or *developmental* aphasias in which speech fails to develop. The boy described by Lenneberg (1962) who by age 8 could not speak but understood language exemplifies developmental expressive aphasia without receptive aphasia.

Like developmental dyslexia, developmental aphasia is assumed to have organic causes, but they are seldom known. No particular organic signs are uniformly present in most cases of aphasia. Goldstein, Landau, and Kleffner (1960), for example, found somewhat more defective motor functions among aphasic children than a control group of deaf children, but little difference in minor neurological signs or abnormal skull x-rays or EEGs. Thirty-two percent of the aphasic children had no detectable neurological abnormalities at all. Similarly, when DiCarlo (1960) examined 67 children diagnosed as having congenital aphasia, he concluded that only four suffered primarily from malfunctioning speech centers of the brain. He ascribed the speech problems of the other children to mental retardation (28 cases), emotional disturbance (20 cases), and defective hearing (15 cases).

Much more common than aphasia are speech dysfluencies collectively designated as *stuttering*. These involve primarily blocking, repetition, prolongation, and interruption of speech sounds. A longitudinal study of British children from birth to age 16 showed that 3 percent stuttered for at least 6 months (Andrews & Harris, 1964). An additional 1.5 percent had brief episodes while acquiring speech. In most cases, stuttering began by age 5, and none began after age 11. About 1 percent were still stuttering at age 15; this is the group for whom it typically remains a permanent affliction. Other surveys show that male stutterers outnumber females by about 5 to 1 (Boberg & Shea, 1978).

The exact cause of stuttering is not known, but family distributions suggest a role for genetic factors (Pauls & Kidd, 1981). Travis (1978) hypothesizes that defective relations between the cerebral hemispheres are involved, although these could arise either from genetic factors or brain damage. Many speech pathologists believe that overly demanding parents can perpetuate speech dysfluencies that normally occur when children first start speaking. If children become too anxious about their efforts to speak, they struggle to avoid failing:

> The efforts to avoid difficulty *are* the stutterings or lead directly to them. Having stuttered, the person is vindicated in the expectation of speech difficulty, and so the cycle continues. (Boberg & Shea, 1978, p. 359)

Behavioral and drug treatments are both reported to diminish stuttering, although neither seems to provide a consistent cure (Boberg & Shea, 1978; Burns, Brady, & Kuruvilla, 1978). A major problem in treating childhood stutterers is to distinguish between those who will improve anyway and those who may become handicapped for life without appropriate help.

The Epilepsies

Epileptic (convulsive) disorders have diverse forms and causes. What they have in common is recurrent disruption of consciousness or activity owing to excessive discharges of electrical energy in nerve cell bodies (gray matter) of the brain. Here's how an authority on epilepsy, Wilder Penfield, describes an attack:

> As long as the gray matter is normal, the energy of the nerve cells is employed only in the coordinated functional mechanisms of the brain. But if some area is injured by

disease or pressure or lack of oxygen, the gray matter, although it may continue to function, may do so with abnormal additions of its own. There seems to be a defect in the regulating mechanisms which normally limit excessive discharge. Thus, sometimes months or years after injury, an abnormal area "ripens" slowly into a self-discharging electrochemical unit. This is called an *epileptic focus*.

In such an area or focus, excess electrical energy is formed and so, from time to time, unruly mass-discharges may be released. Such an explosive discharge produces an *epileptic fit*. The fit is large or small, depending upon the extent and intensity of discharge and the position of the gray matter involved. Consequently, the subject may suddenly make aimless movements over which he has no control, or he may have strange sensations or little dreams or memories. From one point of view these seizures are experiments carried out by disease upon the brain. As each attack unfolds, it may demonstrate to the watchful observer the position of the abnormality and also the functional uses of the area involved. (Penfield & Roberts, 1959, p. 6)

Epileptic attacks have several patterns. Some people show only one, whereas others show multiple patterns. Most can also occur during high fevers, drug and alcohol intoxication, and other temporary states in people not considered epileptic because they do not have persisting attacks.

Grand Mal Epilepsy. This is the best known type. It often starts with an aura: a warning period marked by tension, depression, excitement, or elation. The aura is followed by a brief *tonic* phase: muscles rigidly contract, causing the body to stiffen. Then comes the *clonic* phase: the body jerks rapidly, the tongue may be bitten, and the mouth foams. When the spasms subside, deep sleep often ensues. Unconsciousness seems total during the attack and there are no memories of it, although confusion and headache may follow.

Petit Mal Epilepsy. The petit mal attack (also called an "absence" attack) is most common in childhood (Scott, 1973). It consists of a brief lapse of consciousness, often seen as a fluttering of the eyelids, with no warning or recovery period. It is sometimes accompanied by a slight jerking (*myoclonic jerks*) of the arms and legs, throwing the victim off balance and causing a fall.

Jacksonian Epilepsy. Named for the great British neurologist, J. Hughlings Jackson, this differs from grand and petit mal attacks in that the victim remains conscious. It consists of a tingling or involuntary movement in a particular region, such as a finger. It then spreads to larger and larger areas, often leaving the affected muscles weak for hours or days afterward.

Psychomotor Epilepsy. Psychomotor attacks often start with an odd feeling in the pit of the stomach which rises toward the throat. The victim may experience an unpleasant odor or sounds of voices or bells. Old memories may be vividly relived and organized activities carried out but with little memory of them thereafter. This is a most problematic form of epilepsy, because a person can commit a crime or do something quite out of character during an attack. Since it is hard to verify that a psychomotor attack has occurred, it is sometimes invoked as a legal defense in criminal cases.

Diagnosis and Treatment of Epilepsy

Unlike the "brain-damaged child" syndrome and some of the central processing dysfunctions, persisting epileptic attacks unquestionably involve organic malfunction. However, the exact malfunction is often unknown. Epilepsy having an identified cause is called *symptomatic epilepsy*. An epileptogenic focus in the brain can often be verified via the EEG, as illustrated in Figure 7-8.

Head injuries, tumors, diseases of the brain's blood vessels, encephalitis,

Type of EEG wave	Form and frequency	Conditions of occurrence
Alpha	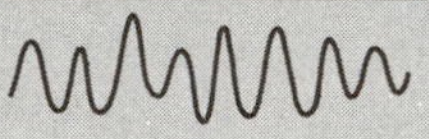 8-14 cycles/sec.	Normal activity seen at back of the head.
Beta	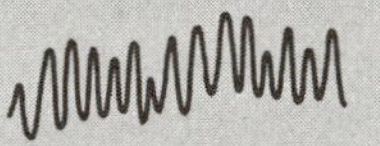 above 14 cycles/sec.	Normal activity. Marked increase with anticonvulsant medicines
Theta	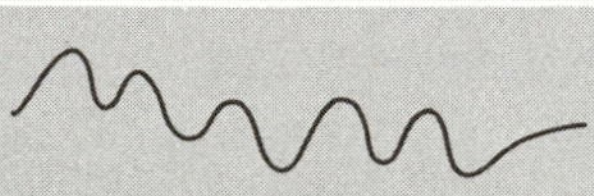 4-7 cycles/sec.	Occurs in drowsiness and many diseases.
Delta	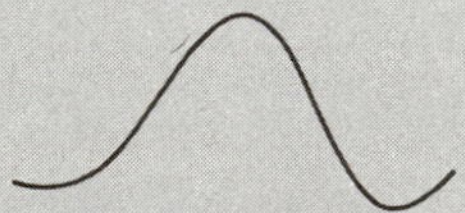 below 4 cycles/sec	Occurs in deep sleep, also in many disorders including brain tumors.
Spikes	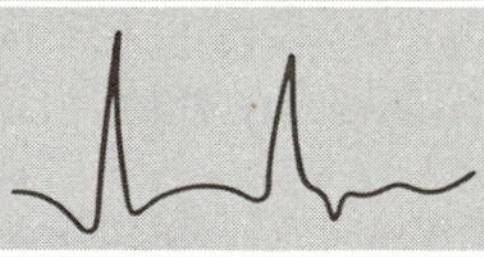	Occurs in patients with epilepsy.
Spike and Wave	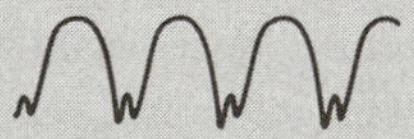	Occurs mainly in children with 'petit mal' attacks.

Figure 7-8. Types of EEG waves. (Adapted from Scott, 1973.)

meningitis, and various congenital and degenerative disorders can cause symptomatic epilepsy. Disorders of other parts of the body can also cause anoxia and toxic states resulting in epileptogenic lesions of the brain; so can poisons such as alcohol, lead, and ergot.

Epileptic attacks can also occur with no other signs of organic abnormality. When no cause is found, it is called *idiopathic, genuine,* or *essential* epilepsy. It has been hypothesized that idiopathic epilepsy results from a general organic, probably hereditary, dysfunction of the brain, rather than from a specific lesion. Consistent with this view, elevated rates of epilepsy and abnormal EEGs are found in families of epileptics (Slater & Cowie, 1971); genetic abnormalities also appear to cause humanlike seizures in mice (Noebels & Sidman, 1979). However, the elevated rates of epilepsy and EEG abnormalities may not reflect specific genetic dispositions to epilepsy but genetically low resistance to seizures once damage has occurred (Metrakos & Metrakos, 1970). Or they may reflect genetic dispositions to perinatal abnormalities which, in turn, cause brain damage leading to epilepsy (Pasamanick & Lilienfeld, 1955).

Once epilepsy is diagnosed, preventing seizures is a major goal. Not only do seizures and the fear of seizures handicap the sufferer, but seizures also risk further brain damage from anoxia, because they increase the brain's oxygen consumption up to 50 percent (Scott, 1973). Fortunately, seizures can usually be prevented with anticonvulsant medication. Biofeedback in which mechanical signals and reinforcements are made contingent on reductions of epileptoid EEG activity can also reduce seizures where medication is ineffective (Olton & Noonberg, 1980).

Even when seizures are controlled, however, epileptics must cope with the fear of further seizures, restrictions on activities like swimming and driving, side effects of medication, and sometimes with other effects of the brain damage causing the seizures. For these reasons, behavioral and educational help is often needed to improve adaptation and avoid psychological stress that may precipitate attacks. (Balaschak & Mostofsky, 1981).

Tourette Syndrome

One of the strangest disorders presumed to have an organic etiology is Gilles de la Tourette syndrome, named for a nineteenth century French neurologist who compiled case histories of it.

> The classical syndrome . . . consists first in the appearance, usually at an early age, of a series of abnormal, uncontrollable involuntary movements, of gradually increasing intensity and frequency. These usually begin in the upper part of the body, in an upper extremity, shoulder or face, and spread in the course of time to involve the head and neck, trunk, and finally the lower extremities, so that eventually there may be widespread involuntary movements of the entire body, including kicking and jumping, twisting of the head and neck, quick movements of all the extremities, blinking of the

eyes, grinding of the teeth, and projection of the tongue. There then appears the involuntary utterance of an inarticulate cry. (Mahler & Rangell, 1943, p. 579)

The most striking hallmark of the syndrome is the involuntary utterance. It is often a grunt, bark, yelp, or shriek, but in about half the cases becomes an obscene word or expression. In a famous nineteenth century case, for example, a French noblewoman, the Marquise de Dampierre, repeatedly cried out "merde" and "foutu cochon." The symptoms usually begin between the ages of 5 and 12 and continue into adolescence, although they often become milder and can sometimes be camouflaged by pretending to clear the throat (Lucas, 1979).

Although tics and nervous movements are reported for about 10 percent of normal children and 30 percent of clinically referred children (Achenbach & Edelbrock, 1981), the complete Tourette syndrome is extremely rare. Even among children referred to psychiatric clinics, the reported incidence ranges from only about 1 in 1000 to 1 in 12,500 (Lucas, 1979). Patterns of tics in the families of people with Tourette syndrome have suggested genetic influences (Pauls & Kidd, 1981). Follow-ups have shown considerable improvement in people taking the drug haloperidol, but side effects including drowsiness, depression, blurred vision, and poor coordination sometimes lead people to quit taking it (Shapiro, Shapiro, Bruun, & Sweet, 1978).

PSYCHOPHYSIOLOGICAL DISORDERS

A distinction is sometimes made between *psychosomatic* and *somatopsychological* disorders: Disorders producing physical symptoms but having important psychological determinants are called *psychosomatic,* whereas those originating with physical dysfunctions but having psychological effects are called *somatopsychological*. In either case, a vicious circle can arise whereby physical symptoms increase psychological stress; the stress, in turn, aggravates the physical symptoms.

The term *psychophysiological* has replaced psychosomatic for the first type of disorder, because psychosomatic refers to a general approach in medicine that emphasizes both the physical and psychological aspects of a patient's condition, no matter what the etiology. Psychosomatic has also come to suggest imaginary physical discomforts. Certain physical malfunctions, called *hysterical,* may indeed have no verifiable organic cause, but psychophysiological disorders involve genuine organic abnormalities, some potentially fatal. Among the most dangerous are *asthma, hypertension* (high blood pressure), *ulcerative colitis* (inflammation of the large intestine), *stomach ulcers,* and *anorexia nervosa* (extreme unwillingness to eat). Others posing significant handicaps include rheumatoid arthritis, vomiting, nausea, skin eruptions, migraine headaches, diarrhea, constipation, pains, muscle cramps, menstrual irregularities, and allergies. Complete physical examination and continuing medical care are often necessary for these disorders.

General Hypotheses about Psychophysiological Disorders

Theories of psychophysiological disorders take many forms. One early theory was that heredity, previous illness, or other factors weaken a particular organ; this weak link later becomes the site of physical reactions to stress. An early psychoanalytic view was that each psychophysiological symptom symbolizes a particular psychological conflict. In an effort to link personality patterns to psychophysiological disorders, it was found that experienced interviewers from whom all medical cues were withheld could rather accurately guess what disorders patients had (Alexander, French, & Pollock, 1968). This suggests consistent relations between personality and psychophysiological disorders, *after* the disorders have developed. However, such relations might reflect *effects* rather than *causes* of the disorders.

Physiological Reaction Patterns. Another approach is to study physiological reactions to stress by people who do not have physical symptoms. Lacey, Bateman, and Van Lehn (1953), for example, tested the hypothesis that people have characteristic reactions to stress which remain consistent across different stresses. They measured galvanic skin responses (GSR), heart rate, and variability of heart rate in college students who experienced four different stressors: fast-paced mental arithmetic, very rapid breathing, being prodded to quickly produce words starting with a particular letter, and having a foot immersed in ice water. Subjects differed markedly in the physiological measures showing the sharpest reactions. Moreover, in each subject, the measure showing the sharpest response to one stress usually showed the sharpest responses to other stresses as well. This suggests that particular psychophysiological symptoms may result from a person's general pattern of physiological functioning, regardless of the particular stress.

Malmo and Shagass (1949) demonstrated a direct relation between specific psychophysiological symptoms and individual reaction patterns. They subjected mental patients to a painful stimulus while heart rate, breathing, and electrical potential in the neck muscles were recorded. Patients who had previously complained of cardiovascular symptoms showed greater changes in heart rate and breathing than patients without these complaints. Likewise, patients who had previously complained of head and neck aches showed more increases in neck muscle potential than other patients. Even though few of the patients were reporting somatic symptoms at the time of the experiment, their physiological reactions to stress were centered at the sites of previous symptoms.

Specificity of Emotion. Ax (1953) used two stress situations to evoke very strong but distinct emotions, fear and anger. Like Lacey, Ax found individual differences in physiological response patterns across both types of stress. However, he also found that fear and anger affected response patterns in distinctive ways that were consistent for most subjects. The individual's preexisting reaction pattern *and* the type of emotion thus appeared to affect physiological responses to stress.

Physiological responses have also been studied by hypnotically inducing specific emotional attitudes (Grace & Graham, 1952). First, psychophysiological patients were asked what they felt was happening to them and what they wanted to do about it when their symptoms occurred. Normal subjects were then hypnotized to experience the stress situation and feelings reported by patients with a particular disorder. Physiological measures were used to determine whether a specific feeling indeed triggered reactions characteristic of a particular disorder.

As an example, hypnotized subjects were induced to imagine that a "Dr. X" was about to burn their hand with a match. Subjects were told they would feel very mistreated but unable to do anything about it, the experience reported by sufferers of *urticaria* (hives). During other sessions subjects were also told they would feel mistreated, but now they would want to hit and strangle Dr. X, the experience reported by people with *Raynaud disease* (a circulatory constriction making the hands cold and oxygen−deficient). It was found that the skin temperature of the subjects' "unburned" hand went *up* when they were given the "hives attitude," as it actually does in hives; but the temperature of their "unburned" hand went *down* when they had the "Raynaud disease attitude," as it does in Raynaud disease (Graham, Stern, & Winokur, 1958).

Conditioning. There is abundant evidence that physiological responses can be conditioned: Conditioning in the form of biofeedback training is used to treat problems as diverse as hypertension, Raynaud disease, headaches, and asthma (Blanchard & Epstein, 1978).

If we can deliberately condition physiological responses, perhaps some psychophysiological disorders result from learning—certain neutral stimuli repeatedly paired with stimuli that naturally elicit physiological responses later elicit the physiological responses by themselves. Early studies seemed to show that asthmatic responses, for example, could indeed be conditioned in animals, but other studies cast doubt on the validity of these findings (Purcell, Weiss, & Hahn, 1972), leaving open the question of whether psychophysiological symptoms actually do result from conditioning.

In short, several theories may shed light on the mechanics of psychophysiological disorders, but none seems to explain them all. We therefore turn to some particularly troublesome disorders of childhood.

SOME PSYCHOPHYSIOLOGICAL DISORDERS OF CHILDHOOD

Certain psychophysiological disorders are concentrated in particular age groups. Hypertension, for example, is most common in adults, whereas anorexia nervosa is most common in adolescents. Beside the three disorders we discuss next, most other psychophysiological disorders also occur in at least a few children. Moreover, certain early problems may precede particular adult psychophysiological disorders. As an example, Steward (1962) found that adults with severe psychophysiological disorders, especially stomach ulcers and hypertension, had showed more depression on personality inventories administered in adolescence than those who were either symptom-free or behaviorally maladjusted.

Anorexia Nervosa

Anorexia nervosa literally means a severe loss of appetite (anorexia) for emotional ("nervous") reasons. Until the 1968 edition of the American Psychiatric Association's *Diagnostic and Statistical Manual,* it was officially classified as a psychophysiological reaction. The 1968 edition classified it as a "special symptom reaction," along with other "feeding disturbances" such as overeating. The 1980 edition classifies it simply as an "eating disorder." Despite this reclassification, we discuss anorexia nervosa here because it is generally viewed as a psychophysiological disorder.

The changing terminology reflects confusion about how to understand and treat such disorders. Because anorexia often comes to professional attention only when severe enough to be life-threatening, clinical views have originated mainly in medical settings where severe anorexics are confined while receiving special feeding. However, studies going beyond single case histories show a variety of personality patterns, precipitating events, and outcomes.

"Anorexia" is a misnomer. Many anorexics do not lose their appetites but fear or avoid eating despite hunger, or gorge only to regret it later.

> Like a creature obsessed, neither tasting nor thinking, I burrowed through cupboards, refrigerator, cookie jar, and freezer. Grabbing fistfuls of Mallomars and brownies, gulping ice cream, Jell-O, and cheese, I was indiscriminate in my gorging. Frenzied, as though possessed by some malevolent phantom. I raced through the larder and could quit only after collapsing in glutted agony. Then, when the spell finally broke, I loathed myself for such weakness and raged at my failure of willpower.
>
> Staggering to the bathroom, I presented myself for penitence. The mirror mercilessly cast its wrath upon me. My reflection resembled that of a bloat-bellied malnutrition victim. I weighed under 90 pounds. My scrawny arms, bony chest, and spindly legs cried out in protest against the distended abdomen of my cruel binge. The sight nauseated me. No doubt about it, eating was evil. My faith in the virtue of abstinence grew the longer I stood examining myself. It sent me into spasms of remorse over my greed and propelled me into a program of redemption.
>
> I began by vomiting. Like yoga, my method relied on muscle contraction and concentrated control. But unable to purge myself completely this way, I worked out a backup maneuver. My magic cure was Ex-Lax, taken at three times the recommended dosage. It was like swallowing Drano. The only problem was that the effects were not instantaneous, and I was desperate for immediate relief. I could feel the calories turning to fat as I waited. My last resort was exercise. Like an expectant mother, I bent over my swollen stomach to touch toes, gasped through hundreds of jumping jacks, and struggled through feverish sit-ups. (Liu, 1979, pp. vii–viii)

It is generally agreed that anorexia is not a unitary disease entity but a symptom having different meanings in different people. Much more common in females than males, it is rare before age 10 and peaks in late adolescence (Halmi, 1974). Refusal or vomiting of food known as *infantile rumination*, however, does occur during the first two years of life.

Among adolescent girls, anorexia may stem from fears of sexual development and menstruation, both of which are inhibited by weight loss. Anorexic adolescents often express fears of becoming fat, but seem unaware of their emaciation.

Treatment has traditionally involved hospitalization and psychotherapy, plus tube feeding when necessary to prevent starvation. Behavioral methods are used to reduce fear of food and to reinforce eating (Geller, Kelly, Traxler, & Marone, 1978). However, helping anorexics maintain normal eating requires long-term changes in the behavior of family members to support more adaptive behavior by the anorexic (Minuchin, Rosman, & Baker, 1978; Van Buskirk, 1977). Efforts to do this via family therapy are reported to bring recovery in 86 percent of young anorexics (Minuchin et al., 1978), as compared to about 50 to 70 percent with other approaches (Rollins & Piazza, 1981). But properly controlled studies are needed to test these claims.

Bronchial Asthma

Asthma involves a contraction of the muscles of the bronchial tubes carrying air from the windpipe to the lungs. This contraction restricts passage of air, causing brain damage or death by suffocation in extreme cases (Dunleavy & Baade, 1980). It can occur as a reflex response to local irritation of the bronchial tubes or as a result of direct innervation by the hypothalamus during emotional states.

Many asthmatic attacks are caused by infections such as whooping cough and by exceptional sensitivity to *allergens,* substances that produce allergic reactions. Although psychological factors do not seem to cause asthma, they can precipitate or intensify attacks in children already having it (Alexander, 1980). Maladaptive behavioral development can also result from severe asthma:

> The early-onset asthma patient and his or her family face some very severe hardships. These youngsters tend to grow up watching the other children play from the livingroom side of the front window. Most have poor self-concepts. Often both academic and social development suffer greatly because of the amount of time lost from school and the restricted and specialized contacts with agemates. They face both peers and adults who are variously overindulgent, or lacking in understanding of their difficulties. Often these children react with shame and embarrassment, and/or demand-ingness to the extreme. At home their asthma may become the sole focus around which all family activities and concerns come to revolve. Their parents may feel responsible, guilty, and helpless; and at other times resentful and angry. Certainly, an asthma sufferer can learn to manipulate others with the disorder, or use it to avoid unpleasant

activities or situations. It is also often difficult for the patient to sort out clearly what he or she can really do, from what is accomplished in the face of asthma. Many maladaptive and inappropriate behavior patterns can develop, as patient and family struggle with the ravages of this disorder. (Alexander, 1980, p. 274)

In assessing psychological factors, Bernstein and Purcell (1963) found that some asthmatic children quickly improve when hospitalized but others do not. An intermediate group improve but continue to require occasional medication. Those improving the most had more neurotic symptoms before admission, and their parents viewed them more negatively than those who failed to improve. When asked to list what brought on their attacks, more of the improved children listed negative emotions, whereas more of the unimproved children listed organic precipitants (Purcell, 1963). Psychological factors thus seemed more crucial in the asthma of the improved than the unimproved children. The particularly crucial effect of the family is underscored by improvements in asthmatic children remaining home exposed to allergens while their families were away (Purcell et al., 1972). Medication is usually essential for treating the impaired pulmonary functioning of severe asthmatics, but behavioral therapies are often used to reduce the fears and other psychological problems associated with asthma (Alexander, 1980).

Gastrointestinal Ulceration

Three kinds of gastrointestinal ulceration are common: *peptic ulcers,* lesions of the stomach's lining; *duodenal ulcers,* lesions of the *duodenum,* the topmost section of the small intestine; and *ulcerative colitis,* lesions in the colon (large intestine).

Peptic and Duodenal Ulcers. These ulcers are popularly associated with hard-driving executives, but children have them too. Research on relations between personality, stress, and physiological mechanisms shows that ulcers involve considerably more than a simple relation between personality and the symptom.

Secretion of stomach acid normally begins when food is eaten and ends when it has been digested. However, excess stomach acid can eat away the linings of the stomach and duodenum, eventually forming ulcers. Many studies have shown high stomach acid levels in people with ulcers. But the most compelling evidence for the causal role of stomach acid comes from longitudinal studies of people who initially had no ulcers but differed in stomach acid levels.

In a massive study of 6000 babies, children, and adults, blood tests were used to measure *pepsinogen,* which is highly correlated with stomach acidity (Mirsky, 1958). Subjects having the most and least pepsinogen were then studied for several years. Ulcers developed *only* in the high pepsinogen group, including 10 percent of the high pepsinogen children. Many showed increases in pepsinogen just before their ulcer symptoms appeared. Three times as many males as females had high pepsinogen levels, corresponding to the 3 to 1 sex ratio prevailing among ulcer patients. Innately high pepsinogen levels, plus further increases, thus seem to dispose people to ulcers.

A related study demonstrated the joint contributions of high pepsinogen, personality characteristics, and situational stress (Weiner, Thaler, Reiser, & Mirsky, 1957). Prior to basic training, 63 draftees with very high pepsinogen levels and 57 with very low levels were administered gastrointestinal x-rays, psychological tests, and interviews by researchers blind to the draftees' pepsinogen level. Three initially had healed duodenal ulcers, while one had an active ulcer. Five more developed active ulcers during basic training. All nine had high pepsinogen levels.

Psychological tests were independently utilized to predict which men were likely to develop ulcers because of their presumed fear of expressing hostility and need to please in order to avoid alienating others. Of the 10 predicted to be the *most* ulcer prone, 9 had high pepsinogen levels, and 7 had ulcers. Hence, the effects of (1) high pepsinogen level, (2) certain personality characteristics, and (3) the stress of basic training all seemed to contribute to ulcer formation.

The psychological tests indicated conflicts over oral dependency among the high pepsinogen men. However, Mirsky (1958) suggested that these conflicts *result* from excessive stomach acid instead of causing it. Being present at birth, high acid levels may prevent a baby from responding to feeding with relaxation. In such cases:

> even the mother with an excellent integrative capacity, i.e., "a strong ego," and without any hostile rejecting attitudes, will be only partially successful in her efforts to provide that physiologic satiation which permits the infant to pass successfully through the purely biologic and into the psychologic phases of dependency. The child's insatiableness may induce frustration in the mother whose need to gratify the infant stems from her own unconscious wishes to be loved and cared for. Hostile and rejecting attitudes may develop in the mother in reaction to the unsatiated and thereby "rejecting" infant. As a result, infantile passive, oral-dependent wishes will persist. (Mirsky, 1958, p. 299)

Even if oral dependency conflicts are found in ulcer victims, this does not mean that these conflicts are the only emotional factor. Acid increases in response to other emotional stresses as well, although oral dependency may make certain events particularly stressful. Observation through a *gastric fistula* (a surgical opening in the stomach), for example, has revealed acid secretion in response to emotions other than those involving dependency (Wolf & Wolff, 1947). By measuring the stomach acid of patients during psychoanalytic therapy hours, Mahl and Karpe (1953) likewise found no exclusive relation between signs of oral dependency and acid secretion.

Ulcerative Colitis. The physiological mechanisms of ulcerative colitis are not as well understood as those of peptic and duodenal ulcers. Stomach acid is unlikely to be involved, because the colon is too far from the stomach. Severe diarrhea or constipation often accompany ulcerative colitis, but probably do not cause it, as rectal bleeding *precedes* diarrhea and constipation in most cases (Fullerton, Kollar, & Caldwell, 1962). Periodic worsening of the ulceration and bleeding often necessitate hospitalization and sometimes surgical removal of some of the colon.

Certain personality traits have been inferred in people with colitis, but a somatic predisposition is also assumed. A study of children hospitalized with colitis revealed neither a specific psychological cause nor much evidence of a familial pattern of predispositions (Finch & Hess, 1962). All the children's fathers were viewed as passive and ineffectual, whereas their mothers were aggressive and domineering. The children were reported to have "primitive fantasies involving the . . . sexual and digestive organs . . . and repeated concern that the body was somehow faulty or defective" (p. 822). Yet, children without colitis may also have passive, ineffectual fathers and aggressive, domineering mothers. And concern about digestive organs and a defective body is not surprising during hospitalization for colitis. In fact, a controlled *comparison* of colitis patients with those having other gastrointestinal disorders showed no differences in psychopathology (Feldman, Cantor, Soll, & Bachrach, 1967). Like other psychophysiological disorders, it thus seems that there is no unique psychological cause and that understanding and treatment requires a comprehensive approach to each affected child and his or her family (Werry, 1979).

PSYCHOPHARMACOLOGY

Psychopharmacology is the study of drug effects on behavior, emotions, and cognition. Drugs producing such effects are called *psychoactive;* their use for therapeutic purposes is called *chemotherapy* or *pharmacotherapy.* Until the rise of illegal drug use, drugs were of interest to mental health workers mainly for their therapeutic value. Sedatives were long used with epileptics and mental patients, and *Benzedrine,* an *amphetamine* drug, was used to treat hyperactive children as early as 1937 (Bradley, 1937).

In the 1950s, tranquilizers revolutionized the care of chronic adult patients. Because they suppressed excitement and violent behavior, tranquilizers made it possible to reduce physical restraints and release many patients to less restrictive settings (Berger, 1978). The success of tranquilizers in calming excited patients was accompanied by the success of antidepressants in stimulating some depressed patients. Tranquilizers and antidepressants soon became popular for outpatient treatment by practitioners of many medical specialities. This was followed by heavily advertised nonprescription versions of these drugs.

The possible effects of drug advertising and prescription of psychoactive drugs have aroused considerable controversy. One target has been advertising to persuade physicians that drugs alleviate the personal and emotional problems of patients, including children (Lennard, Epstein, Bernstein, & Ransom, 1970). An advertisement in the *Journal of the American College Health Association* (1970), for example, portrayed the tranquilizer *Librium* as the solution to a college girl's anxiety when "Exposure to new friends and other influences may force her to reevaluate herself and her goals," and "Her newly stimulated intellectual curiosity may make her more sensitive to and apprehensive about unstable national and world conditions." In another typical ad, a tearful little girl appeared with the caption, "School, the dark, separation, dental visits, 'monsters,' " and a message urging physicians to prescribe *Vistaril* when such anxieties get out of hand (*American Journal of Diseases of Children,* 1969).

Lennard et al. (1970) criticized the tendency of such advertising to relabel normal developmental problems as medical-psychiatric problems to be solved by drugs. The ads seldom offer evidence for the efficacy of such medications. Moreover, even if medication relieves symptoms, the physician prescribing it may unwittingly promote drug use as a solution for everyday problems.

> The contemporary trend of increasing prescription of psychoactive drugs seems to be contributing to the recruitment of more and more persons into a way of life in which the regulation of personal and interpersonal processes is accomplished through the ingestion of drugs. Thus, when a physician prescribes a drug for the control or solution (or both) of personal problems of living, he does more than merely relieve the discomfort caused by the problem. He simultaneously communicates a model for an acceptable and useful way of dealing with personal and interpersonal problems. (Lennard et al., 1970, p. 439)

The spread of psychoactive therapy for childhood behavioral problems is also controversial. One prominent child psychiatrist who has done research on drugs, with both positive and negative outcomes, stated:

> Among the welter of conflicting contentions [about drug effects], the drug house copywriter wanders freely, citing selected references which favor his product and apparently augment its sales. Yet, if the pitch sells, does not a good part of the fault lie with us, the physicians, who are so readily persuaded by so little scholarship?
>
> The remarkably high rate at which drugs are prescribed for the treatment of behavior disorders in children, despite the paucity of evidence to substantiate their efficacy, draws attention immediately to certain features of these disorders and their treatment. Such heavy use implies that complaints about disturbing behavior must be quite common in medical practice. Alternative modes of treatment must be either unfamiliar to physicians, or unsatisfactory in their experience, or considered too burdensome to undertake. (Eisenberg, 1968, p. 625)

On the other hand, another prominent expert on drug therapy for children said:

> . . . there is still a curious reluctance to use drugs in the out-patient psychiatric treatment of children, both in private practice and in many child guidance clinics. Fears

have been raised that drugs will dull perception, stifle learning and destroy the psychotherapeutic relationship (Fish, 1968, p. 60).

Although the total quantity of psychoactive drugs prescribed for children is unknown, about 600,000 American children annually receive stimulant drugs, which are the most commonly prescribed medication for behavior disorders (Sprague & Sleator, 1977). Continuing disagreements over whether rates of this magnitude are "remarkably high" or whether "there is still a curious reluctance . . . " reflect disagreements over how often drugs *should* be used. Eisenberg (1968) implied that they were already used too much, whereas Fish (1968) implied that irrational fears prevented them from being used as much as they should.

The appropriate use of a drug is, of course, determined by knowledge of (1) the short- and long-term effects on specific disorders in particular children, and (2) the effects of other possible treatment options. Inadequate knowledge is partly responsible for controversies over whether drugs are used too much or too little.

Initial clinical enthusiasm for many drugs has worn off when the drugs were later found ineffective or harmful. Although *double-blind placebo controlled* experiments (described in Chapter 5) are needed to assess drug effects, advertising and clinical claims are too seldom based on clearcut results from such studies. Even when good effects are found, drugs should be used clinically with only the types of patients, symptoms, and conditions for which research has demonstrated their effectiveness. Furthermore, all drugs can have harmful side effects in at least some people. These include minor and severe behavioral and physiological reactions, increased susceptibility to the effects of other chemicals, and interference with nutrition (Springer & Fricke, 1975), and impaired cognitive functioning and social responsiveness (Breuning & Davidson, 1981). Some medications are also potentially addictive, and most present risks of overdose, either accidental or deliberate.

Mechanisms of Drug Action

The biochemical details of drug action are beyond the scope of this text. However, most psychoactive drugs seem to affect transmission of impulses across neural synapses by altering the action of chemical neurotransmitters or their receptors. Many drug effects also depend partly on the patient's interpretations of the physiological changes experienced. A drug will thus be most effective when environmental conditions, patients' expectations, and physiological changes are all favorable. Experiments have shown, for example, that physiological symptoms of excitement induced by *epinephrine* can produce very different emotional states, depending on the immediate psychological and social context (Valins, 1970). The emotional effect of the drug is therefore a complex product of physiologic, cognitive, and emotional factors.

Drugs differ greatly in their mode of action. However, it is often assumed that if a disorder responds to drug therapy, it must be caused by organic abnormalities.

Table 7-1 Some Psychoactive Drugs Prescribed for Children and Adolescents

Classification and Primary Use	Generic Name	Trade Name	Side Effects
Anticonvulsants for use with epilepsy	diphenylhydantoin	Dilantin	Softening of gums, nutritional deficits.
	phenobarbital	Luminal	Potential addiction, drowsiness, fatal overdoses.
Antidepressants (imipramine also used for bedwetting)	*Tricyclics* imipramine amitriptyline nortriptyline	Tofranil Elavil Aventyl	Neurological symptoms, speech problems, discoordination, visual hallucinations, hypertension, convulsions, rash, jaundice.
Major tranquilizers for use with psychotic conditions	*Phenothiazines* chlorpromazine thioridazine triflupromazine trifluoperazine fluphenazine	Thorazine Mellaril Vesperin Stelazine Permitil, Prolixin	Drowsiness, lethargy, neurological symptoms (shaking, discoordination), muscle rigidity, hypotension, convulsions, jaundice, sensitivity to light, blurred vision.
	Butyrophenones haloperidol	Haldol	Drowsiness, lethargy, neurological symptoms.

Minor tranquilizers for use with anxiety	*Diphenylmethanes* diphenhydramine hydroxyzine	Benadryl Atarax, Vistaril	Drowsiness, confusion, nervousness, restlessness, nausea, vomiting, rash.
	Substituted Propanediols meprobamate	Equanil, Miltown	Skin reactions, diarrhea
	Benzodiazepine Compounds chlordiazepoxide diazepam	Librium Valium	Drowsiness, discoordination, fainting, hyperexcitement.
Stimulants for use with hyperactivity	*Amphetamines and substitutes* amphetamine dextroamphetamine methamphetamine methylphenidate pemoline	Benzedrine Dexedrine Desocyn Ritalin Cylert	Loss of appetite & weight, insomnia, facial pallor, constriction of veins, irritability, headaches, hallucinations, increased blood pressure & pulse.

Sources: Campbell & Small (1978); Conners & Werry (1979); Honigfeld & Howard (1978).

Wender (1971), for example, argues that if a stimulant reduces a child's hyperactivity, this shows that cerebral dysfunction must cause the hyperactivity. Yet to verify this hypothesis, we need either (1) a better understanding of how stimulants affect behavior, or (2) independent evidence of cerebral dysfunction in children whose hyperactivity is reduced by stimulants and its absence in children whose hyperactivity is not. Arguing against Wender's hypothesis is evidence that *non*hyperactive boys show behavioral, emotional, and cognitive effects of stimulants like the effects found in hyperactive boys (Rapoport et al., 1980).

Use of Psychoactive Drugs with Children and Adolescents

Psychoactive drug treatment of children and adolescents has been handicapped by a lack of controlled studies of effects on groups meeting clearcut diagnostic criteria. Two exceptions are the use of anticonvulsant drugs for epilepsy and stimulant drugs for hyperactivity. There is considerable evidence for drug efficacy in both cases, although, as we will see in Chapter 11, disagreements remain over the diagnosis of hyperactivity, the mechanism of stimulant drug action, the long-term effects of drug therapy, and the relative efficacy of alternative treatments.

Psychoactive drugs developed for adults have often been used secondarily with children, instead of being initially targeted on children's needs. As an example, the major tranquilizers and antidepressants relieve symptoms in adults who have reached plateaus in their biological, cognitive, and psychosocial development, but may hinder the development of disturbed children (Campbell & Small, 1978). Consequently, current practice may not reflect the most appropriate use of psychoactive drugs with youngsters. In the absence of more definitive knowledge, however, Table 7-1 summarizes the major classes and uses of psychoactive drugs prescribed for children and adolescents, along with known side effects.

SUMMARY

By the beginning of the *fetal* period, eight weeks after conception, the child achieves recognizably human form, with a nervous system showing reflexive responses to tactile stimuli. Most nerve cells are present by six months after conception, and nearly all are formed by birth. Later brain growth consists mainly of enlargement of the nerve cell bodies, lengthening of their *dendrites* and *axons*—the fibers carrying impulses toward and away from the cell bodies—and the addition of *glial* cells to the supporting tissue.

Hormones begin to help actualize the genetic growth plan during the fetal period: the *pituitary gland* secretes *growth hormone* by about the eighth week; *testosterone* secreted in the ninth week by the testes of a male fetus instigates development of male genitals and male characteristics of the *hypothalamus* in the brain; *thyroxine* from the *thyroid gland* aids protein synthesis in the brain after the thirteenth week.

Risks to prenatal development include *maternal malnutrition*, factors associated with *maternal age* and *maternal emotions, maternal illness, blood-type incompatibility, drugs,* and *irradiation*.

The birth process can cause neurological damage through direct pressure on the child's head and through *anoxia*. *Apnea* (failure to breathe) immediately after birth can also cause potentially damaging anoxia.

Increased behavioral and neurological abnormalities are found in children of exceptionally low birth weight and/or short gestation. Low birth weight or short gestation may be symptoms of other problems or may increase vulnerability. However, good postnatal environments can reduce the impact of early organic abnormalities on later adaptive behavior.

At birth, the brain is closer to its adult weight than most other organs are, and it grows very quickly during childhood. Much postnatal brain development consists of increases in the physical interconnectedness among nerve cells. The *cerebral cortex* is very immature at birth and early reflexive behavior is controlled mostly by the *brain stem*.

After the age of 1, many functions become relegated to one or the other of the *cerebral hemispheres*. This *lateralization of function* is especially marked for speech, which usually becomes localized in the left hemisphere.

Hormones help regulate development throughout the life cycle. They also affect behavioral tempo and reactions to stress. The *pituitary gland* is the *master gland* of the endocrine system because it produces hormones that stimulate other glands to produce their own hormones. The pituitary and other glands participate in a complex feedback circuit where *sensor* cells, reacting to the level of hormones in the blood, stimulate the production of *releaser* substances that induce the pituitary to produce its hormones. These, in turn, stimulate other glands to produce hormones. Biochemical abnormalities, dietary deficiencies, diseases, and extreme emotional deprivation can disrupt the endocrine system at various points.

Male and female hormones (*androgens* and *estrogens*) instigate the development of adult sexual characteristics at puberty. They also influence cognition and behavior, especially in relation to activation and *automatization*.

Postnatal risks for neurobiological development include malnutrition and brain lesions caused by injury, disease, asphyxiation, and poisoning. Extreme sensory deprivation hinders neurobiological development in animals and might have similar effects in humans. The effects of brain damage depend heavily on the victim's age, general health, and other characteristics.

Certain disorders with presumed organic etiologies are classified according to broad descriptive categories. These include the *brain-damaged child syndrome*, where brain damage is inferred from hyperkinetic behavior, perceptual-motor deficits, and/or "soft" neurological signs; *central processing dysfunctions*, such as *developmental dyslexia* and *aphasia;* and the *epilepsies*.

Numerous hypotheses have been proposed to account for *psychophysiological reactions*. Physiological predispositions, personality characteristics, and precipitating stress are all likely to be involved in many of them and are well-documented for *peptic* and *duodenal ulcers.*

Psychoactive drugs such as *tranquilizers, stimulants,* and *antidepressants* are widely used to treat psychopathology in children, although there is considerable controversy about their value. Many drugs developed for adult disorders have different and even opposite effects on children.

SUGGESTED READING

Neurobiological Development. Tanner (1970) provides an authoritative overview of physical development from conception through maturity with particular implications for developmental psychopathology. In the same volume, Eichorn (1970) reviews relations between the EEG and development. Other useful readings are the chapter on prenatal development in Mussen, Conger, and Kagan (1979), and a paper by Lenneberg (1968) on relations between age and the outcome of central nervous system disease in children.

Brain Function. Gazzaniga (1970) summarizes findings on ''split-brain'' patients (people undergoing surgical severing of the connections between their cerebral hemispheres), shedding light on the lateralization of functions in the brain. Anatomical differences between the two sides of the brain are described by Galaburda, LeMay, Kemper, and Geschwind (1978). Penfield and Roberts' (1959) *Speech and Brain Mechanisms* is a short, nontechnical classic by two of the world's foremost neurologists.

Malnutrition. The effects of malnutrition on brain growth and function are presented from diverse perspectives by Prescott, Read, and Coursin (1975).

Hormones. Leshner (1978) provides an introduction to the study of relations between hormones and behavior. Psychobiological aspects of sex differences are analyzed from several viewpoints in a book edited by Parsons (1980). Hamburg (1977) integrates biological and social variables in analyzing the bases of sex differences in behavior. A special issue of *Science* magazine (1981) has several articles on the development of sex differences.

Brain Damage. Boll and Barth (1981) deal with the neuropsychology of brain damage in children. Goldman and Lewis (1978) document relations between brain damage, development, and experience in monkeys much more precisely than is yet possible in humans. Werner and Smith (1977) report a unique longitudinal study of relations between perinatal abnormalities and later learning disabilities, delinquency, and mental health problems.

Epilepsy. Scott (1973) provides a helpful survey of phenomena, terminology, mythology, theory, and treatment related to epilepsy, while Balaschak and Mostofsky (1981) give an overview of epilepsy in children.

Psychopharmacology. Berger (1978) summarizes drug and related medical treatments of mental illness and their history. A collection of papers edited by Wiener (1978) details clinical psychopharmacology with children and adolescents.

Biofeedback. Diverse approaches to the conditioning of physiological responses for purposes of research and therapy are presented by Olton and Noonberg (1980).

8

Intellectual Development and Retardation

KEVIN

His neonatal course was difficult, with poor feeding and frequent vomiting. During the first two months of life, he sweated excessively and had . . . propulsive vomiting after each feeding. There were repeated respiratory infections during the first months of life; one episode at four months of age was sufficiently severe to require brief hospitalization . . . Kevin did not sit without support until eleven months of age, and did not stand without support until the age of twenty-one months. The parents and pediatrician were concerned with his slow development by the time the child was six months of age. A Gesell evaluation at that time indicated that he had motor and adaptive backwardness. On examination at age twenty-one months, he was found to have . . . behavioral organization appropriate for a child fifteen months of age. . . . Single syllables were not repeated until the child was over two years of age; single words were not used until after he was three . . . and short phrases only appeared between the fourth and fifth years.

Neurological examination at three years eight months indicated a marked disturbance in gait. . . . Swallowing was noted to be poor and drooling excessive.

The first formal psychometric evaluation was carried out when Kevin was four years three months of age. At testing, he was . . . friendly, cheerful, cooperative within limits, but readily distractible and restless. Testing was incomplete because he tired quickly. However, a basal age on the Stanford-Binet of two years six months was established, with some successes occurring at the four-year level. Intelligence testing was repeated at five years one month. . . . A mental age of three years eight months, with an I.Q. score of 72 was recorded.

Kevin, despite his mildly subnormal intelligence, occasional hyperactivity, and prominent motor and speech disorders, was not an excessively difficult child to manage. Although he was moderately active and irregular as an infant, he characteristically tended to approach new situations and to express a positive mood. An early easy distractibility, coupled with a high level of persistence in the first year, came to be replaced after the second year by moderate distractibility but continued high levels of persistence. Perhaps most significantly, from the early months of life onward he was a child whose responses were characterized by a low level of intensity. Thus, even abnormal behaviors were mildly expressed.

From the sixth month of life onward, when they first became convinced of abnormality in his development, his parents accepted the fact that his difficulties in learning and his developmental delays derived from primary neurologic damage. Within this framework they have been highly accepting and very fond of the boy. Demands have usually been appropriate to the level of his intellectual and physical capacities, and efforts at training have been both consistent and patient. Social contact with other children was encouraged and planned for, and the child was placed in a normal nursery school for children one year his junior. Since the age of six he has been in a special school for brain-injured children. Within his limitations, his course in school has shown good social functioning with peers and teachers. Learning has been slow, but progresses. His overall behavior has not presented major problems other than those involving the modifications of management necessary because of his intellectual and physical limitations. At no time has he been considered to present any significant degree of behavioral disturbance. (Thomas, Chess & Birch, 1968, pp. 128–30)

CARL W.

When . . . Carl's father talked about his 10 children, he was not hesitant about singling out one of them as "no good." That child was Carl. Today Carl has similarly rejective feelings about his parents for he does not view them as making any contribution to his life except for providing the basic essentials until he quit school in the third grade. In Carl's eyes he is a self-made man, and he owes all that he is to himself. He taught himself what he needed to know about work, personal appearance, and life in general; he thinks so little of the guidance of his parents that he can no longer remember what his father's occupation was.

Similarly he thinks so little of the contribution of the schools that he can no longer utilize anything that he was taught in the schools or even remember how he felt about them. School for Carl was one frustrating experience after another, for he could not or did not want to learn anything offered by the school. When the expectations became too demanding in the third grade he simply quit attending with no regrets at the time or now. . . .

He says . . . "I quit school while I was in the third grade and grabbed the first train out of here and I've been on my own ever since." Being on his own has meant a succession of jobs in . . . unskilled labor connected with farming, construction, and mining. . . .

In describing himself as a self-made man, Carl says. "I ain't never asked no one for nothin'." He sees no contradiction between his denial of any outside influences or help in his life and his total support today by welfare agencies. . . . Carl continued the pattern characteristic of his parents who relied on welfare support for more than half of their subsistence. Carl claims his right to such support because, "I hurt my back in the mines and two years ago I fell off of a ladder and since then I can't do nothin'. We're getting $254 a month from the government and my lawyers are fighting for the $4000 I got coming from compensation."

Carl is presently living with his second wife in a rented home. They have five children and "Two hundred fifty dollars a month don't go far with these five kids of mine. (Carl's childhood IQ was 54 on the Stanford-Binet test; Baller, Charles, & Miller, 1967, pp. 284−85).

ROCKY F.

Rocky . . . seemed almost completely incapable of reading while he spent eight years in the [special class] and showed only slightly more aptitude in other school subjects. With his fists, however, he displayed a resourcefulness that soon brought him to the attention of boxing promoters not only locally but regionally. An older brother . . . became the manager for a boxing career that established Rocky as one of the very great fighters of his generation.

Earnings as a professional boxer enabled Rocky not only to surround himself with many physical comforts—even luxuries—but to invest in enterprises that became more than adequate replacements monetarily and otherwise for the benefits which were realized from boxing. Doubtless the business acumen of the older brother had much to do with these successes. Rocky and his attractive, musically quite talented wife own a home presently valued above $40,000 [an impressive price in those days]. He has provided generously for the physical comforts of his parents and for other relatives, and he enjoys the close friendship . . . of a number of socially influential persons who for the most part shared vicariously in his triumphs as a boxer and have remained loyal to him. (Rocky's childhood IQ was 66 on the Stanford-Binet; Baller, Charles, & Miller 1967, pp. 281−82).

On the basis of their IQs, Kevin, Carl, and Rocky were eligible for special classes for the retarded in most states. Kevin's IQ was in the "borderline" range (68−83) on the Stanford-Binet test, while Rocky and Carl's scores were in the "mildly retarded" range (52−67). Over 28 million Americans would obtain IQ scores in the borderline range, while about 6 million would score in the mildly retarded range. Another 260,000 would score in the moderately retarded range (36−51), 180,000 in the severely retarded range (19−35), and 110,000 in the profoundly retarded range (0−19) (Grossman, 1977; Haywood, 1979). Between 2 and 6 million Americans are officially classfied as retarded, and about 150,000 of these live in institutions (Heal, Sigelman, & Switzky, 1978).

What are these people like? Kevin, Carl, and Rocky show that their differences are greater than their similarities. They differ enormously in the reasons for their low IQs, their special problems and needs, and the happiness and fulfillment they attain.

Most people who score below the normal range of IQ are not really very far below normal in terms of their potential for adult social and vocational competence in Western society. Only a few are maladapted enough to be recognized as retarded; very few are so handicapped that they need life-long care. Except for this small group, most retarded people can achieve a wide variety of social and vocational roles.

That target of so much controversy, the IQ, is a rather imperfect predictor of life attainment. To the extent that IQ predicts adult vocational abilities, however, people scoring in the upper 40s can be trained as stock clerks, rug weavers, painters' helpers, domestic workers, and operators of many machines. Those scoring in the mid-50s can learn to repair shoes, operate movie projectors and some printing presses, work as short-order cooks, make pottery, and work on assembly lines. Those with IQs in the low 60s can become store clerks, painters, and wood finishers (Rotter, 1971).

Until schooling became compulsory, little notice was taken of most people who today would be classified as retarded. The traditional "village idiot" stereotype included psychotic, delinquent, diseased, brain-damaged, and epileptic people whose oddities may or may not have included poor cognitive ability. As we saw in Chapter 2, the nineteenth century brought the first systematic efforts to distinguish the retarded from the insane and to provide special education for the retarded. The first educational efforts were, however, limited mainly to the severely mentally deficient and physically abnormal. When compulsory schooling imposed age-graded achievement standards, children who fell behind were stigmatized. This change of standards increased the proportion of children considered subnormal.

The discovery that many children fell behind their agemates in school prompted most Western countries to start special classes by 1900 (Kanner, 1964). But how could children unable to profit from regular classes be identified for special help? In 1904, a commission appointed by the French Minister of Public Education asked Alfred Binet and Theophile Simon to identify such children.

THE ASSESSMENT OF INTELLIGENCE

Earlier workers, such as Francis Galton and James McKeen Cattell, had unsuccessfully tried to prove that intelligence was hereditary and unitary. But Binet and Simon had a purely practical goal. As they described it, the Commission:

> . . . decided that no child suspected of retardation should be eliminated from the ordinary school and admitted into a special class, without first being subjected to a pedagogical and medical examination from which it could be certified that because of the state of his intelligence, he was unable to profit, in an average measure, from the instruction given in the ordinary schools.
> But how the examination of each child should be made, what methods should be

followed, what observations taken, what questions asked, what tests devised, how the child should be compared with normal children, the Commission felt under no obligation to decide. . . .

It has seemed to us extremely useful to furnish a guide for future Commissions' examination. . . . It must be made impossible for those who belong to the Commission to fall into the habit of making haphazard decisions according to impressions which are subjective, and consequently uncontrolled. Such impressions are sometimes good, sometimes bad, and have at all times too much the nature of the arbitrary, of caprice, of indifference. Such a condition is quite unfortunate because the interests of the child demand a more careful method. To be a member of a special class can never be a mark of distinction, and such as do not merit it, must be spared the record . . . we are convinced . . . that the precision and exactness of science should be introduced into our practice whenever possible, and in the great majority of cases it is possible (Binet & Simon, 1905b, pp. 9–10).

Binet and Simon argued that the effects of educational and therapeutic interventions could never be judged without standardized objective methods for assessing behavior before and after the intervention.

It is not by means of prior reasonings, of vague considerations, of oratorical displays, that these questions can be solved; but by minute investigation, entering into the details of fact, and considering the effects of the treatment for each particular child. There is but one means of knowing if a child, who has passed six years in a hospital or a special class, has profited from that stay, and to what degree he has profited; and that is to compare his [initial diagnosis] with his [final diagnosis], and by that means ascertain if he shows a special amelioration of his condition beyond that which might be credited simply to the considerations of growth. But experience has shown how imprudent it would be to place confidence in this comparison, when the two [diagnoses] come from different doctors, who do not judge in exactly the same way, or who use different words to characterize the mental status of patients (Binet & Simon, 1905b, p. 12).

Binet and Simon thus stressed the *reliability* and *validity* of assessment (discussed in Chapter 5). They saw that the lack of reliable and valid diagnostic procedures prevented adequate study of epidemiology, etiology, treatment, and prognosis in all forms of psychopathology.

In trying to identify retarded children, Binet and Simon were committed to neither a theory of the cause of intelligence nor a belief in its immutability. They were pragmatists who sought only a reliable and valid measure of children's *current* cognitive functioning.

Our purpose is to be able to measure the intellectual capacity of a child who is brought to us in order to know whether he is normal or retarded. We should, therefore, study his condition at the time and that only. We have nothing to do either with his past history or with his future; consequently we shall neglect his etiology, and we shall make no attempt to distinguish between acquired and congenital idiocy. . . . As to that which concerns his future, we shall exercise the same abstinence; we do not attempt to establish or prepare a prognosis and we leave unanswered the question of whether this retardation is curable, or even improvable. We shall limit ourselves to ascertaining the truth in regard to his present mental state. (Binet & Simon, 1905a, p. 37)

Because they wanted to predict school achievement, Binet and Simon sought to tap the processes actually used in school. Assuming judgment and reasoning to be the basic processes of higher thought, they tried to measure these processes in action. But to minimize the effect of specific previous knowledge, they chose items that did not require academic skills such as reading and writing.

Binet and Simon held that children suspected of subnormal ability should receive a complete medical and achievement assessment, as well as intelligence testing. Medical assessment was to determine whether organic conditions might explain poor performance, while assessment of achievement was to determine current academic knowledge.

Because they wanted to measure cognitive *development*, Binet and Simon tried each test item with normal children of different ages. An item remained a candidate for the final form of their test only if the percentage of children passing it increased sharply with age. If a majority of normal children of a particular age passed an item and the item was passed by fewer children younger than that age and more children older than that age, then the item was deemed to represent the "mental age" (MA) corresponding to that chronological age (CA). For example, an item that was passed by increasing percentages of children at ages 6 through 10, with 8 years being the first age at which a majority passed it, was considered to represent the MA of normal 8-year-olds.

A related principle was that children's performance was not evaluated according to *absolute* standards of ability, but only relative to the performance of their agemates. Consequently, the average performance of 8-year-olds was the norm against which the performance of individual 8-year-olds was judged. Binet and Simon based their norms on small samples of children who were not representative of the entire population, but they were well aware of the relations between test performance and such factors as socioeconomic status (SES). Their normative samples happened to be from the lower SES neighborhoods of Paris. Because upper SES children generally outperform lower SES children, the performance considered typical of a particular age might have been higher if Binet and Simon had used more upper SES subjects.

By 1908, Binet and Simon had assembled their best tests into a complete scale of intelligence. Shortly before Binet's death in 1911, they published a revision that simplified administration and scoring procedures. This scale consisted of five items at nearly every age from 3 to 15 years, plus five at an adult level. Versions of some of these items still appear on the most recent American version (Terman & Merrill,

1973). These include short-term memory for digits; naming common objects; copying a square; putting together two halves of a bisected rectangular card; finding parts missing from familiar figures; solving complex logical problems; and defining abstract words.

When a child passed all items at a certain year level (his or her *basal* level), items at the succeeding levels were given until a level was reached where the child failed all items (the child's *ceiling* level). The child's MA was calculated as the sum of the basal MA, plus one-fifth of a year of MA for each item passed above the basal level.

The current Binet retains this procedure, except that there are six items at most levels and each item counts one-sixth of a year (2 months of MA). Thus, if a child passes all six items at the 6-year level (the child's basal level), four at the 7-year level, three at the 8-year level, and none at the 9-year level (ceiling level), his or her mental age is calculated as follows:

Year Level	Number of Items Passed	MA Credits
VI	6 (basal age)	6 years
VII	4	8 months
VIII	3	6 months
IX	0 (ceiling age)	+ 0

MA = 7 years 2 months

Binet and Simon considered children to need special education if their MAs were more than two years below their CAs.

How valid and reliable were these tests? Just as the available resources and techniques limited the size and adequacy of the normative samples, these factors also limited research on validity and reliability. From their samples of several hundred children, however, Binet and Simon (1908) derived the following evidence for their scale's *validity*:

1. Children who were independently judged by teachers as being very bright all did well on the test.
2. Children who were three or more years behind in their scholastic performance all obtained MAs on the test below their CAs.
3. Most children performing normally in school obtained MAs corresponding to their CAs.
4. Children could rarely pass items located above their ceiling levels—the levels at which they had failed all items.

Test-retest reliability was indicated by consistency of performance by children retested at a two-week interval.

Summary of the Binet-Simon Approach

Binet and Simon established the following ideals for intelligence testing:

1. Their goal was an objective procedure for determining whether a child's cognitive functioning was sufficiently below average to warrant special education or treatment.
2. They viewed test scores as estimates of *current* functioning that proved nothing about the cause (heredity, disease, environment) or immutability of that functioning.
3. The test was to measure thinking-in-action in diverse ways not solely dependent on specific skills or information.
4. The test was to be but one part of a thorough evaluation including a medical assessment of possible organic reasons for poor performance and an assessment of scholastic achievement.
5. The test was to measure attained cognitive *development*, rather than a permanent "state" of intelligence.
6. Levels of cognitive development were defined by the typical performance of normal children of each age, rather than by a theory of development.
7. The *validity* of the test was gauged by (a) external criteria, such as correlations of test scores with teachers' ratings, school performance, and the CAs of normal children; and (b) by internal criteria such as the ordering of successes and failures on items of the test.
8. The *reliability* of the test was gauged by consistency of performance across two testings a short time apart.

Subsequent Developments in Testing

The Binet-Simon scale made an immediate worldwide impact. Henry Goddard translated the scale and began using it in 1908 at the Vineland, New Jersey, Training School, where he was director of one of the first centers for psychological research on retardation. Initially skeptical, he was surprised to find that performance on the scale correlated well with behavior outside the test situation. Another American, Frederick Kuhlmann (1912), showed that the average of several teachers' ratings of retarded children's abilities correlated well with Binet MAs, even though the teachers' ratings correlated poorly with one another.

Goddard proposed classifying retarded adults according to their Binet MAs: Those with MAs below 2 years were "idiots," those with MAs of 3 to 7 years were "imbeciles," and those with MAs of 7 to 12 years were "morons." Widely adopted, this terminology remained in use for many years.

By 1916, Goddard had distributed 88,000 record blanks for his version of the Binet; he reported use of the scale in Canada, England, Australia, New Zealand, South Africa, Germany, Switzerland, Italy, Russia, China, Japan, and Turkey.

Such a response to an admittedly crude attempt at objectively assessing ability was symptomatic of the new interest in the measurement of intelligence for purposes of education, care, and treatment.

The fascination with measuring intelligence had another source as well: the heredity-environment controversy raging since the publication of Darwin's *Origin of Species* (1859) and Galton's *Hereditary Genius* (1869). Binet and Simon did not take sides in this controversy. But hereditarians seized on their test as a measure of innate ability that could demonstrate the dominance of heredity over environment.

Among these hereditarians was Henry Goddard: Beside his work in intelligence testing, he was a leader of the eugenics movement to sterilize the retarded, and he became famous for his book, *The Kallikak Family: A Study in the Heredity of Feeble-mindedness* (1912). In this book, Goddard traced two lines of descendants from a Revolutionary War soldier, Martin Kallikak. One line began when Kallikak fathered a child by a feeble-minded bar maid during the war. The other began with the children Kallikak fathered by the respectable girl he married after the war. Many descendants of the first union were feeble-minded, delinquent, poor, and alcoholic, whereas those of the second were of good reputation. Goddard claimed this as evidence for the inheritance of intelligence, but he neglected the obvious differences in the environments of the two families.

The Stanford-Binet

Binet used the absolute difference between a child's MA and CA as an index of retardation. This implied that a child of 16 with an MA of 12 years was as handicapped as a child of 8 with an MA of 4 years. But because the latter child is really more handicapped than the former, Lewis Terman adopted a *ratio* of MA/CA as an index of ability for his 1916 Stanford revision of the Binet-Simon scale. Terman multiplied this *intelligence quotient* (IQ) by 100 to avoid decimals. This meant that a 16-year-old with an MA of 12 would have an IQ = MA/CA = 12/16 × 100 = 75. An 8-year old with an MA of 6 years would be considered to have a similar degree of handicap, because IQ = MA/CA = 6/8 × 100 = 75.

The Stanford-Binet soon became the most widely used test and the standard against which new tests were validated. The IQ, as an index of presumed *rate* of cognitive development, became both a household word and a focus of the controversy over the inheritance of intelligence. Emphasizing the IQ score, and thus treating test performance as a measure of *rate of development,* also constituted a subtle but significant shift away from Binet and Simon's position that test performance is only an index of *current* cognitive functioning, instead of a long-term prognosticator.

If you know only that an 8-year-old performs like a typical 6-year-old, you are more likely to think about the child's actual current functioning than if you are told, "He has an IQ of 75," which most people view as a permanent inferiority. Indeed, the author has met mental health professionals who, when told a 16-year-old "has an IQ of 75," consider him too retarded for psychotherapy, although they would not reject an average 12-year-old for therapy. Other workers object that the test must be wrong because the youth can read, write, and tell time. Yet, had they realized that the IQ of 75 meant the youth's performance was like an average 12-year-old's (i.e., MA 12), they would not make such misinterpretations, since 12-year-olds participate in therapy, read, write, and tell time.

By the same token, the variety of occupations possible for adults obtaining IQs in the retarded range is not at all surprising when one considers the MAs represented by those IQs. According to norms for the Stanford-Binet, the average adult has an MA of 17 years (Terman & Merrill, 1973). A person 18 years or older who obtains a "moderately retarded" IQ in the upper 40s has an MA of about 8 years. Many occupations require no more than the mental abilities of an 8-year-old with proper training.

To return now to the 1916 Stanford-Binet, Terman started with many new test items and normed them on 1000 children selected to be roughly representative of native-born Americans. He found a nearly normal distribution of IQ scores around the mean of about 100 and high test-retest reliabilities over periods up to four years (Terman et al., 1917). The stability of the IQ and its normal distribution were used to support the hereditarian hypothesis that Terman, like Goddard, held.

Terman also proposed using the "IQ test," as it was now known, to select very bright children for special classes geared to their abilities. He began a longitudinal study that traced the lives of more than a thousand high IQ children for over 50 years (Sears, 1977). Their superior achievement throughout school and adulthood offered additional validation for the IQ as a measure of ability. The adult social success of these children also rebutted the myth that exceptionally high intelligence, or "genius," was typically associated with social maladjustment, or "madness."

By 1920, assorted IQ tests were widely used in education and industry. Children with IQs below a certain cutoff (usually 70 to 80) became eligible for special education, although many states neither required nor guaranteed that it be provided.

Despite the prevailing environmentalist views of personality, there was a strong belief in the genetic determination of IQ. The intelligence test had thus acquired connotations unintended by Binet and Simon, and certainly unjustified by scientific evidence then available.

Later Versions of the Stanford-Binet. Terman and Merrill published a major revision and restandardization of the Stanford-Binet in 1937. They provided alternate forms (L and M) for comparing scores obtained on two occasions without repeating the same items. When given a few days apart, the alternate forms correlated in the .90s for children of nearly all age and IQ levels (McNemar, 1942).

The best items of the 1937 Forms L and M were combined into a single Form L-M published in 1960. The 1960 edition no longer computed IQs as a ratio of MA to CA. Instead, the mean score obtained by the standardization sample of a particular age was defined as an IQ of 100 for that age. Other IQs were then defined in terms of the standard deviation of scores for that age: one standard deviation from the mean was set equal to 16 IQ points. For example, children whose total score on the test is one standard deviation *below* the mean for their age get an IQ of 84. Similarly, children scoring one standard deviation *above* the mean for their age get an IQ of 116. IQs are scored in terms of deviation units to insure that a specific IQ always represents the same distance above or below average at any age.

Figure 8-1 shows the theoretical distribution of deviation IQs. In practice, more children get low IQs than predicted by this distribution. The excess of low IQs has important implications for theories of cultural-familial retardation discussed later in this chapter.

As Figure 8-1 shows, the cut-off points for various degrees of retardation are in terms of standard deviation units below the mean. "Borderline intelligence," for example, includes scores between one and two standard deviations below the mean (68−83). It is obvious from Figure 8-1 that the exact cut-off points for these categories are totally arbitrary.

The Wechsler Tests

Although the Stanford-Binet is still widely used, the tests developed by David Wechsler are also popular. The original Wechsler-Bellevue (W-B) was published in 1939 for use with adults. This test, its later revision—the Wechsler Adult Intelligence Scale-Revised (WAIS-R; 1981)—and its two downward extensions for children—the Wechsler Intelligence Scale for Children (WISC-R; 1974) and the Wechsler Pre-school and Primary Scale of Intelligence (WPPSI; 1967)—were standardized on representative samples of several thousand Americans. Only whites were employed for the original W-B, but nonwhites were included for the others.

The Wechsler tests differ in two major ways from the Binet. First, no MA score is computed from the Wechsler tests. This is largely because adult performance was found to be highest between the ages of 20 and 25 and lower in older adults. The concept of MA as a score that normally increases with CA thus seemed untenable for adults. IQs were therefore defined in terms of standard deviations from the mean of scores in the standardization sample of a given age, the procedure eventually adopted for the Binet. Fifteen IQ points are credited for every standard deviation away from the mean. Accordingly, scores one standard deviation below the mean get an IQ of 85, whereas scores one standard deviation above the mean get an IQ of 115.

The different standard deviations of the Wechsler and Binet tests highlight the arbitrariness of specific IQ scores. Most people obtain somewhat different IQs on

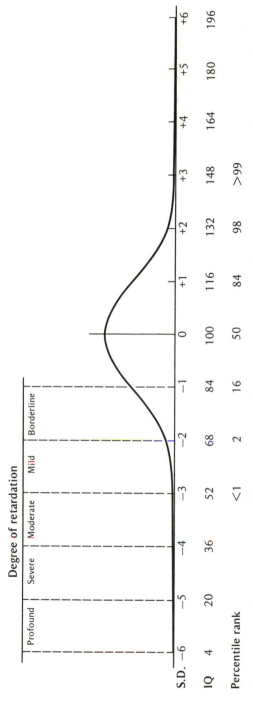

Figure 8-1. Theoretical distribution of scores on which Stanford-Binet IQs are based, together with standard deviations, IQ scores, percentile ranks, and degrees of retardation. The percentage of very low scores has been found to be greater than predicted by this curve (See Fig. 8-7). (From Pinneau, 1961.)

the two tests. For example, a person three standard deviations below the mean obtains an IQ of 52 on the Binet (where each standard deviation equals 16 points) and an IQ of 55 on the Wechsler tests (where each standard deviation equals 15 points).

The second major difference from the Binet is that the Wechsler tests are made up of subtests, each including items of a particular type, instead of diverse items grouped by age levels. A person is given each subtest, beginning with easy items and ending when a certain number are failed in succession. Several of the subtests tap verbal ability and are summed to yield a *Verbal IQ*. The verbal subtests of the WISC-R are:

1. *General Information* (factual knowledge).
2. *General Comprehension* (common sense).
3. *Arithmetic*.
4. *Similarities* (questions of how two things are alike).
5. *Vocabulary*.
6. An optional subtest—*Digit Span* (short-term memory for series of digits).

The remaining subtests tap nonverbal ability and yield a *Performance IQ:*

1. *Picture Completion* (identifying missing parts of common figures).
2. *Picture Arrangement* (putting pictures in sequence to reconstruct cut-up figures or stories).
3. *Block Design* (arranging colored blocks to match designs).
4. *Object Assembly* (putting together puzzlelike pieces to reconstruct objects).
5. *Coding* (quickly and accurately copying symbols).
6. An optional subtest—*Mazes* (tracing pathways through mazes printed on paper).

Scores on all the verbal and performance subtests together yield a *Full Scale IQ*.

Other Types of Intelligence Tests

The Wechsler and Binet tests are the most popular for assessing retardation, but there are numerous other tests of children's ability. Two types often considered in conjunction with the Wechsler and Binet tests are *infant development tests* and *group IQ tests*.

One infant test assesses the sequence of cognitive development hypothesized by Piaget (Uzgiris & Hunt, 1975). It has revealed a *sequence* of cognitive development in very retarded children similar to the sequence followed by normal babies (Kahn, 1976).

Other infant tests use standardized sensory-motor tasks to determine whether a child is progressing at the normal *rate*. These tests yield a *developmental quotient*

(DQ) similar in conception to the IQ. Yet longitudinal studies show little correlation between the infant DQs and later IQs of normal children (McCall, Hogarty, & Hurlburt, 1972). This is not surprising, because IQ tests require symbol manipulation and other complex behavior absent in infants. However, children who have low DQs tend to score low on IQ tests later, evidently because abnormal conditions interfering with infant performance often continue to be detrimental (Rubin & Balow, 1979).

Group IQ tests are paper-and-pencil tests that can be administered by teachers. They are screening devices for identifying pupils whose exceptionally low performance indicates a need for further evaluation. Although these tests give rough estimates of current functioning, the precise scores should not be taken too seriously.

VALIDITY OF IQ TESTS

The value of a psychological test is judged by its accuracy in predicting behavior outside the test situation. Intelligence tests are worthless unless they correlate with important nontest behavior. How well do IQ tests predict academic performance?

Children in Regular Classes

Much of the evidence consists of correlations between the IQs and academic performance of children in regular classes. The correlations of IQ with achievement tests and grade average typically range from the high .40s to the high .70s (Achenbach, 1970b; Stevenson, Hale, Klein, & Miller, 1968).

Because a correlation between two variables depends on the people in whom the variables are measured, it is important to compare the correlations obtained for different groups. As an example, Tulkin and Newbrough (1968) compared correlations between group IQ scores and achievement test scores for several hundred black and white fifth- and sixth-graders. The mean correlation between verbal IQ and achievement tests was .78 for blacks and .75 for whites. When broken down by social class, the correlations were .81 for both black and white upper SES children, .62 for lower SES blacks, and .64 for lower SES whites (Tulkin, 1968). SES differences thus affected the predictive power of IQ more than racial differences did. The correlations can also be affected by sex and linguistic differences within racial and SES groups, however, as well as by the overall range of IQ and achievement within each sample (McCandless, Roberts, & Starnes, 1972).

The long-term predictive power of group IQ tests has been studied by comparing the college records of people who had all attended the same high school (Embree, 1948). Among those who began college, the average childhood IQ was 118; among those who obtained bachelor degrees, 123; among those who obtained advanced degrees, 126; among those who graduated with honors, 133; and among those who were Phi Beta Kappa, 137. This suggests considerable long-term validity for the IQ scores of children having the opportunity and motivation to begin college.

Childhood IQs have also been found to predict adult occupational attainment. As an example, Figure 8-2 shows the correlations between occupational status attained by age 26 and IQs from ages 3 to 18 in the Fels Institute longitudinal study (McCall, 1977). The correlation between *adult IQ* and *occupational status* is generally about .50; the predictive power of the childhood IQs approached this maximum by the elementary school years. Figure 8-2 also shows that the correlation between childhood and adult IQs likewise approaches its maximum (of about .80) by the elementary school years.

Retarded Children

The IQ is seldom the sole criterion for classifying children as retarded. Children doing well in school are unlikely to be considered retarded no matter what their IQ scores. Children who consistently fail *and* get low group test scores are usually retested on an individual test before decisions about special education are made. After special education begins, periodic retesting and evaluation are supposed to insure proper placement, although this is not always done.

Once children are designated as needing special education, their IQs are used to aid in assessing their specific needs. A broad division is usually made between those with IQs of 20 to 50 (designated as *trainable*) and those above 50 (designated

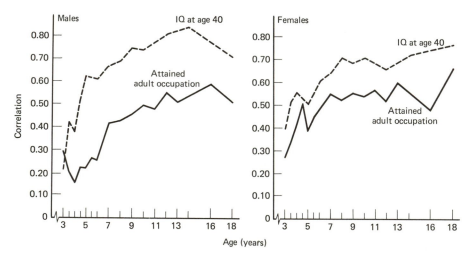

Figure 8-2. Correlations of childhood IQs with adult occupational status (Fels study) and with IQ at age 40 (Berkeley Guidance study). (Adapted from McCall, 1977, p. 482.)

as *educable)*. Surveys have shown that between 74 and 89 percent of retarded children are in the educable range (Farber, 1968; Birch, Richardson, Baird, Horobin, & Illsley, 1970). Correlations between the IQs and achievement test scores of educable children approximate those for normal children, ranging from the upper .40s to the upper .70s (Cochran & Pedrini, 1969; Mueller, 1969).

Social Competence and Adaptive Behavior

Social competence is typically a more important goal of education for the retarded than is academic achievement. A classic measure of social competence in the retarded is the Vineland Social Maturity Scale (Doll, 1965). This is a series of practical behavioral items (e.g., capable of dressing, bathing, and caring for oneself at toilet) arranged in levels according to the ages at which children normally attain them, much as test items are arranged on the Binet. All the items a child can do are scored to yield a social age (SA). This is useful in judging the level of care the child needs.

Social competence measured in this way correlates with intelligence test scores about as well as scholastic performance does. In one study of retarded children, for example, Binet MA correlated .72 with Vineland SA (Saslow, 1961). In a second study, Binet IQ correlated .69 with the Cain-Levin Social Competency Scale (Goldschmid & Domino, 1965). Uzgiris and Hunt's (1975) Piagetian scale of sensory-motor development has also been found to correlate significantly with adaptive behavior (Wachs & DeRemer, 1978). Ratings of retarded adults' personal competencies likewise show substantial correlations with IQ (Reynolds, 1981).

Intelligence tests correlate well enough with academic performance and social competence to justify their use as aids to prediction, but not well enough to be the *only* basis for decisions about children's education. Imagination, artistic and manual abilities, motivation, personality, and other variables affecting adaptation are simply not measured by standard intelligence tests. Furthermore, it has been argued that minority group children, such as Mexican-Americans and blacks, often show more successful adaptive behavior within their own subcultures than their IQs predict. In an effort to take better account of this adaptive behavior, behavioral rating scales have been added to IQ tests as criteria for judging retardation (Mercer, 1979).

Although jobs emphasizing abstract thinking are typically attained only by those with advanced academic training, many jobs do not require academic success. Our responsibility to low IQ children should not, therefore, end with diluted versions of academic curricula, but should include genuine educational opportunities and vocational training often as lengthy as the graduate training offered people of higher IQ. Table 8-1 summarizes the typical behavioral competence of the retarded at ages 0−5, 6−20, and above 21.

Table 8-1 General Behavioral Competency Expected of People with Low IQs at Various Ages. This Table Integrates Chronological Age, Degree of Retardation, and Level of Intellectual, Vocational, and Social Functioning.

Degree of Mental Retardation	Preschool Age 0–5 Maturation and Development	School Age 6–20 Training and Education	Adult 21 and Over Social and Vocational Adequacy
Profound (IQ 0–19)	Gross retardation; minimal capacity for functioning in sensorimotor areas; needs nursing care	Some motor development present; may respond to minimal or limited training in self-help	Some motor and speech development; may achieve very limited self-care; needs nursing care
Severe (IQ 20–35)	Poor motor development; speech minimal; generally unable to profit from training in self-help; little or no communication skills	Can talk or learn to communicate; can be trained in elemental health habits; profits from systematic habit training	May contribute partially to self-maintenance under complete supervision; can develop self-protection skills to a minimal useful level in controlled environment
Moderate (IQ 36–51)	Can talk or learn to communicate; poor social awareness; fair motor development; profits from training in self-help; can be managed with moderate supervision	Can profit from training in social and occupational skills; unlikely to progress beyond 2nd grade level in academic subjects; may learn to travel alone in familiar places	May achieve self-maintenance in unskilled or semiskilled work under sheltered conditions; needs supervision and guidance when under mild social or economic stress
Mild (IQ 52–67)	Can develop social and communication skills; minimal retardation in sensorimotor areas; often not distinguished from normal until later age	Can learn academic skills up to approximately 6th grade level by late teens; can be guided toward social conformity	Can usually achieve social and vocational skills adequate to minimum self-support but may need guidance and assistance when under unusual social or economic stress

Source: Adapted from *Mental Retardation Activities of the U.S. Department of Health, Education, and Welfare,* p. 2. United States Government Printing Office, Washingtion, 1963. (From Millon, 1969.)

LONG-TERM STABILITY AND CHANGE IN IQ

The question of IQ stability is often confused with the "nature-nurture" question. IQ stability has been claimed as evidence for genetic determination of intelligence, whereas IQ changes have been claimed as evidence for environmental determination. Yet neither stability nor instability of IQ automatically supports either of these positions. Consider, for example, that hair color is highly heritable but shows many changes during a lifetime, whereas people's preferred language is not at all heritable but seldom changes.

Empirical Studies

Several longitudinal studies have shown significant correlations between IQs in early childhood, adolescence, and adulthood, as summarized in Figure 8-3. Notice that the one study of infant development tests showed negligible (actually, slightly *negative*) correlations with IQ at age 18. However, the correlations between age 3 and later scores were moderately high in all four studies. By age 9, the correlations were quite substantial.

The age of final testing ranged from 12 years in the Fels Institute study (Sontag, Baker, & Nelson, 1958) to 40 in the Berkeley Guidance Study (Honzik, 1972), but the differences in correlations are not simply a function of the interval between testing, of the amount of practice subjects had with a particular test, or of the overlap in items occurring when the same test is repeated at different ages. As an illustration, the highest correlation between scores at age 3 and a later age, a correlation of .59, was found by Bradway and Thompson. Yet their interval between testings was among the longest (27 years), and they administered the criterion test (Stanford-Binet) only once in the intervening years (at approximately age 12). Furthermore, Bradway and Thompson found an even larger correlation (.64) between the Binet at age 3 and the WAIS, which they administered for the first time at age 30.

Most children retain approximately the same *rank* relative to other children, but the exact IQ does not remain constant. As we saw earlier, differences in scoring systems cause the same person to obtain different scores on different tests. For example, 30-year-olds in the Bradway and Thompson study averaged 124 on the Binet and 110 on the WAIS. When they were retested at age 42, they averaged 130 on the Binet and 118 on the WAIS (Kangas & Bradway, 1971). This increase in adult IQ contradicts the assumption, based on *cross-sectional* samples used to norm the tests, that performance declines after the mid-20s. The mean scores changed less during childhood than adulthood, however, perhaps because the cross-sectional standardization samples were more appropriate for children.

Nevertheless, the IQs of some children in all the studies changed markedly; 42 percent changed more than 10 points and 22 percent more than 15 points between

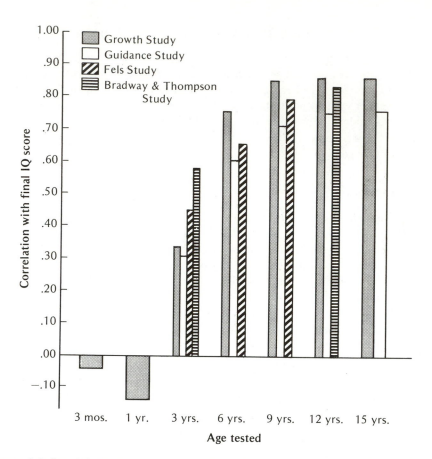

Figure 8-3. Correlations between early and later test scores from four longitudinal studies. 1. Berkeley Growth Study (Bayley, 1949): Correlations of Wechsler Bellevue at age 18 with California Infant and Preschool Tests below age 6, Stanford-Binets at ages 6 to 12, and Terman-McNemar Group Test at age 15. 2. Berkeley Guidance Study (Honzik, 1972): Correlations of WAIS at age 40 with California Preschool Test at age 3 and Stanford-Binets at ages 6 to 15. 3. Fels Institute Study (Sontag, Baker, & Nelson, 1958): Correlations of Stanford-Binet at age 12 with Stanford-Binets at ages 3 to 9. 4. Bradway and Thompson (1962) Study: Correlations of Stanford-Binet at approximately age 30 with Stanford-Binets at approximately ages 3 (actual average age = 4.0) and 12 (actual average age = 13.6).

ages 3 and 12 in the Bradway and Thompson study (Bradway, Thompson, & Cravens, 1958), while 9 percent changed 30 or more points between ages 6 and 18 in the Berkeley Guidance Study (Jones, 1954). Figure 8-4 illustrates typical patterns of variation in the IQs of children in the Fels study. Note that most large changes were gradual rather than sudden. In short, children's IQs tend to maintain a stable rank order, but their exact scores change, sometimes markedly.

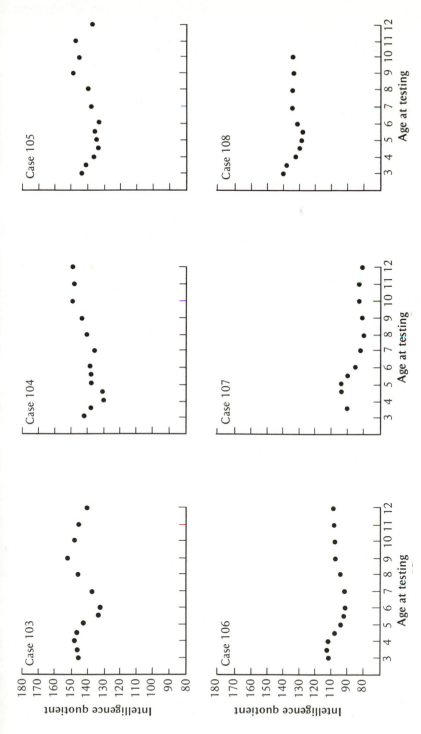

Figure 8-4. Stanford-Binet IQs obtained by six children in the Fels study between the ages of 3 and 12. (From Sontag, Baker, and Nelson, 1958. © 1958 by the Society for Research in Child Development and reprinted by permission.)

ORGANIC ABNORMALITIES CAUSING RETARDATION

Like slow physical growth, slow mental growth has many causes. We turn now to some of the known organic causes.

Genetic Abnormalities

Down Syndrome and Other Chromosomal Abnormalities. In chapter 6 we discussed several syndromes caused by chromosomal abnormalities. One of the best known is *Down syndrome*, which occurred in about 2 out of every 1000 live births (Zarfas & Wolf, 1979), until reductions were brought about by liberalized abortion (Hansen, 1978). This syndrome was described in 1866 by Langdon Down, an Englishman who believed it was an evolutionary throwback to the "Mongol race." However, chromosomal analysis revealed an extra chromosome in people with Down syndrome (Lejeune, Gautier, & Turpin, 1959). In most cases, the extra chromosome results from the failure of the twenty-first pair of the mother's chromosomes to separate during meiosis. When these two chromosomes join with the single twenty-first chromosome from the father, the result is three number twenty-one chromosomes instead of the normal two. Down syndrome is therefore designated as *trisomy 21*.

The extra chromosomal material produces a small skull, large fissured tongue protruding from a small mouth, almond-shaped eyes with sloping eyebrows, flat nasal bridge, short crooked fifth finger, and broad, square hands with a *simian* (monkeylike) crease running straight across the palm. As Figure 8-5 shows, however, the physical features are sometimes inconspicuous and these children can be quite attractive.

IQs vary rather widely, with a few as high as the borderline retarded range. A one-year test-retest reliability of .88 has been found for the Binet IQs of children with Down syndrome, about the same as for normals (Share, Koch, Webb, & Graliker, 1964). However, several studies have shown that their cognitive development advances steadily until it levels off at MAs of about 3½ to 5 years (Cornwell & Birch, 1969; Zeaman & House, 1962). When their MAs level off, the children's IQs begin to drop, not because their ability decreases, but because, as their CAs continue to increase, the gap widens between their performance and that of older normative groups on the IQ test. Although they may continue to acquire simple skills, abstract abilities remain severely limited (Cornwell, 1974).

Another chromosomal abnormality produces *Klinefelter syndrome*, in which a male receives an extra female chromosome. This gives him an XXY karyotype, known as *sex chromosome trisomy* because of the three sex chromosomes. The syndrome includes small testicles, tall and thin bodies, long arms and legs, failure to mature sexually, and, occasionally, mental retardation.

A third chromosomal abnormality produces *Cri-du-Chat* ("cat's cry") syndrome, in which portions of one chromosome are missing. The child has a weak,

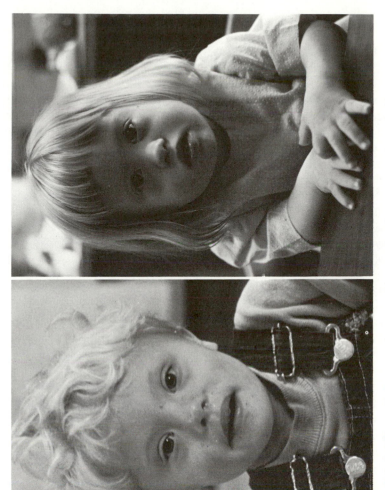

Figure 8-5. Not all children with Down syndrome are this appealing, but many are. (From Smith & Wilson, 1973, p. 25.)

221

catlike cry, plus some mongoloid features but with eyes slanting opposite to those of mongoloids.

Phenylketonuria and Other Single Gene Conditions. Phenylketonuria (PKU) occurs in about 1 out of 20,000 live births (National Research Council, 1975). Unlike the chromosomal abnormalities of Down, Klinefelter, and Cri-du-Chat syndromes, the cause of PKU is a recessive gene transmitted by typical Mendelian mechanisms. Children receiving the gene from both parents (neither of whom need have PKU because they are not homozygous for the gene) lack liver enzymes necessary for converting the amino acid phenylalanine into another essential amino acid, tyrosine. Tyrosine is normally converted into other chemicals needed for physical development.

The failure to metabolize phenylalanine, which is found in many foods, causes it to accumulate and be converted to phenylpyruvic acid and other abnormal metabolites. These cause brain damage, mental retardation, musty body odor, hyperactivity, seizures, and dry, bleached skin and hair. Experiments with monkeys fed phenylalanine show that severe disturbances of social behavior are direct effects (Chamove, Waisman, & Harlow, 1970). Phenylpyruvic acid from the blood of a PKU mother can also cause fetal brain damage and retardation, even though the fetus lacks the genotype for PKU (National Research Council, 1975).

Phenylpyruvic acid can be detected in infancy by routine blood and urine tests. Not all babies with high phenylpyruvic acid levels would develop symptoms of PKU, but low phenylalanine diets are usually prescribed as a precaution against brain damage.

Several factors affect the success of dietary treatment. One is the age at which the low phenylalanine diet is begun: If the diet is not started by 3 months of age, it is unlikely to prevent retardation. Berry (1969), for example, found that the later IQs of children whose dietary treatment began by 3 months ranged from 102 to 118, whereas the IQs of their older PKU siblings whose dietary treatment began after the age of one ranged from 55 to 83. Among still older phenylketonurics, dietary treatment improved behavior somewhat but not intellectual ability.

A second determining factor is whether an appropriate level of phenylalanine and protein can be maintained. At least as late as age 6, increases in phenylalanine cause IQs to drop (Brown & Warner, 1976). But too little causes malnutrition that also interferes with development. Maintenance of an optimal diet requires close supervision by the child's family and medical personnel. The need for rigid dietary control can create secondary problems of personality and social development, however.

Several other syndromes result from genetically based metabolic defects that cause excesses or shortages of certain chemicals. These include *Tay-Sachs disease, gargoylism, Niemann-Pick disease*, and *galactosemia*. In galactosemia, for example, there is a lack of the enzyme required to metabolize galactose, a carbohydrate found in milk. Like PKU, it can often be prevented from causing retardation if a diet low in galactose but rich in substitutes is started early enough.

Cretinism (hypothyroidism), which also results from a genetically based enzyme defect, prevents proper synthesis of the thyroid gland's hormone, thyroxine. Cretinism sometimes stems from congenital absence of the thyroid gland, a damaged thyroid, or iodine deficiencies in the mother's diet during pregnancy or in the child's diet after birth. The cretin's dwarfed stature, thick skin and lips, coarse heavy features, and protruding tongue personify the classic image of the retarded, and cretin was a generic term for the retarded until the mid-nineteenth century. Treatment with thyroid extract can bring marked improvement.

Other genetically transmitted conditions include those where a specific malformation restricts brain development. An example is *microcephaly* ("small headedness"), where the cranium is exceptionally small while the face is close to normal size. Microcephaly is transmitted by a single recessive gene, but may also result from prenatal and perinatal diseases and traumas.

Nongenetic Organic Abnormalities

Many prenatal, perinatal, and postnatal causes of brain damage were discussed in Chapter 7. The degree of initial damage, recovery, and final handicap depends on the developmental level of the nervous system when it is afflicted. For example, *rubella* (German measles) contracted by the mother during the first three months of pregnancy often causes severe defects in the fetus but not when contracted later in the fetal period or after birth. Other diseases causing retardation via brain damage include syphilis, scarlet fever, tuberculosis of the nervous system, degenerative diseases of the nerves, and sometimes measles and mumps.

Retardation can also be caused by x-rays and certain drugs taken by the mother during pregnancy, by mechanical pressure on the child's head during birth, by anoxia owing to delays in breathing at birth, by poisons such as lead and carbon monoxide, and by tumors and cysts in the head. Some early brain infections, tumors, and injuries can cause cerebrospinal fluid to accumulate in the head, a condition known as *hydrocephalus*, where the head is abnormally enlarged. Malnutrition of the mother during pregnancy and of the child during infancy can prevent normal brain development, although the behavioral effects can be lessened by subsequent environmental and nutritional enrichment (McKay et al., 1978). Incompatibility between the blood type of a mother and her fetus is another potential cause of early brain damage, but it can often be averted through blood transfusions (see Chapter 7).

A variety of motor disorders resulting from nonprogressive abnormalities of the brain and sometimes accompanied by low IQ are lumped together under the term *cerebral palsy*. The causes are diverse, but cerebral palsied children are considered together because their problems may necessitate similar treatment, education, and rehabilitation. Because the neurologic causes are so diverse, there is no reason to expect uniformity in the IQs of cerebral palsied children. Several studies have shown average or superior IQs in some, although the majority are below average. Despite the effect of motor problems on test behavior, these studies have also shown that standard IQ tests provide reliable classifications of cerebral palsied children's performance, with test-retest reliabilities as high as for normal children (Klapper & Birch, 1967; Taylor, 1959).

NONORGANIC PATHOLOGICAL CONDITIONS ASSUMED TO CAUSE RETARDATION

Approximately 75 percent of retarded people have no known organic abnormalities to explain their retardation (Zigler, 1967). Their poor cognitive performance may stem from undetected abnormalities but various nonorganic causes are also inferred.

Sensory Deprivation

The taxonomy of the American Association on Mental Deficiency (AAMD) includes retardation arising from "atypical parental-child interactions such as maternal deprivation or severe environmental restrictions such as prolonged isolation during the developing years" (Grossman, 1977, p. 68). Freedman (1969) described two cases of this sort:

> The youngsters are the middle children of a sibship of four. Their parents are intellectually within the normal range . . . . There is no known history of mental deficiency in either of their very large and extended families. The older sibling has been able to maintain himself at expected grade level in a regular school setting . . . . It seems that during her second and third pregnancies the mother developed the conviction that her offspring would be born defective. In the light of this foreordained conclusion, she elected both to keep them isolated from birth on and to devote a minimum of her time to them . . . .
>
> The little girl was confined to a room she shared with her older brother. He had a bed, but she slept on a straw pallet on the floor. He came and went as he pleased, but she remained totally confined to the room. The little boy, by contrast was confined by himself to a room eight by ten feet in size. Aside from a crib and potty, this room was bare of furniture . . . . The only window was covered by burlap sacking.
>
> The following is a description of their behavior when they were found and of its evolution over the next thirty months.
>
> Ann, at age 6, was unable to feed herself or to talk meaningfully although she did repeat some words and sentences in echolalic [echolike] fashion. She displayed no affective reaction either to her mother or to the strangers who came to investigate . . . she ranked below the third percentile in physical development. She was incontinent of urine and feces and indifferent to the overtures of the [hospital] staff. Much of her time she spent sitting up in bed rocking. She was however, able to stand and walk without

assistance. During the . . . 8 weeks hospitalization she is said to have become continent, learned to feed herself, learned to call some objects by name and at times seemed to display affectional responses to members of the staff. She was returned to her family for another nine months before the slowly moving legal process eventuated in placement in a foster home.

The description from the foster mother indicates that the gains made during her hospitalization were short-lived. Although she was able to pass objects from hand-to-hand and to her mouth, this nearly seven-year-old child could neither handle eating utensils nor feed herself by hand. (At home her only food is said to have been moderately thick gruel served in a nursing bottle). She was described as extremely obedient, and it was noted that when told to she would sit for hours in one position. She exhibited no interest either in her environment or in her body . . . .

Ann has progressed from an echolalic, repetitious and meaningless use of a few words to a considerable vocabulary. She now uses some abstract concepts. However, she continues to articulate poorly. She was in foster care a year before she began to use the first person pronoun. Six months later, differentiation of herself from the environment was still incomplete . . . .

The younger sibling, Albert, was isolated *in toto*. Like Ann, he was fed exclusively by bottle . . . . We have reason to believe that his mother only entered the room to feed and diaper him. In his later years we know that it was her wont to place him on the potty where he would, on command, sit for long hours. However, he never learned the intended connection between the potty and excretion.

When he was hospitalized at age four . . . he was well below the third percentile in both weight and height. He walked with a peculiar waddling gait, and he was incapable of even the most elementary use of his hands. Neither the manipulation of objects nor hand-to-mouth activity were present; he was unable to masticate, was incontinent of urine and feces and totally devoid of articulate speech. The only vocalizations recorded were grunting sounds and at times screams.

During the hospitalization locomotion improved, and he became able to hold his cup and clutch toys. He was never observed to play with objects or people. (Freedman, 1969, pp. 247–51)

Considering Ann and Albert's physical retardation, we cannot totally rule out their diet as a cause of their mental retardation. Severe emotional deprivation, however, may hinder pituitary function, reduce the production of growth hormone, and retard growth without malnutrition (see Chapter 7). Moreover, Ann and Albert's growth rates failed to improve after 20 months of ample diet, suggesting that diet alone was not to blame.

On Binet tests at ages 7 and 8, Ann earned IQs of 30, 39, 46, and 40. Albert earned IQs of 36, 42, and 38 at ages 5 and 6. Both children failed to show interest in people and objects long after foster home placement.

In another case, a girl named Isabelle was born to an unmarried woman who was deaf and aphasic due to early brain injury. Totally uneducated, the mother could communicate only by idiosyncratic gestures. When her pregnancy was discovered, the mother was locked in a room with drawn shades. Here she remained with Isabelle until they escaped when Isabelle was 6½.

Extremely malnourished, Isabelle suffered from rickets that bowed her legs until the soles of her shoes came nearly together. She initially earned an MA of 19 months on the Binet and a Social Age of 39 months on the Vineland (cf. Davis, 1947). Her speech therapist, Marie Mason, recounts Isabelle's progress as follows:

11−16−38: Admittance to Children's Hospital, Columbus, Ohio.

11−17−38: Cried almost continuously; would not partake of food except milk and crackers; showed either recoil, disinterest, or fear of everyone with whom she came in contact.

11−20−38: My second visit, Isabelle showed interest in the watch, ring and doll which I brought her. Partook of some food when seated at a small table.

11−25−38: First vocalization. Attempt to say the words "ball" and "car" and "bye" (good-bye).

11−26−38: Repeated the words "baby" and "dirty" in imitation of words spoken to her in the form of play. "Baby" was the most distinct articulation to date.

11−30−38: Said "flower," "one," "two." Jabbered succession of nonsense syllables in imitation of my rather lengthy explanation to Jane that she should not appropriate Isabelle's toys.

12−03−38: Isabelle began to associate the word with its object; does not associate individuals with their names, but recognizes her own name when spoken.

12−08−38: Said: "watch, ring, blue, car, ball, lady, bell, bow-wow, hot, cold, warm, one, two, three, red, dirty, pretty, baby."

1−13−39: Distinguished yellow from the other colors and said "yellow" voluntarily.

2−08−39: Says the following sentences voluntarily: "That's my baby; I love my baby; open your eyes; close your eyes; I don't know; I don't want; that's funny; 'top it—'at's mine [when another child attempted to take one of her toys]."

2−11−39: She now associates people with names.

3−02−39: Isabelle said, "Say please," when I asked her to hand me something. Later said, "I'm sorry," when she accidentally hurt another child's finger.

3−04−39: Isabelle said, "I love you, Miss Mason."

3−09−39: Identified printed form of the words, blue and yellow, and matched the word with the color.

3−10−39: Isabelle matched the printed forms of cow, sheep, dog, and cat with corresponding pictures.

3−13−39: Isabelle pointed to pictures in her book, saying: "This is a boy; this is a baby, etc." Said, "I'm sleepy."

4−01−39: Isabelle goes about humming nursery rhymes, "Here we go round the mulberry bush," and "Baa, baa, black sheep." (Mason, 1942, pp. 301−2)

After a year and a half of education, Isabelle had learned between 1500 and 2000 words. She could count to 100, identify coins, and do arithmetc with numbers up to 10. By the age of 8½, she was described as intellectually normal, imaginative, affectionate, and making an excellent adjustment.

Why was Isabelle's development so different from that of other extremely deprived children? Perhaps social contact was crucial. Despite her restricted environment and lack of exposure to language, Isabelle's interactions with her mother may have helped her take advantage of a better environment when it became available. We cannot be sure, however, as Isabelle's genetic potential and educational program may also have been crucial.

Another girl is of special interest owing to the late age at which she was rescued and the intensive psycholinguistic study made of her. Known as Genie, she was confined to a bedroom from the age of 20 months to 13½ years, strait-jacketed in a harness or sleeping bag much of the time (Curtiss, 1981). She had little to play with, was poorly fed, and experienced only punitive interactions with family members who fed her. After her rescue, she progressed considerably in social and cognitive functioning but remained limited in many ways. Extensive testing and observation revealed cognitive and linguistic functions based mainly in her right cerebral hemisphere. This suggested that the lack of linguistic input during the critical period for language learning—assumed to end at puberty—prevented normal lateralization of symbolic functions to the left hemisphere.

Retardation Accompanying Other Psychopathology

The AAMD taxonomy has a category for retardation following psychiatric disorder "when there is no evidence of cerebral pathology" (Grossman, 1977, p. 67). Most children and adolescents with severe psychopatholology perform poorly on IQ tests. A study of adolescents hospitalized for emotional disturbance, for example, showed that 50 percent were functioning in the retarded range; an additional 32 percent were diagnosed as borderline retarded (Russell & Tanguay, 1981). As we will see in Chapter 12, a basic problem in understanding severe disorders such as autism is to unravel the relations among cognitive, behavioral, and emotional deficiencies.

Case studies of less severely disturbed children demonstrate that their emotional problems can affect cognitive functioning, as illustrated by Danny R.:

> Danny R . . . was found to be such a misfit in Kindergarten that after a few weeks he was offered for a Binet test. . . .
> The first Binet showed such mental immaturity [IQ = 82] that the child was excluded from Kindergarten for a year. The next year Danny moved into another school district . . . . He had seemed so "queer" that the teacher asked for a Binet. This time he tested normal [IQ = 98], so he was placed in the first grade in September in spite of his lack of social adjustment. The mother was called in and only then was light thrown on his peculiarities. The teachers had complained that the boy seemed to live in a little world of his own. . . . He wasn't interested in group activities and was noticeably poor

in his motor coordination. He had a worried look on his face most of the time and watched the clock with undue anxiety.

The mother explained that while Danny was still a baby his father had developed encephalitis. In order for the mother to work they moved to the grandparents' home, where Danny could receive care. Unfortunately, Danny's grandfather was a high-strung, nervous old gentleman who was much annoyed by the child's noise, and expostulated so violently at times that Danny became "petrified" with fear. As a result, he sat on a chair for hours at a time, scarcely breathing, lest it disturb "grandpa". . . . It wasn't until several years had passed that the mother realized her boy was not developing normal habits and interests, and when he was excluded from Kindergarten she decided she must take him away from the grandparents' home. They moved into a different neighborhood and the boy once more entered Kindergarten.

The next few years were a period of educational, social, and emotional growth for the starved child. It is not surprising that the child amazed his teachers with his achievement, for a new world had opened up before him. He became an inveterate reader and could solve arithmetic problems far beyond his grade level. Physically frail, he has been under a doctor's care much of the time, and because of his fear complex, he was also treated by a psychiatrist. He made friends with boys in spite of lack of physical prowess. Recently because of his excellent school work, he was given a fourth Binet [the third had yielded an IQ of 111] and found to have an IQ [132 at age 11] sufficiently high to warrant placement in [an advanced class], where he is now enjoying competition with minds as keen as his own. (Lowell, 1941, pp. 353–55)

A case in which a steady *decline* in IQ may have resulted from an unhealthy relationship with the mother was reported in the Berkeley Guidance study:

Case 764 is an example of a gradual lowering of IQ from 133 [at age 2] to 77 [at age 18]. . . . She is an only child born when the mother was 44, the father 37. The estimated IQ of the mother is 65 to 70. The father is a skilled mechanic. The parents went to school until age 14.

Obesity began in late preschool years and increased steadily until [a diet was instituted] at age 14. . . . Weight was normal at 17. There were, however, no IQ variations in relation to these physical changes. She was always overindulged by the mother, who lived to feed her and keep her young and who was always complaining that her daughter never gave her enough affection. (Honzik et al., 1948, pp. 313–14)

On the other hand, another case from the same study showed a rise in IQ despite continuing stress:

"Case 553 is a boy whose mental test scores increased from a preschool sigma score of −2 [two standard deviations below the mean] to later sigma scores of +2.4 [standard deviations above the mean] in spite of a bad physical history. He is small-statured, thin, with very poor musculature, and presents a history of early ear infections and chronic bronchitis from infancy, headaches (early glasses), stomach pains (appendectomy); he has had three operations and three serious accidents. Only

one 6-month period in his life has been free of illness. In spite of a frail frame, . . . an early strained family situation, and relatively low mental test scores in his early preschool years, his tested ability steadily increased until 9, from which time he has maintained high and fairly stable scores. His mother is a normal-school [teachers' college] graduate; his father completed high school. His greatest security lies in his intellectual interests and achievements, but he has made good social adjustments and an amazingly good adjustment to his handicaps. (Honzik, 1948, p. 314)

Case studies alone cannot decisively confirm whether emotional problems significantly reduce cognitive level. One comparison between the IQs of nonpsychotic children treated for emotional disturbance and their "normal" (untreated) siblings showed no significant differences (Wolf, 1965). Children with IQs in the retarded range and those in slow learning classes, however, were excluded from the study. It is also possible that the untreated siblings, being from families containing a disturbed child, may have had problems that interfered with their cognitive performance too. Hence, while emotional problems no doubt *can* interfere with cognitive functioning, we do not know whether they actually *do* reduce functioning to the retarded range in many cases.

The term *pseudoretardation* has sometimes been used for poor cognitive performance blamed on emotional factors. However, if we focus on the child's actual level of performance—rather than on irrevocable classification as "retarded" or "nonretarded"—we need not increase the ambiguities further with terms like pseudoretardation. Instead, we must always consider the possible role of emotional and environmental stress in each child's functioning and how that functioning can be improved.

CULTURAL-FAMILIAL RETARDATION

Of the 75 percent of people judged retarded without identifiable organic causes, most have IQs above 50 and used to be diagnosed as *cultural-familial* retarded. The 1961 AAMD *Manual* defined this type of retardation as follows:

> In addition to absence of reasonable indication of cerebral pathology, classification in this category requires that there be evidence of retardation in intellectual functioning in at least one of the parents and in one or more siblings where there are [siblings]. . . .
>
> There is no intent in this category to specify either the independent action of, or the relationship between, genetic and cultural factors in the etiology of cultural-familial mental retardation. The exact role of genetic factors cannot be specified since the nature and mode of transmission of genetic aspects of intelligence is not yet understood. Similarly, there is no clear understanding of the specific manner in which environmental factors operate to modify intellectual functioning. (Heber, 1961, p. 40)

Both the term *cultural-familial* and the definition reflect a dilemma raised by this type of retardation. A later AAMD *Manual* (1973) disposed of the dilemma by replacing cultural-familial retardation with retardation ascribed to *psychosocial disadvantage*. By assuming an exclusively environmental etiology, the ambiguity as to whether the cause is mainly cultural (environmental) or familial (genetic) is eliminated. Yet it may be premature to eliminate such ambiguity until we understand the interplay of genetic and environmental factors better.

Cultural-familial retardation has implications far beyond the study of psychopathology: Efforts to help poor children have spawned a host of concepts and controversies rooted in the same ambiguities as the concept of cultural-familial retardation. Intervention programs have often sought to raise IQ, improve school performance, and increase social competence. The intervention programs of the 1960s were based on the assumption that children were "culturally deprived." This asumption is akin to the cultural explanation for cultural-familial retardation. It was then recognized, however, that poor and minority groups, like all other humans, do have cultures, albeit different from those of wealthier people. The term *cultural deprivation* later gave way to terms like *economically deprived, environmentally handicapped,* and *disadvantaged.*

Meanwhile, Arthur Jensen's (1969) interpretations of the heritability of IQ revived the "familial" (genetic) explanation for poor children's lack of school success. The nature-nurture debate was then rekindled in the form it had taken for 70 years before being abandoned in the early 1940s to mental retardation specialists.

Epidemiology of Cultural-Familial Retardation

Before addressing cultural and familial factors in poor school and IQ test performance, let's see whether the actual distribution of retardation warrants a category based on either or both of these concepts.

One of the most thorough studies of the distribution of retardation and its causes was done in Aberdeen, Scotland (Birch et al., 1970). Aberdeen offered an almost ideal site because detailed medical, social, and familial data were available on nearly all births; medical services were available regardless of SES; uniform health and educational records were maintained for all children; public school and health services were provided for virtually all retarded children; the population was ethnically homogeneous and relatively stable with low rates of in- and outmigration; and all children received uniform ability testing at age 7.

All 7-year-olds who obtained a group test IQ below 75 were given individual IQ tests by a school psychologist. The psychologist's findings and recommendations were then combined with a review of each child's medical and social history, general social competence, school achievement, and reports from teachers and other school personnel in deciding on special education. Parents could appeal any decision to higher school and governmental authorities.

Birch et al. studied all 8- to 10-year-olds deemed retarded by the schools. Studying a well-defined age group is essential because only children who are far below average and have organic syndromes are usually identified as retarded at young ages; at later ages many having higher IQs and no physical abnormalities may also be identified. At still later ages, when school performance and IQ are no longer important criteria, some of those earlier deemed retarded make social adaptations that no longer mark them as retarded. For example, statistics from Syracuse, New York, showed that 0.45 percent of children up to age 5, 3.94 percent of children aged 5 to 9, 7.76 percent of children aged 10 to 14, and 4.49 percent of adolescents aged 15 to 19 were considered retarded (New York State Department of Mental Hygiene, 1955).

Birch et al. found that 28 percent of the retarded children had IQs less than 50 and organic abnormalities accounting for their retardation. Another 46 percent had IQs of 50 or more and no evidence of organic cause, while 24 percent had IQs of 50 or more with evidence of organic cause.

Each type and level of retardation were analyzed within five SES groupings: Classes I-IIIa included all nonmanual workers from clerks through professionals; Class IIIb included skilled independent manual workers; Class IIIc other skilled workers; Class IV semiskilled workers; and Class V unskilled workers.

Children with IQs below 50 and organic etiologies were equally common in all social classes. However, children with IQs of 60 or more, whether or not they had signs of organic etiology, increased sharply from 0 in Classes I-IIIa to about 2.6 percent in Class V, as Figure 8-6 shows.

Could the lack of Class I-IIIa children with IQs above 60 reflect school officials' biases against labeling upper-class children retarded unless they had very low IQs? To check this, Birch et al. analyzed the SES distribution of children who scored below 75 at age 7 but were *not* then classified as retarded. They found the same sharp increase in such children from Classes I-IIIa to Class V as among children who were ultimately deemed retarded. Adding these children did not change the pattern seen in Figure 8-6. Other studies of the relations between SES, degree of retardation, and etiology have reported similar findings (Kushlick, 1966; Stein & Susser, 1963).

Compared to Class IV and V children with higher IQs, those diagnosed retarded tended to have families with more than four children, poorer housing (though nearly all lived in public housing), more people per room, and more mothers with low-status premarital occupations. The IQ of children in these families averaged 77 and more than half the siblings of the retarded children had IQs below 75. It is thus clear that most children diagnosed retarded without signs of organic etiology indeed met the criteria for cultural-familial retardation.

Cultural-Familial Retardation as the Low End of the Normal Distribution of IQ

One view is that cultural-familial retardation simply reflects the low end of the normal distribution of IQ and does not stem from pathological causes. According to this view, the *excess* of low IQs over those shown by the normal curve results from

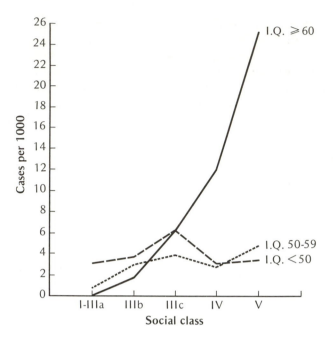

Figure 8-6. The prevalence of different levels of IQ in mentally subnormal children from different social classes. (From Birch et al. 1970. © 1970 by the Williams and Wilkins Company and reprinted by permission.)

organic abnormalities such as those discussed earlier. Figure 8-7 shows that this excess is especially pronounced below IQ 50, where the normal curve predicts very few people and where most of the retarded have organic defects. By contrast, those without organic defects—most of whom have IQs above 50—are assumed to be the recipients of the lower portion of the nonpathological determinants of IQ. If this is true, then cultural-familial retardation reflects the interplay of genetic and environmental factors that determine the IQs of biologically normal people at all points along the distribution.

Genetically Oriented Hypotheses. These hypotheses assume that IQs are to some extent *polygenically* determined. In other words, IQ is affected by several genetic factors (*polygenes*) operating together to yield a broad range of genotypes. These are phenotypically manifested in the normal distribution of IQ. (If the genetic concepts and terminology are unfamiliar, see Chapter 6 for a review.)

Most polygenic hypotheses postulate at least five genes. But for the sake of simplicity, let's suppose that two genes, A and B, affect IQ. Assume that one allele of each gene (designated as A^+ and B^+) enhances IQ test performance, while the other does not (designated as $A°$ and $B°$). Finally, suppose the two alleles ($^+$ and $°$)

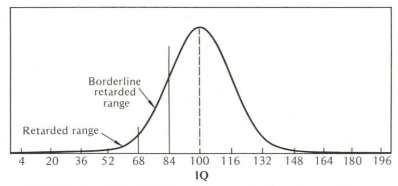

(a) Distribution of Stanford-Binet IQs expected from the normal curve.

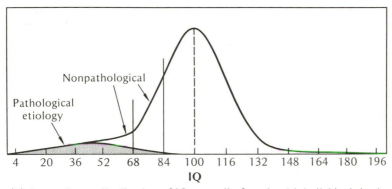

(b) Approximate distribution of IQs actually found, with individuals having
signs of pathological etiology separated from those not having signs of
pathological etiology.

Figure 8-7. Comparison of the theoretical distribution of Stanford-Binet IQs with the approximate form of the distribution actually found. (Based on Penrose, 1963.)

of each gene are not dominant versus recessive, but are additive, that is, people having one $A°$ allele and one A^+ allele are intermediate in IQ between people with two $A°$ alleles and those with two A^+ alleles, all else being equal. Our assumption of polygenes having alleles that function additively is well supported for many human physical characteristics, such as height, which are measurable in gradations and which approximate a normal distribution.

A person *homozygous* for IQ-enhancing alleles has the $A^+ B^+ A^+ B^+$ genotype and a very high IQ. A person *homozygous* for nonenhancing alleles has the $A° B° A° B°$ genotype and a very low IQ.

When two people having these different homozygous genotypes mate, each of their offspring receives an A^+ allele and a B^+ allele from the parent who is homozygous for $^+$ alleles. Each offspring also receives an A° allele and a B° allele from the parent who is homozygous for ° alleles. Consequently, the genotypes of all the offspring have one A$^+$ allele, one A° allele, one B$^+$ allele, and one B° allele. Because the alleles of both the A and B genes are assumed to have equal effects in enhancing IQ, the offspring should have IQs intermediate between those of the A°A°B°B° parent and the A$^+$A$^+$B$^+$B$^+$ parent.

When the heterozygous offspring mate, they can contribute any one of four possible combinations of alleles to each of their children: A°B°; A°B$^+$; A$^+$B°; or A$^+$B$^+$. Since A°B$^+$ has the same effect as A$^+$B° on phenotypic IQ, the parent would contribute an intermediately IQ-enhancing combination to one-half of the offspring, a nonenhancing combination (A°B°) to one-quarter of the offspring, and a highly enhancing combination (A$^+$B$^+$) to the other one-quarter. If the parent's mate likewise has the heterozygous genotype with one A$^+$, one A°, one B$^+$, and one B° allele, the mate can also contribute any of these four possible combinations to their child. Thus, the child could end up with any one of the following 16 combinations, falling into five categories of genotype for IQ, according to the number of $^+$ alleles present:

		A$^+$A$^+$B°B°		
		A$^+$A°B$^+$B°		
	A$^+$A°B°B°	A°A$^+$B$^+$B°	A$^+$A$^+$B$^+$B°	
	A°A$^+$B°B°	A$^+$A°B°B$^+$	A$^+$A$^+$B°B$^+$	
	A°A°B$^+$B°	A°A$^+$B°B$^+$	A$^+$A°B$^+$B$^+$	
A°A°B°B°	A°A°B°B$^+$	A°A°B$^+$B$^+$	A°A$^+$B$^+$B$^+$	A$^+$A$^+$B$^+$B$^+$
0	1	2	3	4

The phenotypic IQs assumed to occur for each of these five categories would be:

0. very low IQ because there are no $^+$ alleles;
1. low because there is only one $^+$ allele;
2. average because there are two $^+$ alleles and two ° alleles;
3. high because there are three $^+$ alleles;
4. very high because all four alleles are $^+$.

Notice that even though there are only five possible categories of genotype resulting from the two genes, the distribution of IQ represented by these genotypes is roughly normal in shape. If the heterozygous parents (each having one A$^+$, one A°, one B$^+$, and one B° allele) produced 16 children, the most likely distribution of the children's genotypes would be that represented above—one child would have each of the possible combinations of the alleles of the A and B genes. In terms of IQ, one child would be very low, four would be low, six would be average, four would be high, and one would be very high.

Since the real distribution of IQs is continuous rather than composed of five distinct steps, such a simple model does not completely explain IQ differences.

However, if we assume that experience, motivation, and other characteristics of the individual, plus inconsistencies in IQ tests, affect the expression of these genotypes in the IQ score, than a continuous distribution of IQs could easily result from the five categories of genotype produced by two genes. Most children without organic syndromes who have IQs from about 50 to 70 might be assumed to have Genotype 0; those with IQs 71 to 90, Genotype 1; those with IQs 91 to 110, Genotype 2; those with IQs of 111 to 130, Genotype 3; and those with IQs above 130, Genotype 4.

Each IQ range would thus represent a possible *reaction range* for one genotype. The exact phenotypic IQ for a given genotype would depend on nongenetic factors, however. If this were the case, the possible phenotypic reaction range for each genotype would overlap with that of the next higher and next lower genotypes; for example, a person with Genotype 1 might attain an IQ over 90 under ideal environmental conditions or below 71 under very poor environmental conditions.

If one adopts the extreme hereditarian hypothesis that nongenetic factors (other than unreliability in IQ tests) have no effect on IQ, it would still take only 12 different genes to account for the continuous distribution of IQs (Gottesman, 1963a). This hypothesis assumes that there are as many different genotypes for IQ as there are "true" phenotypic IQs, and that each genotype, as the sole determinant of IQ, has no reaction range.

The Nongenetic Hypothesis. The view that people who meet the diagnostic criteria for cultural-familial retardation are essentially normal individuals at the low end of the normal distribution does not require us to assume that genotypic differences cause differences in phenotypic IQ. Consider the extreme environmental hypothesis that there is only one genotype for IQ. If this is true, then all (nonpathological) IQ differences are caused by nongenetic factors. If random nongenetic differences cause the differences in phenotypic IQ, the distribution of phenotypic IQs could be as continuous and close to normal as if genetic factors cause IQ differences. Individuals at the low end would be those who encounter only non-IQ enhancing influences. Merely because the distribution of IQs is continuous and normal says nothing about the degree of genetic or environmental influence on them.

Relations Between Phenotypic IQs and Genotypes under Various Hypotheses. Figure 8-8 portrays the relations between phenotypic IQs and genotypes implied by:

1. An extreme hereditarian hypothesis that assumes *no* phenotypic reaction range for each of the possible genotypes.
2. One of the many possible interactionist hypotheses—this one assumes only two genetic factors with large enough phenotypic reaction ranges for the five possible genotypes to account for a continuous distribution.
3. An extreme environmentalist hypothesis that assumes only one genotype

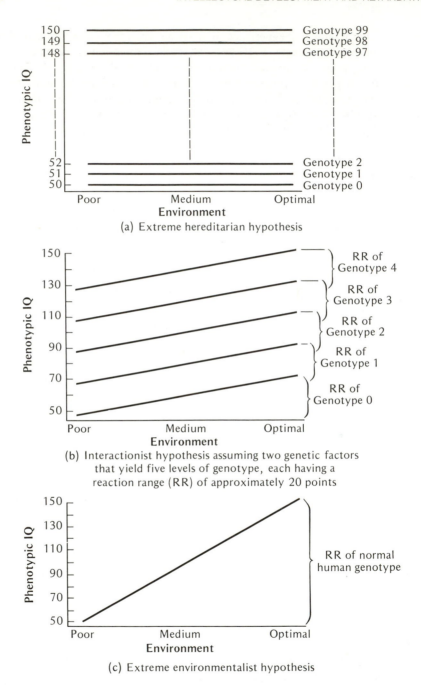

(a) Extreme hereditarian hypothesis

(b) Interactionist hypothesis assuming two genetic factors
that yield five levels of genotype, each having a
reaction range (RR) of approximately 20 points

(c) Extreme environmentalist hypothesis

Figure 8-8. Relations between phenotypic IQ and genotype according to (a) an extreme hereditarian hypothesis, (b) an interactionist hyothesis, and (c) an extreme environmentalist hypothesis.

with a large enough reaction range to account for a continuous distribution.

The extreme hereditarian hypothesis would be tenable only if IQ tests were perfectly reliable, that is, they yielded exactly the same score for an individual on each testing. Since most people's scores change from one testing to the next, the hypothesis that each phenotypic IQ represents a different genotype for IQ seems untenable.

We are then left with this question: Is there one human genotype with a reaction range spanning the distribution of IQs from roughly 50 to its upper limits? Or is there more than one genotype?

Answering this question requires a look at the evidence on the *heritability* of IQ—the proportion of variance in IQ scores attributable to genetic differences. If we find no evidence that genetic differences correlate with phenotypic differences in IQ, then we can reject even the moderate interactionist hypothesis portrayed in Figure 8-8b.

Evidence for Nonpathological Genetic Effects on IQ

Twin Studies. One of the most common approaches to studying nonpathological genetic effects on IQ is to compare the correlations between the IQs of identical (*monozygotic*) twins and same-sex fraternal (*dizygotic*) twins. Because identical co-twins are genetically identical, whereas same-sex fraternal co-twins are identical in only 50 percent of their genes (on the average), higher correlations between the IQs of the identical twins than fraternal twins are assumed to reflect genetic effects (see Chapter 6 for further details).

About 20 studies have compared IQ correlations between identical and fraternal twins in the United States, Britain, Finland, France, Germany, and Sweden; all have shown correlations between the intelligence test scores of identical twins exceeding those of fraternal twins by enough to indicate a considerable genetic influence (Scarr, 1981).

In another type of study, identical twins separated in childhood and raised in different environments are compared to determine how similar their IQs are despite environmental differences. American, British, and Danish studies show correlations of .67 to .78 between the intelligence test scores of identical twins reared apart, although environmental similarities may have increased IQ similarities in some of the twin pairs (Farber, 1981).

Adoption Studies. In the most thorough type of adoption study, the correlations between the abilities of adopted children and those of their *biological* parents are compared with the correlations between the children's abilities and those of their *adoptive* parents. Correlations with biological parents' abilities are assumed to reflect primarily genetic effects, because the parents' influence ended when the children were given up for adoption, usually in early infancy. By contrast, correlations with adoptive parents' abilities are assumed to reflect environmental effects beginning at adoption.

Because most adoptees are born to unwed mothers who give up their babies soon after birth, it is hard to get parental test data. However, the few studies of such data and others estimating parental ability from educational and occupational attainment show considerable consistency: The intelligence test scores of adopted children generally correlate better with the abilities of their *biological* parents than their *adoptive* parents (Horn, Loehlin, & Willerman, 1979; Scarr, 1981). This suggests that genetic factors (and perhaps pre- and perinatal environment) affect the rank ordering of intelligence test scores more than environmental variations resulting from the abilities of adoptive parents. However, this is only part of the story, as we will see later when we consider the effects of environment on IQ levels.

Polygenic Effects on Cultural-Familial Retardation

The twin and adoption studies indicate genetic effects on the rank ordering of IQs among northern Europeans and Americans living in a broad range of environments. It suggests that there is more than one genotype for IQ in this population and that the extreme environmental model positing a single genotype (Figure 8-8c) is inadequate. Since the extreme hereditarian model positing a different genotype for every IQ (Figure 8-8a) also seems untenable, only a model including more than one genotype, each having a phenotypic reaction range (Figure 8-8b) seems plausible. But could IQs as low as the retarded range reflect nonpathological polygenic mechanisms?

Some of the subjects in the twin and adoption studies would be considered cultural-familial retarded. But a more direct approach to nonpathological polygenic effects on retardation is through *family studies*. One of the most thorough assessed the families of 549 people admitted to a Minnesota institution for the retarded between 1911 and 1918. Eleanor and Sheldon Reed (1965) followed up 82,217 descendants of the grandparents of those admitted. They then made family pedigree charts identifying people as retarded (IQs below 70 and/or other other strong signs of retardation) or not retarded.

The subjects included many of average and high IQ as well as the retarded. The mean IQs of children having at least one parent with an extreme IQ were closer to the overall mean than their parents were. For example, the IQs of children having one retarded and one nonretarded parent were closer to the mean of the entire sample than were the IQs of the retarded parents. Furthermore, children with two retarded parents had mean IQs of 74, somewhat above the upper cutoff point of 69 used to define retardation; the IQs of these children extended up into the average and above-average ranges. This tendency for the offspring of extreme parents to be

Table 8-2   IQs of Children of Retarded Parents.

Type of Parents	Percent of children in each IQ range						Average IQ	Percent Retarded
	0−49	50−69	70−89	90−110	111−130	131+		
Retardate × retardate	7	33	40	19	1	0	74	39
Male retardate × normal	0	8	24	49	16	1	95	8
Female retardate × normal	6	14	30	40	9	1	87	20

Source: Adapted from Reed & Reed, 1965.

more like the population average is known as *filial regression*.[1] It has also been found at the high end of the IQ scale: Very high IQ parents have children whose IQs average somewhat lower than those of their parents (Terman & Oden, 1959).

Table 8-2 shows the IQs of children having two retarded parents or one retarded and one nonretarded parent. Not all the retarded parents met the criteria for cultural-familial retardation. But separate analyses of 50 families (18,730 members) who clearly met these criteria revealed patterns like those in Table 8-2.

From a purely environmental viewpoint, it is surprising that low IQ parents, whose SES is also low in most cases, produce children whose IQs are *higher* than their own; it is likewise surprising that high IQ parents, whose SES is high in most cases, produce children with IQs *lower* than their own. Yet these findings are consistent with the polygenic model: People who are phenotypically extreme on a trait nevertheless carry genes for less extreme versions of the trait and pass these genes on to at least some of their offspring.

THE ROLES OF ENVIRONMENT

Polygenic mechanisms seem to affect the *rank ordering* of IQs in the general population and the nonpathologically retarded. But none of the evidence yet cited deals with the determination of phenotypic IQ *levels* or the adaptive behavior of people assumed to have few IQ-enhancing genes. We must therefore ask: Can environmental enrichment raise IQ? And, how does experience shape the adaptive behavior of the retarded?

---

[1] Filial regression is a form of the statistical phenomenon of *regression toward the mean:* Where several determinants, such as polygenes, are involved, extreme scores on one measure tend to be followed by less extreme scores on a second measure related to the first (see Achenbach, 1978b, for a detailed, nontechnical explanation).

Environmental Effects on IQ Level

The Skeels Study. A dramatic demonstration of environmental effects on IQ and adaptive functioning was begun in the 1930s by Harold Skeels (1966). Skeels noticed remarkable improvements in two 1-year-old girls transferred from an Iowa orphanage to an institution for the retarded because they had appeared retarded. Repeated testing in their new environment showed behavioral and intellectual development reaching the normal range. The girls happened to be the only preschoolers in wards with mildly retarded women who "adopted" them and took a warm maternal interest in them. Their experience contrasted sharply with that of children in the orphanage, where busy nurses gave little individual attention and where sensory stimulation was minimal.

Skeels was able to transfer 10 more orphanage children to similar wards in the institution for the retarded. These 10, together with the original two girls and a third previously transferred to another institution for the retarded, formed an *experimental* group of 13. All had been deemed unadoptable because of apparent retardation. Testing just before transfer, at an average age of 19 months, showed mean DQs and IQs of 64.

Each child remained in the institution for the retarded until it was felt he or she had gained maximum benefit. Eleven were then adopted; one remained in the institution because of continued low functioning; one returned to the orphanage.

A *contrast* group of 12 children remaining in the orphanage until at least age 4 was later selected for comparison. Their mean DQs and IQs were 87 when first tested, at an average age of 17 months.

The children had poor family backgrounds, and 10 in each group were born to unwed mothers. Mean IQ of the 5 tested mothers of experimental group children was 70, while a sixth was known to be retarded. Mean IQ of the 9 tested mothers of contrast group children was 63.

After an average of 19 months in the institution for the retarded, the mean IQ of the experimental group children was 92. By the age of 6, their IQs averaged 96. Parallel testing of the contrast children showed IQs of 61 and 66.

The contrasting early life experiences thus seemed to produce major differences in the IQs of the experimental and contrast children. Far more crucial, the "real-life" correlates of IQ bore out the differences in the children's test performance: When followed up in adulthood, the 13 experimental children had educations averaging twelfth grade and all were self-supporting. All had been married, although one was divorced. IQs of their children ranged from 86 to 125, with a mean of 104. Of the 11 who had held jobs (two married women had not), nine had worked at skilled levels or higher. Their incomes exceeded the Iowa state average.

By sad comparison, the contrast group had educations averaging fourth grade. Four were still in institutions, a fifth had died in an institution for the retarded, and six were unskilled. One man, perhaps owing to his good fortune of being placed in a school for the deaf at age 8, was a skilled typesetter. Only the typesetter was married; another had married, but divorced. The only children were four belonging to the typesetter (IQs 103−119) and one belonging to the divorced man (IQ 66).

How do these findings square with the evidence for polygenic influences on IQ? The IQs and other characteristics of the mothers of Skeels's experimental and contrast children, as well as their putative fathers, suggest genetic backgrounds like the cultural-familial retarded. Yet the environmental difference between the experimental and contrast children produced large IQ differences by early childhood and later life differences consistent with the early IQ differences.

The Skodak-Skeels Study. A study by Marie Skodak and Harold Skeels (1949) shows how the environmental and genetic pieces of the puzzle may fit together. The subjects were 100 Iowa orphans adopted before the age of 6 months. As in the Skeels study, the mean IQ of the 63 biological mothers who could be tested was well below that of their children raised in adoptive homes: The mother's mean IQ was 86, with 11 under 70; tested at an average age of 14, their children's mean IQ was 106, with only 1 below 70.

Despite the 20-point difference in mean IQ, the *correlations* of the children's IQs with the IQs and education of their *biological* parents were much *higher* than with the education of their *adoptive* parents. (IQs were not obtained for the biological fathers or adoptive parents, but education correlates well with IQ.) Figure 8-9a shows the correlation of the children's IQs with the IQs and education of their biological mothers and the education of their adoptive mothers; Figure 8-9b shows the correlation of the children's IQs with the education of their biological fathers and adoptive fathers. Corresponding correlations of children's IQs with their biological parents' education are shown from the Berkeley Guidance Study, in which all the children were raised by their biological parents (Honzik, 1957).

Notice that the correlations of children's IQs with their biological mothers' IQs and the education of both biological parents rose along nearly identical paths whether the children were raised by their biological or adoptive parents. The highest correlation of the adopted children's IQs with their adoptive parents' education was about .10. This occurred with adoptive mothers' education when the children were 7 years old. At the final testing, the correlations were only .02 with adoptive mothers' education and .00 with adoptive fathers' education, compared to .44 with biological mothers' IQ; .32 with biological mothers' education; and .42 with biological fathers' education. The correlations of adopted children's IQs with biological mothers' IQs and fathers' education were about the same as the mean of .42 found for correlations between biological parent and child IQs in studies of children raised by their biological parents (Bouchard & McGue, 1981).

The Role of SES. Averaging the IQs of Skodak-Skeels children over all ages having at least 15 scores in each SES shows that children adopted into upper SES homes obtained IQs less than two points higher than children adopted into lower SES

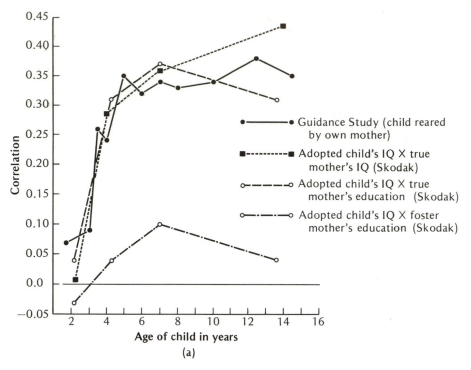

Figure 8-9(a). Correlations of children's IQs with their mothers' education in the Berkeley Guidance Study and with biological mothers' IQ and education and foster mothers' education in the Skodak-Skeels (1949) study. (After Honzik, 1957. © by the Society for Research in Child Development and reprinted by permission.)

homes, despite a detectable bias toward placement of children of better educated mothers in upper SES homes. This finding is important in its own right: It suggests that the correlations typically found between children's IQs and their biological parents' social class owe more to the correlated genotypes of the children and their parents than to the effects of SES on the child, except perhaps at the most impoverished extreme.

Conclusions. We can question the precise size of the correlations between adopted children's abilities and those of their biological and adoptive parents. For example, the correlations may have been higher if the IQs of the offspring had been obtained, like those of their parents, during adulthood when IQs are generally most stable. Greater educational opportunity for the parents might also have raised the correlations between children's IQs and their parents' education.

We can also question the size of the environmental effects reflected in the higher IQs of the adoptees than their biological mothers. The stress of the birth and

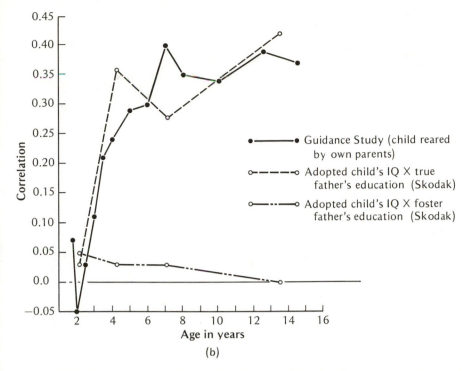

Figure 8-9(b). Correlations of children's IQs with their fathers' education in the Berkeley Guidance Study and with biologic and foster fathers' education in the Skodak-Skeels (1949) study. (After Honzik, 1957. © 1957 by the Society for Research in Child Development and reprinted by permission).

surrender of their babies, for example, may have depressed mothers' IQ test performance. Moreover, *filial regression* would predict somewhat higher IQs in the adoptees than their relatively low-IQ biological mothers.

Despite reservations about the precise *size* of the correlations and environmental effects, the findings nevertheless support the hypothesized interaction between (1) genetic effects on the *rank ordering* of IQs within a particular set of environmental conditions and (2) environmental effects on the actual IQ *levels*. The findings indicate that childrearing conditions considered normal in Western society can yield IQs substantially higher than substandard conditions.

Yet, once "normal" childrearing conditions prevail, it appears that genotypic differences outweigh parental education, occupation, or income in determining phenotypic IQ differences. The evidence for environmental effects on IQ and the correlations between the IQs of adopted children and their biological mothers jointly support the polygenic model, especially since all the adopted children were from the same general population of northern European ancestry on whom the model was based. Similar interactions of genetic and environmental effects have also been found for black children adopted by whites (Scarr & Weinberg, 1977).

If the foregoing analysis is correct, then the term *cultural-familial retardation* need not be an ambiguous cop-out, although a term like *environmental-genetic retardation* might be better. Many of these people may have lower genotypes for IQ than people with higher phenotypic IQs; but postnatal environmental factors also prevent them from maximizing their genetic potentials. A major implication is that enriched environments beginning in infancy can bring many children of low IQ parents above the retarded range; intensive educational programs have, in fact, raised the IQs of such children (Ramey & Campbell, 1979). More importantly, continued enrichment may help them develop the adult adaptive behavior needed for self-sufficiency in western society.

Environmental Shaping of Personality and Behavior

Much maladaptive behavior of the retarded is caused more by specific life experiences than by slow cognitive development. A growing body of research documents the effects of experience on the personality and behavior of the retarded, especially those without significant organic pathology. The research is based on the assumption that cognitive development in nonpathological retardation is deviant primarily in rate and final level rather than in sequence or structure (Weisz & Yeates, 1981; Weisz & Zigler, 1979).

Cognitive Comparability of MA-matched Normal and Retarded Children.
"Level" or "stage" of cognitive development is a *hypothetical construct;* tests are used as operational indices of such constructs. If MA on the Stanford-Binet is used to assess cognitive development, the cognitive level of a 10-year-old having an MA of 6 and an IQ of 60 without organic pathology is assumed to resemble that of a 6-year-old having an MA of 6 and an IQ of 100.

Another way to assess cognitive development is with experimental tasks designed to identify hypothesized stages. Piaget and his co-workers have presented the most comprehensive theory of cognitive development and have devised numerous experimental tasks to test the stages they postulate.

It was long argued that the cognitive levels of retarded and normal children achieving the same MA were not really similar because they pass different items that merely happen to sum to the same MA score. Studies have shown, however, that retarded children without apparent organic abnormalities differ little from MA-matched normal children in the patterns of Binet items they pass and fail (Achenbach, 1970a, 1971a). Piagetian tasks requiring a minimum of motivation and academic skills also show minimal differences between MA-matched normal and retarded children (Achenbach, 1969, 1973; Gruen & Vore, 1972). It therefore appears that the general cognitive competence reflected in the Binet MAs of nonpathologically retarded children is roughly similar to that reflected in the MAs of normal children. If this is so, then the retarded should be able to learn and solve problems as well as MA-matched normals.

Behavioral Differences Between MA-matched Normal and Retarded Children. After early studies showed worse performance by retarded than MA-matched normal children, various cognitive defects were imputed to the retarded. As an example, retarded children were hypothesized to be intrinsically *rigid* in their thinking. This was supported by the finding that (institutionalized) retarded children continued a monotonous repetitive task much longer than (noninstitutionalized) MA-matched normals, even when given the opportunity to switch to something else (Kounin, 1941). Imputing "rigidity" to the "retarded mind" helped stereotype "the retardate" as too rigid to learn, innately liking boring repetitive tasks, and having a wonderful sense of rhythm.

More recent research has revealed that much of the behavior thought to stem from *intrinsic* differences between low and high IQ people can be traced to *experiences* differentiating most retarded children from most normals.

In the case of rigidity, it was found that the amount of social deprivation experienced by retarded children prior to institutionalization correlated with their "rigid" perseveration on experimental tasks (Balla & Zigler, 1979). This suggested that peculiarities of their history, rather than retardation per se, increased perseverative behavior. Other observations suggested that socially deprived institutionalized children's perseveration was reinforced by the supportive attention of the experimenter. Such attention could be especially reinforcing because institutionalized children typically get so little adult attention.

This hypothesis was tested by giving the same tasks to *noninstitutionalized retarded* children and *institutionalized normal* children (mostly orphans). If cognitive rigidity caused perseveration, then the noninstitutionalized retarded children should perseverate as much as the institutionalized retarded; by contrast, institutionalized normal children should not perseverate any more than other normal children. On the other hand, if perseveration by the institutionalized retarded reflected their desire for adult attention instead of cognitive rigidity, then other socially deprived children, including institutionalized normals, would do the same. According to this hypothesis, nondeprived children, including the retarded living at home, should not perseverate.

It was found that institutionalized children of normal IQ showed the same perseveration as institutionalized retarded children. But noninstitutionalized retarded children did not. The history of social deprivation leading to high motivation for supportive adult attention, instead of cognitive rigidity, thus seemed to cause this behavior of institutionalized retarded children. When the effects of social reinforcement are properly controlled, institutionalized retarded children act like noninstitutionalized retarded and normal children of similar MA (Balla & Zigler, 1979).

Other experiential variables have been shown to account for other behavioral peculiarities of the nonpathologically retarded. Some of the most prominent are summarized below.

History of Failure and Low Expectancy of Success. As children grow up, they are often compared to their agemates. By their second or third year, they are not only aware of the comparative judgments others make, but they too make such comparisons. Awareness of the obvious difference between older people's abilities and their own is followed by awareness of more subtle differences between their own abilities and those of the primary reference group that society, especially the school, defines for them. This reference group typically consists of normal agemates.

Many pathologically retarded children may be spared comparison with normals because their physical stigmata mark them as abnormal. However, most non-pathologically retarded and some pathologically retarded children accumulate a history of failing to achieve the norms of their agemates before they are identified as retarded. This history of failure makes them fearful of applying their abilities, even to tasks they can master. They may become more motivated to avoid risking failure than to try new tasks.

Experimental studies have shown that, compared to MA-matched normals, the retarded expect little success, set low goals for themselves, and settle for minimal success where they could do better (MacMillan, 1969). This is especially so when retarded children feel they are competing with normals (Rosen, Diggory, & Werlinsky, 1966; Schwarz & Jens, 1969). Even experimentally contrived failure experiences can increase retardates' expectancy of failure and efforts to avoid risking failure (Balla & Zigler, 1979). This *learned helplessness* may be unwittingly condoned by adults. When told a child is retarded, for example, adults have been found less likely to urge the child to persist following failure than they do for normal children of the same level of cognitive development (Weisz, 1981).

Outer-Directedness and Cue-Dependency. Another aspect of behavioral development is a decreasing reliance on cues from other people. In infancy, imitation is an essential, probably innate, strategy for acquiring new behavior (Yando, Seitz, & Zigler, 1978). Much of the behavior acquired through imitation is reinforced by the success it brings in attaining goals, such as opening forbidden cabinets and cookie jars, providing new ways of communicating desires, and so on.

During early childhood—by about the MA of 1½ to 2 years, according to Piaget (1970)—children become able to construct mental representations of problem situations and possible solutions. They can do this with pictorial mental images, words, or kinesthetic representations. Whichever medium of mental representation they use, the key advance is this: Their behavior comes to be guided by *mental* trial-and-error instead of exclusive reliance on *external* cues such as other people's behavior.

Though powerful, children's thinking during this period is not yet logical. According to Piaget, it remains essentially empirical until it acquires the framework of logical principles that normally develops between about the ages of 5 and 7. Lacking logical principles, the preschool child is dominated by associations among the salient surface characteristics of things and situations.

After the MA of about 7, children—now called *concrete operational* in Piaget's terms—are capable of mental operations based on logical principles. This is manifest in the ability to construct classifications of objects and to understand that superficial changes of appearance do not change quantitative properties unless something is added or taken away.

By the MA of about 11, children become capable of what Piaget calls *formal operational* thinking. This is abstract logical thinking which does not depend on concrete representations, such as quantities and objects. Instead, it can deal with hypothetical constructs of the sort used in science, political theory, law, and theology.

The new abilities emerging in the course of cognitive development make possible many new problem-solving strategies beyond the early strategies of imitation and associative learning, although the early ones remain available; for example, a normal adult unfamiliar with the etiquette of formal state banquets may imitate others rather than trying to deduce by logic which of the many utensils should be used for each course of the dinner.

As children grow up, they acquire higher standards for their own performance. If they succeed in meeting the advancing standards, they are likely to retain confidence in their abilities and use progressively more advanced strategies as they become available. By contrast, children whose abilities lag behind those of their agemates experience failure when relying on their own thinking. They may therefore continue relying on the more primitive strategies of imitation and associative learning whenever possible, even where their own abilities are adequate.

Zigler has described as *outer-directed* the tendency to rely excessively on cues from other people. Research has shown that retarded children are more outer-directed than normals of the same MA and that failure experiences can increase the outer-directedness of normal as well as retarded children (Yando et al., 1978).

It has also been shown that retarded children given an obvious mechanical cue in a problem situation rely much longer on the cue than do MA-matched normals, even though retarded children not given the cue solve the problem as quickly as normals (Achenbach & Zigler, 1968). Retarded children having a teacher who deliberately maximized their success experiences and reinforced them for independent thinking, however, were no more dependent on mechanical cues than MA-matched normals. Excessive dependence on external cues, which often prevents the retarded from using their abilities, can thus be modified through appropriate educational intervention. Reliance on superficial cues has also been shown to interfere with some normal children's thinking as well (Achenbach, 1975), although it can be reduced by interventions designed to promote independent thinking (Salomon & Achenbach, 1974).

CARE AND EDUCATION OF THE RETARDED

Except for the very small percentage whose retardation can be prevented or ameliorated by medical, dietary, or psychotherapeutic means, proper care and education are essential for helping the retarded maximize their potentials. Simply bringing all institutional environments up to fully humane standards could improve the behavior of many of the retarded, even without dramatic breakthroughs in treatment. Just how bad some of these environments are and how change is blocked by purely political and bureaucratic obstacles have been movingly documented by Blatt, Ozolins, and McNally (1979).

Beside humane living conditions, the replacement of large custodial units by social and educational services tailored to the individual needs of the retarded and their families can further aid many retarded people, as well as reducing the number who become institutionalized. Severity of mental and physical disability is a factor in the institutionalization of some children, but behavior problems and lack of family and community resources lead to the institutionalization of others who are not severely disabled (Eyman, O'Connor, Tarjan, & Justice, 1972).

One alternative to the traditional institution is the system of state regional centers begun in Connecticut in 1961. Each center is a relatively small unit that serves a local community. It provides more-or-less permanent accommodations for a few residents who cannot remain in their own or foster homes. More importantly, it offers temporary accommodations for those who can live with their families or in foster homes most of the time, day services for some who go home at night, night care for some who work or study in the community during the day, counseling and referral services for families, sheltered workshops, and educational and recreational programs for residents and nonresidents. It also initiates and coordinates other services and living arrangements, such as group homes and halfway houses.

Normalization and Developmental Programming

Originating in Scandinavia, the ideal of *normalization* has been widely espoused in the care of the retarded (Menolascino, 1977). The essence of this ideal is that the retarded should be helped to lead lives as similar as possible to the nonretarded with respect to living conditions, rights, responsibilities, and privileges. A related ideal is *developmental* service programming for the retarded. Contrasting with the medical model of the retarded as sick people, the developmental model is based on these assumptions: all life involves change; the general sequence of change is similar for all humans; and functioning can vary flexibly within this general sequence (Menolascino, 1977). Accordingly, services should be designed to foster the continued development and progressive normalization of the retarded instead of treating them like chronic invalids.

Coinciding with legislative and judicial mandates on behalf of other handicapped groups, the ideal of normalization has led to placement of retarded children in regular school classes (*mainstreaming*), as well as community placement of the institutionalized retarded. Public Law 94-142, The Education of all Handicapped Children Act of 1975, in particular mandated that children be educated in the least restrictive possible environment. In some cases, efforts to end traditional services have been motivated by the hope of cutting expenditures, just as other reforms have often been perverted (see Chapter 2). Because the circumstances and quality of care accompanying these changes varies so widely, their net impact is difficult to assess. The problem of retardation has certainly not been abolished by efforts at normalization, however. As Ellis (1975) put it:

> The current popular view of retardation suggests that we know how to train, educate and habilitate retarded people and that political action will rid us of the problem. Nothing could be further from the truth. Neither governmental action programs, nor court orders, nor public conscience will wipe out this problem, nor will it disappear with the *re-labeling* of retarded persons. While 'normalization' is a worthy goal, it may blind us to a child's need for *special* help. (p. 2).

Let's look at some of the special help actually provided.

Public School Programs

The public school is the first and only source of education for many borderline, mildly, and moderately retarded children, who together comprise more than 90 percent of the retarded. For educational planning, retarded children are typically divided into the *trainable* (IQs about 20−50) and the *educable* (IQs about 50−70 or 80). The merits of special versus regular class placement for retarded children have long been debated, but less than one-half of American retarded children were actually in special classes even before opposition to such classes mounted in the 1970s (Conley, 1973).

Trainable Children. Classes for trainable children are oriented toward simple self-help skills, safety rules, social adjustment, and rudimentary academic skills such as counting and recognizing words important even in the protected lives the trainable must lead.

The few published studies of classes for the trainable reveal little measurable academic benefit, but are generally inconclusive because of a lack of well-defined curricula, goals, and measuring instruments, and because these children's retardation is due to diverse pathological causes having very different educational prognoses (Kirk, 1964). Such classes, however, may give parents more realistic pictures of their children's limitations. Where there are regional centers or analogous services, classes for the trainable can also prepare children for the vocational and other programs available to retarded adolescents.

Educable Children. Based on their abilities, these are the children for whom the highest goals can be set but to whom the most imagination, resourcefulness, and understanding must be dedicated.

Gunzberg (1975) found that one-half the mildly retarded 16- to 25-year-olds reached a reading level of at least 7 years 9 months, while 10 percent reached the relatively adequate level of 11 years 2 months. More than one-half could tell time adequately and deal with money for bus fares and lunches; 40 percent could fill out employment application forms.

Of the borderline retarded, half reached a reading level of at least 9 years 3 months, while 10 percent reached a level of 12 years 4 months. Nearly all could tell time adequately, while about three quarters could deal with small amounts of money and fill out employment application forms.

There have been several long-term follow-up studies of children classified as educable retarded during their school years. The longest began in 1935 with 206 adults who had childhood IQs of less than 70 and had been in public school special classes between 1916 and 1930 (Baller, 1936). Comparison groups who had borderline (75–85) and average (100–120) IQs were matched to the retarded for sex, nationality of descent, and age. A final follow-up was done when the average age of the retarded subjects was 56 (Baller, Charles, & Miller, 1967).

Attrition was high owing partly to a very high accidental death rate among the retarded, but 119 remained for comparison with the other groups. Only eight of the retarded had been institutionalized, mostly because of physical handicaps; 48 percent were married and living with their spouses, compared to 84 percent of the borderline and 90 percent of the average subjects. Considerably more of the retarded than the other groups had been divorced or never married.

Sixty-five percent of the retarded were entirely self-supporting, compared to 94 percent of the borderline and 96 percent of the average subjects; 72 percent of the retarded, compared to 50 percent of the borderline and less than 1 percent of the average group were semiskilled or unskilled laborers.

About 8 percent of both lower IQ groups had criminal convictions, while there were none in the average group. Social, recreational, and political activities were minimal in the retarded group, higher in the borderline group, and highest in the average group.

A notable finding was that the 15 retarded people retested showed IQ increases from a mean childhood Binet IQ of 60 to a mean WAIS IQ of 75 at age 45 and 82 at age 56. Much of the increase apparently reflected continuing mental development beyond the age that the test makers had assumed it would cease. IQ increases were also found among the 18 borderline subjects retested, from a mean of 81 in the

1920s to 89 in the 1960s. Increases have likewise been found in longitudinal studies of normal adults (Kangas & Bradway, 1971). Early adult IQs thus do not necessarily reflect the limits people will reach.

Other follow-ups of children classified as educable retarded concur that many, usually from 50 to 80 percent, become at least marginally self-supporting. But they are considerably less self-sufficient than people with IQs in the average or even the borderline range growing up in similar socioeconomic conditions (Kennedy, 1966; Skaarbrevik, 1971).

Closer analysis shows that, beside being in the bottom SES and remaining socially isolated, many low IQ people lead insecure lives and are rated by employers as performing worse than other people from the same SES in the same jobs. It also appears that more of their children are academically retarded than children with similar IQs and SES but higher IQ parents (Kennedy, 1966). Furthermore, lack of social awareness and responsibility about interpersonal aspects of work settings often leads to job loss (Greenspan & Shoultz, 1981).

A long-range problem is the progressive decline in the unskilled jobs traditionally filled by the retarded: from about 59 percent of the labor force in 1900 to about 20 percent (Goldstein, 1964). It is therefore imperative that the educable retarded not be left entirely to the mercy of the marketplace.

Improving Education for the Retarded

Although special education for the retarded has been provided on a larger scale and over a longer period than most other helping services for children, the lack of sound outcome studies leaves us with few clues as to the effects of various approaches.

Special Classes and Mainstreaming. Are retarded children helped more by special classes or mainstreaming? Neither the spread of special classes from 1900 through the 1960s nor the shift to mainstreaming in the 1970s have been based on firm knowledge of how the retarded are best helped. This question has several facets. The most obvious concerns the children's academic progress. The effects on retarded children's emotions, attitudes, and self-concepts, however, may be just as crucial for their long-term adaptation. Similarly, various educational options may differentially affect other children's labeling and acceptance of the retarded, which in turn can affect retarded children's social interactions and opportunities.

Goldstein (1967) carried out one of the few studies in which experimental and control groups were initially equated through random assignment to special or regular classes. This was done by randomly assigning 6-year-olds with IQs under 85 to special or regular classes in schools previously without special classes. The new special classes were taught by well-trained teachers using a carefully constructed curriculum guide.

After four years, there was little difference in the academic performance of the two groups, although special class children did better on measures of productive thinking, and they showed less avoidance of difficult questions on a questionnaire administered orally. On the other hand, the special class children interacted less with neighborhood peers than did the low IQ children in regular classes.

Further analyses showed that children with IQs up to 80 did better academically in special classes while those with IQs above 80 did better in regular classes. Since IQs of 70 to 80 are the usual upper cutoff points for special class placement, the results suggest that early special class placement can be beneficial. They do not tell us what happens under the more typical practice of assigning children to special classes after years of failure in regular classes, however.

In one of the few other studies using random assignment, Budoff and Gottlieb (1976) compared special class children who either moved to a special class in a new school or were mainstreamed and attended a remedial learning center in the new school. The findings roughly parallel those of Goldstein (1967): The children of highest ability showed more favorable attitudes when mainstreamed than when in the special class; by contrast, children of lower ability showed more favorable attitudes in the special class than when mainstreamed. In both studies, the effect of regular versus special class placement thus depended on the children's abilities: Children whose abilities were closest to the normal range benefited from regular class placement, whereas less able children did not.

Labeling and Social Acceptance. *Labeling* is one of the most emotional aspects of the controversy over educational integration of the retarded. Mercer (1975), for example, has argued that labeling people as retarded leads to discrimination against them and that removing the label would result in more favorable treatment. Considerable research has shown that normal schoolchildren indeed prefer normal to retarded peers as friends (Corman & Gottlieb, 1978). However, the effects of labeling and integrated versus segregated education are complex.

To study the effects of the label *retarded,* several investigators presented subjects with films or descriptions of a child described as retarded; similar subjects were not told the child was retarded. It was found that the label *retarded* generally leads to more *favorable* responses by other children (Foley, 1979), teachers (Kurtz, Harrison, Neisworth, & Jones, 1977), graduate students and mothers (Seitz & Geske, 1976). However, the effect of the label also depends on the behavior of the labeled person. Normal children react more negatively to *incompetent* behavior by an *unlabeled* child than by a child labeled retarded (Budoff & Siperstein, 1978). Yet they also react more negatively to *aggressive* behavior by a child *labeled retarded* than by an unlabeled child (Gottlieb, 1975). In short, the label *retarded* may help normal children accept the behavior it implies but not other noxious behavior. Slang labels made up by children themselves, such as "retard," also have a more stigmatizing effect than quasi-clinical labels, such as "mentally retarded" (Siperstein, Budoff, & Bak, 1980).

The effects of integrated versus segregated education on normal children's acceptance of retarded peers is harder to evaluate. Prior to the mainstreaming movement, studies had shown that normal children accepted *unlabeled* retarded children in regular classes *less* than retarded children in special classes (Corman & Gottlieb, 1978). After the advent of mainstreaming, elementary schoolchildren in open, ungraded classes were also found to rate retarded mainstreamed classmates more negatively than retarded children in special classes (Gottlieb & Budoff, 1973). Moreover, in an open classroom school without interior walls, retarded children were *better known* by their schoolmates than by normal children in an ungraded school of traditional interior wall design; yet the retarded children were rated more *negatively* than by children in the walled school. This suggests that the closer normal elementary schoolchildren are to their retarded peers, the less they accept them. However, other variables are also relevant, as urban children have been found to rate retarded peers more favorably than suburban children do (Bruininks, Rynders, & Gross, 1974); parental education has been found to correlate *negatively* with children's attitudes toward retarded peers (Peterson, 1974); mainstreaming of retarded adolescents was not found to increase either liking or social contacts by their nonretarded classmates (Stager & Young, 1981); nor were normal preschoolers found to interact favorably with mainstreamed retarded preschoolers (Cavallaro & Porter, 1980). Yet, integration in *nonacademic* activities has improved acceptance of retarded peers by elementary and junior high school pupils (Ballard, Corman, Gottlieb, & Kaufman, 1977; Sheare, 1974).

Behavior Modification. The small differences between school performance by retarded children in regular and special classes do not mean they do well in either setting. Along with the apparent social disadvantages of regular classes for many retarded children, this suggests that educational programs should emphasize the training needed for postschool situations most favorable for the retarded as individuals, instead of hoping that watered-down regular school programs will eventually make them into almost normal adults.

Behavioral principles (detailed in Chapter 10) have been increasingly applied to the education of the retarded. The goals include self-care, language training, and elimination of self-destructive behavior in the severely retarded, as well as academic, social, and vocational training in the more mildly retarded.

Behavioral principles have also been used to reduce disruptive behavior so that more constructive behavior can be taught. Various approaches are possible, including food rewards for single responses, programmed instruction, token rewards, and teaching machines. Because many behavioral techniques are easily taught, parents can be trained to make lasting changes in the behavior of their own retarded children (Baker, Heifetz, & Murphy, 1980).

Another approach has been through *therapeutic pyramids* in which a professional person trains nonprofessional assistants who then supervise retarded assistants in training other retarded people (Whalen & Henker, 1971). Beside being an economical extension of the professional's reach, therapeutic pyramids offer the possibilities of (1) greatly enhancing the self-esteem and functioning of the retarded assistants by giving them meaningful work, and (2) creating self-perpetuating improvement in the behavior of retarded groups. However, continual close supervision is needed to maintain performance (Craighead & Mercatoris, 1973). Furthermore, even highly effective behavioral programs have been destroyed by changes in administrators and government policies (see Thompson & Grabowski, 1977, for a poignant example).

Beside the technology of behavior modification, behavioral approaches have contributed the following guidelines for work with the retarded:

1. Within their biological limits, all people are able to acquire new behavior.
2. Current behavior is largely the result of past and present environmental contingencies.
3. Constructive changes in the behavior of the retarded depend on changes in the environmental contingencies that shape and support it, including contingencies established by the behavior of institutional personnel, family members, teachers, and retarded peers.
4. To be effective, training requires precise behavioral goals that the individual can reach and the environment can support. The kind of self-sufficiency expected of normals is not a realistic goal for most pathologically retarded children and may not be realistic for many nonpathologically retarded children, at least not at the same age as normals.
5. Long-term maintenance of improved behavior requires environmental conditions designed to support it. Retarded children who have learned to use their abilities require continual reinforcement that may not be typical of a world geared to people of greater ability. These assumptions are consistent with the developmental model for services, which stresses the fostering of continual adaptive advances (Menolascino, 1977).

Community Placements

Besides mainstreaming of retarded schoolchildren, community placement of re-tarded adolescents and adults has been a major goal of the normalization ideology. An increasingly community-oriented philosophy of care in the 1960s, followed by the normalization movement and legislative and court mandates for deinstitutionali-zation in the 1970s, greatly reduced the number of retarded living in large institutions (Bruininks, Hauber, & Kudla, 1980). The alternative placements include smaller institutional settings, sheltered villages, dormitory living units affiliated with sheltered workshops, proprietary facilities providing room and board on a fee-for-service basis, group homes ranging from family sized groups to a few dozen residents, and foster family care. Although family living is often considered ideal, it may leave the retarded feeling more isolated than group settings. As one mentally retarded person in a family setting put it: "I'm lonesome all day, with no place to go, no one to talk to. I think only of myself. I got to get out of family care—it's getting on my nerves'' (Gollay, Freedman, Wyngaarden, & Kurtz, 1978, p. 128).

Some forms of community placement have a long history, but the acceleration of efforts to provide small, normalized facilities has raised new problems. One is widespread neighborhood opposition to group homes for the retarded (Heal et al., 1978). This severely limits opportunities for normalized environments and prevents social integration of the retarded when such environments are established, although opposition seems to diminish after a facility opens (Heal et al., 1978). A second problem is the increasing desinstitutionalization of the more severely retarded and those having behavioral or physical problems that would previously have precluded deinstitutionalization. This may explain why people deinstitutionalized through the mid-1950s show higher rates of successful community adaptation than people deinstitutionalized since then: Prior to the intense pressures to deinstitutionalize, only those most likely to adapt well were placed in the community (McCarver & Craig, 1974).

Research on community placements has aimed to find out what characteristics of the retarded, their preplacement preparation, and the placement programs themselves foster successful adaptation. Unfortunately, clearcut answers have been precluded by the lack of studies in which retarded people matched on various characteristics are assigned in a systematic fashion to different preparation and placement programs. Correlational data indicate, however, that the success of community placements depends largely on the quality of family and community support systems and on individual differences in skills and behavior problems (Schalock, Harper, & Genung, 1981). Long-term case studies of the deinstitutionalized retarded show wide variation in adaptive styles and success between individuals and for the same individuals at different times (Edgerton & Bercovici, 1976). Furthermore, variables such as employment, income, marital status, community involvement, friendships, personal satisfaction, use of leisure time, and avoidance of arrest do not necessarily correlate well enough among the retarded to provide a single unitary index of adaptation. Just as the ideology of normalization implies a pluralism of possible life styles, evaluation of outcomes must take account of individual differences in definitions of success (Edgerton & Bercovici, 1976).

SUMMARY

There is tremendous variety among people deemed retarded because of their low IQs and poor social competence. Like growth retardation, mental retardation has many causes, occurs in many different degrees, and has many different consequences.

Mental retardation was first recognized as a social problem in the nineteenth century, beginning with the "discovery" of the severely retarded and followed by "discovery" of the mildly retarded when compulsory schooling imposed age-graded standards of achievement.

The Binet-Simon tests of 1905 to 1911 were the first to be widely accepted for assessing subnormal scholastic aptitude. Although the tests made no assumptions about the determinants or immutability of scholastic aptitude, the evidence that test scores predicted achievement, were roughly normally distributed, and remained fairly stable over several years was cited by hereditarians as proof that "intelligence" is hereditary.

Because IQ scores correlate moderately well with social competence and academic achievement, degrees of retardation are described in terms of IQ intervals: *Borderline* intelligence, IQs 68−83; *mild* retardation, 52−67; *moderate,* 36−51; *severe,* 20−35; *profound,* IQs below 20.

Most retarded people whose IQs are in the profound and severe ranges have definite organic pathology. Organic conditions known to produce retardation include *Down syndrome (mongolism)*, single gene conditions such as *phenylketonuria (PKU)*, and diseases and brain damage resulting from a variety of other causes. Some of these conditions can be treated by medical and dietary means.

There is evidence that other pathological conditions such as extreme environmental isolation and emotional disturbance can also cause mental retardation.

The vast majority of retarded people have IQs above 50 and no known pathological etiologies. Those having close relatives who are similarly retarded have been called *cultural-familial* retarded on the assumption that "cultural deprivation" and/or familial genetic factors limit their cognitive development. Models for understanding the interplay between environmental and genetic factors include: (1) the *extreme hereditarian* model of *polygenic* determination, which posits a different genotype for every phenotypic IQ; (2) an *interactionist* model of *polygenic* determination, which posits a phenotypic *reaction range* for each of several genotypes for IQ; (3) an *extreme environmentalist* model, which posits a single nonpathological genotype and ascribes all phenotypic differences to environmental differences.

Studies of the *heritability* of IQ—based on correlations between IQs of MZ and DZ twins reared together, IQs of MZ twins reared apart, and relations between adopted children's IQs and those of their biological and adoptive parents—support the interactionist model for IQs above 50 in the absence of pathological etiology.

Environmental influences on the level of phenotypic IQ within a genotypic reaction range and on the personalities and behavior of the retarded were documented. Behavior once considered inherent to retardation, such as *rigidity,* seems to arise from retardates' experiential histories, such as *social deprivation.* Similar findings indicated that retardates' *low expectancy of success, outer-directedness,* and *cue-dependency* result from their repeated experiences of failure in meeting standards set for normals of similar chronological age.

Goals for the care and education of the retarded have shifted from medical-custodial models to normalization-developmental models stressing *mainstreaming* and *community placement*. Coupled with legislative and judicial mandates to deinstitutionalize, plus reactions against *labeling*, the change in ideology has reduced the number of retarded people in institutions and special classes. However, the meager research on these changes shows that they may not always bring the intended benefits and that much remains to be learned about how best to meet the varied needs of the retarded.

SUGGESTED READING

Epidemiology of retardation. Birch et al. (1970) report an in-depth study of all children classified as retarded in a community offering nearly ideal conditions for such research. The nature of the community made it especially valuable for studying the nonpathologically retarded without the confounding factors of ethnic differences or differential access to medical, educational, and housing services.

Environmental and Genetic Effects on Intelligence. Despite methodological imperfections, the key studies by Skodak and Skeels (1949) and Skeels (1966) on the relations between IQ and environment and between the IQs of adopted children and their biological and adoptive parents are important milestones in the nature-nurture controversy, as is Honzik's (1957) reanalysis of their and other data. Later adoption studies by Scarr (1981) and Horn, Loehlin, and Willerman (1979) further support hypothesized interactions between genetic and environmental determinants. Wayne Dennis (1973) contrasts the effects of traditional institutional environments, improved institutional environments, and adoption in his book, *Children of the Crèche*.

Institutionalism. Anyone unaware of how poor conditions in institutions for the retarded can be or political obstacles to reform should read Blatt, Ozolins, and McNally (1979), *The family papers: A return to purgatory*. A book by Thompson and Grabowski (1977), *Behavior modification of the mentally retarded*, portrays similar conditions, plus the advantages and limitations of behavioral techniques for improving institutions by changing administrative, staff, and resident behavior. A poignant epilogue tells how a successful behavior modification program was wiped out by political and administrative changes.

Deinstitutionalization and Community Care. Birenbaum and Seiffer (1976) present a detailed case history of Gatewood, a managed community for deinstitutionalized retarded adults. In the *Economics of Mental Retardation,* Conley (1973) provides cost/benefit analyses of various approaches to care, and documents the potential savings achieved through prevention and rehabilitation as compared to other approaches.

Personality and Motivational Factors in the Behavior of the Retarded. Research on the relation of retarded cognitive development to personality and motivational determinants of behavior has been summarized by Balla and Zigler (1979).

Retardation and Public Policy. Sarason and Doris (1979) depict the social and historical context and mythology that have caused and are still causing so much humiliation and unnecessary suffering for the educationally handicapped, including the retarded.

The World of Nigel Hunt (1967). A book by this title is the diary of a boy with Down syndrome. He wrote most of it himself, showing the competencies and charm possible despite what is usually a severely handicapping form of retardation. Nigel's own perspective and commentary by his father also point up some of the cognitive limitations that necessitate continuing help from others.

CHAPTER 9

Psychoanalytic Approaches to Development and Psychopathology

Psychoanalysis originated with Sigmund Freud's efforts to understand psychoneurotic disorders. These efforts spawned multiple theories of psychological functioning and development that have shaped social values and childrearing, as well as views of psychopathology. Although the DSM-III has replaced the term *psychoneurotic disorder* with *anxiety disorder,* analytic theory aims to explain far more than anxiety. To understand analytic approaches, we therefore need to consider the problems they addressed.

FREUD'S FIRST THEORY OF NEUROSIS

Freud's theory of neurosis went through two distinct stages of development. Because the second stage merged with but changed Freud's already well-established theory, we will consider both stages of development.

Charcot and Janet

As a young researcher in neurology, Freud was intrigued by the symptoms of *hysteria.* For no apparent reason, hysterics suffered sudden organic dysfunctions such as paralyses, blindness, and anesthesias (losses of feeling). To learn more, Freud in 1885 studied under Jean-Martin Charcot, a Parisian neurologist famous for his research on hysteria. But Charcot could find no organic causes for hysterical symptoms; they even failed to follow basic anatomical principles. More puzzling yet was that they could be induced and removed through hypnosis.

Impressed by the effects of hypnosis, Charcot's pupil Pierre Janet began studying the *mental* states of hysterics. He found that they often had curious losses of memory. In extreme cases, called *hysterical fugues,* people would suddenly leave home and take up a completely new role, unable to remember their previous life. On "awakening" later, they were oblivious to the period of amnesia. Seeing this "splitting of consciousness" as the crucial feature of hysteria, Janet hypothesized that an innate weakness in the victim's capacity for psychological synthesis allowed groups of thoughts (*complexes*) to become separated (*dissociated*) from one another.

Josef Breuer

Josef Breuer, a Viennese colleague of Freud's, reached a different conclusion: He found that hysterical symptoms could be removed if the hysteric was hypnotized and reexperienced the situation in which the symptom began, freely expressing the accompanying emotion. Breuer also found that the hysteric's memory of the pathogenic situation seemed to explain the symptoms. While hypnotized, for example, a girl suffering from a hysterical disturbance of vision remembered her mortally ill father asking what time it was. The girl, Anna O., had strained to see her watch through her tears so she could reply without betraying her anxiety. Her visual symptoms disappeared when she remembered the situation and vented her suppressed feelings.

Breuer gave the name *hypnoid state* to the period of intense but unexpressed emotion when symptoms were formed. He regarded the suppression of emotion during such a state, rather than an innate defect in psychological synthesis, as the cause of dissociation. He called the therapeutic release of suppressed emotion *abreaction* or *catharsis*.

Breuer's hypothesis that the psychological hypnoid state was primary and the dissociation a byproduct accounted for the hysteric's specific symptoms. It also offered a cure through the abreaction of suppressed emotion. Breuer thus fathered the *psychodynamic* model of conflicts between impulses striving for expression against opposing mental forces. It was this model that Freud developed into psychoanalytic theory.

Studies in Hysteria

Breuer and Freud collaborated on *Studies in Hysteria* (1893−95), which marked the start of the psychoanalytic literature. This was a series of case reports on hysterical women including Anna O., plus Breuer and Freud's hypotheses about hysteria. Freud hypothesized that ideas incompatible with the dominant ideas of a person's ego are forced out of consciousness by a process he called *repression*. The *affective* (emotional) excitation associated with the unacceptable ideas is also forced out of consciousness. However, the excitation remains active and can be *converted* into a somatic form causing bodily dysfunctions. Freud therefore called such disorders *conversion* hysteria.

Freud found that some patients could not recover their repressed memories under hypnosis. Others could not be hypnotized at all. Yet by urging a patient to relax and say whatever came to mind, Freud pieced together fragments of the repressed complex of unconscious thoughts. This psychoanalytic technique became known as *free association*. The patient's resistance to recognizing the repressed thoughts could be overcome if the analyst gradually helped the patient see the unconscious meaning of his or her own words. Symptoms could be relieved if the patient gained enough insight to allow the repressed thoughts and affect into consciousness.

Defense Psychoneuroses

Freud's concept of the *defense psychoneuroses* forms the cornerstone of analytic theory. In his initial version of the theory, he used "defense" as a synonym for "repression." In conversion hysteria, he thought that repression forced both the unacceptable thought and its affect out of consciousness; but the affect was converted into somatic excitation which interfered with bodily organs.

In broadening his theory beyond hysteria, Freud hypothesized that only people predisposed to hysteria could convert affective excitation into somatic forms, even though not everyone with this predisposition developed clinical symptoms. By contrast, obsessional and phobic neurotics seemed to lack the capacity for conversion; they could not repress the affect attached to unacceptable ideas. Instead, they repressed the *connection* between the unacceptable idea and the affect attached to it. For example, unlike hysterics, obsessional and phobic neurotics acknowledged remembering an unacceptable idea; yet they claimed they did not think about it much. The unacceptable idea thus remained accessible to consciousness in a weak, unemotional form. But its affect became attached to more acceptable ideas, causing these to become obsessions. Freud explained phobias by assuming that *anxiety* was separated by repression from its original source. The anxiety then became attached to a new object making the victim fearful (*phobic*) of this object.

Freud thus hypothesized that hysterical, obsessional, and phobic symptoms reflect conflicts between the ego and ideas unacceptable to it. But the consequences of repression differ, partly because of preexisting characteristics of the patient. Freud also hypothesized that psychotic hallucinations are explained by the same principles: In psychoses, however, repression of unacceptable thoughts is so complete that everything associated with them is distorted or forced out of consciousness.

Libido Theory

Freud's conceptual model rested on his hypothetical construct of a quantity of affective excitation. This excitation could be converted into other forms and then displaced, discharged, and attached to new ideas:

> I should like . . . to dwell . . . on the working hypothesis which I have made use of. . . . I refer to the concept that in mental functions something is to be distinguished—a quota of affect or sum of excitation—which possesses all the characteristics of a quantity . . . which is capable of increase, diminution, displacement, and discharge, and which is spread over the memory traces of ideas somewhat as an electric charge is spread over the surface of a body.
>
> This hypothesis . . . can be applied in the same sense as physicists apply the hypothesis of a flow of electric fluid. It is provisionally justified by its utility in co-ordinating and explaining a great variety of psychical states (Freud, 1894).

Where did the affective excitation come from? In every patient analyzed, Freud inferred repressed sexual thoughts. He also found that free association disclosed memories of childhood sexual seductions and that adult symptoms arose in situations stimulating the emotions aroused during the seductions. On further investigation, however, Freud concluded that many of the childhood seductions could not actually have taken place. He decided that they were fantasies motivated by childhood sexual desires.

Following this conclusion, which was radical for his time, Freud sought to deduce from his patients' free associations the psychological aspects of childhood sexuality. In *Three Essays on the Theory of Sexuality* (1905), he presented his conclusions in terms of the psychoanalytic theory of *psychosexual development*, much as it remains today.

First, Freud hypothesized that the affective excitation was biologically based in the sex *Trieb* (the German word for *drive*, often misleadingly translated as "instinct" or "instinctual drive"). His concept of the sex drive extended well beyond genital sexuality, however, as it also encompassed nongenital bodily pleasures, such as oral satisfactions.

Second, he gave the name *libido* to the hypothetical energy arising from the sex drive. The person toward whom a libidinal impulse was directed was called the *object* of the impulse; he coined the term *cathexis* for the investment of libido in the mental representation of the object. Thus, a young child's mother is typically an *object* of *cathexis*.

Third, having assumed a permanent biological source for libido, Freud proposed that all the observed phenomena and inferred processes of neurotic and psychotic disorders are expressed via the distribution of libido. He later proposed that aggressive impulses come from a second instinctual drive, the *death instinct*, but he never elaborated much on this.

Phases of Libidinal Development. Freud hypothesized that libido first centers in one sensitive body area (*erogenous zone*) and then another. At first, during the *oral phase,* children are preoccupied with the mouth, stimulation obtained through it, and activities carried out with it.

During the second phase, called the *anal phase* and lasting from about age 3 to 5, libidinal arousal centers in the penis of the boy and clitoris of the girl. This sets the stage for a drama similar to that of the mythical Greek King Oedipus who killed his father and married his mother: Freud hypothesized that the boy turns against his father in order to possess his mother, while the girl does the opposite. However, fear of punishment by the same-sex parent—castration in the boy and the girl's feeling that she is already castrated—forces the child to repress Oedipal wishes.

Freud credited repression with warding off the libidinal impulses and channeling their energy into learning and socialization during the *latency period,* from about age 5 to puberty. He called this diversion of libido into constructive activity *sublimation.*

At puberty, sexual maturation reactivates the struggle between the ego and resurgent libidinal impulses. Several outcomes are possible: (1) libido can be discharged through sexual relations; (2) there can be *fixation at* or *regression to* infantile modes of libidinal discharge (these infantile modes are viewed as *perversions* in adults); or (3) repression can block libidinal discharge and transform libido into neurotic symptoms—Freud thus viewed neurotic symptoms as *substitute* expressions of libidinal impulses.

Symptom Formation

Because Freud viewed neurotic symptoms as substitutes for repressed impulses, he thought repression was a prerequisite for symptom formation. The content of the repressed impulses, constitutional differences in drive strength and the ability for conversion, and specific experiences all helped determine the form symptoms took. In Freud's words, each symptom was *overdetermined,* that is, determined by multiple factors.

Anxiety

During the first 20 years of psychoanalysis, Freud was preoccupied with demonstrating repressed motives and the roots of adult neurosis in childhood sexuality. He gradually turned to the problem of *anxiety,* however, which was to become the centerpiece of the theory of neurosis he proposed in 1926.

He first hypothesized that impulses threatening to break through repression were converted into neurotic anxiety (Freud, 1915). This he viewed as a toxic end product of blocked libido. His thinking about neurotic anxiety changed, however, as he began to view mental functioning in terms of three distinct entities (Freud,

1923). Most basic was the *id*, embodying instinctual impulses, aggressive as well as sexual. Next was the *ego*, the seat of consciousness and perception, which controls voluntary activity and represses id impulses unacceptable to it. Last, there was the *superego* (or *ego ideal*). This, he thought, was formed from part of the ego when the child's Oedipus complex is resolved by incorporating moral standards and prohibitions associated with the same-sex parent.

Believing that guilt arose when the ego failed to meet the superego's standards, Freud now hypothesized that conflicts between ego and superego were another possible source of neurotic anxiety: Threats of punishment emanating from the superego could therefore augment neurotic anxiety originating from blocked libido.

Summary of Freud's First Theory of Neurosis

We can summarize the main points of Freud's theory prior to his major revision of 1926 as follows:

1.   Freud believed that *defense psychoneuroses* resulted from conflict between the ego and impulses unacceptable to it. He held that the ego defended itself by forcing the impulses out of consciousness via *repression*.
2.   Repression had different consequences in different neuroses: In *hysterical neuroses*, the affective excitation of the unacceptable impulses was *converted* to somatic form, but in *obsessional* and *phobic* neuroses, repression *separated* the affective excitation from the unacceptable impulse, and the affective excitation attached itself to other ideas.
3.   The affective excitation embodied in id impulses was a hypothetical construct that Freud named *libido*. He hypothesized that it was biologically based in the sex drive and that its distribution could explain neurotic and psychotic phenomena.
4.   Freud's *developmental theory* was that libido passed through *oral, anal,* and *phallic* phases, followed by repression during the *latency* period and a renewed upsurge at puberty.
5.   The outcome of the struggle between the ego and libidinal impulses at puberty was crucial for adult personality: It determined whether an adult's libido would be discharged through mature genital sexuality, would regress to or remain fixated at earlier stages (i.e., would be perverted), or would be blocked by excessive repression, resulting in neurotic symptoms. These, Freud thought, were *overdetermined substitutions* for repressed libidinal impulses.
6.   Neurotic anxiety had two sources: Originally Freud thought it was always a toxic end product of blocked libido. As his id-ego-superego theory of personality structure evolved, however, he decided that anxiety in the form of guilt might also arise from superego threats against the ego.

FREUD'S REVISED THEORY OF NEUROSIS

Anxiety

With the publication of *Inhibition, Symptoms, and Anxiety,* Freud (1926a) reassembled his old ideas in new ways. He now hypothesized that anxiety states replicated the physiological and psychological responses triggered during birth. These responses include rapid respiration and heartbeat and a (presumably) overwhelming sense of helplessness owing to sudden separation from the intrauterine environment, mechanical pressures, deprivation of oxygen, and change of temperature. Not only do subsequent danger situations evoke these reactions, but so do stimuli associated with situations that seemed dangerous in childhood.

Typical childhood situations threatening trauma included: (1) *separation from the mother,* threatening the child with unsatisfied biological needs; (2) *upsurges of libidinal drives* that might overwhelm the adaptive mechanisms of the immature ego, for example, when attracted to the opposite-sex parent; and (3) *threats of castration or withdrawal of love* as punishment for libidinal impulses.

Signal Anxiety. Now seeing neurotic anxiety as the ego's response to reactivated childhood dangers, Freud revised his earlier theory of the relations between repression and anxiety. Instead of being a toxic *end product* of repression, Freud conjectured, anxiety is a response to stimuli associated with childhood dangers. This anxiety *instigates* repression by goading the ego into defending against the potentially dangerous impulse or situation before it becomes traumatic. Because it signals impending danger, anxiety that spurs defensive action was dubbed *signal anxiety.*

Defense

Freud made a further innovation. He broadened his concept of defense to include ego techniques other than repression. He had previously mentioned many of these techniques but viewed them as secondary devices for helping prevent repressed impulses from becoming conscious. Besides repression, he now included *reaction formation,* that is, replacment in consciousness of a threatening impulse with its opposite; *undoing,* that is, ritualistic reversal or undoing of acts or events that evoked anxiety; and *isolation*—preventing an anxiety-arousing situation from leading to further anxiety-arousing thoughts or events by interposing after it a period in which nothing must happen. (Isolation also referred to the repression or *isolation of affect* connected with a threatening thought.)

Symptom Formation

If anxiety *instigates* the ego's defensive efforts, how do neurotic symptoms arise? Instead of substituting for libidinal impulses, symptoms were now seen as the ego's way of *avoiding* danger. However, Freud still thought they were overdetermined by the nature of the threatened danger, the strength and nature of the impulses associated with it, constitutional factors, previous experience, and current reality.

The Case of Little Hans. We can contrast Freud's initial and later theories of neurosis by comparing his changing interpretations of his earlier cases. One was his famous case of Little Hans, first published in 1909. The case was crucial because it seemed to show Oedipal dynamics at work in a child instead of through reconstructions from adults' free associations: It revealed the boy's interest in sex, concern about females' lack of a penis, fear of castration as punishment for masturbation and desires toward his mother, and fear and hostility toward his father. Since Hans's parents took part in the treatment, family dynamics and details of his experience were also revealed more directly than through recollections by adult patients.

Long before Hans's symptom, a horse phobia, his parents had made written observations of his behavior, which they later gave Freud. When he was two, Hans showed a lively interest in his "widdler," as he called his penis. He asked his mother if she had one and, seeing a cow milked, he exclaimed, "Oh, look! There's milk coming out of its widdler!" (Freud, 1909, p. 7). More ominiously, when he was 3 his mother threatened to have his penis cut off when she saw him fondling it. Freud interpreted this as the source of Hans's castration complex.

His curiosity about widdlers unquenched, Hans excitedly remarked on the size of animals' widdlers. When asked by his mother why he was so eager to see her undress, he said he wanted to see her widdler—he thought it must be as big as a horse's since she was so big! When Hans saw his baby sister being bathed, he remarked, ". . . her widdler's still quite small. When she grows up it'll get bigger alright." Three months later, he said in a pitying voice, "She *has* got a tiny little widdler," and made a similar observation about a doll he undressed.

Hans became very affectionate toward other children, hugging them and begging to sleep with a particular 14-year-old girl. He also seemed to fall in love with an 8-year-old girl, blushed in her presence, and talked about kissing and sleeping with her.

Hans sometimes fretted about what would happen if his mother went away and he had no mother to "coax with" (caress). On these occasions, his mother often took him into her bed. When Hans was 4, he had a nightmare from which he awoke crying: He told his mother, "When I was asleep I thought you were gone and I had no mummy to coax with."

Some days later, Hans came to his mother's bed, saying, "Do you know what Aunt M. said? She said: 'He *has* got a dear little thingummy (penis),' " which his visiting aunt had indeed remarked when she saw him being bathed. Two days later, on his daily walk with his nursemaid, he cried to be taken home so he could coax with his mother. The next day, his mother took him out herself to see why he now resisted his walk. This time, after much uneasiness, he said he was afraid of being bitten by a horse. At bedtime he again wanted to coax with his mother. He then cried about the prospect of going out the next day and said he was afraid a horse would come into his room. These symptoms continued and grew worse.

Here is Freud's original interpretation:

> The disorder set in with thoughts that were at the same time fearful and tender, and then followed an anxiety dream on the subject of losing his mother and so not being able to coax with her anymore. His affection for his mother must therefore have become enormously intensified. . . . It was this increased affection for his mother which turned suddenly into anxiety. . . . Hans's anxiety, which thus corresponded to a repressed erotic longing, was like every infantile anxiety without an object to begin with; it was still anxiety and not yet fear. The child cannot tell (at first) what he is afraid of. . . .
>
> . . . the states into which he fell . . . before going to sleep . . . were characterized by anxiety with tenderness. These states show that at the beginning of his illness there was as yet no phobia whatever present, whether of streets or of walking or even of horses. If there had been, his evening states would be inexplicable; for who bothers at bedtime about streets and walking? On the other hand it becomes quite clear why he was so fearful in the evening, if we suppose that at bedtime [a time when he had previously admitted to fondling his penis] he was overwhelmed by an intensification of his libido—for its object was his mother, and its aim may perhaps have been to sleep with her. . . .
>
> His anxiety . . . corresponded to repressed longing. But it was not the same thing as the longing. . . . Longing can be completely transformed into satisfaction if it is presented with the object longed for . . . anxiety remains even when longing can be satisfied. . . . It can no longer be completely retransformed into libido; there is something that keeps the libido back under repression. This was shown . . . on the occasion of his next walk when his mother went with him. He was with his mother, and yet he still suffered from the anxiety—that is to say, from an unsatisfied longing for her. . . . But his anxiety had stood the test; and the next thing for it to do was to find an object. It was on this walk that he first expressed a fear that a horse would bite him. Where did the material for this phobia come from? Probably from the complexes . . . which had contributed to the repression and were keeping under repression his libidinal feelings towards his mother. (Freud, 1909)

The rest of Freud's report mainly concerns the selection of horses as the phobic objects that helped Hans justify his anxiety. The choice of horses, according to Freud, was *overdetermined* by Hans's initial interest in their large widdlers; his association of his mother's size with a horse's size and his inference that her penis should therefore be as big as a horse's; his having been upset by seeing a horse fall and seeing a friend playing horsie fall in the same way; his father having been the first to play horsie with him; his association of his father's black mustache with the muzzles worn by horses; and warnings about being bitten by a particular white horse, warnings phrased in the same way as his mother's warning not to touch his penis.

Hans's reaction to analytic interpretations made to him seemed to confirm Freud's theory: It seemed he had indeed projected onto horses the anxiety evoked by repressed libidinal impulses toward his mother and repressed fear and hostility toward his father which accompanied these impulses. In discussing the case, Freud summarized his theory of what he then called "anxiety hysteria" (later known as *phobic neurosis*):

> An anxiety hysteria tends to develop more and more into a phobia. In the end the patient may have got rid of all his anxiety, but only at the price of subjecting himself to all kinds of inhibitions and restrictions. From the outset in anxiety hysteria the mind is constantly at work in the direction of once more psychically binding the anxiety which has become liberated; but this work can neither bring about a retransformation of the anxiety into libido, nor can it establish any contact with the complexes which were the source of libido. Nothing is left for it but to cut off access to every possible occasion that might lead to the development of anxiety, by erecting mental barriers in the nature of precautions, inhibitions, or prohibitions; and it is these defensive structures that appear to us in the form of phobias and that constitute to our eyes the essence of the disease. (Freud, 1909)

The phobic symptom was a *compromise*—it helped Hans justify his anxiety while also holding the repressed impulses in check and permitting some libidinal gratification:

> . . . the essence of Hans's illness was entirely dependent upon the nature of the instinctual components that had to be repulsed. The content of his phobia was such as to impose a very great measure of restriction upon his freedom of movement, and that was its purpose. It was therefore a powerful reaction against the obscure impulses to movement which were especially directed against his mother. For Hans horses had always typified pleasure in movement . . . but since this pleasure in movement included the impulse to copulate, the neurosis imposed a restriction on it and exalted the horse into an emblem of terror. Thus it would seem as though all that the repressed instincts got from the neurosis was the honour of providing pretexts for the appearance of anxiety in consciousness. But however clear may have been the victory in Hans's phobia of the forces that were opposed to sexuality, nevertheless, since such an illness is in its very nature a compromise, this cannot have been all that the repressed instincts obtained. After all, Hans's phobia of horses was an obstacle to his going into the street, and could serve as a means of allowing him to stay at home with his beloved mother. In this way, therefore, his affection for his mother triumphantly achieved its aim. In consequence of his phobia, the lover clung to the object of his love—though to be sure, steps had been taken to make him innocuous. (Freud, 1909)

Revised Interpretation. How did Freud's 1926 theory explain Hans's symptoms? Freud rejected his earlier belief that Hans's anxiety stemmed from repression or from the libido of the repressed impulses. Instead, he now argued that *fear of castration* caused Hans's anxiety. This was what motivated his ego to repress both sexual impulses toward his mother and aggressive impulses toward his father. But when repression failed to blot out the dangerous impulses, Hans responded by blaming his fear on biting horses which served as a symbolic substitute for fear of castration by his father. The choice of horses as the phobic object was overdetermined by many of the factors detailed in the 1909 report, although Freud now held that most children's animal phobias symbolized castration fears.

Substituting fear of being bitten by a horse for fear of castration by his father had two advantages: (1) Fearing horses rather than his father avoided the conflict between Hans's love for his father and the fear and hostility toward his father evoked by his desires on his mother. (2) Thinking of horses as the source of his anxiety enabled Hans to avoid anxiety by avoiding horses. What Hans saw as an objective external danger of castration was thus replaced by the objective external danger of being bitten by a horse.

Summary of Freud's Second Theory of Neurosis

We can summarize Freud's 1926 theory of neurosis as follows:

1. The physiological and psychological aspects of anxiety replicated the birth trauma in miniature.
2. Potentially traumatic danger situations, such as separation from the mother and threats of castration, evoked anxiety reactions resembling responses to the birth trauma.
3. Libidinal impulses and other stimuli previously associated with childhood danger situations triggered *signal anxiety* in the ego; the discomfort of signal anxiety prodded the ego to use its defense mechanisms (*repression, reaction formation, undoing, isolation*) against the threatening stimuli, lest they lead to the previously experienced danger situations.
4. When initial defenses against threatening stimuli failed, the ego formed symptoms to avoid further increases in anxiety.

THE EGO AND THE MECHANISMS OF DEFENSE

In a book bearing the above title, Anna Freud (1936) elaborated on her father's concepts of the ego and its defensive functions. Much of her book was based on analytic work with children. Besides stressing observation of children as a basis for theory, she focused on the ego more than unconscious id impulses. She held that analysis had been unduly restricted to repressed impulses and infantile fantasies. Analysts showed too little concern for their patients' adjustment to current reality. Reflecting a new trend in analytic theory known as *ego psychology,* she emphasized the ego's function as both the medium through which other aspects of personality were revealed and the mediator of id, superego, and reality demands.

Emphasis on the ego did not lessen the need to interpret unconscious mental activity, however. On the contrary, the analyst's task grew larger: now the analyst had to bring unconscious ego activities into consciousness. These unconscious activities were viewed mainly as defenses against anxiety. The analyst could detect them in the ego's efforts to prevent unconscious id impulses from becoming conscious. In adults, interruptions of free association warned that anxiety-arousing thoughts were nearing consciousness. Patients' ploys for avoiding these thoughts revealed the mechanisms by which they controlled forbidden impulses. By exposing defenses, the analyst could deduce how a patient's ego formed neurotic symptoms. The analyst could then help the patient gain insight into his or her defense mechanisms, unconscious impulses, superego prohibitions, and neurotic symptoms.

Children's dreams, daydreams, play, and drawings were thought to reveal id impulses in the same way as adults' free associations. Children cannot free associate well enough to explore their ego defenses during therapy, however. As an alternative, Melanie Klein (1932) observed interruptions and inhibitions in the use of toys provided in the therapy room. She argued that these clues were much like interruptions in the free associations of adults when anxiety-arousing thoughts neared consciousness.

Anna Freud favored a different way of detecting the ego's defensive operations: She noted discordant reactions to events normally expected to make particular emotional impacts. For example, if a child reacted with excessive tenderness where jealousy was expected, she inferred that the ego had intervened; she could then make the child conscious of his or her way of avoiding disturbing thoughts through an appropriate interpretation.

Highlighting the ego's defensive operations, she enumerated the defense mechanisms that were by then part of analytic theory. These included the four mentioned by her father in 1926: *repression, reaction formation, isolation,* and *undoing.* To these four she added:

Denial—of unpleasant facts.

Displacement—of an effect onto an object or person other than the appropriate one; for example, children often displace affects onto imaginary companions.

Identification with the aggressor—mimicking the person, especially a parent, who poses a threat; a conscious use of this mechanism is illustrated by a little girl who overcame her fear of ghosts—"you just have to pretend you're the ghost who might meet you," she explained (A. Freud, 1946, p. 119).

Intellectualization—binding of instinctual drives in intellectual activity, as obsessive-compulsives often do.

Introjection—incorporating the demands of another person, especially a parent, as if they were one's own; one therefore reacts against forbidden impulses as the other person would.

Projection—attributing one's own forbidden impulses to another person; for example, feeling persecuted by another against whom one has hostile impulses.

Reversal—of an impulse into the reaction appropriate if the impulse were directed against oneself; for example, feeling anxious as a response to one's own impulses to harm someone else.

Sublimation—channeling instinctual drives into culturally valued activity, such as artistic creation.

Turning against the self—redirecting against the self the aggressive impulses originally aimed at others, as in masochistic, ascetic, or suicidal behavior.

To illustrate the coordination of multiple defense mechanisms, she returned to Little Hans:

> Here we have a clinical example of simultaneous defensive processes directed respectively inwards and outwards. We are told that the little boy's neurosis was based on impulses quite normally associated with the Oedipus complex. He loved his mother and out of jealousy adopted an aggressive attitude toward his father which, secondarily, came into conflict with his tender affection for him. These aggressive impulses roused his castration-anxiety—which he experienced as objective anxiety—and so the various mechanisms of defense were set in motion. The methods employed by his neurosis were *displacement*—from his father to the anxiety-animal—and *reversal* of his own threat to his father, that is to say, its transformation into anxiety lest he himself should be threatened by his father. Finally, to complete the distortion of the real picture, there was *regression* to the oral level: the idea of being bitten. The mechanisms employed fulfilled their purpose of warding off the instinctual impulses; the prohibited libidinal love for his mother and the dangerous aggressiveness towards his father vanished from consciousness. His castration-anxiety in relation to his father was bound in the symptom of a fear of horses but, in accordance with the mechanism of phobia, anxiety-attacks were avoided by means of a neurotic inhibition—Little Hans gave up going out of doors. (A. Freud, 1936, pp. 75–76)

LATER TRENDS IN EGO PSYCHOLOGY

Analytic ego psychology did not change the basic theory of neurosis, but aimed to broaden analytic theory into a general psychology. It also aimed to modify treatment techniques and goals. We turn now to its implications for development.

As Freud originally saw it, the ego developed solely out of conflicts between id demands and the child's need to adapt to reality in order to survive. Freud hypothesized, for example, that thinking—one of the key functions of the ego—originates when the hungry baby hallucinates its mother's breast as a way of temporarily satisfying id demands for food. In the course of subsequent conflicts between id demands and reality constraints, the hallucinatory process becomes more highly developed and independent of immediate conflict, until it can symbolically represent future possibilities. Thinking becomes rational when the child learns to use words to represent reality. Other ego functions, including memory, perception, and motility, were likewise thought to develop out of conflicts between id demands and reality constraints. To master these conflicts, the child has to develop ways of delaying, deflecting, and circumventing id demands.

Ego Psychology and the Problem of Adaptation

Almost until Freud's death in 1939, analysts concentrated on the expression of the id's power in its conflicts with the ego. The id-ego struggle was repeatedly illustrated by examples from free association, slips of the tongue, dreams, and neurotic symptoms. However, Anna Freud's (1936) book on the ego, Heinz Hartmann's book *Ego psychology and the problem of adaptation* (1939), and related articles (Hartmann, 1950a, 1950b, 1964) helped change this emphasis.

Free association, slips of the tongue, dreams, and symptom formation all reveal conflictual aspects of the ego. Yet, since ego functioning does not usually reveal conflict, Hartmann suggested looking beyond conflictual situations to learn more about the structure and origins of the ego. Specifically, he asked: (1) Does the ego *originate* solely from the conflict between id demands and the need to adapt to reality? (2) What *source of energy* enables the ego to maintain all the complex functions ascribed to it?

Origins of Ego Functions

Ego Functions having Primary Autonomy. Hartmann proposed that many ego functions ordinarily develop and operate independently of id-reality conflicts. He chose the term *conflict-free sphere of the ego* for functions that are normally free of conflict: these include perception, thinking, language, recall, motor development, walking, and many maturational and learning processes. He thought that, instead of originating in conflict, the potential for developing these functions exists from the beginning of life. Moreover, functions such as perception, memory, and associative learning are not byproducts but *prerequisites for* the ego's relationships to instinctual drives and love objects. Hartmann therefore hypothesized that rudimentary forms of these ego functions are, like id drives, genetically based and shaped through evolution to enhance adaptation to the "average expectable environment." He referred to innate ego functions as having *primary autonomy*.

Ego Functions having Secondary Autonomy. Beside those having primary autonomy, Hartmann acknowledged that some ego functions arise from conflicts between id demands and reality constraints, as Freud said. These functions are mainly the ego defenses. Yet even defenses can become general adaptive mechanisms in their own right and function independently of the conflicts spawning them. For example, a child who defends against jealousy over a new sibling by being very loving (*reaction formation*) might continue to be loving because it earns rewards. Functions arising from conflict, but becoming autonomous and joining the conflict-free sphere of the ego, were said to have *secondary autonomy*.

If the ego had conflict-free functions—some autonomous from the beginning and some winning autonomy after originating in conflict—the ego was important in its own right, independent of its conflicts with id impulses. Hartmann (1950b) thought that focusing on normal ego functions would bring analytic theory closer to the subject matter of developmental psychology and require research methods other than those of psychoanalysis.

The Ego's Sources of Energy

Because psychoanalysis retained its model of behavior as motivated by instinctual drive energy, the autonomy now credited to the ego raised a new question: How are the ego's activities energized?

Freud originally theorized that libido powered the mental apparatus. But if libido was the motive force, how could the ego defend *against* id impulses? As a solution, Freud proposed that some libido became temporarily *neutralized*; that is, some became free of its erotic aims and available for other purposes. This *neutralized libidinal energy*, Freud hypothesized, was what powered the ego.

Both Freud and Hartmann suggested that, because ego activities may be pleasurable in their own right, the ego might also have some independent energy of its own (Hartmann, 1964). Hartmann also went a little further: He thought the ego's energy derived from the *aggressive* as well as the sexual drive and that such energy could be *permanently* rather than just temporarily neutralized (Hartmann, Kris, & Loewenstein, 1949).

Because some autonomous functions presumably operate in infancy and because the notion of psychic energy became increasingly incompatible with modern physiology, other theorists have proposed that the ego has its own instinctual energy from the start. Hendrick (1943), for example, proposed an *instinct to master*; Mittelmann, (1954) proposed an *urge to motility*; and White (1963) proposed an *effectance motive* or motive to achieve competence.

David Rapaport took a somewhat different tack. Until his untimely death in 1960, Rapaport sought to extend analytic ego psychology by viewing cognitive functions as if they were independent of drive states altogether and by working out a psychoanalytic theory of learning (Rapaport, 1967, posthumous). He hoped to formulate a cognitive psychology that linked the mental functions highlighted by analytic theory with general cognitive functions such as learning, instead of limiting the cognitive focus to defensive functions.

ERIK ERIKSON'S THEORY OF PSYCHOSOCIAL DEVELOPMENT

One of the best-known contributors to analytic thinking is Erik H. Erikson. Ego psychology has been greatly enriched by his portrayal of the social context of the developing ego, its conflicts, and its sense of identity.

Stages of Psychosocial Development

Based on observations in diverse cultural settings, Erikson (1963, 1980) hypothesized developmental stages representing the ways in which unfolding biological needs and capacities engage children in interactions with adults. He describes these patterns in terms of three components: *zones* of the child's body, roughly corresponding to the erogenous zones of Freud's psychosexual theory; *modes* of action, or types of activity; *modalities* of social interaction, the kinds of social interchanges that children learn as they relate to others via various modes of action. Erikson pictures development as a process by which modes of action centered in particular zones become prototypes for social modalities.

Oral-Sensory Stage I—Getting. Erikson calls the first important zone the *oral-sensory zone*. This includes the facial apertures and upper nutritional organs. The baby's first mode of action is *incorporation,* because its greatest needs are to incorporate input from the world. Food from the mother is the most obvious input, but Erikson stresses that the skin and sense organs also hunger for stimulation. He therefore refers to the first stage as the *oral-sensory stage,* instead of just the "oral phase" as Freud called it.

When all goes well with the child and its relations to caregivers, the incorporative mode remains dominant during this stage and the child learns the basic social modality of *getting*; that is, learning to receive what is given and getting others to provide. When all does not go well, because of caregivers' failure to provide or the child's failure to receive, for physiological or temperamental reasons, other modes may inappropriately dominate. For example, the *eliminative mode,* normally dominant at a later stage, may prematurely dominate in a child who repeatedly thrusts out food after intake. This interferes with learning the social modality of getting and may obstruct later personality development.

Oral-Sensory Stage II—Taking. The second stage is a continuation of the oral-sensory stage, and incorporation remains the dominant mode. However, the incorporative activities are now biting, grasping, and discerning specific stimuli. Erikson calls the social modality arising from this *active incorporative* mode *taking.* Progress through this stage normally involves some trauma for the child, such as the pain of teething, conflict with the mother over weaning, and diminished attention from the mother.

Anal-Urethral-Muscular Stage. The third stage centers in the *anal-urethral zone.* Two conflicting modes of action—*retention and elimination*—become crucial during this stage. Children in all societies are likely to experience this stage when maturation brings well-formed stools, muscles for sphincter control, and the ability to control the environment through holding on and pushing away. Erikson therefore calls this the *anal-urethral-muscular* stage, in contrast to Freud's "anal phase."

Because Western societies impose strict control over when and where feces and urine are voided, they make toilet training a bigger issue than other societies do. Erikson calls the social modalities developed from the retentive and eliminative modes *holding on* and *letting go*. He maintains that social and individual factors affecting the relative balance of these two modalities during this stage affect their relative dominance in later life as well.

Locomotor and Infantile Genital Stage. In the fourth stage, the *genital zone* becomes especially fascinating and sensitive to children of both sexes. Sexual curiosity, erotic sensations, and the Oedipus complex emerge. Yet, because the child's freedom of locomotion also increases markedly, Erikson calls this the *locomotor and infantile genital stage,* instead of the Freudian *"phallic phase."* The dominant mode of action is usually *intrusive,* evident "as the intrusion into space by vigorous locomotion; into other bodies by physical attack; into other people's ears and minds by aggressive sounds; and into the unknown by consuming curiosity." However, the *inclusive* mode may also be expressed "in the often surprising alternation of such aggressive behavior with a quiet, if eager, receptivity in regard to imaginative material and a readiness to form tender and protective relations with peers as well as with smaller children" (Erikson, 1980, p. 24).

At this stage, Erikson sees a decisive divergence between boys and girls:

> Girls often undergo a sobering change at this stage, because they observe sooner or later that although their locomotor, mental, and social intrusiveness is as vigorous as that of the boys', thus permitting them to become perfectly good tomboys, they lack one item, the penis, and, with it, important prerogatives in most cultures and classes. While the boy has this visible, erectable, and comprehensible organ to which he can attach dreams of adult bigness, the girl's clitoris only poorly sustains dreams of sexual equality, and she does not even have breasts as analogously tangible tokens of her future. The idea of her eventual *inception* of the intruding phallus is as yet too frightening, and her maternal drives are relegated to play fantasy or baby tending. On the other hand, where mothers dominate households the boy can develop a sense of inadequacy because he learns at this stage that while he can do well outside in play and work, he will never boss the house, his mother, or his older sisters. His mother and sisters may, in fact, get even with him for their doubts in themselves by making him feel that a boy is really a somewhat repulsive creature. (Erikson, 1968, pp. 117–18)

The social modality of the locomotor and infantile genital stage is *making,* in the sense of "being on the make"—showing "initiative, insistence on goal, pleasure of conquest" (Erikson, 1980, p. 24). For the boy, the emphasis is on "making" by intrusive means. For the girl, by contrast, it changes to "making" by teasing, provoking, or catching through making herself attractive. This represents a partial reversion to the incorporative modes originally developed in oral and sensory areas. Erikson sees the girl as becoming more dependent and demanding and being permitted to do so except in cultures that expect more independent behavior in girls. However, he assumes that both sexes have all modalities at their disposal (Erikson, 1980).

Rudimentary Genital Stage. In this stage, generativity is the normally dominant mode. Male generativity is primarily *intrusive,* whereas female is *inclusive*; both are oriented toward an eventual coming together in procreation. *Genital mutuality* is the social pattern normally developed in this stage. Erikson maintains that the sexual lives of adult neurotics are handicapped by pregenital modes of incorporation, retention, elimination, or intrusion which preempt genital mutuality.

Nuclear Conflicts During Development

Related to the psychosocial stages, Erikson hypothesizes a sequence of psychological conflicts or crises that people typically face. As with the psychosocial stages, the exact resolution of each conflict shapes the next conflict and its possible resolutions. It also shapes the slow process of ego identity formation. Erikson's stress on the interface between the individual and society is evident in his underlying assumptions:

> (1) that the human personality in principle develops according to steps predetermined in the growing person's readiness to be driven toward, to be aware of, and to interact with, a widening social radius; and (2) that society, in principle, tends to be so constituted as to meet and invite this succession of potentialities for interaction and attempts to safeguard and to encourage the proper rate and the proper sequence of their unfolding. (Erikson, 1963, p. 270)

Basic Trust Versus Mistrust. The first nuclear conflict is over a sense of *basic trust* or *mistrust*. Smooth, loving, and mutually regulated interactions with the mother comfortably satisfy basic needs. The result is a sense of basic trust in mother and the world she represents. As this trust develops, the child becomes able to let mother out of sight without undue anxiety, confident that she will return. Inner representations of trusted, predictable people help lay the foundations for ego identity development.

Autonomy Versus Shame and Doubt. The second nuclear conflict arises with the muscular-anal stage. It concerns the development of a sense of autonomy through meeting standards set by parents and oneself, especially in toilet training. Failure to meet these standards—because they are too high, parental criticism is too harsh, or for other reasons—can breed a pervasive sense of shame and doubt.

Initiative Versus Guilt. The third nuclear conflict is linked to the locomotor-genital stage. It involves development of initiative based on confidence in one's autonomy, capacities, and goals. The danger is that aggressive initiatives evoke fear of real or fantasied consequences, leading to guilt over one's destructive powers. This is especially likely when an intense Oedipal situation provokes an extreme castration complex.

Industry versus Inferiority. During latency, children of all cultures receive some form of preparation for mature adult roles. Failure to develop culturally valued skills can inflict a lasting sense of inferiority, hinder further development, and keep the child fixated on infantile conflicts.

Identity Versus Role Confusion. At puberty, formation of an ego identity requires more than a summation of the identities forged in the previous conflicts: The ego must also integrate earlier identities with new libidinal demands, basic aptitudes, and available social-role opportunities. Failure to develop a sense of ego identity undermines the adolescent's confidence in the continiuity of his or her personal sameness. This may be manifest in doubts about sexual identity and in delinquent or psychotic episodes.

Conflicts in Adulthood. Adults typically experience three further conflicts: *intimacy versus isolation, generativity versus stagnation,* and *ego integrity versus despair*. The precise form and resolution of each are assumed to depend on the outcomes of all the preceding conflicts. Table 9-1 shows the relations between these and the earlier stages and conflicts, as well as the circle of social relationships characterizing each stage.

ANNA FREUD'S DEVELOPMENTAL PROFILE

In adapting psychoanalysis to children, Anna Freud advocates diagnosing each child according to the developmental sequence hypothesized by analytic theory. This means assessing the child's progress in terms of *developmental lines,* the step-by-step advances normally occurring in a particular aspect of personality, such as sexual drive (A. Freud, 1980). Beside sexual drive, she urges therapists to assess children in terms of ego and superego development; the stability of borders between id, ego and superego; progress from primitive, id-dominated (*primary process*) thinking to rational, ego-dominated (*secondary process*) thinking; and progress from seeking immediate gratification (the *pleasure principle*) to delaying gratification in favor of adaptation (the *reality principle*).

To facilitate analytic diagnosis, she offers a *developmental profile* for comparing a child with the expected developmental sequence. As summarized in Table 9-2, the profile mirrors the analytic theory of instinctual drives; the id-ego-superego personality structure; the ego's defenses and other functions; the

Table 9-1   Outline of Psychosocial Development Hypothesized by Erik Erikson

Stages	A Psychosexual Stages and Modes	B Psychosocial Crisis	C Radius of Significant Relations
I Infancy	Oral-respiratory, Sensory-kinesthetic (incorporative modes)	Basic trust vs. basic mistrust	Maternal person
II Early childhood	Anal-urethral, Muscular (retentive-eliminative)	Autonomy vs. shame, doubt	Parental persons
III Play age	Infantile-genital, Locomotor (intrusive, inclusive)	Initiative vs. guilt	Basic family
IV School age	"Latency"	Industry vs. inferiority	Neighborhood, school
V Adolescence	Puberty	Identity vs. identity confusion	Peer groups and outgroups; models of leadership
VI Young adulthood	Genitality	Intimacy vs. isolation	Partners in friendship, sex, competition, cooperation
VII Adulthood	(Procreativity)	Generativity vs. stagnation	Divided labor and shared household
VIII Old age	(Generalization of sensual modes)	Integrity vs. despair	"Mankind" "my kind"

Source: Erikson, 1980, p. 21. (Erikson's terminology for stages is not entirely consistent among his publications).

basis of neurosis in libidinal regression and fixation; and the role of dynamic conflict.

Section IV of the profile also lists the child's characteristics thought to bear on prognosis for improvement. Section V outlines diagnostic categories for deciding whether and how the child should be treated.

The profile summarizes Freudian theory pertaining to child analysis. But little has been published on how a child's standing on each variable, such as libido distribution, is to be objectively assessed. Neither reliability of assessment nor validity of the results have been established. Most publications on the profile merely show how it was filled out for a particular child or how it might look for a particular type of child (Yorke, 1980).

Table 9-2   A Summary of Anna Freud's Developmental Profile

I. *Assessments of Development*

A. Drive Development
1. Libido
   a. Phase development—Has child proceeded to age-adequate stage (oral, anal, etc.)? Is appropriate phase dominant? Regressed from his highest level to an earlier one?
   b. Libido distribution—Is self cathected as well as object world? Is narcissism sufficient to insure self-esteem without overestimation of the self and undue independence of others?
   c. Object libido—Have level and quality of object relations proceeded according to age? Regressed from his highest level to an earlier one? Do object relations correspond to the level of phase development?

2. Aggression
   a. Are aggressive expressions present?
   b. Does type of aggressive expression correspond to level of libido development?
   c. Are the expressions directed toward object world or self?

B. Ego and Superego Development
   1. Defects of ego apparatus serving perception, memory, etc.?
   2. Status of ego functions (memory, reality testing, etc.)?
   3. Are defenses directed against individual drives or against drive activity and instinctual pleasure in general? Are defenses age-adequate, too primitive, or too precocious? Is defense balanced, i.e., does ego have many important defenses available, or is it restricted to single ones? Is defense effective, especially in dealing with anxiety? Does it result in equilibrium, or disequilibrium, lability, or deadlock? Is defense against drives dependent on object world or on child's superego?
   4. Any interference of defense activity with ego achievements?

II. *Regressions and Fixation Points*
   Since it is assumed that all infantile neuroses are initiated by libido regressions to early fixation points, the location of these trouble spots in child's history is vital. These are betrayed by:
   A. Forms of behavior which allow conclusions as to the repressed id processes; e.g., obsessional character where cleanliness, orderliness, punctuality, hoarding, doubt, etc. betray difficulty with impulses of anal—sadistic phase.
   B. Fantasy activity revealed in personality tests and psychoanalysis.
   C. Symptoms having known relations to surface and depth determinants, such as symptoms of obsessional neurosis, but not symptoms, such as lying, stealing, and bed-wetting, which have a variety of causes.

III. *Dynamic and Structural Assessments (Conflicts)*
   Behavior is governed by conflicts of internal with external forces or of internal forces with each other. Conflicts should be classified as:
   A. External conflicts between id-ego agencies and object world (arousing fear).
   B. Internalized conflicts between ego-superego and id after ego agencies have taken over in representing to the id the demands of the object world (arousing guilt).
   C. Internal conflicts between incompatible drive representations, such as activ-

Table 9-2   *(Cont.)*

ity vs. passivity, masculinity vs. feminity, etc.

IV. *General Characteristics of the Child*
  A. Level of frustration tolerance.
  B. Degree of sublimation potential.
  C. Overall attitude toward anxiety, e.g., whether child tends to actively master danger situations.
  D. Relative strength of progressive developmental forces vs. regressive tendencies in child's personality.

V. *Diagnosis*
  Based on the foregoing assessments, the clinician must decide among diagnostic categorizations such as the following:
  A. In spite of current behavior disturbance, personality growth is within the wide range of "normality."
  B. Symptoms are of a transitory nature and can be classed as byproducts of developmental strain.
  C. There is a permanent drive regression to fixation points which leads to neurotic conflicts.
  D. There is drive regression plus ego

and superego regressions which lead to infantilisms, borderline psychotic, delinquent, or psychotic disturbances.
  E. There are primary organic deficiencies or early deprivations which distort development and produce retarded, defective, and nontypical personalities.
  F. There are destructive processes at work of organic, toxic, or psychic origin which have caused or are about to cause a disruption of mental growth.

Source: Adapted from A. Freud, 1965, pp. 141–47. © 1965 by International Universities Press and reproduced by permission.

Related Approaches to Developmental Profiling

Because the developmental profile is so elaborate and requires such an intimate knowledge of a child's functioning, other analysts have proposed briefer procedures based on more readily obtainable information. Greenspan, Hatleberg, and Cullander (1980), for example, have prepared the Metapsychological Assessment Profile, consisting of 11 categories to be rated as Good, Fair, Marginal, or Inadequate. The categories include ego flexibility, superego functioning, affects, and defenses. The numerical ratings lend themselves to assessment of reliability and validity more than Anna Freud's developmental profile does, but Greenspan, Hatleberg, and Cullander present only an illustration of their profile with a single case and no reliability or validity data.

Flapan and Neubauer (1975) have also proposed a psychoanalytically oriented assessment procedure. Entitled the Assessment Outline of Early Child Development, it is intended for the evaluation of preschoolers by their teachers. It consists largely of ratings of abilities, behaviors, emotions, and social relations based on the views of Anna Freud and other analysts. As a global assessment, the child is judged as (1) being able to progress developmentally; (2) progressing developmentally despite problems in some areas; (3) not progressing appropriately; or (4) having had problems that interfered with development but currently showing improvement. The authors do not tell how to move from the more specific ratings to the global assessment nor give details of reliability and validity.

OTHER OUTGROWTHS OF PSYCHOANALYTIC THEORY

Beside the efforts to utilize Anna Freud's concepts of developmental assessment, there have been numerous efforts to measure variables suggested by analytic theory. Many of these involve constructs cloaked in analytic terminology without necessarily being part of what analysts regard as their theory. Jane Loevinger (1976), for example, proposed integrating analytic and cognitive developmental concepts into a general paradigm for studying ego development. She also outlined 10 stages according to which character development, interpersonal styles, conscious preoccupations, and cognitive styles can be ordered. Loevinger's lowest level stages—the Presocial, Symbiotic, and Impulsive stages—roughly parallel other stage theories of early development, but her stages do not correspond to particular ages. The more advanced levels differ markedly from other stage theories in that they imply increasingly favorable personality configurations instead of a sequence through which most people pass. These advanced levels include the Self-protective, Conformist, Conscientious, Individualistic, Autonomous, and Integrated stages.

Jeanne and Jack Block (1980) also use analytic ego terminology in formulating two personality constructs: *ego control,* referring to impulse control and modulation; and *ego resiliency,* referring to adaptability to changing circumstances. The Blocks have used composites of observational, self-report, and test data to measure ego control and resiliency in children studied longitudinally from nursery school through adolescence. Correlations between these measures across ages indicate moderate stability in ego control and resiliency.

More radical departures from analytic theory have been proposed by John Bowlby, originally an analyst of the *object relations* school. Unlike the ego analysts who hold that infants' attachment to their mother results from the mother's repeated association with reduction of instinctual drives (A. Freud, 1965), object relations analysts hold that instinctual drives are innately focused toward human objects (Fairbairn, 1952). Although they disagree on the drive mechanisms involved, the ego and object relations analysts do agree that attachment behavior is motivated by instinctual drives.

Bowlby (1980) now differs from both groups, however. He argues that attachment behavior reflects an innately programmed control system whereby loss of proximity to the attachment figure, usually the mother, causes anxiety. This, in turn, activates behavior to restore proximity. Such behavior includes crying, searching, following, and clinging to promote contact with the caretaker. Because proximity-maintaining behaviors protect the young of many species, Bowlby hypothesizes that they have become innately programmed through natural selection. Furthermore, failure to develop a secure sense of attachment may explain much psychopathology. As an example, Bowlby has reinterpreted Freud's case of Little Hans in terms of anxiety over the mother's threats to desert the family:

> . . . the week preceding the onset of the phobia had not been the first time that Hans had expressed the fear that his mother might disappear. Six months earlier . . . he had made remarks such as "Suppose I was to have no Mummy" or "Suppose you were to go away." Looking further back still, . . . when Hanna was born, Hans, aged three and a half, had been kept away from his mother. In father's opinion, Hans's "present anxiety, which prevents him leaving the neighborhood of the house, is in reality the longing for (his mother) which he felt then." Freud endorses that opinion and describes Hans's "enormously intensified affection" for his mother as the "fundamental phenomenon in his condition."
>
> Thus, both the sequence of events leading up to the phobia and Hans's own statements make it clear that, *distinct from and preceding any fear of horses,* Hans was afraid that his mother might go away and leave him. . . .
>
> Early in the record it becomes apparent that mother is inclined to use rather alarming threats. For example, when Hans is only three she is described as having threatened him that, if he touched his penis, she would send for the doctor to cut it off. . . .
>
> Three months later, however, and buried deep in the "analytic" record, Hans lifts the curtain. He had come into father's bed one morning and in the course of talk had told his father: "When you're away I'm afraid you're not coming home." Father expostulates: "And have I ever threatened you that I shan't come home?" "Not you," retorts Hans, "but Mummy. Mummy's told me she won't come back." Father concedes the point, "She said that," he replies, "because you were naughty". . . .
>
> In the passage following father reflects . . . : "His motive for at the most just venturing outside the house but not going away from it, and for turning round at the first attack of anxiety when he is halfway, is his fear of not finding his parents at home because they have gone away." Soon after, however, father reverts to an explanation along Oedipal lines. (Bowlby, 1973, pp. 285–86)

Some analysts reject Bowlby's replacement of drive concepts with more ethologically oriented explanations (Engel, 1971), but certain other shifts in terminology and constructs have generally been accepted. *Instinctual drive,* for example, is increasingly viewed in terms of stable motivational systems instead of biologically based energy impelling behavior toward specific goals. Likewise, *conflicts* are viewed as resulting more from the incompatible goals of competing motivational systems than from the collision of opposing forces such as the ego and id. The explanation of *fixations* as reflecting cathexis of immature modes of functioning is also giving way to explanations in terms of the persistence of early motivational systems into later developmental stages (Rosenblatt & Thickstun, 1977).

CLINICAL APPLICATIONS OF THE PSYCHOANALYTIC APPROACH

Full-scale analysis of children, like that of adults, typically requires four to five sessions a week for several years. Because treatment is so long and costly and because analysts seldom complete their training before age 40 (Goodman, 1977), few children actually receive full-scale analysis. Child analysis is further restricted by the assumptions that a weak ego and excessively delinquent behavior make analysis unfeasible and that preschoolers and adolescents are usually too unstable. Analysis may also be precluded by intense developmental crises, illness, acquisition of a physical handicap, the death of a parent, and environmental interference with development, such as deprivation or disturbed parent behavior. Once these factors are ruled out, Anna Freud (1968) sees the best candidates for child analysis as those whose development is jeopardized by classic neuroses based on the Oedipus complex.

The aim of analysis is to bring greater harmony among intrapsychic forces. With adults, the analyst does this by interpreting ego resistances and id content and by bringing unconscious thoughts into consciousness. The analyst also serves as an object onto which adult patients *transfer* their feelings about their own parents and helps them rework these feelings.

With children, however, the immature ego, inability to introspect and free associate, and tendency to deal with conflict through action instead of thought accentuate other aspects of the analytic relationship. These include clarification of unrepressed thoughts, corrective emotional experience from the child's relationship to the analyst as an understanding adult, and manipulation of the child's environment through the analyst's advice to parents. Yet Anna Freud (1965) warns that allowing these aspects to dominate can undermine the chief goal of relieving intrapsychic conflicts by making them conscious. She contends that reducing neurotic symptoms without relieving these conflicts leads to *symptom substitution*—the production of new and more intractable symptoms by the unrelieved conflicts. However, she also concedes that children suffering from developmental defects might profit more from the relationship aspects of therapy than from interpretation of conflicts (A. Freud, 1974). Furthermore, others extend child analysis to the preschool and adolescent periods that she excludes (Scharfman, 1978), and, as we will see in Chapter 11, her fear of symptom substitution seems unwarranted.

Psychoanalytically Oriented Psychotherapy

Unlike full-scale analysis, most analytically oriented child therapy is done once or twice weekly for a few weeks to a few years by psychiatrists, psychologists, and social workers not necessarily trained as analysts. It deals with more diverse ages and problems than analysis does. It also aims more at clarification of unrepressed thoughts, corrective emotional experience, and advice to parents. In other words, the elements Anna Freud shuns in full-scale analysis.

Despite much wider use than child analysis, analytically oriented child therapy has received less theoretical elaboration. It often seems like a diluted form of analysis aimed at relieving symptoms by solving preconscious rather than unconscious conflicts. In one of the few efforts to distinguish analytically oriented child therapy from full-scale analysis, Brody (1964) lists its aims as:

1. Increasing the capacity for reality testing.
2. Strengthening object relations.
3. Loosening fixations.

However, the theory of analytically oriented child therapy remains largely dependent on the main body of analytic theory.

TYPES OF NEUROSIS

The analytic theory of neurosis centers on three types: phobic, obsessive-compulsive, and hysterical.

Phobic Neuroses

Phobias serve as a good focus for our later comparisons between analytic and behavioral approaches: Phobias can be objectively identified, are relatively common, and get contrasting explanations and treatments from analysts and behavior modifiers. The American Psychoanalytic Association's *Glossary* (Moore & Fine, 1968) defines phobias as follows:

> In phobias the various *ego* defenses against dangerous *instinctual drives* operate in such a way that the inner danger seems to become an outer one. Unacceptable inner strivings of a sexual or aggressive nature have been repressed because of the irrational, unconscious fear of castration by the father. When these impulses threaten to emerge into *consciousness,* intense castration anxiety results in their *projection* and *displacement* onto an outside object or situation. For example, the hatred and fear of a loved father may be shifted finally to some animal. The advantages are evident: the elimination of conscious awareness of the hatred and fear of the father permits continued closeness to him, while the animal, to which the fear is referred, can be avoided. Though unresolved conflicts of the *oedipus complex* contribute in a major way

to phobias, preoedipal problems provide a significant basis for their development. (p. 73)

In this view, the essence of a phobia is not the fear of the phobic object itself, but an unconscious conflict giving rise to fear. The fear, in turn, is *displaced* onto stimuli having a symbolic significance. Treatment, therefore, focuses on the unconscious conflict instead of fear of the phobic object. Unless the unconscious conflict is relieved, new phobias or other symptoms may emerge. Analysts stress that a neurotic phobia is only part of a larger pattern of excessive dependency and avoidance defenses as well as fears other than the main phobia (Kessler, 1972).

Analysis of a Phobic Child. The case of Frankie, a boy analyzed by Berta Bornstein (1949), is a classic of analytic literature. It is an especially revealing example of analytic theory and treatment for three reasons: First, Bornstein, a leader in child analysis, considered it worthy of a 45-page report because she thought the child's apparently simple phobia masked such a complex ego structure. Second, Frankie's fear of school (*school phobia*) is a common one but long disputed as to whether it is really a fear of school or of separation from the mother (Berecz, 1980). Third, Frankie reexperienced school phobic symptoms in his early twenties and was analyzed again by a leading analyst. This analyst's report helps us see the long-term outcome of inferred early psychodynamics and the possible effects of child analysis.

Because analytic theory is based on the behavior of patients during treatment and their responses to interpretations, Bornstein's report is reproduced at length, although still greatly abbreviated from the original.

> Frankie, a 5½-year-old boy of superior intelligence who was eager to learn, was brought into analysis because of a severe school phobia. . . .
>
> His sister Mary was born when Frankie was 3 years and 3 months old. Upon the mother's return from the hospital he displayed marked anxiety. He grew more ill-tempered toward his mother and his coolness toward her increased to such an extent that she became disturbed and made conscious efforts to win the child's affection. Despite her strong urge to devote herself to her little daughter, she left the baby in the care of a second nurse while she and Frankie's nurse were at the boy's disposal. . . .
>
> When she occasionally wanted to leave him, he became violent, panic-stricken, and clung to her desperately. But immediately after, when left alone with the nurse, his outburst subsided, and the tyrannical child became curiously submissive.

What had been mainly a problem at home began to hinder Frankie's development in other arenas:

> The child's anxiety reached its first peak when he was brought to nursery school at the age of 3 years and 9 months. . . . He went to school for only 2 days. Each time, he had to be taken home because of his wild attacks of fear and screaming, and nothing could make him return to school. A second attempt to send him to a different school was

made when he was 4½. Although the mother not only accompanied him to school, but actually stayed in the classroom with him, his anxiety did not subside. . . .

To motivate Frankie for analysis, the analyst encouraged a conscious conflict by allowing him to become positively attached to the school. At the analyst's request, Frankie's teacher then told him his mother could no longer stay but that there was a person—the analyst—who could help him withstand his mother's absence.

His dramatic play during his first session led straight into his conflicts, just as in adult analysis the first dream often leads into the core of the patient's neurosis. . . .

Frankie started his first session by building a hospital which was separated into a "lady department," a "baby department," and a "men's department." In the lobby, a lonely boy of 4 was seated all by himself, on a chair placed in an elevated position. The child's father was upstairs visiting "a lady" who, he informed us, when questioned, "is sick or maybe she's got a baby, maybe—I don't know, never mind." He made the point that newborn babies and mothers were separated in this hospital. Casting himself in the roles of a doctor and a nurse, he attended to the babies in a loving way, fed and cleaned them. However, toward the end of the play, a fire broke out. All the babies were burnt to death and the boy in the lobby was also in danger. He wanted to run home, but remembered that nobody would be there. Subsequently he joined the fire department, but it was not quite clear as to whether the firemen had started the fire or put it out. Frankie announced: "Ladies, the babies are dead; maybe we can save you!" Actually only those lady patients who had no babies were rescued by him. The one whom he several times—by a slip of the tongue—had addressed as "Mommy," however, was killed in the fire. . . .

This game was repeated for many weeks. Bornstein interpreted it as reflecting Frankie's anger at his mother for deserting him by going to the hospital and having another baby. But what were the consequences of Frankie's anger?

Frankie, who so thoroughly punished his mother by the withdrawal of his love, naturally lived in continual fear of retaliation. He could not stay at home or go out without his mother because he needed the presence of just that person against whom his aggressive impulses were directed. The presence of the ambivalently loved person prevents the phobic from being overwhelmed by his forbidden impulses and assures him that his aggressive intentions have not come true. . . .

What could be done about Frankie's unconscious ambivalence?

In order to bring about an *ego change*, we chose for interpretation from the different themes revealed in the child's play that element in which the patient represented his ego. It was evident to us that he himself was the lonely 4-year-old boy in the hospital game, although feelings of sadness and loneliness had not been mentioned by him in his play. On the contrary, in his game he demonstrated only the *defense* against loneliness and sadness. . . . .

We must remember that at the time of the analysis Frankie himself did not know anything of his sadness. . . . He had replaced it by his aggressive and tyrannical demands to which he later reacted with his phobic symptoms. Both aggression and anxiety were the end-product of an initial sadness and without recapturing that initial affect so that the patient was aware of it, no real ego change could be brought about. . . .

In order to introduce this emotion into the child's consciousness without arousing undue resistance, the loneliness of the little boy in his game became the subject of our analytic work for several weeks. The analyst expressed sympathy for the lonely child who is barred from his mother's sickroom and who is too little to understand why his father is admitted. Frankie responded to the analyst's sympathy with growing sadness, which could be discerned only from his facial expression. The analyst's sympathy made it possible for him to tolerate this affect.

Once he had been able to face his sadness, Frankie showed relatively little resistance when his specific situation was examined. We asked whether by any chance he was a child who had been left alone while his mother was in the hospital. . . . He turned to his mother with the question: "Was I alone, Mommy?" and before she could answer, he told about his father and his nurse's presence, adding that his nurse would "never, never leave him alone."

. . . ample material referring to abandonment corroborated the appropriateness of selecting his sadness as the first content of our interpretation. To him, being sent to school was an aggravating repetition of former separations: it happened just after his sister's nurse had left and his own nurse and mother had to share in the care of the baby. Thus, he lost not only his mother but also his nurse "who would never, never leave me alone." *This repetition of the traumatic experience of being abandoned* brought about the climax of his anxiety. . . .

By continually connecting his recent experiences and emotions to . . . his sadness and jealousy, the pathological tie to his nurse was loosened. . . . Only now his own jealousy appeared in its proper place, openly directed against his little sister. . . .

Now that his ambivalence had lessened, what happened to Frankie's symptom? Once the hostility toward his mother was diminished, his relationship to her seemed greatly improved, and his repressed love came to the fore. With this resolution the manifest school phobia subsided. He was able both to stay in school and to attend his analytic sessions without his mother's presence. . . .

Although Frankie's conquest of his aggressiveness toward his mother now made it possible for him to re-experience and to express his normal positive oedipal conflicts, he did so only in the analytic session. At home, the child's reaction to the father seemed to be emotionally neutral. He was, for instance, apparently unaffected by his father's frequent arrivals at and departures from home during war time. . . . Only in his dramatic play and fantasy material did he reveal his hostility toward men. Innumerable play episodes also betrayed Frankie's interest in procreation and his urge to know "what was going on" between his parents. . . .

In the most frequent of his play dramatizations, a father was absent and a mother was alone. Then an apparently friendly man, a butcher, a policeman, or a vegetable man (each impersonated by Frankie), came to dinner. The "friendly" visit always ended with an attack on the mother who was killed. The ending was always the same:

the visitors were taken by the police and sentenced to death by the judge, both of whom were again personified by Frankie.

What could be done about the emerging Oedipal themes? It was our next task to connect these fantasies with his actual experiences. This was achieved by confronting him with a paradox: his lack of emotion about his own father's coming and going, and the excitement the child showed in his play when visitors arrived. The mother had reported that prior to the outbreak of his neurosis, Frankie had shown signs of irritability toward visitors, especially toward his grandfather. . . .

In the course of discussing his irritation toward visitors, Frankie admitted that there was actually no reason for him to assume that visitors would attack his mother. Nevertheless, he felt that he had to guard her against threatening dangers, especially if she were out of his sight. "She might run away," he said. "She might be run over, or her car might break, or men might kill her in the subway." We finally understood that he was afraid that all of these dangers would lead to a second hospitalization, just as when his mother had had her baby.

The circle was closed. The danger which threatened the mother from relations with men would result in what was the gravest danger to him: the arrival of a new baby. He had to guard against a repetition of this traumatic experience. . . .

How were the Oedipal conflicts resolved? With the process of internalization of his conflicts the actually threatening nurse was replaced by imaginary objects, mainly wolves, who stood guard under his bed and kept him from getting up and investigating what might be happening in the parental bedroom. . . .

His configuration of the wolves contained as elements the punitive and protective parent figures as well as his own impulses. The wolves punish his intentions and prevent their fulfillment. Their symbolic role as superego was strikingly confirmed in a drawing which Frankie called the WOLVES' STATUE. It showed an oversized wolf (in human form) with outstretched arms, floating above Frankie in his bed, under which a number of smaller-sized wolves (also in human form) were engaged in mysterious activities, obviously of a sexual nature. . . . Frankie said: "It shows what the wolves hope for, what they will look like some day."

The dread of wolves which had haunted the child for weeks finally led to the analysis of his castration fear. In his stories and in his play, the mother's attackers who previously had been punished by death, now were punished by almost undisguised castration. In his pictures he endowed God with monstrously elongated arms and legs, only to cut off these limbs with scissors. Immediately after such operation he tried to undo this symbolic act of castration by drawing innumerable new arms and legs. . . . Mother's attackers were imprisoned and he, as a doctor, subjected the prisoners to operations which usually threw him into a state of exaltation . . . he exclaimed: "Those criminals, they have to be operated on. Off with their wee-wees. It has to come off!"

The material obtained from his play actions, in which men violently attack women, was interpreted to him in terms of his fantaseis about intercourse. The treatment made it possible for him to re-enter the oedipal phase, and the father then acquired that emotional importance in the child's reality which was due him in terms of the oedipal relationship. . . .

When Frankie's nurse left, his father took over regulating the home. Having previously induced his nurse to provide it, Frankie now sought passive sexual gratification from his father, such as soft patting on the buttocks. His father acquiesced until he recognized Frankie's seductive manner. Frankie then fantasied that passive gratification could be obtained by being a woman, but castration fears spurred him into masculine activities. Yet his passive cravings remained and aroused anxiety manifested in fears of kidnapping.

The essential feature of these new kidnapping fantasies was that they contained an open reference to genital or anal gratifications and that the *factor of passive locomotion was dominant*. As long as these fantasies were of moderate intensity, carrying two toy revolvers sufficed as a magic gesture to ward off anxiety. But whenever his repressed passive desires increased in intensity, the fantasy of being kidnapped lost its playful features, and he went into attacks of violent panic in which he was unable to distinguish between the world of fantasy and reality.

To avoid such states of panic which the intensity of his passive desires repeatedly brought about, Frankie was forced to evolve an entirely new attitude. He began to ignore reality. Signs of passivity were eradicated and were replaced by feelings of omnipotence. He gave his parents nonsensical orders and was greatly annoyed if they were not carried out; he struck his sister and parents for not obeying unspoken orders.

The analyst suggested that he was identifying himself with his tough radio heroes and criminals in order to ward off his passive desires. This interpretation had a negative therapeutic result. He reacted to it by strengthening this particular defense. His demands became even more fantastic, and from time to time his behavior resembled that of a megalomaniacal patient. He claimed that he was actually a king. . . . he called the exalted role he played in the universe, King Boo-Boo.

Frankie's behavior became so bad that it was questionable whether he could remain at home. It was necessary that he be told that his behavior had actually one aim: to be sent away. This would be the realization of the one thing he had dreaded most: to be separated from his parents. We should like to amplify on the session which followed, and which brought about the decisive change in Frankie's attitude.

The analyst found him in the waiting room, the paper basket on his head, hilariously throwing books and blocks at his mother. . . . When alone with him, she asked him what he *really* thought the effect of his actions would be. She conceded that he acted as if he were a great king and as if he expected complete submission from his environment. But she expressed her doubts that he himself really believed in the truth of these ideas. She called to his attention the fact that his behavior would not have the desired effect and that no matter what he did, nobody would accept him as a superman or as King Boo-Boo. Frankie replied quickly: "Oh, they will find out some day, and they will do what I want!"

Referring to several incidents during the analytic sessions in which he had acted out his King Boo-Boo ideas, she told him that even her positive relationship to him was influenced by his "actions." "Even before you enter my office, I can't help thinking: 'For goodness sake, what will Frankie try to do today; what is he going to break and to destroy today?' " He interrupted quickly: "Oh, you shouldn't care. You get paid for that, even more than it costs."

He was then asked whether he knew what had brought about this change in his behavior; after all, there had been a time when he had cared quite a bit for people, and when he had wanted to be with his mother all the time. Frankie replied triumphantly: "So that's fine; now I am cured of my fears, and I don't want to be with Mommy."

The analyst did not agree with him as to his being cured. She thought that he was still very much afraid, just as scared as he was at the time when he did not want to come to his session because he believed the analyst was a kidnapper. Only now he tried to hide his fear even from himself . . . now she was seriously worried about his behavior. Therefore, she must show him that his King Boo-Boo behavior would end in something of which she had always thought he was terribly afraid. . . .

The analyst told him she was compelled to assume that he wanted to create a situation where his being sent away was the only possible outcome. . . .

The child listened calmly, although this was quite unusual in this period of unmanageable wildness. Eventually he asked seriously: "Where can you send me?" . . .

Thereupon the analyst told him about hospitals which specialized in treating children whose sickness led them to behave in unacceptable ways. He interrupted: "But I'm not sick; I have no temperature." The analyst stated that people who seriously believed that the world was divided into camps "of an almighty king and the rest slaves" are seriously ill, even without a temperature and belong in special hospitals. . . . Suddenly realizing that the analyst referred to mental illness, he became quite frightened and asked, "Do you think I'm crazy? Do you think I belong in a crazy house?"

Without waiting for an answer, he wanted to know in detail how those hospitals were run, how children were kept there, whether they were visited by their parents, what kind of toys they had, whether they were permitted to have knives and blocks and whether they were analyzed there. Our answers obviously disappointed him; they did not fit into his picture of exciting fights between attendants and patients and between kidnappers and the kidnapped.

The psychodynamics of this analytic session brought about a decisive therapeutic gain which may be explained as follows:

1) The beginning of the analytic session permitted Frankie to re-experience and to act out the full grandeur of his world of fantasy. He had an opportunity to demonstrate his narcissistic omnipotence, his disdain for reality and his belief in the inferiority and weakness of the analyst.

2) The next analytic step was a thrust into his unconscious, and a demonstration that his unconscious aim was to enforce a separation from home. This was a contradiction of his omnipotence which even the almighty King Boo-Boo could not overlook.

3) He readily picked up the suggestion about enforcing a separation and revealed his unconscious desire by the great interest he showed in the place to which he would be sent. By asking one question after another, he began to consider the reality of what would happen if his unconscious desires were really fulfilled. . . . The ego discovered that fulfillment of these unconscious desires was drab and monotonous if carried out in reality. . . .

Only then did Frankie start to doubt the wisdom of carrying his King Boo-Boo fantasies into reality. . . .

Toward the end of the analysis, Frankie recognized that his megalomaniacal behavior and fantasies were defenses against suffering and death, as well as against passive strivings. Facing the demand that he give up fantasies of King Boo-Boo's immortality, he resorted again to phobic mechanisms, but restricted them to more realistic proportions. Bornstein reviewed the long path to this achievement as follows:

> When Frankie entered his analysis, he was completely enslaved by his symptoms. His preoccupation with his mother and with the need for assurance that he could obtain gratification without endangering his existence, resulted in a constriction of his ego. He had not accepted any external ideals and there were hardly any indications of internal prohibitions. These are the signs of a severe lag in the formation of a superego.
>
> During his oedipal phase, his fears were displaced from real objects such as his mother, his nurse, and his father, to imaginary objects and situations. . . .
>
> Considering what had caused the lag in superego formation, we must refer to two factors. One is that his environment did not provide him with a clear-cut frame of reference as to objects of identification. For example, his mother acted like a child in relation to the nurse, and it was the nurse who exercised authority. Yet he sensed that the nurse took a secondary position whenever his father made his sporadic . . . appearances during wartime. . . . The second and more important factor was that this nurse combined her prohibitions with libidinal gratifications. . . . [I]nstead of forming the basis of a superego, these sexualized prohibitions laid the foundation for a masochistic perversion. . . .
>
> Once he could give up acting out his King Boo-Boo fantasies, he could transfer his omnipotence to others who represented his ego-ideals. He could accept his father as a strong and enviable figure without becoming passively dependent on him. . . .
>
> A prognosis in child analysis is not easy. We are by no means sure that we have forestalled a later recurrence of Frankie's neurosis. But . . . when he could face danger without resorting to pathological anxiety or belief in magic and omnipotence—then we knew that the secondary process had won a victory over the primary process. And this we thought, was the utmost a boy of 8½ can achieve—even with the help of child analysis.

Frankie's Second Analysis. In his early twenties and facing an especially competitive part of his education, Frankie experienced symptoms which led him to seek analysis again. We quote from an unpublished report summarized elsewhere by Ritvo (1966):

> Although his anxiety was fairly well controlled with the aid of the obsessive and compulsive character traits which he developed, he did suffer several attacks of neurotic anxiety during adolescence and in the several years immediately preceding his return to analysis. These outbreaks were accompanied by obsessional symptom formation, and a compulsion to touch things three times and to speak his words in groups of three syllables. If he did not do this the "sanction" would be a poor grade on an examination. The formation of symptoms coincided with the intensification of the old passive

feminine strivings which had required pathological defenses in childhood. In early adolescence they were stirred by homosexual play with peers and in later adolescence by the covert homosexual advances of an older man. Although the patient succeeded in warding off these temptations, it was at the cost of the outbreak of anxiety and symptoms. . . .

How did this young man . . . appear to the world he lived in outside the analysis? His fellow students would probably not be aware of his acute discomfiture and self-consciousness in ordinary social situations which were related to his easily feeling slighted, rebuffed or rejected and to his constant competitive comparison with his fellows. . . . His professors would have found him sometimes active in discussions, sometimes detached, not realizing that this depended on whether he thought the professor had a high regard for him or whether he thought he was out of favor and held in low esteem. He elected courses largely on the basis of whether he thought the professor would like him or would be antagonistic and inclined to attack, punish or harm him. Girls he dated probably found him serious most of the time though capable of a light-hearted playfulness. However, if a girl he had been dating was not in at midnight or two o'clock in the morning to answer his telephone call he could immediately become the Frankie of old who had been so vengeful . . .

He became willful and arbitrary, easily aroused to a petulant and angry jealousy and demanding that his intellectual superiority be recognized. . . .

With his wife . . . he was patient and attentive, and admiring of her endowments and attainments. What may have appeared to the outside as simple devotion could be seen in the transference as a repetition of the situation in childhood when he took revenge on his mother (analyst) by refusing her care and attention and turned to his nurse (wife) instead. In a similar fashion he was solicitous of his wife's jealousy of his exclusive relationship with me in the analysis and warned me repeatedly that he might have to leave me and rebuff my ministrations as he had his mother's, if his wife suffered because of her jealousy. Besides this repetition from childhood, the relationship with his wife also reversed the childhood situation and enabled him to control actively what he had formerly experienced passively. . . . The passive libidinal strivings toward the object which had been so intense in childhood and had been gratified in the toileting experiences with his nurse, remained in his deep-rooted preference for passive manipulation rather than exercising the active role in intercourse, a preference which was reflected in a periodic disturbance of his potency.

Why did Frankie seek analysis again?

When he returned to analysis, the immediate conflict situation was the brilliant conclusion of one phase of his preparation for a career and the decision to start on another more definitive phase. . . . The intense competitiveness of the school situation, the pending irrevocable commitment to a career with its measurement of achievement which might be less than he considered ideal and might tarnish his hitherto bright record, all contributed to the outbreak of anxiety with the feeling of being trapped and wanting to get out. . . .

How did his current problems relate to the earlier ones?

It was the same anxious feeling of being trapped which at the age of five had made it difficult for him to remain in school and had led to his entering analysis. Thus, after a gap of mroe than 15 years one of the immediate reasons for returning to analysis was his difficulty in remaining in school without the help of analysis, certainly a striking demonstration of the tendency of unconscious mental phenomena to repeat themselves quite faithfully.

Equally disturbing at the time of his return were his obsessive doubts about the functioning of his mind. These doubts had an unmistakable similarity to his earlier concern about masturbation and the intactness of his genital. . . .

The same conflicts for which he sought a solution by the formation of phobic symptoms as a child in the phallic-oedipal phase he later tried to cope with by the obsessive doubting about his mind. The fear of erections, the masturbation conflict, the death wishes of the oedipal conflict, the danger of castration were all included in the manifold forms of the preoccupation with the functioning of his mind. . . .

As an adult there were many references in dreams to his unconscious wish for anal and oral homosexual gratifications. . . . One acceptable derivative form of gratification assumed by his oral and anal impulses was enjoying the steady and sure supply of money from his father and anticipating the prospect of eventually having his father's assets as his own. He hungrily desired the respect of his father and other men, but feared there was nothing behind his facade of intelligence and ability for his father and other men to respect. He felt that if he got poor grades, which meant a low evaluation, he would "slip back into a sea of defecation." He linked his revulsion of dirtiness and defecation with a fear of being poor. In early adolescence when he had to defend himself against the homosexual temptations offered by his peers he could not eat in the home of his poor friend because he felt the food was cheap and "defecation-covered". . . . By contrast, the intellectual activities which he idealized were thought of as a type of . . . sterilization. It was a way of keeping things clean and not dirtying them with mushy, soft, fecal emotions. . . .

Whereas the [childhood] fears had placed the focus on what the forces in the outside world might do to him, the doubts [in adulthood] shifted the focus to what he had in him to cope with the dangers outside. . . .

His more highly developed reality-testing capacities could no longer permit his unreasonable fears nor his magic omnipotence (King Boo-Boo) to persist. At the same time his advancing capacity for abstract and logical thinking enabled him to erect a system of thought operations and obsessive doubting, so that the neurotic conflict continued in a form which could not be objectively tested and therefore could pass the scrutiny of the more mature ego. . . .

After 2½ years, Frankie broke off the second analysis because he was leaving the vicinity. The analyst considered him much improved, but did not regard the analysis as complete. Frankie's professional work was successful, but he still felt competitive with his sister and was preoccupied with thoughts of dying. Six years later he again entered analysis with another analyst. No report of this analysis is available, but the Bornstein and Ritvo reports provide what may be a unique record of analysis at two very different developmental stages. They illustrate the process of analysis, the kinds of observations employed by analysts, the interpretations made, and the analytic theory of phobic neuroses in children. We will consider the validity of such interpretations and the efficacy of treatment later.

Obsessive-Compulsive Neuroses

The psychoanalytic *Glossary* defines obsessive-compulsive neurosis as:

> . . . A type of psychoneurosis . . . characterized by obsessional thoughts and compulsive acts. In addition, rumination, doubting and irrational fears are often present. All of these are accompanied by morbid anxiety when the intruding thoughts or repetitive acts are prohibited or otherwise interfered with.
>
> The clinical picture of obsessional neurosis results from both a libidinal regression to the *anal-sadistic phase,* (usually because of severe conflict during the *oedipal phase*) and the ego's defensive activities which . . . include the mechanisms of *isolation, reaction formation,* and *undoing.* Other major characteristics underlying the symptomatology are *ambivalence,* a regression to magical thinking, and indications of rigid and destructive *superego* functioning. The *conflicts* usually involved in this neurosis are closer to those of the prephallic phase of *psycho-sexual development* than to those of the phallic-oedipal period. (Moore & Fine, 1968, p. 65)

The assumption that obsessive-compulsive defenses are based in the anal phase spawned the concept of *anal* or *compulsive character,* a person excessively orderly, obstinate, parsimonious, and concerned with anal functions. Obsessive-compulsive neurosis is not equated with compulsive personality, however, because the anal fixations ascribed to the neurosis are, like those of other neuroses, hypothesized to be *rearoused* by *regression* resulting from unconscious conflicts. Compulsive character traits, by contrast, represent successful defenses (Nagera, 1976). An obsessive-compulsive neurotic may thus be a candidate for analysis while a compulsive personality may not. Despite their excessive concern for cleanliness, order, and conformity, children with compulsive personalities often adapt well and exhibit a lively pseudomaturity, although severe stress intensifies their obsessive-compulsive defenses.

In analyzing Frankie, Ritvo noted that obsessive-compulsive defenses replaced Frankie's phobic defenses as he grew older. The association of phobias with obsessions and compulsions is a common theme in analytic literature, and phobias, obsessions, and compulsions have been found together in empirically derived syndromes of childhood behavioral problems (Achenbach, 1966; Achenbach & Edelbrock, 1979).

Despite frequent references to obsessive-compulsive defenses, the analytic literature offers few detailed reports of these neuroses in children. Because such data were so scarce, Judd (1965) surveyed the clinic records of 405 disturbed children to see how many were obsessive-compulsive. He found 8.4 percent with these symptoms. Eliminating cases in which obsessive-compulsive symptoms were not the most prominent evidence of pathology or were not severe left only 1.2 percent. Twenty-five of the 29 eliminated cases were schizophrenic, while the other four were brain damaged, corroborating an often noted association of obsessive-compulsive symptoms with these disorders. In a sample of 600 disturbed children without evidence of organic pathology, Achenbach (1966) found that 4.7 percent of the boys and 4 percent of the girls manifested a syndrome of obsessions, compulsions, and phobias derived empirically by factor analysis. Other studies have also found low rates of obsessive-compulsive disorders in children and adolescents (Hollingsworth, Tanguay, Grossman, & Pabst, 1980). In both the Judd and Achenbach studies, the obsessive-compulsives averaged considerably higher in IQ than other disturbed children.

The following case illustrates obsessive-compulsive symptoms in a boy diagnosed neurotic by his therapist and schizophrenic by two others. His therapist concluded that her diagnosis was borne out, but she concedes that a break from reality might have occurred without therapy.

> A. S. came to treatment . . . at the age of 9⅓ years, was treated for 2½ years and has made a fairly good adjustment, his progress being followed through his mother's therapist. Diagnosis: *severe obsessive-compulsive neurosis,* although two psychologic tests done at one-year intervals by two independent psychologists formulated a diagnosis of *schizophrenia. . . .*
>
> Complaint, as formulated by the mother at the time of referral, was that "his imagination makes up talks. At school he is said to be a genius, yet his accomplishments fall short of his intelligence. He laughs, giggles. He masturbates extensively, stays in the bathroom a long time, says he does magical things there. He has many compulsions, must square things. Has obsessive thoughts regarding his parents' death."
>
> The father, in his mid-forties, is . . . a passive, ineffectual individual, a poor provider—a schizoid person who "went through several crises, one religious." He is tense and moody.
>
> The mother, in her late thirties, . . . has a severe cleanliness compulsion and, for instance, would sterilize the nursing bottles many times in succession, in the belief that at some point she might have contaminated her hands. As a result of her "germ" phobia, she kept the child from human contacts for several years. She suffered a depression lasting five or six weeks after the birth of the child. She is overanxious and, for instance, said: "It's an abnormal thing with me that I must know every minute where he is."
>
> When seen, the patient was overactive, excitable. He spoke under great pressure, with some incoherence. This was, however, due in large extent to the rush of ideas, and clarification could be obtained. There was a wealth of fantasies regarding his phobias,

some of which were expressed in bizarre manner; for instance, he related his nightmares about bugs: "I found some kind of seeds, buried them, a plant grew and some big giant bugs came out at the ends." . . . his bug phobia and his obsession regarding bugs were such that "I was almost a bug myself." There were similar fantasies about a crocodile in his cellar. Once he had actually pushed his parents on the street, then fantasied them "lying still, dead on the street." However vivid were these fantasies, he knew them to be fantasies; while he was troubled by them, he felt that he got lost in these fantasies because of his intense anxiety. He was much troubled by his constant indecision . . . owing to obsessive thoughts he had about himself, his parents and his friends. "How can I make a decision? I'm never sure. . . ." Many compulsive acts and prayers were carried out in a partly conscious attempt to relieve his guilt: guilt regarding masturbation, guilt regarding death wishes toward the parents. (Despert, 1955, pp. 245−46)

This boy's problems were serious by any criteria. But is the analytic theory of neurosis the only way to explain them? His parents' behavior would have caused trouble for any child. His mother's obsessive-compulsive behavior was likely to shape his behavior directly without regression to the anal-sadistic phase. On the other hand, the severity of the parents' disturbance also raises the possibility of a genetic influence like those evident in some of the severe disorders described in Chapter 12. The interpretation of obsessive-compulsive symptoms in terms of the analytic model may thus help us understand the feelings accompanying certain behavior without necessarily telling us what *causes* the problems or how to alleviate them.

Hysterical Neuroses

The psychoanalytic *Glossary* ascribes both conversion symptoms and dissociative states to a single type of hysterical neurosis:

characterized clinically by 1) conversion symptoms and 2) an apparent affective indifference to the disturbance. . . . Occasionally, either separately or together with the foregoing, there are episodic states or major "hysterical spells," characterized by the *dissociation* of mental functions (e.g., double or multiple personalities, fugue states, somnambulism, major *amnesias,* etc.).

Conversion symptoms are physical manifestations not caused by or related to anatomical or physiological pathology. Among these are symptoms derived from motor, sensory or visceral reactions—anesthesias, pains, paralyses, tremors, deafness, blindness, vomiting, hiccoughing, etc. However, hysterical patients are often convinced their symptoms are due to objective physical disease, although their affective reactions are inappropriate to such conviction.

These syndromes are unique in every individual, and analysis demonstrates that they are historically determined by specific repressed experiences in the individual's past. They represent an expression in "body language" of specific unconscious *fantasies,* developing as a compromise in the conflict between an instinctual wish which has given rise to *anxiety* and the defense against that wish. . . .

Hysterical symptoms occur when there is difficulty at the level of resolution of the *oedipal conflict*. Here the wish for the incestuous love object represents the chief danger. The major defenses used are *repression* and *regression,* leading to dissociated bodily and affective symptomatology that acts as a distorted substitute and compromise for the original infantile sexual gratification. The choice of *symptom* (including affected organ or body zone) is predominantly based on the content of the unconscious fantasy and the ability of the organ to symbolize the unconscious forces involved. These symptoms are thus, par excellence, an example of the "return of the repressed," both the instinctual wish and the defense against it are re-enacted in the symptom . . . (Moore & Fine, 1968, p. 49)

Like the distinction between obsessive-compulsive neurosis and compulsive personality, a distinction is made between hysterical *neurosis* and hysterical *character* or *personality*. The distinction assumes that hysterical neurosis involves regression to earlier conflicts and defenses, whereas hysterical personality is a persistent adaptive style that may or may not lead to symptoms, depending on the stresses encountered.

Hysterical personalities are reported more often among females than males. They are overdramatic, flamboyant, suggestible, coy, seductive, and manipulative in a passive-aggressive way. Despite a veneer of social poise, most are overly dependent on their environments for maintaining their identities. Although they appear to invite heterosexual relationships, they repress sexual impulses and have trouble with sexual relationships (Group for the Advancement of Psychiatry, 1966). Children with hysterical personalities are described as

emotionally labile, overly dramatic, seductive, and generally naive. They are great seekers of attention, often in positive ways, and they love to be on stage. At the same time, they are seemingly unaware that their actions are drawing attention to themselves. After a flirtatious performance, they seem to ask: 'Why is everyone looking at me?' (Finch & Green, 1979, p. 240)

Since the days of Charcot and Freud, dramatic hysterical symptoms seem to have declined, perhaps because more people know that emotions can produce unusual physical symptoms. This may have undermined the effectiveness of dramatic symptoms as solutions to neurotic conflicts. Changes in social mores may also have reduced conflicts over sexual impulses. However, dramatic hysterical symptoms are still sometimes seen in children. Proctor (1958, 1967), for example, found that 13 percent of patients surveyed in a Southern child psychiatry unit met analytic criteria for conversion or dissociative hysteria. Many exhibited dramatic symptoms like those of Freud's day. These included uncontrollable pelvic thrusts, grotesque giant steps, and a dissociative state in which a 12-year-old boy ran about the ward clutching his testicles while screaming in terror. Another boy hid under a bed in fear of his hallucination of a headless man.

Problems arose in differentiating between neurosis and psychosis, but Proctor maintained that hysteria was firmly diagnosed in all his cases. He attributed the abundance of dramatic hysterical symptoms to the children's bible-belt backgrounds: Many were caught in fierce conflicts between repressive religious mores and impulses sparked by seductive and irresponsible adults.

Applying uniform criteria for conversion reactions to children at three other treatment centers, Rae (1977) found rates ranging from 5 to 16 percent. Nearly half had undramatic symptoms such as headaches and abdominal pains that might also be diagnosed as psychophysiological reactions instead of conversion reactions. The rate of undramatic conversion symptoms has likewise been found higher in adults than expected from the classical stereotypes (Watson & Buranen, 1979).

In a study of disturbed children hospitalized in St. Louis, Robins and O'Neal (1953) found that 8.3 percent showed hysterical symptoms. When 37 were followed up at an average of nine years later, 5 (all female) were diagnosed as clear-cut hysterical neurotics; 10 had anxiety neuroses; 4 had other psychiatric or physical afflictions; 12 had symptoms that could not be adequately diagnosed; and 6 were completely well. From the patients' life-history data, Robins and O'Neal concluded that the onset of hysteria was unusual before the age of 9 and rare before 5, and that boys diagnosed hysterical in childhood were not hysterics in later life, but girls more often were.

The onset of dramatic hysterical symptoms is often quite sudden. Such hysterics were the chief subject of Freud's early work and are still considered to be among the best candidates for analytic treatment. When timed well, interpretation of the repressed impulses and defenses is thought to relieve dramatic symptoms, although hypnosis, tranquilizers, and environmental manipulations may also relieve symptoms (Proctor, 1967). Dramatic hysterical symptoms sometimes vanish as quickly as they come, but vague physical complaints often persist for years (Robins & O'Neal, 1953). Because hysterical symptoms in children are occasionally associated with real or possible organic disorders, extensive medical tests to find an organic etiology may inadvertently reinforce the symptoms (Dubowitz & Hersov, 1976).

Here is an example of a classical hysterical reaction in an adolescent:

> Over a two-week period prior to her hospital admission, a robust and vigorously active 14-year-old adolescent had been subject to epileptic-like seizures. Ward observations on these "spells" demonstrated many atypical phenomena not in keeping with a . . . cerebral disorder. During this same period of time she became disinterested in food, complaining of nausea.
>
> Heralding her seizures she experienced a pervading fear of death. She would simultaneously complain of . . . a throbbing sensation involving the whole skin surface [beneath the waist] with a noticeable exception of the genital area. During the course of her seizure the motor phenomena would often be goal-directed; she would involve the attendant, who was close by for protective purposes, in a combative struggle and exclaim "I will break your horns off, you bull."

During her lucid intervals when visited on the ward, she would make an unsuccessfully awkward attempt to cover herself with bed sheets on the approach of the examiner. Quite invariably these attempts at modesty would instead result in a consistent display of parts of her body including the genital region. This sequence represented a clear demonstration of her ambivalent attitudes toward the male—alternately self-protecting and inviting.

The parents described their daughter as a fearless, undaunted, and challenging tom-boy who had "not known fear" until her current illness. She had always been highly contemptuous and disparaging of boys, refusing to associate with them. At the same time her crude and rough demeanor reflected a masculine identification; this largely stemmed from an outspoken envy, the basis of which she listed in outlining their numerous advantages within her subcultural group.

Highly volatile fuel was added to the fire by her parents who were unusually frank in informing their daughter of their deep disappointment when they learned of her sex at birth. Repeated jokes which revolved around the preferential status of boys kept her burning envy stoked.

Psychodynamic Impression: Within the three weeks preceding the onset of her illness, three events seemed psychologically significant in determining her current emotional upheaval:

a. Onset of menarche which served as a reality confirmation of her no longer deniable femininity.
b. She was being given classes on sex education within her parochial school wherein the disastrous consequences of sexuality were underlined.
c. Within the neighborhood a rape-murder incident had been highly publicized and was repetitiously discussed by the mother with a good deal of detail.

Her spell was a dramatization of a sexual assault including the struggle with the assailant. The triple series of events accentuated her feminine role and the dangers inherent therein. Thus her heretofore masculine identification . . . ceased to be able to serve its defensive purposes. The projection of her own destructive and damaging intents (stemming largely from envy of men) onto the male heightened his dangerous qualities for the girl. (Starr, 1953, p. 225)

RESEARCH ON PSYCHOANALYTIC VIEWS OF NEUROTIC DISORDERS

In Chapter 5, we distinguished between two stages in scientific activity. One is the *context of discovery* wherein ideas are generated in whatever subjective, intuitive, creative, or accidental way we happen to think. The second is the *context of confirmation.* To be confirmed, ideas must be communicable to others and testable. When ideas reach this stage, they can be evaluated through experiments or other systematic observation. The more consistently the ideas are corroborated, the more confidence they command. How have psychoanalytic ideas fared?

Their literature is vast, their theory ambitious, and the impact of their views is great. Yet analysts have seldom moved their ideas into the context of confirmation, despite the urging of some such as Kenneth Mark Colby (1958):

we need to make systematic observations of specific phenomena rather than try haphazardly to range over the entirety of complex individual case histories. Most of all, we need systematic experiments designed to ask and answer specific questions.

The lack of controlled experiment in which essential variables are manipulated or held constant constitutes the greatest weakness of psychoanalysis as a science. We cannot advance through thought only, or through waiting to observe nature's experiments. We must actively try to test out which hypotheses fit the empirical facts. For one reason or another . . . psychoanalysts shy away from testing hypotheses. They seem to believe that if a plausible hypothesis can be formulated, it deserves to be considered an explanatory law or principle. They seldom take the next step of testing out which among many plausible hypotheses can be confirmed or disconfirmed.

Finally, besides systematic observations and systematic experiments, we need a careful, logical re-evaluation of our theory construction . . . there exist many logical contradictions and incorrect deductions which should be weeded out. (pp. 9−10)

Why haven't more analysts tested their ideas? Perhaps because, once Freud's work gained a fair hearing, the truth of his most basic discoveries seemed so evident that further research seemed superfluous. Most mental health workers now agree with Freud's assumptions on:

1. Psychological determinism—thoughts and behavior are determined by antecedent events (although there is disagreement about the causal mechanisms).
2. The existence of unconscious mental processes and motives (although not everyone grants as much weight as Freud to the "dynamic" unconscious comprising repressed impulses).
3. The reality of childhood sexuality—prepubertal children have intense sexual curiosity and fantasies, become sexually aroused, and direct sexual desires toward other people, including their parents.

A second possible factor may be Freud's unique role. He was the originator of the basic concepts, inventor of the treatment, leader of the "psychoanalytic movement," and chief revisionist of the theory. Many have written on psychoanalysis, but he remains the authority to whose writings others defer. Most proposed innovations are buttressed with what Freud said or might have said if he had written more about a particular topic. Why such reliance on the words of a long-dead pioneer of the context of discovery? In addressing newly graduated analysts, Colby (1958) says:

It is easy enough to tell young analysts to carry out systematic observation, experiment, and theory reconstruction. Why wouldn't they do so anyway without this tiresome exhortation? In part, because they are afraid. Unfortunately in psychoanalysis there exists an unfavorable atmosphere for change. Physicists are exhilarated by experiments leading to new data and overjoyed when hitherto accepted laws are proved inadequate. . . . But practitioners in psychoanalysis do not always welcome such efforts, and they can make it hard for the young psychoanalyst interested in them. They consider ability in psychoanalysis to be proportionate to familiarity with Freud's writings and skill to consist of adroitness in moving the same old conceptual furniture to new positions in the same old conceptual house. An idea is measured in terms of whether Freud thought of it (legitimate) or whether he didn't (unwarranted). Priority in psychoanalysis is often not a matter of who thought of what first but who knows when Freud thought of it first. (pp. 10−11)

A third factor may be Freud's own attitude toward research, its influence on the analysts he trained, and the continuing transmission of this influence through analytic training programs, societies, and journals. Freud (1940) insisted that the teachings of psychoanalysis could be judged only by those who had repeated its "incalculable number of observations . . . upon himself or upon others (p. 9)." Training is indeed needed to perform psychoanalysis, but there has been a tendency to view analytic training as not only necessary but also *sufficient* to guarantee the validity of observations and hypotheses. As a result, analysts seldom translate personal hunches into testable form.

As Bernard Riess (1972), an analytically oriented psychologist, points out, child analysis has been tested in the context of confirmation even less than adult analysis. However, he defends the lack of research as follows:

> *Research* requires an attitude which in some respects is antagonistic to a fundamental assumption of all analytic therapy, namely, that the therapist maintain an interested, empathic, but nonjudgmental stance vis-a-vis his patient. The therapist-analyst is constantly *searching,* but his interests are not in *re*-searching with his patient, for he is convinced that no situation can be replicated on the same subject and that no two subjects can be adequately matched. Thus the sacred elements of "control" and "repeatability" seem to be beyond the realm of possibility.
> . . . the analyst resists the intrusion of experimentally introduced variables into the treatment process because of concern for the relationship with the patient and for the goal of treatment, which is the increased efficiency of the patient. (pp. 1178−79)

Analysts must certainly assume an attitude of watchful waiting for connections to appear among their patients' free associations and must attend also to their own associations as an intuitive guide to treatment. This process is akin to the search or discovery processes in other fields. Yet it does not preclude testing the hypotheses thus generated.

What about controlled follow-ups to assess the effects of analysis? Riess (1972) objects that such studies present an almost insoluble problem: that of differentiating changes due to maturation from those due to therapy. It is indeed hard to test treatment effects, but maturational change is no more a problem in evaluating analysis than any other treatment, be it nondirective, behavioral, or organic. Control groups receiving no treatment or other treatments enable us to compare changes in them with changes in people receiving a particular treatment, even though all groups may be simultaneously maturing as well.

Despite analysts' failure to move many of their ideas from the context of discovery to the context of confirmation, analytic theory and practice have inspired considerable research. In considering child psychopathology, we need to ask two basic questions of this research: (1) Are what analytic theory defines as neurotic disorders *caused* as the theory implies? (2) Does analytic treatment *relieve* or *cure* such disorders? These are separate questions, because the theory of causation could be correct but the treatment ineffective; or the theory could be wrong but the treatment could work for reasons other than those implied by the theory.

RESEARCH ON PSYCHOANALYTIC VIEWS OF THE CAUSES OF NEUROSIS

Levels of Psychoanalytic Doctrine

Because various conceptual levels are freely intermingled in analytic literature, Robert Waelder (1962), a leading analytic theoretician, tried to clarify them by defining several levels of analytic doctrine. The most fundamental is the *level of observation,* comprising the firsthand observational data analysts obtain from their patients. Such data consist of what patients say and do and how they say and do them.

Second is the *level of clinical interpretation.* This refers to analysts' interpretations of the connections among their observations, that is, their hypotheses about the particular meanings underlying patients' behavior.

Waelder's third level, the *level of clinical generalizations,* refers to "statements regarding a particular type, e.g., a sex, an age group, a psychopathological symptom, a mental or emotional disease, a character type, the impact of a particular family constellation, or of any particular experience, and the like" (p. 620). Such generalizations abound in the analytic literature; many have become standard clinical lore. An example is that the typical mother of an enuretic boy has "depreciatory attitudes toward males that make her demand that her son be both ineffective and rebellious" (Pierce, 1967, p. 1381).

The fourth level is the *level of clinical theory,* comprised of "theoretical concepts which are either implicit in the (clinical) interpretations or to which the interpretations may lead, such as repression, defense, return of the repressed, regression, etc." (p. 620).

Two further levels—which Waelder considers relatively abstract and unimportant for the clinical concepts—are the *level of metapsychology,* including such constructs as cathexis and psychic energy, and the *level of Freud's philosophy.* Freud's personal philosophy need not concern research on neurosis, but his metapsychological constructs are often invoked to explain observations. He defined psychosexual stages, for example, in terms of the distribution of psychic energy, which is a key metapsychological construct. He also defined neuroses in terms of the distribution of psychic energy. However, psychic energy has not been equated with any physical energy (Rapaport, 1959). Apparently destined to remain a metaphor, it has never been objectively defined or measured. Neither have metapsychological constructs like cathexis, id, ego, and superego, although measures of "ego strength" (a general synonym for personality strength) appear on personality tests such as the Minnesota Multiphasic Personality Inventory.

Since Freud's philosophy and metapsychology are probably not testable, we will concentrate on research related to the other levels distinguished by Waelder.

Level of Observation. Although behavior during analytic treatment is the primary data base on which analytic thinking rests, this behavior is seldom recorded. Few therapists even make extensive notes during treatment. This is understandable if note-taking hinders the therapist-patient relationship and the therapist's thinking. But perception and memory are vulnerable to distortion. Do therapists retain accurate mental records of their own and their patients' behavior? Freud stressed how amazing analysts' memories can become for behavior related to themes considered significant in patients' associations. Yet important behavior may well be lost or distorted. We therefore need empirical verification for the observations used to support analytic interpretations, generalizations, and theory.

Patient and analyst behaviors have occasionally been filmed or taped for research purposes. Haggard, Hiken, and Isaacs (1965), for example, studied the effects of filming on three analysts and adult patients. An analyst's extensive notes on another case served as a rough control for comparison with the filmed cases. The therapists in the filmed cases also detailed their own observations and reactions.

From their data and a review of other studies, Haggard, Hiken, and Isaacs drew two major conclusions: First, the research conditions did not disrupt essential therapy processes such as the verbalization of free associations, patients' transference onto the analyst of their feelings toward parents, working-through of intimate emotional conflicts, and personal growth. Second, the research disturbed the analysts more than their patients, but experience eventually reduced most analysts' anxiety about it. Haggard, Hiken, and Isaacs also reported an unpublished study by H. Bolgar in which tapes showed numerous omissions and reorganizations occurring in therapists' summaries, including reversals of therapist-patient sequences.

Level of Clinical Interpretation. Even if patients' behavior is accurately observed, what happens when the observations are transformed into analytic interpretations? The difficulties of moving from observation to interpretation are shown by Wolpe and Rachman's (1960) textual analysis of Freud's (1909) 145-page report of Little Hans.

Wolpe and Rachman found that Freud imputed many behaviors and ideas to Hans that the report itself shows originated with Freud or Hans's father. Right after

Hans become phobic, for example, Freud told Hans's father "that he should tell the boy that all this nonsense about horses was a piece of nonsense and nothing more. The truth was, his father was to say, that he (Hans) was very fond of his mother and wanted to be taken into her bed. The reason he was afraid of horses now was that he had taken so much interest in their widdlers (Freud, 1909, p. 28)."

A second example concerns Freud's contention that, for Hans, a biting white horse symbolized a widdler. Hans's father had repeatedly told him horses don't bite, but Hans told of hearing a friend's father warn her away from a particular white horse lest it bite. Hans's father replied, "I say, it strikes me it isn't a horse you mean, but a widdler, that one mustn't put one's hand to." Hans: "But a widdler doesn't bite." Father: "Perhaps it does, though." Hans then "went on eagerly to try to prove . . . that it really was a white horse." The next day, Hans replied to a remark of his father by saying that his phobia was "so bad because I still put my hand to my widdler every night (Freud, 1909, p. 30)." In a third example, when Hans feared large animals at the zoo, his father said: "Do you know why you're afraid of big animals? Big animals have big widdlers and you're really afraid of big widdlers (Freud, 1909, p. 33)." Hans denied this.

We will never know exactly what Hans really did nor whether Freud's interpretations were correct. But, subsequent studies have shown disagreement among analysts' interpretations of patients' behavior. Seitz (1966), for example, reports that he and other analysts spent three years interpreting observations noted in the course of treatment. The analysts often met to compare their interpretations and improve the reliability of their judgments. Although he reported no reliability figures, Seitz concluded that the results were "strongly negative" in terms of consensus of interpretation.

In a study reporting reliabilities, two graduates of the same analytic institute rated transcripts of Haggard et al.'s (1965) recordings of adult patients' reactions during five-minute periods after important interpretations and other interventions by therapists (Garduk & Haggard, 1972). The ratings were of variables considered crucial in analysis. Table 9-3 lists the variables and the correlations between the ratings. As the table shows, the analysts' agreement did not exceed chance for such key variables as anxiety and blocking of associations, nor did the correlations between their ratings exceed .52 for any of the variables.

Table 9-3 also shows reliabilities of ratings of adult patients during entire tape-recorded therapy sessions (Auerbach & Luborsky, 1968). The correlations between two experienced analytic clinicians' ratings ranged from .26 to .70, with a median of .46. On 9 of the 12 variables, however, one clinician's ratings correlated higher with those of a clinically untrained rater than with those of the other clinician. Analytic training thus did not enhance reliability of judgment. The somewhat higher reliabilities in this study than in Garduk and Haggard's (1972) study may reflect the use of tapes of whole sessions rather than written transcripts of segments.

Table 9-3 Reliability of Psychoanalysts' Ratings of Patient Functioning During Therapy

Garduk & Haggard Study (1972)		Auerbach & Luborsky Study (1968)	
Variable	*Reliability of ratings[a]*	*Variable*	*Reliability of ratings[b]*
1. Anxiety	.11	1. Anxiety	.54
2. Depression	.32	2. Depression	.52
3. Anger, hostility, aggression	.52	3. Hostility to others	.70
4. Defensive and oppositional associations (denial, repudiation, doubt, hostility to therapist; tries to distort, change subject)	.46	4. Hostility to therapist	.47
		5. Quality of experiencing	.42
		6. Warmth to therapist	.46
		7. Guilt and shame	.46
		8. Empathy to therapist	.30
		9. Dependency	.42
5. Presence of affect	.28	10. Activity	.55
6. Pleasant affect	.21	11. Receptiveness	.26
7. Surprise	.30	12. Impact on patient	.47
8. Ego dysfunctioning (disruption, confusion, inability to function)	.04		
9. Symptomatology (alterations or aggravation in symptoms)	.13		
10. Communication of conscious material (factual, objective information)	.35		
11. Communication of deeper-level material	.23		
12. Blocking of associations	.13		
13. Understanding and insight	.37		
14. Transference-related material	.52		

[a]Correlations between two analysts' ratings of 120 5-minute segments of treatment following significant interpretations and noninterpretive interventions. Correlations above .18 are $p < .05$.
[b]Correlations between two analysts' ratings of 60 treatment sessions. Correlations above .25 are $p < .05$.

Despite modest reliabilities, Luborsky (1970) put the recorded therapy data to imaginative use in studying the contexts in which neurotic symptoms are expressed. He located symptomatic expressions (e.g., momentary forgetting, reports of stomach pain and headache) during taped sessions. Then he had raters independently score themes immediately preceding and following the symptom. This revealed particular themes recurring just before a symptom appeared. One patient, for example, momentarily forgot what he intended to say whenever he was about to express a wish for warmth or sexual contact with a woman. Luborsky's technique thus seems to show symptoms being formed as anxiety-arousing thoughts near consciousness. He has also shown similar precursors of petit mal seizures, although some people's seizures seem to have little relation to these psychological factors (Luborsky, et al., 1975).

Level of Clinical Generalizations. Analytic reports often fail to distinguish clinical generalizations from the other levels defined by Waelder. When clinical generalizations are made, their validity is seldom tested.

To test some clinical generalizations, Achenbach and Lewis (1971) searched the psychodynamic literature for generalizations about boys having either enuresis (wetting) or encopresis (bowel incontinence). Eleven generalizations were found for encopresis and 13 for enuresis. For example, "The parents infantilize the boy" was a generalization about encopretics. "The mother emasculates her son" was one about enuretics.

The files of an analytically oriented child clinic were then searched for records of boys who had no evidence of organic pathology and who were treated for either enuresis or encopresis. Boys with learning disorders but without the other two symptoms served as a comparison group. Cases of each type were matched to cases of the other two types in terms of race, socioeconomic status, IQ, and number of clinical interviews. Eighteen triads of cases were thus formed in which all three members were similar on the matching variables but differed in having enuresis, encopresis, or learning disorders. The case histories averaged 37 single-spaced typed pages in length and were based on an average of 38 interviews with the boy, plus more than that with his parents. A child analyst read all the case histories and rated the evidence for each of the 24 statements derived from the clinical generalizations. To prevent contaminating the analyst's judgment with knowledge of which boys had which symptoms, all references to the three symptoms were deleted.

The analyst's ratings showed statistically significant ($p < .05$) support for two of the 24 clinical generalizations. At least one such significant finding is expected by chance, since 24 comparisons were made ($.05 \times 24 = 1.2$).

Could the lack of support for the clinical generalizations reflect randomness in the data or the analyst's interpretations? This was checked by comparing the analyst's ratings on the 24 statements when the cases were grouped according to their *patterns* of symptoms, as identified by factor analysis of behaviors scored by a clinically untrained research assistant. The analyst's ratings significantly differentiated these two groups on 7 of the 24 statements. This indicates that lack of support for the clinical generalizations did not reflect randomness in the analyst's ratings, resulting from either the inadequacy of the records or his judgments. It suggests instead that the clinical generalizations about enuresis and encopresis were invalid.

Several studies have been made of clinical generalizations about antecedents or correlates of oral conflicts. Sewell and Mussen (1952), for example, interviewed mothers of 5- and 6-year-olds to determine whether their children had been breast or bottle fed, fed on demand or on schedule, and gradually or abruptly weaned. These were considered to affect oral conflicts. The children's behavior was assessed in three ways: Mothers' reports of "oral" symptoms, such as stuttering, nail-biting, slowness in acquiring speech, bashfulness about talking, finger-sucking, eating difficulties; a personality test administered by a trained clinician; and teachers' ratings of various traits. No statistically significant relations were found between feeding procedures and behavior or adjustment.

Studies of oral pathology are exemplified by two on relations between oral personality test responses and disorders. In one study, alcoholics were found to prefer soft, sweet, liquid foods suggestive of oral passivity more than did normals, who preferred sour, spicy, crunchy foods (Wolowitz, 1964). In the other study, the Rorschach inkblot responses of alcoholics, stutterers, ulcer patients, and obese people showed more oral imagery than the responses of control subjects (Weiss & Masling, 1970). However, three other "oral" groups—heavy drinkers (not alcoholics), asthmatics, and thumbsuckers (the only group of children)—did not differ significantly from control subjects.

Unfortunately, correlates of pathology do not necessarily show that the pathology *resulted* from particular conflicts or particular stages of psychosexual development. They indicate only that, once people have a particular disorder, they also differ from others on particular correlates. Some of these correlates may be consequences of the disorder instead of causing it. Verifying correlates may help refine causal hypotheses, but does not prove causation.

Studies of antecedents and correlates of "anal" traits have paralleled those for oral traits. Hetherington and Brackbill (1963), for example, sought to determine whether obstinacy, parsimony, and orderliness—three traits imputed to the anal (compulsive) personality—correlated with each other in 5-year-olds and whether toilet training influenced the traits. They gave the children 10 experimental measures of the traits, but did not find the predicted correlations.

The children's parents also filled out lengthy questionnaires tapping their toilet training practices and their own obstinacy, orderliness, and parsimony. No support was found for the analytic hypothesis that too early, too late, or too severe toilet training leads to the anal traits in children. Instead, the children's trait scores correlated with those of their parents. This suggests that the children's personalities were molded by identification with or learning from their parents rather than toilet training per se. Other studies have shown correlations among personality traits like those hypothesized for anal, oral dependent, and hysterical personalities, but little evidence for psychodynamic causation (Kline, 1972; Pollak, 1979).

Level of Clinical Theory. Studies of clinical theory cluster around particular theoretical constructs. Few of the studies deal with children, even though most analytic concepts are assumed to apply equally to children and adults.

Defense mechanisms are among the most studied aspects of clinical theory. One approach is to experimentally manipulate people's defensiveness. For example, negative associations to certain words have been conditioned by pairing the words with ego-threatening experiences, such as social censure or contrived failure on tests. Repression has been inferred from subjects' poor recall of the conditioned words. Furthermore, removing the ego threat by providing success experiences or revealing the deceptions improved recall of the repressed words. Yet most of the findings are also explicable in terms of selective attention: People preoccupied with a stressful experience are less able to focus attention on recalling words. This explanation is borne out by the subjects' poor recall of words not associated specifically with stress, as well as those that were (Holmes, 1974). Some evidence for defensive projection, however, has been found in subjects who deny an unfavorable trait imputed to them through an experimental manipulation. These subjects later ascribed more of the unfavorable trait to a negatively perceived stranger than did subjects who did not deny the trait in themselves (Sherwood, 1979).

A second approach is to examine patients' behavior during therapy to detect defensive processes under the conditions most relevant to analytic theory. The vast material for each patient and the difficulty of obtaining therapist cooperation and reliable ratings have limited this approach. In one study, however, an analyst's treatment notes were used to identify themes that first emerged between the forty-first and one-hundredth hours of a single patient's treatment (Horowitz, Sampson, Siegelman, Wolfson, & Weiss, 1975). Had these themes previously been warded off by the patient?

To test this, 20 clinicians rated the analyst's notes on the first 10 hours of treatment for evidence that the patient was warding off any of the themes. For example, one theme centered on the patient thinking his father was greedy. Each clinician rated the analyst's notes according to whether this theme was too anxiety arousing for the patient to express. Interrater reliabilities were not reported, but when all the clinicians' ratings were averaged for each theme, they correlated .80 with the analyst's ratings of the same themes.

Signs of discomfort, such as slips of the tongue, stammering, and knuckle cracking, were also found most often in tapes of analytic hours containing the themes rated as most strongly warded off. It thus appears possible to detect a patient's discomfort about particular themes, although using a single analyst's notes to rate these themes leaves unanswered many questions of reliability and validity.

A third approach is to assess the correlations between hypothesized defense mechanisms and other variables. Most relevant to developmental psychopathology are relations to developmental level. Children's cognitive levels on Piagetian measures, for example, have been found related to their understanding of defense mechanisms: When defense mechanisms were depicted in tape-recorded stories, preoperational children failed to understand the logical transformations involved in any of the mechanisms. Concrete operational children understood mechanisms involving logical negations of unacceptable feelings, such as repression and denial. But only formal operational children understood more complex mechanisms, such as the projection of one's own motives onto other people (Chandler, Paget, & Koch, 1978). Although inability to explain defense mechanisms does not necessarily mean that children do not *use* such mechanisms, it does imply cognitive developmental constraints on their grasp of interpretations of defenses made in therapy.

Evidence has also been found for sex differences in preferred defense mechanisms. Using the Defense Mechanisms Inventory—a questionnaire on which subjects' defenses are inferred from their responses to hypothetical conflict situations—Cramer (1979) compared the mechanisms characterizing ninth and tenth graders with those characterizing eleventh and twelfth graders. Like adults, boys showed more preference than girls for externalizing conflict through projection and turning against other people. Girls, by contrast, showed a greater preference for turning against the self, intellectualization, and rationalization. These sex differences became more pronounced with age, and older girls' choices resembled those of adult women more than did younger girls' choices. Psychoanalytic theory does not stand or fall on studies like this, but they do help test the viability of analytic constructs.

Are Neurotic Disorders Caused as Implied by Psychoanalysis?

The research cited so far does not tell us whether neuroses are *caused* as analytic theory implies. Certain principles of mental functioning have been supported by research; others have not, and many have not been tested. Perhaps the closest approximation to a test of the cause of neurosis has been to evoke conflicts in animals by rewarding them for learning complex behaviors and then punishing the learned behavior, for example, with electric shock. This has produced symptoms such as compulsions, generalized fear, phobias, and psychophysiological reactions. Jules Masserman (1963), however, a leader in this research and also trained as an analyst, interprets the results as failing to support Freud's theory. He explains neurotic symptoms as conditioned responses to environmental contingencies. He has also removed the symptoms by modifying the incompatible behavior through conditioning.

Comparisons of childhood experiences of neurotic and normal people bring us closer to human neurosis. In a review of 40 years of studies, however, Frank (1965) concluded that no factors were found in the parent-child interactions of neurotics that were unique to them or that distinguished them from other pathological or normal groups. A complementary finding was that people selected for study because of their good mental health had experienced as much trauma, parental discord, tension, illness, and repressiveness as typically ascribed to psychiatric patients (Renaud & Estess, 1961; Schofield & Balian, 1959).

Perhaps the lack of causal evidence reflects insufficient longitudinal study of interactions between children and their parents. Thomas, Chess, and Birch (1968) sought to provide a more precise longitudinal picture of relations between children's temperaments, their parents' behavior, and the development of disorders. One of their key conclusions concerns anxiety:

> in the young child, anxiety has not been evident as an initial factor preceding and determining symptom development. Where anxiety has evolved in the course of the development of a child's behavior disorder, it has been a secondary phenomenon, a consequence rather than a cause of symptom development and expression. Similarly, the removal of symptoms by a successful parent-guidance procedure has had positive consequences for the child's functioning, and has not resulted in the appearance of overt anxiety or of new substitutive symptoms.
>
> We have found it unnecessary to invoke concepts regarding presumed states of intrapsychic conflict or the operation of psychodynamic mechanisms of a purposive ideational character to explain the origins of behavioral disturbances in young children. In each case of an excessively stressful and maladaptive interaction between the child and his environment, a parsimonious formulation in terms of objective and overtly evident characteristics of the child, patterns of parental functioning, and other specific environmental influences has been sufficient to account for the genesis of the problem behavior. However, intrapsychic conflict and psychodynamic defenses, as well as anxiety, have been evident in some older children as later developments in the child's response to the unfavorable and sometimes threatening consequences of an initial maladaptation.
>
> It is, of course, true that once anxiety, intrapsychic conflict, and psychodynamic defense mechanisms appear, they add new dimensions to the dynamics of the child's functioning and contribute to his interactions. When this happens, they may substantially influence the subsequent course of the behavior problem. The painfulness of severe anxiety when it is overt makes it a striking symptom which may dominate our perceptions of the clinical picture. The elaborate psychological techniques utilized to minimize or to avoid distress may also contribute dramatically to the elaboration of pathological patterns of behavior and thought. It is, therefore, not surprising that in retrospective studies that begin when the child already presents with an elaborated psychological disturbance, the prominent phenomena of anxiety and psychodynamic defenses dominate clinical thinking, and come to be labeled as primary, rather than as secondary, influences in the genesis of behavior disturbance. (Thomas et al., 1968, pp. 188–89)

These conclusions do not deny the basic assumptions of psychological determinism, unconscious influences, childhood sexuality, or the meaningfulness of free associations. They do suggest, however, that factors that analysts believe *cause* children's neuroses may in fact be *effects* or may have other nonetiologic significance.

RESEARCH ON THE EFFECTS OF PSYCHOANALYTIC TREATMENT

In Chapter 17, we will examine the general problems of evaluating treatment effects. Because each major viewpoint is closely linked to a method of treatment, however, we need to look at the effects of these treatments in direct relation to their theoretical bases. Few studies of the efficacy of analysis have been published. None has systematically compared its effects with those of a different treatment or no treatment in substantial numbers of patients who were initially well-matched to the analytic patients.

The single study of the effects of child analysis also seems to be the only study comparing analysis with another treatment in patients matched to the analytic patients, although there were only four patients in each group (Heinicke, 1969). In this study, four latency-age boys with learning disorders received four weekly psychoanalytic sessions while four others received analytically oriented therapy once a week. Therapy lasted from 1½ to 2½ years. Mothers of the boys were seen weekly and fathers were seen whenever necessary. Unfortunately, the boys' initial scores on the matching variables were not reported, and the small samples made it difficult to find significant differences. By the end of treatment, ratings on 3 out of 45 clinical dimensions significantly favored the boys receiving analysis, although 2 significant differences would be expected by chance in 45 comparisons.

In ratings 1 and 2 years after treatment, the number of significant differences increased to 6 out of the 45 dimensions. Standardized achievement tests indicated slower improvement in reading and spelling by the analyzed boys during treatment, but faster improvement after treatment, although it is not clear whether they started off and ended up better or worse than the other boys.

Several studies have yielded outcome data for adult analytic patients, but, lacking control groups and objective measures of change, they have generated more argument than evidence. There have, however, been a few comparisons of analytically oriented therapy with other approaches, including behavior modification. Some of the best controlled comparisons have shown little overall difference in outcomes for groups of children or adults receiving the different therapies. Yet, *post hoc* analyses showed that preexisting characteristics of the clients had major impacts on the outcomes: Among phobic children, for example, 6- to 10-year-olds showed much greater improvements than 11- to 15-year-olds (Miller, Barrett, Hampe, & Noble, 1972). Among adults with neuroses or personality disorders, analytically oriented therapy seemed most effective with minimally disturbed people of upper socioeconomic status, whereas behavior therapy seemed effective with a broader range of people (Sloane, Staples, Cristol, Yorkston, & Whipple, 1976). These findings highlight the importance of determining precisely what treatment works best for whom.

SUMMARY

Most *psychodynamically* oriented workers view *psychoneurosis* in terms of Freudian theory. Other theoretical viewpoints, such as the behavioral, portray many of the same disorders in different terms.

In his earliest theory, Freud maintained that neuroses resulted from *conflicts* arising when the ego sought to repress unacceptable *libidinal* impulses. In *hysterical* neuroses, the repressed excitation of the impulses was *converted* into somatic forms producing bodily symptoms. In *obsessional* and *phobic* neuroses, repression separated the excitation from the mental representations of the unacceptable impulses, but the excitation became attached to other thoughts.

The sex drive was hypothesized to be the somatic source of the excitation behind repressed impulses. Freud explained mental functioning in terms of the dynamics of *libido,* a hypothetical quantity of sexual energy. He later postulated an aggressive drive as a second source of psychic energy. Libidinal arousal was hypothesized to be focused successively in the *oral, anal,* and *phallic* regions during early *psychosexual* development. *Neurotic conflicts* were based on *fixations* and *regressions* to conflicts associated with these early phases. *Neurotic symptoms* were viewed as *overdetermined* substitutes for repressed libidinal impulses. Libido blocked by repression was believed to be *transformed* into *neurotic anxiety*.

In 1926, Freud reversed the role ascribed to neurotic anxiety. Rather than being a *toxic end product* of repressed libido, he now regarded anxiety as being aroused in the ego by libidinal impulses associated with traumatic situations in childhood. Resurgence of a dangerous libidinal impulse initially triggered a small amount of anxiety. This *signal anxiety* warned that a danger associated with the impulse in childhood might recur unless defensive measures were taken. The concept of defense was broadened to include *defense mechanisms* other than repression whereby the ego could avoid increases in anxiety. Symptoms were now thought to be formed by the ego to avoid or reduce anxiety, rather than being substitute expressions of libido.

Elaborating on her father's revised ego theory, Anna Freud stated the goal of analysis as not merely to bring repressed id impulses into consciousness, but to provide insight into unconscious ego defenses. She enumerated many defense mechanisms beside those mentioned by her father and was among the first to psychoanalyze children.

In extending *ego psychology,* Heinz Hartmann held that some ego functions have *primary autonomy,* that is, that conflict is not required for their development. Other ego functions arise from conflict as defense mechanisms, but may then achieve *secondary autonomy* and function in the absence of conflict. Hartmann also theorized that the ego was powered by instinctual energy freed (*neutralized*) from its original sexual and aggressive aims.

In his account of *psychosocial development,* Erik Erikson has stressed the ways in which biological development engages children in interactions with other people. Basic to these interactions are the child's *bodily zones,* the *modes of action* focused in the bodily zones, and the *social modalities* arising from the modes of action. Erikson has postulated developmental stages characterized by different modes of action and social modalities, as well as nuclear conflicts related to these stages.

Anna Freud has proposed a *developmental profile* for assessing children's libidinal and aggressive drive development, ego and superego development, regression and fixation points, and conflicts. Although the profile summarizes analytic clinical theory, little has been published on how children are to be assessed on each variable or on the profile's reliability and validity as a guide to prognosis and treatment. Other analysts have published related approaches to developmental profiling but little reliability or validity data. Analytic concepts have also been used to evolve new constructs, such as ego control and ego resiliency, outside the main analytic theory.

Analysis is considered an appropriate treatment for very few disturbed children, primarily those of latency age with classic neurotic conflicts and stable families. The goal is to relieve unconscious conflicts by making them conscious and reworking the feelings connected with them. The child's play is viewed as a partial replacement for the technique of free association so crucial in adult analysis. Some analysts believe that nonanalytic treatments risk *symptom substitution.*

Few analysts have moved their ideas from the *context of discovery* into the *context of confirmation.* Most mental health workers accept unconscious psychological influences, childhood sexuality, and psychological determinism, and evidence supports some other analytic hypotheses. Still others have been contradicted by research findings, but most have never been adequately tested. The few existing studies of analyst's judgments of patient functioning during treatment show minimal reliability.

Research suggests that the analytic theory of childhood neurosis is inaccurate, as anxiety may often *follow* rather than precede symptoms in young children. There is little evidence that analysis is more effective than less time-consuming treatments.

SUGGESTED READING

Development of Freud's Thought. Among the most central works in Freud's theory of neurosis are *Studies in Hysteria* (with Breuer, 1893-95); *The Neuropsychoses of Defense* (1894); *The Interpretation of Dreams* (1900), especially Chapter 7, providing the most complete version of Freud's early model of the mind; *Three*

Essays on the Theory of Sexuality (1905); and his revised theory of neurosis in *Inhibition, Symptoms, and Anxiety* (1926a). Freud's *General Introduction to Psychoanalysis* (1916) and *New Introductory Lectures on Psychoanalysis* (1933) provide especially readable overviews of this thinking. The case of Little Hans (*Analysis of a Phobia in a Five-year-old Boy*, 1909) is also important for its account of the psychodynamics of Oedipal symptom formation. For another view of the case, Wolpe and Rachman's (1960) textual critique should be read with the original. Ernest Jones' three-volume biography of Freud is an "official" biography by one who was close to Freud from the early days of analysis and who had the cooperation of others close to Freud. It is a fascinating aid to understanding the development of psychoanalysis. An excellent one-volume abridgement is available in paperback (1963), but contrasting views should be read as well (e.g., Sulloway, 1980).

Anna Freud. Her own contributions as well as her paternity give Anna Freud a central role in analytic thought, especially concerning children. *The Ego and the Mechanisms of Defense* (1936) is a cornerstone of analytic ego psychology. *Normality and Pathology of Childhood* (1965) is one of the most cited books in the child analytic literature. In "A Psychoanalytic View of Developmental Psychopathology" (1974), she considers general problems of assessing children and treating those falling outside the traditional analytic arena of neurosis.

Psychosocial Development. The best known extension of analytic theory since Freud's death has been Erik Erikson's account of psychosocial development. While their concepts are untested—and perhaps untestable—and their influence on analytic practice is questionable, Erikson's *Childhood and Society* (1963) and *Identity, Youth, and Crisis* (1968) have deeply affected views of children's social development. He also highlights dimensions of development not adequately handled by other theories. A further statement of his psychosocial theory is available in Erikson (1980) "Elements of a psychoanalytic theory of psychosocial development."

Revisionist Views. Building on earlier efforts by Dollard and Miller (1950) and Mahl (1971), Wachtel (1977) offers an imaginative integration of analytic and behavioral approaches to neurosis.

Analytic Treatment. Scharfman (1978) presents an overview of criteria for selecting patients, as well as other considerations in the practice of child analysis. Colby's (1958) short book, *The Skeptical Psychoanalyst*, is recommended as an aid in the self-analysis of anyone considering analysis as a profession.

CHAPTER 10

Behavioral Approaches to Development and Psychopathology

Unlike psychoanalysis, behavioral approaches did not originate with efforts to understand psychopathology. Instead, they arose from efforts to understand the origin of all human knowledge and behavior. Aristotle was an early forerunner of behavioral approaches. He proposed that the child begins life as a *tabula rasa* or unmarked tablet. Development, then, is mainly an accumulation of sensory impressions that write their messages on the unmarked tablet. The view that sensory experience is the main source of thought and behavior was progressively refined by British *empiricist* philosophers of the seventeenth through nineteenth centuries. They were called *empiricist* because they viewed experience as the source of all knowledge and behavior, although their methods involved no more empirical research than those of other philosophers.

Assuming that the environment supplied the raw materials of development, the empiricist philosophers hypothesized that sensory impressions are joined together in the mind by a process of *association*, that is, the linking of impressions according to their contiguity in time, similarity of content, and other shared features. They also hypothesized that complex concepts are merely elaborate combinations of associated sensory impressions.

Associationist theory shaped not only behavioral psychology but Freudian psychology as well. As we have seen in Chapter 9, Freud inferred repressed thoughts by tracing out associations among conscious thoughts. He also hypothesized that repressed thoughts are often disguised in mental symbols; the form these symbols take is shaped partly by sensory associations with the repressed material.

Freud used associationist theory to explain and study mental contents in relation to his drive-based theory of development and psychopathology. His behaviorist contemporaries, by contrast, rejected traditional associationist preoccupations with *mental* life. They focused instead on associationistic mechanisms of behavioral change. Whereas Freud's theory originated with efforts to treat psychopathology, behavioral theory originated with laboratory research on learning.

CONDITIONING

Pavlovian Conditioning

From studies begun in 1899, the Russian physiologist Ivan Pavlov derived certain basic laws of learning. One procedure in his work was to sound a tuning fork as powdered meat was placed on a dog's tongue. The meat, of course, caused the dog to salivate. After several trials, the sound of the tuning fork alone evoked salivation. Salivation to the tone was called a *conditional (conditioned) reflex* because the tone's power to cause salivation was *conditional* on pairing it with a stimulus (food on the tongue) that already caused salivation without prior learning. Food was an *unconditional (unconditioned) stimulus* because it elicited the reflex *unconditionally*, without training. The tone was a *conditional (conditioned) stimulus* because its power to evoke salivation was *conditional* on its prior pairing with food. Pavlov's procedure became known as *Pavlovian, classical,* or *respondent conditioning.*

Operant Conditioning

Another Russian physiologist, Pavlov's rival Bekhterev, concentrated on a second basic form of conditioning, called *operant* or *instrumental conditioning*. In this type of conditioning, a response rewarded under certain circumstances will typically be repeated under those circumstances. For example, a hungry rat receiving food when it operates a lever will continue to operate the lever. Bekhterev (1907) also proposed that complex habits resulted from the *chaining* together of specific rewarded responses.

The Law of Effect. Independently of Bekhterev's work, an American, Edward L. Thorndike, drew similar conclusions. Finding that animals repeated responses that were rewarded but failed to repeat punished responses, Thorndike proposed the Law of Effect. This stated that responses leading to a "satisfying state of affairs" tend to be repeated, while those leading to an "annoying state of affairs" tend not to be repeated (Thorndike, 1913). If the effect a response has previously had determines whether it will be repeated, Thorndike argued, we need not invoke conscious thought as an explanation for the response.

Watsonian Behaviorism

In the same vein, John B. Watson proposed that all human behavior could be analyzed in stimulus-response terms like those applied to animal behavior, without resort to introspection or notions of consciousness. In his 1913 manifesto, "Psychology as the Behaviorist Views It," Watson argued that the proper subject of psychology was observable behavior and how it is learned. After reading translations of Bekhterev's work in 1915, he became convinced that conditioning is the basic process in learning and that chains of conditioned covert vocal responses are the basis of thinking. He insisted that conditioning is responsible for all behavioral and emotional development, abnormal as well as normal.

EARLY BEHAVIOR MODIFICATION

The Case of Albert

The use of learning principles to explain and change undesirable behavior is often dated from Watson, especially his conditioning of a fear in a child named Albert (Watson & Rayner, 1920), although this single-case study was of little scientific value by itself (Samelson, 1980). Albert was described as an especially calm and fearless infant. As documented with films, he responded fearlessly to stimuli including a white rat, rabbit, dog, monkey, masks, cotton, and burning newspapers.

Watson's experiment began when Albert, aged 11 months, was shown a white rat, which he had not previously feared. As Albert reached for the rat, a steel bar was struck with a hammer. Albert jumped violently and fell forward. The bar was struck again whenever Albert reached for the rat. Thereafter, when the rat was presented without the bar being struck, Albert withdrew his hand, whimpered, fell over, and crawled away. He now showed similar but milder reactions to a rabbit, dog, fur coat, cotton, Santa Claus mask, and Watson's hair. But he showed no negative reactions to his blocks. Watson interpreted Albert's fear in terms of classical conditioning: Pairing the previously neutral white rat with the frightening sound caused the emotional response of fear to become *conditioned* to the stimulus of the rat. The transfer of Albert's fear to other objects showed that the fear response *generalized* to similar objects. But this generalization was not indiscriminate, because it did not transfer to objects such as blocks.

Although Watson failed to treat the conditioned fear, he proposed three possible approaches:

1. Repeatedly presenting the feared stimulus without the sound in order to bring about habituation or "fatigue" of the fear response.
2. Reconditioning by evoking positive sensations—stimulating the lips, nipples, or sex organs, or feeding—when the feared stimulus was presented.

3. Building up "constructive" activities around the feared stimulus by getting Albert to imitate unfearful behavior and by using Albert's hand to manipulate the rat.

The Case of Peter and the Rabbit

Mary Cover Jones (1924b) tested some of Watson's proposed treatments with other children. She found that showing a child a feared stimulus in the presence of an unafraid child sometimes prompted imitation by the fearful child and helped reduce fear on later occasions as well. But this method occasionally backfired, when the unafraid child imitated the fearful child!

The most effective method seemed to be reconditioning via pleasurable experience in the presence of the feared stimulus. Jones (1924a) used this method with a boy named Peter whose case is nearly as famous as the case of Albert. Peter is, in fact, often confused with Albert because the presenting symptoms were so similar to the ones Watson conditioned in Albert.

Peter's therapy began when he was 2 years 10 months old. He was very afraid of a white rabbit and slightly less afraid of white rats, fur coats, cotton, feathers, and similar stimuli, but not of objects such as wooden blocks. His behavior during treatment was analyzed into 17 degrees of tolerance of the rabbit. The first step was to put Peter with other children who liked and petted the rabbit. In seven brief sessions spread over several days, Peter progressed nine steps on the scale: From showing fear when the caged rabbit was anywhere in the room to tolerating it at progressively closer distances; tolerating it when uncaged, touching it while the experimenter held it; touching it while it was free in the room; and defying it by spitting and throwing things at it. This sequence is shown in Figure 10-1.

Therapy was interrupted after the seventh session when Peter became ill and was quarantined for nearly two months (point *a* in Figure 10-1). Just before his return, he and his nurse were badly frightened when a large dog jumped at him. On his return, his fear of the rabbit was back to its original level (point *b* in Figure 10-1). Then a new treatment, called "direct conditioning," was started. Peter was fed a favorite food while the experimenter brought the caged rabbit as close as possible without disrupting Peter's eating. Improvements in Peter's tolerance were most apparent in the presence of another child or adult who was either well liked or who showed affection to the rabbit (points *c, d, e, f*). A relapse occurred when Peter was scratched slightly while helping to carry the rabbit (point *g*). But he recovered, and in the forty-fifth session reached the final step on the scale, allowing the rabbit to nibble his fingers. He showed no further fear despite the presence of another child who was very afraid of the rabbit.

When interviewed during therapy, Peter at first said nothing about the rabbit. On later occasions, he said, "I like the rabbit." In a follow-up after treatment, he showed fondness for the rabbit and no fear of cotton, fur coats, or feathers. He was

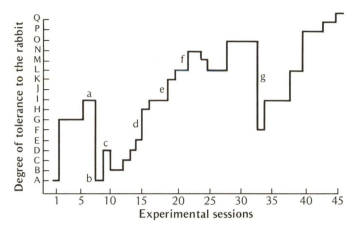

Figure 10-1. The removal of Peter's fear of the rabbit through reconditioning. Point *a* = interruption due to Peter's illness; *b* = renewal of experiment after Peter was frightened by dog; *c, d, e, f* = sessions in which an unafraid child or well-liked adult was present; *g* = Peter scratched while helping to carry the rabbit. (From Jones, in Eysenck, 1960, p. 48. © 1960 by Pergamon Press and reprinted by permission.)

also willing to carry a box of rats and a fur rug with a stuffed head that he previously feared but was not included in treatment.

Jones concluded that her study was incomplete because she had not identified the original feared stimulus and did not know whether removing the rabbit phobia relieved the original fear, if there was one. Moreover, Peter's very bad home situation cast doubt on his future welfare. His disturbed mother often suggested fears to the boy, saying, for example, ''Come in Peter, someone wants to steal you (p. 315).''

As with Freud's case of Little Hans, the case of Peter is important not only as an illustration of a new treatment paradigm, but also because it reveals critical aspects of the paradigm as it has persisted into the present day. Critical features of the behavioral paradigm evident in the case of Peter include:

1. The assumption that fear of a particular class of stimuli, rather than an inferred intrapsychic conflict, was the essential problem.
2. The assumption that the class of feared objects was determined by stimulus generalization, from one object originally associated with pain or fear to similar objects rather than to symbolic representations of the feared situation.
3. The structuring of therapy as an experiment for which data on behavioral change were reported as a function of interventions, rather than as a clinical case history in which events and interpretations are merged.
4. The attribution of behavioral change to a specific learning process

("conditioning"), although other processes could also have been involved, such as imitation and habituation.

5. The tendency to view a specific problem behavior as the focus of
   treatment and the child's life situation as a separate, though admittedly
   ominous, issue.

Holmes's Experiment

Holmes (1936) questioned the utility of Watson and Jones's conditioning methods
because so few children fear objects like white rabbits that can be conveniently
presented while the child eats. Common fears of the dark, heights, and entering the
water, for example, were hard to recondition with food. In place of Watson's
methods, Holmes advocated inducing the child to cope actively with the feared
situation and then rewarding such behavior. In effect, she was proposing an *operant*
conditioning paradigm.

As a demonstration, Holmes induced nursery schoolchildren who feared the
dark to enter a dark room in search of a luminescent light pull that would turn on a
light. If children were too scared to search for the light pull alone, Holmes
accompanied them but urged them to search for the light pull on their own. Holmes
rewarded the children by playing a game with them in the room. Most children
seemed so gratified to find the pull and overcome their fear that the game-playing
was superfluous, however. Thirteen out of 14 children lost their fear after several
experimental trials, although generalization to other situations was not tested.

Mowrer and Mowrer's Treatment of Enuresis

One of the best known studies between the initiation of behavior modification in the
1920s and its revival in the 1950s was an application of conditioning to bedwetting
(Mowrer & Mowrer, 1938). After surveying unsuccessful remedies from many
cultures, the Mowrers concluded that organic and emotional factors might contribute in some cases, but many cases resulted from faulty habit training.

The Mowrers designed an electrically wired pad for the child's bed and a bell
that rang when the pad got wet. The conditioning strategy was as follows: The
stimulus of bladder tension caused the reflex of sphincter relaxation and urination.
The bell served as both an awakening stimulus and a stimulus to sphincter
contraction, which inhibited urination. Pairing the bell with the reflex of sphincter
relaxation over several trials caused the child to awaken and inhibit urination when
bladder tension reached the point where urination had previously begun.

The Mowrers reported 100 percent success with 30 children aged 3 to 13 in a
temporary children's home. They found no evidence of symptom substitution or
negative personality effects, although some children relapsed when they returned to
bad home situations.

LATER DEVELOPMENTS

Government programs for the psychological casualties of World War II sharply increased training and facilities for the treatment of psychopathology during the 1940s. Most treatment followed the medical and psycho-dynamic models, however. Several factors may explain the failure to extend behavioral methods. One is that behavioral methods were developed almost exclusively by specialists in educational and experimental psychology whose work was unknown to clinicians. A second factor is that they were used mainly with children, whereas the new government programs were for treatment of adults. A third factor is that psychotherapy became an enterprise with a life of its own, or *functional autonomy,* as Astin (1961) put it: The professional training, practice, and career system of psychotherapy became independent of its original aim, which was to change pathological behavior. The system functioned autonomously, even without proof that it actually changed behavior.

When efforts were made to bridge the gap between research and therapeutic practice, the efficacy of psychotherapy was not questioned, despite being entirely unproven. Instead, efforts to bridge the gap mainly translated into laboratory terms the prevailing concepts and practices of psychotherapy, especially psychoanalysis. Such efforts were surprisingly numerous (e.g., Cameron & Magaret, 1951; Mowrer, 1950; Shoben, 1949).

Dollard and Miller

The most ambitious effort to bridge the gap between experimental psychology and psychotherapy was *Personality and Psychotherapy,* by John Dollard and Neal Miller (1950). Dedicating their book to "Freud and Pavlov and their students," Dollard and Miller sought "to combine the vitality of psychoanalysis, the rigor of the natural-science laboratory, and the facts of culture (p. 3)." They called psychotherapy a "window to higher mental life" and "the process by which *normality is created* (pp. 3, 5)". They viewed neurotic behavior as learned and psychotherapy as the setting for unlearning neurotic habits and learning normal ones.

Dollard and Miller adopted Freud's definition of neurosis as an unconscious conflict in which (1) repression keeps anxiety-arousing thoughts from consciousness, and (2) symptoms help to avoid further anxiety. However, they translated Freud's concepts into terms derived from laboratory research on animal and human learning, using Clark Hull's (1951) learning theory.

Dollard and Miller stressed four key factors in learning: *drive, response, cue,* and *reinforcement.* Drives were hypothetical constructs resembling Freud's constructs of the instinctual drives of sex and aggression. Hunger, thirst, sex, pain, cold, and other organic need states were *primary drives.* Reduction of a drive was rewarding, so any *response* that reduced a drive was thought to be *reinforced,* that is, the probability increased that the response would be repeated when the drive was again high, especially if the *cue* (stimulus) conditions were similar. Many cue conditions associated with drive reduction could spawn learned motives, called *learned* or *secondary* drives. An excessive urge for wealth, for example, is a learned drive spawned by experiences in which a lack of money causes discomfort and the acquisition of money alleviates the discomfort.

Fear was seen as a learnable drive that motivates behavior which, in turn, is strongly reinforced if it reduces fear. This was demonstrated by shocking rats in one compartment of a box but letting them escape by running to another compartment. The escape behavior continued after shock was no longer administered. When placed in the shock box with the door closed, the rats became agitated and soon learned to turn a wheel that opened the door. Rats repeatedly placed in the box quickly turned the wheel to escape, showing that wheel turning was reinforced by reduction of their learned fear. *Anxiety* was defined as fear for which the specific cues were vague or hidden by repression. *Repression* was defined as avoidance of thinking about a fear, thus preventing verbal labeling of the fear.

Dollard and Miller also reinterpreted specific symptoms and Freudian defense mechanisms in terms of learning theory. Most of their reinterpretations seem true to the psychoanalytic descriptions of such behavior, but dispense with constructs like id, ego, superego, libido, and cathexis. As an example, here's how they illustrated the defense mechanism of projection:

> Mrs. A. . . . had intense anxiety about any verbal expression of sexual desires. On several occasions as a small girl she had "been taken advantage of" by older boys or men. Later she frequently went into situations where she was likely to be taken advantage of. Instead of any thoughts about having sexual desires of her own, she was afraid that the man wanted to do something to her.
>
> According to our analysis, being taken advantage of reduced this girl's fear of sex because it meant that she was not to blame. She was able to get some satisfaction in those situations that she was not able to get otherwise. These experiences attached learned reward value for the sex drive to the cues of being alone with a man in a provocative situation and to the cues produced by the thought "he wants to take advantage of me." This learned reward value reinforced the responses of going into those situations and thinking those thoughts. Since such intense anxiety had been attached to labeling her own sexual desires, any thought that she wanted the man to make advances was repressed. . . . Such a thought might have kept her out of the sex situation entirely. The thought "he wants to do something to me" also helped to . . . keep anxiety-provoking thoughts about her own desires out of her mind. This was an additional source of reinforcement for that thought. (Dollard & Miller, 1950, pp. 182–83)

Beside applying learning theory to Freudian concepts, Dollard and Miller reinterpreted psychotherapy: One facet of therapy consists of helping the patient gain verbal labels for repressed anxiety-arousing thoughts and emotions. The original anxiety can then be unlearned under the guidance of the therapist who encourages the patient to express tabooed feelings and thoughts. Expressing these thoughts and feelings without punishment allows the anxiety responses to extinguish.

Dollard and Miller dubbed a second facet "real-world aspects of therapy." This involves recognizing the distortions neurotic symptoms cause in one's life and efforts to make new responses outside of therapy. To be effective, the therapist must encourage generalization of verbal responses made in treatment to activity outside therapy. But behavior must change at a rate that avoids too great an increase in anxiety while permitting sufficient reinforcement for the new behavior to be learned.

What Impact Did Dollard and Miller Have? *Personality and Psychotherapy* is a *tour de force* in translating psychoanalysis into learning theory language. It showed how psychodynamic lore could be thought of in other terms, and it mapped territory shared by research and therapy. Many of the book's proposals fostered new models, as exemplified in Wachtel's (1977) *Psychoanalysis and Behavior Therapy: Toward an Integration* and Marmor and Woods' (1980) *The Interface between the Psychodynamic and Behavioral Therapies*. Yet the book has not affected analytic theory much. Nor has it spawned new forms of therapy, although it may have helped by (1) popularizing behavioral concepts, and (2) demonstrating that even a highly sophisticated synthesis of psychoanalysis and learning theory could not advance treatment techniques much. As Paul Meehl put it:

> Even such a powerful and illuminating work as Dollard and Miller's *Personality and Psychotherapy* suffers from the traditionalism with which we are all infected. It is a brilliant rendition, in the learning-theory frame, of a fairly orthodox view of therapy. It might be even more illuminating if the authors applied these principles without being constantly guided by the tradition. It seems odd that the learning formulation apparently suggested so few innovations in therapeutic strategy and tactics as appear in that admirable book. (Meehl, 1955, p. 375)

Bandura and Walters (1963) took stronger exception to the "translation" approach:

> The net effect of these translations has . . . been to entrench more firmly assumptions and concepts that have accumulated over the years through the uncontrolled trial-and-error experiences of practicing clinicians. (p. 29)

Nevertheless, continuing efforts at integration help to combat the narrow parochialism arising when therapies develop in isolation from one another.

B. F. Skinner

Starting with his Harvard Ph.D. dissertation in 1931, B. F. Skinner carried on the behaviorist tradition in a style like Watson's. Skinner, however, went further than Watson. He declared that for purposes of psychology the concept of the organism could be replaced by the notion of an unopenable black box. Skinner's psychology was to focus merely on the functional relations between stimuli impinging on this black box (the organism) and responses emitted by it, without any hypotheses about covert activity or internal drives to link the stimuli and responses.

Like Watson, Skinner was eager to extrapolate laboratory behavioral analysis and findings on animal learning to complex human behavior. In "Baby in a box" (1945), he described a boxlike apparatus designed to provide a controlled environment for infants that would avoid the inconvenience and harmful stimulus-response contingencies of ordinary infant care. Skinner's novel, *Walden Two* (1948), depicts a utopia in which the rational programming of reinforcements replaces the haphazard reinforcement contingencies supporting harmful behavior in the real world. In *Beyond Freedom and Dignity* (1971), he argues the need for careful environmental planning. He has also applied operant conditioning principles to the design of teaching machines and programmed educational materials.

Skinner's followers regard his book *Science and Human Behavior* (1953) as a major milestone in the revival of behavioral approaches to psychopathology in the 1950s (Ullmann & Krasner, 1975). It was primarily an extrapolation of Skinnerian principles to broad issues in psychology and society at large, but unsupported by data. Skinner criticized the psychodynamic emphasis on inner illness and its rejection of behavior as a subject matter in its own right. His criticism was more radical than Dollard and Miller's, because he totally denied the need for the psychodynamic constructs that Dollard and Miller translated into learning theory terms.

Yet, even Skinner seemed to accept the efficacy of psychotherapy while explaining it in his own terms. He maintained that its effectiveness depends on the therapist serving as a nonpunishing audience who permits the patient to emit previously punished responses: Emitting such responses without punishment reduces the effects of previous aversive conditioning. Stimuli generated by the patient's behavior become less aversive and generate less negative emotional reactions in the patient. Consequently, patients are less likely to engage in operant behavior designed to escape from their own negative emotional reactions.

WOLPE'S PSYCHOTHERAPY BY RECIPROCAL INHIBITION

The new dawn of behavior modification was heralded mainly by Joseph Wolpe's book, *Psychotherapy by Reciprocal Inhibition* (1958). Seeking alternatives to the repression theory of neurosis, Wolpe provoked experimental neuroses in cats by shocking them under various conditions. The cats responded with anxiety symptoms like those of human neuroses. One cat, for example, showed the "hysterical" symptom of jerking his shoulders every few seconds whenever Wolpe approached. The jerks may have been aborted jumping movements originating on the first shock when the cat jumped through an open hatch in the cage.

After provoking experimental neuroses, Wolpe tried various ways of alleviating the cats' anxiety and symptoms. His basic strategy was to inhibit anxiety responses by conditioning other responses to the same cues. One way was to feed cats in the presence of cues previously associated with shock, much as Jones (1924a) had fed Peter in the presence of the rabbit. Since Wolpe held that two incompatible responses, such as eating and physiologic anxiety reactions, cannot occur simultaneously, he expected vigorous eating responses to cause *reciprocal inhibition* of the old anxiety responses. When the new responses were firmly conditioned to the previously frightening cues, the old anxiety responses might be permanently weakened.

In applying his reciprocal inhibition principles to humans, Wolpe defined neurotic behavior as:

> any persistent habit of unadaptive behavior acquired by learning in a physiologically normal organism. Anxiety is usually the central constituent of this behavior, being invariably present in the causal situation. . . . By anxiety is meant the autonomic response pattern or patterns that are characteristically part of the organism's response to noxious stimulation. (pp. 32–34)

Wolpe viewed human neuroses primarily as conditioned anxiety responses and/or other specific responses such as hysterical symptoms. These were triggered either by stimuli directly evoking anxiety or by ambiguous stimuli that indirectly evoked anxiety. He acknowledged that some people may be especially prone to neurosis either because of physiologically based emotional reactivity or because prior learning had conditioned anxiety responses to stimuli that then became involved in the neurosis-producing situation. Figure 10-2 portrays Wolpe's theory of most human neurotic behavior.

Systematic Desensitization

The successful treatment of cats by feeding them in the presence of increasing doses of anxiety led Wolpe to develop systematic desensitization therapy for humans. First a list is made of everything that makes the patient anxious, ranked in order from most to least anxiety arousing. The patient's *anxiety hierarchy,* as the rank-ordered list is called, is then divided into thematic categories, and the patient ranks the items again within each category. Next, the patient is trained to relax. This is done by tensing the muscles, becoming aware of the accompanying feelings of tension, and then gradually untensing the muscles while concentrating on the

Special predisposing preconditions (not essential)

↓

Subject exposed either to stimuli directly evoking anxiety or to ambivalent stimulation so that anxiety of high intensity is evoked. (Many variables are involved, e.g., degree of constriction of psychological space [limitations of response possibilities], strength of anxiety at each exposure, number of exposures, degree of stimulus constancy at different exposures.)

↓

Conditioning is established
of

high-intensity and/or other responses
anxiety responses   e.g., hysterical responses

to

specific stimuli and/or pervasive stimuli
                        ("free-floating" anxiety)

Secondary anxiety-relieving behavior may ensue:

a) Physical avoidance of stimuli conditioned to anxiety

and/or

b) Displacement of attention

and/or

c) Drug-taking

and/or

d) Anxiety-relieving obsessions

Modifications in the constitution of neurotic responses following their evocation in contiguity with certain other responses

Figure 10-2. Wolpe's theory of most neuroses. (From Wolpe, 1958.)

resulting sensations. Wolpe contends that deep muscle relaxation is antagonistic to anxiety responses.

After several sessions of relaxation training, the patient is hypnotized and induced to relax. While relaxed, the patient is asked to imagine the least threatening scene in one category of the anxiety hierarchy. The patient is to raise a hand if he or she feels disturbed by the scene. This procedure is repeated for several sessions, gradually moving up the anxiety hierarchy as the patient learns to tolerate progressively more threatening scenes. Patients who cannot be hypnotized may progress in a similar but slower fashion without hypnosis. Those who cannot effectively visualize the scenes are asked to verbalize them.

Wolpe's Initial Results. Wolpe's outcome statistics were probably the key to his success in helping revive behavioral approaches. Of 210 adult neurotics getting what Wolpe considered an adequate trial of therapy, he judged 89.5 percent as cured or much improved. Anxiety inventories showed substantial drops in self-reported anxiety, while treatment averaged 34.8 sessions (Lazarus, 1961). Two- to seven-year follow-ups of 45 patients showed only one of the "much improved" relapsing to a moderate degree. The lack of control groups leaves these figures open to the same criticisms as uncontrolled assessments of other therapies, however.

By 1960, enough articles on behavioral approaches were published to fill a book of readings entitled *Behaviour Therapy and the Neuroses* (Eysenck, 1960). Approaches beside Wolpe's were represented, but most of the clinical applications reflected his influence. In fact, his concept of reciprocal inhibition is so general as to explain almost any behavior change (Wolpe, 1976). Other behavioral methods, however, aim to replace maladaptive responses with more adaptive ones rather than reducing the learned fears Wolpe blames for most neuroses. Furthermore, many behavior modifiers disagree with his theory of neurosis, his emphasis on anxiety, and his concept of reciprocal inhibition. Wolpe's conceptual framework and desensitization techniques have nevertheless retained a central place in behavior modification.

Desensitization of Children

Although early behavior modification techniques were tried out mainly on children (e.g., Holmes, 1936; Jones, 1924a; Mowrer & Mowrer, 1938), Wolpe's systematic desensitization is used mainly with adults. This is understandable in light of the need for patients to specify their fears, cooperate in relaxation and desensitization procedures, and accurately report anxiety and the visualized stimulus scenes. Lazarus (1960), however, used reciprocal inhibition techniques with 18 phobic children aged 3 to 12. After treatment averaging 9.4 sessions, he reported all 18 children recovered or were much improved and remained well at follow-ups ranging from 6 months to 2½ years.

An example is Carol, a 9-year-old girl who developed enuresis, fear of the dark, and psychosomatic reactions to school. These symptoms emerged after a friend drowned, a playmate died of meningitis, and she saw a fatal auto accident. In addition, Carol's mother had begun treating her coldly after reading that being affectionate with 9-year-olds could impede their development.

Interviews and projective tests indicated that Carol's chief fear was of separation from her mother because she was afraid the mother might die. Persuading the mother to be affectionate again did not bring improvement. Thereafter, an anxiety hierarchy was constructed with items ranging from imagined separation from the mother for five minutes to one week. Standard relaxation training and desensitization enabled Carol to reach the imagined one-week separation in five sessions spaced over 10 days. Carol then willingly returned to school. A 15-month follow-up revealed occasional enuresis but otherwise satisfactory adjustment.

Fairly orthodox systematic desensitization was used with Carol and many other children's problems (Hatzenbuehler & Schroeder, 1978). Yet many children cannot rank their anxieties, learn relaxation, or vividly imagine anxiety-provoking scenes. Other versions of desensitization have therefore been tried.

Emotive Imagery. One approach is to use anxiety-antagonistic responses other than relaxation. Lazarus and Abramovitz (1962), for example, used *emotive imagery* as a substitute for relaxation in treating children's phobias. After constructing an anxiety hierarchy, the therapist ascertains the child's favorite heroes and fantasy situations The child is then asked to imagine a sequence realistic enough to be credible but involving a favorite hero or fantasy. When the child's emotions reach a highly positive level, the therapist gradually inserts the lowest items in the anxiety hierarchy. The child is told to raise a finger if feeling unhappy, afraid, or uncomfortable. The therapist repeats the procedure until the highest item is reached. Lazarus and Abramovitz described one case as follows:

> Stanley M., aged 14, suffered from an intense fear of dogs, of 2½–3 years duration. He would take two buses on a roundabout route to school rather than risk exposure to dogs on a direct 300-yard walk. He was . . . trying to be cooperative, but sadly unresponsive—especially to attempts at training in relaxation. In his desire to please, he would state that he had been perfectly relaxed even though he had betrayed himself by his intense fidgetiness. Training in relaxation was eventually abandoned, and an attempt was made to establish the nature of his aspirations and goals. By dint of much questioning and after following many false trails because of his inarticulateness, a topic was eventually tracked down that was absorbing enough to form the subject of his fantasies, namely racing motor-cars. He had a burning ambition to own a certain Alfa Romeo sports car and race it at the Indianapolis "500" event. Emotive imagery was induced as follows: "Close your eyes. I want you to imagine, clearly and vividly, that your wish has come true. The Alfa Romeo is now in your possession. . . . It is standing in the street outside your block. . . . Notice the beautiful, sleek lines. You decide to go for a drive with some friends of yours. You sit down at the wheel and you feel a thrill of pride as you realize that you own this magnificent machine. You start up and listen to the wonderful roar of the exhaust. You let the clutch in and the car streaks off. . . . You are out in a clear open road now . . . the speedometer is climbing into the nineties; you have a wonderful feeling of being in perfect control; you look at the trees whizzing by and you see a little dog standing next to one of them—if you feel any anxiety, just raise your finger. . . ." An item fairly high up on the hierarchy: "You stop at a cafe in a little town and dozens of people crowd around to look enviously at this magnificent car and its lucky owner; you swell with pride; and at this moment a large boxer comes up and sniffs at your heels. . . ."
>
> After three sessions using this method he reported a marked improvement in his reaction to dogs. He was given a few field assignments during the next two sessions,

after which therapy was terminated. Twelve months later, reports both from the patient and his relatives indicated that there was no longer any trace of his former phobia. (Lazarus & Abramovitz, 1962, p. 192)

Actual Anxiety Stimuli. Another approach is to use actual anxiety stimuli instead of imagined stimuli. As an example, Wish, Hasazi, and Jurgela (1973) treated an 11-year-old's noise phobia by pairing relaxation with tape recordings of the feared sounds. Actual anxiety stimuli have also been paired with anxiety-antagonistic responses other than relaxation to form yet another variant of desensitization. O'Reilly (1971), for example, treated a first grader's phobia of a school fire bell by pairing taped fire bell sounds with taped children's stories and songs. Over 10 weeks of therapy, the fire bell was made progressively louder. The positive responses to the stories presumably inhibited anxiety responses to the accompanying fire bell sounds. Yet the mere repetition of the fire bell on the tapes and in six fire drills over the course of therapy may also have helped by promoting extinction of fear responses.

Reinforcement of Coping Responses. Consistent with the principles of desensitization but involving more aspects of operant conditioning are approaches that reinforce active coping responses. Recall how Holmes's (1936) treatment of children's fear of the dark differed from Jones's treatment of Peter's rabbit phobia: Rather than merely pairing positive experiences with gradually increasing exposure to the feared stimulus, Holmes *rewarded* children for entering a dark room and finding the light pull. Coping responses were also reinforced in one of the first published cases of desensitization with children. To treat an 8-year-old's fear of moving vehicles after an auto accident, Lazarus (1960) first talked with the child, John, about trains, planes, buses, and other vehicles. Even this evoked anxiety at first, but whenever John made a positive comment, he was casually offered some of his favorite chocolate. The chocolate was thus contingent on John's making a particular type of response, as in operant conditioning.

As John grew less anxious about discussing moving vehicles, Lazarus engaged him in play with toy cars that became involved in accidents. The anxiety evoked by these accidents soom diminished in response to chocolate. Later John sat with the therapist in a stationary car while discussing the original accident and receiving chocolate. Finally, at the seventeenth session (less than six weeks after therapy began), he willingly entered a car accompanied by a complete stranger and rode to a store to buy chocolate. For a short time afterward, he refused to ride with his parents unless given chocolate, but he soon began to enjoy riding for pleasure. Reinforcement for active coping has since been used with desensitization of children for social isolation and refusal to talk (*elective mutism*), as well as for fears of animals, heights, school, and water (Hatzenbuehler & Schroeder, 1978).

A further variant of desensitization is to show children models—either filmed or live—who demonstrate a graduated sequence leading up to the targeted behavioral outcome. The child is then reinforced for imitating the modeled behavior. Although used as an adjunct to desensitization, modeling also has its own independent body of research and theory, to be discussed later in the chapter.

OPERANT APPROACHES

Wolpe's reciprocal inhibiton is rooted in Pavlov's and Hull's "classical" or "respondent" conditioning paradigms. The other most widely used behavioral approach is rooted in the second major conditioning paradigm, *operant* conditioning, as proposed originally by Bekhterev and extended by Skinner. The essence of operant conditioning is summed up by Thorndike's (1913) Law of Effect: A response that produces a satisfying effect will tend to be repeated, while a response that produces an annoying effect will tend not to be repeated. More specifically, an *operant* is a response that *operates* on the environment to produce an effect. A satisfying effect is called a *reinforcer* of the response. A reinforcer is defined as any effect empirically found to strengthen the response that preceded it. Strengthening of a response is reflected by increases in the response's rate, magnitude, or speed of onset.

Operant Techniques

Operant approaches to behavior modification generally involve strengthening behavior by providing reinforcement or *extinguishing* (eliminating) behavior by removing reinforcements. Aversive consequences (punishments) can also reduce behavior, but many operant conditioners view punishment as disrupting or inhibiting behavior rather than extinguishing it (Skinner, 1953). We will discuss punishment further in the section on aversion therapy.

Laboratory research has been a chief source of methods for analyzing complex behaviors into operants and reinforcers. It has also been a source of data on stimulus fading, reinforcement schedules, and the shaping of new operants.

Stimulus Fading. In stimulus *fading*, subjects first learn that they will obtain a reinforcer when they respond to one particular stimulus. The stimulus that signals the availability of a reinforcer is called a *discriminative stimulus*. After a subject learns that reinforcement can be obtained by making a particular response in the presence of the discriminative stimulus, the stimulus is gradually faded out so that another stimulus accompanying it comes to elicit the same response.

As an example, Lovaas (1977) trained psychotic children to attend to and imitate an experimenter. He then began training them to speak words by presenting an object whose name he wanted them to learn. As soon as a child looked at the object, the trainer spoke its name loudly and clearly. Whenever the child imitated the word, the trainer provided food or another reinforcer. The object was then removed and presented again. On later trials, the trainer gradually faded out the prompt by saying the word more softly, whispering it, and eventually making only inaudible mouth movements until the child no longer needed prompting. The object thus came to replace the trainer's prompt as the discriminative stimulus for the child to say the object's name.

Reinforcement Schedules. Laboratory work on *schedules of reinforcement* has shown that *partial* reinforcement (reinforcement after some but not all emissions of an operant) or *intermittent* reinforcement (reinforcement at set time intervals if the operant is being emitted) makes a response more resistant to extinction than does reinforcement every time the response is made. This is crucial in conditioning humans, because even behavior that earns rewards in the real world usually does so on only a partial or intermittent basis.

Shaping. *Shaping* is training new responses by reinforcing successive approximations to them. For example, in teaching retarded children to use eating utensils, they might first be reinforced for picking them up in any manner; then for holding them properly; then for picking up food with them; then for conveying the right amount of food to the mouth, and so on.

Applied Behavior Analysis

The application of operant methods to practical problems of human behavior in the 1960s became known as *applied behavior analysis*. This differed from laboratory operant research in focusing on socially important behaviors in natural settings. Although laboratory standards of experimental control are guiding ideals, practical applications require compromises with these ideals. Dispensing with constructs such as "anxiety," applied behavior analysts try to change behavior by changing its supporting contingencies. Because the target subjects need not cooperate as much as with Wolpe's techniques, these interventions are used more widely with children. Applied behavior analysis has shown, for example, that adult attention can be a powerful reinforcer of children's behavior. Immature, aggressive, and withdrawn behaviors often win extra attention from parents and nursery school teachers. By making adult attention contingent on more appropriate behaviors, we can reduce inappropriate behaviors (Baer & Wolf, 1968). Yet because adult attention can sometimes have negative effects, careful behavioral analysis is always required to assess the actual outcomes (Sajwaj & Dillon, 1977).

ABAB Designs. The effects of making adult attention contingent on appropriate behavior have been shown via *ABAB designs* (also called "reversal" designs): The first *A* signifies an observation period preceding changes of reinforcement contingencies. The rate of the targeted desirable and undesirable behavior is recorded during this period to provide a *baseline* against which to measure change. The first *B* is a period when an intervention is started (if the intervention succeeds, the undesirable behavior decreases while the desirable behavior increases). The second

A is a period when the intervention is temporarily halted. The second *B* is a period when the intervention is reinstated. If the behaviors return to their baseline levels during the second *A* period and return to their first *B* levels during the second *B* period, this shows that the intervention rather than extraneous factors or the passage of time probably caused the behavior change.

In a study that has become a model of the *ABAB* approach, the subject was a 4-year-old nursery school girl named Ann. Ann isolated herself from other children, used elaborate means to get adult attention, and showed mild ticlike behavior (Allen, Hart, Buell, Harris, & Wolf, 1964). As a treatment, Ann was given maximum adult attention whenever she played with another child and minimum attention when she isolated herself or interacted with an adult alone. At 10-second intervals, observers recorded whether Ann was near or interacting with an adult or child.

Baseline percentages of Ann's interactions with children and adults were obtained over five days (the first *A* period). Teachers' attention was then made contingent on interaction with other children for six days (the first *B* period); the contingencies were reversed again for five days (the second *A* period); and the intervention was reinstated for nine days (the second *B* period). To make the new social behavior resistant to extinction, reinforcement during the last nine days was made increasingly intermittent. Figure 10-3 depicts the changes in Ann's behavior under the *ABAB* alternation of reinforcement contingencies. Follow-ups on Days 31, 38, 40, and 51 showed high rates of social interaction, although it dropped on Day 38, a day when Ann's mother was in class. Other effects were a rise in the volume, tempo, and pitch of Ann's speech, a drop in complaints about minor ills, and a general increase in happiness and confidence.

Multiple Baseline Designs. If behavior improves after an intervention, must we suspend the intervention to see whether the improvement will be lost? As an alternative, we can record baseline data for two or more target behaviors. We can then alter environmental contingencies to modify one of the behaviors while we continue to record data on all the behaviors. Once the first behavior has been successfully changed, we can alter contingencies to modify each of the remaining target behaviors in turn. If a target behavior changes only after treatment directed at it, we can credit the treatment with being the cause (Kazdin, 1978).

Token Systems. These involve *token reinforcers* (e.g., poker chips, points on a tally sheet) that are exchangeable for more valuable reinforcers, called *back-up reinforcers*. The basic principles of a token system are like those of the money economies used by most human societies. Under certain circumstances, token reinforcement has several advantages over other forms of reinforcement. One advantage is that the number of tokens (or tokens having different values) can be keyed to particular target behaviors. This permits precise regulation of reinforcement according to the importance or difficulty of specific behaviors. Tokens can

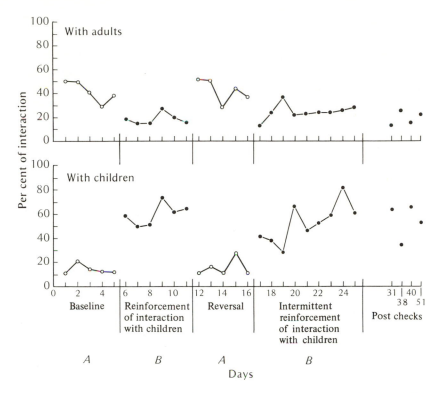

Figure 10-3. Percentage of nursery school time Ann spent in interaction with adults and children during *ABAB* sequence and postintervention follow-ups. (From Allen et al. 1964, p. 515. © 1964 by the Society for Research in Child Development and reprinted by permission.)

also be awarded for each response comprising a *chain* of behavior. Each response is thereby reinforced by the back-up reinforcer for which the accumulated tokens can eventually be exchanged. The power of token systems may be further enhanced by *fines* (deducting tokens) for undesirable behavior. Negative consequences of this sort are called *response costs*.

A second advantage of tokens is that they are more convenient than other forms of reinforcement: They can be easily dispensed (even by machine) and the recipient can store and keep track of them in anticipation of later exchange. This also means that people who dispense the reinforcements need not be well trained or attractive to the recipients; they need only dispense the tokens prescribed for specific behavior, although praise accompanying tokens is often an important component of token systems.

A third advantage is that tokens can be exchanged for reinforcers chosen by the recipient. This means that an effective reinforcer is more apt to be obtained than if the trainer unilaterally determines the reinforcer.

A fourth advantage is that, while emitting the desired behavior, the recipient may also be learning to work toward more distant goals.

Like their advantages, the disadvantages of token systems resemble those of money. For example, theft and hoarding are possible unless tokens are individualized and must be spent at prescribed times. Problems can also arise in replacing tokens with other reinforcement such as social approval to promote generalization to real-world situations where tokens are not dispensed.

Level (Phase) Systems. Token systems have been used in many controlled settings, including schools, institutions for the retarded, correctional facilities, and communes (Kazdin, 1977). An approach designed to make behavior less dependent on continuation of an artificial reinforcing system involves progressive *levels* or *phases*. In such a system, individuals work for reinforcers that may include tokens, but, by maintaining desirable behavior, they earn promotion to more advanced levels that entail higher level reinforcers, plus new standards of conduct. When they meet the new standards, they can work toward still more advanced levels, eventually reaching conditions that are as nearly normal as possible.

The level system has been used at *Achievement Place*, a group home for youths at risk for delinquency (Kirigin, Braukmann, Fixsen, Phillips, & Wolf, 1975). At the first level, youths earned points for appropriate behavior and exchanged them on a daily basis for privileges such as watching television. At the next level, they accumulated and exchanged points for more significant privileges on a weekly basis. If they succeeded at this level, they advanced to a *merit system* in which all privileges were free and only social consequences were applied to behavior. Maintenance of appropriate behavior at this level led to the *homeward-bound level* in which the youths spent increasing amounts of time with their families prior to release from the program.

Biofeedback. Despite Skinner's early emphasis on overt behavior, operant methods have been applied increasingly to the conditioning of physiological responses. The basic procedure is to provide the patient with mechanical feedback about changes in a targeted physiological response and reinforcement for making desired changes. With headache patients, for example, a device for recording electrical activity in forehead muscles is wired to a tone that can vary in pitch. The patient is then trained to relax the muscles while the tone signals the muscle changes. Through the feedback and reinforcement provided by the tone, the patient can learn to relieve headaches by controlling the muscles.

Similar procedures have been used to reduce epileptic seizures by providing feedback on epileptoid EEG activity (Olton & Noonberg, 1980) and to treat high blood pressure and asthma (Blanchard & Epstein, 1978). Although reinforcing successive approximations to the targeted physiological response is an operant strategy, the use of relaxation interfaces with Wolpe's approaches. Most studies have not clearly shown whether feedback or general coping responses or both are essential ingredients of treatment (Andrasik & Holroyd, 1980), and it is not clear whether biofeedback makes a significant independent contribution (Yates, 1980).

AVERSION THERAPY

Owing partly to Skinner's (1953) belief that punishment is ineffective in promoting learning, early behavior modifiers did not use painful stimuli for changing behavior. Various kinds of aversive stimulation have been found effective under certain circumstances, however. Some aversive methods raise ethical issues, but, as in medical treatment, the main question is whether the benefits ultimately justify temporary discomfort. Respondent and operant conditioning paradigms both provide models for aversive stimulation, but the theoretical distinctions among them are less clear than in positive reinforcement techniques. The four chief models of aversive control are:

Model 1. Deprivation of positive reinforcement.

Model 2. Application of aversive stimuli (*punishment*) whenever the target behavior occurs.

Model 3. Removal of aversive stimuli to reinforce an escape or avoidance response.

Model 4. Making neutral or positive stimuli aversive by pairing them with aversive stimuli (*classical aversive conditioning*).

Many aversive techniques can be interpreted in terms of more than one model. For example, *time-out from reinforcement* is widely employed with disruptive children whose behavior is not changed by adult attention or other positive reinforcers. Time-out usually consists of temporarily isolating a child following undesirable behavior.

According to Model 1, the effect of time-out is to cut off all positive reinforcement. Thus, any positive reinforcements supporting the behavior are removed and the behavior should extinguish. Yet the effects of time-out are also interpretable under Model 2, the contingent application of aversive stimuli (punishment): Being closed in a room and losing positive reinforcers are both aversive. And Model 3 implies that time-out may condition nondisruptive responses to the stimuli that evoked disruptive responses: Nondisruptive responses are reinforced by *avoidance* of isolation or *escape* from it if termination of time-out is contingent on cessation of disruptive behavior.

Covert responses, such as anxiety and physiological responses, further complicate the question of how aversive consequences change behavior. Experimental studies have revealed unexpected effects of aversive stimulation, such as increases in some punished behavior (Kanfer & Phillips, 1970), that have not been well explained theoretically. Yet certain aversive methods appear to yield good results, as discussed next.

Time-out from Reinforcement

In a typical application of time-out procedures, Wahler (1969) made *ABAB* analyses of two cases in which parents were trained to use time-out at home. The children were 5- and 6-year-old boys whose parents sought help for severe oppositional and destructive behavior. One of the boys was also oppositional and destructive at school. His parents attributed his behavior to distractibility. The other boy was an only child whose parents acknowledged spoiling him because they had lost several previous babies through miscarriages.

Observers first scored oppositional behavior during baseline sessions in the boys' homes. The parents were then trained to isolate their son in his room for five minutes whenever he was oppositional. If the boy had tantrums while in his room, he was to stay there until the tantrums ceased. The parents were to reinforce the boy with praise and attention whenever he was cooperative. Both boys' oppositional behavior dropped sharply during the first *B* (training) period. A temporary return to pretraining conditions (second *A* period) brought a sudden increase in oppositional behavior, but resumption of the training conditions (second *B* period) eliminated oppositional behavior almost completely.

The parents' effectiveness as reinforcers of their son's behavior was tested with a standardized experimental task after each period in the *ABAB* sequence. In this task, both boys were least responsive to their parents after the first *A* period, and second least responsive after the second *A* period. Their parents' effectiveness as reinforcers rose after the first *B* period and peaked after the second *B* period. This indicated that the intervention increased parental influence on other aspects of the boys' behavior as well as the target behavior.

Electrical Aversive Techniques

Electrical shock has been used in various ways with youngsters, although it is one of the most controversial techniques. Lovaas (1967) used shock for a number of purposes in the conditioning of psychotic children. One purpose was to suppress self-destructive behavior such as self-biting and head-banging so severe as to be life-threatening. Painful shock contingent on these behaviors was found to suppress the behaviors within minutes, with no recurrence for 11 months.

A second use of shock with psychotic children has been to establish social reinforcers by pairing them with pain reduction. For example, shock was administered through an electrified floor and was terminated when the child went to a nearby adult. Lovaas reported that children not only learned to go to the adult and to seek adult contact under other conditions, but they also showed social smiles and molded themselves onto adults' bodies, which they never did before. When adult attention becomes reinforcing through pairing with shock cessation, attention can be used as a reinforcer for new behavior.

A third use of shock has been to train severely disturbed children to respond to speech (Bucher & Lovaas, 1968). This was done by placing children on the electrified floor, commanding them to come to an adult, and terminating the shock when they did so. Other applications to speech training have involved shocking children whenever the word "No!" was given and shocking them for failing to imitate the speech sounds of a trainer. In most of Lovaas's severely disturbed cases, shock has been used mainly at the beginning of training, when other reinforcers were ineffective. Shock is then replaced with food, attention, praise, and other reinforcers as they become effective.

Shock was used in a very different way with a case of *ruminative vomiting* (Lang & Melamed, 1969). In this syndrome, a baby persistently vomits and ruminates (chews) the vomitus. Vomiting began when the baby was 5 months old, and it reached the point where his life was in danger.

After several other treatments failed, aversive conditioning was tried. It involved shocking the boy's leg whenever vomiting activity began, as observed by a nurse and indicated by electromyographic recordings taken around his throat. By the sixth session, the boy no longer vomited during training sessions. A slight recurrence was eliminated in three sessions. The boy's weight and activity increased steadily; he became more interested in his environment; and he smiled and reached out to be held by visitors. Five-month and one-year follow-ups showed normal weight and behavior and no recurrence of vomiting. Figure 10-4 shows the boy before and at two points after treatment.

Covert Sensitization

Reversing Wolpe's desensitization approach, Kolvin (1967) used a technique known as *covert sensitization* with a 14-year-old fetishist and a 15-year-old addicted to sniffing gasoline. In each case, the youth was first asked to list his dislikes. After inducing relaxation, Kolvin told a colorful story leading up to the symptomatic behaviors. When the patient was excitedly enjoying the fantasy, aversive imagery from the patient's list of dislikes was vividly introduced. Follow-ups over a year later revealed no recurrence of the problems in either case.

IMPLOSIVE THERAPY

Stampfl and Levis (1967) proposed "a learning theory-based psychodynamic behavioral therapy." Known as *implosive therapy*, their approach is psychodynamic in that it assumes that neurotic anxiety and symptoms stem from early traumatic experiences which become associated with other thoughts and cues, largely according to psychodynamic principles. The patient's defensive maneuvers are seen as warding off ideas and cues associated with trauma. Anxiety and defense help to explain psychopathology and guide treatment. Yet implosive therapy is behavioral in aiming to extinguish conditioned anxiety by presenting the con-

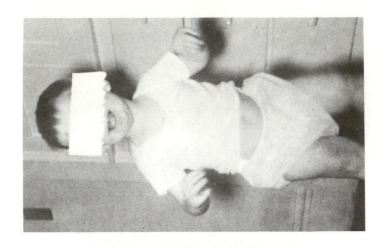

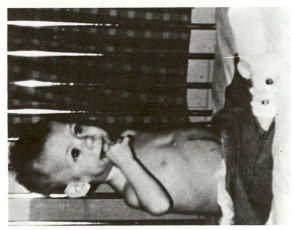

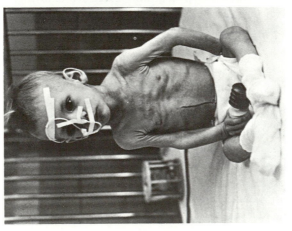

Figure 10-4. Boy suffering from ruminative vomiting. (From Lang & Melamed, 1969, pp. 3, 7.)

ditioned stimuli eliciting it but without the feared painful consequences. Direct exposure to feared stimuli (called *flooding*) has also been used to treat children's animal phobias (Sreenivasan, Manocha, & Jain, 1979) and compulsive behavior in adult obsessive−compulsives (Beech & Vaughn, 1978).

Implosive therapy generally begins with patients reporting what makes them most anxious. It is assumed that the real basis for the anxiety and the cues most strongly associated with it are avoided at first through repression and other defenses. Because avoidance prevents experience with the cues, anxiety to them is unlikely to extinguish without therapy. During therapy, the therapist helps the patient vividly imagine the frightening situations, working up to cues that the therapist believes are even more anxiety provoking than those initially specified by the patient. Repeatedly evoking anxiety responses without painful consequences is expected to extinguish the anxiety responses. The reduction in anxiety is assumed to generalize to real-life situations.

Although resembling desensitization in theory, implosive therapy differs from Wolpe's approach by exposing the patient to intense anxiety without training new responses to inhibit the anxiety. Wolpe (1976) equates it with desensitization that starts with the most potent items in the patient's anxiety hierarchy. Implosive therapy of adult disorders has produced mixed results (Kazdin, 1978), but a few applications to children's phobias appear successful. One case was an 8-year-old boy with a severe phobia for diverse cues associated with injury, especially bleeding (Ollendick & Gruen, 1972). The boy, Tommy, also had insomnia five to seven nights weekly, hives, and asthmatic bronchitis for which no allergen was found. The phobia had apparently begun several years earlier when a retarded sister was born with a disease that prevented her blood from clotting. Tommy's bed had been moved out of his parents' room and the new sister moved in.

After three interviews to establish rapport and elicit relevant fear-provoking cues, Tommy was seen for two therapy sessions in which he was asked to imagine scenes starting with his head being cut by a fall on a rock and climaxing with being attacked by rats that fed on his blood and tore him apart. These scenes evoked extreme anxiety. After each session, Tommy was assured that he was alright and was given brief relaxation training. He was then seen bimonthly for follow-ups.

Despite his grandmother's death during the third posttreatment month and intravenous feeding because of internal injuries suffered in an accident during the fourth month, Tommy's sleepless nights dropped to one per month in the fourth posttherapy month and none in the fifth and sixth posttherapy months. Tommy was also reported to play more with his retarded sister and to have more fun at school, as well as having no recurrence of hives or bronchitis.

Smith and Sharpe (1970) reported similar success in six implosive therapy sessions with a 13-year-old boy whose severe school phobia prevented him from staying in school. The authors of both these studies noted that implosive therapy seemed well suited to children because their high suggestibility made induction of the feared scenes especially effective. Most other views imply, however, that provoking intense fear in children is a very risky procedure. Because implosive therapy has not been shown superior to approaches that minimize anxiety during therapy, it is seldom the treatment of choice (Kazdin, 1978).

SOCIAL LEARNING THEORY: MODELING AND IMITATION

Albert Bandura (1977) has sought to broaden behavioral approaches by stressing the social aspects of learning and by viewing behavior in terms of *reciprocal determinism,* which refers to the mutual effects of behavior, other personal factors, and the environment on one another. Among the important personal factors are cognitive variables which, Bandura contends, play an essential role in the causation of behavior. In fact, he regards observation of behavior modeled by other people as the source of most important learning. Furthermore, he sees modeling as the only possible way to teach children such complex behavior as language.

According to Bandura's learning theory, language and other symbolic activities serve as guides to behavior and give people the ability to regulate their own behavior. Because he accords cognition such a central place in learning, Bandura dismisses the operant view that reinforcement *strengthens* responses. Instead, he views reinforcement as helping to *regulate* behavior through the *feedback* it provides about the consequences of behavior. However, he accords even this aspect of reinforcement a relatively minor role in most real-world behavior, because trial-and-error learning is so much less efficient than observational learning. As summarized in Figure 10-5, his theory of observational learning entails the following four components:

1. *Attentional processes* that determine what will be observed—features of the modeling stimuli and preexisting characteristics of the observer jointly affect attention.
2. *Retention processes* that determine what will be remembered, including mental images, verbal labels, and rehearsal of modeled activity.
3. *Motor reproduction processes* that convert symbolic representations into appropriate actions.
4. *Motivational processes* that determine which modeled behavior will actually be performed.

Bandura also believes that observational learning depends on developmental level: He agrees with Piaget that very young children are restricted to instantaneous imitation, whereas delayed modeling of complex behavior requires symbolic abilities that emerge in the second year of life. He believes, however, that once they have these abilities, children's preexisting mental schemes do not restrict observational learning as much as Piaget believed. Instead, he argues that deficiencies in imitation may be due to inadequate attention to the modeled activities, inadequate retention of the stimuli, motor inadequacies, or lack of motivation, rather than lack

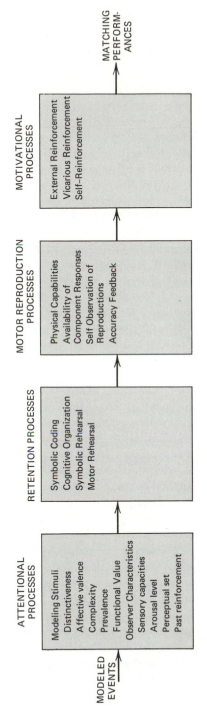

Figure 10-5. Component processes governing observational learning in the social learning analysis. (From Bandura, 1977.)

341

of appropriate mental schemes. While accepting the broad outline of Piagetian theory, Bandura nevertheless focuses mainly on situational determinants of modeling and how modeling can be used to change behavior.

Application to Behavior Problems

Following experimental studies of normal imitative behavior, Bandura extended similar procedures to the treatment of children's phobias. In one study, preschoolers afraid of dogs observed another child approach, pet, feed, and interact with a dog over a series of four sessions (Bandura, Grusec, & Menlove, 1967). Posttreatment and one-month follow-up tests showed that children who had seen the model later interacted better with dogs than control groups who had seen the dog without the model or had enjoyed a party between pretests and posttests but had seen neither the dog nor the model.

In another study, live modeling plus guided participation in handling snakes eliminated snake phobias in nearly all adolescent and adult subjects (Bandura, Blanchard, & Ritter, 1969). (Guided contact with the phobic object is also known as *participant modeling* or *contact desensitization*.) Filmed modeling plus relaxation training was more effective than regular desensitization, although desensitization was significantly better than no treatment. Bandura has since argued that increased feelings of self-efficacy are central to mastering problems such as phobias, and that direct contact procedures maximize such feelings (Bandura, Adams, & Beyer, 1977).

In a study designed to separate the effects of modeling and participation, Lewis (1974) found that participation reduced boys' fear of water more than filmed modeling. The combination of modeling with participation, however, was the most effective treatment of all. The addition of filmed modeling to other procedures designed to reduce anxiety among children facing surgery has also been found to reduce subsequent anxiety and behavior problems (Melamed & Siegel, 1975).

Although spontaneous imitation is common among normal children, its impact on problem behavior depends on many factors. Among these are the model's similarity to the observer. It has been found, for example, that snake phobic elementary school girls were helped more by seeing another girl modeling approach behavior toward snakes than by seeing a woman model the same behavior (Kornhaber & Schroeder, 1975). Reinforcement for imitating several different models has also been found to produce more generalized imitation than reinforcement for imitating a single model (Marburg, Houston, & Holmes, 1977).

In his work with psychotic children who do not readily imitate, Lovaas (1977) has trained imitation of simple tasks by "prompting" the child to follow the trainer's example (e.g., by moving the child's hand through the desired behavior) and then providing food reinforcers for progressively more complete imitation as the prompts are faded on successive trials. Generalized imitative behavior has thus been trained in children who had not previously imitated. Personal hygiene, games, drawing, printing, elementary social skills, and simple speech have then been taught through imitation.

In another application, modeling was used to teach masculine behaviors to Kevin, a 10-year-old boy with gender identity confusion (Hay, Barlow, & Hay, 1981). A multiple-baseline design was used to evaluate the effects of covert modeling in modifying motor behaviors that Kevin performed in a stereotypically feminine way. These behaviors evoked ridicule from peers, making Kevin increasingly isolated and unhappy, as well as leading to disruptive behavior and deteriorating achievement in school. Kevin's therapist taught him to visualize more masculine ways of walking, standing, sitting, gesturing, and carrying books. This was done by having Kevin help formulate fantasies involving the "Six Million Dollar Man," one of his favorite television characters. Kevin was to imagine these fantasy sequences whenever he wanted to remind himself how to perform one of the target behaviors in a more masculine way. Sequences like the following were repeated five times in a therapy session and Kevin practiced them between sessions:

> You are walking out of school onto the playground. You imagine that Steve Austin, the Six Million Dollar Man, is walking ahead of you. You look at how he walks and you want to walk just like him. You see that he takes long, smooth steps and his hips don't swish or move from side to side as he walks. His arms hang loosely at his side. He doesn't move his hands very much when walking and his wrist isn't limp or loose. You catch up with him and ask him if you can walk with him. You continue to look at the way he walks and you try to walk just like he does and you're pretty good at it. As you're walking this new way you see a group of boys from school. They ask you to join them. (Hay et al., 1981, pp. 390—91)

Parent ratings and observers' ratings of videotapes showed large increases in the percentage of masculine behavior, and these were maintained over a 6-month follow-up period.

COGNITIVE-BEHAVIORAL APPROACHES

Bandura's social learning theory gives cognitive variables a central role in behavioral development and change. Several other approaches focus even more strongly on cognition. Called *cognitive-behavioral*, these approaches stress cognitive change as the active ingredient of therapy. Like less cognitive behavioral approaches, they employ structured procedures to alleviate specific problems of current functioning without trying to uncover historical or unconscious determinants. Unlike other behavioral approaches, however, they aim to change behavior by changing cognitions, primarily through the medium of language, rather than changing behavior directly. Because of this focus on cognition, some behavior modifiers do not regard cognitive-behavioral approaches as behavior therapy

(Ledwidge, 1979). Others argue that all behavior therapy involves cognition anyway, but that because "cognitive responses are a subset of behavioral responses, cognition-directed treatment procedures must be a subset of behavioral procedures—and not the other way around" (Wolpe, 1978, p. 444).

Just how similar or different the basic processes are in cognitive-behavioral and other behavioral approaches is an open question. Because they require advanced verbal and cognitive abilities, most cognitive-behavioral techniques have been used mainly with adults.

Beck's Cognitive Therapy

In Aaron Beck's (1976) *cognitive therapy* with depressed adults, the therapist and patient work together to identify distorted cognitions stemming from excessively negative beliefs about the self. The cognitions and beliefs are then analyzed logically and behavioral tasks are assigned through which the patient learns to master previously threatening problems. A controlled comparison has shown this treatment superior to antidepressant drugs with depressed adults (Rush, Beck, Kovacs, & Hollon, 1977).

Ellis's Rational-Emotive Therapy

Albert Ellis (1975) developed a similar approach—known as *rational-emotive therapy*—for changing adults' irrational negative beliefs about themselves. However, (RET) has also been used to treat children's anxiety about taking tests. The theory of RET ascribes the anxiety to irrational statements such as "It would be just *terrible* if I failed the test." "How *stupid* and *worthless* I am if I do poorly." The treatment focuses on changing these beliefs by discussing the nature of emotions, fear of failure, and the substitution of rational self-directed talk for self-deprecation. It also includes practice in taking tests and in rational coping during testing. Test-anxious fifth and sixth graders receiving RET have been found to decline more than an untreated control group on a measure of test anxiety (Warren, Deffenbacher, & Brading, 1976).

Self-instructional Training

In contrast to the Beck and Ellis approaches, Donald Meichenbaum (1977) developed a cognitive-behavioral approach designed for children. Called *self-instruction training,* it entails having a child work tasks with an adult who acts as a model by thinking aloud and saying self-directed statements intended to control behavior. The adult verbalizes self-instructions such as "work slowly," plans for solving the task, and self-praise when the task is mastered. The child is first trained to make the verbalizations aloud and then covertly.

As an example, Kendall and Finch (1978) used six types of tasks to train emotionally disturbed impulsive children. The tasks included identifying matching and dissimilar pictures, completing partial figures, and reproducing designs. The adult trainer first performed a task while talking out loud about possible answers and relevant aspects of the stimuli. The child then performed the task with guidance to talk aloud as the trainer had. The trainer then did the task while whispering to himself, followed by the child doing likewise. Finally, the trainer and the child did the task using covert self-instruction. Response cost was added to self-instruction training by giving the child 10 chips at the beginning of each session and deducting one for each mistake. Children could buy back-up reinforcers if they ended the session with enough chips.

Compared to a control group receiving all but the self-instruction training, the trained group showed greater increases in latency of responses and decreases in errors on the Matching Familiar Figures Test, a measure of impulsivity. Teacher ratings of classroom impulsivity also showed improvements for the trained subjects and worsening for the control subjects, but the children's self-reports of whether they would be impulsive in various situations showed no significant improvement. Despite the cognitive emphasis of the treatment, it thus seemed more effective in modifying overt behavior than self-reported cognitions.

In a further study, Kendall and Wilcox (1980) found that *conceptual* self-instruction, which emphasized general rules, was more effective than concrete self-instruction, which emphasized the task at hand. Self-reports again failed to show significant effects, however.

BEHAVIOR MODIFICATION IN NATURAL ENVIRONMENTS

One of the most promising features of behavioral methods is their use by nonspecialists. Although the design and evaluation of behavioral programs require specialized training and experience, nonspecialists can apply many behavioral procedures and record the relevant data. For example, psychiatric aides, child care workers, volunteers, parents, teachers, and nurses carry out behavioral programs in many settings.

Family Settings

Because most behavioral problems are ascribed at least partly to learning conditions in the home, these conditions are often targeted for change. One approach is via a type of family psychotherapy known as *conjoint family therapy*, which we will discuss in Chapter 17. Here, however, we will focus on behavioral approaches.

In some cases, parents are taught specific procedures such as the time-out technique described earlier (Wahler, 1969). In other cases, efforts are made to change parents' overall behavior toward their families. A common approach is to have parents read behavioral guides to child management. These introduce techniques that are then taught for handling particular problems. Some therapists, however, give more intensive instruction with audio- and videotapes, lectures, role-playing, and tests of parents' knowledge. Adding instruction in learning principles to training in specific techniques can produce better management of children's behavior problems than training specific techniques alone (McMahon, Forehand, & Griest, 1981).

Having the therapist administer the materials usually produces better results than self-administered materials (Glasgow & Rosen, 1978). Instruction in behavioral methods via group counseling has also been found more effective in helping mothers cope with their retarded children than has group counseling aimed at emotional issues (Tavormina, 1975).

A more direct approach was taken in the Family Training Program (Christophersen, Barnard, Ford, & Wolf, 1976). A family was first interviewed to identify problem behaviors, and parents were assigned to read an instruction manual. After the specific problems and likely reinforcers were identified, the program had three phases: In the first phase, the parents watched as the therapist actively intervened with the children and demonstrated intervention techniques in the home. In the second phase, the parents and children practiced the prescribed behaviors while the therapist watched. In the third phase, the therapist periodically contacted the parents to check on behavioral changes.

The parents were trained in operant techniques of providing positive or negative consequences for specific behaviors. Consequences ranged from hugs for toddlers to tokens (poker chips for preschoolers, points for school-aged children) redeemable for back-up reinforcers. Beside receiving negative consequences for problem behavior, the older children were rewarded for positive adaptive behaviors such as practicing time-outs, interacting pleasantly with family members, and assisting with household chores. Parents of Family Training Program children reported a significantly greater decline in problems than parents of a control group treated in a guidance clinic.

If children's behavior problems are at least partly learned at home, what can be done about problem parents? Even when the contingencies supporting a child's behavior are evident, parents may be unwilling or unable to change their own behavior. Marital adjustment, for example, has been found worse in parents of children referred for treatment than in parents of normal children, and severity of marital maladjustment was correlated with severity of the child's problems (Oltmanns, Broderick, & O'Leary, 1977). This does not prove a *causal* relation, but it does warn that we must often contend with parent as well as child problems.

To deal with parent problem behavior, Mealiea (1976) tried an approach called *conjoint behavior modification*. Parents are first trained to modify specific child behavior, but their own interactions are videotaped and are used to shift the focus to themselves. Reinforcement principles learned in relation to their children are then brought to bear on their marital relationship. As an example, 12-year-old Dan was referred for treatment of encopresis. He was also chronically late for breakfast, school, and appointments, and was irresponsible about household chores. An analysis showed that Dan was highly reinforced for these behaviors: He was allowed to leave school whenever he had an "accident," which often enabled him to avoid assignments and exams. His mother collaborated in hiding his soiled pants and kept him supplied with clean ones. When he was late, she drove him the few blocks to school. She and his grandmother did his chores when he did not. Everyone in the family was solicitous of Dan's problems, except his father, who was rejecting him because of his encopresis.

Dan and his parents agreed on a token system for earning rewards, such as time with his father, and avoiding response costs, such as loss of television time, snacks, and movies. His encopresis and tardiness were controlled within five weeks and the increased interaction he earned with his father helped change the father's role in the family.

> The success of the program in changing Dan's behavior helped convince the parents that a similar analysis and program would help their own marital relationship. Dan's mother was very upset by the feedback she received via video of the overwhelming possessive role she played in the family. She became aware of the reinforcement she had been giving Dan for his maladaptive behavior and realized it was serving a need, i.e., having someone depend on her, that compensated for limitations in the relationship with her husband. Mother and father had grown distant from each other; father did not like a son who "shit his pants" and consequently buried himself in the family business. The parents contracted for behavior each wanted the other to exhibit; they rearranged their living schedule to have more private time together. They also clarified and resolved the roles to be played by all family members, particularly that of the grandmother, who tended to ally herself with her daughter and against her son-in-law. After five months of treatment the family had resolved most of the conflicts that had caused friction in the family unit. An 8-month follow-up indicated that Dan's problem behavior had not recurred, and the members of the family felt very good about the family situation. (Mealiea, 1976, pp. 159–160)

As Mealiea illustrates with other case histories, however, successful modification of children's behavior is occasionally undone by insufficient parental change.

Parents' involvement in their children's problems and treatment seems obvious, but their specific impacts and how to change them are not so obvious. Research is needed to determine how best to promote change that is stable and will benefit all the children of a family (Forehand & Atkeson, 1977). The heavy involvement of parents in their child's treatment and occasional disagreement between their judgments and others' judgments of outcome also raise questions of who should determine whether treatment is successful (Atkeson & Forehand, 1978).

School Settings

Like the home, the school provides abundant opportunities for behavioral problems as well as for adaptive learning. Many applications of behavioral methods in schools use time-outs, token reinforcement, differential deployment of teacher attention, and self-control training to reduce disruptive behavior. Numerous studies show that these methods can enhance classroom management (O'Leary & O'Leary, 1977; Rosenbaum & Drabman, 1979). However, behavioral methods are also used to strengthen positive school behaviors more directly. Disruptive behavior in a fifth grade classroom, for example, has been reduced and reading performance improved by using a token economy in which improved reading was the only behavior specifically reinforced (Allyon & Roberts, 1974).

Another use of a token system is to reinforce behaviors incompatible with problem behaviors. Durlak (1977) did this in small groups of second graders who met weekly for arts, crafts, group games, and stories. Praise, attention, and poker chips exchangeable for back-up reinforcers were awarded for target behaviors specified on a chart for each child. Shy, withdrawn children, for example, were reinforced for behaviors such as talking and working with others. Disruptive children, by contrast, were reinforced for waiting their turn and working on their own. Compared to an untreated control group, the participating children showed significant improvements in teacher-rated classroom behavior at the end of the program and at a 7-month follow-up during the next school year.

Because peers often encourage misbehavior in school, efforts have been made to turn peer influence into a more constructive force. In a school for severely disturbed children, for example, a token system was set up in which students approved the rules and elected a captain to award the tokens (Drabman, 1973). This system was as effective as one where the tokens were administered by teachers. Many of the gains made with the token system also survived after back-up reinforcers were no longer offered.

Other Settings

We will discuss behavioral methods in controlled settings such as residential centers for severely disturbed and delinquent children in later chapters. Some applications to more naturalistic settings outside the home and school are worth illustrating here, however.

Mothers participating in the Family Training Program described earlier often complained of difficulty in controlling their children's behavior outside the home (Christophersen et al., 1976). Misbehavior in supermarkets was an especially common problem that was chosen for change. An observer first recorded each episode when a child left his or her mother or disturbed merchandise in the supermarket. The children were then trained by having appropriate behavior demonstrated, practicing these behaviors, and receiving praise and verbal feedback about their performance. Token reinforcement and response cost procedures were used in actual trips to the store. This led to substantial reductions in the target behaviors and more favorable parent ratings of the children's behavior.

A more complex application of behavioral methods to natural settings used indigenous nonprofessionals to help 11- to 17-year-olds with behavior and academic problems (Fo & O'Donnell, 1974). Under the *buddy system,* as it was called, an adult buddy met weekly with three youths to establish a relationship and engage in recreational activities. The buddies were trained in behavioral methods and were to maintain weekly logs of behavioral data and assignments to be carried out with each youth. Youngsters receiving either social approval alone or in combination with material reinforcers for desirable behavior were found to decrease their truancy rates significantly, whereas control groups having a buddy but no contingent rewards or receiving no treatment did not decrease in truancy.

A 3-year follow-up of arrest records for buddy system and control youths revealed a paradoxical outcome, however (O'Donnell, Lydgate, & Fo, 1979): Among youths who had previously committed a major offense (such as auto theft, burglary, or assault), fewer of those participating in the buddy system than of control youth were arrested again. Yet, among youths who had *not* previously committed a major offense, significantly *more* were arrested after participating in the buddy system than in the no-treatment control condition. This suggests that the buddy system was beneficial for those who had previously committed a major offense, but harmful for those who had not, possibly because it brought them in contact with more serious offenders. This again points up the importance of assessing the differential impacts of treatment on different individuals.

BEHAVIORAL APPROACHES TO FEARS AND SOMATIC DYSFUNCTIONS

To illustrate behavioral concepts of specific disorders and permit comparison with psychodynamic views, we now consider two types of disorder that have been of particular interest from both perspectives: fears and somatic dysfunctions. Behavioral approaches to such disorders as learning disability, hyperactivity, bedwetting, and aggression will be discussed in later chapters.

Fears

Like Freud, early behaviorists used children's fears to illustrate their theory of the origin and treatment of behavioral disorders (Jones, 1924b; Watson & Rayner, 1920). As we saw in Chapter 9, Freud (1926) viewed severe fears (*phobias*) as byproducts of repressed intrapsychic conflicts. For example, Little Hans's fear of castration by his father was *displaced* onto horses, which served as symbolic substitutes for his father. Thinking of horses as the source of his anxiety helped

Hans avoid the conflict between his positive and negative feelings toward his father. It also helped him avoid further anxiety by avoiding horses. According to this view, treatment must undo the unconscious causes of the manifest fear.

Behavior modifiers, by contrast, view fears as learned responses to particular stimuli. In some cases, fear responses are generalized from a painful stimulus to others like it. In other cases, fears may be learned by *classical conditioning,* whereby a painful or threatening stimulus is paired with a benign stimulus. If the fear-evoking stimulus is intense or frequently paired with the benign stimulus, then the fear response generalizes to the benign stimulus and others like it. Fear responses to new stimuli are thought to be proportional to the strength of their associations with the original stimulus. A child bitten by a particular dog, for example, may be panicked by that dog and similar dogs, but slightly less afraid of dissimilar dogs; he may be still less afraid of a dog barking in the distance; he may be minimally afraid of other furry animals. The child may also develop elaborate behavior for avoiding dogs, however. This behavior may be *reinforced* (according to *operant* principles) by the relief felt when the child succeeds in avoiding dogs. Although the avoidant behavior relieves fear, it may impede development by preventing the child from playing with other children or visiting new places. This, in turn, can lead to new problems, such as excessive dependency and a pervasive sense of inadequacy.

Children are seldom brought for treatment solely because of a phobia (Graziano & DeGiovanni, 1979). More typically, fears are but one aspect of a general pattern of withdrawn and anxious behavior, although some behavior theorists view the whole pattern as stemming from one or more phobias learned through classical conditioning (Wolpe, 1976). Despite viewing learning as the cause of phobias, some behavior theorists also stress that constitutional differences in anxiety thresholds affect people's susceptibility to phobias. Eysenck, for example, has proposed that two dimensions of personality determine people's susceptibility to phobias (Eysenck & Rachman, 1965). One dimension is *neuroticism,* ranging from normal people whose emotional reactions are relatively stable and weak, to neurotic people whose emotional reactions are labile, intense, and easily aroused. The other dimension is *extroversion-introversion,* ranging from people who are outgoing, sociable, impulsive, optimistic, and not easily conditioned, to people who are quiet, introspective, cautious, serious, and easily conditioned.

Tests that score these two dimensions show that different syndromes represent different positions on the dimensions. Figure 10-6 pinpoints people diagnosed as anxious, obsessional, hysterical, psychopathic (antisocial), and psychosomatic. Note that obsessionals and psychopaths are both high on emotional reactivity (neuroticism), but obsessionals are introverted while psychopaths are extroverted. Obsessionals and anxiety neurotics are viewed as the most susceptible to phobias

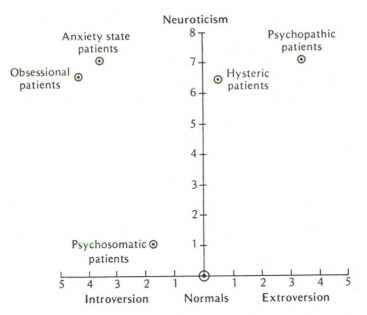

Figure 10-6. The basic dimensions of personality according to Eysenck's theory. Various patient groups are located according to the average scores they obtain on measures of the two dimensions. (Adapted from Eysenck and Rachman, 1965, p. 21. © 1965 by R. R. Knapp and reprinted by permission of the publisher.)

because they are the most reactive *and* the most readily conditioned. When they meet a frightening situation, they are the most likely to learn new fears from it.

Two other questions are not easily answered by conditioning alone: Why do phobias get worse despite nonreinforcing conditions that would extinguish other responses? And why are phobias of snakes and other animals so common?

Eysenck (1976) proposed that constitutional factors may also help to answer these questions. People high in neuroticism and introversion may be especially prone to "incubate" anxiety in response to conditioned fear stimuli even without painful consequences. And the evolutionary process of natural selection may have made our species especially fearful of stimuli associated with threats to survival, such as potential predators. Despite the roles he thus grants to constitutional factors, Eysenck believes that behavior therapy is the best way to treat phobias once they exist.

School Phobia. Most specific fears are not much more common in children referred for mental health services than in normal children, and they decline with age in both groups (Achenbach & Edelbrock, 1981). Marked fear of school (*school phobia*), however, often instigates referral of children who may not show other major problems (Graziano, DeGiovanni, & Garcia, 1979). It is considerably more common among disturbed children than among normals, and its rate does not decline over the school years (Achenbach & Edelbrock, 1981).

Most children are somewhat fearful when starting or changing schools, returning after an absence, and facing difficult classes or exams. Those who become phobic may seem eager to attend but panic when the time comes. They often cry, vomit, and show other somatic reactions. There is a vast literature on school phobia and school refusal from many perspectives: The case of Frankie presented in Chapter 9 illustrates psychoanalytic treatment of a school phobia, while the case of Carol earlier in this chapter illustrates desensitization.

Despite very different approaches to treatment, there is general agreement on three points:

1. The fear is not so much of school itself but of separation from parents.
2. The behavior of the parents is crucial; some may inadvertently encourage the child to stay home.
3. It is essential to return the child to school as soon as possible.

While agreeing that separation rather than school may be feared, most behavior modifiers focus on getting the child into school, reducing anxiety about staying, and eliminating reinforcements for staying home. (Psychoanalysts call these reinforcements *secondary gains,* because they are in addition to the *primary gain* the symptom achieves by solving a neurotic conflict.)

We have already seen how desensitization was used with Carol and how implosive therapy was used with a 13-year-old boy (Smith & Sharpe, 1970). Other behavioral approaches have also been illustrated with case history reports. *In vivo* ("real-life") desensitization, for example, was used with a 9-year-old boy whose therapist arranged gradually increasing exposures to school, supplemented with distraction, humor, emotive imagery, and rewards (Lazarus, Davison, & Polefka, 1965). Taking a different tack with a 7-year-old boy, Patterson (1965) shaped the boy's doll play and conversation by reinforcing him with candy whenever the child dolls left the parent dolls or the boy expressed independence. The mother was also coached in reinforcing the boy for playing outside and increasing his mobility and independence.

Although uncontrolled studies cannot prove that a treatment works, Kennedy (1965) reported a rapid behavioral treatment with 50 school phobic children. The therapist first interviewed the parents to assess the problem and outline the treatment plan. The father was then to take the child to school (by force if necessary), without procrastination or prolonged advance discussion. The school principal or attendance officer insured that the child stayed in class, while the mother remained in the school if necessary. The child was praised for whatever length of time he or she stayed in school. The stay in school was lengthened on the next day, with a goal of cure by the third day. Before or after the first school day, the therapist met with the child to tell stories dramatizing the advantages of going on in the face of fear and to stress the transitory nature of the phobia. Kennedy reports that all 50 children treated in this way lost their symptoms and continued attending school for follow-up periods ranging from two to eight years.

Kennedy made a crucial diagnostic distinction, however, in accepting children for this treatment: He treated children of elementary school age whose main problem was the school phobia and related concerns about their mother's health. Older children who had disturbed parents and previous episodes of school phobia were deemed to need more intensive treatment.

The key role of age in the treatability of phobias was highlighted in a controlled comparison of systematic desensitization with psychodynamically oriented psychotherapy (Miller et al., 1972). The subjects were 6- to 15-year old phobics, most of whom had school phobias. It was found that desensitization and psychotherapy had significantly better outcomes than a no-treatment control condition with 6- to 10-year-olds: 96 percent of the treated children but only 57 percent of the control children showed good outcomes at a 6-week follow-up. Among 11- to 15-year-olds, however, only 45 percent receiving treatment and 44 percent of the untreated controls showed good outcomes. Neither desensitization (with a 56 percent success rate) nor psychotherapy (with a 36 percent success rate) differed significantly from the 44 percent success rate in the no-treatment control condition. A two-year follow-up showed a lessening of phobias for all groups (Hampe, Noble, Miller, & Barrett, 1973). The reasons may be diverse, however, since some youngsters had other treatment after the study, while others reached ages where the original phobias were no longer important, because, for example, they no longer had to attend school.

Somatic Dysfunctions

In Chapter 7, we discussed psychophysiological reactions and other dysfunctions involving a combination of psychological factors and organic abnormalities. In Chapter 9, we discussed psychodynamic views of hysterical disorders in which bodily symptoms arise for psychological reasons without organic abnormalities. Behavioral methods are used to treat both kinds of disorders in children, as exemplified in the following sections. The general application of behavioral psychology to medical problems is known as *behavioral medicine*.

Bronchial Asthma. Despite a large literature on psychological correlates of asthma, there is little evidence that psychological factors actually *cause* asthma (Alexander, 1980). Yet because psychological stresses can help to induce and aggravate asthmatic attacks, it is important to help asthmatic children cope with these stresses and with the consequences of their condition. Behavioral methods are aimed at helping asthmatics by (1) improving breathing, (2) reducing negative emotional responses, and (3) altering maladaptive behaviors and family patterns (Alexander, 1980).

Relaxation and biofeedback have been the chief behavioral methods for improving breathing by preventing bronchial constriction. Relaxation training does this by teaching asthmatics to relax their muscles at will. For example, relaxation training helped 10- to 15-year old asthmatics increase the air flow from their lungs significantly more than control youngsters who merely sat quietly for an equal number of sessions (Alexander, Miklich, & Hershkoff, 1972). The addition of biofeedback has improved the results of relaxation training with mild asthmatics but neither relaxation alone nor accompanied with biofeedback significantly helped children whose asthma was so severe as to require continuous medication (Davis, Saunders, Creer, & Chai, 1973).

Another use of biofeedback is to train dilation of the bronchial passages (Khan, Staerk, & Bonk, 1973). This was done by inducing constriction of the passages and then conditioning dilation responses, using praise and a red light to signal dilation. After training, 8- to 15-year-old asthmatics showed significantly fewer asthmatic attacks, less use of medication, and fewer emergency room visits than control youngsters over an 8- to 10-month follow-up period.

A second aim of behavioral treatment is to alleviate negative emotional reactions to asthma. Because many of these reactions are anxiety responses to cues associated with previous frightening and painful episodes, hierarchies of anxiety cues can be constructed like those used to systematically desensitize other fears (Alexander, 1977). Starting with relatively mild cues, such a hierarchy might include thinking about starting to wheeze and feeling tight; and then progressing to mild wheezing; more severe wheezing; failure to respond to medication; being rushed to the emergency room; and intensive medical treatment. *In vivo* desensitization can also be used by training the asthmatic to make relaxation responses as various symptoms actually occur under medically controlled conditions.

A third aim of behavioral treatment is altering maladaptive behaviors and family patterns arising from asthma. This has been done largely through operant conditioning. In some cases, for example, asthmatic children seek unnecessary hospitalization to avoid school and other stresses. In other cases, symptoms such as coughing in response to ordinary household items arouse excessive family concern that impedes helping the child learn more adaptive behavior. By changing the reinforcement contingencies supporting such behavior, it can often be modified in the same way as other behavioral problems (Alexander, 1977).

Epileptic Seizures. As we saw in Chapter 7, epileptic seizures involve recurrent interruption of normal consciousness or activity owing to excessive electrical discharges in the brain. Although the specific causes are often unknown, seizures must be suppressed in order to prevent seizure-caused injury and anoxia and relieve the anxiety and restrictions on activity that epileptics often face. Because as many as 50 percent of epileptic children continue to have seizures despite anticonvulsive medication, behavioral methods have been increasingly tried (Siegel & Richards, 1978). These take many forms, including operant manipulation of reward and punishment contingencies, relaxation, desensitization, self-control methods, and habituation to precipitating sensory stimuli (Mostofsky & Balaschak, 1977). Biofeedback has also been used to signal and reinforce epileptics for reducing epileptoid EEG activity (Yates, 1980). Although showing positive benefits, most of the published reports are of single cases and small samples.

A case study by Ince (1976) poignantly reveals an epileptic child's anxieties as well as illustrating treatment of the anxiety and the seizures themselves. The patient was a 12-year-old boy who, despite four kinds of medication, continued to have frequent *grand* and *petit mal* seizures. As a consequence, he was teased by classmates, felt rejected, grew fearful of school, and began having headaches, stomachaches, and insomnia, which he used as excuses to stay home. Anxiety about school was the first target of treatment. The anxiety hierarchies in Table 10-1 show in ascending order the boy's fears in four different areas.

Table 10-1   Anxiety Hierarchies Reflecting the Fears of a 12-year-old Epileptic Boy (Higher numbers indicate the boy's greatest fears)

A. Seizures in School

1. Sitting in a classroom and feeling an aura.
2. The classroom environment begins to "fade away."
3. A seizure begins.
4. The teacher is speaking to him but he is unable to respond.
5. Children and teacher gather around him.
6. Seizure is out of control and he feels himself "blacking out."

B. Seizure on Baseball Field

1. Standing on pitcher's mound and feeling an aura.
2. People yelling at him to pitch but he is unable to do so.
3. Other players, coaches, etc. gathering around him.
4. Seizure begins and the environment "fades away."
5. He falls and feels himself "blacking out."

C. Being Ridiculed by Other Children

1. Children laughing at him when he enters school.
2. Children staring at him, pointing at him and laughing in his classroom.
3. Children calling him names.
4. Children telling him that he is "crazy," "retarded," etc., that he belongs in an institution.
5. Children refusing to play with him or come to his house when he asks them to because he has epilepsy.

D. Receiving New Experimental Medication

1. Going with his mother to the physician.
2. Physician gives his mother the medication and informs her of dosages.
3. Physician warns him and his mother of possible negative side effects.
4. At home, his mother calls him to receive his first dose.

Source: Ince, 1976.

After two training sessions in relaxation, it took five sessions of systematic desensitization to eliminate the fears: The boy had no more somatic complaints, and he seemed to function normally. The seizures were then treated by training the boy to relax at home and to use the word "relax" as a conditioned stimulus for relaxation whenever he felt a seizure approaching. This was followed by disappearance of the seizures, with none in the nine months after termination of therapy.

Hysterical Disorders. We saw in Chapter 9 that psychoanalytic theory ascribes hysterical symptoms to conflicts between anxiety-provoking wishes and defenses against these wishes. According to this view, a hysterical symptom is a *compromise* between the forbidden wish and the defense against it that enables the hysteric to avoid further anxiety by preventing further arousal or expression of the wish.

Behavioral and cognitive views agree that hysterics are prone to produce symptoms as a way of avoiding uncomfortable situations (Sackeim, Nordlie, & Gur, 1979; Ullmann & Krasner, 1975). However, rather than ascribing the symptoms to conversion of unconscious conflicts into somatic form, they see parallels between hysterical symptoms and behavior in hypnosis, role playing, placebo treatments, and malingering. Although hysterics are not regarded as deliberately faking organic symptoms, their behavior can be understood as controlled by cues and reinforcers that provide stronger incentives to manifest such symptoms than to avoid them. This implies that hysterical symptoms can be removed by manipulating the relevant cues and reinforcers.

One approach is to attach aversive consequences to hysterical symptoms. Kushner (1970), for example, reported several cases in which termination of small electrical shocks was made contingent on cessation of hysterical symptoms such as paralyses and persistent sneezing. We may need a more comprehensive approach, however, where there are multiple symptoms, firmly embedded in a longstanding life-style. In the case of a 17-year-old girl named Jennifer, for example, electrical shock, psychotherapy, and drug treatments failed to eliminate a hysterical cough (Munford, Reardon, Liberman, & Allen, 1976). The cough, a loud barking sound which occurred 40 to 50 times per minute, was the chief complaint; yet Jennifer also had an extremely rigid posture; complained of headaches, colds, and insomnia; maintained that she could only partially open her mouth; and had not spoken in two years, during which she communicated entirely by writing. Her symptoms led to withdrawal from school and an increasingly reclusive life. Extensive medical procedures revealed no organic causes, although psychological testing showed a hysterical personality structure. Like classic hysterics, Jennifer seemed unconcerned by her symptoms.

After other treatments failed, it was hypothesized that Jennifer's cough was maintained by all the attention it received and by enabling her to avoid the anxiety of leaving home. To test this hypothesis and modify the contingencies, she was hospitalized in an adolescent token economy ward. Observation under various conditions showed her rate of coughing to be lowest when she thought no one was watching and highest when she knew she was observed. Instructing staff and other patients to ignore the coughing while interacting normally with Jennifer led to a diminution of the coughing.

Systematic desensitization was chosen as a way of reducing anxiety about school and other interpersonal situations that presumably helped motivate Jennifer's symptoms. However, her denial of all anxiety made it impossible to construct anxiety hierarchies. As an *in vivo* alternative, she was reinforced for social interaction in the adolescent ward, other areas of the hospital, and recreational and group therapy. She eventually reached the point of taking driving lessons and assuming volunteer jobs as a hospital messenger and teacher's aide. Her mutism was treated by shaping speech, using home visits as reinforcers. The shaping began with behaviors requiring control of the muscles associated with opening her mouth and speaking, followed by appropriate inhaling and exhaling without coughing. Discharge from the hospital was made contingent on appropriate speech.

Family therapy sessions were also used to help generalize Jennifer's successes to the home and increase the family's social activities. Despite Jennifer's initial resistance to treatment and firm denial that her symptoms were psychologically based, she eventually began to accept the idea and was able to talk about her unhappiness and hostility. Follow-ups at 20 and 41 months after discharge showed that she was doing well in college, had a part-time job, and appeared symptom-free. Although largely speculative, the authors provide a detailed reconstruction of the modeling, stresses, and reinforcement contingencies apparently responsible for Jennifer's symptoms.

EVALUATION OF BEHAVIORAL APPROACHES

We have seen that behavioral approaches take many forms and are applied to diverse problems. Although originally grounded in laboratory learning research, practical applications of behavioral theory extend way beyond the laboratory. Much research on behavior modification now consists of trial-and-error experimentation to see which techniques work best under particular applied conditions. Most techniques are traceable to stimulus-response learning theories, but the theoretical underpinnings have proven harder to verify than the effects of specific applications (Kazdin & Wilson, 1978). When, for example, various components of systematic desensitization are applied alone, the results are often as good as if all the components dictated by Wolpe's theory are used together (Kazdin & Wilcoxon, 1976). In other cases, contrasting approaches, such as desensitization and implosive therapy or operant and respondent treatments of phobias, are reported to produce favorable results. We do not know, however, whether different approaches have similar impacts on similar children with similar problems or whether they promote similarly generalizable and durable effects.

Despite the somewhat tenuous relations between laboratory-based stimulus-response theory and many behavioral techniques, behavioral approaches have revolutionized the study and treatment of psychopathology. In addition to providing new treatment methods, they have contributed the following:

1. Explicit efforts to move ideas from the *context of discovery* to the *context of confirmation,* not only in relation to the development of new methods but also in the treatment of individual children.
2. *Precise specification of the target problems,* including baseline data on the rate or intensity of the problem behavior.
3. A search for the *current determinants of the problems,* rather than their historical antecedents.
4. *Aiming treatment at the target problems,* rather than at generalized personality change.
5. *Documentation of changes* in the target problems over the course of treatment and during follow-up periods.
6. A *readiness to help alter the client's real world environment* in order to alter behavior in that environment.
7. The *promotion of clinical research* on diverse problems in diverse settings.

Relationship to Developmental Psychopathology

Beside recognizing the general contributions of behavioral approaches, we also need to view them in the broader context of developmental psychopathology as a field. Prior to the rebirth of behavioral approaches in the late 1950s, the psychodynamic model dominated treatment and theory. As we saw in Chapter 9, there has been little controlled outcome research on psychoanalysis and little research support for the psychoanalytic theory of neurosis. Furthermore, psychodynamic therapy takes place mainly in the offices of mental health professionals treating patients for periods often extending over several years.

Against this background, Wolpe (1958), Lazarus (1960), and others reported substantial cure rates with much briefer behavioral treatments. Their follow-up reports indicated greater efficacy than had ever been obtained with psychoanalysis. Furthermore, their methods were easily explained and taught, applicable under diverse conditions, and seemed firmly based on laboratory research.

Largely in opposition to the psychodynamic tradition, an ideology of behavior modification emerged, which stressed objective assessment, experimental research, and the control of behavior by principles of learning. Following a flood of enthusiastic reports, there has been a more cautious reappraisal of the early claims and ideology. Despite the much greater effort to test and document behavioral than psychodynamic approaches, it is clear that the more sweeping claims for behavior modification were not well supported (Kazdin & Wilson, 1978). As we have seen in this chapter, many single case studies and some control-group comparisons have demonstrated the efficacy of particular behavioral methods under particular conditions. Yet the very few well-controlled *comparisons* of behavioral treatments with *other* treatments in clinical populations have shown minimal differences in outcome (e.g., Miller et al., 1972; Sloane et al., 1975). The transfer and durability of treatment effects also need much further testing.

To draw firmer conclusions about the optimal treatment of particular disorders, we need far better knowledge of the effects of each treatment on children differing in family background, developmental level, and other characteristics. Meanwhile, behavioral approaches offer a rich array of conceptual and practical tools for aiding children's adaptive development. The following case illustrates the use of a behavioral approach in relation to adaptive problems having psychodynamic and cognitive-developmental aspects as well.

Until Kirsten was 3½, she had slept in a room adjoining her parents' room. However, when her mother became pregnant for the second time, Kirsten's parents began to make plans to move Kirsten to an upstairs bedroom. The house had two bedrooms on the first floor and two on the second, making it impossible for both children and the parents to have rooms of their own on the same floor. With Kirsten's help, the upstairs bedroom was decorated and her toys were gradually moved up to it. Some months before the baby's arrival, Kirsten's bed was moved to her new room. The transition was facilitated by the timely arrival of a stray cat which Kirsten adopted and which slept with her at night.

Shortly before the baby's birth, Kirsten began to express fear that the roof beams of the house might break—the house was an old one with exposed beams in Kirsten's room. Kirsten's parents re-assured her about the beams and made a little model of the house to show just how the beams held up the roof.

Just before the baby's arrival, Kirsten was taken to her grandparents. She expressed fear that the beams in their house might break, although they had no exposed beams. Kirsten came home from her grandparents the night before her mother returned from the hospital. Although her other grandparents were now staying in the room next to hers, Kirsten was very reluctant to sleep, expressed fear of the beams, and woke up crying several times. After the baby came home, she continued to express fear of the beams and wanted to sleep downstairs. Whenever she finally did consent to sleep upstairs, she came to her parents' bed during the night crying in fear of the beams.

In view of her distress, Kirsten was allowed to sleep downstairs, first in the baby's room and then in the living room. She was also given extra attention and was allowed to help with the baby as much as possible, although she occasionally betrayed her ambivalence—e.g., by "handing" the baby a toy with considerably more force than necessary and by getting rough with her cat to the point of pushing it down the stairs.

After several weeks, Kirsten appeared to have relaxed about the baby and was in many ways her old self again. Nevertheless, she seemed more determined than ever to keep sleeping downstairs. Since this meant that she often went to sleep quite late, was awakened when her parents got up to tend the baby, and interfered with her parents' use of the living room, her parents tried various methods of reasoning and interpretation to induce her to return to her room. Being quite immovable when determined, Kirsten was not persuaded. Punishment was ruled out because it was recognized that Kirsten was dealing with strong feelings about the baby's arrival and perhaps about the possibility of her parents engendering more babies. On the other hand, her parents felt that allowing Kirsten to have her way over a long period on this issue would create further difficulties for her as well as for them.

After all else failed, it was decided to try a token reinforcement system. A piece of cardboard was ruled off into 30 squares on which Kirsten could paste an S & H Green (trading) Stamp each time she went to bed upstairs without resistance and another stamp each time she stayed there all night, whether or not going to bed had been sufficiently cooperative to earn a stamp. Since she had been wanting a new doll, the doll was to be the back-up reinforcer.

With some trepidation, Kirsten's parents introduced their plan to her, telling her that they wanted to help her overcome her fear. To their relief, she eagerly exclaimed, "You mean I can *earn* stamps for a doll? Can I start tonight?" She did start that night and earned all 30 stamps in slightly more than the 15 days that would have been required for perfect performance. Kirsten was warmly praised whenever she earned a stamp. She expressed no more fear of the beams and proudly showed her stamp card to friends. She also began to ask about the number of stamps, learned to count higher than previously by counting them, and noticed the similar arrangements of the cells of the card and the numbers on her calendar. This prompted curiosity about the days of the months, when to turn the calendar page, etc.

After Kirsten had earned her doll, there were no further problems with fear of going to bed, but she asked if she could go on earning stamps. Her parents offered to let her earn stamps for getting dressed in the morning and undressed at night, with the back-up reinforcer being a doll high chair. When Kirsten wanted to continue the stamp system after that, she was offered a trip to the zoo in return for asking for things nicely rather than whining and for picking up her room. She decided that the latter was more than she cared to bargain for, but the change in her way of asking for things eventually earned her the trip to the zoo. However, both Kirsten and her parents began to lose interest in the stamp system during the last phase. Her parents forgot to award the stamps when they were due and Kirsten did not bother to remind them or to paste the stamps on her card when they were awarded.

Kirsten's beam phobia seemed to emerge as follows: Kirsten's anxiety was due to the arrival of a new sibling, the parents' rejection of her that this signified, the need to compete for parental attention, and, perhaps, the fear that her parents would engender more babies if they were left alone at night to do so. (By cross-examining her parents, she had previously learned exactly how babies are made.) Being alone upstairs in her room at night while the baby was downstairs in her old room near her parents was the most specific focus of her fear.

While visiting friends several months earlier, Kirsten heard them jokingly describe how an exposed beam in their house had once cracked. Kirsten's new room was distinguished from the downstairs rooms by having exposed beams. Thus, the frightening fact that exposed beams sometimes crack and that such beams existed in a setting already frightening to her but not in her old room made the beams good candidates for becoming phobic objects. The role of separation fears in the beam phobia was indicated in two ways: (1) Kirsten's fear of beams at her grandparents' where there were no exposed beams but where she was separated from her parents while they were with the baby, and (2) Kirsten's lack of fear when she could sleep downstairs near her parents, despite the exposed beams upstairs. Once the phobia had developed, it was reinforced by its success in earning Kirsten the privilege of sleeping near her parents.

Even though Kirsten's fear was complex, it did not seem feasible to overcome it through interpretation, working through, and other psychodynamic techniques. Instead, her parents sought to capitalize on Kirsten's ability to look ahead in time and her eagerness to master new skills and responsibilities. The token system meshed well with her abilities. She not only succeeded in mastering her fear, but became very proud of her new accomplishments in "earning" (as she called it), sleeping in her "apartment," counting, and understanding the calendar. In the second phase of the system, she also became very proud of dressing herself.

8-year Follow – up. There were no recurrences of Kirsten's beam phobia, of resistance to sleeping alone in her room, or of other phobic symptoms. She did remain quite rivalrous with her brother, however, and retained personality traits evident long before his birth: A very independent and determined manner (described by her first grade teacher as a "strong sense of self") that reached extremes of stubborn self-rightousness at times. When this produced significant conflicts with her parents over particular issues, other variants of the token system were used again with her assent and considerable success on three occasions. Despite her strong-willed temperament, she also retained an early tenderness for animals and babies. She had many pets, read extensively on animals, and aspired to become a veterinarian. She was also very effective in caring for young children, including her brother when necessary.

The point of Kirsten's case is not to show that token systems are a panacea or that they alter personality or forestall all future problems. On the contrary, the green stamp system might have been a total failure with a younger or older child. As often happens with token systems, it eventually wore out when Kirsten and her parents tired of it. Nor is the point to show that the symptom was merely an outcome of conditioning or that the token system induced new learning: the only new behaviors Kirsten learned (counting higher, calendar reckoning) were inadvertent byproducts of the token system. Instead, the case shows how a typical but troublesome and complex symptom can be handled by motivating the child to resume adaptive development: Kirsten was approached at the level of her conscious understanding of a situation and was helped to direct her behavior toward new conscious goals. Some of the brightest prospects for behavioral approaches appear to be of precisely this sort, where future-oriented behavior is encouraged with children's conscious cooperation in facilitating developmental progress.

SUMMARY

Behavioral approaches arose from *associationist* theories of the development of all human knowledge and behavior, rather than psychopathology in particular. Laboratory research on learning has provided the basic principles of behavioral treatment: Most methods originated with the *classical (Pavlovian, respondent)* and *operant conditioning* paradigms.

Despite experimental demonstrations of behavioral treatment in the 1920s and 1930s, and subsequent translations of psychoanalytic theory into stimulus-response terms, behavioral treatment did not spread until the 1960s. Its spread was initially spurred by Wolpe's (1958) reports of success with *reciprocal inhibition* of neurotic behavior, mainly through *systematic desensitization.* Thereafter, numerous variations of desensitization emerged, including the use of *emotive imagery, desensitization to actual anxiety stimuli,* and *reinforcement of coping responses* during desensitization.

Operant approaches have also proliferated, especially in the form of *applied behavior analysis* to identify and change contingencies supporting problem behavior in its natural setting. Applied behavior analysts have developed *ABAB (reversal) designs* and *multiple baseline designs* for evaluating the effects of interventions. Beside manipulating natural reinforcers such as adult attention, their methods include *token systems, level (phase) systems,* and *biofeedback.*

Although behavior modifiers generally regard punishment as disruptive, some *aversive methods* are used. These include *time-out from reinforcement,* the use of *painful stimuli* such as electric shock, and *covert sensitization. Implosive therapy* uses frightening imagery to extinguish anxiety responses.

Bandura's *social learning theory* stresses *reciprocal determinism:* the mutual effects of behavior, other personal factors, and the environment on one another. Cognitive variables are viewed as central causes of behavior, particularly via *observational learning* and *modeling.* Modeling is used to treat fears alone and in conjunction with *guided participation (contact desensitization).*

Cognitive-behavioral approaches aim to change behavior by changing cognition. They include Beck's *cognitive therapy* for depression, Ellis's *rational-emotive therapy* for irrational negative beliefs about oneself, and Meichenbaum's *self-instructional training* for teaching self-control.

Some of the most innovative applications of behavioral approaches are in natural environments, such as the family, school, and community.

The range of problems treated by behavioral methods is so broad that many will be left to other chapters on specific disorders. However, behavioral approaches to fears and somatic dysfunctions illustrate points of contact and contrast with psychodynamic approaches.

Reappraisal of the early claims of behavior modifiers has led to more modest views of the results and more awareness of the need for much firmer empirical and theoretical support. Nevertheless, behavioral approaches have brought many new emphases and techniques to the treatment of children, far more empirical research than other approaches, and a rich array of tools for aiding children's adaptive development.

SUGGESTED READING

History of Behavior Modification. The history of behavior modification is relatively short but well documented. In *Psychotherapy by Reciprocal Inhibition,* Joseph Wolpe (1958) presents his reasons for trying behavioral methods, the theoretical basis for the methods he evolved, and his report of 90 percent success in treating neurotics. He presents subsequent refinements of his approach (as practiced mainly with adults) in *Theme and Variations: A Behavior Therapy Casebook* (1976). Kazdin's (1978) *History of Behavior Modification: Experimental Foundations of Contemporary Research* offers a comprehensive overview spanning diverse influences from early laboratory research through later applications. London's (1972) article, "The End of Ideology in Behavior Modification," is one of several milestones marking the transition from an ideological emphasis on learning theory to a more pragmatic search for effective treatment regardless of its theoretical origins.

Applications to Children. Despite the experimental demonstration of behavioral methods with children in the 1920s and 1930s, adult treatment received the most attention in the clinical literature after the revival of behavioral approaches in the 1950s. Works focusing on children are increasing, however, and they extend behavioral methods to promotion of new adaptive behaviors in diverse nonclinical as well as clinical settings. Examples include books by Marholin (1978), O'Leary and O'Leary (1977), Ross (1981), and Mash and Terdal (1981).

11

Disorders of Self-Control, Learning, and Affect

In this chapter, we will consider several disorders that have been viewed from perspectives ranging from the purely organic to the purely psychological. The possible mixtures of organic and psychological factors in these disorders present special challenges for a developmental understanding of psychopathology. Although purely organic or psychological explanations may yet be upheld for some of these disorders, such explanations have not been verified to date.

Contrasting therapies have won dedicated advocates, but little proof of long-term superiority. Another feature of these disorders is that they are defined mainly by a particular symptom but are often viewed as reflecting more pervasive underlying pathology. What, then, is the underlying pathology? How should it be treated? How should the overt symptoms be handled? Before we can answer these questions, we need a clearer picture of the problems that bring a child to clinical attention in the first place. The case of Teddy R. illustrates how the problems discussed in this chapter are often intertwined with each other.

TEDDY R.

Nine-year-old Teddy was referred to a community mental health center by his family doctor. His parents reported that he had always been immature, clumsy, and a loner, but during the past year he had become more babyish, bossy, and noisy. He talked constantly without always making sense, flitted from one activity to another, sucked his thumb, was afraid of small animals, imitated his baby sister, and was rivalrous with his 6-year-old sister. He also became uncontrollably excited about special events such as birthdays and became deeply engrossed in television programs, usually identifying with the fall guy. Although IQ testing revealed superior ability, he did not pay attention in school and refused to do oral work.

The primary reason for referral was that Teddy had recently become encopretic. Between the referral and first contacts with the mental health center, he had also wet his pants and hidden them.

When seen at the mental health center, Teddy was a somewhat disheveled blond boy, tall for his age but with a slightly asymmetric head. His speech was pressured, rapid, and slightly confused. In the therapy room, he flitted from one activity to another and often left the room to urinate or get a drink. He seemed to throw himself at the (male) therapist in efforts to be friendly and ingratiating, and said he'd like to lengthen the sessions and come 10 times a week. He also brought the therapist gifts and cards, signing them "Love, Teddy." When his mother asked why, he replied that he wanted the therapist to like him and admitted he was afraid the therapist didn't like him.

Teddy's conversation jumped from things he noticed in the therapy room, to direct statements of things that bothered him, to tales of events at school and home. In the same breath, he would brag and then disparage himself. Besides ambivalence about himself, he showed ambivalence and uncertainty about other personal identities. This was evident in his quickly changing the identities of puppets he used in the therapy room, often explaining the changes in terms of elaborate disguises or bawling out a puppet for doing something inconsistent with its original identity.

Despite Teddy's ingratiating manner, his talk was extremely aggressive when playing with soldiers and board games. He also showed considerable concern about messing, often mentioning messes he had made and dwelling on his mother's anger when he made a mess. His paintings in the therapy room consisted mainly of messing colors together to produce a shapeless brown mass. Despite many direct and oblique references to his problems, Teddy studiously avoided efforts to discuss them more fully. He quickly skipped away from all references to serious emotions, often becoming illogical or abruptly changing the subject to turn a reference to his own feelings into a joke. When the therapist pointed out his evasiveness, he gave the therapist some paper and ordered him to write down his own problems. When the therapist countered that this seemed to be another way of avoiding talk about problems, Teddy used the paper to seal his own mouth. On another occasion, when the therapist mentioned that Teddy held his penis when excited, Teddy replied that it was forbidden to talk about because "the king would kill us."

HYPERACTIVITY

Teddy exemplifies many of the problems discussed in this chapter. He also exemplifies the difficulty of separating them into prevailing diagnostic categories. If we focus on Teddy's activity level, distractibility, noisiness, and impulsivity, he could be diagnosed as hyperactive. According to DSM-II, the *"Hyperkinetic (hyperactive) reaction of childhood . . .* is characterized by overactivity, restlessness, distractibility, and short attention span" (American Psychiatric Association, 1968, p. 50). Reflecting later thinking, the DSM-III gives primary weight to problems in paying attention: It distinguishes between *attention deficit disorder with hyperactivity* and *attention deficit disorder without hyperactivity*, using the criteria shown in Table 11-1.

According to the DSM-III criteria, Teddy could be diagnosed as having an attention deficit disorder with hyperactivity: He showed all five symptoms listed under *Inattention*. Of those listed under *Impulsivity,* he showed symptoms (1) through (4) and (6). Of those listed under *Hyperactivity*, he definitely showed (2) and (3), and could probably be considered to show (5). He also met criteria D, E, and F. Does this make Teddy a *hyperactive child*?

Hyperactivity has been studied more intensively than most childhood disorders. Yet we still know little about its cause and optimal treatment. Why? Let's start with problems of definition and then consider prevalence, developmental course, hypothesized causes, and the outcomes of various treatments.

Problems of Definition

Behavior checklists are often used to identify hyperactive children. Some have been constructed by listing items of behavior thought to characterize hyperactive children. Others include a much broader range of items but have been factor analyzed to determine which items tend to occur together. Both approaches show strong enough relations between overactive and inattentive behaviors to confirm a pattern like the DSM-III's *attention deficit disorder with hyperactivity*. But a separate pattern like the DSM's *attention deficit disorder without hyperactivity* has not been well documented (Achenbach, 1980). And even the inattentive-hyperactive syndrome varies considerably with the rating instrument used, the observers using it, and where the child is observed.

As the DSM states (Table 11-1), the clinician may not see the symptoms at all. One study showed that 58 percent of children referred for hyperactivity were not judged hyperactive by *any* staff members seeing the children in clinical settings and that only 13 percent of the children were judged hyperactive by *all* the staff members who saw them at various times (Kenny et al., 1971). Furthermore, despite adequate agreement between observers seeing each child at the same time, some children deemed hyperactive at school are not deemed hyperactive at home and vice versa (Sandberg, Wieselberg, & Shaffer, 1980). Others may show various problem behaviors beside hyperactivity. For example, factor analysis has revealed separate dimensions of aggressive and hyperactive behavior among boys treated for hyperactivity (Loney, Langhorne, & Paternite, 1978). Some of the boys were both aggressive and hyperactive, whereas others scored high on only one of these dimensions.

Teddy R. was not overtly aggressive, but problems of self-esteem and interpersonal communication were evident, along with inattention, overactivity, impulsivity, and poor self-control. It is often hard to determine which problems are

Table 11-1   DSM-III Diagnostic Criteria for Attention Deficit Disorder with Hyperactivity

The child displays, for his or her mental and chronological age, signs of developmentally inappropriate inattention, impulsivity, and hyperactivity. The signs must be reported by adults in the child's environment, such as parents and teachers. Because the symptoms are typically variable, they may not be observed directly by the clinician. When the reports of teachers and parents conflict, primary consideration should be given to the teacher reports because of greater familiarity with age-appropriate norms. Symptoms typically worsen in situations that require self-application, as in the classroom. Signs of the disorder may be absent when the child is in a new or a one-to-one situation.

The number of symptoms specified is for children between the ages of eight and ten, the peak age range for referral. In younger children, more severe forms of the symptoms and a greater number of symptoms are usually present. The opposite is true of older children.

A. *Inattention.* At least three of the following:
   1. Often fails to finish things he or she starts
   2. Often doesn't seem to listen
   3. Easily distracted
   4. Has difficulty concentrating on schoolwork or other tasks requiring sustained attention
   5. Has difficulty sticking to play activity
B. *Impulsivity.* At least three of the following:
   1. Often acts before thinking
   2. Shifts excessively from one activity to another
   3. Has difficulty organizing work (not due to cognitive impairment)
   4. Needs a lot of supervision
   5. Frequently calls out in class
   6. Has difficulty awaiting turn in games or group situations
C. *Hyperactivity.* At least two of the following:
   1. Runs about or climbs on things excessively
   2. Has difficulty sitting still or fidgets excessively
   3. Has difficulty staying seated
   4. Moves about excessively during sleep
   5. Is always "on the go" or acts as if "driven by a motor"
D. Onset before the age of seven.
E. Duration of at least six months.
F. Not due to Schizophrenia, Affective Disorder, or Severe or Profound Mental Retardation

Attention Deficit Disorder without Hyperactivity

The criteria for this disorder are the same as those for Attention Deficit Disorder with Hyperactivity except that the individual never had signs of hyperactivity (criterion C).

Source: American Psychiatric Association, 1980, pp.43–44.

byproducts of others, however. If children are truly hyperactive to begin with, they often get negative feedback from parents, teachers, and peers. This can, in turn, hurt their self-esteem. On the other hand, children whose self-esteem is already poor may strive excessively for attention, approval, and affection. Teddy's efforts to win his therapist's affection while avoiding discussion of his feelings may have motivated his impulsive and overactive behavior in the therapy room.

Children who feel unliked may use impulsive, disruptive, clowning, or aggressive behavior to get attention. Questionnaires about their school experience show that highly active boys have more negative self-perceptions than less active boys: Significantly more highly active boys said their teachers didn't like their school work or the way they acted; their teachers punished them; and they were unhappy in class (Loney, Whaley-Klahn, & Weissenburger, 1976). But which came first? Did overactive behavior bring disapproval and unhappiness? Or did a sense of disapproval and unhappiness motivate unacceptable behavior?

Because children are seldom identified as needing help until behavior problems have persisted for a long time, it is often hard to see which ones are primary and which ones are byproducts of the original problems. Longitudinal research is needed to answer these questions. Until we have better answers, however, we need to examine all facets of a child's adaptive pattern instead of focusing only on diagnostic categories such as hyperactivity or attention deficit disorders.

How Many Children are Hyperactive?

This question often arises in debates over what hyperactivity is and what should be done about it. The flood of literature on hyperactivity might suggest an epidemic. The much greater attention it has gained in the United States than elsewhere also suggests that it results from conditions here: Psychiatric diagnoses of hyperactivity have ranged from 1 in 1000 children in a British study to 60 times that rate for urban American children (Weiss & Hechtman, 1979). Yet traditional psychiatric diagnoses are a poor source of prevalence data, because diagnostic practices vary and seldom distinguish hyperactivity as a primary disorder from hyperactivity resulting from other disorders or situational factors.

Another approach is to obtain ratings on standardized behavior checklists. Since teachers often make referrals for hyperactivity, their ratings have been used to obtain prevalence estimates. These ratings show that individual component behaviors of the hyperactive syndrome are common, but cutoff points on the distribution of total scores for these behaviors can be used to pick out children considered to show the syndrome. In studies using a standard teacher rating form, the following percentages of boys exceeded a preset cutoff score: 9 percent in a midwestern town; 12 percent in Munich, Germany; 21 percent in Ottawa, Canada; and 22 percent in Auckland, New Zealand. The corresponding figures for girls were 2, 5, 8, and 9 percent (Trites, 1979).

The preponderance of boys scoring above the cutoff in all samples agrees with the higher proportion of boys clinically diagnosed as hyperactive (Weiss & Hechtman, 1979). On the other hand, despite American clinicians' frequent diagnoses of hyperactivity, the teacher ratings show the American sample to have the smallest percentage above the cutoff score. Owing to the American teachers' prior experience with the rating scale and the less urban environment of the American sample, this does not necessarily mean that American children are *less* hyperactive than their German, Canadian, or New Zealand counterparts. Yet it suggests that they are not *more* hyperactive either.

Although the teacher ratings provide an important basis for comparisons among samples, they do not tell us how many children would be clinically diagnosed hyperactive, because many high scorers may be only temporarily or situationally hyperactive. A California study, for example, showed that only 1.2 percent of children were considered hyperactive simultaneously by their teachers *and* their parents *and* their physicians (Sandoval, Lambert, & Sassone, 1980)

Developmental Course of Hyperactivity

The elementary school years are the peak period for clinical referral of hyperactive children. Does this mean that children are not hyperactive before or after this period? How do they start out in life and what typically happens to them?

Longitudinal research is needed to trace the antecedents and outcomes of hyperactivity at various points in the life span. The upsurge of referrals during the elementary school years may reflect conflicts between schools' standards of decorum and children's preexisting behavior more than sudden changes in behavior. Yet because we do not know in advance which children will be judged hyperactive, it is hard to select target groups in whom to study the developmental course of hyperactivity. Finding out what happens to children after they are diagnosed hyperactive is somewhat easier, but the relative recency of this diagnosis, changing diagnostic practices, and variations in treatment have made it hard to form a clear picture of the long-term outcomes. Nonetheless, data from various studies enable us to piece together a tentative picture of the developmental course of hyperactivity.

Antecedents. One way to study antecedents of hyperactivity is to examine large longitudinal samples for early differences between children later identified as hyperactive, those with other disorders, and those considered normal. But this is a difficult strategy, because only a small proportion of children will eventually be considered hyperactive. Besides including enough cases of the target disorder, a sample must include enough children manifesting other disorders for comparison with those having the target disorder. Otherwise, antecedents of psychopathology in general may be thought unique to the target disorder.

A second problem is the many variables that must be assessed to insure detection of antecedents of hyperactivity. If early organic abnormalities are involved, as often hypothesized, then many pregnancy and birth variables must be assessed before studying children's subsequent development. Very few studies of general population samples have assessed a sufficient range of variables over a long enough period in enough children to shed much light on antecedents of hyperactivity. In an Hawaiian study, which started with 698 births, and in the National Perinatal Collaborative Study, which started with over 50,000 pregnancies, perinatal abnormalities were weakly correlated with rough indices of later hyperactivity and other disorders (Nichols, 1976; Werner, 1980). These relations were dwarfed, however, by the relations of social background to the later disorders. Perinatal abnormalities seemed to have less long-term effect on upper socioeconomic children than on lower socioeconomic children, but later disorders were also more common in lower socioeconomic children having no known perinatal abnormalities.

Another strategy is to look for characteristics associated with a disorder and then to study children who show these characteristics early. As an example, certain minor *congenital anomalies* have been found more often in hyperactive than normal boys. The anomalies include such slight peculiarities as malformed and asymmetrical ears; curved fifth finger; third toe longer than the second toe; and a large gap between the first and second toe. Although the reason is unknown, boys diagnosed hyperactive tend to show more anomalies than other boys. Since these anomalies are present at birth, they might give us a *marker* for predicting later hyperactivity.

In a longitudinal study, boys born with many anomalies were rated more difficult on three dimensions of temperament at one year of age than boys born with few anomalies (Rapoport, Quinn, Burg, & Bartley, 1979). The differences concerned poor adaptability, low threshold of response to stimulation, and negative mood, rather than activity level. Elevated rates of difficult behavior were also found in the boys with many anomalies at age 2. Whether the predictive relations between anomalies and behavior will eventually differentiate hyperactive from other difficult children remains to be seen.

Outcomes of Hyperactivity. What happens to hyperactive children? There are many studies of the short-term effects of various treatments (discussed later), but longer-term follow-ups have focused mainly on groups not differing systematically enough in treatment to afford comparisons of treatment effects. One study, for example, compared hyperactive children with normal children at age 4 and again at follow-ups two and three years later (Campbell, Endman, & Bernfeld, 1977; Campbell & Paulauskas, 1979; Campbell, Schleifer, Weiss, & Perlman, 1977). Although the authors hoped to study the long-term effects of stimulant drugs, they abandoned this goal, because the drugs had negative side effects on some of the children. After drugs were terminated, some of the children received a variety of other treatments, but not enough received a particular treatment for a long enough period to permit evaluation of long-term effects.

The children were diagnosed hyperactive mainly on the basis of uncontrolled behavior at home; only a third also showed behavior problems in a research nursery. When followed up at age 6½, the hyperactive group as a whole did not differ much from a control group on measures of cognitive style or mother—child interaction. Those who were initially hyperactive at home *and* school (called *true* hyperactives), however, were generally more deviant than those initially hyperactive only at home (called *situational* hyperactives). Mothers' ratings showed that the situational hyperactives remained the most deviant at home, but teacher ratings and classroom observations at age 7½ suggested that the true hyperactives remained the most deviant in school. Preschoolers identified as hyperactive thus continued to show behavior problems, and there were persisting differences between those initially considered situational versus true hyperactives.

Longer-term follow—ups of children first diagnosed hyperactive in elementary school show decreasing hyperactivity but poorer school achievement and more behavioral problems than normal comparison groups through high school, whether or not medication was used (Weiss & Hechtman, 1979). A generally impulsive life-style appears to continue thereafter, with hyperactives showing more geo-graphic moves, vehicular accidents, inferior performance on cognitive style tests, and impulsive-immature personality traits (Hopkins, Perlman, Hechtman, & Weiss, 1979; Weiss, Hechtman, Perlman, Hopkins, & Wenar, 1980). Employers' ratings showed no significant differences between hyperactives and controls as young adults. Yet, a 25-year follow—up of boys originally seen in a child guidance clinic for symptoms now used to diagnose hyperactivity showed socioeconomic status inferior to that of their brothers and fathers (Borland & Heckman, 1976). As adults, these men also showed more overactivity and restlessness than their brothers, although less than in childhood. Despite declines in acute hyperactivity, problems thus appear to persist well into adulthood. However, we need longitudinal comparisons with other disorders to determine whether these problems are unique to hyperactivity.

Predictors of Outcome. Although we lack definitive long-term comparisons between hyperactivity and other disorders, some predictors of outcome among hyperactive children have been pinpointed. In a five-year follow-up of 6- to 12-year-old hyperactive boys, ratings of aggression and certain aspects of family background (such as socioeconomic status) predicted later problem behavior and poor self-esteem much better than did initial hyperactivity (Langhorne & Loney, 1980; Loney, Kramer, & Milich, 1979). This suggests that subgroups of hyperac-tive boys who differ in initial symptom patterns also differ in outcomes. Those who are initially hyperactive *and* aggressive seem to show the most behavior problems, including hyperactivity, in adolescence. Ratings of initial aggression did *not* predict adolescent *school achievement*, however. Instead, initial hyperactivity, family characteristics, and response to treatment had significant correlations with later school achievement, although these were dwarfed by the correlation between initial and later school achievement. Among boys treated for hyperactivity, early aggressive behavior thus seems more ominous for adolescent behavior than early hyperactivity. Early hyperactivity *does* relate negatively to later school achievement, however.

What Causes Hyperactivity?

Recall from Chapter 7 that early efforts to assess brain damage in children suggested that it produced hyperactivity, distractibility, and perceptual-motor deficits (Strauss & Lehtinen, 1947). Children having these symptoms but no direct evidence of brain damage were thought to have *minimal brain damage* (MBD). The MBD concept, however, was later broadened to include hypothesized abnormalities other than actual damage; MBD therefore came to stand for minimal brain *dysfunction*.

Before considering hypothesized organic causes, let's go back to 9-year-old Teddy R., who we met at the beginning of this chapter. When he was 6 months old, Teddy was badly burned and had to be hospitalized. He also had several high fevers during infancy. Both the burn and the fevers could have caused brain damage (or dysfunction). The asymmetry of Teddy's head also suggested possible brain trauma. Did MBD cause Teddy's hyperactivity?

A complete physical showed no abnormalities. A neurological examination revealed hyperresponsive reflexes but the variability of children's reflexes and Teddy's general tenseness cast doubt on these "soft signs" of dysfunction. An EEG showed no sign of epilepsy, tumors, or other definite abnormalities, but it did show some borderline abnormalities of wave frequency. Like the neurological findings, however, the EEG findings are equivocal because normal children's EEGs vary so widely. Psychological testing showed immaturity in Teddy's drawing of human figures and in copying designs on the Bender Gestalt test of perceptual-motor functioning. This immaturity contrasted with the advanced cognitive development evident in Teddy's superior performance on the Wechsler Intelligence Scale for Children (WISC), but did not strongly suggest dysfunction. His WISC Performance IQ was nine points below his verbal IQ, but it was nevertheless in the superior range, and such a small difference does not indicate specific perceptual-motor problems. Like many hyperactive children, Teddy's past history and current functioning thus hinted at, but did not confirm, slight organic abnormalities. What might these abnormalities be? Most hypotheses about organic causes of hyperactivity implicate *organic deficits, developmental delays,* or *constitutional differences* between hyperactive and other children (Kinsbourne & Swanson, 1979).

Organic Deficits: Brain Damage. To judge the organic deficit hypothesis in its original form, we must ask whether brain damage actually causes hyperactivity. If so, are all hyperactive children brain damaged? Efforts to answer these questions have taken various forms. For example, a follow–up of children known to be brain damaged at birth showed that in early childhood they were rated more *inactive* than control children (Ernhart et al., 1963). This suggests that brain-damaged children are not necessarily hyperactive.

Approaching the question in another way, Shaffer, McNamara, and Pincus (1974) assessed hyperactivity in four groups of 5- to 8-year-old boys: *Group 1* had neither conduct problems nor evidence of brain damage; *Group 2* had conduct problems but no evidence of brain damage; *Group 3* had conduct problems *and* well-documented brain damage; *Group 4* had no conduct problems but had brain damage. If brain damage is the critical factor in hyperactivity, then Groups 3 and 4 should be more hyperactive than Groups 1 and 2. By contrast, if hyperactivity is part of a general behavior disorder not exclusively due to brain damage, then Groups 2 and 3 should be the most hyperactive.

No significant differences were found between the combined brain-damaged groups (3 and 4) and the combined undamaged groups (1 and 2) on a variety of measures of hyperactivity and impulsivity. Ratings of motor activity, the Matching Familiar Figures test of impulsivity, and a direct measure of arm movements in an experimental situation, however, all yielded significantly higher scores for the combined conduct disorder groups (2 and 3) than the nonconduct disorder groups (1 and 4). Hyperactivity and impulsivity were thus more strongly associated with a particular type of behavioral disorder than with brain damage per se. If brain damage as obvious as that suffered by Groups 3 and 4 did not increase activity and impulsivity, then brain damage as subtle as that ascribed to MBD children is unlikely to account for hyperactivity. This does not mean that brain damage cannot increase the risk of behavioral problems—many brain-damaged children have behavioral problems. It seems clear, however, that brain damage does not always cause hyperactivity; nor are all hyperactive children brain damaged. A study of children immediately following head injuries also showed no increase in hyperactivity, although severe damage did lead to other behavioral problems (Brown, Chadwick, Shaffer, Rutter, & Traub, 1981).

Organic Deficits: Neurotransmitter Abnormalities. Other versions of the MBD hypothesis have implicated specific abnormalities of brain function rather than generalized brain damage. Paul Wender, a leading advocate of the MBD concept, argues that:

> In virtually all instances hyperactivity is the result of an *inborn temperamental difference* in the child. How the child is treated and raised can affect the severity of his problem but it cannot cause the problem. Certain types of raising may make the problem worse, certain types of raising may make the problem better. *No* forms of raising can produce (hyperactivity) in a child who is not temperamentally predisposed to them. (Wender & Wender, 1978, p. 21)

Wender describes the cause of hyperactivity as follows:

> [The brain] is in some ways analogous to a telephone network, but there is one major difference. In the telephone network the connections are *electrical*: electricity passes from one wire to another by physical contact. In the brain, however, the connections are *chemical*. One nerve cell releases a small amount of certain chemicals, which are picked up by a second cell, causing it to 'fire.' These chemicals are called 'neurotransmitters.' If there is too little of a particular neurotransmitter, the second cell will not fire because not enough of the neurotransmitter has been released by the first cell. (Wender & Wender, 1978, p. 22)

More specifically, Wender (1978) hypothesizes a deficiency in the functioning of the neurotransmitter *dopamine*. He bases his hypothesis on three arguments: (1) He maintains that behavioral symptoms of MBD resemble those of *von Economo's encephalitis*, in which a virus injures dopaminergic neurons. (2) He credits MBD children's favorable response to stimulant drugs to remediation of deficient dopaminergic activity. (3) He interprets MBD children's behavior as reflecting unresponsiveness to positive and negative reinforcers and interprets animal conditioning evidence as showing enhancement of reinforcement effects by stimulant drugs. Experimental *depletion* of brain dopamine in animals also seems to produce symptoms resembling those of hyperactive children (Shaywitz, Cohen, & Shaywitz, 1978).

Because dopaminergic deficits in children's brains cannot be directly measured, support for Wender's hypothesis is indirect at best. Casting doubt on his hypothesis are findings that normal children respond to stimulant drugs much as hyperactive children do, in terms of behavior, self-ratings, psychological tests, and psychophysiological measures (Rapoport et al., 1980). In rebuttal, Wender argues that continued administration of stimulant drugs would reduce natural dopaminergic activity in normal children, causing the overt effects of the drugs to disappear. In MBD children, by contrast, the drug effects should endure, because the drugs make up for inherently deficient dopaminergic activity. However, Wender notes that ethical considerations preclude long-term administration of stimulant drugs to normal children. The follow-up studies cited earlier nevertheless cast doubt on the long-term effectiveness of stimulant drugs even with hyperactive children, although the difficulty of doing long-term double-blind, placebo-controlled studies makes conclusive tests unlikely.

Organic Deficits: Abnormalities of Arousal. Abnormalities in hyperactive children's arousal level have often been hypothesized. Physiological *over*arousal and *under*arousal have both been implicated. The overarousal hypothesis holds that hyperactive children's physiological functioning makes them overly sensitive to incoming stimuli; this prevents them from modulating their responses to stimuli in a discriminating way. According to this view, hyperactive children need protection from distracting stimuli so they can focus on tasks such as school work. Stemming partly from Strauss and Lehtinen's (1947) findings on brain-damaged children's difficulties in filtering out distracting stimuli, this picture of hyperactive children implies that their favorable response to stimulant drugs is *paradoxical*: If the drugs stimulate physiological arousal, why do they help children who are already overaroused?

The underarousal hypothesis resolves this paradox. If stimulant drugs increase arousal, perhaps hyperactive children suffer from *under*arousal that makes them insensitive to incoming stimuli. Their hyperactivity and distractibility might therefore reflect *stimulus seeking* (or stimulus ''hunger'') instead of overstimulation.

Comparisons of hyperactive and normal children on EEG measures of cortical arousal and GSR measures of autonomic nervous system arousal have partially supported the underarousal hypothesis. But inconsistencies in the findings suggest that underarousal alone is not responsible for most cases of hyperactivity (Hastings & Barkley, 1978; Rosenthal & Allen, 1978). An experimental comparison of the effects of high and low stimulation on the *behavior* of hyperactive children at least shows that high environmental stimulation may not be harmful: Hyperactive children performing academic tasks while exposed to extraneous visual and auditory stimulation showed significantly *less* motor activity than when the stimuli were absent, although task performance was not significantly affected (Zentall & Zentall, 1976). Yet, making academic tasks more stimulating via color, movement, and increased size actually increased activity and lowered performance (Zentall, Zentall, & Booth, 1978). The proper mix of environmental and task-specific stimulation thus remains elusive.

Organic Deficits: Food Sensitivities. Another organic deficit hypothesis concerns abnormal sensitivities to foods. The chief proponent of this hypothesis is an allergist, Dr. Ben Feingold:

> Since it first appeared in 1974, Dr. Ben F. Feingold's great best seller, *Why Your Child is Hyperactive,* has sold hundreds of thousands of copies. In that book the doctor described his findings that hyperactive children could—and should—be helped *without drugs.* Good, healthful, natural food, free from chemical additives and salicylates was the answer, he said.
>
> And now *The Feingold Cookbook* shows you how to prepare an abundance of dishes that contain no harmful chemicals. Food instead of drugs. . . .
>
> And the message from the Feingolds again is one of hope and inspiration. You *can* help your hyperactive child. With love. With care. With *The Feingold Cookbook.* (Advertisement, New York *Times*, 1979).

Although based on clinical impressions rather than controlled research, Feingold's (1975) claims have won a wide following among parents who buy his books and join Feingold associations across the country. He maintains that heightened sensitivity to naturally occurring salicylates and artificial colors, flavors, and other food additives causes hyperactivity in many children. Diets free of these substances are said to produce dramatic improvements in behavior:

> The child who was abusive, disobedient, incorrigible, and disdainful of attention moves toward becoming affectionate, lovable, and responsive to guidance.

> In (mental) retardation the clinical response may be dramatic, as evidenced by improved behavior, better coordination of both fine and gross muscles, and improved learning ability. All of these gains induce a marked transformation in the patient, whose expression becomes more alert and bright, his social adjustment improves, permitting him to function as a self-sufficient person who does not require one-to-one attention or instruction. (Feingold, 1976)

Testing these claims requires controlled studies in which children are assessed when receiving normal and Feingold diets. To control for expectations about the dietary effects, the children and observers must be blind to the dietary conditions. This is hard to arrange, because major changes in diet are obvious. In an exceptionally thorough study, however, elementary school hyperactive boys were assigned randomly to either a Feingold diet or a control diet including ordinary amounts of salicylates and additives (Harley, et al., 1978). The study used a *crossover* design, with half the boys getting the Feingold diet first, followed by the control diet; the other half got the opposite sequence. To insure dietary compliance, the researchers supplied all the families' food, as well as snacks and treats for the boys and their classmates on special occasions at school. Packaging was similar for the Feingold and control diets. Close monitoring showed very few violations of the prescribed diet and no parental awareness of the diet sequence received by any boy.

No significant effects of diet were found on classroom observations of attending to tasks, restless motor activity, or disruptive behavior. Nor were there any significant effects on laboratory observations of motor activity or attention in either free-play or restricted activity conditions. A few significant effects occurred on neuropsychological tests, but most favored the control diet over the Feingold diet. Teacher ratings showed no significant effects of diet. However, parents' ratings showed significant improvements on the Feingold diet when it followed the control diet. Considering that these were the only findings favoring the Feingold diet and that they could arise by chance when so many statistical comparisons were made, the study did not lend much support to Feingold's claims. Yet parent ratings of a small preschool sample receiving the same procedures also significantly favored the Feingold diet.

The marginal support for the Feingold diet suggests *either* a very small effect on hyperactive children in general *or* no effect in most cases but a possibly important effect in a few. If a few hyperactive children in fact show major benefits, this might not be detected in group comparison studies like Harley et al.'s. Another strategy is to find the few who respond favorably and then to observe their responses to the hypothesized offending foods; having the child eat the offending food is called a *challenge*. As a second phase of his study, Harley's group did a challenge experiment in which the boys who seemed to show benefits from the Feingold diet were challenged repeatedly with food additives alternating with additive-free foods according to a double-blind crossover design (Harley, Matthews, & Eichman, 1978). This showed no differences in behavioral problems attributable to the challenge foods, as assessed by parent ratings, teacher ratings, classroom observations, and neuropsychological tests.

Another challenge study found a statistically significant response in 1 out of 22 children, an exceptionally small 34-month-old girl (Weiss et al., 1980). A significant group difference was also found in a study using very large challenge doses of food dyes: Children who had previously shown good responses to stimulant drugs made more errors on a learning task after eating the dyes than children who had not shown good responses to stimulants (Swanson & Kinsbourne, 1980). Behavioral ratings showed no significant effects of the dyes, however.

If the dyes indeed cause behavioral problems in some children, it may thus be due to abnormally large concentrations of the dyes, because of the child's small size or heavy consumption. It has also been found, however, that *sugar* consumption correlated much higher with problem behavior in hyperactive children than Feingold's prohibited foods did (Prinz, Roberts, & Hantman, 1980).

Organic Deficits: Food Allergies. The sensitivity hypothesized by Feingold is not viewed as an allergy, because the body does not seem to produce antibodies or other physical reactions to the offending substances. Instead, behavioral problems are the only putative symptoms. Yet, if the behavioral symptoms have an organic basis, perhaps allergies could be responsible. To test this possibility, Trites, Ferguson, and Tryphonas (1978) did extensive allergy tests on hyperactive, learning disabled, and emotionally disturbed children. They found allergies in 77 percent of the learning disabled, 47 percent of the hyperactive, and 38 percent of the emotionally disturbed group. Most of the allergies were to common meats and cereals. A double-blind crossover study comparing diets with and without the allergens, however, revealed no significant effects on behavioral ratings. The high prevalence of allergies, especially in the learning disabled group, and evidence for correlations between teacher ratings of behavioral problems and the number of allergies per child suggest that allergies may be involved in at least some children's behavior problems. But, like Feingold's hypothesis, allergies do not seem to explain many cases of hyperactivity.

Developmental Delays. Young children's lack of self-control and clinicians' impressions that hyperactive children outgrow their behavioral problems both suggest that hyperactivity reflects a *delay* in development. This hypothesis is not necessarily incompatible with organic deficit hypotheses: Brain damage could cause a developmental delay, for example. Similarly, Wender says that medication is needed to overcome neurotransmitter deficits only until the child's brain develops sufficiently to produce "adequate amounts of the required chemicals" (Wender & Wender, 1978, p. 46). Nor is the developmental delay hypothesis incompatible with the *difference* hypotheses to be discussed later. Constitutional differences could be responsible for developmental delays.

But does hyperactivity typically decline with age? One approach is to look at the proportion of normal and disturbed children reported to show the relevant behaviors at various ages.

Factor analyses of behavioral problems for clinically referred children, grouped by sex at ages 6 to 11 and 12 to 16, have revealed a syndrome resembling the DSM-III's category of attention-deficit disorder with hyperactivity (Achenbach, 1978; Achenbach & Edelbrock, 1979). Although the exact composition of the syndrome varies somewhat by age and sex, all four versions of it include the following items: (1) *acts too young for his/her age;* (2) *can't concentrate, can't pay attention for long;* (3) *can't sit still, restless, or hyperactive;* (4) and *poorly coordinated or clumsy.* If these behaviors represent the common core of a pattern that otherwise differs somewhat with the age and sex of the child, do they typically decline with age?

Figure 11-1 compares the percent of demographically matched normal and clinically referred children for whom each behavior was reported at each age from 4 to 16. Although each item shows a statistically significant decline with age, the graphs show that these drops are neither sharp nor consistent across all ages and groups. It seems unlikely, therefore, that the hyperactive syndrome merely reflects behavior that is later overcome. A closer look at the graphs raises other developmental implications, however. *Can't concentrate, can't pay attention for long,* for example, shows a peak for normal 8- to 9-year-old boys. Boys in this age group are thus generally seen as having trouble paying attention. Since 8- and 9-year-old boys have the highest rate of referral to child clinics, this suggests that attentional problems arising in the course of development may often be involved.

Another approach to the developmental question is to directly assess the activity of children under standardized conditions. For example, when 3- to 9-year-olds were observed in a standardized playroom, gross locomotor activity was found to decline with age (Routh, Schroeder, & O'Tuama, 1974). Hyperactive children were also found to be as active as younger normal children, suggesting a developmental delay (Routh & Schroeder, 1976). A further study (involving only normal 3- to 5-year-olds), showed that the mother's presence in the standardized playroom had a major impact on developmental trends. Whereas activity *declined* with age when the mother was absent, it increased sharply from age 3 to 5 when the mother was in the room (Routh, Walton, & Padan-Belkin, 1978). Activity level is thus not a unitary phenomenon but follows different paths in different contexts. If a

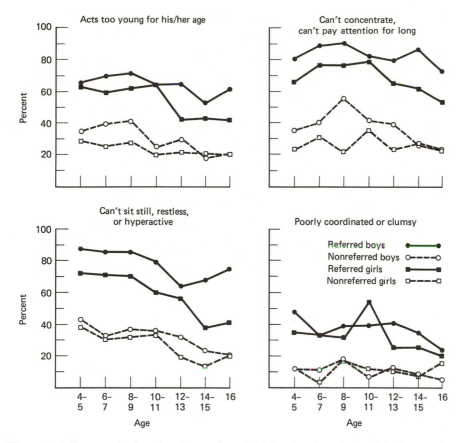

Figure 11-1. Percent of referred and non-referred children for whom items of the hyperactive syndrome were reported. (From Achenbach & Edelbrock, 1981.)

developmental lag underlies hyperactivity, it will probably have to be diagnosed in terms of organic and/or cognitive functioning rather than overt activity levels. Some hyperactive children's brain wave responses to auditory and visual stimuli show signs of immaturity (Buchsbaum & Wender, 1973), but it is not clear that developmental lags play a major role.

Constitutional Differences. Organic deficit hypotheses imply that hyperactive children have a specific organic abnormality, whereas developmental delay hypotheses imply that hyperactive children's development is slow but not defective. A third view is that hyperactive children are merely extreme on certain normal temperamental traits. Kinsbourne and Swanson (1979), for example, hypothesize a cognitive style dimension ranging from insufficient concentration, producing impulsivity at one extreme, to excess concentration, producing overly cautious behavior at the other extreme. Activity level may be an additional dimension of temperament: Kinsbourne and Swanson hypothesize that hyperactive children are extreme in both activity and impulsivity. However, not only the child's position on these dimensions but also the environmental history and the expectations of significant adults determine whether the child is judged hyperactive. Furthermore, the precise effects of such treatments as stimulant drugs will vary with many biological, temperamental, and experiential characteristics of children who happen to be judged hyperactive. Thus, some children's mood and cognitive performance becomes worse on drug doses that improve the mood and performance of other children.

Constitutional determinants of concentration and activity level might involve either genetic factors or organic damage or combinations of them. Thus, certain types of brain damage or experience might precipitate hyperactivity in children who are genetically susceptible, but not in others. Trait ratings of activity level in twins have shown high heritability (Willerman, 1973). Elevated rates of alcoholism, hysteria, and antisocial behavior and of (retrospectively reported) hyperactivity in relatives of hyperactive children have also been thought to show genetic links among these disorders (Cantwell, 1975; Morrison & Stewart, 1974). However, comparison with children having disorders other than hyperactivity shows that the elevated family rates are not unique to hyperactivity (Stewart, DeBlois, & Cummings, 1980). We thus have a wealth of hypotheses about causes for hyperactivity, but no proof that there is any single cause or even any single syndrome.

How can Hyperactive Children be Helped?

Despite uncertainties about its causes, hyperactivity has been treated with stimulant drugs since the 1930s (Bradley, 1937). As controlled studies in the 1960s and 1970s confirmed the effectiveness of stimulant medication, it became the most common treatment. A survey of children identified as hyperactive by their parents, schools, and physicians showed that 85 percent received stimulants at one time or another (Sandoval et al., 1980). Yet, because stimulants are clearly not a cure-all, most of these children received other interventions as well. In contrast to early quests for a single cure, researchers have increasingly sought to identify the specific effects of various approaches and to combine them for greater effectiveness.

Drug Therapy. There have been more double-blind, placebo-controlled studies of drug therapy for hyperactivity than of any other treatment for children's behavioral problems. Most have shown significant behavioral changes with stimulants, typically dextroamphetamine (*Dexedrine*) or methylphenidate (*Ritalin*). However, the drugs do not seem to improve school achievement (Barkley & Cunningham, 1978); nor are long-term behavioral outcomes improved by drug treatment (Weiss & Hechtman, 1979). Why not?

To assess interactions between drug effects and their social-ecological context, 7- to 11-year-old hyperactive boys were studied in a special summer school program (Henker, Whalen, & Collins, 1979). All the boys had previously responded well to Ritalin. Controlled laboratory assessments of the boys' peer interactions, attention, and information-processing styles were made, as well as ratings of their behavior under standardized classroom conditions. The study was not merely double blind, but *triple blind,* in that teachers and other raters did not even know that drug treatment of hyperactivity was under study, much less the sequence of drugs and placebo.

As in other studies, behavioral ratings showed significantly fewer classroom problems on Ritalin than placebo. Interactions between the drug effects and ecological variables were studied by assessing the boys' behavior with peers in a structured communication task and their responses to easy versus difficult academic materials, quiet versus noisy conditions, and working at their own pace versus a pace set by tape-recorded instructions. While on Ritalin, the boys did not show significantly more behavior problems than normal boys under any of these conditions (Whalen, et al., 1978; Whalen, Henker, Collins, Finck, & Dotemoto, 1979). On placebo, by contrast, the hyperactive boys did show more problems on most measures under nearly all conditions. Despite reducing behavioral problems, however, Ritalin did not improve the boys' poor interpersonal communication with peers in a structured communication task (Whalen, Henker, Collins, McAuliffe, & Vaux, 1979). In fact, on Ritalin, the boys showed less verbal interaction, less positive mood, and more negative affect than on placebo. The findings thus suggest that suppression of overt behavioral problems fails to improve interpersonal skills and may depress mood.

Another question is whether drugs affect learning and retention. It has been found that Ritalin improved recall of story content over a 2-hour period but not over a 2-day period (Rie & Rie, 1977). Further research has shown that retention may be affected by whether the child is in the same *state* (drug or nondrug) when tested as when initially learning the materials. Kinsbourne and Swanson (1979), for example, reported that hyperactive children's paired associate learning was best when they were on Ritalin while initially learning and again when tested by relearning the same material. Performance was *worst* when they were on Ritalin while initially learning but on placebo while relearning. As shown in Figure 11-2, learning and relearning on placebo and learning on placebo but relearning on Ritalin were both intermediate between these extremes. Figure 11-2 also shows a different pattern of *state dependent* learning for nonhyperactive children: They made the fewest errors when learning *and* relearning on placebo and the most when learning *and* relearning on Ritalin.

Beside possible state-dependent learning, use of stimulant drugs is complicated by other problems. One is the problem of predicting *which* children will benefit from drugs. Exploration of many organic and behavioral variables has failed to disclose any that consistently discriminate between children who do and do not

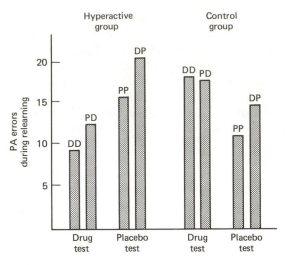

Figure 11-2. Errors made by hyperactive and control children when tested by relearning paired associates. The first letter over each bar indicates drug (D) or placebo (P) condition for initial learning. (From Kinsbourne & Swanson, 1979.)

benefit from stimulants. Instead, follow-up research shows that adolescent outcomes are generally best for unaggressive children having parents who show consistency, firmness, and respect for their child, regardless of drug treatment (Milich & Loney, 1980). These variables may apply not only to outcomes for hyperactivity, however, but other behavioral disorders as well.

A second problem concerns dose levels. Stimulant drugs differ in their potency: Dexedrine is twice as potent as Ritalin, for example. Moreover, *children* also differ in their responsiveness to a particular quantity of a drug. When adjusting dose levels, physicians often rely on reports of school behavior. Yet the quantities needed for favorable school reports may not be optimal for all functions in all children. Sprague and Sleator (1977), for example, found that performance on an information−processing task was optimal at the relatively low dose level of 0.3 milligrams (mg) of Ritalin per kilogram (kg) of the child's weight; performance dropped sharply when dose levels were raised to 1 mg per kg, which is only *half* the 2 mg per kg amount recommended by a standard medical textbook (Goodman & Gilman, 1975).

Another study showed that over 50 percent of children receiving 1 mg per kg had side effects, including loss of appetite, stomachaches, behavioral upsets, and weight loss (Werry & Sprague, 1974). Growth retardation, crying, insomnia, headaches, and psychotic episodes have also been found as side effects, especially on large doses (Barkley, 1977; Roche, Lipman, Overall, & Hung, 1979). Figure 11-3 shows the very different *dose-response curves* obtained for accuracy on

Sprague and Sleator's (1977) information-processing task, teacher ratings of improvements in social behavior, and heart rate (which may correlate with adverse physiological side effects). It is clear from Figure 11-3 that doses yielding the largest improvements in teacher ratings reduce information-processing accuracy and increase heart rates markedly. Some of the difficulty in determining who responds best to stimulants may arise from differences among children in appropriate dosage and in differences in effects on various behaviors. These effects can vary over the 4 to 6 hours that stimulants typically remain active (Kinsbourne & Swanson, 1979).

Behavioral Approaches. As behavioral methods spread in the 1960s, various approaches showed promise with hyperactive children. Tangible reinforcers and teacher attention, for example, were used to increase appropriate behavior in hyperactive school children (Allen, Henke, Harris, Baer, & Reynolds, 1967; Patterson, Jones, Whittier, & Wright, 1965). The apparent success of behavioral methods argued for the importance of environmental influences on hyperactivity (Patterson et al., 1965), just as the apparent success of drug treatment argued for organic influences (Wender, 1971). Yet it became clear that neither environmental nor drug effects prove any particular etiology. It also became clear that suppression of hyperactivity by either approach still leaves hyperactive children with major

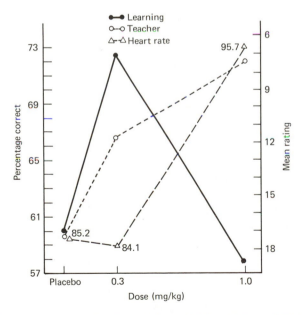

Figure 11-3. Response curves to placebo and doses of 0.3 and 1.0 mg of Ritalin per kg of body weight for percentage of correct responses in a learning task, teacher ratings of social behavior (small numbers = good behavior), and heart beats per minute. (From Sprague & Sleator, 1977.)

adaptive problems: Improvements are often limited to the specific target behaviors, with little generalization to other behavior or situations; reducing hyperactivity does not improve school achievement; and there is little evidence of long-term benefit (Mash & Dalby, 1979). Furthermore, while drug therapy for behavioral problems has been attacked for drugging children into conformity, behavior therapy has come under similar attacks (Schrag & Divoky, 1975). The effort that behavioral intervention requires of parents and teachers is another obstacle, in contrast to the ease with which drugs are dispensed. Arranging double-blind placebo controls is likewise more difficult in behavioral than drug studies.

One approach to obtaining better knowledge of behavioral factors has been to assess the interaction of personality variables with medication and with different behavioral interventions (Bugental, Whalen, & Henker, 1977). This was done by training one group of hyperactive elementary school boys in self-control, using procedures like those of Meichenbaum (1977) described in Chapter 10. A tutor met with each boy twice weekly for eight weeks to model self-controlling speech and self-reinforcement. The boy was to imitate the tutor's behavior by making overt and then covert self-controlling statements. Each boy was also videotaped while using covert speech to control his behavior; the tape was played back to show him his well-controlled behavior. The tutors of a second group of hyperactive boys gave social reinforcement—attention and praise—for working on assigned tasks. Half the boys in each group were taking Ritalin.

The target personality variable was *locus of control,* which is the tendency to view outcomes as due to *external* causes (such as luck or teacher biases) versus *internal* causes (such as one's own effort). It was expected that boys who attributed outcomes to their own efforts would benefit most from the self-control program designed to enhance personal efficacy. The boys' attributions of causality were assessed by asking them to rate the relative importance of luck, studying, and teachers' biases in determining their grades.

As expected, boys who considered their own studying to be most important (*high personal efficacy*) showed the most benefit from self-control training, as measured by impulsivity scores on the Porteus mazes. Boys who considered their own studying least important (*low personal efficacy*) *increased* in impulsivity after self-control training.

In contrast, the social reinforcement program showed better effects on low efficacy boys than on high efficacy boys, although the difference was smaller than for the self-control program. The effects of the programs also depended on the boys' medication status: Among medicated boys, those receiving social reinforcement improved significantly more than those receiving the self-control program; but there was a nonsignificant trend in the *opposite* direction for the unmedicated boys.

A six-month follow-up showed significantly higher personal efficacy scores for the self-control training group than the social reinforcement group (Bugental,

Collins, Collins, & Chaney, 1978). The social reinforcement group showed significantly greater improvement in teacher ratings than the self-control group. Although the findings are complex and statistically marginal, they suggest that different behavioral methods may be needed for children differing in personality and medication status.

Comparisons of Different Approaches. Many studies have compared a particular therapy with a no-treatment or placebo condition. This is an important first step in determining whether a therapy has any benefit at all. Another step is to assess variations in a therapy, such as the effects of dose levels on different aspects of functioning. A further step is to compare the effects of *different* therapies on the same children or on well-matched groups. This has increasingly been done in studies of hyperactive children.

In one study, for example, hyperactive elementary school children were randomly assigned to three treatment conditions: (1) *Placebo drug plus operant behavior therapy* in which contracts between the child, parents, and teacher were used to stipulate target behaviors, token reinforcers, back-up reinforcers, and punishments; (2) *Ritalin therapy* where the dosage was regulated according to parent and teacher reports of behavioral change and side effects; (3) *Ritalin plus operant behavior therapy* (Gittelman, Abikoff, Pollack, Klein, Katz, & Mattes, 1980). After eight weeks of treatment, ratings by teachers, psychiatrists, and classroom observers all showed outcomes to be best for Ritalin plus behavior therapy, second for Ritalin alone, and third for placebo plus behavior therapy. In nearly all comparisons, Ritalin plus behavior therapy was not significantly superior to Ritalin alone, but both were significantly superior to placebo plus behavior therapy. Although there was no control group of untreated hyperactive children, the children receiving Ritalin plus behavior therapy did not differ from *normal* classmates, whereas children receiving placebo plus behavior therapy continued to differ significantly from normals on several measures.

Despite evidence that Ritalin had a more powerful effect on overt problem behavior, other studies have shown that behavioral methods might have more impact on school achievement. As an example, hyperactive children receiving either Ritalin or placebo attended special classes in which a token system was used to reinforce academic performance and appropriate behavior (Wolraich, Drummond, Salomon, O'Brien, & Sivage, 1978). Using an *ABA design* in which two weeks of baseline were followed by two weeks of the token system and then two weeks without it again, it was found that schoolwork was significantly more accurate during the token system than before or after it. Direct observational ratings showed significantly fewer behavioral problems during the token system while the children were doing *group* work, but only in one of the two special classes while they were doing *individual* work. By contrast, the comparison of Ritalin versus placebo showed significantly fewer problems among medicated children doing individual work, but little drug effect on academic tasks or behavioral problems during group work.

The different effects of the two treatments underline again the importance of dissecting the relations between specific interventions and various aspects of outcome: Reducing overt behavior problems does not automatically bring improvement in other areas, such as school work. Drugs offer an easy way to reduce behavioral problems under natural conditions, but additional effort is needed to promote the academic and social skills needed for long-term adaptation.

Summary

Hyperactivity has attracted more attention than almost any other behavior disorder of childhood. Stimulant drugs can reduce overactivity and improve attentiveness in some hyperactive children. It is not clear, however, why the drugs have these effects, what causes hyperactivity, or whether there is any single cause or single syndrome.

Contrary to early hypotheses, most cases of hyperactivity are probably not due to brain damage, although other organic abnormalities have been hypothesized: These include *neurotransmitter abnormalities, abnormalities of arousal, food sensitivities,* and *food allergies.* Developmental delays and constitutional differences have also been hypothesized to cause hyperactivity, but no single cause has been isolated. Because stimulant drugs do not seem to improve hyperactive children's school achievement or long-term adaptation, research is focusing increasingly on *interactions* among biochemical, personality, social, and behavioral variables in treatment.

ENURESIS

Beside being overactive, Teddy R. had also begun wetting his pants. Called *functional enuresis* when no organic cause is found, wetting has received considerable attention in the child clinical literature. Psychoanalytic theorists in particular have viewed it as a symptom of deep-seated psychopathology (see Achenbach & Lewis, 1971). The DSM-III classifies functional enuresis under the heading of *disorders with physical manifestations,* although the DSM states that it is not necessarily associated with mental disorders. Nevertheless, calling enuresis a *disorder with physical manifestations* implies that it is the overt expression of underlying pathology. Just as with hyperactivity, it is therefore important to determine how the overt behavioral problem actually relates to other variables, both developmentally and concurrently.

How many Children are Enuretic?

Teddy wet his pants during the day (*diurnal* enuresis) but bedwetting (*nocturnal* enuresis) is much more common. In a survey of normal boys, for example, the prevalence of day wetting ranged from 7 percent at ages 4 and 5 to less than 1 percent above the age of 9; bedwetting, by contrast, was reported for 26 percent at ages 4 and 5, and still as many as 4 percent at ages 14 and 15, as shown in Figure 11-4.

Although Figure 11-4 shows that enuresis is more common in clinically referred children than normal children, these differences were statistically significant for day wetting only at ages 4 through 7 and for bedwetting only at ages 6 and 7. This means that many of the children who continue wetting beyond the preschool period are not being seen for mental health services. Do they need such services? Is enuresis a sign of psychopathology?

Primary and Secondary Enuresis

Teddy R. had been toilet trained at the age of 2 and had not wet for several years until he began again at the age of 8. However, the majority of children who wet beyond the early preschool period do so continuously, without extended periods of dryness (Doleys, 1981). Because they seem never to have fully learned to stop wetting, they are called *primary* or *continuous* enuretics, whereas those who wet after extended dryness are called *secondary* or *acquired* enuretics. The DSM-III arbitrarily defines enuresis as a *disorder* if it occurs at least twice a month in 5- to

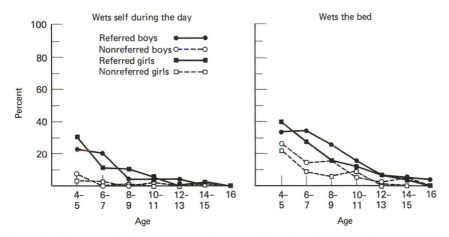

Figure 11-4. Percent of referred and nonreferred children for whom enuresis was reported. (From Achenbach & Edelbrock, 1981.)

6-year-olds and once a month in older children. It designates enuresis as *secondary* if the child has been continent for at least a year before relapsing. The age at which a particular child's wetting is considered a problem typically depends on family expectations, but cultural pressures against wetting mount during the elementary school years. As a result, continued wetting can cause increasing embarrassment and restrictions on activities, such as overnight visiting.

Developmental Course

One of the best sources of longitudinal data on enuresis is a study of Israeli kibbutz children (Kaffman & Elizur, 1977). Because all the children received fairly similar toilet training and could be monitored by their *metaplot* (house mothers), individual differences in the developmental course of wetting could be assessed better than in home-reared children. Failure to achieve bladder control by the age of 4 was found to be correlated with the following variables: (1) enuresis in siblings; (2) high motor activity and aggression; (3) poor adaptability to new situations and routines; (4) low achievement motivation; (5) overly dependent behavior; and (6) a lack of aversion to being wet.

Despite the fact that 70 percent of hyperactive children were enuretic at age 4 and that aggression and masturbation were more common among enuretics, enuretics as a group showed no consistent pattern of behavioral problems. Among children remaining enuretic at ages 6 to 8, 50 percent had behavior disorders, as compared to 12 percent of nonenuretics. However, the enuretics' behavioral problems still showed no consistent pattern. Factor analyses of behavioral problems have also shown that enuresis among disturbed 6- to 11-year-olds is not consistently associated with any particular pattern of problems, although in disturbed 12- to 16-year-olds boys it is associated with immature behaviors, such as excessive crying, whining, overdependency, and preference for younger playmates (Achenbach, 1978; Achenbach & Edelbrock, 1979).

What Causes Enuresis?

Psychodynamic interpretations of enuresis as a symptom of unconscious conflict have not received empirical support (Achenbach & Lewis, 1971). The more general assumption that enuresis is associated with emotional disturbance has received some support in findings of elevated prevalence among children who on other grounds are considered disturbed (Achenbach & Edelbrock, 1981; Kaffman & Elizur, 1977). Yet most enuretic children do not show other signs of disturbance and most disturbed children are not enuretic. We must, therefore, distinguish between enuresis that is linked to emotional disturbance and that which is not.

The distinction between primary enuretics (those who never attained bladder control) and secondary enuretics (those who became enuretic after a period of control) may help. What causes the relapse in secondary enuretics? In the longitudinal study of kibbutz children, five of the six children who started wetting between the ages of 5 and 8 were experiencing significant family stresses. By contrast, children who experienced a variety of stresses during toilet training were no more likely to remain enuretic than children not experiencing stress. An exception to this was that prolonged absence of a parent during toilet training was followed by a somewhat elevated incidence of enuresis (Kaffman & Elizur, 1977). Other studies have also implicated stress in secondary more than primary enuresis, although it is not known whether stress directly causes wetting or simply interferes with poorly learned bladder control (Shaffer, 1977). What, then, affects the acquisition of bladder control?

Acquiring Bladder Control. Organic factors and learning are both likely to be involved in acquiring bladder control. A finding of 68 percent concordance for enuresis in identical twins but only 36 percent in fraternal twins suggests genetic influences (Bakwin, 1971). These could affect many variables, however, including maturation of the urinary system, arousability, responsiveness to cues associated with urination, and learning ability. Enuretics with no known organic disorders have generally been found to have somewhat smaller functional bladder capacities than nonenuretics, as measured by the quantity of urine voided after the child had been asked to wait as long as possible before voiding (Doleys, 1981; Kaffman & Elizur, 1977). Yet this could be due to differences in learned thresholds for voiding as well as organic differences.

Comparisons of bedwetters with nonenuretic children have not shown significant differences in arousability from sleep (Kaffman & Elizur, 1977). General immaturity of functioning has, however, been implicated by findings of delayed development, shorter height, poorer speech, and worse academic performance in enuretics than nonenuretics during the elementary school years (Essen & Peckham, 1976). Essen and Peckham also found an elevated prevalence of enuresis in lower socioeconomic children, but signs of immaturity were more common in enuretics even when socioeconomic differences were controlled. The maturational lags may have affected behavioral interactions involved in socialization more than the ability to control bladder function: Actual delays in ability to control the bladder could not account for many cases of enuresis persisting beyond the preschool period (Essen & Peckham, 1976). Furthermore, Kaffman and Elizur (1977) found that children whose training started between the ages of 15 and 19 months were *less* likely to be enuretic at age 6 than children whose training started between 20 and 26 months. Contrary to prevailing clinical lore, *delayed* training thus seemed to *increase* the risk of later enuresis; this was especially true for children already at risk because of a family history of enuresis, low motivation for achievement, or low adaptability.

In sum, enuresis appears related to general developmental risk factors more than to psychopathology, but appropriate early training can reduce its incidence even in children at risk because of slow development or environmental stress. Stress can contribute, however, especially to secondary enuresis. And enuresis can itself become a source of stress to the child. It is, therefore, important to consider how enuresis can be treated.

How can Enuretics be Helped?

As with hyperactivity, drug and behavior therapies have been the most thoroughly studied treatments for enuresis.

Drug Therapy. Imipramine hydrochloride (*Tofranil*) has been deemed the most effective drug in treating enuretics (Doleys, 1981). Although designed to treat depression in adults, it evidently reduces bedwetting by relaxing the muscles surrounding the bladder, thus allowing greater expansion and delaying voiding. Imipramine has been found superior to placebos, but relapses are common, and seizures and weight loss can occur as side effects. Large doses can be toxic and even fatal (Rapoport & Mikkelsen, 1978). A 10-year follow-up of 29 out of 44 chiidren treated in a controlled study of imipramine showed no negative effects on psychological or physical functioning, however (Bindelglas & Dee, 1978).

Behavioral Therapy. The best researched behavioral treatment for enuresis is the bed pad alarm system developed by Mowrer and Mowrer (1938) and discussed in Chapter 10. When urine activates the alarm by completing a circuit in the electrically wired bed pad, the child is to awaken, shut off the alarm, and go to the toilet. Fourteen consecutive dry nights is the typical criterion for cure. Summarizing studies of 628 children, Doleys (1977) found an overall success rate of 75 percent in treatment lasting from 5 to 12 weeks. Follow−ups showed a relapse rate of 41 percent, although resumption of treatment usually restored continence. Controlled comparisons with psychotherapy, placebo medication, and being awakened by a parent to go to the toilet have shown significant superiority for the alarm method.

A controlled comparison of the alarm with imipramine and a placebo showed the most rapid improvement with the drug; but when treatment ended, relapses reduced the success rate in the drug group to the level of the placebo group (Kolvin, Taunch, Garside, Nolan, & Shaw, 1972). The alarm group remained superior to the placebo group, however. Relapses after alarm treatment have been reduced by using an *intermittent reinforcement* procedure in which not all wetting episodes trigger the alarm and an *overlearning* procedure in which children's bedtime intake of liquids is gradually increased after initial training (Doleys, 1979). Although the exact conditioning mechanisms of the alarm procedure are still unclear, the reduction of relapses with intermittent reinforcement and overlearning are both consistent with learning theory principles for reducing response extinction.

Two other behavioral treatments have shown promise but have not been as extensively tested. One is directed at increasing functional bladder capacity by reinforcing the enuretic for increasing the intervals between voiding during the day (Doleys, 1979). A second method, called *dry bed training,* adds a variety of learning procedures to the alarm system in order to speed and strengthen training (Azrin, Sneed, & Foxx, 1974). Training is concentrated intensively on a single night in which the child first practices getting up and urinating; at bedtime, the child drinks extra fluid and rehearses the training instructions; the child is then awakened hourly and goes to the bathroom but is asked to inhibit urination; the child drinks additional fluid and returns to bed; if the child wets the bed, the alarm sounds and the trainer takes the child to the bathroom, the child changes the sheets, and practices toileting. On subsequent nights, the alarm continues to be used, along with practice in toileting, awakening for toileting when the parents go to bed, and frequent praise for dryness.

In a controlled comparison, Azrin et al. (1974) found that dry bed training eliminated wetting much more quickly and completely than the standard alarm procedure. All children whose wetting was not improved after two weeks of the standard alarm were trained successfully with the dry bed method. In fact, the possible irrelevance of the alarm to training was demonstrated by placing it in the parents' room where the child could not hear it; when the alarm sounded, a parent took the child to the toilet. Children under this condition improved as much as those hearing the alarm, indicating that the social and motivational aspects of training may be more important than Pavlovian conditioning to the noxious stimulus of the alarm.

Family and Child Variables. Even though the standard alarm and dry bed procedures *can* reduce bedwetting, lack of effective parental cooperation reduces their effectiveness (Doleys, 1979). As with hyperactivity, drug treatments may be preferred because they require less effort by the relevant adults. However, the demonstrated superiority of behavioral treatments for bedwetting argues for helping parents make the effort required.

Other factors may also affect the success of behavioral treatments. The training studies, for example, have been designed to *teach* continence, and most of their subjects were primary enuretics. What about secondary enuretics who start wetting after learning continence? Novick (1966) found that more secondary than primary enuretics became dry through supportive encouragement alone and that the alarm method produced quicker results in the remaining secondary enuretics than in primary enuretics. Yet follow-ups showed more relapses, new symptoms, and deterioration of behavior in secondary than primary enuretics. The general behavioral improvement and paucity of new symptoms found in primary enuretics after behavioral treatment contradicts early psychoanalytic warnings that mere symptom removal would result in substitution of new symptoms (Baker, 1969). In secondary enuretics, however, the onset of wetting seems more likely to be related to adaptive problems that need attention in their own right.

Teddy R. was continent before the onset of daytime wetting. He also had problems of self-control in activity, attention, and bowel function. He therefore needed more than treatment of the wetting. This does not necessarily mean that wetting should not be treated in such cases—if it distresses the child, it could serve as an initial focus of treatment in which the child's cooperation can be enlisted and a therapeutic alliance can be established. Although no particular treatment for day wetting has received wide study, the importance of social and motivational factors in continence suggest that reinforcement for dry periods of increasing duration should have high priority.

ENCOPRESIS

Despite other longstanding behavioral problems, it was Teddy's defecation in his pants that ultimately precipitated referral to the mental health center. When not caused by organic abnormalities, uncontrolled defecation is called *functional encopresis*. The DSM-III defines it as a "disorder with physical manifestations" if it occurs at least monthly after the age of 4.

How many Children are Encopretic?

Encopresis is considerably less common than enuresis. As Figure 11-5 shows, a survey of normal children yielded rates ranging from 5 percent for boys and 9 percent for girls at ages 4 and 5, down to no more than 1 percent above the age of 9. Among clinically referred children, the rates ranged from 23 percent for boys and 17 percent for girls at ages 4 to 5, to 2 percent for boys at age 16 and less than 1 percent for girls above the age of 13. Because it is not very common above age 7 even among referred children, the differences between referred and nonreferred children were statistically significant only at ages 4 through 7.

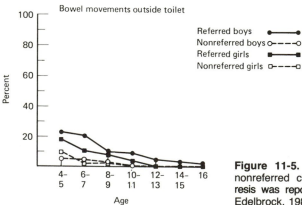

Figure 11-5. Percent of referred and nonreferred children for whom encopresis was reported. (From Achenbach & Edelbrock, 1981.)

Types of Encopresis

Like functional enuresis, encopresis is classified as *primary* or *secondary,* according to whether continence has ever been achieved. Unlike enuresis, however, secondary encopresis is at least as common as primary encopresis (Fisher, 1979). Also unlike enuresis, nocturnal bowel control is usually achieved before daytime control, and daytime encopresis is more common than nocturnal encopresis (Bellman, 1966).

Organic abnormalities, such as a lack of ganglionic cells in the large intestine and rectum (*Hirschsprung disease*), may make it hard for a few children to learn bowel control. Constipation and withholding of bowel movements can also cause impaction of feces which, in turn, stretches the colon. Known as *psychogenic megacolon,* this can lead to encopresis when fecal matter leaks around the blockage or pressure becomes great enough to induce involuntary defecation. Fear of painful bowel movements and fear of using toilets can cause some children to withhold feces until they become encopretic.

Diverse psychodynamic explanations have been proposed, but these have not received empirical support (Achenbach & Lewis, 1971). Nor have factor analyses shown a consistent association with any particular pattern of behavioral problems (Achenbach, 1978; Achenbach & Edelbrock, 1979). Although it has been less well researched than enuresis, encopresis seems similarly multidetermined by inadequate toilet training, stress, and biologic and environmental risk factors. The high proportion of secondary and daytime encopresis, possible fears of defecation, the noxiousness of the problem, and occasional association with constipation and other bowel dysfunctions make it more complex to treat, however.

How can Encopretics be Helped?

The literature on treatment consists largely of clinical descriptions of a particular practitioner's favored method. These can suggest approaches to try, but they do not tell us which method works best. Most approaches have involved a combination of physical treatment of bowel function and behavioral methods for promoting appropriate toilet behavior. Halpern (1977), for example, describes an eclectic approach in which an examination is first performed to rule out physical abnormalities. Then the parents and child are interviewed to obtain data on the symptoms, interpersonal relationships, motivation for change, and potential reinforcers for the child. The physiology of retention and encopresis is explained to the family and child, if he or she is deemed old enough to understand.

A suppository (*Dulcolax*) that induces evacuation within half an hour is inserted once daily for three days to give the child immediate success in defecating in the toilet on a designated schedule. Thereafter, the child is rewarded for bowel movements without the suppository. If the child is afraid of toileting, systematic desensitization is used to reduce fear. Children whose stools are hard enough to cause discomfort are given a stool softener (*Colace*).

A retrospective study of the records of 10 children receiving this treatment showed that seven became continent within four weeks, one became continent before treatment began, and parent and child resistance prevented effective treatment of the other two. Of 10 children treated with psychotherapy in the same clinic, four became continent but took longer than those receiving the eclectic treatment, three failed to become continent but continued in therapy, and three left therapy unimproved. Although there was no controlled assignment to treatment or prospective evaluation, these findings imply reasonable súccess for the combination of the suppository with the behavioral approach. Other studies have likewise reported favorable results with combinations of laxatives, positive reinforcement for toileting, and, in some cases, mild punishment for encopretic episodes (Ashkenazi, 1975; Blechman, 1979; Wright, 1975).

Biofeedback procedures are also used with a few children who lack adequate control of their anal sphincters. For example, a special balloon inserted into the rectum can be attached to a device that signals changes in sphincter pressure (Kohlenberg, 1973). The child is then reinforced for increasing the pressure. The sphincter response seems subject to operant conditioning like other responses, but the elaborateness of the procedure and paucity of outcome data make it a treatment to be tried only after simpler ones have failed. In the case of Teddy R., his long period of continence before becoming encopretic, a lack of organic bowel abnormalities, preoccupation with his mother's anger about messing, and the prominence of other behavioral problems argue for viewing his encopresis as part of a larger picture of maladaptation. Although, like Teddy's enuresis, it might be a good target for behavioral intervention, such interventions should be but one aspect of a coordinated treatment strategy for facilitating adaptive development.

DISORDERS OF LEARNING

Teddy R.'s IQ was in the superior range. Yet his school work was unsatisfactory. In particular, he failed to pay attention and refused to do oral work. School is one of the most crucial areas of adaptation for children in western countries, and it is an area in which most children referred for mental health services have faltered. As Figure 11-6 shows, poor schoolwork is reported for many more referred than nonreferred children at all ages from 6 to 16. There is great diversity in the nature and causes of poor schoolwork, however.

Teddy R. clearly had the ability to master academic skills. He had learned to read, write, and do basic arithmetic. His school problems stemmed more from a failure to behave appropriately than from an inability to learn. Inability to control activity or attention is the main cause of some children's poor school performance. Teddy showed many of the characteristics of such children. Yet he also showed

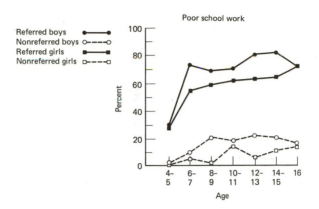

Referred boys ●——●
Nonreferred boys ○----○
Referred girls ■——■
Nonreferred girls □----□

Figure 11-6. Percent of referred and nonreferred children for whom poor school work was reported. (From Achenbach & Edelbrock, 1981.)

other problems of recent origin that suggested increasing emotional stress. Although it may be hard to determine whether longstanding attentional problems or more recent emotional stress interfered most with Teddy's school performance, it at least seemed clear that his school problems were effects rather than causes of his other problems. This does not necessarily mean that his school problems could be ignored or that they would vanish if his other problems were resolved. As we saw earlier, alleviating hyperactivity and inattentiveness via drug and behavior therapies does not automatically improve school achievement. Children who have fallen behind in school, for whatever reasons, usually need help and incentives to catch up.

Learning Disabilities

Unlike Teddy and others whose poor schoolwork does not stem from inability to learn, some children have basic difficulties in learning to read, write, or do arithmetic. When such problems are not due to mental retardation, impairment of sight or hearing, psychological problems, or lack of cultural and educational opportunities, they are called *learning disabilities* (Ross, 1976). Exceptional difficulty with a particular skill is called a *specific learning disability;* the most common ones have acquired technical names of their own, such as *dyslexia, dysgraphia,* and *dyscalculia* for problems in reading, writing, and arithmetic, respectively.

Causal Hypotheses. Such disabilities are often hypothesized to have organic, possibly genetic, causes. Evidence of genetic factors comes from studies showing significantly higher concordance for reading skill and for learning problems in identical than fraternal twins (Bakwin, 1973; Matheny & Dolan, 1974; Matheny, Dolan, & Wilson, 1976). However, this might merely reflect genetic factors in general cognitive ability, rather than anything specific to reading or learning disabilities.

In a study of children having specific reading disabilities despite IQs of at least 100, genetic causes were suggested by elevated rates of reading disabilities in other family members, but pedigree analyses showed no uniform pattern of genetic transmission (Finucci, Guthrie, Childs, Abbey, & Childs, 1976). Males seemed most susceptible, since more male than female family members were affected, a virtually universal finding. However, the diversity of family patterns implied that there are probably several types of reading disability involving different genetic factors.

Inconsistencies are also evident in studies aimed at finding organic abnormalities in specific learning disabilities (Rourke, 1978). Dyslexia is the most common specific learning disability, and the most widely studied. By the time children are diagnosed dyslexic, however, they typically have a host of maladaptive behaviors related to learning. It is, therefore, seldom possible to assess their reading problems in isolation from their other problems. The age at which dyslexics are assessed is also a factor, as different functional deficits are associated with poor reading at different ages: Visual-perceptual deficits have been found in reading disabled 7- to 9-year olds, but linguistic deficits have been found in older learning disabled children. A longitudinal study of the changing relations between reading and other functions in a general population sample showed that visual-perceptual functioning in kindergarten was the best predictor of later reading skill; but by age 11, reading skill correlated higher with linguistic than perceptual functioning (Satz & Fletcher, 1980). This may be because (1) individual differences in visual-perceptual skills affect the initial stages of learning to read, but (2) these differences have less effect when visual-perceptual development levels off after age 9. The later correlation with linguistic functioning may be because higher stages of reading depend more on linguistic skills, or perhaps reading helps *promote* higher level linguistic skills.

It thus seems that different aspects of development are involved in different stages of reading. Poor perceptual functioning may hinder acquisition of the basic mechanics of reading at the normal time, whereas poor linguistic functioning may hinder advances beyond the rudimentary mechanics. Evidence has also been found for at least two distinctive types of dyslexics: *Visual-spatial dyslexics* whose primary weakness is in visual-spatial functioning, and *auditory-linguistic dyslexics* whose primary weakness is in rapid, complex linguistic processing (Pirozzolo, 1979). Possible deficits of right hemisphere functions in visual-spatial dyslexia and left hemisphere functions in auditory-linguistic dyslexia, plus the different developmental courses of these functions, may require very different preventive and treatment approaches. Delaying the teaching of reading until visual-perceptual development is sufficiently advanced may help minimize visual-spatial reading problems, for example. However, the evidence for abnormal asymmetries in the cerebral functioning of poor readers is far from conclusive (Naylor, 1980; Young & Ellis, 1981).

Certain teaching methods may also affect the risk of problems for children having different vulnerabilities. The *sight recognition* method, for example, requires the child to memorize whole words rather than deciphering them by letters and syllables. At the other extreme, the *phonic* method emphasizes sounding out words syllable-by-syllable. The dependence of the sight recognition method on subtle visual discriminations among the shapes of printed words is likely to handicap children with poor visual-perceptual functioning. The phonic method, by contrast, may handicap children with poor auditory-linguistic functioning, especially in a phonetically irregular language like English. Teaching methods that avoid total reliance on any single ability might reduce the risk of severe reading disabilities in many children.

Outcomes of Learning Disorders

Failure to acquire basic academic skills in childhood can produce life-long handicaps that interfere with many aspects of adaptation. Few long-term follow-ups have been done, however, to compare the outcomes of various learning disorders following different interventions. One of the only studies to report long-term outcomes for a specific learning disability showed that dyslexic boys attained adult occupational and educational status equal to a control group who had good early reading skills (Rawson, 1968). Because the boys had very advantaged family backgrounds and received individualized reading instruction, this does not mean that all dyslexics fare so well. Yet it does show that serious reading problems *can* be overcome under optimal conditions.

For most children with learning problems and less privileged backgrounds, the meager existing outcome evidence is not so hopeful (e.g., Ackerman, Dykman, & Peters, 1977). Although intervention programs based on perceptual theories of learning disorders are widely used, most of these programs have not been proven to help very much (Pirozzolo, 1979).

A possible exception is a program called TEACH, developed by Hagin, Silver, and Kreeger (1976). It is designed for elementary school children who are considered at risk for learning problems because of poor perceptual functioning, as identified on a brief battery of tests entitled SEARCH. The SEARCH battery includes tests of visual matching, visual-motor function, auditory discrimination, rote sequencing, verbal expression, and auditory-graphic ability. The TEACH program is designed to train perceptual functioning in the areas found weakest on the SEARCH battery. For example, children who are weak in visual areas are first taught to make simple discriminations among visual stimuli, then to copy such stimuli, and then to recall stimuli with minimal cues from the teacher.

In a controlled study, first graders performing poorly on the SEARCH battery were assigned either to (1) six months of twice-weekly TEACH tutoring; (2) regular academic tutoring in reading and math; or (3) a no-treatment control condition (Arnold et al., 1977). Cognitive, behavioral, and achievement measures showed the most improvement for the TEACH group, with minimal differences between the academic tutoring and no-treatment control groups. A one-year follow-up showed that the TEACH group advanced in nearly all areas, while the other two groups actually grew worse in several areas, including cognitive functioning and behavior problems. These findings support the efficacy of the TEACH program in promoting continued effective learning.

An especially interesting finding was that all three groups improved significantly and similarly on the SEARCH test battery itself. This indicates that the perceptual problems tapped by the SEARCH battery eventually disappear without special intervention. Yet, as Arnold et al. state:

> . . . the "wait and see" attitude toward first-grade perceptual problems is not entirely without foundation; they do tend to improve "by themselves." What this attitude ignores, though, is the academic, behavioral, and emotional sequelae of frustration/failure, with destructive effects on self-esteem, learning attitude, achievement, behavior, and even measurable IQ. The data presented demonstrate that for the children identified as vulnerable, the spontaneous improvement in perceptual skills is not accompanied by an equally spontaneous improvement in behavior, reading achievement, or IQ scores. On the contrary, without some kind of intervention there tends to be deterioration in all three of these areas, sometimes reaching statistical significance, despite the significant improvement in perceptual skills! (p. 1292)

These findings imply that perceptual lags are crucially important in first grade, because they interfere with the basic mechanisms of reading and because the social ecology of our educational system lays so much stress on reading. By the time children catch up perceptually, they may have such negative attitudes about school learning that they cannot put their perceptual abilities to use. Instead, they shirk from learning in many areas and develop behavioral problems as well. The failure of direct academic tutoring in reading and math to prevent these problems in the Arnold et al. study argues that strengthening perceptual processes is a prerequisite to effective first-grade learning in children identified by the SEARCH battery. Further replications and extensions of these findings are needed to determine how schooling can be better coordinated with children's developmental progress in order to prevent learning disabilities.

DISORDERS OF AFFECT

The disorders discussed so far in this chapter consist of specific behaviors hypothesized to involve a combination of organic and psychological determinants. We now turn to debilitating emotional states that have likewise been hypothesized to involve a combination of organic and psychological determinants. Depression is the emotional state currently getting the most attention. Adult depression has long been recognized as a major disorder, potentially culminating in psychosis and/or suicide. Manic-depressive ("bipolar") disorders, in which periods of depression alternate with periods of irrational euphoria, also present striking pictures of psychopathology in adults. Yet depressive disorders in children have been more elusive.

Neither the first, second, nor third edition of the DSM contains any depressive disorders of childhood. Despite early evidence of manic-depressive conditions in a few children (Kasanin & Kaufman, 1929), the psychoanalytic theory dominant from the 1930s through the 1960s implied that true depressive disorders could occur only after the superego was fully internalized during adolescence (see Kashani et al., 1981). Following the success of drug therapies for some adult affective disorders in the 1950s and 1960s, however, the quest for childhood depression was renewed. Since children seldom seek help for depression, speculation has been rife about the forms it might take.

Problems of Definition

One approach was to infer depression from a wide variety of other problems in children. Frommer (1967), for example, maintained that:

> Depression should be suspected in children who complain of non-specific recurrent abdominal pain, headache, sleep difficulties and irrational fears, or mood disturbances such as irritability, unaccountable tearfulness, and associated outbursts of temper. Such children often develop sudden difficulty in social adjustments, which previously were normal; they may either withdraw themselves from the family circle and former friends or display outright aggressive and antisocial behaviour. (p. 729)

In a trial of antidepressant drugs with children she considered depressed, Frommer distinguished two groups: A *phobic group* whose primary symptoms were fears of separation and school, sleep problems, and school failure due to frequent absences, but who "rarely showed a frankly depressive picture or its typical mood disorder, and sometimes even denied any feeling of depression" (p. 730). The others, a *mood disorder group,* "were weepy, irritable, had temper outbursts, and some displayed quite serious antisocial behaviour. A few complained of actually feeling depressed, and one boy made suicidal threats" (p. 730). In a double-blind, crossover trial, Frommer saw significantly greater improvement while the children were taking Nardil (phenelzine) and Librium (chlordiazepoxide) than while taking phenobarbitone with a placebo. No objective assessment of specific symptoms was reported, however.

Another study of antidepressant medication used more explicit diagnostic criteria, but these were so inclusive that 63 percent of a sample of prepubertal children referred to an educational clinic were diagnosed as suffering from a "depressive illness" (Weinberg, Rutman, Sullivan, Penick, & Dietz, 1973).

Children were diagnosed depressed if they showed dysphoric (unhappy, irritable, hypersensitive, or negative) mood and self-deprecatory ideation, plus at least two of the following symptoms: Aggressive behavior, sleep disturbance, change in school performance, diminished socialization, change in attitude toward school, loss of usual energy, unusual change in appetite and/or weight. The symptoms had to represent a change in the child's usual behavior and had to be present for more than a month. They were assessed by a pediatric neurologist informally interviewing the parents and child.

Subsequent interview ratings suggested greater improvement in children who received the antidepressant Elavil (amitriptyline) or Tofranil (imipramine) from their own physicians than in children for whom medication was recommended but not given. However, no objective assessment of symptoms was reported, treatment conditions were not blind nor systematically assigned, and no placebos were used.

The concept of depression was broadened still further by the term *masked depression*. This refers to depression inferred from aggressive, hyperactive, and other troublesome behavior which is used defensively "to ward off the unbearable feelings of dispair" (Cytryn & McKnew, 1979, p. 327). The underlying depression in such cases is said to be evident from "(1) periodic displays of a *purely* depressive picture, which would include sad affect, verbalization of depressive themes, and (2) the existence of depressive themes in dreams, drawings, and other fantasy material" (Cytryn & McKnew, 1979, p. 329). Other authors added signs of masked depression ranging from psychophysiological reactions to truancy, running away, sexual promiscuity, and fire setting (see Kovacs & Beck, 1977). However, the concept of masked depression is generally being dropped in favor of less inferential concepts of depression (Kashani et al., 1981).

Childhood versions of manic-depressive disorders have also been reported and have appeared to benefit from treatment with lithium carbonate, a drug used to treat adult manic conditions (DeLong, 1978); however, such disorders seem rare in prepubertal children (Cytryn & McKnew, 1979). They may be less rare in adolescents, but similar enough to adult versions to be more easily recognized (Carlson & Strober, 1979).

From the varied use of the term *depression*, it should be no wonder that there is little consensus on how to diagnose it in children. The apparent benefits of antidepressant drugs in the questionable studies by Frommer (1967) and Weinberg et al. (1973) are not very informative either, as Cytryn and McKnew (1979) anecdotally report marked improvement when their depressed subjects were merely hospitalized for study. Many of Cytryn and McKnew's cases unexpectedly sustained their improvements over a 5-year follow-up, without treatment.

Conceptual Issues

Several questions arise in determining whether there are coherent syndromes of depression in children. One question is whether some of the behaviors subsumed by the broad concepts of depression are transient developmental phenomena that typically disappear with age, rather than a clinical disorder.

A second question concerns distinctions between unhappiness as a normal reaction to life events and persistent depression not explicable as a normal response. Everyone experiences some unhappiness, and clinical interviews may intensify negative affect in children whose maladaptive behavior gets them referred for mental health services. Furthermore, very negative life situations may explain the misery of some children who look depressed (e.g., Puig-Antich, Blau, Marx, Greenhill, & Chambers, 1978).

A third question is whether depressed affect is a *result* rather than a cause of behavioral problems. Instead of masking or defending against depression, hyperactivity and aggression may earn children negative consequences that make them feel unhappy and worthless. In the case of Teddy R., for example, his negative self-image, lack of friends, and ingratiating manner may have resulted from his being rejected because others found him intolerable. Although the broad concepts of depression imply that such behavior problems result from depression, such problems could help cause depression.

Empirical Approaches

To clarify the conceptual issues, we need to know the prevalence of depressed affect in normal as well as disturbed children, to identify age differences, and to assess relations to other problems of adaptation. Figure 11-7 shows the percent of clinically referred and nonreferred children whose parents described them as *unhappy, sad, or depressed* (Achenbach & Edelbrock, 1981). This item was endorsed for no more than 13 percent of nonreferred children at any age, and there were no marked age differences. For referred children, however, the rates ranged from 43 percent for 4- and 5-year-old boys to 86 percent for 12- and 13-year-old girls. In fact, out of the 118 behavioral problems assessed in this survey, *unhappy, sad, or depressed* showed larger differences between referred and nonreferred children than any other item across all ages (Achenbach & Edelbrock, 1981). It thus appears that depressive affect evident to parents (1) has a fairly constant rate in normal children at ages 4 to 16, and (2) is far more common in children referred for mental health services than in normal children. Depressive affect alone seldom instigates clinical referral of children, but Figure 11-7 shows that it is evident in many who are regarded as needing help for other problems. Is depressive affect then merely a common byproduct of many different problems? Or are there coherent syndromes of depression that distinguish a subset of disturbed children from those whose unhappiness is but one facet of other syndromes?

Factor analyses of the 118 behavior problem items have shown a distinctive syndrome indicative of depression in clinically referred 6- to 11-year-olds of both sexes (Achenbach, 1978; Achenbach & Edelbrock, 1979). Although there were a few differences in the items found on the factors for the two sexes, the 13 items

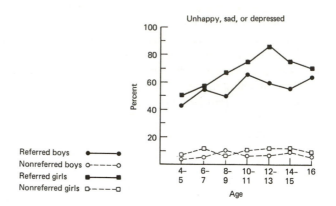

Figure 11-7. Percent of referred and nonreferred children for whom the item *Unhappy, sad or depressed* was reported. (From Achenbach & Edelbrock, 1981.)

shown in Table 11-2 had high loadings on the factor for both sexes. These items certainly seem to reflect a depressive condition. Yet they show minimal overlap with the DSM-III criteria for diagnosing depression, which are shown in Table 11-3. About the only clear overlap between the DSM criteria and the empircally derived syndrome is the presence of depressed mood and excessive guilt feelings, although the boys' version of the empirically derived syndrome also included *deliberately harms self or attempts suicide* and *talks about killing self*, which overlap with DSM criterion B-8.

No such clearcut syndrome of depression was found in factor analyses of problems reported for clinically referred 12- to 16-year-olds (Achenbach & Edelbrock, 1979). Instead, for 12- to 16-year-old boys, three different factors (dubbed *schizoid, uncommunicative,* and *hostile withdrawal*) each included four of the items found on the *depressed* factor for 6- to 11-year-olds. For 12- to 16-year-old girls, more of these items were concentrated on two factors, but one factor featured primarily anxiety, obsessiveness, and self-reproach, whereas the other featured depression and withdrawal.

The differences between the DSM criteria and the syndromes found empirically for different age groups underscore the importance of developmental differences not only in the *incidence* but also the *patterning* of behavioral problems. The lack of a distinctive syndrome of depressive behaviors among disturbed adolescents does not mean such behaviors are rare or unimportant. Instead, they seem to occur with a wider variety of other behavior problems than among younger children, for whom there is a single distinctive syndrome of depressed behaviors.

Table 11-2   Items Appearing on Depressed Factor found for 6-11-year-old Boys and Girls

Complains of loneliness
Fears he/she might think or do something bad
Feels he/she has to be perfect
Feels or complains that no one loves him/her
Feels others are out to get him/her
Feels too guilty
Feels worthless or inferior
Nervous, highstrung, or tense
Self-conscious or easily embarrassed
Sulks a lot
Too fearful or anxious
Unhappy, sad, or depressed
Worrying

Source: Achenbach, 1978; Achenbach & Edelbrock, 1979.

The existence of a syndrome of depressed behaviors in 6- to 11-year-olds does not mean that these behaviors never accompany other behavior problems, however. Cluster analysis of behavior profiles comprising the depressed syndrome and eight other behavioral syndromes found for boys aged 6 to 11 has identified a group having elevated scores on depression, social withdrawal, and aggression, for example (Edelbrock & Achenbach, 1980). Similarly, cluster analysis of 6- to 11-year-old girls' profiles has identified a group having elevated scores on depression and social withdrawal. This means that at least some children manifesting the behavioral syndrome of depression simultaneously manifest other types of behavior problems as well.

Another empirical approach has been to assess relations among several different measures thought to reflect depression in children. Lefkowitz and Tesiny (1980), for example, constructed the Peer Nomination Inventory of Depression (PNID), consisting of 20 items such as "Who often plays alone?" Fourth- and fifth-graders were asked to indicate which of their classmates best fit each item. The children also filled out self-report measures of depression, and their teachers rated them on depression and achievement. Significant but low correlations of .23 and .14 were found between depression scores on the PNID and the two self-report measures. Teacher-rated depression correlated somewhat higher (.41) with the PNID, however. The PNID also showed significant but low negative correlations with measures of ability, achievement, popularity, self-esteem, happiness, and socioeconomic status. Children who tended to have the most signs of depression thus tended to be somewhat worse off in other respects as well. However, the correlations were weak; they do not necessarily shed light on depression of clinical

Table 11-3   DSM-III Diagnostic Criteria for Depressive Episode

Diagnostic criteria for major depressive episode

A. Dysphoric mood or loss of interest or pleasure in all or almost all usual activities and pastimes. The dysphoric mood is characterized by symptoms such as the following: depressed, sad, blue, hopeless, low, down in the dumps, irritable. The mood disturbance must be prominent and relatively persistent, but not necessarily the most dominant symptom, and does not include momentary shifts from one dysphoric mood to another dysphoric mood, e.g., anxiety to depression to anger, such as are seen in states of acute psychotic turmoil. (For children under six, dysphoric mood may have to be inferred from a persistently sad facial expression.)

B. At least four of the following symptoms have each been present nearly every day for a period of at least two weeks (in children under six, at least three of the first four).

1. poor appetite or significant weight loss (when not dieting) or increased appetite or significant weight gain (in children under six, consider failure to make expected weight gains)
2. insomnia or hypersomnia
3. psychomotor agitation or retardation (but not merely subjective feelings of restlessness or being slowed down) (in children under six, hypoactivity)
4. loss of interest or pleasure in usual activities, or decrease in sexual drive not limited to a period when delusional or hallucinating (in children under six, signs of apathy)
5. loss of energy; fatigue
6. feelings of worthlessness, self-reproach, or excessive or inappropriate guilt (either may be delusional)
7. complaints or evidence of diminished ability to think or concentrate, such as slowed thinking, or indecisiveness not associated with marked loosening of associations or incoherence
8. recurrent thoughts of death, suicidal ideation, wishes to be dead, or suicide attempt

C. Neither of the following dominate the clinical picture when an affective syndrome (i.e., criteria A and B above) is not present, that is, before it developed or after it has remitted:

1. preoccupation with a mood-incongruent delusion or hallucination (see definition below)
2. bizarre behavior

D. Not superimposed on either Schizophrenia, Schizophreniform Disorder, or a Paranoid Disorder.

E. Not due to any Organic Mental Disorder or Uncomplicated Bereavement.

Source: American Psychiatric Association, 1980, pp. 213–214.

seriousness; and they do not tell us whether the negative characteristics are uniquely related to signs of depression or maladaptive behavior in general.

Suicide

Probably the gravest consequence of depression is the risk of suicide. Depressed people often harbor suicidal thoughts and sometimes act on them, although not all suicidal acts are preceded by depression. In the factor analyses of behavior problems, the items *deliberately harms self or attempts suicide* and *talks about killing self* were found only in the syndrome for 6- to 11-year-old boys (Achenbach, 1978). For the 6- to 11-year-old girls, these items were associated with a syndrome dubbed *schizoid obsessive*, which included obsessions, compulsions, hallucinations, strange ideas, and strange behavior (Achenbach & Edelbrock, 1979). This indicates that suicidal behavior among girls of this age is more likely to accompany bizarre thinking and behavior than depression. In adolescents, the suicidal items were not consistently associated with any particular syndrome for either sex. This agrees with clinical impressions that adolescent suicidal behavior is often a response to frustrations, interpersonal conflicts, developmental crises, and the breakup of love affairs, rather than clinical depression (Cytryn & McKnew, 1979).

The survey data showed that *talks about killing self* was reported for no more than 6 percent of nonreferred children at any age but for as many as 24 percent of 14- and 15-year-old girls referred for mental health services (Achenbach & Edelbrock, 1981). *Deliberately harms self or attempts suicide* was reported for no more than 5 percent of nonreferred children at any age but up to 19 percent of referred 16-year-old girls. Official statistics show completed suicides rising from less than 1 per 100,000 population among 10- to 14-year-olds to over 7 per 100,000 at ages 15 to 19, and over 16 at ages 20 to 24 (National Center for Health Statistics, 1977). This means about 170 10—14-year-olds, 1600 15—19-year-olds, and 3200 20—24-year-olds kill themselves annually in the United States, making suicide the third most common cause of death in this age range. The even higher accident and homicide rates at these ages may also include deaths due to suicidal behavior (Holinger, 1979). All three types of violent death are far more frequent for males than females, with male suicide rates three to five times as high as female rates at ages 10 to 24. Females make many more suicide attempts than males, however (Shaffer & Fisher, 1981).

The lack of consistent associations between suicidal behavior and signs of depression in adolescents, and recent sharp increases in almost all kinds of violent adolescent deaths make it hard to apportion blame to psychopathology, cultural conditions, and developmental crises. Adolescence is often depicted as a time of turmoil, but there is increasing evidence that such turmoil is neither inevitable nor a common cause of clinical disorders in adolescents (Rutter, 1980). The actual proportion of adolescents who make serious suicide attempts or show other extremely deviant behavior remains fairly low. The motivations and outcomes are also diverse, as illustrated by the following two cases.

LENORE

Everyone at school knew about my father [who had sexually abused her]. It was in the papers. I went into my shell and separated myself from other people. Right through high school I didn't have anything to do with anybody else, and it didn't bother me. I preferred it that way. I was tired of being put down and humiliated by people accepting me and then turning their backs on me when they found out all about my background.

I first knew I was cracking up when I was fourteen. I bit my hand as hard as I could and I drew blood. I called my mom and said, "Look! I need help." And she said, "There's a good movie on downstairs and we have company." At the time I really felt like a fool. But now, looking at it from a different perspective, I could boot her ass for her reaction.

It wasn't long after that I made my first suicide attempt. I remember I was going with my mother and sister to a roadside stand to buy some corn. I had taken two bottles of sleeping pills before we left and I told my mother what I had done a few minutes after we got into the car. She said, "I hope you're happy. Now we can't go to get corn. We'll have to go to the hospital to have your stomach pumped." I said, "Well just forget it then." And she forgot it. I went home and slept it off. I guess the pills weren't too powerful.

The next time I tried it I was going out with a guy. He told me he never wanted to see me again. Nothing else in my life was really worth living for. I think that's really common when you're an adolescent. You don't have the alternatives you have as an adult. Nowadays I think if that happened to me I wouldn't think of killing myself. I'd leave the city, start a new life. When you're an adolescent in high school with your parents controlling you, you don't have the alternatives. Suicide is about the only one. Either continue the way you're going or kill yourself. You can't cope with problems and accept disappointment because past a certain point you don't have the means to cope.

Altogether I made ten suicide attempts. I felt that the only time I would be taken seriously was if I were dead. Even in the hospital no one took me seriously. Last time I was in, the nurse said something like, "We hope you'll think twice before you do this again." Never a matter of them bringing in a psychiatrist. Just "Oh Christ, you again!" Get it out of me and go home. They don't want to see you again. I'm surprised that I kept going through it.

A friend asked my why I used only sleeping pills. I didn't have the courage to do it the painful ways. I also knew if I didn't succeed those ways I'd be in bigger trouble, because I'd have the physical scars. Sleeping pills are convenient; it's not that I thought chances of succeeding with them were less. And sleeping pills are really easy to come by. Many doctors in this city are more than happy to give young people any kind of pill they want. One doctor in particular knew I was suicidal. Had my counsellor not phoned him up and told him not to give me another pill I could still go in there and get anything I wanted. It was common knowledge around the city, but this doctor never lost his licence. Kids in school get to know which doctors will give pills. (Rabkin, 1979, pp. 41–42)

In Lenore's case, sexual abuse by her father, a feeling of being ostracized, and a family history of mental illness and suicides could all have contributed to her suicidal behavior. Yet her suicide attempts seemed motivated more by hopes of concern from others than by a serious wish to die.

PETER

April 14

Hello everyone. My name is Peter Walker. I'm presently fifteen years old, and I'm dead. Yes, dead. I'm trying to figure out how long I've been dead. I think now it's been about six or seven years. Actually, if you looked at me you wouldn't notice anything strange about me. I certainly wouldn't look like a dead person. But I'm convinced that I'm dead. I'm sure that I'm not alive, so I'm either in a state of unbalance or I'm dead. One thing for sure. I am not alive.

When I said I was dead what I really meant was that I don't know what I am, where I am, now and going, what I'm doing here, and in other words, I don't know anything. I'm just one crazy mixed up kid who hasn't got the foggiest idea of what is going on. I don't understand life, love, anything. I just keep asking questions and getting nothing for answers. And it's driving me crazy. I'm not content to live when I don't know what it is to live. I must know all the answers. I will not be satisfied until I know all the answers.

Apr. 20

I don't even know who I am. Something must have created me. But who and why? I am really an agnostic in this area. I say there must have been a creator or supreme being, but then again, did there really have to be one? And I think a creator of something would have control over what he has created. God is supposed to be so kind and right. But what kind of creator would allow such things he has created to kill each other and be so cruel to each other? The situation on earth has gotten out of control and I want to get off.

Dec. 6

To everybody:
Please don't misinterpret what I have done. I want no one person to take the blame. It was my decision, and I am not sad that I did what I did. There are very many reasons why I did this. First, and this may seem strange, I am very curious as to what happens after death. Sorry, Mom, but I can't take what the Bible says as the Gospel Truth (*heh!*). I really am an agnostic.

Secondly, everyone will die sooner or later by old age or an atomic war, so why not sooner.

Thirdly, the pressure of schoolwork and homework were just too much. With six big projects going at the same time I knew I just couldn't take it. And if it's this bad now it sure won't get any better in university.

Fourthly, sorry Mom and Dad, but you must admit we didn't have very good relationships. You drove me nuts sometimes, Mom, and I probably did the same to you.

Fifthly, I see the world turning into an evil place. There is too much corruption, exploitation, misery, and pain. If people say, "Oh, it's too bad he's dead, and I'm happy to be alive and living and well," then the situation might change. I am hopeful.

Sixthly, I am really screwed up in so many areas. I have so many questions about life and no answers. It really got to me. I think I really said this in my poems. My poems and my short story will tell you everything you want to know. The Beatles played the biggest part in my "life." They really helped to relax me. They really did more for me than anything else. Oh, how they would make my body and soul float in the air. And I always cried when I realized that they are no longer producing music together.

I believe that pure Marxism is the best possible society. No class distinction. Everybody at the same level. That's beautiful. So I guess I am like Joan and Craig and am dying for peace and love.

I thought having a religion was important. Mine was a mixture of Buddhism and Christianity, but I could not take all the stuff in the Bible about miracles, etc., which don't seem to be possible. Buddhism tries to eliminate the thought of "I." It appeals to me because it stresses the finding of truth within your own mind.

Dad, I thought you were an okay person. You really tried to get things right for the Indian. I hope you continue and that you are successful. You really amazed me in that you always had a joke for the situation. I think you may come up short this time. You treated me well and I thank you for what you have done for me.

Mother, I know you will rest most of the blame on yourself. Don't. It was my decision. We did argue a lot. I really didn't understand you and I know you didn't understand me. Although I bothered you a lot and vice versa, I realize that you have gone through a lot, and I thank you for the help that you have given me.

Arlene, you were a beautiful person and I hope you continue in that path. You were very close to me and I know this will affect you in many ways. I thought you would answer my poems and was very disappointed when you didn't. I really felt a love between us and it was nice. I loved you in many ways. You always amazed me with your strict belief in God. I will remember you and my mind will think of you often. Remember me. Love, Peter.

Jim, you were a very close friend and I enjoyed your companionship. Try to remember what I have taught you. Try to pick up where I left off. Above all, keep going and fight for betterment. Remember me, Peter.

I want to say thank you to all my teachers over the years. I'm sorry it did not work out better.

"Many times I've been alone and many times I've cried; anyway you'll never know the many ways I've tried." (Beatles)

"Living is easy with eyes closed, misunderstanding all you see. It's getting hard to be someone but it all works out. No one I think is in my tree. I mean it must be high or low." (Beatles)

"All the lonely people, where do they all come from? All the lonely people, where do they all belong?" (Beatles)

Please don't hassle my friends about this. They knew all right, but they sure tried to talk me out of it. My last request is to play *Strawberry Fields Forever*, and *A Day in the Life*, in that order, at my funeral. Please don't deny me that much. Keep trying for peace and love.

Peter Walker

(Rabkin, 1979, pp. 109–111, 123–125)

Fifteen months later, Peter blew off his head with a shotgun, leaving a note indicating where to find his journal and farewell letter, from which the above quotes are taken. Peter had been a high school honor student and athlete whose suicide came as a total surprise to his family. The long period over which he planned suicide and the finality with which he undertook it leave little doubt about his resolve. Yet his suicide seemed related more to normal adolescent doubts and questions than to negative experiences or clinical psychopathology.

Theories of Depression

Abundant research and theory have been devoted to adult depression. Although psychoanalytic theory gave rise to rich speculations on the nature of depression, it implied that clinical depression was not possible in preadolescents and it offered little firm evidence (Kovacs & Beck, 1977). Most recent work has centered instead on biological, behavioral, and cognitive theories of adult depression, with some tentative extensions to children.

Biological Theories. Biological theories of affective disorders focus on abnormalities of monoamine neurotransmitters such as norepinephrine: Depression is hypothesized to reflect inadequate neurotransmitter activity, whereas mania is hypothesized to reflect excess neurotransmitter activity. Antidepressant drugs (such as *imipramine*) and antimanic drugs (lithium) are hypothesized to correct these neurotransmitter abnormalities. Twin and pedigree studies suggest genetically transmitted vulnerabilities (Gershon, Targum, Kessler, Mazure, & Bunney, 1977). However, the picture is clouded by the variety of forms taken by adult depressive disorders and by the lack of established diagnostic criteria for preadolescent and adolescent depression. The lack of diagnostic criteria has not only prevented inclusion of youngsters in pedigree studies, but has also been an obstacle to biochemical studies of depression in youngsters.

Behavioral Theories. Behavioral theorists have often speculated that depression involves a loss of effective reinforcers. However, the most specific and widely tested behavioral theory is Martin Seligman's theory of *learned helplessness*. His theory grew out of observations that laboratory dogs receiving unavoidable shocks later seemed unable to learn responses that would enable them to escape. By contrast, dogs that had not received unavoidable shocks readily learned the escape responses. Seligman (1975) theorized that teaching an organism to expect important events (such as painful shocks) to be uncontrollable produces helpless behavior. Further experiments with animals and humans supported his theory, and the behavior of helpless organisms suggested analogs with human depression. According to the theory, the learned expectation that outcomes are uncontrollable reduces motivation to make new coping responses. This, in turn, prevents learning that other outcomes can be controlled. Depressed affect is hypothesized to be a consequence of generalized expectations that outcomes are uncontrollable.

Later reformulations take more detailed account of people's attributions of the reasons for their helplessness (Abramson, Seligman, & Teasdale, 1978; Miller & Norman, 1979). For example, people attribute the uncontrollability of events to causes that are either stable or unstable, general or specific to those events, and internal or external to themselves. The attributions chosen are hypothesized to influence whether the expectation of future helplessness will be chronic or acute, broad or narrow, and damaging to self-esteem or not. However, persisting individual differences may determine the choice of attributions: Depression-prone people may attribute negative outcomes to general, internal, and stable causes, but positive outcomes to specific, external, and unstable causes. This means that they blame themselves for negative outcomes but fail to take credit or pleasure from favorable outcomes. The more general, internal, and stable the attributions for negative outcomes, the more chronically depressed a person is likely to be.

The learned helplessness theory thus hypothesizes many concomitants of depression, but has not yet led to verified causal explanations nor reliable distinctions among types of depressions. Nor has it received much application to clinical depression in children, although correlations among self-report measures of depression, locus of control, helplessness, self-blame, and self-esteem have been found in normal children (Moyal, 1977).

Cognitive Theories. Cognitive theories stress that depressive affect results from the way people cognitively structure their experience. This view is reminiscent of Seligman's theory, but does not specifically ascribe depressive cognitions to learned helplessness. Aaron Beck's cognitive theory, for example, assigns a central role to a *cognitive triad* of negative attitudes toward the self, the world, and the future: The *self* is viewed as deficient, inadequate, or unworthy because of some presumed defect; the *world* is seen as making exorbitant demands and presenting insurmountable obstacles; and the *future* is anticipated as a continuation of current problems (Kovacs & Beck, 1977). These negative evaluations are unrealistic and illogical, involving distorted interpretations of everyday events.

Although specific etiologies have not been established, Beck has speculated that unfavorable early life experiences such as loss of a parent may make people depression-prone by predisposing them to overreact to analogous conditions in later life. Research has not shown elevated rates of parental death during the childhoods of adult depressives, however (Crook & Eliot, 1980).

Whereas Seligman's initial theory stressed feelings of helplessness and uncontrollability in depressed people's view of events, Beck's theory stresses the depressive's exaggerated sense of *responsibility* and *self-reproach* for negative events. Empirical tests of these contrasting hypotheses have tended to support Beck's view (e.g., Rizley, 1978), and have stimulated revision of Seligman's theory (Abramson et al., 1978). A one-year longitudinal study of adults, however, showed that depression-related cognitions did not predict depressive episodes (Lewinsohn, Steinmetz, Larson, & Franklin, 1981).

A self-report measure of depression, the Beck Depression Inventory, has been used widely in studies of adult depression and is the basis of a children's version, the Children's Depression Inventory (Kovacs, 1981). Kovacs and Beck (1977) found that it correlated negatively with school performance and positively with self-reported adjustment problems in seventh and eighth graders. Their finding that 33 percent of the children scored as high as moderate to severely depressed adults suggests that it exaggerates depression in children, however. In a study of inpatient adolescents, those diagnosed depressed scored significantly higher than those having other diagnoses (Strober, Green, & Carlson, 1981). Further studies are needed to determine whether the kinds of cognitions found in depressed adults also characterize depressed youngsters and distinguish them from other disturbed youngsters.

Therapies for Affective Disorders

Biological, behavioral, and cognitive theories have all spawned therapies for adult affective disorders. Antidepressant and antimanic drugs for altering neurotransmitter activity have proven effective in controlled studies of adult patients, but not all patients seem to benefit. Aside from questionable studies like those described earlier (Frommer, 1967; Weinberg et al., 1973), there has not been much research on drug therapy for childhood depression. Imipramine has shown mixed results in various other childhood behavior disorders, however (Rapoport & Mikkelsen, 1978). For example, imipramine combined with psychosocial interventions helped in returning school phobics to school (Gittelman-Klein & Klein, 1973). However, the large doses used risk serious side effects and may have caused the sudden death of a 6-year-old (Saraf, Klein, Gittelman-Klein, & Groff, 1974). The antimanic drug lithium has had even less adequate testing with children than the antidepressants, partly because the diagnosis of mania in children is even more tenuous (Lena, 1979).

Behavioral and cognitive therapies for childhood affective disorders have not received much study. Cognitive approaches to changing adult depressives' interpretations of their experiences have seemed especially successful when combined with behavioral approaches to reinforcing new behavior (Hollon & Beck, 1979). Applications to children are difficult because childhood depression is so ill-defined and because existing cognitive-behavioral treatments for depression require the active cooperation of cognitively advanced patients. Behavioral methods of the kind described in Chapter 10 have been more successful with children having specific avoidant or withdrawal behavior that could be targeted for change (Richards & Siegel, 1978).

SUMMARY

Disorders of self-control, learning, and affect present similar conceptual and diagnostic problems. Each involves a specific abnormality from which more pervasive pathology is inferred. Such disorders have been viewed from perspectives ranging from the purely organic to the purely experiential.

Hyperactivity has been hypothesized to result from brain damage, neurotransmitter abnormalities, abnormalities of arousal, food sensitivities, allergies, developmental delays, temperament, and cognitive style. Current views stress attention deficits rather than activity level as the central problem. Therapies have ranged from drug to diet to behavioral and cognitive approaches. Although stimulant drugs and some behavioral methods reduce overt behavior problems, they have not led to long-term remediation of academic and social deficits.

Enuresis and *encopresis* have both been theorized to reflect underlying psychopathology, but the causes seem to be diverse. Bedwetting by children who have never had extended dry periods (*primary* enuresis) seems to reflect faulty training, although constitutional and emotional factors may interfere with training in some cases. Behavioral methods have been the most successful in treating primary bedwetting. Day or night wetting beginning after an extended period of continence (*secondary* enuresis) more often reflects current stress that needs attention in its own right, although behavioral treatment of the enuresis may be part of a larger treatment program.

Much less common than enuresis, encopresis is more likely to occur during the day and to be secondary rather than primary. It is often complicated by intestinal blockages formed by withholding of feces, which then seep out around the blockage. There has been little controlled research on treatment, but the most favored approaches involve physical treatment of bowel function combined with behavioral methods for improving toilet behavior.

Disorders of learning range from generalized poor performance reflecting poor motivation, emotional, cognitive, environmental or sensory handicaps, and inadequate instruction, to *specific disabilities* affecting only one skill, such as *dyslexia*. By the time children are diagnosed as having a specific disability, however, they usually have a host of other maladaptive behaviors related to learning. There is some evidence that slow or atypical development of perceptual functioning raises the risk of learning disabilities, but this risk may also be affected by the timing and skills required by different teaching methods.

Disorders of affect, such as depression and manic-depressive conditions, are striking in adults. The quest for analogous disorders in children, however, has led to unvalidated inferences of depression underlying a broad range of behavioral problems. Because behavioral problems often bring unpleasant experiences, it is necessary to distinguish between unhappiness resulting from such experiences and depression that instigates other problems. Factor analyses have identified a syndrome of depressive feelings and behaviors in 6- to 11-year-olds, but these characteristics failed to form a coherent syndrome in adolescents. Instead, depressive items are associated with several different syndromes of adolescent problem behavior. Suicidal behavior also seems to have diverse meanings in adolescents.

Biological, behavioral, and cognitive theories of adult depression are being extended to children, but there is as yet little evidence for the validity of these extensions or the efficacy of adult therapies with children.

SUGGESTED READING

MBD and Hyperactivity. There is a flood of publications on these topics, not only because they may represent important disorders, but also because they have been interpreted so broadly. Minimal brain dysfunction has been given an especially broad role in explaining maladaptive behavior. The *Handbook of minimal brain dysfunctions* (Rie & Rie, 1980) presents diverse interpretations of the MBD construct, along with critical appraisals of its applications to hyperactivity, learning disorders, personality, emotional problems, and social competence. Among the many books on hyperactivity, those by Gadow and Loney (1980), Trites (1979), and Whalen and Henker (1980) give a good flavor of the interplay among developmental, behavioral, and social variables in the definition, diagnosis, and treatment of these disorders.

Depression. Despite mounting interest in childhood depression, there is as yet little definitive research or theory. A sampling of viewpoints can be obtained from Schulterbrandt and Raskin (1977) and Kashani, et al., (1981). A special issue of the *Journal of Abnormal Psychology* (1978) gives a detailed picture of research, theory, and debate on the learned helpless model of depression, especially as it pertains to young adults.

CHAPTER 12

Psychotic and Other Pervasive Developmental Disorders

"Psychotic" means being so severely disturbed that one is "out of contact with reality" or that one's "reality-testing" is so poor that misinterpretations of ordinary situations grossly interfere with adaptation. Adult psychoses, characterized by *delusions* (grossly unrealistic beliefs), *hallucinations* (perceptions of nonexistent objects or sounds), and bizarre behavior, seem to occur in all cultures (World Health Organization, 1979).

EARLY INTEREST IN CHILDHOOD PSYCHOSIS

Although anecdotal reports of so-called insanity in children appeared earlier, it was late in the nineteenth century before interest in child psychopathology rose to the point where the question of childhood psychosis was seriously considered. Reports of childhood psychosis were at first discounted by those who denied that children could be insane, but, by the early twentieth century, there was considerable evidence that children could show psychotic symptoms (cf. Kanner, 1971). As interest in childhood psychosis grew, Kraepelin's taxonomy was simply extrapolated downward to cover children: To Kraepelin's 1893 category of *dementia praecox* ("early insanity," i.e., insanity beginning in adolescence or early adulthood) a new category was added, *dementia praecocissima* ("very early insanity"; DeSanctis, 1906).

Bleuler's "Four A's"

In 1911, the Swiss psychiatrist Eugen Bleuler published his conclusion that *dementia praecox* encompassed several disorders involving a "splitting" or disharmony of feeling and thought. He proposed the name *schizophrenia* (split mind) to denote the inner splitting or coming apart that he inferred in dementia praecox. (Note that schizophrenia does not refer to "split" in the sense of "multiple" personality, although it is often incorrectly used in this way.)

Bleuler listed four fundamental symptoms of schizophrenic disorders, which became known as *Bleuler's four A's:*

1. *Autism:* excessive self-absorption, detached from outer reality.
2. Fragmentation and lack of continuity in mental *associations.*
3. *Affective* disturbance, especially flat or inappropriate affect.
4. Marked *ambivalence* or contradictions in feelings and ideas.

Delusions, hallucinations, and peculiar motor behavior were viewed as more variable than these basic symptoms. Bleuler blamed organic factors for the splitting of feeling and thought in schizophrenia, but he thought the environment shaped the final form of the disorder. Although he had little clinical experience with children, Bleuler reported that 4 percent of adult schizophrenics first showed symptoms during childhood.

Types of Childhood Psychosis

By the 1930s, the concept of childhood schizophrenia had won acceptance, largely as an extension of Bleuler's concept of adult schizophrenia. Howard Potter (1933) offered the following criteria for childhood schizophrenia, which he restricted to disorders beginning before puberty:

1. A generalized retraction of interests from the environment.
2. Unrealistic thinking, feeling, and acting.
3. Disturbances of thought manifested by blocking, condensation, perseveration, incoherence, and diminution of speech, sometimes to the point of mutism.
4. Defects in emotional rapport.
5. Diminution, rigidity, and distortion of affect.
6. Alterations of behavior, with an increase of motility, leading to incessant activity, or a diminution of motility, leading to complete immobility, or bizarre behavior with a tendency to perseveration.

Potter gave several case illustrations, such as the following description of an 11-year-old boy:

About two years prior to admission, when about nine years of age, his sullenness and irritability increased. His talk became so incoherent at times that it was not possible to understand him. He would have outbursts of anger, laughter and grimacing. At times he would refuse to eat. He began complaining of things crawling on his body. He complained that other children made fun of him. He called his mother vile names in fits of anger, would stand for hours before the mirror, stayed in the bath room for prolonged periods, sat by himself in the dark, and some times disappeared from home and would be found in a nearby movie.

During the first 12 months of his stay in the institute, he spent the major part of the time gazing fixedly out of the window with a perplexed frown on his face, and at times would be found under a bed or crouched in a corner behind a piece of furniture. At times there would be periods when he became quite excited and would attack the other children. He mechanically attended school and occupational therapy, but showed little interest. His speech at times was voluble but irrelevant, disconnected and full of neologisms. His replies to most questions were a stereotyped, colorless "I don't know." There was no outstanding mood deviation and his affect was characterized by a combination of disinterest, detachment and perplexity. He sometimes laughed long and loudly for no obvious reason. He spontaneously referred to voices at times but one could not learn their content. Some of his spontaneous productions were as follows: "Do you see the bone" (indicating left shoulder). "I slept on it and now my bowels moved out through it." "I have a red pulse down my neck." "I never breathe." "Look down my throat and you can see a red bone." "Every second the pulse runs through." "I have red pulse sores." "The inside of my skin is bitten." (pp. 1264–65)

A 30-year follow-up of 12 of Potter's cases showed that, as adults, 9 were diagnosed schizophrenic and 3 mentally retarded (Bennet & Klein, 1966). Only one had maintained himself outside a hospital.

Manic-depressive psychosis, an adult disorder involving extreme swings of mood from euphoria to deep depression, was also reported in a few children by the 1930s (e.g., Kasanin & Kaufman, 1929).

Despite Potter's criteria, the term *childhood schizophrenia* soon became a general synonym for *childhood psychosis*. In fact, childhood schizophrenia was the only severe childhood disturbance listed in the 1952 (DSM-I) and 1968 (DSM-II) editions of the American Psychiatric Association's *Diagnostic and Statistical Manual*.

Because many children diagnosed as psychotic do not match Potter's criteria, disagreement about diagnosis has been a source of confusion. Some early efforts were aimed at differentiating among psychotic children on the basis of age and manner of the disorder's onset. A distinction was often made between children who seemed abnormal since infancy, those who had long shown behavioral problems that rather suddenly reached psychotic extremes, and those who seemed fairly normal until they suddenly became psychotic in late childhood or early adolescence (Symonds & Herman, 1957).

Another approach was to specify subtypes of psychotic children within or beside the general category of schizophrenia. Leo Kanner (1943), for example, described a syndrome called *early infantile autism,* which he viewed as "an inborn autistic disturbance of affective contact." Margaret Mahler (1952) proposed the category of *symbiotic psychosis,* which she viewed as a failure of the baby to develop an identity independent of its mother. On the basis of psychological, neurological, and family history data, William Goldfarb (1961) concluded that there are at least two major groups: (1) those with signs of organic dysfunction, and (2) those who lack such signs but come from difficult home situations.

Unfortunately, efforts to distinguish among severely disturbed children were hampered by imprecise use of diagnostic terms. Thus, *autism, schizophrenia,* and *childhood psychosis* were often used almost interchangeably. The confusion was further compounded by a still broader term, *atypical development* (Rank, 1949), for disturbed children who would be called schizophrenic, autistic, or at least psychotic by other workers.

Meanwhile, from about the 1930s through the 1960s, manic-depressive conditions were no longer thought possible in children. This may be partly because the diagnosis of manic-depressive disorders in adults had gone out of fashion, being largely replaced by the schizophrenic and schizoaffective diagnoses. In light of this change, earlier reports of manic-depressive psychosis in children were dismissed (Anthony & Scott, 1960). However, renewed interest in adult manic-depressive disorders and the apparent benefits of antimanic medication (lithium) with a few youngsters having manic symptoms revived interest in manic-depressive conditions beginning before adulthood (Carlson & Strober, 1978).

Disintegrative psychosis is yet another proposed type. This entails a rapid disintegration of emotions, behavior, language, and relationships occurring in early childhood after a period of fairly normal development (Evans-Jones & Rosenbloom, 1978).

PREVALENCE OF CHILDHOOD PSYCHOSIS

The lack of standard diagnostic practices makes it hard to estimate the rate of psychotic disorders in children. Nonetheless, all studies concur that such disorders are rare, occurring in less than 1 in every 1000 children (Werry, 1979). All studies also report an excess of boys over girls judged psychotic, with ratios running from about 1.7 to 9.5:1. Most other psychopathological (and physical) disorders are more common in boys as well, however.

For the sake of comparison, studies in Europe, Asia, and North America show rates of adult psychosis ranging from about 38 per 1000 population in Germany and Taiwan, to 235 per 1000 in rural Sweden (Yolles & Kramer, 1969). The rates for adults are thus many times the rates for children. Since methods for determining the rates of adult psychosis are only slightly better than those for child psychosis, the figures should be taken with a grain of salt. They show that child psychosis is rare not only in absolute terms, however, but also in comparison with adult psychosis.

THE DSM-III: PERVASIVE DEVELOPMENTAL DISORDERS

The first and second editions of the American Psychiatric Association's *Diagnostic and Statistical Manual* (DSM-I, 1952; DSM-II, 1968) contained only one category for psychoticlike disorders of childhood: *Schizophrenia, Childhood Type*. Because the criteria were not clearly spelled out and there were no other official diagnostic categories for severely disturbed children, childhood schizophrenia served largely as a wastebasket term for children having little in common beside the severity of their deviance.

The DSM-III takes a very different approach. Because the severe childhood disorders seem to bear little resemblance to adult psychotic disorders, DSM-III uses the term *pervasive developmental disorders* to emphasize that "many basic areas of psychological development are affected at the same time and to severe degree" (p. 86). Table 12-1 lists the criteria for the two main categories of pervasive developmental disorders, *infantile autism* and *childhood-onset pervasive developmental disorder*. A third category, *atypical pervasive developmental disorder*, is also provided for children having severe distortions of development not corresponding to either of the other two categories.

Although children can also be diagnosed schizophrenic using the adult criteria, DSM-III departs significantly from earlier editions in several ways: First, it adds *autism* as a diagnostic category and gives it the most specific defining criteria among the severe disorders of childhood. This reflects research that has progressively sharpened the distinctions between autism and other severe disturbances. Second, *childhood-onset pervasive developmental disorder* serves as a new general term for most of the remaining severe disorders, defined mainly by onset between 30 months and 12 years of age. Third, to distinguish autism and childhood-onset pervasive developmental disorders from schizophrenia, they both require an "absence of delusions, hallucinations, loosening of associations, and incoherence" (p. 90), which are among the hallmarks of schizophrenia.

The previous use of *schizophrenia* as a blanket term for all severe childhood disturbances exaggerated the similarities between these disorders and adult schizophrenia. However, the exclusion of "delusions, hallucinations, loosening of associations, and incoherence" from pervasive developmental disorders spawns problems of its own: DSM-III lists bizarre ideas and fantasies as "associated features" of childhood-onset pervasive developmental disorders; furthermore, communication with children meeting the criteria for autism or pervasive developmental disorders is often too difficult to rule out delusions, hallucinations, loosening of associations, and incoherence. Another potential weakness of the new category is

Table 12-1   DSM-III Criteria for Autism and Childhood-Onset Pervasive Developmental Disorder

Infantile Autism

A. Onset before 30 months of age.

B. Pervasive lack of responsiveness to other people (autism).

C. Gross deficits in language development.

D. If speech is present, peculiar speech patterns such as immediate and delayed echolalia, metaphorical language, pronominal reversal.

E. Bizarre responses to various aspects of the environment, e.g., resistance to change, peculiar interest in or attachments to animate or inanimate objects.

F. Absence of delusions, hallucinations, loosening of associations, and incoherence as in schizophrenia.

Childhood-Onset Pervasive Developmental Disorder

A. Gross and sustained impairment in social relationships, e.g., lack of appropriate affective responsivity, inappropriate clinging, asociality, lack of empathy.

B. At least three of the following:

(1) Sudden excessive anxiety manifested by such symptoms as free-floating anxiety, catastrophic reactions to everyday occurrences, inability to be consoled when upset, unexplained panic attacks
(2) Constricted or inappropriate affect, including lack of appropriate fear reactions, unexplained rage reactions, and extreme mood lability
(3) Resistance to change in the environment (e.g., upset if dinner time is changed), or insistence on doing things in the same manner every time (e.g., putting on clothes always in the same order)
(4) Oddities of motor movement, such as peculiar posturing, peculiar hand or finger movements, or walking on tiptoe
(5) Abnormalities of speech, such as questionlike melody, monotonous voice
(6) Hyper- or hyposensitivity to sensory stimuli, e.g., hyperacusis
(7) Self-mutilation, e.g., biting or hitting self, head banging

C. Onset of the full syndrome after 30 months of age and before 12 years of age.

D. Absence of delusions, hallucinations, incoherence, or marked loosening of associations.

Source: American Psychiatric Association, 1980, pp. 89–91.

that most severe and pervasive childhood disorders seem to begin either before the age of 2½ or after the age of 12 (Rutter, 1974).

If enough children are nevertheless found to meet the criteria for pervasive developmental disorders, and they are also found to share other important characteristics, then it may become a useful way of grouping severely disturbed children. Until then, however, autism provides us with the clearest focal point among the severe childhood disorders. We will use schizophrenia as a second focal point because of the importance of adolescent and adult schizophrenia and evidence for continuities between at least some childhood disorders and later schizophrenia.

INFANTILE AUTISM

Leo Kanner proposed the syndrome of autism in 1943 after he had seen eleven children described as follows:

1. *Inability to relate* to people from the beginning of life.
2. *Extreme autistic aloneness* that ignored and shut out stimuli by treating them as if they were not there unless they reached painful proportions.
3. *Failure to assume an anticipatory posture* in preparation for being picked up.
4. *Failure to use speech to convey meaning to others*—even in the eight out of eleven autistic children who did speak, language was used primarily for naming objects and repeating phrases, rhymes, songs, etc.
5. *Excellent rote memory* for names, pictures, tunes, etc.
6. *Echolalia*—the literal repetition ("echoing") of phrases the child had heard. When playing with a toy phone, one boy repeatedly sang "He wants the telephone."
7. *Extreme literalness* in the use of words. For example, a child who learned to say "Yes" when his father promised to put him on his shoulders if he said "Yes" then used the word yes only to mean he wanted to be placed on his father's shoulders.
8. *Reversal of personal pronouns* so that the self was called "you" and other people "I". "*You* want candy" was one boy's way of asking for candy.
9. *Eating difficulties,* including vomiting and food refusal, during the first year of life.
10. *Extreme fear of certain loud noises and moving objects* such as vacuum cleaners, egg beaters, tricycles, elevators, etc.
11. *Monotonously repetitious noises and motions by the child.*
12. *Anxious desire for sameness* such that the child became upset when furniture, clothing, etc., was changed.
13. *Minimal variety in spontaneous activity.*

14. *A good relation to objects* such that the child could play happily with them for hours.

15. *Apparently good intellectual potential* as suggested by average or better performance on some items of intelligence tests and by intelligent facial expressions.

16. *Facial expressions* that were typically serious but showed tenseness in the presence of others and placid smiles when alone with objects.

17. *Normal physical condition.*

Kanner presented case histories of the eleven autistic children, as exemplified by the following excerpts from parental reports on Donald, a child Kanner first saw at the age of five:

> At the age of 1 year he could hum and sing many tunes accurately. Before he was 2 years old, he had an unusual memory for faces and names. . . . He was encouraged by the family in learning and reciting short poems, and even learned the Twenty-third Psalm and twenty-five questions and answers of the Presbyterian Catechism. The parents observed that he was not learning to ask questions or to answer questions unless they pertained to rhymes or things of this nature, and often then he would ask no question except in single words. . . . He became interested in pictures and very soon knew an inordinate number of pictures in a set of *Compton's Encyclopedia.* He knew the pictures of the presidents and knew most of the pictures of his ancestors and kinfolks on both sides of the house. He quickly learned the whole alphabet backward as well as forward and to count to 100.
>
> It was observed at an early time that he was happiest when left alone, almost never cried to go with his mother, did not seem to notice his father's homecomings, and was indifferent to visiting relatives. . . . Donald even failed to pay the slightest attention to Santa Claus in full regalia.
>
> He seems to be so self-satisfied. He has no apparent affection when petted. He does not observe the fact that anyone comes or goes, and never seems glad to see father or mother or any playmate. He seems almost to draw into his shell and live within himself. We once secured a most attractive little boy of the same age from an orphanage and brought him home to spend the summer with Donald, but Donald has never asked him a question nor answered a question and has never romped with him in play. . . .
>
> In his second year, he developed a mania for spinning blocks and pans and other round objects. At the same time he had a dislike for self-propelling vehicles . . . tricycles, and swings. He is still fearful of tricycles and seems to have almost a horror of them when he is forced to ride. . . . This summer we bought him a playground slide and on the first afternoon when other children were sliding on it he would not get about it, and when we put him up to slide down it he seemed horror-struck. The next morning when nobody was present, however, he walked out, climbed the ladder, and slid down, and he has slid on it frequently since, but slides only when no other child is present. . . .
>
> When interfered with, he had temper tantrums, during which he was destructive. He was dreadfully fearful of being spanked or switched but could not associate his misconduct with his punishment. (Kanner, 1943, pp. 217−18)

Developmental Course

In trying to grasp a strange new syndrome and seeking the etiology and appropriate treatment, we need to ask, What typically happens as the children grow older? Kanner and his colleagues reported follow-ups of 96 children diagnosed autistic (Eisenberg, 1956; Kanner, 1971; Kanner, Rodrigues & Ashenden, 1972). Most of the children ended up under varying degrees of custodial care, but eleven achieved adequate social adjustment. Three of the eleven obtained college degrees, three junior college educations, one was doing well in college, and the other four did not go beyond high school or special education. Their occupations included bank teller, lab technician, duplicating machine operator, accountant, and several types of unskilled work.

The outcomes showed no relation to psychiatric treatment. The best single predictor of good outcome was the development of useful speech by age five. Neither the ten males nor the one female showed spontaneous interest in the opposite sex or in marriage, although several unsuccessfully experimented with very limited dating.

Kanner interpreted the attempts at dating as reflecting the one thing that seemed to differentiate the eleven from the other autistic children who had useful speech by age five: All eleven underwent an apparent change during their early to middle teens. They all seemed to become aware of their peculiarities and tried to do something about them. Realizing, for example, that young people were expected to have friends, they made use of their obsessive preoccupations and specialized abilities to win approval from others, particularly in hobby clubs and special interest groups. Kanner interpreted their sporadic attempts at dating as stemming from the same sense of obligation to conform, although failures to achieve any real involvement apparently did not cause displeasure.

Donald, who was described above, showed one of the best outcomes of all:

> In 1942 [when he was nine], his parents placed him on a tenant farm. . . . When I visited there in May 1945, I was amazed at the wisdom of the couple who took care of him. They managed to give him goals for his stereotypies. They made him use his preoccupation with measurements by having him dig a well and report on its depth. When he kept collecting dead birds and bugs, they gave him a spot for a "graveyard" and had him put up markers; on each he wrote a first name, the type of animal as a middle name, and the farmer's last name, e.g.: "John Snail Lewis. Born, date unknown. Died, (date on which he found the animal)." When he kept counting rows of corn over and over, they had him count the rows while plowing them. . . . It was obvious that Mr. and Mrs. Lewis [the farm couple] were very fond of him and just as obvious that they were gently firm. He attended a country school where his peculiarities were accepted and where he made good scholastic progress.
>
> The rest of the story is contained in a letter from Donald's mother, dated April 6, 1970:
>
> "Don is now 36 years old, a bachelor living at home with us. . . . Since receiving

his A.B. degree in 1958, he has worked in the local bank as a teller. He is satisfied to remain a teller, having no real desire for promotion. He meets the public there real well. His chief hobby is golf, playing four or five times a week at the local country club. . . . Other interests are Kiwanis Club (served as president one term), Jaycees, Investment Club, Secretary of Presbyterian Sunday School. He is dependable, accurate, shows originality in editing the Jaycee program information, is even-tempered but has a mind of his own. . . . He owns his second car, likes his independence. His room includes his own TV, record player, and many books. In College his major was French and he showed a particular aptitude for languages. Don is a fair bridge player but never initiates a game. Lack of initiative seems to be his most serious drawback. He takes very little part in social conversation and shows no interest in the opposite sex.

"While Don is not completely normal, he has taken his place in society very well, so much better than we ever hoped for. If he can maintain status quo, I think he has adjusted sufficiently to take care of himself." (Kanner, 1971, pp. 121–22)

Kanner remarked that none of his cases had seriously thought of marrying, but DesLauriers (1978) reported that Clarence, described by Kanner et al., (1972) as Case #4, eventually did marry. After graduate training in economics and planning, Clarence was able to hold accounting jobs if he did not have to work closely with people. Like Kanner's other cases having relatively good outcomes, he felt obligated to become involved with people. However, his failures with women seemed to distress him more than Kanner's other cases. After many false starts, he succeeded in sustaining a relationship with a woman. He bought a house, and they ultimately married. DesLauriers ascribed the favorable outcome to Clarence's having a concerned and stable family, being a gifted child, and having therapeutic help with what DesLauriers saw as "the central impairment involved in early autism: a disturbance of affective contact" (DesLauriers, 1978, p. 220). Although we cannot draw causal conclusions from a single case like this, we will consider DesLauriers' hypothesis of an affective deficit later. Other follow-up studies agree with Kanner in finding very few autistic children achieving even marginal social adjustments in later life (Lotter, 1978).

The Problem of Definition

Kanner Syndrome. Strict adherence to Kanner's criteria for autism (also known as *Kanner syndrome*) should have helped clarify the communication needed for research on etiology, prevention, and treatment. This happened with Down syndrome, where workers could at least agree on whether they were discussing children having the same features, even if they disagreed with Langdon Down's theory of the syndrome as an evolutionary throwback to the "mongol race."

Unfortunately, clear communication did not ensue: Many workers used autism as a virtual synonym for childhood schizophrenia and childhood psychosis in general. Kanner (1943) himself mentioned that certain features of autism resembled childhood schizophrenia, but he emphasized its differences from "all other known instances of childhood schizophrenia" (p. 248). These differences included extreme aloneness from the very beginning of life, as contrasted with a *change* from relatively normal behavior preceding schizophrenia; the purposeful and "intelligent" relation to objects but exclusion of people; and the extreme desire for sameness, coupled with extraordinary memories for how things were arranged, no matter how disorganized the arrangements.

One problem with a new syndrome is to determine which features are crucial. In Kanner's syndrome, we must consider the child's age in judging which features are relevant. For example, if the child is less than two, lack of speech cannot be a crucial feature. Above the age of about three, peculiarities of speech such as echolalia and reversal of personal pronouns are relevant criteria only if the child speaks.

Recognizing these problems, Kanner pinpointed two cardinal symptoms of infantile autism:

1. *Extreme self-isolation, present from the first years of life.*
2. *Obsessive insistence on the preservation of sameness* (Eisenberg & Kanner, 1956).

All the children Kanner diagnosed as autistic also showed abnormalities of speech, ranging from lack of speech or delayed onset, through echolalia, pronominal reversal, and highly metaphorical speech, apparently having little communicative intent. But Kanner (1954) viewed speech peculiarities as secondary to the two cardinal symptoms. Another feature of Kanner's cases was that none had organic pathology considered to account for the behavioral syndrome.

Other Attempts to Delineate Infantile Autism. Several checklists have been designed to delineate the autistic syndrome and discriminate autistics from other abnormal children. One of the most widely used was designed by Rimland (1971) to be filled out by the child's parents. Including many variants of the features noted by Kanner, it is scored by subtracting the number of features considered unlike autistic children from the number of features considered to typify them.

In analyzing checklists filled out for 2218 children diagnosed autistic in over 30 countries, Rimland (1971) found that only 215 (9.7 percent) met his criterion for autism, a score of at least 20 (20 more autistic than nonautistic features). His conclusion that only about 10 percent of the children seemed to be truly autistic agreed with Kanner's impression that only about 10 percent of children sent to him as autistic actually fit his syndrome of infantile autism. Many of the children had received diverse diagnoses including deafness, schizophrenia, symbiotic psychosis, retardation, brain damage, and emotionally disturbed, with little agreement among diagnosticians.

Comparisons with other explicit criteria for autism have likewise shown that they identify larger, more heterogeneous groups than Rimland's cutoff score of 20

(Cohen et al., 1978; DeMyer, Churchill, Pontius, & Gilkey, 1971). Although there is moderate agreement among the various criteria, we do not know whether children having only some features of the Kanner syndrome really have the same disorder as those meeting Rimland's stringent criteria. Empirical efforts to determine which features best distinguish autistic children from other severely disturbed children have shown that onset before the age of two, obsessive desire for sameness, presence of special abilities, and skillful manipulation of small objects are among the best discriminators (Prior, Perry, & Gajzago, 1975).

Autistic children also differ from other linguistically handicapped children (dysphasics) in specific aspects of language (Bartak, Rutter, & Cox, 1977). Although often delayed, autistic children seem to acquire rules for forming word sounds (*phonology*) and for linking words to convey meaning (*syntax*). But they seem deficient in the interpersonal use of language (*pragmatics*) and choice of words to symbolize meaning *(semantics)* (Tager-Flusberg, 1981). This suggests that their linguistic peculiarities are intrinsic to autism rather than resembling those of children whose main problem is their inability to acquire language. In reviewing the evidence for a distinctive syndrome of autism, Rutter (1978) concluded that four essential criteria define the syndrome:

1. Onset before the age of 30 months.
2. Social development impaired in ways that are not merely predictable from the child's cognitive retardation.
3. Language development that is delayed and deviant in ways not merely predictable from the child's cognitive retardation.
4. Insistence on sameness, as shown by stereotyped play, abnormal preoccupations, or resistance to change.

Although the DSM-III (Table 12-1) and many researchers now use similar diagnostic criteria, our discussion will show that conclusions are still jeopardized by differences in the stringency with which these criteria are applied. Very stringent use of the criteria produces homogeneous groups that may be too small for comparison with other groups, but lenient use of the criteria risks obscuring true features of autism because nonautistic children are included. Continuing differences in concepts of autism also lead some researchers to use criteria not shared by others. Ritvo (1976), for example, has used perceptual abnormalities as a defining criterion.

Family Characteristics

Kanner was struck by certain uniformities among the parents of autistic children: All seemed highly intelligent, most were very obsessive, and few were really warmhearted. Among the fathers of his first 100 cases were 31 businessmen, 12 engineers, 11 physicians (including 5 psychiatrists), 10 lawyers, 8 tradesmen, 5 chemists, 5 military officers, 5 Ph.D.s in various fields, 4 writers, 2 teachers, 2 rabbis, and 1 psychologist, dentist, publisher, professor of forestry, and photographer (Kanner, 1954).

Kanner also noted a remarkable lack of severe mental disorders in the autistic children's families. As discussed later, the questions of parental intelligence, attainments, and pathology figure prominently in theories of etiology. How well have Kanner's impressions been borne out?

Socioeconomic Status (SES). Several studies show that autistic children tend to have families of higher SES than other severely disturbed children, but not nearly to the degree Kanner reported (see Schopler, Andrews, & Strupp, 1979). Most of the studies that disagree about elevated SES among families of autistic children have used rather idiosyncratic criteria for autism. In one study, for example, a primary diagnostic criterion was "perceptual inconstancy," which the authors hypothesized to characterize a wide range of childhood psychoses (Ritvo et al., 1971). But does SES have any intrinsic relation to the more purely defined forms of autism?

Many biases can affect the selection of children seen in particular clinical settings and the diagnoses they receive. Schopler et al. (1979), therefore, sought to learn whether selective biases could account for the apparent tendency of autistic children to have upper middle class families. They hypothesized seven factors that could increase children's chances of being diagnosed autistic *because of* their parents' SES rather than anything intrinsic to autism: (1) early age of reported onset; (2) age of admission to treatment; (3) evidence for normal cognitive potential; (4) complex rituals and maintenance of sameness; (5) distance traveled to a specialized treatment facility; (6) access to scarce services; and (7) a detailed history of the child's development. SES was thought relevant because high SES parents were expected to notice problems and obtain treatment early, train their children in skills suggestive of normal cognitive potential, permit and recall rituals, travel further and strive more for special services, and provide more detailed histories.

To test their hypotheses, Schopler et al. computed the relations between measures of these factors and parental SES (occupation and education) for 264 children attending programs for autistic and other children with communication handicaps. Finding that reported age of onset, distance traveled, use of scarce services, and detailed histories were significantly related to SES, they inferred that previous conclusions about intrinsic relations between autism and SES were unfounded. Yet the question remains open, as the authors' criterion for autism was merely a rating of "mild" to "severe" on a general scale of behavior problems for which the "terms *autistic* and *psychotic* are used interchangeably" (Schopler et al., 1979, p. 144). Scores on this scale showed little overlap with other researchers' criteria for autism (Schopler, Reichler, DeVellis, & Daly, 1980). Despite the lack of light thrown on more stringently diagnosed autism, the data do illustrate that factors like SES can affect the distribution of cases and information obtained in clinical settings.

Parents' Abilities and Values. Kanner's impression that the parents of autistic children were exceptionally intelligent has been partially borne out by Lotter's (1967) finding that they were superior to parents of nonautistic disturbed children on both a vocabulary test and a nonverbal test. Although the differences were related to the higher SES found for parents of autistic children, test scores also favored the parents of autistic children within SES groups.

In another study, the verbal IQs of autistic children's fathers were nonsignificantly higher (mean IQ = 116) than those of normal children's fathers matched for SES (mean IQ = 108.9), but significantly higher than those of brain-damaged, disturbed children's fathers not matched for SES (mean IQ = 100.5; Allen, DeMyer, Norton, Pontius, & Yang, 1971). Mothers of autistic children did not differ significantly (mean IQ = 109) from mothers of either of the other groups (mean IQ = 108.9, 103.8, respectively). Few of the parents were idea-oriented, intellectual people.

Family Mental Disorders. Kanner's (1954) observation that few of the autistic children's close relatives were psychotic or severely neurotic has been generally supported (e.g., Cox, Rutter, Newman, & Bartak, 1975). A further finding is that schizophrenia is more common in parents of children having later onset psychotic disorders than in parents of children having infantile disorders of the autistic type (Kolvin, Ounsted, Richardson, & Garside, 1971). Because the rate of schizophrenia is also elevated in parents of people who become schizophrenic in adulthood, this suggests that schizophrenia is more closely related to later onset childhood disorders than to infantile disorders.

Child-rearing Practices. Extensive parent interviews on child-rearing practices and early infant characteristics were conducted as part of a comparison between autistic and matched normal and brain-damaged children (DeMyer, Pontius, Norton, Allen, & Steele, 1972). The sample included 26 children diagnosed autistic and 7 diagnosed schizophrenic who developed severe autistic symptoms before their third birthday, although the autistic and schizophrenic cases were not analyzed separately.

All three groups of parents provided their babies with at least average warmth, attention, and stimulation, although the parents of the brain-damaged children provided significantly less than the other two groups. The parents of autistic children were next lowest, but they were more like the parents of normal children than of brain-damaged children and did not differ significantly from parents of normals.

Ratings based on reports of the *children's* early behavior, however, showed significantly less sociability among both the autistic and brain-damaged children than among the normals. The sociability ratings encompassed cuddliness, strength of reaction to weaning, raising arms to be picked up, need for attention, and alertness. Thus, while autistic children's parents evidently behaved like normal children's parents, autistic babies behaved like brain-damaged babies.

Parents' Psychological Characteristics. Singer and Wynne (1963) made an intriguing comparison of the Rorschach and Thematic Apperception Test (TAT) responses of parents of 20 children, most diagnosed as autistic (the rest as schizophrenic) and 20 neurotic children matched to the first group for demographic characteristics. A psychologist blind to which couples had autistic or neurotic children correctly classifed 17 out of 20 couples in each group on the basis of their test responses. The responses of the autistic children's parents seemed to show more cynical outlooks, passivity and apathy about interacting with others, superficiality, obsessive intellectual distance, and dissatisfaction.

Singer and Wynne interpreted their findings as indicating that, when unempathic autistic-type parents have a baby with low innate capacity to elicit attention, a crippling of ego development will begin at birth, resulting in autism. The data are also consistent, however, with at least two other possibilities: (1) that the parents' characteristics do not cause autism but are milder manifestations of a defect in relatedness with which they too were born; or (2) that the negative themes reflect parents' *reactions* to having an autistic child.

Another study showed significant differences between the Rorschach responses of the parents of autistic (and symbiotic) children and the parents of normal children (Ogdon, Bass, Thomas, & Lordi, 1968). The authors conceded, however, that this did not necessarily imply that parental behavior causes autism. In fact, two Rorschach indices showed that parents of autistic children were slightly *less* perfectionistic and obsessive and had *less* interpersonal anxiety and social isolation than the parents of normal children. Furthermore, McAdoo and DeMyer (1978) found somewhat *less* deviance in the MMPI profiles of parents of autistic children than parents of more mildly disturbed outpatient clinic children.

Similarly, parents of autistics scored slightly lower than parents of dysphasic children on questionnaire measures of obsessiveness and neurotic tendencies (Cox et al., 1975). These same two groups of parents received similar ratings of emotional warmth, demonstrativeness, and sociability, although autistic children seemed to have more negative impacts on their parents than dysphasics did. Clinical assessments including personality tests and social histories have also shown negligible psychopathology in parents of children with infantile disorders of the autistic type (Kolvin, Garside, & Kidd, 1971).

Summary of Family Characteristics. Kanner stressed the following characteristics of autistic children's parents: High intelligence, education, and occupational achievement; obsessiveness and coldness; low rates of severe mental disorders. Later studies have confirmed that parents of autistic children tend to be higher in occupation and education, do better on intelligence tests, and have lower rates of severe mental disorders than parents of other severely disturbed children, but not nearly to the degree seen by Kanner. They do not seem to have the personalities he described, and there is no evidence that parental personalities or child-rearing practices cause autism. Certain parental characteristics may reflect the stress of having an autistic child, however.

Organic Abnormalities

In his original report, Kanner (1943) concluded:

> We must . . . assume that these children have come into the world with innate inability to form the usual, biologically provided affective contact with people, just as other children come into the world with innate physical or intellectual handicaps. If this assumption is correct, a further study of our children may help to furnish concrete criteria regarding the still diffuse notions about the constitutional components of emotional reactivity. For here we seem to have pure-culture examples of *inborn autistic disturbances of affective contact.* (p. 250; italics original)

Despite his clear assumption of a biological etiology for autism, Kanner has often been wrongly cited as blaming autism on "refrigerator" parents. Psychogenic theories that blamed autism on parents held sway until the early 1960s (e.g., Despert, 1951; Rank, 1949). Yet the research we have considered does not show that parental behavior causes autism. The fact that autism seldom occurs in more than one child per family casts further doubt on a purely psychogenic hypothesis. Even the most avid proponents of psychogenic hypotheses have conceded that constitutional vulnerabilities may be necessary for autism (e.g., Bettelheim, 1967). Agreement that biological factors may be necessary or that autism stems from some kind of organism-environment interaction, however, does not tell us what the specific etiological factors are, how to prevent them, or how to help the afflicted children.

Brain Damage. Kanner stressed that his cases of autism had no known organic abnormalities accounting for the behavioral syndrome. Later investigators found fewer birth complications, abnormal EEGs, and other signs of brain damage in children like Kanner's than in comparison groups of severely disturbed children (Lotter, 1967; Treffert, 1970). Studies of older and institutionalized autistics have reported more signs of organic abnormalities, but none that seemed peculiar to autism (Lotter, 1974; Schain & Yannet, 1960; Weber, 1970).

Taking another approach, Chess (1971) examined 243 children known to have had rubella (German measles) *in utero.* Most suffered major birth defects, including blindness, deafness, and defects of cardiac and neurological function. Ten children with birth defects were diagnosed autistic, for a rate of 41.2 per 1000—far above the 1 per 1000 generally found for all childhood psychoses (Werry, 1979). Another eight were diagnosed "partially autistic," for a combined rate of 74.1 per 1000. Knobloch and Pasamanick (1975) likewise found elevated rates of autism in infants who had definite central nervous system abnormalities, although the kinds of abnormalities were diverse.

In a four-year follow-up, Chess (1977) found that 3 of her 10 fully autistic children were recovered in social behavior, 1 was improved, and 6 were not improved. Of the 7 partially autistic children followed up, 3 were recovered and 4 were worse. Despite the encouraging improvements in social behavior, all but 2 of the 17 children remained mentally retarded. Furthermore, the follow-up revealed autistic symptoms in four children not initially diagnosed autistic. Follow-ups averaging five years likewise showed improvement in the social behavior but not the cognitive functioning of many of Knobloch and Pasamanick's (1975) cases.

The relatively high rates of autism in children with clearcut organic damage suggest that such damage *can* play a role in the etiology of autism. Yet, since many autistic children do not seem damaged, we do not know whether it is a necessary or sufficient cause of autism. Furthermore, the follow-ups show higher rates of social recovery in organically-damaged children than in those having no known organic damage. This suggests that there may be at least two general types: *Primary autism* not caused by recognized organic damage; and *secondary autism* caused by rubella, perinatal injury, and other abnormalities not specific to autism. While emphasizing that not all cases of autism are caused by viral infections like rubella, Chess illustrates the apparent primacy of organic factors in a rubella-damaged deaf girl who progressed from autism to behavior quite normal for deaf children:

> This dramatic recovery had occurred in spite of a severely traumatic family situation. Her mother had died [a month before the follow-up] of cancer after a long illness with several hospitalizations. Death had actually occurred at home in the girl's presence. Her father was an alcoholic, as observed on the three occasions of our direct contact with him. The neighbors had reported this to the Child Abuse Agency to request that the child be placed in a residential school for the deaf rather than remain at home. Her only stabilizing influence in the immediate family was a normal sister 2 years older. Under these adverse circumstances, and with the continuing presence of both cataract and deafness, it would indeed be difficult to explain this child's recovery as due to any psychological cause. (Chess, 1977, p. 80).

Biochemical Factors. There have been numerous studies of biochemical variables in autistic children (Piggott, 1979). Like other research on autism, however, they have been plagued by a lack of standardized diagnostic criteria. As an example, one study reported that autistic children's blood platelets (colorless discs carried in the blood) gave off a biogenic amine, *serotonin*, at a higher rate than platelets of normal or nonautistic psychotic children (Boullin, Coleman, O'Brien, & Rimland, 1971). A later study failed to replicate this finding (Yuwiler, et al., 1975). Yet, as Rimland (1976) pointed out, Yuwiler et al. diagnosed autism in terms of perceptual inconstancies instead of Boullin et al.'s criterion of a score of 20 on Rimland's checklist. Was the original finding valid but only for the relatively pure autistic children identified by Rimland's stringent criteria? Or was the finding invalid? The extreme sensitivity of biochemical variables to many aspects of human functioning and environment, as well as the scarcity of "pure" autistic children, have made causal interpretations of biochemical findings quite tenuous.

Genetic Factors

Chromosomal analyses have not revealed gross abnormalities of genetic material in most autistic children (Coleman, 1978). The rarity of autism precludes large-scale twin studies to detect more subtle genetic influences, but by searching all over Britain, Folstein and Rutter (1977) found 21 same-sex twin pairs in which at least one twin was autistic. Both members were autistic in 4 of the 11 pairs of identical twins, but none of the 10 pairs of fraternal twins. This difference did not quite reach the conventional .05 level of statistical significance, but the concordance among identical twins far exceeded expectations from general population rates of less than 1 in 1000. Furthermore, five of the nonautistic identical twins showed cognitive or linguistic problems that Folstein and Rutter interpreted as reflecting an inherited "cognitive abnormality which includes but is not restricted to autism" (p. 727). Only one of the nonautistic fraternal twins showed such a disorder.

When both autism and the cognitive/linguistic disorders were considered together, the identical twins showed a significantly higher concordance rate (82 percent) than the fraternal twins (10 percent). In 12 of the 17 discordant pairs, however, the autistic member's perinatal history was suggestive of brain injury. In the remaining five discordant pairs, both members had similar histories. Both genetic factors and organic damage thus seem able to precipitate autism: Among the four concordant identical twin pairs, genetic causes seemed primary, as only one child showed any evidence of organic damage; among the other pairs, organic damage seemed solely responsible in some, whereas a combination of an inherited cognitive defect plus brain damage seemed responsible in others.

Evidence for a genetic mechanism in at least some cases does not tell us what the mechanism is. The lack of autism in parents and very low rates in nontwin siblings argue against single Mendelian genes. Evidence for high intelligence in parents of autistic children has been used to argue that autism may result from an aberration related to genes for high intelligence (Rimland, 1978). Karlsson (1972) has proposed a similar explanation for adult schizophrenia. Reasoning from genealogical studies in Iceland showing elevated rates of schizophrenia and talented people in the same families, Karlsson hypothesized that a portion of the schizophrenic genotype produces exceptional talent, while the full genotype produces schizophrenia. As our discussion of schizophrenia will show, however, many other explanations are possible as well.

Biobehavioral Studies

Autistic children's lack of eye contact, insistence on sameness, and preference for inanimate objects over humans have been studied to determine how they may relate to organic and psychological abnormalities. To minimize confusion, we will consider only those studies in which the subjects approximated Kanner's criteria for autism.

Levels of Physiological Arousal. Sidney and Corinne Hutt have done some of the most extensive biobehavioral studies of children meeting Kanner's criteria. In one study, autistic and nonautistic disturbed children were individually observed under four conditions: (1) when alone in an empty room; (2) when alone with colored blocks; (3) when with the blocks plus a familiar woman who sat passively in a corner; and (4) when the woman tried to engage the child in building a standard design with the blocks (Hutt, Hutt, Lee, & Ounsted, 1965).

Except in the empty room, the autistic children engaged in significantly shorter visual fixations and briefer manipulatory activity than the nonautistic children. The autistic children also spent much of their time scanning the environment rather than fixating on anything in particular; they showed much less constructive block play; and they approached and fixated on the adult less than the nonautistic children did. EEG data transmitted by a tiny radio transmitter on the children's collar revealed increasing arousal as the environment became more complex. They also responded to complexity with more stereotyped behavior.

Hutt and Hutt (1970) later observed the behavior and monitored the EEG of another autistic child as he entered an unfamiliar room. When first placed in the room, the boy "froze" motionless, staring straight ahead. He then made repetitious stereotyped motions with his fingers. After 20 minutes in the room, his flat irregular EEG gave way to a more normal, rhythmic pattern and he began to move slowly around the room. After 10 30-minute sessions in the same situation, more regular EEG activity occurred even when the boy first entered the room; but stereotyped gestures and desynchronized EEG activity reappeared if an adult entered the room.

Autistic children also avoided a new toy and increased their stereotyped behavior when it was placed in a room with them. Retarded children, by contrast, showed *less* stereotyped behavior as complexity increased.

Why do autistic children show stereotyped behaviors and disorganized EEGs in novel situations? The Hutts hypothesized that they are in a chronic state of high physiological arousal and that this is aggravated by novelty. The stereotyped activity may be an attempt to cope with excessive arousal. Their interpretation agrees with the childhood memories of Jerry, one of Kanner's autistic children:

> According to Jerry, his childhood experience could be summarized as consisting of two predominant experiential states: confusion and terror. The recurrent theme that ran through all of Jerry's recollections was that of living in a frightening world presenting

painful stimuli that could not be mastered. Noises were unbearably loud, smells overpowering. Nothing seemed constant; everything was unpredictable and strange. Animate beings were a particular problem. Dogs were remembered as eerie and terrifying. As a child, he believed they were somehow humanoid (since they moved of their own volition, etc.), yet they were not really human, a puzzle that mystified him. They were especially unpredictable; they could move quickly without provocation. To this day, Jerry is phobic of dogs. (Bemporad, 1979, p. 192)

The possibility that autistic children suffer from abnormal arousal has won considerable attention. It has been hypothesized that much of their behavior consists of defensive maneuvers against further arousal. In contrast to the Hutts' overarousal hypothesis, however, it has also been suggested that autistic children are abnormally *hypo*aroused (*under*aroused) owing to a combination of a biological barrier to stimulation and a lack of stimulation from parents (Schopler, 1965). (This is reminiscent of the dichotomy between under- and overarousal hypotheses of hyperactivity that we discussed in Chapter 11).

Combining the two possibilities of over- and underarousal, DesLauriers and Carlson (1969) suggested that *some* autistic children suffer from chronic *hyper*arousal, but others suffer from chronic *hypo*arousal. According to DesLauriers and Carlson, hypoactive autistic children—often described as exceptionally "good" and placid babies—are deficient not only in the arousal system that mediates affect, but in the arousal system that mediates attention and alertness. Both types of children therefore have barriers against normal levels of affective stimulation. *Hyper*aroused children may experience stimulation as excessive, however, while *hypo*aroused children are unaware of stimulation.

Hypoarousal might explain Hutt and Hutt's (1970) finding that, once autistic children approached a novel toy that could be made to emit sounds, they chose to produce the sounds. Likewise, Metz (1967) found that, when left alone with a device that could produce sounds of adjustable volume, autistic children chose significantly higher volumes than schizophrenic or normal children.

Gaze Aversion. One of autistic children's most striking characteristics is their failure to gaze into other people's eyes. On the rare occasions when they do look toward a face, they seem to look "through" or beyond the person.

To determine if certain faces are actively avoided, the five models shown in Figure 12-1 were mounted on stands around an empty room familiar to the subjects (Hutt & Ounsted, 1970). Autistic and nonautistic disturbed children were individually observed in the room with the model faces for a 10-minute session. As Figure 12-1 shows, the autistic children spent significantly less time than the other children looking at the human faces and significantly more time looking at room fixtures—lights, windows, faucets—than at the facial stimuli.

In another experiment, Hutt and Ounsted (1970) found that autistic children made more approaches to a model face having no eyes than one having no mouth.

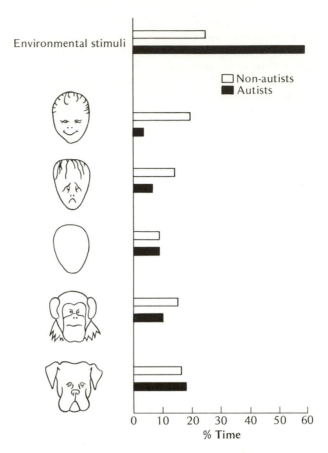

Figure 12.1. Percentage of time spent by autistic and nonautistic disturbed children inspecting face models and environmental stimuli (e.g. room fixtures). (From Hutt and Ounsted, 1970, p. 107. © 1970 by Pergamon Press and reprinted by permission.)

Eye avoidance may thus be another way of avoiding further arousal. Because eye contact is so important for social communication, however, eye avoidance may severely disrupt social development.

Avoidance of eye contact and faces may help explain another interesting finding. Small, DeMyer, and Milstein (1971) recorded the EEGs of autistic and normal children as slide photos of an unfamiliar woman, an unfamiliar child, the subjects' mother, and the subjects themselves were projected. Normal children's EEGs showed different responses to the different stimuli, but autistic children's EEGs did not. The finding was viewed as compatible with both hyper- and hypoarousal hypotheses. Hyperarousal might have precluded further measurable arousal when the stimuli were presented, whereas hypoaroused children were unaware of the stimuli. Another possibility, however, is that the autistic children avoided *attending* to the facial stimuli, although this may in turn have resulted from abnormal arousal.

Perceptual Handicaps. A further line of biobehavioral thinking is that autistic children have perceptual defects. This possibility is suggested by their lack of responsiveness to sounds during infancy, which causes many to be thought deaf. Other autistic children show behavioral mannerisms like those of blind children. Figure 12-2 illustrates mannerisms characteristic of blind children—eye-rubbing, rolling the eyes to the extremes of their sockets, and walking on tip-toe—as shown by a blind child and several autistic children.

Despite similarities to perceptually handicapped children, most autistic children are not impaired on standard tests of hearing and vision. They do, however, seem handicapped by *stimulus overselectivity*—a tendency to "respond to only part of a relevant cue, or even to a minor, often irrelevant feature of the environment without learning about other relevant portions of the environment" (Lovaas, Koegel, & Schreibman, 1979, p. 1237). Whether stimulus overselectivity is a primary factor in autism or secondary to other abnormalities is unknown.

Summary of Biobehavioral Studies. Diverse data suggest that autistic children are in abnormal states of arousal, either hyper- or hypoarousal; or, according to DesLauriers and Carlson, hyperarousal in some and hypoarousal in others. The arousal hypotheses blame odd behaviors on a *blocking out* of normal stimuli, especially social stimuli, although autistic children have been found to select relatively high-volume sounds when given a choice. Systematic aversion to faces and models of faces has been demonstrated. Despite behavioral similarities to blind and deaf children, most autistic children are not defective in vision or hearing, although they are *overselective* in their use of environmental cues.

Cognitive and Linguistic Development

Kanner (1943) believed that autistic children have an inborn defect in affective functioning but normal, possibly superior, cognitive potential. Peculiarities of autistic speech, such as failure to use the pronoun *I*, also suggest an affectively based defect in the sense of self. It was, therefore, assumed that breaking down the barriers to emotional contact would yield great cognitive advances. When research disclosed little evidence of an emotional etiology, however, autistic children's cognitive and linguistic development was examined more closely.

Cognitive Findings. Longitudinal studies have shown that autistic children's IQs maintain stable rank orders over several years. For example, even though several different tests were used and children were not necessarily given the same test at follow-ups, DeMyer found a correlation of .70 between autistic children's IQs at testings averaging six years apart (DeMyer, et al., 1974). The poor performance of

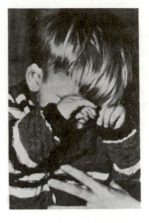

(a) Blind, nonautistic child

(b) Elisabeth, aged 3 years,
7 months, autistic

(c) Diana, aged 5 years,
10 months, autistic

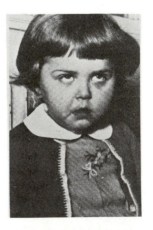

(d) Holger, aged 3 years,
8 months, autistic

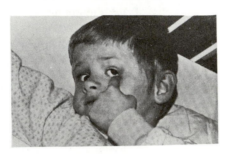

(e) Cornelia, aged 3 years,
2 months, autistic

Figure 12.2. Autistic mannerisms resembling those of blind children. (From Weber, 1970, pp. 55, 56, 63, 74.)

many autistic children used to be blamed on resistance or untestability, but further work showed that their behavior was consistent with the cognitive levels of much younger children. Moreover, the stability of their IQs indicated continuing cognitive development but at a rate like that of nonautistic children having similarly low IQs. Thus, autistic children's low IQs seemed to validly reflect (1) a mental age below their chronological age, and (2) a slow but steady *rate* of development whereby advancing mental age lagged behind chronological age in a constant ratio.

Nearly all of DeMyer's autistic children had IQs in the retarded range. On tests yielding separate verbal and performance scores, autistic children averaged 20 points lower in verbal than performance IQ, but so did nonautistic subnormal children. IQs were also found to be good predictors of work and school placement at follow-up.

Ratings of speech and social functioning were likewise related to IQ in a generally linear fashion. Although "treatment" was evidently quite varied, treated children with IQs over 50 showed significantly greater IQ gains than matched untreated children. Lower IQ children did not seem to benefit from treatment, however.

To examine cognitive developmental sequences more closely, Curcio (1978) administered Piagetian scales of sensory-motor development to nonspeaking autistic boys aged 4 to 12. He found that they were most advanced in object permanence, but least advanced in imitation of gestures. Furthermore, direct observations and teacher reports revealed that none of the boys used *protodeclaratives*, that is, they did not point to or show objects to adults which preverbal normal children often do. All the boys, however, did use *protoimperatives*, that is they used adults to achieve goals, such as gesturing for an adult to open a jar containing a desired object. The autistic boys could thus use gestures to get what they wanted but did not use them for spontaneous communicative interaction the way normal children of similar cognitive levels do.

Linguistic Findings. Autistic children who speak often show echolalia and *pronomial reversal*, especially the substitution of *you* and *me* for *I*. To determine whether these peculiarities reflect systematic avoidance of *I*, Bartak and Rutter (1974) tested autistics with three-word sentences that varied the locations of personal pronouns. Some children echoed the final word of the sentence, while others repeated the whole sentence. When sentence position was varied, there was no consistent tendency to avoid repeating *I*. It thus seems that the failure to use *I* stems from its usual position at sentence beginnings, which are often omitted from echolalic repetitions.

Developmental studies show that normal children learning language also echo and reverse the pronouns *I* and *you* (Fay, 1979). Learning the proper contrasts and shifts between first- and second-person pronouns seems especially hard, since a speaker's first-person pronouns must be recoded in various ways for a hearer to understand or communicate the speaker's meaning. Inability to recall more than the last few words of a speaker's utterance seems to hinder autistic and young normal children's repetition and recoding of first-person pronouns such as *I* that typically begin an utterance. Autistic children whose own utterances are fairly long do not make as many pronoun errors as autistic children whose utterances are short, however (Silberg, 1978). Coupled with Curcio's findings of a lack of protodeclarative gestures, the findings on autistic children's speech suggest a general restriction in communicative capabilities. A long-term follow-up of autistics also underlined the key role of linguistic functioning: Ratings of their speech at ages 8 to 10 were the best predictors of ratings of overall outcome eight years later (Lotter, 1974).

Could autistic children's communication problems reflect abnormal cerebral dominance? To find out, Blackstock (1978) compared the preference of autistic and normal children for hearing sung versus spoken song lyrics. He also compared their ear preference for listening to various kinds of sound. The children were placed in a room with a device they could control to produce music or speech. Figure 12-3 shows that autistic children had a far stronger preference for sung than spoken lyrics. When given a device that permitted listening with only one ear, and the options included several types of music and speech, autistic children showed a general preference for left ear listening, whereas normal children showed no strong ear preference.

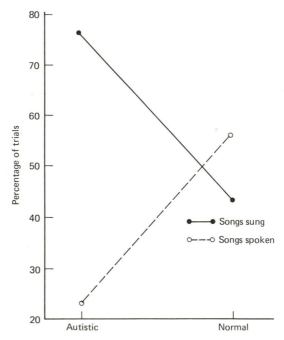

Figure 12.3. Percentage of trials on which spoken and sung songs were chosen by autistic and normal children. (Data from Blackstock, 1978.)

The preferences for music over speech and for left ear listening suggest elevated right hemisphere activity in autistic children, as music and left ear inputs are both subserved by the right hemisphere. Cognitive and EEG measures also suggest a lack of left hemisphere specialization for linguistic functions (Dawson, Warrenburg, & Fuller, 1980). Although the basic puzzle of autism remains unsolved, a fundamental problem in symbolic communication is increasingly implicated.

SCHIZOPHRENIA AND OTHER SEVERE DISORDERS

Unlike infantile autism, schizophrenia typically becomes evident in adulthood. When severe childhood disorders were first recognized, most were viewed as early forms of adult schizophrenia. As we have seen, however, infantile autism seems distinct from schizophrenia in at least three ways: (1) symptoms; (2) presence from infancy rather than being manifest as a decline from attained levels; and (3) lack of elevated rates of schizophrenia in the families of autistic children. As autism has become more clearly distinguished from schizophrenia and the term *childhood schizophrenia* has become less of a blanket term for severe childhood disturbances, questions have arisen as to whether childhood schizophrenia is a single entity. If so, how does it relate to adult schizophrenia?

Diagnostic Problems

Most severe childhood disorders become evident either in infancy or after puberty (Rutter, 1974); those most similar to adult schizophrenia tend to emerge after puberty. The DSM-III handles the question of childhood disorders resembling adult psychoses as follows:

> Because the *essential* features of Affective Disorders and Schizophrenia are the same in children and adults, there are no special [childhood] categories corresponding to these disorders. . . . For example, if a child or adolescent has an illness that meets the criteria for Major Depression, Dysthymic Disorder, or Schizophrenia, these diagnoses should be given regardless of the age of the individual. (American Psychiatric Association, 1980, p. 35)

What, then, are the *essential* features of schizophrenia?

> The essential features of this group of disorders are: the presence of certain psychotic features during the active phase of the illness, characteristic symptoms involving multiple psychological processes, deterioration from a previous level of functioning, onset before age 45, and a duration of at least six months. . . . At some phase of the illness Schizophrenia always involves delusions, hallucinations, or certain disturbances in the form of thought. (American Psychiatric Association, 1980, p. 181)

The DSM then breaks these features down into more specific criteria required for the general diagnosis of schizophrenia and for subtypes including disorganized, catatonic, paranoid, undifferentiated, and residual.

The DSM diagnostic criteria for schizophrenia enjoy several potential advantages over the diagnostic criteria for most childhood disorders. One advantage is the long period over which adult schizophrenia (and its nineteenth century predecessor, *dementia praecox*) has been recognized and studied. A second advantage is that clinical interviews with adults can often reveal the bizarre thoughts that are the hallmarks of schizophrenia. A third advantage is the development of research diagnostic criteria to improve the reliability and validity of the diagnosis and to aid in discriminating schizophrenia from other adult disorders. Several versions of these research diagnostic criteria have become objective enough to permit computer programs to combine clinicians' ratings into diagnostic decisions (Overall & Hollister, 1979). The research diagnostic criteria have also served as prototypes for the DSM-III definitions of the major adult disorders.

Despite the refined diagnostic criteria, experts making diagnoses from standard data about patients often disagree because they hold different concepts of schizophrenia (Hanson, Gottesman, & Meehl, 1977). Furthermore, when a clinician's ratings of a patient's symptoms have been fed into computer programs that make diagnoses according to several versions of research diagnostic criteria, the diagnoses yielded by the different criteria have also shown mediocre agreement (Overall & Hollister, 1979). Thus, even where unreliability does not affect symptom data or translation of these data into diagnoses, differing concepts of schizophrenia lead to diagnostic disagreements. Most of the disagreements stem from differences in the stringency of requirements for the diagnosis of schizophrenia—this is reminiscent of Rimland's (1971) finding that only about 10 percent of children diagnosed autistic by others met his stringent criteria for autism.

The diagnostic dilemma of childhood schizophrenia is worsened by the accumulation of research and clinical literature lacking clear defining criteria. We will deal with this problem in two ways: (1) by considering research on adult schizophrenia that has implications either for childhood schizophrenia or for childhood roots of adult schizophrenia; and (2) by considering theories and findings on severe disorders that have been loosely called childhood schizophrenia.

Family Backgrounds

During the 1940s and 1950s, schizophrenia was blamed on mothers portrayed as immature, narcissistic, overintellectual, and incapable of mature emotional relationships (e.g., Rank, 1949). The *schizophrenogenic mother* became a stereotype invoked even by writers who acknowledged possible constitutional vulnerabilities in psychotic children. The concept was also extended to mothers who "wish that [their] child should not exist" (Bettelheim, 1967, p. 125) and "parents [who] inadvertently hated one another and used the child emotionally'' (Wolman, 1970, p. vii).

Adult Schizophrenics. There are many studies of pathology in the families of adult schizophrenics. To avoid biases inherent in retrospective recall, several have used childhood records of people who later became schizophrenic. Ricks and Berry (1970), for example, compared the child guidance clinic records of people later diagnosed schizophrenic with the records of people who later had other diagnoses or were considered socially adequate. "Schizophrenogenic" mothers were found in all groups but *least* often among those who later became chronic schizophrenics.

Disadvantages such as family poverty and loss of parents through death, divorce, desertion, or illness have not been found unusually common in the childhood histories of adult schizophrenics, although the rate of early parental deaths may be slightly higher than in other abnormal groups (Watt & Nicholi, 1979). The conclusion from diverse studies is that stressful life events probably do not account for schizophrenia but may affect the timing of schizophrenic episodes in some people (Rabkin, 1980).

Childhood Schizophrenics. Klebanoff (1959) assessed the child-rearing attitudes of mothers of schizophrenic, brain-damaged retarded, and normal children by having them fill out the Parental Attitude Research Instrument (PARI), a questionnaire on attitudes related to child-rearing and family life. Mothers of the brain-damaged retarded children expressed significantly more pathological attitudes than mothers of schizophrenic children who, in turn, expressed more pathological attitudes than mothers of normal children. Since the pathological attitudes found among mothers of brain-damaged children could not have caused their children's defects, the mildly pathological attitudes of mothers of schizophrenic children may have been, like the attitudes of mothers of brain-damaged children, *results* rather than causes of their children's problems. Other studies have also failed to find exceptionally pathological attitudes among mothers of schizophrenic or "psychotic" children (e.g., Pitfield & Oppenheim, 1964).

To assess parental personalities, mothers and fathers of schizophrenic (also dubbed "autistic" by the authors) and nonpsychotic neurotic children were given the Rorschach inkblot test, the Minnesota Multiphasic Personality Inventory (MMPI), and the Thematic Apperception Test (Block, Patterson, Block, & Jackson, 1958). The test protocols were evaluated by three clinical psychologists who made Q-sorts describing their impressions of each parent. (In a Q-sort, descriptive statements are sorted into piles ranging from "very like" a person to "very unlike" the person.) No significant differences were found between the Q-sort placements of any of the 108 statements describing the parents of schizophrenics and the parents of neurotic children.

Six psychiatrists also did Q-sorts describing their concepts of the typical schizophrenogenic mother and father. The average correlation between Q-sorts by each pair of psychiatrists for the "typical" schizophrenogenic mother was .56, while for the typical father it was .18. These Q-sorts correlated no better with the Q-sorts of the real parents of schizophrenic children than with the Q-sorts of parents of nonschizophrenic children. The psychiatrists' concepts of typical parents of schizophrenic children thus agreed neither with each other nor with descriptions of parents who really did have schizophrenic children.

Replicating findings that parents of adult schizophrenics showed conceptual disorganization on an object-sorting test, Schopler and Loftin (1969a) found disorganization in the test performance of parents of psychotic children who were undergoing psychodynamic evaluation and treatment. Parents of psychotic children tested in the context of interviews about their *normal* children, however, did *not* show conceptual disorganization (Schopler & Loftin, 1969b). This suggested that parental disorganization might reflect anxiety about being evaluated in relation to their disturbed child. When British researchers administered the same test in parents' homes, they found no differences between parents of autistic and normal boys, nor were there any significant relations to measures of anxiety (Lennox, Callias, & Rutter, 1977).

Family Interactions

Numerous studies have examined interaction patterns in the families of schizophrenics. Some peculiarities have been found (Doane, 1978), but several interpretations are possible: (1) the peculiarities *cause* schizophrenia in the offspring; (2) the peculiarities are merely *symptoms* of the same underlying pathology in several family members; or (3) the peculiarities are *reactions* to the schizophrenic offspring. The first interpretation is difficult to test, because the families are not studied until after their offspring are identified as schizophrenic, and it would be unethical to manipulate family interactions experimentally to see if they can cause schizophrenia. The second interpretation can be tested only if we have a valid sign of the underlying pathology and this sign is independent of the interactional peculiarities shown by family members. The third interpretation is testable, however.

Liem (1974) tested the hypothesis that communications by their schizophrenic offspring adversely affect parents' communications. She studied 11 families having a schizophrenic son aged 17 to 25 and 11 closely matched families free of schizophrenia. Working in separate rooms, parents and their son taped communications describing common objects and concepts, using five separate communications for each item. Parents then responded to the tape made by their own son and tapes made by other normal and schizophrenic sons. The sons responded to tapes made by their own parents and parents of other normal and schizophrenic sons. When serving as respondents, the subjects tried to identify the target item after each communication was played.

Liem found that the schizophrenic sons made far fewer appropriate communications than the normal sons or either group of parents. But there was no significant difference between the two groups of parents. Likewise, the responses of the schizophrenic sons were inferior to those of the other three groups. To clinch the crucial role of the schizophrenic sons' communications: The parents of normal and schizophrenic sons both made fewer misidentifications of the target objects in response to normal sons' communications than schizophrenic sons' communications; yet both sets of sons responded as well to parents of schizophrenic sons as parents of normal sons. The schizophrenic sons were thus inferior to all other groups as both communicators and respondents, whereas their parents were not inferior to the normal sons or parents. Furthermore, the schizophrenic sons' poor communications affected the responses of both sets of parents. Although these findings do not rule out all other interpretations of interactional peculiarities in families of schizophrenics, they do stress that family communication problems can be caused by schizophrenic offspring.

Organic Abnormalities

The search for organic abnormalities has centered mainly on neurological and biochemical factors. These are not mutually exclusive, as a biochemical abnormality may cause neurological damage or vice versa. Nor are they incompatible with research on family characteristics, because the peculiarities of other family members could stem from the same organic abnormality as schizophrenia in the child; or family characteristics could adversely affect an organically vulnerable child.

Neurological Factors. Extending earlier work by Lauretta Bender (Bender & Faretra, 1972), Barbara Fish (1977) has hypothesized an inherited *neurointegrative defect* underlying all schizophrenia, in children as well as adults. She maintains that this defect is manifested in different ways at different developmental periods. Children with psychotic disorders evident in infancy are hypothesized to have the severest defects. Uneven progress on infant development tests is also viewed as symptomatic of the defect in children who do not become psychotic until later. During middle childhood, "soft" (equivocal) signs of neurological dysfunction are assumed to reflect the genetic abnormality, but these signs generally disappear with maturation after the age of 11.

Fish's data come largely from her longitudinal study of 12 babies born to schizophrenic mothers and 12 born to nonpsychotic mothers. Two babies born to schizophrenic mothers were later diagnosed as childhood schizophrenics, while most of the others were diagnosed as having personality disorders. No babies of nonpsychotic mothers were diagnosed schizophrenic by the age of 10, although three had personality disorders. Fish (1977) draws heavily on these samples to illustrate the developmental course of the neurointegrative defect she hypothesizes. However, there were only two schizophrenics, and their perinatal conditions and subsequent environments were very poor. This makes it hard to draw conclusions about causes or predictors of schizophrenia.

William Goldfarb has done some of the most extensive studies of children diagnosed schizophrenic. These included children likely to be diagnosed autistic by others, and Goldfarb ultimately substituted the blanket term *childhood psychosis* for his subjects (Goldfarb, Meyers, Florsheim, & Goldfarb, 1978).

Thorough neurological exams revealed abnormalities in 17 of Goldfarb's (1961) 26 subjects. Elevated rates of pre- and perinatal complications implied that early neurological damage was responsible for these abnormalities (Taft & Goldfarb, 1964). The schizophrenic children diagnosed as organically impaired were inferior to other schizophrenic children on many neurological, perceptual, behavioral, and cognitive measures, including IQ; it averaged 62 in the organically impaired versus 92 in the others. Normal children, in turn, were superior to the "nonorganic" schizophrenics on these measures. Although organic children were functioning worse than nonorganic children at discharge from residential treatment, a follow-up at an average age of 20 showed that close to half of each group attained nearly normal levels of functioning (Goldfarb et al., 1978).

Hypothesizing that childhood schizophrenia can result *either* from organic defects *or* psychosocial adversities, Goldfarb compared the families of normals, organic schizophrenics (those having neurological abnormalities), and nonorganic schizophrenics. Family interactions were rated poorest among the nonorganic schizophrenics, but there was no significant difference beween families of organic schizophrenics and normals.

Meyers and Goldfarb (1961) likewise found the most "maternal perplexity" among mothers of the nonorganic schizophrenics. Ratings of maternal perplexity reflected low spontaneity of maternal interaction, indecisiveness, inconsistency of emotional relatedness, and inappropriateness in relating to the child, control of the child, anticipation of the child's needs, and response to the child's demands. As an illustration, here is the mother rated most perplexed:

> When asked about her maternal feelings, Mrs. A. responded, "My maternal feelings were of responsibility, not of joy, because I was so overanxious. I remember once I was so strict to my schedule that I gave Betty [schizophrenic child] a bath when she was sleeping. . . .
>
> In response to a question about how her husband cooperated in the feeding of the children when they were infants, she said. "We were both afraid to touch her. We thought that she would break. Both of us got up in the night and one gave her the bottle and one held the baby. I put a handkerchief in his hand to hold the baby's head because I was afraid that if he would touch her with his bare hand her head would dilapidate. . . ."
>
> When asked how she handled temper tantrums, Mrs. A. said, "Then I got a temper tantrum too. I don't want to hit Sam because you can sometimes hit him harder than you want. Betty I hit a lot. Now I lock Sam up in a room, but only in the daytime;

if it is in the evening I put on the light, naturally, and I try to make it as short as possible. . . .''

Mrs. A's perplexity over handling sexual play between her children is openly revealed in the following: "Oh yes, she has a terrible effect on him. She plays with his sex organ and then she shows him [her genitals]. Then she plays with his sex organs and he plays with hers and they laugh like it is low, not nice. I just cry that it should be over, but I don't say 'Don't do it.' Am I acting the right way? I don't know why but everything she says [about sex] is like it is low. It is a low thing to own sex organs, the way she puts it. She teaches him low feelings. They laugh together and their laugh is also low, like it wouldn't be nice to have sex organs. . . . He never asked me about sex organs. Just this week he mentioned why did he have them, so I said—I didn't want to name it, I just said—so he asked me, 'Do you use it to urinate with?' and I said yes. I can't tell him this is the way a man has intercourse with his wife because he wouldn't understand. (Meyers & Goldfarb, 1961, pp. 561–62)

To determine the prevalence of schizophrenia among family members, Meyers and Goldfarb (1962) interviewed parents and siblings of 45 children they diagnosed schizophrenic, although others might diagnose some as autistic or symbiotic. Using very liberal diagnostic criteria, they diagnosed as schizophrenic 44 percent of the mothers, 8 percent of the fathers, and 14 percent of the siblings of nonorganic schizophrenic children. By comparison, they diagnosed as schizophrenic 21 percent of the mothers, 15 percent of the fathers, and 4 percent of siblings of organic schizophrenic children. A later study using more objective diagnostic criteria found a lower overall rate of schizophrenia in parents of schizophrenic children (17.9 percent) and negligible differences between parents of organic and nonorganic cases (Goldfarb, Spitzer, & Endicott, 1976).

As shown in Figure 12-4, Goldfarb's model portrays both parental inadequacy *and* organic abnormalities in the child as possible causes of deficient ego development. He argues for an inverse relation between parental perplexity and organic abnormalities, suggesting that both are separate contributors to childhood psychosis. Yet his work does not show that these are either *necessary* or *sufficient causes* of childhood schizophrenia. On the one hand, organic and environmental factors might have a different bearing on different syndromes within the heterogeneous group he called schizophrenic. On the other hand, the organic abnormalities and psychological stresses might merely affect the timing, severity, or form of the disorder in genetically vulnerable children.

Like Goldfarb, others have found poor neurological and cognitive functioning in many children diagnosed schizophrenic (e.g., Pollack, Gittelman, Miller, Berman, & Bakwin, 1970). Despite the variety of dysfunctions and symptoms in these children, their rate of cognitive development seems to be as steady as in normal children: Gittelman and Birch (1967), for example, found a test-retest correlation of .90 for Binet IQ and .82 for WISC IQ among schizophrenic children over intervals averaging 3½ years. In follow-ups averaging six years, children

I.*   Parental inadequacies and perplexity, absence of positive reinforcements, stimulus confusion

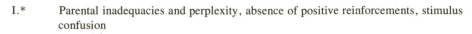

II.*   Deviant child

III.   Ego deficiency with absence of normal guides for self-directed action and self-regulation; and defect in self-identity, diffusion of boundaries of self and nonself

IV.   Absence of predictable expectancies: loss of referents and anchoring

V.   Catastrophic feelings of strangeness and unfamiliarity, and

VI.   Panic (primordial anxiety) with seeking for sameness and constancy

*I and II may be either primary or secondary.

Figure 12.4. Goldfarb's conceptual model for childhood schizophrenia. (From Meyers and Goldfarb, 1961, p. 552. © 1961 by the American Orthopsychiatric Association and reprinted by permission.)

having relatively high initial IQs showed the most improvement. Goldfarb et al. (1978) also found that good outcomes at age 20 were most common among children with the highest initial IQs. IQ thus seems to be a good index of adaptive potential in schizophrenic children.

Biochemical Factors. Since the advent of antipsychotic drugs (called *major tranquilizers* and *neuroleptics*) in the 1950s, there has been a flood of research on biochemical correlates of adult schizophrenia. Much of it focuses on the neuro-transmitter *dopamine*, whose receptors in the synapses of the brain are blocked by neuroleptics. Blockage of dopamine is believed to reduce the schizophrenic's bizarre sensory experiences. Possible causes of excess dopamine have therefore been sought.

One hypothesis is that *monoamine oxidase* (MAO), an enzyme that breaks down neurotransmitters, is deficient in schizophrenia. Low MAO activity has indeed been found in the blood platelets of some adult schizophrenics, especially those with very severe and chronic symptoms (Wyatt et al., 1978). However, low platelet MAO has also been found in nonschizophrenics having problems such as suicide attempts, criminal behavior, and psychiatric hospitalizations (Buchsbaum,

Coursey, & Murphy, 1976). This suggests that low MAO levels are related to psychopathology in general rather than schizophrenia in particular. Extensions of biochemical research to childhood schizophrenia have been hampered by a lack of standardized diagnostic criteria and by uncertainties about the effects of antipsychotic drugs on children (Winsburg & Yepes, 1978).

Genetic Factors

Some of the organic abnormalities implicated in schizophrenia may be genetic. Barbara Fish (1977), for example, hypothesizes that the neurointegrative defect she imputes to schizophrenia is inherited. In addition, Wyatt et al. (1978) have found evidence for genetic influences on the platelet MAO activity they implicated in adult schizophrenia. Extensive pedigree studies have also shown elevated rates of mental disorders in the families of adult schizophrenics (e.g., Reed, Hartley, Anderson, Phillips, & Johnson, 1973).

As we saw in Chapter 6, genetic research requires reliable and valid measures of the trait in question. The lack of objective criteria for childhood schizophrenia makes it hard to test genetic hypotheses, although major chromosomal abnormalities have been pretty well ruled out (Böök, Nichtern, & Gruenberg, 1963). Even for the somewhat better defined adult schizophrenias, it is hard to unravel possible genetic and environmental interactions. The disorders found in close relatives of schizophrenics might reflect shared environmental stresses, for example. We will therefore concentrate on research designed to separate possible genetic and environmental influences. Most of it focuses on adult schizophrenia, but is intended to disclose the developmental roots of schizophrenic disorders.

Twin Studies. As we saw in Chapter 6, twin studies assess genetic effects by comparing *concordance* between identical twins and *concordance* between fraternal twins: If a trait is genetically influenced, it should be significantly more similar in identical twins than in fraternal twins, who inherit only 50 percent of the same genes, on the average. Studies in many countries have shown significantly greater concordance for adult schizophrenia among identical than fraternal twins. Yet the exact concordance rates vary greatly with the age of the twins, the method of finding them, and the diagnostic criteria (Shields & Gottesman 1972). Most studies show from about 20 to 60 percent concordance between identical twins, indicating that genetic factors are not the only cause of schizophrenia.

Identical Twins Discordant for Schizophrenia. The finding that some identical twins are discordant for schizophrenia offers a special opportunity for assessing interactions between genetic and environmental factors: If the twins inherit the same genes but only one twin becomes schizophrenic, what causes the different outcomes? Several studies have shown that twins identified as schizophrenic were usually more submissive, dependent, and socially isolated, and that they evoked more maternal protectiveness in childhood than their co-twins. The differences seemed to emerge very early, but pathological biases in parents' recall cannot be ruled out. Evidence in some studies for low birth weights among the twins who became schizophrenic has been offset by a lack of consistent relations to birth weight in other studies (Shields & Gottesman, 1977). This and other promising leads have also been undermined by follow-ups showing the emergence of schizophrenialike disorders in co-twins initially considered nonschizophrenic (e.g., Belmaker, Pollin, Wyatt, & Cohen, 1974). Nevertheless, assessment of the developmental histories of discordant twins may pinpont factors that shape, moderate, or delay schizophrenia. This strategy has been further extended to a set of genetically identical quadruplets, studied as they showed varying patterns of schizophrenic symptoms over a 20-year period (Rosenthal & Quinn, 1977).

Foster Children. Another strategy for examining the interplay of genetic and environmental effects is to study schizophrenia in people not raised by their biological parents. One way to do this is by starting with children born to schizophrenic parents but raised by others. In a study of this type, Heston (1966) followed up 47 people who had been born to schizophrenic women in mental hospitals. He included only those who seemed normal at birth, were separated from their mothers within three days after birth, and never lived with their maternal relatives. People who as children had been in the same foundling homes were matched to the offspring of schizophrenics for sex, type of foster placement, and length of time in child-care institutions. Heston made first-hand assessments of most subjects, based on personal interviews, Minnesota Multiphasic Personality Inventory (MMPI) scores, IQ, and social class data. Two psychiatrists blind to the subjects' origins made diagnoses and rated psychosocial disability. Complete agreement was obtained on four general diagnostic categories: schizophrenia, mental retardation, sociopathic personality, and neurotic personality disorder.

Table 12-2 shows that substantially more psychopathology, including the only five cases of schizophrenia, occurred in the group having schizophrenic mothers than in the control group. Altogether, 55.3 percent of those with schizophrenic mothers showed serious psychosocial disability, compared to 18 percent of the control group. Yet, among the 44.7 percent having schizophrenic mothers but showing no psychosocial impairment, more had colorful life histories and creative occupations than their controls. Schulsinger (1976) likewise describes her sample of people born to schizophrenic mothers in Denmark as showing "a certain heroism, a spiritual energy and force" (p. 384).

In a further study, Heston and Denney (1968) compared subjects raised in foster families with those raised mainly in child-care institutions. No significant differences were found between institution- and family-reared groups on any of the variables in Table 12-2. Three of the five who developed schizophrenia had been raised primarily in institutions while two had been raised in families. Even the MMPI profiles were nearly identical for the home- and institution-reared groups.

Table 12-2   Characteristics of Foster Children Born to Schizophrenic and Nonschizophrenic Mothers

Characteristics	With Schizophrenic Mothers	With Nonschizophrenic Mothers
Mean psychosocial disability[a]	65.2[c]	80.1
Schizophrenia	10.6%[b]	0%
Mental retardation (IQ < 70)	8.5%[b]	0%
Sociopathic personality disorder	19.1%[b]	4%
Neurotic personality disorder	27.7%[b]	14%
Persons spending > 1 year in penal or psychiatric institution	23.4%[c]	4%
Convicted felons	14.9%[b]	4%
Psychiatric or behavioral discharges from armed forces	17.5%[b]	2%
Mean IQ	94.0	103.7
Never married > 30 years old	19.1%	8%

[a]Low score indicates much disability.
[b]$p \le .05$
[c]$p < .01$ } for difference between groups
Source: From Heston, 1966.

The elevated pathology in the offspring of schizophrenics and the similar outcomes of institution- versus family-rearing suggest that genetic factors definitely play a role in schizophrenia and that other forms of psychopathology also reflect the same genetic factors.

Adoption Studies. Other studies have started with schizophrenic adoptees and then compared psychopathology in their adoptive and biological families. The most extensive studies of this sort have been done in Denmark, where registers of all citizens, adoptions, and mental hospital admissions have been used to compare the family histories of adoptees diagnosed schizophrenic and nonschizophrenic (Kety, Rosenthal, Wender, Schulsinger, & Jacobsen, 1978). Elevated rates of mental disorders were found in the biological families but not the adoptive families of adoptees who became schizophrenic. This again suggested that genetic factors contribute to schizophrenia.

As in the twin studies and Heston's (1966) study of foster children, however, concordance for schizophrenia among close biological relatives was far from perfect: 5.9 percent of the biological relatives of schizophrenic adoptees and 1.0 percent of biological relatives of control adoptees had "schizophrenic spectrum" disorders (including schizoid or inadequate personality, as well as schizophrenia).

Viewed another way, 52 percent of schizophrenic but only 15 percent of nonschizophrenic adoptees had at least one biological relative diagnosed definitely or possibly schizophrenic. Thus, schizophrenia was detected in only a small minority of the biological relatives of schizophrenics, and nearly half the schizophrenics had *no* relatives identified as schizophrenic. Furthermore, exclusion of relatives whose disorders were not clearly schizophrenic made some of the findings statistically nonsignificant (Lidz, Blatt, & Cook, 1981). Other studies have shown schizophrenia in only about 10 percent of people having one schizophrenic parent and about 25 to 35 percent having *two* schizophrenic parents (Kringlen, 1978).

Developmental Course

Findings from studies of twins, foster children, and adoptees generally agree that (1) genetic factors contribute to adult schizophrenia, *but* (2) the genetic factors are not the only cause. The relatively low rates of concordance for schizophrenia among close relatives and the lack of familial patterns corresponding to Mendelian traits suggest that a general vulnerability to schizophrenia rather than the disorder itself is inherited (Gottesman, 1979). It has, therefore, been hypothesized that schizophrenia results when genetically vulnerable people experience precipitating stress. This is called a *diathesis-stress* hypothesis. (*Diathesis* means "a bodily condition predisposing to a disease.")

To detect early signs of vulnerability, researchers have assessed childhood characteristics of people who later became schizophrenic. This has been done largely through *follow-back* studies in which childhood records of adult schizophrenics were compared with childhood records of nonschizophrenic adults. It has been found, for example, that adults hospitalized for schizophrenia showed significantly poorer interpersonal competence in childhood, as rated from teachers' comments in school records, than adults hospitalized for personality disorders, psychotic depression, or neurosis (Lewine, Watt, Prentky, & Fryer, 1980). The future schizophrenics received more teacher's comments indicative of such characteristics as immaturity, unpopularity, and insecurity. Yet they were not inferior in ratings of childhood academic competence.

High-risk Research. To trace the unfolding of schizophrenia, other researchers have undertaken longitudinal studies of children known to be at relatively high risk for schizophrenia because they have a schizophrenic parent. Even though only about 10 percent of children having a schizophrenic parent eventually become schizophrenic, this is ten times the 1 percent risk rate for the general population. Longitudinal study of the unfolding of schizophrenia is far more feasible in samples containing 10 percent future schizophrenics than 1 percent future schizophrenics. Furthermore, specific precursors of schizophrenia may be highlighted by comparing those who do and do not become schizophrenic: Since both groups experience the stress of having a schizophrenic parent and some who presumably have the genetic vulnerability do not become schizophrenic, it may be possible to detect environmental factors that precipitate or prevent schizophrenia.

A most ambitious high-risk study of this sort was begun in Denmark in 1962 (Mednick, Schulsinger, & Venables, 1979). It started with 207 children of schizophrenic mothers and 104 control children of nonschizophrenic parents. Both groups averaged 15 years of age. By the time they reached an average age of 25, some of the high-risk group showed major psychopathology that was diagnosed as schizophrenia. Although the numbers were small, the precursors of schizophrenia seemed different in males and females (Mednick, et al., 1978). In males, the two precursors most strongly related to schizophrenia were (1) the extent the boy was separated from his parents while he was young, and (2) exceptionally quick autonomic nervous system responses and recovery from stress, as shown by galvanic skin responses to standardized stressors. The autonomic nervous responsiveness, in turn, seems to have resulted at least partly from early organic damage due to perinatal complications. In females, by contrast, the most direct precursor of schizophrenia was an especially early onset of schizophrenia in their own mothers.

Although the reason for the sex differences is not known, the possibility that precipitants differ for males and females may help to explain why the puzzle of schizophrenia has been so hard to solve: Because there are no obvious sex differences in the *rate* of schizophrenia, efforts to identify precursors have largely ignored the subjects' sex. In samples including both sexes, the failure to perform separate analyses for each sex may have obscured relations among variables that differed for the two sexes. Likewise, differences in findings may have arisen from sex differences among samples.

Beside highlighting sex differences, high-risk studies have also shown the importance of comparing the developmental course of children at risk for different disorders. If we only study children at risk for schizophrenia, for example, we cannot find out whether the precursors found are exclusive to schizophrenia or characteristic of other psychopathology as well. Several longitudinal high-risk studies have therefore been designed to compare children of schizophrenics with children of other disturbed parents, such as those suffering from severe depressions (e.g., Oltmanns, Weintraub, Stone, & Neale, 1978). Other studies compare children of schizophrenic parents with children whose parents have a severe physical illness, such as tuberculosis. In a study of this type, Anthony (1978) described children who appear invulnerable to severe environmental stress, although their invulnerability may be at the price of an "emotional insulation" from other people. Among the children of schizophrenics who were not so successful at protecting themselves, Anthony (1972) described the following kinds of reactions:

1. *Parapsychotic*—disturbed thinking and behavior occurring in children engaged in an early close relationship with a schizophrenic mother. This syndrome is believed to be determined primarily by the environmental

influence of the disturbed parent and is alleviated by severing the close tie to the parent.

2. *Nonpsychotic*—neurotic and behavior disorders occurring in children as reactions to stress created in the home by the schizophrenic parent, but not reaching bizarre proportions.

3. *Prepsychotic*—hypersensitivity to minor stresses, accompanied by repeated "micropsychotic" episodes in children who appear to be constitutionally vulnerable to psychosis, regardless of which parent is schizophrenic.

Anthony offers this example of a micropsychotic episode:

> . . . a girl of nine . . . noted a small blemish on her skin and became extremely upset. She accused her mother of putting things in her food in order to poison her. She also began to notice that she was becoming forgetful in response to the toxic substance and falling behind in her classwork. She thought that the doctor who examined her with negative findings was in league with the mother, and she observed that some of the patients sitting in his waiting room had similar blemishes so that he was the center of a wider conspiracy. In three months the . . . microparanoidal system cleared up completely, and she was her apparently normal self again. (Anthony, 1972, p. 404)

The absence of clearcut childhood schizophrenia among the offspring of schizophrenics in the high-risk studies raises questions about relations between child and adult disorders that have been labeled "schizophrenia." Even though some studies of childhood schizophrenics have found elevated rates of schizophrenia in adult relatives (e.g., Meyers & Goldfarb, 1962), it seems that most children of schizophrenics are not very deviant. Furthermore, any precursors of adult schizophrenia are quite subtle even in children facing both the environmental and possible genetic disadvantages of having a schizophrenic parent.

TREATMENT

Several approaches to treating severely disturbed children have evolved. These can be roughly categorized as *educational, milieu* (provision of a special environment), *psychoanalytic, behavioral,* and *organic.* We will concentrate on those that have been tested for efficacy in at least a rudimentary way. As we shall see, most treatment programs have not made clear distinctions among disorders such as autism versus schizophrenia.

Educational Approaches

Some approaches focus mainly on the child's education, although education also has a role in each of the other approaches. Most facilities for severely disturbed children are called "schools," but the schooling typically reflects a particular treatment philosophy rather than a purely educational approach.

In assessing a traditional special education approach, Havelkova (1968) found little difference in outcome for schizophrenic and autistic children who received a special nursery school program and those who did not. The special program began with a one-to-one relationship between the child and a nursery therapist. The child's activities included pleasurable contacts with the therapist, instruction in dressing, eating, and toileting, and trips into the community. After one to two years, the child moved gradually into a normal nursery school where the therapist remained as long as necessary. A social worker also met with the parents each week to help them understand their child.

Havelkova concluded that children who were least severely disturbed and began to show improvement before the age of 4½ had the best outcomes, while those who were most severely disturbed and did not improve before the age of 5½ had poor outcomes, regardless of treatment. Cognitive deficits remained even in many of the children whose social behavior improved.

Rutter and Bartak (1973) compared outcomes for autistic children in three contrasting educational units: *Unit A* exemplified a psychodynamic approach aimed at fostering a personal relationship with the child and helping the child regress to the developmental stage at which autism presumably developed. Thereafter, the child was to be helped through the normal stages of social and emotional development, but not taught specific skills. *Unit B* combined regressive techniques with more structured educational methods according to each child's needs. *Unit C* emphasized teaching children specific skills to overcome perceptual, motor, and cognitive handicaps.

Because Rutter and Bartak compared children who happened to be in the different units instead of being systematically assigned, many variables other than the programs themselves might cause differences in outcomes. Among children remaining in the programs over a four-year period, however, those in Unit C showed significantly better reading and arithmetic skills than those in Units A and B. Across all programs, initial IQ was the best predictor of improvement in reading and arithmetic, but Unit C was the only one in which children improved more than their IQs would predict. Figure 12-5 illustrates for reading the pattern that was also found for arithmetic: Children in Unit A fell farthest below the level predicted from their IQs, while those in Unit B were intermediate between A and C.

Ratings for social responsiveness and behavior outside the school situation also correlated significantly with IQ, but did not differ significantly among the programs. Teaching academic skills thus seems to have improved those skills; yet neither academic skills nor the socioemotional emphasis of the other programs seems to have conferred an advantage in behavior outside the school.

Milieu Therapy

Most milieu therapy emphasizes full-time socialization of children by engaging them in interactions with others, helping them adapt to routines, and encouraging

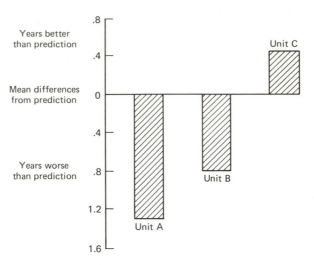

Figure 12.5. Difference between reading scores predicted from IQ and actual reading scores of autistic children in programs emphasizing psychodynamics (Unit A), psychodynamics and structured education (Unit B), and specific skills (Unit C). (From Rutter & Bartak, 1973.)

them to develop educational, creative, and practical skills. Milieu therapy often overlaps with other approaches, however, in that the milieu is designed according to psychoanalytic, behavioral, or organic assumptions. Thus, therapeutic milieux tend to vary along the lines of the other treatment approaches.

Goldfarb, Goldfarb, and Pollack (1966) compared the effects of full-time milieu therapy with the effects of a day-treatment program. The day program resembled the full-time program except that the children spent nights, weekends, and vacations at home. Dividing schizophrenic children into "organic" and "nonorganic" groups according to Goldfarb's (1961) criteria, Goldfarb et al. found that the most severely disturbed children benefitted from neither type of treatment. Among the less severely disturbed children, however, improvements in educational achievement, IQ, and ratings of "ego status" were approximately equal for organic children receiving both kinds of treatment, but better for nonorganic children in residential treatment than day treatment. This suggested that residential treatment protected nonorganic children from harmful family dynamics.

A comparison of autistic children in three milieux produced somewhat different results (Wenar, Ruttenberg, Dratman, & Wolfe, 1967). Children spending a year in a day-treatment program improved in ratings of relationships to people, attempts at mastery, and psychosexual development, while children spending a year in either of two full-time treatment settings actually declined on these measures. One of the two full-time settings, however, was purely custodial and both had older children, poorer child/staff ratios, more staff turnover, and less staff involvement with the children than the day-treatment setting did. The purely custodial institution produced somewhat better results in certain respects than the other residential institution, where there was the most staff turnover and least staff involvement with the children. None of the settings produced much improvement in children's communication, however.

Despite the key role accorded therapists in most treatment settings, workers who directly care for children may have more effect than therapists, who typically see children for only a few hours a week. Portnoy (1973), for example, found that inpatient children imitated child-care workers significantly more than they imitated their therapists. This suggests that more therapeutic leverage can be gained via child-care workers than therapy sessions.

Psychoanalytic Approaches

Psychoanalytic approaches aim to resolve emotional problems via intense relationships with therapists who respond to the child's inner needs. Analysts have portrayed childhood psychosis as defective ego development caused by disturbance of the early mother-child relationship. Most analytic theorists acknowledge possible constitutional vulnerabilities, but they have focused on maternal contributions to psychosis. According to Bettelheim (1967), Rank (1949), and Mahler (Mahler, Pine, & Bergman, 1975), therapy must create a loving relationship with an attentive, permissive mother figure who provides ego support lacking from the child's own mother. Requiring years of therapy, such a relationship is viewed as a prerequisite for later stages of treatment. The later stages involve uncovering and working through unconscious conflicts, as done in analytic treatment of neurotic disorders.

In evaluating analytically oriented treatment, Bettelheim (1967) reported that 42 percent of "autistic" children treated as long-term inpatients at his Orthogenic School showed good improvement. Unfortunately, he did not specify the method of appraisal, and his descriptions suggest that the children did not have either Kanner syndrome or the more broadly defined autistic syndromes described by others.

Brown (1960) followed up children showing "atypical" development (autism or schizophrenia; cf. Rank, 1949) and receiving analytically oriented outpatient therapy. She found that children with the best outcomes did not differ significantly from those with the worst outcomes on any treatment variables, including age of child when starting treatment, number of years of treatment, number or experience of therapists for child or mother, or treatment of father. Instead, children who were the most disturbed before treatment made the least overall progress regardless of treatment variables.

In another follow-up, Brown (1963) compared 15 "atypical" children who received no treatment with 109 who received at least six months of individual therapy or at least a year of small group treatment (e.g., at Bettelheim's Orthogenic School). Again, treatment seemed to have little effect on outcome.

In a study resembling Brown's (1960) first study, the 10 most improved and 10 least improved were selected from a group of 40 schizophrenic children who had received analytic therapy for an average of 4 to 5 years in day care, inpatient, and outpatient settings in conjunction with special schooling and group programs (Kaufman, Frank, Friend, Heims, & Weiss, 1962). Unlike Brown's study, no effect of initial severity was found, although severity in this study was judged according to inferred personality rather than behavior. Length of treatment was *inversely* related to improvement, with the least improved group receiving an average of 58 months of therapy, compared to 36 months in the most improved group.

Behavioral Approaches

Behavioral methods are more recent but have received more extensive assessment than the other major approaches.

Lovaas (1977), for example, assessed operant conditioning with psychotic children rejected for other types of treatment because of their very poor functioning. Self-mutilation and other psychotic behaviors increased whenever demands were made on the children, but removing the demands seemed to reinforce the psychotic behavior. Temporary isolation (*time-out*) was found to suppress self-mutilation in some children, while brief electric shock suppressed it in those whose self-destructive behavior (e.g., biting flesh from their own bodies) was too dangerous to be allowed until the time-out treatment took effect. Case studies have also demonstrated success in eliminating self-destructive behavior with electric shock after other methods had failed (Baroff & Tate, 1968; Risley, 1968). No adverse effects were detected, and the elimination of self-destructive behavior permitted successful treatment of other behavior.

Another way to suppress self-destructive behavior in some children is by reinforcing competing responses. A child who repeatedly poked her eyes, for example, was given a tape recorder that played interesting sounds when she pressed two switches (Carr, 1976). After she figured out how to press the switches with her elbows while still gouging her eyes, however, new switches had to be made that could be pressed only with the fingertips. Nondestructive repetitive behavior has been treated by altering reinforcement contingencies in other ways. Compulsive flicking of light switches—a common autistic behavior—has been eliminated by disconnecting the switches and soundproofing them, for example (Rincover, Newsom, & Carr, 1979).

Positive adaptive behavior has been fostered by reinforcing imitation of self-help skills, athletics, play, drawing, and writing. Training of imitation must sometimes begin with prompts such as moving children through the motions to be imitated and reinforcing them for the slightest attempt at spontaneous imitation.

Generalized imitation has thus been taught to extremely disturbed autistic and schizophrenic children (Lovaas, 1977).

With children who fail to make eye contact, reinforcement of attention and eye contact must precede reinforcement of imitation. Blake and Moss (1967) described a novel procedure in which a child named Dolly was seated in a dark booth. Every five seconds, the trainer opened a shutter to the booth and turned on the lights, saying, "Hi, Dolly—look at me!" Dolly was given a spoonful of ice cream whenever she did look. Within 75 trials, Dolly always responded with eye contact when the trainer said "Look at me!" and continued to make eye contact after the training session.

Token reinforcement of school behavior has shown some success with autistic children (Martin, England, Kaprowy, Kilgour, & Pilek, 1968). Tokens were first given reinforcing value by rewarding children with food whenever they handed a token to the trainer. The tokens were then used to reinforce sitting quietly at a desk, imitating words when prompted, identifying objects, answering simple questions, and matching pictures. It was eventually possible to shift to a group classroom situation in which the children sat quietly and responded to commands and questions from the teacher.

In an extensive study of 17 autistic children having no useful language, operant conditioning was used to establish eye contact and then speech, social behavior, reading, and other school activities (Hamblin, Buckholdt, Ferritor, Kozloff, & Blackwell, 1971). Disruptive and self-injurious behaviors were eliminated by ignoring and then by reinforcing behaviors incompatible with them. Corroborating other findings that high ratios of success to failure reduced disruptive behavior in psychotic children, disruptive behavior was avoided by providing learning conditions geared so closely to the child's abilities that no errors occurred. Nearly all the mothers of the autistic children were successfully trained as assistant teachers.

Preliminary evaluation showed that 35 percent of the children achieved good adjustments—they acquired linguistic syntax and were able to function well in regular or special public school classes; 30 percent achieved fair adjustments—they functioned well in a special lab school and at home and continued to make progress in speech; and 35 percent made poor adjustments. The special significance of age 5 for autistic children was again evident in that only 1 of the 11 children beginning treatment by age 5 showed a poor outcome, while 5 of the 6 children beginning treatment after age 5 showed poor outcomes, and 1 showed a fair outcome.

In one of the very few studies comparing the effects of different types of treatment on well-matched groups of psychotic children, Ney, Palvesky, and Markely (1971) provided 50 sessions of psychoanalytically oriented play therapy, followed by 50 sessions of operant conditioning for schizophrenic boys. The reverse sequence was provided for schizophrenic boys matched to the first group for age, signs of organicity, amount of speech, and Vineland Social Maturity scores. The play therapy was guided by the premise that play activities symbolize the child's conflicts and provide a means for expressing thoughts. A warm, accepting therapist interpreted recurrent play themes to the child. The operant conditioning used candy and verbal reinforcement of behavior related to self-awareness, emotional relationships, imitation of adult behavior, and communication.

Tests of cognitive, communicative, sensory-motor, and personal-social functioning showed significant improvements after operant conditioning but not after play therapy. Direct comparison of the two treatments showed that operant conditioning was superior to play therapy whether it came first or second, but that the difference in favor of operant conditioning was significant only when it came second.

Motivational Factors. The behavior of nearly all children *can* be modified. But positive adaptive behavior usually requires effort on the child's part. Because severely disturbed children seldom make such efforts, behavior modifiers have sought ways to increase motivation. Using an ABAB reversal design, Hung (1978) demonstrated that two autistic boys uttered more spontaneous sentences when rewarded with tokens that could be exchanged for being allowed to engage in self-stimulation activities, such as twiddling objects and flapping hands.

What about motivation to learn new behavior? Autistic children seem to work much more persistently when teachers' prompts facilitate correct responses than when working on their own, where their failure rate is high (Koegel & Egel, 1979). Observational ratings also showed the children to be more enthusiastic when receiving prompts that insured a high success rate.

Motivation has been further manipulated by *reducing* the rate of reinforcement after learning a discrimination under 100 percent reinforcement. As compared to continuing on 100 percent reinforcement, reducing reinforcement to 33 percent of correct responses overcame autistic children's tendency to focus "overselectively" on very limited aspects of stimuli (Koegel, Schreibman, Britten, & Laitinen, 1979). The children seemed to learn more diverse aspects of stimuli because they attended to more cues when they construed omission of reinforcement as signaling an error.

Communicative Behavior. Lovaas (1977) has attempted to teach language to autistic children by first reinforcing imitation of single words spoken by others. After children acquired 10 recognizable words, they were taught nouns and verbs for answering questions about everyday objects and activities, like "What is it?" and "What are you doing?" After mastering this level, children were required to verbalize their wants, such as food, before they would be fulfilled. The next step was to teach abstract words concerning spatial, temporal, and personal relations, as well as properties of objects. Thereafter, training was designed to make speech more complex, grammatical, and spontaneous.

Lovaas (1977) has documented the progress of several autistic children taught with what is basically a discrimination learning procedure. Although progress was slow, most of the children did increase their language skills. Yet, as we will see later, their subsequent progress depended largely on their posttreatment environment. Individual characteristics of the children, especially their initial linguistic competence, also seem to have a big effect on the outcome of operant language training (Howlin, 1981).

An especially intriguing approach has been to teach autistic children sign language, using techniques developed in teaching sign language to chimpanzees. It has been found that some mute autistic children respond much better to signs than spoken language (Carr, 1979) and that most autistic children can learn at least some signs (Bonvillian, Nelson, & Rhyne, 1981). Although the teacher usually speaks while signing, most mute autistics seem to learn little about speech from this procedure. Autistic children who already imitate speech, however, apparently do attend to both the spoken words and signs and improve their speech as a result.

A comparison of signs alone, verbalization alone, and the combination of signs with verbalization showed that the combination approach elicited the most correct responses from a 6-year-old autistic boy who was instructed to perform actions with a set of objects (Brady & Smouse, 1978). Verbalization alone produced the worst results, while signs alone were intermediate. More studies of this sort are needed to determine whether this is a uniform pattern for autistic children and how language teaching can be tailored to autistic children's developmental levels.

Parents as Behavior Modifiers. As mentioned earlier, children's long-term progress after Lovaas's (1977) training program depended on where they went next: Those returning to their parents who had been taught behavior modification did much better than those who went to a state hospital, where many of their gains were lost. Recognizing parents' crucial role in sustaining children's progress, Lovaas (1978) requires parents of children accepted for treatment to sign a legal contract stating what is expected of them. The parents are taught to take reliable data and modify their child's behavior, first in the clinic and then at home under the supervision of Lovaas's staff. At least one parent is required to work with the child for most of every day over at least a year. The specific methods draw on the behavioral technology described in Chapter 10, applied in an exceedingly intensive way.

In a program that shifted behavioral training entirely to the home, it was found that autistic boys' behavior could be markedly improved with much less professional and parental effort than Lovaas (1978) stipulates (Hemsley et al., 1978). In fact, Hemsley et al. "strongly disagree with Lovaas that it is necessary for mothers to give up work and postpone having more offspring to spend most of the day with their autistic children" (p. 405), although their cases may have been initially less handicapped than those Lovaas treated. Parents were trained by clinical psychologists who visited the home once or twice weekly at first, dropping to once a month or less after treatment was well-established. The parents were helped to be more consistent in handling their sons, and they set aside short periods each day to teach specific social and communication skills via behavioral methods adapted to each boy's developmental level.

Compared to control groups receiving other treatments or no treatment, the home-treated boys showed greater advances in speech and decreases in problem behavior without their parents spending more time with them. The *way* in which parents interacted with their sons did change, however, with significant increases in active involvement, total remarks, and differential verbal feedback. Follow-ups after 18 months showed slower progress. Nevertheless, follow-ups over several years showed the home-treated boys to be significantly superior to individually matched control boys in several categories of behavior. Although no cures for autism were claimed, and higher level functioning seemed especially hard to train, the results of this program offer the hope of affordable, practical help for many families of autistic children.

Organic Approaches

Despite an increasing presumption of organic causes for severe disorders, organic treatments of psychotic children have not received much systematic evaluation. After apparent success in the treatment of adults, electroconvulsive shock therapy (ECT) and major tranquilizers were tried with psychotic children. Lauretta Bender (1960) reported that follow-ups of over 500 children treated with ECT between 1942 and 1955 showed no adverse effects. However, she provided no specific data, and ECT is no longer used with children.

Drug Treatments. The major tranquilizers (such as the phenothiazines) used to treat adult psychotics have been widely used with severely disturbed children. Yet there is far less evidence for efficacy with children than with adults, and the negative side effects can be quite different. As one leading drug researcher put it, "Psychopharmacology of autistic and schizophrenic children and adolescents is still in a primitive state. Drug studies with large samples of diagnostically homogeneous populations, controlled for age, IQ, and other pertinent variables, are almost nonexistent" (Campbell, 1978, p. 341). Campbell adds that "in the formative years of the individual, drugs alone never suffice" (p. 346), because other help is needed for the child's specific handicaps.

Campbell herself has done one of the few controlled comparisons between drug treatment and another treatment (Campbell et al., 1978). The subjects were 40 autistic children aged 2 to 7, with no identifiable organic etiology. Children were randomly assigned to receive either haloperidol (trade name Haldol) or a placebo, and either behavioral therapy with reinforcement contingent on correct responses or noncontingent reinforcement under similar conditions. The behavioral therapy began with getting the child to remain seated and make eye contact, followed by speech training.

The results were quite complex in that haloperidol seemed to improve a few specific behaviors but did so only in older children. Contingent reinforcement seemed to improve other behaviors, and learning was best in the group receiving both haloperidol and contingent reinforcement. The unexpected importance of age, the lack of agreement among outcome measures, and numerous side effects (especially oversedation), however, show that far more research is needed before even this potentially promising drug can be fully judged.

Orthomolecular Therapy. Another organic approach that originated with a treatment for adult psychosis is *orthomolecular therapy*. This entails using massive doses of vitamins to overcome presumed deficiencies.

Although the efficacy of orthomolecular therapy even for adult psychosis is still in doubt, Rimland, Callaway, and Dreyfus (1978) studied autistic children whose parents had reported good responses to large doses of vitamin B_6 (pyridoxine). When a placebo was later substituted for vitamin B_6 in a double-blind cross-over design, parent and teacher ratings tended to show more deterioration of behavior during the placebo periods. The results are merely suggestive, however, as the children were selected from a much larger sample because their parents had reported the best responses to vitamin B_6. Furthermore, they were too geographically dispersed to permit close control of many relevant variables, and deterioration in response to *withdrawal* of vitamin B_6 does not prove that vitamin B_6 initially improves behavior; the deterioration could result from a dependency acquired through the previous administration of vitamin B_6 and various other substances the children were receiving.

Reduction of Stimulation. Hypothesizing that autistic behavior defends against exacerbation of a hyperaroused state, Stroh and Buick (1970) tried reducing sensory inputs to two autistic boys. Each boy spent several three- to four-day sessions in a windowless, soundproof room, alternating with four to six days in a condition of graduated stimulation. During the isolation sessions, a child-care worker spent five hours a day caring for the boy, but he was otherwise alone.

Both boys decreased their rocking and running and increased their attention to visual and auditory stimuli. They also explored and vocalized more and sought more contact with the child-care worker. Stroh and Buick concluded that much autistic behavior defends against excessive stimulation.

Theraplay. Agreeing that autistic children are in abnormal states of arousal—some hyperaroused but some *hypo*aroused—DesLauriers and Carlson (1969) adopted the *opposite* treatment strategy. Instead of reducing stimulation, a therapist systematically intruded on the child, attempting to "humanize" the child by maximizing pleasurable sensory and affective stimulation through gamelike activities. Emphasizing the playful aspect of this approach, DesLauriers (1979) calls it *theraplay*.

At first, stimulation is largely tactile, kinesthetic, and proprioceptive, but this is followed by more visual and auditory stimulation. Once the child begins to respond to affective stimulation, the therapist tries to promote reciprocal communication with the child. Eye contact is promoted, for example, through a game in which the therapist repeatedly throws a towel over the child's head and stands so the child looks right into the therapist's eyes when the towel is removed. Although theraplay has an affinity with behavioral approaches, it does not condition discrete bits of behavior. Instead, it aims at affectively "awakening" children, thereby creating opportunities to reinforce spontaneous initiative, curiosity, and mastery that might generalize to new situations. DesLauriers and Carlson argue that effective reinforcement involves organic arousal within the child and is not equivalent to giving specific rewards for specific behavior. As a child improves, parents are encouraged to provide highly affective stimulation at home.

DesLauriers provided an example of how theraplay started with Sammy, a 5-year-old hyperactive autistic boy:

> The therapist began by placing himself in various positions on the floor of the room as a physical obstacle in the path of this rampaging child. Thus, Sammy had to sidestep, go around, or jump over the therapist. This maneuver eventually had the effect of slowing Sammy down sufficiently for the therapist to reach out and grab the child's hand or arm. This was done very quickly and just as quickly the therapist would release the child, the idea being to convey to the child that his "freedom and autonomy" were not in danger; no one would enslave him! Sammy tried various ways, at first, to avoid the therapist (at least he was aware of him!), at one point, even stopping altogether his hyperactivity; but as soon as the therapist got off the floor the race was on again! By this time the therapist knew that Sammy was "with him"; every time Sammy flew by, the therapist would lunge, hold him a second, and let him go. Eventually, Sammy expected the move and imperceptibly slowed down, *in order to be caught.* If, perchance, the therapist, out of breath, would neglect his part of the adventure, Sammy would come to a stop and look as if to say: "Well, what's happening to you?" And so it went for many of the early Theraplay sessions with Sammy, until he, himself, would come spontaneously to the therapist to be held and to sit on his lap for a few minutes!" (DesLauriers, 1979, p. 266)

DesLauriers and Carlson (1969) reported gains in the cognitive and social functioning of five autistic children, but without a control group it is unclear how much reflected spontaneous development or repeated experience with the test items. One-year follow-ups of four children showed that none had regressed into autistic isolation, but all had fairly severe adjustment problems. Neither the parents nor school personnel seemed able to continue the special stimulation and tolerance that DesLauriers and Carlson prescribed.

SUMMARY

Psychosis refers to extreme mental distortions of reality. When severe disturbances were first noticed in children, they were viewed as early forms of adult psychosis, especially schizophrenia. Confusion arose because the terms *childhood schizophre-*

nia, childhood psychosis, autism, and *atypical personality development* were often used interchangeably.

It is now clear that *early infantile autism* (Kanner syndrome) is quite distinct from schizophrenia, which seldom begins before adolescence. Other severe disorders of childhood seem to form less cohesive syndromes, although *symbiotic psychoses* and *disintegrative psychoses* may constitute definite but rare syndromes. Except for schizophrenia, most severe childhood disorders involve failures of appropriate adaptive development more than the systematic distortions of reality seen in adult psychoses.

Among the severe childhood disorders, infantile autism has been the most researched. There has been considerable convergence on the following criteria for diagnosis: onset before age 30 months, impairment of social and linguistic development in ways not ascribable to general cognitive retardation, and obsessive insistence on sameness. Conclusions are still jeopardized, however, by differences in the stringency with which the criteria are applied.

Research has borne out Leo Kanner's early impressions that parents of autistic children tend to be above average in occupation and education, although most are not as exceptional as Kanner reported. There is no evidence that parental behavior or psychological characteristics cause autism. Some organic abnormalities, such as prenatal rubella, apparently increase the risk of autism, and there is evidence of genetic influences, but no specific organic causes have been found. IQ scores are good predictors of overall adaptive development in autistics, but communicative functioning is more deviant than the IQ indicates.

Most severe disorders of childhood were at first called childhood schizophrenia, but there is increasing doubt as to the existence of a distinctly childhood form of schizophrenia. Studies of heterogeneous samples of children diagnosed schizophrenic have not supported early concepts of the *schizophrenogenic* mother. Some peculiarities of communication in the families of schizophrenics also seem to *result* from having a schizophrenic child rather than causing the child's schizophrenia. There is evidence for genetic influences on schizophrenia, but the relatively low rates in close relatives suggests an important role for nongenetic factors, such as brain damage and environmental stress.

Treatment of severe childhood disorders has included *educational, milieu, psychoanalytic, behavioral,* and *organic* approaches. No treatment has brought major improvements in many severely disturbed children. The very few well designed studies show complex interactions between treatment effects and characteristics of individual children, such as developmental level. A repeated finding is that autistic children who show communicative speech by age five have a better prognosis than those who do not.

Behavioral approaches have been most systematically evaluated and have shown that adaptive behavior can be taught most severely disturbed children. Progress is often very slow, but training parents to modify their children's behavior at home seems especially promising.

SUGGESTED READING

Case Histories. *Nadia, a Case of Extraordinary Drawing Ability in an Autistic Child* (Selfe, 1977) presents the case history and numerous drawings of an autistic girl who began drawing with exceptional skill and detail when she was 3, despite a lack of language. The book documents the progress of her drawing and its eventual decline as her speech and other skills slowly improved in a special educational program. T. I. Rubin's (1968) book *Jordi/Lisa and David* poignantly portrays the experience of a schizophrenic boy, Jordi, as inferred by one who has abundant experience with psychotic children. Although fiction, it has a ring of truth about how such a child might experience the world. The other story in the book "Lisa and David," is also worth reading for its picture of two very disturbed adolescents. An excellent movie, entitled "David and Lisa," was made from the story. *I Never Promised You a Rosegarden* (Green, 1964) is also a moving portrayal of the experience of a psychotic adolescent, this time as an autobiographical novel.

Research, Theory, and Treatment. *Autism: A Reappraisal of Concepts and Treatment* (Rutter & Schopler, 1978) provides a comprehensive sampling of research, theory, and treatment pertaining to childhood autism, while a book by Neale and Oltmanns (1980) does likewise for schizophrenia (mainly adult). The *Journal of Autism and Developmental Disorders*, published by Plenum, provides a forum for research, theory, book reviews, and parents' comments on severe disorders of childhood. Brubakken, Derouin, and Morrison (1980) give a detailed account of a multifaceted behavioral systems approach to treatment of severely disturbed children. Schiefelbusch (1980) presents several approaches to nonspeech communication, such as sign language, with severely disturbed children.

Parents of Autistic Children. The National Society for Autistic Children works hard on behalf of these children and their families. John Kysar (1968), a psychiatrist, has described his own ordeals in trying to get help for his autistic son while being blamed for the boy's condition at almost every turn. In *A Child Called Noah* and *A Place for Noah*, novelist Josh Greenfield (1972, 1978) recounts the poignant, painful, and often bitter experiences of (his) autistic child's family. Most painful is the endless search for help and repeated disappointment of learning that nobody really knows how to help very much.

Schizophrenics Anonymous. For adult schizophrenics, there is a mutual aid organization similar to Alcoholics Anonymous, with chapters in many cities. In the absence of firm knowledge about etiology and treatment, such an organization may be of great help to people who might otherwise suffer more than necessary from loneliness, isolation, and despair. Literature can be obtained from Schizophrenics Anonymous, P. O. Box 913, Saskatoon, Saskatchewan, Canada.

CHAPTER 13

The Development of Aggressive and Delinquent Behavior

Most societies try to control harmful behavior and instill certain mores. The difficulty of doing so is a continuing source of conflict between parents and their children and between society and the individual. The developmental course of antisocial behavior is of concern for child rearing, education, and mental health services. As children reach adolescence, antisocial behavior increasingly becomes a matter for law enforcement agencies as well. Much of the research and theory on youthful antisocial behavior concerns juvenile delinquency as defined in legal terms. Legally defined delinquency is, however, a poor starting point for understanding aggression and rule-breaking behavior because it often starts long before legal sanctions are relevant. Furthermore, offenses that come to judicial attention represent only the tip of a very large iceberg of delinquent activity.

We will therefore begin with developmental aspects of antisocial and prosocial behavior. We will then consider behavior that comes to official attention in the form of legally defined juvenile delinquency. As we will see, the legal definitions of offenses will be of little help in understanding the development of delinquent behavior. Prevailing psychiatric diagnoses are likewise of questionable relevance to most of the behavior we will consider. DSM-III categorizes child and adolescent antisocial behavior into four types of *conduct disorders: (a) undersocialized aggressive; (b) undersocialized nonaggressive; (c) socialized aggressive;* and *(d) socialized nonaggressive.* The *undersocialized* types (*a* and *b*) are viewed as failing "to establish a normal degree of affection, empathy, or bond with others" (American Psychiatric Association, 1980, p. 45). The *socialized* types (*c* and *d*) show "social attachment toward others, but may be . . . callous or manipulative toward persons to whom they are not attached and lack guilt when these 'outsiders' are made to suffer'' (American Psychiatric Association, 1980, p. 45). The *aggressive* and *nonaggressive* types (*a* and *c* versus *b* and *d*) differ in the presence or absence of repetitive violence against others. Although these distinctions may reflect actual differences in behavioral patterns, it is not clear that they represent psychiatric disorders. The behavior may be quite normal for youngsters growing up in certain subcultures, for example.

THE DEVELOPMENT OF AGGRESSION

There is a wide range of views on the development of aggression. Freud, for example, once held that it is merely a response to the blocking of libido. Impressed by the violence of World War I, however, he added an aggressive drive to sex as a basic motive. Some analysts still view sex and aggression as the primary motives, but Freud's (1922) elaboration of the aggressive drive into a "death instinct" (*Thanatos*) that competes with the sex or life instinct (*Eros*) is not widely accepted.

At the opposite extreme, John B. Watson's restriction of innate motives to hunger, thirst, sex, and a few specific emotional responses left the explanation for aggression mainly to learning.

The Frustration-Aggression Hypothesis

John Dollard and his colleagues initiated some of the first research on the development of aggression (Dollard, Doob, Miller, Mowrer, & Sears, 1939). They accepted Freud's theory that aggressive impulses can be expressed in various substitute forms, but they rejected Freud's instinct concept. Instead, they hypothesized that aggression is a response to frustration. They defined *frustration* as the blocking of an ongoing goal-directed activity and *aggression* as behavior aimed at inflicting injury. They held that aggression is always a response to frustration— that is, frustration *always* leads to some form of aggression; conversely, *only* frustration instigates aggression. They agreed with Freud that any act of aggression releases energy *(catharsis)*, thereby reducing the strength of other aggressive impulses.

Dollard et al. argued that the frustration-aggression model explains many aspects of criminal behavior. For example, frustrations arise from low economic, educational, and vocational status, youth, minority group disadvantages, and lack of a stable marital relationship. These conditions also minimize fear of punishment because a person has little to lose through punishments like imprisonment. The frustration-aggression model thus seemed to offer a psychological integration of diverse findings.

Frustration is still widely viewed as a cause of aggression, and studies have demonstrated that children may become more aggressive after experimentally induced frustration (e.g., Mallick & McCandless, 1966). Some of these studies also assessed the effect of personality variables on the frustration-aggression relationship. Block and Martin (1955), for example, found that children rated as having weak ego controls indeed responded aggressively to frustration. Yet children rated as "overcontrollers" responded with constructive play. Fitting personality and other variables into the strict frustration-aggression model requires considerable redefinition of both frustration and aggression.

Another kind of problem with the strict frustration-aggression model is as follows: If someone deliberately tromps on my toe, my response may be aggressive, but does the toe-tromping block a goal-directed activity? Efforts to save the frustration-aggression model required elaborate explanations. Berkowitz (1962), for example, explained that the toe-tromping "interfered with the internal response oriented toward the preservation or attainment of security and comfort" (p. 30).

Other questions also arise: How can we *measure* frustration and the strength of anticipated punishment, for example? What individual differences exist in the threshold for frustration? Why is aggression a prepotent response? In at least some species, aggressive responses to noxious stimuli seem to be innate. After no previous rewards for aggression, many animals will attack innocent members of their own species when frustrated, for example (Ribes-Inesta, 1976).

Sears's Studies of Child Aggression. Robert Sears and his colleagues tested the frustration theory of aggressive development by computing correlations between behavioral, fantasy, and teacher ratings of aggression in preschoolers and measures of prior frustration, such as severity of feeding schedule (Sears, Whiting, Nowlis, & Sears, 1953). They found no nonchance relations between the measures of early frustration and later aggression. Nor were there any nonchance relations between aggression and current frustration (eating problems, sickness, danger, maternal demands for orderliness).

Questionnaire measures showed that aggressive 5-year-olds had mothers who permitted aggression but then severely punished it (Sears, Maccoby, & Levin, 1957). Following up the same children at age 12, Sears (1961) found that early maternal permissiveness for aggression predicted later aggression. But *low* punishment rather than severe punishment now correlated with antisocial aggression. Thus, if we can trust the measures of aggression, *low permissiveness* for aggression *inhibits* it throughout childhood. *High punishment encourages* aggression early but *inhibits* it *later*. In a Swedish study, Olweus (1980) likewise found that mothers' reports of their own punishment and permissiveness predicted peer-rated aggression in their sons.

Identification, Imitation, and Modeling. Freud held that children resolve their Oedipal conflicts by *identifying with the aggressor*. By imagining himself to *be* his father, for example, a boy vicariously wins his mother while avoiding his father's wrath. Identification with the aggressor explains the disappearance of Oedipal behavior, the emergence of conscience, and behavioral similarities between children and their same-sex parents. But psychoanalysts also view it as a defense mechanism throughout life (A. Freud, 1936).

From a learning theory perspective, Miller and Dollard (1941) depicted *imitation* as an instrumental response acquired through reinforcement. Seeing an older sibling rewarded for a behavior, a child who imitates the behavior is also apt to be rewarded, for example. This might reinforce not only the specific behavior, but imitation as a generalized response disposition.

In trying to reconcile psychoanalytic and learning theory, Miller and Dollard viewed identification as a persisting disposition or *learned drive* to imitate not only the behavior but the values and feelings of the model, who was usually a parent.

While the instrumental value of imitation may indeed lead to extrinsic reward as Dollard and Miller held, imitation may also have a biological basis. Meltzoff and Moore (1977), for example, showed that two-week old babies seem to imitate an adult's mouth movements long before imitation is likely to have earned extrinsic rewards.

Whatever its origin, imitation helps children acquire many behaviors. Albert Bandura (1977) experimentally demonstrated that children readily imitate the aggressive behavior of live and filmed models, although he prefers the term *modeling* for acquiring behavior by observing and replicating the behavior of another.

Bandura views "identification" as an instance of modeling. In comparing the attitudes and family backgrounds of antisocial aggressive adolescent boys and a control group of unaggressive boys, Bandura and Walters (1959) uncovered numerous differences with which they sought to explain aggressive boys' failure to identify with and internalize societal standards. Two major causes appeared to be (1) the fathers' general hostility toward their sons, and, (2) the mothers' rejection and discouragement of their sons' dependency needs.

Bandura and Walters also found that the aggressive boys' parents had often encouraged aggression and served as aggressive models in their attitudes and use of physical punishment and deprivation of privileges. Parents of the unaggressive boys, by contrast, used more reasoning and withdrawal of love, such as refusing to speak to the boy and ignoring him as punishment. From what could be gleaned about the boys' early development, aggression had long been a problem and had grown more serious because of the boys' increased size, physical maturity, and independence, rather than emerging for the first time in adolescence.

McCord, McCord, and Howard (1961) found nearly all the same differences as Bandura and Walters between aggressive and unaggressive boys living in a high delinquency area. Yet, they found that not only aggressive behavior, but all forms of deviance—including alcoholism, crime, psychosis, sexual promiscuity, and desertion—were more common among the aggressive boys' fathers. Parents of aggressive disturbed children have also been found to show more overt social problems and more deviant MMPI test scores than parents of unaggressive disturbed children (cf. Achenbach & Edelbrock, 1978).

Reinforcement of Aggression. Once aggression begins, what sustains it? Observational studies show abundant natural reinforcement for aggression. Socially active children starting nursery school, for example, progress from being victimized by more aggressive classmates, making counterattacks that are rewarded by the compliance of their victim, and then more freely initiating aggression (Patterson, Littman, & Bricker, 1967). The reactions of the victims help to teach active children which responses and victims to select. Socially inactive children, however, do not follow this escalating sequence. Experimental studies of preschoolers also show that modeling can instigate aggressive behavior but that the responses of the target are more important in sustaining it (Hayes, Rincover, & Volosin, 1980).

Observations of delinquents and the families of aggressive children reveal other reinforcers for aggression (Patterson & Cobb, 1971). Delinquents, for example, regale each other with tales of their misdeeds. Families of aggressive children, on the other hand, provide rich aversive stimulation that can be stopped temporarily by aggressive responses. However, excess aggression may reflect a developmental sequence whereby children and their families reciprocally escalate coercion. Gerald Patterson (1976) proposed that such a sequence begins with innate adaptive behaviors like screaming and kicking that enable babies to get help from their mothers. Most children then learn other skills for getting their needs met. Yet coercive behaviors may remain dominant if parents excessively reinforce them, fail to punish them properly, allow discomforts that are terminated by coercive behavior, or fail to teach prosocial skills. Figure 13-1 illustrates a sequence of interactions that Patterson ascribes to the families of aggressive children. Note that both the children and their parents help perpetuate this vicious circle.

If aggression, like other instrumental responses, is reinforced by its consequences, then it may also be subject to extinction or replacement by other rewarded responses. Several early studies showed that training constructive behavior could reduce aggression in young children, even after frustration (e.g., Brown & Elliot, 1965). On the other hand, the contrasting view held by Freud and Dollard et al. (1939) that freely expressed aggression reduces subsequent aggression has not been supported. Mallick and McCandless (1966), for example, found that children experimentally frustrated and allowed to play aggressively were not then less aggressive toward their frustrator than children not given the opportunity for "cathartic" aggression. Similarly, Kahn (1966) found that experimentally frustrated college students who engaged in cathartic expression of anger later expressed *more* dislike for their frustrator and *higher* physiological arousal than frustrated subjects given no opportunity for catharsis. The minimal support found for catharsis suggests that it operates in an extremely limited fashion, if at all (Baron, 1977).

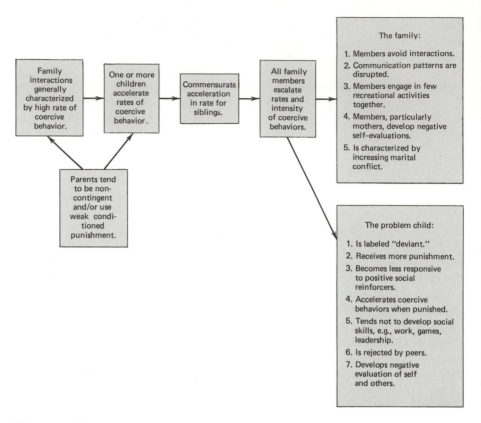

Figure 13.1. Sequence of aggressive development hypothesized by Patterson (1976, p. 287).

The Impact of Television

Since the 1950s, American children have averaged more time watching television than in almost any other activity. Much of what they see is violent and lawless (cf. Cater & Strickland, 1975). Does this affect their behavior?

Several kinds of evidence are relevant. Experimental studies in which children are exposed deliberately to various types of programs show that even brief exposure to violent episodes can increase subsequent aggressive play (e.g., Liebert & Baron, 1972). What happens in real life situations when children regularly watch violent programs by choice? A 10-year follow-up study showed that preference for watching violent television at age 8 was a significant predictor of boys' aggression at ages 18 and 19, according to peer ratings, self-ratings, and MMPI scores (Eron, 1980). Although other early characteristics of the boys and their families also predicted later aggression, preference for violent television remained a significant predictor even after these other variables were partialled out statistically. Yet early preference for violent television did not predict later aggression by girls, perhaps because of the paucity of aggressive female role models on television during the 1960s when the subjects were growing up.

The experimental studies show that violent television *can* instigate aggression, and Eron's (1980) follow-up shows that preference for violent television *predicts* long-term aggression in boys. A thorough study of 1565 English boys, however, pinpointed relations between specific types of television violence and specific types of real life aggression (Belson, 1978). Using intensive interviews with the boys and their mothers and elaborate statistical analyses to rule out alternative explanations, Belson showed that watching a lot of violent television produced serious aggression, especially of an unskilled, unplanned type easily imitated from television. The most potent television stimuli included violence in the context of close personal relations, violence extraneous to a program's plot, realistic violence, violence presented as being in a good cause, and violent Westerns. Because the aggressive boys were no more consciously preoccupied with violence than control boys, and because their aggression was largely unplanned and unskilled, it seemed that violent television broke down inhibitions against violence rather than instilling a fixation on it. It is thus apparent that television violence can be an important factor in the development of aggression, at least by boys.

Cognitive-Behavioral Factors

As pointed out earlier, cognitive and behavioral approaches are increasingly being combined. Research on social cognition in particular may offer insights into relations between cognitive functioning and overt problem behaviors such as aggression.

As an example, Dodge (1980) compared aggressive and unaggressive grade school boys' responses to hostile, benign, and ambiguous cues about another boy's intentions. Dodge hypothesized that aggressive boys fail to respond differentially to hostile versus benign cues. Contrary to his hypothesis, however, he found that aggressive boys discriminated as well as unaggressive boys between hostile and benign cues. In fact, when cues from another boy were benign, the aggressive boys were even more helpful than the unaggressive boys. Yet when the cues were *ambiguous,* the aggressive boys responded much more aggressively than the unaggressive boys. Thus, the aggressive boys did not misinterpret nor respond inappropriately to clearcut cues, but when they lacked clear cues, they ascribed hostile motives to others. (Among *severely disturbed* boys, however, the aggressive ones have been found to exaggerate the hostility of even unambiguous cues [Nasby, Hayden, & DePaulo, 1980]).

Dodge also found that all the boys ascribed more hostile intentions to aggressive than unaggressive peers when cues were ambiguous and that this tendency increased with age. Under ambiguous circumstances then, not only do aggressive boys exaggerate other boys' hostility, but other boys' exaggerate the hostility of boys they view as aggressive. This implies an increasingly vicious circle: Aggressive boys' react with hostility to ambiguous cues from others; others, in turn, react with hostility to ambiguous cues from boys they view as aggressive.

Developmental Stability of Aggression

Several studies show developmental *stability* in aggression, especially among boys (Olweus, 1979). In the Fels Institute longitudinal study, for example, Kagan and Moss (1962) found significant correlations between ratings of aggression at several points in childhood, such as a correlation of .51 between aggression toward peers at ages 3 to 6 and 10 to 14. Some prominent sex differences were evident, however. "Behavioral disorganization" (violent crying, tantrums, uncontrolled destructive activity) at ages 3 to 6 and 10 to 14 correlated .52 for boys, but only −.03 for girls, for example.

Kagan and Moss ascribed the generally poor correlations between early and later aggression in girls to cultural pressures against female aggression. Conversely, significant correlations were found between child and adult *dependency* scores in females but not males. This suggested that cultural pressures censure males for dependency, just as they censure females for direct aggression. Women were also found to be more conflicted about recognizing and showing direct aggression, whereas men were more conflicted about dependency, thus supporting cultural interpretations of the discontinuity between child and adult aggression in females and dependency in males. However, Kagan and Moss acknowledged that constitutional differences could interact with culture to shape the sex differences in aggression and dependency.

Cultural changes may have since made female aggression more stable as reflected in a correlation of .47 between peer ratings of girls' aggression at ages 8 and 19, compared to .38 for boys growing up 30 years after Kagan and Moss's subjects (Eron, 1980). Despite the greater stability of aggression in these girls, however, Figure 13-2 shows that they were rated considerably less aggressive than boys at both ages. Although older studies also showed less overt aggression by girls than boys, this sex difference seems to be decreasing, especially when the provocation to aggression is strong (Baron, 1977). Female crime rates are likewise increasing in many countries (Adler, 1977).

Feshbach (1970) proposed that greater physical aggression by males than females may be partially explained in the same way as positive correlations between muscularity and aggression in boys: Greater muscularity is apt to make physical aggression more successful in achieving the child's goals, thereby reinforcing aggression as an instrumental behavior. Yet, temperamental characteristics correlated with muscularity may also enhance aggressive tendencies (Cortes & Gatti, 1972), and testosterone levels have been found correlated with self-reported

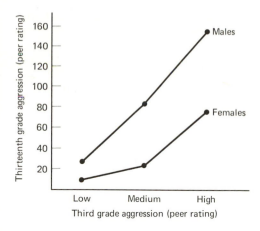

Figure 13.2. Consistency of peer-rated aggression from 3rd grade through age 19 ("13th grade"). (From Eron, p. 245.)

aggression in male adolescents, independent of muscularity (Olweus, Mattson, Schalling, & Löw, 1980). Cultural factors probably contribute to sex differences in aggression, but biological differences between the sexes may lead to differential acculturation (Maccoby & Jacklin, 1980).

PATTERNING AND PREVALENCE OF AGGRESSIVE
AND DELINQUENT BEHAVIOR

How common are aggressive and delinquent behaviors? Most children show at least some of these behaviors at some time in their lives. When serious, they often prompt referral to mental health services. Factor analyses of children's behavioral problems have repeatedly revealed a syndrome comprising aggressive, defiant behaviors and a syndrome comprising delinquent behaviors, such as lying and stealing (Quay, 1979). The composition of these syndromes varies somewhat with age and sex, but Table 13-1 shows behaviors occurring in aggressive and delinquent syndromes found in separate factor analyses of disturbed children of each sex at ages 4 to 5, 6 to 11, and 12 to 16 (Achenbach & Edelbrock, 1982).

Because children showing the delinquent behaviors often have delinquent friends, some authors call the delinquent syndrome "socialized aggressive" or "socialized delinquent," and call the aggressive syndrome "unsocialized aggressive" (Quay, 1979). The question of whether one syndrome reflects more socialization than the other, however, raises issues of causation to be considered later.

Despite the fairly consistent patterning of aggressive and delinquent behaviors, there are age and sex differences in the prevalence of specific behaviors. Figure 13-3 shows the percent of normal and disturbed children whose parents reported certain overtly aggressive behaviors. Most of the behaviors were reported more for

Table 13-1   Behaviors Found in Aggressive and Delinquent Syndromes at Ages 4 to 16

Aggressive Syndrome[a]	*Delinquent Syndrome[b]*
Argues a lot	Hangs around children who get in trouble
Cruelty, bullying, or meanness to others	
Demands a lot of attention	Lying or cheating
Disobedient at home	Runs away from home
Easily jealous	Steals at home
Gets in many fights	Steals outside the home
Physically attacks people	Swearing or obscene language
Screams a lot	
Stubborn, sullen, or irritable	
Sudden changes in mood or feelings	
Teases a lot	
Temper tantrums or hot temper	
Threatens people	
Unusually loud	

[a]Items occurring together in at least five out of six factor analyses of disturbed children of each sex aged 4 to 5, 6 to 11, and 12 to 16.
[b]Items occurring together in at least four out of five factor analyses for boys aged 4 to 5 and both sexes aged 6 to 11 and 12 to 16. (Syndrome not found for girls aged 4 to 5.)
Source: Achenbach & Edelbrock, 1982.

younger than older children. Among children referred for mental health services, the aggressive behaviors were generally reported more for boys than girls, but the differences between nonreferred boys and girls were small (Achenbach & Edelbrock, 1981). This does not necessarily contradict studies reporting more aggressive behavior among boys than girls, because such studies typically sum various aggressive behaviors and fail to separate referred from nonreferred children.

The delinquent behaviors graphed in Figure 13-4 show different patterns, with more increases with age, especially among girls referred for mental health services. Other delinquent behaviors, such as truancy and alcohol or drug use, show even more striking trends of this sort. They rise from negligible levels in early childhood to approximately 60 percent for referred girls and 40 percent for referred boys at age 16 (Achenbach & Edelbrock, 1981).

Although nearly all children show some aggressive and delinquent behaviors at some time, we are concerned mainly with those whose behavior is so deviant as to impede their adaptive development. Some of these children are referred to mental health services, some to juvenile courts, and some to both. To understand these children, we must view their aggressive and delinquent behavior in relation to their other behavior and their social context. Because aggressive and delinquent behavior

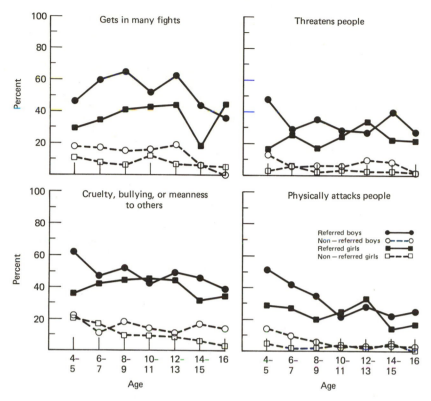

Figure 13.3. Percent of normal and clinically referred children whose parents report particular aggressive behaviors. (From Achenbach & Edelbrock, 1981.)

problems are usually so threatening, adults may ignore a child's problems in other areas and the environmental pressures the child faces. The behavior profiles of adolescent boys having many of the aggressive behaviors listed in Table 13-1, for example, show a subgroup who have numerous immature and hyperactive behaviors. Another aggressive subgroup lacks the immature and hyperactive behaviors but is very uncommunicative (Edelbrock & Achenbach, 1980). On the basis of their aggression, both subgroups might be lumped together as "acting out aggressives." Yet their overall behavior profiles are quite different. The causes of their problems, needs for help, and outcomes may also differ. As we consider aggressive and antisocial behavior, we will therefore look beyond specific acts to find out how youngsters' other characteristics may clarify etiologies, needs, and outcomes.

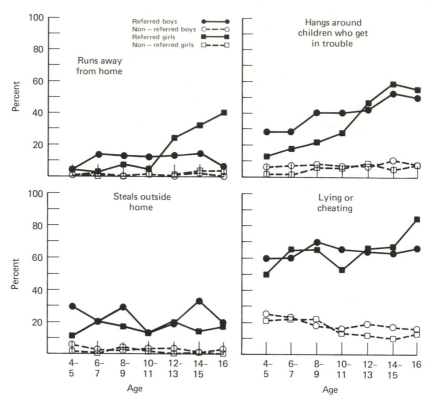

Figure 13.4. Percent of normal and clinically referred children whose parents report particular delinquent behaviors. See Fig 13.3 for key. (From Achenbach & Edelbrock, 1981.)

MORAL AND PROSOCIAL DEVELOPMENT

To understand hurtful behavior, we also need to understand its flip side: Why does helpful behavior occur? Perhaps the *failure* to develop prosocial behavior explains the persistence of antisocial behavior in some children.

Both the psychoanalytic and stimulus-response approaches to development stress children's internalization of behavioral norms from other people, especially their parents. According to psychoanalytic theory, the superego is formed largely through identification with the same-sex parent at the end of the Oedipal period. According to stimulus-response views, the child internalizes social values via reinforcement, punishment, and modeling. Both approaches assume that guilt feelings increasingly help to control behavior.

Early studies revealed little relationship between moral knowledge and ethical behaviors in various situations (Hartshorne & May, 1928–30). Later studies and reanalyses of the early data showed somewhat better consistency in honesty, but situational factors still had a big impact on children's resistance to temptation (e.g., Nelson, Grinder, & Mutterer, 1969).

The study of moral and prosocial behavior in terms of traits expected to remain constant across situations has largely given way to two other approaches: One is the developmental study of *moral reasoning;* the other is the developmental study of *prosocial behavior.*

Development of Moral Reasoning

Piaget's Approach. Jean Piaget (1932) initiated the developmental study of moral reasoning by questioning children to uncover their concepts of justice, punishment, moral dilemmas, and the rules of games. From their answers, he inferred a series of stages corresponding roughly to the stages of cognitive development. The stages mainly reflect a progression in children's grasp of justice and the rules of social order.

At first, children view rules as absolute and unalterable. They view acts as either totally right or wrong and judge the wrongness of an act by the severity of its consequences. In one vignette, for example, Piaget asked, "Who was naughtier? A boy who accidentally broke 15 cups while obeying his mother, or a boy who broke one cup while sneaking some jam?" Children below the age of 8 replied that the boy who broke 15 cups was naughtier, because he did more damage.

Children younger than 8 also seemed to believe in *immanent justice;* that is, punishment or bad luck automatically befalls wrongdoers. Piaget concluded that young children do not distinguish justice from rules that are laid down by adults. Likewise, they believe that unvarying punishment for disobedience is the essence of justice.

By the age of 11 or 12, however, Piaget's subjects began to show more relativistic concepts of rules and justice. Rules were viewed as depending on functional goals and mutual agreements among people; justice was viewed as depending on the intentions of the wrongdoer, the wrongdoer's restitutions to victims, and other mitigating factors.

According to Piaget, the developmental trends in children's moral reasoning reflected decreasingly egocentric and increasingly abstract, logical thought. He concluded that social interaction also stimulates the development of moral reasoning, because it challenges children to see things from others' viewpoints.

To Piaget, moral reasoning was merely one facet of general cognitive structures. But he paved the way for later research on moral development. Some of this research has shown that young children can use more subtle moral reasoning than Piaget thought, at least if the stimulus situations are unambiguous enough (Karniol, 1978). Nevertheless, Piaget's formulation of moral development in terms of *stages* of reasoning and judgment left an indelible mark on subsequent work.

Kohlberg's Approach. Lawrence Kohlberg (1978) has been the most influential proponent of the cognitive-developmental approach pioneered by Piaget. Hypothesizing six stages of moral development, Kohlberg devised rules for scoring responses to moral dilemmas according to these stages. Table 13-2 summarizes the six stages. Kohlberg stresses that the stages represent differing levels of maturity in moral judgment, rather than differing conclusions as to whether a particular act is right or wrong.

Because the different stages do not necessarily dictate different conclusions about particular acts, it is not clear how scores for responses to Kohlberg's vignettes should relate to other behavior. In fact, Kohlberg scores have not been found closely related to specific behaviors, such as resistance to cheating, among normal children. Yet several studies have shown that certain types of delinquents obtain lower scores than other youngsters of similar cognitive and socioeconomic level (Blasi, 1980). Does this mean that retarded development of moral reasoning *causes* these types of delinquency? We cannot be certain from the correlational evidence available. It may be equally plausible that, once youngsters are cast in certain delinquent roles, their conformity to these roles shapes the judgments they express. There will be more on these questions when we compare different delinquent syndromes.

Development of Prosocial Behavior

Research on moral reasoning has focused mainly on rules and prohibitions. Prosocial behavior, by contrast, often consists of active efforts to help others at one's own expense. How does such behavior come about?

One hypothesis is that altruism is a genetically determined tendency resulting from evolutionary selection for behaviors that help the species to survive (Hoffman, 1978). According to this view, humans are biologically programmed not only to promote their own survival but to help members of their species. Others hypothesize that social learning is the main source of concern for others (Yarrow, Scott, & Waxler, 1973). Like their ethical behavior, however, children's prosocial behavior is not very consistent from one situation to another (Payne, 1980).

Direct observation of children has revealed a good deal of spontaneous helping, sharing, and comforting during the preschool years (Eisenberg-Berg & Neal, 1979). Some sharing is evident as early as 18 months (Rheingold, Hay, & West, 1976). When asked about their spontaneous prosocial acts, preschoolers justified them mainly by citing others' needs and practical, nonmoral reasons (Eisenberg-Berg & Hand, 1979). The children said little about the issues of punishment, hedonism, and rules that pervade Kohlberg's theory of early moral judgment. Children who shared a lot, however, did show altruistic reasoning in response to moral dilemmas that posed altruistic versus hedonistic alternatives. Whatever their origin, prosocial tendencies thus seem to emerge early in at least some children. Why antisocial behavior nevertheless dominates in others is a key question that will concern us in the following sections.

Table 13-2   Kohlberg's Definitions of Moral Stages

I. *Preconventional Level*

The child is responsive to cultural rules and labels of good and bad, right or wrong, but interprets these labels either in terms of physical or hedonistic consequences of action (punishment, reward, exchange of favors), or in terms of the physical power of those who enunciate the rules and labels.

Stage 1. The punishment-obedience orientation. The physical consequences of action determine its goodness or badness regardless of the human meaning or value of these consequences. Avoidance of punishment and unquestioning deference to power are valued in their own right, not in terms of respect for an underlying moral order supported by punishment and authority.

Stage 2: The instrumental-relativistic orientation. Right action consists of that which instrumentally satisfies one's own needs and occasionally the needs of others. Reciprocity is a matter of "you scratch my back and I'll scratch yours," not of loyalty, gratitude, or justice.

II. *Conventional level*

Maintaining the expectations of the individual's family, group, or nation is perceived as valuable in its own right, regardless of immediate and obvious consequences. The attitude is not only one of conformity to personal expectations and social order; but of loyalty to it; of actively maintaining, supporting, and justifying the order; and of identifying with persons or groups involved in it.

Stage 3: The interpersonal concordance or "good boy/nice girl" orientation. Good behavior is that which pleases or helps others and is approved by them. There is much conformity to stereotypical images or what is majority or "natural" behavior. Behavior is frequently judged by attention—"he means well" becomes important for the first time. One earns approval by being "nice."

Stage 4: The "law and order" orientation. There is orientation toward authority, fixed rules, and the maintenance of the social order. Right behavior consists of doing one's duty, showing respect for authority, and maintaining the given social order for its own sake.

III. *Postconventional, autonomous, or principled level*

There is a clear effort to define moral values and principles that have validity and application apart from the authority of the groups or persons holding these principles and apart from the individual's own identification with these groups.

Stage 5: The social-contract legalistic orientation. Right action tends to be defined in terms of general individual rights, and standards which have been critically examined and agreed upon by the whole society. There is a clear awareness of the relativism of personal values and opinions and a corresponding emphasis upon procedural rules for reaching consensus. Aside from what is constitutionally and democratically agreed upon, the right is a matter of personal "values" and "opinion." The result is an emphasis upon the "legal point of view," but with an emphasis upon the possibility of changing law in terms of rational considerations of social utility. Outside the legal realm, free agreement and contract is the binding element of obligation. This is the "official" morality of the American government and constitution.

Stage 6: The universal-ethical-principle orientation. Right is defined by the decision of conscience in accord with self-chosen ethical principles appealing to logical

Table 13-2   *(Cont.)*

comprehensiveness, universality, and consistency. These principles are abstract and ethical (the Golden Rule, the categorical imperative); they are not concrete moral rules like the Ten Commandments. At heart, these are universal principles of justice, of the reciprocity and quality of human rights, and of respect for the dignity of human beings as individual persons.

Source: Adapted from Kohlberg (1978), pp. 209–10.

JUVENILE DELINQUENCY

Our discussion so far has centered on antisocial and prosocial behavior in general rather than on the subset of children who happen to get to juvenile court. The findings may therefore fail to reflect factors that distinguish between the minority of youngsters who commit significant crimes and the majority who do not.

Arrests of Juveniles

Children officially judged *(adjudicated)* delinquent represent the small tip of a large iceberg. Even the tip of the iceberg is obscured by inconsistent reporting practices and inconsistent reasons for adjudication, such as the seriousness of the crime versus need for court supervision because of parental neglect.

According to the U.S. Department of Justice (1979), juveniles under 18 are arrested for about 28 percent of the major offenses comprising the FBI's Crime Index. (The major crimes are murder, manslaughter, forcible rape, robbery, aggravated assault, burglary, larceny, and auto theft.) Offenses cleared by arrests of juveniles range from about 5 percent of murders to about 34 percent of burglaries. Many juveniles are also arrested for offenses peculiar to their age group, such as truancy and violation of statutes pertaining to "delinquent tendencies." (Offenses such as truancy that are illegal only at particular ages are called *status offenses.)* For all offenses, over 2 million juveniles are arrested per year. Youngsters aged 16 to 18 show higher arrest rates than any other age group in the population, although 13- to 15-year-olds also rank above most other age groups.

Juvenile Courts

Origins. Until the nineteenth century, most juvenile lawbreakers were treated like adult offenders. During the nineteenth century, many states established reform schools for delinquent youth. These schools became little more than prisons where hard work and rigid discipline were expected to reform the inmates. In 1899, however, Illinois passed a law requiring delinquents to be treated like neglected or dependent children. The law also established a juvenile court in Chicago, the first in the country. The juvenile court was to provide protection and treatment for children who were neglected, dependent on public support, or delinquent.

To reduce the stigma associated with courts, juvenile court proceedings were to be informal and oriented toward investigation, diagnosis, and treatment rather than punishment. The term *petition* was substituted for *complaint, hearing* for *arraignment, adjudication of involvement in delinquency* for *conviction,* and *disposition* for *sentencing.* Judges were given broad discretionary powers to apply laws according to individual circumstances and to work out the best possible arrangements for preventing further misdeeds. An explicitly clinical approach was initiated in 1909, when the Chicago Juvenile Court established the Psychopathic Laboratory to do evaluations of delinquents.

Current Status. Special courts for juveniles eventually spread to all parts of the country. They vary greatly in facilities, procedures, and maximum age limits, however. Most juvenile court records are not supposed to constitute criminal records and are to be destroyed once the child passes the age of the juvenile court's jurisdiction, which is typically 16 to 18 years. There has recently been a strong movement to give juveniles the rights of legal counsel and to apply the standards for evidence and testimony that prevail in adult courts, although most juvenile courts retain informal, discretionary procedures.

Surveys of juvenile courts have revealed that most do not function as intended: they are understaffed, lack psychiatric and psychological services, and have few dispositional options such as foster homes, group homes, and work programs (cf. Gibbons, 1970). The President's Task Force on Juvenile Delinquency (1967) reported that the average probation officer supervised between 71 and 80 cases, plus prehearing case studies that take at least half their time. Juvenile court judges averaged only 10 to 15 minutes on each case.

While it is a truism (perhaps in all societies at all times) that delinquency is getting worse, studies of court statistics show some marked variations in rate. For example, after rises during World War II, there was a marked *drop* in delinquency between 1947 and 1950, although it increased sharply thereafter (U.S. Children's Bureau, 1972; Vedder, 1979). The statistics indicate that about 20 percent of American children are referred to a juvenile court at some time in their lives. As measured by court referrals, delinquency rates have increased steadily since the 1950s in other industrial countries as well.

Analyses of delinquency among various ethnic groups in Chicago have shown that rates tend to be highest among the children of the most recent immigrant group: Germans and Irish in the first decades of this century, followed by Polish, Italian, black, and Spanish-speaking immigrants to the city (Shaw & McKay, 1969).

Looking back further in our history, Tunley (1962) relates accounts of eighteenth- and nineteenth-century delinquency that sound familiar today. In the mid-nineteenth century, however, the youth gangs roaming New York were composed of English, Irish, and German immigrant children, and bore such names as *Plug Uglies, Roach Guards, Slaughter Housers, Dead Rabbits,* and *Forty Thieves.* Contrast these with the more genteel *Young Lords, Viceroys,* and *Crusaders* of today.

Hidden Delinquency

There is no doubt that official statistics underestimate the crime committed by juveniles. A longitudinal study in a high delinquency area, for example, showed that only 40 out of 101 fairly serious delinquents were ever arrested (Murphy, Shirley, & Witmer, 1946). Moreover, out of 616 serious crimes, only 68 (11 percent) were prosecuted and out of 4400 minor offenses, only 27 (0.6 percent) were prosecuted.

Anonymous questionnaire surveys of adolescents also show many illegal acts among those who are not adjudicated delinquent. Table 13-3, for example, presents the responses of high school students in a large Midwestern city (Cernkovich & Giordano, 1979).

DIFFERENCES AMONG DELINQUENTS

It is all too easy to stereotype *The Delinquent:* gang violence, sexual licentiousness, vandalism, mugging, clever burglaries, poor school work, truancy, a bad home in the slums, hate for the police and society at large, alienation, drug addiction, etc. It is also easy to supplement the stereotype with stereotyped explanations for delinquency and the treatment needed. Depending on one's predilections, the assumed causes and treatment might range from moral, genetic, or cultural inferiority treatable only by get-tough policies such as the death penalty or imprisonment, at one extreme, to poverty or discrimination treatable with more boys' clubs, social workers, and jobs at the other extreme.

Those who study delinquency have sometimes cloaked stereotypes in theoretical concepts such as *anomie* (normlessness), gang culture, crime from a sense of guilt, and superego lacunae. However relevant these concepts may be to *some* delinquents, they have not been shown to match many children whose behavior actually is delinquent. To help us resist stereotypes, we will start with research on the actual characteristics of delinquents.

Behavioral Patterns

One approach to identifying patterns of delinquency is to look for statistical associations among characteristics. As an example, a factor analysis of ratings of the behaviors of institutionalized delinquent boys revealed three patterns (Quay, 1964). One, called *socialized-subcultural delinquency,* included the following

Table 13-3 High School Students' Self-Reported Delinquencies

Delinquent Act	Percent Reporting Act		Delinquent Act	Percent Reporting Act	
	Male	Female		Male	Female
1. Drive car without permission	42	25	14. DWI-liquor[a]	38	22
2. Skip school	82	81	15. DWI-marijuana[a]	40	22
3. Run away from home	16	16	16. Burglary-occupied	10	2
4. School probation/suspension/expulsion	32	27	17. Sell hard drugs	12	10
5. Use weapon to attack someone	12	7	18. Robbery	5	1
6. Sex with opposite sex	78	62	19. Theft (over $50)	13	5
7. Gang fight	39	15	20. Property destruction of over $10	20	6
8. Drink alcohol	83	73	21. Burglary-unoccupied	17	4
9. Smoke marijuana	67	59	22. DWI-hard drugs[a]	12	7
10. Theft ($2–$50)	34	26	23. Extortion	14	8
11. Use hard drugs	15	19	24. Theft of car parts	20	3
12. Sell marijuana	35	20	25. Sex for money	5	1
13. Car theft	6	1	26. Carry weapon	34	17

Source: Adapted from Cernkovich & Giordano (1979), pp. 136–137.
[a]Driving while intoxicated.

characteristics: Accepted by delinquent subgroup, bad companions, engages in gang activities, stays out late at night, and strong allegiance to selected peers. A second pattern, called *unsocialized-psychopathic delinquency,* included: Irritable, verbally aggressive, assaultive, feels persecuted and that others are unfair, defies authority, quarrelsome, and unable to profit by praise or punishment. A third pattern, called *disturbed-neurotic delinquency,* included: Sensitive, worries, timid, shy, and has anxiety over own behavior.

Personality Patterns

Factor analyses of delinquents' questionnaire responses have also yielded patterns like those that Quay found in behavior ratings (Peterson, Quay, & Tiffany, 1961). Items representing the socialized-subcultural pattern included:

> When I was going to school, I played hooky quite often. In school I was sometimes sent to the principal for cutting-up. My folks usually blame bad company for the trouble I get into. When I was a little kid, I was always doing things my folks told me not to. (p. 362)

Items representing the unsocialized-psychopathic pattern were:

> The only way to make big money is to steal it. It's dumb to trust older people. A lot of times it's fun to be in jail. The only way to settle anything is to lick the guy. I go out of my way to meet trouble rather than try to escape it. I would have been more successful if people had given me a fair chance. I'm really too tough a guy to get along with most kids. A person is better off if he doesn't trust anyone. I hardly ever get excited or thrilled. (p. 361)

Items representing the neurotic-disturbed pattern were:

> I don't think I'm quite as happy as others seem to be. I just don't seem to get the breaks other people do. It seems as if people are always telling me what to do, or how to do things. I often feel as though I have done something wrong or wicked. It is hard for me to act natural when I am with new people. I seem to do things that I regret more often than other people do. People often talk about me behind my back. I get nervous when I have to ask someone for a job. It seems as if I've been caught in every lie I ever told. (p. 361)

Factor analysis of responses by a broad range of junior high school students has yielded similar patterns, indicating that they are not confined to delinquents, although delinquents show them in more extreme form (Quay & Quay, 1965).

Correlates of the Behavioral and Personality Patterns

Do delinquents showing the different patterns differ in other ways? Several studies have shown that *socialized-subcultural* delinquents have lower IQs, lower socioeconomic status (SES), less overt parental rejection, less adequate father figures, better relations with their mothers, and less deviant MMPI profiles than solitary delinquents (e.g., Brigham, Ricketts, & Johnson, 1967; Jenkins & Boyer, 1968). Studies comparing disturbed-neurotic delinquents and unsocialized-psychopathic delinquents have shown differences between them in MMPI profiles (Shinohara & Jenkins, 1967), in parental attitudes and family interactions (Hetherington, Stouwie, & Ridberg, 1971), and in cheating (Lueger, 1980).

It appears that socialized-subcultural delinquents are relatively normal people who happen to live in an environment that encourages delinquent rather than nondelinquent values and ways of having fun. Unsocialized-psychopathic delinquents, by contrast, may be more abnormal people who do not have good social relations even with delinquent peers and who actively seek trouble rather than adjusting to the environment. After release from reform school, they are more often convicted and incarcerated again than socialized delinquents are (Henn, Bardwell, & Jenkins, 1980). The third pattern, disturbed-neurotic delinquency, has been less studied and may reflect personality and/or organic problems accompanied by high anxiety.

This typology should be taken with a grain of salt, because some offenders manifest aspects of all three patterns. Individual and environmental factors may also interact to produce a particular combination of patterns. A disturbed child living in a high crime neighborhood, for example, might become delinquent, whereas the same child would not in another environment. The strength of cultural factors is illustrated by the extremes of the traditional Eskimo culture, where there is reputedly no delinquency at all, and the Mafia subculture of Sicily, where boys are expected to join in family crime (Cavan & Cavan, 1968).

Beside the three types of male delinquents, female delinquents will be considered together as a group. They may show patterns like males (Hetherington et al., 1971), but there has been less research on female delinquency, perhaps because girls are arrested for less threatening offenses and fewer are brought to court.

There is evidence that a syndrome characterized mainly by drug use has also emerged among delinquents (Stein, Sarbin, & Kulik, 1971), but drug abuse cuts across so many aspects of problem behavior that it will be discussed separately in Chapter 14.

SOCIALIZED-SUBCULTURAL DELINQUENCY

The first cash register I ever rang was in a drugstore on Broadway. There was one man at a long counter. Butch had picked this spot out for me because it was so easy and I hadn't done it before. Butch told me to wait until he did something to make the man come down to the far end of the counter. I watched Butch from inside the telephone booth. He walked up the aisle until he got to the candy display, then he stumbled forward, knocking over the candy and chewing gum display. The man came running out from behind the counter. As he came out, I came out of the telephone booth, went behind the counter, and within a matter of seconds was at the other end of the aisle helping Butch and the counterman pick up the stuff. Butch would pick it up and drop it again until he saw me coming. After we had picked up everything, the man thanked us and went back to his duties, and I walked out with his money. (Brown, 1965, p. 31)

. . . the shoplifting experiences were alluring, exciting, and thrilling. . . . I was in the grip of the bunch and led on by the enticing pleasure which we had together. There was no way out. The feeling of guilt which I had could not overbalance the strong appeal of my chums and shoplifting. At first I did not steal for gain nor out of necessity for food. I stole because it was the most fascinating thing I could do. It was a way to pass the time, for I think I had a keener adventurous spirit than the other boys of my age, sort of more mentally alert. I didn't want to play tame games nor be confined in a schoolroom. I wanted something more exciting. I liked the dare-devil spirit. I would walk down between the third rails on the elevated lines in the same daring spirit that I stole. It gave me a thrill and thrilled my chums in turn. We were all alike, daring and glad to take a chance. (Shaw, 1930, p. 7)

Many high delinquency areas in the United States are slum neighborhoods populated by recent immigrants. Poverty, large families, immigrant parents, crime and other social problems in the family, low IQs, poor school work, and youth gangs are often found in high delinquency areas. Impulsivity, frustration, lack of orientation toward the future, *anomie* (normlessness), and failure to internalize societal standards have been invoked as psychological causes of delinquency in these environments.

Despite the abundance of potential causes, we must distinguish between factors that would make life hard for any child and those that lead to delinquency. Is delinquency specifically *caused* by the hardships of parental inadequacy, poverty, and large families?

Sociological Views

Since most studies of high delinquency areas in the United States concern minority or recent immigrant groups, let's turn for a moment to a study done in England, when most high delinquency groups were neither recent immigrants nor ethnic minorities.

In this study, McDonald (1969) began by asking whether SES differences were as great when delinquency was measured with anonymous questionnaires filled out by adolescents in school as when measured by police and court statistics. He found that more lower SES boys did admit to delinquency and that they admitted to many more delinquent acts than middle SES boys, especially delinquencies involving damage and violence. A study in Germany also showed that lower SES boys admit more delinquencies than their middle SES peers (Remschmidt, Hohner, Merschmann, & Walter, 1977). Similar SES differences are evident in American parents' reports not only of delinquencies but other behavioral problems as well (Achenbach & Edelbrock, 1981).

Across social classes, McDonald found no significant associations between delinquency and several factors assumed to affect delinquency, including broken homes, working mothers, number of siblings, part-time jobs, youth club membership, religion, or church attendance. Thus, while these factors may have differentiated delinquents from nondelinquents *within* SES, they were unlikely to have affected the etiology of delinquency as much as SES did. Something about SES per se seems to affect the risk of delinquency regardless of the other factors. Furthermore, lower SES youngsters seem to view delinquency more favorably than upper SES youngsters. It has been found, for example, that lower SES youngsters popular with their peers had high delinquency rates, whereas the opposite was true of upper SES youngsters (Roff, Sells, & Golden, 1972).

Sociological Theories. McDonald viewed his findings as consistent with two different sociological theories of subcultural delinquency:

1. The *anomie theory*, first proposed by the nineteenth-century French sociologist Emile Durkheim and applied to American society by Robert Merton (1957). This theory holds that lower-class people share the same basic values and material goals as middle-class people . However, when blocked from attaining these goals by legitimate means such as education, they abandon the prescribed social norms for behavior and try to achieve their goals by delinquent means. "Anomie" refers to the state of lawlessness or normlessness characterizing such people. Merton maintained that anomie is an especially critical factor in American society because the goals of material acquisition are held out to everyone in greater measure than in most countries.

2. The *lower-class culture theory* (Miller, 1958) holds that different values and norms are inculcated in lower-class children than in middle-class children. Lack of reward for obeying rules and delaying gratification, less moral training, and high esteem for "toughness" combine to create delinquent rather than nondelinquent norms for behavior.

Merton's version of the anomie theory and Miller's version of the lower-class culture theory represent rather extreme positions. They blame lower-class delinquency exclusively on either normlessness or the delinquent nature of lower-class culture. Yet many other sociological views of delinquency are derived from these positions. For example, in their influential book, *Delinquency and Opportunity,* Cloward and Ohlin (1960) inferred from anomie theory that delinquent subcultures develop as substitutes for the dominant culture which lower class youth reject when they find their access to legitimate means blocked.

According to Cloward and Ohlin, one type of delinquent subculture is the *criminal subculture* organized around stealing and other crime for profit, often in liaison with adult criminals. Members of a criminal subculture pursue the material goals of the larger society—but by illegal means. A second type is the *conflict subculture*, characterized by a quest for status through violence. Cloward and Ohlin hypothesized that the conflict subculture is most common in neighborhoods that are too unstable to support the close social bonds needed for organized crime. Violence is therefore a result of being frustrated in the pursuit of both conventional *and* criminal opportunities for material gain. A third type, the *retreatist subculture*, centered in drug abuse, is hypothesized to be a response to failure either to move on to successful adult crime or to adopt other adult roles once the conflict group activities lose their appeal during late adolescence.

To assess Cloward and Ohlin's anomie-based theory of specialized delinquent subcultures, Short, Tennyson, and Howard (1963) tried to find gangs in Chicago that exemplified each subculture. In over a year of searching, they found no group typifying the criminal subculture and only one group resembling a retreatist subculture, but conflict-oriented gangs were abundant. Workers who infiltrated the gangs were able to get data on 598 members of 16 gangs, although gang structures and definitions of membership were found to be extremely fluid.

Through acquaintance with gang members, the workers could rate each member's participation in certain activities, such as hanging around the street corner, drinking, joy riding, gang fighting, theft, truancy, vandalism, narcotics, and rape. Reliability checks on reports by pairs of workers who infiltrated the same gangs and checks against police records showed consistency in the ratings of each youth.

Factor analysis of the ratings revealed that conflict items defined the primary dimension of behavior, especially individual fighting, group fighting, carrying concealed weapons, and assault. But most other delinquent activities correlated with this dimension as well. The second most prominent dimension encompassed sports, social activities, joy riding, truancy, and hanging around on the corner.

Among the Chicago gangs, there was thus little evidence for the delinquent subcultural specialization hypothesized by Cloward and Ohlin. Instead, the gangs seemed to serve as a focus for adolescent peer group identification and for the organization of fighting among youths who engage in diverse delinquencies independent of, as well as in conjunction with, their gang.

Taking a different approach to the questions of anomie and lower-class culture, Rosenberg and Silverstein (1969) interviewed adolescents in high delinquency slums of New York City, Chicago, and Washington, D.C. In each city, a well-defined neighborhood was chosen where the young people knew one another and expressed a deep sense of localism in that they seldom associated with people from other neighborhoods, even when away from their own. People who moved to other parts of the city often returned to participate in the life of their old neighborhood. The population in New York was mainly Puerto Rican; in Chicago, southern white; and in Washington, southern black.

The interviewees were asked to let their imagination run loose with respect to the job, income, and residence they wanted. Most seemed to have aspirations in line with their realistic expectations, as illustrated by the following examples:

PUERTO RICAN YOUTH IN NEW YORK

Do you want very much to get ahead in the world?
Yeah.
What do you mean by get ahead?
Well, I'd have a good job.
Suppose you had any one of your choice—this is heaven now—any kind of job. What would you pick?
If I had any kind of job?
Yes.
I would get an office job.
You'd like to work in an office? Doing what?
Maybe typing or . . .
That would be the best job you could imagine? Typing?
No, it wouldn't be the best.
What's the best you can imagine? Dream.
That's kind of hard.
Can't you think of any?
No.
Well, what do you think you will wind up doing? . . .
Maybe something that has to do with stock work in department stores and things like that.
How much do you think you'll earn?
I won't make too much. Maybe about eighty or something. (pp. 128–29)

BLACK YOUTH IN WASHINGTON

What kind of work would you like to do for the rest of your life?
Wash dishes.
Wash dishes in a restaurant?
I think that's clean. More clean, like, that's clean work.
Anything else you would like to do?
Cook. Cooks make pretty good money. (p. 129)

WHITE YOUTH IN CHICAGO

What kind of work would you like for the rest of your life?
It's hard to say. I wouldn't mind working . . . I don't even mind pumping gas. I like anything that has to do with a car, put it that way. I'll go sit and look at a car all day long. I'm not sure what I'll do. I may get a job and just keep it, even if I don't like it. I mean if it's easy, I'll keep it. If it isn't, then I'll find a way to get fired. (p. 131)

Less than 25% voiced high aspirations. Of those who did, some were realistically trying to achieve them and engaged in little delinquency. For example, a young black man from Washington said:

Success? That's a very large word as far as I'm concerned. Well, so far, let's just say after I've gotten out of high school, say when I got this job right here, I made a little success in attaining my goal. I have myself a good job now. I can, let's say, more or less get me anything I want because I don't have any responsibilities whatsoever. . . . I think I have been successful. . . . All I have to do is get into college right there. I think that's on the way to success.

What kind of work would you like to be doing the rest of your life?

The rest of my life? Well, that's why I'm trying to go to school now—to be a student first, then a lawyer second. That's what I really want to be—a lawyer. I think I'll be a pretty darn good one . . . I know first it takes four years of college, possibly three or four years of law school—because I want at least three years of law school. (pp. 125–26)

Others with high fantasy aspirations were less optimistic but seemed content to settle for expectations typical of their group, as exemplified by an adolescent in Chicago:

Why would you like to be a lawyer?

I don't know. I guess cause they talk a lot. I fit in there perfectly.

Do you have any idea what a lawyer does?

Yes. I have an idea of what a lawyer does. He makes good money, I can assure you of that.

What kind of thing does he have to do on his job?

He . . . either condemns 'em or. . . . In other words, helps 'em to get locked up, or maybe even sent to the death house, maybe even be the one who executes 'em. Or he could be the one that gets 'em out of an execution. But, it depends on whose side you're on, who hires you for the best price, or whatever. That's just like, say people out here hire you for a job and they don't tell you what you're running up against. That's the same way with a lawyer. He never knows what he runs up against until he's right there.

What kind of work do you think you'll do for the rest of your life?

Digging ditches mostly. . . . Or I'll be running machines. . . . Not too good of jobs, but jobs, you know. Enough today, at least it's a job. (pp. 126–27)

Rosenberg and Silverstein viewed their findings as failing to support the anomie theory that delinquency results from the blocking of legitimate means to fulfilling high aspirations. If anything, there was an inverse relation between high aspiration and delinquency—youth with the highest aspirations were the least delinquent. However, differences in delinquency patterns among the three ethnic groups also cast doubt on the theory that there is any *single* lower class culture that causes delinquency. Furthermore, social class differences in crime rates seem to have decreased in recent years (Tittle, Villemez, & Smith, 1978).

Delinquents and Nondelinquents in High Delinquency Areas

The Glueck Studies. Many children in high delinquency areas do not become delinquent. This weakens explanations resting solely on subcultural hypotheses. But which children become delinquent in a high delinquency area?

To answer this question, Sheldon and Eleanor Glueck (1972) studied 500 persistently delinquent boys and 500 nondelinquent boys from the same high delinquency neighborhoods. The boys were matched for age, IQ, and ethnicity. Through extensive physical and psychological examinations and investigations of home backgrounds, the Gluecks found the following to be more common among delinquents than nondelinquents: mesomorphic (muscular) body build; lower verbal than performance IQ; delinquency, alcoholism, emotional disturbance, or serious physical ailments in parents; family on welfare; poor management of family income; erratic employment of mother; crowded or disorderly home; broken home; lack of family cohesiveness; indifference or hostility of parents or siblings toward the delinquent boy; unsuitable supervision, discipline, or punishment by parents. Other studies have confirmed the higher rates of these characteristics among delinquent than nondelinquent boys in slum neighborhoods (cf. Peterson & Becker, 1965).

From their findings, the Gluecks constructed actuarial tables for predicting who will become delinquent in adolescence. The actuarial tables resemble those used by insurance companies for predicting death rates on which to base insurance premiums. The Glueck prediction tables weight various background factors according to their correlation with delinquency in the original samples of 500 delinquents and 500 nondelinquents. Thus, boys having several of the heavily weighted characteristics get higher scores for potential delinquency than boys having few of the heavily weighted characteristics.

Numerous studies have shown that the Glueck scores of delinquents exceed those of nondelinquents (cf. Glueck & Glueck, 1976). Yet, in one of the few tests of the tables' *predictive* power, predictions from the tables were no more accurate than predictions from base rates for the neighborhood as a whole (Voss, 1963). (In a *base rate prediction,* the proportion becoming delinquent in a neighborhood is used to make predictions for each individual. Thus, if 10 percent of the boys in a neighborhood typically become delinquent, the base rate prediction for each boy is that he will not be delinquent because his probability of delinquency is only 10 percent.)

Another prediction study obtained somewhat better accuracy for modified Glueck tables than base rate predictions (Glick, 1972). Done in an inner city poverty area, this study showed that the individual background variables could potentially improve prediction over local norms for delinquency.

Cambridge-Somerville Youth Study. The Cambridge-Somerville Youth Study was begun in 1935 as an effort to prevent delinquency in the slums of Cambridge and Somerville, Massachusetts (McCord, 1982). Pairs of boys aged 5 to 11 were matched for age, home backgrounds, and delinquency prognosis. One member of each pair was assigned a counselor who visited the boy and his family; took trips with the boy; arranged for medical, dental, welfare, or mental health services; and helped coordinate contacts with various agencies and summer camps. The boys and their families were encouraged to attend church, clergymen were alerted to their problems, and police were kept in touch with the project.

The intervention of World War II, its effects on counselor turnover, and other practical problems prevented the project from being carried out as planned with the entire group. By the end of the project in 1945, only 75 of the original 325 boys remained in the active treatment group. Psychological testing, assessments of school adjustment, police and court records, and juvenile court judges' ratings of the seriousness of the boys' crimes showed little difference between the treatment and control groups at the end of the project or in subsequent follow-ups (Powers & Witmer, 1951).

By 1955, 41 percent of the boys from the intervention group and 37 percent from the control group had court convictions for nontraffic criminal offenses. The numbers and types of convictions were similar, and the tendency for crime to taper off in later years was similar in both groups (McCord, McCord, & Zola, 1959). The negligible benefit of reform school was also evident in both groups: 74 percent of the treated boys and 83 percent of the control boys who had been sent to reform school were later convicted of major crimes. Analysis of numerous child, parent, neighborhood, and treatment variables showed no evidence that treatment was very effective for any particular subgroup of children. The only evidence for positive benefit occurred among 12 boys who had especially intensive relationships with a counselor for at least two years and whose counselor had frequent interviews with parents and had alleviated obvious material, medical, or educational handicaps. Only 6 of these boys became delinquent, as compared to 11 of their 12 control boys ($p < .05$).

A 30-year follow-up, however, showed that the treated group as a whole had worse outcomes than the control group, in terms of criminal convictions, alcoholism, and major mental disorders (McCord, 1982). The poorer outcomes of the treated group seemed unaffected by variations in the intervention, such as age of starting, duration, or type of help received.

The Cambridge-Somerville Study evidently failed to prevent crime, but the vast data accumulated on the boys and their families might shed light on etiological factors (McCord et al., 1959). Certain combinations of home characteristics were found to produce extreme rates of delinquency. For example, all boys whose parents were quarrelsome, neglectful, and lax in discipline became delinquent; but only 14 percent became delinquent among those with quarrelsome, neglectful parents who consistently used withdrawal of love as discipline, such as refusing to speak to the boy. Across all types of homes, the rate of delinquency among boys receiving consistently punitive discipline was lowest (21 percent), with love-oriented discipline next (27 percent), lax discipline next (50 percent), and erratic discipline the worst (56 percent).

The effects of parental deviance and love were examined together by assigning one point for each parent who was overtly deviant (criminal, alcoholic, sexually unfaithful) and one point for each parent who was unloving. A family's score could thus range from zero (neither parent deviant or unloving) to four (both parents deviant *and* unloving. The rate of delinquency showed an increase for each point on this scale: from 28 percent for boys whose parents were both loving and nondeviant, to 81 percent for boys whose parents were both unloving and deviant. The biggest single factor, however, seemed to be the mother's personality. Even when complicated by overprotective attitudes, anxiety, or neurosis, high maternal love generally led to low crime rates.

It is hard to pinpoint a single type of family that produces delinquency in slum areas. Instead, parental laxness, inconsistency, deviance, quarrelsomeness, neglect, and hostility each seem to raise the risk of delinquency among boys living in high delinquency areas. The more factors present, the more likely delinquency becomes. Yet even among boys whose families did not show the delinquency-enhancing conditions, 20 to 30 percent became delinquent anyway. This may reflect the sheer fun of delinquent activities for boys who lack strong scruples against them or competing sources of nondelinquent fun.

The "Good Boy" in High Delinquency Areas. Many boys living in high crime areas do not become delinquent. Why not? In a study designed to find out, teachers were asked to nominate 12-year-olds whom they believed would not get into trouble with the law (Scarpitti, Murray, Dinitz, & Reckless, 1960). Police records were searched to eliminate any who had already been in trouble. Structured questionnaires were then administered to the boys and their mothers.

In a follow-up four years later, teachers were asked to nominate "good boys" from the group who were now 16 years old. Police records were searched and the boys and their mothers were interviewed again. Four of the original 103 "good boys" had acquired police records, although they were for minor offenses. Teachers again nominated nearly all the same boys as likely to stay out of trouble. The new nominations by teachers and the police records thus showed that predictions made at age 12 held good for four years.

The interviews showed that the boys were exceptionally good citizens, admitted very little delinquent behavior of any sort, had favorable attitudes toward the police, felt that they were accepted by parents, and felt that their parents used the right amount of discipline. They were also favorably disposed toward school, were nearly all in academic programs (though not necessarily outstanding in grades or attendance), expected to finish high school, stayed away from delinquents, and said they would give up a friend if he were leading them into trouble. Comparison with classmates nominated by teachers as being headed for trouble at age 12 showed large differences in both the interview measures and police records. Both groups came from the same neighborhoods and SES, yet the latter group committed far more delinquencies over the four-year period (Dinitz, Scarpitti, & Reckless, 1962).

The findings suggest that a firm nondelinquent self-image developed by the age of 12 can insulate a boy against delinquency even in a high delinquency area.

UNSOCIALIZED-PSYCHOPATHIC DELINQUENCY

He lied so plausibly and with such utter equanimity, devised such ingenious alibis or simply denied all responsibility with such convincing appearances of candor that for many years his real career was poorly estimated. Among typical exploits with which he is credited stand these: prankish defecation into the stringed intricacies of the school piano, the removal from his uncle's automobile of a carburetor for which he got 75 cents, and the selling of his father's overcoat to a passing buyer of scrap materials.

Though he often fell in with groups or small gangs, he never for long identified himself with others in a common cause. . . . With several others he broke into a summer cottage . . ., stole a few articles, overturned all the furniture, and threw rugs, dishes, etc., out of the window. He and a few more teenage boys on another expedition smashed headlights and windshields on several automobiles, punctured a number of tires, and rolled one car down a slope, leaving it . . . battered and bogged in a ditch.

At 14 or 15 years of age, having learned to drive, Tom began to steal automobiles with some regularity. Often his intention seemed less that of theft than of heedless misappropriation. A neighbor or friend of the family, going . . . to where the car was parked . . . would find it missing. Sometimes . . . [Tom] would leave the stolen vehicle within a few blocks . . . of the owner, sometimes out on the road where the gasoline had given out. After he had tried to sell a stolen car, his father consulted advisors and, on the theory that he might have some specific craving for automobiles, bought one for him as a therapeutic measure. On one occasion while out driving, he deliberately parked his own car and . . . stole an inferior model which he left slightly damaged on the outskirts of a village some miles away. (Cleckley, 1976, pp. 65−66)

The second behavioral-personality cluster found among delinquents resembles the traditional psychiatric diagnosis of *psychopathic personality*. This diagnosis grew out of the nineteenth century concept of "moral insanity," designating those in whom "the moral and active principles of the mind are strangely perverted and depraved; the power of self-government is lost or greatly impaired; and the individual is . . . incapable, not of talking or reasoning upon any subject proposed to him, but of conducting himself with decency and propriety" (Pritchard, 1835).

By the late nineteenth century, "moral insanity" was replaced by the more clinical terms *psychopathic inferiority* and *constitutional psychopathy*. The term *sociopathic personality* came into use in the twentieth century to avoid the implication of a constitutional etiology. The American Psychiatric Association's (1980) *Diagnostic and Statistical Manual* replaced this term with "antisocial personality," characterized by:

. . . a history of continuous and chronic antisocial behavior in which the rights of others are violated, persistence into adult life of a pattern of antisocial behavior that began before the age of 15, and failure to sustain good job performance over a period of several years . . .

Lying, stealing, fighting, truancy, and resisting authority are typical early childhood signs. In adolescence, unusually early or aggressive sexual behavior, excessive drinking, and use of illicit drugs are frequent. In adulthood, these kinds of behavior continue, with the addition of inability to sustain consistent work performance or to function as a responsible parent and failure to accept social norms with respect to lawful behavior. (American Psychiatric Association, 1980, pp. 317–18)

While the DSM stipulates that this diagnosis is not to be applied before age 18, the behaviors, personality test responses, and MMPI profiles associated with the unsocialized-psychopathic pattern of delinquency have all the earmarks of the adult syndrome, whatever we call it. Not only are the behaviors delinquent, but the lack of sustained relations with others (even other delinquents), persistent defiance of authority, failure to respond to praise or punishment, active seeking of trouble, and lack of strong emotions all resemble adult antisocial personalities.

Developmental Course of Sociopathy

Lee Robins (1974) has demonstrated continuity between child and adult sociopathic behavior. She followed up 524 people 30 years after they had been seen in a child guidance clinic, plus 100 control subjects from the same neighborhoods. Adult data were obtained from family members, neighbors, employers, and police on 98 percent of the sample; interviews were held with 82 percent.

Two psychiatrists diagnosed each subject on the basis of all data available from age 18 until the time of the study, when the subjects averaged 43 years of age. Eighty percent of the former clinic patients were considered to be psychiatrically disturbed; the largest single group (22 percent) was diagnosed as sociopathic. By contrast, only 2 percent of the control group were diagnosed sociopathic. Ninety-four percent of the sociopathic group but only 17 percent of the control group had been arrested for nontraffic offenses. The sociopaths had a median of eight nontraffic arrests.

Ninety-five percent of the sociopaths had originally been referred to the clinic for antisocial behavior. The sheer number of antisocial symptoms listed in the child's clinic record strongly predicted later sociopathy: No child having less than six *kinds* of antisocial behavior, four *episodes* of antisocial behavior, or an episode serious enough to warrant *court referral* was diagnosed sociopathic in adulthood. Thus, *all* the adult sociopaths had shown childhood antisocial childhood behavior and most of it resembled adult sociopathic behavior.

Social class was less strongly related to the later diagnosis of sociopathy than it is to subcultural delinquency. The number of antisocial symptoms shown by the child and diagnosis of the child's father as sociopathic were both far stronger predictors of adult sociopathy than social class was. Moreover, fathers who were rated especially cold had children with exceptionally *low* rates of sociopathy, and broken homes did *not* produce significantly higher rates of sociopathy than of other kinds of disorder. Thus, lack of warm, cohesive family relations did not seem as important in sociopathy as in subcultural delinquency. As with subcultural delinquency, however, good parental discipline produced exceptionally low rates of adult sociopathy.

In reviewing other studies of relations between child and adult antisocial behavior, Robins (1979) concluded that her own findings were amply supported: Antisocial behavior in childhood usually portended antisocial behavior in adulthood, whether or not psychotherapy was obtained. Considerable continuity is thus evident between child and adult antisocial behavior, and sociopathic behavior in childhood is linked to the adult syndrome of sociopathy.

Research on Sociopathic Personalities

Anxiety in Sociopaths. Although there has been little research on unsocialized-psychopathic delinquency in childhood, research on sociopathic (psychopathic, antisocial) adults has revealed a distinctive pattern that originated in childhood. Beginning with a study by David Lykken (1957), it has been repeatedly found that people diagnosed sociopathic show less anxiety on various objective measures than normals or nonsociopathic criminals. Lykken's sociopathic subjects were incarcerated adolescents and young adults. He used a control group of prisoners diagnosed as neurotic and another control group of normal high school and college students.

The subjects filled out a questionnaire requiring preferential choices between frightening activities and onerous activities equated for general unpleasantness (e.g., making a parachute jump versus digging a big garbage pit). The subjects were also given two experimental tasks designed to measure learning as a function of painful consequences. On one task, the subject's job was to learn the correct "path" through a "mental maze" programmed into an apparatus having four switches. Activating the switches in a certain sequence constituted the correct path through the maze. Whenever a subject pressed the correct switch at a choice point, a green light flashed and the program advanced to the next choice point. At each of the choice points, one of the incorrect switches produced a shock. Subjects were not told of the experimenter's interest in seeing how well they learned to avoid the shocked switches.

In the second experimental task, galvanic skin responses (GSRs) were recorded while the subject periodically heard two different buzzers. Unpleasant shocks followed one of the buzzers. Extinction trials then occurred in which no shocks followed the buzzers.

Lykken found that sociopaths differed significantly from normals in several ways: Sociopaths more often chose frightening tasks over onerous tasks, they made proportionally more shocked than nonshocked errors on the mental maze, and they showed smaller GSRs to the shocked buzzer. Neurotic criminals were intermediate between normals and sociopaths on all three measures. Experimental measures employing other noxious stimuli have likewise revealed poor avoidance learning by sociopaths (e.g., Gendreau & Suboski, 1971).

Emotional Reactivity in Sociopaths. Schachter and Latané (1964) directly tested the hypothesis that defects in emotional reactivity underlie sociopaths' failure to learn from painful experience. Sociopathic and nonsociopathic ("normal") prisoners were given Lykken's mental maze task under two conditions, half receiving each condition first. Under one condition, the prisoners were injected with adrenalin (epinephrine), causing increased blood pressure, heart rate, respiration, tremor, and flushing. Under the other condition, they were injected with an inert placebo.

Figure 13-5 shows the results. Under placebo, the normal prisoners showed a marked decline in proportion of shocked errors from the beginning to the end of a session, but the sociopaths did not. Under adrenalin, the groups showed exactly the *reverse* patterns: The normals did *not* reduce their proportion of shocked errors as a session progressed, but the sociopaths markedly decreased their shocked errors.

Schachter (1971) concluded that sociopaths do not learn to avoid normal levels of pain-induced arousal; yet they can learn to avoid pain when adrenalin intensifies

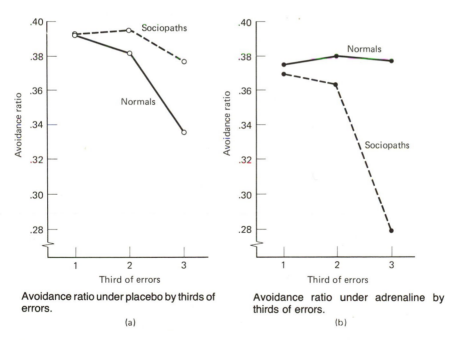

Avoidance ratio under placebo by thirds of errors.

(a)

Avoidance ratio under adrenaline by thirds of errors.

(b)

Figure 13.5. Ratio of shocked/unshocked errors by "normal" and sociopathic prisoners following placebo and adrenalin injections. (Adapted from Schachter, 1971.)

arousal. On the other hand, such high arousal levels disrupt performance by normals, who typically learn to avoid pain when less aroused.

Pain Thresholds in Sociopaths. Could sociopaths' indifference to pain reflect less *perception* of pain? To find out, Robert Hare administered several levels of shock to sociopathic and nonsociopathic prisoners. When a prisoner's threshold for detection of shock had been found, shocks close to that threshold were paired with certain stimuli and the prisoner was to identify the stimulus that had been followed by a shock. Using a boring version of the shock detection task, Hare (1968) found that sociopaths had significantly higher thresholds for the perception of shock than nonsociopaths. When a much less boring version of the task was used, however, Hare and Thorvaldson (1970) found no difference between the shock perception thresholds of sociopaths and nonsociopaths. Antisocial children have likewise been found to be much less attentive than neurotic children to boring stimuli but not to interesting stimuli (DeMyer-Gapin & Scott, 1977).

Hare and Thorvaldson asked their subjects to rate more intense shocks on a scale ranging from 1 for *Uncomfortable or unpleasant but not painful* to 5 for *Stop: don't wish to go any higher*. When Level 5 was reached, the subject was offered two cigarettes for every additional level of shock intensity he was willing to tolerate. There was no significant difference between the groups in the intensities tolerated without incentives (Level 5), but sociopaths tolerated significantly more shock than nonsociopaths when cigarettes were offered. This showed that they were especially willing to face pain to get something they wanted. Hare and Cox (1978) have since hypothesized that sociopaths have an especially efficient coping process that inhibits fear arousal. This, in turn, prevents them from learning to avoid situations that others fear.

Effects of Various Punishments. In a comparison of various punishments, Schmauk (1970) administered Lykken's mental maze task under three punishment conditions to sociopathic prisoners and a normal control group. In the *physical punishment* condition, subjects were shocked for activating the punished switches. In the *social punishment* condition, the experimenter said "wrong" in a disapproving tone when a subject activated a punished switch. In the *tangible punishment* condition, the subject lost a quarter from a pile of 40 quarters whenever he activated a punished switch. Figure 13-6 shows the effects of each punishment on avoidance learning by each type of subject. (The avoidance learning scores were calculated by subtracting the ratio of punished errors from 1, so that a *high* score indicates a *small* ratio of punished to unpunished errors.)

As in other studies, sociopaths did worse in learning to avoid the punished switches when the punishment was shock. Likewise, their avoidance learning was worse than that of normals under the social punishment condition. Yet under the *tangible punishment* condition, the sociopaths' learned slightly *better* than the normals!

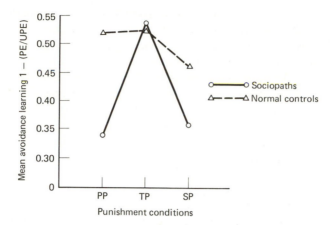

Figure 13.6. Avoidance learning scores for sociopaths and normals under three punishment conditions (PP = physical punishment; TP = tangible punishment; SP = social punishment). (Adapted from Schmauk, 1970.)

Similarly, the sociopaths' GSRs prior to pushing a punished switch were smaller than normals' in the physical and social punishment conditions, but not in the tangible punishment condition. The sociopaths in the tangible punishment condition also rated their anxiety higher and showed more awareness of the punishment contingencies than in either of the other punishment conditions. It thus seems that physical and social punishment had little impact on sociopaths. Yet losing money affected them as much as normals.

The implication is that nothing in sociopaths' nervous systems prevents anxiety. On the contrary, they are fully capable of experiencing anxiety and learning to avoid discomfort. Their values are such that they are not made anxious by the same events as other people, however. On the basis of Schmauk's findings, one kind of punishment that does appear effective is the immediate forfeiture of tangible assets.

Further research has shown, however, that sociopaths avoid this kind of punishment mainly when it is a clearly *inescapable* consequence of a particular act: Where punishment contingencies are more ambiguous, sociopaths engage in superstitious behavior leading to less avoidance of punishment than nonsociopaths (Siegel, 1978).

Moral Development in Sociopathic Children. Although the DSM diagnosis of sociopathy or antisocial personality is not supposed to be made before the age of 18, exploration of the childhood roots of sociopathy has led to studies of moral judgment in children displaying sociopathic behavior. These children have shown lower levels of moral judgment in response to Kohlberg's (1969) moral dilemmas than subcultural and neurotic delinquents or normal children (Campagna & Harter, 1975; Jurkovic & Prentice, 1977). Both studies demonstrated that cognitive development was significantly correlated with moral judgment, but sociopathic children scored lower in moral judgment even when the effects of cognitive level were controlled. Like Siegel's (1978) findings on adult sociopaths' unresponsiveness to subtle contingencies related to punishment, this suggests that sociopathic behavior is associated with failure to use available cognitive processes in certain socially important realms (Jurkovic, 1980).

DISTURBED-NEUROTIC DELINQUENCY

The socialized-subcultural and unsocialized-psychopathic syndromes each seem to represent distinctive groups of delinquents. Delinquents classified as disturbed-neurotic, however, may have little in common with each other beside unhappiness. There is less research on these youngsters, and they probably include neurotic, psychotic, retarded, and brain-damaged children whose personal pathology and environmental circumstances happen to lead to delinquent behavior, but whose delinquency is but one facet of a larger picture of disturbance. Most data on this group are only indirect and include mainly findings of elevated rates of psychopathology and medical problems in heterogeneous samples of delinquents (e.g., Lewis & Balla, 1976).

EEG Findings

EEG abnormalities have often been reported in delinquent and aggressive children. For example, Assael, Kohen-Raz, and Alpern (1967) found that 62.5 percent of fairly severe Israeli delinquents had abnormal EEGs, while Bayrakal (1965) found lying, stealing, and hostility to be more common among disturbed children with abnormal EEGs than disturbed children with normal EEGs. Unfortunately, the lack of a control group in the first study and the lack of matching for age and other characteristics of the two groups in the second study make inferences hazardous.

The 14- and 6-per-Second Spike. High rates of a particular EEG abnormality, known as the *14- and 6-per-second spike*,[1] have also been reported in people with aggressive behavioral disorders (e.g., Kurland, Yeager, & Arthur, 1963). In a controlled comparison of patients aged 5 to 20 having normal EEGs, EEGs with 14- and 6-per-second spikes, EEGs with 14- and 6-per-second spikes plus other abnormalities, or other EEG abnormalities alone, only those with 14- and 6-per-second spikes, *plus* other EEG abnormalities showed significantly more

---

[1]A sharp, spikelike wave suggestive of an epileptic focus and occurring at recording points that normally produce 14 waves and 6 waves per second.

aggressive behavior than those without 14- and 6-per-second spikes (Walter, Colbert, Koegler, Palmer, & Bond, 1960). The children with 14- and 6-per-second spikes plus other EEG abnormalities seemed to be distinguished from socialized-subcultural and sociopathic delinquents especially by their outbursts of extreme rage and violent acts with minimal provocation. As an example:

> . . . this 13-year old boy impulsively shot and killed his mother. There is no history of illness or accidents. His social adjustment and school progress were excellent.
> Prior to the shooting the mother had threatened to deprive this boy of his only meaningful relationship, his boy friend. When studied there was a lack of affect, some confusion, and total lack of ability to describe the tragedy in detail. At the time of the act he stated that he seemed to have to do it and could not resist. While in the detention home there were two aggressive outbursts without obvious cause. One was described as the boy being "at white heat with hands shaking." After he was in the State School there were several violent outbursts which he described as "They are just there. Then they are gone." They occurred when he was frustrated and lost status thereby. (Schwade & Geiger, 1960, p. 618)

The large proportion of normal adolescents with 14- and 6-per-second spikes indicates that these are not very specific to extreme aggression, however (Harris, 1977).

Possible Genetic Influences

The XYY Syndrome. One genetic influence on delinquency may be the XYY chromosome complement found in a few males (detailed in Chapter 6). The incidence of XYYs in the general population is about 0.11 percent, compared to about 2 percent in mental-penal settings (Hook, 1973). This means that an XYY man is 18 times more likely than an XY man to be incarcerated in a mental-penal setting. It has also been found that XYY men tend to have severe acne, below average IQs, and above average height, although the fact that tall XY men are not overrepresented in penal institutions indicates that height alone does not predispose men to crime (Hook & Kim, 1971).

The proportion of XYY men in regular penal settings is lower than in mental-penal institutions; the absolute proportion of XYY men incarcerated is low; the crimes they commit are not especially aggressive; and the total proportion of crime they commit is low. Hence, the XYYs do not play a very big role in the general picture of delinquency. In fact, sensational publicity has grossly exaggerated the XYY phenomenon. For example, press reports repeatedly depicted Richard Speck, convicted of murdering eight nurses, as an XYY, although the only laboratory to analyze his chromosomes found them normal (Engel, 1972). It has also been found that the XYYs' low intelligence may be what accounts for their elevated rates of incarceration (Witkin et al., 1976).

Other Genetic Influences. A few studies have revealed somewhat higher concordance for criminal behavior in identical than in fraternal twins (Cloninger, Christiansen, Reich, & Gottesman, 1978). The adopted-away offspring of criminals also show somewhat higher rates of delinquent behavior than the adopted-away offspring of noncriminals (Mednick & Hutchings, 1978). Based on findings that the GSRs of some delinquents are underresponsive to fear, Mednick and Hutchings hypothesized that this reflects inherited features of the autonomic nervous system and that these in turn, hamper learning from punishment. There is evidence, however, that the unresponsive GSRs reflect a lack of general anxiety or arousal, rather than autonomic characteristics (cf. Raskin, 1979).

Other Findings

Case histories of criminal deviance have sometimes suggested that certain types of crime arise from particular types of psychopathology. For example, in a review of 80 adolescent boys arrested for sexually molesting younger children, "the adolescent child molester" was described as a loner who has no social peer group activity with youths his own age, prefers playing with much younger children, is immature and sexually naive, identifies with an overprotective and dominant mother, has a passive father, and is invariably an underachiever (Shoor, Speed, & Bartelt, 1966). Unfortunately, the lack of adequate control groups in such studies makes it impossible to judge which of the foregoing characteristics are more typical of child molesters than of other adolescent delinquents or nondelinquents. Without such controlled comparisons, little can be concluded about personality or motivation leading to specific crimes. It has been found, in fact, that juveniles who commit assaultive sex crimes commit other sex crimes as well, and show psychopathology like that of other violent juveniles (Lewis, Shanok, & Pincus, 1979).

JUVENILE DELINQUENCY AMONG GIRLS

Perhaps because the offenses are generally less threatening to others, female crime has received less notice than male crime. Since the 1960s, however, juvenile court cases involving girls have been rising faster than those involving boys, causing the former ratio of more than four boys to each girl to drop to three boys for each girl seen in juvenile courts (Vedder, 1979). The disproportionate increase in female cases has occurred in urban, suburban, and rural jurisdictions, and in other countries as well (Adler, 1977). Since such a widespread increase is unlikely to be caused by changes in court or police practices, it may reflect general changes in female role concepts that make delinquent behavior more acceptable.

Girls used to be most often arrested for running away, incorrigibility, and sex delinquency, although the first two were often euphemisms for the third (Wattenberg & Saunders, 1954). Like boys, however, many girls are now arrested for auto theft, burglary, assault, and narcotics (Vedder, 1979). Questionnaire studies have shown similar rankings in the delinquent acts admitted by boys and girls (Cernkovich & Giordano, 1979; see Table 13-3). More boys admit to each act and repetitions of most acts, however.

Sexual Delinquency

Unwed pregnancy causes greater judicial concern over sexual offenses by girls than boys. Many girls adjudicated delinquent are, have been, or soon will be pregnant. Yet, unwed pregnancy may have little more specific significance among adolescent girls than, for example, theft among adolescent boys.

We lack adequate data on the personalities, backgrounds, and subsequent behavior of girls who become pregnant. But the existing data suggest that cultural factors associated with race give unwed pregnancy a different significance among blacks than whites. Rates of unwed pregnancy have been higher among blacks than whites, and a smaller proportion of out-of-wedlock black babies are given up for adoption (Mueller, 1966). This may be partly due to the lack of adoptive families for black babies, but the result is that a much higher proportion of black babies grow up without legally responsible fathers.

A comparison of unwed pregnant black girls under the age of 17 with a control group of nonpregnant black girls showed that about the only evident "pathogenic" factors more characteristic of the pregnant girls was less punishment by parents and more mothers employed outside the home (Gottschalk, Titchener, Piker, & Stewart, 1964). The pregnant black girls had fewer broken homes, less sickness, less problems around menstruation, and fewer neurotic symptoms than the nonpregnant black girls. In a mostly black sample, however, girls who became pregnant had earlier shown more negative attitudes toward school and home than demographically matched nonpregnant girls did (Kaplan, Smith, & Pokorny, 1979).

Among white girls of similar SES and similar neighborhoods, the pregnant ones had also received less punishment from parents, but had more broken homes and more neurotic symptoms than the nonpregnant ones. This suggests that black pregnant girls were more normal than white pregnant girls, as compared to other girls of their race. A study of lower socioeconomic black girls in a special program for unwed adolescents, however, showed that those who became pregnant a second time shortly after their first baby were less well-adjusted and came more often from broken homes than those who did not quickly become pregnant again (Barglow, Bornstein, Exum, Wright, & Visotsky, 1967).

Personality Characteristics

For both sexes, factor analyses show a syndrome of behavioral problems including disobedience, fighting, stealing, and destructiveness (Achenbach & Edelbrock,

1978). This syndrome has been called "conduct disorder," "undercontrolled," and "externalizing" in various studies. For both sexes, a syndrome has also been found that includes phobias, stomachaches, pains, worrying, fearfulness, and vomiting. It has been called "personality disorder," "overcontrolled," and "internalizing" (Achenbach & Edelbrock, 1978). Surveys have shown that normal and disturbed boys have more of the undercontrolled problems, whereas girls have more of the overcontrolled problems (Achenbach & Edelbrock, 1981). Boys also give more physically aggressive responses to projective tests (Brodzinsky, Messer, & Tew, 1979).

At both the levels of overt problems and projective responses, then, physical aggression seems more dominant in boys than girls. Boys' stronger propensity toward aggression, for whatever reasons (cultural and/or biological) may account for some of the sex differences in delinquency. Moreover, emotional difficulties may play a bigger role in delinquency among girls than boys. Broken homes, for example, seem especially common among delinquent girls (Offord, Abrams, Allen, & Poushinksy, 1979). A direct comparison with boy delinquents has shown that more girl delinquents reported marked quarreling at home and intense hostility toward parents (Wattenberg & Saunders, 1954). More girl delinquents were also viewed as friendless "lone wolves," hostile toward teachers and other adults, and unable to get along with their neighbors.

Personality Types

There is some evidence for personality types among female offenders like those found among male offenders (Widom, 1978). Using the same typology for both sexes, Hetherington et al. (1971) divided institutionalized delinquent boys and girls into unsocialized-psychopathic, socialized-subcultural, and neurotic-disturbed on the basis of their personality questionnaire responses. Nondelinquent control groups of each sex were also selected from high delinquency areas. The adolescents and their families were then observed in a structured task where they were to solve hypothetical family problems.

Maternal dominance was found in families of neurotic-disturbed delinquents of both sexes. The neurotic-disturbed delinquents themselves were relatively passive in family interactions. The unsocialized-psychopathic and socialized-subcultural girls were more assertive and disruptive with their parents, especially their fathers, than any of the other groups were, including the boys. The mothers of the unsocialized-psychopathic girls were the weakest in any group, although the fathers did not effectively control their families either. Furthermore, the parents of the unsocialized-psychopathic girls were the least warm of all the parents. We cannot be sure whether the parents' behaviors and attitudes reflected *reactions* to their children's delinquency or *causes* of it. Yet the differences in family constellations support a typology for delinquent girls like the one for boys.

A factor analysis of the personality test responses of girls in a California training school also supported the typology to some extent, although the exclusion of subcultural delinquents from the group precluded a socialized-subcultural syndrome (Butler, 1965). Of the three syndromes identified, one labeled "disturbed-neurotic" clearly resembled the syndrome of this type found for boys and employed for both sexes by Hetherington et al. (1971). The other two syndromes seemed to be subtypes of the psychopathic pattern. One, labeled "immature-impulsive," was characterized mainly by aggression, impulsivity, and overt manipulation. The other, labeled "covert manipulation," was characterized by an externally conforming appearance but continuous covert manipulation, with aggression and hostility when the manipulative activities are discovered. Further refinement of these first attempts at objectively discriminating among types of delinquent girls may help us identify differential etiologies, prognoses, and appropriate treatments.

In the meantime, clinical reports leave little doubt of a female psychopathic type similar to that found among males. In his classic descriptions of psychopathy, Cleckley (1976) includes two females. One, Roberta, is described as having begun her career with repeated thefts, truancy, and straight-faced lying early in childhood. Her family was financially secure and could find no reason for her behavior. Despite her ingenuity in deliberately hiding her misdeeds, she reacted to discovery as if people were just overdoing trivial incidents that she herself did not consider important. Following psychiatric hospitalization and treatment, a series of jobs and placements were obtained for her. Her letters to her psychiatrist portrayed a remarkable cure:

> You and Doctor _____ have given me a new outlook and a new life. This time we have got to the very root of my trouble and I see the whole story in a different light. I don't mean to use such words lightly and, of all things, I want to avoid even the appearance of flattery, but I must tell you how grateful I am, how deeply I admire the wonderful work you are doing. . . . If, in your whole life you had never succeeded with one other patient, what you have done for me should make your practice worthwhile. . . . I wish I could tell you how different I feel. How different I am! But, as I so well realize now, it isn't saying things that counts but what one actually does. I am confident that my life from now on will express better than anything I can say what you have done for me. . . . It is good to feel that as time passes, you can be proud of me and as sure of me as I am sure of myself . . . whether I go on to college or follow up my old impulse and become a nurse; if I become a business girl or settle for being just a normal, happy wife, my life will be fulfilling and useful. . . . If it had not been for you, I shudder to think what I might have become . . . (Cleckley, 1976, p. 54)

Despite her letters, Roberta was continually getting into trouble as serious as before, including theft, turning her quarters into a brothel, and obtaining money under false pretenses. She even requested letters of recommendation from her psychiatrist whom she knew had been told of her continuing escapades. She seemed blissfully certain that he would recommend her in the most glowing terms!

TREATMENT

The traditional "treatment" for crime has been punishment. The traditional motive for punishment has probably been revenge more than anything else, although it may be rationalized as deterrence, protection for society, correction, or rehabilitation.

Since the advent of juvenile courts at the turn of the century, judges' main options have been informal supervision by a caseworker or probation officer, official supervision in the form of probation, and incarceration. Because courts seldom have enough caseworkers and probation officers to provide more than token supervision, the basic form of treatment for juvenile delinquents, as for adult criminals, is incarceration and the threat of incarceration.

Long-term incarceration of juveniles has declined steadily since the 1960s as more emphasis has been placed on community alternatives (Rector, Barth, & Ingram, 1980). This trend was reinforced by the Juvenile Justice and Delinquency Act of 1974, which mandates deinstitutionalization of youth who have not committed criminal acts, mainly status offenders. Nevertheless, over 20,000 youth remain in state institutions and hundreds of thousands more are temporarily held in detention centers and jails each year (Rector et al., 1980). Imprisonment rates for the American population as a whole are more than three times as high as for most western countries and *10 times* as high as some countries, such as the Netherlands (Goldstein, 1978).

Traditional Institutionalization

Most institutions for juvenile offenders are "open" in that they are not walled and escape is relatively easy (and common). Superintendents are often appointed through the political spoils system. Token educational, vocational, and psychotherapeutic programs exist, but the orientation is primarily custodial. Officials try to keep costs down and avoid disturbances and escapes that might bring community and political repercussions. There are tacit agreements between the staff and inmate power structures dominated by the tougher, more experienced juveniles who control other inmates for purposes of extortion, homosexual activity, and scapegoating. The regimented institutional mentality frequently afflicts the staff as well as inmates, and there is little sensitivity to individual inmate differences that may affect rehabilitation (Gibbons, 1970). The difficulties of truly reforming such systems have been well documented (see Miller & Ohlin, 1981).

Inmates are seldom prepared for noncriminal occupations and life-styles. Minute regulation of their daily lives leaves them with little need for constructive thinking or initiative. Instead of providing positive socialization, the negative approach of traditional penal institutions leaves to the inmate subculture the task of socializing new arrivals. A delinquent's account of his incarcerations illustrates this socialization process as it functioned long ago and continues today:

> In the Detention Home, and in every institution where criminals are confined, the inmates always talk about their experiences in crime. That is the main topic of conversation. . . . Every fellow tries to impress upon everybody else what a great criminal he is and how many big deals in crime he has pulled off. Anything in the underworld like scandals, murders, robberies is interesting and talked about. Every fellow tries to tell the biggest exploit and make the other fellows look up to him as a big shot and a daring gunman.
>
> They talk about the outside and how they're going to get by the next time. They talk against the police, and the older guys tell the young fellows how to get by in the racket and not get caught. The fellow who is timid and cries is razzed and made fun of. If there's anything that makes a young crook miserable, it's to be razzed by a big shot for being a coward. (Shaw, 1930, p. 12)

It should not be surprising that traditional treatment for delinquency has a low "cure" rate. Follow-ups of boys released from training schools generally show that only 20 to 30 percent avoid rearrest within the next few years (Cohen & Filipczak, 1971; Gibbons, 1970). Boys seen in juvenile court also have elevated rates of later psychiatric hospitalization (Balla, Lewis, Shanok, Snell, & Henisz, 1974). There are less data on girls, but as many as 80 percent may avoid rearrest within a few years after release, perhaps because they reach ages where the behavior for which most of them were incarcerated is no longer of concern to the law. The sex difference and lengthy preincarceration police records suggest that the schools themselves may not be the cause of further delinquency, but they do not seem to prevent it either.

In one of the few controlled comparisons between community treatment and incarceration, California delinquents eligible for training schools were instead kept in the community to receive either individual therapeutic and vocational counseling or group therapy and supervision. Twenty-nine percent of those in the community groups had their paroles revoked within 14 months, compared to 48 percent of the matched controls released from a state training school. Yet the community groups committed an average of 2.81 known offenses, compared to 1.61 for the training school group. The higher rate among the community groups may have reflected their parole officers' better knowledge of their offenses than of those committed by the training school group. However, comparison of the seriousness of offenses showed that training school parollees were more likely to have their paroles revoked for less serious offenses, while the community group had their paroles revoked only for serious offenses (Gibbons, 1970; Lerman, 1968). In short, it appears that community treatment affected relationships with parole officers, but there was no clear evidence that training school placement actually increased crime over community treatment. On the other hand, it seems clear that traditional methods do little to prevent subsequent crime.

Psychotherapy. The addition of more than token psychotherapy to traditional training school programs has produced mixed results. Guttman (1970) compared parole violations by boys receiving psychiatric treatment in two California training schools with violations by boys from the same schools receiving no therapy. Treated boys from one school had fewer violations than untreated boys, but treated boys from the other school had more violations than untreated boys. The apparently negative effect of psychotherapy in the second school was attributed to the older age of the boys and staff hostility toward the psychiatric units in that school.

Another California training school provided intensive individual and group therapy for high and low anxious boys (Adams, 1962). At follow-up, treated high anxious boys had the fewest parole violations, whereas treated low anxious boys had more than untreated boys. Taken together, these studies suggest that psychotherapy may help some boys in training schools but is harmful to others. Other studies suggest moderate benefits from various forms of psychotherapy with incarcerated male and female delinquents, but the therapies have not been defined specifically enough to permit clear conclusions about their effective ingredients (see Tramontana, 1980). A community-based approach featuring psychotherapy, remedial education, and job placement has also shown somewhat superior outcomes over a 15-year follow-up for a small group of delinquents as compared to an untreated control group (Shore & Massimo, 1979).

Therapeutic Milieux

A British psychiatrist, Maxwell Jones (1953), advocated "therapeutic communities" in which mental patients participate in continuous group therapy and self-government of the institution. Other forms of therapeutic milieux stress democratic self-government less than Jones's model, but they share an emphasis on socialization via group interaction. Redl and Wineman's (1957) Pioneer House, for example, was intended as a therapeutic milieu for delinquent children. Lack of funds brought Pioneer House to a premature end, and no outcome evaluations were made, but Redl and Wineman's descriptions of their impulse-ridden children have become classics.

The Balderton Hospital Study. A self-governing therapeutic milieu like Jones's was compared with a more standard authoritarian system at Balderton Hospital in England (Crafts, Stephenson, & Granger, 1964). The subjects were sociopathic males, aged 13 to 26, who were under court orders to have residential treatment. A council composed of all the youth and staff ran the self-governing unit. Each youth also joined an intensive therapy group.

In the more authoritarian unit, by contrast, the youths were told they would receive a therapy program designed for their needs. Noise and disarray were not allowed, and offenders were put to bed, fined, or deprived of privileges. The youth had to stand up when senior staff entered, and there were monthly convocations at which offenders were sentenced. Not enough professional time was available for more than superficial psychotherapy. The rules made visits to nearby towns much more difficult than for youth in the self-governing unit.

Tests showed that the youths in the authoritarian unit improved significantly in IQ and in Porteus Maze measures of impulsivity and carelessness, typically found to be high in delinquents. Overall personality profiles did not change in either group, although the test results and test-taking behavior suggested that the youths in the authoritarian unit became more concerned with making a good impression, whereas those in the self-governing unit became more carefree and abusive.

During follow-up periods averaging 14 months, the youths from the self-governing unit committed more offenses, more often needed reinstitutionalization, and were rated less improved than those from the authoritarian unit. The groups showed no differences in neurotic traits, however. Contrary to their predictions, the authors' concluded that the authoritarian unit produced better results than the self-governing unit. For this particular group, then, the milieu providing less psychotherapy and self-government seemed the most effective.

In a less adequate study of sociopathic American youth, however, a program designed to maximize excitement, novelty, and action within a controlled setting seemed to produce better institutional behavior than an ordinary authoritarian program (Ingram, Gerard, Quay, & Levinson, 1970).

Highfields. The Highfields program was set up in New Jersey to try out *guided group interaction* in the treatment of delinquents (McCorkle, Elias, & Bixby, 1958). About 20 boys were housed in the mansion of Charles Lindbergh's former estate, known as Highfields. Rules were minimal, but staff could mete out extra work during leisure hours as punishment and boys could be returned to court if they misbehaved. On weekdays the boys worked as laborers at a nearby mental hospital. Weekends were taken up with house chores, recreation, and visitors.

Guided group interaction was centered in group therapy sessions held five nights a week. The sessions focused on each boy's "problem" and the progress he was making on it. The group interaction was guided toward socializing experiences enabling delinquents to discuss, examine, and understand their problems, free of the threats they had previously faced.

The effects were evaluated by comparing Highfields boys with state training school boys who met criteria for admission to Highfields (Weeks, 1958). Unfortunately, the groups were not entirely comparable, because those who went to Highfields did so at the discretion of judges and as a voluntary condition of probation.

The results showed that 63 percent of the Highfields boys completed their stays (typically four months) and were not reinstitutionalized for at least a year following discharge. This contrasted with 47 percent of training school boys not being reinstitutionalized within eight months of discharge. (The difference in follow-up intervals is partly due to the longer terms spent in the training school.) The difference in recidivism (relapse into crime) was especially pronounced for blacks: 59 percent of those from Highfields completed their stay and were not reinstitutionalized, compared to 33 percent from the training school; for whites, the corresponding figures were 64 percent and 59 percent.

Personality and attitude tests administered at admission and discharge did not show major differences. In both facilities, however, boys initially showing the most positive attitudes toward law enforcement had the best long-term outcomes.

Essexfields. The apparently better results of Highfields in shorter time and at lower cost than the training school led New Jersey to start other group homes with similar programs. Another variant, known as Essexfields, was situated in an urban area and the boys returned home at night.

Boys who went to Essexfields were compared with similar boys on probation, sent to Highfields or other group homes, or sent to the training school. Recidivism during a two-year follow-up was 15 percent for probation, 41 percent for group homes, 45 percent for Essexfields, and 53 percent for the training school (Stephenson & Scarpitti, 1969). When "treatment failures" (mainly those who recidivated before their treatment was finished) were included, the recidivism rate rose to 32 percent for probation, but it is not clear what it was for Essexfields and the group homes. In a somewhat similar comparison of a private institution (Boys Republic) and a group home where boys went home on weekends, Empey and Lubeck (1971) found 12-month recidivism rates of 44 percent for the institution boys and 40 percent for the group home.

The small differences among recidivism rates for the treatments other than probation imply that none is much more successful than the others. Yet in analyzing predictor variables such as socioeconomic status, delinquency record, and race, Stephenson and Scarpitti found that high-risk boys often did better at Essexfields and group homes than elsewhere. This was especially true for lower SES blacks with long delinquency records. It suggests that funneling certain types of high-risk delinquents into Essexfields and group homes may improve the success rate with this group.

Behavior Modification

Behavioral methods reward prosocial behavior as an antidote to antisocial behavior. This use of positive rewards should not be confused with approaches that offer reward or freedom noncontingently, as in Balderton Hospital's self-governing unit for sociopathic adolescents (Crafts et al., 1964). Instead, rewards are offered on an explicit contractual basis to motivate behavior. Behavioral approaches to antisocial behavior also use punishment, especially through deprivation of reward. Instead of indiscriminately punishing delinquents, however, behavioral approaches use specific punishments to reduce specifically targeted behaviors. Various behavioral techniques, especially token systems, are applied to antisocial behavior among institutionalized delinquents (Holt & Hobbs, 1979) and noninstitutionalized aggressive children (Horne & Patterson, 1980). Behaviorally oriented family therapy for delinquents has also shown a significant reduction of recidivism as compared to client-centered or psychodynamic family therapy or no treatment, and has prevented delinquency among the siblings of the treated delinquents (Klein, Alexander, & Parsons, 1977).

CASE-II-MODEL Project. One of the most thorough applications of behavioral methods with hardcore delinquents was undertaken at the National Training School (NTS), a Federal reform school (Cohen & Filipczak, 1971). Known as the CASE-II-MODEL Project (Contingencies Applicable to Special Education-Motivationally Oriented Designs for an Ecology of Learning), it was implemented for one year following a pilot test (CASE-I).

A point system was set up in which each point was worth one cent. On arrival, a new inmate, called a "student educational researcher," was temporarily given a private sleeping room and was tested for IQ and achievement. The student was paid one point for every correct answer on the tests. Thereafter, he could earn more points for studying and passing tests. Points tallied by staff members were used instead of tokens, which were vulnerable to theft.

The points could purchase entrance to the recreational lounge, better food than the usual institutional fare, clothes, items in the store ranging up to TV sets, merchandise from mail-order catalogues, telephone calls, transportation home, and—after a free introductory period—continued use of a private sleeping room and private shower. Not being required to work for points, students could choose to go on "relief," which meant regular NTS treatment such as sleeping in a group room and receiving standard institutional food and clothing.

The program aimed to develop adaptive academic skills in boys who were too academically deficient to get jobs. Unlike the isolation and punishment philosophy of traditional institutions, CASE-II sought to motivate delinquents to learn behavior needed for success in the outside world. Most educational instruction used programmed materials and teaching machines, enabling students to advance at their own rates. They earned points for passing tests more advanced than the level at which they began.

Normal social behavior was also encouraged. Over the objection of the Chief Chaplain of the Federal Bureau of Prisons, the boys were allowed to buy magazines like Playboy and to hang pin-ups in their rooms. They could also purchase admission to coed social events and could earn weekend passes during which they were encouraged to date. Unlike the traditional NTS policy of discouraging, ridiculing, and punishing masturbation and preventing solitude when it might occur, private rooms (when earned) made masturbation as acceptable as for noninstitutionalized boys.

Most CASE students improved several grade levels on achievement measures, and their mean IQs increased from 93 to 105.

Follow-ups showed that students who had spent at least 90 days in CASE and were released directly from CASE had a recidivism rate of 27 percent in the first year and 36 percent by the end of two years. Of the students who had gone to other penal programs after CASE was terminated, 63 percent were arrested in their first year out, and 69 percent by the end of two and one-half years. Previous NTS data had indicated a recidivism rate of 76 percent for similar juveniles in the first year, although no matched control group was evaluated.

Teaching Family Homes. In Chapter 10, we discussed Achievement Place, a Kansas group home founded in 1967 to apply behavioral principles to the education and socialization of youth at risk for delinquency. It has evolved into the Teaching Family Model which is now used in over 150 group homes for youth needing special care (Jones, 1979). In this model, a small group of 12- to 18-year-olds live in a homelike environment with house parents who use behavioral principles to teach adaptive behavior. To encourage uniformity of procedures, standardized training is required for certification as teaching family house parents.

Token reinforcement starts with points awarded for specific behaviors and exchangeable for privileges on a daily basis. Success at the first level leads to higher levels that culminate in a merit system without points. School performance as well as behavior in the house is targeted for reinforcement. Counseling and direct teaching of new skills are also emphasized, however.

There is abundant evidence for improved behavior and decreased delinquencies while youth are in teaching family programs (Quay, 1979). Effects on later delinquency are less clear, because they have been assessed by comparing outcomes for youth who were not assigned to other programs in a randomized or matched fashion. In comparisons between teaching family and other types of group homes, similar reductions of offense rates have been found for both. Youths from teaching family homes improved more in school performance, however. These homes are also rated more favorably by court and social agency personnel, and they generally cost only about two-thirds as much per youth as other group home programs (Jones, 1979).

Cognitive-Behavioral Approaches. Efforts to blend cognitive and behavioral approaches to problem behavior have been extended to delinquency as well (Little & Kendall, 1979). Delinquents' conspicuous deficits in handling social situations (Freedman, Rosenthal, Donahoe, Schlundt, & McFall, 1978) have prompted programs for improving social skills through role playing and modeling. Chandler (1973), for example, randomly assigned 11- to 13-year-old noninstitutionalized delinquent boys to one of three groups: A group designed to train role-playing by writing, performing, and videotaping skits about boys their own age; a group that likewise spent a half day per week for 10 weeks making films about their neighborhood; and a no-treatment control group. The role-taking group not only improved more than the others in role-taking ability, but also showed a significantly greater decline in delinquencies over the following 18 months.

Using incarcerated 15- to 18-year-old boys, Sarason (1978) similarly found improvements on self-report measures and recidivism following 16-session programs that featured either modeling or discussion of ways to handle real-life situations such as job interviews. The modeling program, which, like Chandler's (1973) program, aimed to teach effective role playing, seemed to have a better effect on the delinquents' attitudes, especially those of neurotic, socially inadequate delinquents. Both programs showed similar recidivism rates of about 25 percent over five years, however, as compared to about 50 percent for untreated control delinquents.

DIFFERENTIAL TREATMENT

We have seen evidence for different personality types among delinquents and the low success rate of most treatment programs that do not differentiate among them. Yet there have been few attempts to tailor treatments to the different personality types. Juvenile court judges may try to individualize the justice they dispense, but their limited range of options, lack of objective criteria for identifying personality types, and lack of follow-ups make this haphazard at best, although judges are loath to give it up (cf. Dean & Repucci, 1973).

California Youth Authority Studies

The California Youth Authority has made the most ambitious efforts to evaluate differential treatment. These efforts were guided largely by Marguerite Warren's (1969, 1972) concepts of interpersonal maturity. According to Warren, there are seven levels of interpersonal maturity. These range from the interpersonal reactions of the newborn baby, to an ideal of social maturity seldom attained in our culture. Most adolescent delinquents range from Level 2 to Level 4. People at Maturity Level 2 demand that the world take care of them; they see others as either "givers" or "withholders"; they cannot effectively explain, understand, or predict the behavior of others; and they are not interested in things outside themselves except as sources of supply.

Within each level are subtypes characterized by specific behavioral reactions. The subtypes at Level 2, for example, are the *Asocial Aggressive,* who reacts to frustration with active demands and open hostility, and the *Asocial Passive,* who reacts with whining, complaining, and withdrawal.

People at Maturity Level 3 understand others better, but they perceive the world on a power dimension and manipulate their environments for short-term gains. The subtypes at Level 3 are the *Immature Conformist,* who responds with immediate compliance to whomever holds sway at the moment; the *Cultural Conformist,* who conforms to delinquent peers; and the *Manipulator,* who tries to undermine authority figures and gain the upper hand.

Individuals at Maturity Level 4 have internalized standards by which they judge behavior. They are concerned about status and have rigid "good-bad" standards with no tolerance of ambiguity. The subtypes at Level 4 are the *Neurotic Acting-Out* delinquent who responds to underlying guilt with efforts to avoid conscious anxiety; the *Neurotic Anxious* delinquent who shows symptoms of emotional disturbance in response to feelings of inadequacy and guilt; the *Situational Emotional Reaction* subtype who responds to crises by acting out; and the *Cultural Identifier,* who identifies with deviant values and deliberately lives out these values (Warren, 1969, 1972). Note that Maturity Level 2 is somewhat analogous to the psychopathic personality-behavioral cluster, Level 3 to the subcultural cluster, and the first two Level 4 subtypes to the neurotic-disturbed cluster.

In a test of various treatments, delinquents committed to the California Youth Authority were first sent to diagnostic centers for classification on the basis of interviews and observations. The delinquents were then assigned to treatments, many of which were community-based programs.

One finding was that careful matching of delinquent subtypes with group home workers having styles appropriate to those subtypes reduced recidivism during a two-year follow-up. A second finding was that grouping by subtypes within a living unit resulted in fewer rule infractions, peer problems, and transfers to closer confinement, especially for Manipulators, Cultural Conformists, and Acting Out Neurotics. These same groups also did best in a community program, while Cultural Identifiers were more effectively handled by incarceration. Another finding was that behavior modification was best for the two types of asocial delinquents and for the Cultural Conformists. On the other hand, guided group interaction worked best for Acting Out Neurotics. Later research showed that seriously disturbed Neurotic (or "conflicted") youth benefitted most from community placement if they had a short residential placement first (Warren, 1977).

Behavior Modification Versus Transactional Analysis. In an exceptionally thorough comparison of two treatment programs, Jesness (1975) appraised differences in outcomes for 15- to 17-year-old delinquents showing different maturity levels as well as comparing the programs' net effect across various types of delinquents. One program featured a token economy like that of the CASE-II project described earlier (Cohen & Filipczak, 1971). The other program was based on principles of transactional analysis: Each boy was given a primer on transactional analysis, and his counselor held a "life script" interview with him. The interview was used to negotiate a verbal contract specifying how the boy would like to change. Counselors then met with their boys twice weekly for group therapy. Transactional analysis principles were also used in everyday management, classrooms, and large group meetings held two or three times a week. Each program operated at one California Youth Authority institution.

What were the outcomes? Questionnaire self-reports and behavior ratings by staff showed that boys in the transactional analysis program had more positive attitudes toward themselves and the treatment program. But the boys in the behavioral program showed more overt behavioral improvement. These differences in immediate effects thus reflected the different foci of the programs.

Follow-ups over 24 months showed virtually identical rates of parole violations among boys from the two programs, although these rates were significantly lower than for boys not in the programs (approximately 33 percent versus 42 percent, respectively). The absence of a matched control group weakens this finding somewhat, but it does suggest an overall favorable impact on recidivism.

Classification of boys according to maturity level showed the clearest differential responses for Level 3 Manipulators: Those receiving the transactional analysis program achieved significantly greater attitudinal and behavioral gains, as well as less recidivism than those receiving the behavioral program. Other differences in responsiveness were less clearcut, although the least mature boys (Level 2) seemed to profit more from the behavioral program. Analysis of the differential effects indicated that each type of program could benefit from certain features of the other: The transactional analysis program might profit from more explicit behavioral goals and performance criteria, whereas the behavioral program might profit from negotiating goals with the boys rather than imposing them from without.

Kennedy Youth Center

Another approach to differential treatment was taken at the Robert F. Kennedy Youth Center, the successor to the National Training School. The physical plant, located in Morgantown, West Virginia, was specially designed to facilitate the CASE-II system. A behavior checklist, self-report questionnaire, and life history checklist were used to classify delinquents as inadequate-immature, neurotic-disturbed, unsocialized-psychopathic, or socialized-subcultural (Cavior & Schmidt, 1978).

An overall token economy was based on the CASE-II model, but youths of each type were assigned to cottages having staff suited to their type. Treatment goals and point payoffs were worked out by each youth with his cottage staff. Various other treatments, such as transactional analysis, were employed according to each youth's characteristics. The token economy had three levels: *trainee, apprentice,* and *honors.* To be promoted to a higher level, a youth had to attain the goals set for the preceding level. Pay and privileges were greater at the higher levels, but fines for violations were also greater. Prior to release, honors level youths moved to prerelease cottages where they gained additional privileges.

Although no definitive comparison with other well-matched groups was possible, three-year follow-ups of youths released from the Kennedy Center and another federal institution showed reincarceration rates of about 42 percent for both (Cavior & Schmidt, 1978). A tendency for Kennedy Center unsocialized-psychopathic youths to have better outcomes was a hopeful sign, but termination of the program prevented further study of differential treatment.

In summary, outcome studies have shown promising effects of some well-focused treatments in particular delinquent populations. But increasing the precision of treatment requires sustained funding and close collaboration between researchers, practitioners, and public officials.

PREVENTION

Effective treatment programs for delinquents are hard to create and evaluate, but prevention programs are still harder, because the target populations include potential nondelinquents as well as potential delinquents and the subjects may see no reason to participate. Nonetheless, one of the first large-scale efforts to deal with delinquency was an attempt at prevention, the Cambridge-Somerville Youth Project, described earlier in the chapter (McCord, 1982).

The basic strategy was to compare later delinquency in matched boys receiving either no intervention or the long-term assistance of an adult counselor. The specific interventions varied from boy to boy, but these variations were considered less important than the benefit of the relationship provided. Yet the 30-year follow-up finding of significantly *poorer* outcomes for the treated group shows that well-intentioned preventive efforts may actually have negative impacts. School-based preventive programs have also failed to reduce delinquency in boys (Reckless & Dinitz, 1972) or girls (Meyer, Borgatta, & Jones, 1965), although no negative impacts were evident over short follow-up periods.

Taking gangs as his prevention target, Miller (1962) asssessed efforts of streetcorner workers to influence seven adolescent gangs receiving intensive attention and seven superficial attention. Seven others got no attention. A follow-up showed almost identical rates of court appearances for all three groups of gangs.

Targeting High-Risk Individuals

It seems clear that preventive efforts focused on broad populations containing only some future delinquents have not reduced subsequent delinquency. Because even in the worst neighborhoods many children do not become delinquent, population-focused preventive programs must have very strong benefits to improve outcome rates for the target population as a whole. Furthermore, McCord's (1982) finding that a population-focused program seems to have *worsened* the outcomes raises further cautions about such efforts.

But what if we could identify youth who are quite certain to be delinquent? There is evidence that interventions with youth who are individually at high risk for crime can be more effective than interventions focused on groups containing only a few individuals who are genuinely at risk. As an example, a preventive effort in Hawaii used a "buddy system" whereby indigenous nonprofessionals served as buddies for 10- to 17-year-olds referred by schools, police, courts, social agencies, and community residents (O'Donnell, Lydgate, & Fo, 1979). The adult buddy met frequently with the youngster and used contingency management procedures to reinforce school attendance, academic performance, and nondelinquent behavior.

Among youngsters who were previously arrested for criminal offenses, the buddy system significantly reduced arrests over a three-year follow-up, as compared to an untreated control group. Buddy system participants, however, who had *not* previously been arrested for criminal offenses were subsequently arrested *more* than control youngsters without previous offenses. Furthermore, the participants without previous arrests who remained longest in the buddy system showed the greatest increase in subsequent arrests!

The authors interpreted this disappointing finding as reflecting the influence of the more serious delinquent participants on the participants who had not previously been arrested, many of whom were probably not actually at high risk for delinquency.

Another effort may owe its more successful preventive consequences to its focus on the *families* of youngsters at especially high risk because they had an older sibling who was delinquent (Klein, Alexander, & Parsons, 1977). Court-referred delinquents and their families were assigned to one of three family therapy treatments or a no-treatment control group. One type of family therapy was behaviorally oriented. It aimed to improve clarity of communication, reciprocity of social reinforcement, and contingency contracting that emphasized equivalence of rights and responsibilities for all family members. A second type of family therapy was client-centered, while a third was psychodynamically oriented.

Follow-ups of the target delinquents showed significantly less recidivism (26 percent) following the behaviorally oriented family therapy than the other conditions (47 to 73 percent). Moreover, 2½- to 3½-year follow-ups of the *siblings* of the target delinquents showed that significantly fewer of those whose families received the behaviorally oriented therapy had court contacts (20 percent) than those receiving the other conditions (40 to 63 percent). The types of family interaction targeted by the behavioral therapy were also found to be better in the families whose children remained free of court involvement.

As a byproduct of a remediation effort, prevention in this case seems to have succeeded for three reasons:

1. It focused on youngsters who were genuinely at high risk (they had a delinquent sibling).

2. It dealt with variables having a direct impact on the youngsters' behavior (family interactions).
3. It used a treatment with a documented impact on these variables.

The failure of population-focused preventive efforts could reflect their failure to do 1 and 2. Yet the poor performance of the client-centered and psychodynamic family therapy shows that 1 and 2 are not enough for successful prevention: In fact, because both the client-centered and psychodynamic therapies were followed by *higher* rates of sibling court contacts (59 percent and 63 percent, respectively) than the no-treatment control (40 percent), they may have had adverse effects like those McCord (1982) and O'Donnell et al. (1980) found for other preventive efforts. Thus, preventive efforts must not only be accurately aimed at appropriate individuals and variables, but they must also have the power to affect those variables favorably. And to find out which methods actually have this power, we need careful comparative studies like that of Klein, Alexander, and Parsons.

SUMMARY

Early psychological explanations for aggression included Freud's concept of an aggressive instinctual drive and Dollard et al.'s hypothesis that frustration causes aggression. Dollard's hypothesis generated research showing that frustration often leads to aggression, but that there are other reactions to frustration and other instigations to aggression.

Children's aggression is increased by parental permissiveness and encouragement of aggression; reinforcement of aggression by compliance of the victim; imitation of aggressive models; parental deviance, quarrelsomeness, and rejection; and preference for violent television programs. Severe punishment for aggression is positively correlated with aggression in early childhood but negatively correlated with aggression in later childhood. "Cathartic" aggression does not seem to reduce subsequent aggression and may increase it. Aggressiveness is relatively stable from childhood to adulthood in males and seems increasingly so in females.

Children's moral *behavior* is strongly affected by situational variables, but their moral *judgments* are closely related to their level of cognitive development. Prosocial behavior seems to arise spontaneously at early ages in at least some children. Its relation to antisocial behavior and moral judgment is as yet unclear.

Juvenile crime has risen steadily since about 1950. Three personality-behavioral patterns have been repeatedly replicated in studies of male delinquents: *Socialized-subcultural* delinquency is especially characteristic of lower SES boys from broken, disorganized homes with deviant parents; *unsocialized-psychopathic* delinquency occurs in all social classes and is characterized by poor peer relations, low fear of punishment, and chronic misbehavior; *disturbed-neurotic* delinquency probably encompasses a diverse group of disturbed and organically-damaged youth.

Female delinquency has risen faster than male delinquency since about 1965, although more boys than girls are still arrested. Girls show less physical aggression than boys, but there is evidence for three personality-behavioral patterns among females like those among males.

Informal supervision, probation, and incarceration are the treatment options typically open to juvenile courts. Recidivism following incarceration generally runs between 70 and 80 percent. Psychotherapy and various therapeutic milieux have produced mixed results. Compared to incarceration, group homes may cut recidivism somewhat for certain types of delinquents and are much cheaper.

Efforts to tailor treatments to particular subtypes of delinquents have shown that some treatments help certain subtypes while harming others. Preventive efforts aimed at general population groups have not been successful, although modification of family interactions may prevent delinquency in youngsters who are at especially high risk.

SUGGESTED READING

Development of Aggression. Baron (1977) gives an overview of theories and research on the development of aggression. Most empirical research on variables affecting childhood aggression has approached it from the learning point of view. Examples include Bandura and Walters' (1959) comparison of aggressive and nonaggressive boys and their parents; Eron, Walder, and Lefkowitz's (1971) study of family characteristics relating to aggression; and Patterson's (1980) analysis of reinforcement for aggression occurring in children's interpersonal relations. Redl and Wineman (1957) provide a classic psychoanalytic picture of extremely aggressive children.

Subcultural Delinquency. Good pictures of what it's like to be young in a high delinquency slum can be found in Claude Brown's (1965) autobiographical book, *Manchild in the Promised Land,* and in Rosenberg and Silverstein's (1969) accounts of youth attitudes in three ethnically different high delinquency communities.

Psychopathy. Cleckley's, *The Mask of Sanity* (1976), is a classic on psychopathy (sociopathy, antisocial personality). Cleckley recounts many fascinating case histories including those of a psychopathic scientist, businessman, physician, and psychiatrist, along with his hypothesis as to the underlying nature of psychopathy. Reid (1978) provides an extensive review of theories and empirical research on psychopathy.

Treatment. Street et al. (1966) made a sociological comparison of six residential settings for delinquents, including traditional penal settings, educational settings, and treatment-oriented settings. An extensive description of the Highfields guided group interaction program can be found in McCorkle et al (1958) and an evaluation of this program in Weeks (1958). Cohen and Filipczak (1971) describe in detail the

CASE-II behavioral program at the National Training School. Warren (1977) presents the rationale for her system of differential diagnosis and treatment of delinquents by the California Youth Authority. Jesness (1975) reports a careful comparison of behavioral and transactional analysis programs for delinquents, plus findings according to the California Youth Authority typology.

Chronic Offenders. There is growing evidence that most serious crimes are the work of a small proportion of delinquent youth and that these few commit a truly impressive volume of crime, much of it violent. Reforming or incapacitating this small group could therefore have a great impact on crime rates. They may also be the hardest to influence, however. Building on previous research, *The Violent Few*, by Hamparian, Schuster, Dinitz, and Conrad (1978), offers a detailed study of these youth and what might be done about them.

CHAPTER 14

Drug Abuse

Alcohol and other drugs have long been used for nonmedicinal purposes. What some may view as a scourge unique to the youth of our times is a form of behavior manifested by people of many ages in many societies and historical epochs. However, Figure 14-1 shows that, among today's adolescents, there is a fairly strong relation between referral for mental health services and illict drug and alcohol use: At age 16, 59 percent of clinically referred girls and 44 percent of clinically referred boys were reported to use drugs or alcohol, as compared to only about 10 percent of demographically matched nonreferred 16-year-olds (Achenbach & Edelbrock, 1981). Factor analyses of behavior problems for the referred group showed that alcohol and drug use was correlated primarily with the syndrome of delinquent behavior shown in Table 13-1 (Achenbach, 1978; Achenbach & Edelbrock, 1979).

To understand the popularity of drugs for pleasure, the drugs selected, the social significance of use, and the nonphysiological consequences, we need to consider the psychosocial context. As an example, in early nineteenth century England, an opiate-based patent medicine, *Dr. Godfrey's Cordial,* was widely recommended for young children "that are weakly and restless . . . and those that are greatly troubled with gripes, vomitings, or loosenesses" (Wilson, 1968, p. 141). A large teaspoonful was prescribed for one-year-olds, half that for six-month-olds, and so forth according to age. Contemporary accounts tell of the cordial's huge sales and its obviously addictive effects. A surgeon of the time reported that such drugs were a common cause of death among children and that he considered

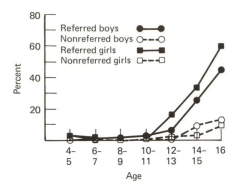

Figure 14.1. Percent of children referred for mental health services whose parents reported drug or alcohol use, as compared to demographically similar children not referred for services. (From Achenbach & Edelbrock, 1981.)

informing the coroner of the deaths he knew they caused, but their use was so widespread he doubted he could make an impression (Wilson, 1968).

At the turn of this century, the United States had an estimated 240,000 opiate addicts (Boyd, 1971)—a far larger share of the population than now addicted. Many addicts were women who took opiate-based medicines like *Dr. Godfrey's Cordial* for their aches and ailments. Little social censure or crime was associated with such medicines despite their physiological and behavioral effects. In fact, opiate addiction was regarded as less serious than alcoholism, and some physicians proposed opium as a cure for alcoholism. Heroin was considered still less harmful, as it seemed to cure morphine addiction and was substituted for other opiates in tonics and cough medicines. Medical journals stressed its nonaddictive properties (Nyswander, 1963). Following the ban on nonmedical opiate use by the Harrison Narcotics Act of 1914, the number of addicts dropped markedly, especially among women. Yet the association between crime and narcotics increased, because many remaining addicts were men who turned to crime to get their now illicit drugs.

TYPES OF DRUGS AND THEIR EFFECTS

Before examining psychosocial factors related to drug abuse in today's adolescents, we must distinguish among types of drugs and their effects. The biochemical and pharmacological properties of the drugs are beyond the scope of this book, but Table 14-1 outlines the major categories of habit-forming drugs subject to widespread abuse, their effects, and current beliefs as to whether they cause physical as well as psychological dependence.

All the drugs in Table 14-1 are *psychoactive;* that is, they alter subjective feeling states via the central nervous system. A drug is usually considered to cause *physiological dependence* if it evokes a physiological state that requires continued ingestion of the drug to prevent physiological withdrawal symptoms. Some drugs, whether or not they cause physiological dependence, induce *physical tolerance,*

Table 14-1   Some Commonly Abused Drugs

Type of Dependence	Drug	Effect on Central Nervous system
A. Psychological	1. Organic solvents[a] (e.g., acetone, benzene contained in glue)	Depressant
	2. Mescaline (peyote)	Hallucinogenic
	3. Psilocybin	Hallucinogenic
	4. Cocaine	Stimulant
	5. LSD (lysergic acid diethylamide)	Hallucinogenic
	6. PCP (phencyclidine)	Hallucinogenic
B. Psychological and mild or questionable physiological dependence	1. Amphetamines (e.g., Benzedrine, Dexedrine)	Stimulant
	2. Methylphenidate (Ritalin)	Stimulant
	3. Cannabis	Hallucinogenic
C. Psychological and physiological dependence	1. Alcohol	Depressant
	2. Tobacco	Depressant
	3. Sleeping pills (e.g., methaqualone, ethchlorvynol)	Depressant
	4. Barbiturates (e.g., secobarbital, pentobarbital, phenobarbital)	Depressant
	5. "Minor" tranquilizers (e.g., Librium, Valium, Equanil)	Depressant
	6. Opiates (e.g., opium, heroin, morphine)	Depressant
	7. Synthetic opiate-like drugs (e.g., methadone, pethidine)	Depressant

[a] Pharmacological properties of solvents give them potential for physiological dependence, but type of use, typically by young boys, makes physiological dependence unlikely.
Source: From American Psychiatric Association (1980) and Schnoll (1979).

meaning that increasing doses are needed to get a particular subjective effect. LSD and related drugs, for example, produce marked tolerance without physiological dependence. Amphetamines produce marked tolerance accompanied by a questionable type of physiological dependence. Opiates produce enormous tolerance, plus strong physiological and psychological dependence, goading users to increase their consumption.

Physiological withdrawal symptoms used to be the criterion for classifying a drug as addictive, but *psychological dependence* appears more crucial to addiction than physiological dependence. Some drugs such as cocaine, cause no physiological dependence or tolerance, but very strong psychological dependence. Moreover, the physiological dependence and tolerance evoked by drugs such as the opiates seem to sustain addiction more through psychological than physiological mechanisms: After physiological addiction is established, drug-taking behavior is reinforced by avoidance of withdrawal symptoms. But even after complete physiological withdrawal, stimuli such as the sight of another addict can trigger conditioned withdrawal-type symptoms in an ex-addict, thus reactivating the habit (Isbell, 1972). Physical withdrawal is thus often followed by readdiction, because the old conditioned cues and reinforcers for drug taking retain their potency.

LICIT DRUGS

Tobacco

We need to pinpoint specific patterns of drug use, because generalizations about one drug may not hold for others. Licit drugs enjoying social support—such as alcohol and tobacco—do not involve the same patterns as illegal drugs, such as heroin. Yet, in terms of sheer quantity of harm, alcohol and tobacco are more dangerous than illicit drugs. Many states prohibit tobacco sales to minors under a stipulated age, often 16 or 18 years. Most parents and school officials also object to young people smoking, and illicit use of tobacco by juveniles has many earmarks of other early delinquencies—it often starts as a sign of toughness and rebellion. Because tobacco is so widely condoned and causes slow death rather than intoxication, however, its use is seldom considered a serious delinquency. Even anonymous questionnaire studies of self-admitted offenses omit questions on tobacco (e.g., Cernkovich & Giordano, 1979). Nevertheless, smoking at an early age is predictive of later use of illicit drugs (Green, 1979), and tobacco addiction closely resembles other addictions (Jaffe & Kanzler, 1980).

Alcohol

Alcohol is in some ways intermediate between tobacco and harder addictive drugs. Like tobacco, it is used illicitly by many youngsters, but its greater cost and more stringent control make it more likely to be obtained illegally, and its intoxicating effects are more conspicuously related to antisocial behavior. It is therefore of greater concern in relation to juvenile delinquency. Alcohol abuse is also a far larger problem than abuse of illegal drugs. There are an estimated 9 million alcohol abusers in the United States (DuPont, 1979). It has been estimated that over 50 percent of fatal traffic accidents involve at least one drunken driver. Adding the many crimes committed under the influence of alcohol to the 25,000 annual traffic deaths involving drink, the birth defects occurring in babies born to alcoholic mothers, the personal grief brought to families of alcoholics, and the physical debilitation resulting from alcoholism shows that alcohol abuse is our number 1 drug problem. Early alcohol use is also correlated with use of illicit drugs (Green, 1979).

Arrest statistics suggest that alcohol abuse presents a numerically larger problem than other drug abuse by juveniles. In a typical year, for example, there are about 190,000 arrests of youth under 18 for violations of liquor laws and drunkenness, compared to 174,000 for all violations of narcotic drug laws (U.S. Department of Justice, 1979). Because simple possession of alcohol is less likely to bring arrest than possession of other drugs, the arrest statistics probably underestimate the disparity in usage; however, arrests for drug offenses have risen much faster than alcohol arrests. Between 1969 and 1979, for example, drug arrests rose 93 percent, whereas arrests for violation of alcohol laws rose only 19 percent, and arrests for drunkenness declined (U.S. Department of Justice, 1979).

ILLICIT DRUGS

Even though alcohol offenses are more common among the young and abuse of alcohol may cost our society more than drug addiction, abuse of other drugs is of greater current concern and probably bears more directly on serious youth crime. Moreover, the tremendous rise in the extent and variety of drug abuse has ramifications at every level of our society. National surveys show that roughly 60 percent of high school seniors report illicit drug experiences (Green, 1979).

Drug Abuse in Other Developed Countries

The total quantity of drug abuse among young Americans appears higher, or at least better publicized, than in most other countries, but drug abuse has risen in other developed countries as well. The United Kingdom, which long permitted physicians to prescribe opiates and cocaine for addicts, witnessed an increase from 437 to 2,782 known addicts during the 1960s, for example (Beedle, 1972).

Why the sudden rise? It seemed due largely to a new drug culture among youths who first got narcotics from addicts and others posing as addicts who obtained prescriptions from physicians (James, 1969). The "British system" of prescribing drugs for addicts had successfully stabilized the number of addicts for four decades, but was unsuccessful when new values arose among the young. This shows the impact of cultural factors on drug use regardless of official drug policies. Nevertheless, treatment programs, compulsory registration of addicts, and curtailment of prescriptions reduced known British addicts to 1,430 in 1970. In West Germany, however, where drug policies more closely resemble those of the United States, rising supplies of potent heroin from Afghanistan, Pakistan, and Iran led to a big increase in heroin addiction and deaths from overdoses in the late 1970s (Lentz, 1979).

Cannabis

Marijuana is the most widely used illicit drug and the crux of the greatest controversy. Much that is said of marijuana can also be said for hashish, which comes from the same plant *(Cannabis sativa,* "Indian hemp"). Marijuana—also known as "grass," "pot," "tea," "joint," "boo," "Mary Jane," and "dope"— is typically a mixture of crushed cannabis leaves, flowers, and twigs; hashish ("hash") is made from the more potent resin of the plant. The principal active chemical compound is *tetrahydrocannabinol* (THC), which is sometimes taken in pure form to get stronger effects than smoking cannabis. Many cultures have used cannabis for medicinal, ceremonial, and intoxicating purposes. Marijuana smoking spread in the southwestern United States and especially New Orleans around 1910, largely as a result of contact with Mexicans, who started using it widely in the late nineteenth century. The word marijuana is Mexican. Black jazz musicians, their fans, and lower income urban blacks were the first in the United States known to use marijuana on a large scale. During the 1920s and 1930s, New Orleans served as the major distribution center from which marijuana was shipped up the Mississippi to other urban areas. In 1944, a committee appointed by New York Mayor LaGuardia reported that there were at least 500 individual marijuana peddlers in Harlem and 500 "tea pads" where marijuana was sold (Commission of Inquiry into the Nonmedical Use of Drugs, 1972—hereafter cited as CINUD).

White middle class use of marijuana rose after World War II when soldiers who started using it in the service returned to college campuses under the G.I. Bill. Its spread was further encouraged in the 1950s by popular Beat writers William Burroughs, Allen Ginsberg, and Jack Kerouac.

In the 1960s, burgeoning use reflected the psychedelic youth culture in which popular rock groups touted drug-induced ecstasies. Drugs also became a prominent youth symbol in intergenerational conflicts, heightened enormously by the Vietnam war. The war itself helped spread marijuana use among American servicemen who first began using it in Vietnam, where it is abundantly available in potent form (Robins, 1978). It was estimated that 50 to 60 percent of soldiers had at least experimented with marijuana while stationed in Vietnam (U.S. House Committee on Armed Services, 1971).

Over 15 million Americans smoke marijuana at least weekly and 60 percent of high school seniors have tried it (Johnston, Bachman, & O'Malley, 1979). The easy availability of marijuana makes it unnecessary to become part of a special group to get the drug. Most Americans first try marijuana out of curiosity at the urging of friends (CINUD, 1972).

Marijuana is classed as a hallucinogen in Table 14-1 because heavy doses induce hallucinations, thought disorder, and delusions. In the more typical smaller doses, the subjective effects are a feeling of being high, mild intoxication, loosening of inhibitions, increased self-confidence, and uncontrollable hilarity or crying. Under intermediate doses, there is a rush of thoughts. Sights and sounds seem more vivid, and there may be an illusion that one is thinking better. Judgment and memory become impaired, and confusion, disorientation, and mood variation occur. Acute panic reactions and fear of going crazy also occur (Jones, 1978).

As with most psychoactive drugs, the effects of marijuana depend on the user's circumstances, personality, and expectations. Initial use seldom offers positive experiences. These usually come only after training in inhalation procedures and guidance by veteran users as to the drug's effects. Between 20 and 50 percent of users are estimated to discontinue after a few trials (CINUD, 1972). Those who continue moderate to heavy use appear to restrict their associations to other users, partly in order to maintain secrecy, although the need for special contacts with dealers and fear of arrest now appear minimal. Heavy long-term users show many of the characteristics of mental inertia found in chronic alcoholics (Boyd, 1971), and emotionally vulnerable individuals may suffer panic, paranoia, or psychosis.

Although there are signs of greater psychopathology in chronic users than nonusers, it is not known whether cannabis leads to psychopathology through neurological, emotional, or psychosocial effects, or whether psychopathology contributes to chronic usage (Jones, 1978). The same question as to causal direction arises with respect to statistical associations between cannabis use and other forms of crime. It is unknown whether such associations arise because someone willing to break one law (e.g., by using cannabis) is more likely than average to commit other offenses, or whether a lessening of inhibitions through cannabis consumption makes a person more inclined to crime. There are a few reports of crimes committed under the influence of cannabis and of crimes committed in order to obtain it (CINUD, 1972). Furthermore, the younger the age at first marijuana use, the more likely a person is to sell drugs and engage in other crimes (O'Donnell & Clayton, 1979).

Marijuana has several short-term physiological effects, such as increased pulse rate; bloodshot eyes; puffing around the eyes; drying of the mouth, throat, and nasal passages; stimulation of the appetite; nausea; and drowsiness. Long-term effects have not been well studied, although the carcinogenic potential of marijuana smoking probably equals that of tobacco. Both yield similar amounts of tar, and the typically lower frequency of marijuana than tobacco smoking is offset by the deeper inhalation and longer retention of marijuana smoke. Studies of long-term hashish users have not revealed organic pathology specifically attributable to the drug (Stefanis, Dornbush, & Fink, 1977).

Marijuana, Hard Drugs, and Social Problems. A common argument against legalizing marijuana is that its use "leads to" use of more dangerous drugs, especially heroin, amphetamines, and LSD. Marijuana is usually the first illicit drug tried by eventual hard drug users, although they are also heavy consumers of tobacco and alcohol (O'Donnell & Clayton, 1979).

There is longitudinal evidence on relations between marijuana and hard drug use by urban black males who were adolescents when marijuana was already plentiful in their neighborhoods. In a follow-up of youth growing up in St. Louis, over 200 black men were interviewed at an average age of about 33 (Robins, Darvish, & Murphy, 1970). Police, Federal Bureau of Narcotics, and hospital records also supplied data on the men. Almost half the men reported using marijuana at some time, and a third had begun before they were 20.

Comparisons of the marijuana users with nondrug users showed that more of the users (1) failed to graduate from high school and college; (2) married spouses who had previous marriages or illegitimate children; (3) reported their own marital infidelity and the fathering of illegitimate children; (4) earned less than $4000 per year; (5) worked at low-status jobs; (6) were unemployed; (7) received financial aid; (8) had adult police records for nondrug offenses; (9) drank heavily enough to create social or medical problems; and (10) reported violent behavior. Even when dropping out of high school, nondrug juvenile delinquency, and early drinking were controlled for, the differences between users and nonusers remained significant on the other variables.

Although it could not be conclusively proved that adolescent marijuana use was the *cause,* more subjects who began using marijuana in adolescence than in adulthood eventually went on to amphetamines, barbiturates, and opiates, to opiate addiction, heavy drinking, and medical or social problems with alcohol and alcoholism. Of youth who began using marijuana in adolescence, those who continued for more than five years also showed higher rates of nearly all the social problems studied than those who used it for less than five years.

From Robins's study, we cannot be sure if adolescent marijuana use *results from* other personal problems or *causes* problems. Yet the strong relation between early marijuana use and later social problems seems well established for this group of black urban males. Moreover, the evidence conclusively shows that marijuana does not function as a substitute for alcohol or other drugs and that users are not less violent than comparable nonusers. In fact, marijuana use was positively correlated with alcohol and other drug use and with violent behavior. Other studies also show high rates of tobacco, alcohol, and other drug use by frequent marijuana users (Johnston, 1980). Early marijuana use also seemed to impede solving typical adolescent social problems, making the users less prepared for adulthood and more likely to continue seeking refuge in drugs, including alcohol and hard drugs.

Other Hallucinogens

LSD (lysergic acid diethylamide, "acid") has probably been the most widely used hallucinogen beside cannabis. Like LSD, mescaline ("peyote") and psilocybin ("mushrooms") were also popular in the middle class drug culture of the 1960s. Their use has diminished since then, perhaps in response to stricter controls, fears of organic damage, and growing awareness of the harm done by bad trips. The decline of the psychedelic youth culture and their diminishing availability, as well as the lack of much sentiment for legalization, have generally reduced concern about these drugs (Schnoll, 1979).

Replacing LSD as a vicious hallucinogen, however, has been the animal tranquilizer phencyclidine (PCP, "angel dust," "crystal," "Pea Ce Pill"). Illegally sold in many forms under many different names, it is taken orally, smoked on parsley leaves, snorted, injected, and sometimes taken as eye drops. Because it is cheap and easy to make, it has become widely available and often mixed with or substituted for other drugs.

Although PCP evokes intense perceptual experiences resembling those of LSD, its side effects and mechanisms of action are quite different. Schizophrenialike psychoses have resulted, even in previously normal people. Feelings of depersonalization, isolation, and dependency occur, along with changes in the body image. Thought and learning are disrupted, and long-term speech and memory deficits emerge after chronic use. Chromosomal abnormalities and fetal mortality and defects appear to be elevated among PCP users. Bizarre, violent, and suicidal behavior has also led to accidental deaths (Lerner & Burns, 1979). Despite these risks, PCP has apparently been tried on an experimental basis by many youth and then become the preferred drug of small groups of chronic users. Young users have been found to believe that it is much safer than LSD (Lerner & Burns, 1979). The following is an example of PCP effects:

> A 15-year-old Caucasian male was found by police in a field with no clothes on, hanging on to a barbed-wire fence. He was distorted and incoherent upon questioning. A physical examination revealed a confused, disoriented youth with inflamed eyes, bloody mouth with an upper incisor missing, multiple scratches of the trunk, and scratches and lacerations of the extremities. Fluctuations in orientation were observed over the next 7 hours ranging from cooperative and alert to unarousable. Prior to being discharged the patient stated that he "smoked some phencyclidine and got awfully stoned." (Lerner & Burns, 1979, p. 337)

Some regular users, however, seem able to control their dosages sufficiently to enjoy the drug's bizarre effects (Feldman, Agar, & Beschner, 1979).

Stimulants

The most widely abused stimulants are amphetamines and cocaine. Methylpheni-date (Ritalin)—an amphetaminelike drug often prescribed for hyperactive children—has also become popular as a street drug. However, follow-ups of children for whom Ritalin was prescribed do not show elevated rates of stimulant or other drug abuse among them (Beck, Langford, MacKay, & Sum, 1975).

Amphetamines. Until about 1970, amphetamines ("speed," "pep pills," "up-pers") were among the most abundant drugs in the United States. They were legally prescribed for conditions ranging from hyperactivity, obesity, and depression, to stuffiness caused by head colds. As widespread abuse became evident, however, federal regulations drastically curtailed permitted uses. The most commonly abused amphetamines are Benzedrine ("bennies"), Dexedrine, and Methedrine.

Small doses produce feelings of self-confidence, alertness, and well-being for a few hours. As doses increase, repetitive activities, such as picking at the skin or trying to disassemble and assemble objects, may result (Schnoll, 1979). Heavy doses produce withdrawal, irritability, disorganized thinking, seizures, and paranoid psychoses. Not limited merely to vulnerable individuals, these psychoses are toxic reactions to the drug and can lead to murderous violence (Schnoll, 1979).

Because of increasing tolerance for amphetamines, users tend to progressively increase their doses. Withdrawal produces depression that can reach suicidal intensity. Increasing tolerance and the negative effects of withdrawal combine to drive heavy users toward continuous direct dosing, especially intravenous injection ("shooting speed"), and use of barbiturates or heroin to blot out the "crash" that comes when amphetamines wear off.

The social support of other users seems to enhance the pleasure of large doses and to encourage escalation. Adolescent users in the Haight-Ashbury district of San Francisco, for example, were found to progress rapidly from initial curiosity about diverse drugs, to abandonment of old life-styles, and adoption of the alliances, rhetoric, and attitudes of the speed culture, along with the crime required to get their drugs (Smith, 1972). Whether amphetamines contribute similarly to crime and violence outside subcultures like Haight-Ashbury is not known, although their potentially disastrous effects make them very risky.

Cocaine. In its stimulant effects, cocaine resembles amphetamines, but it is physiologically more toxic. During the 1970s, snorting cocaine became popular among middle class adults. When snorted, it produces a short, intense high. Long-term snorting can destroy the mucuous membranes of the nose (Schnoll, 1979). Other effects of heavy use include confusion, headache, nausea, vomiting, abdominal pain, aggression, and psychosis with delerium, convulsions, and coma. Especially risky is the "speedball"—cocaine mixed with heroin.

Opiates

Since about 1910, western countries have considered opiate addiction the most serious form of drug abuse. Opium comes from the juice of the poppy seed and has served as a pain killer and narcotic for thousands of years. Each grain of opium contains a tiny bit of morphine. Heroin ("H," "horse," "junk," "joy powder"), made by heating morphine in acetic acid, is the most widely abused derivative of opium, although morphine, paregoric, and codeine are also abused. Opiate addiction sometimes starts with oral ingestion, sniffing, and injection under the skin, but intravenous injection ("mainlining") of heroin is by far the most common and serious form.

The effects of opiates include reduction of the hunger, thirst, and sex drives; a relaxed, worry-free euphoria; and a high in which the user feels very self-confident. The high is followed by a period of inactivity bordering on stupor. Physical dependence, enormous increases in tolerance, pleasant feelings, fear of withdrawal symptoms, assimilation into the subculture of users, and the need for continuous criminal activity to raise funds all contribute to a tremendous psychological dependence. This dependence is not erased by withdrawal, even though physiological withdrawal from opiates is safer and quicker than withdrawal from barbiturates or alcohol. The extreme psychological dependence can be understood in terms of conditioning: Because heroin anesthesizes drive stimuli, any increase in a drive— including hunger and thirst—becomes a conditioned stimulus for the response of taking heroin (Platt & Labate, 1976). However, the discovery of specific receptors in the brain for opiates suggests a direct, physiologically based reinforcement mechanism as well.

Physical illness is endemic among heroin addicts, because hunger and thirst are abnormally suppressed, withdrawal effects and overdoses are common consequences of street heroin's varying purity, and unsterile needles transmit tetanus and hepatitis. An especially cruel side effect is the physiological addiction of babies born to addicted women. At birth, these babies go through withdrawal that can be fatal without proper treatment.

National and international restrictions on opiates early in this century greatly cut addiction in the United States. Most of the remaining addicts are concentrated in large urban areas. The number of American opiate addicts reached a low of about 43,000 in 1958, which was down from about 240,000 in 1900, but it rose to an estimated 550,000 in the 1970s (McCoy, McBride, Russe, Page, & Clayton, 1979). The age of addiction also dropped during that period, and heroin became the leading cause of death among 15- to 35-year-olds in New York City (Boyd, 1971). Many heroin deaths were also reported among children under 15. However, the addict population then stabilized and heroin deaths declined as supplies of high grade heroin from Turkey, Mexico, and the Far East were reduced (New York *Times*, 1980a). Nevertheless, some of the reduction in heroin deaths may reflect shifts to abuse of legally obtainable drugs such as methadone, pentazocaine (Talwin), and tripelenamine (Pyribenzamine). When taken together, the latter two drugs ("Ts" and "Blues") produce many of the same physical and psychological effects as heroin and methadone. Widely prescribed separately, they have been illegally diverted for street use by certain pharmacists and clinics (Scott, 1979).

The exact reasons for the sharp rise in addiction during the 1970s are not known, although some of the increase among middle-class youth may have resulted from the psychedelic pop culture. The role of cultural factors of this sort seems quite apparent in Britain and there is no reason to absolve them in the United States, As with marijuana, many American servicemen also began using cheap and potent heroin in Vietnam (Robins, Helzer, Hesselbrock, & Wish, 1980).

Sedative-Hypnotics

These are the most widely prescribed drugs in the world, and are among the most widely abused (Schnoll, 1979). They include minor tranquilizers such as Valium and Librium; barbiturates such as Seconal, Nembutal, Equanil, and Phenobarbital; and prescription sleeping pills, such as Doriden, Placidyl, and Quaalude (now restricted from general use). Their primary effect in small doses is sedative. In higher doses, however, they cause intoxication, confusion, staggering, anger, irritability, and impairment of thought and emotional control. Combining them with alcohol or other drugs intensifies their effects.

Overdoses of barbiturates ("barbs," "goof balls," "candy") cause many deaths, both accidental and deliberate. All of the sedative-hypnotics induce physical tolerance and dependence (Schnoll, 1979). Withdrawal from barbiturates is more severe than with any other drugs and can be fatal. It must therefore be gradual or mitigated by other drugs. Many abusers are adults whose physicians prescribe the drugs and who typically commit little drug-related crime. Yet they risk auto accidents and death via overdose. Younger abusers often obtain them illegally and combine them with stimulants, heroin, or alcohol, thus multiplying their intrinsic risks.

Inhalants and Solvents

Inhalation of common chemical substances, aerosols, and fumes is widespread among youngsters who lack ready access to psychoactive drugs. Small doses usually do not have long-lasting effects, although deep or prolonged inhalation of many substances can cause brain damage or death. Mild asphyxiation is usually responsible for the "high" sought by users. Mustard and other unpleasant additives are now mixed in many solvents to deter sniffing, but other common substances, such as gasoline, also serve the purpose.

Although most youngsters are merely experimenters or casual users, some "heads" develop a high tolerance and become psychologically dependent on daily use. Among the hundreds of deaths occurring in users, a variety of causes appear, including suffocation inside bags or closets filled with inhalant, falling unconscious on a rag containing the inhalant, and heart failure, evidently owing to the inhalent's direct effect on the heart (Cohen, 1979).

PSYCHOSOCIAL CHARACTERISTICS OF DRUG ABUSERS

There are abundant studies of the personalities and backgrounds of drug abusers. Unfortunately, because most of their subjects had already become abusers, it is hard to distinguish the *results* of drug abuse from its antecedents. Nevertheless, an increasing longitudinal data base and certain consistencies among findings permit tentative conclusions about developmental course.

Adolescent Alcohol Abusers

Several studies have linked childhood and early adolescent data to problem drinking in later adolescence and adulthood. Because most adult alcoholism begins with problem drinking during adolescence, the predictive relations between marked alcohol abuse in adolescence and adulthood are generally similar.

There is consistency across studies in finding poor early management of impulsivity and aggression among future alcoholics, plus early delinquent behavior and externalizing, "acting out," behavioral problems. Heavy drinking among family members and peers have also been found (Zucker, 1979). Moreover, alcoholism in fathers raises not only the risks of alcoholism in their children, but the risk of other problems as well, including school truancy and dropping out of school (Robins, West, Ratcliff, & Herjanic, 1978). Conflicts over dependency needs and efforts to conform to traditional masculine roles also seem to encourage alcohol abuse by boys, whereas rejection of traditional feminine roles is correlated with alcohol abuse by girls (Wilsnack & Wilsnack, 1979).

Because depression and "oral" traits (pessimism, self-doubt, passivity, and dependence) have often been found in adult alcoholics, the "oral-dependent personality" has sometimes been inferred as an antecedent of alcoholism. A 40-year longitudinal study of college men, however, showed that early oral dependent behavior predicted early instability and adult personality disorder but *not* adult alcohol abuse (Vaillant, 1980). Unfavorable childhood environments were not predictive of adult alcohol abuse either. On the other hand, depression emerged *after* the development of alcoholism in adulthood. Alcoholics evidently become depressed as a *result* of their inability to control their drinking, rather than depression causing alcoholism.

Adolescent Abusers of Illicit Drugs

As the problem of drug abuse grew in the 1960s and 1970s, several longitudinal studies were launched in which questionnaires were periodically readministered to school and college students as they traversed the years of increasing risk for illicit drug use. Such studies depend heavily on the candor of the respondents, although some of the studies also obtained data from parents, peers, schools, and other sources. It became apparent, however, that understanding the progression of drug-related behavior required not only valid data, but developmental analyses like those needed to grasp the development of other important behaviors. As analyses of drug-related behavior became more sophisticated, they showed that most drug use and its consequences depend jointly on individual developmental course, specific environmental factors, and rapidly changing drug fads and availability. The converging results of several longitudinal studies offer the following tentative conclusions about drug use among young Americans (Kandel, 1980):

1. A high proportion of youth who try marijuana eventually try other illicit drugs, although they do not necessarily become habitual users.
2. The later the onset of drug abuse, the less eventual involvement with drugs and the greater the probability of stopping.
3. Drug use shows a fairly uniform developmental sequence, starting with beer or wine, followed by cigarettes or hard liquor, then marijuana, and culminating with other illicit drugs. Almost no youth use hard drugs who have not already used alcohol, tobacco, and marijuana. Sequences of hard drug use are highly variable, however, depending on availability, peer culture, and individual user characteristics.
4. Different psychosocial characteristics predict advances to the various stages of drug use: Minor delinquencies and use of cigarettes, beer, and wine are good predictors of adolescent hard liquor use; beliefs and values favorable to marijuana and association with peer users are good predictors of marijuana use; poor relations with parents, feelings of depression, and exposure to drug-using peers predict use of other illicit drugs.
5. Several personality factors predict early marijuana and other drug use, although they are less predictive of marijuana in the college years, when it becomes normative in many groups. The following personality factors correlate with early onset and amount of drug use: Rebelliousness, emphasis on personal independence, poor sense of psychological well-being, low self-esteem, and low academic aspirations and motivation.
6. Low grades and frequent absences from school are predictive of drug use.
7. Attitudes and values favorable to deviance and nonconformity predict drug use.
8. Parents' behavior, attitudes, and closeness to their children predict some

aspects of drug use: Parents' use of hard liquor predicts adolescent use of hard liquor and illict drugs; parents' use of psychoactive drugs, tolerance of marijuana, belief in the harmlessness of drugs, and lack of closeness to their children all predict use of illict drugs by their children.

9. Social settings favorable to drug use greatly accelerate and increase it, especially in individuals already predisposed. This was most strikingly demonstrated in Robins's (1978) study of American soldiers in Vietnam.

10. Nonaddictive drug use does not generally lead to criminality or an overall loss of motivation. Instead, willingness to engage in deviant behavior and low achievement motivation both appear to *precede* drug use. As an illustration, Figure 14-2 shows parallel rates of self-reported theft and vandalism for youth who were not drug users in 1970 and remained nonusers in 1974, versus youths who began using marijuana only and youths who began using other drugs. A 10-year longitudinal study also showed that first-grade boys rated as aggressive were more likely to use tobacco, alcohol, and marijuana in their teens than boys initially rated shy (Kellam, Brown, & Fleming, 1982).

These data, however, do not reflect alcohol *abuse* and drug *addiction*—both are more likely to increase criminal behavior than the casual use of marijuana and other drugs reflected in Figure 14-2 (Johnston, O'Malley, & Eveland, 1978).

Heroin Addicts

The longitudinal studies show that some occasional users of heroin do not become addicted (Kandel, 1978). Furthermore, some who do become addicted are able to

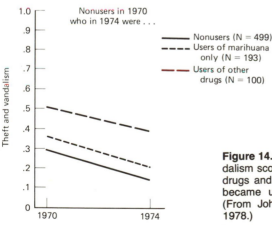

Figure 14.2. Self-reported theft and van-dalism scores for youth who did not use drugs and either remained nonusers or became users over a 4-year period. (From Johnston, O'Malley, & Eveland, 1978.)

overcome their addiction without treatment. This seems especially true of those whose addiction stems from unusual conditions that are then terminated, such as soldiers who became addicted in Vietnam but kicked the habit after returning home (Robins et al., 1980).

Nevertheless, the hundreds of thousands of heroin users who become long-term addicts pose major social problems beyond most other drug abusers: Criminal activities to pay for their drugs, crime networks supplying them, the need for frequent fixes, interference with normal diet and hygiene, prenatal addiction of babies born to addicted mothers, neglect of children by addict parents—these are some of the most obvious problems associated with heroin addiction.

What are heroin addicts like? From the strict control of opiates in 1914, until the rise of the youth drug culture of the 1960s, adolescent heroin use became concentrated mainly in low-income, high-delinquency urban ghettoes (Braucht, Brakarsh, Follingstad, & Berry, 1973). Users' family environments were typically unstable, with high rates of psychiatric, physical, and interpersonal problems among parents (Platt & Labate, 1976).

Comparison of white, Puerto Rican, and black adolescent heroin users and nonusers from similar neighborhoods in New York has shown that the users in each ethnic group had less cohesive families, as judged by family quarreling, joint participation in celebrations and mealtimes, and behavior when a family member was ill (Chein, Gerard, Lee, & Rosenfeld, 1964). Only among blacks were users more economically deprived than nonusers, however. Among whites and Puerto Ricans, users were *less* deprived than nonusers.

Chein found that most of the nonusers had known of heroin in their neighborhoods and had been offered the chance to try it, but they did not accept it, whereas the users did. Moreover, the nonusers deliberately avoided peers who used drugs. Boys who were nonusers and not delinquent in other respects were clearly "square" by their neighborhood standards. They expressed more interest in books, school, organized activities, future plans, and long-term friendships than those who tried drugs. The "cats" who tried drugs engaged in other delinquency, spent most of their time hanging around, and were preoccupied with immediate acquisition of cars, clothes, and other goods.

Most of the boys who became regular users had been casually offered heroin by peers at around the age of 15 or 16. Very few had spontaneously sought it out. The age of 16 seemed especially critical, as more boys accepted heroin and became addicted at that age than younger or older. Most 16-year-olds who tried it had quit school, acquired working papers, and thought of themselves as more independent at that point. These factors probably made 16-year-olds especially vulnerable.

Most boys who tried heroin had positive reactions on their first try; 90 percent of those who eventually became regular users did so within one year of the first try, the rest within two years. Among a group of 50 delinquents in Chein's study who were nonusers, four had tried heroin but stopped after the first try. It thus appears that, for most (but not all) of the youth in the areas studied, the first try quickly led to regular use.

Personality tests generally show opiate addicts to be immature, insecure, irresponsible, and egocentric (Braucht et al., 1973). Very few normal MMPI profiles have been found among known addicts, although the types of psychopathology are diverse, including mainly character disorders, sociopathy, psychosis, and—to a lesser extent—neurosis. Similar personality characteristics have also been found in nonaddicted prisoners whose backgrounds resemble those of addicts (Platt & Labate, 1976). This suggests that the deviant personality characteristics are not uniquely associated with addiction. The spread of heroin among soldiers and other nonghetto groups in the 1960s and 1970s led to further diversification of psychosocial characteristics. However, the apparent end of the rapid spread of addiction (New York *Times,* 1980a) suggests that addiction may once again become confined largely to certain subcultural groups.

WHAT SHOULD BE DONE ABOUT DRUG ABUSE?

Treatment for drug abuse raises medical, legal, and ethical questions more than most other problems we have considered. In no other area of psychopathology do public passions run higher in support of so many opposing viewpoints. Other forms of delinquent behavior raise some of the same questions about prevention, punishment, treatment, deterrence, and self-protection. But drug abuse also evokes fear of epidemic contagion to one's own children, irrational violence, the weakening of the nation, and intergenerational conflict, not to mention questions about such cornerstones of adult social customs as tobacco and alcohol. Considering the disagreements on whether drug abuse is a medical, legal, behavioral, moral, or social problem, and considering the vicissitudes of public policy and funding, we should not be surprised at the lack of agreement on remedies.

Reducing Alcohol Abuse

Alcoholism has the longest history of treatment efforts, but most have been geared toward older, chronic alcoholics (Miller, 1979). These efforts have ranged from aversive conditioning, in which noxious stimuli are paired with drinking, to mutual aid groups like Alcoholics Anonymous. Some alcoholics can be taught to control their drinking (Sobell & Sobell, 1978). But most programs for chronic alcoholics have not shown high success rates. Furthermore, these programs are seldom applicable to the young, for whom prevention of episodic abuse and later dependence are the main aims.

Because behavioral analyses show that situational cues play a large role in social drinking behavior, interventions have increasingly aimed to train more adaptive responses to these cues (Miller, 1979). *Skills training* approaches, for example, teach specific drinking skills, such as taking small, infrequent sips rather than the large, frequent gulps characteristic of alcoholics. *Operant conditioning* is also used by pairing positive reinforcers with responsible drinking behavior, often as prescribed in a written behavioral contract signed by the problem drinker.

A more complex approach has been to train people to *discriminate their blood alcohol levels* in the following way: As they drink alcohol mixed in another drink, such as orange juice, they are periodically asked to estimate their blood alcohol level based on a list of bodily sensations associated with various levels. A breath test is then used to determine the actual level, and discrepancies between the estimated and actual level are discussed to sharpen awareness of internal cues. Several studies have shown that young social drinkers can learn to discriminate their blood alcohol levels, although confirmed alcoholics seem less successful (Miller, 1979).

Aversive conditioning has also been used to teach alcoholics more responsible drinking by shocking their fingertips when they show "alcoholic" drinking behaviors, such as rapid gulping of drinks. The improved drinking behavior, however, seldom lasts when the aversive stimuli are gone (Miller, 1979).

Although not originating as antidotes to alcohol abuse, certain popular "healthy habits" seem to reduce alcohol consumption among adolescents and young adults. Several studies have shown decreased drinking by people practicing transcendental meditation and various forms of relaxation, for example (Miller, 1979). Regular running and other strenuous activity have been found to improve functioning in alcoholics and nonalcoholics alike, although research on the impact of exercise on alcohol consumption is meager.

Reducing Abuse of Illicit Drugs

Treatment programs and services proliferated in response to the drug epidemics of the 1960s and 1970s. These include crisis intervention centers, telephone hotlines, counseling and psychotherapy for drug users and their families, peer counseling, runaway houses, group homes, supervised work experience, halfway houses, therapeutic communities, and administration of alternative drugs such as methadone (Smith, Levy, & Striar, 1979). As with alcohol abuse, "healthy habits" such as transcendental meditation have also been cultivated as antidotes to drugs, and there is some indication that meditation may increase motivation to abstain from at least the softer drugs (Benson & Wallace, 1972). For youthful abusers of harder drugs, however, therapeutic communities, methadone maintenance, and detoxification programs have dominated (Sells & Simpson, 1979). After describing these approaches, we will consider the outcome of a nationwide comparison of outcomes.

Therapeutic Communities. The first and best known American therapeutic community for drug addicts is *Synanon*. It was started in Santa Monica, California, by Charles Dederich, an ex-alcoholic, in 1958. Many other therapeutic communities trace their origins to Synanon, either because they were started by members of Synanon or borrowed some of its principles (Brook & Whitehead, 1980).

From a mutual aid group resembling Alcoholics Anonymous, Synanon rapidly became a national organization with local residential units run by ex-addicts. The word "Synanon" was coined by Dederich for the "Synanon game"—a kind of group encounter session led by a "Synanist," an addict who has given up drugs or is making good progress toward that goal. Synanon sessions are held regularly to confront addicts with their defenses and manipulations. The sessions are intended to provide an emotional catharsis and trigger an atmosphere of truth seeking.

As Dederich described it, Synanon communities have a "family structure" that provides social support but also demands that members take directions from supervisors—ex-addicts who try to implant values of self-reliance. Rather than aiming to return addicts to their old environments, Synanon creates new social roles for many of its members as Synanon executives and business people, Synanists, and workers with addicts. By thus offering upward mobility within the organization, Synanon helps addicts find new identities after they give up the drug culture.

Another facet of Synanon's resocialization regimen is its stressful entrance "exam." When an addict arrives begging for help, token roadblocks, such as appointment times, fees, and ridicule, are engineered by ex-addict "experts." Addicts are treated as emotional infants whose silly plots and rationalizations need to be exposed and who need jobs commensurate with their limited ability. As an example, here is an interview with an addict prospect whom Synanon had decided to accept. "J.H." is ex-addict Jack Hurst, Resident Director of the Westport, Connecticut, Synanon House.

J.H.: You'll be the new element in the family. You'll be kind of like the new baby. . . . You'll be told when to get up, you'll be told what to do when you do get up. You'll be told when to go to Synanon, what kind of work to do, when to go to seminars. You'll be told when to talk and when not to talk. . . .

I guarantee you that if you go through the motions that we describe and prescribe for you you'll end up being a man, not the sniveling whining brat that you are now. You'll be a man!

Prospect: What makes you think I'm a sniveling brat? You only know me for five minutes and . . .

J.H.: You see, people that use drugs, people that live with their sisters, people that steal hubcaps, people that go in and out of jails, the people that go to nut houses for help, these are sniveling brats in my opinion and my opinion carries a lot of weight in this house. Get that gut level. My opinion is pretty Goddamn certain to be valid as a salad. Try to understand that, if you don't understand it, act as if you understand.

When you make a lot of noise in our environment it's not very nice to listen to. Arguments are something we save for Synanons. You can argue your ass off in a Synanon. When you're being talked to around here, and when you're in my office or in my dining room you kind of behave yourself and keep your big mouth shut. Listen to what's going on around you, you might learn something. Don't be so frightened to learn something. You see, you almost learned something a moment ago—the fact that you are a whining, sniveling brat. But you fight it. . . .

Now you're not going to be expected for a couple of, three-four months, to do our banking, for instance. This would be like asking a four-year-old child to carry a hundred-pound suitcase like a man. You're not going to be expected to do our shopping. You're not going to be expected to get into our car and go to Bridgeport to pick up donations. . . . What you're going to be expected to do is wash the toilets, wash the floors, do the dishes, anything that we feel that you should be doing. As you learn how to do these things *well, well* mind you, then you will gradually get to more and better things, or let's say, more responsible jobs. You'll graduate up the power structure, pretty soon you know in a couple of years, maybe even a year, you just might be a big shot around here—or Santa Monica or Reno. (Yablonsky & Dederich, 1965, pp. 201−2)

One effect of the initial reception may be to increase the motivation of some addicts:

I couldn't figure it out. I figured there must be a gimmick. I didn't really want to stop being a dope fiend. I wanted to rest awhile. First, I began to look for the connection in the joint. They laughed at me. I think I stuck around at the beginning cause I couldn't believe it was true. Live dope fiends not shooting dope—behind an open door, with no screws to keep them locked up! (Yablonsky & Dederich, 1965, p. 200)

Another effect of the entrance hurdles and the three-month trial period may be to exclude addicts who are poor prospects. This makes the overall effectiveness of the Synanon model hard to evaluate as a treatment for addiction.

As Synanon grew, it attracted national publicity and contributions that helped it become a wealthy, tax-exempt organization with extensive real estate holdings and several communelike ranches (Synanon, 1977). It also attracted nonaddicts who helped operate communal facilities, including schools and collective living quarters for members' children. Synanon's leader, Charles Dederich, became increasingly authoritarian, however, and was eventually convicted of conspiring with members of his security force, the Imperial Marines, to murder a critic of Synanon with a rattlesnake (New York *Times,* 1980b). The transformation of Synanon reached the point where it declared itself a religion (New York *Times,* 1980c).

Other therapeutic communities have diverged from the original Synanon model in various ways. New York City's *Phoenix House* program, for example, admits addicts after a 1- to 3-month detoxification period elsewhere (Platt & Labate, 1976). The 12- to 18-month Phoenix House stay incorporates many Synanon principles but is oriented toward eventual reentry into the community. When ready to reenter, the addict moves to a Phoenix Reentry House for 6 to 12 months.

Odyssey House places still stronger emphasis on reentry into the mainstream of community life. It provides more differentiated program options for different kinds of addicts and employs professional staff to render specialized therapeutic services (Brook & Whitehead, 1980). Odyssey House also differs from the others in admitting more young addicts—a survey of 2500 early Odyssey House clients showed that 1000 were between 9 and 18 years of age (Rohrs, Murphy, & Densen-Gerber, 1972).

Methadone Maintenance. Methadone is a synthetic opiatelike drug that blocks heroin's euphoric effect and the craving for heroin. It is highly addictive, but can be cheaply made. Its effects continue for 24 hours, compared with 2 to 4 hours for heroin. Because it is effective when taken orally, it also avoids the medical complications risked with intravenous injection of heroin.

Although used mainly with addicts over the age of 18, methadone maintenance has become one of the most widespread treatments for heroin addiction. It is not without its problems, however, as users have sold excessive amounts obtained from private physicians, and deaths from overdoses occur. A significant number of heroin addicts apparently switched to methadone as their drug of choice (Platt & Labate, 1976). To prevent illegal sales, private physicians' access to methadone has been limited, and many programs require participants to consume their daily dose at a clinic. Methadone maintenance alone does not usually change addicts' life-styles, and some may continue their criminal activities and abuse of nonopiates. The goal of methadone maintenance, however, is to make addicts accessible to other forms of help toward more adequate psychosocial functioning despite their dependence on methadone.

Detoxification Programs. These are designed mainly to break the physical dependence on drugs by inducing withdrawal. Detoxification typically takes place in an inpatient medical setting employing drugs and other procedures to lessen the physiological hazards. The classic detoxification program in this country was started in 1935 at the U.S. Public Health Service Hospital in Lexington, Kentucky. Treatment at Lexington has consisted mainly of physical detoxification, plus short-term vocational rehabilitation and psychotherapy aimed at helping addicts meet stress without drugs. Thereafter, the addicts usually return to their home communities—many to become re-addicted, as follow-up studies show (Platt & Labate, 1976). Contrary to the assumption that early treatment should be the most effective, these studies show that young adult addicts have worse relapse rates than older ones.

Comparison of Outcomes. Rigorous assessment of the effects of treatment for illicit drug abuse faces all the hurdles of other outcome research, plus additional problems arising from the illicit nature of the target behavior and the heterogeneity and instability of the programs as well as their participants. Even where efforts have been made to randomly assign drug abusers to different treatments, the vicissitudes of the target population have hampered rigorous comparisons of treatment effects (e.g., Brook & Whitehead, 1980). We are, therefore, left largely with outcome data based on a mixture of differing programs, differing clients, and different forms of drug abuse.

The federal Drug Abuse Reporting Program (DARP) provided outcome data on 44,000 clients admitted to 52 treatment centers (Sells & Simpson, 1980). The following treatment modalities were compared: methadone maintenance, therapeutic communities, detoxification, and outpatient drug-free programs featuring counseling and rehabilitation services. Clients who went through the intake procedures of a program but did not receive treatment were used as a no-treatment comparison group. Follow-ups obtained self-report data on employment, opiate use, use of nonopiate drugs other than marijuana, alcohol use, crime, and return to treatment. Sells and Simpson defined a highly favorable outcome as drug abstinence, plus high ratings on all but employment or return to treatment.

How many drug abusers achieved favorable outcomes? Follow-ups 4 to 6 years after intake into the programs showed the following success rates: methadone maintenance 29.5 percent; therapeutic communities 36.9 percent; drug-free outpatient programs 34.4 percent; detoxification 19.1 percent; and intake only (i.e., no treatment) 21 percent. Although none of the treatments produced high rates of favorable outcomes, all but detoxification produced significantly better outcomes than no treatment.

Other analyses showed that young clients (under age 19) had the best overall outcomes after drug-free outpatient programs and the best employment records after therapeutic community and drug-free outpatient programs (Sells & Simpson, 1979). Note, however, that the type of treatment was based at least partly on the type and degree of drug abuse, with some treatments reserved for one type of abuser—methadone maintenance for opiate addicts, for example. Furthermore, there is evidence that certain personality types benefit more than others from a particular type of program. Within a methadone program, for example, opiate addicts whose MMPI profiles indicated the most stable personalities had the best outcomes (Ottomanelli, Wilson, & Whyte, 1978).

PREVENTION OF DRUG ABUSE

Education

Preventive education is one of the most talked about but least evaluated approaches to drug abuse. Abundant films, lectures, and literature have been devoted to heading off drug abuse by the young.

Chein et al. (1964) found that fewer adolescent heroin users than nonusers within a neighborhood reported knowing the dangers of drugs before they tried them. The subjects were growing up in the 1950s before publicity about drugs had reached its later crescendo, but it is hard to believe that the nonusers were so much better informed than those who tried drugs, when almost all of both groups reported seeing addicts in their neighborhood. Casting further doubt on the role of ignorance is the tremendous growth of abuse during the 1960s and 1970s when knowledge of its dangers became more widespread than ever.

In one of the most comprehensive studies of drug education, Blum (1976) found that the effects varied greatly with the type of program and age of the pupils: In a high drug area of California, the major benefit was to retard the increase and intensity of drug use among children in the middle elementary school grades. It seemed, however, to have no impact in grades 2 to 3 and 9 to 12, and actually accelerated use in grades 6 to 8, when it was already rising rapidly. Other evidence suggests that some youngsters are first attracted to drugs by newspaper and television reports (Beschner & Friedman, 1979). As a result, a moratorium was imposed on federally supported prevention programs until guidelines for preventive materials were established. The guidelines stress that prevention messages must be nonglamorous, realistic, and factual (Beshner & Friedman, 1979).

One benefit of drug education programs, whether or not they prevent drug use, may be to make young people more discriminating and cautious in their choice of drugs. Thus, the decline of LSD and growth of marijuana use may be partly thanks to increasing awareness of the dangers of LSD and the relative safety of marijuana. Drug education may also help stem abuse of legal drugs. Some abuse of barbiturates, amphetamines, and tranquilizers almost certainly results from public ignorance of their dangers, for example. Unless the prescription, production, and advertising of commercial psychoactive drugs are stringently controlled, public wariness will be the only way to reduce abuse encouraged by massive advertising of these drugs.

Law

Stricter laws, law enforcement, and penalties are probably the most commonly advocated weapons against drug abuse. They seem to have worked in some situations, but not others. In World War II Japan, for example, amphetamines were widely used to ward off pilot and worker fatigue. By 1954, two million Japanese were using amphetamines intravenously and 600,000 were chronic users. Strict laws and an all-out educational campaign reduced arrests from 55,000 in 1954 to 271 in 1958, and there has been no recurrence of epidemic amphetamine abuse. A heroin epidemic in Japan was controlled by similar measures between 1955 and 1962. American legal efforts against opiates also reduced addiction considerably after 1914. Despite strict laws, however, addicts have remained so numerous that a purely legal approach seems unlikely to succeed here. The foothold given criminal syndicates via prohibition-era liquor sales also suggests that a purely legal approach may do more harm than good.

Socioeconomic Changes

Could improvement in the living conditions of the disadvantaged reduce drug abuse? Perhaps, but Chein et al. (1964) found that white and Puerto Rican heroin users were somewhat more economically advantaged than their nonuser peers from the same neighborhoods, although black users were more deprived than black nonusers. Also, most of the growth in nonopiate abuse has been among relatively advantaged youth. They, too, may be suffering from the lack of family cohesiveness that appears to be the most critical factor in drug abuse among disadvantaged adolescents (Chein et al., 1964), but no foreseeable socioeconomic changes are likely to remove this contributor to drug abuse. Just as massive drug use grew partly out of a new cultural ethos, future fads will no doubt bring other expressions of adolescents' desires to form new identities for themselves.

SUMMARY

The implications of psychoactive drug use depend on how society views it. All psychoactive drugs, licit as well as illicit, are potentially harmful. *Physical dependence,* most strongly induced by alcohol, barbiturates, and opiates, is typically a less significant factor in addictions than *psychological dependence,* which may cause readdiction even after physical dependence ends. *Physical tolerance,* produced by LSD, amphetamines, marijuana, and opiates, requires a user to increase the dose needed to obtain a particular effect.

Adolescents often begin using tobacco and alcohol in the same manner as illicit drugs. The enormous volume of abuse, traffic deaths, and crime associated with alcohol make it the most problematic drug in the United States. Hard drugs typically culminate a developmental sequence progressing from beer or wine, to tobacco, hard liquor, and marijuana.

Adolescent abuse of illicit drugs spiraled in many developed countries during the 1960s and 1970s. *Cannabis* is the most controversial, because it is the most widely used and seems the least harmful of the illicit drugs. It is not clear whether statistical associations between psychopathology and cannabis use arise because cannabis causes psychopathology or vice versa, or whether both have similar causes. Heavy cannabis users also tend to be heavy users of tobacco, alcohol, and other drugs. There is evidence that chronic use of cannabis by black urban males during adolescence increases the risk of later social problems, including excess use of alcohol and other drugs, although the relations between cannabis and later problems are less clear in other groups. LSD, PCP, and other potent hallucinogens produce serious psychopathological reactions, as well as possible organic damage.

Amphetamines, legally prescribed for children's hyperactivity, are taken intravenously in large doses to get very strong stimulant effects. These effects are often followed by suicidal depression, disorganized thinking, and paranoid psychosis. Groups of amphetamine users seem especially prone to violence. *Cocaine* produces similar but more potent and toxic stimulant effects.

Sniffing of *organic solvents* in household products can depress central nervous system functioning enough to cause mild intoxication, although large doses can be fatal. High doses of *barbiturates* and *"minor" tranquilizers* cause more extreme central nervous system depression. Their effects become especially potent when mixed with alcohol or other drugs.

Opiates, especially *heroin*, foster severe addiction by anesthesizing organic drive stimuli and producing euphoria. Even after physical dependence is ended through withdrawal, new withdrawal symptoms can be triggered by cues previously associated with drug use. The number of heroin users rose sharply from the 1950s through the 1970s, and the age of addiction became progressively younger, although the addict population then seemed to level off.

Adolescent alcohol abuse tends to be preceded by poor control of aggression and impulsivity, early delinquency, and heavy alcohol use by parents and peers. Depression appears to be a result rather than a cause of alcoholism. No clear-cut personality patterns have been verified for most other drug users, but they have fairly high rates of psychopathology.

Heroin users tend to be minority group members from ghetto neighborhoods and broken homes, whose peers readily provide drugs. Lack of family cohesiveness seems especially pronounced among users, although socioeconomic deprivation is not necessarily greater than among nonusers from the same neighborhoods. Most users quickly become addicts after their first experience with heroin. Personality tests reveal elevated psychopathology, immaturity, irresponsibility, insecurity, and egocentrism among heroin addicts, although no particular personality characteristics seem unique to addicts.

Traditional detoxification treatments are typically followed by relapses. Synanon, Phoenix House, and other therapeutic communities offer the addict new social roles. Odyssey House is intermediate between traditional treatment and the community-of-addicts approach in that it has a staff of professional therapists and tries to return addicts to the outside world. *Methadone* is being widely used to block the craving for heroin, although methadone is addictive and does not directly alter the addict's life style. Methadone maintenance, therapeutic communities, and outpatient drug-free programs appear to produce better outcomes than detoxification or no treatment, but no approach has shown very high success rates with serious drug abusers.

Like treatment, preventive efforts have not shown strong results. Strict legal approaches have cut drug abuse greatly in some countries, but the example of Prohibition suggests that they cannot be completely successful in the United States.

SUGGESTED READING

A major problem in studying drug abuse is to keep up with the latest fads and literature. Since the burgeoning of illict drug use by the young of many countries, numerous conferences and publications have sprung forth. However, rapidly changing drug preferences prevent programmatic research from keeping pace and often make conclusions obsolete before they are published. A book edited by Kandel (1978) details the problems and accomplishments of much-needed longitudinal research on drug abuse.

Overviews. Although adolescent drug use has sparked the greatest concern, many reports and programs either do not distinguish between older and younger users, or are generally oriented toward older users. Beschner and Friedman (1979) have edited an exceptionally comprehensive collection of papers focused specifically on youth drug abuse. The contributions deal with pharmacological aspects, determinants of use, patterns of use among various American youth groups, links to delinquency, and treatment programs and outcomes. Robins's (1978) study of drug use among American soldiers nicely illustrates the interplay among personal and situational factors in determining the onset and course of drug use (see also Robins et al., 1980). Blum's (1976) research and review of other work shows that hopes for prevention through drug education may be unjustified.

Alcohol. In *Youth, Alcohol, and Social Policy,* Blane and Chafetz (1979) present research on youthful drinking, its relations to later alcohol problems, and policy implications, including the effects of changing the drinking age.

Hallucinogens. An ethnographic study of PCP users entitled *Angel Dust* (Feldman, Agar, & Beschner, 1979) affords glimpses of youth attitudes and subcultures related to what seems to be one of the most irrational of drug fads.

Opiates. Before the blossoming of the drug culture in the 1960s and 1970s, heroin was the illicit drug commanding the most attention. Chein et al.'s (1964) book, *The Road to H,* gives a good picture of adolescent addiction in the slums of New York, although the data are sometimes buried in the verbiage. Platt and Labate (1976) and Wikler (1980) have written exceptionally thorough books on theory, research, and treatment relating to heroin addiction.

Therapeutic Communities. Because they seek to stimulate pervasive personality changes through resocialization of addicts, therapeutic communities entail much more intensive personal involvement by staff and clients than most other approaches. The prototype and sparkplug for most American therapeutic communities was Synanon. Despite its evolution into a cultlike movement in the 1980s, Synanon's early history (Yablonsky, 1965) shows the fervor that attracted many addicts. Brook and Whitehead (1980) have provided a more research-oriented (and pessimistic) picture of a therapeutic community, along with appraisals of others.

CHAPTER 15

Taxonomic Aspects of Developmental Psychopathology

We have repeatedly faced the need to make distinctions among syndromes of behavior, individual adaptive patterns, and etiological factors. These are problems of *taxonomy,* that is, of grouping together individuals having something important in common, whether it is behaviors, IQ scores, genetic abnormalities, or heroin addiction, for example. Most of the groupings we used were painfully inadequate as guides to etiology, treatment, or prognosis, but they reflect current customs in the mental health fields. In this chapter, we will compare these customs with alternative approaches.

THE DIAGNOSTIC AND STATISTICAL MANUAL OF MENTAL DISORDERS

Chapter 4 outlined the third edition of the American Psychiatric Association's (1980) *Diagnostic and Statistical Manual* (DSM-III). In other chapters, we have taken a close look at the DSM's criteria for particular disorders, such as Attention Deficit Disorders and Depressive Disorders in Chapter 11. Here we will consider the DSM as a general approach and how other approaches could lead to different results.

Medical Origins

The DSM is a descendant of nineteenth century organic medicine. As research on mental disorders emerged during the nineteenth century, organic disease served as the taxonomic model. According to this model, each symptom syndrome has a specific organic cause. In mental disorders, the underlying pathology was assumed to be brain disease (Griesinger, 1845). In order to discover the specific brain disease responsible in each case, it was first necessary to form a clear picture of the symptoms. The most compelling example was *general paralysis* (later called *paresis):* As we saw in Chapter 2, progress in describing the syndrome of paresis as a combination of mental derangement and physical impairment was followed by the post mortem discovery of inflammation in the brains of paretics. Further research isolated syphilis as the cause. This success fueled hopes that taxonomic advances would spur discovery of organic causes for other mental disorders as well.

Convinced that accurate description would lead to the discovery of a specific organic etiology for each disorder, Emil Kraepelin (1883) devised a comprehensive taxonomy for the hodgepodge of disorders proposed by various authorities. Over the next 40 years, successive editions of Kraepelin's taxonomy shaped the classification of mental disorders. Although initially assuming an organic cause for all disorders, Kraepelin (1915) eventually included disorders viewed as psychological in origin, as well as personality disorders viewed as bordering between illness and eccentricity.

The DSM is a direct descendant of Kraepelin's taxonomy. It retains many of the same disorders and avows a descriptive approach to disorders of unknown etiology. The first and second editions of the DSM (1952 and 1968) incorporated psychodynamic theory and Adolf Meyer's concept of *reaction types of the psychobiologic unit* but implicitly retained the organic disease model. DSM-III shed most of the Freudian and Meyerian concepts and reemphasized the organic disease model; an early draft of DSM-III even held that all mental disorders are medical disorders.

Although this claim was moderated in the final version, DSM-III nevertheless repeatedly refers to disorders as illnesses. Furthermore, the DSM-III committee regarded each disorder as a diseaselike entity. Their approach

> starts with a clinical concept for which there is some degree of face validity. Face validity is the extent to which the description of a particular category seems on the face of it to describe accurately the characteristic features of persons with a particular disorder. It is the result of clinicians agreeing on the identification of a particular syndrome or pattern of clinical features as a mental disorder. Initial criteria are generally developed by asking the clinicians to describe what they consider to be the most characteristic features of the disorder. (Spitzer & Cantwell, 1980, p. 369)

Most clinical concepts of adult disorders, such as schizophrenia and affective disorders, date from Kraepelin's time. The architects of DSM-III drew on previously developed research diagnostic criteria for their definitions of these disorders.

Unlike the adult disorders, however, many of the child and adolescent disorders had *no* counterparts in previous editions of the DSM. Moreover, there were *no* preexisting research diagnostic criteria for the child or adolescent disorders. In the passage just quoted from Spitzer and Cantwell, "face validity" therefore concerns clinical concepts held by DSM-III's contributors. The DSM taxonomy of child and adolescent disorders was not validated in any other way. We do have data on its reliability, however.

Reliability of the DSM-III Taxonomy of Child and Adolescent Disorders

The DSM-III manual reports reliability figures for several diagnostic categories. These figures were based on data submitted by pairs of clinicians who made independent diagnoses of cases they saw in their own clinical settings. The DSM committee provided general instructions, but the exact procedures varied among participating clinicians. For example, some subjects were jointly interviewed by the two clinicians of a pair; other subjects were seen separately by two clinicians. Many biases may have affected the self-selection of clinicians who submitted data, the cases they chose to include, and the conditions under which their diagnoses were made. We cannot, therefore, take the specific reliability figures very seriously. Nevertheless, these figures suggest three conclusions:

1. *The overall agreement between clinicians' diagnoses of children and adolescents was poor*
   a. Within broad categories of disorders on DSM-III's Axis I *(psychiatric syndromes)*, the overall agreement was .52, as shown by a statistic *(kappa)* that indicates the percentage of agreement, corrected for chance. Even this rate of agreement was obtained only by counting diagnoses as agreeing if they fell within a single broad category. For example, two diagnoses of conduct disorder were counted as agreeing, even though one of the diagnoses was of *undersocialized aggressive* and the other was of *socialized nonaggressive* conduct disorder. Because DSM-III specifies four different types of conduct disorder but no overarching diagnosis of conduct disorder, counting all diagnoses of conduct disorder as agreements could mask many disagreements.
   b. As an even more extreme example, all the following specific diagnoses were considered equivalent to each other within the broad category of *other disorders of infancy, childhood, or adolescence: Reactive attachment disorder of infancy; schizoid disorder of childhood or adolescence; elective mutism; oppositional disorder;* and *identity disorder.*
   c. On the DSM's Axis II *(developmental and personality disorders)*, all of the 18 specific disorders were lumped into the two general categories of *developmental disorders* and *personality disorders.*

Despite the masking of disagreements among specific diagnoses by grouping within broad categories, the overall rate of agreement still only attained a *kappa* of .55.

2. *Agreement was better for diagnosis of adults than children and adolescents.* On Axis I, the overall *kappas* were .72 for adults and .52 for children and adolescents; on Axis II, they were .64 versus .55; on Axis IV *(severity of psychosocial stressors),* the intraclass correlation was .66 versus .59; and on Axis V *(highest level of attained functioning)* .80 versus .52.

3. *Agreement on child and adolescent diagnoses declined from an early draft of DSM-III to the latest draft used in the reliability study.* On Axis I, *kappa* declined from .68 to .52; on Axis II, from .66 to .55; on Axis IV, the correlation declined from .75 to .59; and on Axis V, from .77 to .52. This consistent deterioration of reliability for assessment of children and adolescents contrasted with improving reliability in the assessment of adults on all four axes.

Could unknown biases in the data account for the poor reliability of the DSM-III child and adolescent categories? Or for the deterioration of reliability from early to later drafts? Two studies report the reliability of diagnoses made from children's case histories according to DSM-II and DSM-III criteria (Mattison, Cantwell, Russell, & Will, 1979; Mezzich & Mezzich, 1979). By providing clinicians with the same materials, these studies insured a more uniform data base for making diagnoses than the DSM-III reliability study did. Yet they also showed poor agreement on the DSM-III diagnoses: For Axis I diagnoses, Mattison et al. found 54 percent agreement (uncorrected for chance); Mezzich and Mezzich found a *kappa* of .23. Moreover, both studies showed somewhat better agreement between DSM-II diagnoses than DSM-III Axis I diagnoses, which are the most comparable to DSM-II's single axis: 57 percent agreement for DSM-II diagnoses in the Mattison et al. study and a *kappa* of .26 for DSM-II diagnoses in the Mezzich and Mezzich study. (Mezzich and Mezzich also reported *kappas* of .33 and .27 for DSM-III Axes II and III, and intraclass correlations of .25 and .58 for Axes IV and V, respectively.)

If users of a taxonomy like DSM-III disagree in their diagnoses, then the taxonomy is of little help in grouping children who share important features. Possible sources of unreliability include:

1. Imprecise criteria for determining which diagnosis a case warrants.
2. Inadequate rules for deciding between diagnoses.
3. Users' failure to master the criteria and rules.
4. Problems in assessing the characteristics of individual cases needed to make the diagnosis.
5. Mismatches between the taxonomy's categories and the phenomena to be categorized.

DSM-III provides much more specific criteria and explicit decision rules than earlier editions of the DSM did. In DSM-III's own reliability study, the users were supposed to be experienced with the taxonomy before participating. Most of Mezzich and Mezzich's diagnosticians had moderate to extensive experience, while Mattison's had studied but not previously used DSM-III.

Even those diagnosticians using DSM-III for the first time reported few difficulties, however. Better training might improve the reliability of DSM-III, but inadequate training does not explain the declining reliability of the child diagnoses. Indeed, the opposite trends for the child and adult categories suggest that revisions which improved the reliability of adult diagnoses made child diagnoses less reliable. Why?

The match between the DSM taxonomy and the actual disorders of children has had far less attention than DSM's match to adult disorders. DSM-III's child and adolescent disorders and the criteria for diagnosing them were established through the consensus of the DSM committee members rather than empirical research or cumulative trial-and-error in clinical practice. Perhaps the organic disease model that has been rejuvenated in DSM-III is simply inappropriate for childhood disorders. What are the alternatives?

THE GAP TAXONOMY

Dissatisfied with the neglect of children in the then prevailing taxonomy, the Committee on Child Psychiatry of the Group for the Advancement of Psychiatry (GAP) proposed an ambitious alternative system for children's disorders (GAP, 1966). The GAP committee followed the traditional procedure of starting with clinical concepts of disorders, but they tried to incorporate developmental considerations more than the DSM has. For example, they proposed a category of *healthy responses* to encompass normal reactions to developmental crises, such as the separation anxiety 6-month-old babies show whenever their mothers leave; phobias among preschool children; the compulsive behavior of school-aged children; identity crises in adolescents; and grief reactions to the death of loved ones. Table 15-1 outlines the diagnostic categories of the GAP taxonomy.

The GAP committee held that its definitions of disorders were as operational as possible, involving an irreducible minimum of inference. Some of the GAP categories require quite a bit of inference, however. Category IV, *Psychoneurotic Disorders,* for example, is defined almost exclusively in psychoanalytic terms as

> . . . disorders based on unconscious conflicts over the handling of sexual and aggressive impulses which, though removed from awareness by the mechanism of repression, remain active and unresolved. . . . The anxiety, acting as a danger signal to the ego, ordinarily sets into operation certain defense mechanisms, in addition to repression, and leads to the formation of psychological symptoms which symbolically deal with the conflict, thus achieving a partial though unhealthy solution. (GAP, 1966, pp. 229–30)

Table 15-1   Outline of the GAP (1966) Taxonomy

I. Healthy Responses
  A. Developmental crisis
  B. Situational crisis
  C. Other responses

II. Reactive Disorders

III. Developmental Deviations
  A. Deviations in maturational patterns
  B. Deviations in specific dimensions
     of development (Motor, sensory,
     speech, cognitive, social,
     psychosexual, affective, or integ-
     rative)

IV. Psychoneurotic Disorders
  A. Anxiety
  B. Phobic
  C. Conversion
  D. Dissociative
  E. Obsessive-compulsive
  F. Depressive
  G. Other

V. Personality Disorders
  A. Compulsive
  B. Hysterical
  C. Anxious
  D. Overly dependent
  E. Oppositional
  F. Overly inhibited
  G. Overly independent
  H. Isolated
  I. Mistrustful
  J. Tension-discharge disorders
     1. Impulse-ridden
     2. Neurotic personality
  K. Sociosyntonic
  L. Sexual deviation
  M. Other

VI. Psychotic Disorders
  A. Psychoses of infancy and early
     childhood
     1. Early infantile autism
     2. Interactional psychotic disorder
     3. Other
  B. Psychoses of later childhood
     1. Schizophreniform psychotic
        disorder
     2. Other
  C. Psychoses of adolescence
     1. Acute confusional state
     2. Schizophrenic disorder, adult
        type
     3. Other

VII. Psychophysiologic Disorders
   (Specific sites are listed)

VIII. Brain Syndromes
    (Acute, chronic)

IX. Mental Retardation

X. Other Disorders

Nonanalysts might well question whether this reflects an irreducible minimum of inference.

Reliability of the GAP System

Studies of the GAP system's reliability have been done in Australia (Freeman, 1971) and the United States (Beitchman, Dielman, Landis, Benson, & Kemp, 1978). In both studies, diagnoses were based on case history materials read by the diagnosticians. Freeman found 59 percent agreement (uncorrected for chance) in the use of broad categories analogous to those of the DSM reliability studies. Beitchman et al. found 40 percent agreement (uncorrected for chance) for broad diagnostic categories and 23 percent for more specific diagnoses. Despite its explicit orientation toward children, the GAP taxonomy thus does not offer greater reliability than the DSM. Furthermore, Freeman found that disagreement among diagnosticians was not the only source of unreliability; when he had his diagnosticians reassess the same case materials three months later, only 72 percent of their second diagnoses agreed with their own original broad-category diagnoses. Thus, inconsistency in the diagnosticians' own judgments of the materials probably contributed to the overall lack of agreement.

MULTIVARIATE APPROACHES

Both the DSM and GAP taxonomies were formulated by committees of psychiatrists through negotiation and the polling of colleagues. The categories involving organic abnormalities are defined largely in terms of those abnormalities, such as brain damage due to toxic substances. Most organic syndromes are diagnosable via tests of physical functioning, observable physical signs, and/or events such as head trauma.

Mental retardation is categorized in terms of degree of intellectual impairment, from mild to profound, based largely on IQ. It is diagnosable via IQ tests and developmental history.

Because the criteria for organic disorders and mental retardation are fairly objective, there has been little reason to propose major departures from these categories. The reliability studies, show, however, that these relatively reliable categories account for only a small minority of children's disorders (American Psychiatric Association, 1980; Beitchman, 1978; Freeman, 1971; Mattison et al., 1979). It is in the diagnosis of the remaining majority of disturbed children that the most problems arise and that alternatives have been most sought.

Both the DSM and GAP committees espoused *description* as the basis for classifying disorders of unknown etiology. Yet, they did not obtain descriptions of actual children with which to form their categories. Instead, as our earlier quote from Spitzer and Cantwell (1980) illustrates, the committees described their own *concepts* of the disorders they imputed to children. The low reliability of both taxonomies of children's disorders indicates that they do not serve as objective descriptions of children's disorders. This could reflect a lack of congruence with the actual disorders or problems in clinically applying what may be valid descriptions.

For behavioral disorders of unknown etiology, an alternative to the DSM and GAP approach is to determine empirically what characteristics tend to occur with what other characteristics. The rationale is that diagnostic categories should embody objectively identified syndromes instead of clinical concepts that lack empirical support.

A great many characteristics of children are potentially relevant to psychopathology. Few of these characteristics are as blatantly pathognomonic as those used to diagnose classic adult disorders such as schizophrenia, depressive conditions, or antisocial personality. Furthermore, unlike adults who assume the role of patients, children seldom contribute to the diagnostic process by spontaneously recounting relevant thoughts, feelings, and experiences. To identify all but the most blatant children's syndromes, we therefore have to sift through an immense variety of behaviors, most of which are displayed to some extent by most children. The diversity of potentially relevant behaviors, complicated further by the variability of each child's behavior, poses a much more massive information-processing task than the detection of blatant focal abnormalities.

To cope with the information-processing task, researchers on child and adolescent psychopathology have turned to statistical methods for summarizing relations among children's problem behaviors. In the first studies of this sort, behavioral problems were scored from the case histories of children seen in mental health settings. Correlations were then computed between each item and every other item. This amounted to a very large number of correlations. Having scored 125 behavior problem items, Ackerson (1942), for example, computed 7750 correlations among the items, separately for each sex, for a total of 15,500 correlations!

To derive *syndromes* from this bewildering array of correlations, Jenkins and Glickman (1946) picked out pairs of highly correlated items and then added items that correlated highest with each member of the highly correlated pairs. They then used a combination of statistical criteria and clinical judgment to decide when to stop adding items to each syndrome. A similar study by Hewitt and Jenkins (1946) and subsequent reanalyses of the same data yielded syndromes that ultimately served as prototypes for some of the DSM-II categories of childhood disorders (American Psychiatric Association, 1968). Yet even though empirical research did contribute in this case to the clinical concepts embodied in the official taxonomy, the research data themselves were second-hand reports in case histories from a very restricted range of settings. Furthermore, the derivation of syndromes from correlations was largely subjective and did not lead to clinically applicable operational definitions. When the DSM-II committee incorporated the results of this work, it was by describing in a narrative fashion *their* clinical concepts of the disorders they inferred from the findings.

Multivariate Methods

As electronic computers and more powerful statistical techniques became available, multivariate analyses were applied to an increasing range of data on child psychopathogy. Most analyses use correlations to measure the tendency of specific behaviors or other characteristics to occur together. Correlations can be computed on qualitative as well as quantitative data if the items are at least scored as 0 for *absent* and 1 for *present*. Analyses can be made more sensitive by scoring items in gradations, even as coarse as 0 for *never*, 1 for *sometimes*, and 2 for *often*.

Once correlations among items have been computed, multivariate statistical analyses of these correlations can detect groups of items that tend to occur together. Multivariate analyses do this by applying preselected mathematical criteria to the correlations among a large number of items. Subjective decisions are involved in selecting the mathematical criteria, but once we choose the criteria, the analyses derive groups of items in a rigorous and perfectly reliable fashion; that is, given scores for a sample of children, a particular multivariate analysis will always produce the same results, no matter who does the analysis. This eliminates unreliability that could arise in mentally combining data into syndromes, even if human minds could somehow process the many interrelations among potentially important items.

One type of multivariate statistical method for deriving syndromes is *factor analysis*. Factor analysis derives vectors or dimensions, called *factors*, from correlations among items. A *factor* consists of a list of *loadings* for all the items analyzed. A loading is like a correlation coefficient that can range from -1.00 to $+1.00$. An item's loading on a factor shows how strongly the item correlates with the dimension defined by the factor. The items having the highest loadings on the factor can be collectively regarded as a syndrome. Each item has a loading on every factor, but it usually has a high loading on only one or two factors. This indicates that it is strongly related only to those one or two syndromes.

Cluster analysis is another type of multivariate method for deriving syndromes. Cluster analysis forms groups *(clusters)* of items that are mutually exclusive. Each item can therefore be a member of only one cluster. Because they are not dimensional like factors are, clusters may intuitively seem more like traditional syndromes of psychopathology. Yet, because each item can belong to only one cluster, clusters may obscure the tendency of some items to occur with two or more groups of items. Factor analysis, by contrast, reveals such tendencies, because each item has a loading on every factor. As a result, some items can be associated with more than one syndrome derived through factor analysis, just as a fever may be associated with more than one organic disease.

Multivariate Findings

What have multivariate studies found? The specific analyses, rating instruments, and subject samples have varied from study to study. Nevertheless, when allowance is made for these differences, there is considerable convergence in the identification of numerous syndromes. In a review of 27 studies, 18 syndromes were found that had clear counterparts in two or more of the studies (Achenbach & Edelbrock, 1978). These could be divided into "broad band" and "narrow band" syndromes, somewhat analogous to the broad and more specific diagnostic categories of the DSM and GAP taxonomies. Table 15-2 shows the number of studies in which each broad and narrow band syndrome was found in ratings of behavior reported in case histories and direct ratings of children's behavior by mental health workers, parents, and teachers.

The broad band syndromes called *overcontrolled* and *undercontrolled* in Table 15-2 were found in almost all studies. The overcontrolled syndrome typically

Table 15-2 Number of Studies in which Syndromes have been Identified through Multivariate Analyses

Syndrome	Case Histories	Mental Health Workers	Teachers	Parents	Total
Broad Band					
Overcontrolled	2	1	5	6	14
Undercontrolled	3	3	5	7	18
Pathological Detachment	3	—	1	—	4
Learning problems	—	—	1	1	2
Narrow Band					
Academic Disability	—	1	—	3	4
Aggressive	3	4	1	8	16
Anxious	1	2	1	2	6
Delinquent	3	1	—	7	11
Depressed	2	1	—	5	8
Hyperactive	3	2	1	7	13
Immature	—	1	—	3	4
Obsessive-Compulsive	1	—	—	2	3
Schizoid	3	4	—	5	12
Sexual Problems	1	2	—	3	6
Sleep Problems	—	—	—	3	3
Social Withdrawal	1	1	1	5	8
Somatic Complaints	1	—	—	7	8
Uncommunicative	—	1	—	2	3

Source: From Achenbach & Edelbrock, 1978, plus syndromes subsequently identified in factor analyses of the Child Behavior Checklist for boys and girls aged 4 to 5 (see Table 15-4).

includes fearfulness, somatic complaints, and unhappiness, and has been given such labels as inhibited, internalizing, shy—anxious, and personality disorder. The undercontrolled syndrome, by contrast, typically includes fighting, destructiveness, and disobedience, and has been given such labels as aggressive, externalizing, acting out, and conduct disorder. The broad band syndrome called *pathological detachment* in Table 15-2 was found in only four studies and was not very uniform among these four. It was characterizied mainly by withdrawal and strange behavior. The other syndromes listed in Table 15-2 are self-explanatory.

How well do the DSM syndromes match the empirically derived syndromes? Although the precise composition of the empirically derived syndromes varies from study to study, Table 15-3 shows the approximate correspondence between them and those DSM syndromes that are defined largely in terms of observable behavior. The DSM-III syndromes intended primarily for children and adolescents are first listed on the left. The empirically derived syndromes corresponding closest to the DSM syndromes are listed on the right. Thereafter, the remaining empirically derived syndromes are listed with any roughly corresponding DSM syndrome listed in parentheses, even if the DSM syndrome was not primarily intended for children or adolescents.

Several DSM syndromes correspond roughly to empirically derived syndromes, but others do not. The DSM's *Attention deficit disorder without hyperactivity,* for example, did not have a clear counterpart among the empirically derived syndromes, although inattention was found in other syndromes without hyperactivity. Other DSM syndromes not found in the empirical studies include undersocialized conduct disorders without aggression, separation and avoidant disorders other than generalized withdrawal and anxiety; oppositional disorders other than the aggressive; identity disorders; and childhood-onset pervasive developmental disorders. If these syndromes really exist, it may be possible to find them through multivariate analyses of samples and items specifically chosen to manifest them. If such syndromes are truly distinct from those already identified, however, they may be rare or restricted to unusual groups.

Just as several DSM syndromes have no counterparts in the multivariate findings, several syndromes found in the multivariate studies have no clear counterparts in the DSM, as shown in Table 15-3. Some of these seem restricted to one sex or a particular developmental period, as discussed next.

Age and Sex Differences

Most of the multivariate studies have combined children of both sexes and diverse ages. This may obscure syndromes that occur in only one sex or age group. For example, items that correlate positively with each other at one age may not correlate at all or may even have negative correlations with each other at another age. If both age groups are combined in the same analysis, the positive correlations for children

Table 15-3 **Approximate Relations between DSM-III and Empirically Derived Syndromes of Childhood Behavior Disorders**

DSM-III	*Empirically Derived Narrow-Band Syndromes*
Attention deficit disorders	
314.01 With hyperactivity	Hyperactive
314.00 Without hyperactivity	—
314.80 Residual type	—
Conduct disorders	
312.00 Undersocialized, aggressive	Aggressive
312.10 Undersocialized, nonaggressive	—
312.23 Socialized, aggressive	Delinquent (boys)
312.21 Socialized, nonaggressive	Delinquent (girls)
312.90 Atypical	—
Anxiety disorders of childhood or adolescence	
309.21 Separation anxiety disorder	—
313.21 Avoidant disorder	—
313.00 Overanxious disorder	Anxious
Other disorders of childhood or adolescence	
313.22 Schizoid disorder	Social withdrawal (?)
313.23 Elective mutism	Uncommunicative
313.81 Oppositional disorder	—
313.82 Identity disorder	—
Pervasive developmental disorders	
299.8 Childhood onset pervasive developmental	—
299.9 Atypical	—
302.60 Gender identity disorder of childhood	Sex problems (boys 4−5)
V62.30 Academic problem	Academic disability
Disorders not specific to childhood or adolescence	
300.30 Obsessive-compulsive disorder	Obsessive-compulsive
300.81 Somatization disorder	Somatic complaints
309.00 Adjustment disorder with depressed mood (?)	Depressed
301.22 Schizotypal personality disorder (?)	Schizoid
—	Immature
—	Sexual problems
—	Sleep problems
	Cruel (girls)

Source: Achenbach, 1980, p. 410. Numbers are DSM-III statistical codes.

of one age may be cancelled out by the null or negative correlations for children of other ages.

In studies designed to detect age and sex differences in the patterning of behavioral problems, some syndromes have shown considerable similarity across groups, whereas others have been found for only one sex or age group. Table 15-4 lists syndromes found when parents' ratings on a single instrument, the Child Behavior Checklist, were factor analyzed separately for disturbed boys and girls at ages 4 to 5, 6 to 11, and 12 to 16. These age intervals were chosen because they mark changes in cognitive, biological, and psychosocial functioning, as well as major transitions in schooling. The parents scored each of 118 behavior problem items as 0 if the item was *not true* of their child; 1 if it was *somewhat or sometimes true;* and 2 if it was *very true or often true.*

The names given the syndromes are intended to summarize the behavioral problems found to occur together. Traditional clinical terms were chosen for syndromes approximating established clinical concepts. A syndrome designated as *schizoid,* for example, was found that included such items as *hears things that aren't there* and *sees things that aren't there.* On the other hand, some of the syndromes had no clear counterparts in either traditional taxonomies or multivariate studies that lumped together children of both sexes and diverse ages. The syndrome designated as *cruel,* for example, was found only for girls aged 6 to 11 and girls aged 12 to 16. For both groups of girls, this syndrome included *cruel to animals; cruelty, bullying, or meanness to others; destroys things belonging to his/her family;* and *physically attacks people.* This was not just a syndrome of aggression, because a separate syndrome of diverse aggressive behaviors was found for girls, as well as for boys, in all age groups. The cruel syndrome contradicts sex stereotypes, as these behaviors are more often imputed to boys than girls (Achenbach & Edelbrock, 1981). Yet for disturbed boys, the behaviors do not *occur together* to form a syndrome as they do for girls. The tendency for these behaviors to occur together among girls in a discriminating way distinct from other aggressive behaviors would have been obscured if boys and girls were analyzed together.

A syndrome that showed distinctive *age* differences across both sexes was the one designated in Table 15-4 as *depressed.* For both sexes at ages 4 to 5 and 6 to 11, numerous items grouped together with high loadings on the depressed factor. Yet at ages 12 to 16, no such factor was found for boys. For 12- to 16-year-old girls, a factor having several depressive items was found but it also had several items that formed a separate syndrome of withdrawal in all the other groups. It was therefore designated as *depressed withdrawal.*

Even though depressive items are reported for more adolescents than younger children (Achenbach & Edelbrock, 1981), these items do not occur together in a discriminating fashion to the same extent for adolescents as for younger children. Instead, signs of unhappiness accompany a more diverse array of adolescent problem behaviors. When the 6- to 11- and 12- to 16-year-old samples were combined for analysis, the depressed syndrome found for the younger groups alone disappeared

Table 15-4 Syndromes Found Through Factor Analysis of the Child Behavior Checklist

Group	Internalizing Syndromes[a]	Mixed Syndromes	Externalizing Syndromes[a]
Boys aged 4–5	1. Social withdrawal 2. Somatic complaints 3. Immature 4. Depressed	1. Sex problems	1. Delinquent 2. Aggressive 3. Schizoid
Boys aged 6–11	1. Schizoid 2. Depressed 3. Uncommunicative 4. Obsessive compulsive 5. Somatic complaints	1. Social withdrawal	1. Delinquent 2. Aggressive 3. Hyperactive
Boys aged 12–16	1. Somatic complaints 2. Schizoid 3. Uncommunicative 4. Immature 5. Obsessive compulsive	1. Hostile withdrawal	1. Hyperactive 2. Aggressive 3. Delinquent
Girls aged 4–5	1. Depressed 2. Somatic complaints 3. Schizoid 4. Social withdrawal	1. Sex problems	1. Obese 2. Aggressive 3. Hyperactive
Girls aged 6–11	1. Depressed 2. Social withdrawal 3. Somatic complaints 4. Schizoid obsessive		1. Cruel 2. Aggressive 3. Delinquent 4. Sex Problems 5. Hyperactive
Girls aged 12–16	1. Anxious obsessive 2. Somatic complaints 3. Schizoid 4. Depressed withdrawal	1. Immature hyperactive	1. Cruel 2. Aggressive 3. Delinquent

[a]Syndromes are listed in descending order of their loadings on the second-order internalizing and externalizing factors.
Source: Achenbach & Edelbrock, 1982.

(Achenbach & Edelbrock, 1979). This underlines the importance of developmental differences in the patterning of psychopathology.

Broad Band versus Narrow Band Syndromes

The syndromes listed in the body of Table 15-4 are *narrow band* syndromes; that is, they reflect relatively numerous (8 or 9) specific disorders for each sex/age group. How do the narrow band syndromes relate to the more general broad band syndromes shown in Table 15-2?

One way of finding out is too perform *second order* factor analyses of the narrow band syndromes. In the studies summarized in Table 15-4, this was done by first computing children's scores on all the syndromes found for their sex/age group: To obtain a 4-year-old boy's score on the Social Withdrawal syndrome, for example, his parent's ratings of 0, 1, or 2 on each of the 12 items of this syndrome were summed. The boy's score could thus range from 0 (if all 12 items were scored 0) to 24 (if all 12 items were scored 2). The boy's scores on the other seven narrow band syndromes found for 4- to 5-year-old boys were computed in the same way. After scores were computed on all eight syndromes for all the 4- and 5-year-old boys in the sample, correlations were computed among the eight syndromes. These correlations were then factor analyzed to obtain *second-order factors;* these are factors that show which of the narrow band syndromes group together to form broad band syndromes.

For each sex/age group, two second-order factors were obtained that resembled the broad band overcontrolled and undercontrolled syndromes found in many other studies. A look back at Table 15-4 shows which of the narrow band syndromes had high loadings on the overcontrolled (''internalizing'') second-order factor and which ones had high loadings on the undercontrolled (''externalizing'') second-order factor. Those listed in the center column under the heading *mixed syndromes* had moderate loadings on both second-order factors; they did not, therefore, seem to be integral components of either.

These findings show that the empirically identified broad and narrow band syndromes are not mutually contradictory. Instead, they form a hierarchy: Many of the narrow band syndromes can be viewed as *subtypes* of the broad band syndromes. This hierarchy of broad and narrow band syndromes differs in a crucial way from the relation between broad and narrow diagnostic categories in the DSM and GAP taxonomies: The relations between the broad and narrow band syndromes are derived empirically, whereas the hierarchies postulated by the DSM and GAP committees lack an empirical basis for linking particular narrow categories to the broad categories.

The Child Behavior Profile

Many multivariate studies have identified factors or clusters of items but have not provided ways to assess individual children. How can we apply the multivariate findings to actual children? Several steps are needed. These will be illustrated with the steps taken to apply the multivariate syndromes shown in Table 15-4. (The identification of these syndromes was itself a lengthy process that will not be detailed here but that involved several factor analyses of each sex/age sample to determine which factors were most robust despite changes in statistical criteria.)

The behavior problem items loading highest on a factor were used to define the syndrome represented by that factor. For example, the *Cruel* syndrome described earlier was defined by items such as *cruel to animals* that grouped together with high loadings on a particular factor. To provide a comprehensive overview of a child's behavior problems, all the items of each syndrome are displayed in a profile format, called the Child Behavior Profile. Because the syndromes vary among the sex/age groups, a separate edition of the Profile was constructed for each group.

Figure 15-1 illustrates the edition of the Profile for 6- to 11-year-old boys, as it has been filled out for 9-year-old Bobby S. Bobby's total score for each syndrome is the sum of his parent's 0, 1, and 2 ratings on the items of the syndrome. Behavioral problems that did not load highly on any of the factors retained as syndromes are displayed on the Profile under the heading of *Other Problems*. Because data on all the items and syndromes are retained on the Profile, we do not need to make a forced choice among categorical alternatives as required by traditional taxonomies. Instead, Bobby's standing on all the syndromes and specific problems can be viewed simultaneously.

Quantitative Scoring. Bobby is scored quantitatively on each syndrome; the more items ascribed to him and the higher the ratings, the higher his total score for the syndrome. We do not, therefore, need to decide in a yes-or-no fashion whether Bobby is well versus sick or normal versus abnormal.

Children tend to differ from one another in the *degree* to which they manifest each syndrome, not in an all-or-none fashion. Quantitative scoring reflects variations in degree better than the categorical judgments required by the DSM and GAP taxonomies. Although the DSM and GAP permit multiple diagnoses, their categorical structure may be a source of unreliability in assessing characteristics that do not really occur in categorical form. Quantitative scoring can also provide a more sensitive index of change in problem behavior than all-or-none diagnostic judgments do.

Comparison with Normative Groups. How does Bobby compare with other boys his age? Percentiles listed on the left of the Profile reflect scores found for children not receiving mental health services. Their parents filled out the Child Behavior Checklist as part of a home interview survey. Thus, the peaks on the profile in Figure 15-1 show that Bobby S. scored considerably higher on the *Depressed, Social Withdrawal,* and *Aggressive* syndromes than typical 6- to 11-year-old boys. His scores were well above the 99th percentile of the normative groups on all three of these syndrome scales. (The scores to the right of the Profile are standard

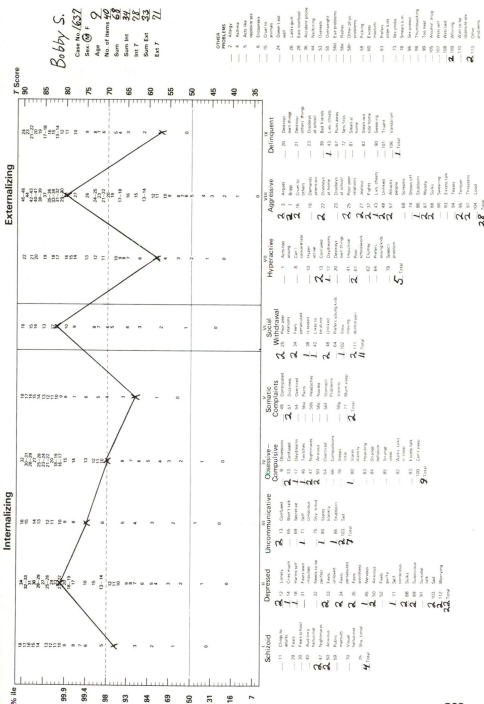

Figure 15.1. Example of the behavior problem portion of the Child Behavior Profile for boys aged 6 to 11.

563

scores—*T* scores—that translate the syndrome scores into standard deviation units for purposes of statistical analysis.)

Broad Band Syndromes. Beside reflecting a child's scores on specific behavioral problems and narrow band syndromes, the Child Behavior Profile is also designed to assess broad band internalizing and externalizing syndromes. Another look at Figure 15-1 shows that the narrow band syndromes are grouped according to the second-order internalizing and externalizing factors. Bobby's Profile has peaks on one internalizing syndrome *(Depressed)*, one mixed syndrome *(Social Withdrawal)*, and one externalizing syndrome *(Aggressive)*. Bobby's internalizing score can be computed by adding up his scores on the items of all five internalizing scales. His externalizing score can likewise be computed by adding up his scores on the items of the three externalizing scales. These internalizing and externalizing scores can then be converted to standard scores *(T* scores) by reference to a table that accompanies the Profile. The *T* scores show how much Bobby differs from the normative group of 6- to 11-year-old boys. He happens to have considerably more problems of both types than normal boys, but many disturbed children score high in only one area or the other. Children can thus be assessed quantitatively in terms of the broad internalizing versus externalizing distinction as well as in terms of their standing on the more specific narrow band syndromes.

Social Competence. Because children's competencies may be as important as their deficits in determining their developmental prospects, the Child Behavior Checklist includes items tapping the amount and quality of children's participation in sports, nonsports activities, organizations, jobs and chores, and social relations, as well as their school performance. These are scored on three scales entitled *Activities, Social,* and *School,* as shown in Figure 15-2.

Like the behavior problem scales, the social competence scales in Figure 15-2 show how Bobby S. compares with normative groups of boys in terms of percentiles and standard scores. Unlike the behavior problem scales, however, for which *high* scores indicate clinically significant deviance, exceptionally low scores, showing a lack of competencies, are of clinical importance on the social competence scales. As Figure 15-2 shows, Bobby S. scores at about the second percentile on the Activities scale; at less than 1/10 of the first percentile on the Social scale; and at almost the thirty-first percentile on the School scale.

Child Behavior Profile Patterns

The Child Behavior Profile provides a comprehensive picture of parent-reported competencies and problems, grouped according to dimensions that quantitatively reflect a child's deviance from normative groups. The behavior problem dimensions and the norms reflect the patterning and prevalence of behaviors characteristic of the child's age and sex. The narrow band behavior problem

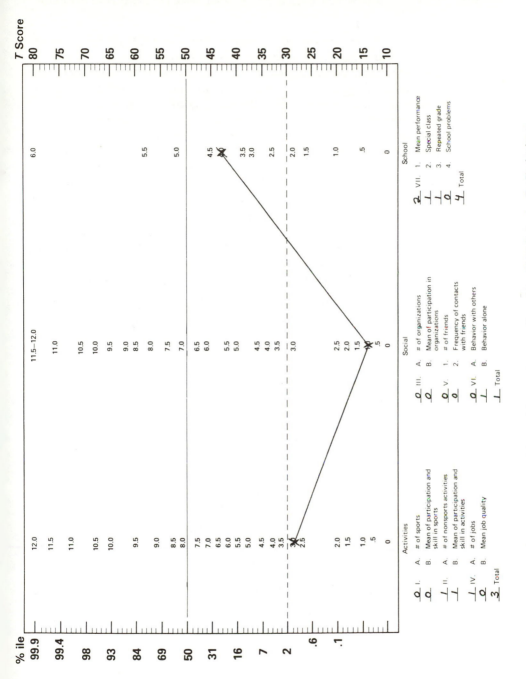

Figure 15.2. Example of the social competence portion of the Child Behavior Profile for boys aged 6 to 11, as filled out for 9-year old Bobby S.

syndromes are analogous to syndromes found within such DSM-III categories as attention deficit disorders, conduct disorders, and anxiety disorders. The syndromes of both the DSM and the Profile are intended to depict naturally occurring groups of behavioral problems. Furthermore, both the DSM and the Profile embody a hierarchy of general and more specific syndromal categories. The DSM's general categories of attention deficit, conduct, and anxiety disorders each comprise from three to five specific syndromes; likewise, the Profile's broad band internalizing and externalizing categories comprise from three to five narrow band syndromes.

Despite certain similarities between the DSM and the Profile, there are also important differences: The DSM syndromes form a categorical taxonomy of individuals. A child is diagnosed as either having or not having an attention deficit disorder with hyperactivity, for example. If we use the DSM to group children for purposes of finding etiologies, testing the effects of treatments, or determining prognosis, we must group children in categories such as the attention deficit disorders. In effect, DSM's syndromes are equivalent to a taxonomy of *children,* even though some children may be diagnosed as having more than one syndrome.

A Taxonomy of Profile Patterns. Unlike the DSM syndromes, the syndromes of the Profile are not intended as a taxonomy of children. They were derived as a taxonomy of *behaviors* and are intended to serve only as a taxonomy of behaviors. A high score on the Schizoid scale, for example, is not equivalent to a diagnostic categorization such as the DSM's *Schizoid disorder of childhood or adolescence.* Instead, the score merely shows the degree of deviance on a particular syndrome of behaviors. Some of the children having a high score on this scale may have still higher scores on all the other scales of the Profile; others may have a high score on one or no other scales.

If we categorize children solely on the basis of a particular syndrome, we may be neglecting potentially important differences on other syndromes. To avoid this problem, the overall Profile patterns have been used to generate a taxonomy of individuals. This was done by cluster analyzing the Profiles of children who were referred for mental health services (Edelbrock & Achenbach, 1980).

In using cluster analysis to identify groups of children having similar behavior patterns, we began with the Profiles of a large sample of children. The cluster analysis then formed groups of Profiles that were most similar to one another. This was done in a hierarchical fashion: Small groups having very similar Profiles were formed first; then larger groups were formed from the small groups that were most alike. Figure 15-3 shows the hierarchical relations between the small, differentiated groups and larger, more global groups of Profile patterns found for 6- to 11-year-old boys. For girls, an additional global grouping was found that was designated as mixed.

The Profile type represented by each box in Figure 15-3 is named according to the syndrome scales having the highest scores on that Profile type. For example, the box labelled *Depressed-Social Withdrawal-Aggressive* represents a Profile pattern

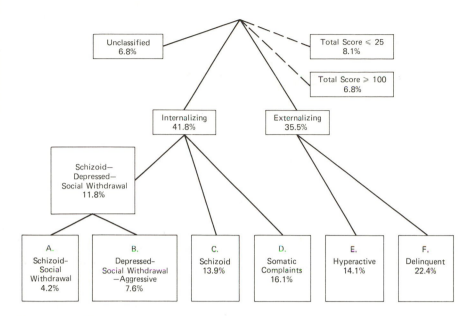

Figure 15.3. Distribution of Child Behavior Profile patterns found for 6- to 11-year-old boys (n=1050) referred for mental health services. Each box indicates the percentage of boys grouped in that category. Those with exceptionally low scores (⩽ 25) or high scores (⩾ 100) were excluded. (From Edelbrock & Achenbach, 1980, p. 452.)

like that of Bobby S. (Fig. 15-1) on which the highest scores are on the Depressed, Social Withdrawal, and Aggressive scales. However, each Profile type is defined not just by its peaks on these scales but by its entire pattern, including intermediate and low scores on some scales. Basing a taxonomy on the entire Profile pattern thus preserves a more comprehensive picture of behavior than categorization according to single syndromes.

As Figure 15-4 shows, some Profile patterns are characterized by exceptionally high scores on one syndrome and low scores on the others. Some of these patterns happen to correspond to taxonomies based on single syndromes: the Profile pattern characterized by a high score on only the *Hyperactive* syndrome, for example, resembles DSM-III's *Attention deficit disorder with hyperactivity.*

Despite the correspondence of some Profile types to categorization in terms of single DSM-III syndromes, other Profile types embody more complex patterns that have no counterparts in single DSM syndromes. Bobby S., for example, had exceptionally high scores on the Depressed, Social Withdrawal, and Aggressive syndromes of the Profile. This was a pattern that characterized 7.6 percent of 6- to 11-year-old boys in our clinical sample. Because even normal 6- to 11-year-old boys show numerous behaviors of the aggressive syndrome and most clinically referred

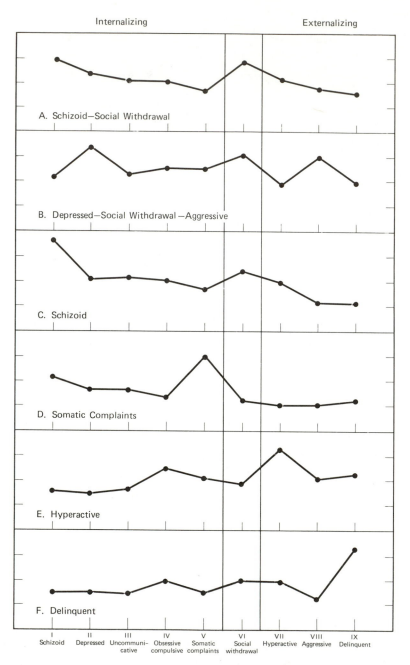

Figure 15.4. Profile types identified for 6- to 11-year-old boys. (Edelbrock & Achenbach, 1980, p. 448.)

boys show even more, boys whose Profiles match this pattern are very aggressive indeed. Their aggressive behavior is typically the reason for referral and the focus of greatest concern. Using the DSM, such an aggressive boy would be diagnosed as having an *undersocialized aggressive conduct disorder*. Yet, if he is scored on the Child Behavior Profile, it would be clear that he is equally deviant on the Depressed and Social Withdrawal scales as well.

Reliability of the Profile Taxonomy. Unlike traditional categorical taxonomies, individual Profiles can be assigned to the cluster-based taxonomy in a purely quantitative way. Because each category is defined by a particular Profile pattern, a correlation can be computed between a child's Profile and the pattern defining each category. (Unlike the commonly used Pearson correlation, which indicates the relation between two variables measured in several people, the correlation between a child's Profile and one defining a Profile category is computed between the child's scores on all scales of his or her Profile and the scores of the Profile defining the category. The resulting correlation coefficient thus shows how closely the child's Profile resembles the Profile category. This correlation can range from −1.00 to +1.00.)

We can then categorize the child's Profile with the Profile type with which it correlates best. If it does not correlate highly with any type, we can leave it uncategorized. We can use the same procedure for categorizing Profiles in terms of the differentiated Profile types shown in Figure 15-3 or the more global internalizing, mixed, and externalizing Profiles that subsume these, as shown in Figure 15-4. This procedure is not affected by disagreements among diagnosticians, because the correlation indicates the *degree* of resemblance to a category. Diagnosticians may disagree about how strongly a child's Profile *should* correlate with a Profile type to warrant placing the child in that category, but different cut-off criteria for correlations can be empirically compared with respect to their impact on the homogeneity of groups created.

Assigning individual Profiles to the taxonomy is thus completely objective. But unreliability might affect the behavior ratings from which Profiles are scored. Unreliability in the data gathering process was ignored by the DSM and GAP reliability studies where diagnosticians were given identical data. Yet it should be assessed to give a truer picture of taxonomic reliability than that based merely on agreements between diagnoses from identical data. The reliability of the data used in the Profile has been assessed in several ways.

First, with regard to the scoring of specific items: Mothers' and fathers' ratings of their children showed an overall correlation *(interparent reliability)* of .99 for the behavior problems and .98 for the social competence items; mothers' ratings of their children at one-week intervals *(test-retest reliability)* showed an overall correlation of .95 for behavior problems and .99 for social competence items; in the home interview survey in which data were obtained on normal children, parents' ratings obtained by different interviewers on demographically matched children *(inter-interviewer reliability)* showed overall intraclass correlations of .96 for behavior problems and .93 for social competence items (Achenbach & Edelbrock, 1981). These figures all show good agreement in the rating of specific items as measured by intraclass correlations, which reflect a combination of the rank of the child's score within the entire sample and the actual size of each score (e.g., 0, 1, or 2 for behavior problems).

The total scores for each syndrome scale can vary over a much wider range than the 0-1-2 ratings of individual items. Separate assessment of the reliability of rank ordering of scores within a sample and the actual sizes of scores were therefore made. Reliability in the rank ordering of scores was assessed by Pearson correlations. These showed an average correlation of .69 for agreement between mothers' and fathers' ratings and an average correlation of .88 for test-retest reliability of mothers' ratings across a one-week interval (Achenbach, 1979). Good reliability in the actual size of scores was also found: The mean of mothers' ratings did not differ significantly from the mean of fathers' ratings on most scales; nor did mothers' scores change significantly over one-week intervals on most scales (Achenbach, 1979).

To assess agreement in the *categorization* of children's Profiles from Child Behavior Checklist data, Profiles were scored from Checklists filled out by mothers of children referred to a community mental health center and by a psychologist who interviewed the child and family and examined Checklist ratings by parents and teachers. Having the psychologist examine ratings by mothers, fathers, and teachers gave her a picture of their perceptions of the child's behavior, although she also used all she knew about the family to correct errors and biases that she detected. The Profiles based on the mothers' and psychologist's ratings were then categorized according to the Profile types found through cluster analysis. For the differentiated Profile types, agreement between categorization of Profiles scored from the mothers' and psychologist's ratings averaged 74 percent across the sex/age groups. For the more global internalizing, mixed, and externalizing Profile types, agreement averaged 83 percent. This is a more stringent test of agreement than used by the DSM and GAP reliability studies, because it reflects agreement between non-professionals (mothers) and a clinician who did not use identical data the way the DSM and GAP diagnosticians did. Yet, for both the differentiated and global categories, the percent of agreement is higher than in studies reporting percent of agreement for global categories of the DSM or GAP taxonomies (Beitchman et al., 1978; Freeman, 1971; Mattison et al., 1979). The *kappa* statistic that corrects for chance agreements was also higher for both the differentiated categories *(kappa = .64)* and global categories *(kappa = .62)* than in studies reporting *kappas* for the DSM child and adolescent syndromes (American Psychiatric Association, 1980; Mezzich & Mezzich, 1979).

Validity of Multivariate Approaches

Recall Spitzer and Cantwell's (1980) statement quoted earlier concerning the *face validity* of DSM-III's diagnostic categories:

Face validity is the extent to which the description of a particular category seems on the face of it to describe accurately the characteristic features of persons with a particular disorder. It is the result of clinicians agreeing on the identification of a particular syndrome or pattern of clinical features as a mental disorder (p. 359).

Where the target variables are self-evident, face validity is indeed worthwhile. For example, if an achievement test is supposed to determine whether students know the names of the American presidents, having them list the presidents would be a *face valid* test item needing no other kind of validation. Although some of the DSM's target disorders may seem so self-evident that face validity suffices, its behavior disorders of childhood and adolescence are not. Other forms of validation are therefore needed.

What about the validity of multivariate syndromes? Because we lack well-validated diagnostic constructs for children's behavior disorders, we cannot assess multivariate syndromes via either face validity or correlations with diagnoses made by other means. Instead, to validate the empirically derived syndromes, we need to rely mainly on *bootstrapping;* that is, "lifting ourselves by our own bootstraps" by finding relations among measures that we know are imperfect. As we improve our measures and find out how well they correlate with each other, we can use the best measures as validating criteria for new measures.

One way to validate multivariate syndromes is to see how well syndrome scores obtained with different instruments agree with each other. Several studies show significant correlations between similar syndromes scored on different instruments. Where a single instrument was factor analyzed for several different populations, similar factors have also been found (see Achenbach & Edelbrock, 1978). Cross-validation of this sort, however, has been confined largely to the broad band syndromes.

Another way to validate multivariate syndromes is to find out whether individuals who score high on one syndrome differ in other respects from individuals who score high on another syndrome. Also confined largely to the broad band syndromes, this work has shown that children manifesting mostly undercontrolled, externalizing problems have less adequate families, are less socially competent, have worse prognoses, and are less appropriate candidates for traditional mental health services than children manifesting overcontrolled, internalizing problems (see Achenbach & Edelbrock, 1978).

A third way to validate multivariate syndromes is to see whether children diagnosed disturbed according to other criteria have more features of the syndromes than children considered normal. Where children referred for mental health services have been compared to demographically matched normal children, the referred children have shown significantly higher scores on all the narrow band and broad band syndromes (Achenbach, 1978; Achenbach & Edelbrock, 1979). Although this does not prove that the different syndromes represent different disorders, it does show that they validly discriminate between disturbed and normal children. Where narrow band syndromes have been cluster analyzed to form taxonomies of children, those classified by different Profile types have been found to differ in social competencies and demographic characteristics (Edelbrock & Achenbach, 1980; Langner, Gersten, Eisenberg, Greene, & Herson, in press). Programmatic research is needed, however, to determine whether the different syndromes and Profile patterns are related to differences in etiology, prognosis, or responsiveness to treatment.

OTHER APPROACHES TO TAXONOMY

Several other approaches to taxonomy of child and adolescent disorders have been tried. We will consider three that illustrate directions other than those taken by the DSM, GAP, and multivariate approaches.

World Health Organization

The World Health Organization (WHO) proposed a multiaxial taxonomy for children's disorders (Rutter, Shaffer, & Shepherd, 1975). Like the DSM and GAP approaches, the WHO started with clinical concepts and then formulated categories to represent each concept. The axes selected by the WHO differ from those of the DSM, however. The four WHO axes are *psychiatric syndromes; level of intellectual functioning; biological factors;* and *psychological and social factors.*

Separating intellectual functioning from the psychiatric syndromes avoids problems arising from DSM-III's inclusion of mental retardation as an Axis I psychiatric syndrome. For example, DSM-III states that certain diagnoses, such as attention deficit disorders, should not be made if the condition is due to severe mental retardation. This implies that retardation per se causes these disorders. Yet many retarded children do not manifest them, whereas some nonretarded children do. Furthermore, clinicians who make an Axis I diagnosis of mental retardation sometimes assume that this completes their Axis I work, thereby omitting other relevant Axis I diagnoses (Rutter & Shaffer, 1980).

The WHO categories seem to be more reliable than the DSM-III categories of child and adolescent disorders: 67 percent agreement (uncorrected for chance) was found among psychiatrists' diagnoses made from case histories in terms of five broad categories of the WHO system (Rutter et al., 1975).

Anna Freud's Developmental Profile

In Chapter 9, we discussed Anna Freud's (1965) Developmental Profile for psychoanalytic assessment of development. It provides an outline for inferences about psychoanalytic constructs such as libido, aggressive drive, ego, superego, defenses, regressions, and fixations. After assessing a child in terms of these constructs, the clinician must decide among diagnostic categorizations such as the following:

A. In spite of current behavior disturbance, personality growth is within the wide range of ''normality.''

B. Symptoms are of a transitory nature and can be classed as byproducts of developmental strain.

C. There is a permanent drive regression to fixation points which leads to neurotic conflicts.

D. There is drive regression plus ego and superego regressions which lead to infantilisms, borderline psychotic, delinquent, or psychotic disturbances.

E. There are primary organic deficiencies or early deprivations which distort development and produce retarded defective, and nontypical personalities.

F. There are destructive processes at work of organic, toxic, or psychic origin which have caused or are about to cause a disruption of mental growth. (Adapted from A. Freud, 1965, p. 147)

Efforts have been made to use the Profile in psychoanalytic settings, and there are some published illustrations of the Profile's use with single cases (e.g., Nagera, 1981). Efforts have also been made to construct categories for rating the characteristics implied by the Profile. One set of categories, for example, includes ego flexibility, superego functioning, affects, and defenses (Greenspan, Hatleberg, & Cullander, 1980). The child's functioning in each category is rated as good, fair, marginal, or inadequate. Although the reliability of these ratings could easily be tested, Greenspan et al. present only an illustration of their profile for a single case, with no reliability data. Validity would be much harder to test, because the diagnostic distinctions apply to a network of inferences about psychoanalytic constructs that require validation themselves.

Anthony's Diagnostic Classification

E. James Anthony (1970) proposed to integrate a variety of developmental concepts into a taxonomy for developmental psychopathology. His aim was to portray disorders ''in terms of the psychosexual, psychosocial, psychocognitive, and psychoaffective operations at work during any particular stage'' (p. 371). As shown in Table 15-5, he did this by listing the roughly parallel stages proposed by Freud, Erikson, Piaget, and Jersild, plus the approximate ages and pathology thought to characterize each stage.

Anthony acknowledged that his schema could do no more than generate hypotheses, but he offered it as a way of summarizing important dimensions of development. As with our own efforts in Chapter 3 to integrate the many factors needed for a developmental understanding of psychopathology, it is now necessary to move beyond these rough parallels between theories that have each highlighted a different aspect of development. For each construct and disorder, we need reliable measures with which to link development in one domain with development in other domains. In this chapter, we have considered advances in assessing psychopathol-

Table 15-5　Anthony's Proposed Diagnostic Classification for Developmental Psychopathology.

Ages	Psychosexual stages (Freud)	Psychosocial stages (Erikson)	Cognitive stages (Piaget)	Affective stages (Jersild)	Psychopathology
0–1½	Oral	Basic trust vs. Mistrust	Sensorimotor	Fears of: Dark, Strangers, Aloneness, Sudden noise, Loss of support	Autism, Anaclitic depression, Feeding and sleeping problems
1½–3	Anal	Autonomy vs. Doubt, shame	Symbolic	Separation, Desertion, Sudden movements	Symbiosis, Negativism, Constipation, Shyness & withdrawal, Night terrors
3–5	Genital Oedipal	Initiative vs. Guilt	Intuition, Representational	Animals, Imaginary creatures, Injury	Phobias, Nightmares, Speech problems, Enuresis, Encopresis, Anxiety states
6–11	Latency	Industry vs. Inferiority	Concrete operational	School failure, Ridicule, Loss of possessions, Disfigurement, Disease, Death	School problems, School phobias, Obsessions, Conversion symptoms, Tics
12–17	Adolescent—recapitulation of earlier conflicts	Identity vs. Role confusion	Formal operational	Being different physically, socially, intellectually, Sexual fears, Loss of face	Identity diffusion, Anorexia nervosa, Delinquency, Schizophrenia

Source: Adapted from Anthony, 1970, p. 730. © 1970 by John Wiley & Sons and reproduced by permission.

ogy of childhood and adolescence, but much remains to be done in order to link assessment across domains and periods of development.

SUMMARY

The lack of an adequate taxonomy has handicapped the search for etiologies and optimal treatments for child and adolescent psychopathology. The traditional approach has been to base taxonomy on a medical model whereby disorders are viewed as disease entities, each with a specific organic cause. Contemporary psychiatric taxonomy—embodied in the American Psychiatric Association's Diagnostic and Statistical Manual (DSM)—is a direct descendant of Kraepelin's taxonomy, which translated psychiatric disorders into a nineteenth-century organic disease model. The third edition of the DSM (DSM-III) provides more explicit criteria for diagnosis than previous editions have. For adult disorders, these criteria are based on well-established clinical concepts and on previously tested research diagnostic criteria. Most of the child and adolescent disorders have no such basis, however. As a result, DSM-III's child and adolescent categories are less reliable than its adult categories, and they lack firm links to actual distinctions among child and adolescent disorders.

Also starting with clinical concepts of disorders, the Group for the Advancement of Psychiatry (GAP) proposed a taxonomy of children's disorders designed to incorporate developmental factors more than the DSM has. Although the GAP taxonomy was intended to provide operational criteria for disorders, some of its categories require extensive theoretical inference. Like the DSM's child and adolescent categories, its reliability is inadequate.

The lack of well-established clinical concepts of children's disorders has spurred efforts to identify syndromes empirically through multivariate analyses of behavioral ratings. Despite differences in rating instruments, samples, and methods of analysis, these have shown considerable convergence in identifying a few broad band and more plentiful narrow band syndromes. Some of these syndromes correspond to DSM-III syndromes, but others do not. Some syndromes are quite uniform across both sexes and diverse ages, whereas others are restricted to one sex or developmental period.

Although many multivariate studies have not yielded procedures for assessing individual children, steps for translating multivariate findings into clinical assessment and taxonomic procedures were illustrated with the Child Behavior Profile. The Profile comprises behavior problem scales derived from factor analyses of behavior problems reported by parents of children referred for mental health services. Social competence scales are also included for children's positive adaptive behaviors. Children are scored on each scale of the Profile to show how their problems and competencies compare with those of their normal peers. Cluster analyses of the overall Profile patterns provide a taxonomy by which children can be grouped with children having similar Profile patterns. A child's Profile can be categorized according to the Profile type it correlates best with, thereby avoiding unreliability arising from clinical judgments. The reliability of the data from which Profiles are scored is quite satisfactory. Validity has been demonstrated via significant discrimination between referred and nonreferred children on all scales of the Profile and some significant correlates of particular Profile types.

Other approaches to the taxonomy of child and adolescent disorders include those of the World Health Organization's multiaxial taxonomy; Anna Freud's Developmental Profile; and E. James Anthony's schema for depicting parallel concepts of psychosexual, psychosocial, cognitive, and affective stages. However, all taxonomies need further tests of their ability to index such important variables as etiology, prognosis, and responsiveness to treatment.

SUGGESTED READING

Taxonomies. As examples of American psychiatry's official taxonomy, the three editions of the American Psychiatric Association's *Diagnostic and Statistical Manual* (DSM-I, 1952; DSM-II, 1968; DSM-III, 1980) are worth perusing to gain a glimpse of changing attitudes and customs. DSM-III in particular represents a break with the past in greatly expanding the number of child and adolescent disorders, providing multiple diagnostic axes, and specifying explicit diagnostic criteria. The DSM-III *Manual* is also worth reading for the background it provides on the committee process by which psychiatric taxonomy has been developed. Two taxonomies devised especially for child and adolescent disorders illustrate other directions psychiatric committee work can take: These are embodied in the Group for the Advancement of Psychiatry's (1966) *Psychopathological Disorders of Childhood: Theoretical Considerations and a Proposed Classification,* and the World Health Organization's *A Multiaxial Classification of Child Psychiatric Disorders: An Evaluation of a Proposal* (Rutter et al., 1975). Reviews of child and adolescent syndromes derived empirically through multivariate research have been compiled by Achenbach and Edelbrock (1978) and Quay (1979). Clinical and research applications of multivariate syndromes are detailed by Achenbach and Edelbrock (1982).

Conceptual Issues. From an international perspective, Rutter and Shaffer (1980) provide a detailed critique of DSM-III as compared to their vision of a more ideal system for children's disorders. Achenbach (1981) analyzes the role of taxonomy in developmental psychopathology. Hobbs (1975) has edited a massive work dealing with issues in the classification of children from diverse perspectives.

16

Diagnostic Assessment of Psychopathology

"To diagnose" literally means "to distinguish" or "to know apart" (from Greek *dia* = "apart," *gignoskein* = "to know"). In its narrow sense, *diagnosis* is almost synonymous with *classification*. Thus, a leading psychiatric diagnostician calls diagnosis "the medical term for classification" (Guzé, 1978, p. 53). In a broader sense, *diagnosis* means an "investigation or analysis of the cause or nature of a condition, situation, or problem," and "a statement or conclusion concerning the nature or cause of some phenomenon" (Woolf, 1977, p. 313).

A medical diagnosis in the narrow sense is called a *formal diagnosis* or *differential diagnosis*. This is the sense in which the term is used in the DSM. In deciding that a boy meets the criteria for Attention Deficit Disorder with Hyperactivity, for example, we are making a *formal* diagnosis of this disorder; it is a *differential* diagnosis in the sense that assignment to this particular category involves *differentiating* the boy's disorder from other disorders in the DSM.

A medical diagnosis in the broad sense, by contrast, is called a *diagnostic formulation* or *diagnostic work-up*. This refers to the process of gathering the information needed to understand an individual's problems and formulating conclusions in a comprehensive fashion. The diagnostic formulation often includes the individual's history, possible etiology, strengths and vulnerabilities, treatment options, and prognosis. Thus, although a boy's differential diagnosis is Attention Deficit Disorder with Hyperactivity, the diagnostic formulation should include information on the course and duration of problems, description of the specific

577

problem behaviors, family and school environment, adaptive assets, and the expected prognosis under various conditions.

The diagnostic formulation provides an idiographic picture of the boy in all his uniqueness, a picture that can help guide interventions. Yet, to optimize interventions, we need to identify individuals who share certain important characteristics— these are the characteristics embodied in the differential diagnosis. It is only by linking each new case to previous cases that we can bring accumulated knowledge to bear on the new case. Thus, even though the diagnostic formulation provides a more comprehensive picture than the differential diagnosis, it rests on the taxonomic distinctions embodied in the differential diagnosis.

As we saw in Chapter 15, different types of taxonomic distinctions may be relevant in different cases. For disorders having known organic etiologies, identifying the specific organic etiology is an important aspect of the formal diagnosis, although other taxonomic distinctions may also be important, such as specific type or degree of impairment. For disorders without known organic etiologies, taxonomic distinctions among behavior problem patterns may be primary. In all cases, however, some sort of taxonomic structure is needed to provide a focus for diagnosis in both its broad and narrow sense.

Neither diagnosis nor taxonomy is an end in itself. Each should facilitate services to children and their families. Approaches to diagnosis and taxonomy typically reflect the users' concepts of psychopathology and treatment. Broadening conceptions of psychopathology and treatment have led to widespread use of the term *assessment* in preference to *diagnosis,* which connotes organic disease concepts. Because the target phenomena are so diverse and no single viewpoint can encompass them all, the more general term *assessment* does not imply a rejection of medical diagnosis for disorders where organic factors are important. The main question is whether particular assessment (diagnostic) procedures discriminate among children in ways that help to serve the children.

To make useful and valid discriminations, a procedure must reveal something about the child that could not be learned more easily in other ways; this "something" must distinguish between the target child and other children so as to help us tailor services to this particular child. Yet, we do not know how best to serve the particular child unless we have previously evaluated the effects of efforts to help similar children.

Notice that we have returned full circle to the problem of taxonomy again: The need to link new cases to previous cases forces us to link assessment to taxonomy. Assessment and taxonomy are but two phases of a continuous process that should also encompass treatment and the evaluation of outcomes. The procedures employed in each phase of the process should be determined in part by what we learn from the other phases. As we will see, the links between assessment, taxonomy, treatment, and the evaluation of outcomes need strengthening in order to advance assessment.

We now turn to the major foci in the assessment of children and adolescents: infant development, cognitive functioning, personality, family functioning, behavioral assessment, and organic dysfunction. Thereafter, we will discuss questions of cultural influences that cut across all assessment.

ASSESSMENT OF INFANT DEVELOPMENT

Some early revisions of the Binet intelligence scale included items for testing infants, but Gesell's (1925) was the first test designed specifically for infant development. Most subsequent infant tests have been modeled on the Gesell scales, which consist of motor, adaptive, language, and personal-social items assessed by eliciting behavior from the child in a standardized manner (Knobloch & Pasamanick, 1974). They are supplemented by parental reports on behavior that is not readily elicited in the test situation. Norms are provided for four-week intervals up to the age of one year, three-month intervals to the age of two years, and six-month intervals to the age of three years. Four Developmental Quotients (DQs) are computed by dividing the child's scores on each of the four types of items by the child's chronological age and multiplying by 100, analogous to the IQ score on early IQ tests.

Other infant scales include the Brazelton Neonatal Behavioral Assessment Scale (1973), Uzgiris and Hunt's (1975) Piagetian scales, the Bayley Scales of Infant Development (1969), and the Denver Developmental Screening Test (Frankenburg & Dodds, 1968), which is a quick screening inventory rather than a comprehensive measure of development.

Developed by Nancy Bayley, the Bayley Scales provide the most thoroughly standardized omnibus measure of infant behavioral development. The Scales include items representative of behavior at ages 1 through 30 months, divided into a Mental Scale and a Motor Scale. On each scale, a child's total score is converted into a standard score that shows how the child compares with normative groups of agemates. Called a Development Index, this score is analogous to the deviation type of IQ employed on current IQ tests (explained in Chapter 8). Table 16-1 lists Bayley items typically passed by children at the ages of about 1 month, 6 months, 12 months, and 2 years.

At first it was hoped that infant test scores would predict later IQs, but longitudinal studies have repeatedly demonstrated little correlation between test scores before the age of about 18 months and the later IQs of normal children (McCall, Hogarty, & Hurlburt, 1972). Since IQ tests mainly measure manipulation of symbols (especially linguistic symbols), which infants appear totally incapable of, it is not surprising that infant tests do not accurately predict later IQs. Infants who score exceptionally low, however, tend to have low IQs later, because some abnormal conditions interfering with infant functioning continue to interfere later as well (Rubin & Balow, 1979).

Table 16-1 Examples of Infant Test Items from the Bayley (1969) Scales of Infant Development

Approximate Age (mos.)	Mental Scale Items	Motor Scale Items
1	Vocalizes once or twice	Thrusts legs in play
	Follows red ring with eyes	Head erect
6	Looks for fallen spoon	Rotates wrist
	Playful response to mirror	Sits alone 30 seconds or more
12	Jabbers expressively	Stands alone
	Turns pages of book	Walks alone
24	Names 4 pictures	Walks on line
	Names 3 objects	Stands on walking board with both feet

Infant tests are used mainly as screening devices. Exceptionally *low* scores may indicate organic damage, disease, or severe environmental deprivation which might be remediable; *uneven* performance, such as large disparities between motor, language, and social development, may indicate specific handicaps, such as deafness, emotional disturbance, or autism. Uneven infant test performance has also been found related to psychopathology evident much later (Fish, 1977), although further tests of these relationships are needed.

ASSESSMENT OF COGNITIVE FUNCTIONING

IQ Tests

The most widely used individual IQ tests are the Stanford-Binet and the Wechsler tests: the Wechsler Preschool and Primary Scale of Intelligence (WPPSI), the Wechsler Intelligence Scale for Children-Revised (WISC-R), and the Wechsler Adult Intelligence Scale-Revised (WAIS-R). These were reviewed in Chapter 8, as was evidence on the stability of IQs and their ability to predict academic performance. The evidence shows that the rank ordering of most children's IQs on the individual tests becomes fairly stable by about the age of 6, although the precise scores continue to fluctuate a bit for most children and a great deal for some children. The evidence also shows that both individual and group test scores predict academic grades fairly well and predict achievement test scores quite well.

Clinical-Diagnostic Use of IQ Tests

Beside yielding an estimate of a child's academic potential and mental age, individual IQ tests are used diagnostically to form hypotheses about specific problem areas. Such hypotheses are based on observation of the ways in which a child deviates from the responses typically given by a normative sample of agemates.

Response Style. Children's approach to IQ test items and their style of responding may be as informative as the content of their answers. For example, if a child gives several wrong answers without stopping to think, the examiner may ask the child to stop, think, and see if he or she can give another answer after each quick but wrong answer. If the child gives correct answers on the second try, it may be inferred that impulsivity rather than lack of ability was at fault. This can be noted in the test report and one IQ score can be computed on the basis of the child's initial answers, while a second is computed on the basis of the second answers. The two can be contrasted in the test report to demonstrate the possible difference between the child's typical current functioning and potential functioning when impulsivity is reduced.

In contrast to impulsivity, a response style characterized by unusually lengthy and detailed answers may suggest an obsessive-compulsive concern with knowledge and correctness. Inferences of this sort, however, should be viewed as tentative hints rather than definitive conclusions about a child's personality.

Patterns of Performance. Another diagnostic use of the IQ test is to compare the child's performance on various types of items. The Wechsler tests lend themselves to this especially well, because they are divided into subtests, each of which is administered and normed separately. The WISC-R, for example, includes Vocabulary, Arithmetic, Information, Comprehension, and Similarities subtests, which together yield the Verbal IQ score. The WISC-R Picture Completion, Picture Arrangement, Object Assembly, Block Design, and Coding subtests yield the Performance IQ (see Chapter 8 for details).

All children show some disparity among their scores on the various subtests. For children in the WISC-R standardization sample, the average difference between their highest and lowest subtest was 7 points (subtests' standard scores can range from a low of 1 to a high of 19; Kaufman, 1980). This means that an average child could have one or more scores as low as 7 and other scores as high as 14, where 10 is average.

Where scatter exceeds about 12 points, the child's lowest subtests may reflect weakness in particular areas, while the child's highest subtests reflect a special strength (Kaufman, 1980). Because very large disparities may be caused by chance or momentary factors, these disparities should be the basis for *hypotheses*, not *conclusions*, about the child. The hypotheses should be tested by gathering other data about the child from parent and school reports, medical examinations, observation of the child, and other tests to see whether the child is consistently weak in a particular area and whether the reason can be found.

One pattern of IQ test performance that often alerts examiners is a markedly poorer performance on items requiring visual-motor coordination than on verbal items. Examples are the copying of a square and diamond on the Stanford-Binet and the puzzlelike tasks on the Block Design and Object Assembly subtests of the WISC-R. If a child does much worse on these items than on the rest of the test and does not improve when asked to repeat them more slowly, the examiner might hypothesize that the child's visual-motor coordination is below his or her verbal functioning. However, unless a discrepancy between WISC-R Verbal and Performance IQs exceeds 26 points, it is not a statistically significant deviation from the normal range of discrepancies (Kaufman, 1980).

If a discrepancy exceeds 26 points, the hypothesis of a weakness in visual-motor functioning can be further tested with other measures of visual-motor functioning and by observing how the child walks and grasps objects in order to detect peculiarities of coordination. Specific hypotheses as to etiology might include poor vision, slow perceptual-motor maturation, damage or disease in the nervous system, or excessive anxiety about physical activity. The organic possibilities can be tested by vision, neurological, and medical exams, and by gathering developmental history data to identify any events responsible for organic damage. The anxiety hypothesis can be tested by observing the child in various situations, administering personality tests, obtaining parent and teacher ratings on behavior checklists, and interviewing the child and family.

Another potentially significant pattern involves exceptionally low scores on the information and arithmetic subtests. Such a pattern may suggest environmental deprivation or poor school learning in a child whose ability is adequate. Exceptionally high scores on these subtests may reflect environmental enrichment in a child whose basic ability is not especially high. These subtests, however, should be singled out for interpretation only if they differ by more than 3 points from the average of the scaled scores of all the subtests on the Verbal IQ scale of which they are a part (Kaufman, 1980).

Nature of Incorrect Responses. Besides subtest patterning, the nature of a child's wrong responses may also be informative. As Piaget noted long ago, children's incorrect answers to adult questions do not merely reflect ignorance. Instead, children's answers often reflect a way of thinking and a set of assumptions different from those of adults. While most IQ test items are not explicitly designed to reveal the qualitative levels of children's thought, certain incorrect answers are characteristic of children whose overall level of thinking is developmentally below that required for a correct answer. On the Binet, for example, the question, "What makes a sailboat move?" is often answered "The water," by children below the mental age of 7. This reflects their failure to apply a form of causal reasoning that becomes common after the mental age of 7.

A child whose wrong answers are consistently like those of other children is probably thinking in a way that is normal for a cognitive level below that required for correct answers. However, answers that are not only incorrect but extremely unusual may suggest that the child has a peculiar and possibly bizarre way of thinking. The response, "A unit in the sky," to the Binet vocabulary word "Mars," for example, was peculiar enough to alert one psychologist to a thought disorder in a person later diagnosed schizophrenic.

Wrong answers to easy items interspersed with right answers to difficult items also suggest that anxiety or some other factor is hindering the child's cognitive functioning.

Specialized Tests of Ability

Raven's Progressive Matrices (1960) is a widely used nonverbal test that can be administered in any language and even to deaf mutes. The matrices consist of designs and patterns from which one component is missing. The subject is to select the missing component for each item from a multiple-choice array. The test's major clinical function is to provide a quick estimate of intellectual level, especially with people who are linguistically handicapped on IQ tests. A group form has been widely used in cross-cultural research on cognitive functioning.

Other tests designed to minimize the influence of linguistic factors include the Leiter International Scale (1948), the Porteus Mazes (1965), and the Goodenough Draw-a-Person Test. In the Goodenough, the child is merely asked to draw a person and the drawing is scored according to norms for children aged 3 to 14 (Harris, 1963). Scores correlate about .50 with individual IQ tests, although they tend to be lower than IQ scores and do not predict academic performance anywhere near as well as IQ does (Scott, 1981). The draw-a-person is often used only as an "ice-breaker" at the beginning of testing, as a very rough index of ability, and as a basis for general inferences about personality.

At the other extreme from the nonverbal tests are the Peabody Picture Vocabulary Test (Dunn & Dunn, 1981), which requires the child to point to a picture corresponding to a word spoken by the examiner, and the Illinois Test of Psycholinguistic Abilities (ITPA; Kirk, McCarthy, & Kirk, 1968), which yields several indices of verbal functioning in children aged 2 to 10. The ITPA has been used as an educational diagnostic instrument and for evaluating the progress of children in special educational programs for the disadvantaged, especially those designed to enhance linguistic skills. One study found that the ITPA correlated higher with achievement tests administered two years later ($r = .72$) than the Stanford-Binet did ($r = .60$; Hirshoren, 1969).

IQ tests and most other ability tests measure the *end-products* of cognitive functioning. Koppitz (1977) designed a test to tap specific *processes* that she hypothesized to be deficient in learning disabled children. Called the Visual Aural Digit Span Test (VADS), it presents series of digits aurally (read aloud by the examiner) and visually (printed on cards). The child is asked to recall each type of input either orally or by writing out the stimulus digits. The four combinations of input and output form four subtests: aural input-oral output; visual input-oral output; aural input-written output; and visual input-written output.

By testing immediate recall via spoken and written modalities and combinations of the two, the VADS aims to detect weaknesses in intersensory integration (sound to sight and sight to sound) and sequencing and accuracy of recall. Normative data are available for children aged 5½ to 12, and several studies have shown significantly poorer performance by children independently identified as learning disabled than by normative groups. More importantly, all four subtests discriminate significantly between learning disabled and normal children who are matched for chronological age and IQ (Koppitz, 1977). This indicates that the VADS taps learning problems not revealed by IQ alone.

Achievement Tests

Although most children seen in mental health settings have school problems, their academic strengths and weaknesses are seldom assessed very precisely. Individual tests, such as the Wide-Range Achievement Test (Jastak & Jastak, 1978) and Peabody Individual Achievement Test (Dunn & Markwardt, 1970), give global indices of achievement in several areas, but diagnosis often focuses on "clinically relevant" characteristics rather than on specific academic weaknesses that may contribute to overall maladjustment. Even the diagnosis of "learning disability" is often a global one implying a fundamental block in learning that must be overcome by therapeutic measures, after which the child is expected to progress normally in school. Yet, whatever the original reason for children's poor school progress, gaps between their skills and those of their agemates are unlikely to be closed merely by a new surge of psychological health. Instead, they need specific help from teachers, tutors, or parents in addition to therapeutic measures. In some cases, enhancing school progress may have a direct therapeutic effect, both by improving children's self-esteem and by helping them cope in developmentally more mature ways.

For the foregoing reasons, precise assessment of academic weaknesses and precise techniques for remedying them deserve more attention than they typically get. Highly detailed individual tests of academic functioning are available. An example is the *Woodcock-Johnson Psychoeducational Battery* (1977), which includes 12 subtests of cognitive abilities, 10 achievement subtests, and 5 tests of interests in academic and nonacademic areas. Much needs to be done by way of tailoring psychoeducational remediation to specific deficits, however.

Behavior modifiers have sought to remedy specific skills deficits by using programmed teaching materials in conjunction with achievement tests. A continuous process of diagnosis and remediation is established by rewarding children for learning the answers to progressively more advanced items on achievement tests (e.g., Cohen & Filipczak, 1971). The Vineland Social Maturity Scale, described in

Chapter 8, is also used as an index of deficits and progress in self-help skills, especially with the retarded, although more detailed behavioral guides are now available for training the retarded (e.g., Baker, 1980).

ASSESSMENT OF PERSONALITY

"Personality" was once the dominant concept linking views of psychopathology, assessment, and psychotherapy. Aside from mental retardation and organic dysfunction, it was the child's personality that was typically regarded as malfunctioning, that was the object of assessment, and that therapists tried to modify. Unfortunately, a lack of consensus on what personality is precludes a single definition beyond, perhaps, "the total functioning of the person."

Psychodynamic and *trait* concepts have dominated personality assessment. The main source of psychodynamic concepts is, of course, psychoanalytic theory. In the psychodynamic view, behavior reflects the interplay between motives and defenses that oppose and modify expression of the motives. The favorite diagnostic tools of the psychodynamic approach are unstructured situations in which motives, conflicts, and defenses can be freely exposed. Unstructured interviews that encourage free association, unstructured play sessions intended to function for children like unstructured interviews for adults, and projective tests, such as the Rorschach and TAT, are the most common psychodynamic assessment techniques.

In contrast to psychodynamic concepts, *trait theories* portray personality in terms of a person's dispositions to act in certain ways (Cattell & Dreger, 1977). Traits are usually assessed by psychometric methods, including standardized personality tests and structured interviews from which the client's responses can be quantified. Quantified response measures on projective tests, such as the Rorschach and TAT, and structured observations from free play are occasionally used as well. How extreme a person is on a trait is best judged from scores over several measures, although the more typical clinical procedure is to judge a person's standing from scores on one or two tests. Anxiety is perhaps the most commonly inferred and measured personality trait, but introversion-extroversion, aggression, hostility, depression, and traits corresponding to diagnostic categories such as hysteria are also of widespread interest.

Global Personality Assessment

In clinical practice, psychodynamically oriented assessments are often integrated with trait measures to give the diagnostician a feeling that he or she understands the client. Unfortunately, this feeling is difficult to validate. One approach, called *personal validation,* is to have subjects judge the validity with which their own personalities are portrayed. In one study, for example, a trait measure (Bell Adjustment Inventory) and a projective measure (House-Tree-Person Test) were administered to college students (Ulrich, Stachnik, & Stainton, 1963). The students were later given a psychologist's written interpretation of their personalities, such as the following:

> You have a strong need for other people to like you and for them to admire you. You have a tendency to be critical of yourself. You have a great deal of unused capacity which you have not turned to your advantage. While you have some personality weaknesses, you are generally able to compensate for them. Your sexual adjustment has presented some problems for you. Disciplined and controlled on the outside, you tend to be worrisome and insecure inside. At times you have serious doubts as to whether you have made the right decision or done the right thing. You prefer a certain amount of change and variety and become dissatisfied when hemmed in by restrictions and limitations. You pride yourself as being an independent thinker and do not accept others' opinions without satisfactory proof. You have found it unwise to be too frank in revealing yourself to others. At times you are extroverted, affable, sociable, while at other times you are introverted, wary, and reserved. Some of your aspirations tend to be pretty unrealistic. (p. 832)

The students rated the interpretations of their own personalities on a 5-point scale of accuracy, from Excellent to Very Poor. Fifty-three of the 57 students rated the interpretations as either good or excellent, the top two steps on the scale; three rated the interpretations as average, one rated them as poor, and none rated them as very poor. Here are some typical comments:

> ". . . I agree with almost all your statements and think they answer the problems I may have."

> "On the nose! Very good. I wish you had said more, but what you did mention was all true without a doubt. I wish you could go further into this personality sometime."

> "The results have brought out several points which have worried me because I was not sure if I had imagined these to be personality traits of mine. Tests like this could be valuable to an individual in helping him to solve some of his own problems."

> "The interpretation is surprisingly accurate and specific in description. I shall take note of many of the things said."

> "I feel that the interpretation does apply to me individually. For the first time things that I have been vaguely aware of have been put into concise and constructive statements which I would like to use as a plan for improving myself" (Ulrich et al., 1963, p. 833).

The agreement between the test interpretations and the students' feelings about themselves seems to validate the tests, unless you are troubled by the fact that all the students received *exactly the same interpretation,* the one quoted above. Other studies show similar results (Snyder, Shenkel, & Lowery, 1977).

The Barnum Effect. The students may have accepted the generalized personality interpretations because almost everybody has most personality characteristics in *some* degree and certain statements are probably true of almost everybody. The compelling plausibility of generalized personality interpretations has been dubbed the *Barnum Effect* in honor of P. T. Barnum, the famous showman who enthralled customers with his off-the-cuff personality interpretations.

The power of the Barnum Effect should warn us that the intrinsic plausibility of personality interpretations is not a test of their validity for discriminating among children with respect to characteristics related to etiology, treatment, or prognosis. Satisfying as a personality description may seem, it is useless unless it helps us discriminate the characteristics and needs of a specific child from children in general.

Illusory Correlation. Beside the Barnum Effect, another pitfall of global personality assessment is the tendency to infer correlations between characteristics that are not in fact correlated. Called *illusory correlation,* this tendency has been demonstrated in many experiments where people are presented with information on a series of individual cases. For example, after being shown a series of Rorschach responses *randomly* paired with alleged characteristics of the respondents, expert diagnosticians and naive judges alike inferred that certain Rorschach signs were correlated with homosexuality. Conversely, when certain responses actually *were* correlated 100 percent with imputed homosexuality, the judges did *not* detect the correlation (Kurtz & Garfield, 1978).

The tendency to infer correlations where none exist and to miss actual correlations seems to result from the observers' own mental associations among stimuli. That is, the mental set of the observer to aggregate certain information outweighs the observer's ability to mentally tabulate the actual covariation between variables. Explicit warnings to beware of illusory correlation did not reduce it, even with observers who were already skeptical of the Rorschach (Kurtz & Garfield, 1978). It is thus clear that clinical inferences about correlations among various characteristics cannot be taken at face value without systematic empirical testing.

The personality assessments discussed in the following sections will be evaluated in terms of the functions assigned them by the varying approaches. Besides the psychodynamic and trait approaches, the behavioral approach employs some of the personality measures to be described, although the behavioral approach emphasizes specific facts about a child rather than global conceptions of personality.

Interview Procedures

Of all methods of assessment, the interview is the most universal and the one considered most indispensible by clinicians. Indeed, it is unlikely that the interview will ever by wholly supplanted as a source of assessment data. But what do interviews tell us? Basic facts about interviewees' appearance, manner of speaking, their views of their problems (insofar as they are willing and able to share them), demographic data (age, education, family constellation) if they are competent to report them, and arrangements for further procedures are obtained through face-to-face interviews.

Behaviorally oriented interviewers generally ask structured questions about the client's specific problems, their duration and cause, and the client's readiness to accept behavioral methods. Psychodynamically oriented interviewers usually obtain a sketch of the client's life history and an impression of underlying dynamics based on the client's free associations and emphasis on or avoidance of certain topics. Psychodynamically oriented assessment interviews resemble the uncovering process in psychoanalysis, although interpretations are seldom given except perhaps as "trial balloons" to see how the client reacts. Trait-oriented interviewers may use both the behavioral and psychodynamic approaches to rate the client on traits such as anxiety and to decide what personality measures to use. The different approaches to interviewing inevitably elicit different behavior from interviewees (cf. Cox & Rutter, 1976).

Despite the use of interviews by all assessment approaches, we saw in Chapter 15 that interviews have not typically yielded reliable psychiatric diagnoses of children (American Psychiatric Association, 1980). Furthermore, interviewers' expectations can shape their impressions. For example, the expectation that a client is disturbed can impose a *pathological bias* on interviewers' observations, as well as on their diagnostic conclusions. In one study, McCoy (1976) asked clinical trainees to rate (normal) children's adjustment and need for treatment. For each child, half the judges saw a film of negative behavior and half saw a film of positive behavior. Half of each group of judges received positive parental reports about each child and half received negative parental reports. It was found that the parental reports had significantly more influence on the judges' ratings than the films of the children's actual behavior, even when the behavior directly contradicted the parental reports.

In another study, Langer and Abelson (1974) showed a videotaped interview of a young job applicant to clinicians who were told either that he was a job applicant or a patient. Both groups received otherwise identical instructions to write brief descriptions of the interviewee, his gestures, attitudes, and the factors that explained his outlook on life. Their descriptions were later rated on a scale of 1 ("very disturbed") to 10 ("very well adjusted") by raters blind to the conditions.

Where the interviewee was described as a job applicant, descriptions by behavioral and psychodynamic clinicians both received mean ratings of 6.3 on the 10-point scale, indicating good adjustment. Where the interviewee was described as a patient, however, psychodynamic clinicians' descriptions were rated significantly lower (mean = 3.8), while behavioral clinicians' descriptions were rated nonsignificantly lower (mean = 6.1). The behavioral orientation toward describing the interviewee's overt behavior may have thus protected clinicians against a pathological bias better than the psychodynamic orientation did.

Interviews Designed for Children

Children seldom have either the motivation or ability to contribute spontaneously to diagnostic interviews. Interviewing children therefore requires departures from adult interview models. The most standard departure is to provide a play setting designed to encourage spontaneous expression.

The interviewer should have a thorough knowledge of normative behavior typical of the child's developmental level and cultural background. How children do things, such as separating from their parents and handling toys, is just as important as what they say. The effects of the unfamiliar situation must also be considered. Otherwise, normal withdrawal, anxiety, or boisterousness may be mistaken for pathological symptoms.

Rutter and Graham (1968) assessed the reliability and validity of standardized playroom interviews for children aged 7 to 12. Interviews began in an unstructured fashion to get the child relaxed and talking freely. Thereafter, the children were systematically asked about their fears, worries, unhappiness, irritability, and peer relationships. Although the exact wording was left to the interviewers, they were to record their observations in predetermined categories. Attention span, persistence, and distractability were assessed with age-appropriate tasks, such as drawing a person, naming the days of the week forward and backward, and doing simple arithmetic.

When different interviewers assessed normal children on two occasions averaging 12 days apart, their ratings correlated .84 for the categories *no* psychiatric normality, *some* abnormality, and *definite* abnormality. Similar 3-point ratings showed much lower agreement on specific items, however, especially emotions.

Higher agreement on specific items was obtained when one rater interviewed disturbed children while the other rater watched, but the correlations between ratings on overall abnormality dropped to .74. When disturbed children were interviewed by different psychiatrists at 1- to 4-week intervals, agreement on specific items was lower and the correlations between ratings on overall abnormality dropped to .61. Although adequate reliability could be obtained for ratings of three degrees of abnormality, reliability was thus worse for disturbed children than normals.

Rutter and Graham also assessed the validity of their procedure on children judged either normal or disturbed on the basis of teacher and parent reports. Blind to the teacher and parent reports, the interviewers diagnosed as abnormal only 25 percent of the boys and 43 percent of the girls in the "abnormal" group, although this was significantly more than the proportion they diagnosed abnormal in the "normal" group (3 percent of the boys and none of the girls).

A more structured interview composed of yes-or-no questions has also been assessed for reliability and for agreement between answers given by clinic children aged 6 to 16 and their mothers (Herjanic, Herjanic, Brown, & Wheatt, 1975). Interrater reliability averaged 84 percent agreement, and test-retest reliability averaged 89 percent agreement where the same psychiatrist saw the child at two- to three-month intervals. Overall agreement between mothers and children was 80 percent, with the highest agreement (84 percent) being for factual items such as age, address, and reason for referral. Agreement was almost as good (83 percent) for symptoms, such as phobias, obsessions, and somatic complaints, but worse (69 percent) for ratings of mental status, including memory, insight, impulse control, and ability, based on the child and mother interviews.

The percentage of agreement may be inflated by failure to correct for the large proportion of problems denied by the children and their mothers. For example, the child agreeing best with her mother denied all problems as did her mother. Another study has shown, however, that the interview can discriminate psychiatrically referred from nonreferred children (Herjanic & Campbell, 1978).

Projective Techniques

Freud's concept of *projection* referred to the defensive process whereby one imputes one's own unconscious motives to other people. Projective assessment techniques were devised to encourage the projection of unconscious material onto ambiguous stimuli. They were welcomed as analogous to techniques in the physical sciences and medicine, such as x-rays, that reveal hidden structures without dissecting or oversimplifying them (Frank, 1939). With the justification that they function like x-rays of the personality, projective techniques quickly became the most popular and glamorous assessment tools. They are still among the most widely used methods of clinical assessment (O'Leary & Johnson, 1979).

As some specialists in projective techniques have pointed out, the aspects of people's private worlds revealed by their responses to test stimuli may not be unconscious, unacceptable, negative, nor entirely concerned with their own characteristics (Murray, 1959). Instead, projective tests may merely evoke "images, fantasies of interactions, and dramatic improvisation . . . (which) constitute one of several forms of behavior"—only certain parts of the responses elicited by a projective technique can "be called projective, *grain* for the analyst of personality. The rest is *chaff* . . . Hence, the great question is this: By what signs can one differentiate grain from chaff?" (Murray, 1951, p. xiii—xiv).

Separating the grain from the chaff remains a central problem in projective techniques. Users of these techniques assume that a subject's responses are neither random nor expressions of free will, but are determined by underlying characteristics from which other behavior can be predicted. Like other assessment procedures, projective techniques must therefore be evaluated according to the reliability and validity of the predictions they yield.

The Rorschach Technique. Interest in responses to inkblots has a long history. During the 1890s, Binet used the number and type of responses to inkblots as measures of imagination. In the United States, Dearborn used them to study the contents of consciousness, while others used them to study perceptual development (cf. Zubin, Eron, & Schumer, 1965).

In 1911, a Swiss psychiatrist, Hermann Rorschach, began experimenting with colored geometric cutouts to test fantasy, but he found that inkblots yielded better results. By the time he died in 1922, he was concentrating on the perceptual aspects of inkblot responses rather than on their content. The Rorschach Test, consisting of ten standard inkblots printed on cards, became popular in the United States during the 1920s and soon spawned an enormous literature. By the 1940s, great confidence was placed in the Rorschach test for revealing the way people see the world. It was also thought to reveal their anxieties, needs, hurts, likes and dislikes, motivations, cognitive efficiency, emotional maturity, acceptance of reality, and the organic versus nonorganic basis for their problems (e.g., Lindner & Seliger, 1945).

In the 1950s, researchers sought to relate Rorschach responses to perceptual and personality functioning, but the lack of standardized administration, scoring, and interpretation has made it difficult to reconcile conflicting findings. The typical clinical procedure is to hand the cards to the client, one at a time in a standardized order, and to write down each response, the response time, and any turning of the card. After responding to all the cards, the client is asked to indicate where he or she saw each percept. With young children, the inquiry as to response locations is usually done right after the child responds. The examiner marks the location of each percept on reproductions of the blots printed on a record sheet. The instructions and depth of inquiry about the responses vary greatly.

Rorschach responses can be scored according to various systems based on the number of percepts involving human or animal movement, dominance of color versus form, reliance on the whole blot versus small details, and well-differentiated versus global images (e.g., Exner, 1978). Children's responses can be judged for developmental level by comparing them with responses given by normative groups of children at various ages (e.g., Ames, Metraux, & Walker, 1977).

Hypotheses abound about the meaning of the various scores, relations among them, and the content of the responses. Clinicians vary in the way they make personality interpretations from the Rorschach. Full scoring and interpretation of a Rorschach protocol often takes several hours.

In its typical unstandardized clinical application, the Rorschach is hard to evaluate for reliability or validity. Despite its orientation toward idiographic portrayal of personality, its reliability and validity have been evaluated largely in terms of quasi-psychometric scoring systems. Some of these systems yield substantial inter-rater and test-retest reliabilities for selected scores (e.g., Exner, 1978). These scores, however, do not directly reflect personality or psychopathology but aspects of the responses themselves, such as form, color, and animate movement. Testing the reliability and validity of the Rorschach's ability to discriminate underlying personality and psychopathology is a far different task.

Among the thousands of publications on the Rorschach, few report evidence for valid discriminations among children or adolescents (Gittelman, 1980). Although the Rorschach is considered to be especially good for detecting incipient thought disorders, adolescents whose Rorschach protocols were interpreted as indicative of prepsychotic states have later been found to be especially well-adjusted adults (Vaillant, 1980). Several scoring systems focus on the developmental level of responses, and there is no doubt that responses clearly change with development (Weisz, Quinlan, O'Neill, & O'Neill, 1978). It is unknown, however, whether developmental trends reflected in the Rorschach tell us any more about developmental level than global indices such as chronological or mental age.

The Thematic Apperception Test (TAT). The TAT stimuli are pictures for which the subject is to make up stories. The subject is thus to *apperceive* (interpret) the TAT stimuli in terms of dramatic themes.

Although there were other early efforts to use pictures as projective stimuli, Henry Murray's TAT was the first complete test of this type (Morgan & Murray, 1935). The final version (Murray, 1943) consists of 30 black-white reproductions of paintings and drawings, plus one blank card. On one card, for example, a boy sits looking toward a violin in front of him, while another card shows a woman opening a door with a surprised look. Only about ten cards are usually used. Some are especially intended for boys, girls, men, or women, but the examiner decides which cards to administer on the basis of expectations about the client. The client is asked to make up a story about each card, telling who the people are; what they are doing, thinking, and feeling; what led up to the current situation; and what the outcome will be.

Murray assumed that the stories reveal needs or motives. He postulated several basic needs, such as achievement, affiliation, and power, to be inferred from TAT stories. Later research has produced fairly reliable systems for scoring the strength of some of these motives in TAT responses (Atkinson & Raynor, 1978). David McClelland (1961), in particular, stimulated a great deal of research on need for achievement (*n* Achievement) as scored from TAT protocols. This research demonstrated statistically significant but modest relations between TAT scores for *n* Achievement and behavior in other situations.

As the research became more sophisticated, however, concern arose about motives to *avoid* certain situations as well as to achieve. For example, achievement *behavior* could be viewed as a joint function of *n* Achievement and need to avoid failure. McClelland (1966) concluded that TAT imagery is an index of a person's *concern* with a particular topic rather than a direct index of needs to strive in a particular direction. Thus, high achievement imagery might indicate high concern about achievement, but does not necessarily indicate whether a person will engage in achievement activity or avoid it.

Findings that adolescent *activities* rather than adolescent TAT imagery predicted adult TAT imagery in a longitudinal study indicate that a particular type of activity may increase imagery related to that activity rather than the other way around. Consequently, McClelland suggested that TAT imagery may be a better index of a person's previous activity than future activity. This hypothesis is not incompatible with the theory of projective tests, which implies merely that a person's mental concerns are revealed in responses to ambiguous stimuli.

Although the goal of clinical projective testing has been to make *predictions* about people, there is no reason to believe that fantasies, even if accurately tapped by projective tests, portend future behavior. Thus, the low predictive validity found for projective measures may be because people's fantasies stem at least partly from their past behavior rather than their future behavior stemming from their current fantasies. Furthermore, several motives operating together may reduce the correlation between any one motive and overt behavior (Atkinson, 1981). If this is so, projective measures are unlikely to be powerful predictors of behavior, although they may help in classifying people on the basis of their concerns with certain issues. If such classification is related to different etiologies and/or to differing prognoses under various treatments, then projective measures might validly improve diagnostic classification.

Clinical Use of the TAT. Much of the TAT research, especially the formal scoring of motives, has been more sophisticated than Rorschach research. In clinical practice, however, the TAT is often used to infer themes and conflicts in a person's fantasies without being formally scored for specific needs. The clinical-diagnostic use of the TAT has received considerably less validation than its use as a research instrument for measuring *n* Achievement and other formally scored needs. Among the findings that have been validated, however, is that the number of aggressive stories, aggressive stories to cards rarely eliciting them, and aggressive impulses were more common in the TAT responses of overtly aggressive and delinquent adolescents than of nonaggressive adolescents in several studies (Suinn & Oskamp, 1969). Unfortunately, the picture is clouded by findings of an *inverse* relation between TAT and overt aggression *within* clinical samples (Goldberg & Wilensky, 1976; Matranga, 1976).

In a rough comparison of clinical and statistical approaches to the TAT, Cox and Sargent (1950) applied fairly objective scoring rules to the TAT responses of emotionally disturbed and normal boys. Surprisingly, the normals had significantly *higher* scores in most categories, including feelings of frustration, anxiety, negativism, and depression; need for security; fears of death, disaster, and domination; and story outcomes involving failure. The disturbed boys, by contrast, more often showed an *absence* of feelings, needs, fears, and outcomes involving either success or failure. The greater expressiveness of normal boys may explain why clinicians given the protocols of 15 normals judged 11 of them as disturbed. This points up the tendency of clinicians who lack an objective baseline to focus on signs of negative emotions, which were indeed abundant in the normal boys' protocols.

Variants of the TAT for Children. One of the best known TAT-type tests for children is the Children's Apperception Test (CAT; Bellak & Bellak, 1974). The CAT has 10 pictures of animals in situations suggestive of psychosexual conflicts assumed important for children aged 3 to 10. One picture, for example, shows an adult dog raising its paw above the rear of a puppy stretched over the adult dog's knee, with a toilet nearby. Animals were used in the belief that children would identify more closely with them than with the mostly adult figures of the TAT.

Normative data have been collected, although there is little evidence to support interpretations made from the CAT (Gittelman, 1980). Several studies show that children tell longer stories, express more feelings, and give other evidence of greater identification in their responses to human pictures than the CAT, thus casting doubt on the clinical value of animal pictures (Zubin et al., 1965). A version using human pictures (CAT-H; Bellak & Bellak, 1965) was therefore produced for children for whom animal pictures may be ineffective.

The Michigan Picture Test is another alternative to the TAT for children (Hutt, 1980). Nearly a thousand pictures were pretested with children aged 8 to 14 in order to obtain a final set of 14 pictures, plus a blank card. The pictures are photos that are much more realistic than other projective test stimuli. They portray scenes such as a schoolroom, a family engaged in various activities at a table, and a streak of lightening on a black background. Analysis of normative samples has identified MPT response variables that correlate with teacher ratings and other criteria of maladjustment. For example, the Tension Index is based on the relative frequency of verbally expressed needs in responses to the pictures. Children rated by teachers as poorly adjusted expressed significantly more needs than children rated as well adjusted.

Another variation of the TAT is the Make-A-Picture Story (MAPS) Test (Shneidman, 1960). The child selects figures from an array of 67 cutouts to make a scene against each of 22 background pictures and tells a story for each scene. Unfortunately, the intended strength of the test in allowing great freedom as to the stimuli has proved to be a weakness for norming and the assessment of reliability and validity. Some clinical signs have been found to discriminate among certain groups in some studies, but, because every subject responds to different stimuli, generalizations and cross-validation are nearly impossible (Zubin et al., 1965).

Rosenzweig Picture-Frustration Study. The Rosenzweig (1978) Picture Frustration Study (P-F Study) has a children's form, an adolescent form, and an adult form. Each form consists of 24 cartoonlike pictures, each portraying two people in a frustrating situation. One figure is shown as saying something that is either frustrating to the second figure or describes the frustration of the second figure. One picture, for example, shows a person telling another, ''You're a liar and you know it!'' The subject is instructed to write in or tell what words should fill the empty ''balloon'' above the second figure.

Direction of aggression is scored as *extraggression* (directing aggression outward), *intraggression* (directing against the self), or *imaggression* (no aggression is expressed). Type of aggression is scored as *obstacle-dominance* (responses focusing on the barrier that causes frustration), *ego-defense* (responses referring to ego threats in the situation), or *need-persistence* (responses emphasizing the solution of the frustrating problem). Samples from many countries show that extraggression declines with age, while intraggression and imaggression increase, suggesting that direction of aggression represents a general developmental dimension.

The P-F Study is psychometrically better than most other projective tests. Administration procedures are standardized; rules for scoring are explicit; interscorer agreement has been over 80 percent in several studies; the results can be compared with normative samples by age; and specific inferences are derived from the results. Test-retest reliability has generally ranged between about .30 and .60. Because projective techniques may be susceptible to short-term changes in the subject, it is not certain whether higher test-retest reliability would be considered an unmitigated blessing. Yet if a projective technique reflects transitory states, what useful information can it provide about more stable characteristics that may need to be known in order to predict behavior or plan treatment?

Extensive research on the validity of the P-F Study does not resolve this dilemma. Several studies have shown no difference in P-F scores of normals and assaultive or delinquent subjects (cf. Zubin et al., 1965), and at least one study found significantly *lower* aggression scores for delinquents than normal boys (Lindzey & Goldwyn, 1954). Rosenzweig (1978) has tried to account for these negative findings by arguing that level of personality and degree of overtness in the subjects' responses were not taken into consideration. Yet, this does not tell us *how* to determine the relation between a momentary measure of fantasy and important behavior outside the test situation.

One of the most likely avenues for future research with the P-F Study would be to determine the basis for the consistent decline with age in extraggression and increases in intraggression and imaggression found in cultures as diverse as American, French, Italian, German, Japanese, Indian, Congolese, Finnish, Sicilian, and Dutch. Perhaps this developmental trend reflects cognitive changes like those revealed by measures of moral development.

Drawing Techniques. One of the simplest projective techniques is the Draw-A-Person test. According to Machover's (1949) procedure, the child is first asked to draw a person and then a second person of the sex opposite the first. Machover

(1960) also suggests 33 questions to be asked about each figure, such as, "What is he/she doing?" "How old is he/she?" "Is he/she married?" The questions provide opportunities to explore the child's thinking beyond what is inferred from the drawings.

In her interpretations, Machover assumes that the drawings represent projections of children's images of their own bodies and various concerns and ideals. She gives composite descriptions of typical drawings for each sex from age 4 through 12, but no systematic way to assess deviations from these descriptions.

Research on human figure drawings has shown that clinical judges could not discriminate between drawings by normal and physically handicapped children, suggesting that the drawings do not reflect children's body images (Silverstein & Robinson, 1956). Moreover, drawing skill appears to be a significant determinant of the features included (Woods & Cook, 1954), and interpretations of personality from human figure drawings have not correlated well with other data (Gittelman, 1980; Suinn & Oskamp, 1969).

Taking a different approach, Koppitz (1968) has distinguished between *development items* and *emotional indicators*. The development items are major features, such as head, eyes, legs, and clothing, that show a steady increase with children's age and IQ. The emotional indicators are not closely correlated with age, but are thought to reflect anxieties, concerns, and attitudes. They include *quality signs,* such as broken or sketchy lines, shading of the face, and slanting figures; *special features,* such as a tiny head, large head, and crossed eyes; and *omissions* of important features, such as eyes, nose, and legs. Koppitz has shown that disturbed children tend to produce more emotional indicators than normal children of the same developmental level, although specific clinical interpretations have not been firmly supported.

In the slightly more elaborate House-Tree-Person test, the child is asked to draw a house, then a tree, then a person, and, last, a person of the sex opposite that of the first person (Buck, 1966). The drawings are followed by questions such as "What is the person doing?" "How old is the tree?" "Is the tree alive?" The house is interpreted as revealing children's thoughts about their family. Smoke pouring from the chimney, for example, represents a hot and turbulent home situation. The tree is believed to portray children's deeper unconscious feelings about themselves, while the person reveals children's more conscious views of themselves and their relations to their environment (Hammer, 1960). The failure of the H-T-P to differentiate between physically handicapped and normal children again casts doubt on interpretations in terms of self-images, however (Wawrzaszek, Johnson, & Sciera, 1958).

Sentence Completion Tests. In the early 1900s, Carl Gustave Jung made up a list of words to which clients were to respond with their first associations. From the responses and variations in reaction times to each stimulus word, Jung inferred the respondent's unconscious complexes in psychoanalytic fashion. Word association tests of this sort are still used, but they have generally been replaced by tests in which the client is asked to provide endings for incomplete sentences. The advantage of the incomplete sentence method is that the stimuli can be more precisely focused on specific problem areas and the responses are likely to be more revealing with less inference than simple word associations. Some typical incomplete sentence items are: "I am . . ." "I wish my father . . ." "People always . . ."

Even with stimuli more focused than word association tests, sentence completion tests suffer the typical problems of projective techniques for assessing reliability and validity and for comparing responses with normative data. On Rotter's Incomplete Sentence Blank (ISB), however, each item is scored on a seven-point scale for degree of conflict (Rotter & Rafferty, 1958). Scores on this test have been fairly successful in discriminating between maladjusted and normal children (Suinn & Oskamp, 1969). Since the test is designed to be administered in group form, it may be useful for picking out children for further diagnostic screening.

Objectively Scored Measures

Objectively scored measures include true-false, multiple-choice, and other structured instruments that provide predetermined response categories. Since it is seldom known whether subjects' responses accurately reflect their true behavior or feelings outside the assessment situation, the "objectivity" of these instruments does not lie in their assessment of personality. Instead, their objectivity is in the *scoring* of responses according to predetermined rules insuring that all scorers obtain the same results (barring clerical errors). The ultimate question to be asked of objective tests is, therefore, the same as what we ask of projective tests: Do responses correlate with anything meaningful about the respondents that could not be learned more easily in other ways?

Certain tests using projective-type stimuli are "objective" because they offer objectively scored response choices. The Blacky Test (Blum, 1960), for example, consists of cartoon pictures of dogs drawn to suggest psychosexual conflicts, such as castration fears suggested by a puppy about to have its tail cut off. The subject is asked to choose from a multiple-choice array of answers describing each scene. These answers are scored objectively for various personality traits. TAT pictures have also been administered in multiple-choice formats. Even though the rationale of the stimulus materials is "projective," the scoring system makes these tests "objective."

Most objectively scored measures constrain the individuality of responses more than projective techniques do. However, some projective tests, such as Rotter's Incomplete Sentence Blank, likewise constrain individuality, because they yield a dimensional score intended to discriminate between adjusted and maladjusted subjects. Likewise, the Rorschach test is often used to make a single distinction, such as psychotic versus nonpsychotic. On the other hand, the most widely used objectively scored personality test, the Minnesota Multiphasic Personality Inventory, yields numerous dimensional scores whose *configuration* is *interpreted* to provide a diagnostic picture of the subject. Thus, objective scoring does not necessarily prevent analysis of individual response patterns.

Children's Anxiety Scales. Several anxiety tests for children have been modeled on adult tests. The Children's Manifest Anxiety Scale (CMAS; Castaneda, McCandless, & Palermo, 1956; revised by Reynolds & Richmond, 1978), for example, was modeled on the adult Taylor Manifest Anxiety Scale. A similar test is the General Anxiety Scale for Children (GASC; Sarason, Davidson, Lighthall, Waite, & Ruebush, 1960). The CMAS contains items such as, "I blush easily" and "I worry most of the time." The GASC has items like, "Are you afraid of spiders?" and "Do you worry that you are going to get sick?" Another version of the GASC is the Test Anxiety Scale for Children, designed to identify children whose anxiety about being tested may interfere with their school performance (Sarason et al., 1960). A more elaborate measure—also derived from adult tests—is the State-Trait Anxiety Inventory for Children (STAIC; Spielberger, 1973). The STAIC yields separate scores for the child's current anxiety *state* and a more enduring anxiety *trait*.

Unfortunately, the self-report anxiety scores do not agree well with other indices of anxiety, such as ratings by psychiatrists (Hafner, Quast, Speer, & Grams, 1964) or teachers (Wirt & Broen, 1956), or behavior such as nailbiting (Finch & Kendall, 1979). Czech researchers even found that *high* CMAS scores were related to *low* heart rate under anxiety-provoking conditions (Kutina & Fischer, 1977).

The lack of agreement with other indices of anxiety suggests that the questionnaires reflect "willingness to say deviant things about the self" (Wirt & Broen, 1956), rather than clinical anxiety. Hafner et al. (1964) reported two positive findings consistent with this view: (1) Children's CMAS and GASC scores correlated significantly with the number of symptoms psychiatrists noted (but not with the psychiatrists' ratings of the children's anxiety); and (2) the CMAS and GASC filled out by children correlated significantly with those filled out by parents to describe their children. Because the anxiety scores consist of the sum of "yes" responses to deviant self-descriptions, the children's own scores, those based on parent descriptions, and the symptom scores from the psychiatrists may all reflect acknowledgement of problems rather than anxiety per se.

More promising results have been obtained with a scale for rating observable signs of anxiety in preschoolers (Glennon & Weisz, 1978). Called the Preschool Observation Scale of Anxiety (POSA), it consists of 30 specific behaviors, such as trembling voice, very soft speech, lip licking, extraneous body movements, and rigid posture. Ratings by two observers correlated .78, and total scores correlated significantly with parent and teacher ratings of the children's anxiety. Scores were also significantly higher when anxiety was deliberately heightened than when it was minimized. Children's self reports of feeling scared and a psychological examiner's global ratings of anxiety, however, did not correlate significantly with the other indices of anxiety or with each other. This indicates that applying objective, psychometric procedures to the scoring of overt behaviors may be a more effective way to assess children than depending on self-reports or global ratings of inferred states.

Minnesota Multiphasic Personality Inventory (MMPI). The MMPI is the most widely used objectively scored personality test. Designed primarily for adults, it contains 566 items chosen mainly for their ability to discriminate between normal adults and psychiatric patients diagnosed according to Kraepelinian categories such as hysteria, depression, psychopathy, schizophrenia, and mania. The items are statements scored as *true, false,* or *cannot say.* Each item is scored on one or more scales arranged in a profile format.

A score on a particular scale is regarded as abnormally high if it exceeds the 98th percentile of the normative sample. On the Depression scale, for example, a woman must answer at least 30 of the 60 items in the direction scored for depression to reach the 98th percentile. (The distributions of scores differ for males and females on several MMPI scales.)

The 98th percentile cutoff point is not diagnostic of psychopathology by itself, however. Instead, particular *configurations* of scores on the various scales correlate better with some diagnoses than do scores on individual scales. For example, profiles having high scores on both the Psychopathic Deviate and Manic scales correlate better with diagnoses of psychopathy (antisocial personality) than elevations on the Psychopathic scale alone (Dahlstrom, Welsh, & Dahlstrom, 1972). Here is how one guide to the MMPI describes people with high scores on these two scales (the scales are numbered 4 and 9):

> The most salient characteristic of 49/94 individuals is a marked disregard for social standards and values. They frequently get into trouble with the environment because of antisocial behavior. They have poorly developed consciences, easy morals, and fluctuating ethical values. Alcoholism, fighting, marital problems, sexual acting out, and a wide array of delinquent acts are among the difficulties in which they may be involved.
>
> 49/94 individuals are narcissistic, selfish, and self-indulgent. They are quite impulsive and are unable to delay gratification of their impulses. They show poor judgment, often acting without considering the consequences of their acts, and they fail to learn from experience. They are not willing to accept responsibility for their own behavior, rationalizing shortcomings and failures and blaming difficulties on other people. They have a low tolerance for frustration, and they often appear to be moody, irritable, and caustic. They harbor intense feelings of anger and hostility, and these feelings get expressed in occasional emotional outbursts.

49/94 persons tend to be ambitious and energetic, and they are restless and overactive. They are likely to seek out emotional stimulation and excitement. In social situations they tend to be uninhibited, extroverted, and talkative, and they create a good first impression. However, because of their self-centeredness and distrust of people, their relationships are likely to be superficial and not particularly rewarding. They seem to be incapable of deep emotional ties, and they keep others at an emotional distance. Beneath the facade of self-confidence and security, the 49/94 individuals are immature, insecure, and dependent persons who are trying to deny these feelings. A diagnosis of antisocial personality or emotionally unstable personality is usually associated with the 49/94 code, although patients with the code occasionally are diagnosed as having manic-depressive psychosis. (Graham, 1977, pp. 74–75)

The MMPI's value for children is limited by its length, the morbid and sexual content of some items, and its focus on adult psychiatric categories. Norms and profile configurations have been documented for adolescents (Marks, Seeman & Haller, 1974), however, and a tape-recorded version has been used with nonreaders (Baughman & Dahlstrom, 1968). Ninth graders' MMPI scores have been found to predict later delinquency (Monachesi & Hathaway, 1969), and the MMPIs of parents of disturbed children correlate with their children's behavior problem patterns: Boys with predominantly aggressive, externalizing symptoms, for example, have fathers with higher scores on the Psychopathic Deviate scale than the fathers of boys with internalizing symptoms (Anderson, 1969).

The Personality Inventory for Children (PIC). In an effort to extend the MMPI approach to children, Wirt and Broen (1958) constructed the Personality Inventory for Children. The original version had 550 true-false items intended to tap clinically important dimensions. Like the MMPI, the items include deliberate ambiguities and mixtures of past and present tenses on the assumption that "item content is not a central issue, and is in fact incidental to the predictive ability of the scale" (Wirt, Lachar, Klinedinst, & Seat, 1977, p. 9).

Despite the effort to emulate the MMPI, two major differences prevent the PIC from being a junior MMPI. One difference is that the basic source of data is not the target subjects themselves, but their mothers, who fill out the PIC. The second major difference is that most PIC items were not selected according to their ability to discriminate among groups diagnosed in terms of an established psychiatric taxonomy, because there was no taxonomy of children's disorders. Both these factors affect most other approaches to assessment of children as well, but they mean that the PIC cannot be expected to do for child assessment what the MMPI does for adult assessment.

There is no doubt that the mother is a key person in the assessment of almost every child. She can often provide more comprehensive information than anyone else and her views are crucial in determining what will be done to help the child. As the authors intended, however, many of the PIC items are ambiguous, are probes of the mother's personality, involve mothers' judgments of people other than the child, or are descriptions of family circumstances. Some examples include: *The child's mother or father have never been divorced. The child's mother can't stand to stay home all day. A mother's place is in the home. The child's father doesn't understand the child.* Of the items that do refer directly to the child, some require recall of historical facts, such as *Delivery of my child was with instruments.* Others are descriptions of current characteristics, such as *My child is worried about sin.* Still others require inferential judgments about the child, such as *My child could do better in school if he (she) tried.* If the PIC is a measure of personality at all, it may thus be the mother's personality more than the child's.

The questions of whose personality is being measured and the factual basis for responses to specific items might be less problematic if items could be validated against well-established criteria. The taxonomy against which the MMPI items were validated left much to be desired, but it was better than nothing, perhaps. Even though we do not know the factual basis for people's responses to particular MMPI items, their correlation with other indices of personality or psychopathology support their inclusion in the test.

Lacking a taxonomy of children's disorders, Wirt and Broen (1958) initially wrote 50 items to cover each of 11 areas that they deemed important, including withdrawal, excitement, reality distortion, aggression, somatic concern, anxiety, social skills, family relations, physical development, intellectual development, and asocial behavior. Fifty more items were added later to strengthen certain areas, and items deemed offensive were replaced with other items expected to reveal lying.

Scales were constructed partly by having clinical judges nominate items to measure predetermined constructs and partly by identifying items that discriminated criterion groups, such as delinquents, from normative groups of school children (Wirt et al., 1977). Twelve clinical scales were ultimately included on the PIC profile, but only five of these correspond to content areas for which items were originally written. Lachar and Gdowski (1979) have since produced an array of interpretive statements based on characteristics found to correlate with PIC scores of children seen at an inner city Detroit clinic. However, it remains to be seen how valid the interpretive statements are across both sexes, the age range covered by the PIC (6 to 16 years), and other clinical populations.

ASSESSMENT OF FAMILY FUNCTIONING

Most children are dependent on their families, directly involved in their conflicts, and shaped by the models, rewards, and punishments they provide. The family context of children's problems has long been emphasized in the child guidance "team" approach where a social worker sees parents while a therapist sees the child. This enables the social worker to obtain information from the parents and to advise and treat them in relation to the child's problems.

Family systems therapists view the family as the primary unit of analysis. A leading family therapist, Nathan Ackerman (1968), even maintained that "The emergence of psychiatric disorder in a child is regularly preceded by family conflict (p. 513)." Because family therapists believe that children's problems can only be understood as an integral part of the family system, Ackerman argued that assessment must focus on the entire family's capacity for change and growth, including:

1. Fulfillment of strivings and values.
2. The stability, maturity, and realism of the family.
3. The presence or absence of regressive and disintegrative trends.
4. The quality and degree of successful adaptation. (Ackerman & Behrens, 1974, p. 45)

Although Ackerman outlined data that should be obtained for family assessment, he did not offer specific procedures for obtaining the data, nor any findings on reliability or validity. Few techniques have actually been developed for objective clinical assessment of the relations between family dynamics and children's problems. Although many techniques focus on children's feelings and fantasies about their families, they do not assess the actual events that foster these feelings and fantasies, nor do they pinpoint family interactions that can be modified.

Careful standardized interviews can obtain good interparent agreement and interrater reliability on parents' reports of some aspects of family functioning (Brown & Rutter, 1966), but these reports are still quite remote from the ongoing family interactions stressed by family therapists. Even where family interactions are studied directly, the observers and the observation setting affect the interaction patterns (Hetherington & Martin, 1979). Furthermore, there is evidence that interviewing families together produces higher dropout rates from therapy than individual approaches do (Shapiro & Budman, 1973).

Research on family interactions shows that healthy versus unhealthy family functioning can be reliably rated. In an especially thorough study, for example, observers rated the interactions of families who were videotaped as they worked together on a variety of tasks designed to expose positive and negative family characteristics (Lewis, Beavers, Gossett, & Phillips, 1976). In one task, the family listened to a recorded vignette in which an unidentified family member appears to be in danger of dying. The vignette stopped on an ambiguous note, and the family was asked to make up an ending to the story. In other tasks, they were asked to discuss the strengths and weaknesses of their family and to plan something together.

Adequate reliability was obtained on a global health versus pathology scale and other scales indicative of the family's overall mood, invasiveness (speaking for one another), and permeability (receptiveness to each other's statements). Ratings also discriminated well between families with and without a disturbed adolescent and even between normal families who were considered to be functioning either optimally or only adequately. This indicated that family systems concepts can be translated into reliable and discriminating assessment. It was also found that family strengths were at least as important in overall functioning as the presence of family problems or "pain." The family measures did not correlate well with independent assessments of psychopathology in individual family members, however. Firmer links thus need to be established between family assessment and the assessment and treatment of children's problems.

BEHAVIORAL ASSESSMENT

As behavioral methods spread, behavior modifiers sought to distinguish their approach to assessment from what they called "traditional" assessment, meaning mainly psychodynamic, medically oriented, and trait approaches. The following contrasts were typically made (cf. Mash & Terdal, 1981):

1. On the assumption that behavior is maintained by the current environment, behavioral assessment dispenses with the inferred constructs on which traditional assessment focuses.

2. Behavioral assessment views behavior as situationally specific, whereas traditional assessment assumes consistency across situations.

3. Behavioral assessment views stability and change across time as a function of stability and change in the environment, whereas traditional assessment views it as a function of internal causes.

4. Behavioral assessment views responses as samples of behavior, whereas traditional assessment views responses as clues to underlying attributes.

5. Behavioral assessment focuses on characteristics involved directly in treatment, whereas traditional assessment seeks to diagnose an underlying condition and evaluate its prognosis.

6. Behavioral assessment seeks observations of problem behavior in its natural environment, whereas traditional assessment is done in clinical settings.

7. Behavioral assessment is a continuous process integrated into treatment, whereas traditional assessment is a separate process that precedes treatment.

Consistent with these principles, published examples of behavioral approaches often report direct observations of problem behavior in its natural setting, together with interobserver reliabilities. Cost and other practical obstacles, however, often preclude having multiple trained observers record problem behavior for routine clinical assessment. As a result, there is often a gap between the idealized model of behavioral assessment and what behavioral clinicians really do (Wade, Baker, & Hartmann, 1979). This is reminiscent of the gap between the formalized and reliable scoring of projective tests for research purposes and their typical clinical applications. Yet, because the target variables of behavioral assessment are more closely related to the target variables of most child treatment, there may be a greater potential for adapting the strengths of behavioral assessment to everyday clinical realities. Rather than defining behavioral assessment by negating "traditional" assessment, it may be more useful to consider how to do this.

Reliability and Validity Issues in Direct Observations

Early behavior modifiers argued that they avoided problems of reliability and validity raised by indirect measures, because they directly observed the problem behavior itself. Yet, if behavior is as situationally specific as behavior modifiers claim, then clinicians will never observe many of the problems they are asked to treat. Few children are likely to engage in stealing, firesetting, and fighting under the eyes of trained observers, for example. Other problems, such as sleep disturbances, bedwetting, and nightmares, are not very convenient to observe. Observation by the clinician is not the only option, however, as parents, teachers, and other "natural observers" can often report these problems. On the other hand, many behavioral problems arise mainly in interactions with a particular adult, such as a parent or teacher. Reports by the adult in question may not yield a complete picture in such cases. Direct observation in the home or school may therefore be essential. It has been unduly neglected by other assessment approaches.

Even though direct observation may sometimes be necessary for proper assessment, an observer's presence may affect the target behavior. Furthermore, it is seldom possible to arrange observations with appropriate reliability checks before, during, and after interventions in all situations where the target behavior might occur. We therefore have to rely on people in the child's environment for at least some of the relevant data.

Direct observation is limited in other ways as well. Although training and frequent reliability checks can produce satisfactory reliability, this does not insure that reliability will remain high under the typical conditions of clinical assessment. Reliability has been found to deteriorate when observers do not expect it to be checked, for example (O'Leary & Johnson, 1979). Nor are direct observational ratings immune to the effects of observer biases, as expectations that a child is hyperactive have been shown to increase observers' ratings of activity as compared to ratings of the same child by observers who did not expect hyperactivity (Neisworth, Kurtz, & Jones, 1974). Structured ratings of specific behaviors are less vulnerable to observer biases than unstructured description or global judgments, however (O'Leary & Johnson, 1979).

A further issue concerns the standardization of observational procedures. Problem behavior might seem easy to describe, but methodological questions arise. In order to determine whether a particular behavior occurs, and with what intensity or frequency, we need an operational definition and rules for recording its occurrence within specified observational intervals.

Because behavioral assessment focuses not only on problem behaviors but on environmental contingencies supporting them, events preceding and following children's problem behaviors must be recorded and analyzed to reveal contingent relationships. In one of the most thorough efforts to do this, Gerald Patterson (1981) developed procedures whereby observers record specific behaviors by a target child and others in the home. Contingent relations between the behavior of the child and other people are then computed in terms of the conditional probabilities that one will follow the other. Table 16-2 shows some of the behavioral categories that Patterson employs.

Patterson has obtained adequate reliability among observers recording behavior in the homes of aggressive children and has demonstrated contingent relations between some behaviors by family members and aggressive behaviors by their children. However, observers require lengthy training, families must confine their activities to certain parts of their home while multiple observers record their behavior on repeated occasions, and extensive analyses are needed to identify contingent relations. Patterson's work thus represents a tour-de-force of direct observational technology. Yet, even this impressive effort taps only a small subset of aggressive behavior in exceptionally cooperative families, and in situations not fully representative of the target child's behavior problems. Furthermore, the procedures are far too costly and time-consuming to use for routine assessment of even those cases that have problems and families like Patterson's subjects.

Like the observations of family interactions favored by family therapists, observations for behavioral assessment also face the "problem of how to reduce the plethora of fine objective behavioral categories into fewer, more meaningful and interpretable categories" (Hetherington & Martin, 1979, p. 254). This is, once again, the problem of relating assessment to meaningful taxonomic distinctions among children's disorders. A further hurdle is to relate behavioral assessment to developmentally appropriate norms for particular categories of behavior.

Table 16-2   Examples of Behaviors Scored from Direct Observations

---

Command Negative
Cry
Disapproval
Destructive
Humiliate
Ignore
Noncomply
Negativism
Tease
Whine
Yell

Source: From Patterson, 1981.

Behavioral Ratings by Significant Others

Because they cannot rely solely on observations by trained observers, behavior modifiers must obtain data from other sources as well. Like other clinicians, they use interviews with children and parents, although the focus is more on specific behavior and its contingencies than on past history. Additional precision may be added by asking parents to keep log books for recording the occurrence of target behaviors.

Parent and Teacher Ratings. Ratings by parents and teachers on behavior checklists are also widely used. Table 16-3 shows an example of a behavior problem checklist designed to be filled out by parents.

A general advantage of checklists is that they can quickly and economically provide a picture of the child's behavior in a standardized format from the perspective of people who are involved with the behavior in its natural setting. Parents' perspectives are especially important, because they are typically crucial in determining what will de done to help the child, if anything. Checklists can be readministered to assess behavioral change as perceived by the informant. Checklists can also cover a much wider range of behaviors, occasions, and settings than direct observations, and data on normative samples can be used to assess children's deviation from their agemates. Furthermore, as we saw in Chapter 15, factor analyses of checklists show that the items form syndromes on which taxonomies can be based.

Potential disadvantages of parent and teacher checklists are that the informants vary in objectivity and sophistication and that their ratings do not directly reflect predefined behavior samples, such as event samples or time samples rated by trained observers. Because it is clear that no procedure—including direct observation by trained observers—can provide a totally objective and representative picture of children's problem behavior, the main question is whether checklists add reliable and valid data not easy to get otherwise.

Test-retest reliability correlations in the .80s and .90s have been found for syndromes scored from parent and teacher checklists (cf. Achenbach & Edelbrock, 1978). Correlations between mothers and fathers and between pairs of teachers have been somewhat lower, but have nevertheless ranged from the .70s through the .90s in several studies. Long-term stability of ratings over periods of up to five years has also been quite satisfactory (Achenbach & Edelbrock, 1978, 1981).

Despite satisfactory reliabilities, agreement between different types of informants seeing children in different settings is more variable. Good agreement can be obtained between clinicians and parents (Edelbrock & Achenbach, 1980) and between trained observers and teachers (Bolstad & Johnson, 1977) who focus on the same behaviors. Correlations between parent and teacher ratings tend to be in the .30s and .40s, however (Achenbach & Edelbrock, 1978). This reflects children's different responses to home and school (Bernal, Delfini, North, & Kreutzer, 1976), as well as the different standards by which parents and teachers judge behavior. A boy rated as overactive because he does not sit attentively at his desk, for example, may not be rated as overactive by parents who never see him in situations where long periods of sedentary concentration are required. Similarly, even though mothers and fathers generally report about the same number and type of behavioral problems (Achenbach & Edelbrock, 1979), disagreements between parents can reveal differences in their tolerance, perspectives, or effects on the child that should be explored clinically. In some cases, a parent's idiosyncratic views or behavior may need changing, and not the child's behavior.

The point is that a comprehensive picture of a child's behavior requires data from multiple sources that can be compared in assessing the problems, targets for change, and effects of interventions. Because children's behavior is variable and the perspectives of important adults also differ, disagreements in ratings can be as informative as agreements.

Numerous studies have demonstrated the ability of checklist ratings to discriminate significantly between clinically referred and normal children, both in terms of specific items and syndrome scores (Achenbach & Edelbrock, 1978, 1981). As we saw in Chapter 15, specific syndrome scores have also been found to discriminate among disturbed children who differ in other ways. Moreover, checklist ratings can reflect the effects of treatment for specific syndromes, such as behavior modification and stimulant drugs for hyperactivity (Gittelman et al., 1980). Nevertheless, it is important to view scores on specific syndromes in relation to one another in order to form a comprehensive picture of individual children. As illustrated in Chapter 15, profiles of checklist scores on empirically derived syndromes can provide a basis for directly linking assessment and taxonomy.

Peer Ratings. Sociometric procedures designed to obtain evaluations of children by their peers have also been used in research on behavior disorders. In one sociometric format, children are asked to indicate which of their classmates they would most like to join in certain activities. In another format, a list of descriptions is provided, such as "Who often looks sad?" (Lefkowitz & Tesiny, 1980). Each child is to name a classmate who fits the description. A child's score for an item is the number of times he or she is nominated for that characteristic.

A variant of this is to provide a list of roles for a hypothetical class play, with children writing in the names of classmates for each role. Several studies have shown that scores derived from sociometric procedures correlate with other indices of psychopathology and are predictive of continuing problems over several years (Bower, 1969). The need for cooperation from schools, and often from the parents of all the participating children, limits this approach for the clinical assessment of individual children, however.

Behavioral Competencies

Although the focus of clinical assessment is mainly on *problems,* behavioral *competencies* are at least as crucial for long-term adaptation. In fact, the *failure* to

Table 16-3 Examples of Behavior Problems from the Child Behavior Checklist

Below is a list of items that describe children. For each item that describes your child *now* or *within the past 6 months*, please circle the 2 if the item is *very true* or *often true* of your child. Circle the *1* if the item is *somewhat* or *sometimes true* or your child. If the item is *not true* of your child, circle the *0*.

0 1 2	1.	Acts too young for his/her age
0 1 2	2.	Allergy (describe): _____
0 1 2	3.	Argues a lot
0 1 2	4.	Asthma
0 1 2	5.	Behaves like opposite sex
0 1 2	6.	Bowel movements outside toilet
0 1 2	7.	Bragging, boasting
0 1 2	8.	Can't concentrate, can't pay attention for long
0 1 2	9.	Can't get his/her mind off certain thoughts; obsessions (describe): _____
0 1 2	10.	Can't sit still, restless, or hyperactive
0 1 2	11.	Clings to adults or too dependent
0 1 2	12.	Complains of loneliness
0 1 2	13.	Confused or seems to be in a fog
0 1 2	14.	Cries a lot
0 1 2	15.	Cruel to animals
0 1 2	16.	Cruelty, bullying, or meanness to others
0 1 2	17.	Day-dreams or gets lost in his/her thoughts
0 1 2	18.	Deliberately harms self or attempts suicide

0 1 2	31.	Fears he/she might think or do something bad
0 1 2	32.	Feels he/she has to be perfect
0 1 2	33.	Feels or complains that no one loves him/her
0 1 2	34.	Feels others are out to get him/her
0 1 2	35.	Feels worthless or inferior
0 1 2	36.	Gets hurt a lot, accident-prone
0 1 2	37.	Gets in many fights
0 1 2	38.	Gets teased a lot
0 1 2	39.	Hangs around with children who get in trouble
0 1 2	40.	Hear things that aren't there (describe): _____
0 1 2	41.	Impulsive or acts without thinking
0 1 2	42.	Likes to be alone
0 1 2	43.	Lying or cheating
0 1 2	44.	Bites fingernails
0 1 2	45.	Nervous, highstrung, or tense
0 1 2	46.	Nervous movements or twitching (describe): _____

0	1	2	19.	Demands a lot of attention
0	1	2	20.	Destroys his/her own things
0	1	2	21.	Destroys things belonging to his/her family or other children
0	1	2	22.	Disobedient at home
0	1	2	23.	Disobedient at school
0	1	2	24.	Doesn't eat well
0	1	2	25.	Doesn't get along with other children
0	1	2	26.	Doesn't seem to feel guilty after misbehaving
0	1	2	27.	Easily jealous
0	1	2	28.	Eats or drinks things that are not food (describe): ___
0	1	2	29.	Fears certain animals, situations, or places, other than school (describe): ___
0	1	2	30.	Fears going to school

0	1	2	47.	Nightmares
0	1	2	48.	Not liked by other children
0	1	2	49.	Constipated, doesn't move bowels
0	1	2	50.	Too fearful or anxious
0	1	2	51.	Feels dizzy
0	1	2	52.	Feels too guilty
0	1	2	53.	Overeating
0	1	2	54.	Overtired
0	1	2	55.	Overweight
			56.	Physical problems without known medical cause:
0	1	2	a.	Aches or pains
0	1	2	b.	Headaches
0	1	2	c.	Nausea, feels sick
0	1	2	d.	Problems with eyes (describe): ___
0	1	2	e.	Rashes or other skin problems
0	1	2	f.	Stomachaches or cramps
0	1	2	g.	Vomiting, throwing up
0	1	2	h.	Other (describe): ___

609

develop adaptive competencies may account for the persistence of immature behaviors in some children. Because behavior modification often involves teaching new skills to supplant problem behaviors, it is important to assess existing skills and skills deficits.

The importance of adaptational competencies is increasingly recognized from many perspectives. Waters and Sroufe (1981), for example, proposed social competence as a central developmental construct for integrating the study of individual differences across ages, situations, and behavioral domains. It remains to be seen whether such a powerful construct will emerge and whether measures of it will have clinical relevance, however.

Measures of accomplishment such as achievement tests and the Vineland Social Maturity Scale (Doll, 1965) were previously discussed. Another approach poses hypothetical situations in order to determine how skillfully subjects react. This has been done in the evaluation of adolescent delinquents with items like the following:

> You're visiting your aunt in another part of town, and you don't know any of the guys your age there. You're walking along her street, and some guy is walking toward you. He is about your size. As he is about to pass you, he deliberately bumps into you, and you nearly lose your balance. What do you say or do now? (Freedman, Rosenthal, Donahoe, Schlundt, & McFall, 1978).

Responses were rated for degree of competency, based on rules derived from the reactions of various criterion groups. It was found that school leaders scored significantly better than ordinary nondelinquent boys who, in turn, scored better than delinquents. A correlation of .70 with IQ, however, suggests that the test was largely measuring cognitive ability.

As an alternative to the test approach, the behavior checklist approach has been extended to include parents' reports of their children's participation in sports, nonsports activities, organizations, jobs and chores, friendships, other social relations, and school performance. The example shown in Table 16-4 is from the social competence portion of the Child Behavior Checklist. The social competence items are scored on scales entitled Activities, Social, and School, which are normed like scales comprising behavior problem syndromes identified through factor analysis. The individual social competence items and the three scales have been found to discriminate well between demographically matched normal and clinically referred children (Achenbach & Edelbrock, 1981). Combining social competence scores with behavior problem scores also increases the accuracy of discrimination between referred and nonreferred children somewhat, but clinical application of social competence assessment is still in its infancy.

Multimethod Behavioral Assessment

As it became clear that assessment could not rely solely on direct observation of problem behavior in its natural setting, behavior modifiers began to emphasize multiple methods of assessment, just as they did multiple approaches to treatment (Nay, 1979). The methods of child assessment include interviews, standardized tests, checklists, log books, observations in natural settings, observations of play in clinical settings, and simulation of problem situations. Other methods are also devised to suit particular cases.

As an example, consider the assessment of Kay, a 7-year-old girl referred for school problems of inattention, walking around the classroom, climbing on tables, tantrums, and poor achievement (McCammon & Palotai, 1978). At home, Kay's grandparents (Peter and Suzanne, with whom she lived) reported frequent tantrums, noncompliance, and babyish behaviors, including sucking her thumb, using baby talk, and having to be dressed in the morning. The following assessment methods were used:

I. *Interviews*
   A. At clinic
      1. Initial interview at which grandparents specified referral problems (Feb. 13).
      2. Interviews following structured clinic observation (March 5).
   B. At home following observation periods (Feb. 15 and 23)
   C. With teachers (Feb. 19, 23, March 8)

II. *Observations*
   A. At home
      1. Qualitative observations (Feb. 15).
      2. Structured observations using coding system adapted from Patterson (Feb. 23).
   B. At school
      1. In classroom using coding system adapted from Patterson (Feb. 19, 23, March 8).
      2. In cafeteria but behaviors were not coded, as the teacher had isolated Kay from other students (Feb. 19).
   C. At clinic—situations were set up to sample family interactions and antecedents of problem behavior (March 5).
      1. Free play: Grandparents were to play with Kay and her sister in games of their choice.
      2. Attention withdrawal: Grandparents were to agree between themselves on the meaning of "A rolling stone gathers no moss," and to ignore the children.
      3. Grandparents as teachers: They were to teach the girls the meaning of the above proverb.
      4. Planning an activity: Peter was to plan an activity with the girls while Suzanne was out of the room. Then Suzanne and the girls planned an outing while Peter was out. Then they all planned an activity together.

Table 16-4 Examples of Social Competence Items from the Child Behavior Checklist

I. Please list the sports your child most likes to take part in. For example: swimming, baseball, skating, skate boarding, bike riding, fishing, etc.

□ None

	Compared to other children of the same age, about how much time does he/she spend in each?				Compared to other children of the same age, how well does he/she do each one?			
	Don't Know	Less Than Average	Average	More Than Average	Don't Know	Below Average	Average	Above Average
a. _____	□	□	□	□	□	□	□	□
b. _____	□	□	□	□	□	□	□	□
c. _____	□	□	□	□	□	□	□	□

II. Please list your child's favorite hobbies, activities, and games, other than sports. For example: stamps, dolls, books, piano, crafts, singing, etc. (Do not include T.V.)

□ None

	Compared to other children of the same age, about how much time does he/she spend in each?				Compared to other children of the same age, how well does he/she do each one?			
	Don't Know	Less Than Average	Average	More Than Average	Don't Know	Below Average	Average	Above Average
a. _____	□	□	□	□	□	□	□	□
b. _____	□	□	□	□	□	□	□	□
c. _____	□	□	□	□	□	□	□	□

III. Please list any organizations, clubs, teams, or groups your child belongs to.

☐ None

Compared to other children of the same age, how active is he/she in each?

	Don't Know	Less Active	Average	More Active
a. _____	☐	☐	☐	☐
b. _____	☐	☐	☐	☐
c. _____	☐	☐	☐	☐

IV. Please list any jobs or chores your child has. For example: paper route, babysitting, making bed, etc.

☐ None

Compared to other children of the same age, how well does he/she carry them out?

	Don't Know	Below Average	Average	Above Average
a. _____	☐	☐	☐	☐
b. _____	☐	☐	☐	☐
c. _____	☐	☐	☐	☐

613

III. *Tantrum records*

The grandparents were to keep a log of Kay's tantrums, their antecedents and consequences. They were provided with forms for indicating the date, how the conflict arose, when it occurred, how long it lasted, and what the resolution was. Clinic personnel picked up the forms at the grandparents' work to obtain an informal sample of their work environment (Feb. 18 to March 5).

IV. *Cassette tapes*

A cassette recorder was provided to enable the grandparents to record interactions during a particularly problematic time, driving home after picking up the girls at daycare. They were also to record any situation they felt would lead to a tantrum.

In drawing conclusions from these assessment procedures, McCammon and Palotai (1978) used a combination of narrative descriptions and quantitative data, such as the number of tantrums during an observation period and the ratio of compliance to noncompliance in response to commands. It was clear that Kay indeed showed the problems reported by her parents and teachers. It likewise seemed clear that the grandparents' inconsistency in dealing with the problem behavior provided intermittent reinforcement, which is known to make behavior very resistant to extinction. That they were poor disciplinarians is also suggested by the behavior of their own daughter, Kay's mother, who was too irresponsible to care for Kay and her sister.

The potential modifiability of relevant behavior is typically an important aspect of assessment of children's behavior disorders. Peter's failure to keep a log after agreeing to do so; Suzanne's lapse after a short period of record keeping; and both grandparents' unwillingness to rearrange their schedules to keep clinic appointments boded ill for change. Consequently, beside making recommendations for changing Kay's behavior, McCammon and Palotai recommended a therapist-client contract whereby Peter and Suzanne would initially make a payment that they could earn back for keeping records and clinic appointments.

ASSESSMENT OF ORGANIC DYSFUNCTION

In Chapter 7, we saw that one-to-one relations are seldom found between behavioral abnormalities and organic damage. The behavioral effects of a particular type of damage to a particular area of the brain depend on the age at which the damage occurs and many other organic and psychological factors. The effects can also change over the course of development. Some are severe during early childhood and diminish later; others show the reverse pattern.

Organic Assessment Techniques

Assessment of organic damage is usually imprecise, because autopsy findings are often the only firm criterion against which to validate assessment procedures, and even autopsies cannot pinpoint subtle organic anomalies. The precision of organic assessment can be increased through computerized aggregation of multiple variables that diagnosticians would otherwise have to combine mentally. Computerized axial tomography *(CAT scanning),* for example, has greatly increased the precision of x-ray diagnosis of the nervous system, while computerized analysis of EEGs *(neurometrics)* shows promise of identifying patterns of brain function associated with developmental level and certain behavior disorders (Baird, John, Ahn, & Maisel, 1980).

Efforts have also been made to improve the reliability and precision of neurological examinations of children, especially with respect to ''soft'' (equivocal) signs of dysfunction. An example is a standardized neurological examination called the Physical and Neurological Examination for Soft Signs (PANESS). Items include having the child touch one heel to the other, recognize by feel a common object placed in the hand, walk on tiptoe, hop, and stand straight with eyes closed.

Of the 56 PANESS items analyzed in a reliability study, only two showed correlations of .70 or higher between two pediatricians examining the same children (Werry & Aman, 1976). The average number of signs did not differ much between normal, hyperactive, and neurologically impaired children either. Agreement on overall degree of neurological abnormality, however, showed a correlation of .76 between the two examiners. This suggested that they were responding consistently to characteristics of the children that were not accurately reflected in the specific items of the exam. Although soft signs may be viewed as indicators of dysfunction, they also show developmental trends, with the number decreasing with age for most children (Hertzig, 1980).

Psychological Tests

Organic assessment procedures are often used in conjunction with cognitive and perceptual-motor performance on psychological tests, behavioral observations, interviews, and developmental histories to assess possible organic dysfunctions. Conclusions are usually based on a composite of the findings.

The possibility of organic dysfunction should be considered in every child referred for psychological assessment. Children's problems may be affected by organic dysfunction evident in their performance on psychological tests and other behavior during assessment. In some cases, the dysfunction may be a sign of vision or hearing defects that can be pinpointed and remedied by appropriate specialists. In other cases, the dysfunction may be an early sign of a progressive disease. In most cases, however, specific organic causes are not found for dysfunctions detected by psychological assessment. Instead, the results are combined with developmental history and medical data to infer that brain damage, slow maturation, or poor neural organization may handicap the child and that expectations for the child should take account of the potential handicap.

Assessment of organic dysfunction should not merely label a child as damaged or intact, but should specify strengths and weaknesses that can guide help for the child. Most tests have been validated only against gross diagnoses of damage versus no damage, however.

Halstead-Reitan Neuropsychological Test Battery. Originally developed for adults, the Halstead-Reitan Battery includes a variety of measures for various aspects of perceptual-motor functioning (Reitan & Davison, 1974). Many of the measures require mechanical equipment for presenting visual and auditory stimuli and recording the subject's responses. A summary Impairment Index is computed by counting the number of subtests on which a subject's performance falls in the range characteristic of brain damaged rather than normal adults.

The test battery has been simplified somewhat for administration to 9- to 14-year-olds, and a much simpler version is available for 5- to 8-year-olds. Although it can discriminate significantly between brain-damaged and normal children, many of the children's measures remain experimental and are not recommended for routine clinical use (Boll, 1981). Furthermore, particular patterns of test performance may have very different implications for children and adults, as those Wechsler IQ subtests that Reitan considers *most* sensitive to brain damage in children are the ones he considers *least* sensitive to brain damage in adults (Reitan & Davison, 1974).

Bender Gestalt Test. The most widely used test of visual-motor dysfunction, the Bender-Gestalt Test, consists of nine figures printed on separate cards. Lauretta Bender (1938) selected the figures from configurations designed by the *Gestalt* psychologist Max Wertheimer to illustrate various principles of perceptual organization. Bender hypothesized that children's ability to copy the various *Gestalten* (configurations) reflects their levels of perceptual-motor maturation. The figures include a circle attached to a diamond, a straight line of dots, a series of small circles arranged in short parallel lines, complex patterns of dots, and straight and wavy lines.

The child is asked to copy each of the designs in succession. Children who rotate the figures, seem confused, make major alterations, or produce inferior copies for their age may be asked to repeat their drawings in order to see whether they can recognize and correct their errors.

Bender provided no norms or scoring criteria, but Elizabeth Koppitz (1975) devised a Developmental Scoring System based on specific distortions, rotations, failures of integration, and other errors by children aged 5 to 10. Inter-rater reliabilities are in the .90s and test-retest reliabilities are generally in the .80s over periods of a few weeks. Normative data show steady improvement in scores from the ages of 5 to about 9. The developmental nature of Koppitz's scoring is also reflected in correlations of up to .85 with MA.

Because Bender performance correlates so well with cognitive development, children's general cognitive ability must be considered when evaluating their perceptual-motor handicaps. Children with low MAs, for example, cannot be expected to perform well on the Bender even if they have no perceptual-motor or emotional problems. In studies controlling for MA, however, Koppitz's scoring, combined with assessment of the qualitative nature of children's errors and their ability to correct them has effectively identified children diagnosed as brain-damaged by a consensus of other criteria (see Koppitz, 1975). Koppitz stresses that low scores for a given MA merely *suggest* brain damage and that all other data about a child should be considered in making a diagnosis.

Graham-Kendall Memory-for-Designs Test. The Graham-Kendall Test (Graham & Kendall, 1960) is fairly similar to the Bender, except that the subject draws each design from memory after having seen it for five seconds. The designs are all straight-line figures selected for ease of scoring and ability to discriminate between normal and brain-damaged people in the standardization samples. Scoring is highly reliable and data on a variety of groups show that the scores discriminate fairly well between normal and brain-damaged subjects ranging in age from 9 to 60. For this age range, cognitive development seems to have less impact than on Bender performance for ages 5 to 9. Normative data on both tests suggest that cognitive development beyond an MA of about 10 does not improve perceptual-motor functioning much. The Graham-Kendall's scoring system, however, does permit a correction for developmental level by subtracting a subject's age and vocabulary level.

Frostig Developmental Test of Visual Perception. The Frostig Test provides a profile across five areas believed to reflect organic dysfunction (Maslow, Frostig, Lefever, & Whittlesey, 1964). The five areas are eye-hand coordination, figure-ground perception, form constancy, position in space, and spatial relations. Drawing tasks tapping the five areas have been standardized on large samples of children aged 3 to 9. A perceptual age level and a perceptual quotient (PQ), analogous to the IQ, are calculated in each of the five areas. Scoring is objective and test-retest reliabilities for PQs over several weeks have been about .80 (Frostig & Orpet, 1972).

As to validity, significant correlations have been found between Frostig scores and teacher ratings of classroom adjustment, motor coordination, and intellectual functioning, Goodenough Draw-a-Man scores, and reading scores. Marked scatter among scores and low total scores have also been found in children diagnosed as neurologically impaired. One purpose of the profile is to guide Frostig's educational program for improving perceptual-motor functioning. Controlled studies have shown that Frostig's procedures do improve PQ scores on her test, but that they do not necessarily improve reading or other school performance (Hammill, 1975).

CULTURAL INFLUENCES ON ASSESSMENT

We have stressed the multiplicity of influences on children's behavior in assessment situations. Among the influences that cut across all types of assessment are those related to cultural differences. Research on psychological differences between people living in different societies has a long history. Yet it was only in the 1960s and 1970s that civil rights issues sparked much concern for the effects of cultural differences on psychological development and functioning within our own society.

At first, differences in language, test performance, and attitudes were regarded merely as deficits to be remediated through early intervention programs. As it was recognized, however, that not all differences were deficits and that acceleration toward middle class norms might not be either feasible or desirable, there was a reaction against assessment oriented toward special services for children (Oakland, 1977). As we saw in Chapter 8, IQ testing and classes for the retarded became key targets. "Mainstreaming" became a favored solution that was applied not only to the retarded but other handicapped groups as well. As the research reviewed in Chapter 8 showed, however, mainstreaming has not overcome the problems of stigma or educational handicap suffered by the retarded, and efforts to tailor special help still require appropriate assessment of children's strengths and deficits. The question is how to do this without mistaking cultural differences for deficits simply because they deviate from majority values.

One approach to broadening cognitive assessment has been to integrate test data with questions about children's performance of social roles; measures of social, cultural, and economic characteristics of children's families; and health history data relevant to children's learning difficulties. The most ambitious effort of this sort has been Jane Mercer's (1975) System of Multicultural Pluralistic Assessment (SOMPA). As illustrated in Figure 16-1, the SOMPA is intended to give the examiner a context for evaluating cognitive performance in relation to the child's nontest behavior, family, cultural milieu, and medical status.

Another approach has been to study the effects of specific task variables on the performance of minority group children. For example, a comparison of various conditions of reinforcement has shown marked differences in the WISC IQs obtained by black children: Those receiving no special reinforcement obtained a mean IQ of 81.55; those receiving verbal praise, such as "good" and "fine," obtained a mean of 84.85; those receiving candy after each correct response obtained a mean of 92.85; and those receiving "culturally relevant praise," such as "good job, blood," obtained a mean of 99.15 (Terrell, Taylor, & Terrell, 1978).

In addition to studies of the effects of cultural influences on test performance, comparisons have been made between behavioral problems and competencies

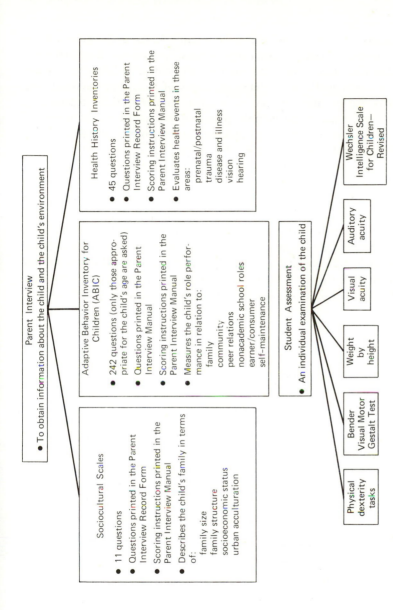

Figure 16.1. Outline of Mercer's (1975) System of Multicultural Pluralistic Assessment.

reported by parents of normal and clinically referred black and white children (Achenbach & Edelbrock, 1981). Differences in the socioeconomic distributions of blacks and whites make it essential to control for socioeconomic differences. When this was done, it was found that the rates and types of behavioral problems and competencies reported by black parents were quite similar to those reported by white parents of the same socioeconomic status. *Within* racial group, however, lower socioeconomic parents generally reported more problems and fewer competencies than middle and upper socioeconomic parents. Socioeconomic differences thus seem much more strongly related to parent-reported behavior than racial differences do. Nevertheless, the difference in problems and competencies reported for clinically referred versus nonreferred children was much greater across all socioeconomic strata than the differences between socioeconomic strata. In other words, lower socioeconomic nonreferred children were reported to be much more like upper socioeconomic nonreferred children than either group were to referred children of any socioeconomic status. Although many possible effects of cultural differences remain to be explored, there does appear to be a large common ground among parents' perceptions of their children's behavioral problems and competencies.

SUMMARY

The terms *formal diagnosis* and *differential diagnosis* signify diagnosis in its narrow sense, which refers to the classification of disorders. The terms *diagnostic formulation* and *diagnostic work-up* signify diagnosis in its broad sense, which refers to the process of gathering diagnostic information and formulating comprehensive conclusions. The term *assessment* encompasses the broader meaning of diagnosis but avoids connotations of organic disease.

The most valuable assessment procedures are those that distinguish a particular child from other children in ways that will help tailor services to the particular child. This requires linking assessment to a taxonomy that highlights differences in the etiology, prognosis, and/or optimal treatments for particular disorders. When this is done, assessment should be one phase of a continuous process that also encompasses taxonomy, treatment, and the evaluation of outcomes.

Infant development tests are used primarily to identify babies who are organically damaged, diseased, deprived, or suffering from severe emotional disturbance. Although constructed on the same principles as IQ tests, infant development tests do not predict later IQs among normal children. Babies who score very low, however, tend to have low IQs later, because some abnormal conditions interfere with functioning throughout the course of development.

Beside yielding global scores predictive of school achievement, individually administered IQ tests can provide clues to a child's response style, patterns of cognitive performance, and characteristic errors. Achievement tests and specialized ability tests can be used to pinpoint more precisely the relations between a child's knowledge, learning, and developmental level.

Personality has been a primary focus of clinical assessment, although there is little agreement on what personality is. Most personality assessment draws on *psychodynamic* and *trait* concepts. However, the global picture of personality derived from these approaches to assessment is hard to validate and may yield a false sense of understanding, thanks to factors like the *Barnum effect* and *illusory correlations*.

Interviews are the most universal assessment procedures, but inferences from unstructured interviews are unreliable and vulnerable to the effects of biasing expectations. More structured interviews employing predetermined rating categories can yield adequate reliability with children and their parents.

Projective techniques have enjoyed great popularity, but there is little evidence of reliability or validity for most of the personality interpretations made from them. The most reliable and best validated findings have been obtained by scoring them in a structured fashion to make specific predictions rather than global personality inferences.

The few existing *objectively scored* personality tests for children have been modeled on adult tests such as the MMPI, which is itself used with adolescents. Although objective scoring eliminates the problem of interscorer unreliability, these tests have not yet demonstrated much clinical validity with preadolescents.

Family therapists have stressed assessment of families as functioning systems, and research has shown that family interactions can be reliably rated under experimental conditions. Links to child psychopathology and clinically useful discriminations have not been verified, however.

Behavioral assessment seeks to *sample* behavior as accurately as possible in situations where change is desired. Although direct observations epitomize behavioral assessment, practical obstacles to reliable and representative observation have spurred development of alternative methods. Behavior ratings by significant others, such as parents and teachers, can provide reliable data from the perspectives of those most involved with the problem behavior. These ratings validly discriminate among children, can be directly related to empirically derived taxonomies, and can be repeatedly obtained to assess change. Efforts are also being made to assess behavioral competencies via tests and ratings. Because no single method can provide comprehensive, unbiased data, behavioral assessment is increasingly characterized by a *multimethod* approach.

Psychological tests often contribute to the assessment of central nervous system dysfunction in children. Patterns of performance on cognitive and perceptual motor tests provide clues to organic deficits that may be inferred from a combination of the test findings, neurological examinations, and organic diagnostic procedures.

Cutting across all approaches to assessment are issues of cultural differences that may be misinterpreted as deficits in functioning. Insofar as assessment involves comparing individual children with normative groups, it is essential that majority group norms not obscure cultural differences in what is normative and adaptive in the assessment situation as well as in real life.

SUGGESTED READING

Cognitive Assessment. Kaufman (1979) provides a detailed appraisal of variables influencing children's performance on the WISC-R, as well as analyses of the clinical implications of various patterns of scores.

Projective Techniques. Despite the lack of research support for the validity of projective techniques with children (Gittelman, 1980), they are still widely used. Perhaps the best way to gain a developmental perspective on children's responses to projective tests is to study the responses characterizing children grouped by age. Louise Bates Ames and her colleagues from the Gesell Institute have provided some raw material for developmental study of the Rorschach responses of children aged 2 to 10 (Ames, Metraux, Rodell, & Walker, 1974) and adolescents aged 10 to 16 (Ames, Metraux, & Walker, 1977).

Family Assessment. *No Single Thread: Psychological Health in Family Systems* (Lewis, et al., 1976) is a good example of what can be done to assess family interactions through observational ratings. Despite the success of the research in developing reliable and discriminating ratings, however, it also shows that much remains to be done to link these to assessment and treatment of psychopathology in children.

Behavioral Assessment. Numerous publications are available on behavioral assessment, although only a few, such as Mash and Terdal (1981), provide detailed applications to children's disorders. Nay (1979) illustrates the broadening scope of multimethod behavioral assessment.

Neuropsychological Assessment. Reitan and Davison (1974) and Boll (1981) present overviews of neuropsychological assessment, plus details of specific tests.

CHAPTER 17

Issues in the Prevention and Treatment of Psychopathology

Our ultimate goal is, of course, to find effective methods of prevention and treatment. In this chapter, we will discuss approaches not detailed earlier in the book. We begin with therapies focusing on the individual child and then consider approaches that focus on group dynamics, family systems, educational settings, the community at large, and children at risk. Thereafter, we will consider issues that cut across all approaches to prevention and treatment.

NONDIRECTIVE PLAY THERAPY

In nearly all nonorganic therapies for preadolescent children, the therapist provides play materials and the opportunity to play. The assumption is that children feel more comfortable and can express themselves better in play than in purely verbal interviews. Psychoanalytically oriented therapists regard children's play as symbolically expressing unconscious thoughts and conflicts, just as adult free association does. Some behavior therapists also use the play situation to get at problems the child is not willing or able to discuss. But they often use play as a way of trying to change other behavior. They may, for example, reinforce the child for overcoming specific fears through play. Neither the psychoanalytic nor the behavioral approach, however, view play per se as *therapy*. In both, play serves as a medium of communication between child and therapist. In nondirective play therapy, by contrast, the child's play is the essential instrument of therapy.

Nondirective play therapy extends Carl Rogers' (1951) nondirective client-centered therapy to children. A leader of nondirective play therapy, Virginia Axline (1969), explains its basic assumptions as follows: All behavior is caused by a "drive for complete self-realization." When external pressures block this drive, children either fight outwardly to establish their self-concept in external reality or turn their struggle inward and begin separating themselves from reality. Children are maladjusted when they lack the self-confidence to grow in self-realization and fail to channel this drive into constructive, positive directions. Axline regards daydreaming, withdrawal, compensation, identification, projection, regression, and repression as means by which children who are turning inward try to fulfill their self-concept. The greater the disparity between the inner self-concept and the outer behavior, the greater the maladjustment.

As with most extensions of adult therapy to children, play in nondirective therapy is assumed to function like words do for adults. Thus, the play therapist's role is to create conditions under which children can express their feelings in play, face them, and learn to control or abandon them. The playroom is a secure place where the child is the most important person. Here, children can achieve a sense of power to be individuals in their own right. Since the child's self-directed expressive activity is considered crucial, Axline provides simple toys that children can use creatively, rather than mechanical toys or competitive games.

According to Axline, play therapy can help a child even without accompanying changes in the adults who contribute to the child's problems. Although counseling or therapy for the significant adults in a child's life may be helpful, the play therapist's primary alliance is with the child. The therapist, therefore, does not work with the parents. If play therapy is successful, the child may develop new and effective ways of coping with the negative influences of adults. As an example of what play therapists hope to do, here is a therapy session with a 12-year-old delinquent named John:

> In the preceeding session, he had asked the therapist to get him a penknife so that he could carve some balsa wood. . . .
>
> When John came into the playroom, he immediately looked on the table, found the knife, picked it up, snapped open the blade.
>
> "Oh, you fool, you," he cried. "I asked you to get me a knife to carve with, and you walked into the trap. Now you've given me a knife, and I'll cut your wrists." He suddenly reached out, grabbed the therapist's hand and placed the open blade against the vein. "Now what are you going to do?" he demanded.
>
> "It seems to me that is my question," the therapist replied. "You're the one with the knife. What are *you* going to do?"
>
> "You wonder what?" John asked.
>
> "I certainly do," the therapist said.
>
> "What are you going to do?" John demanded.
>
> "What would you suggest?" the therapist inquired.

"You know what will happen if I get mad enough right now?" John asked threateningly.

"What will?" asked the therapist.

"I'd cut your damn wrists. Then how would you like that? I'd cut that vein right there. What would you do? Tell me that. What would you do?"

"I'd probably bleed," the therapist answered, after some quick thinking.

"And *then* what would happen?" John demanded.

"I don't know," the therapist said. "That would be your problem."

"*My* problem? You'd be the one bleeding to death!" John yelled.

"You'd be the one who did it, though," the therapist said.

"Why don't you try to pull loose?" John demanded.

"Why don't you let go and put away the knife?"

"You were a fool to get me this knife for in here, you know," John said. "You realize what a fool you were? You brought this all on yourself."

"You asked for the knife to carve balsa wood," the therapist replied.

"And *you* turn out to be the balsa wood," shrieked John, laughing hilariously. "So you'll bleed to death. Then what will you do? Tell me. What do you do then?"

"I don't know" the therapist said. "I've never bled to death before."

John suddenly released the therapist's wrist, closed up the knife, tossed it on the table.

"Some people are too damn dumb to be turned loose," he said. "You're so stupid you could get your very throat cut and wouldn't know what happened. Why did you get this knife? Why did you give it to me?"

"You said you wanted to carve wood. I believe what you say."

Suddenly he sat down with his back to the therapist.

"Some people shouldn't be let out alone," he said. "Some people are too damn dumb. How can I fight you if you won't fight back? How can I cut your wrists if you won't even struggle? All the time here it's like this. It's not *me* against all the people in the world that I hate and despise. You make it turn out again and again that it's me against myself. All of a sudden I feel all my feelings—and sudden like I just wish I'm not the way I am. I wish I had a feeling of being strong deep inside of me without threats and being afraid really. I feel like I'm too little for too big a world. I don't want to always make war with myself."

John, in his way, indicated what therapists hope to induce in every child with whom they work—an increased awareness of his feelings, a sense of measuring himself against himself, a seeking for an understanding of himself that will bring with it inner peace, and a feeling of being at one with the world. (Axline, 1955, pp. 625–626)

Effects of Nondirective Play Therapy

While developing nondirective therapy for adults, Carl Rogers stressed the need for evaluating the effects of therapy and he coordinated research that showed benefits from client-centered therapy (Rogers & Dymond, 1954). To some extent, concern for research carried over into the early development of play therapy. Controlled studies showed greater improvement on personality measures by children receiving play therapy than by untreated control children, even without parental involvement (e.g., Seeman, Barry, & Ellingwood, 1964). A controlled comparison, however, showed that boys with conduct disorders improved more after behavior modification than play therapy (Perkins, 1967).

Filial Therapy

In an approach called *filial therapy*, the principles of nondirective play therapy are taught to parents (Guerney, 1976). The goal is not only to facilitate children's development through play therapy, but also to make therapy skills a part of parents' permanent behavioral repertoire. Groups of parents are trained to conduct play sessions with their own children. Principles of social reinforcement and parent effectiveness training (PET; Gordon, 1970) are also used to help parents toward specific behavioral goals and improve communications between them and their children. Guerney (1976) reports a study in which parent and therapist ratings showed significant improvement in target children from intake to the termination of their parents' participation. Exclusion of the 25 percent who dropped out and the lack of an appropriate control group make the results hard to judge, however. We thus need firmer evidence for the efficacy of play therapy, whether administered by parents or therapists.

GROUP THERAPY

From a focus on treating the individual child, we turn now to approaches that emphasize group dynamics. J. L. Moreno is often credited with initiating group psychotherapy in Vienna about 1911. He began by having children act out dramatic plays, but soon allowed them to act out their problems without prepared scripts. After moving to the United States in 1927, Moreno applied his technique, known as *psychodrama*, with prisoners and reform school inmates. His work sparked a tremendous interest in group therapy, which is assumed to be especially good for stimulating social behavior, encouraging efforts to share problems, and providing mutual support for reality testing. Group therapy is also used to supplement individual therapy or as a substitute when a client's finances or a shortage of therapists preclude individual therapy.

Several types of group therapy are used with children too young for adolescent-adult forms of discussion group therapy. One is the *activity group* in which up to eight children are free to pursue their own interests, but they also have a refreshment period and may take trips together. The therapist exerts as little leadership or control as possible, but praises good work and behavior and provides a model of thoughtfulness, courtesy, and self-control with which the children can identify (Slavson & Schiffer, 1975).

Another variant is the *activity-interview group*, which combines the activity group with the approach taken in individual psychoanalytically oriented therapy. Beside permitting the children to behave as they wish, the therapist encourages communication and interprets the children's behavior to them, with the goal of promoting insight.

A third variant of child group therapy is *nondirective group play therapy*, which generally follows the principles of individual play therapy, except that the children meet in groups. An early report showed a positive effect of nondirective group play therapy on retarded readers (Bills, 1950), but a much better controlled study showed no differences between treated and untreated control children at the end of therapy or after a one-year follow-up, either in social adjustment or reading scores (Elliot & Pumfrey, 1972). An eclectic combination of group play and discussion has been found about as effective as individual therapy with boys considered to have high ego strength, but neither group nor individual therapy significantly improved the behavior of boys low in ego strength (Novick, 1965).

Behavioral methods are also used in group therapy. Group modeling, desensitization, and reinforcement techniques have all shown significant effects on children (Clement, Roberts, & Lantz, 1970; Ritter, 1968). Rose (1972) presents a variety of child therapy groups in which small group dynamics and behavioral methods are combined to achieve well-defined goals. The children's behavior outside the group is also monitored to determine whether goals are being met. An advantage of this approach is that treatment effects can be evaluated in terms of specific goals for each child, although there have been few systematic comparisons between Rose's procedures and other treatments or no treatment.

CONJOINT FAMILY THERAPY

Most therapies for children emphasize the need for working with the child's family. The child guidance approach, in which a social worker sees the parents while a therapist sees the child, is sometimes called "family therapy." In the 1950s, however, *conjoint family therapy* emerged, in which all members of a family meet together with one or two therapists. This reflects a view of the family as a social system in which each member's behavior is a function of pressures existing in the whole system (Goldenberg & Goldenberg, 1980). A child's problems are thus viewed as symptoms of family stress. Moreover, the child's symptoms are seen as serving a definite function for the family, so that their removal without other changes in the family may produce symptoms in other members or a dissolution of the family system. Consequently, the child is called the "identified patient"—the one identified as a patient by the other family members—but the family system is viewed as the target of treatment.

Conjoint family therapists sometimes use psychodynamic concepts, but they apply them to the family rather than individuals. They may also use behavioral concepts, but seek to change the interactions among all family members rather than only the identified patient or the one-to-one interaction between the patient and other family members. The following reinterpretation of Freud's (1909) case of Little Hans illustrates contrasts between a family therapist's views and those of Freud and the behavior modifiers whose interpretations we presented in Chapter 9 (Wolpe & Rachman, 1960):

> If we view Hans' family as a gestalt, we will then not only analyze Hans' oedipal fantasies but also attempt to understand what impact his parents had on their development. . . .
>
> Children's developmental problems activate unresolved childhood conflicts of their parents so that when a parent seeks assistance from a therapist in relation to his child, he is also presenting a part of himself which seeks help. When Hans' father went to Freud, he may have been unconsciously communicating that "I, Hans' father, have Oedipal difficulties of my own which I can't resolve. They are being stimulated constantly by my son. Please help me." It is of interest that concurrent with Hans' developing sexual curiosity, we find his father curious about the sexual theories of Freud and attending his lectures on sex. . . . Based on his quests for sexual information . . . one may reasonably speculate that the father was having some sexual difficulties of his own.
>
> If our hypothesis concerning the sexual difficulties that Father was experiencing with his wife is correct, and if we consider the dearth of communication that transpired between the mother and father throughout the case, it would follow that Hans' sexual curiosity could not be discussed by Mama and Papa together, either with or without Hans present. Apparently, Hans' burgeoning sexual curiosity and attendant fantasies induced considerable anxiety in both parents and, in turn, exacerbated their withdrawal from each other. Intensified were Hans' erotic desires towards Mother because he sensed an increased availability of her by virtue of Father's withdrawal from her. Furthermore, Father, who attended lectures on sex in his spare time and did not spend very much time with his wife, emerged throughout the story as a tender, maternal man, one whose lack of aggressiveness could strengthen a boy's Oedipal guilt. Hence, Papa and Mama avoided each other, avoided discussing sexual questions about Hans with each other, and interestingly, Hans developed a symptom which had as its major feature, avoidance. Because there was a dearth of verbal communication in the interdependent triangular relationship of sex, Hans squelched his feelings and thoughts on the subject and displaced his conflicts on to an object that could not verbally communicate at all, namely, a horse.
>
> The relationship between Hans' father and Freud became recapitulated in the father's treatment of Hans; childhood sexuality was again the topic of discussion. Since the therapeutic encounters transpired almost daily, we can tentatively conclude that the sexual discussion provided both partners with some sexual stimulation and gratification. . . . As Freud, himself, has taught us, when an Oedipal conflict in a boy is strong, a common defense is to repress his competitive aggression toward the father and deny the love attachment towards the mother. The boy then submits to father in a homosexual manner, his hostility goes underground, and a love and beloved relationship between father and son is formed. Father's sexual talks with Hans apparently seduced the boy into a submissive relationship with him, and Hans became more and more positively

suggestible to his father's interpretations. To please his father, Hans gave up the fear of horses, which was Father's main objective. It will be recalled that as the case material unfolded, and not prior to the therapy, Hans became increasingly effeminate and submissive. He began to have fantasies of becoming a woman and dreamed that he had given birth to a baby. Like his mother who had given birth to Hans' baby sister during his pre-Oedipal phase, Hans became, psychologically, his father's wife and surrendered his own virility.

As we know, Mother was excluded and probably excluded herself from the consultations with Freud. . . . Is there a possibility that the rage she felt in being a loner was conveyed to Hans when she admonished him for his masturbatory activity by threatening him with the loss of his "widdler"? . . .

As family therapists have demonstrated, when the family member with the presenting problem improves, other family members exhibit distress and/or the family unit can possibly be threatened with dissolution. Hans' phobia was the displayed expression of family conflict and held the family together, preserving its equilibrium. When Hans, the family member with the presenting problem, improved, the parents' marriage soon after was dissolved. The mutual avoidance pattern of both parents towards each other reinforced Father's attachment to his son wherein Hans became his father's wife. As mother became further alienated from her husband and son, Hans and his father drew closer. Father evolved into both a mother and father for Hans, was ascribed strong omnipotence by the latter, and the patient was cured through love. Hans, in his submission to father, complied with his father's prescription that was received from Freud, namely, that "the phobia is nonsense and ridiculous to keep." (Strean, 1967, pp. 230–32)

Application of Conjoint Family Therapy

Family therapy techniques vary greatly. Some therapists, such as Virginia Satir (1967), see the parents first for a couple of sessions and then the children with their parents for most other sessions, unless the children are under 4. Satir also takes an extensive family history to learn about the family and provide initial structure to reduce their fears of the therapy situation. Other therapists see all family members from the beginning to the end of therapy, while still others see only the parents and the child who is the identified patient. Many shun detailed family histories, because they believe this sets a pattern of having the therapist ask questions and the family answer them.

Nearly all family therapists agree on the need to avoid taking sides with particular family members. Most therapists also lay down certain rules. A cardinal rule is that family members can say anything they want without being punished afterward, but that they do not have to say anything unless they want to. There is disagreement, however, on whether the therapist should interpret individual psychopathology or should respond instead only to family dynamics. A questionnaire survey of 300 family therapists of various professions revealed such diversity in this respect that it was decided to order therapists along a dimension from A to Z (Group for the Advancement of Psychiatry, 1970).

A therapists use family therapy only as a supplement or occasional substitute for individual therapy. *Z* therapists, at the other extreme, think in terms of family systems for all emotional problems and see several family members together in all their work. The *Z* therapists are the purest family therapists, but they are a small minority.

In one of the first case illustrations of conjoint family therapy, John E. Bell (1961) outlined several phases he viewed as typical, The first is the *child-centered phase* in which the therapist builds a relationship with the children by being especially attentive to them, supporting their requests for changes in parental behavior, and tending to ignore parental criticism. In the *parent-child interaction phase*, parental complaints about the children are prominent and the parents and children tend to talk *about* each other rather than *to* each other. In the *father-mother interaction phase*, the parents begin to express their conflicts with each other. These conflicts are assumed to be the cause of the identified patient's problems. As therapy progresses toward the *termination phase*, emphasis on the identified patient and parental interaction gives way to a focus on the interaction of all family members with one another.

There is no doubt that conjoint family therapy brings a family's attitudes and interactions into much sharper focus than can ever be achieved through individual therapy with some or even all the family members. Not only can the behavior of each family member be observed, but the stimuli each family member provides to the others, the responses of family members to these stimuli, and the continuing succession of stimuli and responses can be observed. In fact, observations on families in therapylike situations are often used for research on relations between child psychopathology and family dynamics (e.g., Lewis et al., 1976).

Effects of Conjoint Family Therapy

When children's disorders stem from family pressures, family therapy might reduce those pressures more effectively than one-to-one treatment in which changes in the child or parent alone cannot improve family dynamics. In conjoint family therapy, the presence of several family members and the focus on family interaction would seem better able to promote complementary and lasting changes. Yet, so many variables are involved, including the therapist's ability to respond effectively to entire families, that the efficacy of family therapy must be tested empirically rather than being accepted merely for its intuitive appeal.

In one of the few well-designed comparisons of individual and family therapy, hospitalized adolescents from intact families were randomly assigned to one treatment or the other (Wellisch, Vincent, & Ro-Trock, 1976). Each treatment was brief, comprising only eight 90-minute sessions, and was conducted by the same therapists. Extensive self-report and observational measures showed minimal differences in outcome, but the adolescents receiving family therapy returned to work or school significantly faster than those receiving individual therapy, and significantly fewer were rehospitalized over a three-month follow-up (none of 14 receiving family therapy versus 6 of 14 receiving individual therapy).

In a study that we discussed briefly in chapter 13, adolescent delinquents and their families were assigned to one of four treatment conditions (Klein, Barton, & Alexander, 1980):

1. Behavioral family therapy in which therapists prompted and reinforced all family members for clearly communicating the substance as well as the affect of their thoughts, for clearly presenting their "demands," and for negotiating contractual compromises, for example, through use of token systems.
2. Client-centered family therapy.
3. Psychodynamically oriented family therapy.
4. No-treatment control.

Six- to 18-month follow-ups showed a recidivism rate of 26 percent for adolescents in the behavioral condition, significantly less than for the client-centered condition (47 percent), psychodynamic condition (73 percent), and no-treatment condition (50 percent). It thus appears that behavioral family therapy reduced recidivism while the more traditional forms did not.

There was also striking evidence for the preventive effects of behavioral therapy: Significantly fewer siblings of the target adolescents in the behavioral group had court contacts (20 percent) than in the no-treatment (40 percent), client-centered (59 percent), or psychodynamic (63 percent) groups over a three-year follow-up period. Within the behavioral approach, however, good therapist skills in interpersonal relations further improved outcomes (Alexander, Barton, Schiavo, & Parsons, 1976). This indicates that not only the method of therapy but the therapist's skills in dealing with families are important.

PSYCHOEDUCATIONAL APPROACHES

We turn now to agencies having the greatest responsibility for the most children over the longest periods: the schools. Almost every child attends school; educational failure often precludes normal adaptation in Western society; and most children referred for mental health services have problems in school. Furthermore, the general quality of the school's educational and social processes significantly affect children's adaptive behaviors as well as their academic achievement (Rutter, Maughn, Mortimore, Ouston, & Smith, 1979).

The role of the school was recognized early in the development of mental health services for children. Founded by Lightner Witmer in 1896, the first psychological clinic in America aimed to help children with school problems and to train practitioners for work with children in their schools. Furthermore, the cornerstone of psychological assessment—the intelligence test—was developed to improve educational placements.

Special education for the mildly retarded became a school responsibility around the turn of the century. Problem behavior not due to retardation, however, was blamed largely on emotional disturbance. Theories of psychopathology implied that school behavior problems were symptoms of personality disorder and that treating the personality disorder would cure them. Because treating emotional disorders was considered to be no more a responsibility of schools than treating organic disease, the label *emotionally disturbed* often absolved schools of further responsibility. As a result, schools often avoided dealing with disturbed children's problem behavior, partly out of fear of aggravating it.

The label *emotionally disturbed* also justified excluding children from school; or, if a school continued to tolerate them, it stopped trying to educate them. Another consequence was that "treatment" was seen as a panacea that would enable the child to rejoin the ranks of normal children and require no further special attention in school. Legislation passed during the 1960s and 1970s, however, required public schools to educate all children, unless more appropriate services were provided. This meant that labels such as *emotional disturbance* could not justify exclusion. On the other hand, it led to considerable confusion about how to educate disturbed children.

Special Classes for the Emotionally and Behaviorally Handicapped

Making schools officially responsible for the emotionally and behaviorally hand-icapped was a great step forward. Now, according to the law, nonretarded children who did not cope well in regular classes must not be excluded from the educational process. Yet, the available options remained limited, as few teachers were trained to teach disturbed children, and there were few private educational facilities for use by communities willing to pay. A common outcome was that extreme cases who could not be tolerated in school received a few hours a week of homebound instruction from an itinerant teacher; less extreme cases were kept in regular classes but were no longer labeled emotionally disturbed, lest the gap between the mandate and its fulfillment become too obvious.

As more teachers were certified to teach these children, more of the most difficult ones were handled in special classes. There is evidence that such classes can be beneficial, both educationally and behaviorally. Vacc (1968), for example, found that disturbed children in special classes improved significantly more on achievement tests and behavior checklists from the beginning to the end of a school year than well-matched disturbed children in regular classes. According to the behavior checklists, the disturbed children in regular classes actually grew some-what worse. A sociometric measure in which children chose classmates for positive and negative roles in a hypothetical class play also showed that the disturbed children in regular classes were selected for positive roles less often and for negative roles more often than their normal peers.

A five-year follow-up of children who had been back in regular classes for at least two years showed that they no longer differed from the disturbed children who had never been in special classes (Vacc, 1972). Both groups remained poorly accepted by classmates. This suggests that the benefits of special classes do not automatically immunize children against later problems, but that mainstreaming does not make disturbed children more acceptable to their peers either.

In an exceptionally thorough comparison of structured but individualized special class programs with regular class placement for matched groups of disturbed children, Rubin, Simson, and Betwee (1966) found only small advantages for the special classes. In analyzing diagnostic variables, however, they found that special classes were very helpful for certain types of children, especially those with perceptual-motor weaknesses and excessive inhibition and withdrawal. These findings underline the need for precise assessment of children to tailor special programs to their specific needs.

Behavioral techniques for modifying disturbed school behavior were described in Chapter 10. Frank Hewett (1968) assembled these into a detailed behavioral program for educating emotionally disturbed children, including methods for controlling problem behavior, teaching specific subject matter, promoting social behavior, and evaluating results. He provides specialized physical layouts, desensitization procedures for reducing anxiety about school failure prior to operant conditioning of new skills, and detailed lesson plans to aid teachers in their role as "learning specialist." Children receiving Hewett's (1972) tangible reinforcement procedures have improved in attention and arithmetic more than children not receiving tangible reinforcement.

Special Schools

As we saw in Chapter 12, some day and residential treatment centers for severely disturbed children are known as schools and provide educationally oriented programs. A broader educational approach for a wider range of disturbed children has been developed under the name of Project Re-ED (Hobbs, 1979). Project Re-ED serves as a model for residential schools in which new concepts of reeducation can be tried out. It trains a new type of mental health professional—the teacher/counselor—and evaluates the effectiveness of reeducation.

The children in Re-ED are usually lagging in academic achievement and too severely disturbed for ordinary community services. The goal of Re-ED is to provide about six months of reeducation that enables children to return to own homes and schools.

The main "treatment" is not therapy intended to "cure" children, but ecological structuring intended to help them adapt to the outside world and to help their families reestablish them in their own home, school, and community as quickly as possible. Controlling overt behavior problems, building trust and a sense of competence, and enhancing cognitive control of behavior are key goals. To maintain and strengthen relations with the world to which they will return, children spend weekends at home, their parents participate in school discussion groups and activities, and liaison teacher-counselors help smooth the way back to the public school and community. Behavior modification is used, but is not considered sufficient for promoting maturity, especially among adolescents. Costs of the Re-ED schools are well below those of long-term residential institutions emphasizing psychotherapy.

In an 18-month follow-up, children discharged from a Re-ED program showed more gains than comparison children on ratings by regular teachers and parents, as well as in achievement. The groups did not differ in peer ratings, however (Hobbs, 1979).

Other Psychoeducational Approaches

The high cost of special educational settings restricts their availability. Furthermore, court decisions and legislation in the 1970s required that children be cared for in the least restrictive possible environment. This was generally construed as a mandate for mainstreaming. For many children who have school problems, therefore, special educational placement is not a viable option.

Just how many children need special help is suggested by a finding that 41 percent of a broad sample of children in kindergarten through third grade had already repeated a grade, been placed in a special class, received special assistance from a school psychologist, social worker, speech therapist, or tutor, or had been rated by their teacher as having attitudinal or behavioral problems (Rubin & Balow, 1971). Although this 41 percent included some children considered to be retarded and some with sensory-motor handicaps, it was only a portion of those who *at some time* in their school careers would have significant problems.

The Resource Room. One approach to integrating educational and mental health services for children not placed in full-time special settings is the "resource room." This is a room to which children go during times when they function least well in regular classes. Although resource room programs vary greatly, one of the only controlled studies of their effects has been with a behavioral resource room program employing token and time-out procedures (Quay, Glavin, Annesley, & Werry, 1972). Disturbed children attending the resource room for one or two periods daily showed significantly greater gains in reading and arithmetic achievement, but no more behavioral improvement while in regular classes than control children not receiving the resource room program.

Classroom Consultants. A broader-gauged program of school mental health services was developed by the Yale Psychoeducational Clinic (Sarason, Levine,

Goldenberg, Cherlin, & Bennett, 1966). Classroom consultants—psychologists who observed problem children in classrooms—served as links between interventions in the school and clinic. After a child was identified by a teacher or the consultant as having problems, the consultant first observed classroom influences on the child's behavior. The consultant then met with the teacher to discuss ways of altering class conditions to help the child. If the classroom situation was basically sound or if the teacher was unable to improve it, the consultant met directly with the child and, occasionally, with the child's parents to discuss ways of altering the problem behavior. As a last resort, the child was seen at the Psychoeducational Clinic.

The clinic contact was worked out by the therapist and child with the parents' permission. Unlike most clinic contacts, the child was fully involved in planning it, and the clinic was explained by the consultant in advance. In many cases, the consultant drove the child to the clinic in order to prevent missing appointments, which is otherwise common among the inner-city children served by the clinic. The clinic contact focused on the child's school behavior. Nondirective therapy and help in schoolwork were used to identify the precise nature of the child's problem and to build up more adaptive school behavior. The clinic was also the site of ongoing group meetings between psychologists and teachers to resolve day-to-day school problems.

Although the variety of problems and interventions precluded controlled evaluation, Sarason et al. reported that only one child was expelled from the four inner-city schools served by the clinic, a rate significantly below the rate for ten neighboring schools. Other localities have since used classroom consultants to help with problems in a variety of ways.

Preventive Measures. Just as schools can aid in treating many children, they can also help identify and prevent psychopathology before it becomes severe. In one effort to utilize this potential, all children scheduled to begin school were seen for an evaluation by a psychologist while their parents were interviewed by a psychiatric social worker (Newton & Brown, 1967). The aims of this evaluation were to identify techniques teachers might use with specific children, to make predictions about the children's adaptation to school, to advise the parents, and to provide interventions when necessary before the group actually entered school. Preschool interventions included arranging for medical care, food from the welfare department, supervised group experience, and therapeutic interviews. After the children entered school, a stand-by interventionist was available to help as soon as problems became apparent.

Although not directly providing services, a study by Bower (1969) was designed to provide tools for mass screening of elementary schoolchildren to identify maladjustment which could, in turn, lead to intervention. Bower first had school psychologists and psychiatrists pick out children they believed to be disturbed. Personality and sociometric measures were then filled out by all the children in the classes of those identified as disturbed, and teachers rated their adjustment.

Of the children identified in advance by the psychologists and psychiatrists, teachers rated 87 percent as poorly adjusted. Peer ratings on the sociometric measure showed that the disturbed children were perceived more negatively than their classmates. A five-year follow-up showed that, compared to classmates selected by teachers as having average adjustment, the disturbed children had significantly more police contacts; more referrals to guidance clinics, health services, and school guidance personnel; more school disciplinary actions; and more absences.

One of the lengthiest prevention projects started in the Rochester, New York, public schools in the 1950s. Known as the Primary Mental Health Project (PMHP), it uses homemakers as child aides who meet periodically with primary graders identified as having problems of aggression, withdrawal, or learning (Cowen, Gesten, & Weissberg, 1980). The children are referred by teachers who report their problems on a behavior checklist. The aides meet with the children individually or in small groups at school, typically once a week for one to two years. They engage in structured or unstructured interactions geared to the child's needs for academic or interpersonal help. The PMHP model has been widely disseminated through workshop and training programs, and several studies have examined relations between characteristics at referral and program variables (e.g., Cowen, Orgel, Gesten, & Wilson, 1979). An adaptation of the PMHP using behavioral techniques yielded significantly greater improvements in school behavior ratings of participants than of untreated children at another school, although Hawthorne (placebo) effects and rater biases could not be ruled out in this study (Durlak, 1977).

COMMUNITY MENTAL HEALTH CENTERS

The 1960s and 1970s brought an upsurge in community approaches to mental health. Rather than discussing everything that has been tagged with the "community" label, we will focus on the most central achievement of the community approaches: the community mental health centers initiated by the federal government.

Origin of the Centers

The concept of community mental health centers originated with the recommendations of the Joint Commission on Mental Illness and Health, established by Congress in 1955. After a five-year study of mental health needs, the Commission recommended that reliance on large mental hospitals be replaced by a flexible array of local services for the mentally ill (Joint Commission on Mental Illness and Health, 1961). These services were intended to minimize disruptions in patients' ties to their family and community.

Several factors helped to promote this goal. One was the advent of tranquilizing drugs that now enabled many patients to return home quickly rather than being chronically institutionalized. Although the drugs did not bring about cures, and relapses occurred, links to home, job, and family could be sustained better than when major disorders were treated mainly through continued incarceration. A second factor was the advent of new concepts of treatment that emphasized the therapeutic effects of the social milieu and the negative effects of "hospitalism."

A third factor was the Commission's finding that mental health facilities were pathetically inadequate for all but the very wealthy living in certain favored areas. For example, a survey showed that *half* the counties in the United States had *no* mental health services for children! Less than one-quarter had child guidance clinics, most of the existing clinics had long waiting lists, and there was little coordination among the available services (Robinson, DeMarche, & Wagle, 1960). The recognition that only federal initiatives could tackle such a massive problem was fostered by precedents set when the government assumed responsibility for the millions of emotional casualties among servicemen of World War II and the Korean War and established the National Institute of Mental Health in 1949.

A fourth factor was the sheer arithmetic of numbers revealed in the Commission's surveys. The gap between the number needing help and the projected supply of mental health workers demonstrated conclusively that traditional one-to-one therapy could never meet much of the need. As a result of the Commission's recommendations, President Kennedy in 1963 became the first American President to address Congress on the mental health of the nation. Congress responded by providing up to two-thirds of the costs of building and staffing comprehensive community mental health centers operated by the states. The goal was to provide one community mental health center for every 100,000 citizens, a total of 2000 centers by 1975. The centers were to offer inpatient and outpatient care and partial hospitalization in the form of night care for people who could work during the day, short-term hospitalization, and after-care for people who had been hospitalized. The centers were also to aid other agencies in education, research, and prevention.

To staff the centers, the National Institute of Mental Health sponsored a program that by the late 1960s provided up to 10,000 stipends yearly for graduate training in mental health professions. Funds were also provided for basic research and evaluation of programs. The vision of a coordinated national effort to reform the piecemeal and inequitably distributed efforts of the past seemed on the verge of realization. The Nixon administration sharply curtailed federal support for these efforts in the early 1970s, however, and the Reagan administration vowed to end support entirely in the 1980s.

Despite threats to their continuation, it is worthwhile to consider the centers that were put into operation. The Commission's original recommendations said little about children. At that time, 85 percent of child clinics had waiting lists, as compared to 42 percent of adult clinics (Rosen, Wiener, Hench, Willner, & Bahn, 1966), and over two-thirds of the 1.5 million children needing immediate care were not getting it (Joint Commission on Mental Health of Children, 1969). Nevertheless, the centers were to treat adults, who were already served in far greater proportions than children.

The emphasis on adults is understandable if we view mental health problems in terms of the number of existing patients, how they were being treated, and how much it was all costing. One-half of the hospital beds in the United States were occupied by mental patients. The Joint Commission estimated the direct cost of mental disorders at a billion dollars a year in 1960 and the indirect costs at two billion dollars, far above the costs of any other form of illness. Yet, the most conspicuous costs were for adult patients. Very few children occupy mental hospital beds (partly because few are available); few children receive expensive private treatment; no wages are lost by disturbed children; the immediate crime and welfare costs of childhood disorders are minimal; and child psychopathology does not cause the break-up or destitution of families in such obvious ways as adult psychopathology (although a disturbed child *can* severely disrupt a family). Moreover, mental health training and practice have been oriented toward adults to such a degree that many professionals were simply unaware of children's unmet needs.

Thus, in a spirit of "first things first," the community mental health centers focused mainly on adults. Even where centers were viewed as a resource for children, chidlren's services were among the first frills to be eliminated when the planning got down to dollars and cents.

In practice, some centers, especially those serving as the sole resource in a community, offer help for children as well as adults. Furthermore, Congress in 1975 mandated that all centers serve children, along with several other new target groups. In 1978, President Carter's Commission on Mental Health singled out children as an especially needy group. Yet, the failure to earmark funds for children left them essentially unserved by many centers. The gap between needs and services thus remained much greater for children than adults (Rosen, 1979).

Evaluation of the Centers

It is hard to objectively evaluate the impact of a mental health center on an entire community, but many centers seem to have succeeded in their original mission of preventing long-term hospitalization. As droves of mental patients were released from hospitals, the centers often became their only source of help. The location of some centers in poor neighborhoods, their use of indigenous paraprofessional staff, and their orientation outward toward the community-at-large have enabled them to stimulate community programs. Some centers have even served as refuges for neighborhood people during riots. They have also operated educational and preventive programs in mental health, drug abuse, and alcoholism.

Another achievement of the centers is the fostering of new models for staffing mental health systems. Partly by design and partly because of the realities encountered, many centers replaced the traditional medical model for delivery of mental health services with one in which medicine coexists among other specialities relevant to helping disturbed people. Thus, the administrators of many centers are nonphysicians, such as psychiatric social workers, nurses, and psychologists, while physicians are employed to serve functions that specifically require medical training, such as prescribing drugs. Choosing administrators according to their skills rather than according to a predefined hierarchy of professional titles has greatly expanded the pool of potential administrators. This practice has spread to other mental health systems, such as state hospitals and departments of mental health, which were once headed exclusively by physicians.

While some centers have suffered from uncertainty and turmoil, and federal policies may doom them, the original federal initiative was a success. Yet, since children were minimally served, new efforts should be directed more intensively toward children, both by applying the knowledge we already have and by seeking more effective ways to improve social systems that affect children's development.

HIGH-RISK GROUPS

Just as it would be folly to treat all disorders the same way, preventive efforts must be tailored to specific preventable conditions. This requires knowledge of the causes of particular disorders.

One way to target preventive efforts is by identifying groups who are at especially high risk for psychopathology because of certain predisposing conditions. As we saw in Chapter 12, for example, the children of schizophrenic parents have higher rates of psychopathology in adulthood than the children of nonschizophrenic parents. Even though many offspring of schizophrenics are normal, their statistically elevated risk rate makes them a more appropriate group for the study of etiology and prevention than groups having lower rates. Not only schizophrenic parents, but those suffering from any major adaptive problems may subject their children to stress that warrants preventive efforts (Cohler, Grunebaum, Weiss, Hartman, & Gallant, 1975).

Other disorders that show elevated risk rates in certain groups include Down syndrome, which is elevated in births to women over 40, and Tay-Sachs disease, a genetic disorder elevated in births to couples who carry the recessive Tay-Sachs gene. People whose offspring are at high risk for these disorders can prevent the birth of affected children by avoiding pregnancy or aborting if amniocentesis shows a fetus to be affected.

In addition to the statistically verified risks of particular disorders, there are conditions that may predispose children to a broader array of developmental problems. In Chapter 7, for example, we saw that various perinatal organic abnormalities raise the risk of later learning and behavior problems. However, many organic abnormalities raise these risks more for children growing up in poor psychosocial circumstances than children blessed with good environments (Werner & Smith, 1977).

Because the quality of the psychosocial environment seems critical for many aspects of adaptive development, various psychosocial disadvantages are assumed to elevate the risk of psychopathology. These include poverty, neglectful and abusive parents, adolescent parents, loss of parents, and foster care. Although each of these disadvantages has been viewed categorically as a causative factor, each is often associated with several others that may collectively do far more harm than any one alone.

Economically Disadvantaged Children

Poverty can entail a long series of risks, such as poor nutrition in the mother, which gives her child a poor start in life; high rates of teenage and unmarried pregnancy; poor nutrition of the child after birth; large families living in poor housing; high rates of accidents and disease; poor schooling with insufficient family support for academic achievement; and few opportunities for economic advancement. Yet, low income is not always accompanied by all these risk factors, and psychosocial strengths in the family or community can offset the effects of economic deprivation. A British study, for example, showed that childhood disorders are much more common in low socioeconomic environments with high rates of parental social problems than in other low socioeconomic environments (Rutter, Yule, Quinton, Rowlands, Yule, & Berger, 1975).

The concentration of social problems and other risk factors in many poverty areas of the United States has stimulated efforts to break the poverty cycle. The most ambitious originated in the 1960s under the banner of the War on Poverty. Because it was clear that poor school achievement hindered later economic advancement, Project Head Start became a cornerstone of antipoverty programs.

Head Start was launched on the assumption that a brief nursery school experience would give poor children the head start they needed to succeed in school (Zigler & Valentine, 1980). When it was found that quick, simple remedies of this sort did not produce lasting jumps in ability or achievement, it became clear that intensive research was needed to develop and validate sustained intervention efforts and that poor children also needed medical and nutritional help.

Some traditional philosophies of early childhood education proved impossible to translate into effective programs. But follow-ups of intervention efforts extending downward to infancy and upward through the elementary school grades have shown significant impacts on adaptive behavior as well as school progress (Lazar, Royce, Murray, Snipper, & Darlington, 1982; Zeskind & Ramey, 1981). Comparisons of approaches have made it possible to identify especially effective instructional methods for certain skills, such as particular behavioral programs for teaching initial reading and arithmetic (Becker & Carnine, 1980). Behavioral programs have also been shown to improve the reading skills of low achieving inner-city adolescents, but a program emphasizing parental involvement continued to produce improvements during a follow-up period when the effects of the behavioral program were declining (Roderick & Hengeler, 1980).

Unwanted, Abused, and Neglected Children

At times, most parents feel ambivalent or angry toward their children. What happens when these feelings reach the point where children are genuinely unwanted, abused, or neglected?

Epidemiological studies reveal widespread and serious neglect and abuse of children (Baldwin & Oliver, 1979). In some cases, problems begin with the birth of a child who was not wanted in the first place. Studies in countries where abortions must be approved by state officials have shown higher rates of later behavioral, peer, and academic problems in children whose mothers were refused abortions than in control children (e.g., Matejcek, Dytrych, & Schuller, 1979).

Beside the fact that some are unwanted in the first place, abused children often become victims of circumstances after they are born. It is easy to blame pathological aberrations in the parents or situational stresses that drive parents to abuse, but this does not explain why not all children in a particular family or a stressful environment are abused. Transactional research on relations between child, parent, and situational variables shows that all three can contribute (Frodi, 1981).

Children who are developmentally deviant, handicapped, or hard to manage are the most likely to be abused. Why? Compared to normal babies, the deviant cries and appearance of premature babies, for example, elicit more annoyance and less sympathy from nonabusing as well as abusing parents. Yet abusing parents show more negative and less positive responses to normal children as well (Frodi, 1981).

Certain ecological factors in the larger social environment also seem to raise the risk of abuse. Garbarino and Sherman (1980), for example, compared two lower socioeconomic neighborhoods differing markedly in abuse rates. When interviewed, neighborhood parents, police, letter carriers, visiting nurses, and school officials all reported more stresses and other negative features in the high abuse neighborhood. According to mothers, some of the biggest differences were in availability of child care, quality of the neighborhood as a place to raise children, and ease of rearing children.

A prospective study, however, has shown that among mothers living in high stress environments, the minority who eventually neglected or abused their infants initially scored high on anxiety and aggression and low on measures of succorance (Egeland, Breitenbucher, & Rosenberg, 1980). These mothers also showed poorer patterns of interaction with their infants, and the infants themselves showed less optimal functioning on neonatal measures than those in mother-infant pairs where care remained adequate despite stressful environments. It is thus clear that no one factor accounts for neglect and abuse, but that a combination of environmental stress, maternal characteristics, and infant characteristics combine to raise the risks.

What are the effects of abuse on children? It has often been noted that abusing parents were themselves abused as children and that extremely aggressive children have been abused. Although a causal relation is hard to prove, it should not be surprising that children who suffer abuse from their parents fail to learn more positive ways of relating to people, including their own children.

Efforts to document specific child behaviors related to abuse have shown that abuséd children as young as 1 to 3 years old already show more deviant behavior than those whose families were under stress but not abusive (George & Main, 1979). In particular, the abused toddlers more often assaulted peers, harassed caregivers, and assaulted or threatened to assault them. They also failed to respond to friendly overtures and showed mixed approach-avoidance movements. For example, they approached caregivers to the side, the rear, or by turning about and backstepping. It thus appears that their early behavior already bears the mark of problems likely to interfere with future social development.

Children Who Lose a Parent

Losing a parent can be one of the most stressful experiences children suffer. In fact, elementary schoolchildren rated it the *most* stressful on a list of twenty possible life events, even more stressful than going blind (Yamamoto, 1979). Loss of a parent by any means is likely to cause grief, family disruption, increased burdens on the remaining parent, and a threat to a family's economic security. As mortality rates have declined and divorce rates have risen, an increasing proportion of parental loss is accompanied by the added stress of family conflict, divided loyalties, and ambivalence about adult role models. The tendency of divorcing parents to use their children as pawns can worsen an already stressful situation and encourage behavioral problems in the children on behalf of their parents. Remarriage and adaptation to a step parent can create additional stress.

How big is the problem? It is estimated that 40 to 50 percent of children born in the 1970s will spend some of their childhood in a single parent family and that this period will average 6 years (Hetherington, 1979). Studies of the impact of divorce reveal a sequence of experiences accompanied by anger, fear, depression, and guilt on children's part. Although a divorce may ultimately result in less stress than a conflictual nuclear family, conflict usually escalates in the first year following divorce.

The specific effects of divorce vary with the developmental level, temperamental style, competencies, and other characteristics of the child. Young children, for example, are least able to understand the situation. Their greater dependence on the family also restricts compensating social relationships more than for older children.

The sex of the child is an additional factor, as boys show more behavioral problems and are viewed more negatively than girls by their mothers, peers, and teachers following divorce (Hetherington, 1979). This could be due jointly to separation from the father in most divorces, the greater exposure of boys to parental battles and other harmful behavior, the less postdivorce support given boys than girls, and the more harmful effects on boys of a loss of firm parental discipline. However, the presence of another adult in the home—especially a grandmother—reduces the risks of behavior disorders below those in mother-only families (Kellam, Ensminger, & Turner, 1977). Recognition of the difficulties faced by divorcing and single parents has led to counseling and therapy programs designed to help them and their children cope realistically with the stresses involved.

Among the most unfortunate aspects of divorce are the legal struggles over child custody and visiting rights. Although courts have traditionally decided such issues in terms of parental "rights" and a presumption in favor of the mother's preeminent claim on her child, there has been a move toward making the child's interests paramount (Goldstein, Freud, & Solnit, 1979). This means considering the continuity and strength of a child's attachment to particular adults and the possibility that a child's "psychological parent" is not the biological mother or father.Because children in custody cases are usually at risk already, Goldstein, Freud, and Solnit advocate phrasing the goal of child placement as finding "the least detrimental available alternative for safeguarding the child's growth and development" (p. 53).

Foster Care

Discrepancies between the psychological and biological parent are especially likely where children are placed in the care of people other than their biological parents. Some of the saddest cases concern children raised from infancy by couples who become the child's psychological parents, only to have a biological parent reclaim the child later. Even when the foster parents are the child's psychological parents, courts have sometimes favored biological parents in these cases (Goldstein et al., 1979).

More numerous are children temporarily placed with foster parents because their own parents are incapacitated, incompetent, abusive, or rejecting. In a typical year, about 500,000 American children are in foster placements (National Commission on Children in Need of Parents, 1979). Such children often have behavioral problems before being placed in foster care, and the severity of these problems is sometimes the reason for placement. They also have elevated rates of behavior disorders after leaving foster placement, especially antisocial behavior among boys (Wolkind & Rutter, 1973).

Although state agencies are typically responsible for placement and support of the children, there is a great variety of arrangements. Furthermore, these arrangements are subject to frequent change because of court decisions, changing availability of placement settings, and even state policies against long-term placements to prevent children from becoming attached to foster parents. The insecurity and flux are major threats to adaptive development, as 18-year-old Jay's experiences show:

> I remember in one home I was told not to play football, or any rough sport at school because we were supposed to keep our clothes clean and wear our pants for three days before washing them. In the next home, they scolded me for not going out to play. In one home we watched TV a lot; in another that was considered bad. In my last foster home they corrected my manners and the way I spoke English. This had never been important before. They told me to bring friends home. I was confused and didn't know where to begin. In the previous home I had to come home after school and clean the barns. I wasn't allowed to have friends over. Really, I didn't have any friends. At age 11, in my last home they signed me up for soccer and basketball and taught me how to swim. It was hard for me. The other kids had been playing for years while I had been moving, and cleaning barns.
>
> I never really felt any home was permanent. I felt that if I didn't do what the foster parents asked me to do and do it promptly, I would have to leave. I don't know why I thought that, but I was always afraid. A temporary family doesn't try to teach you their morals and values; they don't really discipline you. You know they get money for keeping you and you know you don't really belong to them. (National Commission on Children in Need of Parents, 1979, p. 5)

Although such children's lives could be stabilized through adoption or permanent placements, courts have often been loathe to permit this as long as a biological parent is potentially available. The result is that children continue to be shifted around much longer than they would if clearcut decisions were made on the basis of the child's interests. Because foster care is regarded as welfare, it is also a favorite target for budget cutting politicians. It is therefore hard to maintain stable cadres of professional placement workers and well-trained foster parents (Fanshel & Shinn, 1978). Efforts to improve foster care, however, show that foster parents' child-rearing attitudes and behavioral management can be significantly improved through relatively brief special training (Guerney & Wolfgang, 1981; Hampson & Tavormina, 1980).

EVALUATING INTERVENTIONS

We have repeatedly stressed the need to evaluate efforts at prevention and treatment. Although theories often seem compelling and people feel confident that they are helping, we cannot really know whether an intervention works without controlled studies of outcomes, conducted according to the principles of scientific confirmation outlined in Chapter 5. This means comparing changes in children who receive a particular intervention with similar children who receive no intervention or different interventions.

In regard to almost every disorder, we have been left with unanswered questions because we lack adequate outcome studies. The lack of outcome studies is understandable in light of the sophisticated research skills needed to conduct them; the need for cooperation from diverse participants, including therapists, parents, and children; and the length of time required to accumulate large enough subject samples, conduct interventions, and provide adequate follow-up periods. Such studies require intensive and long-term commitments by those who conduct them.

An additional stumbling block to research on interventions aimed at altering personality has been a lack of operational outcome criteria. It is especially hard to evaluate effects on children's personality, because, unlike adults, children do not seek therapy for subjective discomforts that can then be targeted for outcome evaluations. With the broadening of treatment approaches to include drug, behavioral, and psychoeducational interventions, however, outcome evaluations have increasingly focused on objectively scorable criteria. There is a large core of implicit agreement on problems for which children need help, even though there may be disagreements on *what else* should be accomplished.

As an example, Table 17-1 lists problems that were reported much more often by parents of children referred for mental health services than for demographically similar normal children. These problems are fairly easy to ascertain, and changes in them can usually be judged by parents and others who know a child well. They illustrate behavioral characteristics on which evaluations of almost any type of intervention can focus, although other characteristics are also relevant in many cases. An intervention failing to ameliorate problems of this sort that damage children's self-esteem or adaptive development cannot be considered successful, no matter what else it accomplishes. The total numbers of behavioral problems and

Table 17-1 Behavior Problems Showing the Greatest Differences Between Normal and Disturbed Children Aged 4 to 16, as Reported by their Parents

Problem	Normal (%)	Disturbed (%)
Can't concentrate, can't pay attention for long	32	75
Demands a lot of attention	33	74
Disobedient at home	35	81
Disobedient at school	14	59
Doesn't get along with other children	12	57
Feels worthless or inferior	13	58
Lying or cheating	18	64
Nervous, highstrung, or tense	21	71
Poor school work	13	68
Sudden changes in mood or feelings	21	65
Unhappy, sad, or depressed	9	63

Source: Data from Achenbach & Edelbrock, 1981.

competencies reported by parents are even more powerful discriminators between referred and nonreferred children than any specific behaviors taken alone (Achenbach & Edelbrock, 1981). Total scores of this sort can therefore serve as global indices of outcome. So can standardized tests of behavior targeted for change, such as school achievement.

Research Designs for Evaluating Interventions

Since it is not hard to specify desirable outcomes for interventions with children, it should be possible to compare the effectiveness of interventions using preintervention, postintervention, and follow-up assessments as outlined in Figure 17-1. The specific measures and follow-up periods depend on the target problems, developmental level of the children, type of intervention, and other factors. Children should be randomly assigned to the different interventions to insure that those receiving each intervention are initially as similar as possible with respect to potentially important variables such as developmental level and socioeconomic status.

The design outlined in Figure 17-1 is called a *single factor* design, because it compares results only among different types or levels of one dimension or factor—that of intervention. Group 1 receives Intervention A, Group 2 receives Intervention B, and Group 3 is a no-intervention control group. Each intervention can be tailored to the needs of each child somewhat, but the aim is to determine whether Intervention A or Intervention B is more effective and whether each is better than no intervention at all.

Many variations of the single factor evaluation design are possible, such as comparing more or fewer intervention groups with each other or with a no-intervention control group. Related designs involve alternating interventions in opposite orders for two groups (the *cross-over design*) and repeatedly starting and stopping an intervention (the *ABAB design*) to see if problems rise and fall in response to the intervention condition.

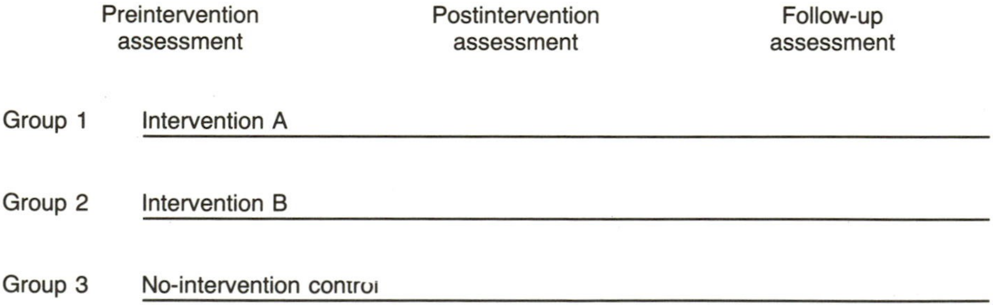

	Preintervention assessment	Postintervention assessment	Follow-up assessment
Group 1	Intervention A		
Group 2	Intervention B		
Group 3	No-intervention control		

Figure 17.1. Single factor design for comparing the effects of two interventions and no intervention.

Many factors can influence the outcome of an intervention. Certain characteristics of the children—such as their sex, developmental level, cognitive ability, socioeconomic status, or social competence—may determine which intervention works best for them, for example. Or certain characteristics of the children's families, such as intact versus single parent, or characteristics of the interveners, such as male versus female, may affect the outcomes of interventions. It is therefore important to assess the effects of interventions in relation to other factors, such as types of children, families, or interveners. This can be done by combining two or more factors in a *multifactorial design*. Figure 17-2 illustrates a two-factor design for simultaneously assessing the effects of two interventions and a no-intervention control condition with three "types" of children (see Cronbach & Snow, 1977, for details of designs for detecting interactions).

Multifactorial designs represent an ideal that can seldom be used to assess very many of the potentially relevant factors. Yet, when such designs are carried out, the results are often surprising and underscore the fallacy of applying a single intervention to broad categories of children. In one of the few multifactorial studies of child treatment, for example, Lovick Miller found that systematic desensitization and psychodynamic psychotherapy, with a relatively inexperienced as well as a very experienced therapist, were significantly more effective than no treatment for 6- to 10-year-old phobic children. Yet, *neither* treatment with *either* therapist was more effective than *no* treatment with 11- to 15-year-olds (Miller et al., 1972; discussed in more detail in Chapter 10).

In one of the few other multifactorial studies of interventions with children, three methods of treatment were assigned to children of three socioeconomic strata

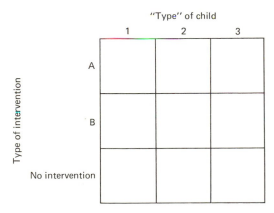

Figure 17.2. Multifactorial design for comparing the effects of two interventions and no intervention with three "types" of children. The "types" can represent age, socioeconomic status, IQ, symptom pattern, degree of parental involvement, or the like.

who were having school problems (Love & Kaswan, 1974). The three methods of treatment were:

1. Child psychotherapy in which the therapists also met with parents and school personnel as they deemed necessary;
2. Parent counseling in which only the parents were seen following one initial interview with the child and testing if the clinician felt test information would help the parents;
3. Information feedback, in which the parents and school personnel provided their views to a counselor, the family was fed back similarities and differences among themselves and the school in their perceptions of their child, they watched videotapes of their own meetings with the counselor, and they met jointly with school personnel.

Figure 17-3 shows changes in grade averages for children in each socioeconomic group receiving each treatment: Parent feedback helped upper socioeconomic children, did not affect middle-class children, and may have harmed lower socioeconomic children. Parent counseling showed *exactly the reverse* pattern, while grades declined for children of all three socioeconomic classes receiving psychotherapy.

The study lacked a true no-treatment control group. However, a group of the children's classmates not referred for treatment but participating in a research project at the same clinic showed no changes in grade average. The results show

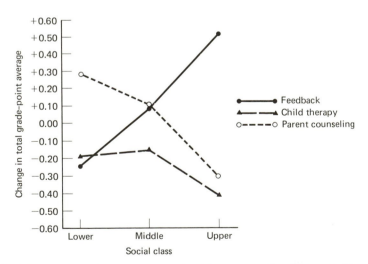

Figure 17.3. Effects of social class and type of treatment on school performance. (From Love and Kaswan, 1974, p. 173.)

that psychotherapy did not help school performance and that the effects of the other treatments depended heavily on the socioeconomic status of the recipients.

Because multifactorial designs can never include all possible variables, other approaches are necessary to assess the effects of multiple variables. Multivariate statistics, such as *multiple regression, discriminant analysis,* and *path analysis,* are increasingly used to examine interactions among variables that cannot be assessed via experimental manipulation (see Achenbach, 1978, for a nontechnical introduction to these approaches). In some cases, categorizing children prior to an intervention on the basis of measurable characteristics and then determining which ones have the best and worst outcomes can help to identify groups who are not benefitting from existing interventions. Close study of these groups may lead to new interventions designed specifically for them. Although a few disorders, such as infantile autism, are already recognized as refractory to most standard interventions, we need far closer study of the factors that predict good and poor outcomes under specific interventions. This is necessary not only to concentrate interventions on those who will benefit and to find alternatives for those who will not, but also to prevent interventions from being used with those who might be harmed. Whereas it was once thought that mental health interventions were either helpful or ineffective, there is also evidence that they may be harmful in some cases (Strupp, Hadley, & Gomes-Schwartz, 1977).

SUMMARY

Nondirective-play therapy is an extension to children of Carl Rogers' client-centered therapy for adults. Controlled studies have demonstrated some improvements in children receiving play therapy without the involvement of their parents. *Filial therapy* is a variant of play therapy in which parents are trained to conduct play sessions with their own children.

Group therapies with children include *psychodrama, activity groups, activity-interview groups,* and *nondirective group play therapy. Behavior modification* in group situations has been shown to have significant benefits, but there is little evaluative research on more traditional forms of child group therapy.

In *conjoint family therapy,* an entire family meets together for therapy sessions. Based on the assumption that a child's symptoms reflect pressures within the family system, conjoint family therapy aims to modify the behavior of the family rather than that of the *identified patient* alone. Although controlled research on family therapy is meager, there is some evidence for efficacy. Behaviorally oriented family therapy has also been found superior to client-centered and psychodynamically oriented family therapy.

Psychoeducational approaches include special classes, special schools, resource rooms, classroom consultants, and screening for early identification of adaptive problems in school. Evaluative research has demonstrated that some of the psychoeducational approaches are effective and that schools can play an important role in prevention and treatment of child psychopathology.

In the 1960s and 1970s, *community mental health centers* became a central focus of mental health services. Several hundred centers were established under a federal program before it was prematurely curtailed. The centers offer a variety of preventive and short-term treatment programs aimed at avoiding long-term hospitalization, mainly for adults.

Preventive efforts are increasingly targeted on groups believed to be at high risk for psychopathology. The risks are often multiple, but some that have been singled out as especially needing preventive efforts are those associated with parental mental disorders, economic disadvantage, abuse and neglect, and loss of parents.

Research designs for evaluating the effectiveness of interventions include the *single factor, cross-over, ABAB,* and *multifactorial* designs. The multifactorial design is typically the most powerful for identifying effective combinations of treatment, child, problem, intervener, and other factors. The few well-controlled multifactorial studies of child treatment have exposed the fallacy of applying a single type of treatment to broad categories of children.

SUGGESTED READING

Nondirective Play Therapy. One of its chief, proponents, Virginia Axline, has written a detailed exposition of play therapy in diverse contexts (1969) and a full-length case history poignantly portraying a particularly successful case (1964). Schaefer (1979) has compiled illustrations of other variants of play therapy.

Group Therapy. Rose (1972) offers an extensive guide to behavioral methods for use with groups of disturbed children. Slavson and Schiffer (1976) describe other approaches to group therapy with children.

Family Therapy. There are many zealous and fascinating works on conjoint family therapy, althouth they are short on objective evaluation of its effects. Goldenberg and Goldenberg (1980) provide a good overview, while Klein, Barton, and Alexander (1980) deal with research issues.

Children at Risk. For economically disadvantaged children, Project Head Start has been the centerpiece of intervention efforts. A book edited by Edward Zigler, one of Head Start's leaders, and Jeannette Valentine (1980) gives an overview of its aims, history, and outcome. Other preventive efforts are the subject of volumes compiled from the annual Vermont Conference on the Primary Prevention of Psychopathology (e.g., Albee & Joffe, 1977; Forgays, 1978; Kent & Rolf, 1979; Bond & Rosen, 1980). Garbarino and Gilliam (1980) focus on understanding

abusive families, while Scott, Field, and Robertson (1981) present the consequences of teenage pregnancy for the teenagers and their offspring.

Evaluation of Interventions. Among the many works on evaluation, a chapter by
Hartmann, Roper, and Gelfand (1977) offers a good appraisal of research issues in
therapies for children. A book edited by Price and Politser (1980) covers more
general issues in evaluation research, plus several specific programs for children.

Epilogue: Where do We Go from Here?

Having studied so many aspects of children's problems, we must at last find a vantage point from which to view prospects for the future. In some ways, the prospects for helping troubled children have grown brighter. Adults have become more aware of children's needs, and there are numerous efforts to find new ways of helping. On the other hand, cultural and economic conditions continue to spawn developmental risks that demand attention. Without national leadership, it is unlikely that much progress can be made in helping the most needy of our children.

If children's services receive adequate support, we can continue to develop and test new methods of prevention and treatment. A major innovation has been the growth of behavioral approaches. Although behavioral methods may not fulfill all the hopes of their proponents, and they will not eradicate mental disorders, behavioral viewpoints have brought a new emphasis on *specificity* and *observability* in the definition, assessment, and treatment of problems. They have thereby dispelled much of the mystique from psychopathology and its treatment and have challenged other approaches to demonstrate their cost/effectiveness.

The benefits of behavioral approaches should not, however, obscure the need for continuous testing to determine which methods are most effective, with whom, and under what conditions. We saw in Chapter 10 that, despite the much greater attention to evaluation than has characterized other approaches, only a few behavioral methods have been tested adequately for efficacy. Unless behavioral methods are tested and subjected to long-term follow-ups, their net effect may be to add a new jargon more than to help children. Furthermore, like drugs and other powerful therapies, they are easily perverted if used merely to suppress noxious behavior without fostering adaptive development.

Beside behavior modification, contributions from other sources are likely to play increasing roles in helping children. One source is the study of genetics. Research in genetics has already shed light on syndromes associated with mental retardation and may enhance our understanding of some forms of psychotic and delinquent behavior. Of more general significance, however, is the light genetic research may shed on normal development and on the interactions between organic and experiential determinants of behavior. Studies of genetic effects on cognitive ability, extroversion-introversion, anxiety, and schizophrenia, for example, may tell us more about *environmental* influences than purely environmental studies will. Thus, comparisons of the environmental histories of people who are believed to be genetically vulnerable to schizophrenia may tell us what *non*genetic factors lead to schizophrenic and nonschizophrenic outcomes. These factors may include biochemical and other physical characteristics, as well as life events that shape children's coping styles and strategies.

The Developmental Framework

In Chapter 3, we surveyed development from diverse perspectives. To integrate these perspectives, we need a conceptual framework for understanding each child as a whole, integrated, living organism—this is the essential reality with which we deal. Any child is far more than the sum of the identifiable influences on him or her. Even when troubled, children are highly adaptive organisms whose troublesome behavior represents a complex adaptation to their situation and their concept of it.

The study of normal development provides a framework within which to understand specific deviations. We already know enough about normal cognitive and socioemotional development to show that much "disturbed" behavior can be understood in terms of normal adaptive mechanisms that change as development proceeds. Erikson's (1963) outline of psychosocial development highlights the qualitatively different tasks and methods of coping that children display at various ages. Behavior that seems abnormal to uninformed observers may be quite typical of children wrestling with developmental tasks at the interface between societal mores and their own unfolding desires, abilities, and fantasies. Much behavior that *is* indeed abnormal, in the sense that it deviates markedly from the typical developmental course or interferes with development, may be an *exaggeration* of normal coping behavior, owing to deviations in the child or environment.

Just as Erikson outlines the dialectic between social mores and the psychosocial development of the individual, Piaget (1970) outlines the developmental changes and continuities in children's ways of knowing about themselves and the world. The basic biological push of all living things to adapt by modifying the self (*accommodation*) and modifying the environment (*assimilation*) is so basic in children as to be often overlooked. Children's need to grasp the world at their own level and the constant changes in their systems of knowing are basic aspects of their development.

What are the implications for modifying behavior? One of the most important implications is that step-by-step mastery of developmental tasks is essential to children's long-term well-being. These tasks include resolving psychosocial conflicts like those outlined by Erikson, such as trust versus mistrust, autonomy versus shame and doubt, and initiative versus guilt. They also include the maintenance of a sense of competence and pleasure in constructive advance—abundantly evident in the delight healthy infants and children take in novelty and in meeting the cognitive challenges they create for themselves. Specific developmental tasks include mastery of the developmentally graded skills needed for adaptation in a child's society: appropriate toileting, speaking, dressing, academic skills, and social skills such as making friends, dealing with strong emotions, and carrying out cooperative efforts.

Although developmental processes can go awry at many points—owing to organic and experiential factors, parental behavior, lack of appropriate models and incentives, and unfortunate combinations of vulnerabilities and risks—the goal of a developmental approach is to help children adapt and advance through developmental tasks in the best way possible. Helpful interventions can include environmental changes, family changes, organic treatments, prosthetic techniques to enable a child to advance despite handicaps, modification of behavior that may alienate others or prevent a child from advancing developmentally, and verbal counseling or therapy. Nevertheless, any intervention should take account of children's conceptions of themselves, their competencies and their problems, as well as their potential for striving toward solutions to developmental tasks.

Cognitive Aspects. Many approaches to psychopathology neglect children's capacities for constructive cognitive adaptation and reorganization. This neglect has resulted from assuming that cognition mainly reflects reinforcement histories or psychodynamics. As we saw in Chapter 10, behavior modifiers have taken account of thinking by including symbolic mediation, cognitive behavioral techniques, and self-control techniques in their paradigms. Some psychodynamic theorists have sought to do likewise by invoking a conflict-free sphere of the ego to explain higher thought processes. These are essentially *translations* of cognitive concepts into behavioral or psychoanalytic theory, however. While translation can facilitate communication among diverse viewpoints, translation alone will not provide an adequate paradigm from which research on the role of thinking can proceed.

It may be far more profitable to study thinking as an independent variable that is correlated with other kinds of independent variables or can itself provide a basis for predicting important behavior. For example, a child's symptom pattern may represent a strategy for coping with reality as that child sees it. The child's mental representations are end-products of many organic and experiential factors, but these mental representations may yield better predictions of behavior than all the separate determinants would. Modification of the mental representations may therefore be an important step in promoting more adaptive development.

One means of preventive intervention is by formally teaching children to solve problems that arise in social interactions. Shure and Spivak (1978), for example, have tried this by preparing extensive training "scripts" for use with children by their mothers and teachers. Children may also be helped to reorient their mental representations away from the past in which they were shaped and toward present and future developmental goals. Another line of intervention may be through direct amelioration of fears and social or academic deficits that otherwise hinder a constructive orientation toward further development. In most cases, a combination of methods may be needed to encourage children to change their coping strategies, help them actually make the changes, and help them acquire new skills that make new strategies viable as they face other developmental tasks.

The essential point is that children are biologically and cognitively designed for adaptation and change. Interventions should aim to reduce obstacles to development and provide support for it. The best way to help children may therefore be to build on their existing adaptive strategies and capacities and their cognitive representations of their current status in such a way as to facilitate developmental advancement.

REFERENCES

Abel, E. L. Fetal alcohol syndrome: Behavioral teratology. *Psychological Bulletin,* 1980, *87,* 29−50.

Abramson, L. Y., Seligman, M. E. P., & Teasdale, J. D. Learned helplessness in humans: Critique and reformulation. *Journal of Abnormal Psychology,* 1978, *87,* 49−74.

Achenbach, T. M. The classification of children's psychiatric symptoms: A factor-analytic study. *Psychological Monographs,* 1966, *80*(Whole No. 615).

Achenbach, T. M. Conservation of illusion distorted identity: Its relation to MA and CA in normals and retardates. *Child Development,* 1969, *40,* 663−679.

Achenbach, T. M. Comparison of Stanford-Binet performance of nonretarded and retarded persons matched for MA and sex. *American Journal of Mental Deficiency,* 1970, *74,* 488−494.(a)

Achenbach, T. M. The Children's Associative Responding Test: A possible alternative to group IQ tests. *Journal of Educational Psychology,* 1970, *61,* 340−348.(b)

Achenbacn, T. M. Stanford-Binet Short-Form performance of retarded and nonretarded persons matched for MA. *American Journal of Mental Deficiency,* 1971, *76,* 30−32.

Achenbach, T. M. Surprise and memory as indices of concrete operational development. *Psychological Reports,* 1973, *33,* 47−57.

Achenbach, T. M. A longitudinal study of relations between associative responding, IQ changes, and school performance from grades 3 to 12. *Developmental Psychology,* 1975, *11,* 653−654.

Achenbach, T. M. Psychopathology of childhood: Research problems and issues. *Journal of Consulting and Clinical Psychology,* 1978, *46,* 759−776.(a)

Achenbach, T. M. *Research in developmental psychology. Concepts, strategies, methods.* New York: Free Press, 1978.(b)

Achenbach, T. M. The Child Behavior Profile: I. Boys aged 6−11. *Journal of Consulting and Clinical Psychology,* 1978, *46,* 478−488.(c)

Achenbach, T. M. The Child Behavior Profile: An empirically based system for assessing children's behavioral problems and competencies. *International Journal of Mental Health,* 1979, *7,* 24−42.

Achenbach, T. M. Developmental perspectives: II. Methodology and research. In M. H. Bornstein (Ed.), *The comparative method in psychology.* Hillsdale, NJ: Erlbaum, 1980.

Achenbach, T. M. DSM-III in light of empirical research on the classification of child psychopathology. *Journal of the American Academy of Child Psychiatry,* 1980, *19,* 395−412.

Achenbach, T. M. The role of taxonomy in developmental psychology. In M. E. Lamb, & A. L. Brown (Eds.), *Advances in developmental psychology (Vol. 1).* Hillsdale, NJ: Erlbaum, 1981.

Achenbach, T. M., & Edelbrock, C. S. The classification of child psychopathology: A review and analysis of empirical efforts. *Psychological Bulletin,* 1978, *85,* 1275−1301.

Achenbach, T. M., & Edelbrock, C. S. Behavioral problems and competencies reported by parents of normal and disturbed children aged 4 through 16. *Monographs of the Society for Research in Child Development,* 1981, *46,* Serial No. 188.

Achenbach, T. M., & Edelbrock, C. S. *Manual for the Child Behavior Checklist and Child Behavior Profile.* Burlington, VT: Child Psychiatry, University of Vermont, 1982.

Achenbach, T. M., & Lewis, M. A proposed model for clinical research and its application to encopresis and enuresis. *Journal of the American Academy of Child Psychiatry,* 1971, *10,* 535−554.

Achenbach, T. M., & Weisz, J. R. Impulsivity-reflectivity and cognitive development in preschoolers: A longitudinal analysis of developmental and trait variance. *Developmental Psychology,* 1975, *11,* 413−414.

Achenbach, T. M., & Zigler, E. Social competence and self-image disparity in psychiatric and nonpsychiatric patients. *Journal of Abnormal and Social Psychology,* 1963, *67,* 197−205.

Achenbach, T. M., & Zigler, E. Cue-learning and problem-learning strategies in normal and retarded children. *Child Development,* 1968, *39,* 827−848.

Ackerman, N. W. The role of the family in the emergence of child disorders. In E. Miller (Ed.), *Foundations of child psychiatry.* New York: Pergamon Press, 1968.

Ackerman, N. W., & Behrens, M. L. Family diagnosis and clinical process. In S. Arieti (Ed.), *Handbook of American Psychiatry (Vol. 2).* New York: Basic Books, 1974.

Ackerman, P. T., Dykman, R. A., & Peters, J. E. Teenage status of hyperactive and nonhyperactive learning disabled boys. *American Journal of Orthopsychiatry,* 1977, *47,* 577−596.

Ackerson, L. *Children's behavior problems (Vol. 2).* Chicago: University of Chicago Press, 1942.

Adams, P. L. *Obsessive children: A sociopsychiatric study.* New York: Brunner/Mazel, 1973.

Adams, S. The PICO project. In N. Johnston, L. Savitz, & M. E. Wolfgang (Eds.), *The sociology of punishment and correction.* New York: Wiley, 1962.

Adler, F. The interaction between women's emancipation and female criminality: A cross-cultural perspective. *International Journal of Criminology and Penology*, 1977, *5*, 101−112.

Albee, G. W., & Joffe, J. M. (Eds.). *Primary prevention of psychopathology. Vol. I: The issues*. Hanover, NH: University Press of New England, 1977.

Aleksandrowicz, M. K. The effect of pain relieving drugs administered during labor and delivery on the behavior of the newborn: A review. *Merrill-Palmer Quarterly*, 1974, *20*, 121−141.

Alexander, A. B. Chronic asthma. In R. B. Williams, Jr., & W. D. Gentry (Eds.), *Behavioral approaches to medical treatment*. Cambridge, MA: Ballinger, 1977.

Alexander, A. B. The treatment of psychosomatic disorders: Bronchial asthma in children. In B. B. Lahey & A. E. Kazdin (Eds.), *Advances in clinical child psychology (Vol. 3)*. New York: Plenum, 1980.

Alexander, A. B., Miklich, D. R., & Hershkoff, H. The immediate effects of systematic relaxation training on peak expiratory flow rates in asthmatic children. *Psychosomatic Medicine*, 1972, *34*, 388−394.

Alexander, F., French, T. M., & Pollack, G. H. *Psychosomatic specificity, Vol. 1*. Chicago: University of Chicago Press, 1968.

Alexander, J. F., Barton, C., Schiavo, R. S., & Parsons, B. V. Systems-behavioral intervention with families of delinquents: Therapist characteristics, family behavior, and outcome. *Journal of Consulting and Clinical Psychology*, 1976, *44*, 656−664.

Allen, J., DeMyer, M. K., Norton, J. A., Pontius, W., & Yang, E. Intellectuality in parents of psychotic, subnormal and normal children. *Journal of Autism and Childhood Schizophrenia*, 1971, *1*, 311−326.

Allen, K. E., Hart, B., Buell, J. S., Harris, F. R., & Wolf, M. M. Effects of social reinforcement on isolate behavior of a nursery school child. *Child Development*, 1964, *35*, 511−518.

Allen, K. E., Henke, L. B., Harris, F. R., Baer, D. M., & Reynolds, N. J. Control of hyperactivity by social reinforcement of attending behavior. *Journal of Educational Psychology*, 1967, *50*, 231−237.

Allport, G. W. *Personality: A psychological interpretation*. New York: Holt, 1937.

Allyon, T., & Roberts, M. D. Eliminating discipline problems by strengthening academic performance. *Journal of Applied Behavior Analysis*, 1974, *7*, 71−76.

American Journal of Diseases of Children. 1969, *118*(2), 22−23.

American Psychiatric Association. *Diagnostic and statistical manual of mental disorders*. Washington, DC: American Psychiatric Association, (1st ed.), 1952; (2nd ed.), 1968; (3rd ed.), 1980.

Ames, L. B., Gillespie, C., Haines, J., & Ilg, F. L. *The Gesell Institute's child from one to six: Evaluating the behavior of the preschool child*. New York: Harper & Row, 1979.

Ames, L. B., Metraux, R. W., Rodell, J. L., & Walker, R. N. *Children's Rorschach responses. Developmental trends from 2 to 10 years*. New York: Brunner/Mazel, 1974.

Ames, L. B., Metraux, R. W., & Walker, R. N. *Adolescent Rorschach responses: Developmental trends from ten to sixteen years (Rev. ed.)*. New York: Brunner/Mazel, 1977.

Anderson, L. M. Personality characteristics of parents of neurotic, aggressive, and normal preadolescent boys. *Journal of Consulting and Clinical Psychology*, 1969, *33*, 575−582.

Andrasik, F., & Holroyd, K. A. A test of specific and nonspecific effects in the biofeedback treatment of tension headache. *Journal of Consulting and Clinical Psychology,* 1980, *48,* 575—586.

Andrews, G., & Harris, M. *The syndrome of stuttering.* London: Heinemann, 1964.

Anthony, E. J. The behavior disorders of childhood. In P. H. Mussen (Ed.), *Carmichael's manual of child psychology (Vol. 1).* New York: Wiley, 1970.

Anthony, E. J. A clinical and experimental study of high risk children and their schizophrenic parents. In A. R. Kaplan (Ed.), *Genetic factors in "schizophrenia."* Springfield, IL: Thomas, 1972.

Anthony, E. J. High risk and premorbid development. In L. C. Wynne, R. L. Cromwell, & S. Matthyse (Eds.), *The nature of schizophrenia: New approaches to research and treatment.* New York: Wiley, 1978.

Anthony, E. J., & Scott, P. Manic-depressive psychosis in childhood. *Journal of Child Psychology and Psychiatry,* 1960, *1,* 53—72.

Arnold, L. E., Barnebey, N. E., McManus, J., Smeltzer, D. J., Conrad, A., Winer, G., & Desgranges, L. Prevention by specific perceptual remediation for vulnerable first-graders. *Archives of General Psychiatry,* 1977, *34,* 1279—1294.

Ashkenazi, Z. The treatment of encopresis using a discriminative stimulus and positive reinforcement. *Journal of Behavior Therapy and Experimental Psychiatry,* 1975, *6,* 155—157.

Assael, M., Kohen-Raz, R., & Alpern, S. Developmental analysis of EEG abnormalities in juvenile delinquents. *Diseases of the Nervous System,* 1967, *28,* 49—54.

Astin, A. The functional autonomy of psychotherapy. *American Psychologist,* 1961, *16,* 75—78.

Atkeson, B. M., & Forehand, R. Parent behavioral training for problem children: An examination of studies using multiple outcome measures. *Journal of Abnormal Child Psychology,* 1978, *6,* 449—460.

Atkinson, J. W. Studying personality in the context of an advanced motivational psychology. *American Psychologist,* 1981, *36,* 117—128.

Atkinson, J. W., & Raynor, J. O. *Personality, motivation, and achievement.* Washington, DC: Hemisphere, 1978.

Auerbach, A. H., & Luborsky, L. Accuracy of judgments and the nature of the "good hour." In J. M. Shlien (Ed.), *Research in psychotherapy (Vol. III).* Washington, DC: American Psychological Association, 1968.

Ax, A. F. The physiological differentiation between fear and anger in humans. *Psychosomatic Medicine,* 1953, *15,* 433—442.

Axline, V. M. Play therapy procedures and results. *American Journal of Orthopsychiatry,* 1955, *25,* 618—626.

Axline, V. M. *Dibs: In search of self.* New York: Houghton-Mifflin, 1964.

Axline, V. M. *Play therapy (Rev. ed.).* New York: Ballantine Books, 1969.

Azrin, N. H., Sneed, T. J., & Foxx, R. M. Dry-bed training: Rapid elimination of childhood enuresis. *Behavior Research and Therapy,* 1974, *12,* 147—156.

Baekgaard, W., Nyborg, H., & Nielsen, J. Neuroticism and extroversion in Turner's syndrome. *Journal of Abnormal Psychology,* 1978, *87,* 583—586.

Baer, D. M., & Wolf, M. M. The reinforcement contingency in preschool and remedial education. In R. D. Hess & R. M. Baer (Eds.), *Early education: Current theory, research and action.* Chicago: Aldine, 1968.

Baird, H. W., John, E. R., Ahn, H., & Maisel, E. Neurometric evaluation of epileptic children who do well and poorly in school. *Electroencephalography and Clinical Neurophysiology,* 1980, *48,* 683−693.

Baker, B. L. Symptom treatment and symptom substitution in enuresis. *Journal of Abnormal Psychology,* 1969, *74,* 42−49.

Baker, B. L. Training parents as teachers of their developmentally disabled children. In S. Salzinger, J. Antrobus, & J. Glick (Eds.), *The ecosystem of the "sick" child.* New York: Academic Press, 1980.

Baker, B. L., Heifetz, L. J., & Murphy, D. M. Behavioral training for parents of mentally retarded children: One-year follow-up. *American Journal of Mental Deficiency,* 1980, *85,* 32−38.

Bakwin, H. Enuresis in twins. *American Journal of Diseases of Childhood,* 1971, *121,* 222−225.

Bakwin, H. Reading disability in twins. *Developmental Medicine and Child Neurology,* 1973, *15,* 184−187.

Balaschak, B. A., & Mostofsky, D. I. Seizure disorders. In E. J. Mash & L. G. Terdal (Eds.), *Behavioral assessment of childhood disorders.,* New York: Guilford Press, 1981.

Baldwin, J. A., & Oliver, J. E. Severe child abuse: Implications of the epidemiology. *International Journal of Mental Health,* 1979, *7,* 78−95.

Baldwin, J. A., Robertson, N. C., & Satin, D. G. The incidence of reported deviant behavior in children. *International Psychiatry Clinics,* 1971, *8,* 161−175.

Balla, D., Lewis, D. O., Shanok, S., Snell, L., & Henisz, J. Subsequent psychiatric treatment and hospitalization in a delinquent population. *Archives of General Psychiatry,* 1974, *30,* 243−245.

Balla, D., & Zigler, E. Personality development in retarded persons. In N. R. Ellis (Ed.), *Handbook of mental deficiency: Psychological theory and research (2nd ed.).* Hillsdale, NJ: Erlbaum, 1979.

Ballard, M., Corman, L., Gottlieb, J., & Kaufman, M. J. Improving the social status of mainstreamed retarded children. *Journal of Educational Psychology,* 1977, *69,* 605−611.

Baller, W. R. A study of the present social status of a group of adults who, when they were in elementary school, were classified as mentally deficient. *Genetic Psychology Monographs,* 1936, *18,* 165−244.

Baller, W. R., Charles, D. C., & Miller, E. L. Mid-life attainment of the mentally retarded: A longitudinal study. *Genetic Psychology Monographs,* 1967, *75,* 235−329.

Baltes, P. B., Reese, H. W., & Nesselroade, J. R. *Life-span developmental psychology: Introduction to research methods.* Monterey, CA: Brooks/Cole, 1977.

Bandura, A. *Social learning theory.* Englewood Cliffs, NJ: Prentice-Hall, 1977.

Bandura, A., Adams, N. E., & Beyer, J. Cognitive processes mediating behavioral change. *Journal of Personality and Social Psychology,* 1977, *35,* 125−139.

Bandura, A., Blanchard, E. B., & Ritter, B. Relative efficacy of desensitization and modeling approaches for inducing behavioral, affective, and attitudinal changes. *Journal of Personality and Social Psychology,* 1969, *13,* 173−199.

Bandura, A., Grusec, J. E., & Menlove, F. L. Vicarious extinction of avoidance behavior. *Journal of Personality and Social Psychology,* 1967, *5,* 16−23.

Bandura, A., & Walters, R. *Adolescent aggression.* New York: Ronald Press, 1959.

Bandura, A., & Walters, R. *Social learning and personality development*. New York: Holt, Rinehart, & Winston, 1963.

Barglow, P., Bornstein, M. B., Exum, D. B., Wright, M. K., & Visotsky, H. M. Some psychiatric aspects of illegitimate pregnancy during early adolescence. *American Journal of Orthopsychiatry*, 1967, *37*, 266—267.

Barkley, R. A. A review of stimulant drug research with hyperactive children. *Journal of Child Psychology and Psychiatry*, 1977, *18*, 137—165.

Barkley, R. A., & Cunningham, C. E. Do stimulant drugs improve the academic performance of hyperkinetic children?: A review of outcome research. *Clinical Pediatrics*, 1978, *17*, 85—93.

Baroff, G. S., & Tate, B. G. The use of aversive stimulation in the treatment of chronic self-injurious behavior. *Journal of the American Academy of Child Psychiatry*, 1968, *7*, 454—470.

Baron, R. A. *Human aggression*. New York: Plenum, 1977.

Bartak, L., & Rutter, M. The use of personal pronouns by autistic children. *Journal of Autism and Childhood Schizophrenia*, 1974, *4*, 217—222.

Bartak, L., Rutter, M., & Cox, A. A comparative study of infantile autism and specific developmental language disorders. III. Discriminant function analysis. *Journal of Autism and Childhood Schizophrenia*, 1977, *7*, 383—396.

Basser, L. S. Hemiplegia of early onset and the faculty of speech with special reference to the effects of hemispherectomy. *Brain*, 1962, *85*, 427—460.

Bauer, S. R., & Achenbach, T. M. Self-image disparity, repression-sensitization, and extraversion-introversion: A unitary dimension? *Journal of Personality Assessment*, 1976, *40*, 46—51.

Baughman, E. E., & Dahlstrom, W. G. *Negro and white children: A psychological study in the rural South*. New York: Academic Press, 1968.

Bayley, N. Consistency and variability in the growth of intelligence from birth to eighteen years. *Journal of Genetic Psychology*, 1949, *75*, 165—196.

Bayley, N. Behavioral correlates of mental growth: Birth to thirty-six years. *American Psychologist*, 1968, *23*, 1—17.

Bayley, N. *Bayley Scales of Infant Development*. New York: Psychological Corporation, 1969.

Bayrakal, S. The significance of EEG abnormality in behavior problem children. *Canadian Psychiatric Association Journal*, 1965, *10*, 387—391.

Beck, A. T. *Cognitive therapy and the emotional disorders*. New York: International Universities Press, 1976.

Beck, L., Langford, W., Mackay, M., & Sum, G. Childhood chemotherapy and later drug abuse and growth curve: A follow-up study of 30 adolescents. *American Journal of Psychiatry*, 1975, *132*, 436—438.

Becker, B. A. Exogenous drug influences on the developing nervous system: Teratology and perinatal toxicology. In W. A. Himwich (Ed.), *Developmental neurobiology*. Springfield, IL: Thomas, 1970.

Becker, W. C., & Carnine, D. W. Direct instruction: An effective approach to educational intervention with the disadvantaged and low performers. In B. B. Lahey & A. E. Kazdin (Eds.), *Advances in clinical child psychology (Vol. 3)*. New York: Plenum, 1980.

Beckwith, D., Elseviers, L., Gorin, C., Mandansky, L., Osouka, J., & King, J. Harvard XYY study. *Science,* 1975, *187,* 298.

Beech, H. R., & Vaughn, M. *Behavioral treatment of obsessional states.* New York: Wiley, 1978.

Beedle, P. The patterns of drug abuse in the United Kingdom. In S. Btesh (Ed.), *Drug abuse: Nonmedical use of dependence-producing drugs.* New York: Plenum Press, 1972.

Beers, C. W. *A mind that found itself.* New York: Longmans, Green, 1908; reprinted by Doubleday, 1966.

Beitchman, J. H., Dielman, T. E., Landis, J. R., Benson, R. M., & Kemp, P. L. Reliability of the Group for the Advancement of Psychiatry diagnostic categories in child psychiatry. *Archives of General Psychiatry,* 1978, *35,* 1461–1466.

Bekhterev, V. W. *Objektive Psychologie oder Psychoreflexologie* (1907). German translation. Leipzig: Teubner, 1913.

Bell, J. E. Family group therapy. *Public health monograph.* Washington, DC: United States Department of Health, Education, and Welfare, 1961, No. 64.

Bell, R. Q., & Harper, L. V. *Child effects on adults.* Hillsdale, NJ: Erlbaum, 1977.

Bellak, L., & Bellak, S. S. *Children's Apperception Test (Human Figures).* Larchmont, NY: C. P. S., Inc., 1965.

Bellak, L., & Bellak, S. S. *Children's Apperception Test (6th and rev. ed.).* Larchmont, NY: C. P. S., Inc., 1974.

Bellman, M. Studies on encopresis. *Acta Paediatrica Scandinavica,* 1966, Supplement 170.

Belmaker, R., Pollin, W., Wyatt, R. J., & Cohen, S. A follow-up of monozygotic twins discordant for schizophrenia. *Archives of General Psychiatry,* 1974, *30,* 219–222.

Belson, W. A. *Television violence and the adolescent boy.* Farnborough, England: Teakfield, 1978.

Bemis, K. M. Current approaches to the etiology and treatment of anorexia nervosa. *Psychological Bulletin,* 1978, *85,* 593–617.

Bemporad, J. R. Adult recollections of a formerly autistic child. *Journal of Autism and Developmental Disorders,* 1979, *9,* 179–197.

Bender, L. A visual motor Gestalt test and its clinical use. *The American Orthopsychiatric Association Research Monographs,* 1938, No. 3.

Bender, L. Treatment in early schizophrenia. *Progress in Psychotherapy,* 1960, *5,* 177–184.

Bender, L., & Faretra, G. The relationship between childhood schizophrenia and adult schizophrenia. In A. R. Kaplan (Ed.), *Genetic factors in "schizophrenia".* Springfield, IL.: Thomas, 1972.

Bennett, S., & Klein, H. Childhood schizophrenia: 30 years later. *American Journal of Psychiatry,* 1966, *122,* 1121–1124.

Benson, H., & Wallace, R. K. Decreased drug abuse with transcendental meditation: A study of 1,862 subjects. In C. J. D. Zarafonetis (Ed.), *Drug abuse: Proceedings of the International Conference.* Philadelphia: Lea & Febiger, 1972.

Benton, J., Moser, H. W., Dodge, P. R., & Carr, S. Modification of the schedule of myelinization in the rat by early nutritional deprivation. *Pediatrics,* 1966, *38,* 801–804.

Berecz, J. M. Treatment of school phobia. In G. P. Sholevar, R. M. Benson, & B. J.

Blinder (Eds.), *Emotional disorders of children and adolescents. Medical and psychological approaches to treatment.* Larchmont, NY: SP Medical and Scientific Books, 1980.

Berger, P. A. Medical treatment of mental illness. *Science,* 1978, *200,* 974−981.

Bergland, R. M., & Page, R. B. Pituitary-brain vascular relations: A new paradigm. *Science,* 1979, *204,* 18−24.

Berkowitz, L. *Aggression: A social psychological analysis.* New York: McGraw-Hill, 1962.

Berkun, M., Bialek, H., Kern, R., & Yagi, K. Experimental studies of psychological stress in man. *Psychological Monographs,* 1962, *76*(Whole No. 534).

Berlyne, D. E. *Conflict, arousal, and curiosity.* New York: McGraw-Hill, 1960.

Bernal, M. E., Delfini, L. F., North, J. A., & Kreutzer, S. L. Comparison of boys' behaviors in homes and classrooms. In E. J. Mash, L. A. Hamerlynck, & L. C. Handy (Eds.), *Behavior modification and families.* New York: Brunner/Mazel, 1976.

Bernstein, L., & Purcell, K. Institutional treatment of asthmatic children. In H. I. Schneer (Ed.), *The asthmatic child: Psychosomatic approach to problems and treatment.* New York: Harper, 1963.

Berry, H. K. Phenylketonuria: Diagnosis, treatment and long-term management. In G. Farrell (Ed.), *Congenital mental retardation.* Austin, Texas: University of Texas Press, 1969.

Beschner, G. M., & Friedman, A. S. (Eds.). *Youth drug abuse. Problems, issues, and treatment.* Lexington, MA: Lexington Books, 1979.

Bettelheim, B. *The empty fortress.* New York: Free Press, 1967.

Bills, R. E. Nondirective play therapy with retarded readers. *Journal of Consulting Psychology,* 1950, *14,* 140−149.

Bindelglas, P. M., & Dee, G. Enuresis treatment with imipramine hydrochloride: A 10-year follow-up study. *American Journal of Psychiatry,* 1978, *135,* 1549−1551.

Binet, A., & Simon, T. New methods for the diagnosis of the intellectual level of subnormals. *L'Annee Psychologique,* 1905 (a). Translated and reprinted in A. Binet & T. Simon, *The development of intelligence in children.* Baltimore: Williams & Wilkins, 1916.

Binet, A., & Simon, T. Upon the necessity of establishing a scientific diagnosis of inferior states of intelligence. *L'Annee Psychologique,* 1905 (b). Translated and reprinted in A. Binet & T. Simon, *The development of intelligence in children.* Baltimore: Williams & Wilkins, 1916.

Binet, A., & Simon, T. The development of intelligence in the child. *L'Annee Psychologique,* 1908. Translated and reprinted in A. Binet & T. Simon, *The development of intelligence in children.* Baltimore: Williams & Wilkins, 1916.

Birch, H. G. The problem of "brain damage" in children. In H. G. Birch (Ed.), *Brain damage in children: The biological and social aspects.* Baltimore: Williams & Wilkins, 1964.

Birch, H. G., & Gussow, J. D. *Disadvantaged children: Health, nutrition, and school failure.* New York: Grune & Stratton, 1970.

Birch, H. G., Richardson, S. A., Baird, D., Horobin, G., & Illsley, R. *Mental subnormality in the community: A clinical and epidemiologic study.* Baltimore: Williams & Wilkins, 1970.

Birenbaum, A., & Seiffer, S. *Resettling retarded adults in a managed community.* New York: Praeger, 1976.

Blackstock, E. G. Cerebral asymmetry and the development of early infantile autism. *Journal of Autism and Childhood Schizophrenia,* 1978, *8,* 339–353.

Blake, P., & Moss, T. The development of socialization skills in an electively mute child. *Behavior Research and Therapy,* 1967, *5,* 349–356.

Blanchard, E. B. Behavioral medicine: A perspective. In R. B. Williams, Jr., & W. D. Gentry (Eds.), *Behavioral approaches to medical treatment.* Cambridge, MA: Ballinger, 1977.

Blanchard, E. B., & Epstein, L. H. *A biofeedback primer.* Reading, MA: Addison-Wesley, 1978.

Blane, H. T., & Chafetz, M. E. (Eds.). *Youth, alcohol, and social policy.* New York: Plenum, 1979.

Blasi, A. Bridging moral cognition and moral action: A critical review of the literature. *Psychological Bulletin,* 1980, *88,* 1–45.

Blatt, B., Ozolins, A., & McNally, J. *The family papers: A return to purgatory.* New York: Longman, 1979.

Blechman, E. A. Short- and long-term results of positive home-based treatment of childhood chronic constipation and encopresis. Unpublished manuscript. Wesleyan University, Middleton, CT, 1979.

Bleuler, E. *Dementia Praecox or the group of schizophrenias* (1911). New York: International Universities Press, 1950.

Block, J. H., & Block, J. The role of ego-control and ego-resiliency in the organization of behavior. In W. A. Collins (Ed.), *Minnesota symposia on child psychology (Vol. 13).* New York: Erlbaum, 1980.

Block, J., & Martin, B. Predicting the behavior of children under frustration. *Journal of Abnormal and Social Psychology,* 1955, *51,* 281–285.

Block, J., Patterson, V., Block, J., & Jackson, D. D. A study of the parents of schizophrenic and neurotic children. *Psychiatry,* 1958, *21,* 387–397.

Blum, G. S. The Blacky Pictures with children. In A. I. Rabin & M. R. Haworth (Eds.), *Projective techniques with children.* New York: Grune & Stratton, 1960.

Blum, R. H. *Drug education: Results and recommendations.* Lexington, MA: Heath, 1976.

Boberg, E., & Shea, R. Stuttering: Recent developments in theory and in therapy. *Canadian Medical Association Journal,* 1978, *119,* 357–360.

Bockoven, J. S. *Moral treatment in American psychiatry (2nd ed.).* New York: Springer, 1963, 1972.

Boll, T. J. The Halstead-Reitan Neuropsychology Battery. In S. B. Filskov & T. J. Boll (Eds.), *Handbook of clinical neuropsychology.* New York: Wiley, 1981.

Boll, T. J., & Barth, J. T. Neuropsychology of brain damage in children. In S. B. Filskov & T. J. Boll (Eds.), *Handbook of clinical neuropsychology.* New York: Wiley, 1981.

Bolstad, O. D., & Johnson, S. M. The relationship between teachers' assessment of students and the students' actual behavior in the classroom. *Child Development,* 1977, *48,* 570–578.

Bond, L. A., & Rosen, J. C. (Eds.). *Competence and coping during adulthood.* Hanover, NH: University Press of New England, 1980.

Bonvillian, J. D., Nelson, K. E., & Rhyne, J. M. Sign language and autism. *Journal of Autism and Childhood Schizophrenia,* 1981, *11,* 125–137.

Böök, J. A., Nichtern, S., & Gruenberg, E. Cytogenetical investigations in childhood schizophrenia. *Acta Psychiatrica Scandinavica,* 1963, *39,* 309–323.

Borland, B. L., & Heckman, H. K. Hyperactive boys and their brothers. *Archives of General Psychiatry,* 1976, *33,* 669–675.

Bornstein, B. Analysis of a phobic child. *Psychoanalytic Study of the Child,* 1949 *(Vol. III–IV),* 181–226.

Bouchard, T. J., & McGue, M. Familial studies of intelligence: A review. *Science,* 1981, *212,* 1055–1059.

Boullin, D. J., Coleman, M., O'Brien, R. A., & Rimland, B. Laboratory predictions of infantile autism based on 5-Hydroxtryptamine efflux from blood platelets and their correlation with the Rimland E-2 score. *Journal of Autism and Childhood Schizophrenia,* 1971, *1,* 63–71.

Bower, E. M. *Early identification of emotionally handicapped children in school (2nd ed.).* Springfield, IL: Thomas, 1969.

Bowlby, J. *Attachment and loss (Vol. 2). Separation anxiety and anger.* New York: Basic Books, 1973.

Bowlby, J. The making and breaking of affectional bonds. I. Aetiology and psychopathology in light of attachment theory. *British Journal of Psychiatry,* 1977, *130,* 201–210.

Bowlby, J. *Attachment and loss (Vol. 3). Loss.* New York: Basic Books, 1980.

Boyd, P. R. Drug abuse and addiction in adolescents. In J. G. Howells (Ed.), *Modern perspectives in adolescent psychiatry.* New York: Brunner/Mazel, 1971.

Bradley, C. The behavior of children receiving benzedrine. *American Journal of Psychiatry,* 1937, *94,* 577–585.

Bradway, K. P., & Thompson, C. W. Intelligence at adulthood: A twenty-five year follow-up. *Journal of Educational Psychology,* 1962, *53,* 1–14.

Bradway, K. P., Thompson, C. W., & Cravens, R. B. Preschool IQs after twenty-five years. *Journal of Educational Psychology,* 1958, *49,* 278–281.

Brady, D. O., & Smouse, A. D. A simultaneous comparison of three methods for language training with an autistic child: An experimental single case analysis. *Journal of Autism and Childhood Schizophrenia,* 1978, *8,* 271–279.

Braid, J. *Neurypnology or the rationale of nervous sleep, considered in relation with animal magnetism.* London: J. Churchill, 1843.

Braucht, G. N., Brakarsh, D., Follingstad, D., & Berry, K. L. Deviant drug use in adolescence: A review of psychosocial correlates. *Psychological Bulletin,* 1973, *79,* 92–106.

Brazelton, T. B. *Neonatal Behavioral Assessment Scale.* London: Spastics International Medical Publications, 1973.

Breuer, J., & Freud, S. Studies in hysteria (1893–1895). In *Standard edition of the complete psychological works of Sigmund Freud.* London: Hogarth, 1955.

Breuning, S. E., & Davidson, N. A. Effects of psychotrophic drugs on intelligence test performance of institutionalized mentally retarded adults. *American Journal of Mental Deficiency,* 1981, *85,* 575–579.

Brigham, J. C., Ricketts, J. L., & Johnson, R. C. Reported maternal and paternal behaviors of solitary and social delinquents. *Journal of Consulting Psychology,* 1967, *31,* 420–422.

Broadhurst, P. L. Studies in psychogenetics: The quantitative inheritance of behavior in rats investigated by selective and cross-breeding. *Bulletin of the British Psychological Society,* 1958, *34(2A).*

Brody, S. Aims and methods in child psychotherapy. *Journal of the American Academy of Child Psychiatry,* 1964, *3,* 385–412.

Brodzinsky, D. M., Messer, S. B., & Tew, J. D. Sex differences in children's expression and control of fantasy and overt aggression. *Child Development,* 1979, *50,* 372–379.

Broman, S. H. Perinatal anoxia and cognitive development in early childhood. In T. M. Field (Eds.), *Infants born at risk: Behavior and development.* Larchmont, NY: SP Medical & Scientific Books, 1979.

Brook, R. C., & Whitehead, P. C. *Drug-free therapeutic community. An evaluation.* New York: Human Sciences Press, 1980.

Broverman, D. M., Klaiber, E. L., & Vogel, W. Gonadal hormones and cognitive functioning. In J. E. Parsons (Eds.), *The psychobiology of sex differences and sex roles.* Washington, DC: Hemisphere, 1980.

Brown, C. *Manchild in the promised land.* New York: Signet, 1965.

Brown, E. S., & Warner, R. Mental development of phenylketonuric children on or off diet after the age of six. *Psychological Medicine,* 1976, *6,* 287.

Brown, G., Chadwick, O., Shaffer, D., Rutter, M., & Traub, M. A prospective study of children with head injuries. III. Psychiatric sequelae. *Psychological Medicine,* 1981, *11,* 63–78.

Brown, G. W., & Rutter, M. The measurement of family activities and relationships: A methodological study. *Human Relations,* 1966, *19,* 241–263.

Brown, J. L. Prognosis from presenting symptoms of preschool children with atypical development. *American Journal of Orthopsychiatry,* 1960, *30,* 382–390.

Brown, J. L. Follow-up of children with atypical development (infantile psychosis). *American Journal of Orthopsychiatry,* 1963, *33,* 855–861.

Brown, P., & Elliott, R. Control of aggression in a nursery school class. *Journal of Experimental Child Psychology,* 1965, *2,* 103–107.

Brubakken, D. M., Derouin, J. A., & Morrison, H. L. *Treatment of psychotic and neurologically impaired children: A systems approach.* New York: Van Nostrand, 1980.

Bruininks, R. H., Hauber, F. A., & Kudla, M. J. National survey of community residential facilities: A profile of facilities and residents in 1977. *American Journal of Mental Deficiency,* 1980, *84,* 470–478.

Bruininks, R. H., Rynders, J. E., & Gross, J. C. Social acceptance of mildly retarded pupils in resource rooms and regular classes. *American Journal of Mental Deficiency,* 1974, *78,* 377–383.

Bucher, B., & Lovaas, O. I. Use of aversive stimulation in behavior modification. In M. R. Jones (Ed.), *Miami Symposium on the Prediction of Behavior, 1967: Aversive Stimulation.* Coral Gables, FL: University of Miami Press, 1968.

Buchsbaum, M., & Wender, P. Averaged evoked responses in normal and minimally brain dysfunctioned children treated with amphetamine. A preliminary report. *Archives of General Psychiatry,* 1973, *29,* 764–770.

Buchsbaum, M. S., Coursey, R. S., & Murphy, D. L. The biochemical high-risk paradigm: Behavioral and familial correlates of low platelet monoamine oxidase activity. *Science,* 1976, *194,* 339–341.

Buck, J. N. *The House-Tree-Person technique (Revised Manual)*. Beverly Hills. CA: Western Psychological Services, 1966.

Budoff, M., & Gottlieb, J. Special-class EMR children mainstreamed: A study of an aptitude (learning potential) x treatment interaction. *American Journal of Mental Deficiency*, 1976, *81*, 1−11.

Budoff, M., & Siperstein, G. N. Low income children's attitudes toward mentally retarded children: Effects of labeling and academic behavior. *American Journal of Mental Deficiency*, 1978, *82*, 474−479.

Bugental, D. B., Collins, S., Collins, L., & Chaney, L. A. Attributional and behavioral changes following two behavior management interventions with hyperactive boys: A follow-up study. *Child Development*, 1978, *49*, 247−250.

Bugental, D. B., Whalen, C. K., & Henker, B. Causal attributions of hyperactive children and motivational assumptions of two behavior-change approaches: Evidence for an interactionist position. *Child Development*, 1977, *48*, 874−884.

Burns, D., Brady, J. P., & Kuruvilla, K. The acute effect of haloperidol and apomorphine on the severity of stuttering. *Biological Psychiatry*, 1978, *13*, 255−264.

Buss, D. M. Predicting parent-child interactions from children's activity level. *Developmental Psychology*, 1981, *17*, 59−65.

Butler, E. W. Personality dimensions of delinquent girls. *Criminologica*, 1965, *3*, 7−10.

Cameron, N. A., & Magaret, A. *Behavior pathology*. New York: Houghton, 1951.

Campagna, A. F., & Harter, S. Moral judgment in sociopathic and normal children. *Journal of Personality and Social Psychology*, 1975, *31*, 199−205.

Campbell, M. Pharmacotherapy. In M. Rutter & E. Schopler (Eds.), *Autism: A reappraisal of concepts and treatment*. New York: Plenum, 1978.

Campbell, M., Anderson, L. T., Meier, M., Cohen, I. L., Small, A. M., Samit, C., & Sachar, E. J. A comparison of haloperidol and behavior therapy and their interaction in children. *Journal of the American Academy of Child Psychiatry*, 1978, *17*, 640−655.

Campbell, M., & Small, A. M. Chemotherapy. In B. B. Wolman, J. Egan, & A. O. Ross (Eds.), *Handbook of treatment of mental disorders in childhood and adolescence*. Englewood Cliffs, NJ: Prentice-Hall, 1978.

Campbell, S. B., Endman, M., & Bernfeld, G. A three-year follow-up of hyperactive preschoolers into elementary school. *Journal of Child Psychology and Psychiatry*, 1977, *18*, 239−249.

Campbell, S. B., & Paulauskas, S. Peer relations in hyperactive children. *Journal of Child Psychology and Psychiatry*, 1979, *20*, 233−246.

Campbell, S. B., Schleifer, M., Weiss, G., & Perlman, T. A two-year follow-up of hyperactive preschoolers. *American Journal of Orthopsychiatry*, 1977, *47*, 149−162.

Cantwell, D. P. A model for the investigation of psychiatric disorders of childhood. Its application in genetic studies of the hyperkinetic syndrome. In E. J. Anthony (Eds.), *Explorations in child psychiatry*. New York: Plenum, 1975.

Caplan, A. I., & Ordahl, C. P. Irreversible gene repression model of development. *Science*, 1978, *201*, 120−130.

Carlson, G. A., & Strober, M. Manic-depressive illness in early adolescence: A study of clinical and diagnostic characteristics in six cases. *Journal of the American Academy of Child Psychiatry*, 1978, *17*, 138−153.

Carlson, G., & Strober, M. Affective disorders in adolescence. *Psychiatric Clinics of North America*, 1979, *2*, 511−526.

Carr, E. G. Teaching autistic children to use sign language: Some research issues. *Journal of Autism and Childhood Schizophrenia*, 1979, *9*, 345–359.

Carr, J. The severely retarded autistic child. In L. Wing (Ed.), *Early childhood autism: clinical, educational, and social aspects (2nd ed.)*. New York: Pergamon Press, 1976.

Casler, L. Perceptual deprivation in institutional settings. In G. Newton & S. Levine (Eds.). *Early experience and behavior*. Springfield, IL: Thomas, 1968.

Cater, D., & Strickland, S. *TV violence and the child: The evolution and fate of the Surgeon General's Report*. New York: Russell Sage Foundation, 1975.

Cattell, R. B. *Personality*. New York: McGraw-Hill, 1950.

Cattell, R. B., & Dreger, R. M. (Eds.). *Handbook of modern personality theory*. Washington DC: Hemisphere, 1977.

Cavallaro, S. A., & Porter, R. H. Peer preferences of at-risk and normally developing children in a preschool mainstream classroom. *American Journal of Mental Deficiency*, 1980, *84*, 357–366.

Cavan, R. S., & Cavan, J. T. *Delinquency and crime: Cross-cultural perspectives*. Philadelphia: J. B. Lippincott, 1968.

Cavior, H. E., & Schmidt, A. A test of the effectiveness of a differential treatment strategy at the Robert F. Kennedy Center. *Criminal Justice and Behavior*, 1978, *5*, 131–139.

Cernkovich, S. A., & Giordano, P. C. A comparative analysis of male and female delinquency. *Sociological Quarterly*, 1979, *20*, 131–145.

Cerreto, M. C., & Tuma, J. M. Distribution of DSM-II diagnoses in a child setting. *Journal of Abnormal Child Psychology*, 1977, *5*, 147–155.

Chalfant, J. C., & Scheffelin, M. A. *Central processing dysfunctions in children*. Washington, D.C.: United States Government Printing Office, 1969.

Chamove, A. S., Waisman, H. A., & Harlow, H. F. Abnormal social behavior in phenylketonuric monkeys. *Journal of Abnormal Psychology*, 1970, *76*, 62–68.

Chandler, M. J. Egocentrism and antisocial behavior: The assessment and training of social perspective-taking skills. *Developmental Psychology*, 1973, *9*, 326–332.

Chandler, M. J., Paget, K. F., & Koch, D. A. The child's demystification of psychological defense mechanisms: A structural and developmental analysis. *Developmental Psychology*, 1978, *14*, 197–205.

Chassan, J. B. *Research design in clinical psychology (2nd ed.)*. New York: Irvington Publishers, 1978.

Chein, I., Gerard, D. L., Lee, R. S., & Rosenfeld, E. *The road to H: Narcotics, delinquency, and social policy*. New York: Basic Books, 1964.

Chess, S. Autism in children with congenital rubella. *Journal of Autism and Childhood Schizophrenia*, 1971, *1*, 33–37.

Chess, S. Follow-up report on autism in congenital rubella. *Journal of Autism and Childhood Schizophrenia*, 1977, *7*, 69–81.

Chess, S., Thomas, A., & Birch, H. G. Distortions in developmental reporting made by parents of behaviorally disturbed children. *Journal of the American Academy of Child Psychiatry*, 1966, *5*, 226–234.

Christophersen, E. R., Barnard, J. D., Ford, D., & Wolf, M. M. The Family Training Program: Improving parent-child interaction patterns. In E. J. Mash, L. C. Handy, & L. A. Hamerlynck (Eds.), *Behavior modification approaches to parenting*. New York: Brunner/Mazel, 1976.

Claridge, G., Hume, W. I., & Canter, S. *Personality differences and biological variations: A study of twins.* Oxford: Pergamon, 1973.

Clark, R. W. *Freud: The man and the cause—A biography.* New York: Random House, 1980.

Clarke, A. M., & Clarke, A. D. B. *Early experience: Myth and evidence.* New York: Free Press, 1976.

Clayton, B. E. (Ed.). *Mental retardation: environmental hazards.* London: Butterworth, 1973.

Cleckley, H. *The mask of sanity (5th ed.).* St. Louis: Mosby, 1976.

Clement, P. W., Anderson, E., Arnold, J., Butman, R., Fantuzzo, J., & Mays, R. Self-regulation training for undercontrolled children. In L. Oettinger & L. V. Majovski (Eds.), *The psychologist, the school, and the child with MBD/LD.* New York: Grune & Stratton, 1978.

Clement, P. W., Roberts, P. V., & Lantz, C. E. Social models and token reinforcements in the treatment of shy withdrawn boys. *Proceedings, 78th Annual Convention, American Psychological Association,* 1970, 515—516.

Cloninger, C. R., Christiansen, K. O., Reich, T., & Gottesman, I. I. Implications of sex differences in the prevalence of antisocial personality, alcoholism, and criminality for familial transmission. *Archives of General Psychiatry,* 1978, *35,* 941—951.

Cloward, R., & Ohlin, L. *Delinquency and opportunity.* Glencoe, IL: Free Press, 1960.

Cochran, M. L., & Pedrini, D. T. The concurrent validity of the 1965 WRAT with adult retardates. *American Journal of Mental Deficiency,* 1969, *73,* 654—656.

Cohen, D. J., Caparulo, B. K., Gold, J. R., Waldo, M. C., Shaywitz, B. A., Ruttenberg, B. A., & Rimland, B. Agreement in diagnosis: Clinical assessment and behavior rating scales for pervasively disturbed children. *Journal of the American Academy of child Psychiatry,* 1978, *17,* 589—603.

Cohen, H. L., & Filipczak, J. *A new learning environment.* San Francisco: Jossey-Bass, 1971.

Cohen, S. Inhalants and solvents. In G. M. Beschner & A. S. Friedman (Eds.), *Youth drug abuse. Problems, issues, and treatment.* Lexington, MA: Heath, 1979.

Cohler, B. J., Grunebaum, H. U., Weiss, J. L., Hartman, C. R., & Gallant, D. H. Perceived life-stress and psychopathology among mothers of young children. *American Journal of Orthopsychiatry,* 1975, *45,* 58—73.

Colby, K. M. *The skeptical psychoanalyst.* New York: Ronald Press, 1958.

Coleman, M. Biochemical and organic abnormalities associated with the cognitive defects of infantile autism. In G. Serban (Ed.), *Cognitive defects in the development of mental illness.* New York: Brunner/Mazel, 1978.

Collins, W. A. (Ed.). *Development of cognition, affect, and social relations. Minnesota symposia on child psychology (Vol. 13).* Hillsdale, NJ: Erlbaum, 1980.

Commission of Inquiry into the Non-Medical Use of Drugs. *Cannabis.* Ottawa: Information Canada, 1972.

Conley, R. W. *The economics of mental retardation.* Baltimore: Johns Hopkins University Press, 1973.

Conners, C. K., Goyette, C. H., Southwick, D. A., Lees, J. M., & Andrulonis, P. A. Food additives and hyperkinesis: A controlled double-blind experiment. *Pediatrics,* 1976, *58* 154—166.

Conners, C. K., & Werry J. S. Pharmacotherapy. In H. C. Quay & J. S. Werry (Eds.), *Psychopathological disorders of childhood (2nd ed.)*. New York: Wiley, 1979.

Connolly, J. A. Intelligence levels of Down's syndrome children. *American Journal of Mental Deficiency*, 1978, *83*, 193−196.

Cooper, R. M., & Zubek, J. P. Effects of enriched and restricted early environments on the learning ability of bright and dull rats. *Canadian Journal of Psychology*, 1958, *12*, 159−164.

Corah, N. L., Anthony, E. J., Painter, P., Stern, J. A., & Thurston, D. Effects of perinatal anoxia after 7 years. *Psychological Monographs*, 1965, *79*, 1−34 (Whole No. 596).

Corman, L., & Gottlieb, J. Mainstreaming mentally retarded children: A review of research. In N. R. Ellis (Ed.), *International review of research in mental retardation (Vol. 9)*. New York: Academic Press, 1978.

Cornwell, A. C. Development of language, abstraction, and numerical concept formation in Down's syndrome children. *American Journal of Mental Deficiency*, 1974, *79*, 179−190.

Cornwell, A. C., & Birch, H. G. Psychological and social development in home-reared children with Down's syndrome (mongolism). *American Journal of Mental Deficiency*, 1969, *74*, 341−350.

Cortés, J. B., & Gatti, F. M. *Delinquency and crime: A biopsychosocial approach*. New York: Seminar Press, 1972.

Cott, A., Pavloski, R. P., & Black, A. M. Reducing epileptic seizures through operant conditioning of central nervous system activity: Procedural variables. *Science*, 1979, *203*, 73−75.

Cowen, E. L., Gesten, E. L., & Weissberg, R. P. An integrated network of preventively oriented school-based mental health approaches. In R. H. Price & P. E. Polister (Eds.), *Evaluation and action in the social environment*. New York: Academic Press, 1980.

Cowen, E. L., Orgel, A. R., Gesten, E. L., & Wilson, A. B. The evaluation of an intervention program for young school children with acting-out problems. *Journal of Abnormal Child Psychology*, 1979, *7*, 381−396.

Cox, A., & Rutter, M. Diagnostic appraisal and interviewing. In M. Rutter & L. Hersov (Eds.), *Child psychiatry. Modern approaches*. Philadelphia: Lippincott, 1976.

Cox, A., Rutter, M., Newman, S., & Bartak, L. A comparative study of infantile autism and specific developmental receptive language disorders. II. Parental Characteristics. *British Journal of Psychiatry*, 1975, *126*, 146−159.

Cox, B., & Sargent, H. TAT responses of emotionally disturbed and emotionally stable children: Clinical judgement versus normative data. *Journal of Projective Techniques*, 1950, *14*, 61−74.

Crafts, M., Stephenson, G., & Granger, C. A controlled trial of authoritarian and self-governing regimes with adolescent psychopaths. *American Journal of Orthopsychiatry*, 1964, *34*, 543−554.

Craighead, W. E., & Mercatoris, M. Mentally retarded residents as paraprofessionals: A review. *American Journal of Mental Deficiency*, 1973, *78*, 339−347.

Cramer, P. Defense mechanisms in adolescence. *Developmental Psychology*, 1979, *15*, 476−477.

Critchley, M. *The dyslexic child*. Springfield, IL: Thomas, 1970.

Cronbach, L. J., & Snow, R. E. *Aptitudes and instruction methods: A handbook for research on interactions*. New York: Irvington Publications, 1977.

Crook, T., & Eliot, J. Parental death during childhood and adult depression: A critical review of the literature. *Psychological Bulletin*, 1980, *87*, 252−259.

Curcio, F. Sensorimotor functioning and communication in mute autistic children. *Journal of Autism and Childhood Schizophrenia*, 1978, *8*, 281−292.

Curtiss, S. Dissociations between language and cognition: Cases and implications. *Journal of Autism and Developmental Disorders*, 1981, *11*, 15−30.

Cytryn, L., & McKnew, D. H. Affective disorders. In J. Noshpitz (Ed.), *Basic handbook of child psychiatry (Vol. 2)*. New York: Basic Books, 1979.

Cytryn, L., McKnew, D. H., & Bunney, W. E. Diagnosis of depression in children: A reassessment. *American Journal of Psychiatry*, 1980, *137*, 22−25.

Dahlstrom, W. G., Welsh, G. S., & Dahlstrom, L. E. *An MMPI handbook: Vol. 1. Clinical interpretation*. Minneapolis: University of Minnesota Press, 1972.

Darwin, C. *Origin of species*. London: J. Murray, 1859.

Darwin, C. A biographical sketch of an infant. *Mind*, 1877, *2*, 286−294.

Davids, A., & DeVault, S. Maternal anxiety during pregnancy and childbirth abnormalities. *Psychosomatic Medicine*, 1962, *24*, 464−470.

Davids, A., DeVault, S., & Talmadge, M. Anxiety, pregnancy, and childbirth abnormalities. *Journal of Consulting Psychology*, 1961, *25*, 74−77.

Davie, R., Butler, N., & Goldstein, H. *From birth to seven*. London: Longman, 1972.

Davis, K. Final note on a case of extreme isolation. *American Journal of Sociology*, 1947, *52*, 432−437.

Davis, M. H., Saunders, D., Creer, T., & Chai, H. Relaxation training facilitated by biofeedback apparatus as a supplemental treatment in bronchial asthma. *Journal of Psychosomatic Research*, 1973, *17*, 121−128.

Dawson, G., Warrenburg, S., & Fuller, P. *Cerebral lateralization in individuals diagnosed as autistic in early childhood*. Presented at Western Psychological Association, Honolulu, Hawaii, 1980.

Dawson, J. L. M. Effects of sex hormones on cognitive style in rats and men. *Behavior Genetics*, 1972, *2*, 21−42.

Dean, C. W., & Repucci, N. D. Juvenile correctional institutions. In D. Glaser (Ed.), *The handbook of criminology*. Chicago: Rand McNally, 1973.

DeFries, J. C., & Plomin, R. Behavioral genetics. In M. R. Rosenzweig & L. W. Porter (Eds.), *Annual Review of Psychology (Vol. 29)*. Palo Alto, CA: Annual Reviews, 1978.

Dekker, H. S. Freud in Germany. Revolution and reaction in science, 1893−1907. *Psychological Issues*, 1977, *11*, Monograph 41.

DeLong, G. R. Lithium carbonate treatment of selected behavior disorders in children suggesting manic-depressive illness. *Journal of Pediatrics*, 1978, *93*, 689−694.

DeMyer, M. K., Barton, S., Alpern, G. D., Kimberlin, C., Allen, J., Yang, E., & Steele, R. The measured intelligence of autistic children. *Journal of Autism and Childhood Schizophrenia*, 1974, *4*, 42−60.

DeMyer, M. K., Churchill, D. W., Pontius, W., & Gilkey, K. M. A comparison of five diagnostic systems for childhood schizophrenia and autism. *Journal of Autism and Childhood Schizophrenia*, 1971, *1*, 175−189.

DeMyer, M. K., Pontius, W., Norton, J. A., Barton, S., Allen, J., & Steele, R. Parental practices and innate activity in normal, autistic, and brain-damaged infants. *Journal of Autism and Childhood Schizophrenia*, 1972, *2*, 49−66.

DeMyer-Gapin, S., & Scott, T. J. Effects of stimulus novelty on stimulation seeking in antisocial and neurotic children. *Journal of Abnormal Psychology*, 1977, *86*, 96−98.

Denenberg, V. H., Garbanati, J., Sherman, G., Yutzey, D. A., & Kaplan, R. Infant stimulation induces brain lateralization in rats. *Science*, 1978, *201*, 1150−1152.

Dennis, W. *Children of the Creche*. New York: Appleton-Century-Crofts, 1973.

Dennis, W., & Najarian, P. Infant development under environmental handicap. *Psychological Monographs*, 1957, *71*(Whole No. 436).

DeSanctis, S. On some varieties of dementia praecox. In S. A. Szurek & I. N. Berlin (Eds.), *Clinical studies in childhood psychosis*. New York: Brunner/Mazel, 1973. (Originally published in Italian, 1906).

DesLauriers, A. M. The cognitive-affective dilemma in early infantile autism: The case of Clarence. *Journal of Autism and Childhood Schizophrenia*, 1978, *8*, 219−229.

DesLauriers, A. M. Early infantile autism and theraplay. In A. J. Finch & P. C. Kendall (Eds.), *Clinical treatment and research in child psychopathology*. Larchmont, NY: SP Medical & Scientific books, 1979.

DesLauriers, A. M., & Carlson, C. F. *Your child is asleep*. Homewood, IL: Dorsey, 1969.

Despert, J. L. Some considerations relating to the genesis of autistic behavior in children. *American Journal of Orthopsychiatry*, 1951, *21*, 335−350.

Despert, J. L. Differential diagnosis between obsessive-compulsive neurosis and schizophrenia in children. In P. H. Hoch & J. Zubin (Eds.), *Psychopathology of childhood*. New York: Grune & Stratton, 1955.

Deutsch, A. *The mentally ill in America (2nd ed.)*. New York: Columbia University Press, 1949.

DiCarlo, L. M. Differential diagnosis of congenital aphasia. *Volta Review*, 1960, *62*, 361−364.

Dinitz, S., Scarpitti, F. R., & Reckless, W. C. Delinquency vulnerability: A cross group and longitudinal analysis. *American Sociological Review*, 1962, *27*, 515−517.

Doane, J. A. Family interaction and communication deviance in disturbed and normal families: A review of research. *Family Process*, 1978, *17*, 357−376.

Dodge, K. A. Social cognition and children's aggressive behavior. *Child Development*, 1980, *51*, 162−170.

Doleys, D. M. Behavioral treatments for nocturnal enuresis in children: A review of the literature. *Psychological Bulletin*, 1977, *84*, 30−54.

Doleys, D. M. Assessment and treatment of childhood enuresis. In A. J. Finch & P. C. Kendall (Eds.), *Clinical treatment and research in child psychopathology*. Larchmont, NY: SP Medical and Scientific Books, 1979.

Doleys, D. M., Schwartz, M. S., & Ciminero, A. R. Elimination problems: Enuresis and encopresis. In E. J. Mash & L. G. Terdal (Eds.), *Behavioral assessment of childhood disorders*. New York: Guilford, 1981.

Doll, E. A. *Vineland Social Maturity Scale*. Circle Pines, Minn.: American Guidance Service, 1965.

Dollard, J., Doob, L. W., Miller, N. E., Mowrer, O. H., & Sears, R. R. *Frustration and aggression*. New Haven: Yale University Press, 1939.

Dollard, J., & Miller, N. *Personality and psychotherapy*. New York: McGraw-Hill, 1950.

Douglas, J. W. B. The age at which premature children walk. *Medical Officer*, 1956, *95*, 33–35.

Drabman, R. S. Child versus teacher-administered token programs in a psychiatric hospital school. *Journal of Abnormal Psychology*, 1973, *1*, 68–87.

Dreifuss, S. E. Delayed development of hemispheric dominance. *Archives of Neurology*, 1963, *8*, 510–514.

Dubowitz, V., & Hersov, L. Management of children with non-organic (hysterical) disorders of motor functions. *Developmental Medicine and Child Neurology*, 1976, *18*, 358–368.

Dugdale, R. L. *The Jukes* (1877). New York: Putnam, 1910.

Dunleavy, R. A., & Baade, L. E. Neuropsychological correlates of severe asthma in children 9–14 years old. *Journal of Consulting and Clinical Psychology*, 1980, *48*, 214–219.

Dunn, L. M., & Dunn, L. M. *Peabody Picture Vocabulary Test-Revised*. Circle Pines, MN: American Guidance Service, 1981.

Dunn, L. M., & Markwardt, F. C. *Peabody Individual Achievement Test*. Circle Pines, Minn: American Guidance Service, 1970.

DuPont, R. L. Marihuana: A review of the issues regarding decriminalization and legalization. In G. M. Beschner & A. S. Friedman (Eds.), *Youth drug abuse. Problems, issues, and treatment*. Lexington, MA: Heath, 1979.

Durlak, J. A. Description and evaluation of a behaviorally oriented school-based preventive mental health program. *Journal of Consulting and Clinical Psychology*, 1977, *45*, 27–33.

Dworkin, R. H., Burke, B. W., Maher, B. A., & Gottesman, I. I. A longitudinal study of the genetics of personality. *Journal of Personality and Social Psychology*, 1976, *34*, 510–518.

Edelbrock, C., & Achenbach, T. M. A typology of Child Behavior Profile patterns: Distribution and correlates in disturbed children aged 6 to 16. *Journal of Abnormal Child Psychology*, 1980, *8*, 441–470.

Edgerton, R. B., & Bercovici, S. M. The cloak of competence: Years later. *American Journal of Mental Deficiency*, 1976, *80*, 485–497.

Egeland, B., Breitenbucher, M., & Rosenberg, D. A prospective study of the significance of life stress in the etiology of child abuse. *Journal of Consulting and Clinical Psychology*, 1980, *48*, 195–205.

Ehrhardt, A. A. Prenatal hormonal exposure and psychosexual differentiation. In E. J. Sachar (Ed.), *Topics in psychodendocrinology*. New York: Grune & Stratton, 1975.

Ehrhardt, A. A., & Meyer-Bahlburg, H. F. L. Psychological correlates of abnormal pubertal development. *Clinics in Endocrinology and Metabolism*, 1975, *4*, 207–222.

Ehrhardt, A. A., & Meyer-Bahlburg, H. F. L. Effects of prenatal sex hormones on gender-related behavior. *Science*, 1981, *211*, 1312–1318.

Eibl-Eibesfeldt, I. *Ethology: The biology of behavior (2nd ed.)*. New York: Holt, Rinehart & Winston, 1975.

Eichorn, D. Physiological development. In P. H. Mussen (Ed.), *Carmichael's manual of child psychology (Vol. I)*. New York: Wiley, 1970.

Eisenberg, L. Psychopharmacology in childhood: A critique. In E. Miller (Ed.), *Foundations of child psychiatry*. New York: Pergamon Press, 1968.

Eisenberg, L., & Kanner, L. Early infantile autism, 1943–1955. *American Journal of Orthopsychiatry*, 1956, *26*, 556–566.

Eisenberg-Berg, N., & Hand, M. The relationship of preschoolers' reasoning about prosocial moral conflicts to prosocial behavior. *Child Development*, 1979, *50*, 356–363.

Eisenberg-Berg, N., & Neal, C. Children's moral reasoning about their own spontaneous prosocial behavior. *Developmental Psychology*, 1979, *15*, 228–229.

Elkind, D. *The child and society: Essays in applied child development*. New York: Oxford University Press, 1979.

Elliot, C. D., & Pumfrey, P. D. The effects of nondirective play therapy on some maladjusted boys. *Educational Research*, 1972, *14*, 157–161.

Ellis, A. Rational-emotive therapy and the school counselor. *The School Counselor*, 1975, *22*, 236–242.

Ellis, N. R. Current issues in mental retardation. *Division 33 Newsletter, American Psychological Association*, 1975, *2*, 1–2.

Elmer, E., Gregg, G. S., & Ellison, P. Late results of the 'failure to thrive' syndrome. *Clinical Pediatrics*, 1969, *8*, 584–589.

Embree, R. B. The status of college students in terms of IQs determined during childhood. *American Psychologist*, 1948, *3*, 259.

Empey, L. T., & Lubeck, S. G. *The Silverlake experiment: Testing delinquency theory and community intervention*. Chicago: Aldine, 1971.

Engel, E. Guest editorial: The making of an XYY. *American Journal of Mental Deficiency*, 1972, *77*, 123–127.

Engel, G. L. Attachment behavior, object relations and the dynamic-economic points of view. Critical review of Bowlby's Attachment and Loss. *International Journal of Psycho-Analysis*, 1971, *52*, 183–196.

Erikson, E. H. *Childhood and society. (2nd ed.)*. New York: Norton, 1963.

Erikson, E. H. *Identity, Youth, and Crisis*. New York, Norton, 1968.

Erikson, E. H. Elements of a psychoanalytic theory of psychosocial development. In S. I. Greenspan & G. H. Pollock (Eds.), *The course of life: Psychoanalytic contributions toward understanding personality development (Vol. I). Infancy and early childhood*. Adelphi, MD.: NIMH Mental Health Study Center, 1980.

Ernhart, C. B., Graham, F. K., Eichman, P. L., Marshall, J. M., & Thurston, D. Brain injury in the preschool child: Some developmental considerations: II. Comparison of brain injured and normal children. *Psychological Monographs*, 1963, *77* (Whole No. 573). pp. 17–33.

Ernhart, C. B., Graham, F. K., & Thurston, D. Relationship of neonatal apnea to development at three years. *Archives of Neurology*, 1960, *2*, 504–510.

Eron, L. D. Prescription for reduction of aggression. *American Psychologist*, 1980, *35*, 244–252.

Eron, L. D., Walder, L. O., & Lefkowitz, M. M. *Learning of aggression in children*. Boston: Little, Brown, 1971.

Essen, J., & Peckham, C. Nocturnal enuresis in childhood. *Developmental Medicine and Child Neurology,* 1976, *18,* 577–589.

Evans-Jones, L. G., & Rosenbloom, L. Disintegrative psychosis in childhood. *Developmental Medicine and Child Neurology,* 1978, *20,* 462–470.

Exner, J. E. *The Rorschach: A comprehensive system.* New York: Wiley, 1978.

Eyman, R. K., O'Connor, G., Tarjan, G., & Justice, R. S. Factors determining residential placement of mentally retarded children. *American Journal of Mental Deficiency,* 1972, *76,* 692–698.

Eysenck, H. J. The inheritance of extraversion-introversion. *Acta Psychologica,* 1956, *12,* 95–110.

Eysenck, H. J. (Ed.). *Behavior therapy and the neuroses.* New York: Pergamon Press, 1960.

Eysenck, H. J. *Eysenck on extraversion.* New York: Wiley, 1973.

Eysenck, H. J. The learning theory model of neurosis—a new approach. *Behavior Research and Therapy,* 1976, *14,* 251–267.

Eysenck, H. J. *You and neurosis.* London: Temple Smith, 1977.

Eysenck, H. J., & Prell, D. B. The inheritance of neuroticism: An experimental study. *Journal of Mental Science,* 1951, *97,* 441–465.

Eysenck, H. J., & Rachman, S. *The causes and cures of neurosis.* San Diego: R. R. Knapp, 1965.

Fairbairn, W. R. D. *Psycho-analytic studies of the personality.* London: Tavistock, 1952.

Fanshel, D., & Shinn, E. *Children in foster care: A longitudinal investigation.* New York: Columbia University Press, 1978.

Farber, B. *Mental retardation. Its social context and social consequences.* Boston: Houghton-Mifflin, 1968.

Farber, S. L. *Identical twins reared apart. A reanalysis.* New York: Basic Books, 1981.

Fay, W. H. Personal pronouns and the autistic child. *Journal of Autism and Developmental Disorders,* 1979, *9,* 247–260.

Fechter, L. D., & Annau, Z. Toxicity of mild prenatal carbon monoxide exposure. *Science,* 1977, *197,* 680–682.

Feingold, B. F. *Why your child is hyperactive.* New York: Random House, 1975.

Feingold, B. F. Hyperkinesis and learning disabilities linked to the ingestion of artificial food colors and flavors. *Journal of Learning Disabilities,* 1976, *9,* 551–559.

Feldman, F., Cantor, D., Soll, S., & Bachrach, W. Psychiatric study of a consecutive series of 34 patients with ulcerative colitis. *British Medical Journal,* 1967, *3,* 14–17.

Feldman, H. W., Agar, M. H., & Beschner, G. M. *Angel dust.* Lexington, MA: Heath, 1979.

Ferreira, A. *Prenatal environment.* Springfield, IL: Thomas, 1970.

Feshbach, S. Aggression. In P. H. Mussen (Ed.), *Carmichael's manual of child psychology (Vol. I).* New York: Wiley, 1970.

Finch, A. J., & Kendall, P. C. The measurement of anxiety in children: Research findings and methodological problems. In A. J. Finch & P. C. Kendall (Eds.), *Clinical treatment and research in child psychopathology.* Larchmont, NY: SP Medical and Scientific Books, 1979.

Finch, S. M., & Green, J. M. Personality disorders. In J. Noshpitz (Ed.), *Basic handbook of child psychiatry (Vol. 2).* New York: Basic Books, 1979.

Finch, S. M., & Hess, J. M. Ulcerative colitis in children. *American Journal of Psychiatry,* 1962, *118,* 819–826.

Finucci, J. M., Guthrie, J. T., Childs, A. L., Abbey, H., & Childs, B. The genetics of specific reading disability. *Annals of Human Genetics,* 1976, *40,* 1–23.

Fish, B. Drug therapy in children's psychiatric disorders. *Clinical Psychopharmacology. Modern Problems of Pharmacopsychiatry,* 1968, *1,* 60–72.

Fish, B. Neurobiologic antecedents of schizophrenia in children. *Archives of General Psychiatry,* 1977, *34,* 1297–1313.

Fisher, S. M. Encopresis. In J. Noshpitz (Ed.). *Basic handbook of child psychiatry (Vol. 2).* New York: Basic Books, 1979.

Flapan, D., & Neubauer, P. B. *The assessment of early child development.* New York: Aronson, 1975.

Flavell, J. H., & Ross, L. (Eds.). *Social cognitive development: Frontiers and possible futures.* New York: Cambridge University Press, 1981.

Floeter, M. K., & Greenough, W. T. Cerebellar plasticity: Modification of Purkinje cell structure by differential rearing in monkeys. *Science,* 1979, *206,* 227–229.

Fo, W. S. O., & O'Donnell, C. R. The buddy system: Relationship and contingency conditions in a community intervention program for youth with professionals as behavior change agents. *Journal of Consulting and Clinical Psychology,* 1974, *42,* 163–169.

Foley, J. M. Effect of labeling and teacher behavior on children's attitudes. *American Journal of Mental Deficiency,* 1979, *83,* 380–384.

Folstein, S., & Rutter, M. Genetic influences and infantile autism. *Nature,* 1977, *265,* 726–728.

Ford, F. R. *Diseases of the nervous system in infancy, childhood, and adolescence (6th ed.).* Springfield, IL: Thomas, 1973.

Forehand, R., & Atkeson, B. M. Generality of treatment effects with parents as therapists: A review of assessment and implementation procedures. *Behavior Therapy,* 1977, *8,* 575–593.

Forgays, D. G. (Ed.). *Environmental influences on the development and prevention of psychopathology.* Hanover, NH: University Press of New England, 1978.

Fraiberg, S. H. *The magic years.* New York: Scribners, 1959.

Frank, G. H. The role of the family in the development of psychopathology. *Psychological Bulletin,* 1965, *64,* 191–205.

Frank, L. K. Projective methods for the study of personality. *Journal of Psychology,* 1939, *8,* 389–413.

Frankenburg, W. K., & Dodds, J. B. *The Denver Developmental Screening Test Manual.* Denver: University of Colorado Press, 1968.

Freedman, B. J., Rosenthal, L., Donahoe, C. P., Schlundt, D. G., & McFall, R. M. A social-behavioral analysis of skill deficits in delinquent and nondelinquent adolescent boys. *Journal of Consulting and Clinical Psychology,* 1978, *46,* 1448–1462.

Freedman, D. A. The role of early mother/child relations in the etiology of some cases of mental retardation. In G. Farrell (Ed.), *Congenital mental retardation.* Austin: University of Texas Press, 1969.

Freedman, D. G. An ethological approach to the genetical study of human behavior. In S. G. Vandenburg (Ed.), *Methods and goals in human behavior genetics.* New York: Academic Press, 1965.

Freedman, D. G. *Human infancy: An evolutionary perspective.* Hillsdale, NJ: Erlbaum, 1974.

Freeman, H. E., Klein, R. E., Townsend, J. W., & Lechtig, A. Nutrition and cognitive development among rural Guatemalan children. *American Journal of Public Health,* 1980, *70,* 1277−1285.

Freeman, M. A reliability study of psychiatric diagnosis in childhood and adolescence. *Journal of Child Psychology and Psychiatry,* 1971, *12,* 43−54.

Freud, A. *The ego and the mechanisms of defense* (1936). Translated by Cecil Baines. New York: International Universities Press, 1946.

Freud, A. *Normality and pathology in childhood.* New York: International Universities Press, 1965.

Freud, A. Indications and contraindications for child analysis. *Psychoanalytic Study of the Child,* 1968, *23,* 37−46.

Freud, A. A psychoanalytic view of developmental psychopathology. *Journal of the Philadelphia Association for Psychoanalysis,* 1974, *1,* 7−17.

Freud, A. Child analysis as the study of mental growth. In S. I. Greenspan & G. H. Pollock (Eds.), *The course of life: Psychoanalytic contributions toward understanding personality development (Vol. I): Infancy and early childhood.,* Adelphi, MD: NIMH Mental Health Study Center, 1980.

Freud, S. *New introductory lectures on psychoanalysis.* New York: Norton, 1933.

Freud, S. *An outline of psychoanalysis,* New York: Norton, 1940.

Freud, S. *A general introduction to psychoanalysis* (1916). New York: Permabooks, 1953.

Freud, S. The interpretation of dreams (1900). In *Standard edition of the complete psychological works of Sigmund Freud (Vol. 4).* London: Hogarth Press, 1953.

Freud, S. Three essays on the theory of sexuality (1905). In *Standard edition of the complete psychological works of Sigmund Freud (Vol. 7).* London: Hogarth Press, 1953.

Freud, S. Analysis of a phobia in a five-year-old boy. In *Standard edition of the complete works of Sigmund Freud (Vol. 7).* London: Hogarth Press, 1953.

Freud, S. Beyond the pleasure principle (1922). In *Standard edition of the complete psychological works of Sigmund Freud (Vol. 18).* London: Hogarth Press, 1955.

Freud, S. On the history of the psychoanalytical movement (1914). In *Standard edition of the complete psychological works of Sigmund Freud (Vol. 14).* London: Hogarth Press, 1957.

Freud, S. Repression (1915). In *Standard edition of the complete psychological works of Sigmund Freud (Vol. 14).* London: Hogarth Press, 1957.

Freud, S. Inhibition, symptoms, and anxiety (1926a). In *Standard edition of the complete psychological works of Sigmund Freud (Vol. 20).* London: Hogarth Press, 1959.

Freud, S. The question of lay analysis (1926b). In *Standard edition of the complete psychological works of Sigmund Freud (Vol. 20).* London: Hogarth Press, 1959.

Freud, S. The ego and the id (1923). In *Standard edition of the complete psychological works of Sigmund Freud (Vol. 19).* London: Hogarth, 1961.

Freud, S. The neuro-psychoses of defence (1894). In *Standard edition of the complete psychological works of Sigmund Freud (Vol. 3).* London: Hogarth, 1962.

Frodi, A. M. Contribution of infant characteristics to child abuse. *American Journal of Mental Deficiency,* 1981, *85,* 341−349.

Fromm, E. *Man for himself.* New York: Holt, 1947.

Frommer, E. A. Treatment of childhood depression with antidepressant drugs. *British Medical Journal,* 1967, *1,* 729−732.

Frostig, M., & Orpet, R. E. Cognitive theories and diagnostic procedures for children with learning difficulties. In B. B. Wolman (Ed.), *Manual of child psychopathology*. New York: McGraw-Hill, 1972.

Fuller, J. L., & Thompson, W. R. *Foundations of behavior genetics*. St. Louis: Mosby, 1978.

Fullerton, D. T., Kollar, E. J., & Caldwell, A. B. A clinical study of ulcerative colitis. *Journal of the American Medical Association*, 1962, *181*, 463–471.

Gadow, K., & Loney, J. (Eds.). *Psychological aspects of drug treatment for hyperactivity*. Boulder, CO.: Westview Press, 1980.

Galaburda, A. M., LeMay, M., Kemper, T. L., & Geschwind, N. Right-left asymmetries in the brain. *Science*, 1978, *199*, 852–856.

Galton, F. *Hereditary genius*. London: Macmillan, 1869.

Garbarino, J., & Gilliam, G. *Understanding abusive families*. Lexington, MA: Lexington Books, 1980.

Garbarino, J., & Sherman, D. High risk neighborhoods and high-risk families: The human ecology of child maltreatment. *Child Development*, 1980, *51*, 188–198.

Garduk, E. L., & Haggard, E. A. Immediate effects on patients of psychoanalytic interpretations. *Psychological Issues*, 1972, *7*, Monograph 28.

Gazzaniga, M. S. *The bisected brain*. New York: Appleton-Century-Crofts, 1970.

Geller, M. I., Kelly, J. A., Traxler, W. T., & Marone, F. J. Behavioral treatment of an adolescent female's bulimic anorexia: Modification of immediate consequences and antecedent conditions. *Journal of Clinical Child Psychology*, 1978, *7*, 138–142.

Gellis, S. S., & Hsia, D. Y. The infant of the diabetic mother. *American Journal of the Diseases of Children*, 1959, *97*, 1–41.

Gendreau, P., & Suboski, M. D. Classical discrimination eyelid conditioning in primary psychopaths. *Journal of Abnormal Psychology*, 1971, *77*, 242–246.

George, C., & Main, M. Social interactions of young abused children: Approach, avoidance, and aggression. *Child Development*, 1979, *50*, 306–318.

Gershon, E. S., Targum, S. D., Kessler, L. R., Mazure, C. M., & Bunney, W. E. Genetic studies and biologic strategies in the affective disorders. In A. G. Steinberg, A. G. Bearn, & B. Childs (Eds.), *Progress in Medical Genetics (Vol. 2)*. Philadelphia: Saunders, 1977. New Series.

Gesell, A. *The mental growth of the preschool child*. New York: Macmillan, 1925.

Gesell, A. A decade of progress in the mental hygiene of the preschool child. *Annals of the American Academy of Political and Social Science*, 1930, *151*, 143–148.

Gesell, A. The stability of mental growth careers. In G. M. Whipple (Ed.), *Intelligence: Its nature and nurture. Thirty-Ninth Yearbook of the National Society for the Study of Education. Part III*. Bloomington, IL: Public School Publishing Co., 1940, pp. 149–160.

Gesell, A. The autogenesis of behavior. In L. Carmichael (Ed.), *Manual of child psychology*. New York: Wiley, 1954.

Gesell, A., & Ilg, F.L. *Infant and child in the culture of today*. New York: Harper, 1943.

Gibbons, D. C. *Delinquent behavior*. Englewood Cliffs, NJ: Prentice-Hall, 1970.

Ginsburg, H., & Opper, S. *Piaget's theory of intellectual development (2nd Ed.)*. Englewood Cliffs, NJ: Prentice-Hall, 1979.

Gittelman, M., & Birch, H. G. Childhood schizophrenia: Intellect, neurologic status, perinatal risk, prognosis, and family pathology. *Archives of General Psychiatry,* 1967, *17,* 16−25.

Gittelman, R. The role of psychological tests for differential diagnosis in child psychiatry. *Journal of the American Academy of Child Psychiatry,* 1980, *19,* 413−438.

Gittleman, R., Abikoff, H., Pollack, E. G., Klein, D. F., Katz, S., & Mattes, J. A controlled trial of behavior modification and methylphenidate in hyperactive children. In C. K. Whalen & B. Henker (Eds.), *Hyperactive children. The social ecology of identification and treatment.* New York: Academic Press, 1980.

Gittleman-Klein, R., & Klein, D. F. School phobia: Diagnostic considerations in the light of imipramine effects. *Journal of Nervous and Mental Disease,* 1973, *156,* 199−215.

Glasgow, R. E., & Rosen, G. M. Behavioral bibliotherapy: A review of self-help behavior therapy manuals. *Psychological Bulletin,* 1978, *85,* 1−23.

Glennon, B., & Weisz, J. R. An observational approach to the assessment of anxiety in young children. *Journal of Consulting and Clinical Psychology,* 1978, *46,* 1246−1257.

Glick, S. J. First follow-up study of Glueck Table to identify predelinquents at school entrance. In S. Glueck & E. Glueck (Eds.), *Identification of predelinquents. Validation studies and some suggested uses of Glueck Table.* New York: Intercontinental Medical Book Corp., 1972.

Glueck, S., & Glueck, E. *Towards a typology of juvenile offenders: Implications for therapy and prevention.* New York: Grune & Stratton, 1970.

Glueck, S., & Glueck, E. *Identification of pre-delinquents: Validation studies and some suggested uses of Glueck Table.* New York: Intercontinental Medical Book Corp, 1972.

Goddard, H. H. *The Kallikak family: A study in the heredity of feeble-mindedness.* New York: Macmillan, 1912.

Goldberg, L., & Wilensky, H. Aggression in children in an urban clinic. *Journal of Personality Assessment,* 1976, *40,* 73−80.

Goldenberg, I., & Goldenberg, H. *Family therapy: An overview.* Monterey, CA: Brooks/ Cole 1980.

Goldfarb, W. *Childhood schizophrenia.* Cambridge: Harvard University Press, 1961.

Goldfarb, W., Goldfarb, N., & Pollack, R. A. Treatment of childhood schizophrenia: A three-year comparison of day and residential treatment. *Archives of General Psychiatry,* 1966, *14,* 119−128.

Goldfarb, W., Meyers, D. I., Florsheim, J., & Goldfarb, N. Psychotic children grow up: A prospective follow-up study in adolescence and adulthood. *Issues in Child Mental Health,* 1978, *5,* 108−172.

Goldfarb, W., Spitzer, R. L., & Endicott, J. A. A study of psychopatholoy of parents of psychotic children by structured interview. *Journal of Autism and Childhood Schizophrenia,* 1976, *6,* 327−338.

Goldman, P. S., & Lewis, M. E. Developmental biology of brain damage and experience. In C. W. Cotman (Ed.), *Neuronal plasticity.* New York: Raven Press, 1978.

Goldschmid, M. L., & Domino, G. Some para-diagnostic implications of the IQ among mentally retarded patients. *Training School Bulletin,* 1965, *61,* 178−83.

Goldsmith, H. H., & Gottesman, I. I. Origins of variations in behavioral style: A longitudinal study of temperament in young twins. *Child Development,* 1981, *52,* 91−103.

Goldstein, H. Social and occupational adjustment. In H. A. Stevens & R. Heber (Eds.), *Mental retardation: A review of research*. Chicago: University of Chicago Press, 1964.

Goldstein, H. The efficacy of special classes and regular classes in the education of educable mentally retarded children. In J. Zubin & G. A. Jervis (Eds.), *Psychopathology of mental development*. New York: Grune & Stratton, 1967.

Goldstein, T. America is fresh out of prisons. *New York Times,* 1978, *127,* 16E.

Goldstein, J., Freud, A., & Solnit, A. J. *Beyond the best interests of the child (New ed. with epilogue)*. New York: Free Press, 1979.

Goldstein, R., Landau, W. M., & Kleffner, F. R. Neurologic observations in a population of deaf and aphasic children. *Annals of Otology, Rinology, and Laryngology,* 1960, *69,* 756–767.

Gollay, E., Freedman, R., Wyngaarden, M., & Kurtz, N. R. *Coming back: The community experiences of deinstitutionalized mentally retarded people*. Cambridge, MA: Abt Books, 1978.

Goodenough, F. L. Trends in modern psychology. *Psychological Bulletin,* 1934, *31,* 81–97.

Goodman, S. (Ed.). *Psychoanalytic education and research: The current situation and future possibilities*. New York: International Universities Press, 1977.

Goodman, L. S., & Gilman, A. *The pharmacological basis of therapeutics (5th ed.)*. New York: Macmillan, 1975.

Gordon, T. *Parent effectiveness training*. New York: Peter H. Wyden, 1970.

Gottesman, I. I. Heritability of personality: A demonstration. *Psychological Monographs,* 1963, *77*(Whole No. 572).

Gottesman, I. I. Personality and natural selection. In S. G. Vandenberg (Ed.), *Methods and goals in human behavior genetics*. New York: Academic Press, 1965.

Gottesman, I. I. Genetic variance in adaptive personality traits. *Journal of Child Psychiatry and Psychology,* 1966, *7,* 199–208.

Gottesman, I. I. Beyond the fringe—Personality and psychopathology. In D. C. Glass (Ed.), *Genetics*. New York: Rockefeller University Press, 1968.

Gottesman, I. I. Schizophrenia and genetics: Toward understanding uncertainty. *Psychiatric Annals,* 1979, *9,* 1–12.

Gottesman, I. I., & Shields, J. *Schizophrenia and genetics. A twin study vantage point*. New York: Academic Press, 1972.

Gottlieb, J. Attitudes toward retarded children: Effects of labeling and behavioral aggressiveness. *Journal of Educational Psychology,* 1975, *67,* 581–585.

Gottlieb, J., & Budoff, M. Social acceptability of retarded children in nongraded schools differing in architecture. *American Journal of Mental Deficiency,* 1973, *78,* 15–19.

Gottschalk, L. A., Titchener, J. L., Piker, H. N., & Stewart, S. S. Psychosocial factors associated with pregnancy in adolescent girls: A preliminary report. *Journal of Nervous and Mental Disease,* 1964, *138,* 524–534.

Gouin-Décarie, T. A study of the mental and emotional development of the thalidomide child. In B. M. Foss (Ed.), *Determinants of infant behavior*. Vol. IV. London: Methuen, 1961.

Gouin-Décarie, T. *Intelligence and affectivity in early childhood*. New York: International Universities Press, 1965.

Goy, R. W. Organizing effects of androgen on the behavior of rhesus monkeys. In R. P. Michael (Ed.), *Endocrinology and human behavior*. London: Oxford University Press, 1968.

Goyette, C. H., Conners, C. K., Petti, T. A., & Curtis, L. E. Effects of artificial colors on hyperkinetic children: A double-blind challenge study. *Psychopharmacology Bulletin,* 1978, *14,* 39–40.

Grace, W. J., & Graham, D. T. Relationship of specific attitudes and emotions to certain bodily diseases. *Psychosomatic Medicine,* 1952, *14,* 242–251.

Graham, D. T., Stern, J. A., & Winokur, G. Experimental investigation of the specificity of attitude hypothesis in psychosomatic disease. *Psychosomatic Medicine,* 1958, *20,* 446–457.

Graham, F. K., & Kendall, B. S. Memory-for-designs test: Revised general manual. *Perceptual and Motor Skills,* 1960, *11,* (Part VII) 147–188.

Graham, G. G. Effect of infantile malnutrition on growth. *Federation Proceedings,* 1967, *26,* 139–143.

Graham, J. R. *The MMPI: A practical guide.* New York: Oxford University Press, 1977.

Graziano, A. M., & DeGiovanni, I. S. The clinical significance of childhood phobias: A note on the proportion of child-clinical referrals for the treatment of children's fears. *Behavior Research and Therapy,* 1979, *17,* 161–162.

Graziano, A. M., DeGiovanni, I. S., & Garcia, K. A. Behavioral treatment of children's fears: A review. *Psychological Bulletin,* 1979, *86,* 804–830.

Green, H. *I never promised you a rose garden.* New York: Signet, 1964.

Green, J. Overview of adolescent drug use. In G. M. Beschner & A. S. Friedman (Eds.), *Youth drug abuse. Problems, issues, and treatment.* Lexington, MA: Heath, 1979.

Greenfield, J. *A child called Noah.* New York: Holt, Rinehart, and Winston, 1972.

Greenfield, J. *A place for Noah.* New York: Holt, Rinehart, and Winston, 1978.

Greenspan, S. I. An integrated approach to intelligence and adaptation. A synthesis of psychoanalytic and Piagetian developmental psychology. *Psychological Issues,* 1979, Monograph 47/48.

Greenspan, S. I., Hatleberg, J. L., & Cullander, C. C. H. A developmental approach to systematic personality assessment: Illustrated with the case of a six year old child. In S. I. Greenspan & G. H. Pollock (Eds.), *The course of life: Psychoanalytic contributions toward understanding personality development (Vol. II): Latency, Adolescence, and youth.* Adelphi, MD: NIMH Mental Health Study Center, 1980.

Greenspan, S., & Shoultz, B. Why mentally retarded adults lose their jobs: Social competence as a factor in work adjustemnt. *Applied Research in Mental Retardation,* 1981, *2,* 23–38.

Griesinger, W. *Die Pathologie und Therapie der psychischen Krankheiten* (1845). Translated as *Mental pathology and therapeutics* by C. L. Robertson & J. Rutherford. London: New Sydenham Society, 1867.

Grob, G. N. *Mental institutions in America: Social policy to 1875.* New York: Free Press, 1973.

Grossman, H. J. *Manual on terminology and classification in mental retardation.* Washington, DC: American Association on Mental Deficiency, 1977.

Group for the Advancement of Psychiatry. Psychopathological disorders in childhood: Theoretical considerations and a proposed classification. *GAP Report No. 62,* 1966.

Group for the Advancement of Psychiatry. The field of family therapy. *GAP Report No. 78,* 1970.

Gruen, G. E., & Vore, D. A. Development of conservation in normal and retarded children. *Developmental Psychology,* 1972, *6,* 146−157.

Guerney, L. F. Filial therapy program. In D. H. L. Olson (Ed.), *Treating relationships.* Lake Mills, IA: Graphic Publishing, 1976.

Guerney, L. F., & Wolfgang, G. Long-range evaluation of effects on foster parents of a foster parent skills training program. *Journal of Clinical Child Psychology,* 1981, *10,* 33−37.

Gunzberg, H. C. *Social competence and mental handicap: An introduction to social education (2nd ed., revised reprint).* Baltimore: Williams & Wilkins, 1975.

Guttman, E. S. Effects of short-term psychiatric treatment for boys in two California Youth Authority Institutions. Cited by D. C. Gibbons, *Delinquent behavior.* Englewood Cliffs, NJ: Prentice-Hall, 1970.

Guzé, S. Validating criteria for psychiatric diagnosis: The Washington University approach. In M. S. Akiskal & W. L. Webb (Eds.), *Psychiatric diagnosis: Exploration of biological predictors.* New York: Spectrum, 1978.

Haberman, C. Cocaine may be chic, booze is the big worry. *New York Times,* December 30, 1979.

Hafner, A. J., Quast, W., Speer, D. C., & Grams, A. Children's anxiety scales in relation to self, parental, and psychiatric ratings of anxiety. *Journal of Consulting Psychology,* 1964, *28,* 255−558.

Haggard, E. A., Hiken, J. R., & Isaacs, K. S. Some effects of recording and filming on the psychotherapeutic process. *Psychiatry,* 1965, *28,* 169−191.

Hagin, R. A., Silver, A. A., & Kreeger H. *TEACH: A preventive approach for potential learning disability.* New York: Walker Educational Book Corp., 1976.

Hall, G. S. *Adolescence.* New York: Appleton, 1904.

Halmi, K. Anorexia nervosa: Demographic and clinical features in 94 cases. *Psychosomatic Medicine,* 1974, *36,* 18−25.

Halpern, W. I. The treatment of encopretic children. *Journal of the American Academy of Child Psychiatry,* 1977, *16,* 478−499.

Hamblin, R. L., Buckholdt, D., Ferritor, D., Kozloff, M., & Blackwell, L. *The humanization processes: A social, behavioral analysis of children's problems.* New York: Wiley-Interscience, 1971.

Hamburg, B. A. The biosocial bases of sex difference. In S. Washburn & P. Dolhinow (Eds.), *Perspectives on human evolution (Vol. 13)* Palo Alto, CA: W. A. Benjamin, 1977.

Hammer, E. F. The House-Tree-Person drawings as a projective technique with children. In A. I. Rabin & M. R. Haworth (Eds.), *Projective techniques with children.* New York: Grune & Stratton, 1960.

Hammill, D. D. Assessing and training perceptual motor processes. In D. D. Hammill & N. R. Badte (Eds.), *Teaching children with learning and behavior problems.* Boston: Allyn & Bacon, 1975.

Hamparian, D. M., Schuster, R., Dinitz, S., & Conrad, J. P. *The violent few: A study of dangerous juvenile offenders.* Lexington, MA: Lexington Books, 1978.

Hampe, E., Noble, H., Miller, L. C., & Barrett, C. L. Phobic children one and two years posttreatment. *Journal of Abnormal Psychology*, 1973, *82*, 446–453,

Hampson, R. B., & Tavormina, J. B. Relative effectiveness of behavioral and reflective group training with foster mothers. *Journal of Consulting and Clinical Psychology*, 1980, *48*, 294–295.

Handlon, J. H. Hormonal activity and individual responses to stresses and easements in everyday living. In R. Roessler & N. S. Greenfield (Eds.), *Physiological correlates of psychological disorder*. Madison: University of Wisconsin Press, 1962.

Hansen, H. Decline of Down's syndrome after abortion reform in New York State. *American Journal of Mental Deficiency*, 1978, *83*, 185–188.

Hanson, D. R., Gottesman, I. I., & Meehl, P. E. Genetic theories and the validation of psychiatric diagnoses: Implications for the study of children of schizophrenics. *Journal of Abnormal Psychology*, 1977, *86*, 575–588.

Hare, R. D. Detection threshold for electric shock in psychopaths. *Journal of Abnormal Psychology*, 1968, *73*, 268–272.

Hare, R. D., & Cox, D. N. Psychophysiological research on psychopathy. In W. H. Reid (Ed.), *The psychopath*. New York: Brunner/Mazel, 1978.

Hare, R. D., & Thorvaldson, S. A. Psychopathy and response to electrical stimulation. *Journal of Abnormal Psychology*, 1970, *76*, 370–374.

Harley, J. P., Matthews, C. G., & Eichman, P. Synthetic food colors and hyperactivity in children: A double-blind challenge experiment. *Pediatrics*, 1978, *62*, 975–983.

Harley, J. P., Ray, R. S., Tomasi, L., Eichman, P. L., Matthews, C. G., Chun, R., Cleeland, C. S., & Straisman, E. Hyperkinesis and food additives: Testing the Feingold hypothesis. *Pediatrics*, 1978, *61*, 818–828.

Harms, E. *Origins of modern psychiatry*. Springfield, IL: Thomas, 1967.

Harper, P. A., Fischer, K., & Rider, R. V. Neurological and intellectual status of prematures at three to five years of age. *Journal of Pediatrics*, 1959, *55*, 679–690.

Harris, D. B. *Children's drawings as measures of intellectual maturity*. New York: Harcourt Brace Jovanovich, 1963.

Harris, R. The EEG. In M. Rutter & L. Hersov (Eds.), *Child Psychiatry. Modern Approaches*. Philadelphia: Lippincott, 1977.

Harris, R. Relationship between EEG abnormality and aggressive and antisocial behavior—A critical appraisal. In L. A. Hersov, M. Berger, & D. Shaffer (Eds.), *Aggression and antisocial behavior in childhood and adolescence*. Oxford, England: Pergamon, 1978.

Hartmann, D. P., Roper, B. L., & Gelfand, D. M. An evaluation of alternative modes of child psychotherapy. In B. B. Lahey & A. E. Kazdin (Eds.), *Advances in clinical child psychology (Vol. 1)*. New York: Plenum Press, 1977.

Hartmann, H. *Ego psychology and the problem of adaptation*. New York: International Universities Press, 1939.

Hartmann, H. Comments on the psychoanalytic theory of the ego. *Psychoanalytic Study of the Child*, 1950, *5*, 74–96. (a)

Hartmann, H. Psychoanalysis and developmental psychology. *Psychoanalytic Study of the Child*, 1950, *5*, 7–17. (b)

Hartmann, H. *Essays on ego psychology*. New York: International Universities Press, 1964.

Hartmann, H., Kris, E., & Lowenstein, R. M. Notes on the theory of aggression. *Psychoanalytic Study of the Child*, 1949, *3*, 9–36.

Hartshorne, H., & May, M. *Studies in the nature of character*. New York: Macmillan, 1928–1930. 3 vols.

Hastings, J. E., & Barkley, R. A. A review of psychophysiological research with hyperkinetic children. *Journal of Abnormal Child Psychology*, 1978, *6*, 413–447.

Hatzenbuehler, L. C., & Schroeder, H. E. Desensitization procedures in the treatment of childhood disorders. *Psychological Bulletin*, 1978, *85*, 831–844.

Havelkova, M. Follow-up study of 71 children diagnosed as psychotic in preschool age. *American Journal of Orthopsychiatry*, 1968, *38*, 846–857.

Hay, W. M., Barlow, D. H., & Hay, L. R. Treatment of stereotypic cross-gender motor behavior using covert modeling in a boy with gender identity confusion. *Journal of Consulting and Clinical Psychology*, 1981, *49*, 388–394.

Hayes, S. C., Rincover, A., & Volosin, D. Variables influencing the acquisition and maintenance of aggressive behavior: Modeling versus sensory reinforcement. *Journal of Abnormal Psychology*, 1980, *89*, 254–262.

Haywood, H. C. What happened to mild and moderate mental retardation? *American Journal of Mental Deficiency*, 1979, *83*, 429–431.

Heal, L. W., Sigelman, C. K., & Switzky, H. N. Research on community residential alternatives for the mentally retarded. In N. R. Ellis (Ed.), *International review of research in mental retardation (Vol. 2)*. New York: Academic Press, 1978.

Heber, R. A manual on terminology and classification in mental retardation *(2nd ed.)*. *American Journal of Mental Deficiency, Monograph Supplement*, 1961.

Hechtman, L., Weiss, G., Finkelstein, J., Werner, A., & Benn, R. Hyperactives as young adults: Preliminary report. *Canadian Medical Journal*, 1976, *115*, 625–630.

Heinicke, C. M. Frequency of psychotherapeutic session as a factor affecting outcome: Analysis of clinical ratings and test results. *Journal of Abnormal Psychology*, 1969, *74*, 553–560.

Heinstein, M. *Behavior problems of young children in California*. Berkeley, CA.: California Department of Public Health, 1969.

Hemsley, R., Howlin, P., Berger, M., Hersov, L., Holbrook, D., Rutter, M., & Yule, W. Treating autistic children in a family context. In M. Rutter & E. Schopler (Eds.), *Autism: A reappraisal of concepts and treatment*. New York: Plenum, 1978.

Hendrick, I. Discussion of the "instinct to master." *Psychoanalytical Quarterly*, 1943, *12*, 561–565.

Henker, B., Whalen, C. K., & Collins, B. E. Double-blind and triple-blind assessments of medication and placebo responses in hyperactive children. *Journal of Abnormal Child Psychology*, 1979, *7*, 1–13.

Henn, F. A., Bardwell, R., & Jenkins, R. L. Juvenile delinquents revisited. Adult criminal activity. *Archives of General Psychiatry*, 1980, *37*, 1160–1163.

Herjanic, B., & Campbell, W. Differentiating psychiatrically disturbed children on the basis of a structured interview. *Journal of Abnormal Child Psychology*, 1977, *5*, 127–134.

Herjanic, B., Herjanic, M., Brown, F., & Wheatt, T. Are children reliable reporters? *Journal of Abnormal Child Psychology*, 1975, *3*, 41–48.

Hertzig, M. E. *Stability and change in non-focal neurological signs*. Presented at American Academy of Child Psychiatry Meetings, Chicago: October, 1980.

Hess, E. H. Ethology and developmental psychology. In P. H. Mussen (Ed.), *Carmichael's manual of child psychology (3rd ed., Vol. 1)*. New York: Wiley, 1970.

Heston, L. L. Psychiatric disorders in foster home reared children of schizophrenic mothers. *British Journal of Psychiatry,* 1966, *112,* 819−825.

Heston, L. L., & Denney, D. Interactions between early life experience and biological factors in schizophrenia. In D. Rosenthal & S. Kety (Eds.), *The transmission of schizophrenia.* New York: Pergamon, 1968.

Hetherington, E. M. Divorce: A child's perspective. *American Psychologist,* 1979, *34,* 851−858.

Hetherington, E. M., & Brackbill, Y. Etiology and covariation of obstinacy, orderliness, and parsimony in young children. *Child Development,* 1963, *34,* 919−943.

Hetherington, E. M., & Martin, B. Family interaction. In H. C. Quay & J. S. Werry (Eds.), *Psychopathological disorders of childhood (2nd ed.).* New York: Wiley, 1979.

Hetherington, E. M., Stouwie, R. J., & Ridberg, E. H. Patterns of family interaction and child-rearing attitudes related to three dimensions of juvenile delinquency. *Journal of Abnormal Psychology,* 1971, *78,* 160−176.

Hewett, F. M. *The emotionally disturbed child in the classroom.* Boston: Allyn & Bacon, 1968.

Hewett, F. M. Educational programs for children with behavior disorders. In H. C. Quay & J. S. Werry (Eds.), *Psychopathological disorders of childhood.* New York: Wiley, 1972.

Hewitt, L. E., & Jenkins, R. L. *Fundamental patterns of maladjustment: The dynamics of their origin.* Springfield, IL: State of Illinois, 1946.

Hirshoren, A. A comparison of the predictive validity of the Revised Stanford−Binet Intelligence Scale and the Illinois Test of Psycholinguistic Abilities. *Exceptional Children,* 1969, *35,* 517−521.

Hobbs, N. *Issues in the classification of children.* San Francisco: Jossey-Bass, 1975.

Hobbs, N. *Helping disturbed children and their families. Project Re-ED twenty years later.* Nashville, TN: Center for the Study of Families and Children, 1979.

Hockman, C. H. Prenatal maternal stress in the rat: Its effect on emotional behavior in the offspring. *Journal of Comparative and Physiological Psychology,* 1961, *54,* 679−684.

Hoffman, M. L. Psychological and biological perspectives on altruism. *International Journal of Behavioral Development,* 1978, *1,* 323−329.

Holinger, P. C. Violent deaths among the young: Recent trends in suicide, homocide, and accidents. *American Journal of Psychiatry,* 1979, *136,* 1144−1147.

Hollingsworth, C. E., Tanguay, P. E., Grossman, L., & Pabst, P. Long-term outcome of obsessive-compulsive disorder in childhood. *Journal of the American Academy of Child Psychiatry,* 1980, *19,* 134−144.

Hollon, S. D., & Beck, A. T. Cognitive therapy of depression. In P. C. Kendall & S. D. Hollon (Eds.), *Cognitive-behavioral interventions. Theory, research, and procedures.* New York: Academic Press, 1979.

Holmes, D. S. Investigations of repression: Differential recall of material experimentally or naturally associated with ego threat. *Psychological Bulletin,* 1974, *81,* 632−653.

Holmes, F. B. An experimental investigation of a method of overcoming children's fears. *Child Development,* 1936, *7,* 6−30.

Holt, L. E. *The care and feeding of children: A catechism for the use of mothers and children's nurse.* New York: Appleton, 1929.

Holt, M. M., & Hobbs, T. R. Problems of behavioral interventions with delinquents in an institutional setting. In A. J. Finch & P. C. Kendall (Eds.), *Clinical treatment and research in child psychopathology.* Larchmont, NY: SP Medical and Scientific Books, 1979.

Holt, R. R. *Methods in clinical psychology (Vol. 2). Prediction and research.* New York: Plenum, 1978.

Honigfeld, G., & Howard, A. *Psychiatric drugs. A desk reference (2nd ed.).* New York: Academic Press, 1978.

Honzik, M. P. Developmental studies of parent-child resemblance in intelligence. *Child Development,* 1957, *28,* 215–228.

Honzik, M. P. Consistency and change in intellectual functioning and personality characteristics during the life-span. International Congress of Psychology, Tokyo, Japan, 1972. *Proceedings of the XXth International Congress of Psychology,* pp. 224–225.

Honzik, M. P., MacFarlane, J. W., & Allen, L. The stability of mental test performance between two and eighteen years. *Journal of Experimental Education,* 1948, *17,* 309–324.

Hook, E. B. Behavioral implications of the human XYY genotype. *Science,* 1973, *179,* 139–150.

Hook, E. B., & Kim, D. S. Height and antisocial behavior in XY and XYY boys. *Science,* 1971, *172,* 284–286.

Hopkins, J., Perlman, T., Hechtman, L., & Weiss, G. Cognitive style in adults originally diagnosed as hyperactive. *Journal of Psychology and Psychiatry,* 1979, *20,* 209–216.

Horn, J. M., Loehlin, J. C., & Willerman, L. Intellectual resemblance among adoptive and biological relatives: The Texas Adoption Project. *Behavior Genetics,* 1979, *9,* 177–207.

Horne, A. M., & Patterson, G. R. Working with parents of aggressive children. In R. R. Abidin (Ed.), *Parent education and intervention handbook,* Springfield, IL: Thomas, 1980.

Horney, K. *Neurosis and Human Growth.* New York: Norton, 1950.

Horowitz, L., Sampson, H., Siegelman, E., Wolfson, A., & Weiss, J. On the identification of warded-off mental contents: An empirical and methodological contribution. *Journal of Abnormal Psychology,* 1975, *84,* 545–558.

Howlin, P. A. The effectiveness of operant language training with autistic children. *Journal of Autism and Developmental Disorders,* 1981, *11,* 89–105.

Hull, C. L. *Principles of behavior.* New York: Appleton-Century-Crofts, 1943.

Hull, C. L. *Essentials of behavior.* New Haven: Yale University Press, 1951.

Hull, C. L. *A behavior system: An introduction to behavior theory concerning the individual organism.* New Haven: Yale University Press, 1952.

Hung, D. W. Using self-stimulation as reinforcement for autistic children. *Journal of Autism and Childhood Schizophrenia,* 1978, *8,* 355–366.

Hunt, N. *The world of Nigel Hunt: The diary of a mongoloid youth.* New York: Garrett, 1967.

Hutt, C., & Ounsted, C. Gaze aversion and its significance in childhood autism. In S. J. Hutt & C. Hutt (Eds.), *Behavior studies in psychiatry.* New York: Pergamon Press, 1970.

Hutt, M. L. *The Michigan Picture Test-Revised.* New York: Grune & Stratton, 1980.

Hutt, S. J., & Hutt, C. (Eds.). *Behavior studies in psychiatry.* New York: Pergamon, 1970.

Hutt, S. J., Hutt, C., Lee, D., & Ounsted, C. A behavioral and electroencephalographic study of autistic children. *Journal of Psychiatric Research,* 1965, *3,* 181–197.

Ince, L. P. The use of relaxation training and a conditional stimulus in the elimination of epileptic seizures in a child: A case study. *Journal of Behavior Therapy and Experimental Psychology,* 1976, *7,* 39—42.

Inglis, J., & Lawson, J. S. Sex differences in the effects of unilateral brain damage on intelligence. *Science,* 1981, *212,* 693—695.

Ingram, G. L., Gerard, R. E., Quay, H. C., & Levinson, R. B. An experimental program for the psychopathic delinquent. *Journal of Research in Crime and Delinquency,* 1970, *7,* 24—30.

Isbell, H. Pharmacological factors in drug dependence. In S. Btesh (Ed.), *Drug abuse: Nonmedical use of dependence-producing drugs.* New York: Plenum Press, 1972.

Jacobs, P. A., Brunton, M., Melville, M. M., Brittain, R. P., & McClement, W. F. Aggressive behavior, mental subnormality, and the XXY male. *Nature,* 1965, *208,* 1351—1352.

Jacobson, M. *Developmental neurobiology (2nd ed.).* New York: Plenum, 1978.

Jaffe, J. H., & Kanzler, M. Tobacco use as drug abuse. In L. Brill & C. Winick (Eds.), *The yearbook of substance use and abuse.* New York: Human Sciences Press, 1980.

James, I. P. Delinquency and heroin addiction in Britain. *British Journal of Criminology,* 1969, *9,* 108—124.

Jastak, J. F., & Jastak, S. R. *Wide Range Achievement Test.* Wilmington, Del.: Jastak Associates, 1978.

Jenkins, R. L., & Boyer, A. Types of delinquent behavior and background factors. *International Journal of Social Psychiatry,* 1968, *14,* 65—76.

Jenkins, R. L., & Glickman, S. Common syndromes in child psychiatry. *American Journal of Orthopsychiatry,* 1946, *16,* 244—261.

Jensen, A. R. How much can we boost IQ and scholastic achievement? *Harvard Educational Review,* 1969, *39,* 1—123.

Jesness, C. Comparative effectiveness of behavior modification and transactional analysis programs for delinquents. *Journal of Consulting and Clinical Psychology,* 1975, *43,* 758—779.

Johnston, L. D. *The daily marijuana user.* Presented at National Alcohol and Drug Coalition, Washington, D. C., 1980.

Johnston, L. D., Bachman, J. G., & O'Malley, P. M. *Drugs and the nation's high school students. Five year national trends.* Rockville, MD: National Institute on Drug Abuse, 1979.

Johnston, L. D., O'Malley, P. M., & Eveland, L. K. Drugs and delinquency: A search for causal connections. In D. B. Kandel (Ed.), *Longitudinal research on drug use. Empirical findings and methodological issues.* Washington, DC: Hemisphere, 1978.

Joint Commission on Mental Health of Children. *Crisis in child mental health: Challenge for the 1970s.* New York: Harper, 1968.

Joint Commission on Mental Health and Illness. *Action for mental health.* New York: Science Editions, 1961.

Jones, E. *The life and work of Sigmund Freud.* New York: Basic Books, *Vol. 1,* 1953; *Vol. 2,* 1955; *Vol. 3,* 1957; abridged version: Anchor, 1963.

Jones, H. E. The environment and mental development. In L. Carmichael (Ed.), *Manual of child psychology.* New York: Wiley, 1954.

Jones, M. C. A laboratory study of fear: The case of Peter. *Pedagogical Seminary,* 1924, *31,* 308—315. (a).

Jones, M. C. The elimination of children's fears. *Journal of Experimental Psychology*, 1924, *7*, 382–390. (b)

Jones, R. R. *Therapeutic effects of the Teaching Family Group Home model*. Presented at the American Psychological Association, New York, September, 1979.

Jones, R. T. Marihuana: Human effects, In L. I. Iversen, S. D. Iversen, & S. H. Snyder (Eds.), *Drugs of abuse (Vol. 12)*. New York: Plenum, 1978.

Journal of the American College Health Association, 1970, *18, i*.

Journal of Abnormal Psychology, 1978, *87(1)*, Special issue: Learned helplessness as a model of depression.

Judd, L. L. Obsessive compulsive neurosis in children. *Archives of General Psychiatry*, 1965, *12*, 136–143.

Jung, R., & Hassler, R. The extrapyramidal motor system. In J. Field (Ed.), *Handbook of neurophysiology. Section I: Neurophysiology. Vol. II*. Washington, DC: American Physiological Society, 1960.

Jurkovic, G. J. The juvenile delinquent as a moral philosopher: A structural-developmental perspective. *Psychological Bulletin*, 1980, *88*, 709–727.

Jurkovic, G. J., & Prentice, N. M. Relation of moral and cognitive development to dimensions of juvenile delinquency. *Journal of Abnormal Psychology*, 1977, *86*, 414–420.

Kaffman, M., & Elizur, E. Infants who became enuretic: A longitudinal study of 161 Kibbutz children. *Monographs of the Society for Research in Child Development*, 1977, *42* (Serial No. 170).

Kagan, J., & Kogan, N. Individuality and cognitive performance. In P. H. Mussen (Ed.), *Carmichael's manual of child psychology. (Vol. 1, 3rd Ed.)*. New York: Wiley, 1970.

Kagan J., & Moss, H. A. *Birth to maturity*. New York: Wiley, 1962.

Kahn, J. V. Utility of the Uzgiris and Hunt scales of sensorimotor development with severely and profoundly retarded children. *American Journal of Mental Deficiency*, 1976, *80*, 663–665.

Kahn, M. The physiology of catharsis. *Journal of Personality and Social Psychology*, 1966, *3*, 278–286.

Kallmann, F. J., & Roth, B. Genetic aspects of preadolescent schizophrenia. *American Journal of Psychiatry*, 1956, *112*, 599–606.

Kandel, D. B. *Longitudinal research on drug use. Empirical findings and methodological issues*. Washington, DC: Hemisphere, 1978.

Kandel, D. B. Convergences in prospective longitudinal surveys of drug use in normal populations. In S. B. Sells, R. Crandall, M. Roff, J. S. Strauss, & W. Pollin (Eds.), *Human functioning in longitudinal perspective*. Baltimore: Williams & Wilkins, 1980.

Kanfer, F. H., & Phillips, J. S. *Learning foundations of behavior therapy*. New York: Wiley, 1970.

Kangas, J., & Bradway, K. Intelligence at middle age: A thirty-eight year follow-up. *Developmental Psychology*, 1971, *5*, 333–337.

Kanner, L. Autistic disturbances of affective contact. *Nervous Child*, 1943, *2*, 217–250.

Kanner, L. To what extent is early infantile autism determined by constitutional inadequacies? *Association for Research on Nervous and Mental Diseases, Proceedings*, (1953), 1954, *33*, 378–385.

Kanner, L. *Child psychiatry (3rd ed.)* Springfield, IL: Thomas, 1957.

Kanner, L. *A history of the care and study of the mentally retarded*. Springfield, IL: Thomas, 1964.

Kanner, L. Childhood psychosis: A historical overview. *Journal of Autism and Childhood Schizophrenia,* 1971, *1,* 14–19. (a)

Kanner, L. Follow-up study of eleven autistic children originally reported in 1943. *Journal of Autism and Childhood Schizophrenia,* 1971, *1,* 119–145. (b)

Kanner, L., Rodrigues, A., & Ashenden, B. How far can autistic children go in matters of social adaptation? *Journal of Autism and Childhood Schizophrenia,* 1972, *2,* 9–33.

Kaplan, A. R. (Ed.). *Human behavior genetics.* Springfield, IL: Thomas, 1976.

Kaplan, H. B., Smith, P. B., & Pokorny, A. D. Psychosocial antecedents of unwed motherhood among indigent adolescents. *Journal of Youth and Adolescence,* 1979, *8,* 181–207.

Karlsson, J. L. A two-locus hypothesis for inheritance of schizophrenia. In A. R. Kaplan (Ed.), *Genetic factors in "schizophrenia."* Springfield, IL: Thomas, 1972.

Karniol, R. Children's use of intention cues in evaluating behavior. *Psychological Bulletin,* 1978, *85,* 76–85.

Kasanin, J., & Kaufman, M. R. A study of the functional psychoses in childhood. *American Journal of Psychiatry,* 1929, *9,* 307–384.

Kashani, J. M., Husain, A., Shekim, W. O., Hodges, K. K., Cytryn, L., & McKnew, D. H. Current perspectives on childhood depression: An overview. *American Journal of Psychiatry,* 1981, *138,* 143–153.

Katz, P., & Zigler, E. Self-image disparity: A developmental approach. *Journal of Personality and Social Psychology,* 1967, *5,* 186–195.

Kaufman, A. S. *Intelligent testing with the WISC-R.* New York: Wiley, 1979.

Kaufman, A. S. Interpreting the WISC-R intelligently. In B. B. Lahey & A. E. Kazdin (Eds.), *Advances in clinical child psychology (Vol. 3),* New York: Plenum, 1980.

Kaufman, I. et al Success and failure in the treatment of childhood schizophrenia. *American Journal of Psychiatry,* 1962, *118,* 909–913.

Kazdin, A. E. *The token economy.* New York: Plenum, 1977.

Kazdin, A. E. *History of behavior modification: Experimental foundations of contemporary research.* Baltimore: University Park Press, 1978.

Kazdin, A. E. *Research design in clinical psychology.* New York: Harper & Row, 1980.

Kazdin, A. E., & Wilcoxon, L. A. Systematic desensitization and nonspecific treatment effects: A methodological evaluation. *Psychological Bulletin,* 1976, *83,* 729–758.

Kazdin, A. E., & Wilson, G. T. *Evaluation of behavior therapy: Issues, evidence, and research strategies.* Cambridge, MA: Ballinger, 1978.

Kellam, S. G., Brown, C. H., & Fleming, J. P. The prevention of teenage substance use: Longitudinal research and strategy. In T. J. Coates, A. C. Peterson, & C. Perry (Eds.), *Adolescent health: Crossing the barriers.* New York: Academic Press, 1982.

Kellam, S. G., Ensminger, M. E., & Turner, R. J. Family structure and the mental health of children. *Archives of General Psychiatry,* 1977, *34,* 1012–1022.

Kendall, P. C., & Finch, A. J. A cognitive-behavioral treatment for impulsivity: A group comparison study. *Journal of Consulting and Clinical Psychology,* 1978, *46,* 110–118.

Kendall, P. C., & Wilcox, L. E. Cognitive-behavioral treatment for impulsivity: Concrete versus conceptual training on non-self controlled problem children. *Journal of Consulting and Clinical Psychology,* 1980, *48,* 80–91.

Kendler, H. H., & Guenther, K. Developmental changes in classifactory behavior. *Child Development,* 1980, *51,* 339–348.

Kennedy, R. J. R. *A Connecticut community revisited: A study of the social adjustment of a group of mentally deficient adults in 1948 and 1960.* Hartford: Connecticut State Department of Health, Office of Mental Retardation, 1966.

Kennedy, W. A. School phobia: Rapid treatment of 50 cases. *Journal of Abnormal Psychology,* 1965, *70,* 285–289.

Kenny, T. J., Clemmens, R. L., Hudson, B. W., Lentz, G. A., Cicci, R., & Nair, P. Characteristics of children referred because of hyperactivity. *Journal of Pediatrics,* 1971, *79,* 618–622.

Kent, M. W., & Rolf, J. E. (Eds.). *Primary prevention of psychopathology. Vol. 3: Social competence in children.* Hanover, NH: University Press of New England, 1979.

Kessen, W. *The child.* New York: Wiley, 1965.

Kessen, W., Haith, M. M., & Salapatek, P. H. Human infancy: A bibliography and guide. In P. H. Mussen (Ed.), *Carmichael's manual of child psychology (Vol. 1).* New York: Wiley, 1970.

Kessler, J. W. Neurosis in childhood. In B. B. Wolman (Ed.), *Manual of child psychopathology.* New York: McGraw-Hill, 1972.

Kety, S. S., Rosenthal, D., Wender, P. H., Schulsinger, F., & Jacobsen, B. The biologic and adoptive families of adopted individuals who became schizophrenic: Prevalence of mental illness and other characteristics. In L. C. Wynne, R. L. Cromwell, & S. Matthysse (Eds.), *The nature of schizophrenia: New approaches to research and treatment.* New York: Wiley, 1978.

Khan, A. U., Staerk, M., & Bonk, C. Role of counter-conditioning in the treatment of bronchial asthma. *Journal of Psychosomatic Research,* 1973, *17,* 389–392.

Kinsbourne, M., & Swanson, J. M. Models of hyperactivity. Implications for diagnosis and treatment. In R. L. Trites (Ed.), *Hyperactivity in children. Etiology, measurement, and treatment implications.* Baltimore: University Park Press, 1979.

Kirigin, K. A., Braukmann, C. J., Fixsen, D. L., Phillips, E. L., & Wolf, M. M. *Is community based corrections effective?: An evaluation of Achievement Place.* Presented at the American Psychological Association, Chicago, 1975.

Kirk, S. A. Research in education. In H. A. Stevens & R. Heber (Eds.), *Mental retardation: A review of research.* Chicago: University of Chicago Press, 1964.

Kirk, S. A., McCarthy, J. J., & Kirk, W. D. *Illinois Test of Psycholinguistic Abilities.* Urbana: University of Illinois Press, 1968.

Klapper, Z. S., & Birch, H. G. A fourteen-year follow-up study of cerebral palsy: Intellectual change and stability. *American Journal of Orthopsychiatry,* 1967, *37,* 540–547.

Klebanoff, L. B. Parental attitudes of mothers of schizophrenic, brain-injured and retarded, and normal children. *American Journal of Orthopsychiatry,* 1959, *29,* 445–454.

Klein, M. *The psychoanalysis of children.* London: International Psychoanalytic Library, 1932.

Klein, N. C., Alexander, J. F., & Parsons, B. V. Impact of family systems intervention on recidivism and sibling delinquency: A model of primary prevention and program evaluation. *Journal of Consulting and Clinical Psychology,* 1977, *45,* 469–474.

Klein, N. C., Barton, C., & Alexander, J. F. Intervention and evaluation in family settings. In R. H. Price & P. E. Polister (Eds.), *Evaluation and action in the social environment.* New York: Academic Press, 1980.

Kline, P. *Fact and fantasy in Freudian theory.* London: Methuen, 1972.

Knobloch, H., & Pasamanick, B. (Eds.). *Gesell and Amatruda's Developmental Diagnosis: The evaluation and management of normal and abnormal development in infancy and early childhood (3rd ed.)*. Hagerstown, MD: Harper & Row, 1974.

Knobloch, H., & Pasamanick, B. Some etiological and prognostic factors in early infantile autism. *Pediatrics,* 1975, *55,* 182−191.

Koegel, R. L., & Egel, A. L. Motivating autistic children. *Journal of Abnormal Psychology,* 1979, *88,* 418−426.

Koegel, R. L., Schreibman, L., Britten, K., & Laitinen, R. The effects of schedule of reinforcement on stimulus overselectivity in autistic children. *Journal of Autism and Childhood Schizophrenia,* 1979, *9,* 383−397.

Kohlberg, L. Stage and sequence: The cognitive developmental approach to socialization. In D. A. Goslin (Ed.), *Handbook of socialization theory and research*. Chicago: Rand McNally, 1969.

Kohlberg, L. Moral stages and moralization: The cognitive developmental approach. In T. Lickona (Ed.), *Moral development and moral behavior*. New York: Holt, Rinehart, & Winston, 1976.

Kohlberg, L. The cognitive developmental approach to behavior disorders: A study of the development of moral reasoning in delinquents. In G. Serban (Ed.), *Cognitive defects in the development of mental illness*. New York: Brunner/Mazel, 1978.

Kohlberg, L., LaCrosse, J., & Ricks, D. The predictability of adult mental health from childhood behavior. In B. B. Wolman (Ed.), *Manual of child psychopathology*. New York: McGraw-Hill, 1972.

Kohlenberg, R. J. Operant conditioning of human anal and sphincter pressure. *Journal of Applied Behavior Analysis,* 1973, *6,* 201−208.

Kolvin, I. Aversive imagery treatment in adolescents. *Behavior Research and Therapy,* 1967, *5,* 245−248.

Kolvin, I., Garside, R. F., & Kidd, J. S. H. Studies in the childhood psychoses. IV. Parental personality and attitude and childhood psychoses. *British Journal of Psychiatry,* 1971, *118,* 403−406.

Kolvin, I., Ounsted, C., Richardson, L. M., & Garside, R. F. Studies in the childhood psychoses: III. The family and social background in childhood psychoses. *British Journal of Psychiatry,* 1971, *118,* 396−402.

Kolvin, I., Taunch, J., Currah, J., Garside, R. F., Nolan, J., & Shaw, W. B. Enuresis: A descriptive analysis and a controlled trial. *Developmental Medicine and Child Neurology,* 1972, *14,* 715−726.

Koppitz, E. M. *Psychological evaluation of children's human figure drawings*. New York: Grune & Stratton, 1968.

Koppitz, E. M. *The Bender Gestalt Test for young children (Vol. II)*. New York: Grune & Stratton, 1975.

Koppitz, E. M. *The Visual Aural Digit Span Test*. New York: Grune & Stratton, 1977.

Kornhaber, R. C., & Schroeder, H. E. Importance of model similarity in extinction of avoidance behavior in children. *Journal of Consulting and Clinical Psychology,* 1975, *43,* 601−607.

Kotses, H., Glaus, K. D., Crawford, P. L., Edwards, J. E., & Scherr, M. S. Operant reduction of frontalis EMG activity in the treatment of asthma in children. *Journal of Psychosomatic Research,* 1976, *20,* 453−459.

Kounin, J. Experimental studies of rigidity: I. The measurement of rigidity in normal and feebleminded persons. *Character and Personality, 1941, 9,* 251–272.

Kovacs, M. Rating scales to assess depression in school-aged children. *Acta Paedopsychiatrica, 1981, 46,* 305–315.

Kovacs, M., & Beck, A. T. An empirical-clinical approach toward a definition of childhood depression. In J. G. Schulterbrandt & A. Raskin (Eds.), *Depression in childhood: Diagnosis, treatment, and conceptual models.* New York: Raven Press, 1977.

Kraepelin, E. *Compendium der Psychiatrie.* Leipzig: Abel, 1883; 1893; 1899; 1915.

Kraus, P. E. *Yesterday's children: A longitudinal study of children from kindergarten into adult years.* New York: Wiley, 1973.

Kringlen, E. Adult offspring of two psychotic parents with special reference to schizophrenia. In L. C. Wynne, R. L. Cromwell, & S. Matthysse (Eds.), *The nature of schizophrenia. New approaches to research and treatment.* New York: Wiley, 1978.

Kronstadt, D., Oberlaid, F., Ferb, T. E., & Swartz, J. P. Infant behavior and maternal adaptations in the first six months of life. *American Journal of Orthopsychiatry, 1979, 49,* 454–464.

Kuhlmann, F. The Binet and Simon tests of intelligence in grading feebleminded children. *Journal of Psycho-asthenics, 1912, 16,* 173–193.

Kuhn, T. S. *The structure of scientific revolutions (2nd ed.).* Chicago: University of Chicago Press, 1970.

Kuhn, T. S. *The essential tension.* Chicago: University of Chicago Press, 1977.

Kurland, H. D., Yeager, C. T., & Arthur, R. J. Psychophysiologic aspects of severe behavior disorders. *Archives of General Psychiatry, 1963, 8,* 599–604.

Kurtz, P. D., Harrison, M., Neisworth, J. T., & Jones, R. T. Influence of 'mentally retarded' label on teachers' nonverbal behavior toward preschool children. *American Journal of Mental Deficiency, 1977, 82,* 204–206.

Kurtz, R. M., & Garfield, S. L. Illusory correlation: A further exploration of Chapman's paradigm. *Journal of Consulting and Clinical Psychology, 1978, 46,* 1009–1015.

Kushlick, A. Assessing the size of the problem of subnormality. In J. E. Meade & A. S. Parkes (Eds.), *Genetic and environmental factors in human ability.* Edinburgh: Oliver & Boyd, 1966.

Kushner, M. Faradic aversive controls in clinical practice. In C. Neuringer & J. L. Michael (Eds.), *Behavior modification in clinical psychology.* New York: Appleton-Century-Crofts, 1970.

Kutina, J., & Fischer, J. Anxiety, heart rate, and their interrelation at mental stress in school children. *Activitas Nervosa Superior, 1977, 19,* 89–95.

Kysar, J. E. The two camps in child psychiatry: A report from a psychiatrist father of an autistic and retarded child. *American Journal of Psychiatry, 1968, 125,* 103–109.

Lacey, J. I., Bateman, D. E., & VanLehn, R. Autonomic response specificity: An experimental study. *Psychosomatic Medicine, 1953, 15,* 8–21.

Lachar, D., & Gdowski, C. L. *Actuarial assessment of child and adolescent personality: An interpretive guide for the Personality Inventory for Children Profile.* Los Angeles, CA: Western Psychological Services, 1979.

Lahey, B. B., & Kazdin, A. E. *Advances in clinical psychology (Vol. 5).* New York: Plenum, 1982.

Lancioni, G. E. Infant operant conditioning and its implications for early intervention. *Psychological Bulletin*, 1980, *88*, 516−534.

Lang, P. J., & Melamed, B. G. Case report: Avoidance conditioning therapy of an infant with chronic ruminative vomiting. *Journal of Abnormal Psychology*, 1969, *74*, 1−8.

Langer, E. J., & Abelson, R. P. A patient by any other name . . .: Clinician group difference in labeling bias. *Journal of Consulting and Clinical Psychology*, 1974, *41*, 4−9.

Langhorne, J., & Loney, J. A four-fold model for subgrouping the hyperkinetic/MBD syndrome. *Child Psychiatry and Human Development*, 1979, *9*, 153−159.

Langner, T. S., Gersten, J. C., Eisenberg, J. G., Greene, E. L., & Herson, J. H., *Children under stress: Family and social factors in the behavior of urban children and adolescents*. New York: Columbia University Press, in press.

Lazar, I., Royce, J. M., Murray, H. M., Snipper, A. S., & Darlington, R. B. The lasting effects of early education. *Monographs of the Society for Research in Child Development*, 1982, 47(Serial No. 195).

Lazarus, A. A. The elimination of children's phobias by deconditioning. In H. J. Eysenck (Ed.), *Behavior therapy and the neuroses*. New York: Pergamon Press, 1960.

Lazarus, A. A. Group therapy of phobic disorders by systematic desensitization. *Journal of Abnormal and Social Psychology*, 1961, *63*, 504−510.

Lazarus, A. A., & Abramovitz, A. The use of "emotive imagery" in the treatment of children's phobias. *Journal of Mental Science*, 1962, *108*, 191−195.

Lazarus, A. A., Davison, G. C., & Polefka, D. A. Classical and operant factors in the treatment of a school phobia. *Journal of Abnormal Psychology*, 1965, *70*, 225−229.

Leahy, R. L., & Huard, C. Role taking and self-image disparity in children. *Developmental Psychology*, 1976, *12*, 504−508.

Ledwidge, B. Cognitive behavior modification or new ways to change minds: Reply to Mahoney and Kazdin. *Psychological Bulletin*, 1979, *86*, 1050−1053.

Lefkowitz, M. M., & Tesiny, E. P. Assessment of childhood depression. *Journal of Consulting and Clinical Psychology*, 1980, *48*, 43−50.

Leiter, R. G. *Leiter International Performance Scale*. Chicago: C. H. Stoelting, 1948.

Lejeune, J., Gautier, M., & Turpin, R. Study of the somatic chromosomes of nine mongoloid idiot children, 1959. In S. H. Boyer (Ed.), *Papers on human genetics*. Englewood Cliffs, N.J.: Prentice-Hall, 1963.

Lena, B. Lithium in child and adolescent psychiatry. *Archives of General Psychiatry*, 1979, *36*, 854−855.

Lennard, H. L., Epstein, L. J., Bernstein, A., & Ransom, D. C. Hazards implicit in prescribing psychoactive drugs. *Science*, 1970, *169*, 438−441.

Lenneberg, E. H. Understanding language without the ability to speak. *Journal of Abnormal and Social Psychology*, 1962, *65*, 419−425.

Lenneberg, E. H. *Biological foundations of language*. New York: Wiley, 1967.

Lenneberg, E. H. The effect of age on the outcome of central nervous system disease in children. In R. L. Isaacson (Ed.), *The neuropsychology of development*. New York: Wiley, 1968.

Lennox, C., Callias, M., & Rutter, M. Cognitive characteristics of parents of autistic children. *Journal of Autism and Childhood Schizophrenia*, 1977, *7*, 243−261.

Lentz, E. West Germany now discovers a deadly monkey on its back. *New York Times*, October 21, 1979, p. 10E.

Lerman, D. Evaluative studies of institutions for delinquents: Implications for research and social policy. *Social Work*, 1968, *13*, 55–64.

Lerner, S. E., & Burns, R. S. Youthful phencyclidine (PCP) users. In G. M. Beschner & A. S. Friedman (Eds.), *Youth drug abuse. Problems, issues, and treatment*. Lexington, MA: Lexington Books, 1979.

Leshner, A. I. *An introduction to behavioral endocrinology*. New York: Oxford University Press, 1978.

Levine, S., & Mullins, R. F. Hormones in infancy. In G. Newton & S. Levine (Eds.), *Early experience and behavior*. Springfield, IL.: Thomas, 1968.

Levy, F., Dumbrell, S., Hobbes, G., Ryan, M., Wilton, N., & Woodhill, J. M. Hyperkinesis and diet: A double-blind crossover trial with a tartrazine challenge. *Medical Journal of Australia*, 1978, *1*, 61–64.

Lewine, R. R. J., Watt, N. F., Prentky, R. A., & Fryer, J. H. Childhood social competence in functionally disordered psychiatric patients and in normals. *Journal of Abnormal Psychology*, 1980, *89*, 132–138.

Lewinsohn, P. M., Steinmetz, J. L., Larson, D. W., & Franklin, J. Depression-related cognitions: Antecedent of consequence? *Journal of Abnormal Psychology*, 1981, *90*, 213–219.

Lewis, S. A comparison of behavior therapy techniques in the reduction of fearful avoidance behavior. *Behavior Therapy*, 1974, *5*, 648–655.

Lewis, D. O., & Balla, D. A. *Delinquency and psychopathology*. New York: Grune & Stratton, 1976.

Lewis, D. O., Shanok, S. S., & Pincus, J. H. Juvenile male sexual assaulters. *American Journal of Psychiatry*, 1979, *136*, 1194–1196.

Lewis, J. M., Beavers, W. R., Gossett, J. T., & Phillips, V. A. *No single thread: Psychological health in family systems*. New York: Brunner/Mazel, 1976.

Lezak, M. D., & Dixon, H. The brain-injured child in a clinic population. A statistical description. *Exceptional Children*, 1964, *30*, 237–240.

Lidz, T., Blatt, S., & Cook, B. Critique of the Danish-American studies of the adopted away offspring of schizophrenic parents. *American Journal of Psychiatry*, 1981, *138*, 1063–1068.

Lieberman, A. E. Preschoolers' competence with a peer: Influence of attachment and social competence. *Child Development*, 1977, *48*, 1277–1287.

Liebert, R. M., & Baron, R. A. Some immediate effects of televised violence on children's behavior. *Developmental Psychology*, 1972, *6*, 469–475.

Liebman, R., Minuchin, S., Baker, L., & Rosman, B. Chronic asthma: A new approach to treatment. In M. F. McMillan & S. Henao (Eds.), *Child psychiatry: treatment and research*, New York: Brunner/Mazel, 1977.

Lief, A. *The commonsense psychiatry of Dr. Adolf Meyer*. New York: McGraw-Hill, 1948.

Liem, J. H. Effects of verbal communications of parents and children: A comparison of normal and schizophrenic families. *Journal of Consulting and Clinical Psychology*, 1974, *42*, 438–450.

Lindner, R. M., & Seliger, R. V. Projective techniques and the medical psychologist. *Southern Medicine and Surgery*, 1945, *107*, 355–356.

Lindzey, G., & Goldwyn, R. M. Validity of the Rosenzweig Picture-Frustration Study. *Journal of Personality*, 1954, *22*, 519–547.

Little, V. L., & Kendall, P. C. Cognitive-behavioral interventions with delinquents:

Problem solving, role-taking, and self-control. In P. C. Kendall & S. D. Hollan (Eds.), *Cognitive-behavioral interventions: Theory, research, and methods.* New York: Academic Press, 1979.

Liu, A. *Solitaire.* New York: Harper & Row, 1979.

Loehlin, J. C., & Nichols, R. C. *Heredity, environment, and personality. A study of 850 sets of twins.* Austin, TX: University of Texas Press, 1976.

Loevinger, J. *Ego development: Conceptions and theories.* San Francisco: Jossey-Bass, 1976.

London, P. The end of ideology in behavior modification. *American Psychologist,* 1972, *27,* 913–920.

Loney, J., Kramer, J., & Milich, R. *The hyperkinetic child grows up: Predictors of symptoms, delinquency, and achievement at follow-up.* American Association for the Advancement of Science, Houston, TX, 1979.

Loney, J., Langhorne, J. E., & Paternite, C. E. An empirical basis for subgrouping the hyperkinetic/minimal brain dysfunction syndrome. *Journal of Abnormal Psychology,* 1978, *87,* 431–441.

Loney, J., Whaley-Klahn, M. A., & Weissenburger, F. E. Responses of hyperactive boys to a behaviorally focused school attitude questionnaire. *Child Psychiatry and Human Development,* 1976, *6,* 123–133.

Longstreth, L. E. Revisiting Skeels' final study: A critique. *Developmental Psychology,* 1981, *17,* 620–625.

Lotter, V. Epidemiology of autistic conditions in young children. II. Some characteristics of the parents and children. *Social Psychology,* 1967, *1,* 163–173.

Lotter, V. Factors related to outcome in autistic children. *Journal of Autism and Childhood Schizophrenia,* 1974, *4,* 263–277.

Lotter, V. Follow-up studies. In M. Rutter & E. Schopler (Eds.), *Autism: A reappraisal of concepts and treatment.* New York: Plenum, 1978.

Lovaas, O. I. A behavior therapy approach to the treatment of childhood schizophrenia. In J. P. Hill (Ed.), *Minnesota Symposium on Child Psychology,* Vol. I. Minneapolis: University of Minnesota Press, 1967.

Lovaas, O. I. *The autistic child. Language development through behavior modification.* New York: Irvington, 1977.

Lovaas, O. I. Parents as therapists. In M. Rutter & E. Schopler (Eds.), *Autism: A reappraisal of concepts and treatment.* New York: Plenum, 1978.

Lovaas, O. I., Koegel, R. L., & Schreibman, L. Stimulus overselectivity in autism: A review of research. *Psychological Bulletin,* 1979, *86,* 1236–1254.

Love, L. R., & Kaswan, J. W. *Troubled children: their families, schools, and treatments.* New York: Wiley, 1974.

Lowell, F. E. A study of the variability of IQs in retest. *Journal of Applied Psychology,* 1941, *25,* 341–356.

Luborsky, L. New directions in research on neurotic and psychosomatic symptoms. *American Scientist,* 1970, *58,* 661–668.

Luborsky, L., Docherty, J., Todd, T., Knapp, P., Mirsky, A., & Gottschalk, L. A context analysis of psychological states prior to petit-mal seizures. *Journal of Nervous and Mental Disease,* 1975, *160,* 282–298.

Lubs, H. A., & Ruddle, F. H. Chromosomal abnormalities in the human population:

Estimation of rates based on New Haven newborn study. *Science*, 1970, *169*, 495–497.

Lucas, A. R. Treatment in child psychiatry. In R. L. Jenkins & E. Harms (Eds.), *Understanding disturbed children*. Seattle, WA: Special Child Publications, 1976.

Lucas, A. R. Gilles de la Tourette's syndrome. In J. D. Noshpitz (Ed.), *Basic handbook of child psychiatry. Vol. III. Disturbances in development*. New York: Basic Books, 1979.

Lueger, R. J. Person and situation factors influencing transgression in behavior-problem adolescents. *Journal of Abnormal Psychology*, 1980, *89*, 453–458.

Lykken, D. T. A study of anxiety in the sociopathic personality. *Journal of Abnormal and Social Psychology*, 1957, *55*, 6–10.

Lyle, O. E., & Gottesman, I. I. Subtle cognitive deficits as 15–20 year precursors of Huntington's disease. In T. N. Chase, N. Wexler, & A. Barbeau (Eds.), *Huntington's disease*. New York: Raven Press, 1980.

Lytton, H. Do parents create or respond to differences in twins? *Developmental Psychology*, 1977, *13*, 456–459.

Maccoby, E. E. *Social development, psychological growth, and the parent-child relationship*. New York: Harcourt, Brace, Jovanovich, 1980.

Maccoby, E. E., & Jacklin, C. N. Sex differences in aggression: A rejoinder and reprise. *Child Development*, 1980, *51*, 964–980.

MacFarlane, J. W., Allen, L., & Honzik, M. P. *A developmental study of the behavior problems of normal children between twenty-one months and fourteen years*. Berkeley: University of California Press, 1954.

Machover, K. *Personality projection in the drawing of the human figure*. Springfield, IL.: Thomas, 1949.

Machover, K. Sex differences in the developmental pattern of children as seen in human figure drawings. In A. I. Rabin & M. R. Haworth (Eds.), *Projective techniques with children*. New York: Grune & Stratton, 1960.

MacMillan, D. L. Motivational differences: Cultural-familial retardates vs. normal subjects on expectancy for failure. *American Journal of Mental Deficiency*, 1969, *74*, 254–258.

Maher, B. *Principles of psychopathology*. New York: McGraw-Hill, 1966.

Maher, B. A., & Maher, W. B. Psychopathology. In E. Hearst (Ed.), *The first century of experimental psychology*. Hillsdale, NJ: Erlbaum, 1979.

Mahl, G. *Psychological conflict and defense*. New York: Harcourt Brace Jovanovich, 1971.

Mahl, G. F., & Karpe, R. Emotions and hydrochloric acid secretion during psychoanalytic hours. *Psychosomatic Medicine*, 1953, *15*, 312–327.

Mahler, M. On child psychosis and schizophrenia: Autistic and symbiotic infantile psychosis. *Psychoanalytic Study of the Child*, 1952, *7*, 286–305.

Mahler, M., Pine, F., & Bergman, A. *The psychological birth of the human infant*. New York: Basic Books, 1975.

Mahler, M. S., & Rangell, L. A psychosomatic study of Maladie des Tics (Gilles de la Tourette's disease). *Psychiatric Quarterly*, 1943, *17*, 579–603.

Mallick, S. K., & McCandless, B. R. A study of catharsis of aggression. *Journal of Personality and Social Psychology*, 1966, *4*, 591–596.

Malmo, R. B., & Shagass, C. Physiologic study of symptom mechanisms in psychiatric patients under stress. *Psychosomatic Medicine*, 1949, *11*, 25–29.

Marburg, C. C., Houston, B. K., & Holmes, D. S. Influence of multiple models on the behavior of institutionalized retarded children: Increased generalization to other models and other behaviors. *Journal of Consulting and Clinical Psychology*, 1976, *44*, 514–519.

Marholin, D. (Ed.). *Child behavior therapy*. New York: Gardner, 1978.

Marks, P. A., Seeman, W., & Haller, D. L. *The actuarial use of the MMPI with adolescents and adults*. Baltimore: Williams & Wilkins, 1974.

Marmor, J., & Woods, S. M. (Eds.). *The interface between the psychodynamic and behavioral therapies*. New York: Plenum, 1980.

Martin, G. L., England, G., Kaprowy, E., Kilgour, K., & Pilek, V. Operant conditioning of kindergarten-class behavior in autistic children. *Behavior Research and Therapy*, 1968, *6*, 281–294.

Mash, E. J., & Dalby, J. T. Behavioral interventions for hyperactivity. In R. L. Trites (Ed.), *Hyperactivity in children. Etiology, measurement, and treatment implications*. Baltimore: University Park Press, 1979.

Mash, E. J., & Terdal, L. G. (Eds.). *Behavioral assessment of childhood disorders*. New York: Guilford Press, 1981.

Maslow, P., Frostig, M., Lefever, D. W., & Whittlesey, J. R. B. The Marianne Frostig developmental test of visual perception in 1963 standardization. *Perceptual and Motor Skills*, 1964, *19*, 463–499.

Mason, M. K. Learning to speak after six and one-half years of silence. *Journal of Speech Disorders*, 1942, *7*, 295–304.

Masserman, J. H. Ethology, comparative biodynamics, and psychoanalytic research. In J. Scher (Ed.), *Theories of the mind*. New York: Free Press, 1963.

Matejcek, Z., Dytrych, Z., & Schuller, V. The Prague study of children born from unwanted pregnancies. *International Journal of Mental Health*, 1979, *7*, 63–77.

Matheny, A. P. Bayley's Infant Behavior Record: Behavioral components and twin analyses. *Child Development*, 1980, *51*, 1157–1167.

Matheny, A. P., & Dolan, A. B. Twin study of genetic influences in reading achievement. *Journal of Learning Disabilities*, 1974, *7*, 99–102.

Matheny, A. P., Dolan, A. B., & Wilson, R. S. Twins with academic learning problems: Antecedent characteristics. *American Journal of Orthopsychiatry*, 1976, *46*, 464–469. (a)

Matheny, A. P., Dolan, A. B., & Wilson, R. S. Twins: Within-pair similarity on Bayley's Infant Behavior Record. *Journal of Genetic Psychology*, 1976, *128*, 263–270. (b)

Matranga, J. T. The relationship between behavioral indices of aggression and hostile content on the TAT. *Journal of Personality Assessment*, 1976, *40*, 130–234.

Mattison, R., Cantwell, D. P., Russell, A. T., & Will, L. A comparison of DSM-II and DSM-III in the diagnosis of childhood psychiatric disorders. *Archives of General Psychiatry*, 1979, *36*, 1217–1222.

Mattson, A., Schalling, D., Olweus, D., Low, H., & Svenson, J. Plasma testosterone, aggressive behavior, and personality in young male delinquents. *Journal of the American Academy of Child Psychiatry*, 1980, *19*, 476–490.

Maugh, T. H. LSD and the drug culture: New evidence of hazard. *Science*, 1973, *179*, 1221–1222.

McAdoo, W. G., & DeMyer, M. K. Personality characteristics in parents. In M. Rutter &

E. Schopler (Eds.), *Autism: A reappraisal of concepts and treatment*. New York: Plenum, 1978.

McCall, R. B. Childhood IQs as predictors of adult educational and occupational status. *Science*, 1977, *197*, 482–483.

McCall, R. B., Hogarty, P. S., & Hurlburt, N. Transitions in infant sensorimotor development and the prediction of childhood IQ. *American Psychologist*, 1972, *27*, 728–748.

McCammon, S., & Palotai, A. Behavioral assessment of a seven-year-old girl with behavior problems at school and at home. In S. N. Haynes (Ed.), *Principles of behavioral assessment*. New York: Gardner Press, 1978.

McCandless, B. R., Roberts, A., & Starnes, T. Teachers' marks, achievement test scores, and aptitude relations with respect to social class, race, and sex. *Journal of Educational Psychology*, 1972, *63*, 153–159.

McCarver, R. B., & Craig, E. M. Placement of the retarded in the community: Prognosis and outcome. In N. R. Ellis (Ed.), *International review of research in retardation (Vol. 7)*. New York: Academic Press, 1974.

McClearn, G. E. Genetic influences on behavior and development. In P. H. Mussen (Ed.), *Carmichael's manual of child psychiatry*. New York: Wiley, 1970.

McClearn, G. E., & DeFries, J. C. *Introduction to behavioral genetics*. San Francisco: Freeman, 1973.

McClelland, D. C. *The achieving society*. Princeton, NJ: Van Nostrand, 1961.

McClelland, D. C. Longitudinal trends in the relation of thought to action. *Journal of Consulting Psychology*, 1966, *30*, 479–483.

McCord, J. The Cambridge-Somerville Youth study: A sobering lesson on treatment, prevention, and evaluation. In A. J. McSweeny, W. J. Fremouw, & R. P. Hawkins (Eds.), *Practical program evaluation for youth treatment*. Springfield, IL: Thomas, 1982.

McCord, W., McCord, J., & Howard, A. Familial correlates of aggression in non-delinquent male children. *Journal of Abnormal and Social Psychology*, 1961, *62*, 79–83.

McCord, W., McCord, J., & Zola, I. K. *Origins of crime*. New York: Columbia University Press, 1959.

McCorkle, L., Elias, A., & Bixby, F. *The Highfields Story: A unique experiment in the treatment of juvenile delinquency*. New York: Holt, 1958.

McCoy, C., McBride, D. C., Russe, B. R., Page, J. B., & Clayton, R. R. Youth opiate use. In G. M. Beschner & N. S. Friedman (Eds.), *Youth drug abuse. Problems, issues, and treatment*. Lexington, MA: Heath, 1979.

McCoy, S. A. Clinical judgments of normal childhood behavior. *Journal of Consulting and Clinical Psychology*, 1976, *44*, 710–714.

McDonald, L. *Social class and delinquency*. London: Faber & Faber, 1969.

McKay, H., Sinisterra, L., McKay, A., Gomez, H., & Lloreda, P. Improving cognitive ability in chronically deprived children. *Science*, 1978, *200*, 270–278.

McMahon, R. J., Forehand, R., & Griest, D. L. Effects of knowledge of social learning principles on enhancing treatment outcome and generalization in a parent training program. *Journal of Consulting and Clinical Psychology*, 1981, *49*, 526–532.

McMillen, M. M. Differential mortality by sex in fetal and nonfetal deaths. *Science,* 1979, *204,* 89—91.

McNemar, Q. *The revision of the Stanford-Binet Scale.* Boston: Houghton-Mifflin, 1942.

McNemar, Q. *Psychological statistics (4th ed.).* New York: Wiley, 1969.

Mealiea, W. L. Conjoint-behavior therapy: The modification of family constellations. In E. J. Mash, L. C. Handy, & L. A. Hamerlynck (Eds.), *Behavior modification approaches to parenting.* New York: Brunner/Mazel, 1976.

Mednick, S. A., & Hutchings, B. Genetic and psychophysiological factors in asocial behavior. In R. D. Hare & D. Schalling (Eds.), *Psychopathic behavior: Approaches to research.* New York: Wiley, 1978.

Mednick, S. A., Schulsinger, F., Teasdale, T. W., Schulsinger, H., Venables, P. H., & Rock, D. R. Schizophrenia in high risk children: Sex differences in predisposing factors. In G. Serban (Ed.), *Cognitive defects in the development of mental illness.* New York: Brunner/Mazel, 1978.

Mednick, S. A., Schulsinger, F., & Venables, P. H. Risk research and primary prevention of mental illness. *International Journal of Mental Health,* 1979, *7,* 150—164.

Meehl, P. E. *Clinical versus statistical prediction.* Minneapolis: University of Minnesota Press, 1954.

Meehl, P. E. Psychotherapy. In C. P. Stone & Q. McNemar (Eds.), *Annual Review of Psychology (Vol. 6).* Stanford, CA: Annual Reviews, 1955.

Meehl, P. E. Specific etiology and other forms of strong inference: Some quantitative meanings. *Journal of Medicine and Philosophy,* 1977, *2,* 33—35.

Meichenbaum, D. H. *Cognitive-behavior modification.* New York: Plenum, 1977.

Melamed, B. G., & Siegel, L. J. Reduction of anxiety in children facing hospitalization and surgery by use of filmed modeling. *Journal of Consulting and Clinical Psychology,* 1975, *43,* 511—521.

Meltzoff, A. N., & Moore, M. K. Imitation of facial and manual gestures by human neonates. *Science,* 1977, *198,* 75—78.

Menolascino, F. Children with disorders of the central nervous system. In R. L. Jenkins & E. Harms (Eds.), *Understanding disturbed children.,* Seattle, WA: Special Child Publications, 1976.

Menolascino, F. J. *Challenges in mental retardation: Progressive ideology and services.* New York: Human Sciences Press, 1977.

Mercer, J. R. Psychological assessment and the rights of children. In N. Hobbs (Eds.), *Issues in the classification of children (Vol. I).* San Francisco: Jossey-Bass, 1975.

Mercer, J. *Technical manual: SOMPA.* New York: Psychological Corporation, 1979.

Merton, R. K. Social structure and anomie. In R. K. Merton (Ed.), *Social theory and social structure (Rev. ed.).* New York: Free Press, 1957.

Metrakos, J. D., & Metrakos, K. Genetic factors in epilepsy. In E. Niedermeyer (Ed.), *Epilepsy. Modern problems of pharmopsychiatry (Vol. 4).* New York: Karger, 1970.

Metz, J. R. Stimulation preferences of autistic children. *Journal of Abnormal Psychology,* 1967, *72,* 529—535.

Meyer, H. J., Borgatta, E. F., & Jones, W. C. *Girls at Vocational High: An experiment in social work intervention.* New York: Russell Sage Foundation, 1965.

Meyers, D. I., & Goldfarb, W. Studies of perplexity in mothers of schizophrenic children. *American Journal of Orthopsychiatry,* 1961, *31,* 551—564.

Meyers, D. I., & Goldfarb, W. Psychiatric appraisal of parents and siblings of schizophrenic children. *American Journal of Psychiatry,* 1962, *118,* 902–908.

Mezzich, A. C., & Mezzich, J. E. Diagnostic reliability of childhood and adolescent behavior disorders. Presented at American Psychological Association, New York, September, 1979.

Milich, R., & Loney, J. The role of hyperactive and aggressive symptomatology in predicting adolescent outcome among hyperactive children. *Journal of Pediatric Psychology,* 1979, *4,* 93–112.

Miller, A. D., & Ohlin, L. E. The politics of secure care in youth correctional reform. *Crime and Delinquency,* 1981, *27,* 449–467.

Miller, I. W., & Norman, W. H. Learned helplessness in humans: A review and attributional model. *Psychological Bulletin,* 1979, *86,* 93–118.

Miller, L. C., Barrett, C. L., & Hampe, E. Phobias in childhood in a prescientific era. In A. Davids (Ed.), *Child personality and psychopathology: Current topics (Vol. 1).* New York: Wiley, 1974.

Miller, L. C., Barrett, C. L., Hampe, E., & Noble, H. Comparison of reciprocal inhibition, psychotherapy, and waiting list control for phobic children. *Journal of Abnormal Psychology,* 1972, *79,* 269–279.

Miller, N. E. Biofeedback and visceral learning. *Annual Review of Psychology,* 1978, *29,* 373–404.

Miller, N. E., & Dollard, J. *Social learning and imitation.* New Haven: Yale University Press, 1941.

Miller, P. M. Behavioral strategies for reducing drinking among young adults. In H. T. Blane & M. E. Chafetz (Eds.), *Youth, alcohol, and social policy.* New York: Plenum, 1979.

Miller, W. B. Lower-class culture as a generating milieu of gang delinquency. *Journal of Social Issues,* 1958, *14,* 5–19.

Miller, W. B. The impact of a "total community" delinquency control project. *Social Problems,* 1962, *10,* 168–191.

Millon, T. *Modern psychopathology: A biosocial approach to maladaptive learning and functioning.* Philadelphia: Saunders, 1969.

Minuchin, S., Rosman, B. L., & Baker, L. *Psychosomatic anorexia nervosa in context.* Cambridge, MA: Harvard University Press, 1978.

Mirsky, I. A. Physiologic, psychologic, and social determinants in the etiology of duodenal ulcer. *American Journal of Digestive Diseases,* 1958, *3,* 285–314.

Mittelmann, B. Motility in infants, children, and adults. *Psychoanalytic Study of the Child,* 1954, *9,* 142–177.

Monachesi, E. D., & Hathaway, S. R. The personality of delinquents. In J. N. Butcher (Ed.), *MMPI: Research developments and clinical applications.* New York: McGraw-Hill, 1969.

Mönckeberg, F. The effect of malnutrition on physical growth and brain development. In J. W. Prescott, M. S. Read, & D. B. Coursin (Eds.), *Brain function and malnutrition. Neuropsychological methods of assessment.* New York: Wiley, 1975.

Money, J. Behavior genetics: Principles, methods, and examples from XO, XXY, and XYY syndromes. *Seminars in Psychiatry,* 1970, *2,* 11–29.

Money, J. The syndrome of abuse dwarfism (psychosocial dwarfism or reversible hyposomatotropism). Behavioral data and a case report. *American Journal of Diseases of Children*, 1977, *131*, 508−513.

Money, J. Behavior genetics: Principles, methods, and examples from XO, XXY, and XYY syndromes. *Seminars in Psychiatry*, 1979, *2*, 11−29.

Money, J., & Ehrhardt, A. A. *Man and woman. Boy and girl. The differentiation and dimorphism of gender identity from conception to maturity*. Baltimore: Johns Hopkins, 1972.

Money, J., & Mittenthal, S. Lack of personality pathology in Turner's syndrome: Relation to cytogenetics, hormones, and physique. *Behavior Genetics*, 1970, *1*, 43−56.

Money, J., & Russo, A. J. Homosexual outcome of discordant gender-identity/role in childhood: Longitudinal follow-up. *Journal of Pediatric Psychology*, 1979, *4*, 29−41.

Montagu, M. F. A. *Prenatal influences*. Springfield, IL: Thomas, 1962.

Moore, B. E., & Fine, B. D. *A glossary of psychoanalytic terms (2nd ed.)*. New York: American Psychoanalytic Association, 1968.

Morgan, C. D., & Murray, H. A. A method for investigating fantasies: The Thematic Apperception Test. *Archives of Neurology and Psychiatry*, 1935, *34*, 289−306.

Morris, L. W. *Extraversion and introversion: An interactional perspective*. New York: Halsted Press, 1979.

Morrison, J. R., & Stewart, M. A. Bilateral inheritance as evidence for polygenicity in the hyperactive child syndrome. *Journal of Nervous and Mental Diseases*, 1974, *158*, 226−228.

Mostofsky, D. I., & Balaschak, B. A. Psychobiological control of seizures. *Psychological Bulletin*, 1977, *84*, 723−750.

Mowrer, O. H. *Learning theory and personality dynamics*. New York: Ronald Press, 1950.

Mowrer, O. H., & Mowrer, W. M. Enuresis: A method for its study and treatment. *American Journal of Orthopsychiatry*, 1938, *8*, 436−459.

Moyal, B. R. Locus of control, self-esteem, stimulus appraisal, and depressive symptoms in children. *Journal of Consulting and Clinical Psychology*, 1977, *45*, 951−952.

Mueller, K. H. Programs for deviant girls. In W. W. Wattenberg (Ed.), *Social deviancy among youth. Sixty-fifth Yearbook of the National Society for the Study of Education*. Chicago: National Society for the Study of Education, 1966.

Mueller, M. W. Prediction of achievement of educable mentally retarded children. *American Journal of Mental Deficiency*, 1969, *73*, 590−596.

Mumpower, D. L. Sex ratios found in various types of referred exceptional children. *Exceptional Children*, 1970, *36*, 61−62.

Munford, P. R., Reardon, D., Liberman, R. P., & Allen, L. Behavioral treatment of hysterical coughing and mutism: A case study. *Journal of Consulting and Clinical Psychology*, 1976, *44*, 1008−1014.

Munsinger, H. Reply to Kamin. *Psychological Bulletin*, 1978, *85*, 202−206.

Murphy, F. J., Shirley, M. M., & Witmer, H. L. The incidence of hidden delinquency. *American Journal of Orthopsychiatry*, 1946, *16*, 686−695.

Murray, A. D., Dolby, R. M., Nation, R. L., & Thomas, D. B. Effects of epidural anesthesia on newborns and their mothers. *Child Development*, 1981, *52*, 71−82.

Murray, H. A. *Thematic Apperception Test*. Cambridge: Harvard University Press, 1943.

Murray, H. A. Foreword. In H. & G. Anderson (eds.), *An introduction to projective techniques*. Englewood Cliffs, N.J.: Prentice−Hall, 1951.

Murray, H. A. Preparations for the scaffold of a comprehensive system. In S. Koch (Ed.), *Psychology: A study of science (Vol. 3)*. New York: McGraw-Hill, 1959.

Mussen, P. H., Conger, J. J., & Kagan, J. *Child development and personality (5th ed.)*. New York: Harper & Row, 1979.

Myers, R. E. Maternal psychological stress and fetal asphyxia: A study in the monkey. *American Journal of Obstetrics and Gynecology*, 1975, *122*, 47–59.

Nagera, H. *Obsessional neuroses: Developmental psychopathology*. New York: Aronson, 1976.

Nagera, H. *The developmental approach to childhood psychopathology*. New York: Aronson, 1981.

Nasby, W., Hayden, B., & DePaulo, B. M. Attributional bias among aggressive boys to interpret unambiguous social stimuli as displays of hostility. *Journal of Abnormal Psychology*, 1980, *89*, 459–468.

National Center for Health Statistics. *Table 292. Deaths by suicide for 5-year age groups*. Hyattsville, MD: Health Resources Administration, 1977.

National Commission on Children in Need of Parents. *Who knows? Who cares? Forgotten children in foster care*. New York: Child Welfare League of America, 1979.

National Research Council. *Genetic screening: Programs, principles, and research*. Washington, DC: National Academy of Sciences, 1975.

Nay, W. R. *Multimethod clinical assessment*. New York: Gardner Press, 1979.

Naylor, H. Reading disability and lateral asymmetry: An information-processing analysis. *Psychological Bulletin*, 1980, *87*, 531–545.

Neale, J. M., & Oltmanns, T. F. *Schizophrenia*. New York: Wiley, 1980.

Neissworth, J. T., Kurtz, P. D., Jones, R. T., & Madle, R. A. Biasing of hyperkinetic behavior ratings by diagnostic reports. *Journal of Abnormal Child Psychology*, 1974, *2*, 323–330.

Nelson, E. A., Grinder, R. E., & Mutterer, M. L. Sources of variance in behavioral measures of honesty in temptation situations: Methodological analyses. *Developmental Psychology*, 1969, 1, 265–279.

Nesselroade, J. R., & Baltes, P. B. Adolescent personality development and historical change. *Monographs of the Society for Research in Child Development*, 1974, *39* (Serial No. 154).

Neugebauer, R. Medieval and early modern theories of mental illness. *Archives of General Psychiatry*, 1979, *36*, 477–483.

New York State Department of Mental Hygiene. A special census of suspected and referred mental retardation, Onondaga County, New York. In *Technical Report of the Mental Health Research Unit*. Syracuse: Syracuse University Press, 1955.

New York Times Book Review, Advertisement. April 8, 1979, 21.

New York Times, The sad story of Synanon's founder. July 20, 1980, 22E.(a)

New York Times, Heroin availability indicators. August 24, 1980, 4E.(b)

New York Times, Synanon real estate deals disturb Lake Havasu. November 16, 1980, 36.(c)

Newman, H. H., Freeman, F. N., & Holzinger, K. *Twins, a study of heredity and environment*. Chicago: University of Chicago Press, 1937.

Newton, M. R., & Brown, R. D. A preventive approach to developmental problems in school children. In E. M. Bower & W. G. Hollister (Eds.), *Behavioral science frontiers in education*. New York: Wiley, 1967.

Ney, P. G., Palvesky, A. E., & Markely, J. Relative effectiveness of operant conditioning and play therapy in childhood schizophrenia. *Journal of Autism and Childhood Schizophrenia,* 1971, *1,* 337–349.

Nichols, P. *Minimal brain dysfunction: Associations with perinatal complications.* Presented at Society for Research in Child Development, New Orleans, 1976.

Noebels, J. L., & Sidman, R. L. Inherited epilepsy: Spike-wave and focal motor seizures in the mutant mouse tottering. *Science,* 1979, *204,* 1334–1336.

Novick, J. I. Comparison between short-term group and individual psychotherapy in effecting change in nondesirable behavior in children. *International Journal of Group Psychotherapy,* 1965, *15,* 366–373.

Novick, J. Symptomatic treatment of acquired and persistent enuresis. *Journal of Abnormal Psychology,* 1966, *77,* 363–368.

Nyswander, M. History of a nightmare. In D. Wakefield (Ed.), *The addict.* Greenwich, CT: Fawcett, 1963.

O'Donnell, C. R., Lydgate, T., & Fo, W. S. O. The buddy system: Review and follow-up. *Child Behavior Therapy,* 1979, *1,* 161–169.

O'Donnell, J. A., & Clayton, R. R. Determinants of early marihuana use. In G. M. Beschner & A. S. Friedman (Eds.), *Youth drug abuse. Problems, issues, and treatment.* Lexington, MA: Heath, 1979.

O'Leary, K. D., & Johnson, S. B. Psychological assessment. In H. C. Quay & J. S. Werry (Eds.), *Psychopathological disorders of childhood (2nd ed.).* New York: Wiley, 1979.

O'Leary, K. D., & O'Leary, S. G. *Classroom management: The successful use of behavior modification (2nd ed.).* New York: Pergamon Press, 1977.

O'Leary, K. D., & Turkewitz, H. Methodological errors in marital and child treatment research. *Journal of Consulting and Clinical Psychology,* 1978, *46,* 747–758.

Oakland, T. *Psychological and educational assessment of minority children.* New York: Brunner/Mazel, 1977.

Offer, D., & Offer, J. B. *From teenage to young manhood.* New York: Basic Books, 1975.

Offord, D. R., Abrams, N., Allen, N., & Poushinsky, M. Broken homes, parental psychiatric illness, and female delinquency. *American Journal of Orthopsychiatry,* 1979, *49,* 252–264.

Ogdon, D. P., Bass, C. L., Thomas, E. R., & Lordi, W. Parents of autistic children. *American Journal of Orthopsychiatry,* 1968, *38,* 653–658.

Ollendick, T., & Gruen, G. E. Treatment of a bodily injury phobia with implosive therapy. *Journal of Consulting and Clinical Psychology,* 1972, *38,* 389–393.

Oltmanns, T. F., Broderick, J. E., & O'Leary, K. D. Marital adjustment and the efficacy of behavior therapy with children. *Journal of Consulting and Clinical Psychology,* 1977, *45,* 724–729.

Oltmanns, T. F., Weintraub, S., Stone, A. A., & Neale, J. M. Cognitive slippage in children vulnerable to schizophrenia. *Journal of Abnormal Child Psychology,* 1978, *6,* 237–245.

Olton, D. S., & Noonberg, A. R. *Biofeedback. Clinical applications in behavioral medicine.* Englewood Cliffs, NJ: Prentice-Hall, 1980.

Olweus, D. Stability of aggressive reaction patterns in males: A review. *Psychological Bulletin,* 1979, *86,* 852–875.

Olweus, D. Familial and temperamental determinants of aggressive behavior in adolescent boys: A causal analysis. *Developmental Psychology*, 1980, *16*, 644−660.

Olweus, D., Mattson, A., Schalling, D., & Löw, H. Testosterone, aggression, physical, and personality dimensions in normal adolescents. *Psychosomatic Medicine*, 1980, *42*, 253−269.

Omenn, G. S. Prenatal diagnosis of genetic disorders. *Science*, 1978, *200*, 952−958.

O'Reilly, P. P. Desensitization of fire bell phobia. *Journal of School Psychology*, 1971, *9*, 55−57.

Oster, H. Facial expression and affect development. In M. Lewis & L. A. Rosenblum (Eds.), *The development of affect*. New York: Plenum, 1978.

Ottomanelli, G., Wilson, P., & Whyte, R. MMPI evaluation of 5-year methadone treatment status. *Journal of Consulting and Clinical Psychology*, 1978, *46*, 579−581.

Overall, J. E., & Hollister, L. E. Comparative evaluation of research diagnostic criteria for schizophrenia. *Archives of General Psychiatry*, 1979, *36*, 1198−1205.

Owen, D. R. The 47 XYY male: A review. *Psychological Bulletin*, 1972, *78*, 209−233.

Parlee, M. B. Comments on "Roles of activation and inhibition in sex differences in cognitive abilities" by D. M. Broverman, E. L. Klaiber, Y. Kobayshi, & W. Vogel. *Psychological Review*, 1971, *79*, 180−184.

Parsons, J. E. (Ed.). *The psychobiology of sex differences and sex roles*. Washington, DC: Hemisphere, 1980.

Pasamanick, B., & Knobloch, H. Retrospective studies on the epidemiology of reproductive casuality: old and new. *Merrill-Palmer Quarterly*, 1966, *12*, 7−26.

Pasamanick, B., & Lilienfeld, A. M. Maternal and fetal factors in the development of epilepsy. Relationship to some clinical features of epilepsy. *Neurology*, 1955, *5*, 77−83.

Pascual-Leone, J. A view of cognition from a formalist's perspective. In K. F. Riegel (Ed.), *Current issues in developmental psychology*. Basel: Karger, 1974.

Patterson, G. R. A learning theory approach to the treatment of the school phobic child. In L. P. Ullmann & L. Krasner (Eds.), *Case studies in behavior modification*. New York: Holt, Rinehart, & Winston, 1965.

Patterson, G. R. The aggressive child: Victim and architect of a coercive system. In L. A. Hamerlynck, E. J. Mash, & L. C. Handy (Eds.), *Behavior modification and families*. New York: Brunner/Mazel, 1976.

Patterson, G. R. Mothers: the unacknowledged victims. *Monographs of the Society for Research in Child Development*, 1980, *45*(Serial No. 186).

Patterson, G. R., & Cobb, J. A. A dyadic analysis of "aggressive" behaviors. In J. P. Hill (Ed.), *Minnesota Symposia on Child Psychology (Vol. 5)*. Minneapolis: University of Minnesota Press, 1971.

Patterson, G. R., Jones, R., Whittier, J., & Wright, M. A. A behavior modification technique for the hyperactive child. *Behavior Research and Therapy*, 1965, *2*, 217−226.

Patterson, G. R., Littman, R. A., & Bricker, W. Assertive behavior in children: A step toward a theory of aggression. *Monographs of the Society for Research in Child Development*, 1967, *32*(Serial No. 113).

Pauls, D. L., & Kidd, K. K. Genetics of childhood behavior disorders. In B. B. Lahey & A.

E. Kazdin (Eds.), *Advances in clinical child psychology (Vol. 4).* New York: Plenum, 1981.

Payne, F. D. Children's prosocial conduct in structured situations and as viewed by others: consistency, convergence, and relationships with person variables. *Child Development,* 1980, *51,* 1252−1259.

Peiper, A. *Cerebral function in infancy and childhood.* New York: Consultants Bureau, 1963.

Penfield, W., & Roberts, L. *Speech and brain mechanisms.* Princeton: Princeton University Press, 1959.

Penrose, L. S. *Recent advances in human genetics.* London: Churchill, 1961.

Penrose, L. S. *The biology of mental defect (3rd ed.).* London: Sidgwick and Jackson, 1963.

Perkins, M. J. *Effects of play therapy and behavior modification approaches with conduct problem boys.* (Doctoral dissertation, University of Illinois, 1967) *Dissertation Abstracts,* 1968, *28* (8-B), 3478−3479.

Peskin, H. Multiple prediction of adult psychological health from preadolescent and adolescent behavior. *Journal of Consulting and Clinical Psychology,* 1972, *38,* 155−160.

Petersen, A. C., & Wittig, M. A. Differential cognitive development in adolescent girls. In M. Sugar (Ed.), *Female adolescent development.* New York: Brunner/Mazel, 1979.

Peterson, D. R., & Becker, W. C. Family interaction and delinquency. In H. C. Quay (Ed.), *Juvenile delinquency: Research and theory.* Princeton, NJ: Van Nostrand, 1965.

Peterson, D. R., Quay, H. C., & Tiffany, T. L. Personality factors related to juvenile delinquency. *Child Development,* 1961, *32,* 355−372.

Peterson, G. F. Factors related to the attitudes of nonretarded children toward their EMR peers. *American Journal of Mental Deficiency,* 1974, *79,* 412−416.

Piaget, J. *The moral judgment of the child.* New York: Harcourt, 1932.

Piaget, J. *Play, dreams, and imitation in childhood.* New York: Norton, 1962.

Piaget, J. Development and learning. In R. E. Ripple & V. N. Rockcastle (Eds.), *Piaget rediscovered.* Ithaca, NY: Cornell University Press, 1964.

Piaget, J. Piaget's theory. In P. E. Mussen (Ed.), *Carmichael's manual of child psychology. (Vol. 1, 3rd ed.).* New York: Wiley 1970.

Piaget, J. *The development of thought. Equilibration of cognitive structures.* New York: Viking Press, 1977.

Pierce, C. M. Enuresis. In A. M. Freedman & H. I. Kaplan (Eds.), *Comprehensive textbook of psychiatry.* Baltimore: Williams & Wilkins, 1967.

Piggott, L. R. Overview of selected research in autism. *Journal of Autism and Developmental Disorders,* 1979, *9,* 199−216.

Pinneau, S. R. *Changes in intelligence quotient: Infancy to maturity.* Boston: Houghton-Mifflin, 1961.

Pirozzolo, F. J. *The neuropsychology of developmental reading disorders.* New York: Praeger, 1979.

Pitfield, M., & Oppenheim, A. Child-rearing attitudes of mothers of psychotic children. *Journal of Child Psychology and Psychiatry,* 1964, *5,* 51−57.

Platt, J. J., & Labate, C. *Heroin addiction: Theory, research, and treatment.* New York: Wiley, 1976.

Plomin, R. Ethological behavioral genetics and development. In K. Immelmann, G. W.

Barlow, L. Petrinovich, & M. Main (Eds.), *Behavioral Development*, NY: Cambridge University Press, 1982.

Plomin, R., & Rowe, D. C. Genetic and environmental etiology of social behavior in infancy. *Developmental Psychology*, 1979, *15*, 62–72.

Pollack, J. M. Obsessive-compulsive personality: A review. *Psychological Bulletin*, 1979, *86*, 225–241.

Pollack, M., Gittelman, M., Miller, R., Berman, P., & Bakwin, R. A developmental, pediatric, neurological, psychological, and psychiatric comparison of psychotic children and their sibs. *American Journal of Orthopsychiatry*, 1970, *40*, 329–330.

Pollin, W. Genetic and environmental determinants of neurosis. In A. R. Kaplan (Ed.), *Human behavior genetics*. Springfield, IL: Thomas, 1976.

Popper, K. R. *The logic of scientific discovery*. New York: Science Editions, 1961.

Porteus, S. D. *Porteus Maze Test: Fifty years' application*. Palo Alto, CA: Pacific Books, 1965.

Portnoy, S. M. Power of child care worker and therapist figures and their effectiveness as models for emotionally disturbed children in residential treatment. *Journal of Consulting and Clinical Psychology*, 1973, *40*, 15–19.

Potter, H. W. Schizophrenia in children. *American Journal of Psychiatry*, 1933, *12*, 1253–1270.

Powers, E., & Witmer, H. *An experiment in the prevention of delinquency*. New York: Columbia University Press, 1951.

Prescott, J. W., Read, M. S., & Coursin, D. B. (Eds.). *Brain function and malnutrition. Neuropsychological methods of assessment*. New York: Wiley, 1975.

President's Commission on Law Enforcement and Administration of Justice. *Task Force Report: Juvenile Delinquency and Youth Crime*. Washington, DC: U.S. Government Printing office, 1967.

Price, R. H., & Polister, P. E. (Eds.). *Evaluation and action in the social environment*. New York: Academic Press, 1980.

Prinz, R. J., Roberts, W. A., & Hantman, E. Dietary correlates of hyperactive behavior in children. *Journal of Consulting and Clinical Psychology*, 1980, *48*, 760–769.

Prior, M., Perry, D., & Gajzago, C. Kanner's syndrome or early-onset psychosis: A taxonomic analysis of 142 cases. *Journal of Autism and Childhood Schizophrenia*, 1975, *5*, 71–80.

Pritchard, J. A. *A treatise on insanity*. Philadelphia: Haswell, Barrington, & Haswell, 1835.

Proctor, J. T. Hysteria in childhood. *American Journal of Orthopsychiatry*, 1958, *28*, 394–407.

Proctor, J. T. The treatment of hysteria in childhood. In M. Hammer & A. M. Kaplan (Eds.), *The practice of psychotherapy with children*. Homewood, IL: Dorsey, 1967.

Provence, S., & Lipton, R. C. *Infants in institutions*. New York: International Universities Press, 1962.

Puig-Antich, J., Blau, S., Marx, N., Greenhill, L., & Chambers, W. Prepubertal major depressive disorder. *Journal of the American Academy of Child Psychiatry*, 1978, *17*, 695–707.

Purcell, K. Distinctions between subgroups of asthmatic children: Children's perceptions of events associated with asthma. *Pediatrics*, 1963, *31*, 486–494.

Purcell, K., Weiss, J., & Hahn, W. Certain psychosomatic disorders. In B. B. Wolman

(Ed.). *Manual of child psychopathology*. New York: McGraw-Hill, 1972.

Quay, H. C. Personality dimensions in delinquent males as inferred from the factor analysis of behavior ratings. *Journal of Research in Crime and Delinquency*, 1964, *1*, 33–36.

Quay, H. C. Residential treatment. In H. C. Quay & J. Werry (Eds.), *Psychopathologial disorders of childhood (2nd ed.)*. New York: Wiley, 1979.

Quay, H. C., Glavin, J. P., Annesley, R. F., & Werry, J. S. The modification of problem behavior and academic achievement in a resource room. *Journal of School Psychology*, 1972, *10*, 187–197.

Quay, H. C., & Quay, L. C. Behavior problems in early adolescence. *Child Development*, 1965, *36*, 215–220.

Quigley, M. E., Sheehan, K. L., Wilkes, M. M., & Yen, S. S. C. Effects of maternal smoking on circulating catecholamine levels and fetal heart rates. *American Journal of Obstetrics and Gynecology*, 1979, *133*, 685–690.

Quinton, D., & Rutter, M. Early hospital admissions and later disturbances of behaviour: An attempted replication of Douglas' findings. *Developmental Medicine and Child Neurology*, 1976, *18*, 447–459.

Rabkin, B. *Growing up dead*. Nashville, TN: Abingdon, 1979.

Rabkin, J. G. Stressful life events and schizophrenia: A review of the research literature. *Psychological Bulletin*, 1980, *87*, 408–425.

Rae, W. A. Childhood conversion reactions: A review of incidence in pediatric settings. *Journal of Clinical Child Psychology*, 1977, *6*, 69–72.

Ramey, C. T., & Campbell, F. A. Early childhood education for psychosocially disadvantaged children: Effects on psychological processes. *American Journal of Mental Deficiency*, 1979, *83*, 645–648.

Rank, B. Adaptation of the psychoanalytic technique for the treatment of young children with atypical development. *American Journal of Orthopsychiatry*, 1949, *19*, 130–139.

Rapaport, D. *Organization and pathology of thought*. New York: Columbia University Press, 1951.

Rapaport, D. The structure of psychoanalytic theory: A systematizing attempt. In J. S. Koch (Ed.), *Psychology: A study of science*. New York: McGraw-Hill, 1959.

Rapaport, D. *Collected papers of David Rapaport*. Merton Gill (Ed.). New York: Basic Books, 1967.

Rapoport, J. L., Buchsbaum, M. S., Weingartner, H., Zahn, T. P., Ludlow, C., & Mikkelsen, E. J. Dextroamphetamine. Its cognitive and behavioral effects in normal and hyperactive boys and normal men. *Archives of General Psychiatry*, 1980, *37*, 933–943.

Rapoport, J. L., & Mikkelsen, E. J. Antidepressants. In J. S. Werry (Ed.), *Pediatric psychopharmacology: The use of behavior modifying drugs in children*. New York: Brunner/Mazel, 1978.

Rapoport, J. L., Quinn, P. O., Burg, C., & Bartley, C. Can hyperactives be identified in infancy? In R. L. Trites (Ed.), *Hyperactivity in children*. Baltimore: University Park Press, 1979.

Raskin, D. C. What makes Sammy steal: Nature or Nurture? Review of S. A. Mednick & K. O. Christiansen (Eds.), Biosocial bases of criminal behavior. *Contemporary Psychology*, 1979, *24*, 787–788.

Raven, J. C. *Progressive matrices*. New York: Psychological Corporation, 1960.

Rawson, M. B. *Developmental language disability*. Baltimore: Johns Hopkins Press, 1968.

Reckless, W., & Dinitz, J. *The prevention of juvenile delinquency*. Columbus, OH: Ohio State University Press, 1972.

Rector, M. G., Barth, S. M., & Ingram, G. The juvenile justice system. In M. Johnson (Ed.), *Toward adolescence: The middle school years. 79th Yearbook of the National Society for the Study of Education. Part I*. Chicago: University of Chicago Press, 1980.

Redl, F., & Wineman, D. *The aggressive child*. New York: Free Press, 1957.

Reed, E. W. Genetic anomalies in development. In F. D. Horowitz (Ed.), *Review of child development research (Vol. 4)*. Chicago: University of Chicago Press, 1975.

Reed, E. W., & Reed, S. C. *Mental retardation. A family study*. Philadelphia: Saunders, 1965.

Reed, S. C., Hartley, C., Anderson, V. E., Phillips, V. P., & Johnson, N. *The psychoses: Family studies*. Philadelphia: Saunders, 1973.

Reese, M. W., & Lipsitt, L. P. (Eds.). *Advances in child development and behavior. Vol. 13*. New York: Academic Press, 1979.

Reid, W. H. (Ed.). *The psychopath*. New York: Brunner/Mazel, 1978.

Reinisch, J. M. Prenatal exposure to synthetic progestin increases potential for aggression in humans. *Science*, 1981, *211*, 1171–1173.

Reitan, R. M., & Davison, L. A. (Eds.). *Clinical neuropsychology: Current status and applications*. Washington, D. C.: Winston, 1974.

Rekers, G. A. Psychosexual and gender problems. In E. J. Mash & L. G. Terdal (Eds.), *Behavioral assessment of childhood disorders*. New York: Guilford Press, 1981.

Remschmidt, H., Hohner, G., Merschmann, W., & Walter, R. Epidemiology of delinquent behavior in children. In P. J. Graham (Ed.), *Epidemiological approaches in child psychiatry*. New York: Academic Press, 1977.

Renaud, H., & Estess, F. Life history interviews with one hundred normal American males: "Pathogenicity" of childhood. *American Journal of Orthopsychiatry*, 1961, *31*, 786–802.

Reynolds, C. R., & Richmond, B. O. What I Think and Feel: A revised measure of children's manifest anxiety. *Journal of Abnormal Child Psychology*, 1978, *6*, 271–280.

Reynolds, W. M. Measurement of personal competence of mentally retarded individuals. *American Journal of Mental Deficiency*, 1981, *85*, 368–376.

Reznikoff, M., & Honeyman, M. S. MMPI profiles of monozygotic and dizygotic twin pairs. *Journal of Consulting Psychology*, 1967, *31*, 100.

Rheingold, H. L., Hay, D. F., & West, M. J. Sharing in the second year of life. *Child Development*, 1976, *47*, 1148–1158.

Ribes-Inesta, E. Some social considerations of aggression. In E. Ribes-Inesta & A. Bandura (Eds.), *Analysis of delinquency and aggression*. Hillsdale, NJ: Erlbaum, 1976.

Richards, C. S., & Siegel, L. J. Behavioral treatment of anxiety states and avoidance behaviors in children. In D. Marholin (Ed.), *Child behavior therapy*. New York: Gardner, 1978.

Ricks, D. F., & Berry, J. C. Family and symptom patterns that precede schizophrenia. In M. Roff & D. F. Ricks (Eds.), *Life history research in psychopathology*. Minneapolis: University of Minnesota Press, 1970.

Rie, E. D., & Rie, H. E. Recall, retention, and Ritalin. *Journal of Consulting and Clinical Psychology*, 1977, *45*, 967–972.

Rie, H. E., & Rie, E. D. (Eds.), *Handbook of minimal brain dysfunctions: A critical view*. New York: Wiley, 1980.

Riess, B. F. Psychoanalytic theory and related approaches. In B. B. Wolman (Ed.), *Manual of child psychopathology*. New York: McGraw-Hill, 1972.

Rimland, B. The differentiation of childhood psychoses: An analysis of checklists for 2218 psychotic children. *Journal of Autism and Childhood Schizophrenia*, 1971, *1*, 161–174.

Rimland, B. Platelet uptake and efflux of serotonin in subtypes of psychotic children. *Journal of Autism and Childhood Schizophrenia*, 1976, *6*, 379–382.

Rimland, B. Savant capabilities of autistic children and their cognitive implications. In G. Serban (Ed.), *Cognitive defects in the development of mental illness*. New York: Brunner/Mazel, 1978.

Rimland, B., Callaway, E., & Dreyfus, P. The effect of high doses of Vitamin B6 on autistic children: A double-blind crossover study. *American Journal of Psychiatry*, 1978, *135*, 472–475.

Rincover, A., Newsom, C. D., & Carr, E. G. Using sensory extinction procedures in the treatment of compulsivelike behavior of developmentally disabled children. *Journal of Consulting and Clinical Psychology*, 1979, *47*, 695–701.

Risley, T. R. The effects and side effects of punishing the autistic behaviors of a deviant child. *Journal of Applied Behavior Analysis*, 1968, *1*, 21–34.

Ritter, B. The group desensitization of children's snake phobias using vicarious and contact desensitization procedures. *Behavior Research and Therapy*, 1968, *6*, 1–6.

Ritvo, E. R., Cantwell, D., Johnson, E., Clements, M., Benbrook, F., Slagle, S., Kelly P., & Ritz, M. Social class factors in autism. *Journal of Autism and Childhood Schizophrenia*, 1971, *1*, 297–310.

Ritvo, E. R. *Autism—diagnosis, current research, management*. New York: Spectrum Publications, 1976.

Ritvo, S. Correlation of a childhood and adult neurosis: Based on the adult analysis of a reported childhood case. *International Journal of Psychoanalysis*, 1966, *47*, 130–131.

Rizley, R. Depression and distortion in the attribution of causality. *Journal of Abnormal Psychology*, 1978, *87*, 32–48.

Roazen, P. *Freud and his times*. New York: Meridian, 1975.

Robbins, E., & O'Neal, P. Clinical features of hysteria in children. *Nervous Child*, 1953, *10*, 246–271.

Robins, L. The accuracy of parental recall of aspects of child development and of child rearing practices. *Journal of Abnormal and Social Psychology*, 1963, *66*, 261–270.

Robins, L. N. *Deviant children grown up (2nd ed.)*. Huntington, NY: Krieger, 1974.

Robins, L. N. The interaction of setting and predisposition in explaining novel behavior: Drug initiations before, in, and after Vietnam. In D. B. Kandel (Ed.), *Longitudinal research on drug use: Empirical findings and methodological issues*. Washington, DC: Hemisphere, 1978.

Robins, L. N. Follow-up studies. In H. C. Quay & J. S. Werry (Eds.), *Psychopathological disorders of childhood (2nd ed)*. New York: Wiley, 1979.

Robins, L. N. Longitudinal methods in the study of normal and pathological development. In

F. Earls (Ed.), *Studies of Children. Monographs in Psychosocial Epidemiology, No. 1,* New York: Prodist, 1980.

Robins, L. N., Darvish, H. S., & Murphy, G. E. The long-term outcome for adolescent drug users: A follow-up study of 76 users and 146 nonusers. In J. Zubin & A. M. Freedman (Eds.), *The psychopathology of adolescence.* New York: Grune & Stratton, 1970.

Robins, L. N., Helzer, J. E., Hesselbrock, M., & Wish, E. Vietnam veterans three years after Vietnam. How our study changed our view of heroin. In L. Brill & C. Winick (Eds.), *The yearbook of substance use and abuse (Vol. II).* New York: Human Sciences Press, 1980.

Robins, L. N., West, P. A., Ratcliff, K. S., & Herjanic, B. M. Father's alcoholism and children's outcomes. In F. A. Seixas (Ed.), *Currents in alcoholism, Vol. IV: Psychiatric, psychological, social, and epidemiological studies.* New York: Grune & Stratton, 1978.

Robinson, R., DeMarche, D. F., & Wagle, M. *Community resources in mental health.* New York: Basic Books, 1960.

Roche, A., Lipman, R., Overall, J., & Hung, W. The effects of stimulant medication on the growth of hyperkinetic children. *Pediatrics,* 1979, *63,* 847−850.

Rodick, J. D., & Henggeler, S. W. The short-term and long-term amelioration of academic and motivational deficiencies among low-achieving inner-city adolescents. *Child Development,* 1980, *51,* 1126−1132.

Roff, M., Sells, S. B., & Golden, M. M. *Social adjustment and personality development in children.* Minneapolis: University of Minnesota Press, 1972.

Rogers, C. R. *Client-centered therapy: Its current practice, implications, and theory.* Boston: Houghton-Mifflin, 1951.

Rogers, C. R. Persons or science? A philosophical question. *American Psychologist,* 1955, *10,* 267−278.

Rogers, C. R., & Dymond, R. F. (Eds.). *Psychotherapy and personality change.* Chicago: University of Chicago Press, 1954.

Rohrs, C. C., Murphy, J. P., & Densen-Gerber, J. The therapeutic community: The Odyssey House concept. In C. J. D. Zarefonetis (Ed.), *Drug abuse: Proceedings of the International Conference.* Philadelphia: Lea & Febiger, 1972.

Rollins, N., & Piazza, E. Anorexia nervosa. A quantitative approach to follow-up. *Journal of the American Academy of Child Psychiatry,* 1981, *20,* 167−183.

Rose, S. D. *Treating children in groups. A behavioral approach.* San Francisco: Jossey-Bass, 1972.

Rosen, B. M. Distribution of child psychiatric services. In I. N. Berlin & L. A. Stone (Eds.), *Basic handbook of child psychiatry. Vol. 4: Prevention and current issues.* New York: Basic Books, 1979.

Rosen, B. M., Bahn, A. K., & Kramer, M. Demographic and diagnostic characteristics of psychiatric clinic outpatients in the U. S. A., 1961. *American Journal of Orthopsychiatry,* 1964, *34,* 455−468.

Rosen, B. M., Wiener, J., Hench, C. L., Willner, S. G., & Bahn, A. K. A nationwide survey of outpatient psychiatric clinic functions, intake policies, and practices. *American Journal of Psychiatry,* 1966, *122,* 908−915.

Rosen, M., Diggory, J. C., & Werlinsky, B. E. Goal-setting expectancy of success in institutionalized and noninstitutionalized mental sub-normals. *American Journal of Mental Deficiency,* 1966, *71,* 249−255.

Rosenbaum, M. S., & Drabman, R. S. Self-control training in the classroom: A review and critique. *Journal of Applied Behavior Analysis,* 1979, *12,* 467−485.

Rosenberg, B., & Silverstein, H. *The varieties of delinquent experience.* Waltham, MA: Blaisdell, 1969.

Rosenblatt, A. D., & Thickstun, J. T. Modern psychoanalytic concepts in a general psychology. *Psychological Issues,* 1977, *11,* Monographs 42/43.

Rosenthal, D. *The design of studies to evaluate hereditary and environmental contributions to the etiology of behavioral disorders.* Presented at American Psychological Association, Miami Beach, 1970.

Rosenthal, D. *Genetics of psychopathology.* New York: McGraw-Hill, 1971.

Rosenthal, D., & Quinn, O. W. Quadruplet hallucinations. Phenotypic variations of a schizophrenic genotype. *Archives of General Psychiatry,* 1977, *34,* 817−827.

Rosenthal, R. H., & Allen, T. W. An examination of attention, arousal, and learning dysfunctions of hyperkinetic children. *Psychological Bulletin,* 1978, *85,* 689−715.

Rosenzweig, M. R. Effects of environment on brain and behavior in animals. In E. Schopler & R. J. Reichler (Eds.), *Psychopathology and child development. Research and treatment.* New York: Plenum, 1976.

Rosenzweig, M. R. Responsiveness of brain size to individual experience: Behavioral and evolutionary implications. In M. E. Hahn, C. Jensen, & B. C. Dudek (Eds.), *Development and evolution of brain size. Behavioral implications.* New York: Academic Press, 1979.

Rosenzweig, S. *Aggressive behavior and the Rosenzweig Picture-Frustration Study.* New York: Praeger, 1978.

Ross, A. O. *Psychological aspects of learning disabilities and reading disorders.* New York: McGraw-Hill, 1976.

Ross, A. O. *Child behavior therapy: Principles, procedures, and empirical basis.* New York: Wiley, 1981.

Ross, D. M., & Ross, S. A. *Hyperactivity.* New York: Wiley, 1976.

Ro-Trock, G. K., Wellisch, D., & Schoolar, J. A family therapy outcome study in an inpatient setting. *American Journal of Orthopsychiatry,* 1977, *47,* 514−522.

Rotter, J. B. *Clinical psychology.* (2nd ed.) Englewood Cliffs, NJ: Prentice-Hall, 1971.

Rotter, J., & Rafferty, J. *Manual for the Rotter Incomplete Sentence Blank.* New York: Psychological Corporation, 1958.

Rourke, B. P. Reading, spelling, arithmetic disabilities: A neuropsychological perspective. In H. R. Myklebust (Ed.), *Progress in learning disabilities (Vol. IV).* New York: Grune & Stratton, 1978.

Routh, D. K., & Schroeder, C. S. Standardized playroom measures as indices of hyperactivity. *Journal of Abnormal Child Psychology,* 1976, *4,* 199−207.

Routh, D. K., Schroeder, C. S., & O'Tuama, L. A. Development of activity level in children. *Developmental Psychology,* 1974, *10,* 163−168.

Routh, D. K., Walton, M. D., & Padan-Belkin, E. Development of activity level in children revisited: Effects of mother presence. *Developmental Psychology,* 1978, *14,* 571−581.

Rubin, E. Z., Simson, C. B., & Betwee, M. C. *Emotionally handicapped children and the elementary school.* Detroit: Wayne State University Press, 1966.

Rubin, R., & Balow, B. Learning and behavior disorders: A longitudinal study. *Exceptional Children,* 1971, *38,* 293–299.

Rubin, R. A., & Balow, B. Perinatal influences on the behavior and learning problems of children. In B. B. Lahey & A. E. Kazdin (Eds.), *Advances in clinical child psychology (Vol. 1).* New York: Plenum Press, 1977.

Rubin, R. A., & Balow, B. Measures of infant development and socioeconomic status as predictors of later intelligence and school achievement. *Developmental Psychology,* 1979, *15,* 225–227.

Rubin, T. I., *Jordi/Lisa and David.* New York: Ballantine, 1968.

Rush, A. J., Beck, A. T., Kovacs, M., & Hollon, S. Comparative efficacy of cognitive therapy and pharmacotherapy in the treatment of depressed outpatients. *Cognitive Therapy and Research,* 1977, *1,* 17–37.

Rush, B. *Medical inquiries and observations upon the diseases of the mind.* Philadelphia: Kimber & Richardson, 1812. Reprinted by New York: Hafner Publishing Co., 1962.

Russell, A. T., & Tanguay, P. E. Mental illness and mental retardation: Cause or coincidence? *American Journal of Mental Deficiency,* 1981, *85,* 570–574.

Rutter, M. Relationships between child and adult psychiatric disorders: some research considerations. *Acta Psychiatrica Scandinavica,* 1972, *48,* 3–21.

Rutter, M. The development of infantile autism. *Psychological Medicine,* 1974, *4,* 147–163.

Rutter, M. Diagnosis and definition of childhood autism. *Journal of Autism and Childhood Schizophrenia,* 1978, *8,* 139–161.

Rutter, M. *Changing youth in a changing society.* Cambridge, MA: Harvard University Press, 1980.

Rutter, M., & Bartak, L. Special educational treatment of autistic children: A comparative study. II. Follow-up findings and implications for services. *Journal of Child Psychology and Psychiatry,* 1973, *14,* 241–270.

Rutter, M., Chadwick, O., Shaffer, D., & Brown, G. A prospective study of children with head injuries: I. Design and methods. *Psychological Medicine,* 1980, *10,* 663–645.

Rutter, M., & Graham, P. The reliability and validity of the psychiatric assessment of the child: I. Interview with the child. *British Journal of Psychiatry,* 1968, *114,* 563–579.

Rutter, M., Graham, P., Chadwick, O. F. D., & Yule, W. Adolescent turmoil: Fact or fiction? *Journal of Child Psychology and Psychiatry,* 1976, *17,* 35–56.

Rutter, M., Maughn, B., Mortimore, P., Ouston, J., & Smith. A. *Fifteen thousand hours: Secondary schools and their effects on children.* Cambridge, MA: Harvard University Press, 1979.

Rutter, M., & Schopler, E. (Eds.). *Autism: A reappraisal of concepts and treatment.* New York: Plenum, 1978.

Rutter, M., & Shaffer, D. DSM-III. A step forward or back in terms of the classification of child psychiatric disorders? *Journal of the American Academy of Child Psychiatry,* 1980, *19,* 371–394.

Rutter, M., Shaffer, D., & Shepherd, M. *A multiaxial classification of child psychiatric disorders, An evaluation of a proposal.* Geneva, Switzerland: World Health Organization, 1975.

Rutter, M., Tizard, J., & Whitmore, K. (Eds.). *Education, health, and behavior.* London: Longman, 1970.

Rutter, M., Yule, B., Quinton, D., Rowlands, O., Yule, W., & Berger, M. Attainment and adjustment in two geographical areas. III. Some factors accounting for area differences. *British Journal of Psychiatry,* 1975, *126,* 520−533.

Sackeim, H. A., Nordlie, J. W., & Gur, R. C. A model of hysterical and hypnotic blindness: Cognition, motivation, and awareness. *Journal of Abnormal Psychology,* 1979, *88,* 474−489.

Sager, R. Genes outside the chromosomes. *Scientific American,* 1965, *212,* 70−81.

Sajwaj, T., & Dillon, A. Complexities of an 'elementary' behavior modification procedure: Differential adult attention used for children's behavior disorders. In B. C. Etzel, J. M. LeBlanc, & D. M. Baer (Eds.), *New developments in behavioral research: Theory, methods, and applications.* Hillsdale, NJ: Erlbaum, 1977.

Salomon, M. K., & Achenbach, T. M. The effects of four kinds of tutoring experience on associative responding in children. *American Educational Research Journal,* 1974, *11,* 395−405.

Samelson, F. J. B. Watson's Little Albert, Cyril Burt's twins, and the need for a critical science. *American Psychologist,* 1980, *35,* 619−625.

Sandberg, A. A., Koepf, G., Ishihara, T., & Hauschka, T. S. XYY human male. *Lancet,* 1961, *2,* 488−489.

Sandberg, S. T., Wieselberg, M., & Shaffer, D. Hyperkinetic and conduct problem children in a primary school population: Some epidemiological considerations. *Journal of Child Psychology and Psychiatry,* 1980, *21,* 293−311.

Sandoval, J., Lambert, N. M., & Sassone, D. The identification and labeling of hyperactivity in children: An interactive model. In C. K. Whalen & B. Henker (Eds.), *Hyperactive children: The social ecology of identification and treatment.* New York: Academic Press, 1980.

Saraf, K., Klein, D., Gittleman-Klein, R., & Groff, S. Imipramine side-effects in children. *Psychopharmacologia,* 1974, *37,* 265−274.

Sarason, I. G. A cognitive social learning approach to juvenile delinquency. In R. D. Hare & D. Schalling (Eds.), *Psychopathic behavior: Approaches to research.* New York: Wiley, 1978.

Sarason, S. B., Davidson, K. S., Lighthall, F. F., Waite, P. R., & Ruebush, B. K. *Anxiety in elementary school children: A report of research.* New York: Wiley, 1960.

Sarason, S. B., & Doris, J. *Educational handicap, public policy, and social history. A broadened perspective on mental retardation.* New York: Free Press, 1979.

Sarason, S. B., Levine, M., Goldenberg, I. I., Cherlin, D. L., & Bennett, E. M. *Psychology in community settings: Clinical, educational, vocational, social aspects.* New York: Wiley, 1966.

Saslow, H. L. The comparability of the Peabody Picture Vocabulary Test and the Revised Stanford-Binet, Form L-M, with cerebral palsied children. *American Psychologist,* 1961, *16,* 377.

Satir, V. M. *Conjoint family therapy.* Palo Alto, CA: Science and Behavior Books, 1967.

Satz, P. Incidence of aphasia in left-handers: A test of some hypothetical models of cerebral speech organization. In J. Herron (Ed.), *Neuropsychology of left-handedness.* New York: Academic Press, 1980.

Satz, P., & Fletcher, J. M. Minimal brain dysfunctions: An appraisal of research concepts and methods. In H. E. Rie & E. D. Rie (Eds.), *Handbook of minimal brain dysfunctions: A critical view.* New York: Wiley, 1980.

Sawyer, J. Measurement *and* prediction, statistical *and* clinical. *Psychological Bulletin,* 1966, *66,* 178–200.

Sayegh, Y., & Dennis, W. The effect of supplementary experiences upon the development of infants in institutions. *Child Development,* 1965, *36,* 81–90.

Scarpitti, F. R., Murray, E., Dinitz, S., & Reckless, W. C. The "good" boy in a high delinquency area: Four years later. *American Sociological Review,* 1960, *25,* 555–558.

Scarr, S. Environmental bias in twin studies. In S. G. Vandenberg (Ed.), *Progress in human behavior genetics.* Baltimore: Johns Hopkins University Press, 1968.

Scarr, S. Social introversion-extroversion as a heritable response. *Child Development,* 1969, *40,* 823–832.

Scarr, S. *Race, social class, and individual differences in IQ. New studies of old issues.* Hillsdale, NJ: Erlbaum, 1981.

Scarr, S., & Carter-Saltzman, L. Twin method: Defense of a critical assumption. *Behavior Genetics,* 1979, *9,* 527–542.

Scarr, S., & Weinberg, R. A. Intellectual similarities within families of both adopted and biological children. *Intelligence,* 1977, *1,* 170–191.

Schachter, S. *Emotion, obesity, and crime.* New York: Academic Press, 1971.

Schachter, S., & Latané, B. Crime, cognition, and the autonomic nervous system. In D. Levine (Ed.), *Nebraska Symposium on Motivation.* Lincoln: University of Nebraska Press, 1964.

Schaefer, C. (Ed.). *The therapeutic use of child's play.* New York: Aronson, 1979.

Schaffer, H. R., & Emerson, P. E. The development of social attachments in infancy. *Monographs of the Society for Research in Child Development,* 1964, *29,* (Serial No. 94).

Schaie, K. W., Anderson, V. E., McClearn, G. E., & Money, J. (Eds.). *Developmental human behavior genetics.* Lexington, MA: Lexington Books, 1975.

Schain, R. J., & Yannet, H. Infantile autism: An analysis of 50 cases and a consideration of certain neurophysiologic concepts. *Journal of Pediatrics,* 1960, *57,* 560–567.

Schalock, R. L., Harper, R. S., & Genung, T. Community integration of mentally retarded adults: Community placement and program success. *American Journal of Mental Deficiency,* 1981, *85,* 478–488.

Scharfman, M. A. Psychoanalytic treatment. In B. B. Wolman, J. Egan, & A. O. Ross (Eds.), *Handbook of treatment of mental disorders in childhood and adolescence.* Englewood Cliffs, NJ: Prentice-Hall, 1978.

Schiefelbusch, R. *Nonspeech language and communications.* Baltimore: University Park Press, 1980.

Schmauk, F. J. Punishment, arousal, and avoidance learning in sociopaths. *Journal of Abnormal Psychology,* 1970, *76,* 325–335.

Schnoll, S. H. Pharmacological aspects of youth drug abuse. In G. M. Beschner & A. S. Friedman (Eds.), *Youth drug abuse. Problems, issues, and treatment.* Lexington, MA: Heath, 1979.

Schofield, W., & Balian, L. A comparative study of the personal histories of schizophrenics and nonpsychiatric patients. *Journal of Abnormal and Social Psychology,* 1959, *59,* 216–225.

Schopler, E. Early infantile autism and receptor processes. *Archives of General Psychiatry,* 1965, *13,* 327–335.

Schopler, E., & Loftin, J. Thinking disorders in parents of young psychotic children. *Journal of Abnormal Psychology*, 1969, *74*, 281–287. (a)

Schopler, E., & Loftin, J. Thought disorders in parents of psychotic children: A function of test anxiety. *Archives of General Psychiatry*, 1969, *20*, 174–181. (b)

Schopler, E., Andrews, C. E., & Strupp, K. Do autistic children come from upper-middle class parents? *Journal of Autism and Developmental Disorders*, 1979, *9*, 139–152.

Schopler, E., Reichler, R. J., DeVellis, R. F., & Daly, K. Toward objective classification of childhood autism: Childhood Autism Rating Scale (CARS). *Journal of Autism and Developmental Disorders*, 1980, *10*, 91–103.

Schrag, P., & Divoky, D. *The myth of the hyperactive child*. New York: Pantheon, 1975.

Schulsinger, H. A. A ten-year follow-up of children of schizophrenic mothers clinical assessment. *Acta Psychiatrica Scandinavica*, 1976, *53*, 371–386.

Schulterbrandt, J. G., & Raskin, A. *Depression in childhood: Diagnosis, treatment, and conceptual models*. New York: Raven, 1977.

Schwade, E. D., & Geiger, S. G. Severe behavior disorders with abnormal electroencephalograms. *Diseases of the Nervous System*. 1960, *11*, 616–620.

Schwarz, R. H., & Jens, K. G. The expectation of success as it modifies the achievement of mentally retarded adolescents. *American Journal of Mental Deficiency*, 1969, *73*, 946–949.

Science, March 20, 1981, *211*, Special issue on development of sex differences.

Scott, C. *Alcohol, Drug, and Mental Health Administration News*, February 9, 1979, 1 & 4.

Scott, D. *About epilepsy. (Rev. ed.)*. New York: International Universities Press, 1973.

Scott, K. G., Field, T., & Robertson, E. G. *Teenage parents and their offspring*. New York: Grune & Stratton, 1981.

Scott, L. H. Measuring intelligence with the Goodenough-Harris drawing test. *Psychological Bulletin, 1981, 89*, 483–505.

Searle, L. V. The organization of hereditary maze-brightness and maze-dullness. *Genetic Psychology Monographs*, 1949, *39*, 279–325.

Sears, R. R. Relation of early socialization experiences to aggression in middle childhood. *Journal of Abnormal and Social Psychology*, 1961, *63*, 466–492.

Sears, R. R. Sources of life satisfaction of the Terman gifted men. *American Psychologist*, 1977, *32*, 119–128.

Sears, R. R., Maccoby, E. E., & Levin, H. *Patterns of child rearing*. New York: Harper, 1957.

Sears, R. R., Whiting, J. W. M., Nowlis, V., & Sears, P. S. Some child-rearing antecedents of aggression and dependency in young children. *Genetic Psychology Monographs*, 1953, *47*, 135–234.

Sechzer, J. A., Faro, M. D., & Windle, W. F. Studies of monkeys asphyxiated at birth: Implications for minimal cerebral dysfunction. *Seminars in Psychiatry*, 1973, *5*, 19–34.

Seeman, J., Barry, E., & Ellingwood, C. Interpersonal assessment of play therapy outcome. *Psychotherapy: Theory, Research, and Practice*, 1964, *1*, 64–66.

Seitz, P. F. D. The consensus problem in psychoanalytic research. In L. Gottschalk & A. Auerbach (Eds.), *Methods of research in psychotherapy*. New York: Appleton-Century-Crofts, 1966.

Seitz, S., & Geske, D. Mothers' and graduate trainees' judgments of children: Some effects of labeling. *American Journal of Mental Deficiency*, 1976, *81*, 362–370.

Selfe, L. *Nadia. A case of extraordinary drawing ability in an autistic child*. New York: Academic Press, 1977.

Seligman, M. E. P. *Helplessness: On depression, development, and death*. San Francisco: Freeman, 1975.

Sells, S. B., & Simpson, D. D. Evaluation of treatment outcomes for youths in the drug abuse reporting program (DARP): A follow-up study. In G. M. Beschner & A. S. Friedman (Eds.), *Youth drug abuse. Problems, issues, and treatment*. Lexington, MA: Heath, 1979.

Sells, S. B., & Simpson, D. D. The case for drug abuse treatment effectiveness, based on the DARP research program. *British Journal of Addiction*, 1980, *75*, 117−131.

Sewell, W. H., & Mussen, P. H. The effects of feeding, weaning, and scheduling procedures on childhood adjustment and the formation of oral symptoms. *Child Development*, 1952, *23*, 185−191.

Shaffer, D. Brain injury. In M. Rutter & L. Hersov (Eds.), *Child psychiatry. Modern approaches*. Philadelphia: Lippincott, 1977. (a)

Shaffer, D. The association between enuresis and emotional disorder: A review of the literature. In M. Rutter & L. Hersov (Eds.), *Child psychiatry: Modern approaches*. Philadelphia: Lippincott, 1977. (b)

Shaffer, D., & Fisher, P. Suicide in children and young adolescents. In C. F. Wells & I. R. Stuart (Eds.), *Self-destructive behavior in children and adolescents*. New York: Van Nostrand, 1981.

Shaffer, D., McNamara, N., & Pincus, J. H. Controlled observations on patterns of activity, attention, and impulsivity in brain-damaged and psychiatrically disturbed boys. *Journal of Psychological Medicine*, 1974, *4*, 4−18.

Shapiro, R. J., & Budman, S. H. Defection, termination, and continuation in family and individual therapy. *Family Process*, 1973, *12*, 55−67.

Shapiro, A. K., Shapiro, E. S., Bruun, R. D., & Sweet, R. D. *Gilles de la Tourette syndrome*. New York: Raven Press, 1978.

Share, J., Koch, R., Webb, A., & Graliker, B. The longitudinal development of infants and young children with Down's syndrome (mongolism). *American Journal of Mental Deficiency*, 1964, *68*, 685−692.

Shaw, B. F. Comparison of cognitive therapy and behavior therapy in the treatment of depression. *Journal of Consulting and Clinical Psychology*, 1977, *45*, 543−551.

Shaw, C. R. *The Jack Roller*. Chicago: University of Chicago Press, 1930.

Shaw, C. R., & McKay, H. D. *Juvenile delinquency and urban areas. (Rev. ed.)*. Chicago: University of Chicago Press, 1969.

Shaywitz, S. E., Cohen, D. S., & Shaywitz, B. A. The biochemical basis of minimal brain dysfunction. *Journal of Pediatrics*, 1978, *92*, 179−187.

Sheare, J. B. Social acceptance of EMR adolescents in integrated programs. *American Journal of Mental Deficiency*, 1974, *78*, 678−682.

Sherwood, G. G. Classical and attributive projection: Some new evidence. *Journal of Abnormal Psychology*, 1979, *88*, 635−640.

Shields, J. Personality differences and neurotic traits in normal twin school children. A study in psychiatric genetics. *Eugenics Review*, 1954, *45*, 213−246.

Shields, J. *Monozygotic twins*. London: Oxford University Press, 1962.

Shields, J., & Gottesman, I. I. Cross-national diagnosis of schizophrenia in twins. *Archives of General Psychiatry*, 1972, *27*, 725−730.

Shinohara, M., & Jenkins, R. L. MMPI study of three types of delinquents. *Journal of Clinical Psychology*, 1967, *23*, 156–163.

Shneidman, E. S. The MAPS Test with children. In A. I. Rubin & M. R. Haworth (Eds.), *Projective techniques with children*. New York: Grune & Stratton, 1960.

Shoben, E. J., Jr. Psychotherapy as a problem in learning theory. *Psychological Bulletin*, 1949, *46*, 366–392.

Shoor, M., Speed, M. H., & Bartelt, C. Syndrome of the adolescent child molester. *American Journal of Psychiatry*, 1966, *122*, 783–789.

Shore, M. F., & Massimo, J. L. Fifteen years after treatment: A follow-up study of comprehensive vocationally-oriented psychotherapy. *American Journal of Orthopsychiatry*, 1979, *49*, 240–245.

Short, J. F., Tennyson, R. A., & Howard, K. I. Behavior dimensions of gang delinquency. *American Sociological Review*, 1963, *28*, 411–428.

Shure, M. B., & Spivack, G. *Problem solving techniques in childrearing*. San Francisco: Jossey-Bass, 1978.

Siegel, L. J., & Richards, C. S. Behavioral intervention with somatic disorders in children. In D. Marholin, II (Ed.), *Child behavior therapy*. New York: Gardner, 1978.

Siegel, R. A. Probability of punishment and suppression of behavior in psychopathic and nonpsychopathic offenders. *Journal of Abnormal Psychology*, 1978, *87*, 514–522.

Silberg, J. L. The development of pronoun usage in the psychotic child. *Journal of Autism and Childhood Schizophrenia*, 1978, *8*, 413–425.

Silberman, C. *Crisis in the classroom*. New York: Random House, 1970.

Silbert, A., Wolff, P. H., & Lilienthal, J. Spatial and temporal processing in patients with Turner's syndrome. *Behavior Genetics*, 1977, *7*, 11–21.

Silverstein, A., & Robinson, H. The representation of orthopedic difficulties in children's figure drawings. *Journal of Consulting Psychology*, 1956, *20*, 333.

Singer, M., & Wynne, L. C. Differentiating characteristics of parents of childhood schizophrenics, childhood neurotics, and young adult schizophrenics. *American Journal of Psychiatry*, 1963, *120*, 234–243.

Siperstein, G. N., Budoff, M., & Bak, J. J. Effects of the labels 'mentally retarded' and 'retard' on the social acceptability of mentally retarded children. *American Journal of Mental Deficiency*, 1980, *84*, 596–601.

Skaarbrevik, K. J. A follow-up study of educable mentally retarded in Norway. *American Journal of Mental Deficiency*, 1971, *75*, 560–565.

Skeels, H. M. Adult status of children with contrasting early life experiences. *Monographs of the Society for Research in Child Development*, 1966, *31*(Serial No. 105).

Skinner, B. F. Baby in a box. *Ladies Home Journal*, October, 1945.

Skinner, B. F. *Walden two*. New York: Macmillan, 1948.

Skinner, B. F. *Science and human behavior*. New York: Macmillan, 1953.

Skinner, B. F. *Beyond freedom and dignity*. New York: Knopf, 1971.

Skodak, M., & Skeels, H. M. A final follow-up study of one hundred adopted children. *Journal of Genetic Psychology*, 1949, *75*, 85–125.

Slater, E., & Cowie, V. *The genetics of mental disorders*. London: Oxford University Press, 1971.

Slavson, S. R., & Schiffer, M. *Group psychotherapies for children. A textbook*. New York: International Universities Press, 1975.

Sloane, R. B., Staples, F. R., Cristol, A. H. Yorkston, N. J., & Whipple, K. *Psychotherapy versus behavior therapy.* Cambridge, MA: Harvard University Press, 1975.

Sloane, R. B., Staples, F. R., Cristol, A. H., Yorkston, N. J., & Whipple, K. Patient characteristics and outcome in psychotherapy and behavior therapy. *Journal of Consulting and Clinical Psychology*, 1976, *44*, 330−339.

Small, J. G., DeMyer, M. K., & Milstein, V. CNV responses of autistic and normal children. *Journal of Autism and Childhood Schizophrenia*, 1971, *1*, 215−231.

Smith, D., Levy, S. J., & Striar, D. E. Treatment services for youthful drug users. In G. M. Beschner & A. S. Friedman (Eds.), *Youth drug abuse. Problems, issues and treatment.*, Lexington, MA: Heath, 1979.

Smith, D. W., & Wilson, A. *The child with Down's syndrome (mongolism). Causes, characteristics and acceptance.* Philadelphia: Saunders, 1973.

Smith, R. C. Speed and violence: Compulsive methamphetamine abuse and criminality in the Haight-Ashbury district. In C. J. D. Zarafonetis (Ed.), *Drug abuse: Proceedings of the International Conference.* Philadelphia: Lea & Febiger, 1972.

Smith, R. E., & Sharpe, T. M. Treatment of a school phobia with implosive therapy. *Journal of Consulting and Clinical Psychology*, 1970, *35*, 239−243.

Smith, R. T. A comparison of socio-environmental factors in monozygotic and dizygotic twins, testing an assumption. In S. G. Vandenberg (Ed.), *Methods and goals in human behavior genetics.* New York: Academic Press, 1965.

Snyder, C. R., Shenkel, R. J., & Lowery, C. R. Acceptance of personality interpretations: The 'Barnum effect' and beyond. *Journal of Consulting and Clinical Psychology*, 1977, *45*, 104−114.

Sobell, M. B., & Sobell, L. C. *Behavioral treatment of alcohol problems.* New York: Plenum, 1978.

Solomon, P., Kubzansky, P. E., Leiderman, P. H., Mendelson, J. H., Trumbull, R., & Wexler, D. (Eds.), *Sensory deprivation.* Cambridge: Harvard University Press, 1961.

Sontag, L. W., Baker, C. T., & Nelson, V. L. Mental growth and personality development: A longitudinal study. *Monographs of the Society for Research in Child Development*, 1958, *23*(Serial No. 68).

Sostek, A. M., Quinn, P. O., & Davitt, M. K. Behavior, development, and neurologic status of premature and full-term infants with varying medical complications. In T. M. Field (Ed.), *Infants born at risk: Behavior and development.* Larchmont, NY: SP Medical and Scientific Books, 1979.

Spielberger, C. D. *Preliminary Manual for the State-Trait Anxiety Inventory for Children.* Palo Alto, CA: Consulting Psychologists Press, 1973.

Spitz, R. A. Possible infantile precursors of psychopathology. *American Journal of Orthopsychiatry*, 1950, *20*, 240−248.

Spitzer, R. L., & Cantwell, D. P. The DSM-III classification of the psychiatric disorders of infancy, childhood, and adolescence. *Journal of the American Academy of Child Psychiatry*, 1980, *19*, 356−370.

Spock, B. *Baby and child care. (2nd ed.)* New York: Pocket Books, 1968.

Sprague, R. L., & Sleator, E. K. Methylphenidate in hyperkinetic children: Differences in dose effects on learning and social behavior. *Science*, 1977, *198*, 1274−1276.

Springer, N. S., & Fricke, N. L. Nutrition and drug therapy for persons with developmental disabilities. *American Journal of Mental Deficiency,* 1975, *80,* 317−322.

Sreenivasan, U., Manocha, S. N., & Jain, V. K. Treatment of severe dog phobia in childhood by flooding: A case report. *Journal of Child Psychology and Psychiatry,* 1979, *20,* 255−260.

St. James-Roberts, B. Neurological plasticity, recovery from brain insult, and child development. In H. W. Reese & L. P. Lipsitt (Eds.), *Advances in child development and behavior (Vol. 14).* New York: Academic Press, 1979.

Stager, S. F., & Young, R. D. Intergroup contact and social outcomes for mainstreamed EMR adolescents. *American Journal of Mental Deficiency,* 1981, *85,* 497−503.

Stampfl, T. G., & Levis, D. J. Essentials of implosive therapy: A learning theory-based psychodynamic behavioral therapy. *Journal of Abnormal Psychology,* 1967, *72,* 496−503.

Stanbury, J. B. The role of the thyroid in the development of the human nervous system. In L. S. Greene (Ed.), *Malnutrition, behavior, and social organization.* New York: Academic Press, 1977.

Starr, P. H. Some observations on the diagnostic aspects of childhood hysteria. *Nervous Child,* 1953, *10,* 214−231.

Stefanis, C., Dornbush, R., & Fink, M. *Hashish: Studies of long-term use.* New York: Raven Press, 1977.

Stein, K. B., Sarbin, T. R., & Kulik, J. A. Further validation of antisocial personality types. *Journal of Consulting and Clinical Psychology,* 1971, *36,* 177−182.

Stein, Z., & Susser, M. The social distribution of mental retardation. *American Journal of Mental Deficiency,* 1963, *67,* 811−821.

Stein, Z., Susser, M., Saenger, G., & Marolla, F. *Famine and human development: The Dutch hunger winter of 1944−1945.* New York: Oxford University Press, 1975.

Stephenson, R., & Scarpitti, F. Essexfields: A nonresidential experiment in group-centered rehabilitation of delinquents. *American Journal of Corrections,* 1969, *31,* 12−18.

Stevenson, H. W., Hale, G. A., Klein, R. E., & Miller, L. K. Interrelations and correlates in children's learning and problem solving. *Monographs of the Society for Research in Child Development,* 1968, *33*(Serial No. 123).

Stewart, L. H. Social and emotional adjustment during adolescence as related to the development of psychosomatic illness in adulthood. *Genetic Psychology Monographs,* 1962, *65,* 175−215.

Stewart, M. A., DeBlois, S., & Cummings, C. Psychiatric disorders in the parents of hyperactive boys and those with conduct disorders. *Journal of Child Psychology and Psychiatry,* 1980, *21,* 283−292.

Stoch, M. B., & Smythe, P. M. Undernutrition during infancy, and subsequent brain growth and intellectual development. In N. S. Scrimshaw & J. E. Gordon (Eds.), *Malnutrition, learning, and behavior.* Cambridge: M.I.T. Press, 1968.

Strauss, A. A., & Lehtinen, L. E. *Psychopathology and education of the brain-injured child.* New York: Grune & Stratton, 1947.

Strauss, M. E., Lessen-Firestone, J. K., Starr, R. H., & Ostrea, E. M. Behavior of narcotics addicted newborns. *Child Development,* 1975, *46,* 877−893.

Strean, H. S. A family therapist looks at "Little Hans." *Family Process,* 1967, *6,* 227−234.

Street, D., Vinter, R., & Perrow, C. *Organization for treatment: A comparative study of institutions for delinquents.* New York: Free Press, 1966.

Streissguth, A. P., Landesman-Dwyer, S., Martin, J. C., & Smith, D. W. Teratogenic effects of alcohol in humans and laboratory animals. *Science,* 1980, *209,* 353–361.

Strober, M., Green, J., & Carlson, G. Utility of the Beck Depression Inventory with psychiatrically hospitalized adolescents. *Journal of Consulting and Clinical Psychology,* 1981, *49,* 482–483.

Stroh, G., & Buick, D. The effect of relative sensory isolation on the behavior of two autistic children. In S. J. Hutt & C. Hutt (Eds.), *Behavior studies in psychiatry.* New York: Pergamon Press, 1970.

Strupp, H. H., Hadley, S. W., & Gomes-Schwartz, B. *Psychotherapy for better or worse: The problem of negative effects.* New York: Aronson, 1977.

Stuart, R. B. Teaching facts about drugs: Pushing or preventing? *Journal of Educational Psychology,* 1974, *66,* 189–201.

Suinn, R. M., & Oskamp, S. *The predictive validity of projective measures.* Springfield, IL.: Thomas, 1969.

Sullivan, H. S. *The interpersonal theory of psychiatry.* New York: Norton, 1953.

Sulloway, F. J. *Freud, Biologist of the mind. Beyond the psychoanalytic legend.* New York: Basic Books, 1979.

Sulzer-Azaroff, B., & Mayer, G. R. *Applying behavior-analysis procedures with children and youth.* New York: Holt, Rinehart, & Winston, 1977.

Sundby, H. S., & Kreyberg, P. C. *Prognosis in child psychiatry.* Baltimore: Williams & Wilkins, 1968.

Suskind, R. M. Characteristics and causation of protein-calorie malnutrition in the infant and preschool child. In L. S. Greene (Ed.), *Malnutrition, behavior and social organization.* New York: Academic Press, 1977.

Swanson, J. M., & Kinsbourne, M. Artificial color and hyperactive behavior. In R. M. Knights & D. Bakker (Eds.), *Rehabilitation, treatment, and management of learning disorders.* Baltimore: University Park Press, 1980.

Sweetster, W. *Mental hygiene.* New York: Putnam, 1843.

Symonds, A., & Herman, M. The patterns of schizophrenia in adolescence: A report on 50 cases of adolescent girls. *Psychiatric Quarterly,* 1957, *31,* 521–530.

Synanon. *Fact sheet: Synanon: The people business.* Marshall, CA: Synanon, 1977.

Szasz, T. *The manufacture of madness: A comparative study of the inquisition and the mental health movement.* New York: Harper, 1970.

Taft, L. T., & Goldfarb, W. Prenatal and perinatal factors in childhood schizophrenia. *Developmental Medicine and Child Neurology,* 1963, *6,* 32–43.

Tager-Flusberg, H. On the nature of linguistic functioning in early infantile autism. *Journal of Autism and Developmental Disorders,* 1981, *11,* 45–56.

Tanner, J. M. Physical growth. In P. H. Mussen (Ed.), *Carmichael's manual of child psychology (3rd ed., Vol. 1).* New York: Wiley, 1970.

Tarler-Benlolo, L. The role of relaxation in biofeedback training: A critical review of the literature. *Psychological Bulletin,* 1978, *85,* 727–755.

Tavorimina, J. B. Relative effectiveness of behavioral and reflective group counseling with parents of mentally retarded children. *Journal of Consulting and Clinical Psychology,* 1975, *43,* 22–31.

Taylor, E. M. *Psychological appraisal of children with cerebral defects.* Cambridge: Harvard University Press, 1959.

Templin, M. C. *Certain language skills in children. Their development and interrelationships*. Minneapolis: University of Minnesota Press, 1957.

Terestman, N. Mood quality and intensity in nursery school children as predictors of behavior disorders. *American Journal of Orthopsychiatry*, 1980, *50*, 125–138.

Terman, L. M. *The measurement of intelligence*. Boston: Houghton-Mifflin, 1916.

Terman, L., Lyman, G., Ordahl, G., Ordahl, L. E., Galbreath, N., & Talbert, W. *The Stanford revision and extension of the Binet-Simon Measuring Scale of Intelligence*. Baltimore: Warwick and York, 1917.

Terman, L. M., & Merrill, M. A. *Stanford-Binet Intelligence Scale. Manual for the third revision, Form L-M*. Boston: Houghton-Mifflin, 1960; 1973.

Terman, L. M., & Oden, M. H. *Genetic studies of genius, V: The gifted group at mid-life*. Stanford, CA: Stanford University Press, 1959.

Terrell, F., Taylor, J., & Terrell, S. L. Effects of type of social reinforcement on the intelligence test performance of lower-class black children. *Journal of Consulting and Clinical Psychology*, 1978, *46*, 1538–1539.

Teuber, H. L., & Rudel, R. G. Behavior after cerebral lesions in children and adults. *Developmental Medicine and Child Neurology*, 1962, *4*, 3–20.

Thomas, A., & Chess, S. *Temperament and development*. New York: Brunner/Mazel, 1977.

Thomas, A., & Chess, S. *The dynamics of psychological development*. New York: Brunner/Mazel, 1980.

Thomas, A., Chess, S., & Birch, H. G. *Temperament and behavior disorders in children*. New York: New York University Press, 1968.

Thompson, T., & Grabowski, J. (Eds.). *Behavior modification of the mentally retarded (2nd ed.)*. New York: Oxford University Press, 1977.

Thompson, W. R. Influence of prenatal maternal anxiety on emotionality in young rats. *Science*, 1957, *125*, 698–699.

Thorndike, E. L. *Educational psychology, Vol. II: The psychology of learning*, New York: Teacher's College, Columbia University, 1913.

Tittle, C. R., Villemez, W. J., & Smith, D. A. The myth of social class and criminality: An empirical assessment of the empirical evidence. *American Sociological Review*, 1978, *43*, 643–656.

Tizard, B., & Rees, J. The effect of early institutional rearing on the behavior problems and affectual relationships of four-year-old children. *Journal of Child Psychology and Psychiatry*, 1975, *16*, 61–73.

Tomlinson-Keasey, C., Kelly, R. R., & Burton, J. K. Hemispheric changes in information processing during development. *Developmental Psychology*, 1978, *14*, 214–223.

Torgerson, A. M., & Kringlen, E. Genetic aspects of temperamental differences in twins. A study of same-sexed twins. *Journal of the American Academy of Child Psychiatry*, 1978, *17*, 433–444.

Townsend, J. W., Klein, R. E., Irwin, M., Yarbrough, C., Lechtig, A., Delgado, H., Martorell, R., & Engel, P. L. Malnutrition and mental development: Some longitudinal perspectives. In G. Serban (Ed.), *Cognitive defects in the development of mental illness*. New York: Brunner/Mazel, 1978.

Tramontana, M. G. Critical review of research on psychotherapy outcome with adolescents: 1967–1977. *Psychological Bulletin*, 1980, *88*, 429–450.

Travis, L. E. The cerebral dominance theory of stuttering: 1931–1978. *Journal of Speech and Hearing Disorders*, 1978, *43*, 278–281.

Treffert, D. A. Epidemiology of infantile autism. *Archives of General Psychiatry*, 1970, *22*, 431–438.

Trilling, L., & Marcus, S. (Eds.). *The life and work of Sigmund Freud (Abridged ed.)*. New York: Anchor, 1963.

Trites, R. L. (Ed.). *Hyperactivity in children. Etiology, measurement, and treatment implications*. Baltimore: University Park Press, 1979.

Trites, R., Ferguson, B., & Tryphonas, H. *Food allergies and hyperactivity*. Presented at American Psychological Association, Toronto, Ontario, August 1978.

Tryon, R. C. Individual differences. In F. A. Moss (Ed.), *Comparative psychology*. New York: Prentice-Hall, 1934.

Tuber, D. S., Berntson, G. G., Bachman, D. S., & Allen, J. N. Associative learning in premature hydranencephalic and normal twins. *Science*, 1980, *210*, 1035–1037.

Tuchmann-Duplessis, H. *Drug effects on the fetus*. Littleton, MA.: Publishing Sciences Group, 1975.

Tulkin, S. R. Race, class, family and school achievement. *Journal of Personality and Social Psychology*, 1968, *9*, 1–37.

Tulkin, S. R., & Newbrough, J. R. Social class, race, and sex differences on the Raven (1956) Standard Progressive Matrices. *Journal of Consulting and Clinical Psychology*, 1968, *32*, 400–406.

Tunley, R. *Kids, crimes, and chaos*. New York: Harper, 1962.

Ullmann, L. P., & Krasner, L. *A psychological approach to abnormal behavior (2nd ed.)*. Englewood Cliffs, N.J.: Prentice-Hall, 1975.

Ulrich, R. E., Stachnik, T. J., & Stainton, N. R. Student acceptance of generalized personality interpretations. *Psychological Reports*, 1968, *13*, 831–834.

U. S. Children's Bureau. *Infant care*. Washington, DC: U.S. Government Printing Office, 1914; 1929; 1963.

U.S. Children's Bureau. *Juvenile court statistics*. Washington, DC: U.S. Department of Health, Education, and Welfare, Children's Bureau, 1972.

U.S. Department of Justice. *Crime in the United States, 1978*. Washington, DC: U. S. Government Printing Office 1979.

U.S. House Committee on Armed Services. Inquiry into alleged drug abuse in the armed services: Report of a special subcommittee, 92nd Congress, second session, 1971. HASC, 92–94.

Uzgiris, I. D., & Hunt, J. M. *Assessment in infancy. Ordinal scales of psychological development*. Urbana, IL: University of Illinois Press, 1975.

Vacc, N. A. A study of emotionally disturbed children in regular and special classes. *Exceptional Children*, 1968, *35*, 197–204

Vacc, N. A. Long-term effects of special class intervention for emotionally disturbed children. *Exceptional Children*, 1972, *39*, 15–22.

Vaillant, G. E. Natural history of alcoholism. I. A preliminary report. In S. B. Sells, R. Crandall, M. Roff, J. S. Strauss, & W. Pollin (Eds.), *Human functioning in longitudinal perspective*. Baltimore: Williams & Wilkins, 1980. (a)

Vaillant, G. E. Natural history of male psychological health: VIII. Antecedents of alcoholism and 'orality.' *American Journal of Psychiatry*, 1980, *137*, 181–186. (b)

Valins, S. The perception and labeling of bodily changes as determinants of emotional behavior. In P. Black (Ed.), *Physiological correlates of emotion*. New York: Academic Press, 1970.

Van Buskirk, S. S. A two-phase perspective on the treatment of anorexia nervosa. *Psychological Bulletin*, 1977, *84*, 529–538.

Vandenberg, S. G. Hereditary factors in normal personality traits as measured by inventories. In J. Wortis (Eds.), *Recent Advances in biological psychiatry (Vol. 9)*. New York: Plenum, 1967.

Vandenberg, S. G. Twin studies. In A. R. Kaplan (Ed.), *Human behavior genetics*. Springfield, IL: Thomas, 1976.

Vedder, C. B. *Juvenile offenders (rev. 6th printing)*. Springfield, IL: Thomas, 1979.

Vogel, W., Broverman, D. M., Klaiber, E. L., Kobayshi, Y., & Clarkson, F. E. A model for the integration of hormonal, behavioral, EEG, and pharmacological data in psychopathology. In T. M. Itil, G. Laudahn, & W. M. Hermann (Eds.), *Psychotropic action of hormones*. New York: Spectrum, 1976.

Voss, H. L. The predictive efficiency of the Glueck Social Prediction Table. *Journal of Criminal Law, Crime, and Police Science*, 1963, *54*, 421–430.

Wachs, T. D., & DeRemer, P. Adaptive behavior and Uzgiris-Hunt performance of young, developmentally disabled children. *American Journal of Mental Deficiency*, 1978, *83*, 171–176.

Wachtel, P. L. *Psychoanalysis and behavior theory: Toward an integration*. New York: Basic Books, 1977.

Wade, T. C., Baker, T. B., & Hartmann, D. P. Behavior therapists' self-reported views and practices. *The Behavior Therapist*, 1979, *2*, 3–6.

Waelder, R. Review of *Psychoanalysis, scientific method, and philosophy*, by S. Hook. *Journal of the American Psychoanalytic Association*, 1962, *10*, 617–637.

Wahler, R. G. Oppositional children: A quest for parental reinforcement control. *Journal of Applied Behavioral Analysis*, 1969, *2*, 159–170.

Walter, R. D., Colbert, E. G., Koegler, R. R., Palmer, J. O., & Bond, P. M. A controlled study of the 14 and 6 per-second EEG pattern. *American Medical Association Archives of General Psychiatry*, 1960, *2*, 559–566.

Walzer, S., Wolff, P. H., Bowen, D., Silbert, A. R., Bashir, A. S., Gerald, P. S., & Richmond, J. B. A method for the longitudinal study of behavioral development in infants and children: The early development of XXY children. *Journal of Child Psychology and Psychiatry*, 1978, *19*, 213–229.

Ward, I. L., & Weisz, J. Maternal stress alters plasma testerone in fetal males. *Science*, 1980, *207*, 328–329.

Warren, M. Q. The case for differential treatment of delinquents. *Annals of the American Academy of Political and Social Science*, 1969, *381*, 47–59.

Warren, M. Q. Classification for treatment. Presented at National Institute of Law Enforcement and Criminal Justice Seminar on the classification of criminal behavior: Uses and the state of research. Washington, DC: May 4, 1972.

Warren, M. Q. Correctional treatment and coercion: The differential effectiveness perspective. *Criminal Justice and Behavior*, 1977, *4*, 355–376.

Warren, R., Deffenbacher, J. L., & Brading, P. Rational-emotive therapy and the reduction of test anxiety in elementary school students. *Rational Living*, 1976, *11*, 26–29.

Waterman, A. S., Geary, P. S., & Waterman, C. K. Longitudinal study of changes in ego identity status from the freshman to the senior year at college. *Developmental Psychology*, 1974, *10*, 387–392.

Waters, E., & Sroufe, L. A. Social competence as a developmental construct: Perceiving the coherence of individual differences across age, across situations, and across behavioral domains. Unpublished manuscript, University of Minnesota, 1981.

Watson, C. G., & Buranen, C. The frequencies of conversion reaction symptoms. *Journal of Abnormal Psychology*, 1979, *88*, 209–211.

Watson, J. B. Psychology as the behaviorist views it. *Psychological Review*, 1913, *20*, 158–177.

Watson, J. B. *Psychology from the standpoint of a behaviorist*. Philadelphia: J. B. Lippincott, 1919.

Watson, J. B. *Behaviorism*. New York: People's Publishing Co., 1924.

Watson, J. B., & Rayner, R. Conditioned emotional reactions. *Journal of Experimental Psychology*, 1920, *3*, 1–14.

Watson, J. D., & Crick, F. H. C. Molecular structure of nucleic acids—a structure for deoxyribose nucleic acid. *Nature*, 1953, *171*, 737–738.

Watt, N. F., & Nicholi, A. Early death of a parent as an etiological factor in schizophrenia. *American Journal of Orthopsychiatry*, 1979, *49*, 465–473.

Wattenberg, W. W., & Saunders, F. Sex differences among juvenile offenders. *Sociology and Social Research*, 1954, *39*, 24–31.

Wawrzaszek, F., Johnson, O. G., & Sciera, J. L. A comparison of H-T-P responses of handicapped and non-handicapped children. *Journal of Clinical Psychology*, 1958, *14*, 160–162.

Weber, D. *Der frühkindliche Autismus unter dem Aspekt der Entwicklung*. Bern: Verlag Hans Huber, 1970.

Wechsler, D. *Wechsler Preschool and Primary Scale of Intelligence*. New York: Psychological Corporation, 1967.

Wechsler, D. *Wechsler Intelligence Scale for Children-Revised*. New York: Psychological Corporation, 1974.

Wechsler, D. *Wechsler Adult Intelligence Scale-Revised*. New York: Psychological Corporation, 1981.

Weeks, H. *Youthful offenders at Highfields*. Ann Arbor: University of Michigan Press, 1958.

Weinberg, W. A., Rutman, J., Sullivan, L., Penick, E. C., & Dietz, S. G. Depression in children referred to an educational diagnostic center: Diagnosis and treatment. *Journal of Pediatrics*, 1973, *83*, 1065–1072.

Weiner, D. B. The apprenticeship of Phillipe Pinel: A new document, 'Observations of Citizen Pussin on the insane.' *American Journal of Psychiatry*, 1979, *136*, 1128–1134.

Weiner, H., Thaler, M., Reiser, M. F., & Mirsky, I. A. Etiology of duodenal ulcer. I. Relation of specific psychological characteristics to rate of gastric secretion (Serum pepsinogen). *Psychosomatic Medicine*, 1957, *19*, 1–10.

Weintraub, S. A. Self-control as a correlate of an internalizing-externalizing symptom dimension. *Journal of Abnormal Child Psychology*, 1973, *1*, 292–307.

Weiss, B., Williams, J. H., Margen, S., Abrams, B., Caan, B., Citron, L. J., Cox, C., McKibben, J., Ogar, D., & Schultz, S. Behavioral responses to artificial food colors. *Science*, 1980, *207*, 1487–1489.

Weiss, G., & Hechtman, L. The hyperactive child syndrome. *Science*, 1979, *205*, 1348–1354.

Weiss, G., Hechtman, L., Perlman, T., Hopkins, J., & Wener, A. Hyperactive children as young adults: A controlled 10-year follow-up of the psychiatric status of 75 hyperactive children. *Archives of General Psychiatry*, 1979, *36*, 675–681.

Weiss, G., Kruger, E., Danielson, U., & Elman, M. Effect of long-term treatment of hyperactive children with methylphenidate. *Canadian Medical Journal*, 1975, *112*, 159–165.

Weiss, L., & Masling, J. Further validation of a Rorschach measure of oral imagery. A study of six clinical groups. *Journal of Abnormal Psychology*, 1970, *76*, 83–87.

Weisz, J. R. Effects of the 'mentally retarded' label on adult judgments about child failure. *Journal of Abnormal Psychology*, 1981, *90*, 371–374.

Weisz, J. R., O'Neill, P., & O'Neill, P. C. Field dependence-independence on the children's Embedded Figures Test: Cognitive style or cognitive level? *Developmental Psychology*, 1975, *11*, 539–540.

Weisz, J. R., Quinlan, D. M., O'Neill, P., & O'Neill, P. C. The Rorschach and structured tests of perception as indices of development in mentally retarded and nonretarded children. *Journal of Experimental Child Psychology*, 1978, *25*, 326–336.

Weisz, J. R., & Yeates, K. O. Cognitive development in retarded and nonretarded persons: Piagetian tests of the similar structure hypothesis. *Psychological Bulletin*, 1981, *90*, 153–178.

Weisz, J. R., & Zigler, E. Cognitive development in retarded and nonretarded persons: Piagetian tests of the similar sequence hypothesis. *Psychological Bulletin*, 1979, *86*, 831–851.

Wellisch, D. K., Vincent, J., & Ro-Trock, G. K. Family therapy versus individual therapy: A study of adolescents and their parents. In D. H. L. Olson (Ed.), *Treating relationships*. Lake Mills, IO: Graphic Publications, 1976.

Wenar, C., Ruttenberg, B. A., Dratman, M. L., & Wolfe, E. G. Changing autistic behavior. The effectiveness of three milieus. *Archives of General Psychiatry*, 1967, *17*, 26–35.

Wenar, C., & Ruttenberg, B. A. The use of BRIAC for evaluating therapeutic effectiveness. *Journal of Autism and Childhood Schizophrenia*, 1976, *6*, 175–191.

Wender, P. *Minimal brain dysfunction in children*. New York: Wiley-Interscience, 1971.

Wender, P. H. The etiology of MBD: Evidence for genetic and biochemical factors. In N. A. Reatig (Ed.), *Proceedings of the National Institute of Mental Health Workshop on the Hyperkinetic Behavior Syndrome*. Rockville, MD: NIMH, 1978.

Wender, P., & Wender, E. *The hyperactive child and the learning disabled child. A handbook for parents*. New York: Cramm, 1978.

Werner, E. E. Environmental interaction in minimal brain dysfunctions. In H. E. Rie & E. D. Rie (Eds.), *Handbook of minimal brain dysfunctions. A critical view*. New York: Wiley, 1980.

Werner, E., & Smith, R. S. *Kauai's children come of age*. Honolulu: University of Hawaii Press, 1977.

Werry, J. S. Psychosomatic disorders, psychogenic symptoms, and hospitalization. In H. C. Quay & J. S. Werry (Eds.), *Psychopathological disorders of childhood (2nd ed.)* New York: Wiley, 1979.

Werry, J. S., & Aman, M. G. The reliability and diagnostic validity of the physical and neurological examination for soft signs (PANESS). *Journal of Autism and Childhood Schizophrenia*, 1976, *6*, 253−262.

Werry, J. S., & Sprague, R. L. Methylphenidate in children: effect of dosage. *Australian and New Zealand Journal of Psychiatry*, 1974, *8*, 9−19.

Whalen, C. K., Collins, B. E., Henker, B., Alkus, S. R., Adams, D., & Stapp, J. Behavior observations of hyperactive children and methylphenidate (Ritalin) effects in systematically structured classroom environments: Now you see them, now you don't. *Journal of Pediatric Psychology*, 1978, *3*, 177−187.

Whalen, C. K., & Henker, B. A. Pyramid therapy in a hospital for the retarded: Methods, program evaluation, and long term effects. *American Journal of Mental Deficiency*, 1971, *75*, 414−434.

Whalen, C. K., & Henker, B. (Eds.). *Hyperactive children: The social ecology of identification and treatment*. New York: Academic Press, 1980.

Whalen, C. K., Henker, B., Collins, B. E., Finck, D., & Dotemoto, S. A social ecology of hyperactive boys: Medication effects in structured classroom environments. *Journal of Applied Behavior Analysis*, 1979, *12*, 65−81.

Whalen, C. K., Henker, B., Collins, B. E., McAuliffe, S., & Vaux, A. Peer interaction in a structured communication task: Comparisons of normal and hyperactive boys and of methylphenidate (Ritalin) and placebo effects. *Child Development*, 1979, *50*, 388−401.

White, R. W. Motivation reconsidered: The concept of competence. *Psychological Review*, 1959, *66*, 297−333.

White, R. W. Ego and reality in psychoanalytic theory. *Psychological Issues*, 1963, *3*, (Monogr. 11).

Widom, C. Toward an understanding of female criminality. In B. A. Maher (Ed.), *Progress in experimental personality research (Vol. 8)*. New York: Academic Press, 1978.

Wiener, J. M. *Psychopharmacology in childhood and adolescence*. New York: Basic Books, 1978.

Wiesel, T. N., & Hubel, D. H. Effects of visual deprivation on morphology and physiology of cells in the cat's lateral geniculate body. *Journal of Neurophysiology*, 1963, *26*, 978−993.

Wiggins, J. S. Clinical and statistical prediction: Where are we and where do we go from here? *Clinical Psychology Review*, 1981, *1*, 3−18.

Wikler, A. *Opiod dependence*. New York: Plenum, 1980.

Willerman, L. Activity level and hyperactivity in twins. *Child Development*, 1973, *44*, 288−293.

Wilsnack, S. C., & Wilsnack, R. W. Sex roles and adolescent drinking. In H. T. Blane & M. E. Chafetz (Eds.), *Youth, alcohol, and social policy*. New York: Plenum, 1979.

Wilson, C. W. M. (ed.), *The pharmacological and epidemiological aspects of adolescent drug dependence*. Oxford: Pergamon, 1968.

Wilson, R. S. Synchronies in mental development: An epigenetic perspective. *Science*, 1978, *202*, 939−948.

Winick, M., & Rosso, P. Malnutrition and central nervous system development. In J. W. Prescott, M. S. Read, & D. B. Coursin (Eds.), *Brain function and malnutrition. Neuropsychological methods of assessment*. New York: Wiley, 1975.

Winsberg, B. G., & Yepes, L. E. Antipsychotics (major tranquilizers, neuroleptics). In J. S.

Werry (Ed.), *Pediatric psychopharmacology: The use of behavior modifying drugs in children*. New York: Brunner/Mazel, 1978.

Wirt, R. D., & Broen, W. E. The relation of the Children's Manifest Anxiety Scale to the concept of anxiety as used in the clinic. *Journal of Consulting Psychology*, 1956, *20*, 482.

Wirt, R. D., & Broen, W. E. *Personality Inventory for Children*. Minneapolis: University of Minnesota, 1958.

Wirt, R. D., Lachar, D., Klinedinst, J. K., & Seat, P. D. *Multidimensional description of personality*. Los Angeles: Western Psychological Services, 1977.

Wish, P. A., Hasazi, J. E., & Jurgela, A. R. Automated direct deconditioning of a childhood phobia. *Journal of Behavior Therapy and Experimental Psychiatry*, 1973, *4*, 279–283.

Witelson, S. F. Developmental dyslexia: Two right hemispheres and none left. *Science*, 1977, *195*, 309–311.

Witelson, S. F. Neuroanatomical asymmetry in left-handers: A review and implications for functional asymmetry. In J. Herron (Ed.), *Neuropsychology of left-handedness*. New York: Academic Press, 1980.

Witkin, H. A., Mednick, S. A., Schulsinger, F., Bakkestrom, E., Christiansen, K. O., Goodenough, D. R., Hirschhorn, K., Lundsteen, C., Owen, D. R., Philip, J., Rubin, D. B., & Stocking, M. Criminality in XYY and XXY men. *Science*, 1976, *193*, 547–555.

Witkin, H. A. Socialization, culture, and ecology in the development of group and sex differences in cognitive style. *Human Development*, 1979, *22*, 358–372.

Wolf, M. G. Effects of emotional disturbance in childhood on intelligence. *American Journal of Orthopsychiatry*, 1965, *35*, 906–908.

Wolf, S., & Wolff, H. G. *Human gastric function*. New York: Oxford University Press, 1947.

Wolfenstein, M. Trends in infant care. *American Journal of Orthopsychiatry*, 1953, *23*, 120–130.

Wolkind, S., & Rutter, M. Children who have been 'In care'—an epidemiological study. *Journal of Child Psychology and Psychiatry*, 1973, *14*, 97–105.

Wolman, B. B. *Children without childhood.* New York: Grune & Stratton, 1970.

Wolowitz, H. Food preferences as an index of orality. *Journal of Abnormal and Social Psychology*, 1964, *69*, 650–654.

Wolpe, J. *Psychotherapy by reciprocal inhibition*. Stanford, CA: Stanford University Press, 1958.

Wolpe, J. *Theme and variations: A behavior therapy casebook*. New York: Pergamon Press, 1976.

Wolpe, J. Cognition and causation in human behavior and its therapy. *American Psychologist*, 1978, *33*, 437–446.

Wolpe, J., & Rachman, S. Psychoanalytic 'evidence': A critique based on Freud's case of Little Hans. *Journal of Nervous and Mental Disease*, 1960, *131*, 135–148.

Wolraich, M., Drummond, T., Salomon, M., O'Brien, M., & Sivage, C. Effects of methylphenidate alone and in connection with behavior modification procedures on the behavior and performance of hyperactive children. *Journal of Abnormal Child Psychology*, 1978, *6*, 149–161.

Woodcock, R. W., & Johnson, M. B. *Woodcock-Johnson Psychoeducational Battery.* Hingham, MA: Teaching Resources Corp., 1977.

Woods, W. A., & Cook, W. E. Proficiency in drawing and placement of hands in drawings of the human figure. *Journal of Consulting Psychology,* 1954, *18,* 119–121.

Woolf, H. B. (Ed.). *Webster's new collegiate dictionary.* Springfield, MA: Merriam, 1977.

World Health Organization. *Schizophrenia. An international follow-up study.* New York: Wiley, 1979.

Wright, L. Outcome of a standardized program for treating psychogenic encopresis. *Professional Psychology,* 1975, *6,* 453–456.

Wyatt, R. J., Potkin, S. G., Walls, P. D., Nichols, A., Carpenter, W., & Murphy, D. Clinical correlates of low platelet monoamine oxidase in schizophrenic patients. In H. S. Akiskal & W. L. Webb (Eds.), *Psychiatric diagnosis: Exploration of biological predictors.* New York: Spectrum, 1978.

Wynne, L., Cromwell, R. L., & Matthyse, S. (Eds.). *The nature of schizophrenia: New approaches to research and treatment.* New York: Wiley, 1978.

Yablonsky, L. *The tunnel back: Synanon.* New York: Macmillan, 1965.

Yablonsky, L., & Dederich, C. E. Synanon: An analysis of some dimensions of the social structure of an antiaddiction society. In D. M. Wilner & G. G. Kassebaum (Eds.), *Narcotics.* New York: McGraw-Hill, 1965.

Yamamoto, K. Children's ratings of the stressfulness of experience. *Developmental Psychology,* 1979, *15,* 581–582.

Yando, R., Seitz, V., & Zigler, E. *Imitation: A developmental perspective.* Hillsdale, NJ: Erlbaum, 1978.

Yang, R. K., Zweig, A. R., Douthitt, T. C., & Federman, E. J. Successive relationships between maternal attitudes during pregnancy, analgesic medication during labor and delivery, and newborn behavior. *Developmental Psychology,* 1976, *12,* 6–14.

Yarrow, M. R., Campbell, J. D., & Burton, R. V. A study of the retrospective method. *Monographs of the Society for Research in Child Development,* 1970, *35*(Serial No. 138).

Yarrow, M. R., Scott, P. M., & Waxler, C. Z. Learning concern for others. *Developmental Psychology,* 1973, *8,* 240–260.

Yarrow, M. R., Waxler, C. Z., & Scott, P. M. Child effects on adult behavior. *Developmental Psychology,* 1971, *5,* 300–311.

Yates, A. J. *Biofeedback and the modification of behavior.* New York: Plenum Press, 1980.

Yolles, S. F., & Kramer, M. Vital statistics. In L. Bellak & L. Loeb (Eds.), *The schizophrenic syndrome.* New York: Grune & Stratton, 1969.

Yorke, C. The contributions of the Diagnostic Profile and the assessment of developmental lines to child psychiatry. *Psychiatric Clinics of North America,* 1980, *3,* 593–603.

Young, A. W., & Ellis, A. W. Asymmetry of cerebral hemispheric function in normal and poor readers. *Psychological Bulletin,* 1981, *89,* 183–190.

Yuwiler, A., Ritvo, E., Geller, E., Glousman, R., Schneiderman, G., & Matsuno, D. Uptake and efflux of serotonin from platelets of autistic and nonautistic children. *Journal of Autism and Childhood Schizophrenia,* 1975, *5,* 83–98.

Zarfas, D. E., & Wolf, L. C. Maternal age patterns and the incidence of Down's syndrome. *American Journal of Mental Deficiency,* 1979, *83,* 353–359.

Zeaman, D. T., & House, B. J. Mongoloid MA is proportional to log CA. *Child Development*, 1962, *33*, 481–488.

Zentall, S. S., & Zentall, T. R. Activity and task performance of hyperactive children as a function of environmental stimulation. *Journal of Consulting and Clinical Psychology*, 1976, *44*, 693–697.

Zentall, S., Zentall, T. R., & Booth, M. E. Within-task stimulation: Effects on activity and spelling performance in hyperactive and normal children. *Journal of Educational Research*, 1978, *71*, 223–230.

Zeskind, P. S., & Ramey, C. T. Preventing intellectual and interactional sequelae of fetal malnutrition: A longitudinal, transactional, and synergistic approach to development. *Child Development*, 1981, *52*, 213–218.

Zigler, E. Familial mental retardation: A continuing dilemma. *Science*, 1967, *155*, 292–298.

Zigler, E., & Balla, D. Motivational aspects of mental retardation. In R. Koch & J. C. Dobson (Eds.), *The mentally retarded child and his family. A multidisciplinary handbook (2nd ed.)*. New York: Brunner/Mazel, 1976.

Zigler, E., & Balla, D. A. Impact of institutional experience on the behavior and development of retarded persons. *American Journal of Mental Deficiency*, 1977, *82*, 1–11.

Zigler, E., & Valentine, J. *Project Head Start: A legacy of the war on poverty*. New York: Free Press, 1980.

Zubin, J., Eron, L., & Schumer, F. *An experimental approach to projective techniques*. New York: Wiley, 1965.

Zucker, K. J., Doering, R. W., Bradley, S. J., & Finegan, J. K. Sex-typed play in gender-disturbed children: A comparison to sibling and psychiatric controls. *Archives of Sexual Behavior*, 1982, in press.

Zucker, R. A. Developmental aspects of drinking through the young adult years. In H. T. Blane & M. E. Chafetz (Eds.), *Youth, alcohol, and social policy*. New York: Plenum, 1979.

Source Notes

p. 33, Quotation   Thomas, A., Chess, S., & Birch, H. G. *Temperament and behavior disorders in children.* New York University Press, 1968. Reprinted by permission of New York University Press. Copyright © 1968 by New York University.

p. 34, Quotation   Thomas, A., Chess, S., & Birch, H. G. *Temperament and behavior disorders in children.* New York University Press, 1968. Reprinted by permission of New York University Press. Copyright © 1968 by New York University.

p. 35, Quotation   Thomas, A., Chess, S., & Birch, H. G. *Temperament and behavior disorders in children.* New York University Press, 1968. Reprinted by permission of New York University Press. Copyright © 1968 by New York University.

p. 46, Figure 3.1   Schaffer, H. R., & Emerson, P. E. The development of social attachments in infancy. *Monographs of the Society for Research in Child Development,* 1964, *29,* Serial No. 94. © The Society for Research in Child Development, Inc.

p. 52, Figure 3.2   Oster, H. Facial expression and affect development. In M. Lewis & L. A. Rosenblum (Eds.), *The development of affect.* New York: Plenum, 1978.

p. 70, Figure 3.4   Baldwin, J. A., Robertson, N. C., & Satin, D. G. The incidence of reported deviant behavior in children. *International Psychiatry Clinics,* 1971, *8,* 161–175. Little, Brown, & Co.

p. 93, Table 4.2   American Psychiatric Association. *Diagnostic and statistical manual of mental disorders. Third Edition.* Washington, DC, APA, 1980.

p. 111, Table 5.1   Achenbach, T.M. *Research in developmental psychology: Concepts, strategies, methods.* Copyright © 1978 by The Free Press, A Division of Macmillan Publishing Co., Inc.

p. 115, Table 5.2   Sawyer, J. Measurement *and* prediction, clinical *and* statistical. *Psychological Bulletin,* 1966, *66,* 178–200. Copyright © 1966 by the American Psychological Association. Adapted by permission of the publisher and author.

p. 124, Figure 6.1   Penrose, L. S. *Recent advances in human genetics.* London: Churchill, 1961. Copyright Longman Group Limited.

p. 128, Figure 6.3   McClearn, G. E. Genetic influences on behavior and development. In P. H. Mussen (Ed.), *Carmichael's Manual of Child Psychology, Vol. 1, 3rd. ed.* New York: Wiley, 1970.

p. 131, Figure 6.4   Cattell, R. B. *Personality.* New York: McGraw-Hill, 1950. Used by permission of R. B. Cattell, *The inheritance of personality and ability.* New York: Academic Press, 1982.

p. 134, Figure 6.5   Tryon, R. C. Individual differences. In F. A. Moss (Ed.), *Comparative psychology.* New York: Prentice-Hall, 1934.

p. 142, Table 6.1   Vandenberg, S. G. Hereditary factors in normal personality traits as measured by inventories. In J. Wortis (Ed.), *Recent advances in biological psychiatry. Vol. 9.* New York: Plenum, 1967.

p. 144, Figure 6.7   Rosenthal, D. The design of studies to evaluate hereditary and environmental contributions to the etiology of behavioral disorders. Paper presented at the American Psychological Association Convention, Miami Beach, Sept. 5, 1970. Uncopyrighted paper by government employee.

p. 146, Figure 6.8   Freedman, D. G. An ethological approach to the genetical study of human behavior. In S. G. Vandenburg (Ed.), *Methods and goals in human behavior genetics*. New York: Academic Press, 1965.

p. 147, Table 6.3   Plomin, R., & Rowe, D. C. Genetic and environmental etiology of social behavior in infancy. *Developmentul Psychology*, 1979, *15*, 62−72. Copyright 1979 by the American Psychological Association. Adapted by permission of the publisher and author.

p. 148, Table 6.4   Eysenck, H. J. The inheritance of extroversion-introversion. *Acta Psychologica*, 1956, *12*, 95−110.

p. 162, Figure 7.2   Davie, E., Butler, N., & Goldstein, H. *From birth to seven: The second report of the National Child Development Study*. London: Longman, 1972. Courtesy of Longman and the National Children's Bureau.

p. 163, Figure 7.3   Penfield, W., & Roberts, L. *Speech and brain mechanisms*. Princeton, NJ: Princeton University Press, 1959. Reprinted by permission of Princeton University Press.

p. 164, Figure 7.4   Scott, D. P. *About Epilepsy*. New York: International Universities Press, 1973.

p. 167, Figure 7.5   Maher, B. *Principles of psychopathology*. New York: McGraw-Hill, 1966. Copyright © 1966 by McGraw-Hill. Used with the permission of McGraw-Hill Book Company.

p. 175, Figure 7.6   Teuber, H. L., & Rudel, R. G. Behavior after cerebral lesions in children and adults. *Developmental Medicine and Child Neurology*, 1962, *4*, 3−20. Copyright by Spastics International Medical Publications.

p. 176, Figure 7.7   Strauss, A. A., & Lehtinen, L. E. *Psychopathology and education of the brain-injured child*. New York: Grune & Stratton, 1947.

p. 182, Figure 7.8   Scott, D. P. *About Epilepsy*. New York: International Universities Press, 1973.

pp. 200−201, Quotations   Thomas, A., Chess, S., & Birch, H. G. *Temperament and behavior disorders in children*. New York University Press, 1968. Reprinted by permission of New York University Press. Copyright © 1968 by New York University.

pp. 201−202, Quotations   Baller, W. R., Charles, D. C., & Miller, E. L. Mid-life attainment of the mentally retarded: a longitudinal study. *Genetic Psychology Monographs*, 1967, *75*, 235−329.

pp. 203−205, Quotations   Binet, A., & Simon, T. *The development of intelligence in children*. Baltimore: Williams & Wilkins, 1916.

p. 211, Figure 8.1   Pinneau, S. R. *Changes in intelligence quotient: Infancy to maturity*. Boston: Houghton Mifflin, 1961. Figure from Pinneau, S.R., *Changes in intelligence* *quotient: Infancy to maturity*. Boston: Houghton Mifflin Company, 1961. Reproduced with permission from The Riverside Publishing Company.

p. 214, Figure 8.2   McCall, R. B. Childhood IQs as predictors of adult educational and occupational status. *Science*, 1977, *197*, 482−483. Copyright © 1977 by the American Association for the Advancement of Science.

p. 216, Table 8.1   Millon, T. *Modern psychopathology: A biosocial approach to maladaptive learning and functioning*. Philadelphia: Saunders, 1969. Used by permission of Holt, Rinehart, & Winston.

p. 219, Figure 8.4   Sontag, L. W., Baker, C. T., & Nelson, V. L. Mental growth and personality development: A longitudinal study. *Monographs of the Society for Research in Child Development*, 1958, *23*, Serial #68. Copyright © the Society for Research in Child Development, Inc.

p. 221, Figure 8.5   Smith, D. W., & Wilson, A. *The child with Down's syndrome (mongolism)*. Philadelphia: Saunders, 1973.

pp. 224−225, Quotations   Freedman, D. A. The role of early mother/child relations in the etiology of some cases of mental retardation. In G. Farrell (Ed.), *Congenital mental retardation*. Austin, TX: University of Texas Press, 1969.

p. 232, Figure 8.6   Birch, H. G., Richardson, S. A., Baird, D., Horobin, G., & Illsley, R. *Mental subnormality in the community: A clinical and epidemiological study*. Baltimore: Williams & Wilkins, 1970.

p. 239, Table 8.2   Reed, E. W., & Reed, S. C. *Mental retardation. A family study*. Philadelphia: Saunders, 1965.

pp. 242−243, Figures 8.9 a,b   Honzik, M. P. Developmental studies of parent-child resemblance in intelligence. *Child Development*, 1957, *28*, 215−228. © The Society for Research in Child Development, Inc.

p. 262, Quotation   Freud, S. *Standard edition of the complete psychological works of Sigmund Freud*. London: Hogarth Press, *Vol. 10*, 1955; *Vol. 3*, 1962. Sigmund Freud Copyrights, Ltd., The Institute of Psycho-Analysis, and The Hogarth Press, Ltd. for permission to quote from *The Complete Psychological Works of Sigmund Freud* translated and edited by James Strachey.

p. 267, Quotation   From *The Collected Papers of Sigmund Freud, Vol. 1*, edited by Ernest Jones, M.D. Authorized translation under the supervision of Joan Riviere. Published by Basic Books, Inc. by arrangement with The Hogarth Press Ltd. and The Institute of Psycho-Analysis London. Used by permission of Basic Books, Inc., Publishers, New York.

p. 268, Quotation   From *The Collected Papers of Sigmund Freud, Vol. 3*, edited by Ernest Jones, M.D. Authorized translation by Alex and James Strachey. Published by Basic Books, Inc. by arrangement with The Hogarth Press Ltd. and the Institute of Psycho-Analysis, London. Used by permission of Basic Books, Inc., Publishers, New York.

p. 278, Table 9.1   Erikson, E. H. Elements of a psychoanalytic theory of psychosocial development. In S. I. Greenspan & G. H. Pollock (Eds.), *The course of life: Psychoanalytic* *contributions toward understanding personality development, Vol. 1*. Adelphi, MD: NIMH, Mental Health Study Center, 1980. Chapter copyright E. H. Erikson. Used by permission of author and W. W. Norton.

p. 279, Table 9.2 Freud, A. *Normality and pathology in childhood*. New York: International Universities Press, 1965.

pp. 285−291, Quotations Bornstein, B. Analysis of a phobic child. *Psychoanalytic Study of the Child*, 1949, 3−4, 181−226.

pp. 291−293, Quotation Ritvo, S. Unpublished, uncopyrighted report.

pp. 295−296, Quotations Despert, J. L. Differential diagnosis between obsessive-compulsive neurosis and schizophrenia in children. In P. H. Hoch & J. Zubin (Eds.), *Psychopathology of childhood*. New York: Grune & Stratton, 1955. Used by permission of Grune & Stratton.

pp. 298−299, Quotations Starr, P. H. Some observations on the diagnostic aspects of childhood hysteria. *Nervous Child*, 1953, *10*, 214−231.

p. 310, Quotation Thomas, A., Chess, S., & Birch, H. G. *Temperament and behavior disorders in children*. New York University Press, 1968. Reprinted by permission of New York University Press. Copyright © 1968 by New York University.

p. 319, Figure 10.1 Eysenck, H. J. *Behavior therapy and the neuroses*. New York: Pergamon, 1960.

p. 326, Figure 10.2 Wolpe, J. *Psychotherapy by reciprocal inhibition*. Stanford, CA: Stanford University Press, 1958.

p. 333, Figure 10.3 Allen, K. E., Hart, B., Buell, J. S., Harris, R. R., & Wolf, M. M. Effects of social reinforcement on isolate behavior of a nursery school child. *Child Development*, 1964, *35*, 511−518. The Society for Research in Child Development, Inc.

p. 338, Figure 10.4 Lang, P. J., & Melamed, B. Avoidance conditioning therapy of an infant with chronic ruminative vomiting. *Journal of Abnormal Psychology*, 1969, *74*, 1−8. Copyright 1969 by the American Psychological Association. Reprinted by permission of the publisher and author.

p. 341, Figure 10.5 Bandura, A. *Social learning theory*. Englewood Cliffs, NJ: Prentice-Hall, 1977. Albert Bandura, *Social Learning Theory*, © 1977, p. 23. Reprinted by permission of Prentice-Hall, Inc.

p. 351, Figure 10.6 Eysenck, H. J., & Rachman, S. *The causes and cures of neurosis*. San Diego: R. R. Knapp, 1965.

p. 355, Table 10.1 Ince, L. P. The use of relaxation training and a conditioned stimulus in the elimination of epileptic seizures in a child. *Behavior Therapy and Experimental Psychiatry*, 1976, *7*, 39−42. Reprinted with permission from *Behavior Therapy and Experimental Psychiatry*. Copyright 1976, Pergamon Press, Ltd.

p. 367, Quotation American Psychiatric Association. *Diagnostic and statistical manual of mental disorders. Third Edition*. Washington, DC, APA, 1980.

p. 382, Figure 11.2 Kinsbourne, M., & Swanson, J. M. Models of hyperactivity. In R. L. Trites (Ed.), *Hyperactivity in children.* Baltimore: University Park Press, 1979. © 1979 University Park Press, Baltimore.

p. 383, Figure 11.3 Sprague, R. L. & Sleator, E. K. Methylphenidate in hyperkinetic children: Differences in dose effects on learning and social behavior. *Science,* Vol. 198, pp. 1274−1276, 23 December 1977. Copyright 1977 by the American Association for the Advancement of Science.

p. 404, Quotation American Psychiatric Association. *Diagnostic and statistical manual of mental disorders. Third Edition.* Washington, DC, APA, 1980.

pp. 406−408, Quotations Rabkin, B. *Growing up dead.* Nashville, TE: Abingdon, 1979. Reprinted by permission of The Canadian Publishers, McClelland and Stewart Limited, Toronto.

p. 419, Table 12.1 American Psychiatric Association. *Diagnostic and statistical manual of mental disorders. Third Edition.* Washington, DC, APA, 1980.

p. 421, Quotation Kanner, L. Autistic disturbances of affective contact. *Nervous Child,* 1943, 2.

p. 429, Quotation Kanner, L. Autistic disturbances of affective contact. *Nervous Child,* 1943, 2.

p. 434, Figure 12.1 Hutt, C., & Ounsted, C. Gaze aversion and its significance in childhood autism. In S. J. Hutt & C. Hutt (Eds.), *Behavior studies in psychiatry.* New York: Pergamon Press, 1970.

p. 436, Figure 12.1 Weber, D. *Der frühkindliche Autismus unter dem Aspekt der Entwicklung.* Bern: Verlag Hans Huber, 1970.

p. 439, Quotation American Psychiatric Association. *Diagnostic and statistical manual of mental disorders. Third Edition.* Washington, DC, APA, 1980.

p. 446, Figure 12.4 Meyers, D. I., & Goldfarb, W. Studies of perplexity in mothers of schizophrenic children. *American Journal of Orthopsychiatry,* 1961, *31,* 551−564. Reprinted, with permission, from the *American Journal of Orthopsychiatry.* Copyright 1961 by the American Orthopsychiatric Association, Inc.

p. 449, Table 12.2 Heston, L. L. Psychiatric disorders in foster home reared children of schizophrenic mothers. *British Journal of Psychiatry,* 1966, *112,* 819−825.

p. 454, Figure 12.5 Rutter, M., & Bartak, L. Special educational treatment of autistic children. *Journal of Child Psychology and Psychiatry,* 1973, *14,* 241−270. Reprinted with permission from the *Journal of Child Psychology and Psychiatry.* Copyright 1973, Pergamon Press, Ltd.

p. 470, Figure 13.1 Patterson, G. R. The aggressive child: Victim and architect of a coercive system. In L. A. Hamerlynck, E. J. Mash, & L. C. Handy (Eds.), *Behavior Modification and Families.* New York: Brunner/Mazel, 1976. Reprinted with permission from L. A. Hamerlynck, E. J. Mash, & L. C. Handy.

p. 473, Figure 13.2   Eron, L. D. Prescription for reduction of aggression. *American Psychologist*, 1980, *35*, 244–252. Copyright 1980 by the American Psychological Association. Reprinted by permission of the publisher and author.

p. 479, Table 13.2   Kohlberg, L. The cognitive developmental approach to behavior disorders. In G. Serban (Ed.), *Cognitive defects in the development of mental illness*. New York: Brunner/Mazel, 1978, p. 209. Adapted with permission from G. Serban.

p. 483, Table 13.3   Cernkovich, S. A., & Giordano, P. C. A comparative analysis of male and female delinquency. *Sociological Quarterly*, 1979, *20*, 131–145.

pp. 489–490, Quotations   Rosenberg, B., & Silverstein, H. *The varieties of delinquent experience*. Blaisdell: 1969. Reprinted by permission of John Wiley & Sons, Inc.

p. 494, Quotation   Cleckley, H. *The mask of sanity, 5th edition*. St. Louis! Mosby, 1976.

pp. 494–495, Quotations   American Psychiatric Association. *Diagnostic and statistical manual of mental disorders. Third Edition*. Washington, DC, APA, 1980.

p. 497, Figure 13.5   S. Schachter. *Emotion, obesity, and crime*. New York: Academic Press, 1971.

p. 499, Figure 13.6   Schmauk, F. J. Punishment, arousal, and avoidance learning in sociopaths. *Journal of Abnormal Psychology*, 1970, *76*, 325–335. Copyright 1970 by the American Psychological Association. Adapted by permission of the publisher and author.

p. 505, Quotation   Cleckley, H. *The mask of sanity. 5th edition*. St. Louis: Mosby, 1976.

p. 535, Figure 14.2   Johnston, L. D., O'Malley, & Eveland, L. K. Drugs and delinquency: A search for causal connections. In D. B. Kandel (Ed.), *Longitudinal research on drug use*. Washington, DC: Hemisphere, 1978.

pp. 539–540, Quotations   Yablonsky, L., & Dederich, C. E. Synanon: An analysis of some dimensions of the social structure of an antiaddiction society. In D. M. Wilner & G. G. Kassebaum (Eds.), *Narcotics*. New York: McGraw-Hill, 1965. From *Narcotics*, edited by D. M. Wilner & G. G. Kassebaum. Copyright © 1965, by McGraw-Hill. Used with the permission of McGraw-Hill Book Company.

p. 574, Figure 15.5   Anthony, E. J. The behavior disorders of childhood. In P. H. Mussen (Ed.), *Carmichael's Manual of Child Psychology, 3rd ed., vol. 1*. New York: Wiley, 1970.

p. 619, Figure 16.1   Psychological Corporation Advertisement. System of Multicultural Pluralistic Assessment. Copyright © 1977 by The Psychological Corporation, New York, New York. All rights reserved.

pp. 628–629, Quotations   Axline, V. M. Play therapy procedures and results. *American Journal of Orthopsychiatry*, 1955, *25*, 618–626. Reprinted, with permission, from the *American Journal of Orthopsychiatry*. Copyright 1955 by the American Orthopsychiatric Association, Inc.

pp. 628–629, Quotations   Strean, H. S. A family therapist looks at "Little Hans." *Family Process*, 1967, *6*, 227–234.

p. 648, Figure 17.3   Love, L. R., & Kaswan, J. W. *Troubled children, Their families, schools, and treatments*. New York: Wiley, 1974.

NAME INDEX

Abbey, H., 396
Abel, E. L., 158
Abelson, R. P., 84, 588
Abikoff, H., 385
Abramowitz, A., 328, 329
Abrams, N., 504
Abramson, L. Y., 410
Achenbach, T. M., 35–38, 47, 57, 60, 64–69,
    82–85, 90, 95, 110–111, 117–118, 184, 213,
    239, 244, 247–248, 294–295, 306, 351–352,
    366, 378–379, 386, 388, 392–395, 401–405,
    469, 473–476, 486, 503, 521–522, 556–576,
    606–613, 620, 645–646, 649
Ackerman, N. W., 397, 602
Ackerson, L., 554
Adams, N. E., 342
Adams, S., 508
Adler, A., 18–19
Adler, F., 71, 472, 502
Agar, M. H., 529, 546
Ahn, H., 165, 615
Aichorn, A., 19
Albee, G. W., 650
Alexander, A. B., 188–189, 353–354, 511,
    517
Alexander, F., 185
Alexander, J. F., 518, 631, 650
Allen, J,. 427
Allen, J. N., 165
Allen, K. E., 332–333, 383
Allen, L., 56, 356
Allen, N., 504
Allen, T. W., 375
Allport, G. W., 82–83
Allyon, T., 348
Alpern, S., 500
Aman, M. G., 615
Ames, L. B., 31, 591, 622
Anderson, L. M., 600
Anderson, V. E., 151, 447
Andrasik, F., 335
Andrews, C. E., 426
Andrews, G., 180

Annau, Z., 158
Annesley, R. F., 634
Anthony, E. J., 417, 451–452, 573–574, 576
Aristotle, 315
Arnold, L. E., 398
Arthur, R. J., 500
Ashenden, B., 422
Ashkenazi, Z., 394
Assael, M., 500
Astin, A., 321
Atkeson, B. M., 347
Atkinson, J. W., 592–593
Auerbach, A. H., 304–305
Ax, A. F., 185
Axline, V. M., 80, 95, 624–625, 650
Azrin, N. H., 391

Baade, L. E., 188
Bachman, D. S., 165
Bachman, J. G., 527
Bachrach, W., 191
Baekgaard, W., 137
Baer, D. M., 26, 331, 383
Bahn, A. K., 59, 90, 637
Baird, D., 215
Baird, H. W., 165, 615
Bak, J. J., 252
Baker, B. L., 253, 391, 585
Baker, C. T., 217–219
Baker, L., 188
Baker, T. B., 603
Bakwin, H., 389, 396
Bakwin, R., 445
Balaschak, B. A., 183, 198, 355
Baldwin, J. A., 68, 70, 641
Balian, L., 310
Balla, D., 245–246, 258, 500, 507
Ballard, M., 253
Baller, W. R., 202, 250
Balow, B., 162, 213, 579, 634
Baltes, P. B., 109–110, 117
Bandura, A., 26, 323, 340–343, 362, 468, 519
Bardwell, R., 485

737

SUBJECT INDEX